Ford Focus
Owners Workshop Manual

Peter T Gill

(6417 - 384)

Models covered

Hatchback & Estate

Petrol: 1.0 litre (998cc) 3-cyl & 1.6 litre (1596cc) 4-cyl
Turbo-diesel: 1.5 litre (1499cc) & 1.6 litre (1560cc)

Does NOT cover 1.5, 2.0 or 2.3 litre petrol engines, Flexfuel models or 2.0 litre diesel engine
Does NOT cover ST or RS models, 4WD, automatic or 'Powershift' transmissions

ABCDE
FGHIJ
KLMNO
PQRST

A book in the **Haynes Owners Workshop Manual Series**

ISBN **978 1 78521 417 2**

British Library Cataloguing in Publication Data
A catalogue record for this book is available from the British Library.

Printed in Malaysia

Haynes Publishing
Sparkford, Yeovil, Somerset BA22 7JJ, England

Haynes North America, Inc
859 Lawrence Drive, Newbury Park, California 91320, USA

Printed using NORBRITE BOOK 48.8gsm (CODE: 40N6533) from NORPAC; procurement system certified under Sustainable Forestry Initiative standard. Paper produced is certified to the SFI Certified Fiber Sourcing Standard (CERT - 0094271)

Contents

Contents

REPAIRS & OVERHAUL

Engine and associated systems

Transmission

Brakes and suspension

Body equipment

Wiring diagrams

REFERENCE

Index

First Introduced to the UK In 1998, this manual covers the latest version Introduced in January 2015. The latest Focus builds on Ford's 'kinetic' design concept with a low profile bonnet and wrap around lights. The new range shares many of the attributes of its ancestors, but with improved refinement and performance, coupled with lower emissions.

The Ford Focus model range covered by this manual was introduced in January 2015, superseding the previous Focus range. It is available in 5-door Hatchback, and Estate versions with 1.0 litre EcoBoost (turbocharged) engines and 1.6 litre Duretec petrol engines, and 1.5 and 1.6 litre Duratorq TDCi diesel engines.

The 1.0 litre petrol engine is a 3-cylinder design, the 1.6 litre engine has 4 cylinders. All petrol engines are 4-valves per cylinder, with Double OverHead Camshafts (DOHC). All engines are mounted transversely at the front of the car.

The Duratorq diesel engines all feature state-of-the art common-rail injection which meet or exceed the latest emissions standards. Both the 1.5 and 1.6 litre diesel engines are 4-cylinder, Single OverHead Camshaft (SOHC) design, with 2-valves per cylinder. All engines are mounted transversely at the front of the car. All diesel are fitted with a diesel particulate filter (DPF) to ensure compliance with European emissions regulations.

Safety features include door side impact bars, airbags for the driver and front seat passenger, side airbags, head airbags, whiplash protection system (front seats), and an advanced seat belt system with pretensioners and load limiters. Vehicle security is enhanced, with an engine immobiliser, shielded locks, and security-coded audio equipment being fitted as standard, as well as double-locking doors on most models.

The transversely-mounted engines drive the front roadwheels through either a five- or six-speed manual transmission with a hydraulically-operated clutch. An electronically-controlled six-speed automatic transmission is also available, but is not covered by this manual.

The fully-independent suspension is by MacPherson struts and transverse lower arms at the front, with multilink independent suspension at the rear; anti-roll bars are fitted at front and rear.

The vacuum servo-assisted brakes are disc at the front, and either disc or drum at the rear. An electronically-controlled Anti-lock Braking System (ABS) is fitted on all models, with Dynamic Stability and Traction Control System (DSTC) also available.

Power-assisted steering is standard on all models. The Mark 3 Focus was the first Ford to feature electric power steering, with a steering rack mounted electric motor providing the power. Some earlier models still retain standard power steering with a belt driven hydraulic pump.

Air conditioning is standard on all models, with full climate control fitted to many of the higher trim level models. The interior has been fully updated from previous versions with an ergonomically-designed passenger cabin with high levels of safety and comfort for all passengers.

Provided that regular servicing is carried out in accordance with the manufacturer's recommendations, the Focus should prove a reliable and economical car. The engine compartment is well-designed, and most of the items needing frequent attention are easily accessible.

Your Ford Focus manual

The aim of this manual is to help you get the best value from your vehicle. It can do so in several ways. It can help you decide what work must be done (even should you choose to get it done by a garage). It will also provide information on routine maintenance and servicing, and give a logical course of action and diagnosis when random faults occur. However, it is hoped that you will use the manual by tackling the work yourself. On simpler jobs it may even be quicker than booking the car into a garage and going there twice, to leave and collect it. Perhaps most important, a lot of money can be saved by avoiding the costs a garage must charge to cover its labour and overheads.

The manual has drawings and descriptions to show the function of the various components so that their layout can be understood. Tasks are described and photographed in a clear step-by-step sequence. The illustrations are numbered by the Section number and paragraph number to which they relate – if there is more than one illustration per paragraph, the sequence is denoted alphabetically.

References to the 'left' or 'right' of the vehicle are in the sense of a person in the driver's seat, facing forwards.

Acknowledgements

Thanks are due to AST Tools and Draper Tools Limited, who provided some of the workshop tools, and to all those people at Sparkford who helped in the production of this manual.

Working on your car can be dangerous. This page shows just some of the potential risks and hazards, with the aim of creating a safety-conscious attitude.

General hazards

Scalding

• Don't remove the radiator or expansion tank cap while the engine is hot.

• Engine oil, transmission fluid or power steering fluid may also be dangerously hot if the engine has recently been running.

Burning

• Beware of burns from the exhaust system and from any part of the engine. Brake discs and drums can also be extremely hot immediately after use.

Crushing

• When working under or near a raised vehicle, always supplement the jack with axle stands, or use drive-on ramps. ***Never venture under a car which is only supported by a jack***.

• Take care if loosening or tightening high-torque nuts when the vehicle is on stands. Initial loosening and final tightening should be done with the wheels on the ground.

Fire

• Fuel is highly flammable; fuel vapour is explosive.

• Don't let fuel spill onto a hot engine.

• Do not smoke or allow naked lights (including pilot lights) anywhere near a vehicle being worked on. Also beware of creating sparks (electrically or by use of tools).

• Fuel vapour is heavier than air, so don't work on the fuel system with the vehicle over an inspection pit.

• Another cause of fire is an electrical overload or short-circuit. Take care when repairing or modifying the vehicle wiring.

• Keep a fire extinguisher handy, of a type suitable for use on fuel and electrical fires.

Electric shock

• Ignition HT and Xenon headlight voltages can be dangerous, especially to people with heart problems or a pacemaker. Don't work on or near these systems with the engine running or the ignition switched on.

• Mains voltage is also dangerous. Make sure that any mains-operated equipment is correctly earthed. Mains power points should be protected by a residual current device (RCD) circuit breaker.

Fume or gas intoxication

• Exhaust fumes are poisonous; they can contain carbon monoxide, which is rapidly fatal if inhaled. Never run the engine in a confined space such as a garage with the doors shut.

• Fuel vapour is also poisonous, as are the vapours from some cleaning solvents and paint thinners.

Poisonous or irritant substances

• Avoid skin contact with battery acid and with any fuel, fluid or lubricant, especially antifreeze, brake hydraulic fluid and Diesel fuel. Don't syphon them by mouth. If such a substance is swallowed or gets into the eyes, seek medical advice.

• Prolonged contact with used engine oil can cause skin cancer. Wear gloves or use a barrier cream if necessary. Change out of oil-soaked clothes and do not keep oily rags in your pocket.

• Air conditioning refrigerant forms a poisonous gas if exposed to a naked flame (including a cigarette). It can also cause skin burns on contact.

Asbestos

• Asbestos dust can cause cancer if inhaled or swallowed. Asbestos may be found in gaskets and in brake and clutch linings. When dealing with such components it is safest to assume that they contain asbestos.

Special hazards

Hydrofluoric acid

• This extremely corrosive acid is formed when certain types of synthetic rubber, found in some O-rings, oil seals, fuel hoses etc, are exposed to temperatures above 4000C. The rubber changes into a charred or sticky substance containing the acid. *Once formed, the acid remains dangerous for years. If it gets onto the skin, it may be necessary to amputate the limb concerned*.

• When dealing with a vehicle which has suffered a fire, or with components salvaged from such a vehicle, wear protective gloves and discard them after use.

The battery

• Batteries contain sulphuric acid, which attacks clothing, eyes and skin. Take care when topping-up or carrying the battery.

• The hydrogen gas given off by the battery is highly explosive. Never cause a spark or allow a naked light nearby. Be careful when connecting and disconnecting battery chargers or jump leads.

Air bags

• Air bags can cause injury if they go off accidentally. Take care when removing the steering wheel and trim panels. Special storage instructions may apply.

Diesel injection equipment

• Diesel injection pumps supply fuel at very high pressure. Take care when working on the fuel injectors and fuel pipes.

Warning: Never expose the hands, face or any other part of the body to injector spray; the fuel can penetrate the skin with potentially fatal results.

Remember...

DO

• Do use eye protection when using power tools, and when working under the vehicle.

• Do wear gloves or use barrier cream to protect your hands when necessary.

• Do get someone to check periodically that all is well when working alone on the vehicle.

• Do keep loose clothing and long hair well out of the way of moving mechanical parts.

• Do remove rings, wristwatch etc, before working on the vehicle – especially the electrical system.

• Do ensure that any lifting or jacking equipment has a safe working load rating adequate for the job.

DON'T

• Don't attempt to lift a heavy component which may be beyond your capability – get assistance.

• Don't rush to finish a job, or take unverified short cuts.

• Don't use ill-fitting tools which may slip and cause injury.

• Don't leave tools or parts lying around where someone can trip over them. Mop up oil and fuel spills at once.

• Don't allow children or pets to play in or near a vehicle being worked on.

The following pages are intended to help in dealing with common roadside emergencies and breakdowns. You will find more detailed fault finding information at the back of the manual, and repair information in the main chapters.

If your car won't start and the starter motor doesn't turn

- ☐ Open the bonnet and make sure that the battery terminals are clean and tight (unclip the battery cover for access), also check the earth lead from the battery to the inner wing panel.
- ☐ Switch on the headlights and try to start the engine. If the headlights go very dim when you'r e trying to start, the battery is probably flat. Get out of trouble by jump starting (see next page) using a friend's car.

If your car won't start even though the starter motor turns as normal

- ☐ Is there fuel in the tank?
- ☐ Has the engine immobiliser been deactivated? This should happen automatically, on inserting the ignition key. However, if a replacement key has been obtained (other than from a Ford dealer), it may not contain the transponder chip necessary to deactivate the system. Even 'proper' replacement keys have to be coded to work properly – a procedure for this is outlined in the vehicle handbook.
- ☐ Is there moisture on electrical components under the bonnet? Switch off the ignition, then wipe off any obvious dampness with a dry cloth. Remove the plastic cover on the top of the engine (where applicable). Spray a water-repellent aerosol product (WD-40 or equivalent) on ignition and fuel system electrical connectors like those shown in the photos. Pay special attention to the ignition coil wiring connectors (petrol models).

A Check the security and condition of the battery connections. Remove the cover for access

B Check the crankshaft sensor wiring plug – (Diesel engine shown)

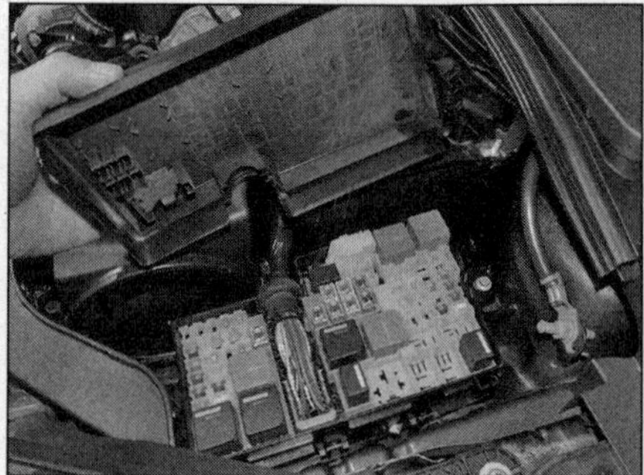

C Check that none of the engine compartment fuses have blown

Check that electrical connections are secure (with the ignition switched off) and spray them with a water-dispersantspray like WD-40 if you suspect a problem due to damp.

Jump starting

Jump starting will get you out of trouble, but you must correct whatever made the battery go flat in the first place. There are three possibilities:

1 The battery has been drained by repeated attempts to start, or by leaving the lights on.

2 The charging system is not working properly (alternator drivebelt slack or broken, alternator wiring fault or alternator itself faulty).

3 The battery itself is at fault (electrolyte low, or battery worn out).

When jump-starting a car, observe the following precautions:

- ✓ Before connecting the booster battery, make sure that the ignition is switched off.
- ✓ Ensure that all electrical equipment (lights, heater, wipers, etc) is switched off.
- ✓ Take note of any special precautions printed on the battery case.
- ✓ Make sure that the booster battery is the same voltage as the one recommended for the vehicle.
- ✓ If the battery is being jump-started from the battery in another vehicle, the two vehicles MUST NOT TOUCH each other.
- ✓ Make sure that the transmission is in neutral (or PARK, in the case of automatic transmission).

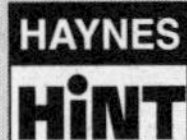

Budget jump leads can be a false economy, as they often do not pass enough current to start large capacity or diesel engines. They can also get hot.

1 Connect one end of the red jump lead to the positive (+) terminal of the flat battery

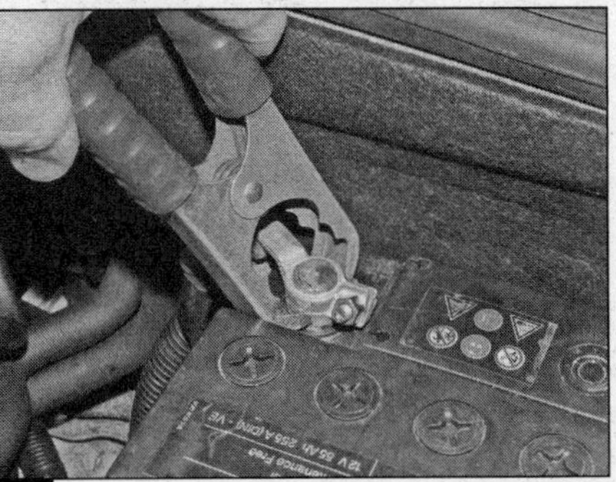

2 Connect the other end of the red lead to the positive (+) terminal of the booster battery.

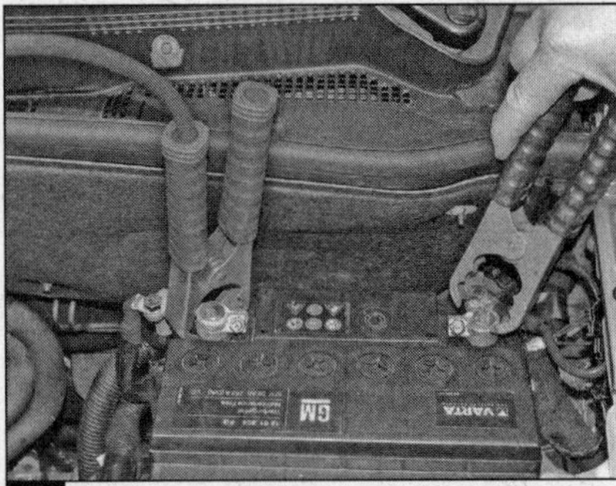

3 Connect one end of the black jump lead to the negative (-) terminal of the booster battery

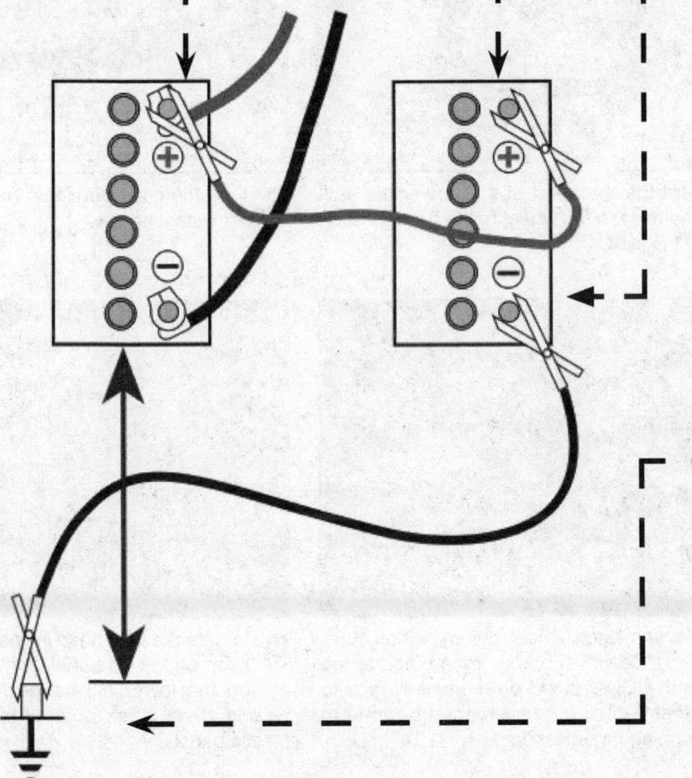

4 Connect the other end of the black jump lead to a bolt or bracket on the engine block, well away from the battery, on the vehicle to be started.

5 Make sure that the jump leads will not come into contact with the fan, drive-belts or other moving parts of the engine.

6 Start the engine using the booster battery and run it at idle speed. Switch on the lights, rear window demister and heater blower motor, then disconnect the jump leads in the reverse order of connection. Turn off the lights etc.

Wheel changing

Warning: Do not change a wheel in a situation where you risk being hit by other traffic. On busy roads, try to stop in a lay-by or a gateway. Be wary of passing traffic while changing the wheel – it is easy to become distracted by the job in hand.

Preparation

- ☐ When a puncture occurs, stop as soon as it is safe to do so.
- ☐ Park on firm level ground, if possible, and well out of the way of other traffic.
- ☐ Use hazard warning lights if necessary.
- ☐ If you have one, use a warning triangle to alert other drivers of your presence.
- ☐ Apply the handbrake and engage first or reverse gear (or P on models with automatic transmission).
- ☐ Chock the wheel diagonally opposite the one being removed – a couple of large stones will do for this.
- ☐ If the ground is soft, use a flat piece of wood to spread the load under the jack.

Changing the wheel

1 The spare wheel and tools are stored under the floor in the luggage compartment.

2 Remove the polystyrene round spacer, then unscrew the plastic retaining nut, and lift out the spare wheel.

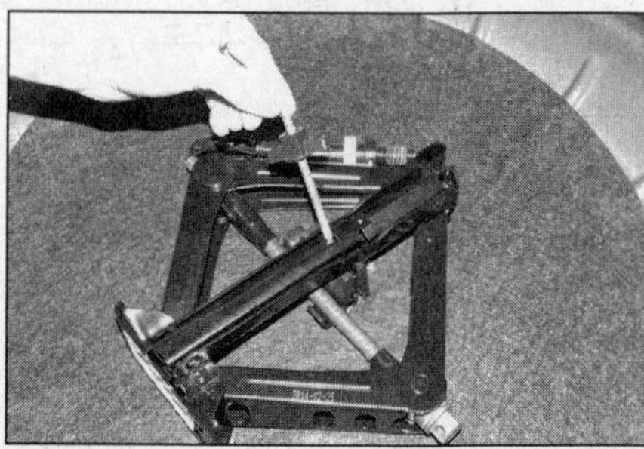

3 Undo the retaining screw to remove the jack and wheel brace.

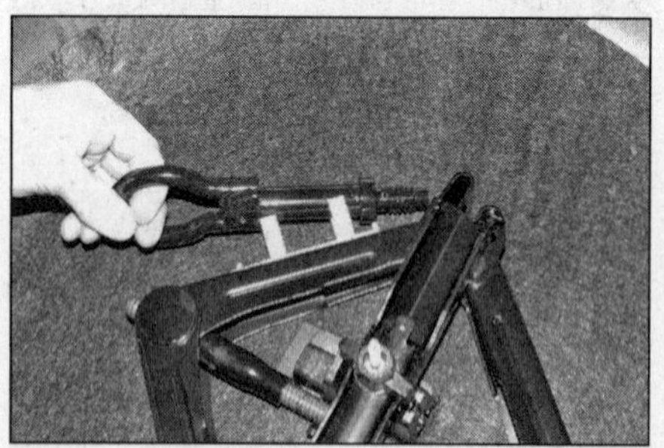

4 The screw-in towing eye is located on clips on the side of the vehicle jack.

5 Turn the threaded bolt to lower the jack and release the wheel brace from the side of the jack.

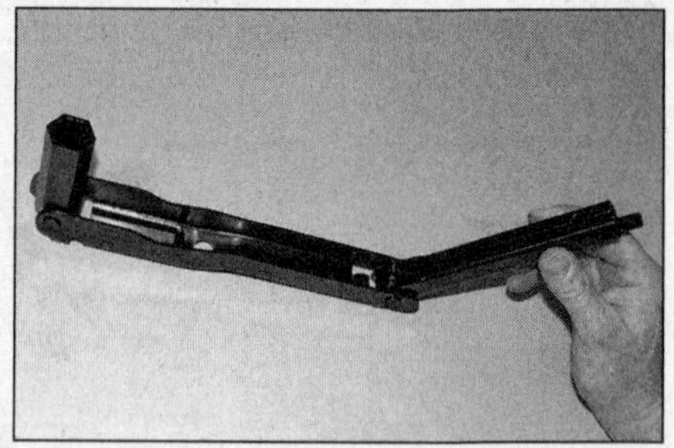

6 Fold the ends outwards to be able to use the wheel brace.

7 Models with alloy wheels may have special locking nuts – these are removed with a special tool, which should be provided with the wheel brace (or it may be in the glovebox). Where applicable, using the flat end of the wheel brace, prise off the wheel trim or centre cover for access to the wheel nuts.

8 Slacken each wheel nut by a half turn, using the wheel brace. If the nuts are too tight, DON'T stand on the wheelbrace to undo them – call for assistance from one of the motoring organisations.

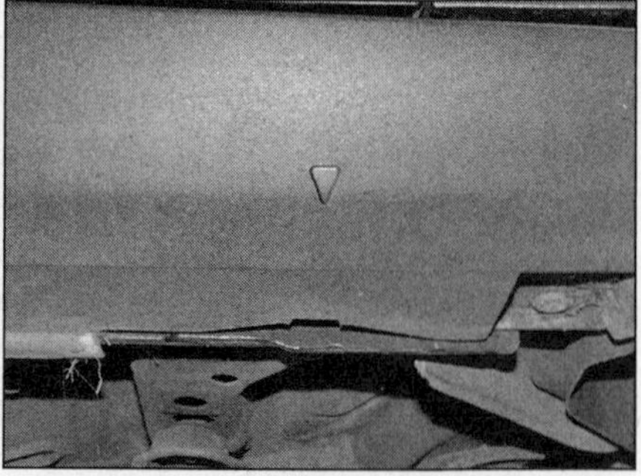

9 Locate the jack head in line with the arrow head on the sill panel, at the jacking point on the lower sill flange (don't jack the vehicle at any other point of the sill, nor on a plastic panel).

10 Two jacking points are provided on each side – use the one nearest the punctured wheel. Turn the jack handle clockwise until the wheel is raised clear of the ground.

11 Unscrew the wheel nuts and remove the wheel.

12 Fit the spare wheel, and screw on the nuts. Lightly tighten the nuts with the wheel brace, then lower the vehicle to the ground. Securely tighten the wheel nuts, then where applicable, refit the wheel trim or centre cover.

Finally . . .

☐ Remove the wheel chocks. Stow the punctured wheel and tools back in the luggage compartment, and secure them in position.

☐ Check the tyre pressure on the tyre just fitted. If it is low, or if you don't have a pressure gauge with you, drive slowly to the next garage and inflate the tyre to the correct pressure. In the case of the narrow 'space-saver' spare wheel this pressure is much higher than for a normal tyre.

☐ The wheel nuts should be slackened and retightened to the specified torque at the earliest possible opportunity.

☐ Have the punctured wheel repaired as soon as possible, or another puncture will leave you stranded.

Note: *All models that have a spare wheel, are supplied with a special lightweight 'space-saver' spare wheel, the tyre being narrower than standard. The 'space-saver' spare wheel is intended only for temporary use, and must be replaced with a standard wheel as soon as possible. Drive with particular care with this wheel fitted, especially through corners and when braking; do not exceed 50 mph.*

Note: *Models that do not have a spare wheel are supplied with a small compressor and a bottle of leak sealing solution. Full instructions for the use of the compressor and sealant are supplied with the kit.*

Towing

When all else fails, you may find yourself having to get a tow home – or of course you may be helping somebody else. Long-distance recovery should only be done by a garage or breakdown service. For shorter distances, DIY towing using another car is easy enough, but observe the following points:

☐ Use a proper tow-rope – they are not expensive. The vehicle being towed must display an ON TOW sign in its rear window.

☐ Always turn the ignition key to the 'On' position when the vehicle is being towed, so that the steering lock is released, and the direction indicator and brake lights work.

☐ The towing eye is of the screw-in type, and is found in the spare wheel well with the jack and wheel brace. The towing eye screws into a threaded hole, accessible after prising out a cover on the right-hand side of the front and rear bumper covers. Use the end of the wheel brace to unclip the plastic covers if required **(see illustrations)**. **Note:** *The towing eye has a left-hand thread – rotate it anti-clockwise to install it, using the wheel brace to make sure it is secure.*

☐ Before being towed, release the handbrake and make sure the transmission is in neutral. On models with automatic transmission, special precautions apply – do not exceed 30 mph or travel further than 30 miles, and the wheels must always roll forwards.

☐ Note that greater-than-usual pedal pressure will be required to operate the brakes, since the vacuum servo unit is only operational with the engine running.

☐ The driver of the car being towed must keep the tow-rope taut at all times to avoid snatching.

☐ Make sure that both drivers know the route before setting off.

☐ Only drive at moderate speeds and keep the distance towed to a minimum. Drive smoothly and allow plenty of time for slowing down at junctions.

Unclip the cover...

...and secure the rear towing eye

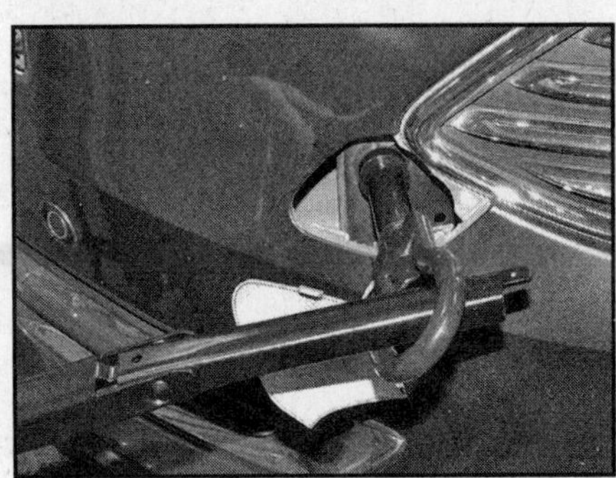

Fitting the front towing eye

Identifying leaks

Puddles on the garage floor or drive, or obvious wetness under the bonnet or underneath the car, suggest a leak that needs investigating. It can sometimes be difficult to decide where the leak is coming from, especially if an engine undershield is fitted. Leaking oil or fluid can also be blown rearwards by the passage of air under the car, giving a false impression of where the problem lies.

Most automotive oils and fluids are poisonous. Wash them off skin, and change out of contaminated clothing, without delay.

The smell of a fluid leaking from the car may provide a clue to what's leaking. Some fluids are distinctively coloured. It may help to remove the engine undershield, clean the car carefully and to park it over some clean paper overnight as an aid to locating the source of the leak. Remember that some leaks may only occur while the engine is running.

Sump oil

ngine oil may leak from the drain plug...

Oil from filter

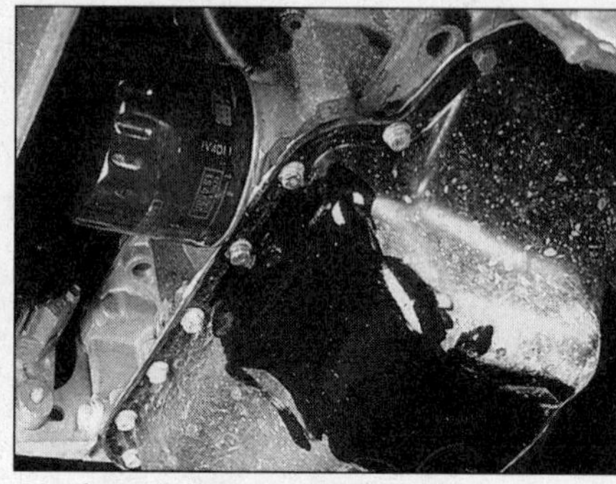

...or from the base of the oil filter.

Gearbox oil

Gearbox oil can leak from the seals at the inboard ends of the driveshafts.

Antifreeze

Leaking antifreeze often leaves a crystalline deposit like this.

Brake fluid

A leak occurring at a wheel is almost certainly brake fluid.

Power steering fluid

Power steering fluid may leak from the pipe connectors on the steering rack.

Introduction

There are some very simple checks which need only take a few minutes to carry out, but which could save you a lot of inconvenience and expense.

These checks require no great skill or special tools, and the small amount of time they take to perform could prove to be very well spent, for example:

☐ Keeping an eye on tyre condition and pressures, will not only help to stop them wearing out prematurely, but could also save your life.

☐ Many breakdowns are caused by electrical problems. Battery-related faults are particularly common, and a quick check on a regular basis will often prevent the majority of these.

☐ If your car develops a brake fluid leak, the first time you might know about it is when your brakes don't work properly. Checking the level regularly will give advance warning of this kind of problem.

☐ If the oil or coolant levels run low, the cost of repairing any engine damage will be far greater than fixing the leak, for example.

Underbonnet check points

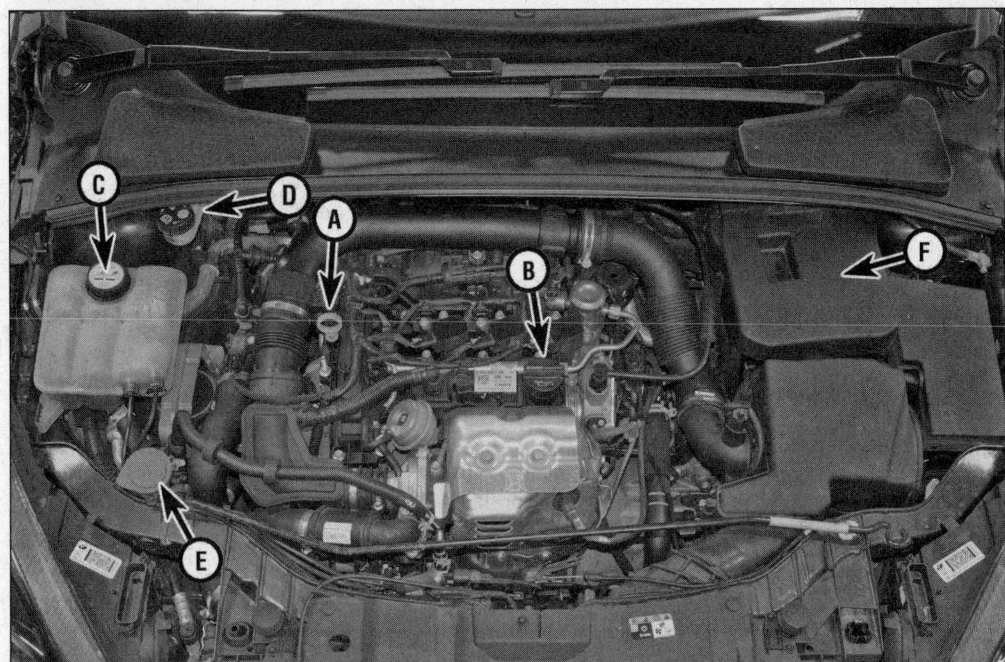

◀ 1.0 litre petrol engine

A *Engine oil level dipstick*
B *Engine oil filler cap*
C *Coolant expansion tank*
D *Brake and clutch fluid reservoir*
E *Screen washer fluid reservoir*
F *Battery*

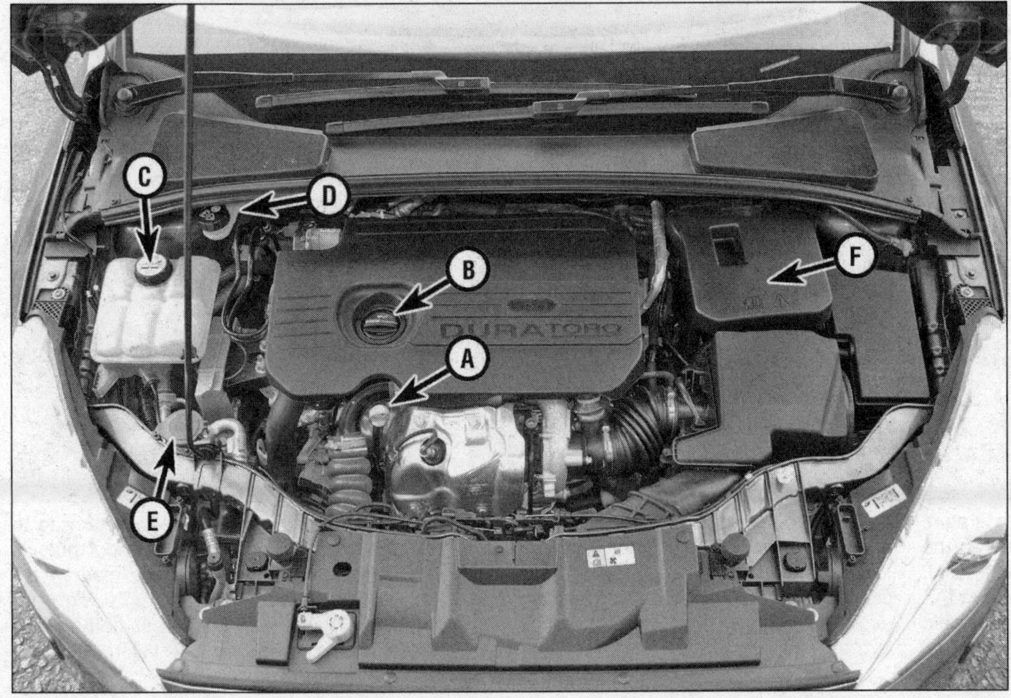

◀ 1.5 litre diesel engine

A *Engine oil level dipstick*
B *Engine oil filler cap*
C *Coolant expansion tank*
D *Brake and clutch fluid reservoir*
E *Screen washer fluid reservoir*
F *Battery*

Engine oil level

Before you start

✔ Make sure that the car is on level ground.
✔ Check the oil level before the car is driven, or at least 5 minutes after the engine has been switched off.

If the oil is checked immediately after driving the vehicle, some of the oil will remain in the upper engine components, resulting in an inaccurate reading on the dipstick.

The correct oil

Modern engines place great demands on their oil. It is very important that the correct oil for your car is used (see *Lubricants and fluids*).

Car care

- If you have to add oil frequently, you should check whether you have any oil leaks. Place some clean paper under the car overnight, and check for stains in the morning. If there are no leaks, then the engine may be burning oil.
- Always maintain the level between the upper and lower dipstick marks (see photo 2). If the level is too low, severe engine damage may occur. Oil seal failure may result if the engine is overfilled by adding too much oil.

1 Withdraw the dipstick and using a clean rag or paper towel, remove all oil from the dipstick. The dipstick has a brightly coloured top for easy identification (see Underbonnet check points for exact location depending on engine).

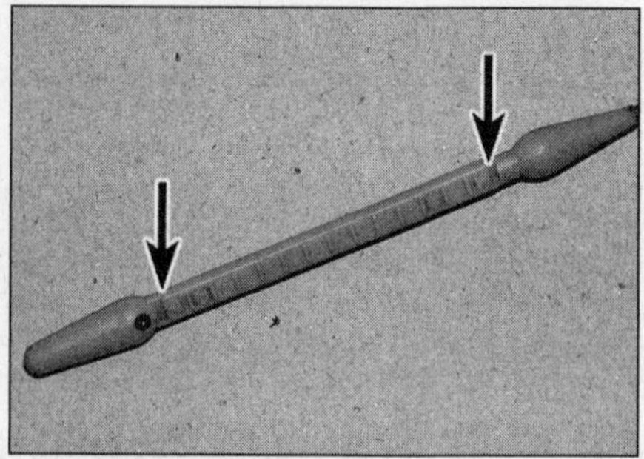

2 Insert the dipstick into the tube as far as it will go, then withdraw it again. Note the oil level on the end of the dipstick, which should be between the MAX and MIN marks. If the oil level is only just above, or below, the MIN mark, topping-up is required.

3 Oil is added through the filler cap. Unscrew the filler cap and then top up the level of the oil (1.5 litre diesel engine shown).

4 Add the oil slowly, checking the level on the dipstick often, and allowing time for the oil to run to the sump; a funnel may be useful to prevent any spillage. Add oil until the level is just up to the MAX mark on the dipstick – DO NOT overfill (see *Car care*)

Coolant level

Warning: Do not attempt to remove the expansion tank pressure cap when the engine is hot, as there is a very great risk of scalding. Do not leave open containers of coolant about, as it is poisonous.

Car care

- With a sealed-type cooling system, adding coolant should not be necessary on a regular basis. If frequent topping-up is required, it is likely there is a leak. Check the radiator, all hoses and joint faces for signs of staining or wetness, and rectify as necessary
- It is important that antifreeze is used in the cooling system all year round, not just during the winter months. Don't top up with water alone, as the antifreeze will become diluted.

1 Coolant level varies with the temperature of the engine, and is visible through the expansion tank. When the engine is cold, the coolant level should be between the MAX and MIN marks on the front of the reservoir. When the engine is hot, the level may rise slightly above the MAX mark.

2 If topping-up is necessary, wait until the engine is cold. Slowly unscrew the expansion tank cap, to release any pressure present in the cooling system, and remove it.

3 Add a mixture of water and antifreeze to the expansion tank until the coolant level is halfway between the levelmarks. Use only the specified antifreeze – if using Ford antifreeze, make sure it is the same type and colour as that already in the system. Refit the cap and tighten it securely.

Brake and clutch fluid level

Note: *All manual transmission models have a hydraulically-operated clutch, which uses the same fluid as the braking system.*

Warning:

- ***Brake fluid can harm your eyes and damage painted surfaces, so use extreme caution when handling and pouring it.***
- ***Do not use fluid that has been standing open for some time, as it absorbs moisture from the air, which can cause a dangerous loss of braking effectiveness.***
- ***The fluid level in the reservoir will drop slightly as the brake pads wear down, but the fluid level must never be allowed to drop below the MIN mark.***

Before you start

✔ Make sure that your car is on level ground.

Safety first!

● If the reservoir requires repeated topping-up this is an indication of a fluid leak somewhere in the system, which should be investigated immediately.

● If a leak is suspected, the car should not be driven until the braking system has been checked. Never take any risks where brakes are concerned.

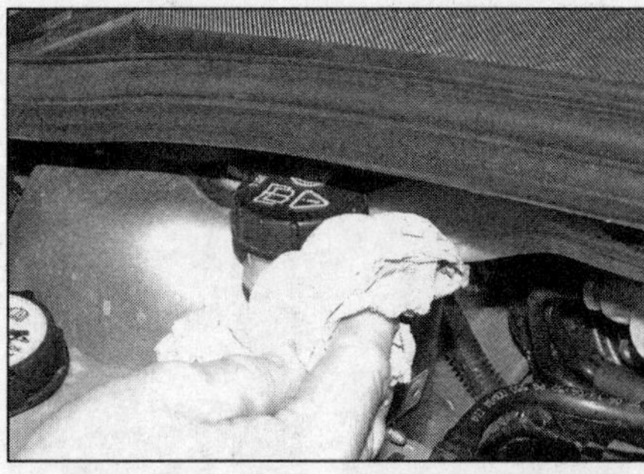

1 The brake fluid reservoir is located on the right-hand side of the engine compartment. Wipe clean the area around the filler cap, before removing the cap

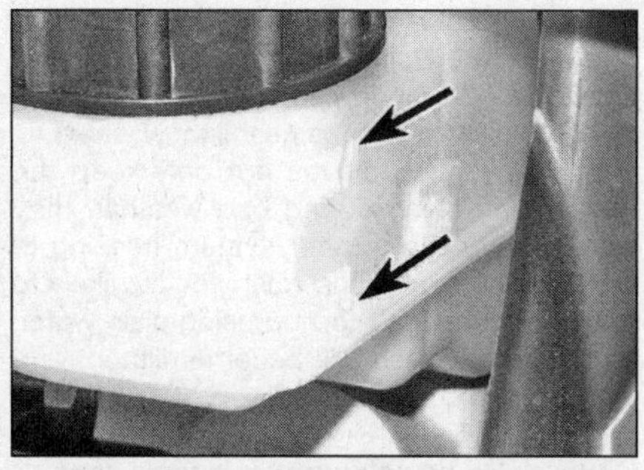

2 The MAX and MIN marks are indicated on the front of the reservoir. The fluid level must be kept between the marks at all times.

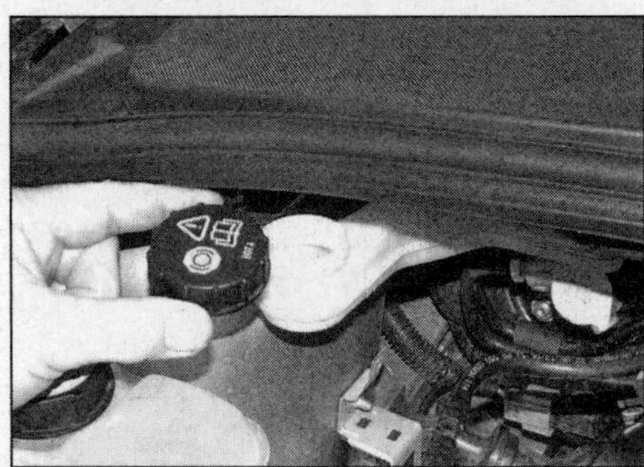

3 If topping-up is necessary, first wipe clean the area around the filler cap to prevent dirt entering the hydraulic system. Unscrew the reservoir cap and carefully lift it out of position, holding the wiring connector plug and taking care not to damage the level sender float. Inspect the reservoir; if the fluid is dirty, the hydraulic system should be drained and refilled (see Chapter 1).

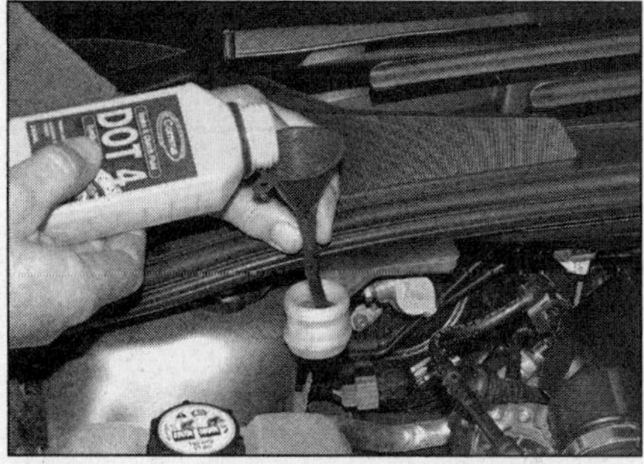

4 Carefully add fluid, taking care not to spill it onto the surrounding components. Use only the specified fluid;mixing different types can cause damage to the system. After topping-up to the correct level, securely refit the cap and wipe off any spilt fluid.

Power steering fluid level

✔ Park the vehicle on level ground.
✔ Set the steering wheel straight-ahead.
✔ The engine should be turned off.

For the check to be accurate, the steering must not be turned while the level is being checked.

Safety first!

● The need for frequent topping-up indicates a leak, which should be investigated immediately.

1 The reservoir is mounted at the front right-hand side of the engine compartment. The fluid level can be viewed through the reservoir body, and should be between the MIN and MAX marks when the engine is cold. If the level is checked when the engine is running or hot, the level may rise slightly above the MAX mark.

2 If topping-up is necessary, use the specified type of fluid – do not overfill the reservoir. Undo the reservoir cap. Take care not to introduce dirt into the system when topping-up. When the level is correct, securely refit the cap.

Washer fluid level

● The windscreen washer reservoir also supplies the tailgate washer jet, where applicable. On models so equipped, the same reservoir also serves the headlight washers.
● Screenwash additives not only keep the windscreen clean during bad weather, they also prevent the washer system freezing in cold weather – which is when you are likely to need it most. Don't top-up using plain water, as the screenwash will become diluted, and will freeze in cold weather.

Caution: On no account use engine coolant antifreeze in the screen washer system – this may damage the paintwork.

1 The washer fluid reservoir filler neck is located at the front of the engine compartment. The washer level cannot easily be seen. Remove the filler cap, and look down the filler neck – if fluid is not visible, topping-up may be required.

2 When topping-up the reservoir, add a screenwash additive in the quantities recommended on the additive bottle.

Wiper blades

● Only fit good-quality wiper blades.
● When removing an old wiper blade, note how it is fitted. Fitting new blades can be a tricky exercise, and noting how the old blade came off can save time.
● While the wiper blade is removed, take care not to knock the wiper arm from its locked position, or it could strike the glass.
● Offer the new blade into position the same way round as the old one. Ensure that it clicks home securely, otherwise it may come off in use, damaging the glass.
Note: *Fitting details for wiper blades vary according to model, and according to whether genuine Ford wiper blades have been fitted. Use the procedures and illustrations shown as a guide for your car.*

If smearing is still a problem despite fitting new wiper blades, try cleaning the glass with neat screenwash additive or methylated spirit.

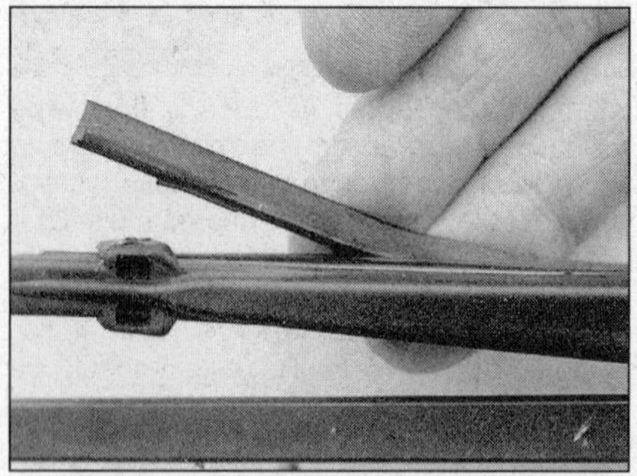

1 Check the condition of the wiper blades; if they are cracked or show any signs of deterioration, or if the glass swept area is smeared, renew them. It is recommended that the wiper blades be renewed annually, regardless of their apparent condition.

2 To remove a windscreen wiper blade, pull the arm fully away from the glass and depress the square locking button.

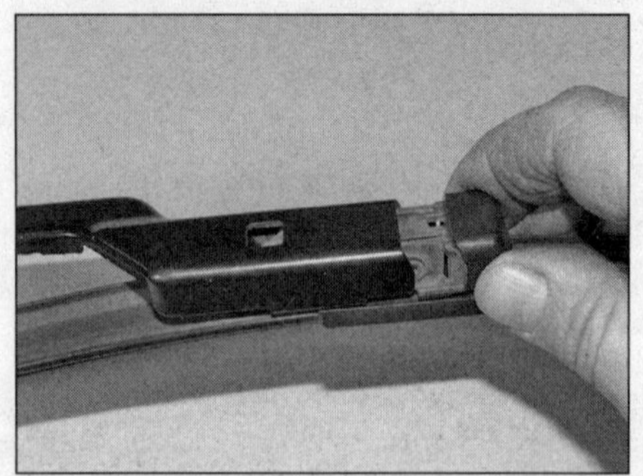

3 Slide the blade upwards...

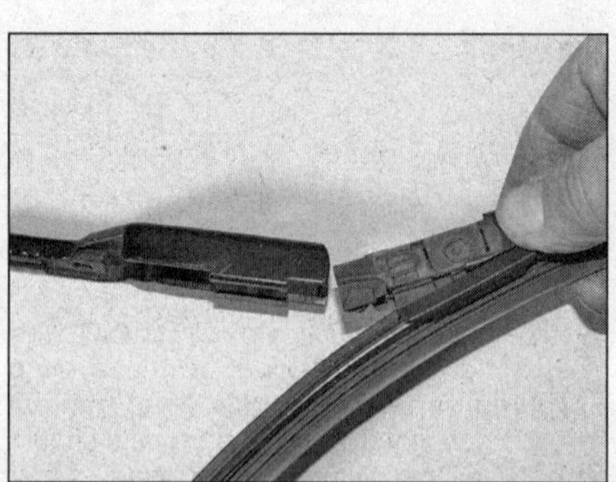

4 ...and release it from the wiper arm

5 To remove the tailgate blade, lift the arm from the rear screen, then tilt the blade and pull it from the arm.

Tyre condition and pressure

It is very important that tyres are in good condition, and at the correct pressure - having a tyre failure at any speed is highly dangerous.
Tyre wear is influenced by driving style - harsh braking and acceleration, or fast cornering, will all produce more rapid tyre wear. As a general rule, the front tyres wear out faster than the rears. Interchanging the tyres from front to rear ("rotating" the tyres) may result in more even wear. However, if this is completely effective, you may have the expense of replacing all four tyres at once!
Remove any nails or stones embedded in the tread before they penetrate the tyre to cause deflation. If removal of a nail does reveal that the tyre has been punctured, refit the nail so that its point of penetration is marked. Then immediately change the wheel, and have the tyre repaired by a tyre dealer.
Regularly check the tyres for damage in the form of cuts or bulges, especially in the sidewalls. Periodically remove the wheels, and clean any dirt or mud from the inside and outside surfaces. Examine the wheel rims for signs of rusting, corrosion or other damage. Light alloy wheels are easily damaged by "kerbing" whilst parking; steel wheels may also become dented or buckled. A new wheel is very often the only way to overcome severe damage.
New tyres should be balanced when they are fitted, but it may become necessary to re-balance them as they wear, or if the balance weights fitted to the wheel rim should fall off. Unbalanced tyres will wear more quickly, as will the steering and suspension components. Wheel imbalance is normally signified by vibration, particularly at a certain speed (typically around 50 mph). If this vibration is felt only through the steering, then it is likely that just the front wheels need balancing. If, however, the vibration is felt through the whole car, the rear wheels could be out of balance. Wheel balancing should be carried out by a tyre dealer or garage.

1 *Tread Depth - visual check*
The original tyres have tread wear safety bands (B), which will appear when the tread depth reaches approximately 1.6 mm. The band positions are indicated by a triangular mark on the tyre sidewall (A).

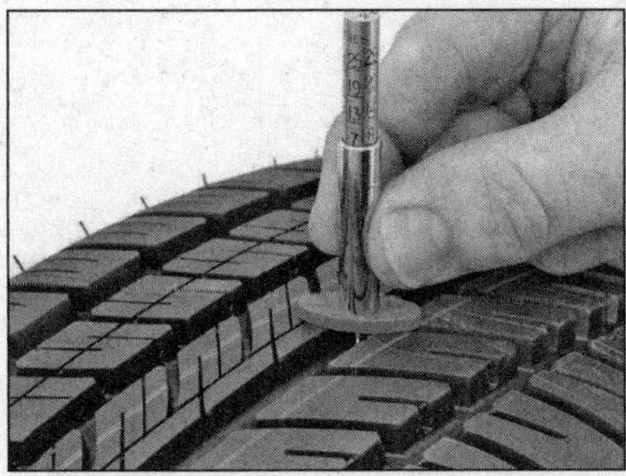

2 *Tread Depth - manual check*
Alternatively, tread wear can be monitored with a simple, inexpensive device known as a tread depth indicator gauge.

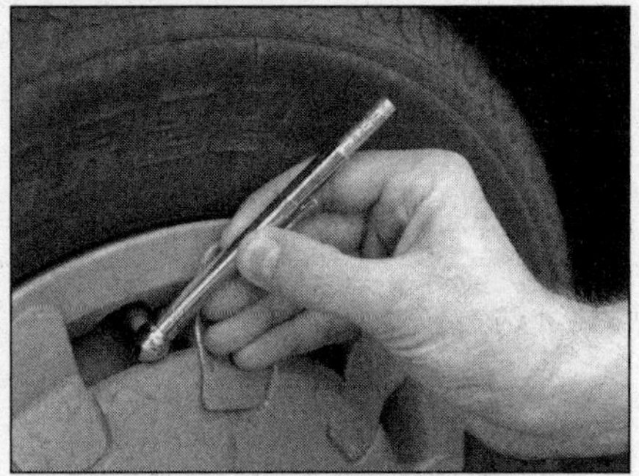

3 *Tyre Pressure Check*
Check the tyre pressures regularly with the tyres cold. Do not adjust the tyre pressures immediately after the vehicle has been used, or an inaccurate setting will result.

Tyre tread wear patterns

Shoulder Wear

Underinflation (wear on both sides)
Under-inflation will cause overheating of the tyre, because the tyre will flex too much, and the tread will not sit correctly on the road surface. This will cause a loss of grip and excessive wear, not to mention the danger of sudden tyre failure due to heat build-up.
Check and adjust pressures
Incorrect wheel camber (wear on one side)
Repair or renew suspension parts
Hard cornering
Reduce speed!

Centre Wear

Overinflation
Over-inflation will cause rapid wear of the centre part of the tyre tread, coupled with reduced grip, harsher ride, and the danger of shock damage occurring in the tyre casing.
Check and adjust pressures

If you sometimes have to inflate your car's tyres to the higher pressures specified for maximum load or sustained high speed, don't forget to reduce the pressures to normal afterwards.

Uneven Wear

Front tyres may wear unevenly as a result of wheel misalignment. Most tyre dealers and garages can check and adjust the wheel alignment (or "tracking") for a modest charge.
Incorrect camber or castor
Repair or renew suspension parts
Malfunctioning suspension
Repair or renew suspension parts
Unbalanced wheel
Balance tyres
Incorrect toe setting
Adjust front wheel alignment
Note: *The feathered edge of the tread which typifies toe wear is best checked by feel.*

Battery

Caution: Before carrying out any work on the vehicle battery, read the precautions given in 'Safety first!' at the start of this manual.

✔Make sure that the battery tray is in good condition, and that the clamp is tight. Corrosion on the tray, retaining clamp and the battery itself can be removed with a solution of water and baking soda. Thoroughly rinse all cleaned areas with water. Any metal parts damaged by corrosion should be covered with a zinc-based primer, then painted.

✔Periodically (approximately every three months), check the charge condition of the battery, as described in Chapter 5A Section 2.

✔If the battery is flat, and you need to jump start your vehicle, see Roadside repairs Section 4.

✔Battery corrosion can be kept to a minimum by applying a layer of petroleum jelly to the clamps and terminals after they are recommended.

1 The battery is located in the left-hand rear corner of the engine compartment.

2 Unclip and remove the battery cover to gain access. The exterior of the battery should be inspected periodically for damage such as a cracked case or cover.

3 Check the tightness of battery clamps to ensure good electrical connections. You should not be able to move them. Also check each cable for cracks and frayed conductors.

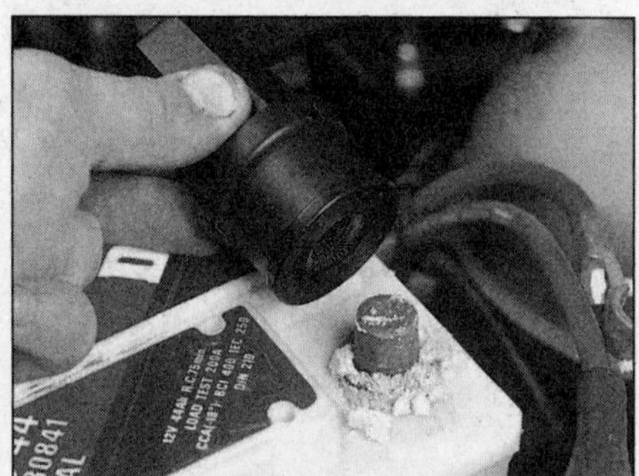

4 If corrosion (white, fluffy deposits) is evident, remove the cables from the battery terminals, clean them with a small wire brush, then refit them. Automotive stores sell a tool for cleaning the battery post…

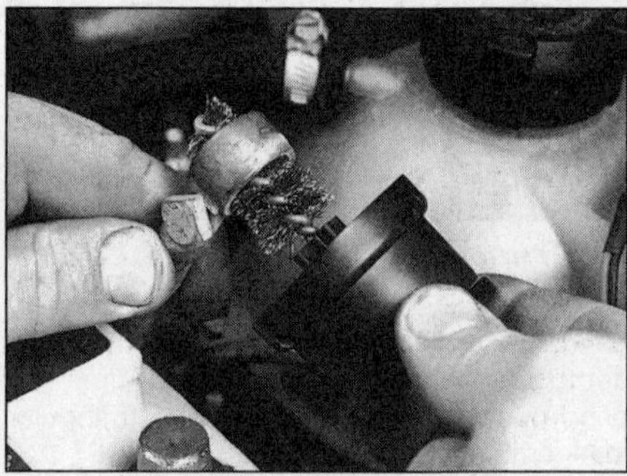

5 …as well as the battery cable clamps

Bulbs and fuses

✔ Check all external lights and the horn. Refer to Chapter 12 Section 2 for details if any of the circuits are found to be inoperative.

✔ Visually check all accessible wiring connectors, harnesses and retaining clips for security, and for signs of chafing or damage.

If you need to check your brake lights and indicators unaided, back up to a wall or garage door and operate the lights. The reflected light should show if they are working properly.

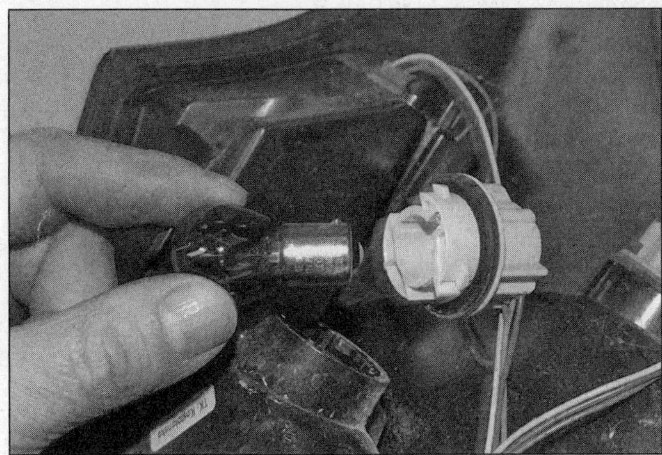

1 If a single indicator light, stop-light or headlight has failed, it is likely that a bulb has blown and will need to be renewed. Refer to Chapter 12 for details. If both stop-lights have failed, it is possible that the switch has failed (see Chapter 9).

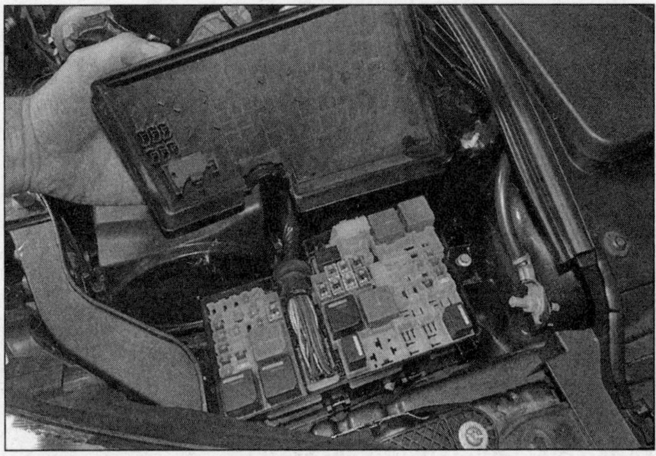

2 If more than one indicator light or tail light has failed, it is likely that either a fuse has blown or that there is a fault in the circuit. The main fusebox is located in the engine compartment on the left-hand side. Unclip and remove the cover for access. Refer to the wiring diagrams at the end of this manual for details of fuse locations and circuits protected.

3 Additional fuses are located in the passenger compartment fuse/relay box which is located behind the glovebox.

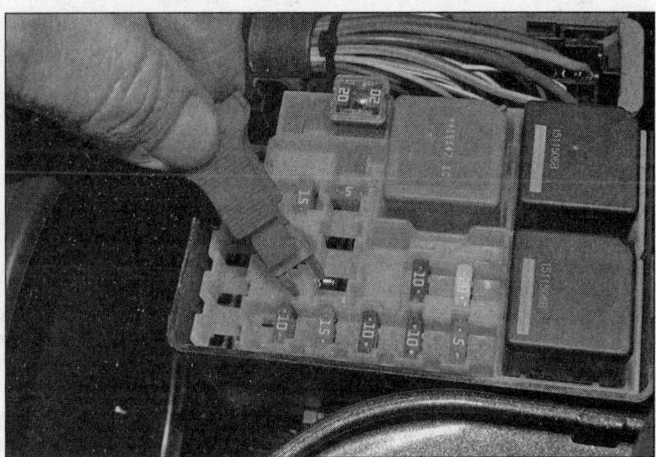

4 To renew a blown fuse, simply pull it out and fit a new fuse of the correct rating. A fuse removal tool, is provided on the inside of the fusebox lid in the engine compartment. If the fuse blows again, it is important that you find out why – a complete checking procedure is given in Chapter 12.

Lubricants and fluids

Engine:	
Petrol engines	
1.0 litre engines	Multigrade engine oil, viscosity SAE 5W/20 to Ford specification WSS-M2C948-B
1.6 litre engines	Multigrade engine oil, viscosity SAE 5W/20 to Ford specification WSS-M2C948-B or alternatively 5W/30 to Ford specification WSS-M2C913-D
Diesel engines	
1.5 litre engines	Multigrade engine oil, viscosity 0W/30 engine oil to Ford specification WSS-M2C950-A or alternatively 5W/30 engine oil to Ford specification WSS-M2C913-C/D
1.6 litre engines	Multigrade engine oil, viscosity 5W/30 engine oil to Ford specification WSS-M2C913-C/D
Cooling system	Motorcraft SuperPlus antifreeze to Ford specification WSS-M97B44-D
Manual transmission	SAE 75W FE gear oil to Ford specification WSD-M2C200-D2
Brake and clutch hydraulic system	Hydraulic fluid to Ford specification WSS-M6C65-A2 (ISO 4925, Class 6) Super DOT 4
Power steering	Ford or Motorcraft power steering fluid to Ford specification WSS-M2C204-A2

Tyre pressures

The tyre pressures for your vehicle are given on a label affixed to the drivers door pillar **(see illustration).**

Note: *Pressures apply to original-equipment tyres, and may vary if any other make of tyre is fitted; check with the tyre manufacturer or supplier for the correct pressures if necessary.*

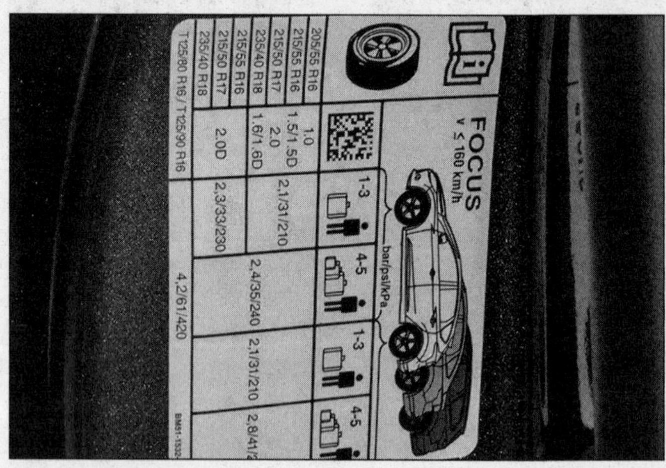

Tyre pressures label on the door pillar – (1.5 diesel engine model shown)

Chapter 1 Part A
Routine maintenance and servicing – petrol models

Contents

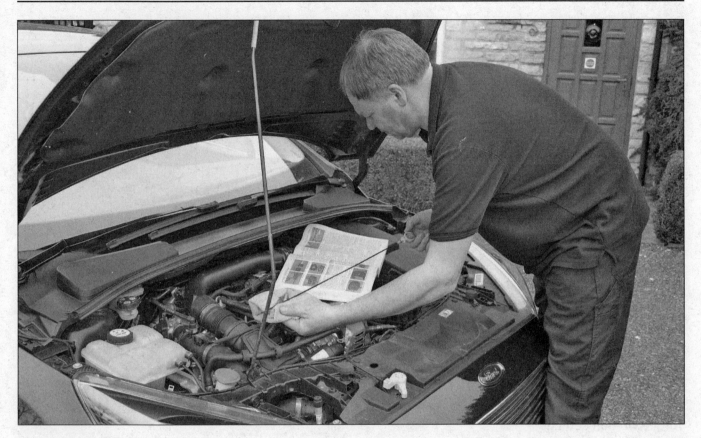

Degrees of difficulty

Easy, suitable for novice with little experience 	**Fairly easy,** suitable for beginner with some experience	**Fairly difficult,** suitable for competent DIY mechanic	**Difficult,** suitable for experienced DIY mechanic	**Very difficult,** suitable for expert DIY or professional 

1 Servicing specifications

Lubricants and fluids	Refer to end of *Weekly checks*	
Capacities		
Engine oil (including filter)		
1.0 litre engines	4.6 litres	
1.6 litre engines	4.6 litres	
Cooling system (approximate)	6.0 litres	
Manual transmission:		
5 speed (B5/IB5)	2.3 litres	
6 speed (B6)	1.67 litres	
Washer fluid reservoir		
Without headlamp washers	3.0 litres	
With headlamp washers	4.5 litres	
Fuel tank – all models	55.0 litres	
Cooling system		
Antifreeze mixture:		
50% antifreeze	Protection down to –37°C	
55% antifreeze	Protection down to –45°C	
Note: *Refer to antifreeze manufacturer for latest recommendations.*		
Ignition system		
Spark plugs type	Refer to Ford dealer or parts specialist	
Spark plug gap		
1.0 litre	0.7 mm	
1.6 (Ti-VCT)	1.2 mm	
1.6 (EcoBoost)	0.8 mm	
Brakes		
Friction material minimum thickness:		
Front or rear brake pads	1.5 mm	
Rear brake shoes	1.0 mm	
Remote control battery		
Type	CR2032, 3V	
Torque wrench settings	**Nm**	**lbf ft**
Drivebelt automatic tensioner bolts (1.6 EcoBoost engines)	48	35
Engine mounting bolts (right-hand, 1.6 EcoBoost engines):		
To engine	90	66
To chassis	80	60
Engine mounting damper (1.6 EcoBoost engines)	90	66
Engine oil drain plug:		
1.0 litre engines	25	18
1.6 litre engines	28	21
Ignition coil retaining bolts	10	7
Manual transmission oil level/filler plug	35	26
Roadwheel nuts	135	100
Spark plugs:		
1.0 litre models	13	10
1.6 litre models	15	11

2 Maintenance schedule

The maintenance intervals in this manual are provided with the assumption that you, not the dealer, will be carrying out the work. These are the minimum maintenance intervals recommended by us for vehicles driven daily. If you wish to keep your vehicle in peak condition at all times, you may wish to perform some of these procedures more often. We encourage frequent maintenance, because it enhances the efficiency, performance and resale value of your vehicle.

If the vehicle is driven in dusty areas, used to tow a trailer, or driven frequently at slow speeds (idling in traffic) or on short journeys, more frequent maintenance intervals are recommended.

When the vehicle is new, it should be serviced by a dealer service department (or other workshop recognised by the vehicle manufacturer as providing the same standard of service) in order to preserve the warranty. The vehicle manufacturer may reject warranty claims if you are unable to prove that servicing has been carried out as and when specified, using only original equipment parts or parts certified to be of equivalent quality.

Every 250 miles or weekly

- ☐ Refer to *Weekly checks*

Every 12 500 miles or 12 months, whichever comes first

- ☐ Renew the engine oil and oil filter (Section 6)
- ☐ Check the condition of the auxiliary drivebelt (Section 23)
- ☐ Check the operation of the lights and the horn (Section 7)
- ☐ Check under the bonnet for fluid leaks and hose condition (Section 8)
- ☐ Check the condition of the engine compartment wiring (Section 9)
- ☐ Check the condition of the brake pads, shoes and discs (Section 10)
- ☐ Check the exhaust system (Section 11)
- ☐ Check the steering and suspension components for condition and security (Section 12)
- ☐ Check the condition of the driveshaft joints and gaiters (Section 13)
- ☐ Check the underbody and all fuel/brake lines (Section 14)
- ☐ Lubricate all hinges and locks (Section 15)
- ☐ Roadwheel nuts tightness check (Section 16)
- ☐ Carry out a road test (Section 17)
- ☐ Check and if necessary adjust the handbrake (Section 18)
- ☐ Check the condition of the seat belts (Section 19)
- ☐ Check the antifreeze/inhibitor strength (Section 28)

Every 37 500 miles or 3 years, whichever comes first

In addition to the items listed above, carry out the following:

- ☐ Renew the air filter (Section 20)*
- ☐ Renew the spark plugs (Section 21)

* **Note:** *If the vehicle is used in dusty conditions, the air filter should be renewed more frequently.*

Every 80 000 miles

- ☐ Renew the timing belt and tensioners – 1.6 engines (Section 22)

Note: *The Ford interval for belt renewal is actually at a much higher mileage than this (100 000 miles or 8 years on Ti-VCT engines and 125 000 on miles or 10 years on EcoBoost engines). It is strongly recommended, however, that the interval is reduced to 80 000 miles, particularly on vehicles which are subjected to intensive use, ie, mainly short journeys or a lot of stop-start driving. The actual belt renewal interval is therefore very much up to the individual owner, but bear in mind that severe engine damage will result if the belt breaks*

Every 100 000 miles or 8 years, whichever comes first

- ☐ Renew the auxiliary belt (Section 23)
- ☐ Renew the timing belt and tensioners – 1.0 litre engines (Section 24)

Note: *The Ford interval for belt renewal is actually at a much higher mileage than this (150 000 miles or 10 years). It is strongly recommended, however, that the interval is reduced to 100 000 miles, particularly on vehicles which are subjected to intensive use, ie, mainly short journeys or a lot of stop-start driving. The actual belt renewal interval is therefore very much up to the individual owner, but bear in mind that severe engine damage will result if the belt breaks.*

Every 2 years, regardless of mileage

- ☐ Renew the pollen filter (Section 25)
- ☐ Renew the brake fluid (Section 26)
- ☐ Renew remote control battery (Section 27)
- ☐ Renew the coolant (Section 28)

Note: *If the vehicle is used in dusty conditions, the pollen filter should be renewed more frequently.*

Note: *If Ford 'Superplus' antifreeze is used, the coolant can then be left for a maximum of ten years, providing the strength of the mixture is checked every year. If any antifreeze other than Ford's is to be used, the coolant must be renewed at regular intervals to provide an equivalent degree of protection; the conventional recommendation is to renew the coolant every two years.*

3 Component location

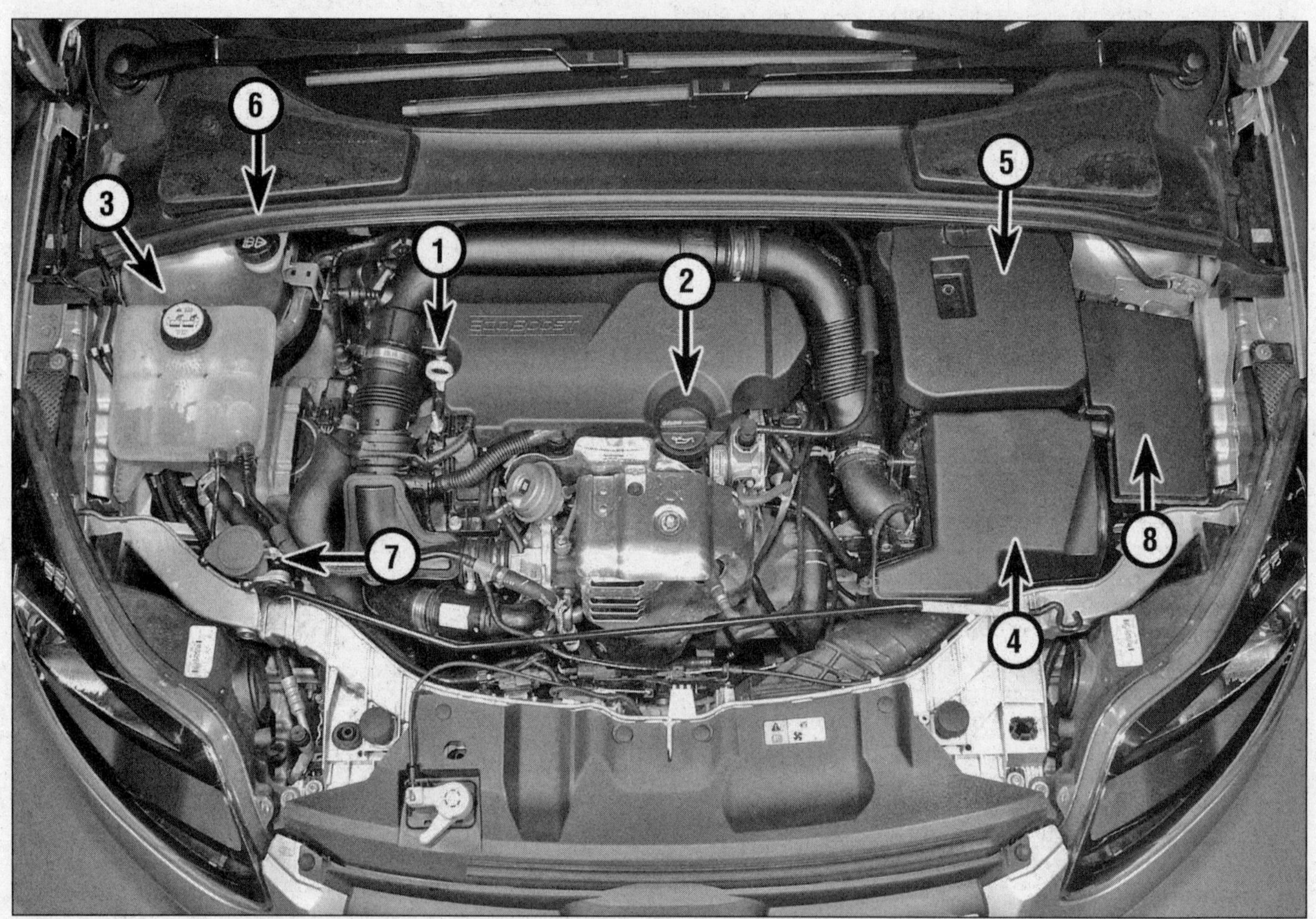

Underbonnet view of a 1.0 litre model

1 Engine oil level dipstick
2 Oil filler cap
3 Coolant expansion tank cap
4 Air filter element cover
5 Battery cover
6 Brake and clutch fluid reservoir
7 Washer fluid reservoir cap
8 Fuse/relay box

Front underbody view

1 Oil filter
2 Engine oil drain plug
3 Suspension control arm
4 Transmission drain plug
5 Right-hand driveshaft
6 Air conditioning compressor
7 Oxygen sensor
8 Starter motor

Rear underbody view

1 Anti-roll bar
2 Handbrake cable
3 Fuel tank
4 Silencer
5 Shock absorber
6 Lateral link
7 Lower control arm
8 Tie rod

4 General Information

1 This Chapter is designed to help the home mechanic maintain his/her vehicle for safety, economy, long life and peak performance.
2 The Chapter contains a master maintenance schedule, followed by Sections dealing specifically with each task in the schedule. Visual checks, adjustments, component renewal and other helpful items are included. Refer to the accompanying illustrations of the engine compartment and the underside of the vehicle for the locations of the various components.
3 Servicing your vehicle in accordance with the mileage/time maintenance schedule and the following Sections will provide a planned maintenance programme, which should result in a long and reliable service life. This is a comprehensive plan, so maintaining some items but not others at the specified service intervals, will not produce the same results.
4 As you service your vehicle, you will discover that many of the procedures can – and should – be grouped together, because of the particular procedure being performed, or because of the proximity of two otherwise-unrelated components to one another. For example, if the vehicle is raised for any reason, the exhaust can be inspected at the same time as the suspension and steering components.
5 The first step in this maintenance programme is to prepare yourself before the actual work begins. Read through all the Sections relevant to the work to be carried out, then make a list and gather all the parts and tools required. If a problem is encountered, seek advice from a parts specialist, or a dealer service department.

5 Regular maintenance

1 If, from the time the vehicle is new, the routine maintenance schedule is followed closely, and frequent checks are made of fluid levels and high-wear items, as suggested throughout this manual, the engine will be kept in relatively good running condition, and the need for additional work will be minimised.
2 It is possible that there will be times when the engine is running poorly due to the lack of regular maintenance. This is even more likely if a used vehicle, which has not received regular and frequent maintenance checks, is purchased. In such cases, additional work may need to be carried out, outside of the regular maintenance intervals.
3 If engine wear is suspected, a compression test (refer to Chapter 2A or 2B, as applicable) will provide valuable information regarding the overall performance of the main internal components. Such a test can be used as a basis to decide on the extent of the work to be carried out. If, for example, a compression test indicates serious internal engine wear, conventional maintenance as described in this Chapter will not greatly improve the performance of the engine, and may prove a waste of time and money, unless extensive overhaul work is carried out first.
4 The following series of operations are those most often required to improve the performance of a generally poor-running engine:

Primary operations

a) Clean, inspect and test the battery (refer to 'Weekly checks').
b) Check all the engine-related fluids (refer to 'Weekly checks').
c) Check the condition and tension of the auxiliary drivebelt (Section 23).
d) Renew the spark plugs (Section 21).
e) Check the condition of the air filter, and renew if necessary (Section 20).
f) Check the condition of all hoses, and check for fluid leaks (Section 8).

5 If the above operations do not prove fully effective, carry out the following secondary operations:

Secondary operations

6 All items listed under Primary operations, plus the following:
a) Check the charging system (refer to Chapter 5A).
b) Check the ignition system (refer to Chapter 5B).
c) Check the fuel system (refer to Chapter 4A).

6 Engine oil and filter renewal

1 Frequent oil and filter changes are the most important preventative maintenance procedures which can be undertaken by the DIY owner. As engine oil ages, it becomes diluted and contaminated, which leads to premature engine wear.
2 Before starting this procedure, gather together all the necessary tools and materials. Also make sure that you have plenty of clean rags and newspapers handy, to mop-up any spills. Ideally, the engine oil should be warm, as it will drain more easily, and more built-up sludge will be removed with it.
3 Take care not to touch the exhaust (especially the catalytic converter) or any other hot parts of the engine when working under the vehicle. To avoid any possibility of scalding, and to protect yourself from possible skin irritants and other harmful contaminants in used engine oils, it is advisable to wear gloves when carrying out this work.
4 If not already done, firmly apply the handbrake, then jack up the front of the vehicle and support it on axle stands (see

6.4a Where fitted, remove the air deflector trim along the front edge...

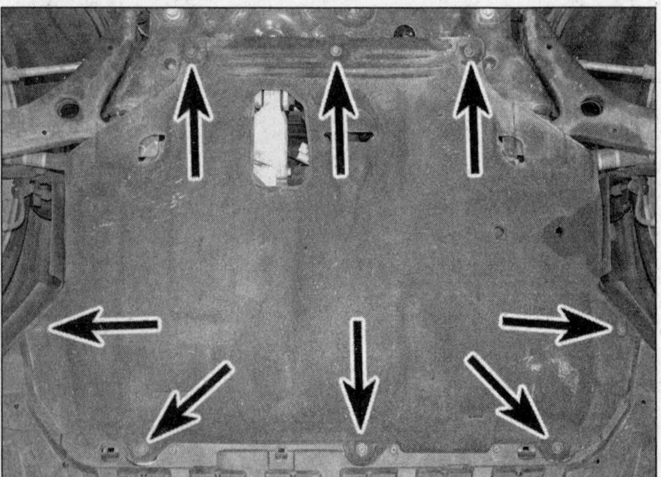

6.4b then remove the undershield fasteners (arrowed)

6.6a Slacken the engine oil sump drain plug...

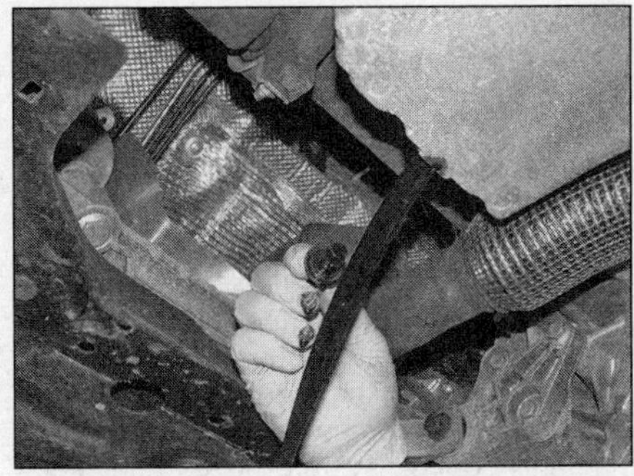
6.6b ...and then remove it completely (1.0 litre engine shown)

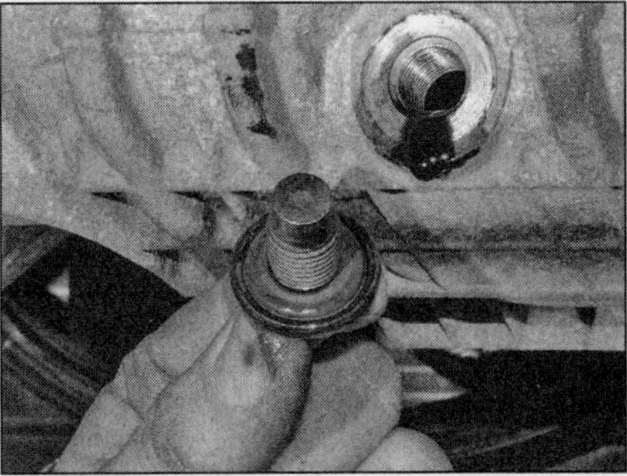
6.8 The seal is integral with the drain plug

Jacking and vehicle support). Where fitted, unscrew the three screws and remove the plastic air deflector trim from along the front edge of the engine undershield. Remove the 8 fasteners to remove the undershield from below the engine compartment **(see illustrations)**.

5 Open the bonnet and remove the oil filler cap from the top of the camshaft cover. If required, remove the plastic engine cover.

6 Using a spanner, or preferably a socket and bar, slacken the sump drain plug about half a turn. Position the draining container under the drain plug, then remove the plug completely **(see illustrations)**.

7 Allow some time for the oil to drain, noting that it may be necessary to reposition the container as the oil flow slows to a trickle.

8 After all the oil has drained, wipe the drain plug with a clean rag. Examine the condition of the drain plug sealing ring, and renew it if it shows signs of flattening or other damage which may prevent an oil-tight seal (it is generally considered good practice to fit a new seal every time. Note that the seal is integral with the drain plug **(see illustration)**. Clean the area around the drain plug opening, and refit the plug complete with the seal and tighten it to the specified torque.

9 Move the container into position under the oil filter, which is located on the front of the cylinder block on 1.6 litre engines and at the rear (above the driveshaft) on 1.0 litre engines **(see illustrations)**.

10 Use an oil filter removal tool if necessary to slacken the filter initially, then unscrew it by hand the rest of the way. Empty the oil from the old filter into the container, then puncture the top of the filter, and allow the remaining oil to drain from the filter into the container.

11 Use a clean rag to remove all oil, dirt and sludge from the filter sealing area on the engine.

12 Apply a light coating of clean engine oil to the sealing ring on the new filter, then screw the filter into position on the engine **(see illustrations)**. Wipe clean any oil around the filter and tighten the filter firmly by hand only – do not use any tools.

13 Remove the old oil and all tools from under the car, then lower the car to the ground.

6.9a Oil filter cartridge (arrowed) on 1.0 litre engines...

6.9b ...and on 1.6 litre engines

14 Fill the engine, using the correct grade and type of oil (refer to *Weekly checks* for details of topping-up). An oil can spout or funnel may help to reduce spillage. Pour in half the specified quantity of oil first, then wait a few minutes for the oil to run to the sump.

15 Continue adding oil a small quantity at a time until the level is up to the MIN mark on the dipstick. Adding around 0.5 litre of oil will now bring the level up to the MAX on the dipstick – do not worry if a little too much goes in, as some of the excess will be taken up in filling the oil filter. Refit the dipstick and the filler cap.

16 Start the engine and run it for a few minutes; check for leaks around the oil filter and the sump drain plug. Note that there may be a few seconds delay before the oil pressure warning light goes out when the engine is started, as the oil circulates through the engine oil galleries and the new oil filter before the pressure builds-up.

17 Switch off the engine, and wait a few minutes for the oil to settle in the sump once more. With the new oil circulated and the filter completely full, recheck the level on the dipstick, and add more oil as necessary. Where applicable, refit the engine undershield when all work is completed.

18 Dispose of the used engine oil and the old oil filter safely, with reference to *General repair procedures* in the Reference section of this manual. Many local recycling points have containers for waste oil, with oil filter disposal receptacles alongside.

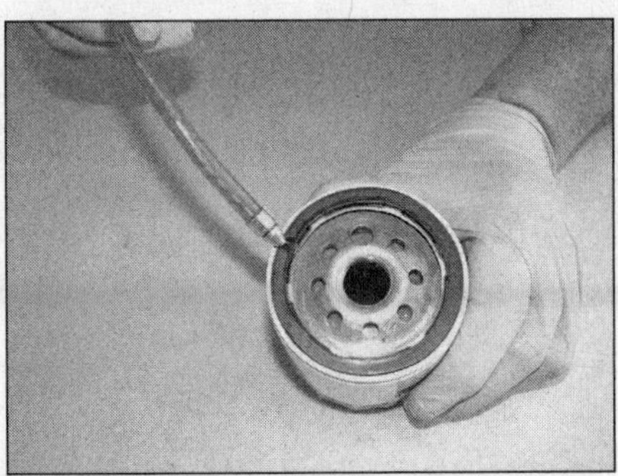
6.12a Apply a light coating of clean engine oil to the sealing ring...

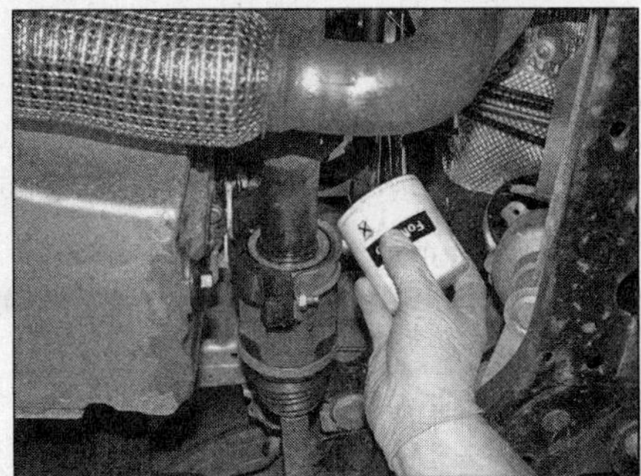
6.12b ...and screw the cartridge into place by hand

7 Lights and horn operation check

1 With the ignition switched on where necessary, check the operation of all exterior lights.
2 Check the brake lights with the help of an assistant, or by reversing up close to a reflective door. Make sure that all the rear lights are capable of operating independently, without affecting any of the other lights – for example, switch on as many rear lights as possible, then try the brake lights. If any unusual results are found, this is usually due to an earth fault or other poor connection at that rear light unit.
3 Again with the help of an assistant or using a reflective surface, check as far as possible that the headlights work on both main and dipped beam.
4 Renew any defective bulbs with reference to Chapter 12.
5 Check the operation of all interior lights, including the glovebox and luggage area illumination lights. Switch on the ignition, and check that all relevant warning lights come on as expected – the vehicle handbook should give details of these. Now start the engine, and check that the appropriate lights go out. When you are next driving at night, check that all the instrument panel and facia lighting works correctly. If any problems are found, refer to Chapter 12
6 Finally, choose an appropriate time of day to test the operation of the horn.

8 Underbonnet check for fluid leaks and hose condition

Warning: Renewal of air conditioning hoses must be left to a dealer service department or air conditioning specialist who has the equipment to depressurise the system safely. Never remove air conditioning components or hoses until the system has been depressurised.

General

1 Visually inspect the engine joint faces, gaskets and seals for any signs of water or oil leaks. Pay particular attention to the areas around the cylinder head cover, cylinder head, oil filter and sump joint faces. Bear in mind that, over a period of time, some very slight seepage from these areas is to be expected – what you are really looking for is any indication of a serious leak. Should a leak be found, renew the offending gasket or oil seal by referring to the appropriate Chapters in this manual.
2 High temperatures in the engine compartment can cause the deterioration of the rubber and plastic hoses used for engine, accessory and emission systems operation. Periodic inspection should be made for cracks, loose clamps, material hardening and leaks.
3 When checking the hoses, ensure that all the cable-ties or clips used to retain the hoses are in place, and in good condition. Clips which are broken or missing can lead to chafing of the hoses, pipes or wiring, which could cause more serious problems in the future.
4 Carefully check the large top and bottom radiator hoses, along with the other smaller-diameter cooling system hoses and metal pipes; do not forget the heater hoses/pipes which run from the engine to the bulkhead. Inspect each hose along its entire length, replacing any that is cracked, swollen or shows signs of deterioration. Cracks may become more apparent if the hose is squeezed, and may often be apparent at the hose ends.
5 Make sure that all hose connections are tight. If the large-diameter air hoses from the air cleaner are loose, they will leak air, and upset the engine idle quality **(see illustration)**. If the spring clamps that are used to secure some of the hoses appear to be slackening, they should be updated with worm-drive clips to prevent the possibility of leaks.
6 Some other hoses are secured to their fittings with clamps. Where clamps are used, check to be sure they haven't lost their tension, allowing the hose to leak. If clamps aren't used, make sure the hose has not expanded and/or hardened where it slips over the fitting, allowing it to leak.
7 Check all fluid reservoirs, filler caps, drain plugs and fittings, etc, looking for any signs of leakage of oil, transmission and/or brake hydraulic fluid, coolant and power steering fluid. Also check the clutch hydraulic fluid lines which lead from the fluid reservoir and slave cylinder (on the transmission).
8 If the vehicle is regularly parked in the same place, close inspection of the ground underneath it will soon show any leaks; ignore the puddle of water which will be left if the air conditioning system is in use. Place a clean piece of cardboard below the engine, and examine it for signs of contamination after the vehicle has been parked over it overnight – be aware, however, of the fire risk inherent in placing combustible material below the catalytic converter.
9 Remember that some leaks will only occur with the engine running, or when the engine is hot or cold. With the handbrake firmly applied, start the engine from cold, and let the engine idle while you examine the underside of the engine compartment for signs of leakage.
10 If an unusual smell is noticed inside or around the car, especially when the engine is thoroughly hot, this may point to the presence of a leak.
11 As soon as a leak is detected, its source must be traced and rectified. Where oil has been leaking for some time, it is usually necessary to use a steam cleaner, pressure washer or similar, to clean away the accumulated dirt, so that the exact source of the leak can be identified.

Vacuum hoses

12 It's quite common for vacuum hoses, especially those in the emissions system, to be colour-coded, or to be identified by coloured stripes moulded into them. Various systems require hoses with different wall thicknesses, collapse resistance and temperature resistance. When renewing hoses, be sure the new ones are made of the same material.
13 Often the only effective way to check a hose is to remove it completely from the vehicle. If more than one hose is removed, be sure to label the hoses and fittings to ensure correct installation **(see illustration)**.
14 When checking vacuum hoses, be sure to include any plastic 'T' fittings in the check. Inspect the fittings for cracks, and check the hose where it fits over the fitting for distortion, which could cause leakage.
15 A small piece of vacuum hose (quarter-inch inside diameter) can be used as a stethoscope to detect vacuum leaks. Hold one end of the hose to your ear, and probe around vacuum hoses and fittings, listening for the 'hissing' sound characteristic of a vacuum leak.

Warning: When probing with the vacuum hose stethoscope, be very careful not to come into contact with moving engine components such as the auxiliary drivebelt, radiator electric cooling fan, etc.

8.5 Check the security of the air intake pipes

8.13 Check the security of the various vacuum hoses

Fuel hoses

Warning: There are certain precautions which must be taken when inspecting or servicing fuel system components. Work in a well-ventilated area, and do not allow open flames (cigarettes, appliance pilot lights, etc) or bare light bulbs near the work area. Mop-up any spills immediately, and do not store fuel-soaked rags where they could ignite.

16 Check all fuel hoses for deterioration and chafing. Check especially for cracks in areas where the hose bends, and also just before fittings, such as where a hose attaches to the fuel rail or pump **(see illustration)**.

17 High-quality fuel line, usually identified by the word 'Fluoroelastomer' printed on the hose, should be used for fuel line renewal. Never, under any circumstances, use non-reinforced vacuum line, clear plastic tubing or water hose as a substitute for fuel lines.

18 Spring type clamps may be used on fuel lines. These clamps often lose their tension over a period of time, and can be 'sprung' during removal. Renew all spring - type clamps with proper petrol pipe clips whenever a hose is renewed.

Metal pipes

19 Sections of metal piping are often used for fuel line between the fuel filter and the engine, and for some power steering and air conditioning applications. Check carefully to be sure the piping has not been bent or crimped, and that cracks have not started in the line; also check for signs of excessive corrosion.

20 If a section of metal fuel line must be renewed, only seamless steel piping should be used, since copper and aluminium piping don't have the strength necessary to withstand normal engine vibration.

21 Check the metal lines where they enter the brake master cylinder, ABS hydraulic unit or clutch master/slave cylinders (as applicable) for cracks in the lines or loose fittings. Any sign of brake fluid leakage calls for an immediate and thorough inspection.

9 Engine compartment wiring check

1 With the vehicle parked on level ground, apply the handbrake firmly and open the bonnet. Using an inspection light or a small electric torch, check all visible wiring within and beneath the engine compartment.

2 What you are looking for is wiring that is obviously damaged by chafing against sharp edges, or against moving suspension/transmission components and/or the auxiliary drivebelt, by being trapped or crushed between carelessly-refitted components, or melted by being forced into contact with the hot engine castings, coolant pipes, etc.

8.16 Check the security of the fuel supply pipe. EcoBoost fuel supply pipe to the high pressure pump shown (arrowed)

In almost all cases, damage of this sort is caused in the first instance by incorrect routing on reassembly after previous work has been carried out.

3 Depending on the extent of the problem, damaged wiring may be repaired by rejoining the break or splicing-in a new length of wire, using solder to ensure a good connection, and remaking the insulation with adhesive insulating tape or heat-shrink tubing, as appropriate. If the damage is extensive, given the implications for the vehicle's future reliability, the best long-term answer may well be to renew that entire section of the loom, however expensive this may appear.

4 When the damage has been repaired, ensure that the wiring loom is re-routed correctly, so that it is clear of other components, and not stretched or kinked, and is secured out of harm's way using the plastic clips, guides and ties provided.

5 Check all electrical connectors, ensuring that they are clean, securely fastened, and that each is locked by its plastic tabs or wire clip, as appropriate **(see illustration)**. If any connector shows external signs of corrosion (accumulations of white or green deposits, or streaks of 'rust'), or if any is thought to be dirty, it must be unplugged and cleaned using electrical contact cleaner. If the connector pins are severely corroded, the connector must be renewed; note that this may mean the renewal of that entire section of the loom – see your local Ford dealer for details.

6 If the cleaner completely removes the corrosion to leave the connector in a satisfactory condition, it would be wise to pack the connector with a suitable material which will exclude dirt and moisture, preventing the corrosion from occurring again; a Ford dealer may be able to recommend a suitable product.

7 Check the condition of the battery connections – remake the connections or renew the leads if a fault is found (see Chapter 5A). Use the same techniques to ensure that all earth points in the engine compartment provide good electrical contact through clean, metal-to-metal joints, and that all are securely fastened.

10 Brake pads, shoes and discs check

1 The work described in this Sectionshould be carried out at the specified intervals, or whenever a defect is suspected in the braking system. Any of the following symptoms could indicate a potential brake system defect:

a) *The vehicle pulls to one side when the brake pedal is depressed.*
b) *The brakes make squealing, scraping or dragging noises when applied.*
c) *Brake pedal travel is excessive, or pedal feel is poor.*
d) *The brake fluid requires repeated topping-up. Note that, because the hydraulic clutch shares the same fluid as the braking system (see Chapter 6), this problem could be due to a leak in the clutch system.*

Front disc brakes

2 Apply the handbrake, then loosen the front wheel nuts. Jack up the front of the vehicle, and support it on axle stands (see *Jacking and vehicle support*).

3 For better access to the brake calipers, remove the wheels.

4 Look through the inspection window in the caliper, and check that the thickness of the friction lining material on each of the pads is not less than the recommended minimum thickness given in the Specifications **(see illustration)**.

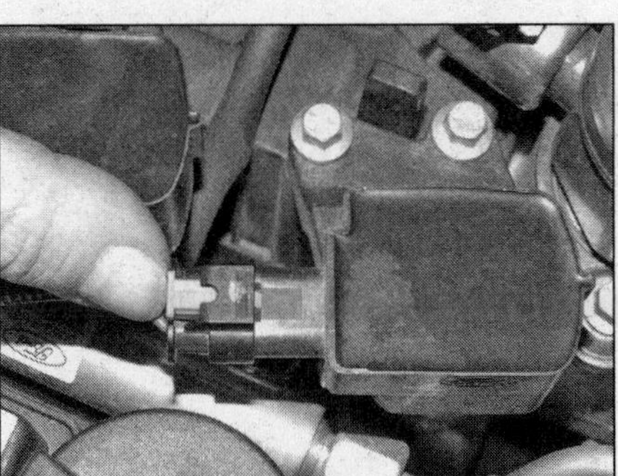

9.5 Ensure all electrical connector clips are securely clipped together

10.4 Measure the thickness of the brake pad friction material (arrowed)

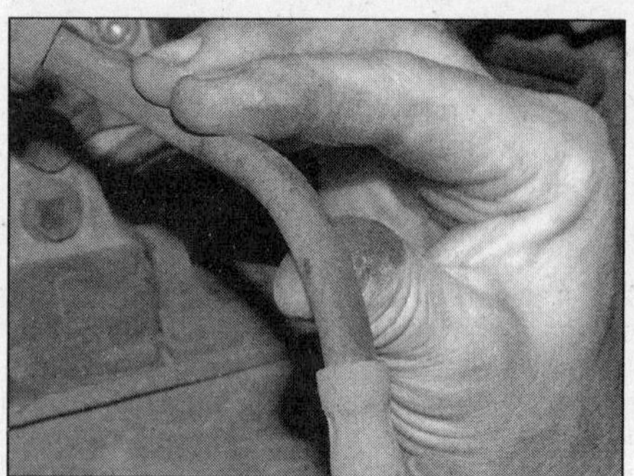

10.12 Check the condition of the rubber brake hoses by bending them slightly and looking for cracks

5 If it is difficult to determine the exact thickness of the pad linings, or if you are at all concerned about the condition of the pads, then remove them from the calipers for further inspection (refer to Chapter 9 Section 3 or 9).

6 Check the other caliper in the same way.

7 If any one of the brake pads has worn down to, or below, the specified limit, all four pads at that end of the car must be renewed as a set. If the pads on one side are significantly more worn than the other, this may indicate that the caliper pistons have partially seized – refer to the brake pad renewal procedure in Chapter 9 Section 2, and push the pistons back into the caliper to free them.

8 Measure the thickness of the discs with a micrometer, if available, to make sure that they still have service life remaining. Do not be fooled by the lip of rust which often forms on the outer edge of the disc, which may make the disc appear thicker than it really is – scrape off the loose rust if necessary, without scoring the disc friction (shiny) surface.

9 If any disc is thinner than the specified minimum thickness, renew it (refer to Chapter 9 Section 4, 10).

10 Check the general condition of the discs. Look for excessive scoring and discolouration caused by overheating. If these conditions exist, remove the relevant disc and have it resurfaced or renewed (refer to Chapter 9 Section 4)

11 Make sure that the handbrake is firmly applied, then check that the transmission is in neutral. Spin the wheel, and check that the brake is not binding. Some drag is normal with a disc brake, but it should not require any great effort to turn the wheel – also, do not confuse brake drag with resistance from the transmission.

12 Before refitting the wheels, check all brake lines and hoses (refer to Chapter 9). In particular, check the flexible hoses in the vicinity of the calipers, where they are subjected to most movement **(see illustration)**. Bend them between the fingers (but do not actually bend them double, or the casing may be damaged) and check that this does not reveal previously-hidden cracks, cuts or splits.

13 On completion, refit the wheels and lower the car to the ground. Tighten the wheel nuts to the specified torque.

Rear disc brakes

14 Loosen the rear wheel nuts, then chock the front wheels. Jack up the rear of the car, and support it on axle stands. Release the handbrake and remove the rear wheels.

15 The procedure for checking the rear brakes is much the same as described in paragraphs 2 to 13 above. Check that the rear brakes are not binding, noting that transmission resistance is not a factor on the rear wheels. Abnormal effort may indicate that the handbrake needs adjusting – see Section 18.

Rear drum brakes

16 Loosen the rear wheel nuts, then chock the front wheels. Jack up the rear of the car, and support on axle stands (see *Jacking and vehicle support*). Release the handbrake and remove the rear wheels.

17 Spin the wheel to check that the brake is not binding. A small amount of resistance from the brake is acceptable, but no great effort should be required to turn the wheel hub. Abnormal effort may indicate that the handbrake needs adjusting – see Section 18.

18 To check the brake shoe lining thickness without removing the brake drums, prise the rubber plugs from the backplates, and use an electric torch to inspect the linings of the leading brake shoes. Check that the thickness of the lining material on the brake shoes is not less than the recommendation given in the Specifications.

19 If it is difficult to determine the exact thickness of the brake shoe linings, or if you are at all concerned about the condition of the shoes, then remove the rear drums for a more comprehensive inspection (refer to Chapter 9 Section 5).

20 With the drum removed, check the shoe return and hold-down springs for correct installation, and check the wheel cylinders for leakage of brake fluid. Apart from fluid being visible, a leaking wheel cylinder may be characterised by an excessive build-up of brake dust (stuck to the fluid which has leaked) at the cylinder seals.

21 Check the friction surface of the brake drums for scoring and discoloration. If excessive, the drum should be resurfaced or renewed.

11.2 Check the condition of the exhaust rubber mountings

22 Before refitting the wheels, check all brake lines and hoses. On completion, apply the handbrake and check that the rear wheels are locked. The handbrake can be adjusted as described in Chapter 9 Section 22.

23 On completion, refit the wheels and lower the car to the ground. Tighten the wheel nuts to the specified torque.

11 Exhaust system check

1 With the engine cold (at least three hours after the vehicle has been driven), check the complete exhaust system, from its starting point at the engine to the end of the tailpipe. Ideally, this should be done on a hoist, where unrestricted access is available; if a hoist is not available, raise and support the vehicle on axle stands (see *Jacking and vehicle support*).

2 Make sure that all brackets and rubber mountings are in good condition, and tight; if any of the mountings are to be renewed, ensure that the new ones are of the correct type – in the case of the rubber mountings, their colour is a good guide. Those nearest to the catalytic converter are more heat-resistant than the others **(see illustration)**.

3 Check the pipes and connections for evidence of leaks, severe corrosion, or damage. One of the most common points for a leak to develop is around the welded joints between the pipes and silencers. Leakage at any of the joints or in other parts of the system will usually show up as a black sooty stain in the vicinity of the leak. **Note:** *Exhaust sealants should not be used on any part of the exhaust system upstream of the catalytic converter (between the converter and engine) – even if the sealant does not contain additives harmful to the converter, pieces of it may break off and foul the element, causing local overheating.*

4 At the same time, inspect the underside of the body for holes, corrosion, open seams, etc, which may allow exhaust gases to enter the passenger compartment. Seal all body openings with silicone or body putty.

5 Rattles and other noises can often be traced to the exhaust system, especially the rubber mountings. Try to move the system, silencer(s), heat shields and catalytic converter. If any components can touch the body or suspension parts, secure the exhaust system with new mountings.

6 Check the running condition of the engine by inspecting inside the end of the tailpipe; the exhaust deposits here are an indication of the engine's state of tune. The inside of the tailpipe should be dry, and should vary in colour from dark grey to light grey/brown; if it is black and sooty, or coated with white deposits, this may indicate the need for a full fuel system inspection.

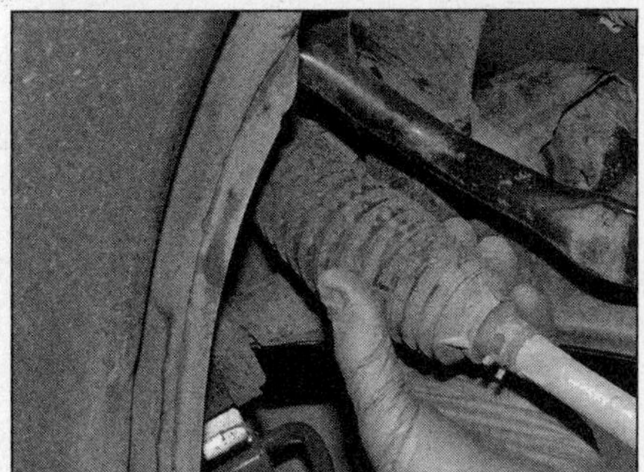
12.2 Check the condition of the steering rack gaiters

12.4 Check for wear in the wheel bearing by grasping the wheel and trying to rock it

12.5 Check for wear in the steering rack-track rod balljoints

12 Steering, suspension and roadwheel check

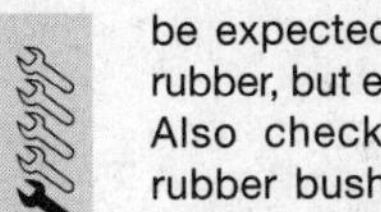

Front suspension and steering

1 Apply the handbrake, then raise the front of the vehicle and support it on axle stands (see *Jacking and vehicle support*).

2 Visually inspect the balljoint dust covers and the steering rack gaiters for splits, chafing or deterioration **(see illustration)**. Any wear of these components will cause loss of lubricant, together with dirt and water entry, resulting in rapid deterioration of the balljoints or steering gear.

3 Where fitted, check the power-assisted steering fluid hoses for chafing or deterioration, and the pipe and hose unions for fluid leaks. Also check for signs of fluid leakage under pressure from the steering gear rubber gaiters, which would indicate failed fluid seals within the steering gear.

4 Grasp the roadwheel at the 12 o'clock and 6 o'clock positions, and try to rock it **(see illustration)**. Very slight free play may be felt, but if the movement is appreciable, further investigation is necessary to determine the source. Continue rocking the wheel while an assistant depresses the footbrake. If the movement is now eliminated or significantly reduced, it is likely that the hub bearings are at fault. If the free play is still evident with the footbrake depressed, then there is wear in the suspension joints or mountings.

5 Now grasp the wheel at the 9 o'clock and 3 o'clock positions, and try to rock it as before**(see illustration)**. Any movement felt now may again be caused by wear in the hub bearings or the steering track rod balljoints. If the outer track rod balljoint is worn, the visual movement will be obvious. If the inner joint is suspect, it can be felt by placing a hand over the rack-and-pinion rubber gaiter, and gripping the track rod. If the wheel is now rocked, movement will be felt at the inner joint if wear has taken place.

6 Using a large screwdriver or flat bar, check for wear in the suspension mounting and subframe bushes by levering between the relevant suspension component and its attachment point. Some movement is to be expected as the mountings are made of rubber, but excessive wear should be obvious. Also check the condition of any visible rubber bushes, looking for splits, cracks or contamination of the rubber.

7 With the vehicle standing on its wheels, have an assistant turn the steering wheel back-and-forth, about an eighth of a turn each way. There should be very little, if any, lost movement between the steering wheel and roadwheels. If this is not the case, closely observe the joints and mountings previously described, but in addition, check the steering column joints for wear, and also check the rack-and-pinion steering gear itself.

Rear suspension

8 Chock the front wheels, then raise the rear of the vehicle and support it on axle stands (see *Jacking and vehicle support*).

9 Check the rear hub bearings for wear, using the method described for the front hub bearings (paragraph 4).

10 Using a large screwdriver or flat bar, check for wear in the suspension mounting bushes by levering between the relevant suspension component and its attachment point. Some movement is to be expected as the mountings are made of rubber, but excessive wear should be obvious.

Roadwheel check and balancing

11 Periodically remove the roadwheels, and clean any dirt or mud from the inside and outside surfaces. Examine the wheel rims for signs of rusting, corrosion or other damage. Light alloy wheels are easily damaged by 'kerbing' whilst parking, and similarly, steel wheels may become dented or buckled. Renewal of the wheel is very often the only course of remedial action possible.

12 The balance of each wheel and tyre assembly should be maintained, not only to avoid excessive tyre wear, but also to avoid wear in the steering and suspension components. Wheel imbalance is normally signified by vibration through the vehicle's bodyshell, although in many cases it is particularly noticeable through the steering wheel. Conversely, it should be noted that wear or damage in suspension or steering components may cause excessive tyre wear. Out-of-round or out-of-true tyres, damaged wheels and wheel bearing wear/maladjustment also fall into this category. Balancing will not usually cure vibration caused by such wear.

13 Wheel balancing may be carried out with the wheel either on or off the vehicle. If balanced on the vehicle, ensure that the wheel-to-hub relationship is marked in some way prior to subsequent wheel removal, so that it may be refitted in its original position.

13 Driveshaft rubber gaiter and joint check

1 The driveshaft rubber gaiters are very important, because they prevent dirt, water and foreign material from entering and damaging the joints. External contamination can cause the gaiter material to deteriorate prematurely, so it's a good idea to wash the gaiters with soap and water occasionally.

2 With the vehicle raised and securely supported on axle stands (see *Jacking and vehicle support*), turn the steering onto full-lock, then slowly rotate each front wheel in turn. Inspect the condition of the outer constant velocity (CV) joint rubber gaiters, squeezing the gaiters to open out the folds. Check for signs of cracking, splits, or deterioration of the rubber, which may allow the escape of grease, and lead to the ingress of water and grit into the joint. Also check the security and condition of the retaining clips. Repeat these checks on the inner tripod joints **(see illustration)**. If any damage or deterioration is found, the gaiters

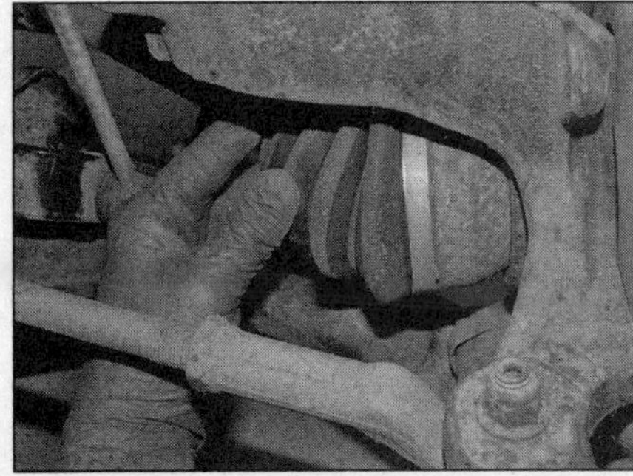
13.2 Squeeze the driveshaft gaiters and check for cracks

should be renewed as described in Chapter 8 Section 3, or 4.

3 At the same time, check the general condition of the outer CV joints themselves, by first holding the driveshaft and attempting to rotate the wheels. Repeat this check on the inner joints, by holding the inner joint yoke and attempting to rotate the driveshaft.

4 Any appreciable movement in the joint indicates wear in the joint, wear in the driveshaft splines, or a loose driveshaft retaining bolt.

14 Underbody and fuel/brake line check

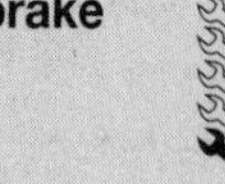

1 With the vehicle raised and supported on axle stands or over an inspection pit, thoroughly inspect the underbody and wheel arches for signs of damage and corrosion. In particular, examine the bottom of the side sills, and any concealed areas where mud can collect.

2 Where corrosion and rust is evident, press and tap firmly on the panel with a screwdriver, and check for any serious corrosion which would necessitate repairs.

3 If the panel is not seriously corroded, clean away the rust, and apply a new coating of underseal. Refer to Chapter 11 Section 4 or 5 for more details of body repairs.

4 At the same time, inspect the lower body panels for stone damage and general condition.

5 Inspect all of the fuel and brake lines on the underbody for damage, rust, corrosion and leakage, checking the PVC coating on the lines for damage, where applicable. Also make sure that the pipes/hoses are correctly supported in their clips **(see illustrations)**. Where fitted, remove the plastic covers from under the vehicle to check the underbody.

15 Hinge and lock lubrication

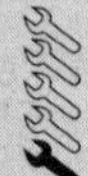

1 Work around the vehicle and lubricate the hinges of the bonnet, doors and tailgate with a light machine oil.

2 Check carefully the security and operation of all hinges, latches and locks, adjusting them where required. Check the operation of the central locking system (if fitted).

3 Where applicable, check the condition and operation of the tailgate struts, renewing them if either is leaking or no longer able to support the tailgate securely when raised.

16 Roadwheel nut tightness check

1 Checking the tightness of the wheel nuts is more relevant than you might think. Apart from the obvious safety aspect of ensuring they are sufficiently tight, this check will reveal whether they have been overtightened, as may have happened the last time new tyres were fitted, for example. If the car suffers a puncture, you may find that the wheel nuts cannot be loosened with the wheel brace.

2 Apply the handbrake, chock the wheels, and engage 1st gear.

3 Remove the wheel cover (or wheel centre cover), using the flat end of the wheel brace supplied in the tool kit.

4 Loosen the first wheel nut, using the wheel brace if possible. If the nut proves stubborn, use a close-fitting socket and a long extension bar.

Warning: Do not use makeshift means to loosen the wheel nuts if the proper tools are not available. If extra force is required, make sure that the tools fit properly, and are of good quality. Even so, consider the consequences of the tool slipping or breaking, and take precautions – wearing stout gloves is advisable to protect your hands. Do not be tempted to stand on the tools used – they are not designed for this, and there is a high risk of personal injury if the tool slips or breaks. If the wheel nuts are simply too tight, take the car to a garage equipped with suitable power tools.

5 Once the nut has been loosened, remove it and check that the wheel stud threads are clean. Use a small wire brush to clean any rust or dirt from the threads, if necessary. **Note:** *Only remove one wheel nut at a time, unless the vehicle has been jacked up and placed on axle stands.*

6 Refit the nut, with the tapered side facing inwards. Tighten it fully, using the wheel brace alone – no other tools. This will ensure that the wheel nuts can be loosened using the wheel brace if a puncture occurs. However, if a torque wrench is available, tighten the nut to the specified torque wrench setting.

7 Repeat the procedure for the remaining nuts, then refit the wheel cover or centre cover, as applicable.

8 Work around the car, checking and retightening the nuts for all four wheels.

17 Road test

Braking system

1 Make sure that the vehicle does not pull to one side when braking, and that the wheels do not lock when braking hard.

2 Check that there is no vibration through the steering when braking. As all models are equipped with ABS brakes, if vibration is felt through the pedal under heavy braking, this is a normal characteristic of the system operation, and is not a cause for concern.

3 Check that the handbrake operates correctly, without excessive movement of the lever, and that it holds the vehicle stationary on a slope, in both directions (facing up and down a slope).

4 With the engine switched off, test the operation of the brake servo unit as follows. Depress the footbrake four or five times to exhaust the vacuum, then start the engine. As the engine starts, there should be a noticeable 'give' in the brake pedal as vacuum builds-up. Allow the engine to run for at least two minutes, and then switch it off. If the brake pedal is now depressed again, it should be possible to detect a hiss from the servo as the pedal is depressed. After about four or five applications, no further hissing should be heard, and the pedal should feel considerably harder.

Steering and suspension

5 Check for any abnormalities in the steering, suspension, handling or road 'feel'.

6 Drive the vehicle, and check that there are no unusual vibrations or noises.

7 Check that the steering feels positive, with no excessive sloppiness or roughness, and check for any suspension noises when cornering and driving over bumps.

Drivetrain

8 Check the performance of the engine, transmission and driveshafts.

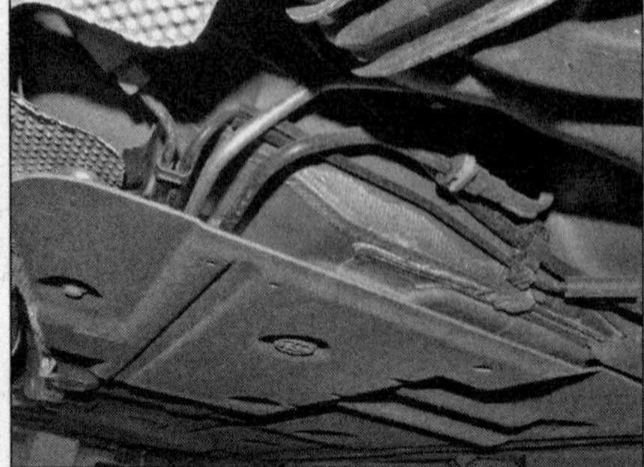

14.5a Remove the plastic shields (where fitted)...

14.5b ...and check the fuel and brake pipes are clipped to the vehicle body

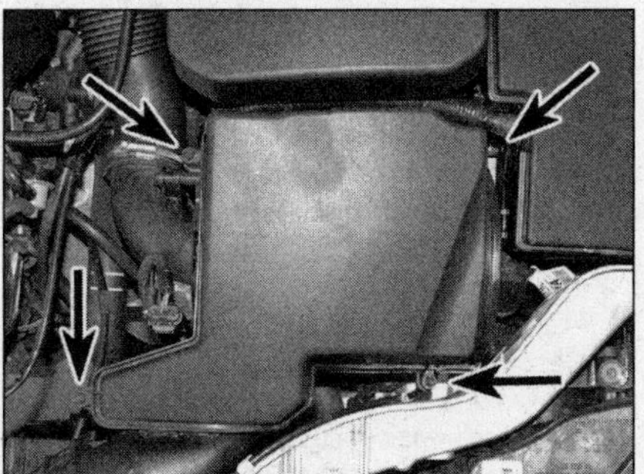

20.2 Remove the screws (arrowed)

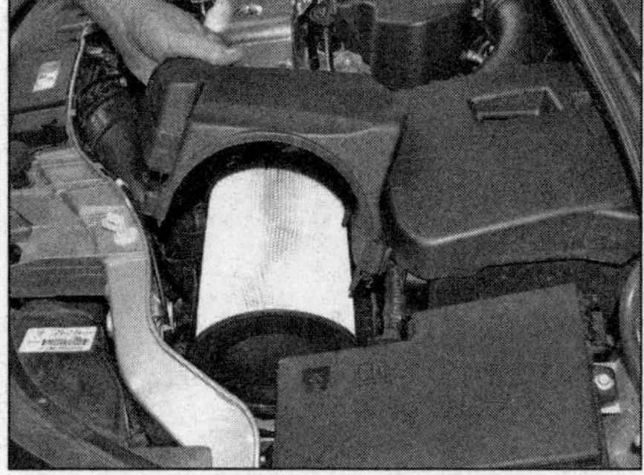

20.3a Lift off the cover...

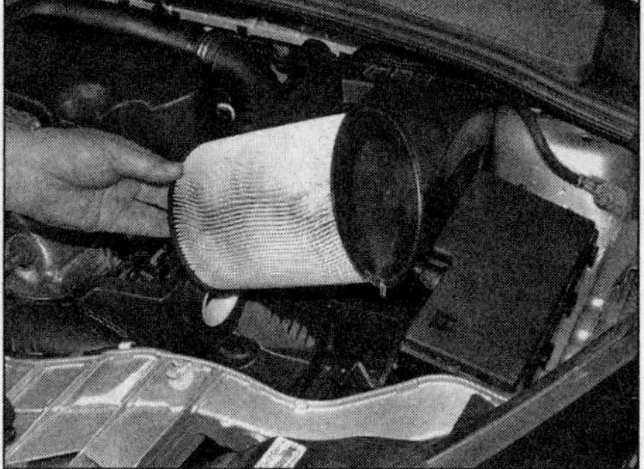

20.3b ...and remove the filter

9 Check that the engine starts correctly, both when cold and when hot.

10 Listen for any unusual noises from the engine and transmission.

11 Make sure that the engine runs smoothly when idling, and that there is no hesitation when accelerating.

12 Check that all gears can be engaged smoothly without noise, and that the gear lever action is smooth and not abnormally vague or 'notchy'.

13 Listen for a metallic clicking sound from the front of the vehicle as the vehicle is driven slowly in a circle with the steering on full-lock. Carry out this check in both directions. If a clicking noise is heard, this indicates wear in a driveshaft joint, in which case renew the joint if necessary.

Clutch

14 Check that the clutch pedal moves smoothly and easily through its full travel, and that the clutch itself functions correctly, with no trace of slip or drag.

15 If the clutch is slow to release, it is possible that the system requires bleeding (see Chapter 6 Section 5). Also check the fluid pipes under the bonnet for signs of leakage.

16 Check the clutch as described in Chapter 6 Section 1.

Instruments and electrical equipment

17 Check the operation of all instruments and electrical equipment.

18 Make sure that all instruments read correctly, and switch on all electrical equipment in turn, to check that it functions properly.

18 Handbrake check and adjustment

1 In service, the handbrake should be fully applied within 3 to 5 clicks of the handbrake lever ratchet. Should adjustment be necessary, refer to Chapter 9 Section 21, for the full procedure description.

19 Seat belt check

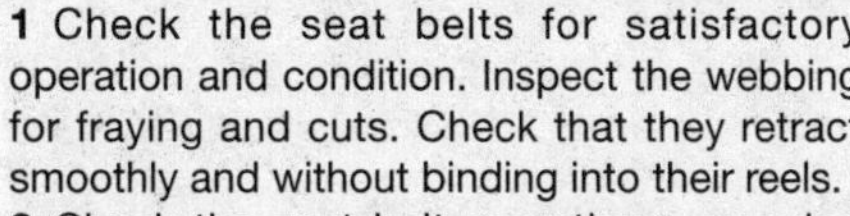

1 Check the seat belts for satisfactory operation and condition. Inspect the webbing for fraying and cuts. Check that they retract smoothly and without binding into their reels.

2 Check the seat belt mountings, ensuring that all the bolts are securely tightened.

20 Air filter element renewal

Caution: Never drive the vehicle with the air filter element removed. Excessive engine wear could result, and backfiring could even cause a fire under the bonnet.

1 On all models the air filter element is located in the air cleaner assembly on the left-hand side of the engine compartment.

2 Remove the four torx head screws securing the cover to the air cleaner housing **(see illustration)**.

3 The cover can now be lifted, and the filter element removed **(see illustrations)**.

4 If carrying out a routine service, the element must be renewed regardless of its apparent condition.

5 If you are checking the element for any other reason, inspect its lower surface; if it is oily or very dirty, renew the element. If it is only moderately dusty, it can be re-used by blowing it clean from the upper to the lower surface with compressed air. Because it is a pleated-paper type filter, it cannot be washed. If it cannot be cleaned satisfactorily with compressed air, discard and renew it.

Caution: Wear eye protection when using compressed air.

6 Where the air cleaner cover was removed, wipe out the inside of the housing. Check that no foreign matter is visible, either in the air inlet or in the air mass meter.

7 Refitting is the reverse of the removal procedure, making sure the peg on the lower part of the filter, aligns with the locating point in the housing **(see illustration)**.

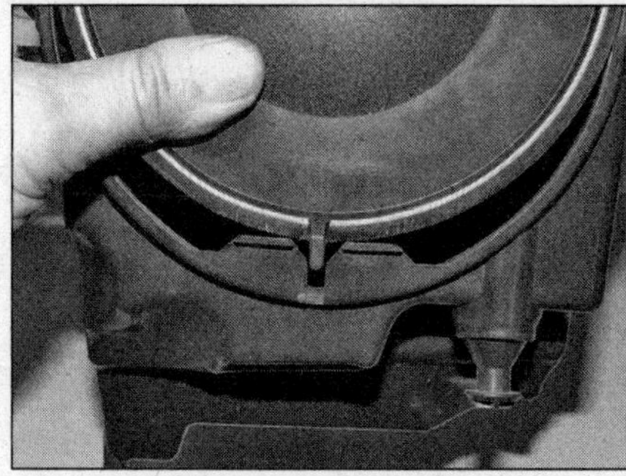

20.7 Align the locating peg

21 Spark plug renewal

1 The correct functioning of the spark plugs is vital for the correct running and efficiency of the engine. It is essential that the plugs fitted are appropriate for the engine.

2 If the correct type is used and the engine is in good condition, the spark plugs should not need attention between scheduled intervals. Spark should not be attempted.

3 Spark plug removal and refitting requires a spark plug socket, with an extension which can be turned by a ratchet handle or similar. This socket is lined with a rubber sleeve, to protect the porcelain insulator of the spark plug, and to hold the plug while you insert it into the spark plug hole. You will also need feeler blades, to check and adjust the spark plug electrode gap, and (ideally) a torque wrench to tighten the new plugs to the specified torque.

4 Open the bonnet and disconnect the battery – see Disconnecting the battery in Chapter 5A.

5 If fitted, pull up and remove the engine cover.

6 'EcoBoost' models have individual coils fitted to each plug – often referred to as a 'coil on plug' (COP) ignition system. Ti-VCT models have a standard 'wasted spark' coil, with individual HT leads fitted.

7 On the 'coil on plug' (COP) system, release the locking clips and disconnect the wiring plugs from the coils. Then remove the bolts

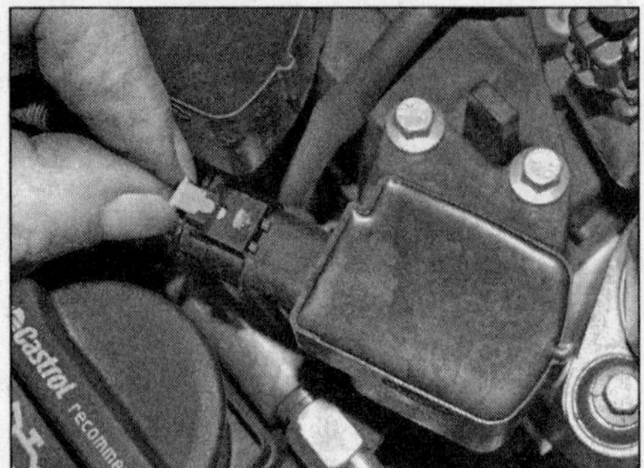
21.7a Release the locking clip...

21.7b ...disconnect the wiring plug...

21.7c ...remove the mounting bolts...

21.7d ...and then remove the ignition coil

from each coil and pull the coil from the plug to access the spark plug **(see illustrations)**.

8 On engines fitted with conventional HT leads, note how the spark plug leads are routed and secured by the clips on the cylinder head cover; unclip the leads as necessary, to provide enough slack in the lead. To prevent the possibility of mixing up spark plug (HT) leads, it is a good idea to try to work on one spark plug at a time.

9 If the marks on the original-equipment spark plug (HT) leads cannot be seen, mark the leads 1 to 4, to correspond to the cylinder the lead serves (No 1 cylinder is at the timing belt end of the engine). Pull the leads from the plugs by gripping the rubber boot sealing the cylinder head cover opening, not the lead, otherwise the lead connection may be fractured **(see illustration)**.

10 Unscrew the spark plugs, ensuring that the socket is kept in alignment with each plug – if the socket is forcibly moved to either side, the porcelain top of the plug may be broken off. Remove the plug from the engine **(see illustration)**.

11 If any undue difficulty is encountered when unscrewing any of the spark plugs, carefully check the cylinder head threads and sealing surfaces for signs of wear, excessive corrosion or damage; if any of these conditions is found, seek the advice of a Ford dealer as to the best method of repair.

12 As each plug is removed, examine it as follows – this will give a good indication of the condition of the engine:

a) If the insulator nose of the spark plug is clean and white, with no deposits, this is indicative of a weak mixture.

b) If the tip and insulator nose are covered with hard black-looking deposits, then this is indicative that the mixture is too rich.

c) Should the plug be black and oily, then it is likely that the engine is fairly worn, as well as the mixture being too rich.

d) If the insulator nose is covered with light tan to greyish-brown deposits, then the mixture is correct, and it is likely that the engine is in good condition.

e) Inspect the main ceramic body of the plug. Check carefully for pitting and any tracking marks running down the side of the insulator.

13 If you are renewing the spark plugs, purchase the new plugs, then check each of them first for faults such as cracked insulators or damaged threads. New plugs are supplied with a preset gap. Do not attempt to adjust the gap.

14 If the plugs were removed to inspect them, then the gap can be checked **(see illustration)**. If the gap is not as specified do not attempt to adjust the gap or clean the spark plug. If there is any doubt as to the condition of the spark plugs they should be replaced.

15 Before fitting the spark plugs, check that the threaded connector sleeves at the top of the plugs are tight (where fitted), and that the plug exterior surfaces and threads are clean. Brown staining on the porcelain, immediately above the metal body, is quite normal, and does not necessarily indicate a leak between the body and insulator.

16 On installing the spark plugs, first check that the cylinder head thread and sealing surface are as clean as possible; use a clean rag wrapped around a paintbrush to wipe clean the sealing surface. Apply a smear of copper-based grease or anti-seize compound to the threads of each plug, and screw them in by hand where possible. Take extra care to enter the plug threads correctly, as the cylinder head is made of aluminium alloy – it's often difficult to insert spark plugs into their holes without cross - threading them (see **Haynes Hint**).

17 When each spark plug is started correctly on its threads, screw it down until it just seats lightly, then tighten it to the specified torque wrench setting. If a torque wrench is not available – and this is one case where the use of a torque wrench is strongly recommended – tighten each spark plug through no more than 1/16th of a turn. Do not exceed the specified torque setting, and NEVER overtighten spark plugs.

21.9 Pull the HT leads from the top of the spark plug

21.10 Unscrew each spark plug carefully

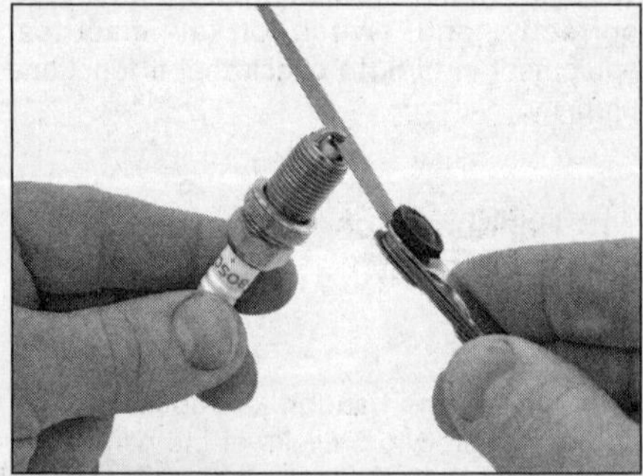
21.14 Check the electrode gap with a set of feeler gauges

HAYNES HiNT

It is often difficult to insert spark plugs into their holes without dross-threading them. To avoid this possibility, fit a short length of rubber or plastic hose over the end of the spark plug. The flexible hose acts as a universal joint, to help align the plug with the plug hole. Should the plug begin to cross thread, the hose will slip on the spark plug, preventing thread damage to the cylinder head.

18 Refit the coils (in the correct order) and tighten the retaining bolts or reconnect the HT leads (in their correct order), using a slight twisting motion.

19 On 'coil on plug' models reconnect the wiring plugs, making sure the locking clips are secure**(see illustration)**.

20 Reconnect the battery -see Disconnecting the battery in Chapter. 5A Section 3

22 Timing belt renewal

1 The procedure (applicable only to 1.6 litre engines) is described in Chapter 2B Section 8.

23 Auxiliary drivebelt check and renewal

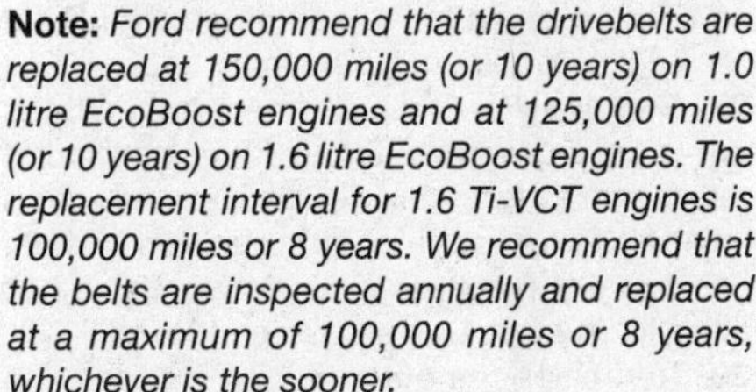

Note: *Ford recommend that the drivebelts are replaced at 150,000 miles (or 10 years) on 1.0 litre EcoBoost engines and at 125,000 miles (or 10 years) on 1.6 litre EcoBoost engines. The replacement interval for 1.6 Ti-VCT engines is 100,000 miles or 8 years. We recommend that the belts are inspected annually and replaced at a maximum of 100,000 miles or 8 years, whichever is the sooner.*

Drivebelt check

Note: *On all engines only rotate the engine in the normal clockwise direction.*

1 All models except some 1.6 Ti-VCT engines have a single drivebelt fitted. Two belts are fitted only to 1.6 Ti-VCT models that have conventional power steering fitted.

2 'EcoBoost' engines (1.0 litre and 1.6 litre) have an automatic belt tensioner fitted. 1.6 Ti-VCT engines use 'stretch' belts.

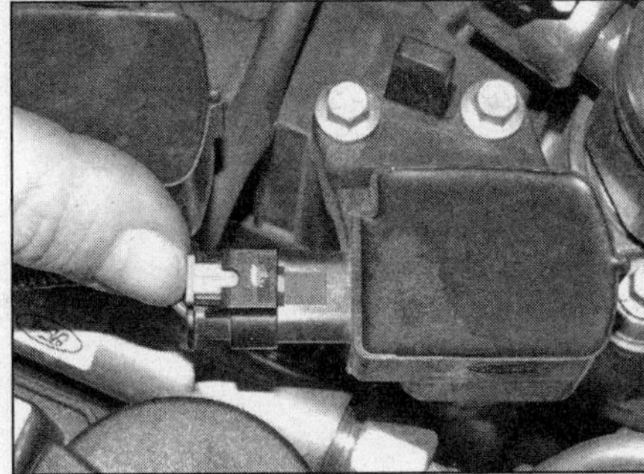

21.19 Secure the locking clip

Replacement of these belts requires the use of special tools.

3 Due to their function and material make-up, drivebelts are prone to failure after a long period of time, and should therefore be inspected regularly.

4 Since the drivebelt is located very close to the right-hand side of the engine compartment, it is possible to gain better access by raising the front of the vehicle and removing the right-hand wheel, then undoing the fasteners and removing the engine undershield (where fitted).

5 With the engine stopped, inspect the full length of the drivebelt for cracks and separation of the belt plies. It will be necessary to turn the engine (using a spanner or socket and bar on the crankshaft pulley bolt) in order to move the belt from the pulleys so that the belt can be inspected thoroughly. Twist the belt between the pulleys so that both sides can be viewed. Also check for fraying, and glazing which gives the belt a shiny appearance. Check the pulleys for nicks, cracks, distortion and corrosion.

6 Note that it is not unusual for a ribbed belt to exhibit small cracks in the edges of the belt ribs, and unless these are extensive or very deep, belt renewal is not essential.

Renewal 1.0 litre engines

7 If not already done so, jack up and support the front of the vehicle (see *Jacking and vehicle support* in the reference section). Remove the right-hand wing liner and the engine undershield.

8 If the belt is to be refitted mark the direction of rotation on the belt.

23.9 Lock the tensioner with a suitable drill bit

9 Using a suitable socket and short extension rotate the tensioner upwards (anti-clockwise) until it is possible to fit an 4.5mm drill bit into the hole provided in the tensioner to lock the tensioner in position **(see illustration)**.

10 Note the routing of the belt and then remove it **(see illustration)**.

11 Fit the replacement belt and carefully release the tensioner sufficiently to remove the drill bit. With the drill bit removed slowly release the tensioner. Align the belt with all the pulleys and fully release the tensioner.

12 Using a suitable spanner or socket on the crankshaft pulley, rotate the engine twice in the normal (clockwise) direction, checking that the belt is correctly located on all the pulleys as the engine is rotated.

Renewal 1.6 EcoBoost engines

13 If not already done so, jack up and support the front of the vehicle (see *Jacking and vehicle support* in the reference section). Remove the right-hand wing liner and the engine undershield.

14 If the belt is to be refitted mark the direction of rotation on the belt.

15 Using a suitable jack and a block of wood to spread the load support the engine from below.

16 Release the coolant expansion tank and move it to one side. There is no need to drain the coolant.

17 Unbolt and remove the damper from the right-hand engine mounting.

18 Unbolt and then remove the engine mounting.

19 Note the routing of the drivebelt **(see**

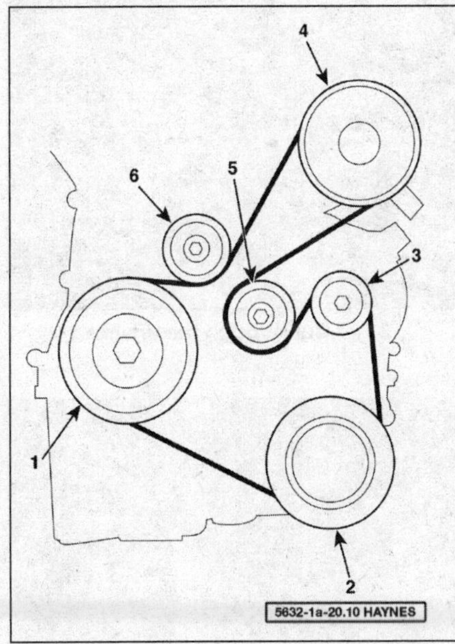

23.10 Auxiliary belt routing 1.0 EcoBoost models

1 Crankshaft pulley
2 AC Compressor
3 Alternator
4 Waterpump
5 Tensioner
6 Idler pulley

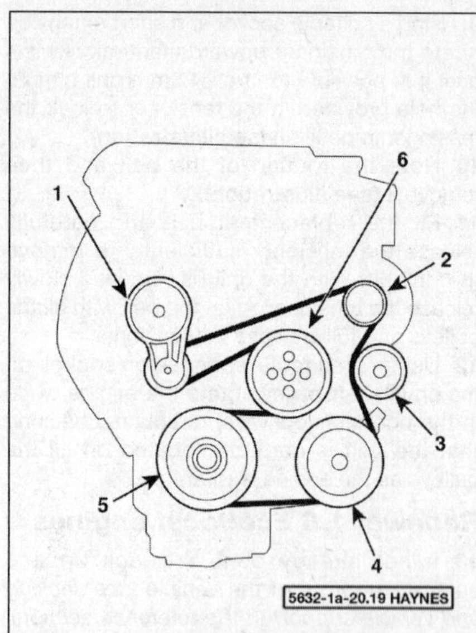

23.19 Auxiliary belt routing 1.6 EcoBoost models

1 Tensioner
2 Alternator
3 Idler pulley
4 Ac Compressor
5 Crankshaft pulley
6 Waterpump

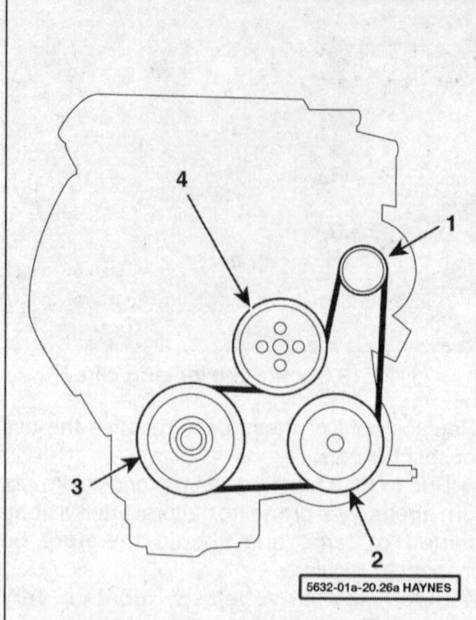

23.26a Auxillary belt routing 1.6 models with electric power steering

1 Alternator
2 AC Compressor
3 Crankshaft pulley
4 Waterpump

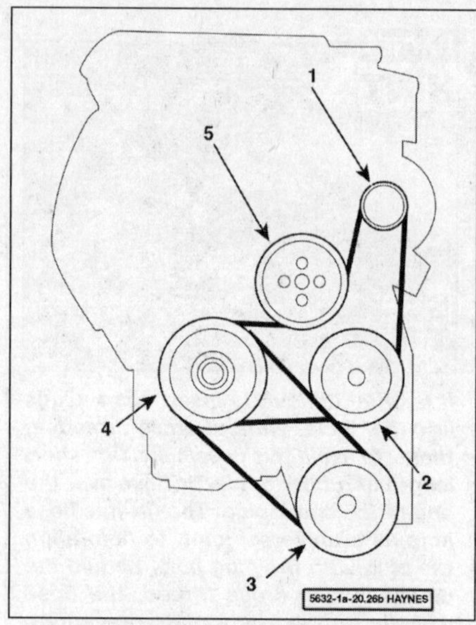

23.26b Auxiliary drivebelt routing – 1.6 models with standard power steering

1 Alternator
2 Power steering pump
3 AC Compressor
4 Crankshaft pulley
5 Waterpump

illustration) and then using a suitable spanner release the tension from the drivebelt. With the tension released, slip the drivebelt off the waterpump pulley and then slowly release the automatic tensioner.

20 Remove the spanner and then unbolt and remove the tensioner. Remove the drivebelt.

21 Fit the new drivebelt around all the pulleys except the waterpump pulley and then refit the automatic tensioner.

22 Fit the drivebelt over the tensioner and then use a spanner to rotate the tensioner clockwise sufficiently to slip the drivebelt over the waterpump pulley. Slowly release the tensioner to take up the slack in the drivebelt.

23 Using a suitable spanner or socket on the crankshaft pulley, rotate the engine twice in the normal (clockwise) direction, checking that the belt is correctly located on all the pulleys as the engine is rotated.

24 Refit the components in reverse order.

23.27 Cut through the drivebelt

23.30a Fit the installation tool (arrowed) to the coolant pump pulley

23.30b Fit the tool to the crankshaft pulley in the 12 o'clock position...

23.30c ...with the curved side (arrowed) of the tool towards the engine

Renewal 1.6 Ti-VCT engines

25 If not already done so, jack up and support the front of the vehicle (see *Jacking and vehicle support* in the reference section). Remove the right-hand wing liner and the engine undershield.

26 Note the routing of the belt (s) before removing them **(see illustrations)**.

27 Where two belts are fitted (models with hydraulic power steering) cut off the outer belt first with a sharp knife **(see illustration)** and then cut off and remove the inner belt.

28 Genuine Ford replacement main belts are supplied with a fitting kit. Aftermarket replacement belts may not be supplied with a fitting kit. Where no fitting kit is supplied it will be necessary to purchase a 'universal' stretch belt fitting kit (such as Draper tools part No EABT-1).

29 To replace the outer belt on models with two belts, Ford special tool 303-1288 or a universal stretch belt tool will be required.

30 To replace the main belt, locate the special tool on the waterpump pulley and then fit the second part of the special tool over the crankshaft pulley. Route the belt over the pulleys and then onto the special tool **(see illustrations)**.

31 Using a suitable spanner on the special tool rotate the waterpump pulley and stretch the belt over the tool and onto the pulley **(see**

23.31a Rotate the coolant pump pulley/tool by hand until it catches the belt...

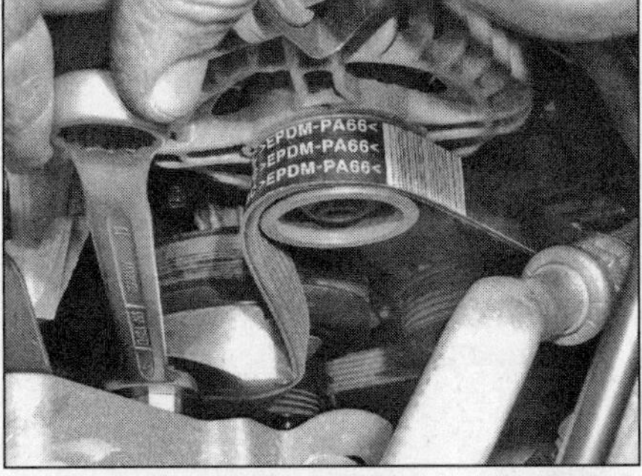

23.31b ...then use a spanner to fully rotate the pulley/tool

23.33a Fit the compressor drivebelt installation tool in the 7 o'clock position

23.33b Fit the belt around the tool...

23.33c ...then rotate the crankshaft pulley clockwise

illustrations). Check that the belt is correctly located on all the pulleys. Remove the tools.

32 Using a suitable spanner or socket on the crankshaft pulley, rotate the engine twice in the normal (clockwise) direction, checking that the belt is correctly located on all the pulleys as the engine is rotated.

33 Where a second belt is fitted, fit Ford special 303-1288 (or suitable universal belt tool) to the crankshaft pulley. Locate the drivebelt over the AC compressor and then over the special tool. Use a suitable spanner or socket on the crankshaft pulley and rotate the engine approximately 180 degrees, allowing the special tool to lift the belt up and over the crankshaft pulley as the engine is rotated **(see illustrations)**.

34 Check that the belt is correctly located and then rotate the engine twice in the normal direction of rotation, checking that the new belt is correctly located as the engine is rotated.

35 Refit the remaining components in reverse order.

24 Timing belt renewal

1 The procedure (applicable only to 1.0 litre engines) is described in Chapter 2A Section 8.

25 Pollen filter renewal

1 To make access easier, remove the glovebox assembly, as described in Chapter 11 Section 29.

2 Working under the passengers side of the facia, inside the footwell, reach up and unclip the wiring loom securing clip from the lower part of the pollen filter trim cover **(see illustration)**.

3 Compress the locking clips on the lower part of the trim cover to release it from the heater housing, and then remove the cover **(see illustration)**.

4 Pull the filter free from the housing, noting any directional arrows, as it is removed **(see illustration)**. The filter will need to be squeezed together to remove it completely from the heater housing.

5 Fit the new filter using a reversal of the removal procedure, ensuring that the filter is fitted with the airflow arrows pointing in the correct direction, as noted on removal. Refit the wiring loom securing clip back to the lower part of the housing, once filter trim cover has been refitted.

26 Brake fluid renewal

Warning: Brake hydraulic fluid can harm your eyes and damage painted surfaces, so use extreme caution when handling and pouring it. Do not use fluid that has been standing open for some time, as it absorbs moisture from the air. Excess moisture can cause a dangerous loss of braking effectiveness. Brake fluid is also highly flammable – treat it with the same respect as petrol.

1 The procedure is similar to that for the bleeding of the hydraulic system in Chapter. 9 Section 14

2 Reduce the fluid level in the reservoir (by syphoning), but do not allow the fluid level to drop far enough to allow air into the system.

Warning: Do not syphon the fluid by mouth; it is poisonous.

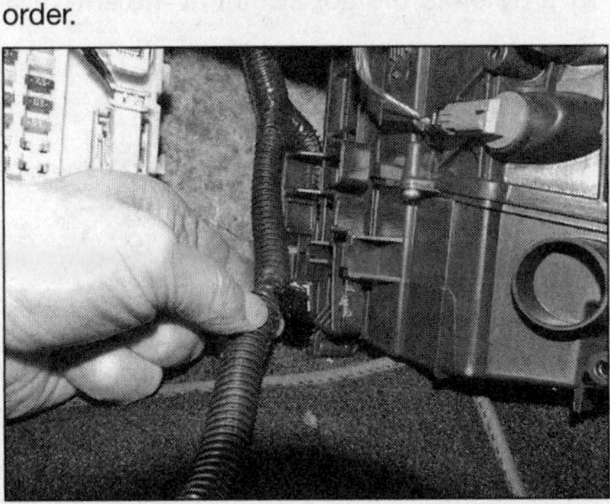
25.2 Unclip the wiring loom securing clip

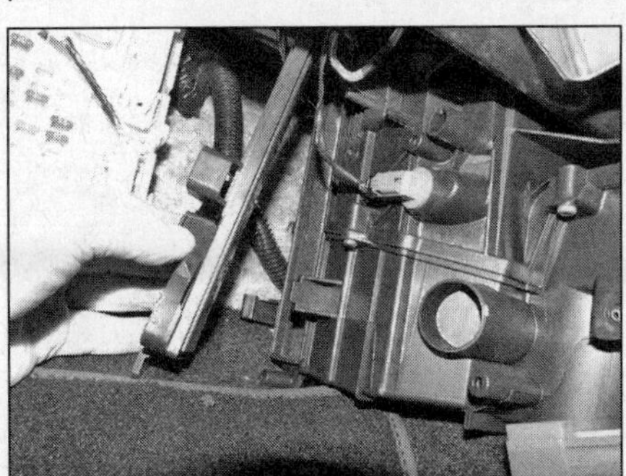
25.3 Remove the trim cover

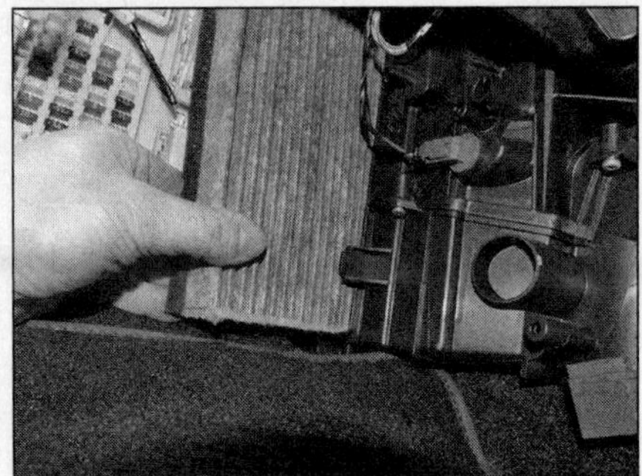
25.4 Remove the pollen filter

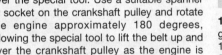

3 Working as described in Chapter 9, open the first bleed screw in the sequence, and pump the brake pedal gently until nearly all the old fluid has been emptied from the master cylinder reservoir. Top-up to the MAX level with new fluid, and continue pumping until only the new fluid remains in the reservoir, and new fluid can be seen emerging from the bleed screw. Tighten the screw, and top the reservoir level up to the MAX level line. Old hydraulic fluid is invariably much darker in colour than the new, making it easy to distinguish the two.

4 Work through all the remaining bleed screws in the sequence until new fluid can be seen at all of them. Be careful to keep the master cylinder reservoir topped-up to above the MIN level at all times, or air may enter the system and greatly increase the length of the task.

5 When the operation is complete, check that all bleed screws are securely tightened, and that their dust caps are refitted. Wash off all traces of spilt fluid, and recheck the master cylinder reservoir fluid level.

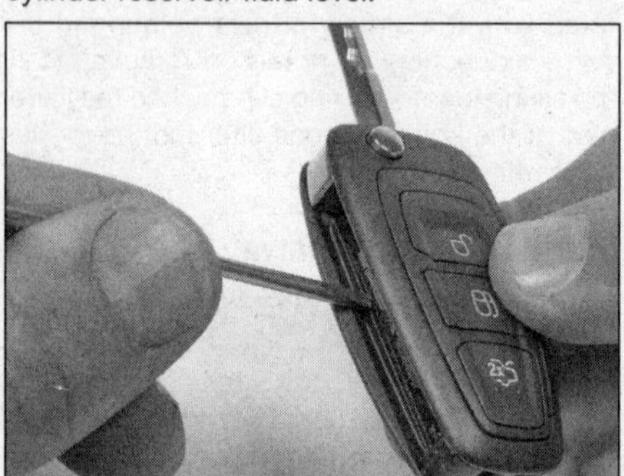

27.3a Insert a screwdriver into the slot ...

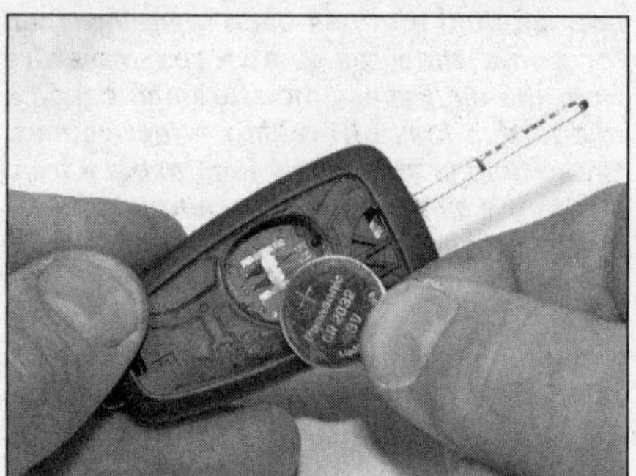

27.5 The battery fits positive side up

27.9a Separate the 2 halves and...

6 Check the operation of the brakes before taking the car on the road.

7 Finally, check the operation of the clutch. Since the clutch shares the same fluid reservoir as the braking system, it may also be necessary to bleed the clutch as described in Chapter 6 Section 5.

27 Remote control battery renewal

1 Although not in the Ford maintenance schedule, we recommend that the battery is changed every 2 years, regardless of the vehicle's mileage. However, if the door locks repeatedly fail to respond to signals from the remote control at the normal distance, change the battery in the remote control before attempting to troubleshoot any of the vehicle's other systems.

Models with a folding key blade

2 Press the button to release the key blade.

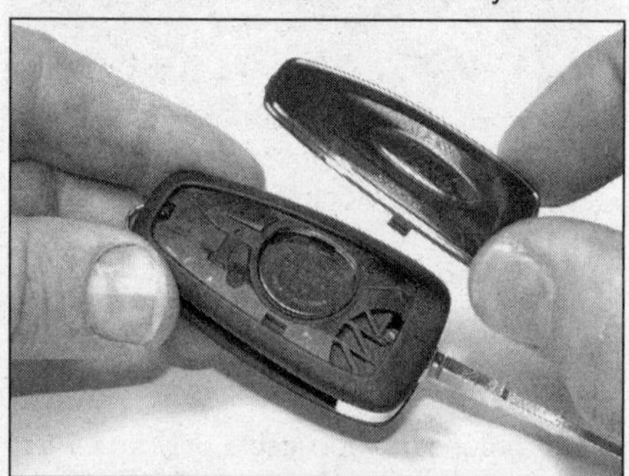

27.3b ... and prise off the cover

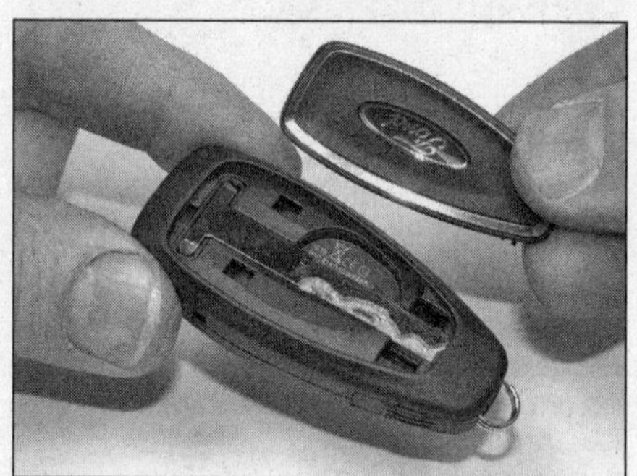

27.7 Release the key cover

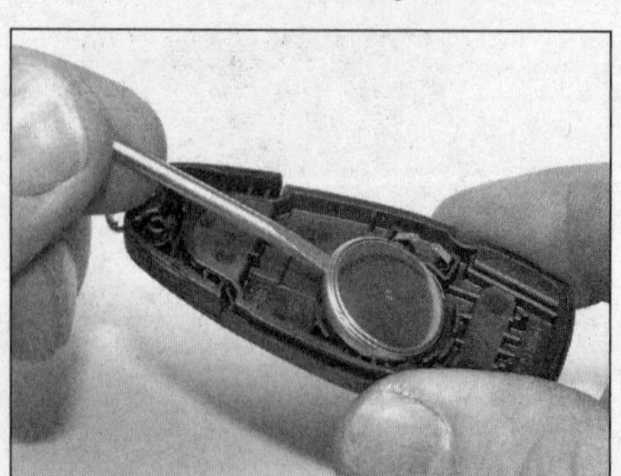

27.9b ...remove the battery

3 Use a small screwdriver and release the battery cover **(see illustrations)**.

4 Fully remove the battery cover and then remove the battery.

5 Fit a new battery – the '+' (positive) side of the battery must face up **(see illustration)**.

6 Refit the battery compartment cover and check the operation of the remote.

Models without a key blade

7 The emergency key blade is located under a cover. Press and hold the small buttons on the side of the remote to release the cover **(see illustration)**.

8 Remove the key blade and then use a small screwdriver, first at the end of the narrow end of the key blade compartment and then on the side of the remote **(see illustration)**.

9 Fully separate the two halves of the remote and then use the screwdriver to remove the battery **(see illustrations)**.

10 Fit a new battery – the '+' (positive) side of the battery must face down **(see illustration)**.

11 Reassemble the two halves of the remote and refit the emergency key blade. Refit the blade compartment cover and check the operation of the remote.

28 Coolant strength check and renewal

Warning: Do not allow antifreeze to come in contact with your skin or painted surfaces of the vehicle. Flush contaminated areas immediately with plenty of water. Don't store new coolant, or leave old coolant lying around,

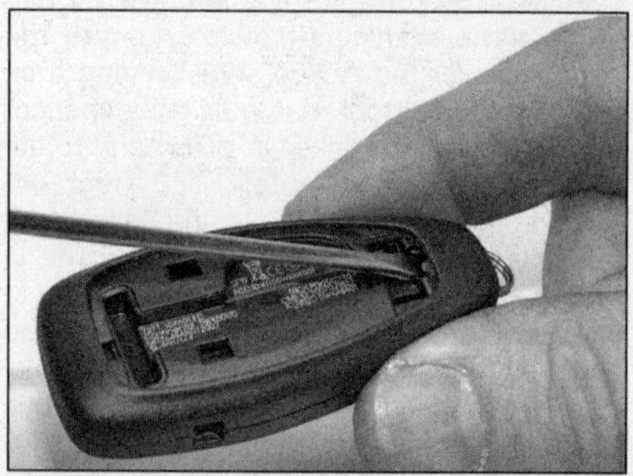

27.8 Release the upper half at the end first

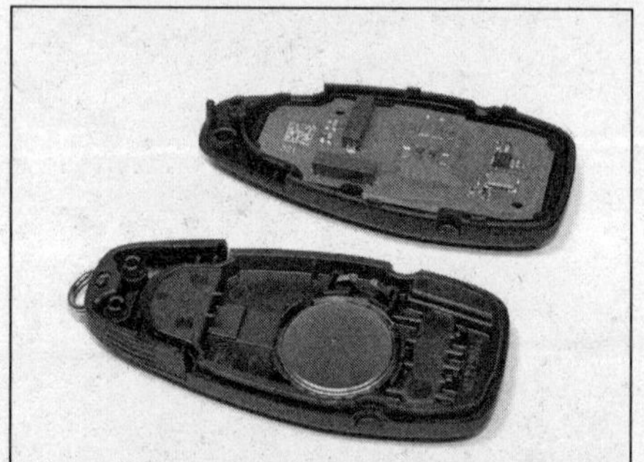

27.10 The battery fits positive side down

where it's accessible to children or pets – they're attracted by its sweet smell. Ingestion of even a small amount of coolant can be fatal. Wipe up garage-floor and drip-pan spills immediately. Keep antifreeze containers covered, and repair cooling system leaks as soon as they're noticed.

Warning: Never remove the expansion tank filler cap when the engine is running, or has just been switched off, as the cooling system will be hot, and the consequent escaping steam and scalding coolant could cause serious injury.

Warning: Wait until the engine is cold before starting these procedures.

Note: *If Ford 'Superplus' antifreeze is used, the coolant can then be left indefinitely, providing the strength of the mixture is checked every year. If any antifreeze other than Ford's is to be used, the coolant must be renewed at regular intervals to provide an equivalent degree of protection; the conventional recommendation is to renew the coolant every two years.*

Strength check

1 Use a hydrometer to check the strength of the antifreeze. Follow the instructions provided with your hydrometer. The antifreeze strength should be approximately 50%. If it is significantly less than this, drain a little coolant from the radiator (see this Section), add antifreeze to the coolant expansion tank, then recheck the strength.

Coolant draining

2 To drain the system, first remove the expansion tank filler cap.

3 If the additional working clearance is required, raise the front of the vehicle and support it securely on axle stands (see *Jacking and vehicle support*). Where fitted, undo the fasteners and remove the engine undershield **(see illustrations 7.4a & 7.4b)**.

4 Place a large drain tray underneath, and unscrew the radiator drain tap, which is located at the lower left-hand corner of the radiator. Fit a length of hose to the pipe at the side of the drain tap to help direct the flow of coolant into the drain tray **(see illustrations)**.

5 Once the coolant has stopped draining from the radiator, close the drain plug.

System flushing

6 With time, the cooling system may gradually lose its efficiency, as the radiator core becomes choked with rust, scale deposits from the water, and other sediment. To minimise this, as well as using only good-quality antifreeze and clean soft water, the system should be flushed as follows whenever any part of it is disturbed, and/or when the coolant is renewed.

7 With the coolant drained, refit the drain plug and refill the system with fresh water. Refit the expansion tank filler cap, start the engine and warm it up to normal operating temperature, then stop it and (after allowing it to cool down completely) drain the system again. Repeat as necessary until only clean water can be seen to emerge, then refill finally with the specified coolant mixture.

28.4a Fit a length of hose to the side of the drain tap...

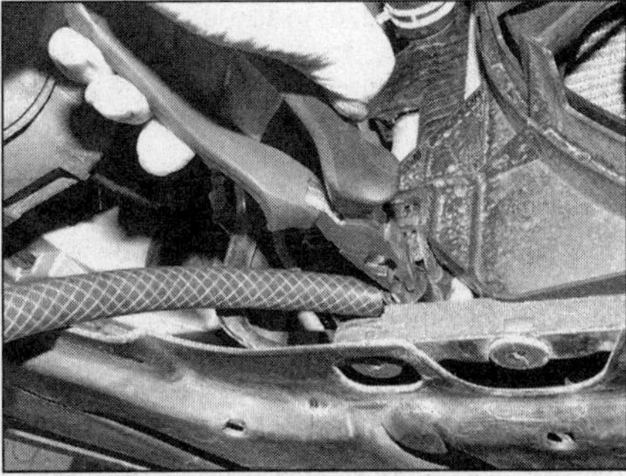

28.4b ...then unscrew the radiator drain tap

8 If only clean, soft water and good-quality antifreeze (even if not to Ford's specification) has been used, and the coolant has been renewed at the suggested intervals, the above procedure will be sufficient to keep clean the system for a considerable length of time. If, however, the system has been neglected, a more thorough operation will be required, as follows.

9 First drain the coolant, then disconnect the radiator top and bottom hoses. Insert a garden hose into the radiator top hose connection, and allow water to circulate through the radiator until it runs clean from the bottom outlet.

10 To flush the engine, insert the garden hose into the radiator bottom hose, wrap a piece of rag around the garden hose to seal the connection, and allow water to circulate until it runs clear.

11 Try the effect of repeating this procedure in the top hose, although this may not be effective, since the thermostat will probably close and prevent the flow of water.

12 In severe cases of contamination, reverse-flushing of the radiator may be necessary. This may be achieved by inserting the garden hose into the bottom outlet, wrapping a piece of rag around the hose to seal the connection, then flushing the radiator until clear water emerges from the top hose outlet.

13 If the radiator is suspected of being severely choked, remove the radiator (Chapter 3 Section 7), turn it upside-down, and repeat the procedure described in paragraph 12.

14 Flushing the heater matrix can be achieved using a similar procedure to that described in paragraph 12, once the heater inlet and outlet hoses have been identified. These two hoses will be of the same diameter, and pass through the engine compartment bulkhead (refer to the heater matrix removal procedure in Chapter 3 Section 9 for more details).

15 The use of chemical cleaners is not recommended, and should be necessary only as a last resort; the scouring action of some chemical cleaners may lead to other cooling system problems. Normally, regular renewal of the coolant will prevent excessive contamination of the system.

Coolant filling

16 With the cooling system drained and flushed, ensure that all disturbed hose unions are correctly secured, and that the radiator/engine drain plug(s) is securely tightened. Refit the engine undershield (where applicable). If it was raised, lower the vehicle to the ground.

17 Set the heater temperature control to maximum heat, but ensure the blower is turned off.

18 Prepare a sufficient quantity of the specified coolant mixture (see below); allow for a surplus, so as to have a reserve supply for topping-up.

19 Slowly fill the system through the expansion tank. Since the tank is the highest point in the system, all the air in the system should be displaced into the tank by the rising liquid. Slow pouring reduces the possibility of air being trapped and forming airlocks. On some models, there are bleed screws fitted, to allow the air out from the system **(see illustration)**, place a container/cloth below the bleed screw, then remove the cap and release the air until there is a flow of coolant. Clean up any spilt coolant when completed.

20 Continue filling until the coolant level reaches the expansion tank MAX level line (see *Weekly checks*), then cover the filler opening to prevent coolant splashing out.

21 Start the engine and run it at 2500 rpm for

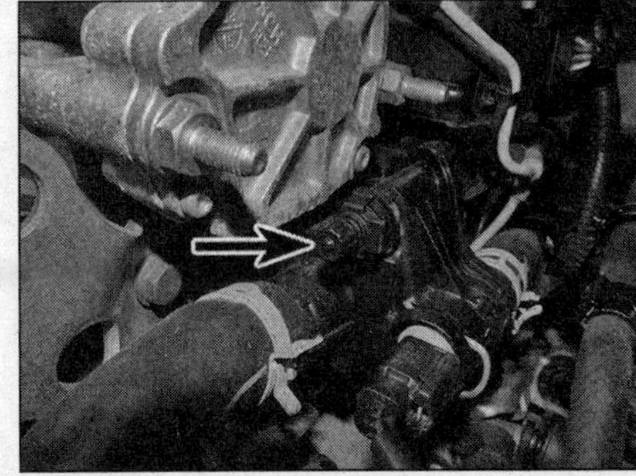

28.19 Bleed screw fitted to coolant housing on some models

2 minutes. If the level in the expansion tank drops significantly, top-up to the MAX level line, to minimise the amount of air circulating in the system.

22 Fill the expansion tank to the MAX level line, refit the expansion tank cap, and run the engine at 2500 rpm until the thermostat opens and the engine is at normal operating temperature. Check this by feeling the radiator bottom hose – if it's hot, then the thermostat has opened.

23 Briefly run the engine at 4000 rpm, then run it at 2500 rpm for approximately 3 minutes.

24 Stop the engine, wash off any spilt coolant from the engine compartment and bodywork, then leave the car to cool down completely (overnight, if possible).

25 With the system cool, open the expansion tank, and top-up the tank to the MAX level line. Refit the filler cap, tightening it securely, and clean up any further spillage.

26 After refilling, always check carefully all components of the system (but especially any unions disturbed during draining and flushing) for signs of coolant leaks. Fresh antifreeze has a searching action, which will rapidly expose any weak points in the system.

Antifreeze type and mixture

Note: *Do not use engine antifreeze in the windscreen/tailgate washer system, as it will damage the vehicle's paintwork. A screenwash additive should be added to the washer system in its maker's recommended quantities.*

27 If the vehicle's history (and therefore the quality of the antifreeze in it) is unknown, owners are advised to drain and thoroughly reverse-flush the system, before refilling with fresh coolant mixture.

28 If the antifreeze used is to Ford's specification, the levels of protection it affords are indicated in the coolant packaging.

29 To give the recommended standard mixture ratio for antifreeze, 50% (by volume) of antifreeze must be mixed with 50% of clean, soft water; if you are using any other type of antifreeze, follow its manufacturer's instructions to achieve the correct ratio.

30 You are unlikely to fully drain the system at any one time (unless the engine is being completely stripped), and the capacities quoted in Specifications are therefore slightly academic for routine coolant renewal. As a guide, only two-thirds of the system's total capacity is likely to be needed for coolant renewal.

31 As the drained system will be partially filled with flushing water, in order to establish the recommended mixture ratio, measure out 50% of the system capacity in antifreeze and pour it into the hose/expansion tank as described above, then top-up with water. Any topping-up while refilling the system should be done with water – for *Weekly checks* use a suitable mixture.

32 Before adding antifreeze, the cooling system should be drained, preferably flushed, and all hoses checked for condition and security. As noted earlier, fresh antifreeze will rapidly find any weaknesses in the system.

33 After filling with antifreeze, a label should be attached to the expansion tank, stating the type and concentration of antifreeze used, and the date installed. Any subsequent topping-up should be made with the same type and concentration of antifreeze.

General cooling system checks

34 The engine should be cold for the cooling system checks, so perform the following procedure before driving the vehicle, or after it has been shut off for at least three hours.

35 Remove the expansion tank filler cap, and clean it thoroughly inside and out with a rag. Also clean the filler neck on the expansion tank. The presence of rust or corrosion in the filler neck indicates that the coolant should be changed. The coolant inside the expansion tank should be relatively clean and transparent. If it is rust-coloured, drain and flush the system, and refill with a fresh coolant mixture.

36 Carefully check the radiator hoses and heater hoses along their entire length; renew any hose which is cracked, swollen or deteriorated.

37 Inspect all other cooling system components (joint faces, etc) for leaks. A leak in the cooling system will usually show up as white- or antifreeze-coloured deposits on the area adjoining the leak (see Haynes Hint). Where any problems of this nature are found on system components, renew the component or gasket with reference to Chapter 3.

A leak in the cooling system will usually show up as white or antifreeze coloured deposits on the areas adjoining the leak.

38 Clean the front of the radiator with a soft brush to remove all insects, leaves, etc, embedded in the radiator fins. Be careful not to damage the radiator fins, or cut your fingers on them. To do a more thorough job, remove the front bumper cover, as described in Chapter 11 Section 6.

Airlocks

39 If, after draining and refilling the system, symptoms of overheating are found which did not occur previously, then the fault is almost certainly due to trapped air at some point in the system, causing an airlock and restricting the flow of coolant; usually, the air is trapped because the system was refilled too quickly.

40 If an airlock is suspected, first try gently squeezing all visible coolant hoses. A coolant hose which is full of air feels quite different to one full of coolant when squeezed. After refilling the system, most airlocks will clear once the system has cooled, and been topped-up.

41 While the engine is running at operating temperature, switch on the heater and heater fan, and check for heat output. Provided there is sufficient coolant in the system, lack of heat output could be due to an airlock in the system.

42 Airlocks can have more serious effects than simply reducing heater output – a severe airlock could reduce coolant flow around the engine. Check that the radiator top hose is hot when the engine is at operating temperature – a top hose which stays cold could be the result of an airlock (or a non-opening thermostat).

43 If the problem persists, stop the engine and allow it to cool down completely, before unscrewing the expansion tank filler cap or loosening the hose clips and squeezing the hoses to bleed out the trapped air. In the worst case, the system will have to be at least partially drained (this time, the coolant can be saved for re-use) and flushed to clear the problem. If all else fails, have the system evacuated and vacuum filled by a suitably-equipped garage.

Expansion tank pressure cap check

44 Wait until the engine is completely cold – perform this check before the engine is started for the first time in the day.

45 Place a wad of cloth over the expansion tank cap, then unscrew it slowly and remove it.

46 Examine the condition of the rubber seal on the underside of the cap. If the rubber appears to have hardened, or cracks are visible in the seal edges, a new cap should be fitted.

47 If the car is several years old, or has covered a large mileage, consider renewing the cap regardless of its apparent condition – they are not expensive. If the pressure relief valve built into the cap fails, excess pressure in the system will lead to puzzling failures of hoses and other cooling system components.

Chapter 1 Part B
Routine maintenance and servicing – diesel models

Contents

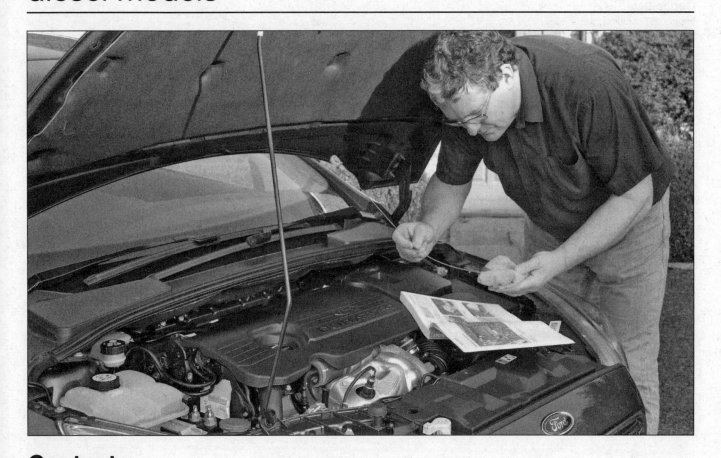

Degrees of difficulty

Easy, suitable for novice with little experience 	**Fairly easy,** suitable for beginner with some experience	**Fairly difficult,** suitable for competent DIY mechanic	**Difficult,** suitable for experienced DIY mechanic 	**Very difficult,** suitable for expert DIY or professional 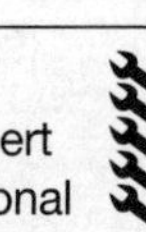

1 Servicing specifications

Lubricants and fluids	Refer to end of Weekly checks	
Capacities		
Engine oil (including filter)	3.85 litres	
Manual transmission:		
5 speed (B5/IB5)	2.3 litres	
6 speed (B6)	1.67 litres	
Cooling system (approximate)	7.3 litres	
Washer fluid reservoir:		
With headlight washer system	4.5 litres	
Without headlight washer system	3.0 litres	
Fuel tank	55.0 litres	
Cooling system		
Antifreeze mixture:		
50% antifreeze	Protection down to –37°C	
55% antifreeze	Protection down to –45°C	
Note: *Refer to antifreeze manufacturer for latest recommendations.*		
Brakes		
Friction material minimum thickness:		
Brake pads	1.5 mm	
Brake shoes	1.0 mm	
Torque wrench settings	**Nm**	**lbf ft**
Engine oil drain plug	34	25
Engine oil filter housing cap:	24	18
Roadwheel nuts	135	100

2 Maintenance schedule

The maintenance intervals in this manual are provided with the assumption that you, not the dealer, will be carrying out the work. These are the minimum maintenance intervals recommended by us for vehicles driven daily. If you wish to keep your vehicle in peak condition at all times, you may wish to perform some of these procedures more often. We encourage frequent maintenance, because it enhances the efficiency, performance and resale value of your vehicle.

If the vehicle is driven in dusty areas, used to tow a trailer, or driven frequently at slow speeds (idling in traffic) or on short journeys, more frequent maintenance intervals are recommended.

When the vehicle is new, it should be serviced by a dealer service department (or other workshop recognised by the vehicle manufacturer as providing the same standard of service) in order to preserve the warranty. The vehicle manufacturer may reject warranty claims if you are unable to prove that servicing has been carried out as and when specified, using only original equipment parts or parts certified to be of equivalent quality.

Every 250 miles or weekly

- ☐ Refer to *Weekly checks*

Every 12 500 miles or 12 months, whichever comes first

In addition to the items listed above, carry out the following:

- ☐ Renew the engine oil and filter (Section 6)
- ☐ Drain the fuel filter (Section 7)
- ☐ Check the condition of the auxiliary drivebelt (Section 24)
- ☐ Check the operation of the lights and the horn (Section 8)
- ☐ Check under the bonnet for fluid leaks and hose condition (Section 9)
- ☐ Check the condition of the engine compartment wiring (Section 10)
- ☐ Check the condition of the seat belts (Section 11)
- ☐ Check the condition of the brake pads, shoes and discs (Section 12)
- ☐ Check the exhaust system (Section 13)
- ☐ Check the steering and suspension components for condition and security (Section 14)
- ☐ Check the condition of the driveshaft joints and gaiters (Section 15)
- ☐ Check the underbody and all fuel/brake lines (Section 16)
- ☐ Lubricate all hinges and locks (Section 17)
- ☐ Check roadwheel nut tightness (Section 18)
- ☐ Carry out a road test (Section 19)
- ☐ Check and if necessary adjust the handbrake (Section 20)
- ☐ Check the antifreeze/inhibitor strength (Section 28)

Every 37 500 miles or 3 years, whichever comes first

In addition to the items listed above, carry out the following:

- ☐ Renew the fuel filter (Section 21)
- ☐ Renew the air filter (Section 22)*
- ☐ Renew the pollen filter (Section 25)*

Note: **If the vehicle is used in dusty conditions, the air filter and pollen filter should be renewed more frequently.*

Every 100 000 miles or 8 years, whichever comes first

- ☐ Renew the auxiliary belt (Section 24)
- ☐ Renew the timing belt and tensioner (Section 23)

Note: *The Ford interval for belt renewal (timing and auxiliary drive) is actually at a much higher mileage than this (125 000 miles or 10 years). It is strongly recommended, however, that the interval is reduced to 100 000 miles or 8 years, particularly on vehicles which are subjected to intensive use, ie, mainly short journeys or a lot of stop-start driving. The actual belt renewal interval is therefore very much up to the individual owner, but bear in mind that severe engine damage will result if the belt breaks.*

Every 2 years, regardless of mileage

- ☐ Renew the brake fluid (Section 26)
- ☐ Renew the remote control battery (Section 27)
- ☐ Renew the coolant (Section 28)*

Note: **If Ford 'Superplus' antifreeze is used, the coolant can then be left for a maximum of 10 years, providing the strength of the mixture is checked every year. If any antifreeze other than Ford's is to be used, the coolant must be renewed at regular intervals to provide an equivalent degree of protection; the conventional recommendation is to renew the coolant every two years.*

3 Component location

Underbonnet view

1 Engine oil level dipstick
2 Oil filler cap
3 Coolant expansion tank cap
4 Washer fluid reservoir cap
5 Brake/clutch fluid reservoir cap
6 Air filter element cover
7 Fuel filter
8 Battery cover
9 Fuse/relay box cover

Front underbody view

1 *Engine oil sump drain plug*
2 *Air conditioning compressor*
3 *Right-hand driveshaft intermediate bearing*
4 *Lower control arm*
5 *Track rod end*
6 *Front subframe*
7 *Catalytic converter*
8 *Front brake caliper*

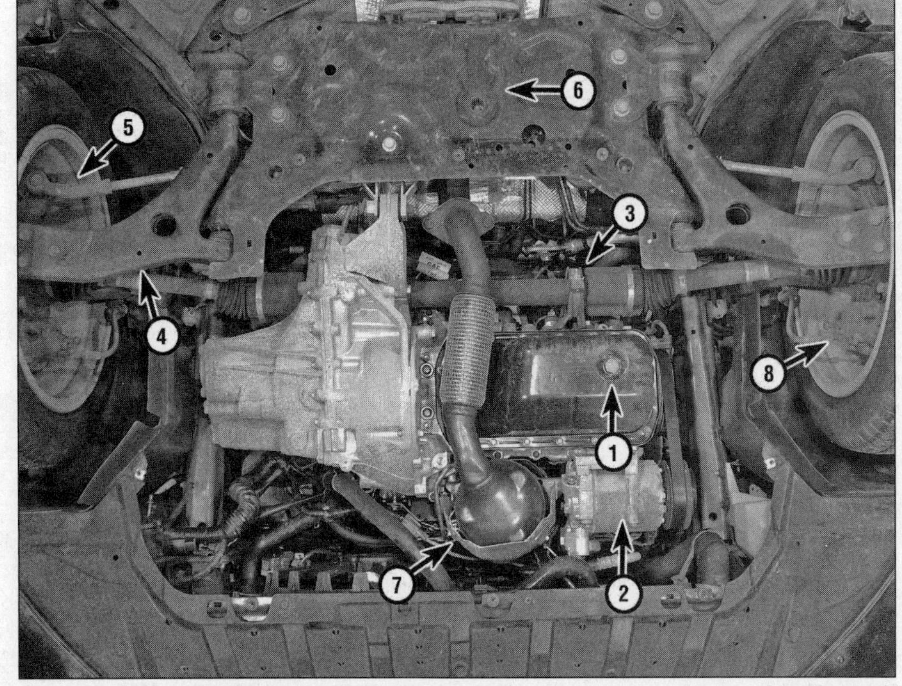

Rear underbody view

1 *Anti-roll bar*
2 *Shock absorber*
3 *Middle silencer*
4 *Handbrake cable*
5 *Fuel filler pipe*
6 *Lower control arm*
7 *Tie rod*
8 *Fuel tank*

4 General Information

1 This Chapter is designed to help the home mechanic maintain his/her vehicle for safety, economy, long life and peak performance.

2 The Chapter contains a master maintenance schedule, followed by Sections dealing specifically with each task in the schedule. Visual checks, adjustments, component renewal and other helpful items are included. Refer to the accompanying illustrations of the engine compartment and the underside of the vehicle for the locations of the various components.

3 Servicing your vehicle in accordance with the mileage/time maintenance schedule and the following Sections will provide a planned maintenance programme, which should result in a long and reliable service life. This is a comprehensive plan, so maintaining some items but not others at the specified service intervals will not produce the same results.

4 As you service your vehicle, you will discover that many of the procedures can – and should – be grouped together, because of the particular procedure being performed, or because of the proximity of two otherwise-unrelated components to one another. For example, if the vehicle is raised for any reason, the exhaust can be inspected at the same time as the suspension and steering components.

5 The first step in this maintenance programme is to prepare yourself before the actual work begins. Read through all the Sections relevant to the work to be carried out, then make a list and gather all the parts and tools required. If a problem is encountered, seek advice from a parts specialist, or a dealer service department.

5 Regular maintenance

1 If, from the time the vehicle is new, the routine maintenance schedule is followed closely, and frequent checks are made of fluid levels and high-wear items, as suggested throughout this manual, the engine will be kept in relatively good running condition, and the need for additional work will be minimised.

2 It is possible that there will be times when the engine is running poorly due to the lack of regular maintenance. This is even more likely if a used vehicle, which has not received regular and frequent maintenance checks, is purchased. In such cases, additional work may need to be carried out, outside of the regular maintenance intervals.

3 If engine wear is suspected, a compression test or leakdown test (refer to the relevant part of Chapter 2A) will provide valuable information regarding the overall performance of the main internal components. Such a test can be used as a basis to decide on the extent of the work to be carried out. If, for example, a compression or leakdown test indicates serious internal engine wear, conventional maintenance as described in this Chapter will not greatly improve the performance of the engine, and may prove a waste of time and money, unless extensive overhaul work is carried out first.

4 The following series of operations are those most often required to improve the performance of a generally poor-running engine:

Primary operations

a) Clean, inspect and test the battery (refer to 'Weekly checks').
b) Check all the engine-related fluids (refer to 'Weekly checks'[).
c) Check the condition and tension of the auxiliary drivebelt (Section 24).
d) Check the condition of the air filter, and renew if necessary (Section 22).
e) Renew the fuel filter (Section 21).
f) Check the condition of all hoses, and check for fluid leaks (Section 9).

5 If the above operations do not prove fully effective, carry out the following secondary operations:

Secondary operations

6 All items listed under Primary operations, plus the following:

a) Check the charging system (refer to Chapter 5A).
b) Check the preheating system (refer to Chapter 5A).
c) Check the fuel system (refer to Chapter 4B).

6 Engine oil and filter renewal

1 Frequent oil and filter changes are the most important preventative maintenance procedures which can be undertaken by the DIY owner. As engine oil ages, it becomes diluted and contaminated, which leads to premature engine wear.

2 Before starting this procedure, gather together all the necessary tools and materials. Also make sure that you have plenty of clean rags and newspapers handy, to mop-up any spills. Ideally, the engine oil should be warm, as it will drain more easily, and more built-up sludge will be removed with it. Take care not to touch the exhaust or any other hot parts of the engine when working under the vehicle. To avoid any possibility of scalding, and to protect yourself from possible skin irritants and other harmful contaminants in used engine oils, it is advisable to wear gloves when carrying out this work.

3 If required, remove the plastic cover on the top of the engine. Pull up the right-hand rear corner and the front edges, then pull the cover forwards to release it **(see illustration)**.

4 Remove the air cleaner assembly, as described in Chapter 4B Section 2.

5 Using a socket on an extension bar, undo

6.3 Remove the plastic cover by pulling it upwards starting at the front edge

6.5a Location of the engine oil filter – 1.6 litre engines

6.5b Location of the engine oil filter – 1.5 litre engines

6.5c Unscrew the cap and remove it complete with filter element

6.6a Where fitted, remove the air deflector trim along the front edge...

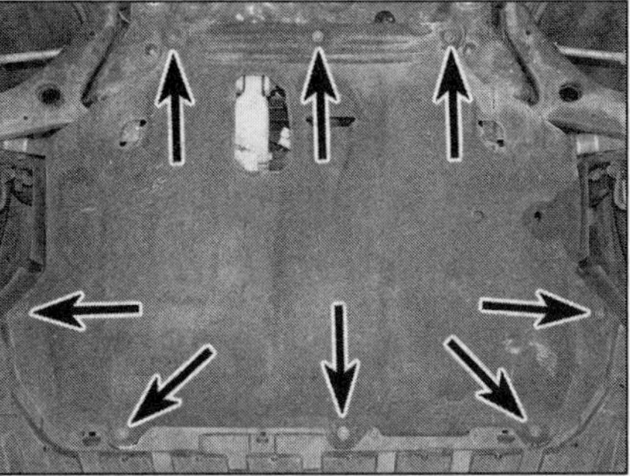
6.6b ...then remove the undershield fasteners (arrowed)

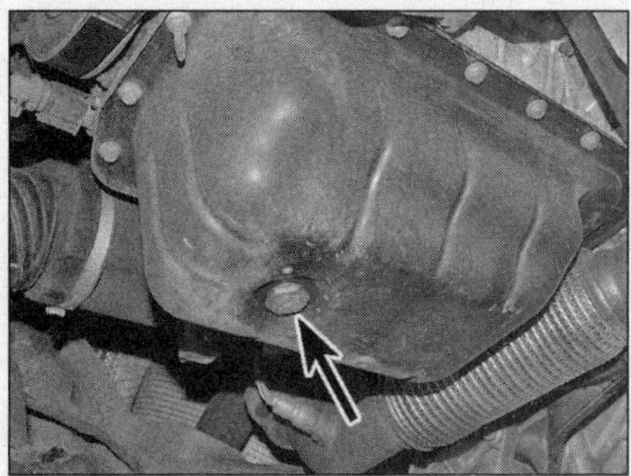
6.7 Undo the engine oil drain plug

the oil filter housing cap. Lift the cap up, with the filter element inside it. Discard the filter and the O-ring seal around the circumference of the cap **(see illustrations)**.

6 If not already done, firmly apply the handbrake, then jack up the front of the vehicle and support it on axle stands (see *Jacking and vehicle support*). Where fitted, unscrew the three screws and remove the plastic air deflector trim from along the front edge of the engine undershield. Undo the 8 fasteners to remove the engine undershield from below the engine compartment **(see illustrations)**.

7 Using a spanner, socket or Allen key as applicable, slacken the drain plug about half a turn **(see illustration)**. Position the draining container under the drain plug, then remove the plug completely (see **Haynes Hint**).

8 Allow some time for the oil to drain, noting that it may be necessary to reposition the container as the oil flow slows to a trickle.

9 After all the oil has drained, wipe the drain plug and the sealing washer (where fitted) with a clean rag. Examine the condition of the sealing washer, and renew it if it shows signs of scoring or other damage which may prevent an oil-tight seal (it is generally considered good practice to fit a new washer every time). Clean the area around the drain plug opening, and refit the plug complete with the washer and tighten it to the specified torque **(see illustration)**.

10 Remove the old oil and all tools from under the vehicle, refit the undershield, then lower the vehicle to the ground.

11 Ensure the oil filter housing and cap are clean, then fit a new O-ring seal to the cap **(see illustration)**.

12 Fit the new filter element into the cap, then fit the cap to the housing and tighten it to the specified torque **(see illustration)**.

13 With the car on level ground, fill the engine, using the correct grade and type of oil (refer to *Weekly checks* for details of topping-up). An oil can spout or funnel may help to reduce spillage. Pour in half the specified quantity of oil first, then wait a few minutes for the oil to run to the sump.

14 Continue adding oil a small quantity at a time until the level is up to the MIN mark on the dipstick. Adding around 1.0 litre of oil will now bring the level up to the MAX on the dipstick – do not worry if a little too much goes in, as some of the excess will be taken up in filling the oil filter. Refit the dipstick and the filler cap.

15 Start the engine and run it for a few minutes, while checking for leaks around the oil filter seal and the sump drain plug. Note that there may be a delay of a few seconds before the low oil pressure warning light goes out when the engine is first started, as the oil circulates through the new oil filter and the engine oil galleries before the pressure builds-up.

16 Stop the engine, and wait a few minutes for the oil to settle in the sump once more. With the new oil circulated and the filter now completely full, recheck the level on the dipstick, and add more oil as necessary.

17 Dispose of the used engine oil and the old oil filter safely, with reference to *General repair procedures* in the Reference section of this manual. Many local recycling points have containers for waste oil with oil filter disposal receptacles alongside.

HAYNES HiNT

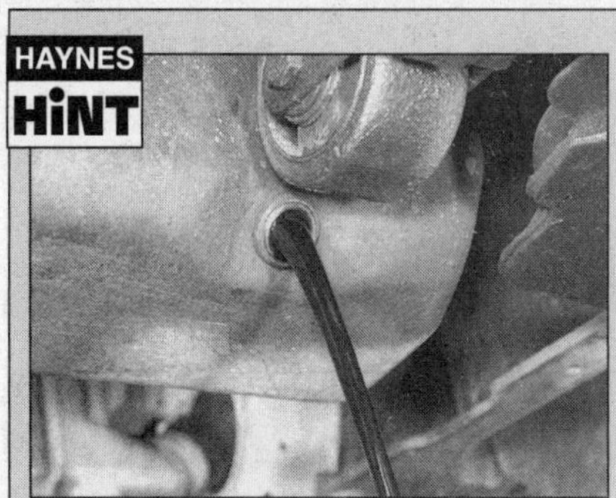

As the drain plug releases from the threads, move it away sharply so the stream of oil issuing from the sump runs into the container, not up your sleeve.

7 Fuel filter water draining

Note: *Various types of fuel filters are fitted to these engines depending on model year and territory. Not all filters may be fitted with a drain facility.*

1 The fuel filter is located at the rear left-hand side of the engine compartment next to the battery.

2 Pull up the plastic cover and remove it from the top of the engine.

6.9 Renew the sump plug sealing washer

6.11 Fit a new O-ring

6.12 Fit a new paper element to the cap

7.3a Fuel drain pipe attached to underside of filter mounting bracket...

7.3b ...and drain tube coming out at rear of transmission

7.4a Using a Tox key...

7.4b ...slacken the water drain screw

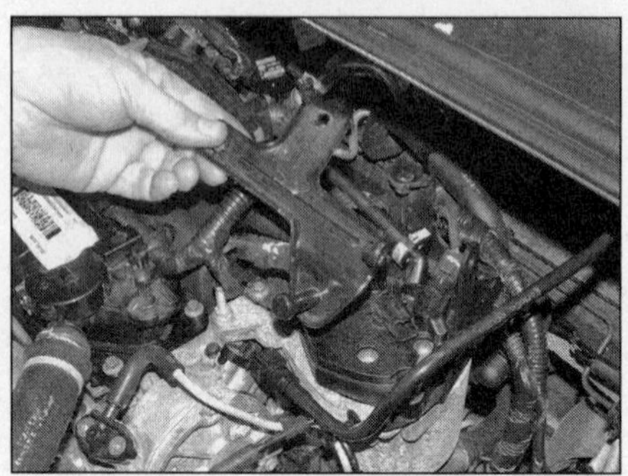
7.6 Remove the bracket

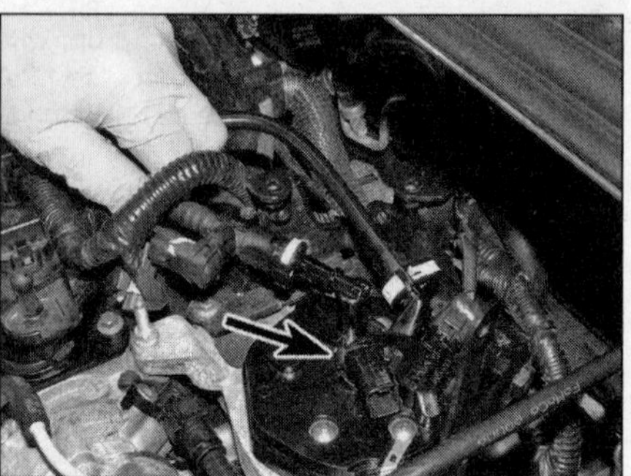
7.8 Remove the sensor (arrowed)

1.5 litre engines

3 A drain pipe is attached to the underside of the filter housing, which exits at the rear of the transmission **(see illustrations)**. To prevent fuel spillage, position a suitable container under the back of the transmission, on the left-hand side.

4 Using a Torx key unscrew the drain screw to allow the water to drain out from the fuel filter housing **(see illustrations)**. As soon as water-free fuel emerges from the pipe, tighten the drain screw.

5 With the drain screw secure, refit the engine cover and start the engine. If difficulty is experienced, bleed the fuel system (Chapter 4B Section 6).

1.6 litre engines

6 Remove the crash protection bracket from the top of the filter **(see illustration)**.

7 Position a container or cloth beneath the filter housing.

8 Disconnect the wiring plug from the water sensor, rotate the sensor and lift it from the fuel filter top cover **(see illustration)**.

9 Rotate the centre fitting on the top of the filter clockwise slightly and lift it. This opens the drain tap, and allows the fuel/water to drain from the filter. As soon as water-free fuel emerges from the pipe, press down the fitting and rotate it anti-clockwise to secure it.

10 Allow diesel to drain into the container or onto the cloth. Note that there is no need to remove a large amount of fuel.

11 Refit the sensor and reconnect the wiring plug. Fit the crash protection bracket.

12 Start the engine and check for leaks. Refit the engine cover.

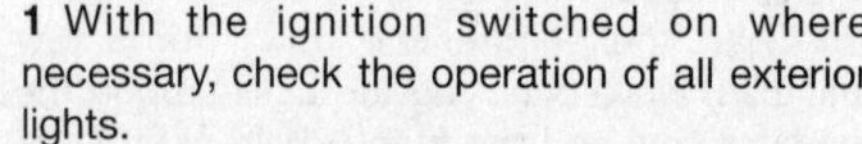

8 Lights and horn operation check

1 With the ignition switched on where necessary, check the operation of all exterior lights.

2 Check the brake lights with the help of an assistant, or by reversing up close to a reflective door. Make sure that all the rear lights are capable of operating independently, without affecting any of the other lights – for example, switch on as many rear lights as possible, then try the brake lights. If any unusual results are found, this is usually due to an earth fault or other poor connection at that rear light unit.

3 Again with the help of an assistant or using a reflective surface, check as far as possible that the headlights work on both main and dipped beam.

4 Renew any defective bulbs with reference to Chapter 12.

5 Check the operation of all interior lights, including the glovebox and luggage area illumination lights. Switch on the ignition, and check that all relevant warning lights come on as expected – the vehicle handbook should give details of these. Now start the engine, and check that the appropriate lights go out. When you are next driving at night, check that all the instrument panel and facia lighting works correctly. If any problems are found, refer to Chapter 12

6 Finally, choose an appropriate time of day to test the operation of the horn.

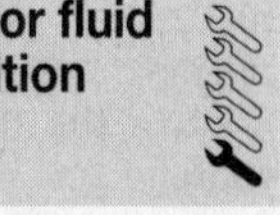

9 Underbonnet check for fluid leaks and hose condition

Warning: Renewal of air conditioning hoses must be left to a dealer service department or air conditioning specialist who has the equipment to depressurise the system safely. Never remove air conditioning components or hoses until the system has been depressurised.

1 Visually inspect the engine joint faces, gaskets and seals for any signs of water or oil leaks. Pay particular attention to the areas around the cylinder head cover, cylinder head, oil filter and sump joint faces. Bear in mind that, over a period of time, some very slight seepage from these areas is to be expected – what you are really looking for is any indication of a serious leak. Should a leak be found, renew the offending gasket or oil seal by referring to the appropriate Chapters in this manual.

2 High temperatures in the engine compartment can cause the deterioration of the rubber and plastic hoses used for engine, accessory and emission systems operation. Periodic inspection should be made for cracks, loose clamps, material hardening and leaks.

3 When checking the hoses, ensure that all the cable-ties or clips used to retain the hoses are in place, and in good condition. Clips which are broken or missing can lead to chafing of the hoses, pipes or wiring, which could cause more serious problems in the future.

4 Carefully check the large top and bottom radiator hoses, along with the other smaller-diameter cooling system hoses and metal pipes; do not forget the heater hoses/pipes which run from the engine to the bulkhead. Inspect each hose along its entire length, replacing any that is cracked, swollen or shows signs of deterioration. Cracks may become more apparent if the hose is squeezed, and may often be apparent at the hose ends.

5 Make sure that all hose connections are tight. If the large-diameter air hoses from the air cleaner are loose, they will leak air, and upset the engine idle quality. If the spring clamps that are used to secure many of the hoses appear to be slackening, they should be updated with worm-drive clips to prevent the possibility of leaks.

6 Some other hoses are secured to their fittings with clamps. Where clamps are used, check to be sure they haven't lost their tension, allowing the hose to leak. If clamps aren't used, make sure the hose has not expanded and/or hardened where it slips over the fitting, allowing it to leak.

7 Check all fluid reservoirs, filler caps, drain plugs and fittings, etc, looking for any signs of leakage of oil, transmission and/or brake hydraulic fluid, coolant and power steering fluid. Also check the clutch hydraulic fluid lines which lead from the fluid reservoir and slave cylinder (on the transmission).

8 If the vehicle is regularly parked in the same place, close inspection of the ground underneath it will soon show any leaks; ignore the puddle of water which will be left if the air conditioning system is in use. Place a clean piece of cardboard below the engine, and examine it for signs of contamination after the vehicle has been parked over it overnight.

9 Remember that some leaks will only occur with the engine running, or when the engine is hot or cold. With the handbrake firmly applied, start the engine from cold, and let the engine idle while you examine the underside of the engine compartment for signs of leakage.

10 If an unusual smell is noticed inside or around the car, especially when the engine is thoroughly hot, this may point to the presence of a leak.

11 As soon as a leak is detected, its source must be traced and rectified. Where oil has been leaking for some time, it is usually necessary to use a steam cleaner, pressure washer or similar to clean away the accumulated dirt, so that the exact source of the leak can be identified.

Vacuum hoses

12 It's quite common for vacuum hoses, especially those in the emissions system, to be colour-coded, or to be identified by coloured stripes moulded into them. Various systems require hoses with different wall thicknesses, collapse resistance and temperature resistance. When renewing hoses, be sure the new ones are made of the same material.

13 Often the only effective way to check a hose is to remove it completely from the vehicle. If more than one hose is removed, be sure to label the hoses and fittings to ensure correct installation.

14 When checking vacuum hoses, be sure to include any plastic T-fittings in the check. Inspect the fittings for cracks, and check the hose where it fits over the fitting for distortion, which could cause leakage.

15 A small piece of vacuum hose (quarter-inch inside diameter) can be used as a stethoscope to detect vacuum leaks. Hold one end of the hose to your ear, and probe around vacuum hoses and fittings, listening for the 'hissing' sound characteristic of a vacuum leak.

Warning: When probing with the vacuum hose stethoscope, be very careful not to come into contact with moving engine components such as the auxiliary drivebelt, radiator electric cooling fan, etc.

Fuel hoses

Warning: There are certain precautions which must be taken when inspecting or servicing fuel system components. Work in a well-ventilated area, and do not allow open flames (cigarettes, appliance pilot lights, etc) or bare light bulbs near the work area. Mop-up any spills immediately, and do not store fuel-soaked rags where they could ignite.

16 Check all fuel hoses for deterioration and chafing. Check especially for cracks in areas where the hose bends, and also just before fittings, such as where a hose attaches to the fuel filter.

17 It is not unusual for a high-mileage diesel engine to exhibit a 'film' of diesel fuel around the injectors, resulting in an oily appearance. Unless there is clear evidence of a significant fuel leak, this is not normally a matter for concern. The best course of action would be to first clean the engine thoroughly; then, after several more miles have been covered, the source of the leak can be identified and its severity assessed.

18 High-quality fuel line, usually identified by the word 'Fluoroelastomer' printed on the hose, should be used for fuel line renewal. Never, under any circumstances, use non-reinforced vacuum line, clear plastic tubing or water hose as a substitute for fuel lines.

19 Springtype clamps are commonly used on fuel lines. These clamps often lose their tension over a period of time, and can be 'sprung' during removal. Renew all spring-type clamps with proper petrol pipe clips whenever a hose is renewed.

Metal lines

20 Sections of metal piping are often used for fuel line between the fuel filter and the engine. Check carefully to be sure the piping has not been bent or crimped, and that cracks have not started in the line.

21 If a section of metal fuel line must be renewed, only seamless steel piping should be used, since copper and aluminium piping don't have the strength necessary to withstand normal engine vibration.

22 Check the metal lines where they enter the brake master cylinder, ABS hydraulic unit or clutch master/slave cylinders (as applicable) for cracks in the lines or loose fittings. Any sign of brake fluid leakage calls for an immediate and thorough inspection.

10 Engine compartment wiring check

1 With the vehicle parked on level ground, apply the handbrake firmly and open the bonnet. Using an inspection light or a small electric torch, check all visible wiring within and beneath the engine compartment. Make sure that the ignition is switched off – take out the key.

2 What you are looking for is wiring that is obviously damaged by chafing against sharp edges, or against moving suspension/transmission components and/or the auxiliary drivebelt, by being trapped or crushed between carelessly-refitted components, or melted by being forced into contact with the hot engine castings, coolant pipes, etc. In almost all cases, damage of this sort is caused in the first instance by incorrect routing on reassembly after previous work has been carried out.

3 Depending on the extent of the problem, damaged wiring may be repaired by rejoining the break or splicing-in a new length of wire, using solder to ensure a good connection, and remaking the insulation with adhesive insulating tape or heat-shrink tubing, as appropriate. If the damage is extensive, given the implications for the vehicle's future reliability, the best long-term answer may well be to renew that entire section of the loom, however expensive this may appear.

4 When the actual damage has been repaired, ensure that the wiring loom is re-routed correctly, so that it is clear of other components, and not stretched or kinked, and is secured out of harm's way using the plastic clips, guides and ties provided.

5 Check all electrical connectors, ensuring that they are clean, securely fastened, and that each is locked by its plastic tabs or wire clip, as appropriate. If any connector shows external signs of corrosion (accumulations of white or green deposits, or streaks of 'rust'), or if any is thought to be dirty, it must be unplugged and cleaned using electrical contact cleaner. If the connector pins are severely corroded, the connector must be renewed; note that this may mean the renewal of that entire section of the loom – see your local Ford dealer for details.

6 If the cleaner completely removes the corrosion to leave the connector in a satisfactory condition, it would be wise to pack the connector with a suitable material which will exclude dirt and moisture, preventing the corrosion from occurring again; a Ford dealer may be able to recommend a suitable product.

7 Check the condition of the battery connections – remake the connections or renew the leads if a fault is found (see Chapter 5A). Use the same techniques to ensure that all earth points in the engine compartment provide good electrical contact through clean, metal-to-metal joints, and that all are securely fastened.

8 Check the wiring to the glow plugs, referring to Chapter if necessary.

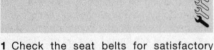

11 Seat belt check

1 Check the seat belts for satisfactory operation and condition. Inspect the webbing for fraying and cuts. Check that they retract smoothly and without binding into their reels.

2 Check the seat belt mountings, ensuring that all the bolts are securely tightened.

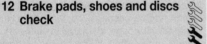

12 Brake pads, shoes and discs check

1 The work described in this Sectionshould be carried out at the specified intervals, or whenever a defect is suspected in the braking system. Any of the following symptoms could indicate a potential brake system defect:

a) *The vehicle pulls to one side when the brake pedal is depressed.*
b) *The brakes make squealing, scraping or dragging noises when applied.*
c) *Brake pedal travel is excessive, or pedal feel is poor.*
d) *The brake fluid requires repeated topping-up. Note that, because the hydraulic clutch shares the same fluid as the braking system (see Chapter 6), this problem could be due to a leak in the clutch system.*

Front disc brakes

2 Apply the handbrake, then loosen the front wheel nuts. Jack up the front of the vehicle, and support it on axle stands (see *Jacking and vehicle support*).

3 For better access to the brake calipers, remove the wheels.

4 Look through the inspection window in the caliper, and check that the thickness of the friction lining material on each of the pads is not less than the recommended minimum thickness given in the Specifications **(see illustration)**.

5 If it is difficult to determine the exact thickness of the pad linings, or if you are at all concerned about the condition of the pads, then remove them from the calipers for further inspection (refer to Chapter 9 Section 2).

6 Check the other caliper in the same way.

7 If any one of the brake pads has worn down to, or below, the specified limit, all four pads at that end of the car must be renewed as a set. If the pads on one side are significantly more worn than the other, this may indicate that the caliper pistons have partially seized – refer to the brake pad renewal procedure in Chapter 9 Section 2, and push the pistons back into the caliper to free them.

8 Measure the thickness of the discs with a micrometer, if available, to make sure that they still have service life remaining. Do not be fooled by the lip of rust which often forms on the outer edge of the disc, which may make the disc appear thicker than it really is – scrape off the loose rust if necessary, without scoring the disc friction (shiny) surface.

9 If any disc is thinner than the specified minimum thickness, renew it (refer to Chapter 9 Section 4).

10 Check the general condition of the discs. Look for excessive scoring and discolouration caused by overheating. If these conditions exist, remove the relevant disc and have it resurfaced or renewed (refer to Chapter 9 Section 4).

11 Make sure that the handbrake is firmly applied, then check that the transmission is in neutral. Spin the wheel, and check that the brake is not binding. Some drag is normal with a disc brake, but it should not require any great effort to turn the wheel – also, do not confuse brake drag with resistance from the transmission.

12 Before refitting the wheels, check all brake lines and hoses (refer to Chapter 9). In particular, check the flexible hoses in the vicinity of the calipers, where they are subjected to most movement **(see illustration)**. Bend them between the fingers (but do not actually bend them double, or the casing may be damaged) and check that this does not reveal previously-hidden cracks, cuts or splits.

13 On completion, refit the wheels and lower the car to the ground. Tighten the wheel nuts to the specified torque.

Rear disc brakes

14 Loosen the rear wheel nuts, then chock the front wheels. Jack up the rear of the car, and support it on axle stands. Release the handbrake and remove the rear wheels.

15 The procedure for checking the rear brakes is much the same as described in paragraphs 2 to 13 above. Check that the rear brakes are not binding, noting that transmission resistance is not a factor on the rear wheels. Abnormal effort may indicate that the handbrake needs adjusting – see Chapter 9 Section 22.

Rear drum brakes

16 Loosen the rear wheel nuts, then chock the front wheels. Jack up the rear of the car, and support on axle stands (see *Jacking and vehicle support*). Release the handbrake and remove the rear wheels.

17 Spin the wheel to check that the brake is not binding. A small amount of resistance from the brake is acceptable, but no great effort should be required to turn the wheel hub. Abnormal effort may indicate that the handbrake needs adjusting – see Chapter 9 Section 21.

18 To check the brake shoe lining thickness without removing the brake drums, prise the rubber plugs from the backplates, and use an electric torch to inspect the linings of the leading brake shoes. Check that the thickness of the lining material on the brake shoes is not less than the recommendation given in the Specifications.

19 If it is difficult to determine the exact thickness of the brake shoe linings, or if you are at all concerned about the condition of the shoes, then remove the rear drums for a more comprehensive inspection (refer to Chapter 9 Section 5).

20 With the drum removed, check the shoe return and hold-down springs for correct installation, and check the wheel cylinders for leakage of brake fluid. Apart from fluid being visible, a leaking wheel cylinder may be characterised by an excessive build-up of brake dust (stuck to the fluid which has leaked) at the cylinder seals.

21 Check the friction surface of the brake drums for scoring and discoloration. If excessive, the drum should be resurfaced or renewed.

12.4 Check the brake pad friction material thickness (arrowed)

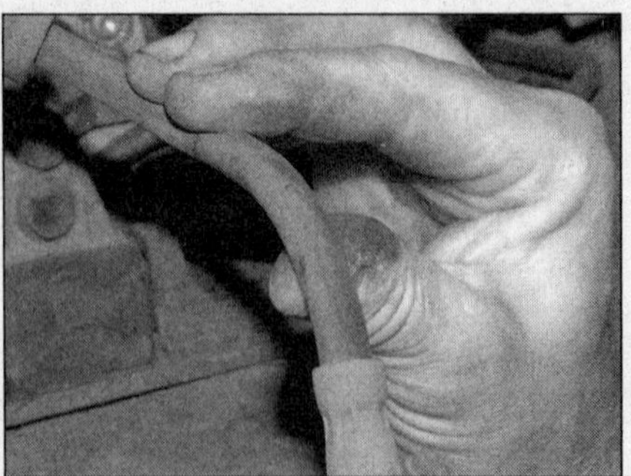

12.12 Bend the flexible hoses and check for cracks

22 Before refitting the wheels, check all brake lines and hoses (refer to Section 16). On completion, apply the handbrake and check that the rear wheels are locked. The handbrake can be adjusted as described in Chapter 9 Section 21.

23 On completion, refit the wheels and lower the car to the ground. Tighten the wheel nuts to the specified torque.

13 Exhaust system check

1 With the engine cold (at least three hours after the vehicle has been driven), check the complete exhaust system, from its starting point at the engine to the end of the tailpipe. Ideally, this should be done on a hoist, where unrestricted access is available; if a hoist is not available, raise and support the vehicle on axle stands.

2 Make sure that all brackets and rubber mountings are in good condition, and tight; if any of the mountings are to be renewed, ensure that the new ones are of the correct type – in the case of the rubber mountings, their colour is a good guide. Those nearest to the catalytic converter are more heat-resistant than the others.

3 Check the pipes and connections for evidence of leaks, severe corrosion, or damage. Leakage at any of the joints or in other parts of the system will usually show up as a black sooty stain in the vicinity of the leak. **Note:** *Exhaust sealants should not be used on any part of the exhaust system upstream of the catalytic converter (between the engine and the converter) – even if the sealant does not contain additives harmful to the converter, pieces of it may break off and foul the element, causing local overheating.*

4 At the same time, inspect the underside of the body for holes, corrosion, open seams, etc, which may allow exhaust gases to enter the passenger compartment. Seal all body openings with silicone or body putty.

5 Rattles and other noises can often be traced to the exhaust system, especially the rubber mountings **(see illustration)**. Try to move the system, silencer(s) and catalytic converter. If any components can touch the body or suspension parts, secure the exhaust system with new mountings.

13.5 Check the condition of the rubber mountings

14 Steering, suspension and roadwheel check

Front suspension and steering

1 Apply the handbrake, then raise the front of the vehicle and support it on axle stands.

2 Visually inspect the balljoint dust covers and the steering gear gaiters for splits, chafing or deterioration **(see illustration)**. Any wear of these components will cause loss of lubricant, together with dirt and water entry, resulting in rapid deterioration of the balljoints or steering gear.

3 Check the power-assisted steering fluid hoses for chafing or deterioration, and the pipe and hose unions for fluid leaks. Also check for signs of fluid leakage under pressure from the steering gear rubber gaiters, which would indicate failed fluid seals within the steering gear.

4 Grasp the roadwheel at the 12 o'clock and 6 o'clock positions, and try to rock it **(see illustration)**. Very slight free play may be felt, but if the movement is appreciable, further investigation is necessary to determine the source. Continue rocking the wheel while an assistant depresses the footbrake. If the movement is now eliminated or significantly reduced, it is likely that the hub bearings are at fault. If the free play is still evident with the footbrake depressed, then there is wear in the suspension joints or mountings.

5 Now grasp the wheel at the 9 o'clock and 3 o'clock positions, and try to rock it as before **(see illustration)**. Any movement felt now may again be caused by wear in the hub bearings or the steering track rod balljoints. If the outer track rod balljoint is worn, the visual movement will be obvious. If the inner joint is suspect, it can be felt by placing a hand over the rack-and-pinion rubber gaiter, and gripping the track rod. If the wheel is now rocked, movement will be felt at the inner joint if wear has taken place.

6 Using a large screwdriver or flat bar, check for wear in the suspension mounting and subframe bushes by levering between the relevant suspension component and its attachment point. Some movement is to be expected as the mountings are made of rubber, but excessive wear should be obvious. Also check the condition of any visible rubber bushes, looking for splits, cracks or contamination of the rubber.

7 With the vehicle standing on its wheels, have an assistant turn the steering wheel back-and-forth, about an eighth of a turn each way. There should be very little, if any, lost movement between the steering wheel and roadwheels. If this is not the case, closely observe the joints and mountings previously described, but in addition, check the steering column joints for wear, and also check the rack-and-pinion steering gear itself.

Rear suspension

8 Chock the front wheels, then raise the rear of the vehicle and support it on axle stands.

9 Check the rear hub bearings for wear, using the method described for the front hub bearings (paragraph 4).

10 Using a large screwdriver or flat bar, check for wear in the suspension mounting bushes by levering between the relevant suspension component and its attachment point. Some movement is to be expected as the mountings are made of rubber, but excessive wear should be obvious.

Roadwheel check and balancing

11 Periodically remove the roadwheels, and clean any dirt or mud from the inside and

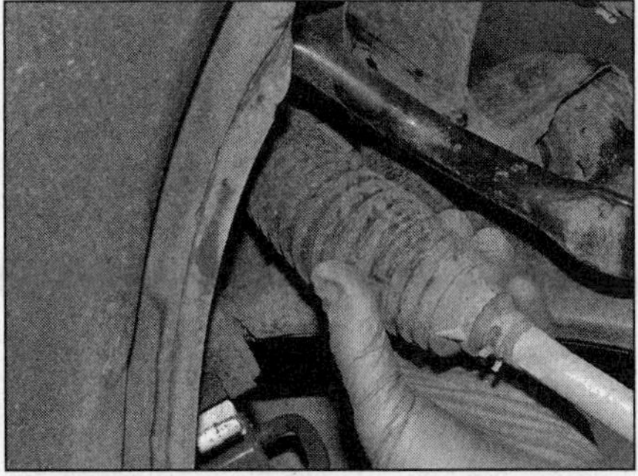

14.2 Check the condition of the steering rack gaiters

14.4 Grasp the roadwheel at the 12 o'clock and 6 o'clock positions, and try to rock it

14.5 Check for wear in the steering rack-track rod balljoints

outside surfaces. Examine the wheel rims for signs of rusting, corrosion or other damage. Light alloy wheels are easily damaged by 'kerbing' whilst parking, and similarly, steel wheels may become dented or buckled. Renewal of the wheel is very often the only course of remedial action possible.

12 The balance of each wheel and tyre assembly should be maintained, not only to avoid excessive tyre wear, but also to avoid wear in the steering and suspension components. Wheel imbalance is normally signified by vibration through the vehicle's bodyshell, although in many cases it is particularly noticeable through the steering wheel. Conversely, it should be noted that wear or damage in suspension or steering components may cause excessive tyre wear. Out-of-round or out-of-true tyres, damaged wheels and wheel bearing wear/maladjustment also fall into this category. Balancing will not usually cure vibration caused by such wear.

13 Wheel balancing may be carried out with the wheel either on or off the vehicle. If balanced on the vehicle, ensure that the wheel-to-hub relationship is marked in some way prior to subsequent wheel removal, so that it may be refitted in its original position.

15 Driveshaft rubber gaiter and joint check

1 The driveshaft rubber gaiters are very important, because they prevent dirt, water and foreign material from entering and damaging the joints. External contamination can cause the gaiter material to deteriorate prematurely, so it's a good idea to wash the gaiters with soap and water occasionally.

2 With the vehicle raised and securely supported on axle stands, turn the steering onto full-lock, then slowly rotate each front wheel in turn. Inspect the condition of the outer constant velocity (CV) joint rubber gaiters, squeezing the gaiters to open out the folds. Check for signs of cracking, splits, or deterioration of the rubber, which may allow the escape of grease, and lead to the ingress of water and grit into the joint. Also check the security and condition of the retaining clips.

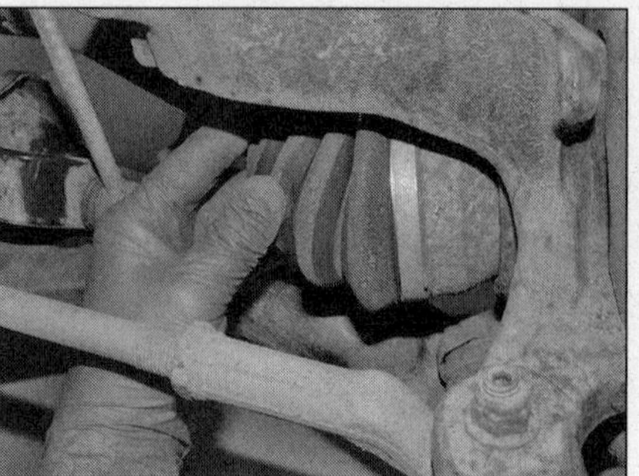

15.2 Check the condition of the driveshaft gaiters

Repeat these checks on the inner joints **(see illustration)**. If any damage or deterioration is found, the gaiters should be renewed as described in Chapter 8 Section 3 or 4.

3 At the same time, check the general condition of the outer CV joints themselves, by first holding the driveshaft and attempting to rotate the wheels. Repeat this check on the inner joints, by holding the inner joint yoke and attempting to rotate the driveshaft.

4 Any appreciable movement in the joint indicates wear in the joint, wear in the driveshaft splines, or a loose driveshaft retaining bolt.

16 Underbody and fuel/brake line check

1 With the vehicle raised and supported on axle stands or over an inspection pit, thoroughly inspect the underbody and wheel arches for signs of damage and corrosion. In particular, examine the bottom of the side sills, and any concealed areas where mud can collect.

2 Where corrosion and rust is evident, press and tap firmly on the panel with a screwdriver, and check for any serious corrosion which would necessitate repairs.

3 If the panel is not seriously corroded, clean away the rust, and apply a new coating of underseal. Refer to Chapter 11 Section 4 or 5 for more details of body repairs.

4 At the same time, inspect the lower body panels for stone damage and general condition.

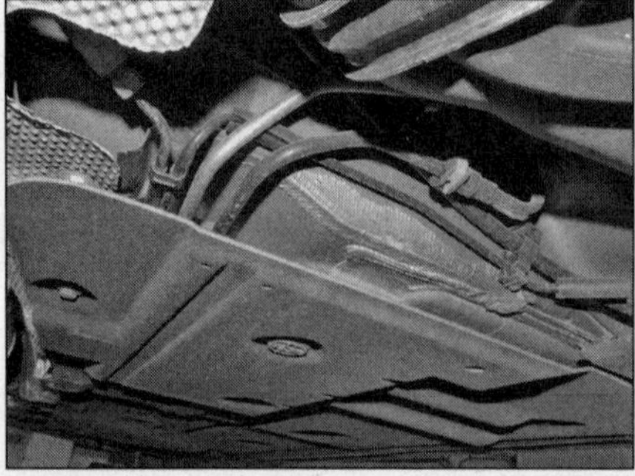

16.5a Remove the plastic shields (where fitted)...

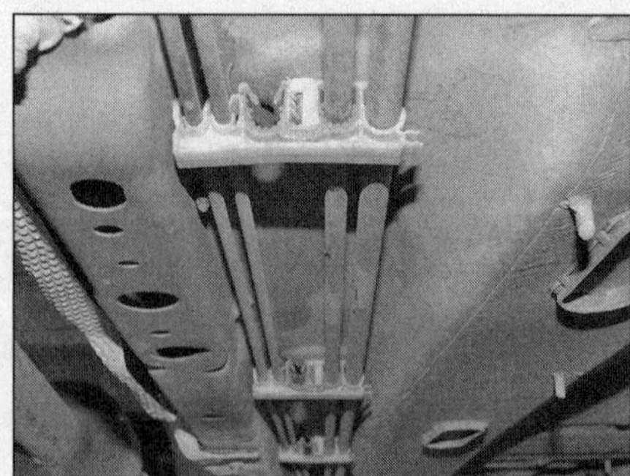

16.5b ...and check the fuel and brake pipes are clipped to the vehicle body

5 Inspect all of the fuel and brake lines on the underbody for damage, rust, corrosion and leakage, checking the PVC coating on the lines for damage, where applicable. Also make sure that the pipes/hoses are correctly supported in their clips **(see illustrations)**. Where fitted, remove the plastic covers from under the vehicle to check the underbody.

17 Hinge and lock lubrication

1 Work around the vehicle and lubricate the hinges of the bonnet, doors and tailgate with a light machine oil.

2 Check carefully the security and operation of all hinges, latches and locks, adjusting them where required. Check the operation of the central locking system (if fitted).

3 Where applicable, check the condition and operation of the tailgate struts, renewing them if either is leaking or no longer able to support the tailgate securely when raised.

18 Roadwheel nut tightness check

1 Checking the tightness of the wheel nuts is more relevant than you might think. Apart from the obvious safety aspect of ensuring they are sufficiently tight, this check will reveal whether they have been overtightened, as may have happened the last time new tyres were fitted, for example. If the car suffers a puncture, you may find that the wheel nuts cannot be loosened with the wheel brace.

2 Apply the handbrake, chock the wheels, and engage 1st gear.

3 Remove the wheel cover (or wheel centre cover), using the flat end of the wheel brace supplied in the tool kit.

4 Loosen the first wheel nut, using the wheel brace if possible. If the nut proves stubborn, use a close-fitting socket and a long extension bar.

Warning: Do not use makeshift means to loosen the wheel nuts if the proper tools are not available. If extra force is required, make sure that the tools fit properly, and are of good quality. Even so, consider the consequences of the tool slipping or breaking, and take precautions – wearing stout gloves is advisable to protect your hands. Do not be tempted to stand on the tools used – they are not designed for this, and there is a high risk of personal injury if the tool slips or breaks. If the wheel nuts are simply too tight, take the car to a garage equipped with suitable power tools.

5 Once the nut has been loosened, remove it and check that the wheel stud threads are clean. Use a small wire brush to clean any rust or dirt from the threads, if necessary. **Note:**

Only remove one wheel nut at a time, unless the vehicle has been jacked up and placed on axle stands.

6 Refit the nut, with the tapered side facing inwards. Tighten it fully, using the wheel brace alone – no other tools. This will ensure that the wheel nuts can be loosened using the wheel brace if a puncture occurs. However, if a torque wrench is available, tighten the nut to the specified torque wrench setting.

7 Repeat the procedure for the remaining nuts, then refit the wheel cover or centre cover, as applicable.

8 Work around the car, checking and retightening the nuts for all four wheels.

19 Road test

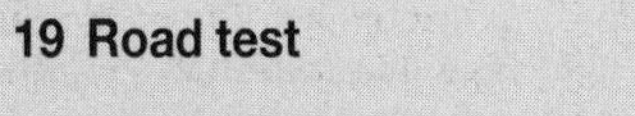

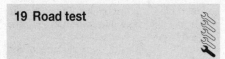

Braking system

1 Make sure that the vehicle does not pull to one side when braking, and that the wheels do not lock when braking hard.

2 Check that there is no vibration through the steering when braking. On models equipped with ABS brakes, if vibration is felt through the pedal under heavy braking, this is a normal characteristic of the system operation, and is not a cause for concern.

3 Check that the handbrake operates correctly, without excessive movement of the lever, and that it holds the vehicle stationary on a slope, in both directions (facing up and down a slope).

21.1 Remove the cover locating peg

4 With the engine switched off, test the operation of the brake servo unit as follows. Depress the footbrake four or five times to exhaust the vacuum, then start the engine. As the engine starts, there should be a noticeable 'give' in the brake pedal as vacuum builds-up. Allow the engine to run for at least two minutes, and then switch it off. If the brake pedal is now depressed again, it should be possible to detect a hiss from the servo as the pedal is depressed. After about four or five applications, no further hissing should be heard, and the pedal should feel considerably harder.

Steering and suspension

5 Check for any abnormalities in the steering, suspension, handling or road 'feel'.

6 Drive the vehicle, and check that there are no unusual vibrations or noises.

7 Check that the steering feels positive, with no excessive sloppiness or roughness, and check for any suspension noises when cornering and driving over bumps.

Drivetrain

8 Check the performance of the engine, transmission and driveshafts.

9 Check that the engine starts correctly, both when cold and when hot. Observe the glow plug warning light, and check that it comes on and goes off correctly.

10 Listen for any unusual noises from the engine and transmission.

11 Make sure that the engine runs smoothly when idling, and that there is no hesitation when accelerating.

12 Check that all gears can be engaged smoothly without noise, and that the gear lever action is smooth and not abnormally vague or 'notchy'.

13 Listen for a metallic clicking sound from the front of the vehicle as the vehicle is driven slowly in a circle with the steering on full-lock. Carry out this check in both directions. If a clicking noise is heard, this indicates wear in a driveshaft joint, in which case renew the joint if necessary.

Clutch

14 Check that the clutch pedal moves smoothly and easily through its full travel, and that the clutch itself functions correctly, with no trace of slip or drag.

15 If the clutch is slow to release, it is possible that the system requires bleeding (see Chapter 6 Section 5). Also check the fluid pipes under the bonnet for signs of leakage.

16 Check the clutch as described in Chapter 6.

Instruments and electrical equipment

17 Check the operation of all instruments and electrical equipment.

18 Make sure that all instruments read correctly, and switch on all electrical equipment in turn, to check that it functions properly.

20 Handbrake check and adjustment

1 In service, the handbrake should be fully applied within 3 to 5 clicks of the handbrake lever ratchet. Should adjustment be necessary, refer to Chapter 9 Section 21 ; for the full procedure description.

21 Fuel filter renewal

1 Remove the engine cover from the top of the engine, and then slacken and remove the cover locating peg **(see illustration)**, from the top of the fuel filter bracket.

2 Release the locking clip and disconnect the wiring plug from the sensor on the top of the filter **(see illustration)**.

3 Undo the two retaining nuts and disconnect the the wiring loom mounting brackets from the top of the fuel filter housing **(see illustration)**.

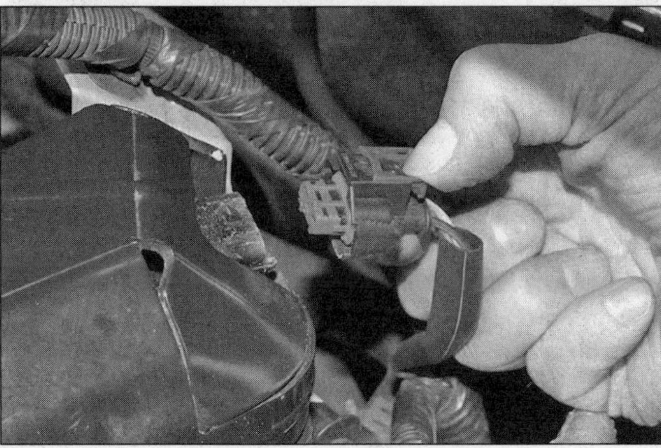

21.2 Disconnect the wiring plug

21.3 Disconnect the wiring loom brackets

21.4a Slacken and remove...

21.4b ...the two retaining studs...

21.4c ...then remove the metal bracket

4 Undo the two retaining nuts/studs, and then remove the metal bracket from over the top of the fuel filter **(see illustrations)**.

5 Place a piece of cloth around the filter housing, under the fuel pipes to catch any spilt fuel **(see illustration)**.

6 Release the locking clip, then press down on the securing clip and release the fuel supply pipe from the top of the fuel filter **(see illustrations)**. Plug the opening to prevent contamination.

7 Press the locking clips at each side of the fuel feed pipe and disconnect it from the top of the fuel filter **(see illustrations)**. Plug the opening to prevent contamination.

8 Using a ratchet and socket slacken and remove the upper part of the filter housing **(see illustrations)**.

21.5 Place cloth around filter housing

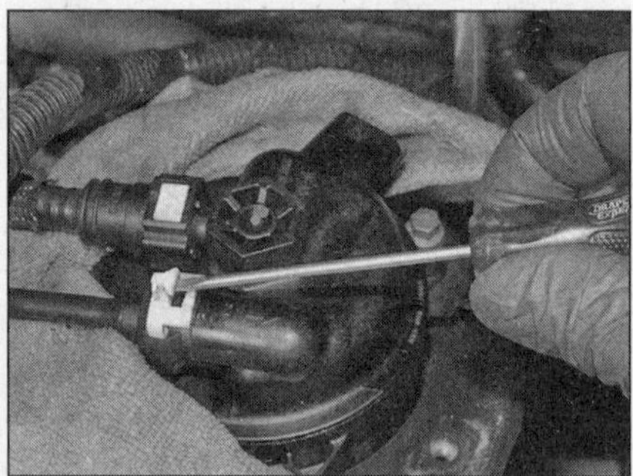
21.6a Release the locking clip...

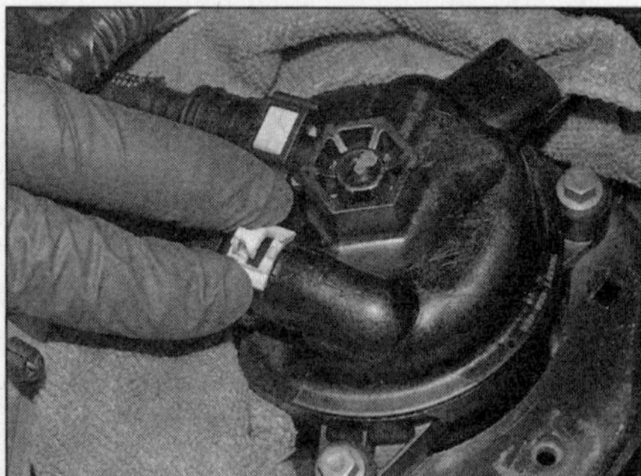
21.6b ...press down on the securing clip...

21.6c ...and disconnect the fuel supply pipe

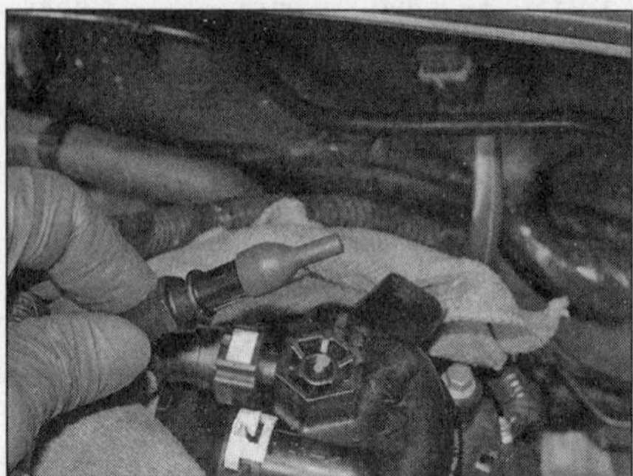
21.6d Plug the end of the fuel pipe

21.7a Release the locking clips to disconnect the fuel hose

21.7b Plug the end of the fuel pipe

21.8a Slacken the top of the fuel filter housing...

21.8b ...and unscrew it from the lower housing

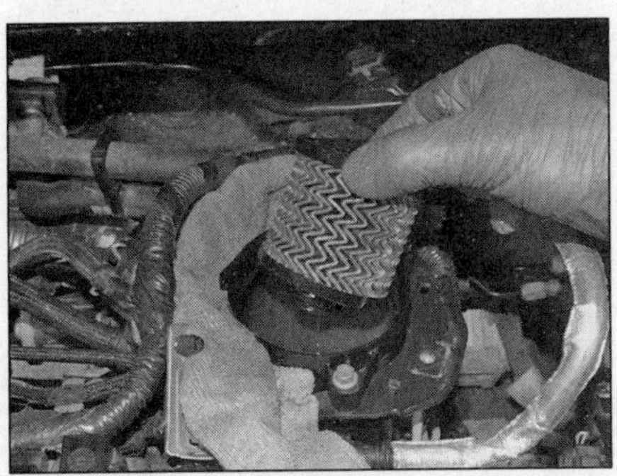
21.9 Lift out the old filter element

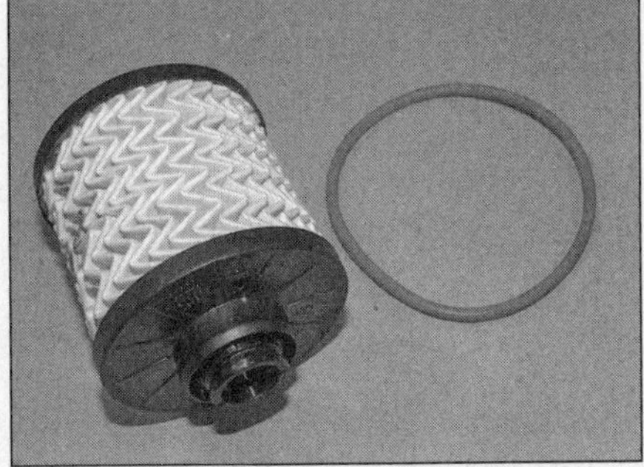
21.11 New filter and O-ring seal

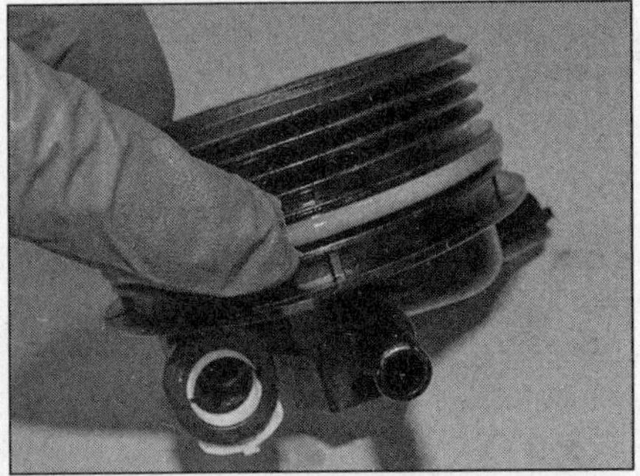
21.13 Fit the new seal to the upper housing

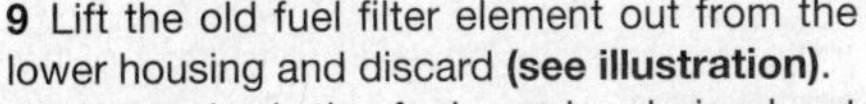
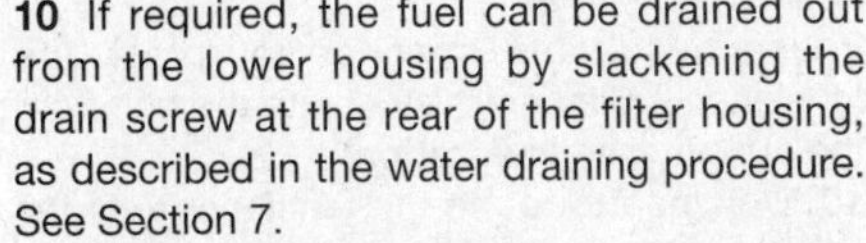

9 Lift the old fuel filter element out from the lower housing and discard **(see illustration)**.

10 If required, the fuel can be drained out from the lower housing by slackening the drain screw at the rear of the filter housing, as described in the water draining procedure. See Section 7.

11 Insert the new filter element into the lower housing, pressing it down fully into position **(see illustration)**.

12 If the lower part of the housing has been drained previously, after the new filter element is fitted, poor some clean diesel back into the lower housing, making sure it is not contaminated with dirt or water. This will aid the starting procedure, so that the system does not require bleeding.

13 Fit a new seal to the filter upper housing, making sure it is located correctly in the groove in the housing **(see illustration)**.

14 Refit the upper housing and tighten it until the stepped edge on the outer circumference of the upper housing contacts the stepped edge on the outer circumference of the lower housing **(see illustrations)**.

15 Refit the fuel supply and feed pipes to the top of the fuel filter housing, making sure the locking/securing clips hold the pipes in position securely.

16 Refit the upper metal bracket over the top of the fuel filter, refitting the wiring loom mounting brackets.

17 Reconnect the wiring connector to the sensor on the top of the fuel filter, making sure the locking clip is secured.

18 Refit the locating peg to the stud on the top of the filter housing and then refit the engine cover.

19 If necessary, bleed the fuel system as described in Chapter 4B Section 6.

21.14a Refit the upper housing...

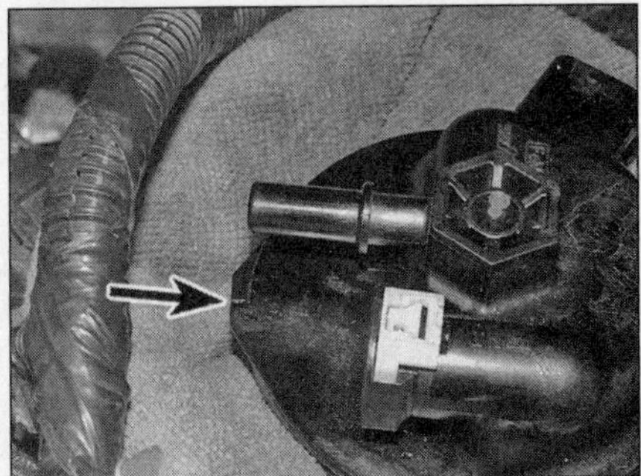
21.14b ...until the stepped edges meet

22 Air filter element renewal

Caution: Never drive the vehicle with the air cleaner filter element removed. Excessive engine wear could result, and backfiring could even cause a fire under the bonnet.

1 On all models the air filter element is located in the air cleaner assembly on the left-hand side of the engine compartment.

2 Remove the four torx head screws securing the cover to the air cleaner housing **(see illustration)**.

3 The cover can now be lifted, and the filter element removed **(see illustrations)**.

4 If carrying out a routine service, the element must be renewed regardless of its apparent condition.

5 If you are checking the element for any other reason, inspect its lower surface; if it is oily or very dirty, renew the element. If it is only moderately dusty, it can be re-used by blowing it clean from the upper to the lower surface with compressed air. Because it is a pleated-paper type filter, it cannot be washed. If it cannot be cleaned satisfactorily with compressed air, discard and renew it.

Caution: Wear eye protection when using compressed air.

6 Wipe out the inside of the housing, checking that no foreign matter is visible, either in the air inlet or in the air mass meter.

7 Refitting is the reverse of the removal

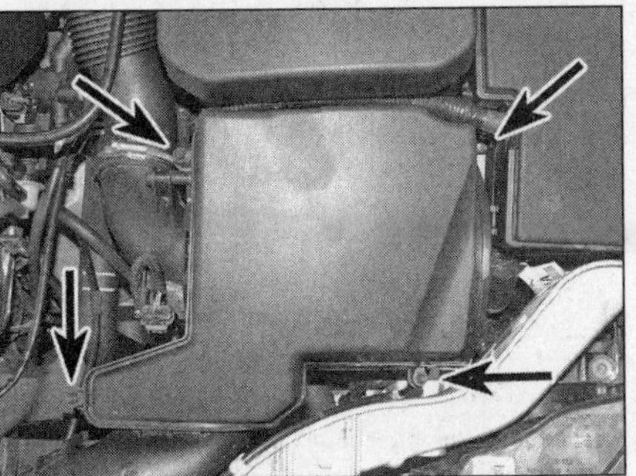
22.2 Remove the screws (arrowed)

22.3a Lift off the cover...

22.3b ...and remove the filter

22.7a Locate the inner part of the filter element on the collar...

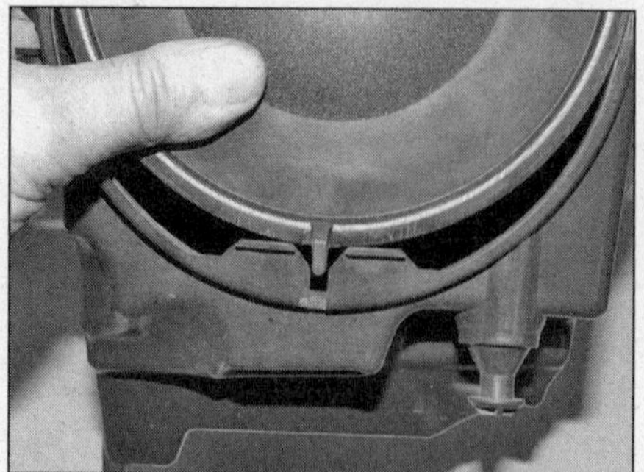

22.7b ...and align the locating peg on the outside – removed for clarity

24.1 Auxiliary belt routing – 1.5 litre engine

procedure, making sure the filter element locates on the collar inside the filter lower housing, and also the locating peg on the outside of the filter element locates in the lower housing **(see illustrations)**.

23 Timing belt renewal

1 The procedure is described in the relevant part of Chapter 2C Section 7 on 1.5 litre engines or Chapter 2D Section 7 on 1.6 litre engines.

24 Auxiliary drivebelt check and renewal

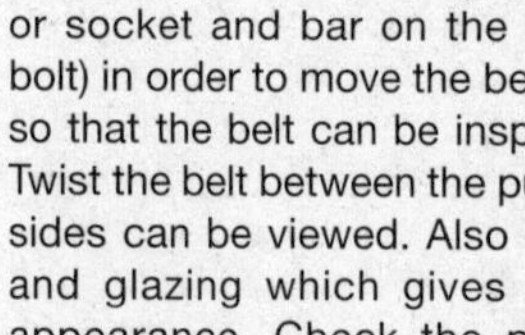

Note: *Only rotate the engine in the normal (clockwise) direction.*

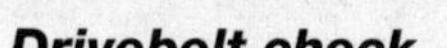

Drivebelt check

1 A single auxiliary drivebelt is fitted at the right-hand side of the engine **(see illustration)**. An automatic adjuster is fitted, so checking the drivebelt tension is unnecessary.

2 Due to their function and material make-up, drivebelts are prone to failure after a long period of time, and should therefore be inspected regularly.

3 Since the drivebelt is located very close to the right-hand side of the engine compartment, it is possible to gain better access by raising the front of the vehicle, undoing the fasteners and removing the engine undershield **(see illustration 3.6)**.

4 Some models have a protective cover fitted to protect the crankshaft pulley and belt assembly. Where fitted remove the 2 bolts that secure the protective cover, and then remove the cover

5 With the engine stopped, inspect the full length of the drivebelt for cracks and separation of the belt plies. It will be necessary to turn the engine (using a spanner or socket and bar on the crankshaft pulley bolt) in order to move the belt from the pulleys so that the belt can be inspected thoroughly. Twist the belt between the pulleys so that both sides can be viewed. Also check for fraying, and glazing which gives the belt a shiny appearance. Check the pulleys for nicks, cracks, distortion and corrosion.

6 Note that it is not unusual for a ribbed belt to exhibit small cracks in the edges of the belt ribs, and unless these are extensive or very deep, belt renewal is not essential.

Drivebelt renewal

7 To remove the drivebelt, first raise the front of the vehicle and support on axle stands (see *Jacking and vehicle support*). Remove the right-hand road wheel. Undo the fasteners and remove the engine undershield **(see illustration 3.6)**. Followed by the wheel arch liner and (where fitted) the crankshaft pulley cover.

8 Depending on model, it may be helpful to remove the plastic cover from the top of the engine.

9 Use a suitable spanner to rotate the tensioner, while an assistant lifts the belt from the pulleys **(see illustration)**.

10 Continue to rotate the tensioner until the tensioner arm passes the hole in the housing, and a 4.5 mm drill bit can be inserted, locking the tensioner in position **(see illustration)**.

11 Note how the belt is routed, then remove the belt from the pulleys **(see illustration)**.

12 Fit the new drivebelt onto the crankshaft, air conditioning compressor, alternator and tensioner/idler pulleys. Fit the tool to the tensioner arm, hold the tensioner stationary with the tool and remove the locking drill bit. Slowly allow the tensioner arm to rotate and tension the belt. Remove the tool.

13 Using a suitable socket on the crankshaft pulley, rotate the engine twice in the normal (clockwise) direction of rotation, checking that the belt is correctly located as the engine is rotated

14 Refit the engine top cover, undershield, wheel arch liner and (where fitted) the crankshaft pulley cover. Refit the road wheel and lower the car to the ground lower the car to the ground. Tighten the roadwheel bolts to the specified torque.

24.9 Use a 15 mm open-ended spanner to rotate the tensioner clockwise

24.10 Insert a 5.0 mm drill bit/rod into the hole (arrowed) in the tensioner housing

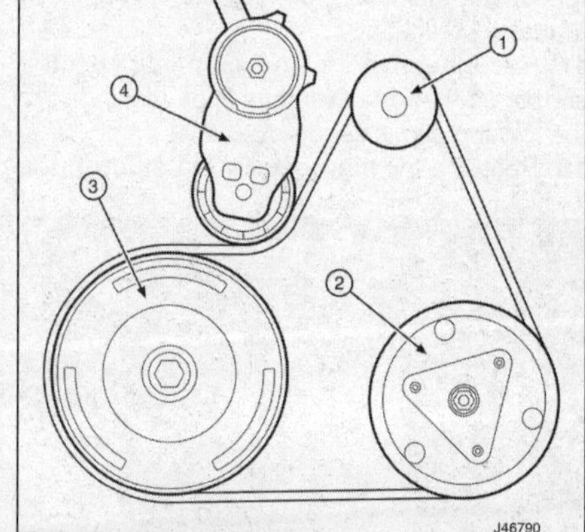

24.11 Auxiliary belt routing

1 Alternator pulley
2 Air conditioning compressor
3 Crankshaft pulley
4 Tensioner

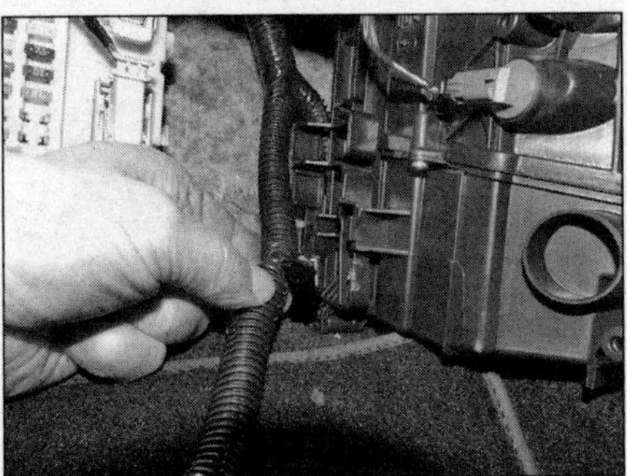
25.2 Unclip the wiring loom securing clip

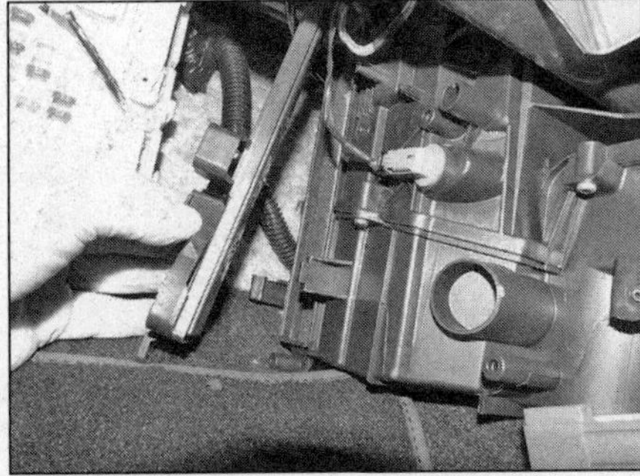
25.3 Remove the trim cover

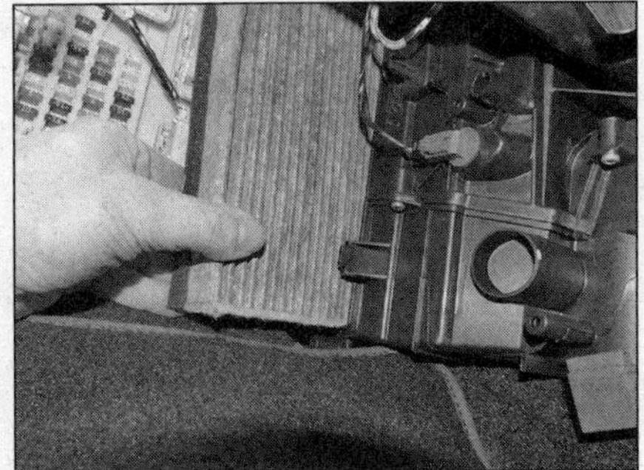
25.4 Remove the pollen filter

25 Pollen filter renewal

1 To make access easier, remove the glovebox assembly, as described in Chapter 11 Section 29.

2 Working under the passengers side of the facia, inside the footwell, reach up and unclip the wiring loom securing clip from the lower part of the pollen filter trim cover **(see illustration)**.

3 Compress the locking clips on the lower part of the trim cover to release it from the heater housing, and then remove the cover **(see illustration)**.

4 Pull the filter free from the housing, noting any directional arrows, as it is removed **(see illustration)**. The filter will need to be squeezed together to remove it completely from the heater housing.

5 Fit the new filter using a reversal of the removal procedure, ensuring that the filter is fitted with the airflow arrows pointing in the correct direction, as noted on removal. Refit the wiring loom securing clip back to the lower part of the housing, once filter trim cover has been refitted.

26 Brake fluid renewal

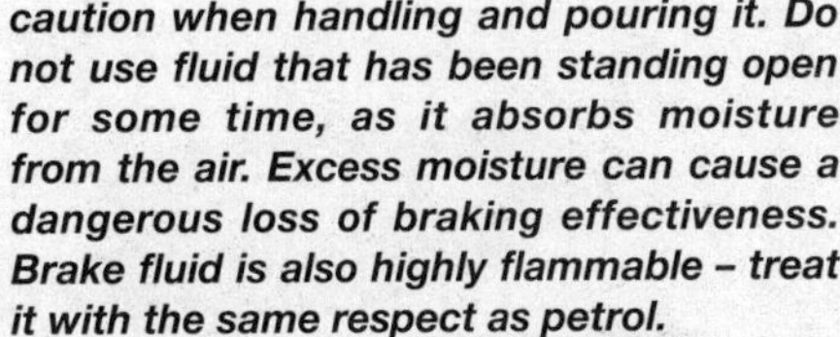

Warning: Brake hydraulic fluid can harm your eyes and damage painted surfaces, so use extreme caution when handling and pouring it. Do not use fluid that has been standing open for some time, as it absorbs moisture from the air. Excess moisture can cause a dangerous loss of braking effectiveness. Brake fluid is also highly flammable – treat it with the same respect as petrol.

1 The procedure is similar to that for the bleeding of the hydraulic system as described in Chapter 9 Section 14.

2 Reduce the fluid level in the reservoir (by syphoning or using a poultry baster), but do not allow the fluid level to drop far enough to allow air into the system – if air enters the ABS hydraulic unit, the unit may need be bled using special Ford test equipment (see Chapter 9).

Warning: Do not syphon the fluid by mouth; it is poisonous.

3 Working as described in Chapter 9, open the first bleed screw in the sequence, and pump the brake pedal gently until nearly all the old fluid has been emptied from the master cylinder reservoir. Top-up to the MAX level with new fluid, and continue pumping until only the new fluid remains in the reservoir, and new fluid can be seen emerging from the bleed screw. Tighten the screw, and top the reservoir level up to the MAX level line. Old hydraulic fluid is invariably much darker in colour than the new, making it easy to distinguish the two.

4 Work through all the remaining bleed screws in the sequence until new fluid can be seen at all of them. Be careful to keep the master cylinder reservoir topped-up to above the MIN level at all times, or air may enter the system and greatly increase the length of the task.

5 When the operation is complete, check that all bleed screws are securely tightened, and that their dust caps are refitted. Wash off all traces of spilt fluid, and recheck the master cylinder reservoir fluid level.

6 Check the operation of the brakes before taking the car on the road.

7 Finally, check the operation of the clutch. Since the clutch shares the same fluid reservoir as the braking system, it may also be necessary to bleed the clutch as described in Chapter 6 Section 5.

27 Remote control battery renewal

1 Although not in the Ford maintenance schedule, we recommend that the battery is changed every 2 years, regardless of the vehicle's mileage. However, if the door locks repeatedly fail to respond to signals from the remote control at the normal distance, change the battery in the remote control before attempting to troubleshoot any of the vehicle's other systems.

Models with a folding key blade

2 Press the button to release the key blade.

3 Use a small screwdriver and release the battery cover **(see illustrations)**.

4 Fully remove the battery cover and then remove the battery.

5 Fit a new battery – the '+' (positive) side of the battery must face up **(see illustration)**.

27.3a Insert a screwdriver into the slot ...

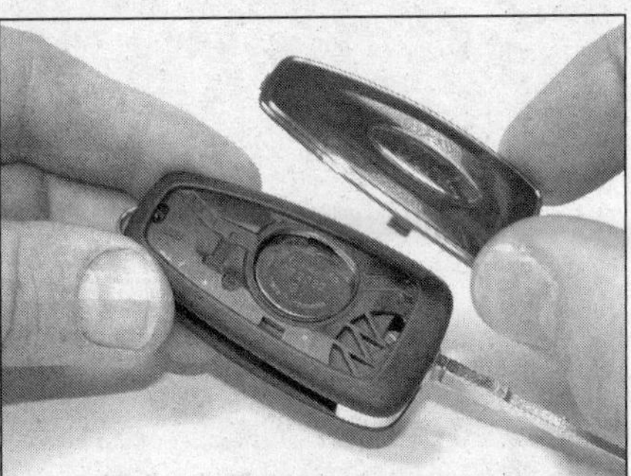
27.3b ... and prise off the cover

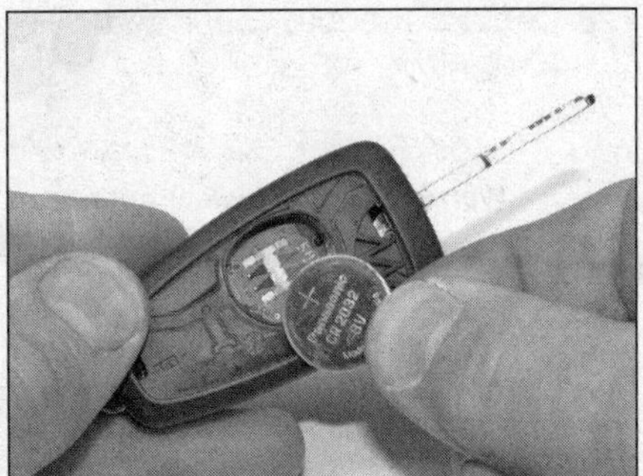
27.5 The battery fits positive side up

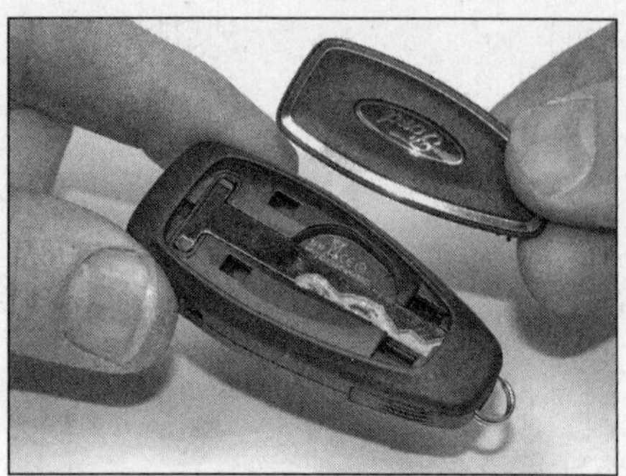

27.7 Release the key cover

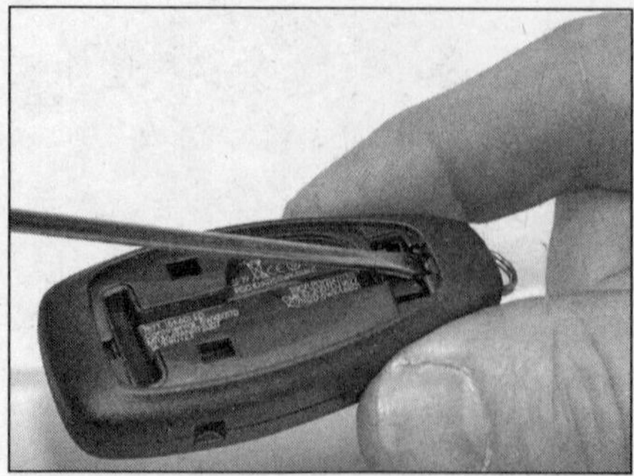

27.8 Release the upper half at the end first

27.9a Separate the 2 halves and...

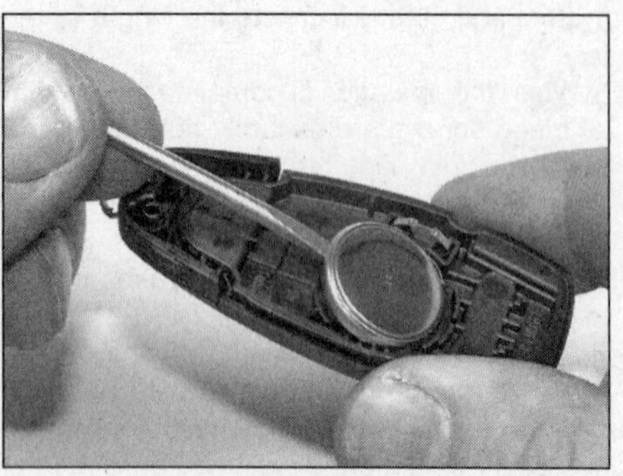

27.9b ...remove the battery

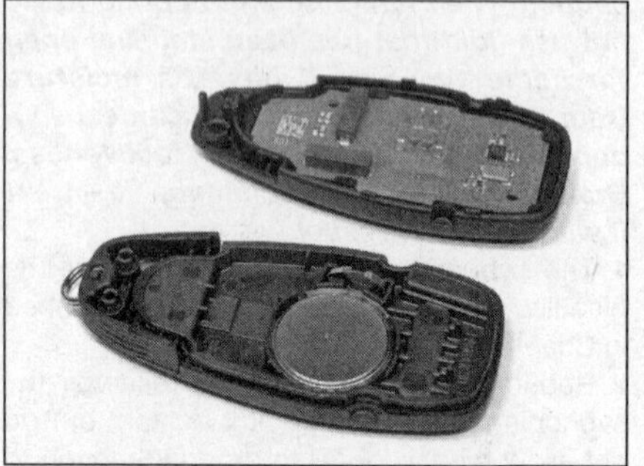

27.10 The battery fits positive side down

6 Refit the battery compartment cover and check the operation of the remote.

Models without a key blade

7 The emergency key blade is located beneath a cover. Press and hold the small buttons on the side of the remote to release the key cover **(see illustration)**.

8 Remove the key blade and then use a small screwdriver, first at the end of the narrow end of the key blade compartment and then on the side of the remote **(see illustration)**.

9 Fully separate the two halves of the remote and then use the screwdriver to remove the battery **(see illustrations)**.

10 Fit a new battery – the '+' (positive) side of the battery must face down **(see illustration)**.

11 Reassemble the two halves of the remote and refit the emergency key blade. Refit the blade compartment cover and check the operation of the remote.

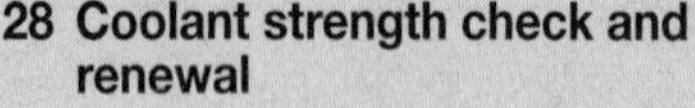

28 Coolant strength check and renewal

Warning: Do not allow antifreeze to come in contact with your skin or painted surfaces of the vehicle. Flush contaminated areas immediately with plenty of water. Don't store new coolant, or leave old coolant lying around, where it's accessible to children or pets – they're attracted by its sweet smell. Ingestion of even a small amount of coolant can be fatal. Wipe up garage-floor and drip-pan spills immediately. Keep antifreeze containers covered, and repair cooling system leaks as soon as they're noticed.

Warning: Never remove the expansion tank filler cap when the engine is running, or has just been switched off, as the cooling system will be hot, and the consequent escaping steam and scalding coolant could cause serious injury.

Warning: Wait until the engine is cold before starting these procedures.

Note: *If Ford 'Superplus' antifreeze is used, the coolant can then be left indefinitely, providing the strength of the mixture is checked every year. If any antifreeze other than Ford's is to be used, the coolant must be renewed at regular intervals to provide an equivalent degree of protection; the conventional recommendation is to renew the coolant every two years.*

Strength check

1 Use a hydrometer to check the strength of the antifreeze. Follow the instructions provided with your hydrometer. The antifreeze strength should be approximately 50%. If it is significantly less than this, drain a little coolant from the radiator (see this Section), add antifreeze to the coolant expansion tank, then recheck the strength.

Coolant draining

2 To drain the system, first remove the expansion tank filler cap.

3 If the additional working clearance is required, raise the front of the vehicle and support it securely on axle stands (see *Jacking and vehicle support*). Where fitted, undo the fasteners and remove the engine undershield **(see illustrations 3.6a & 3.6b)**.

4 Place a large drain tray underneath, and unscrew the radiator drain tap, which is located at the lower left-hand corner of the radiator. Fit a length of hose to the pipe at the side of the drain tap to help direct the flow of coolant into the drain tray **(see illustrations)**.

5 Once the coolant has stopped draining from the radiator, close the drain plug.

System flushing

6 With time, the cooling system may gradually lose its efficiency, as the radiator core becomes choked with rust, scale

28.4a Fit a length of hose to the side of the drain tap...

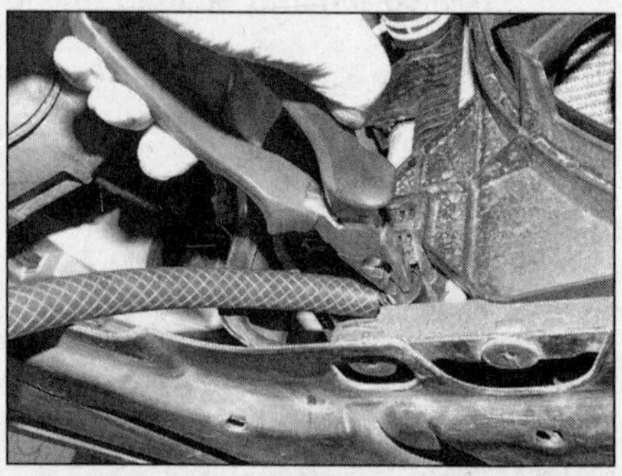

28.4b ...then unscrew the radiator drain tap

deposits from the water, and other sediment. To minimise this, as well as using only good-quality antifreeze and clean soft water, the system should be flushed as follows whenever any part of it is disturbed, and/or when the coolant is renewed.

7 With the coolant drained, refit the drain plug and refill the system with fresh water. Refit the expansion tank filler cap, start the engine and warm it up to normal operating temperature, then stop it and (after allowing it to cool down completely) drain the system again. Repeat as necessary until only clean water can be seen to emerge, then refill finally with the specified coolant mixture.

8 If only clean, soft water and good-quality antifreeze (even if not to Ford's specification) has been used, and the coolant has been renewed at the suggested intervals, the above procedure will be sufficient to keep clean the system for a considerable length of time. If, however, the system has been neglected, a more thorough operation will be required, as follows.

9 First drain the coolant, then disconnect the radiator top and bottom hoses. Insert a garden hose into the radiator top hose connection, and allow water to circulate through the radiator until it runs clean from the bottom outlet.

10 To flush the engine, insert the garden hose into the radiator bottom hose, wrap a piece of rag around the garden hose to seal the connection, and allow water to circulate until it runs clear.

11 Try the effect of repeating this procedure in the top hose, although this may not be effective, since the thermostat will probably close and prevent the flow of water.

12 In severe cases of contamination, reverse-flushing of the radiator may be necessary. This may be achieved by inserting the garden hose into the bottom outlet, wrapping a piece of rag around the hose to seal the connection, then flushing the radiator until clear water emerges from the top hose outlet.

13 If the radiator is suspected of being severely choked, remove the radiator (Chapter 3 Section 7), turn it upside-down, and repeat the procedure described in paragraph 12.

14 Flushing the heater matrix can be achieved using a similar procedure to that described in paragraph 12, once the heater inlet and outlet hoses have been identified. These two hoses will be of the same diameter, and pass through the engine compartment bulkhead (refer to the heater matrix removal procedure in Chapter 3 Section 9 for more details).

15 The use of chemical cleaners is not recommended, and should be necessary only as a last resort; the scouring action of some chemical cleaners may lead to other cooling system problems. Normally, regular renewal of the coolant will prevent excessive contamination of the system.

Coolant filling

16 With the cooling system drained and flushed, ensure that all disturbed hose unions are correctly secured, and that the radiator/engine drain plug(s) is securely tightened. Refit the engine undershield (where applicable). If it was raised, lower the vehicle to the ground.

17 Set the heater temperature control to maximum heat, but ensure the blower is turned off.

18 Prepare a sufficient quantity of the specified coolant mixture (see below); allow for a surplus, so as to have a reserve supply for topping-up.

19 Slowly fill the system through the expansion tank. Since the tank is the highest point in the system, all the air in the system should be displaced into the tank by the rising liquid. Slow pouring reduces the possibility of air being trapped and forming airlocks. On some models, there are bleed screws fitted, to allow the air out from the system **(see illustration)**, place a container/cloth below the bleed screw, then remove the cap and release the air until there is a flow of coolant. Clean up any spilt coolant when completed.

20 Continue filling until the coolant level reaches the expansion tank MAX level line (see *Weekly checks*), then cover the filler opening to prevent coolant splashing out.

21 Start the engine and run it at 2500 rpm for 2 minutes. If the level in the expansion tank drops significantly, top-up to the MAX level line, to minimise the amount of air circulating in the system.

22 Fill the expansion tank to the MAX level line, refit the expansion tank cap, and run the engine at 2500 rpm until the thermostat opens and the engine is at normal operating temperature. Check this by feeling the radiator bottom hose – if it's hot, then the thermostat has opened.

23 Briefly run the engine at 4000 rpm, then run it at 2500 rpm for approximately 3 minutes.

24 Stop the engine, wash off any spilt coolant from the engine compartment and bodywork, then leave the car to cool down completely (overnight, if possible).

25 With the system cool, open the expansion tank, and top-up the tank to the MAX level line. Refit the filler cap, tightening it securely, and clean up any further spillage.

26 After refilling, always check carefully all components of the system (but especially any unions disturbed during draining and flushing) for signs of coolant leaks. Fresh antifreeze has a searching action, which will rapidly expose any weak points in the system.

Antifreeze type and mixture

Note: *Do not use engine antifreeze in the windscreen/tailgate washer system, as it will damage the vehicle's paintwork. A screenwash additive should be added to the washer system in its maker's recommended quantities.*

27 If the vehicle's history (and therefore the quality of the antifreeze in it) is unknown, owners are advised to drain and thoroughly reverse-flush the system, before refilling with fresh coolant mixture.

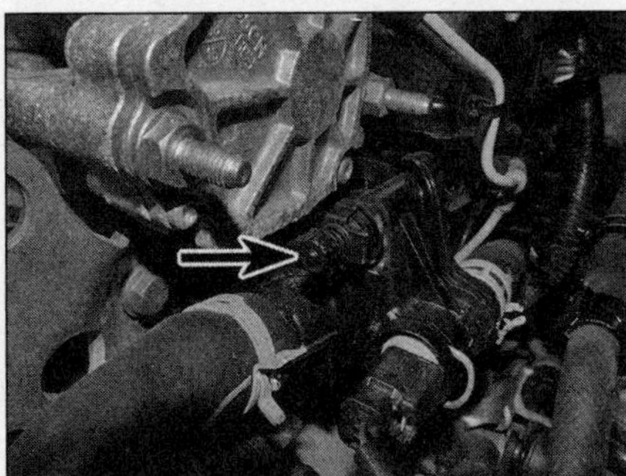

28.19 Bleed screw fitted to coolant housing – 1.5 litre model shown

28 If the antifreeze used is to Ford's specification, the levels of protection it affords are indicated in the coolant packaging.

29 To give the recommended standard mixture ratio for antifreeze, 50% (by volume) of antifreeze must be mixed with 50% of clean, soft water; if you are using any other type of antifreeze, follow its manufacturer's instructions to achieve the correct ratio.

30 You are unlikely to fully drain the system at any one time (unless the engine is being completely stripped), and the capacities quoted in Specifications are therefore slightly academic for routine coolant renewal. As a guide, only two-thirds of the system's total capacity is likely to be needed for coolant renewal.

31 As the drained system will be partially filled with flushing water, in order to establish the recommended mixture ratio, measure out 50% of the system capacity in antifreeze and pour it into the hose/expansion tank as described above, then top-up with water. Any topping-up while refilling the system should be done with water – for *Weekly checks* use a suitable mixture.

32 Before adding antifreeze, the cooling system should be drained, preferably flushed, and all hoses checked for condition and security. As noted earlier, fresh antifreeze will rapidly find any weaknesses in the system.

33 After filling with antifreeze, a label should be attached to the expansion tank, stating the type and concentration of antifreeze used, and the date installed. Any subsequent topping-up should be made with the same type and concentration of antifreeze.

General cooling system checks

34 The engine should be cold for the cooling system checks, so perform the following procedure before driving the vehicle, or after it has been shut off for at least three hours.

35 Remove the expansion tank filler cap, and clean it thoroughly inside and out with a rag. Also clean the filler neck on the expansion tank. The presence of rust or corrosion in the filler neck indicates that the coolant should be changed. The coolant inside the expansion tank should be relatively clean and transparent. If it is rust-coloured, drain and flush the system, and refill with a fresh coolant mixture.

36 Carefully check the radiator hoses and heater hoses along their entire length; renew any hose which is cracked, swollen or deteriorated.

37 Inspect all other cooling system components (joint faces, etc) for leaks. A leak in the cooling system will usually show up as white- or antifreeze-coloured deposits on the area adjoining the leak (see Haynes Hint). Where any problems of this nature are found on system components, renew the component or gasket with reference to Chapter 3.

A leak in the cooling system will usually show up as white- or antifreeze-coloured deposits on the areas adjoining the leak.

38 Clean the front of the radiator with a soft brush to remove all insects, leaves, etc, embedded in the radiator fins. Be careful not to damage the radiator fins, or cut your fingers on them. To do a more thorough job, remove the front bumper cover, as described in Chapter 11 Section 6.

Airlocks

39 If, after draining and refilling the system, symptoms of overheating are found which did not occur previously, then the fault is almost certainly due to trapped air at some point in the system, causing an airlock and restricting the flow of coolant; usually, the air is trapped because the system was refilled too quickly.

40 If an airlock is suspected, first try gently squeezing all visible coolant hoses. A coolant hose which is full of air feels quite different to one full of coolant when squeezed. After refilling the system, most airlocks will clear once the system has cooled, and been topped-up.

41 While the engine is running at operating temperature, switch on the heater and heater fan, and check for heat output. Provided there is sufficient coolant in the system, lack of heat output could be due to an airlock in the system.

42 Airlocks can have more serious effects than simply reducing heater output – a severe airlock could reduce coolant flow around the engine. Check that the radiator top hose is hot when the engine is at operating temperature – a top hose which stays cold could be the result of an airlock (or a non-opening thermostat).

43 If the problem persists, stop the engine and allow it to cool down completely, before unscrewing the expansion tank filler cap or loosening the hose clips and squeezing the hoses to bleed out the trapped air. In the worst case, the system will have to be at least partially drained (this time, the coolant can be saved for re-use) and flushed to clear the problem. If all else fails, have the system evacuated and vacuum filled by a suitably-equipped garage.

Expansion tank pressure cap check

44 Wait until the engine is completely cold – perform this check before the engine is started for the first time in the day.

45 Place a wad of cloth over the expansion tank cap, then unscrew it slowly and remove it.

46 Examine the condition of the rubber seal on the underside of the cap. If the rubber appears to have hardened, or cracks are visible in the seal edges, a new cap should be fitted.

47 If the car is several years old, or has covered a large mileage, consider renewing the cap regardless of its apparent condition – they are not expensive. If the pressure relief valve built into the cap fails, excess pressure in the system will lead to puzzling failures of hoses and other cooling system components.

Chapter 2 Part A
1.0 litre petrol engines in-car repair procedures

Contents

Degrees of difficulty

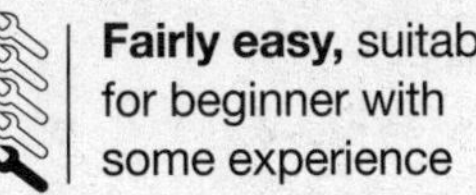

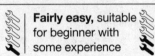

Easy, suitable for novice with little experience	**Fairly easy,** suitable for beginner with some experience	**Fairly difficult,** suitable for competent DIY mechanic	**Difficult,** suitable for experienced DIY mechanic	**Very difficult,** suitable for expert DIY or professional

Specifications

General

Engine type	Three-cylinder, in-line, double overhead camshafts, with variable valve timing
Designation	EcoBoost
Engine codes	M1DA, M1DC, M1DD, M2DA, M2DB, M2DC and SFDB
Capacity	998 cc
Bore	71.9 mm
Stroke	81.9 mm
Compression ratio:	
SFDB engines	10.5: 1
All except SFDB engines	10: 1
Output:	
Power:	
SFDB, M2DA, M2DB and M2DC	74 kW (100 PS)
M1DA, M1DC and M1DD	92 kW (125 PS)
Torque:	
All engines	170 Nm
Firing order	1-2-3 (No 1 cylinder at timing belt end)
Direction of crankshaft rotation	Clockwise (seen from right-hand side of car)

Valves

Valve clearances (cold)	
Inlet	0.21 to 0.30 mm
Exhaust	0.38 to 0.47 mm

Lubrication

Oil pressure (minimum, warm engine) at 2000 rpm	2.0 bars
Pressure relief valve opens at	Not specified
Oil pump clearances	Not specified

Torque wrench settings	Nm	lbf ft
Air conditioning compressor mounting bolts	25	18
Alternator mounting bolts	48	35
Auxiliary drivebelt belt idler pulley bolt	25	18
Auxiliary drivebelt tensioner bolts	25	18
Camshaft bearing caps	10	7
Camshaft position sensors	10	7
Camshaft sprocket bolts		
Stage 1	30	22
Stage 2	50	37
Stage 3	95	70
Stage 4	Angle-tighten a further 45°	
Coolant outlet to cylinder head	10	7
Coolant outlet at rear of the waterpump	10	7
Crankshaft position sensor	10	7
Crankshaft oil seal carrier	10	7
Crankshaft pulley/vibration damper: *		
Stage 1	25	18
Stage 2	70	52
Install Torque multiplier**		
Stage 1	60	44
Stage 2	Angle-tighten a further 90°	
Stage 3	Angle-tighten a further 90°	
Stage 4	Angle-tighten a further 90°	
Stage 5	Angle-tighten a further 90°	
Stage 6	Angle-tighten a further 90°	
Cylinder head bolts: *		
Stage 1	10	7
Stage 2	40	29
Stage 3 (slacken)	Loosen 45°	
Stage 4	30	22
Stage 5	Angle-tighten a further 90°	
Stage 6	Angle-tighten a further 90°	
Cylinder head cover	10	7
Engine mountings:		
Right-hand mounting retaining bolts	90	66
Right-hand mounting bracket-to-engine bolts	80	59
Right-hand mounting studs (on engine)	10	7
Left-hand mounting nuts	48	35
Left-hand mounting bracket to transmission	82	61
Left-hand mounting centre bolt*	148	109
Lower-rear torque rod bolts:		
To transmission	46	34
To subframe		
Stage1	30	22
Stage 2	Angle-tighten a further 270°	
Engine lifting eye	22	16
Exhaust flexible section-to-catalytic converter nuts	25	18
Exhaust manifold heat shield bolts	10	7
Exhaust manifold nuts/bolts	25	18
Fuel pump bolts:		
Stage 1	5	3
Stage 2	13	9
Flywheel bolts*		
Stage 1	10	7
Stage 2	25	18
Stage 3	50	37
Stage 4	Angle-tighten a further 90°	
Inlet manifold-to-block bolt	10	7
Oil drain plug	25	18
Oil filter connector (to block)	55	41
Oil pressure switch	15	11
Oil pressure control solenoid	10	7
Oil pump to cylinder block	25	18
Spark plugs	15	11
Sump bolts:		
Sump-to-block bolts	10	7
Sump-to-transmission bolts	48	35

Torque wrench settings (continued)

	Nm	lbf ft
TDC pin hole blanking plug	20	15
Timing belt cover bolts*		
First stage:		
Bolts 1-2	5	3
Bolts 3-6	10	7
Bolts 7-16	5	3
Bolts 17-19	5	3
Bolts 20	5	3
Second stage:		
Bolts 3-6	40	30
Bolts 3-4		
Stage 1	70	52
Stage 2	Angle-tighten a further 90°	
Bolts 5-6		
Stage 1	70	52
Stage 2	Angle-tighten a further 90°	
Bolts 1-2		
Stage 1	9	6.5
Stage 2	Angle-tighten a further 90°	
Bolts 7-20		
Stage 1	15	11
Stage 2	Angle-tighten a further 90°	
Timing belt tensioner bolt	25	18
Variable valve timing solenoid	7	6
Variable valve timing units		
Stage 1	30	22
Stage 2	50	37
Stage 3	95	70
Stage 4	Angle-tighten a further 45°	

**Use new fasteners*

***See the text for an alternative method, that does not require the use of a torque multiplier*

1 General Information

How to use this Chapter

1 This Part of Chapter 2 is devoted to in-car repair procedures on the 1.0 litre 3 cylinder petrol engine. All procedures concerning engine removal and refitting, and engine block/cylinder head overhaul can be found in Chapter 2E.

2 Refer to Vehicle identification numbers in the Reference Section at the end of this manual for details of engine code locations.

3 Most of the operations included in this Chapter are based on the assumption that the engine is still installed in the car. Therefore, if this information is being used during a complete engine overhaul, with the engine already removed, many of the steps included here will not apply.

Engine description

4 The EcoBoost engine is a twelve-valve, double overhead camshaft (DOHC), three-cylinder engine, mounted transversely at the front of the car, with the transmission on its left-hand end. The engine features an aluminium cylinder head with an integral exhaust manifold, a cast iron cylinder block and an aluminium sump.

Caution: When tightening bolts into aluminium castings, it is important to adhere to the specified torque wrench settings, to avoid stripping threads.

5 The crankshaft runs in four main bearings. Due to the very fine bearing clearances and bearing shell tolerances incorporated during manufacture, it is not possible to renew the crankshaft separate to the cylinder block; in fact it is not possible to remove and refit the crankshaft accurately using conventional tooling. This means that if the crankshaft is worn excessively, it must be renewed together with the cylinder block.

Caution: Do not unbolt the main bearing caps from the cylinder block, as it is not possible to refit it accurately using conventional tooling. Additionally, the manufacturers do not supply torque settings for the main bearing cap/ladder retaining bolts.

6 The connecting rods rotate on horizontally-split bearing shells at their big-ends. The pistons are attached to the connecting rods by gudgeon pins which are an interference fit in the connecting rod small-end eyes. The aluminium alloy pistons are fitted with three piston rings: two compression rings and an oil control ring. After manufacture, the cylinder bores and pistons are measured and classified. These are then matched together, to ensure the correct piston/cylinder clearance. No oversizes or replacement parts are available to rectify any faults with the pistons, piston rings, connecting rods or big end bearings. If there is any fault with the crankshaft, pistons or cylinder bores, a replacement 'short' engine must be fitted.

Caution: Do not unbolt the big end bearing caps from the crankshaft, as it is not possible to refit them accurately using conventional tooling. Additionally, the manufacturers do not supply torque settings or replacement parts.

7 The inlet and exhaust valves are each closed by coil springs; they operate in guides which are shrink-fitted into the cylinder head, as are the valve seat inserts. The exhaust valves are hollow sodium filled valves.

8 Both camshafts are driven by the same toothed timing belt, each operating six valves via bucket tappets. Each camshaft rotates in four main bearings that are line-bored directly in the cylinder head and the (bolted-on) bearing caps; this means that the bearing caps are not available separately from the cylinder head, and must not be interchanged with caps from another engine.

9 All engines are fitted with variable valve timing on the both the inlet and exhaust camshafts. Engine oil pressure is used to vary the positions of the camshaft sprocket in relation to the camshafts, thus varying the valves opening and closing times. Control of the oil flow is achieved using solenoid valves, which in turn are controlled by the engine management electronic control module (ECM). Varying the valve timing is this manner results in improved driveability and output, whist reducing fuel consumption and exhaust emissions.

10 The timing belt features an automatic tensioner and runs in an oil bath. This reduces noise and frictional loses, thus contributing to improved fuel consumption.

11 The coolant pump is bolted to the right-hand end of the cylinder block and is driven by the auxiliary drivebelt from the crankshaft pulley. Separate cooling circuits for the cylinder head and block enable a faster warm up time.

12 Lubrication is by means of a vane type oil pump with an adjustable outer ring. The oil pump has a variable output, controlled by the ECU, via a solenoid valve. The oil pump is mounted is mounted below the crankshaft right-hand end. The oil pump is belt driven and draws oil through a strainer located in the sump. The pump forces oil through an externally-mounted full-flow cartridge-type filter.

Operations with engine in car

13 The following work can be carried out with the engine in the car:

a) Cylinder head cover – removal and refitting.
b) Timing belt – renewal.
c) Timing belt tensioner and sprockets – removal and refitting.
d) Camshaft oil seals – renewal.
e) Camshafts, tappets and shims – removal and refitting.
f) Cylinder head – removal and refitting.
g) Sump – removal and refitting.
h) Crankshaft oil seals – renewal.
i) Oil pump – removal and refitting.
j) Flywheel/driveplate – removal and refitting.
k) Engine/transmission mountings – removal and refitting.

Note: *It is possible to remove the pistons and connecting rods (after removing the cylinder head and sump) without removing the engine. However, this is not recommended. Work of this nature is more easily and thoroughly completed with the engine on the bench, as described in Chapter 2E.*

2 Compression test – description and interpretation

Note: *Cranking the engine with the coils removed will set a DTC (Diagnostic Trouble Code). Completing several drive cycles after carrying out a compression test may erase the fault codes. If the EML (Engine Management Light) remains illuminated, suitable diagnostic equipment will be required to erase the fault codes.*

1 When engine performance is down, or if misfiring occurs which cannot be attributed to the ignition or fuel systems, a compression test can provide diagnostic clues as to the engine's condition. If the test is performed regularly, it can give warning of trouble before any other symptoms become apparent.

2 The engine must be fully warmed-up to operating temperature, the oil level must be correct and the battery must be fully-charged. The help of an assistant will also be required.

3 Remove fuse number 56 from the passenger compartment fusebox, which is located behind the glovebox **(see illustration)**. This is the fuse for the fuel pump – further details are to be found in Chapter 12. Now start the engine and allow it to run until it stalls.

4 Remove the engine cover and the with reference to Chapter 1A Section 21 remove the ignition coils and the spark plugs.

5 Fit a compression tester to the No 1 cylinder spark plug hole – the type of tester which screws into the spark plug thread is preferable.

6 Arrange for an assistant to hold the accelerator pedal fully depressed to the floor, while at the same time cranking the engine over for several seconds on the starter motor. Observe the compression gauge reading. The compression will build-up fairly quickly in a healthy engine. Low compression on the first stroke, followed by gradually-increasing pressure on successive strokes, indicates worn piston rings. A low compression on the first stroke which does not rise on successive strokes, indicates leaking valves or a blown head gasket (a cracked cylinder head could also be the cause). Deposits on the underside of the valve heads can also cause low compression. Record the highest gauge reading obtained, then repeat the procedure for the remaining cylinders.

7 Due to the variety of testers available, and the fluctuation in starter motor speed when cranking the engine, different readings are often obtained when carrying out the compression test. For this reason, actual compression pressure figures are not quoted by Ford. However, the most important factor is that the compression pressures are uniform in all cylinders, and that is what this test is mainly concerned with.

8 Add some engine oil (about three squirts from a plunger type oil can) to each cylinder through the spark plug holes, and then repeat the test.

9 If the compression increases after the oil is added, the piston rings are probably worn. If the compression does not increase significantly, the leakage is occurring at the valves or the head gasket. Leakage past the valves may be caused by burned valve seats and/or faces, or warped, cracked or bent valves.

10 If two adjacent cylinders have equally low compressions, it is most likely that the head gasket has blown between them. The appearance of coolant in the combustion chambers or on the engine oil dipstick would verify this condition.

11 If one cylinder is about 20 percent lower than the other, and the engine has a slightly rough idle, a worn lobe on the camshaft could be the cause.

12 On completion of the checks, refit the spark plugs and ignition coils. Refit the fuel pump fuse to the fusebox.

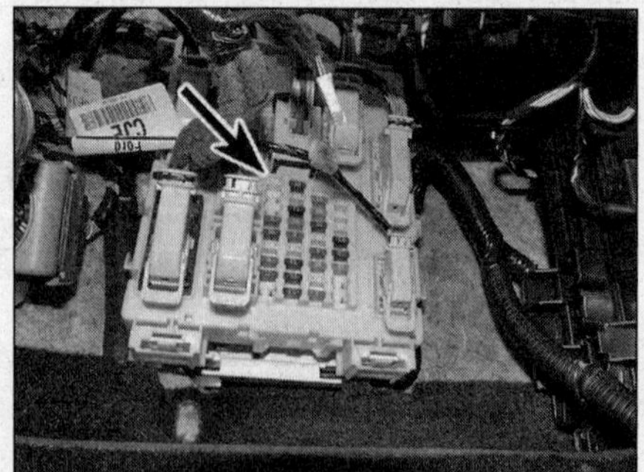

2.3 Fuel pump fuse 56 – upper left-hand side fuse

3 Top Dead Centre (TDC) for No 1 piston – locating

Note: *The engine must only be rotated in the normal direction of rotation (clockwise).*

1 Top dead centre (TDC) is the highest point of the cylinder that each piston reaches as the crankshaft turns. Each piston reaches its TDC position at the end of its compression stroke, and then again at the end of its exhaust stroke. For the purpose of engine timing, TDC on the compression stroke for No 1 piston is used. No 1 cylinder is at the timing belt end of the engine. Proceed as follows.

2 Disconnect the battery negative (earth) lead (see Chapter 5A Section 3). Remove the spark plugs as described in Chapter 1A Section 21.

3 Apply the handbrake and then slacken the driveshaft retaining nut. Jack up the front of the vehicle and support it on axle stands (see *Jacking and vehicle support*). Remove the right-hand road wheel

4 Undo the fasteners, remove the engine undershield, then remove the wheel arch liner to improve access to the crankshaft pulley and bolt.

5 With reference to Chapter 8 Section 2 remove the right-hand driveshaft.

6 Remove the blanking plug from the rear of the engine block – next to the oil pump control solenoid **(see illustration)**.

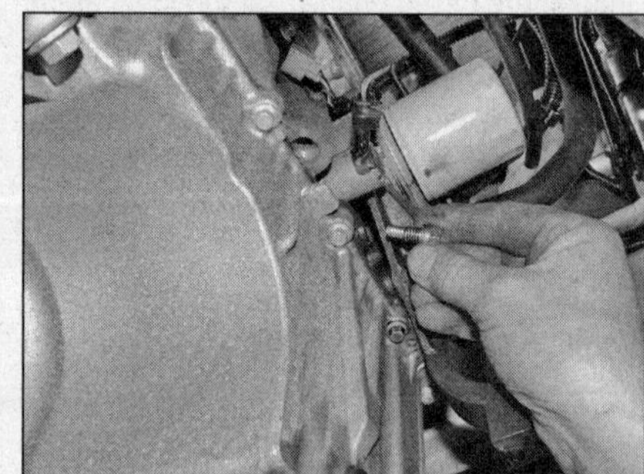

3.6 Remove the blanking plug

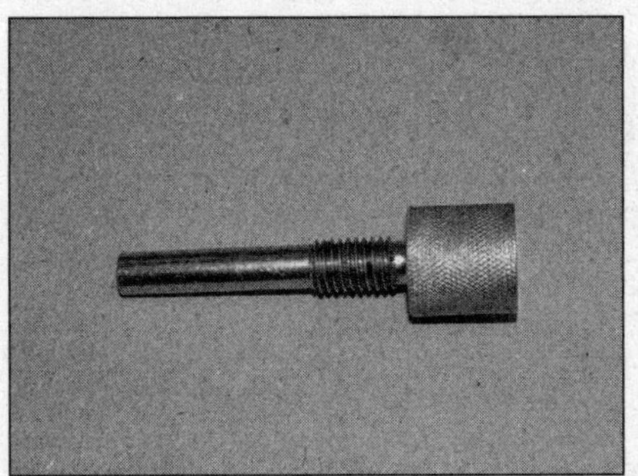
3.7 The TDC locating pin

3.8 Remove the control solenoids

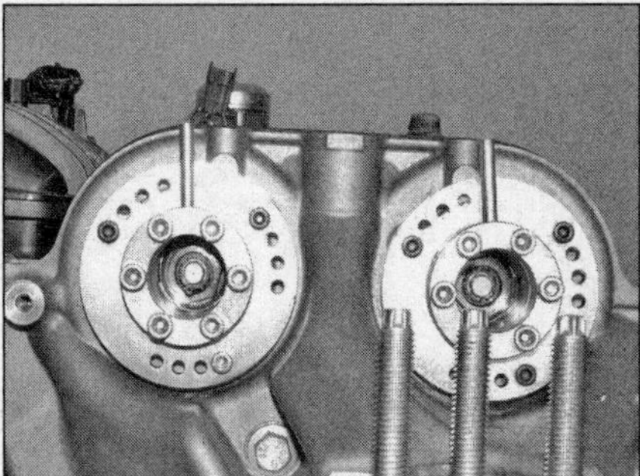
3.9 Fit the special tools.

7 Install the Top Dead Centre (TDC) locating pin. This is Ford special tool 303-1604 **(see illustration)** or equivalent from a reputable manufacturer such as Draper or AST.

8 Remove the wiring plugs from the variable valve timing control solenoids and then remove the solenoids **(see illustration)**. Recover the O-ring seals.

9 Rotate the crankshaft pulley slowly clockwise until the crankshaft stops against the locating pin. Install Ford special tool 303-1606 to the camshaft Variable Valve Timing units (VVT). If the engine is at TDC with cylinder number 1 on the firing stroke, the tool can easily be fitted and the pointers on the VVT timing tools will be vertical **(see illustration).** If this is not the case, remove the TDC locating pin and rotate the crankshaft approximately 340 degrees and then refit the TDC locating pin. Fully rotate the crankshaft until the crankshaft locks against the TDC locating pin. The VVT locking tools should now fit.

10 Once the work requiring the TDC setting has been completed, remove the special tool from the camshaft VVT units and refit the control solenoids – the O-rings can be reused if they are in good condition. Unscrew the TDC locating pin and refit the blanking plug. Refit the driveshaft as described in Chapter 8 Section 2. Refit the engine undershield, wing liner and roadwheel. Lower the vehicle to the ground. Refit the spark plugs (Chapter 1A Section 21).and reconnect the battery negative lead (see Chapter 5A Section 3).

4 Cylinder head cover – removal and refitting

Removal

1 Remove fuse number 56 from the passenger compartment fusebox, which is located behind the glovebox **(see illustration 2.3)**. This is the fuse for the fuel pump – Now start the engine and allow it to run until it stalls.

2 Disconnect the battery negative (earth) lead (see Chapter 5A Section 3).

3 Disconnect and then remove the fuel rail as described in Chapter 4A Section 13.

4 Release the hose clamps from the turbocharger intake pipe, disconnect the wiring plug from the Manifold Absolute Pressure (MAP) sensor and then release the engine breather pipe **(see illustration)**. Remove the mounting bolts and then remove the pipe.

5 Disconnect the wiring plugs from the camshaft position sensors.

6 Disconnect the wiring plug from the evaporative emissions control solenoid and then remove the pipe from the top of the engine **(see illustrations)**.

7 Place a cloth beneath the fuel pipes and then disconnect the fuel supply pipe from the high pressure fuel pump. Ford list a special tool (310-137) for this procedure, but it is not required if the fuel line is disconnected at the point where the metal fuel line meets the plastic fuel line and not at the pump **(see illustration)**.

4.4 Remove the breather pipe

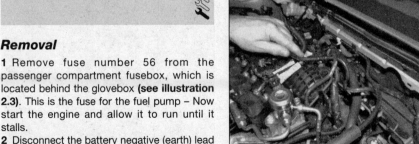

4.6b ...then remove the pipes

8 Disconnect the wiring plug from the fuel pump and then remove the securing bolts from the fuel pump. Remove each bolt one turn at a time. Remove the fuel pump from the engine.

9 Disconnect the wiring plugs from the ignition coils and then unclip the wiring loom from the engine.

10 Note the location of the vacuum pipes and then remove them from the waste gate and control valve.

11 Remove the bolt and 2 nuts from the small heat shield - located between the cover and the turbocharger. Remove the heat shield.

12 Disconnect the breather pipe and then in reverse order to that shown **(see illustration 4.17)**, slacken the cover bolts in turn.

13 Remove the cover from the engine.

Refitting

14 Clean the mating surfaces of the cylinder head and the cover gasket. Inspect the

4.6a Disconnect the wiring plug and...

4.7 Disconnect the fuel supply line (arrowed)

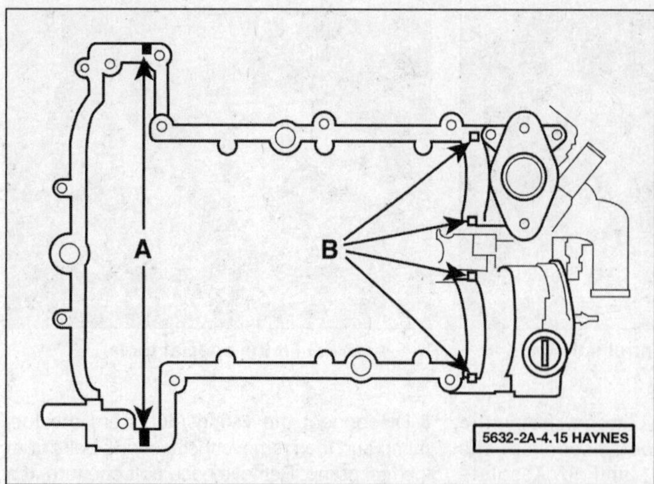

4.15 Apply a 5mm diameter bead of sealant at (A) and a 4mm diameter bead at (B)

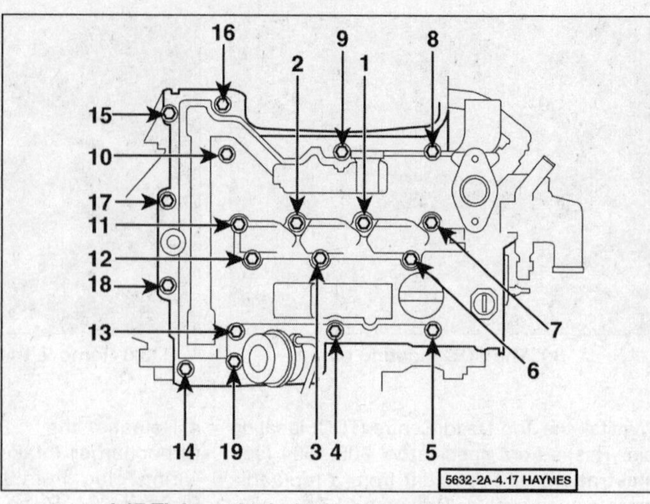

4.17 Tighten the bolts in the sequence shown

gasket, if it is in good condition it can be reused.

15 Apply sealant at the points shown **(see illustration)**. Note that Ford list 2 different sealants for this application. Ford WSE-M4G323-A4 should be applied at the timing belt end of the engine and Ford WSE-M2G348-A5 should be applied at the fuel pump end of the engine.

16 Lower the cover onto the cylinder head, ensuring that the gasket stays in place.

17 Tighten the bolts in the correct sequence, finger tight at first and then to the specified torque **(see illustration)**.

18 Fit a new O-ring to the high pressure fuel pump and lubricate the O-ring with clean engine oil before refitting. Tighten the bolts half a turn at time to the specified torque.

19 When refitting the camshaft position sensors lubricate the O-rings with clean engine oil and tighten to the specified torque

20 The remainder of refitting is a reversal of removal.

5 Valve clearances – checking and adjustment

Note: *The valve clearances will not normally require checking or adjustment during the life of the vehicle. Checking and adjustment should only be required when work has been undertaken on the cylinder head or the camshafts.*

Note: *If checking the valve clearances with the timing belt removed (eg, after refitting the camshafts), rotate the crankshaft 90° anti-clockwise back from TDC on No 1 cylinder so the pistons are halfway down the cylinder bores. Verify this by inserting a long screwdriver down the spark plug holes.*

1 Remove the cylinder head cover as described in Section 4.

2 Remove the spark plugs (Chapter 1A Section 21) in order to make turning the engine easier. The engine may be turned using a spanner on the crankshaft pulley bolt or by raising the front right-hand roadwheel clear of the ground, engaging top gear and turning the wheel. If the former method is used, jack up and support the front of the car (see *Jacking and vehicle support*) then remove the engine undershield for access to the pulley bolt; if the latter method is used, apply the handbrake then jack up the front right-hand side of the car until the roadwheel is clear of the ground and support with an axle stand.

3 Draw the valve positions on a piece of paper, numbering them 1 to 12 inlet and exhaust, from the timing belt (right-hand) end of the engine (ie, 1E, 1I, 2E, 2I and so on). As there are two inlet and two exhaust valves for each cylinder, draw the cylinders as large circles and the four valves as smaller circles. The inlet valves are at the rear of the cylinder head, and the exhaust valves are at the front. As the valve clearances are checked, cross them off.

Note: *The engine should only ever be turned in the normal (clockwise) direction of rotation.*

4 Turn the engine in a clockwise direction until both inlet valves of No 1 cylinder are fully shut and the apex of the camshaft lobes are pointing upwards away from the valve positions.

5 Insert a feeler blade of the correct thickness (see Specifications) between the heel of the camshaft lobe and the tappet **(see illustration)**. It should be a firm sliding fit. If this is the case, the clearance is correct and the valve position can be crossed off. If the clearance is not correct, use feeler blades to determine the exact clearance and record this on the drawing. From this clearance it will be possible to calculate the thickness of the new tappet to be fitted. Note that no shims are fitted between the camshaft and tappet – the complete tappet must be renewed.

6 Check the clearance of the second inlet valve for No 1 cylinder, and if necessary record the existing clearance on the drawing.

7 Now turn the engine until the inlet valves of No 2 cylinder are fully shut and the camshaft lobes pointing away from the valve positions. Check the clearances as described previously, and record any that are incorrect.

8 After checking all of the inlet valve clearances, check the exhaust valve clearances in the same way, but note that the clearances are different.

9 Where adjustment is required, the procedure is to remove the camshafts as described in Section 11.

10 If the recorded clearance was too small, a thinner tappet must be fitted, and conversely if the clearance was too large, a thicker tappet must be fitted. To calculate the thickness of the new tappet, first use a micrometer to measure the thickness of the existing tappet (C) and add this to the measured clearance (B) **(see illustration)**. Deduct the desired

5.5 Checking the valve clearances

5.10 Measure the thickness of the tappets with a micrometer

clearance (A) to provide the thickness (D) of the new tappet. The thickness of the tappet should be etched on the downward facing surface, however use the micrometer to verify this. The formula is as follows.

11 New tappet thickness D = Existing tappet thickness C + Measured clearance B – Desired clearance A

Sample calculation
Desired clearance (A) = 0.20
Measured clearance (B) = 0.15
Existing tappet thickness (C) = 2.725
Tappet thickness required (D) = C+B-A = 2.675
All measurements in mm

12 The tappets are available in varying thicknesses in increments of 0.025 mm. Note that tappets are only marked with the digits after the decimal point e.g. a 2.625 will be marked 625 **(see illustration)**.

13 It will be helpful for future adjustment if a record is kept of the thickness of tappet fitted at each position.

14 When all the clearances have been checked and adjusted, refit the camshafts and valve cover. Refit the engine undershield and lower the car to the ground.

5.12 The thickness of each tappet should be etched on its underside

6.7 Install the flywheel locking tool

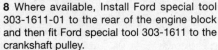

6 Crankshaft pulley/vibration damper – removal and refitting

Note: *The crankshaft pulley/ vibration damper retaining bolt may only be used once. Obtain a new bolt for the refitting procedure.*

Removal

1 Remove the auxiliary drivebelt as described in Chapter 1A Section 23.

2 Set the engine to the top dead centre (TDC) position as described in Section 3. Fully tighten both the inner and outer sections of the VVT locating tool.

3 Remove the starter motor as described in Chapter 5A Section 7.

4 Jack up and support the front of the vehicle (see *Jacking and vehicle support* in the reference section). Remove the right-hand road wheel.

5 If the correct Ford special tools are available unbolt the driveshaft bearing support bracket from the block.

6 If not already done so, remove the blanking plug and install the crankshaft locating pin (303-1604).

7 Ford tool 303-1602 (or equivalent) must now be fitted to lock the crankshaft in position. This tool bolts across the starter motor aperture in the transmission bellhousing, and engages with the teeth of the starter ring gear on the flywheel/driveplate **(see illustration)**. The tool must be firmly locked in position. Do not attempt to improvise this tool, the correct tool must be used due to the high torque figure required to retain the crankshaft pulley bolt

8 Where available, Install Ford special tool 303-1611-01 to the rear of the engine block and then fit Ford special tool 303-1611 to the crankshaft pulley.

9 If the correct Ford tools are not available it is possible to remove the pulley using conventional methods. Note however that the bolt is extremely tight and a very long knuckle bar and a best quality socket will be required.

10 Loosen the crankshaft pulley bolt and discard it. A new one must be used.

11 Remove the crankshaft pulley. Note that Ford recommend that whenever the pulley is removed, then the crankshaft oil seal should also be replaced. See Section 15 of this Chapter for replacement of the oil seal.

Refitting

Caution: The crankshaft pulley locating pin and the crankshaft locating pin are not designed to lock the pulley or the crankshaft in position. The crankshaft must be locked in place with the correct tool (303-1602) fitted to the flywheel ring gear.

Refitting with the Ford special tools

12 Refit the crankshaft pulley and then loosely fit the new bolt. Fit Ford special tool 303-732 and lock the crankshaft pulley in position.

13 The crankshaft pulley bolt requires a very high torque to fully tighten it. Tighten the bolt through the first 2 stages given in the specifications and then remove the crankshaft pulley locating pin.

14 Install the torque multiplier and fully tighten the crankshaft pulley bolt to the specified torque and then through the angle tightening stages given in the specifications.

15 Check that the crankshaft pulley locating pin can be fitted. Note that if the pulley has moved in relation to the crankshaft, the bolt will have to be removed (and replaced) and the procedure repeated.

16 Remove the crankshaft locating pin, the VVT locking tools and the flywheel locking tool and then rotate the engine clockwise 2 complete revolutions. Refit the locating tools and check that they fit. If the crankshaft pulley, crankshaft and VVT locating tools do not fit the procedure must be repeated. A replacement crankshaft pulley bolt will be required

17 Refit the remaining components in the reverse order of removal.

Refitting without the Ford special tools

Note: *The crankshaft locating pin, the crankshaft pulley locating pin, the VVT locating tools and the flywheel locking tool will be still be required.*

18 Refit the crankshaft pulley and then loosely fit the new bolt. Fit Ford special tool 303-732 and lock the crankshaft pulley in position **(see illustrations)**.

19 The crankshaft pulley bolt requires a very high torque to fully tighten it. Tighten the bolt through the first 2 stages given in the specifications and then remove the crankshaft pulley locating pin.

6.18a Using a new bolt fit the pulley...

6.18b ...and then install the special tool (arrowed)

6.21a Use an angle gauge or...

6.21b ...alternatively mark the bolt and the pulley (arrowed). This Is also useful as a back up In case the gauge moves

20 The torque multiplier specified is a 5: 1 multiplier, so the crankshaft pulley is effectively tightened to 300Nm using conventional tools. A best quality socket and long knuckle bar will be required. Ideally this will be a ¾ drive socket set.

21 Tighten the crankshaft pulley bolt to 300Nm and then fit an angle gauge to the crankshaft pulley bolt **(see illustrations)**. Tighten the bolt through 90 degrees. Note that unless the vehicle is raised sufficiently it will be impossible to attain the required 90 degrees in one movement. A less than ideal solution will be to tighten the bolt 45 degrees and then another 45 degrees.

22 Check that the crankshaft pulley locating pin can be fitted. Note that if the pulley has moved in relation to the crankshaft, the bolt will have to be removed (and replaced) and the procedure repeated.

23 Remove the crankshaft locating pin, the VVT locking tools and the flywheel locking tool and then rotate the engine clockwise 2 complete revolutions. Refit the locating tools and check that they fit. If the crankshaft pulley, crankshaft and VVT locating tools do not fit the procedure must be repeated. A replacement crankshaft pulley bolt will be required

24 Refit the remaining components in the reverse order of removal.

7 Timing belt cover – removal and refitting

Removal

1 Disconnect the battery as described in Chapter 5A Section 3, then drain the cooling system as described in Chapter 1A Section 28.

2 Remove the cylinder head cover (Section 4) and then remove the auxiliary drivebelt (as described in Chapter 1A Section 23) and drivebelt tensioner.

3 Remove the crankshaft pulley as described in Section 6 of this Chapter.

4 With reference to Chapter 4C Section 5 remove the catalytic converter.

5 At the right-hand end of the engine the air intake pipe must be removed. To remove, release the hose clips, disconnect the wiring plug, and release the breather pipe. Remove the single retaining bolt from the inner wing. Remove the intake pipe.

6 Disconnect the wiring loom from the alternator, variable valve control solenoids and the top dead centre (TDC) sensor **(see illustrations)**. Release the loom from the wiring clips and remove it from the front cover. Secure the loom out of harms way at the rear of the engine.

7 Remove the alternator mounting bolts and then remove the alternator as described in Chapter 5A Section 5.

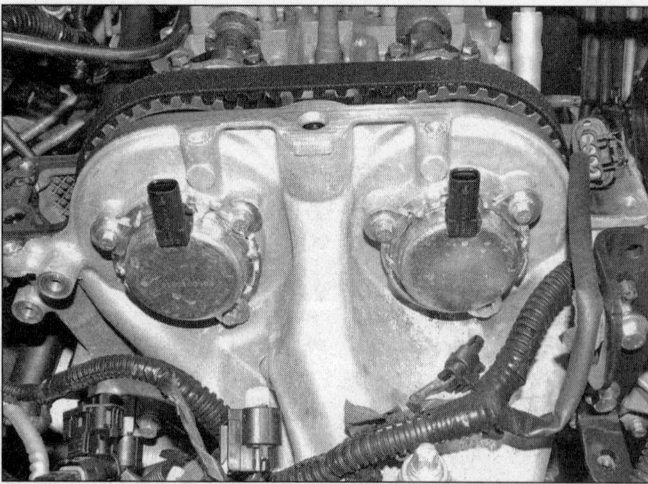

7.6a Disconnect the wiring plugs from the VVT units and...

7.6b ...the TDC sensor

7.12 Remove the control solenoids and recover the O-rings

7.14 Remove the idler pulley

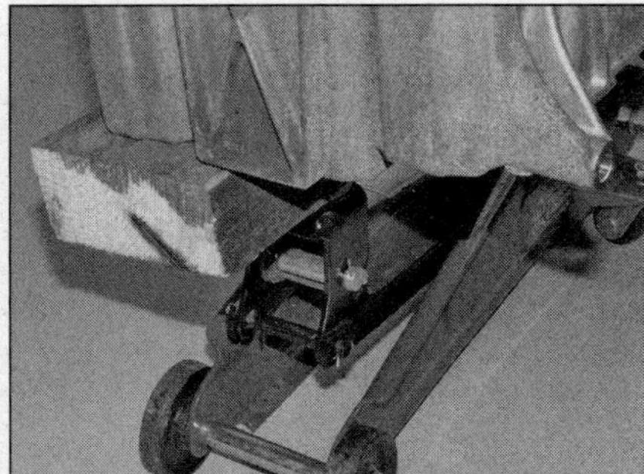
7.16 Support the engine from below

8 At the inlet manifold release the wiring loom and the breather pipe.

9 Mark the locations of the various vacuum pipes and release then from the cylinder head and inlet manifold. Unbolt and then remove the vacuum solenoid (2 nuts and 1 bolt).

10 At the rear of the engine disconnect the wiring loom from oil pressure sensor the knock sensor and the oil pump control solenoid

11 Remove the coolant hose at the rear of the engine. Check that inlet manifold is free of all hoses and wiring and then remove the inlet manifold – as described in Chapter 4A Section 14.

12 Unbolt and remove the TDC sensor and then unbolt and remove the variable valve timing control solenoids **(see illustration)**.

13 Disconnect the wiring plugs from the AC compressor. Unbolt the compressor and secure it to one side.

14 At the cover remove the auxiliary drivebelt idler pulley **(see illustration)** and then at the rear of the cover remove the 2 bolts from the coolant distribution pipe.

15 Release and remove the coolant expansion tank from the inner wing.

16 The engine must now be supported from below. Using a suitable jack and a block of wood to spread the load, raise the engine slightly **(see illustration)**.

17 With the engine supported from below remove the left-hand engine mount as described in Section 17 of this Chapter.

18 Remove the engine lifting eye from the cover.

19 The cover can now be removed. It is held in place with a total of 20 bolts that are of varying lengths. Note position of each bolt as it is removed and remove them in reverse order to that shown **(see illustration 7.22)**. The cover is secured to the engine and sump with sealant. Do not use any metal tools to separate the cover. Small wooden wedge can be used at strategic points around the cover to free it from the engine.

Refitting

20 Clean the gasket material from both surfaces using a plastic or wooden scraper. Do not use a metal scraper or the machined surfaces will be damaged.

21 Apply silicone gasket and sealant (Ford WSE-M4G323-A4) as shown **(see illustrations)**. The sealant must be applied 1mm from the inner edge and must go all the way around the mating surface. Note that the cover must be installed within 10 minutes of applying the sealant.

22 Fit the new bolts to the cover and tighten them finger tight in the order shown. Torque them to the settings given in the specifications in the order shown **(see illustration)**.

23 Refit the remaining components in reverse order.

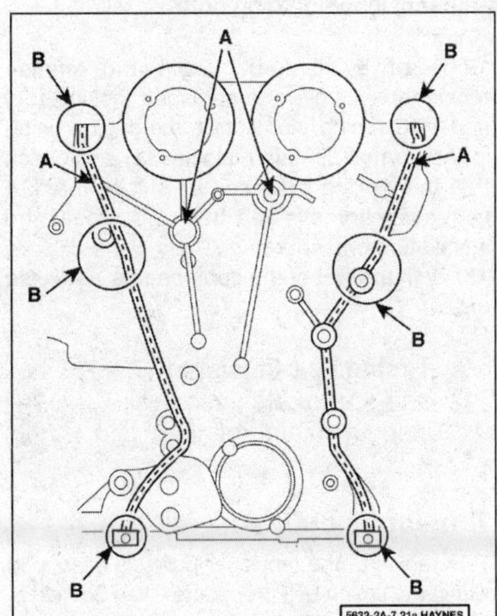

7.21a Apply a 4mm diameter bead of sealant at (A) and a 6mm diameter bead of sealant at (B)

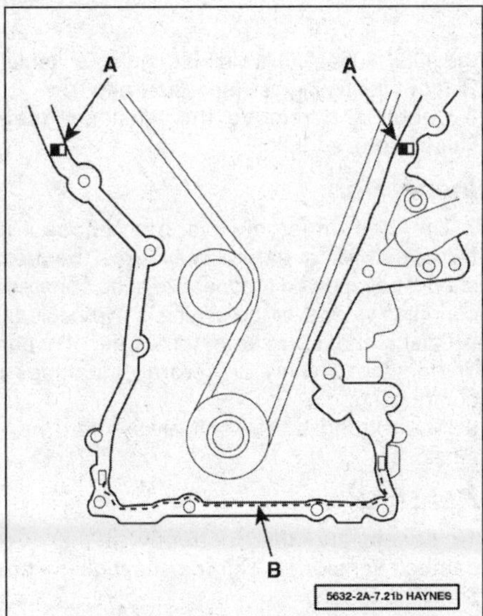

7.21b Add a 4mm bead of sealant at the join between the cylinder head and block (A) and a 4mm run of sealant along the sump (B)

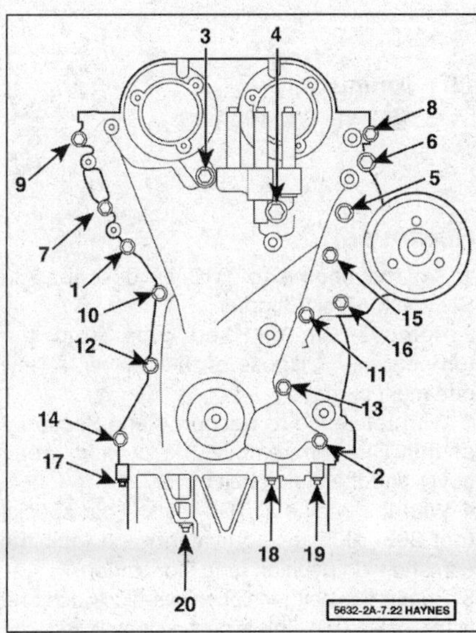

7.22 Tighten the bolts in the order shown

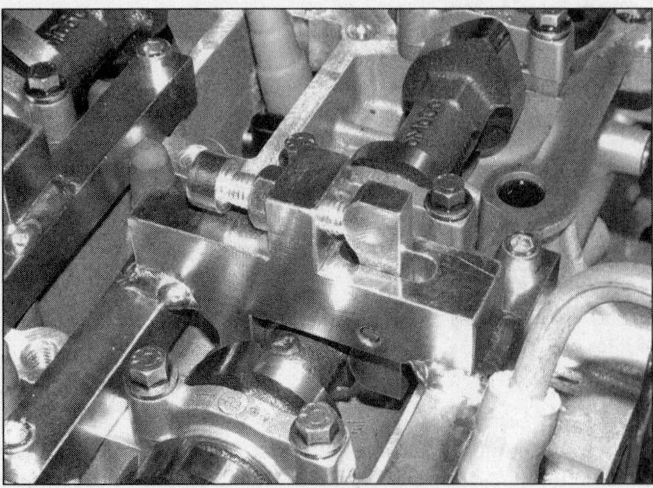

8.4 Lock the camshafts in position with the special tools

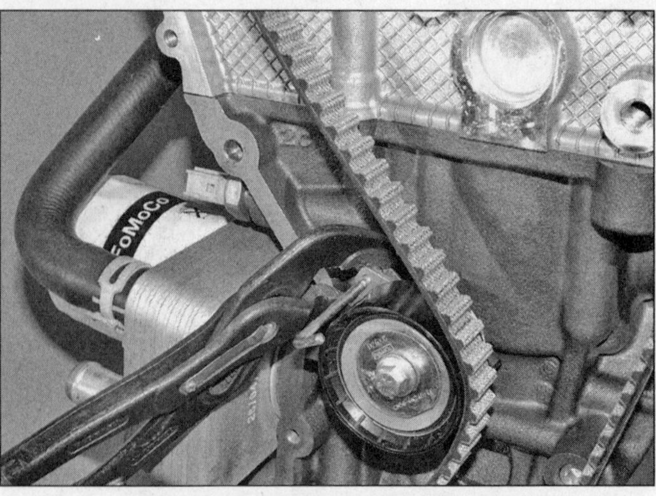

8.5a Lock the tensioner in position and...

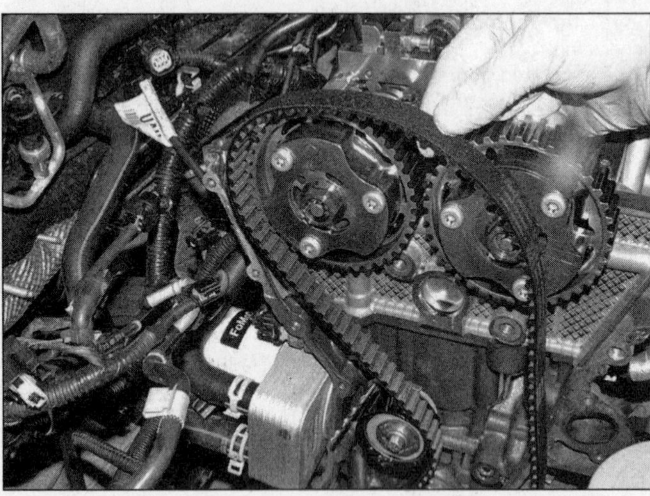

8.5b ...then remove the belt

8.6 Note how the tensioner locates on the engine block, then remove the tensioner locating bolt

8 Timing belt – removal and refitting

Removal

1 Set the engine to TDC as described in Section 3 of this Chapter.

2 Remove the oil feed pipe from the turbocharger. Dispose of the washer. A new one must be used.

3 With reference to Section 4 and Section 7 of this Chapter remove the cylinder head cover and the timing belt cover.

4 With the engine at TDC install Ford special tool 303-1605 (or equivalent) and lock the camshafts in position **(see illustration)**.

5 Rotate the belt tensioner anti-clockwise and fit the locking pin. This is best accomplished with the aid of an assistant pulling on the long run of the timing belt. Use a pair of waterpump pliers to finally rotate the tensioner and fit the locking pin **(see illustration)**. Ford list a special tool for this (303-1054) but a drill bit is also suitable. Remove the timing belt **(see illustration)**.

6 Unbolt and remove the tensioner **(see illustration)**.

Inspection

7 The belt must always be replaced if removed. As a safety measure, the belt should be renewed irrespective of its apparent condition whenever the engine is overhauled.

8 Check the sprockets for signs of wear or damage. Renew any worn or damaged components.

9 When fitting a new belt always fit a new tensioner.

Refitting

10 Locate and then correctly fit the new cambelt tensioner. Tighten the bolt to the specified torque.

11 Locate the timing belt on the crankshaft sprocket, then feed it first over the exhaust camshaft sprocket and then the inlet camshaft sprocket. Finally fit the belt over the tensioner pulley.

12 Remove the locking pin and release tensioner. Remove the camshaft locking tool and TDC timing pin. Rotate the engine twice in the normal direction (clockwise) and check that the locking tools can be still be fitted. If necessary remove the belt and repeat the installation procedure

13 Refit the rest of the components in reverse order.

9 Timing belt tensioner and sprockets – removal, inspection and refitting

Tensioner pulley

1 Removal of the tensioner pulley is described within the timing belt procedure – see Section 8.

Camshaft sprockets (VVT units)

Removal

2 Remove the timing belt and cylinder head cover as described in Section 8 and Section 4.

9.3 Hold the camshaft on the flats provided with an open ended spanner

9.4a Unbolt and then...

9.4b ...remove the sprockets

Caution: Do not use the camshaft locking tools (303-1605) to restrain the camshafts whilst the VVT sprockets are removed.

3 Use a suitable extra long open ended spanner on the camshafts to prevent them from turning, and then with the aid of an assistant remove the camshaft sprocket bolts **(see illustration)**. Note that the bolts are also the control valves for the variable valve timing.

4 Mark the position of the sprockets and then remove them **(see illustrations)**. Inspect them for damage and replace them if necessary.

Refitting

5 Fit the camshaft locking tools (303-1605, or equivalent) and lock the camshafts in position **(see illustration)**.

6 Refit the sprockets and then install Ford special tool 303-1606 (or equivalent). Tighten the bolts on the tool finger tight only at this point.

7 Install the camshaft sprocket special bolts – finger tight only at this stage. Position the special tools (303-1606) so that the lever arms on the special tool are approximately vertical **(see illustration)**. Remove the special tools.

8 With reference to Section 8 fit a new timing belt and tensioner. Refit the timing belt cover.

9 With the camshaft locking tool still in position, install special tool 303-1606 to the camshaft sprockets. Using the tool rotate the camshaft sprockets anti-clockwise until resistance is felt. Tighten the 6 central bolts and lock the tool in position **(see illustration 3.9)**.

10 Use an open ended spanner on the camshaft flats and tighten the camshaft sprocket bolts to the first stage in the bolt tightening procedure. Do not use the camshaft locking tool to prevent the camshafts from turning, a spanner must be used on the flat section provided on each camshaft.

11 Use an open ended spanner on the camshaft flats and tighten the camshaft sprocket bolts to the specified torque (stages 2, 3 and 4). Note to prevent any possibility of the camshafts moving it is recommended that an assistant holds the camshaft in position whilst the bolts are tightened.

12 Remove the special tool from the sprockets and then refit the control solenoids to the timing belt cover.

13 Remove the camshaft locking tool (303-1605) and then (using a new washer) refit the oil feed banjo bolt. Tighten the bolt to the specified torque.

14 Refit the rest of the components in reverse order.

Crankshaft sprocket

15 Remove the timing belt as described in Section 8.

16 Slide the sprocket off the end of the crankshaft.

17 Examine the teeth of the sprocket for wear and damage, and renew if necessary.

18 Wipe clean the end of the crankshaft, then slide on the sprocket.

19 Refit the timing belt as described in Section 8.

10 Camshafts and tappets – removal, inspection and refitting

Removal

1 Disconnect the battery – see Disconnecting the battery in Chapter 5A Section 3.

2 Remove the cylinder head cover as described in Section 4 of this Chapter.

3 Before removing the camshafts, it may be useful to check and record the valve clearances as described in Section 5. If any clearance is not within limits, new tappets can be obtained and fitted.

4 Remove the timing belt as described in

9.5 Lock the camshafts in position

9.7 Fit the special tools

10.6a Remove the camshafts...

10.6b ...and then the tappets

10.13 The camshafts are position with the 'QR' code uppermost (arrowed)

Section 8 and then remove the camshaft sprockets/variable valve timing control units as described in Section 9.

5 Note the positions of the camshaft bearing caps (mark them if necessary) and then slacken them in the reverse order to that shown **(see illustration 10.15)**. Each bolt should be slackened one turn only initially. Repeat this a second time for all 22 bolts and then finally fully slacken the bolts and remove the bearing caps. Keep the caps in the correct order for refitting.

6 Remove the camshafts and then remove the tappets **(see illustrations)**. Store them in the correct order – ideally obtain 12 small containers and label each one appropriately.

Inspection

7 With the camshafts and tappets removed, check each for signs of obvious wear (scoring, pitting, etc) and for ovality, and renew if necessary.

8 Visually examine the camshaft lobes for score marks, pitting, and evidence of overheating (blue, discoloured areas). Look for flaking away of the hardened surface layer of each lobe. If any such signs are evident, renew the component concerned.

9 Examine the camshaft bearing journals and the cylinder head bearing surfaces for signs of obvious wear or pitting. If any such signs are evident, renew the component concerned.

10 To check camshaft endfloat, remove the tappets, clean the bearing surfaces carefully, and refit the camshafts and bearing caps. Tighten the bearing cap bolts to the specified torque wrench setting, then measure the endfloat using a dial gauge mounted on the cylinder head so that its tip bears on the camshaft right-hand end.

11 Tap the camshaft fully towards the gauge, zero the gauge, then tap the camshaft fully away from the gauge, and note the gauge reading. At the time of writing no camshaft endfloat specifications were available from Ford, however and play in excess of 0.2mm will require further investigation.

Refitting

12 Clean all the gasket material from the bearing caps and cylinder head before refitting the camshafts.

13 Lubricate the tappets with clean engine oil and refit them. Refit the camshafts **(see illustration)**. Apply engine oil to the camshaft lobes and bearing journals. To avoid any possibility of the valves contacting the pistons rotate the crankshaft anti-clockwise so that the pistons are halfway up (or down) the bores.

14 Each end bearing cap must be have a 3mm bead of Ford sealant (WSK-M2G348-A5) applied to the cap surface. **(see illustrations)**. The camshaft caps must then be fitted within 5 minutes of applying the sealant.

15 With all the caps in position tighten the bolts in the order shown **(see illustration)**. Tighten each bolt finger tight and then each bolt should be tightened two turns only to start with – in the order shown. Finally tighten the bolts to the specified torque.

16 Refit the remaining components in reverse order of removal.

10.14a Applying sealant to the fuel pump housing/bearing cap

10.14b A 3mm diameter bead of sealant must be applied as shown

10.14c Follow the same procedure for the vacuum pump housing

10.14d Fit the cap/housing within 5 minutes of applying the sealant

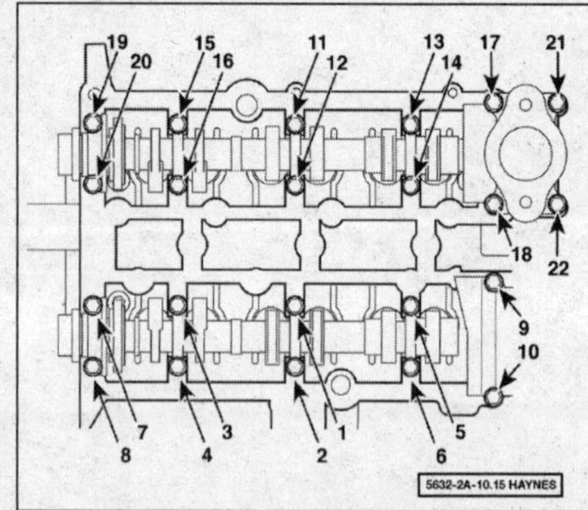

10.15 Tighten the bolts in the order shown

11 Cylinder head – removal, inspection and refitting

Note: *The cylinder head bolts require a suitable 'Ribe' socket to remove them.*

Removal

1 Depressurise the fuel system as described in Chapter 4A Section 13.

2 Jack up and support the front of the vehicle (see *Jacking and vehicle support* in the reference section).

3 Drain the cooling system and the engine oil as described in Chapter 1A Section 28.

4 Disconnect the battery negative lead as described in Chapter 5A Section 3.

5 Remove the inlet manifold and the turbocharger as described in Chapter 4A.

6 Remove the camshafts and tappets as described in Section 10.

7 Remove the inlet manifold support bolt from the front of the engine at the timing belt end.

8 At the left-hand end of the cylinder head unbolt and remove both coolant hoses and then unbolt the coolant outlet from the cylinder head (4 bolts) **(see illustrations)**.

11.8a Remove the coolant hoses and...

11.8b ...then the coolant outlet

9 At the rear of the cylinder head remove the mounting plate that holds the vacuum solenoid in place (3 bolts).

10 Lower the vehicle to the ground.

11 Make a note of their fitted locations and the harness routing, then disconnect any wiring plugs attached to components on the cylinder head. Label the plugs if necessary to aid refitting.

12 Make a last check round the cylinder head, to ensure that nothing remains connected or attached which would prevent the head from being lifted off. Prepare a clean surface to lay the head down on once it has been removed.

13 Working in the reverse of the tightening sequence **(see illustration 11.27)**, slacken the ten cylinder head bolts progressively and by half a turn at a time; a Torx key (TX 55 size) will be required. Remove all the bolts and dispose of them.

14 Lift off the cylinder head away. Remove the gasket, noting the two dowels **(see illustrations)**. Although the gasket cannot be re-used, it is advisable to retain it for comparison with the new one, to confirm that the right part has been supplied.

11.14a Remove the cylinder head and...

11.14b ...recover the gasket

Inspection

15 The mating faces of the cylinder head and cylinder block must be perfectly clean before refitting the head. Use a hard plastic or wood scraper to remove all traces of gasket and carbon; also clean the piston crowns. Take particular care during the cleaning operations, as aluminium alloy is easily damaged.

16 Make sure that the carbon is not allowed to enter the oil and coolant passages – this is particularly important for the lubrication system, as carbon could block the oil supply to the engine's components. Using adhesive tape and paper, seal the coolant, oil and bolt holes in the cylinder block. To prevent carbon entering the gap between the pistons and bores, smear a little grease in the gap. After cleaning each piston, use a small brush to remove all traces of grease and carbon from the gap, then wipe away the remainder with a clean rag.

17 Check the mating surfaces of the cylinder block and the cylinder head for nicks, deep scratches and other damage. If slight, they may be removed carefully with a file, but if excessive, renewal is necessary as it is not permissible to machine the surfaces.

18 If warpage of the cylinder head gasket surface is suspected, use a straight-edge to check it for distortion **(see illustration)**. Refer to Part E of this Chapter if necessary.

19 If possible, clean out the bolt holes in the block using compressed air, to ensure no oil or coolant is present. Screwing a bolt into an oil- or coolant-filled hole can (in extreme cases) cause the block to fracture, due to the hydraulic pressure created.

20 Although not essential, if a suitable tap-and-die set is available, it's worth running the correct-size tap down the bolt threads in the cylinder block. This will clean the threads of any debris, and go some way to restoring any damaged threads. Make absolutely sure the tap is the right size and thread pitch, and lightly oil the tap before starting.

21 Ford insist that the cylinder head bolts must be renewed.

Refitting

22 Wipe clean the mating surfaces of the cylinder head and cylinder block, and check that the two locating dowels are in position in the block **(see illustration)**.

23 Turn the crankshaft anti-clockwise so that pistons are halfway up (or down) the cylinder

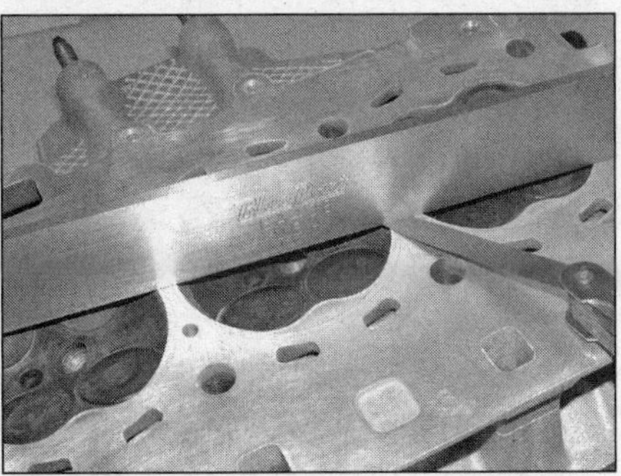

11.18 Check the cylinder head for distortion with a straight edge and a feeler gauge

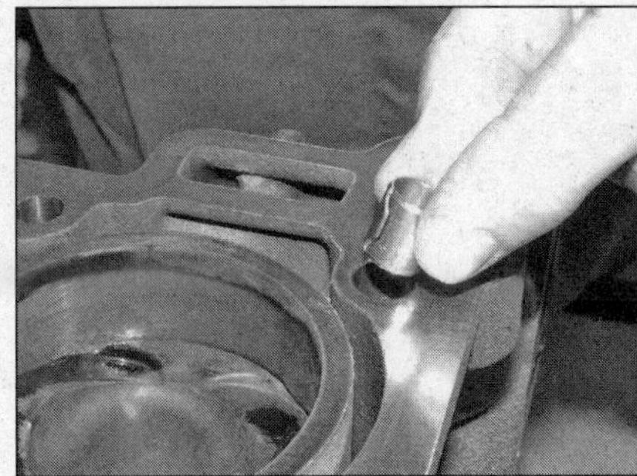

11.22 Check that the dowels are secure

11.24 Fit the new gasket

bores, in order to avoid the risk of valve/piston contact. Turn the crankshaft using a spanner on the pulley bolt.

24 If the old gasket is still available, check that it is identical to the new one. Position the new gasket over the dowels on the cylinder block surface. It can only be fitted one way round – check carefully that the holes in the gasket align with the holes in the block surface, and that none are blocked **(see illustration)**.

25 It is useful when refitting a cylinder head to have an assistant on hand to help guide the head onto the dowels. Take care that the gasket does not get moved as the head is lowered into position. To confirm that the head is aligned correctly, once it is in place, temporarily slide in two or more of the head bolts, and check that they fit into the block holes.

26 Fit the new head bolts carefully, and screw them in by hand only until finger-tight.

27 Working progressively and in sequence, tighten the cylinder head bolts to their Stage 1 torque setting **(see illustration)**.

28 Next, go around again in the same sequence, and tighten the bolts to the Stage 2 setting.

29 Stage 3 requires all the bolts to be loosened by 45 degrees – an 'angle tightening gauge' will be required.

30 Next (stage 4) tighten the bolts in sequence to the specified torque.

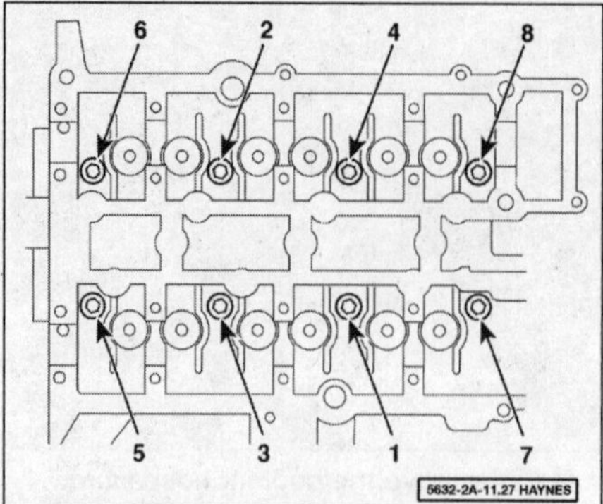

11.27 Tighten the bolts to the specified torque

31 Stage 5 is to tighten all the bolts through 90 degrees in correct order.

32 Finally (stage 6), the bolts should be angle-tightened further, by the specified amount.

33 The remainder of refitting is a reversal of removal, noting the following points:

a) *Refit the camshafts as described in Section 10, and the timing belt as described in Section 8.*
b) *Tighten all fasteners to the specified torque, where given.*
c) *Ensure that all hoses and wiring are correctly routed, and that hose clips and wiring connectors are securely refitted.*
d) *Refill the cooling system as described in Chapter 1A Section 28.*
e) *Replace the engine oil. An oil and filter change is recommended.*
f) *Check all disturbed joints for signs of oil or coolant leakage once the engine has been restarted and warmed-up to normal operating temperature.*

12 Sump – removal and refitting

Removal

1 Apply the handbrake, then jack up the front of the car and support it on axle stands (see *Jacking and vehicle support*).

2 Drain the engine oil, then check the drain plug sealing washer and renew if necessary. Clean and refit the engine oil drain plug together with the washer, and tighten it to the specified torque wrench setting. Although not strictly necessary, as the oil is being drained, it makes sense to fit a new oil filter at the same time (see Chapter 1A Section 6).

3 With reference to Chapter 4A Section 15 remove the catalytic converter.

4 Remove the auxiliary drivebelt as described in Chapter 1A Section 23.

5 Disconnect the wiring plugs from the AC compressor and secure them out of harms way.

6 Unbolt the AC compressor and secure it using stout cord or cable ties to the bonnet slam panel or other suitable location **(see illustration)**. Do not disconnect the refrigerant pipes.

7 Remove the sump retaining bolts in the reverse order to that shown **(see illustration 12.13)**. Note the location of each bolt, as they are of different lengths.

8 A traditional sump gasket is not used – sealant is used instead. Unfortunately, the use of sealant makes removal of the sump more difficult. There are several points around the sump where it is possible to insert a screwdriver or wooden wedges to break the seal and release the sump **(see illustration)**.

9 On no account lever between the mating faces, as this will almost certainly damage them, resulting in leaks when finished.

Refitting

10 Thoroughly clean the contact surfaces of the sump and crankcase. Use a plastic or wooden scraper only. Do not use metal tools or the machined surfaces may be damaged.

11 Apply a 3 to 4 mm diameter bead of sealant (Ford WSE M4G323-A4, or equivalent) to the sump pan, to the inside of the bolt holes **(see illustration)**. The sump bolts must be fitted and tightened within 10 minutes of applying the sealant.

12 Offer the sump up into position and fit all the sump bolts finger tight.

13 Tighten the bolts to the specified torque in

12.6 Secure the compressor to the side

12.8 Gently lever the sump free

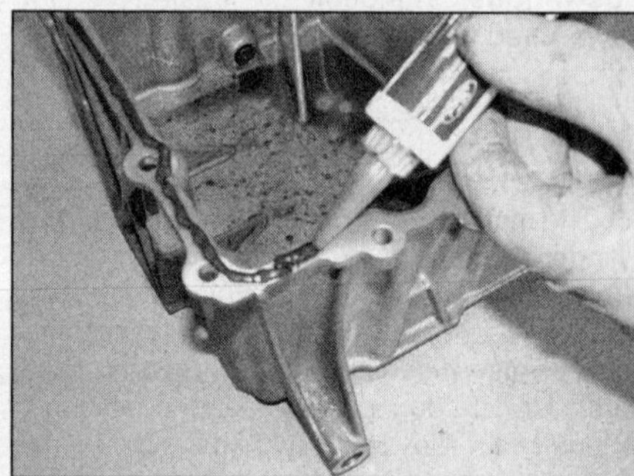
12.11 Apply sealant

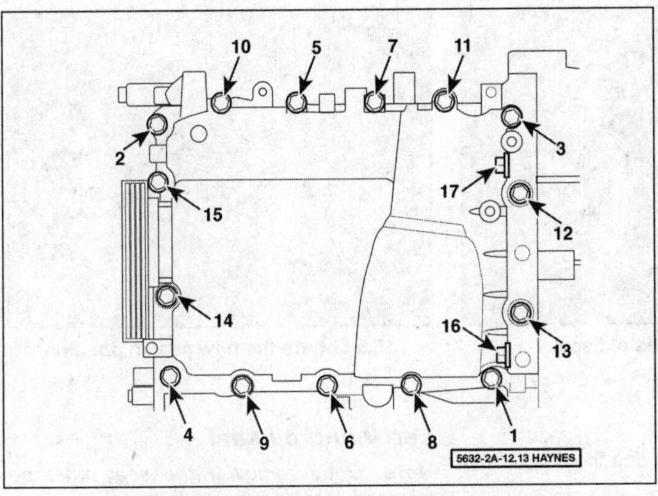

12.13 Tighten the bolts in the order shown

13.2 Remove the cover

the order shown **(see illustration)**. Note that the 2 sump to transmission bolt have a higher torque value than the sump to block bolts.

14 Refit the remaining components in reverse order of removal.

15 Lower the car to the ground. To be on the safe side, wait a further 30 minutes for the sealant to cure before filling the sump with fresh oil, as described in Chapter 1A Section 6.

16 Finally start the engine and check for signs of oil leaks.

13 Oil pump – removal and refitting

Removal

1 Remove the sump as described in Section 12.

2 Unclip the cover plate from the oil pump and remove it **(see illustration)**.

3 Unscrew the 3 bolts securing the oil pump to the block and then rotate the pump towards the timing belt, to enable it to be unhooked from the drive belt **(see illustrations)**.

4 If required the oil pump drive sprocket can now be removed **(see illustration)**.

5 Individual parts are not available for the oil pump. If the oil pump is faulty it must be replaced.

Refitting

6 If the oil pump has been replaced it should be primed with fresh engine before being fitted.

7 Refitting is a reversal of removal, but note that the oil pump cover must be clipped in place and then rotated into position. An audible click will be heard when the cover is correctly positioned **(see illustration)**.

8 Refit the sump and change the oil and filter as described in Chapter 1A Section 6.

9 Ensure that the oil pressure warning light is illuminated before starting the engine. Restart the engine whilst watching the oil pressure warning light. It should go out as soon as the engine starts. Stop the engine immediately if the oil pressure warning light does not go out.

14 Oil pressure switch – removal and refitting

1 The oil pressure switch is a vital early warning of low oil pressure. The switch operates the oil warning light on the instrument panel – the light should come on with the ignition, and go out almost immediately when the engine starts.

2 If the light does not come on, there could be a fault on the instrument panel, the switch wiring, or the switch itself. If the light does not go out, low oil level, worn oil pump (or sump pick-up blocked), blocked oil filter, or worn main bearings could be to blame – or again, the switch may be faulty.

3 If the light comes on while driving, the best advice is to turn the engine off immediately, and not to drive the car until the problem has been investigated – ignoring the light could mean expensive engine damage.

13.3a Remove the pump...

13.3b ...and recover the belt

13.4 Note the orientation of the drive sprocket (arrowed)

13.7 The cover must clip into place correctly (arrowed)

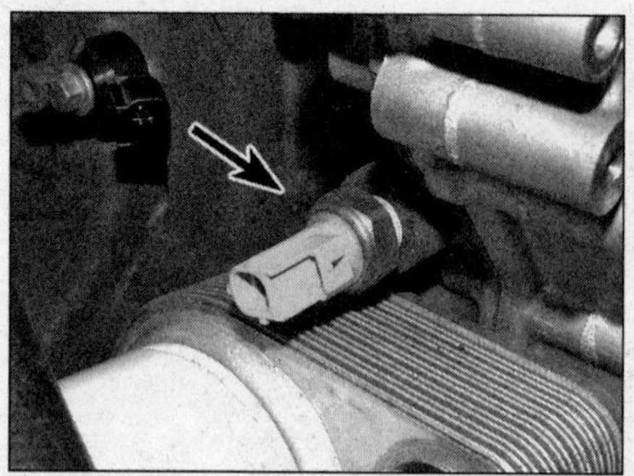

14.4 The oil pressure switch (arrowed)

15.3 Remove the old seal

15.5 Locate the new seal in position

Removal

4 The oil pressure switch is located on the rear face of the engine, above the oil filter **(see illustration)**.

5 Disconnect the wiring plug from the switch.

6 Unscrew the switch from the block, and remove it. There should only be a very slight loss of oil when this is done.

Inspection

7 Examine the switch for signs of cracking or splits. If the top part of the switch is loose, this is an early indication of impending failure.

8 Check that the wiring terminals at the switch are not loose, then trace the wire from the switch connector until it enters the main loom – any wiring defects will give rise to apparent oil pressure problems.

Refitting

9 Refitting is the reverse of the removal procedure, noting the following points:

a) Coat the switch with thread lock (Loctite 243, Ford WSK-M2G349-A7 or equivilant)

b) Tighten the switch securely.

c) Reconnect the switch connector, making sure it clicks home properly. Ensure that the wiring is routed away from any hot or moving parts.

d) Check the engine oil level and top-up if necessary (see 'Weekly checks').

e) Check for signs of oil leaks once the engine has been restarted and warmed-up to normal operating temperature.

15 Crankshaft oil seals – renewal

Right-hand oil seal

1 Remove the crankshaft pulley as described in Section 6.

2 Note the fitted depth of the oil seal as a guide for fitting the new one.

3 Using a small pry bar or (ideally) an oil seal removal tool, prise the old oil seal from the timing cover **(see illustration)**. Take great care not to damage the timing belt cover or the nose of the crankshaft.

4 Wipe clean the seating and the nose of the crankshaft.

5 Apply a little clean engine oil to the inner lip of the seal, then locate it in position. Make sure that the closed end of the oil seal faces outwards **(see illustration)**.

6 Using a socket or length of metal tubing, drive the oil seal squarely into position to the previously-noted depth. The Ford installation tool (303-1603) can be used together with an old crankshaft pulley bolt to press the oil seal into position **(see illustrations)**. Do not use a new crankshaft pulley bolt, as it is only permissible to use the bolt once. With the oil seal in position, wipe away any excess oil.

7 Refit the crankshaft pulley with reference to Section 6.

15.6a Use the correct Ford tool or alternatively...

15.9a Remove the bolts (arrowed)...

Left-hand oil seal

Note: *Once removed the seal must be replaced. It can not be refitted.*

8 Remove the flywheel/driveplate as described in Section 16.

9 Unscrew the 8 bolts (2 from the sump-upwards) and withdraw the oil seal carrier from the end of the crankshaft **(see illustrations)**. Note that the seal and carrier are made as one unit – it is not possible to obtain the seal separately.

10 Clean the carrier contact surface on the cylinder block, and the end of the crankshaft.

11 The new oil seal carrier is supplied complete with a fitting sleeve, which ensures that the oil seal lips are correctly located on the crankshaft. Ford state that neither the crankshaft nor the new oil seal should be lubricated before fitting.

15.6b ...drive the seal home with a large socket

15.9b ...and withdraw the seal

16.2 The correct Ford tool locking the flywheel

16.5 Mark the inner and outer sections (arrowed) and check for excessive play

12 Locate the oil seal carrier and fitting sleeve over the end of the crankshaft. Press the carrier into position, noting that the centre bolt holes are formed into locating dowels.
13 Insert the retaining bolts and progressively tighten them to the specified torque.
14 Remove the fitting sleeve and check that the oil seal lips are correctly located.
15 Refit the flywheel/driveplate as described in Section 16.

16 Flywheel/driveplate – removal, inspection and refitting

Removal

1 Remove the transmission as described in Chapter 7 Section 7 and the clutch as described in Chapter 6 Section 6.
2 Hold the flywheel/driveplate stationary using one of the following methods:

a) If an assistant is available, insert one of the transmission mounting bolts into the cylinder block and have the assistant engage a wide-bladed screwdriver with the starter ring gear teeth while the bolts are loosened. Alternatively, a piece of angle-iron can be engaged with the ring gear and located against the transmission mounting bolt

b) A further method is to fabricate a piece of flat metal bar with a pointed end to engage the ring gear – fit the tool to the transmission bolt and use washers and packing to align it with the ring gear, then tighten the bolt to hold it in position.

c) Fit Ford tool 303-1602 (or equivalent) and lock the flywheel in position **(see illustration)**.

3 Unscrew and remove the bolts, then lift the flywheel/driveplate off the locating dowel on the crankshaft. Dispose of the bolts. New ones must be used

Inspection

4 Clean the flywheel/driveplate to remove grease and oil. Inspect the surface for cracks, rivet grooves, burned areas and score marks. Light scoring can be removed with emery cloth. Check for cracked and broken ring gear teeth. Lay the flywheel/driveplate on a flat surface, and use a straight-edge to check for warpage.
5 Where a dual mass flywheel is fitted check for excessive play between the stationary section and the movable section. Make paint marks on the inner and outer sections and then rotate the secondary section of the flywheel. Note the amount of rotation between the two sections **(see illustration)**. As a rule of thumb anything greater than 15mm should be considered excessive. If in doubt (and given the amount of work required to remove the flywheel) a second opinion from a Ford dealer or suitably equipped garage should be sought. Note that special tools are available to accurately asses the condition of the flywheel. If the service history of the vehicle is known and the clutch is being replaced for the second time, then the dual mass flywheel should always be replaced.
6 Clean and inspect the mating surfaces of the flywheel/driveplate and the crankshaft. If the crankshaft oil seal is leaking, renew it (see Section 15) before refitting the flywheel/ driveplate. In fact, given the large amount of work needed to remove the flywheel/ driveplate, it's probably worth fitting a new seal anyway, as a precaution.

Refitting

7 Make sure that the mating faces of the flywheel/driveplate and crankshaft are clean, then locate the flywheel/driveplate on the crankshaft – it will only fit in one position.
8 Insert the new retaining bolts finger-tight **(see illustration)**.
9 Lock the flywheel/driveplate (see paragraph 2), then tighten the bolts in a diagonal sequence to the specified torque.
10 Refit the clutch with reference to Chapter 6 Section 6, and the transmission as described in Chapter 7 Section 7.

17 Engine/transmission mountings – inspection and renewal

General

1 The engine/transmission mountings seldom require attention, but broken or deteriorated mountings should be renewed immediately, or the added strain placed on the driveline components may cause damage or wear.
2 While separate mountings may be removed and refitted individually, if more than one is disturbed at a time – such as if the engine/transmission unit is removed from its mountings – they must be reassembled and their fasteners tightened in the position marked on removal.
3 On reassembly, the complete weight of the engine/transmission unit must not be taken by the mountings until all are correctly aligned with the marks made on removal. Tighten the engine/transmission mounting fasteners to their specified torque wrench settings.

16.8 Fit the new bolts

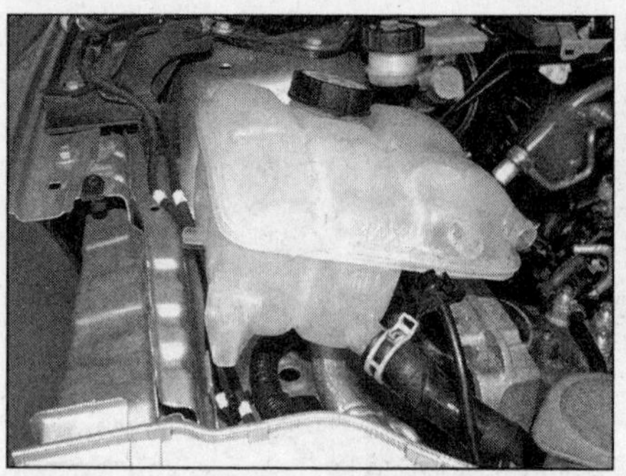
17.8 Move the coolant expansion bottle to the side

17.10 Remove the mounting

17.14 Remove the battery support tray

Inspection

4 During the check, the engine/transmission unit must be raised slightly, to remove its weight from the mountings.

5 Raise the front of the vehicle, and support it securely on axle stands. Position a jack under the sump, with a large block of wood between the jack head and the sump, then carefully raise the engine/transmission just enough to take the weight off the mountings.

Warning: DO NOT place any part of your body under the engine when it is supported only by a jack.

6 Check the mountings to see if the rubber is cracked, hardened or separated from the metal components. Sometimes the rubber will split right down the centre.

7 Check for relative movement between each mounting's brackets and the engine/transmission or body (use a large screwdriver or lever to attempt to move the mountings). If movement is noted, lower the engine and check-tighten the mounting fasteners.

Renewal

Note: *The following paragraphs assume the engine is supported beneath the sump as described earlier.*

Right-hand mounting

8 Lift up the coolant expansion tank and position it to one side **(see illustration)**. Note there is no need to disconnect the coolant pipes. On some models a vibration damper is fitted to the rear of the mounting. Where fitted unbolt and remove the damper.

9 Mark the position of the mounting on the vehicle on the right-hand inner wing panel, and then undo the 2 bolts securing the mounting.

10 Undo the 3 retaining bolts from the engine side of the mounting and then remove the mounting **(see illustration)**.

11 Re-align the marks made on removal. Tighten all fasteners to the torque wrench settings specified.

Left-hand mounting

12 Remove the air filter housing as described in Chapter 4A Section 5.

13 Remove the battery as described in Chapter 5A Section 3, then undo the 3 bolts and remove the battery tray. Disconnect any wiring as the tray is withdrawn.

14 Unclip the wiring loom from the battery tray support panel, remove the 4 bolts and withdraw the support panel **(see illustration)**.

15 With the transmission supported, note the position of the mounting then unscrew the centre retaining bolt to release the upper half of the mounting from the transmission **(see illustration)**.

16 On six speed transmissions, lower the transmission slightly to access the 3 mounting bolts on the transmission **(see illustration)**. On five speed transmission access the bolts from the engine bay. Remove the bolts and recover the mounting.

17 Refitting is a reversal of removal. Re-align the mounting in the position noted on removal, then tighten all fasteners to the specified torque wrench settings.

Rear mounting (roll restrictor)

18 Remove the 3 mounting bolts from the transmission. Note, that the bolts are different lengths on five speed transmissions. Remove the single bolt from the subframe **(see illustration)**.

19 With the aid of an assistant pivot the engine (assuming the two main engine mountings are in position) and work the mounting free.

20 On refitting, ensure that the bolts are securely tightened to the specified torque wrench setting.

17.15 Remove the bolt (arrowed)

17.16 Lower the transmission to access the mounting bolts

17.18 Remove the mounting bolts (arrowed)

Chapter 2 Part B
1.6 litre petrol engines in-car repair procedures

Contents

Degrees of difficulty

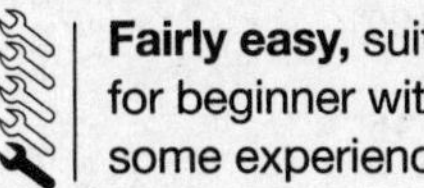

Easy, suitable for novice with little experience	**Fairly easy,** suitable for beginner with some experience	**Fairly difficult,** suitable for competent DIY mechanic	**Difficult,** suitable for experienced DIY mechanic	**Very difficult,** suitable for expert DIY or professional

Specifications

General

Engine type	Four-cylinder, in-line, double overhead camshafts, with variable valve timing. EcoBoost model has turbocharging and direct petrol injection	
Designation	1.6 Duratec 16V Ti-VCT	
Engine codes	IQDA, IQDB, IQDC, PNDD, XTDA and XTDB	
Capacity	1596 cc	
Bore	79.0 mm	
Stroke	81.4 mm	
Compression ratio	11: 1	
Output:	**Power**	**Torque**
IQDA, XTDA and XTDB engines	63 KW (85 PS)	141 Nm at 2500 rpm
IQDB and IQDC engines	77 KW (105 PS)	150 Nm at 4000 rpm
PNDD 92 KW (125 PS)	159 Nm at 4000 rpm	
Firing order	1-3-4-2 (No 1 cylinder at timing belt end)	
Direction of crankshaft rotation	Clockwise (seen from right-hand side of car)	

Valves

Valve clearances (cold)	
Inlet	0.14 to 0.23 mm
Exhaust	0.28 to 0.37 mm

Camshafts

Camshaft bearing journal diameter	Unavailable at time of writing
Camshaft bearing journal-to-cylinder head running clearance	Unavailable at time of writing
Camshaft endfloat (typical)	0.05 to 0.13 mm

Lubrication

Oil pressure (minimum temp of 80°):	
Idling (800 rpm)	1.0 bar
At 2000 rpm	2.0 bars
Oil pressure relief valve opening pressure	4 ± 0.4 bar

Torque wrench settings	Nm	lbf ft
Air conditioning compressor mounting bolts	25	18
Alternator mounting nuts	48	35
Auxiliary drivebelt tensioner bolts	48	35
Camshaft bearing cap:		
EcoBoost engines: *		
Stage 1 (bolts 1-16)	7	5
Stage 2 (bolts1-16)	Angle-tighten a further 45°	
Stage 3 (bolts 17 and 18)	10	7
Stage 4 (bolts 17 and 18)	Angle-tighten a further 70°	
Stage 5 (bolts 19 and 20)	10	7
Stage 6 (bolts 19 and 20)	Angle-tighten a further 53°	
Ti-VCT engines:		
Stage 1 (bolts 1-16)	7	5
Stage 2 (bolts 17-20)	10	7
Stage 3 (bolts 1-16)	Angle-tighten a further 45°	
Stage 4 (bolts 17 and 19)	Angle-tighten a further 70°	
Stage 5 (bolts 18 and 20)	Angle-tighten a further 53°	
Camshaft position sensor	10	7
Coolant outlet to cylinder head	10	7
Coolant outlet on cylinder block	18	14
Coolant pump pulley bolts	24	17
Crankcase breather to cylinder block	10	7
Crankshaft position sensor	8	6
Crankshaft oil seal carrier	10	7
Crankshaft pulley/vibration damper: *		
Stage 1	100	74
Stage 2	Angle-tighten a further 90°	
Stage 3	Wait 20 seconds	
Stage 4	Angle-tighten a further 15°	
Cylinder head bolts: *		
EcoBoost engines:		
Stage 1	5	3
Stage 2	15	11
Stage 3	35	26
Stage 4	Angle-tighten a further 90°	
Stage 5	Angle-tighten a further 90°	
Ti-VCT engines:		
Stage 1	5	3
Stage 2	15	11
Stage 3	35	26
Stage 4	Angle-tighten a further 75°	
Cylinder head cover	10	7
Driveshaft support bracket to engine block bolts	48	35
Driveshaft bearing support nuts:		
Stage 1	6	4
Stage 2	25	18
Engine mountings:		
Left-hand mounting nuts	48	35
Left-hand mounting bracket to transmission	82	60
Left-hand mounting centre bolt*	148	109
Lower-rear torque rod bolts:		
On transmission	63	46
On subframe:		
Stage 1	30	22
Stage 2	Angle-tighten a further 270°	
Right-hand mounting retaining bolts	90	66
Right-hand mounting bracket-to-engine bolts	55	41
Right-hand mounting harmonic damper	90	66
Exhaust flexible section-to-catalytic converter nuts	48	35
Exhaust manifold nuts/bolts	21	15
Flywheel bolts: *		
EcoBoost engines		
Stage 1	15	11
Stage 2	25	18
Stage 3	30	22
Stage 4	Angle-tighten a further 90°	

Torque wrench settings (continued)

	Nm	lbf ft
Flywheel bolts (continued): *		
Ti-VCT engines:		
Stage 1	30	22
Stage 2	ngle-tighten a further 80°	
Fuel pump bolts (EcoBoost engines)	13	10
Fuel pump high pressure fuel lines (EcoBoost engines):		
Stage 1	21	15
Stage 2	Wait 5 minutes	
Stage 3	21	15
Fuel pump housing bolts (EcoBoost engines):		
Stage 1 (bolts 1-10)	3	2
Stage 2 (bolts 1-10)	9	7
Stage 3 (bolts 1-10)	11	8
Stage 4 (bolts 1,2,5,6,7,8,9,10 only)	14	10
Fuel pump housing bolts (EcoBoost engines – 6 bolt type)	10	7
Fuel rail bolts (EcoBoost engines)	23	17
Inlet manifold:		
Lower bolts (EcoBoost engines only)	10	7
Upper bolts	18	13
Oil baffle to cylinder block	9	7
Oil drain plug	27	21
Oil filter connector (cooler)	55	41
Oil intake pipe to oil baffle	9	7
Oil pressure switch	15	11
Oil pump to cylinder block	9	7
Spark plugs	15	11
Sump bolts:		
Sump-to-block bolts	19	14
Sump-to-transmission bolts	48	36
TDC pin hole blanking plug	20	15
Timing belt cover bolts	10	7
Timing belt tensioner bolt	25	15
Turbocharger oil pipe banjo bolts*	20	15
VVT solenoid	10	6
Intercooler pipe (to sump) bolts	20	15
Vacuum pump housing	10	7
VVT unit blanking plugs	16	12
VVT unit retaining bolts:		
Stage 1	25	18
Stage 2	Angle-tighten a further 75°	

Use new fasteners

1 General Information

How to use this Chapter

1 This Part of Chapter 2 is devoted to in-car repair procedures on the 1.6 litre petrol engine. All procedures concerning engine removal and refitting, and engine block/cylinder head overhaul can be found in Chapter 2E.

2 Refer to Vehicle identification numbers in the Reference Section at the end of this manual for details of engine code locations.

3 Most of the operations included in this Chapter are based on the assumption that the engine is still installed in the car. Therefore, if this information is being used during a complete engine overhaul, with the engine already removed, many of the steps included here will not apply.

Engine description

4 The engine is a sixteen-valve, double overhead camshaft (DOHC), four-cylinder, in-line unit. The engine is mounted transversely at the front of the car, with the transmission on its left-hand end.

5 Apart from the plastic timing belt covers, plastic cylinder head cover, plastic inlet manifold, and the cast-iron cylinder liners, the main engine components (including the sump) are manufactured entirely of aluminium alloy.

Caution: When tightening bolts into aluminium castings, it is important to adhere to the specified torque wrench settings, to avoid stripping threads.

6 The crankshaft runs in five main bearings, the centre main bearing's upper half incorporating thrustwashers to control crankshaft endfloat. Due to the very fine bearing clearances and bearing shell tolerances incorporated during manufacture, it is not possible to renew the crankshaft separate to the cylinder block; in fact it is not possible to remove and refit the crankshaft accurately using conventional tooling. This means that if the crankshaft is worn excessively, it must be renewed together with the cylinder block.

Caution: Do not unbolt the main bearing cap/ladder from the cylinder block, as it is not possible to refit it accurately using conventional tooling. Additionally, the manufacturers do not supply torque settings for the main bearing cap/ladder retaining bolts.

7 The connecting rods rotate on horizontally-split bearing shells at their big-ends, however the big-ends are of unusual design in that the caps are sheared from the rods during manufacture thus making each cap individually matched to its own connecting rod. The big-end bearing shells are also unusual in that they do not have any locating tabs and must be accurately positioned during refitting. The pistons are attached to the connecting rods by gudgeon pins which are an interference fit in the connecting rod small-end eyes. The aluminium alloy pistons are fitted with three piston rings: two compression rings and an oil control ring. After manufacture, the cylinder bores and pistons are measured and classified into three grades, which must be carefully matched together, to ensure the correct piston/cylinder clearance; no oversizes are available to permit reboring.

8 The inlet and exhaust valves are each closed by coil springs; they operate in guides which are shrink-fitted into the cylinder head, as are the valve seat inserts.

9 Both camshafts are driven by the same toothed timing belt, each operating eight valves via bucket tappets. Each camshaft rotates in five bearings that are line-bored directly in the cylinder head and the (bolted-on) bearing caps; this means that the bearing caps are not available separately from the cylinder head, and must not be interchanged with caps from another engine.

10 All engines feature variable valve timing on the both the inlet and exhaust camshafts. Engine oil pressure is used to vary the positions of the camshaft sprocket in relation to the camshafts, thus varying the valves' opening and closing times. Control of the oil flow is achieved using solenoid valves, which in turn are controlled by the engine management electronic control module (ECM). Varying the valve timing is this manner results in improved driveability and output, whist reducing fuel consumption and exhaust emissions.

11 The coolant pump is bolted to the right-hand end of the cylinder block, beneath the front run of the timing belt, and is driven by the auxiliary drivebelt from the crankshaft pulley.

12 Lubrication is by means of an eccentric-rotor trochoidal pump on Ti-VCT engines and by a variable output vane type oil pump on EcoBoost engines. On EcoBoost engines, the output of the oil pump can be altered by adjusting the outer ring of the pump, so that the output can be matched to the engines demands. Use of a variable output oil pump can reduce mechanical loss in the engine by up to 10%. The oil pump is mounted on the crankshaft right-hand end, and draws oil through a strainer located in the sump. The pump forces oil through an externally-mounted full-flow cartridge-type filter.

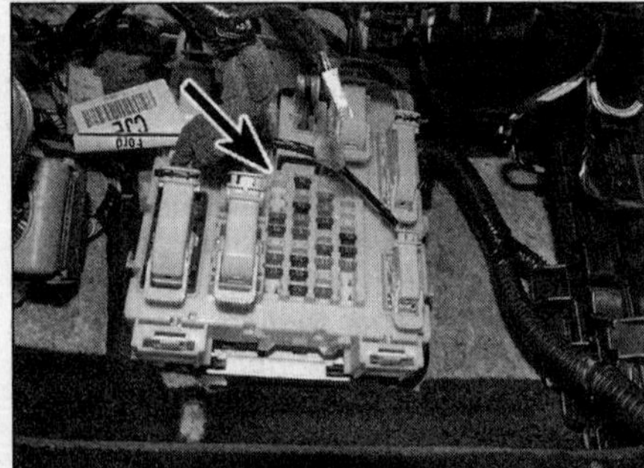

2.3 Fuel pump fuse 56 – upper left-hand side fuse

Operations with engine in car

13 The following work can be carried out with the engine in the car:

a) Cylinder head cover – removal and refitting.
b) Timing belt – renewal.
c) Timing belt tensioner and sprockets – removal and refitting.
d) Camshaft oil seals – renewal.
e) Camshafts, tappets and shims – removal and refitting.
f) Cylinder head – removal and refitting.
g) Sump – removal and refitting.
h) Crankshaft oil seals – renewal.
i) Oil pump – removal and refitting.
j) Flywheel/driveplate – removal and refitting.
k) Engine/transmission mountings – removal and refitting.

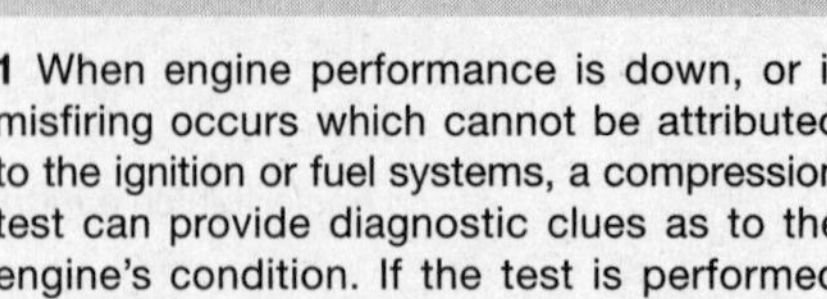

2 Compression test – description and interpretation

1 When engine performance is down, or if misfiring occurs which cannot be attributed to the ignition or fuel systems, a compression test can provide diagnostic clues as to the engine's condition. If the test is performed regularly, it can give warning of trouble before any other symptoms become apparent.

2 The engine must be fully warmed-up to operating temperature, the oil level must be correct and the battery must be fully-charged. The help of an assistant will also be required.

3 Remove fuse number 56 from the passenger compartment fusebox, which is located behind the glovebox **(see illustration)**. This is the fuse for the fuel pump – further details are to be found in Chapter 12. Now start the engine and allow it to run until it stalls.

4 On EcoBoost engines, disable the ignition system by disconnecting the multiplugs from the individual ignition coils. Remove all ignition coils and the spark plugs with reference to Chapter 1A Section 21.

5 On Ti-VCT engines disable the ignition system by disconnecting the multiplug from the DIS ignition coil. Remove all the spark plugs with reference to Chapter 1A Section 21.

6 Fit a compression tester to the No 1 cylinder spark plug hole – the type of tester which screws into the spark plug thread is preferable.

7 Arrange for an assistant to hold the accelerator pedal fully depressed to the floor, while at the same time cranking the engine over for several seconds on the starter motor. Observe the compression gauge reading. The compression will build-up fairly quickly in a healthy engine. Low compression on the first stroke, followed by gradually-increasing pressure on successive strokes, indicates worn piston rings. A low compression on the first stroke which does not rise on successive strokes, indicates leaking valves or a blown head gasket (a cracked cylinder head could also be the cause). Deposits on the underside of the valve heads can also cause low compression. Record the highest gauge reading obtained, then repeat the procedure for the remaining cylinders.

8 Due to the variety of testers available, and the fluctuation in starter motor speed when cranking the engine, different readings are often obtained when carrying out the compression test. For this reason, actual compression pressure figures are not quoted by Ford. However, the most important factor is that the compression pressures are uniform in all cylinders, and that is what this test is mainly concerned with.

9 Add some engine oil (about three squirts from a plunger type oil can) to each cylinder through the spark plug holes, and then repeat the test.

10 If the compression increases after the oil is added, the piston rings are probably worn. If the compression does not increase significantly, the leakage is occurring at the valves or the head gasket. Leakage past the valves may be caused by burned valve seats and/or faces, or warped, cracked or bent valves.

11 If two adjacent cylinders have equally low compressions, it is most likely that the head gasket has blown between them. The appearance of coolant in the combustion chambers or on the engine oil dipstick would verify this condition.

12 If one cylinder is about 20 percent lower than the other, and the engine has a slightly rough idle, a worn lobe on the camshaft could be the cause.

13 On completion of the checks, refit the spark plugs and reconnect the HT leads and the DIS ignition coil plug. Refit the fuel pump relay to the fusebox.

3 Top Dead Centre (TDC) for No 1 piston – locating

1 Top dead centre (TDC) is the highest point of the cylinder that each piston reaches as the crankshaft turns. Each piston reaches its TDC position at the end of its compression stroke, and then again at the end of its exhaust stroke. For the purpose of engine timing, TDC on the compression stroke for No 1 piston is used. No 1 cylinder is at the timing belt end of the engine. Proceed as follows.

2 Disconnect the battery negative (earth) lead and remove the spark plugs as described in Chapter 1A Section 21.

3 Apply the handbrake, then jack up the front of the vehicle and support it on axle stands (see *Jacking and vehicle support*).

4 Undo the fasteners and remove the engine undershield. Remove the wheel arch liner, and auxiliary drivebelt lower cover (where fitted) for access to the crankshaft pulley and bolt.

5 Remove the engine cover and then on EcoBoost engines remove the air inlet pipe from the top of the engine.

6 Position a trolley jack under the engine. Use a block of wood on the jack head to spread the load and prevent damage to the sump. Take the weight of the engine.

7 Make alignment marks between the right-hand engine mounting bracket and the cylinder head bracket/vehicle body, then undo the nuts/bolts and remove the mounting. Discard the nuts – new ones must be fitted.

8 Slacken the 4 mounting bolts on the waterpump pulley and then remove the auxiliary drivebelt as described in Chapter 1A Section 23.

9 Remove the waterpump pulley and then remove the timing belt cover as described in Section 7.

10 To fit the TDC locating tool remove the right-hand drive shaft as described in Chapter 8 Section 2.

11 Remove the engine mounted section of the support bracket and then remove the blanking plug from the engine block.

12 Rotate the crankshaft pulley clockwise until the marks on the camshaft variable valve timing (VVT) units are approaching the 11 o'clock position.

13 A TDC timing pin must now be inserted and tightened into the hole **(see illustrations)**. It is highly recommended that the Ford timing pin 303-748 is obtained, or alternatively, a timing pin from a reputable tool manufacturer such as Draper or AST.

14 With the timing pin in position, turn the crankshaft slowly clockwise until the specially machined surface on the crank web just touches the timing pin. No 1 piston is now at TDC on its compression stroke.

15 With the engine at TDC fit Ford special tool 303-1097 over the VVT units on the ends of the camshafts. Note that the tool is marked with a line to indicate the exhaust side, a dot to indicate the inlet side, and an arrow which must point upwards **(see illustrations)**.

16 Once the work requiring the TDC setting has been completed, remove the special tool from the camshaft VVT units then unscrew the timing pin and refit the blanking plug.

17 Refit the remaining components in reverse order of removal.

3.13a Undo the blanking plug from the right-hand rear corner of the cylinder block...

3.13b ...and screw-in the timing pin

3.15a Fit the special tool over the Ti-VCT units

3.15b The tool is marked with a dot (1) for the inlet camshaft, a line (2) for the exhaust camshaft, and an arrow (3) which must point upwards

4 Cylinder head cover – removal and refitting

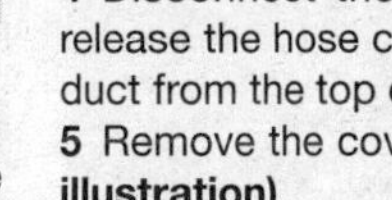

Removal

1 Remove fuse number 56 from the passenger compartment fusebox, which is located behind the glovebox **(see illustration 2.3)**. This is the fuse for the fuel pump – Now start the engine and allow it to run until it stalls.

2 Disconnect the battery negative (earth) lead.

3 Pull up and remove the engine cover.

EcoBoost models

4 Disconnect the crankcase breather pipe, release the hose clips and remove the ait inlet duct from the top of the engine.

5 Remove the cover from the fuel pump **(see illustration)**.

6 Disconnect the wiring plugs from the ignition coils, the fuel pump, the MAP sensor, the camshaft sensor and the VVT control solenoids.

7 Unclip the wiring loom and move it to one side **(see illustration)**.

8 Unbolt and remove the ignition coils and

4.5 Remove the cover from the fuel pump

4.7 A trim tool can be used to release the wiring loom clips

4.8 Remove the coil mounting plate

4.15a Remove the fuel pump and...

4.15b ...recover the bucket tappet

then unbolt and remove the coil mounting plate **(see illustration)**.

9 Anticipating some fuel spillage unbolt the fuel pipe from between the high pressure pump and the fuel rail. Dispose of the pipe. A new one must be fitted.

10 Disconnect the wiring plugs from the fuel injectors and the main section of the wiring loom. Remove the wiring loom from the vehicle.

11 Unbolt the fuel rail and pull it up evenly. from the cylinder head. Anticipate some fuel spillage. Note that some of the injectors may come out with the fuel rail. Any injectors left in the cylinder head should now be remove and the holes sealed.

12 Disconnect the breather pipe and then unbolt the main section of the cover in reverse order to that shown **(see illustration 4.29)**. Carefully lift the cover from the top of the cylinder head. Recover the gasket – this may be re-used if it is not damaged.

13 To completely expose the camshafts the high pressure fuel pump and the vacuum pump must be removed next.

14 Anticipating some fuel spillage, disconnect the fuel pump inlet pipe. This can be released at the connection with the plastic fuel supply line If the pipe is disconnected at the fuel pump it must be replaced.

15 Disconnect the wiring plug and then unbolt the high pressure pump by releasing each bolt a turn at a time. Recover the bucket tappet from beneath **(see illustrations)**.

16 Disconnect the wiring plug from the camshaft position sensor and then slacken the cover mounting bolts in reverse order to that shown **(see illustrations 4.26a or 4.26b)** Recover the o-ring (where fitted).

17 At the inlet camshaft (and with reference to Chapter 9 Section 23) remove the vacuum pump. Disconnect the wiring plug from the camshaft position sensor and then unbolt the vacuum pump housing.

Ti-VCT models

18 Disconnect the breather pipe from the front of the cover.

19 Disconnect the HT leads from the spark plugs, unclip them from the cover, and position them to the left-hand side of the engine compartment.

20 Disconnect the wiring plugs from the camshaft position sensors and VCT solenoids on the cylinder head cover, clean around the area, then undo the retaining bolts and remove both VCT oil control solenoids from the top, right-hand end of the cylinder head **(see illustrations)**. Plug the openings to prevent contamination. Examine the O-ring seals, and renew if necessary.

21 Where fitted, undo the nut and bolt and move the wiring connector bracket at the left-hand rear corner of the cylinder head cover to one side.

22 The cylinder head cover is secured by a total of twelve bolts. Note their fitted locations and remove the bolts in the reverse order to that shown **(see illustration 4.35)**. On some models the bolts are integral with the cover.

23 Carefully lift the cover from the top of the cylinder head, unclipping any wiring as necessary. Recover the gasket – this may be re-used if it is not damaged.

4.20a Disconnect the camshaft position sensors wiring plugs

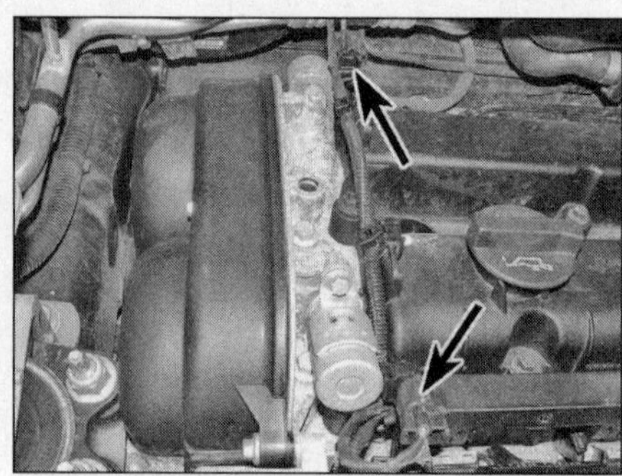
4.20b Disconnect the VCT solenoid wiring plugs (arrowed)

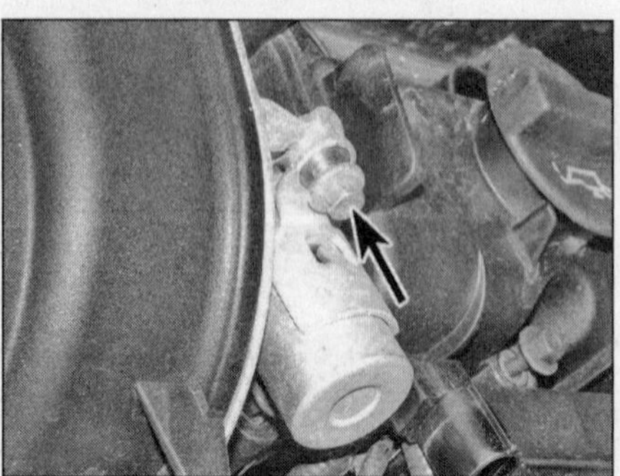
4.20c Then undo the bolt (arrowed)...

4.20d ...and pull the solenoids from place

Refitting

EcoBoost models

24 Clean the mating surfaces of the cylinder head and the cylinder head cover. Examine the condition of the gasket – it may be reused if it is in good condition.

25 Apply sealant to the area shown (Ford WSS-M2G348-A11 or equivalent) on the vacuum pump housing and the fuel pump

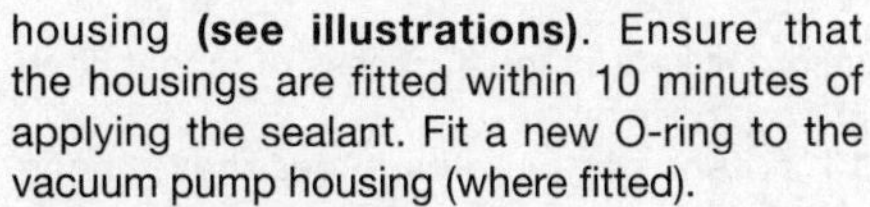

4.25a Apply a 1.5mm diameter bead of sealant...

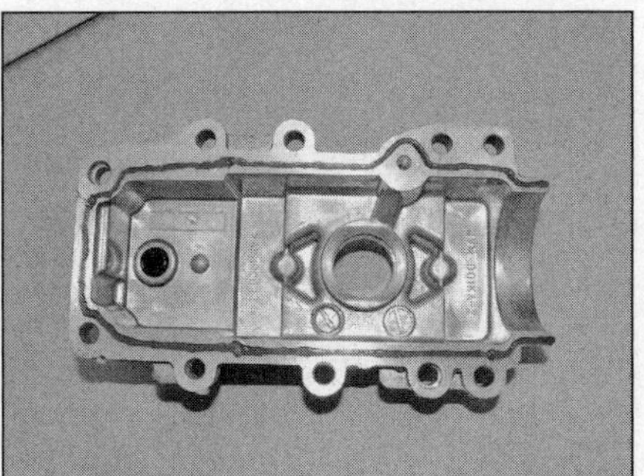

4.25b ...to the fuel pump housing...

4.25c ...and the vacuum pump housing as shown

housing **(see illustrations)**. Ensure that the housings are fitted within 10 minutes of applying the sealant. Fit a new O-ring to the vacuum pump housing (where fitted).

26 Fit the bolts to the fuel pump housing and tighten in the order shown to the specified torque. Note that one of two different fuel pump housings may be fitted **(see illustrations)**.

27 Lubricate the bucket tappet and refit it. Check the condition of the fuel pump O-ring. Renew it if necessary. Lubricate the O-ring with clean engine oil and refit the pump.

28 Tighten the fuel pump bolts evenly, 2 turns at a time. Fully tighten to the specified torque setting.

29 Refit the main section of the cylinder head cover (ensuring that the gasket stays in place), and tighten the bolts to the specified torque in the order shown **(see illustration)**.

30 Refit the fuel rail and then fit a new fuel pipe between the rail and the pump. Tighten to the specified torque.

31 Fit a new fuel pipe to the inlet side of the high pressure pump. Tighten to the specified torque.

32 The remainder of refitting is a reversal of removal.

Ti-VCT models

33 Clean the mating surfaces of the cylinder head and the cover gasket.

34 Lower the cover onto the cylinder head, ensuring that the gasket stays in place.

35 Tighten bolt number 1 first 3 to 4 turns only and then progressively tighten all bolts in the correct order to the specified torque **(see illustration)**.

36 The remainder of refitting is a reversal of removal.

5 Valve clearances – checking and adjustment

1 Remove the cylinder head cover as described in Section 4.

Note: *If checking the valve clearances with the timing belt removed (eg, after refitting the camshafts), rotate the crankshaft 90° anti-clockwise back from TDC on No 1 cylinder so the pistons are halfway down the cylinder bores. Verify this by inserting a long screwdriver down the spark plug holes.*

2 Remove the spark plugs (Chapter 1A Section 21) in order to make turning the engine easier. The engine may be turned using a spanner on the crankshaft pulley bolt or by raising the front right-hand roadwheel clear of the ground, engaging top gear and turning the wheel. If the former method is used, jack up and support the front of the car (see *Jacking and vehicle support*) then unbolt the lower cover for access to the pulley bolt; if the latter method is used, apply the handbrake then jack up the front right-hand side of the car until the roadwheel is clear of the ground and support with an axle stand.

3 Draw the valve positions on a piece of paper, numbering them 1 to 8 inlet and exhaust, from the timing belt (right-hand) end of the engine (ie, 1E, 1I, 2E, 2I and so on). As

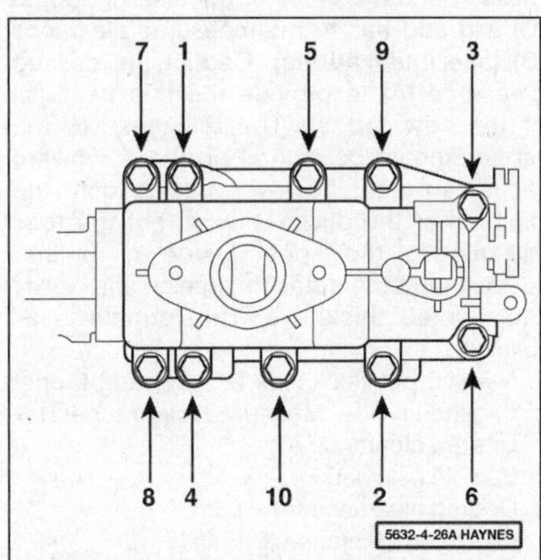

4.26a Tighten the bolts in the order shown (Type 1 housing)

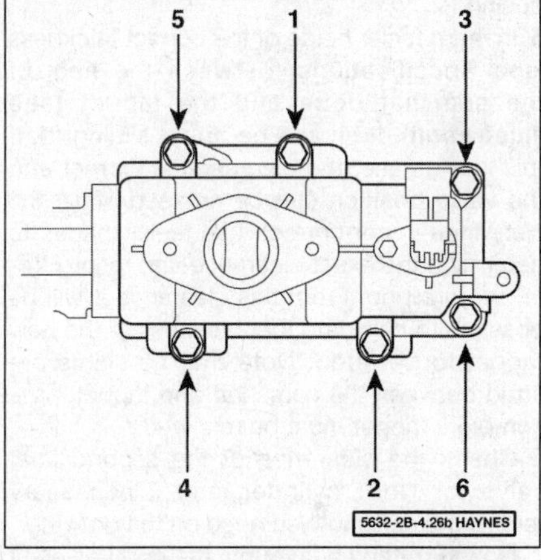

4.26b Tighten the bolts in the order shown (Type 2 housing)

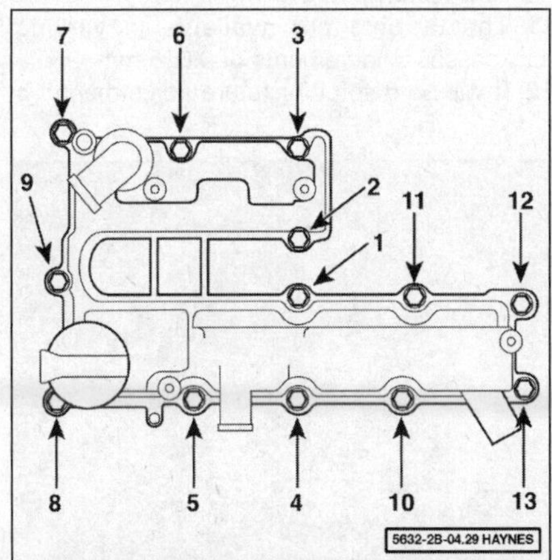

4.29 Tighten the bolts in the order shown

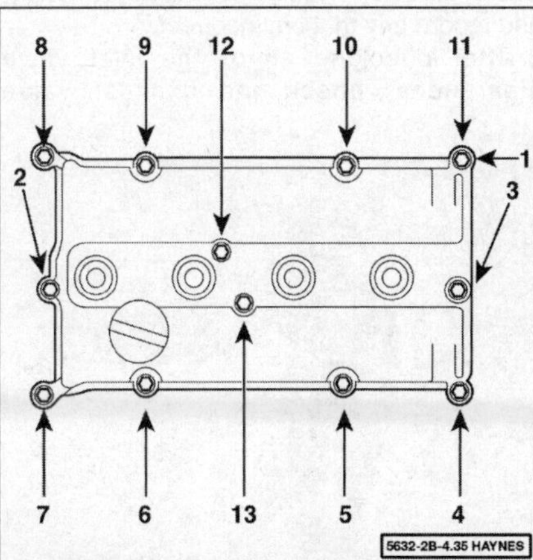

4.35 Tighten the bolts in the order shown

5.5 Insert a feeler gauge between the heel of the camshaft lobe and the tappet

5.10a Measure the thickness of the tappets with a micrometer

5.10b The thickness of each tappet should be etched on its underside

there are two inlet and two exhaust valves for each cylinder, draw the cylinders as large circles and the four valves as smaller circles. The inlet valves are at the front of the cylinder head, and the exhaust valves are at the rear. As the valve clearances are adjusted, cross them off.

4 Turn the engine in a clockwise direction until both inlet valves of No 1 cylinder are fully shut and the apex of the camshaft lobes are pointing upwards away from the valve positions.

5 Insert a feeler blade of the correct thickness (see Specifications) between the heel of the camshaft lobe and the tappet **(see illustration)**. It should be a firm sliding fit. If this is the case, the clearance is correct and the valve position can be crossed off. If the clearance is not correct, use feeler blades to determine the exact clearance and record this on the drawing. From this clearance it will be possible to calculate the thickness of the new tappet to be fitted. Note that no shims are fitted between the camshaft and tappet – the complete tappet must be renewed.

6 Check the clearance of the second inlet valve for No 1 cylinder, and if necessary record the existing clearance on the drawing.

7 Now turn the engine until the inlet valves of No 2 cylinder are fully shut and the camshaft lobes pointing away from the valve positions. Check the clearances as described previously, and record any that are incorrect.

8 After checking all of the inlet valve clearances, check the exhaust valve clearances in the same way, but note that the clearances are different.

9 Where adjustment is required, the procedure is to remove the camshafts as described in Section 11.

10 If the recorded clearance was too small, a thinner tappet must be fitted, and conversely if the clearance was too large, a thicker tappet must be fitted. To calculate the thickness of the new tappet, first use a micrometer to measure the thickness of the existing tappet (C) and add this to the measured clearance (B) **(see illustrations)**. Deduct the desired clearance (A) to provide the thickness (D) of the new tappet. The thickness of the tappet should be etched on the downward facing surface, however this is only the digits after the decimal point, not the total thickness of the tappet. Use a micrometer to measure the total thickness and verify the marked thickness. The formula is as follows.

New tappet thickness D = Existing tappet thickness C + Measured clearance B – Desired clearance A

Sample calculation
Desired clearance (A) = 0.20
Measured clearance (B) = 0.15
Existing tappet thickness (C) = 2.725
Tappet thickness required (D) = C+B-A = 2.675
All measurements in mm

11 The tappets are available in varying thicknesses in increments of 0.025 mm.

12 It will be helpful for future adjustment if a record is kept of the thickness of tappet fitted at each position.

13 When all the clearances have been checked and adjusted, refit the lower cover (where removed), lower the car to the ground and refit the cylinder head cover.

6 Crankshaft pulley/vibration damper – removal and refitting

Caution:** **Removal of the crankshaft pulley effectively loses the valve timing setting, and it will be necessary to reset the timing.

Note: *The vibration damper/crankshaft pulley retaining bolt may only be used once. Obtain a new bolt for the refitting procedure.*

Removal

1 Remove the auxiliary drivebelt as described in Chapter 1A Section 23.

2 Set the engine to the top dead centre (TDC) position as described in Section 3.

3 Remove the starter motor as described in Chapter 5A Section 7, then use Ford tool 303-393A and 303-393-02 (or equivalent) to lock the crankshaft in position. This tool bolts across the starter motor aperture in the transmission bellhousing, and engages with the teeth of the starter ring gear on the flywheel/driveplate **(see illustrations)**.

4 With the tool installed slacken the bolt and remove the pulley. If necessary a suitable

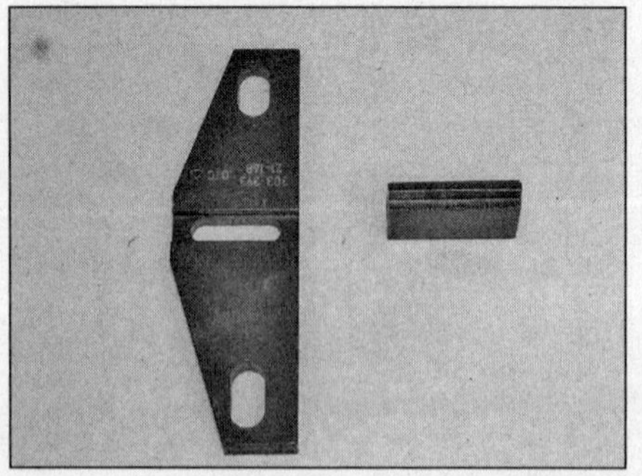
6.3a Ford tool No 303-393 and 303-393-02

6.3b The assembled tools bolt across the starter motor aperture ...

6.3c ... and engages with the teeth on the flywheel ring gear

pulley can be used to pull the pulley off the crankshaft.

5 Clean the end of the crankshaft and the pulley.

Refitting

6 Ensure that the crankshaft is in the Top Dead Centre (TDC) position and that the camshafts are set in the correct position.

7 On EcoBoost models, if not already done so remove the TDC sensor and install Ford special tool 303-1550 (or equivalent) **(see illustration)**.

8 Refit the pulley and on EcoBoost models rotate the pulley until the tool locates correctly in the slot in the rear of the pulley.

9 Tighten the bolt by hand and then remove the special tool. Note that the special tool is not designed to hold the pulley in position, it is designed only to locate the pulley correctly.

10 Ensuring that the pulley does not move, tighten the pulley to the specified torque.

11 Remove the crankshaft locating pin, the crankshaft locking tool, the camshaft timing tool and (on EcoBoost models) the crankshaft pulley locating tool. Rotate the engine at least twice in the normal (clockwise) direction of rotation. Refit the TDC locating tool, the camshaft timing tool and (on EcoBoost models) the crankshaft pulley locating tool. If the timing and pulley position are correct, they should all fit easily, if not recheck the timing and position of the crankshaft pulley. Note that if the crankshaft pulley bolt is slackened it must be replaced again.

12 Refit the remaining components in reverse order of removal.

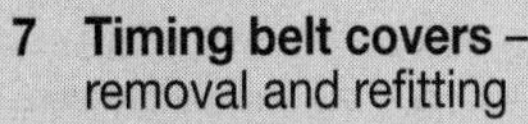

7 Timing belt covers – removal and refitting

Removal

EcoBoost models

1 Remove the engine cover by pulling it upwards.

2 Release the coolant expansion bottle from the inner wing and secure it to one side.

3 Remove the breather pipe from the air intake duct and then unbolt and remove the air inlet duct from the top of the engine.

6.7 On EcoBoost models fit the crankshaft pulley locating tool

4 Ford recommend removing the turbocharger oil return pipe, however with care it is possible to remove the cover without removing the oil feed pipe. Note that if the pipe is removed it must be replaced with a new one.

5 Position a trolley jack under the engine. Use a block of wood on the jack head to spread the load and prevent damage to the sump. Take the weight of the engine on the jack.

6 Make alignment marks between the right-hand engine mounting bracket and the cylinder head bracket/vehicle body, then undo the nuts/bolts and remove the mounting **(see illustration)**.

7 Slacken the 4 mounting bolts on the waterpump pulley and then remove the auxiliary drivebelt as described in Chapter 1A Section 23.

8 Remove the waterpump pulley and then remove the auxiliary belt tensioner.

9 Unclip (and unbolt) the wiring loom from the side of the cover and move it to one side.

10 At the rear of the cover (close to the wiring loom) is a flexible auxiliary cover. If the oil feed pipe has been left in position this needs to be released and worked free around the oil filler pipe and the rear of the main cover.

11 Remove the cover retaining bolts (7) and then remove the cover **(see illustration)**.

Ti-VCT models

12 Pull the coolant expansion tank upwards and move it to one side.

13 Slacken the coolant pump pulley bolts, then remove the auxiliary drivebelt(s) as described in Chapter 1A Section 23.

7.6 Remove the engine mounting

14 Unscrew the 4 bolts and remove the coolant pump pulley.

15 Some models feature a mounting bracket for the wiring loom. Where fitted, unbolt and remove the bracket from the cover.

16 Remove the 8 timing belt upper cover retaining bolts **(see illustration)**.

17 Manoeuvre the timing cover from the engine compartment.

Refitting

18 Refitting is a reversal of removal. Inspect the auxiliary drivebelt and fit a new one if necessary.

Lower cover – Ti-VCT models only

Removal

19 The timing belt lower cover is located around the crankshaft. First remove the crankshaft pulley/vibration damper as described in Section 6.

20 Working beneath the right-hand wheel arch, unscrew the retaining bolts and withdraw the timing cover **(see illustration)**.

Refitting

21 Refitting is a reversal of removal.

8 Timing belt – removal and refitting

Removal

1 Disconnect the battery – see Disconnecting the battery in Chapter 5A Section 3.

7.11 Remove the cover

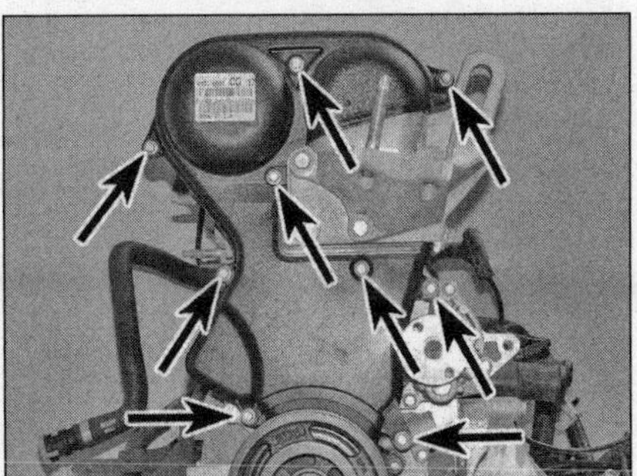

7.16 Timing belt upper cover bolts (arrowed)

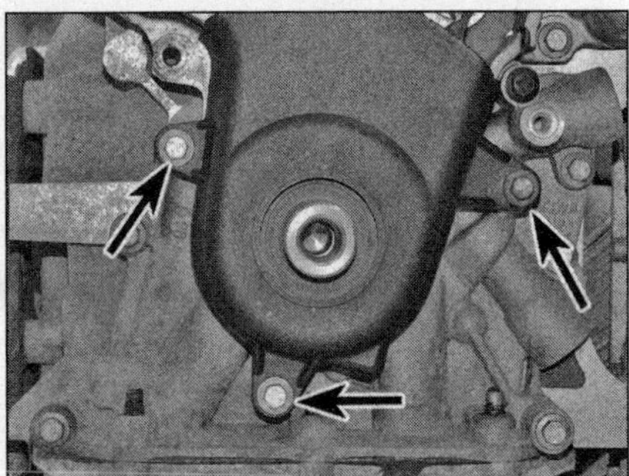

7.20 Timing belt lower cover bolts (arrowed)

8.3 Support the engine with a trolley jack and block of wood under the sump

8.8 Remove the bracket

8.11 Remove the timing belt guide disc (where fitted)

8.12 Fit the camshaft locking tool

2 Jack up and support the front of the vehicle (see *Jacking and vehicle support* in the reference section). Remove the right-hand road wheel.

3 Remove the engine undershield and then using a block of wood to spread the load on the sump, use a trolley jack to support the engine **(see illustration)**.

4 Remove the Alternator as described in Chapter 5A Section 5.

5 Mark the position of the right-hand engine mounting and then remove it.

6 Loosen the four bolts securing the coolant pump pulley and then remove the auxiliary drivebelt as described in Chapter 1A Section 23.

7 Remove the coolant pump pulley and then remove the drivebelt tensioner.

8 Unbolt and remove the engine mounting from the cylinder head **(see illustration)**.

9 Remove the timing belt covers as described in Section 7.

10 Set the engine at TDC as described in Section 3.

11 Remove the crankshaft pulley/vibration damper as described in Section 6. Dispose of the bolt. A new one must be fitted. Where fitted remove the timing belt guide disc **(see illustration)**.

12 Install Ford special service tool 303-1097 (or equivalent) between the camshaft sprockets **(see illustration)**.

13 Push the timing belt eccentric tensioner pulley rearwards to detension the belt, then insert Ford tool No 303-1054 or a suitable drill bit into the pulley hub to lock it in position **(see illustration)**.

14 Remove the belt and then remove the automatic tensioner. **Note:** *The tensioner should always be renewed along with the timing belt.*

Inspection

15 Once the belt is removed it should always be replaced. As a safety measure, the belt should be renewed irrespective of its apparent condition whenever the engine is overhauled.

16 Check the sprockets for signs of wear or damage, and replace the tensioner. This should be standard practise, as most manufacturers will not guarantee a belt against failure if the tensioner is not replaced at the same time as the timing belt. Ford dealers (and many motor factors) now only supply 'cambelt kits', consisting of the belt itself and a new tensioner.

17 If signs of oil or coolant contamination are found on the old belt, trace the source of the leak and rectify it, then wash down the engine timing belt area and related components to remove all traces of oil or coolant.

Refitting

18 Fit a new tensioner pulley and insert the locking pin (Ford 3030-1054) to hold the tensioner in position.

19 Ensure the engine is still set to TDC on No 1 cylinder (Section 3), then working anti-clockwise, locate the timing belt on the crankshaft sprocket and then over the camshaft sprockets **(see illustrations)**. Finally fit the belt over the tensioner.

20 Remove the locking pin and slowly allow the tensioner to take up the slack in the new timing belt.

21 Temporarily fit the crankshaft pulley (use the old bolt). Remove the TDC locating pin, the flywheel locking tool and the camshaft timing tool.

22 Rotate the engine in the normal direction of rotation (clockwise) at least twice and refit the timing tools. If the belt has been correctly fitted the tools will fit easily. Refit the flywheel locking tool and remove all the other timing tools.

23 Refit the timing belt cover and tighten the bolts to the specified torque.

24 Locate the crankshaft pulley/vibration damper on the end of the crankshaft, and press it squarely onto the shaft as far as

8.13 Insert a 4 mm drill bit or rod into the tensioner arms (arrowed)

8.19a Fit the belt over the crankshaft sprocket...

8.19b ...and then around the camshaft sprockets

9.5 Counterhold the camshaft with a spanner on the hexagonal section, then unscrew the blanking plug from the VCT unit

9.6a Unscrew the Torx bolt ...

9.6b ... and pull the VCT unit from the camshaft

it will go. Insert the new bolt and follow the procedure given in Section 6 to align and tighten the crankshaft pulley.

25 The remainder of refitting is a reversal of removal.

9 Timing belt tensioner and sprockets – removal, inspection and refitting

Tensioner pulley

1 Removal of the tensioner pulley is described within the timing belt procedure – see Section 8.

Camshaft sprockets

2 Remove the timing belt as described in Section 8.

3 Remove the cylinder head cover as described in Section 4.

4 On EcoBoost models, remove the vacuum pump, vacuum pump housing, fuel pump and fuel pump housing. (as described in Section 4).

5 Counterhold the camshafts using an open-ended spanner on the hexagonal sections, then unscrew the blanking plugs from the centre of the variable valve timing (VVT) units **(see illustration)**.

6 Still counterholding the camshafts, slacken and remove the VVT units centre Torx bolts **(see illustrations)**. Remove the VVT units from the ends of the camshafts. Dispose of the bolts – new ones must be fitted.

7 Examine the teeth of the sprockets for wear and damage, and renew them if necessary.

8 Insert Ford tool 303-1552 (EcoBoost models) or Ford tool 303-376B (Ti-VCT models) into the slots in the left-hand ends of the camshafts. If the Ford setting tools are notavailable, a home-made versions can be fabricated out of a length of flat metal bar 5 mm thick **(see illustrations)**.

9 Locate the VVT units on the ends of the camshafts, but only finger-tighten the retaining bolts at this stage. Ensure the timing marks on the VVT units (dot on the inlet sprocket, groove on the exhaust sprocket) are at the 12 o'clock position **(see illustration)**.

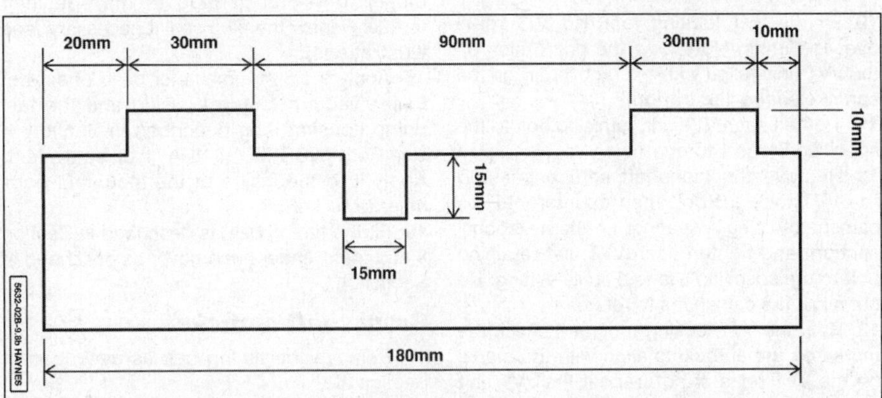

9.8a Camshaft setting tool dimensions – EcoBoost models

Drawing not to scale

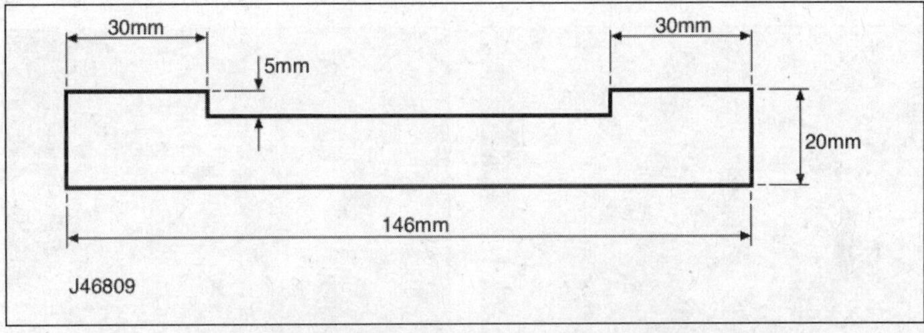

9.8b Camshaft setting tool – Ti-VCT models

Drawing not to scale

9.8c Fit the setting tool into the slots in the end of the camshafts

9.9 Ensure the groove (1) on the exhaust VCT unit and the dot (2) on the inlet unit are at the 12 o'clock position

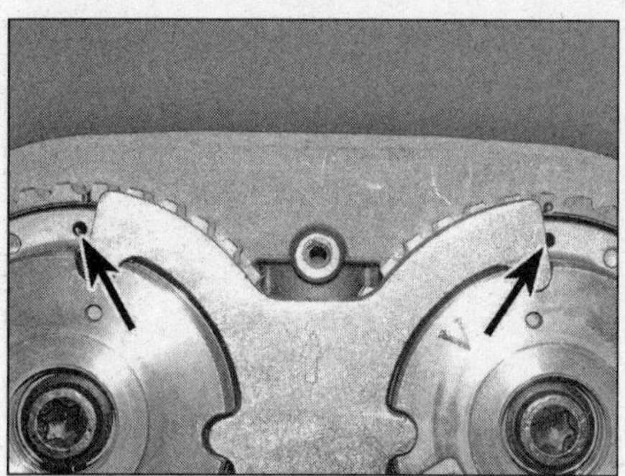

9.10 Note how the dots/holes on the VCT units align with the groove/dot on the sprockets (arrowed)

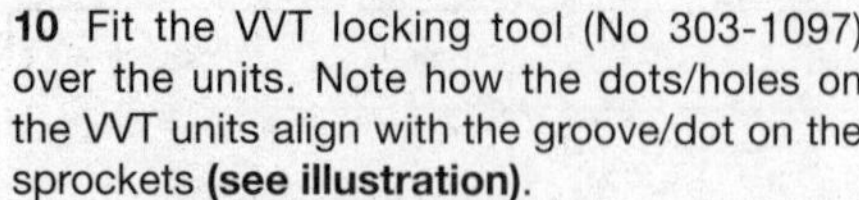

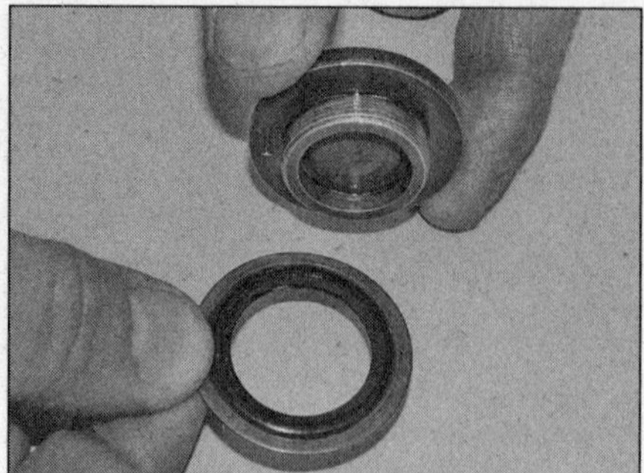

9.14a Renew the seal if necessary ...

9.14b ... then refit the plugs to the VCT units

10 Fit the VVT locking tool (No 303-1097) over the units. Note how the dots/holes on the VVT units align with the groove/dot on the sprockets **(see illustration)**.

11 Tighten each VVT unit retaining bolt to the specified Stage 1 torque.

12 Remove the camshaft setting bar and the VVT locking tool, then counterhold the camshafts using a spanner on the hexagonal section, and tighten each VVT unit retaining bolt to the specified Stage 2 angle setting. Do not allow the camshafts to rotate.

13 Refit the VVT locking tool, and check the marks on the sprockets align with the marks on the VVT units. If not, repeat the VVT unit refitting procedure.

14 If the timing is correct, counterhold the camshafts using a spanner on the hexagonal section, and fit the each VVT unit blanking plug. Tighten each plug to the specified torque. Renew the plug seal if necessary **(see illustrations)**.

15 Apply a 1.5 mm diameter bead of sealant to the vacuum pump housing and the fuel pump housing – as described in Section 4. Use Ford WSS-M2G348-A11 or equivalent. Apply it to the inside of the mounting bolts holes only.

16 Fit the timing belt as described in Section 8 and the cylinder head cover as described in Section 4.

Crankshaft sprocket

17 Remove the timing belt as described in Section 8.

18 Slide the sprocket off the end of the crankshaft **(see illustration)**.

19 Examine the teeth of the sprocket for wear and damage, and renew if necessary.

9.18 Slide the crankshaft sprocket from place

20 Wipe clean the end of the crankshaft, then slide on the sprocket.

21 Refit the timing belt as described in Section 8.

10 Camshaft oil seals – renewal

10.3a Drill a small hole and insert a self-tapping screw ...

10.3b ... then pull out the oil seal using a pair of pliers

10.5 Locate the new oil seal into the cylinder/camshaft bearing cap

10.6 Drive the new seal into position with a socket

1 Remove the camshaft sprockets or VVT units as described in Section 9.

2 Note the fitted depths of the oil seals as a guide for fitting the new ones.

3 Using a screwdriver or similar tool, carefully prise the oil seals from the cylinder head/ camshaft bearing caps. Take care not to damage the oil seal contact surfaces on the ends of the camshafts or the oil seal seatings. An alternative method of removing the seals is to drill a small hole, then insert a self-tapping screw and use pliers to pull out the seal **(see illustrations)**.

4 Wipe clean the oil seal seatings and also the ends of the camshafts.

5 Apply a little clean engine oil to the seal lip, then locate it over the camshaft and into the cylinder head/camshaft bearing cap. Make sure that the closed end of the oil seal faces outwards **(see illustration)**.

6 Using a socket or length of metal tubing, drive the oil seals squarely into position to the previously-noted depths. Wipe away any excess oil **(see illustration)**.

7 Refit the camshaft sprockets as described in Section 9.

11.4 Number the bearing caps with paint if they are not clearly marked

11.7a Undo the camshaft bearing cap bolts...

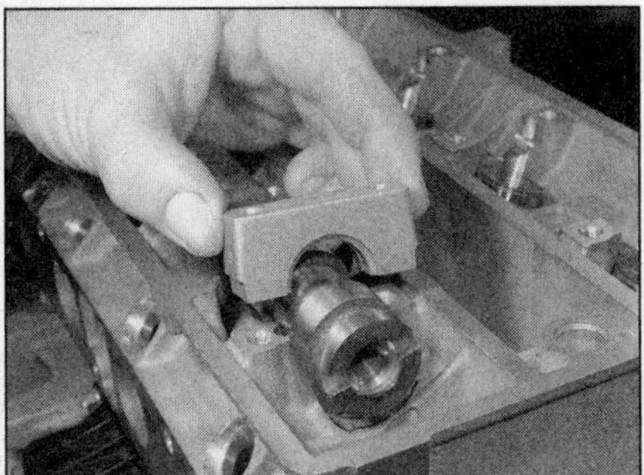
11.7b ...withdraw the caps

11 Camshafts and tappets – removal, inspection and refitting

Removal

1 Disconnect the battery (see Disconnecting the battery in Chapter 5A Section 3) and then jack up and support the front of the vehicle (see *Jacking and vehicle support*in the reference section).

2 Remove the cylinder head cover (Section 4), the timing belt (Section 8), the camshaft sprockets/VVT units (Section 9) and the camshaft oil seals (Section 10).

3 Before removing the camshafts, it may be useful to check and record the valve clearances as described in Section 5. If any clearance is not within limits, new tappets can be obtained and fitted.

4 The camshaft bearing caps may be marked for position – the inlet caps have the letter I and exhaust caps have the letter E. Where no marks are visible, mark the caps using paint or a marker pen. **(see illustration)**.

5 Position the crankshaft so that No 1 piston is approximately 25 mm before TDC. This can be done by starting from the TDC position; carefully insert a large screwdriver down No 1 cylinder spark plug hole until the tip touches the top of the piston, and turn the engine anti-clockwise until the screwdriver shaft has descended 25 mm.

6 Position the camshafts so that none of the valves are at full lift (ie, fully-open, being heavily pressed down by the cam lobes). To do this, turn each camshaft using a spanner on the hexagon flats provided.

7 Progressively loosen the camshaft bearing cap retaining bolts, working in the reverse order shown for tightening **(see illustration 11.21)**. Work only as described to release gradually and evenly the pressure of the valve springs on the caps **(see illustrations)**. On EcoBoost engines dispose of the bolts. New ones must be fitted.

8 At the timing belt end of the engine remove the bearing cap and recover the O-ring **(see illustration)**.

9 Withdraw the remaining caps, keeping them in order to aid refitting, then lift the camshafts from the cylinder head **(see illustration)**. On EcoBoost engines the exhaust camshaft has an extra lobe for the fuel pump drive. On Ti-VCT models make sure they are identified for inlet and exhaust camshafts – mark them if necessary

10 Obtain sixteen small, clean containers, and number them 1 to 8 for both the inlet and exhaust camshafts. Lift the tappets one by one from the cylinder head.

Inspection

11 With the camshafts and tappets removed, check each for signs of obvious wear (scoring, pitting, etc) and for ovality, and renew if necessary.

12 Visually examine the camshaft lobes for score marks, pitting, and evidence of overheating (blue, discoloured areas). Look for flaking away of the hardened surface layer of each lobe. If any such signs are evident, renew the component concerned.

13 Examine the camshaft bearing journals and the cylinder head bearing surfaces for signs of obvious wear or pitting. If any such signs are evident, renew the component concerned.

14 To check camshaft endfloat, remove the tappets, clean the bearing surfaces carefully, and refit the camshafts and bearing caps. Tighten the bearing cap bolts to the specified torque wrench setting, then measure the endfloat using a dial gauge mounted on the cylinder head so that its tip bears on the camshaft right-hand end.

11.8 Recover the O-ring seal under the right-hand (No 1) bearing cap

11.9 Remove the camshafts

11.17 The slots in the end of the camshafts should be just above, and approximately parallel to the cylinder head upper surface

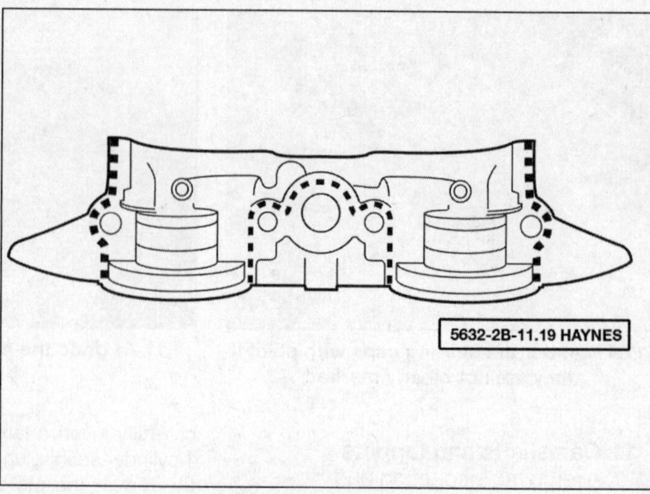

11.19 Apply a 1.5mm diameter bead of sealant to the underside of the No 1 bearing cap as shown

15 Tap the camshaft fully towards the gauge, zero the gauge, then tap the camshaft fully away from the gauge, and note the gauge reading. If the endfloat measured is found to be more than the typical value given, fit a new camshaft and repeat the check; if the clearance is still excessive, the cylinder head must be renewed.

Refitting

16 Lubricate the cylinder head tappet bores and the tappets with engine oil. Carefully refit the tappets to the cylinder head, ensuring each tappet is refitted to its original bore. Some care will be needed to enter the tappets squarely into their bores.

17 Liberally oil the camshaft bearings and lobes. Ensuring that each camshaft is in its original location, refit the camshafts, locating each so that the slot in its left-hand end is approximately parallel to, and just above, the cylinder head mating surface **(see illustration)**. At this stage, position the camshafts so that none of the valves are at full lift.

18 Clean the mating faces of the cylinder head and camshaft bearing caps.

19 Apply a 1.5 mm bead of sealant (Ford recommend WSS-M2G348-A11 or equivalent) to the No 1 camshaft bearing caps at the oil seal ends only **(see illustration)**. Renew the O-ring seal beneath the No 1 bearing cap.

20 Oil the bearing surfaces, then locate the camshaft bearing caps on the camshafts and insert the retaining bolts loosely. Make sure that each cap is located in its previously-noted position **(see illustration)**.

21 Ensuring each cap is kept square to the cylinder head as it is tightened down, and working in sequence **(see illustration)**, tighten the camshaft bearing cap bolts slowly and by one turn at a time, until each cap touches the cylinder head. Next, go round again in the same sequence, tightening the bolts to the specified Stage 1 torque wrench setting specified.

22 Finally, still working in the tightening sequence, tightening the bolts further to the Stage 2 angle. It is recommended that an angle gauge is used for this, to ensure accuracy.

23 Wipe off all surplus sealant, and check the valve clearances as described in Section 5.

24 Fit new camshaft oil seals as described in Section 10.

25 Refit the remaining components in the reverse order of removal.

12 Cylinder head – removal, inspection and refitting

Removal

1 Depressurise the fuel system as described in Chapter 4A.

2 Drain the cooling system as described in Chapter 1A Section 28.

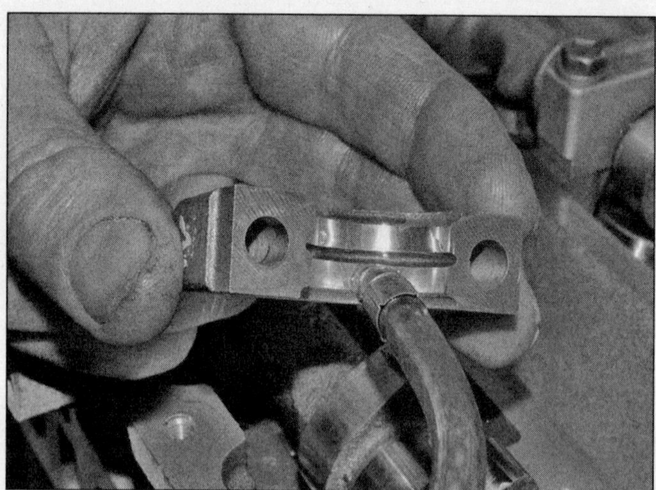

11.20 Oil the camshaft bearing surfaces

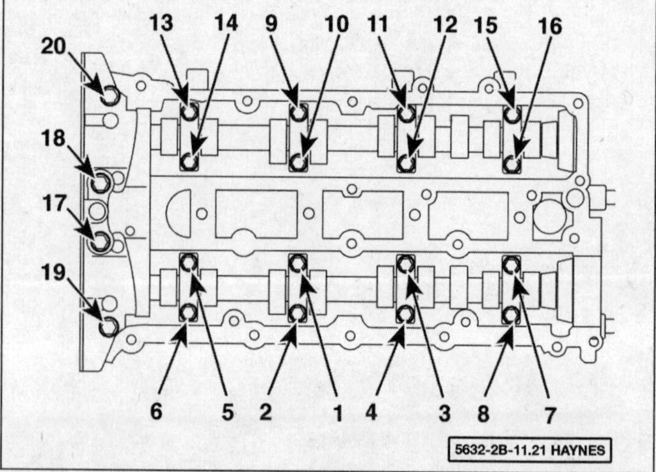

11.21 Camshaft bearing cap bolt slackening and tightening sequence

3 Disconnect the battery negative lead as described Chapter 5A Section 3.
4 Remove the inlet manifold and exhaust manifold (with the turbocharger) as described in Chapter 4A Section 14.
5 Remove the camshafts and tappets as described in Section 11.
6 Remove the inlet manifold support bolt from the front of the engine at the timing belt end.
7 Lower the car to the ground.
8 Make a note of their fitted locations and the harness routing, then disconnect any wiring plugs attached to components on the cylinder head. Label the plugs if necessary to aid refitting.
9 Release the spring-type clip and disconnect the coolant pipe from the left-hand rear of the cylinder head.
10 Make a last check round the cylinder head, to ensure that nothing remains connected or attached which would prevent the head from being lifted off. Prepare a clean surface to lay the head down on once it has been removed.
11 Working in the reverse of the tightening sequence **(see illustration 12.25)**, slacken the ten cylinder head bolts progressively and by half a turn at a time – a TX 55 Torx key will be required. Remove all the bolts and dispose of them. New ones will be required.
12 Lift the cylinder head away; use assistance if possible, as it is a heavy assembly. Remove the gasket, noting the two dowels. Although the gasket cannot be re-used, it is advisable to retain it for comparison with the new one, to confirm that the right part has been supplied.

Inspection

13 The mating faces of the cylinder head and cylinder block must be perfectly clean before refitting the head. Use a hard plastic or wood scraper to remove all traces of gasket and carbon; also clean the piston crowns. Take particular care during the cleaning operations, as aluminium alloy is easily damaged.
14 Make sure that the carbon is not allowed to enter the oil and coolant passages – this is particularly important for the lubrication system, as carbon could block the oil supply to the engine's components. Using adhesive tape and paper, seal the coolant, oil and bolt holes in the cylinder block. To prevent carbon entering the gap between the pistons and bores, smear a little grease in the gap. After cleaning each piston, use a small brush to remove all traces of grease and carbon from the gap, then wipe away the remainder with a clean rag. Note that there is a filter fitted into the oil supply galleries feeding the VVT system. This filter is permanently installed and cannot be removed.
15 Check the mating surfaces of the cylinder block and the cylinder head for nicks, deep scratches and other damage. If slight, they may be removed carefully with a file, but if excessive, renewal is necessary as it is not permissible to machine the surfaces.

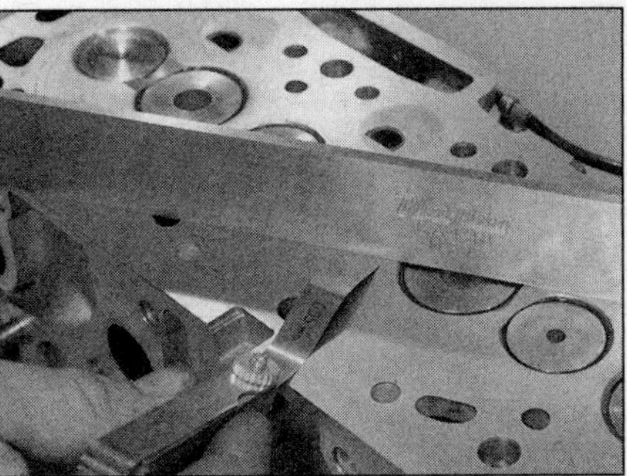
12.16 Check the cylinder head gasket face for distortion using a straight-edge

16 If warpage of the cylinder head gasket surface is suspected, use a straight-edge to check it for distortion **(see illustration)**. Refer to Part D of this Chapter if necessary.
17 If possible, clean out the bolt holes in the block using compressed air, to ensure no oil or coolant is present. Screwing a bolt into an oil- or coolant filled hole can (in extreme cases) cause the block to fracture, due to the hydraulic pressure created.
18 Although not essential, if a suitable tap-and-die set is available, it's worth running the correct-size tap down the bolt threads in the cylinder block. This will clean the threads of any debris, and go some way to restoring any damaged threads. Make absolutely sure the tap is the right size and thread pitch, and lightly oil the tap before starting.
19 Ford insist that the cylinder head bolts must be renewed.

Refitting

20 Wipe clean the mating surfaces of the cylinder head and cylinder block, and check that the two locating dowels are in position in the block.
21 Turn the crankshaft anti-clockwise so that pistons 1 and 4 are approximately 25 mm before TDC, in order to avoid the risk of valve/piston contact. Turn the crankshaft using a spanner on the pulley bolt.
22 If the old gasket is still available, check that it is identical to the new one. Position the new

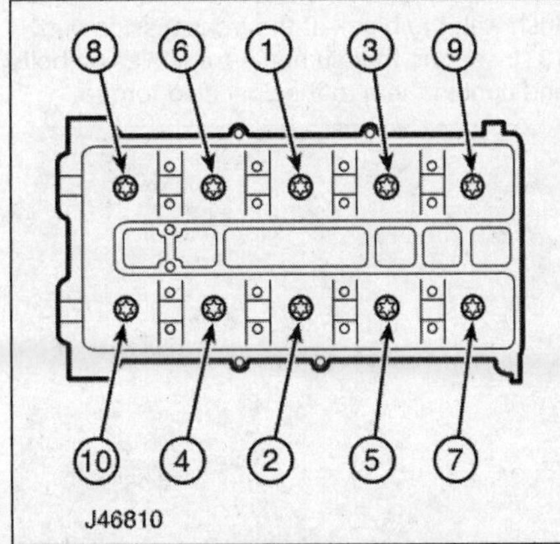

12.25 Cylinder head bolt tightening sequence

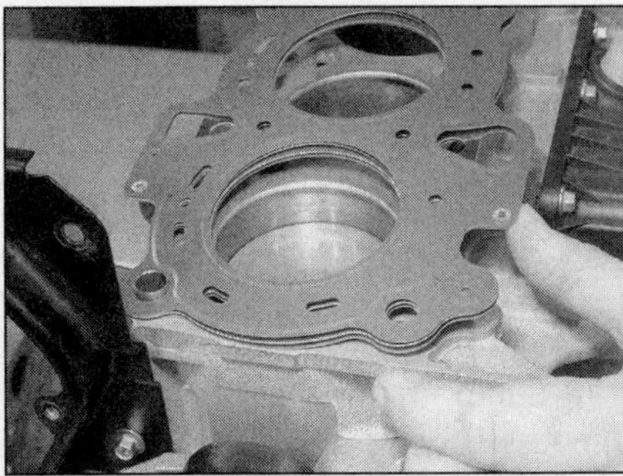
12.22 Locate the new cylinder head gasket over the dowels

gasket over the dowels on the cylinder block surface. It can only be fitted one way round – check carefully that the holes in the gasket align with the holes in the block surface, and that none are blocked **(see illustration)**.
23 It is useful when refitting a cylinder head to have an assistant on hand to help guide the head onto the dowels. Take care that the gasket does not get moved as the head is lowered into position. To confirm that the head is aligned correctly, once it is in place, temporarily slide in two or more of the head bolts, and check that they fit into the block holes.
24 Fit the new head bolts carefully, and screw them in by hand only until finger-tight.
25 Working progressively and in sequence, tighten the cylinder head bolts to their Stage 1 torque setting **(see illustration)**.
26 Next, go around again in the same sequence, and tighten the bolts to the Stage 2 setting. Repeat the procedure again for Stage 4.
27 The bolts should now be angle-tightened by the specified Stage 4 amount (in sequence) and again angle-tightened for the final Stage 5. This means simply that each bolt in the sequence must be turned through the stated angle. A special 'angle gauge' will be required to for Stages 4 and 5 **(see illustration)**. These are widely available.
28 The remainder of refitting is a reversal of removal, noting the following points:

a) *Refit the camshafts as described in Section 11, and the timing belt as described in Section 8.*
b) *Tighten all fasteners to the specified torque, where given.*

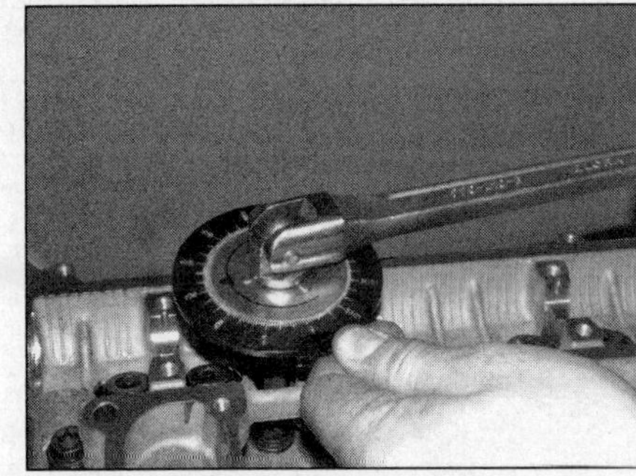
12.27 Use an angle-gauge for the final stage

c) *Ensure that all hoses and wiring are correctly routed, and that hose clips and wiring connectors are securely refitted.*

d) *Refill the cooling system as described in Chapter 1A Section 28.*

e) *Check all disturbed joints for signs of oil or coolant leakage once the engine has been restarted and warmed-up to normal operating temperature.*

13 Sump – removal and refitting

Removal

1 Apply the handbrake, then jack up the front of the car and support it on axle stands (see *Jacking and vehicle support*).

2 Unbolt and then remove the engine undershield.

3 Drain the engine oil, then check the drain plug sealing washer and renew if necessary. Clean and refit the engine oil drain plug together with the washer, and tighten it to the specified torque wrench setting. Although not strictly necessary, as the oil is being drained, it makes sense to fit a new oil filter at the same time (see Chapter 1A Section 6).

4 On EcoBoost models, release the hose clips from the intercooler pipe and then remove the 2 bolts that secure the pipe to the sump. Remove the pipe from the vehicle.

5 Unscrew the bolts securing the transmission to the sump, then progressively unscrew the sump-to-block bolts **(see illustration)**.

6 On all models, a sump gasket is not used, and sealant is used instead. Unfortunately, the use of sealant makes removal of the sump more difficult. If care is taken not to damage the surfaces, the sealant can be cut around using a sharp knife.

7 On no account lever between the mating faces, as this will almost certainly damage them, resulting in leaks when finished. Ford technicians have a tool comprising a metal rod which is inserted through the sump drain hole, and a handle to pull the sump downwards. Providing care is taken not to damage the threads, a large screwdriver could be used in the drain hole to prise down the sump.

8 While the sump is removed, take the opportunity to remove the oil pump pick-up/strainer pipe, and clean it with reference to Section 14.

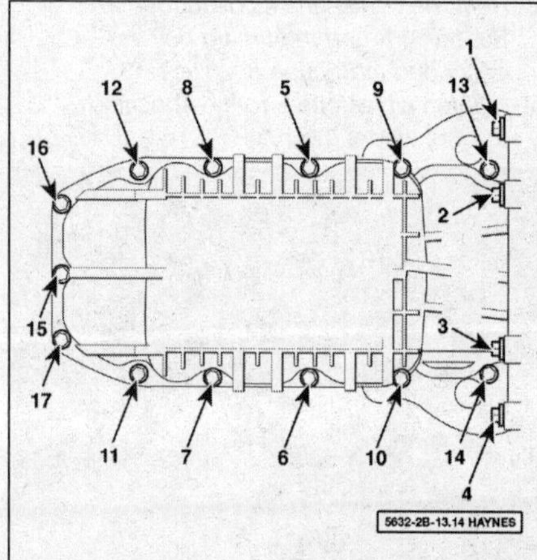

13.14 Sump bolt tightening sequence.

13.5 Sump viewed from below, showing the engine and transmission bolts

Refitting

9 Thoroughly clean the contact surfaces of the sump and crankcase. Take care not to damage the oil pump gasket or the crankshaft oil seal, both of which are partially exposed when the sump is removed. If necessary, use a cloth rag to clean inside the sump and crankcase. If the oil pump pick-up/strainer pipe was removed, fit a new O-ring and refit the pipe with reference to Section 14.

10 To aid aligning the sump fit 2 studs (M8 X 20 mm) to engine block (at the centre and opposite each other). Cut a slot across the end of each stud, to make removal easier when the sump is in place.

11 Apply a 3 to 4 mm diameter bead of sealant (Ford recommend WSE M4G323-A4, or equivalent) to the sump pan, to the inside of the bolt holes **(see illustration)**. The sump bolts must be fitted and tightened within 10 minutes of applying the sealant.

12 Offer the sump up into position over the studs, and fully refit the remaining bolts by hand. Unscrew the studs, and refit the sump bolts in their place. The sump should be fitted flush with the block at the transmission end.

13 Insert the four sump-to-transmission bolts and tighten them to the specified torque.

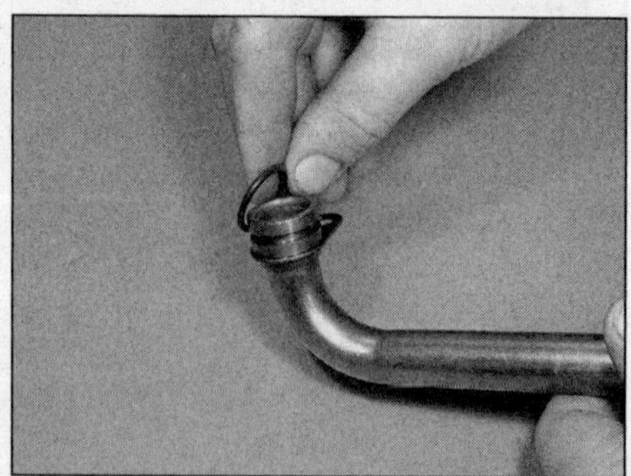

14.6 Remove the O-ring seal from the oil pump pick-up/strainer pipe

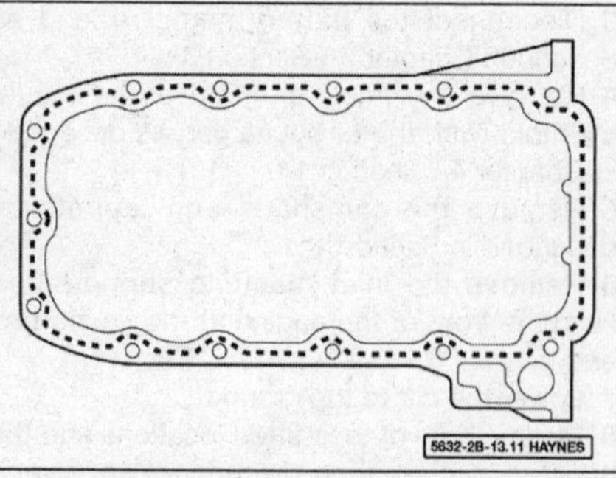

13.11 Apply a 3-4mm bead of sealant to the sump mating surface as shown

14 Tighten the main sump bolts to the specified torque in the order shown **(see illustration)**.

15 Refit the intercooler pipe and the engine undershield.

16 Lower the car to the ground. To be on the safe side, wait a further 30 minutes for the sealant to cure before filling the sump with fresh oil, as described in Chapter 1A Section 6.

17 Finally start the engine and check for signs of oil leaks.

14 Oil pump – removal, inspection and refitting

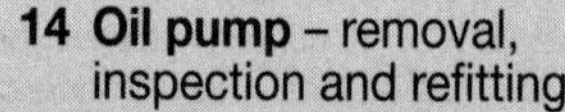

Removal

1 Remove the crankshaft right-hand oil seal as described in Section 16.

2 Remove the sump as described in Section 13.

3 On EcoBoost models, remove the TDC (Top Dead Centre) sensor.

4 Undo the timing belt rear cover lower 2 bolts.

5 Unscrew the bolts securing the oil pump pick-up/strainer pipe to the baffle plate/main bearing cap.

6 Unscrew the bolt securing the oil pump pick-up/strainer pipe to the oil pump, then withdraw the pipe and recover the sealing O-ring **(see illustration)**. If it is in good condition the O-ring can be reused.

7 Unscrew the bolts securing the oil pump to the cylinder block/crankcase **(see illustration)**. Note that the bolts are different

14.7 Remove the oil pump-to cylinder block/crankcase bolts

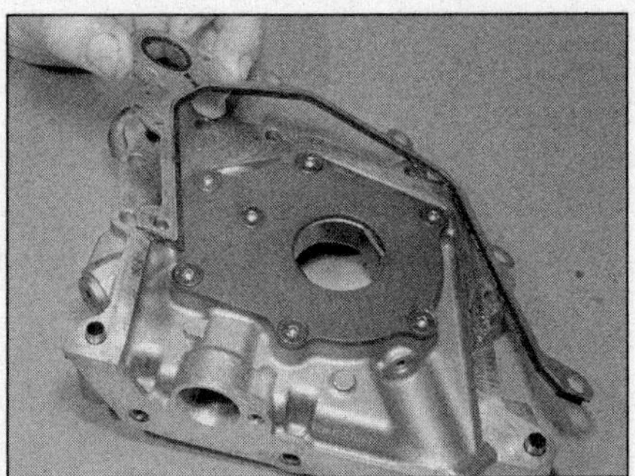

14.8 Remove the oil pump gasket

14.9 Unbolt the baffle plate from the main bearing cap/ladder

15.4 Oil pressure switch (arrowed)

lengths. Withdraw the pump over the nose of the crankshaft.

8 Recover then discard the gasket **(see illustration)**.

9 If necessary, unbolt and remove the baffle plate from the main bearing cap/ladder **(see illustration)**. Thoroughly clean all components, particularly the mating surfaces of the pump, the sump, and the cylinder block/crankcase.

Inspection

10 It is not possible to obtain individual components of the oil pump, furthermore, there are no torque settings available for tightening the pump cover plate bolts. However, the following procedure is provided for owners wishing to dismantle the oil pump for examination.

11 Take out the bolts, and remove the pump cover plate; noting any identification marks on the rotors, withdraw the rotors.

12 Inspect the rotors for obvious signs of wear or damage, and renew if necessary; if either rotor, the pump body, or its cover plate are scored or damaged, the complete oil pump assembly must be renewed.

13 The oil pressure relief valve can be dismantled as follows.

14 Unscrew the threaded plug, and recover the valve spring and plunger. If the plug's sealing O-ring is worn or damaged, a new one must be obtained, to be fitted on reassembly.

15 Reassembly is the reverse of the dismantling procedure; ensure the spring and valve are refitted the correct way round, and tighten the threaded plug securely.

Refitting

16 If removed, refit the oil baffle plate to the crankcase and tighten the bolts.

17 The oil pump must be primed on installation, by pouring clean engine oil into it and rotating its inner rotor a few turns.

18 Use a little grease to stick the new gasket in place on the cylinder block/crankcase.

19 Offer the oil pump over the nose of the crankshaft, and turn the inner rotor as necessary to align its flats with the flats on the crankshaft. Insert the retaining bolts finger tight only, and then using a straight edge along the bottom of the engine block (to ensure the that the pump is flush with the block), progressively tighten the oil pump bolts. Fully tighten them to the specified torque.

20 Locate the O-ring (dipped in oil) on the pick-up/strainer pipe, then locate the pipe in the oil pump and insert the retaining bolts. Insert the bolts retaining the pipe on the baffle plate/main bearing cap. Tighten the bolts to the specified torque.

21 Where removed, refit the air conditioning compressor, tightening the bolts to the specified torque.

22 Refit the sump as described in Section 13.

23 Fit a new crankshaft oil seal as described in Section 16.

24 Refit the remaining components in the reverse order of removal.

15 Oil pressure switch – removal and refitting

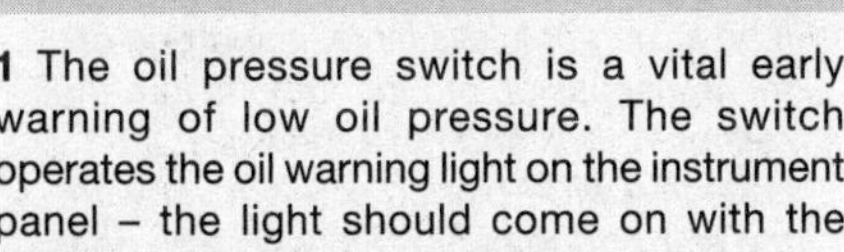

1 The oil pressure switch is a vital early warning of low oil pressure. The switch operates the oil warning light on the instrument panel – the light should come on with the ignition, and go out almost immediately when the engine starts.

2 If the light does not come on, there could be a fault on the instrument panel, the switch wiring, or the switch itself. If the light does not go out, low oil level, worn oil pump (or sump pick-up blocked), blocked oil filter, or worn main bearings could be to blame – or again, the switch may be faulty.

3 If the light comes on while driving, the best advice is to turn the engine off immediately, and not to drive the car until the problem has been investigated – ignoring the light could mean expensive engine damage.

Removal

4 The oil pressure switch is located on the front face of the engine, above the oil filter **(see illustration)**.

5 Disconnect the wiring plug from the switch.

6 Unscrew the switch from the block, and remove it. There should only be a very slight loss of oil when this is done.

Inspection

7 Examine the switch for signs of cracking or splits. If the top part of the switch is loose, this is an early indication of impending failure.

8 Check that the wiring terminals at the switch are not loose, then trace the wire from the switch connector until it enters the main loom – any wiring defects will give rise to apparent oil pressure problems.

Refitting

9 Refitting is the reverse of the removal procedure, noting the following points:

a) Tighten the switch securely.

b) Reconnect the switch connector, making sure it clicks home properly. Ensure that the wiring is routed away from any hot or moving parts.

c) Check the engine oil level and top-up if necessary (see ' Weekly checks0,5 ').

d) Check for signs of oil leaks once the engine has been restarted and warmed-up to normal operating temperature.

16 Crankshaft oil seals – renewal

Right-hand oil seal

1 Remove the crankshaft sprocket as described in Section 9.

2 As a safety precaution, refit the engine right- hand mounting upper section and mounting bracket, and tighten the mounting bolts/nuts.

3 Note the fitted depth of the oil seal as a guide for fitting the new one.

4 Using a screwdriver, prise the old oil seal from the oil pump housing. Take great care not to damage the seal contact surface on the nose of the crankshaft, or the seating in the housing.

5 Wipe clean the seating and the nose of the crankshaft.

6 Apply a little clean engine oil to the inner lip of the seal, then locate it over the crankshaft and into the oil pump housing. Make sure that

16.6 Locate the new right-hand oil seal over the crankshaft

16.14 Locate the new oil seal housing (complete with fitting sleeve) over the end of the crankshaft

16.16 With the oil seal housing bolted into position, remove the fitting ring

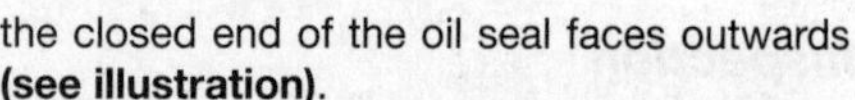

the closed end of the oil seal faces outwards **(see illustration)**.

7 Using a socket or length of metal tubing, drive the oil seal squarely into position to the previously-noted depth. The Ford installation tool (303-395) is used together with an old crankshaft pulley bolt to press the oil seal into position. The same idea may be used with metal tubing and a large washer – do not use a new crankshaft pulley bolt, as it is only permissible to use the bolt once. With the oil seal in position, wipe away any excess oil.

8 With the weight of the engine once more supported, unscrew the nuts and bolts and remove the engine right-hand mounting upper section and mounting bracket.

9 Refit the crankshaft sprocket with reference to Section 9.

Left-hand oil seal

10 Remove the flywheel/driveplate as described in Section 17.

11 Unscrew the six bolts and withdraw the oil seal carrier from the end of the crankshaft. Note that the seal and carrier are made as one unit – it is not possible to obtain the seal separately.

12 Clean the carrier contact surface on the cylinder block, and the end of the crankshaft.

13 The new oil seal carrier is supplied complete with a fitting sleeve, which ensures that the oil seal lips are correctly located on the crankshaft. Ford state that neither the crankshaft nor the new oil seal should be lubricated before fitting.

14 Locate the oil seal carrier and fitting sleeve over the end of the crankshaft. Press the carrier into position, noting that the centre bolt holes are formed into locating dowels **(see illustration)**.

15 Insert the retaining bolts and progressively tighten them to the specified torque.

16 Remove the fitting sleeve and check that the oil seal lips are correctly located **(see illustration)**.

17 Refit the flywheel/driveplate as described in Section 17.

17.2 Home-made flywheel locking tool

17 Flywheel/driveplate – removal, inspection and refitting

Removal

1 Remove the transmission as described in Chapter 7 Section 7 and the clutch as described in Chapter 6 Section 6.

2 Hold the flywheel/driveplate stationary using one of the following methods:

a) *If an assistant is available, insert one of the transmission mounting bolts into the cylinder block and have the assistant engage a wide-bladed screwdriver with the starter ring gear teeth while the bolts are loosened. Alternatively, a piece of angle-iron can be engaged with the ring gear and located against the transmission mounting bolt.*

b) *A further method is to fabricate a piece of flat metal bar with a pointed end to engage the ring gear – fit the tool to the transmission bolt and use washers and packing to align it with the ring gear, then tighten the bolt to hold it in position* **(see illustration)**.

c) *Fit Ford special tool 303-939A (or equivalent) and lock the flywheel in position.*

17.5 Mark the inner and outer sections (arrowed) and check for excessive play

3 Unscrew and remove the bolts, then lift the flywheel/driveplate off the locating dowel on the crankshaft. Dispose of the bolts. New ones must be used.

Inspection

4 Clean the flywheel/driveplate to remove grease and oil. Inspect the surface for cracks, rivet grooves, burned areas and score marks. Light scoring can be removed with emery cloth. Check for cracked and broken ring gear teeth. Lay the flywheel/driveplate on a flat surface, and use a straight-edge to check for warpage.

5 Where a dual mass flywheel is fitted check for excessive play between the stationary section and the movable section. Make paint marks on the inner and outer sections and then rotate the secondary section of the flywheel. Note the amount of rotation between the two sections **(see illustration)**. As a rule of thumb anything greater than 15mm should be considered excessive. If in doubt (and given the amount of work required to remove the flywheel) a second opinion from a Ford dealer or suitably equipped garage should be sought. Note that special tools are available to accurately asses the condition of the flywheel. If the service history of the vehicle is known and the clutch is being replaced for the second time, then the dual mass flywheel should always be replaced.

6 Clean and inspect the mating surfaces of the flywheel/driveplate and the crankshaft. If the crankshaft oil seal is leaking, renew it (see Section 16) before refitting the flywheel/driveplate. In fact, given the large amount of work needed to remove the flywheel/driveplate, it's probably worth fitting a new seal anyway, as a precaution.

Refitting

7 Make sure that the mating faces of the flywheel/driveplate and crankshaft are clean,

then locate the flywheel/driveplate on the crankshaft – it will only fit in one position.
8 Insert the new retaining bolts finger-tight **(see illustration)**.
9 Lock the flywheel/driveplate (see paragraph 2), then tighten the bolts in a diagonal sequence to the specified torque.
10 Refit the clutch with reference to Chapter 6 Section 6, and the transmission as described in Chapter 7 Section 7.

18 Engine/transmission mountings – inspection and renewal

General

1 The engine/transmission mountings seldom require attention, but broken or deteriorated mountings should be renewed immediately, or the added strain placed on the driveline components may cause damage or wear.
2 While separate mountings may be removed and refitted individually, if more than one is disturbed at a time – such as if the engine/transmission unit is removed from its mountings – they must be reassembled and their fasteners tightened in the position marked on removal.
3 On reassembly, the complete weight of the engine/transmission unit must not be taken by the mountings until all are correctly aligned with the marks made on removal. Tighten the engine/transmission mounting fasteners to their specified torque wrench settings.

Inspection

4 During the check, the engine/transmission unit must be raised slightly, to remove its weight from the mountings.
5 Raise the front of the vehicle, and support it securely on axle stands. Position a jack under the sump, with a large block of wood between the jack head and the sump, then carefully raise the engine/transmission just enough to take the weight off the mountings.

Warning: DO NOT place any part of your body under the engine when it is supported only by a jack.

6 Check the mountings to see if the rubber is cracked, hardened or separated from the metal components. Sometimes the rubber will split right down the centre.
7 Check for relative movement between each mounting's brackets and the engine/transmission or body (use a large screwdriver or lever to attempt to move the mountings). If movement is noted, lower the engine and check-tighten the mounting fasteners.

Renewal

Note: *The following paragraphs assume the engine is supported beneath the sump as described earlier.*

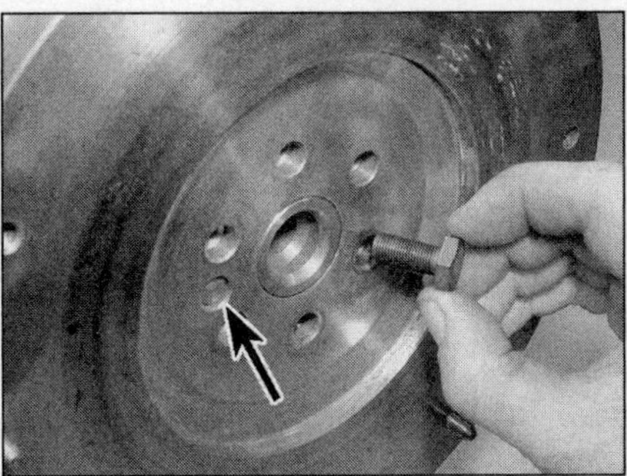

17.8 Fit the new flywheel retaining bolts. Note the dowel (arrowed) in the end of the crankshaft

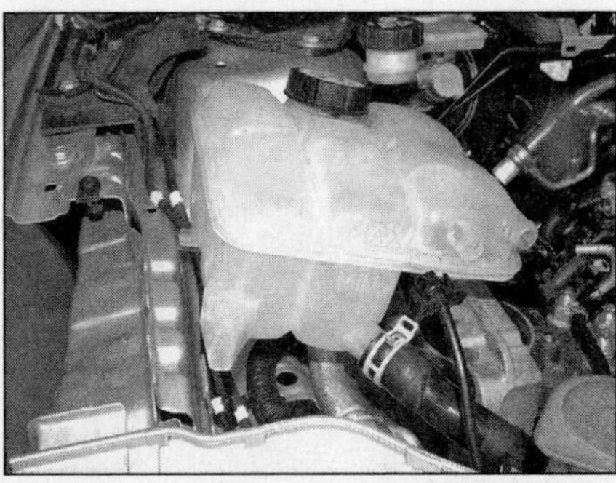

18.8 Move the coolant expansion bottle to the side

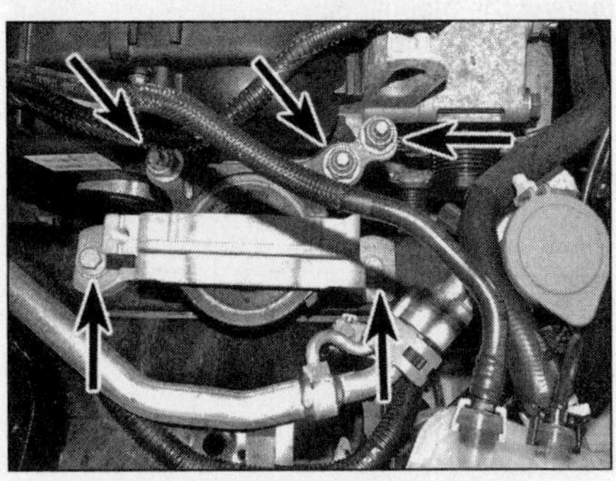

18.10a Undo the bolts (arrowed)...

18.10b ...and remove the mounting

Right-hand mounting

8 Lift up the coolant expansion tank and position it to one side **(see illustration)**. Note there is no need to disconnect the coolant pipes. On some models a vibration damper is fitted to the rear of the mounting. Where fitted unbolt and remove the damper.
9 Mark the position of the mounting on the vehicle on the right-hand inner wing panel, and then undo the 2 bolts securing the mounting.
10 Undo the 3 retaining bolts from the engine side of the mounting and then remove the mounting **(see illustrations)**.
11 Re-align the marks made on removal. Tighten all fasteners to the torque wrench settings specified.

Left-hand mounting

12 Remove the air filter housing as described in Chapter 4A Section 5.
13 Remove the battery as described in Chapter 5A Section 3, then undo the 3 bolts and remove the battery tray. Disconnect any wiring as the tray is withdrawn.
14 Unclip the wiring loom from the battery tray support panel, remove the 4 bolts and withdraw the support panel **(see illustration)**.
15 With the transmission supported, note the position of the mounting then unscrew the centre retaining bolt to release the upper half of the mounting from the transmission **(see illustration)**.
16 On six speed transmissions, lower the

18.14 Remove the battery support panel

18.15 Remove the centre bolt (arrowed)

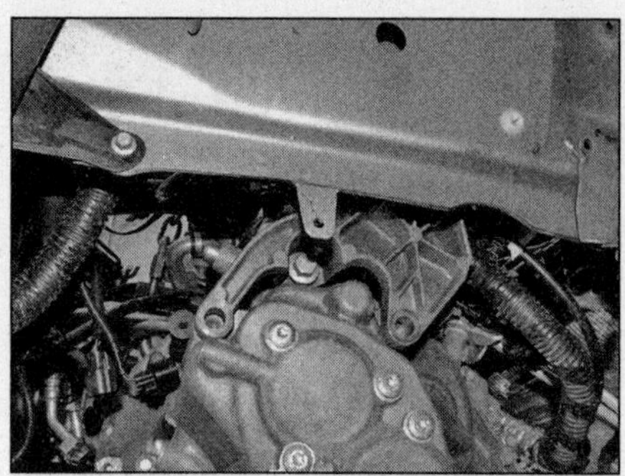

18.16 Lower the transmission and remove the bolts

18.18 Remove the bolts (arrowed)

transmission slightly to access the 3 mounting bolts on the transmission **(see illustration)**. On five speed transmission access the bolts from the engine bay. Remove the bolts and recover the mounting.

17 Refitting is a reversal of removal. Re-align the mounting in the position noted on removal, then tighten all fasteners to the specified torque wrench settings.

Rear mounting (roll restrictor)

18 Remove the 3 mounting bolts from the transmission. Note, that the bolts are different lengths on five speed transmissions. Remove the single bolt from the subframe **(see illustration)**.

19 With the aid of an assistant pivot the engine (assuming the two main engine mountings are in position) and work the mounting free.

20 On refitting, ensure that the bolts are securely tightened to the specified torque wrench setting.

Chapter 2 Part C
1.5 litre SOHC diesel engine in-car repair procedures

Contents

Degrees of difficulty

Easy, suitable for novice with little experience 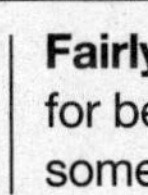	**Fairly easy,** suitable for beginner with some experience	**Fairly difficult,** suitable for competent DIY mechanic	**Difficult,** suitable for experienced DIY mechanic	**Very difficult,** suitable for expert DIY or professional

Specifications

General

Designation	Duratorq-TDCi
Engine codes*	XWDA, XWDB, XWDC, XWDD, XXDA, XXDB and XXDC
Capacity	1499 cc
Bore	73.5 mm
Stroke	88.3 mm
Direction of crankshaft rotation	Clockwise (viewed from the right-hand side of vehicle)
No 1 cylinder location	At the transmission end of block
Maximum power output:	
Engine codes XXDA and XXDC	70 kW (95 PS)
Engine code XXDB	77 kW (105 PS)
Engine codes XWDA, XWDB, XWDC and XWDD	88 kW (120ps)
Maximum torque output:	
Engine codes XXDA, XXDC, XXDB, XWDC and XWDD	270 Nm
Engine codes XWDA and XWDB	300 Nm
Emissions level	Stage 6
Compression ratio	16: 1

**The engine code is stamped on a plate attached to the front of the cylinder block, next to the oil filter*

Valves

Valve clearances (cold)	
Inlet	0.103 to 0.118 mm
Exhaust	0.113 to 0.128 mm

Compression pressures (engine hot, at cranking speed)

Normal	20 ± 5 bar
Minimum	15 bar
Maximum difference between any two cylinders	5 bar

Camshaft

Camshaft end float	0.195 – 0.3 mm

Lubrication system

Oil pump type	Gear-type, driven directly by the right-hand end of the crankshaft, by two flats machined along the crankshaft journal
Minimum oil pressure at 80°C:	
Idle speed	1.0 to 2.0 bar
2000 rpm	2.3 to 3.7 bar

Torque wrench settings

	Nm	lbf ft
Ancillary drivebelt tensioner roller	20	15
Big-end bolts: *		
Stage 1	10	7
Stage 2	Slacken 180°	
Stage 3	10	7
Stage 4	Angle-tighten a further 130°	
Camshaft bearing caps	10	7
Camshaft bearing ladder:		
Studs	10	7
Bolts	10	7
Camshaft position sensor bolt	5	4
Camshaft sprocket bolt		
Stage 1	20	15
Stage 2	Angle-tighten a further 50°	
Coolant outlet housing bolts	8	6
Crankshaft position/speed sensor bolt	10	7
Crankshaft pulley/sprocket bolt: *		
Stage 1	35	26
Stage 2	Angle-tighten a further 190°	
Cylinder head bolts: *		
Stage 1	20	15
Stage 2	40	30
Stage 3	Angle-tighten a further 260°	
Cylinder head cover	10	7
EGR valve	10	7
Engine-to-transmission fixing bolts	47	35
Flywheel bolts: *		
Stage 1	25	18
Stage 2	Slacken 1 turn	
Stage 3	8	6
Stage 4	18	13
Stage 5	Angle-tighten a further 75°	
Fuel pump sprocket	50	37
Left-hand engine/transmission mounting:		
Mounting-to-bracket centre nut	148	109
Mounting-to-bracket outer nuts	48	35
Mounting bracket to transmission	80	59
Main bearing ladder outer seam bolts:		
Stage 1	5	4
Stage 2	10	7
Main bearing ladder to cylinder block:		
Stage 1	10	7
Stage 2	Slacken 180°	
Stage 3	30	22
Stage 4	Angle-tighten a further 140°	
Piston oil jet spray tube bolt	20	15

Torque wrench settings (continued)	Nm	lbf ft
Oil cooler retaining bolts	10	7
Oil filter cover	25	18
Oil pick-up pipe	10	7
Oil pressure switch	30	22
Oil pump to cylinder block:		
Stage 1	5	4
Stage 2	9	7
Rear engine mounting:		
Rear through-bolt	70	52
Mounting bracket-to-transmission bolts	63	46
Right-hand engine mounting:		
Mounting to inner wing and mounting bracket (nuts/bolts)	48	35
Mounting bracket to engine block	55	41
Sump drain plug	35	26
Sump bolts/nuts	12	8
Timing belt idler pulley	37	27
Timing belt tensioner pulley	30	22
Timing cover bolts	5	4
Vacuum pump bolts	20	15

**Do not re-use*

1 General Information

How to use this Chapter

1 This Part of Chapter 2 describes the repair procedures that can reasonably be carried out on the engine while it remains in the vehicle. If the engine has been removed from the vehicle and is being dismantled as described in Part E, any preliminary dismantling procedures can be ignored.

2 Note that, while it may be possible physically to overhaul items such as the piston/connecting rod assemblies while the engine is in the car, such tasks are not usually carried out as separate operations. Usually, several additional procedures are required (not to mention the cleaning of components and oilways); for this reason, all such tasks are classed as major overhaul procedures, and are described in Part E of this Chapter.

3 Part E describes the removal of the engine/transmission from the car, and the full overhaul procedures that can then be carried out.

4 The 1.5 litre Duratorq-TDCi engine is a 4-cylinder, turbocharged, single overhead cam (SOHC) 8-valve design, with direct injection. The engine is mounting transversely, with the transmission mounted on the left-hand side.

5 A toothed timing belt drives the camshaft, high-pressure fuel pump and coolant pump. The camshaft operates the inlet and exhaust valves via rocker arms which are supported at their pivot ends by hydraulic self-adjusting tappets. The camshaft Is supported by bearings machined directly in the cylinder head and camshaft bearing housing.

6 The high-pressure fuel pump supplies fuel to the fuel rail, and subsequently to the electronically-controlled injectors which inject the fuel direct into the combustion chambers. This design differs from the previous type where an injection pump supplies the fuel at high pressure to each injector. The earlier, conventional type injection pump required fine calibration and timing, and these functions are now completed by the high-pressure pump, electronic injectors and engine management ECM.

7 The crankshaft runs in five main bearings of the usual shell type. Endfloat is controlled by thrustwashers either side of No 2 main bearing.

8 The pistons are selected to be of matching weight, and incorporate fully-floating gudgeon pins retained by circlips.

Repair operations precaution

9 The engine is a complex unit with numerous accessories and ancillary components. The design of the engine compartment is such that every conceivable space has been utilised, and access to virtually all of the engine components is extremely limited. In many cases, ancillary components will have to be removed, or moved to one side, and wiring, pipes and hoses will have to be disconnected or removed from various cable clips and support brackets.

10 When working on this engine, read through the entire procedure first, look at the car and engine at the same time, and establish whether you have the necessary tools, equipment, skill and patience to proceed. Allow considerable time for any operation, and be prepared for the unexpected.

11 Because of the limited access, many of the engine photographs appearing in this Chapter were, by necessity, taken with the engine removed from the vehicle.

Warning: It is essential to observe strict precautions when working on the fuel system components of the engine, particularly the high-pressure side of the system. Before carrying out any engine operations that entail working on, or near, any part of the fuel system, refer to the special information given in.

12 Operations with engine in vehicle

a) Compression pressure – testing.
b) Cylinder head cover – removal and refitting.
c) Crankshaft pulley – removal and refitting.
d) Timing belt covers – removal and refitting.
e) Timing belt – removal, refitting and adjustment.
f) Timing belt tensioner and sprockets – removal and refitting.
g) Camshaft oil seal – renewal.
h) Camshaft, rocker arms and hydraulic tappets – removal, inspection and refitting.
i) Sump – removal and refitting.
j) Oil pump – removal and refitting.
k) Crankshaft oil seals – renewal.
l) Engine/transmission mountings – inspection and renewal.
m) Flywheel – removal, inspection and refitting.

2 Compression and leakdown tests – description and interpretation

Compression test

Note: *A compression tester specifically designed for diesel engines must be used for this test.*

1 When engine performance is down, or if misfiring occurs which cannot be attributed to the fuel system, a compression test can provide diagnostic clues as to the engine's condition. If the test is performed regularly, it can give warning of trouble before any other symptoms become apparent.

2 A compression tester specifically intended for diesel engines must be used, because of the higher pressures involved. The tester is connected to an adapter which screws into the glow plug or injector hole. On this engine, an adapter suitable for use in the glow plug holes will be required, so as not to disturb the fuel system components. It is unlikely to be worthwhile buying such a tester for occasional use, but it may be possible to borrow or hire one – if not, have the test performed by a garage.

3 Unless specific instructions to the contrary are supplied with the tester, observe the following points:

a) *The battery must be in a good state of charge, the air filter must be clean, and the engine should be at normal operating temperature.*
b) *All the glow plugs should be removed, and the glow plug module disconnected as described in Chapter 5A Section 9 before starting the test.*

4 The compression pressures measured are not so important as the balance between cylinders. Values are given in the Specifications.

5 The cause of poor compression is less easy to establish on a diesel engine than on a petrol one. The effect of introducing oil into the cylinders ('wet' testing) is not conclusive, because there is a risk that the oil will sit in the swirl chamber or in the recess on the piston crown instead of passing to the rings. However, the following can be used as a rough guide to diagnosis.

6 All cylinders should produce very similar pressures; any difference greater than that specified indicates the existence of a fault. Note that the compression should build-up quickly in a healthy engine; low compression on the first stroke, followed by gradually-increasing pressure on successive strokes, indicates worn piston rings. A low compression reading on the first stroke, which does not build-up during successive strokes, indicates leaking valves or a blown head gasket (a cracked head could also be the cause). Deposits on the undersides of the valve heads can also cause low compression.

7 A low reading from two adjacent cylinders is almost certainly due to the head gasket having blown between them; the presence of coolant in the engine oil will confirm this.

8 If the compression reading is unusually high, the cylinder head surfaces, valves and pistons are probably coated with carbon deposits. If this is the case, the cylinder head should be removed and decarbonised.

Note: *After performing this test, a fault code may be generated and stored in the PCM memory. Have the PCM self-diagnosis facility interrogated by a Ford dealer or suitably-equipped specialist, and the fault code erased. Inexpensive diagnostic code scanners are readily available.*

Leakdown test

9 A leakdown test measures the rate at which compressed air fed into the cylinder is lost. It is an alternative to a compression test, and in many ways it is better, since the escaping air provides easy identification of where pressure loss is occurring (piston rings, valves or head gasket).

10 The equipment needed for leakdown testing is unlikely to be available to the home mechanic. If poor compression is suspected, have the test performed by a suitably-equipped garage.

3 Engine assembly/valve timing holes – general information and usage

Note: *Do not attempt to rotate the engine whilst the crankshaft and camshaft are locked in position. If the engine is to be left in this state for a long period of time, it is a good idea to place suitable warning notices inside the vehicle, and in the engine compartment. This will reduce the possibility of the engine being accidentally cranked on the starter motor, which is likely to cause damage with the locking pins in place.*

1 Timing holes or slots are located in the crankshaft pulley flange and camshaft sprocket hub. This will ensure that the valve timing is maintained during operations that require removal and refitting of the timing belt. When the holes/slots are aligned with their corresponding holes in the cylinder block and cylinder head, suitable diameter bolts/pins can be inserted to lock the crankshaft and camshaft in position, preventing rotation.

2 Note that the fuel system used on these engines does not have a conventional diesel injection pump, but instead uses a high-pressure fuel pump. However, the fuel pump sprocket must be pegged in position in a similar fashion to the camshaft sprocket.

3 To align the engine assembly/valve timing holes, proceed as follows.

4 Apply the handbrake, then jack up the front of the vehicle and support it on axle stands (see *Jacking and vehicle support*). Remove the right-hand front roadwheel.

5 To gain access to the crankshaft pulley, to enable the engine to be turned, the wheel arch plastic liner must be removed. The liner is secured by several plastic expanding rivets/nut/bolts. To remove the rivets, push in the centre pins a little, then prise the clips from place. Remove the liner from under the front wing.

6 Remove the crankshaft pulley as described in Section 5.

7 Remove the upper and lower timing belt covers as described in Section 6.

8 Temporarily refit the crankshaft pulley bolt (without the crankshaft pulley) and then remove the crankshaft locking tool.

9 Turn the crankshaft until the timing hole in the crankshaft sprocket aligns with the hole in the oil pump casing (this is at the 12 o'clock position). Fit the special tool 303-732, or a suitable alternative (5.0 mm drill bit or rod) and lock the crankshaft in position **(see illustration)**.

10 With the crankshaft locked in position fit the camshaft locking tool (303-735 or similar). The hole in the camshaft sprocket should be at approximately the 1 o'clock position **(see illustration)**. If this is not the case remove the

3.9 Insert the special tool (or a 5.0 mm drill bit/bolt) through the round hole in the sprocket flange into the hole in the oil pump housing

3.10 Insert the special tool (or an 8.0 mm bolt/rod) through the hole in the camshaft sprocket into the corresponding hole in the cylinder head

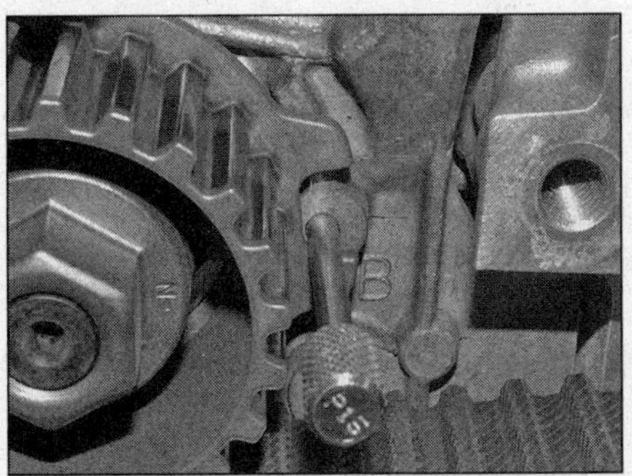

3.11 Insert a 5.0 mm rod (or similar) through the slot in the fuel pump sprocket flange

4.1 Pull up and remove the plastic cover

4.2a Release the clamp, undo the bracket nut...

4.2b ...undo the bolts and remove the charge air pipe

4.3 Throttle body retaining bolts

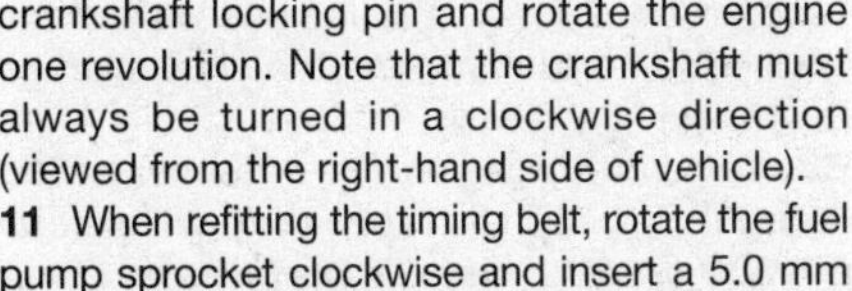

crankshaft locking pin and rotate the engine one revolution. Note that the crankshaft must always be turned in a clockwise direction (viewed from the right-hand side of vehicle).

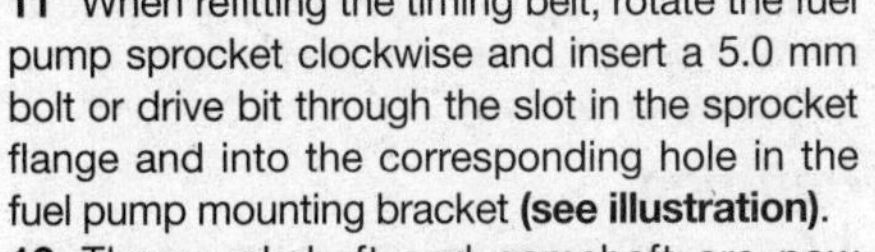

11 When refitting the timing belt, rotate the fuel pump sprocket clockwise and insert a 5.0 mm bolt or drive bit through the slot in the sprocket flange and into the corresponding hole in the fuel pump mounting bracket **(see illustration)**.

12 The crankshaft and camshaft are now locked in position, preventing unnecessary rotation.

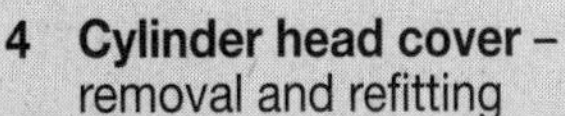

4 Cylinder head cover – removal and refitting

Removal

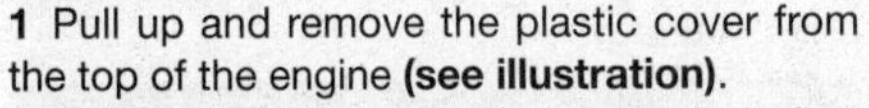

1 Pull up and remove the plastic cover from the top of the engine **(see illustration)**.

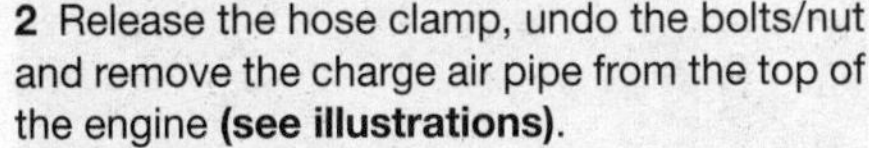

2 Release the hose clamp, undo the bolts/nut and remove the charge air pipe from the top of the engine **(see illustrations)**.

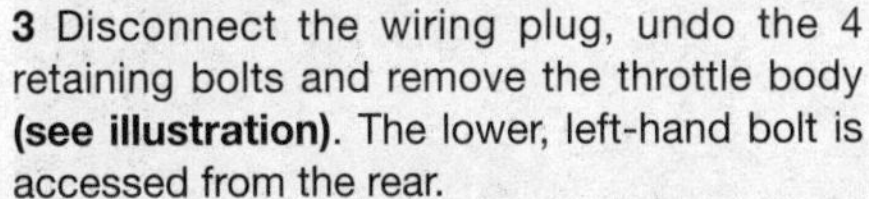

3 Disconnect the wiring plug, undo the 4 retaining bolts and remove the throttle body **(see illustration)**. The lower, left-hand bolt is accessed from the rear.

4 Disconnect the wiring plugs from the fuel injectors, then undo the retaining bolt and unclip the wiring harness duct from the top of the engine **(see illustrations)**.

5 Release the clips and disconnect the breather hose from the cylinder head cover.

6 Unclip the wiring harness, then unbolt and then remove the timing belt upper cover as described in Section 6.

7 Prise up and remove fuel return pipe assembly plastic rivet **(see illustration)**.

8 Remove the 11 bolts and then remove the cover **(see illustrations)**. Recover the rubber seal. Examine the seal and renew it if there are any signs of deterioration or damage.

4.4a Disconnect the injector wiring plugs

4.4b Undo the bolt and unclip the wiring harness duct

4.7 Prise up the rivet securing the fuel return pipe assembly

4.8a Undo the 9 bolts at the top...

4.8b ...and the 2 bolts at the right-hand end of the cover

4.9a Gently push back the clips to release the seal

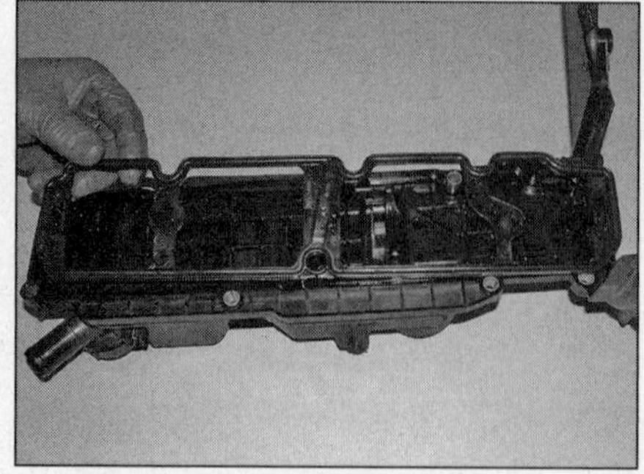
4.9b Ensure the seal is correctly seated

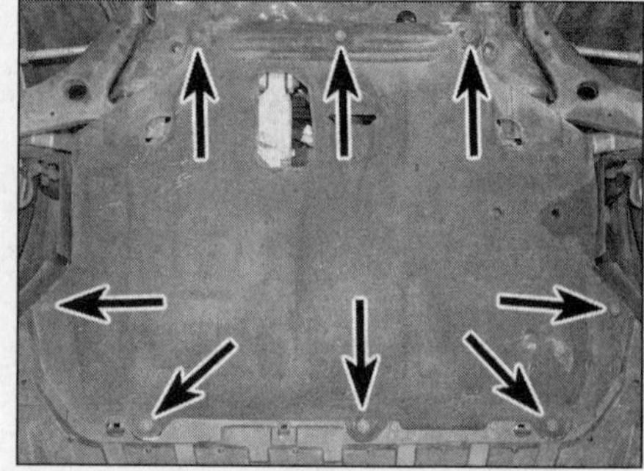
5.1 Engine undershield fasteners

Refitting

9 Refitting is a reversal of removal, but ensure that the seal is correctly located **(see illustrations)**.

5 Crankshaft pulley – removal and refitting

Removal

1 Jack up and support the front of the vehicle (see *Jacking and vehicle support*) then undo the fasteners and remove the engine undershield **(see illustration)**.

2 Remove the auxiliary drivebelt as described in Chapter 1B Section 24.

3 To prevent accidental damage, undo the lower timing belt cover lower rear bolt 1.5 turns, then undo the retaining bolt and move the crankshaft position sensor to one side **(see illustrations)**.

4 To lock the crankshaft, working underneath the engine, insert Ford tool No. 303-734 or a 12 mm diameter rod into the hole in the engine block casting over the lower section of the flywheel **(see illustration)**. Note that the hole in the casting and flywheel is provided purely to lock the crankshaft whilst the pulley bolt it undone – it does not position the crankshaft at TDC. Rotate the crankshaft clockwise until the tool engages in the hole in the flywheel – don't rotate the crank pulley anti-clockwise.

5 Pull the central cover from the pulley **(see illustration)**.

6 Using a suitable socket and extension bar, unscrew the retaining bolt, remove the washer, then slide the pulley off the end of the crankshaft **(see illustrations)**. If the pulley is tight fit, it can be drawn off the crankshaft using a suitable puller. If a puller is being used, refit the pulley retaining bolt without the washer, to avoid damaging the crankshaft as the puller is tightened.

Caution: Do not touch the outer magnetic sensor ring of the sprocket with your fingers, or allow metallic particles to come into contact with it.

Refitting

7 Refit the pulley to the end of the crankshaft.

8 Refit the crankshaft pulley. Fit a new bolt and retaining washer. Tighten the bolt to the specified torque, then through the specified angle.

9 Refit the cover to the centre of the pulley.

10 Remove the locking tool.

11 Refit the crankshaft position sensor and tighten the retaining bolt to the specified torque.

12 Refit and tension the auxiliary drivebelt as described in.

13 Refit the remaining components in reverse order of removal.

5.3a Undo the lower cover rear bolt 1.5 turns

5.3b Note the sensor locating dowel and pin

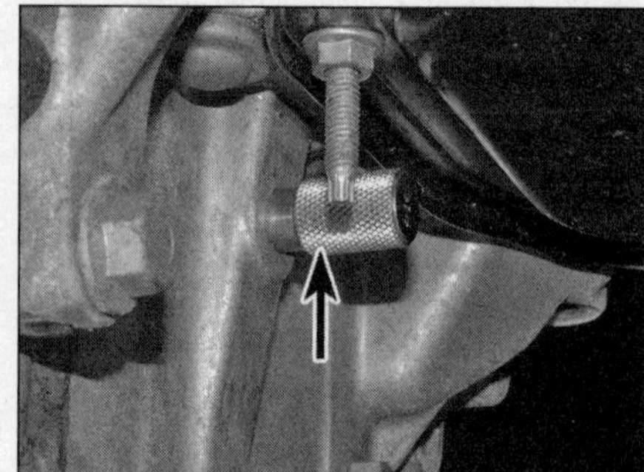
5.4 Install the flywheel locking tool

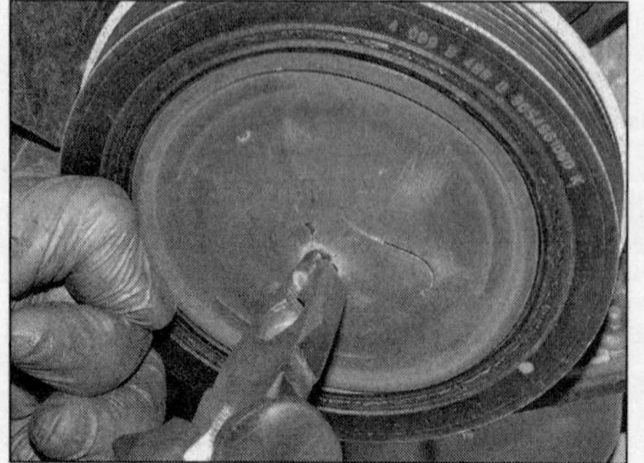
5.5 Pull the cover from the pulley

5.6a Remove the bolt and washer

5.6b The key on the crankshaft engages with the slot in the pulley

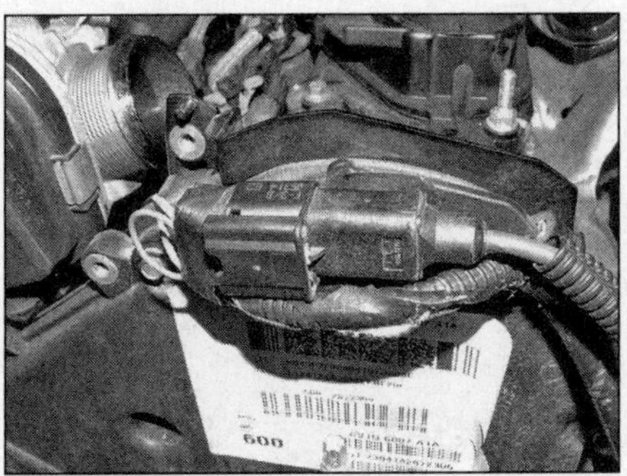
6.2 Release the clips securing the wiring loom

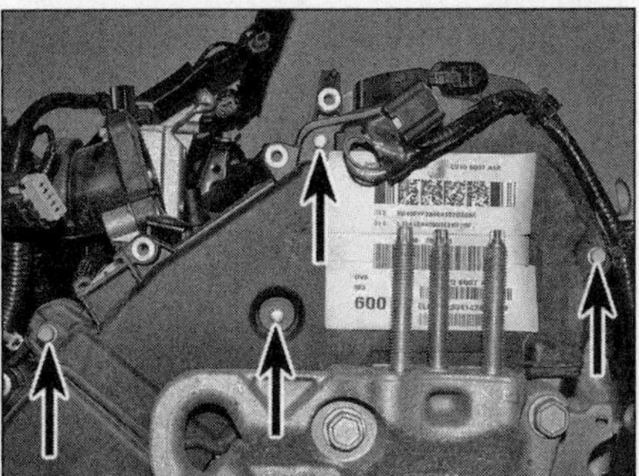
6.3 Upper cover bolts

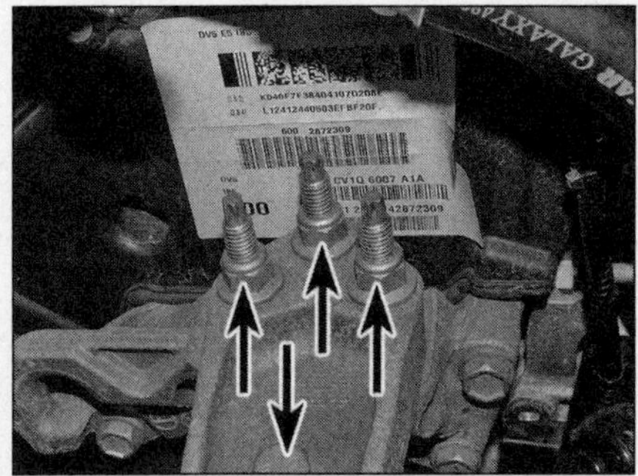
6.7 Engine mounting nuts/bolt

6.8a Undo the 2 bolts above the auxiliary drivebelt tensioner...

6.8b ... and the bolt at the rear

6.10 Lower timing belt cover bolts

6 Timing belt covers – removal and refitting

Warning: Refer to the precautionary information contained in Section 1 before proceeding.

Removal

Upper cover

1 Pull the plastic cover on the top of the engine upwards from its' mountings.

2 Unclip the wiring loom from the cover **(see illustration)**.

3 Undo the 4 bolts and remove the timing belt upper cover **(see illustration)**.

Lower cover

4 Remove the crankshaft pulley as described in Section 5.

5 Position a trolley/workshop jack under the engine. Place a block of wood on the jack head (to help spread the load on the sump), then take the weight of the engine.

6 Prise up the coolant expansion tank and move it to one side – there is no need to drain the coolant.

7 Undo the nuts/bolt, and remove the right-hand engine mounting **(see illustration)**.

8 Undo the 3 retaining bolts and move the wiring harness guide away from the engine **(see illustrations)**. The rear bolt is accessible from underneath the vehicle.

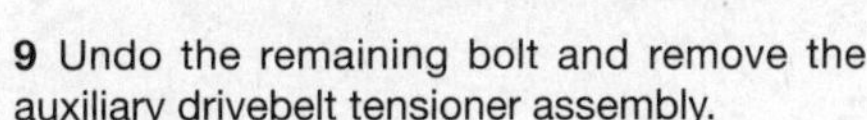

9 Undo the remaining bolt and remove the auxiliary drivebelt tensioner assembly.

10 Undo the 5 bolts and remove the lower cover **(see illustration)**.

Refitting

11 Refitting of all the covers is a reversal of the relevant removal procedure, ensuring that each cover section is correctly located, and that the cover retaining bolts are securely tightened. Ensure that all disturbed hoses are reconnected and retained by their relevant clips.

7 Timing belt – removal, inspection, refitting and tensioning

General

1 The timing belt drives the camshaft, high-pressure fuel pump, and coolant pump from a toothed sprocket on the end of the crankshaft. If the belt breaks or slips in service, the pistons are likely to hit the valve heads, resulting in expensive damage.

2 The timing belt should be renewed at the specified intervals, or earlier if it is contaminated with oil, or at all noisy in operation (a 'scraping' noise due to uneven wear).

3 If the timing belt is being removed, it is a wise precaution to renew the coolant pump at the same time. This may avoid the need to remove the timing belt again at a later stage, should the coolant pump fail. The timing belt tensioner should always be replaced when a new timing belt is fitted.

Removal

4 Remove the upper and lower timing belt covers, as described in Section 6.

5 Undo the bolts and remove the mounting bracket from the engine **(see illustration)**.

6 Lock the crankshaft and camshaft in the correct position as described in Section 3. If necessary, temporarily refit the crankshaft pulley bolt to enable the crankshaft to be rotated.

7 Insert a hexagon key into the belt tensioner pulley centre, slacken the pulley bolt, and allow

7.5 Undo the bolts and remove the bracket

7.7 Slacken the bolt and allow the tensioner to rotate, relieving the tension on the belt

the tensioner to rotate clockwise, relieving the belt tension **(see illustration)**. With belt slack, temporarily tighten the pulley bolt.

8 Note its routing, then remove the timing belt from the sprockets.

Inspection

9 Renew the belt as a matter of course, regardless of its apparent condition. The cost of a new belt is nothing compared with the cost of repairs should the belt break in service. If signs of oil contamination are found, trace the source of the oil leak and rectify it. Wash down the engine timing belt area and all related components, to remove all traces of oil. The tensioner must always be replaced. Check that the idler pulleys rotate freely without any sign of roughness, and also check that the coolant pump pulley rotates freely. It is highly recommended that both the coolant pump and the idler pulley are replaced at the same time as the timing belt and tensioner.

Refitting and tensioning

10 Commence refitting by ensuring that the crankshaft, camshaft and fuel pump sprocket timing pins are in position as described in Section 3.

11 Locate the timing belt on the crankshaft sprocket, then keeping it taut, locate it around the idler pulley, camshaft sprocket, high-pressure pump sprocket, coolant pump sprocket, and the tensioner roller **(see illustration)**.

12 Slacken the tensioner pulley bolt, and using a hexagonal key, rotate the tensioner anti-clockwise, which moves the index arm clockwise, until the index arm is aligned as shown **(see illustration)**.

13 Remove the camshaft, crankshaft and fuel pump sprocket (where applicable) timing pins and, using a socket on the crankshaft pulley bolt, rotate the crankshaft clockwise 6 complete revolutions. Refit the crankshaft and camshaft locking pins.

14 Check that the tensioner index arm is still aligned **(see illustration 7.12)**. If it is not, remove and belt and begin the refitting process again, starting at Paragraph 11.

15 The remainder of refitting is a reversal of removal. Tighten all fasteners to the specified torque where given.

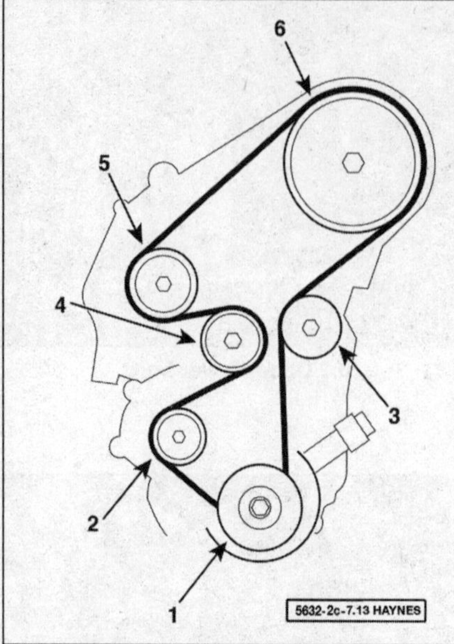

7.11 Timing belt routing

1 Crankshaft
2 Waterpump
3 Idler
4 Tensioner
5 Fuel pump
6 Camshaft

8 Timing belt sprockets and tensioner – removal and refitting

Camshaft sprocket

Removal

1 Remove the timing belt as described in Section 7.

2 Remove the locking tool from the camshaft sprocket/hub. Slacken the sprocket hub retaining bolt. To prevent the camshaft rotating as the bolt is slackened, a sprocket holding tool will be required. In the absence of the special Ford tool, an acceptable substitute can be fabricated at home (see **Tool Tip**). Do not attempt to use the engine assembly/valve timing locking tool to prevent the sprocket from rotating whilst the bolt is slackened.

3 Remove the sprocket hub retaining bolt, and slide the sprocket and hub off the end of the camshaft.

4 Clean the camshaft sprocket thoroughly, and renew it if there are any signs of wear, damage or cracks.

Refitting

5 Refit the camshaft sprocket to the camshaft **(see illustration)**.

6 Refit the sprocket hub retaining bolt. Tighten the bolt to the specified torque, preventing the camshaft from turning as during removal.

7 Align the engine assembly/valve timing slot in the camshaft sprocket hub with the hole in the cylinder head and refit the timing pin to lock the camshaft in position.

8 Fit the timing belt around the pump sprocket and camshaft sprocket, and tension the timing belt as described in Section 7.

TOOL TIP

A sprocket holding tool can be made from two lengths of steel strip bolted together to form a forked end. Drill holes and insert bolts in the ends of the fork to engage with the sprocket spokes.

7.12 The index arm must align with the lug

Crankshaft sprocket

Removal

9 Remove the timing belt as described in Section 7.

10 Check that the engine assembly/valve timing holes are still aligned as described in Section 3, and the camshaft sprocket and flywheel are locked in position.

8.5 Ensure the lug on the sprocket hub engages with the slot on the end of the camshaft

8.11a Slide the sprocket from the crankshaft...

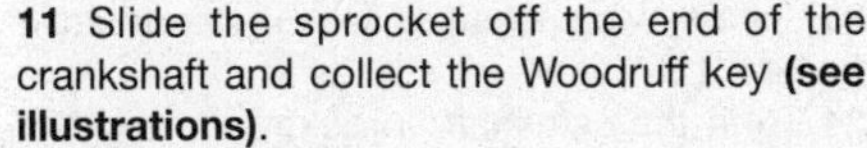

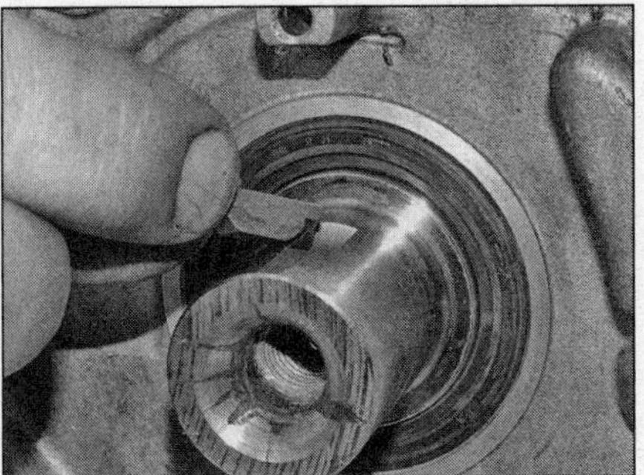

8.11b ...and recover the Woodruff key

8.31 Timing belt idler pulley retaining nut

11 Slide the sprocket off the end of the crankshaft and collect the Woodruff key **(see illustrations)**.

12 Examine the crankshaft oil seal for signs of oil leakage and, if necessary, renew it as described in Section 13.

13 Clean the crankshaft sprocket thoroughly, and renew it if there are any signs of wear, damage or cracks. Recover the crankshaft locating key.

Refitting

14 Refit the key to the end of the crankshaft, then refit the crankshaft sprocket (with the flange facing the crankshaft pulley).

15 Fit the timing belt around the crankshaft sprocket, and tension the timing belt as described in Section 7.

Fuel pump sprocket

Removal

16 Remove the timing belt as described in Section 7.

17 Using a suitable socket, undo the pump sprocket retaining nut. The sprocket can be held stationary by inserting a suitably-sized locking pin, drill or rod through the slot in the sprocket flange, and into the corresponding hole in the backplate.

18 The pump sprocket is a taper fit on the pump shaft and it will be necessary to use a two-legged puller to release if from the taper.

19 Partially unscrew the sprocket retaining nut, fit the puller and release the sprocket from the taper.

20 Clean the sprocket thoroughly, and renew it if there are any signs of wear, damage or cracks.

Refitting

21 Refit the pump sprocket and retaining nut, and tighten the nut to the specified torque.

22 Refit the timing belt as described in Section 7.

Coolant pump sprocket

23 The coolant pump sprocket is integral with the pump, and cannot be removed. Coolant pump removal is described in Chapter 3 Section 8.

Tensioner pulley

Removal

24 Remove the timing belt as described in Section 7.

25 Remove the tensioner pulley retaining bolt, and then remove the tensioner.

26 Clean the tensioner pulley, but do not use any strong solvent which may enter the pulley bearings. Check that the pulley rotates freely, with no sign of stiffness or free play. The pulley should always be replaced when the timing belt is replaced.

27 Examine the pulley mounting stud for signs of damage and if necessary, renew it.

Refitting

28 Refitting is a reversal of removal.

29 Refit the timing belt as described in Section 7.

Idler pulley

Removal

30 Remove the timing belt as described in Section 7.

31 Undo the retaining bolt/nut and withdraw the idler pulley from the engine **(see illustration)**.

32 Clean the idler pulley, but do not use any strong solvent which may enter the bearings. Check that the pulley rotates freely, with no sign of stiffness or free play. Renew the idler pulley if there is any doubt about its condition, or if there are any obvious signs of wear or damage.

Refitting

33 Locate the idler pulley on the engine, and fit the retaining bolt/nut. Tighten the bolt/nut to the specified torque.

34 Refit the timing belt as described in Section 7.

9 Camshafts, rocker arms and hydraulic tappets – removal, inspection and refitting

Removal

1 Remove the cylinder head cover as described in Section 4.

2 Remove the camshaft position sensor as described in Chapter 4B Section 12.

3 Remove the camshaft sprocket as described in Section 8.

4 Refit the right-hand engine mounting, but only tighten the bolts moderately; this will keep the engine supported during the camshaft removal.

5 Undo the bolts and remove the vacuum pump as described in Chapter 9 Section 23. Recover the pump O-ring seals.

6 Unbolt the fuel filter (see Chapter 1B Section 21) and move it to one side.

7 Working in reverse order to that shown **(see illustration 9.22)** remove the retaining bolts and then remove camshaft bearing cap ladder **(see illustration)**.

8 Lift out the camshaft **(see illustration)** and dispose of the oil seal. A new one will be required.

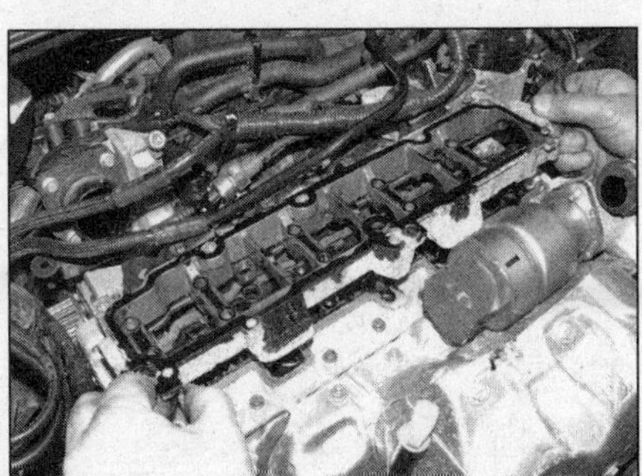

9.7 Remove the bearing ladder

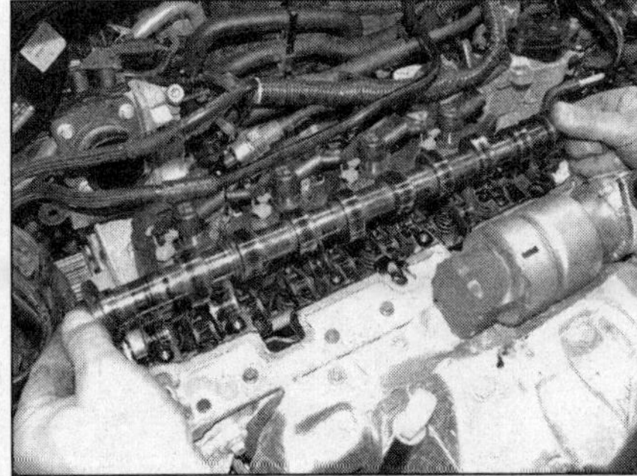

9.8 Remove the camshaft

9.10 Remove the rocker arms (cam followers)

9.11 Use long nose pliers to remove the hydraulic tappets

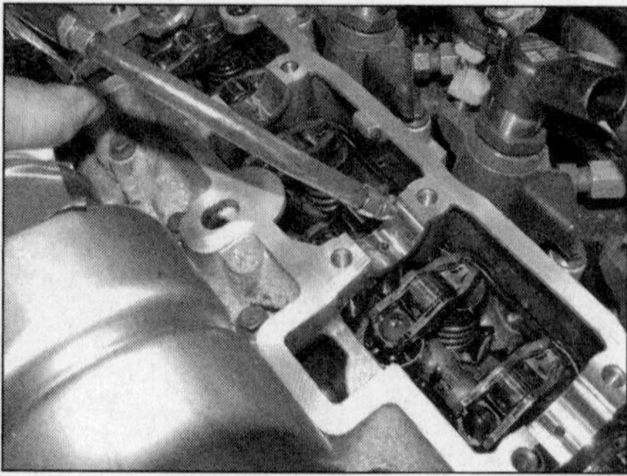

9.19 Lubricate the bearing surfaces

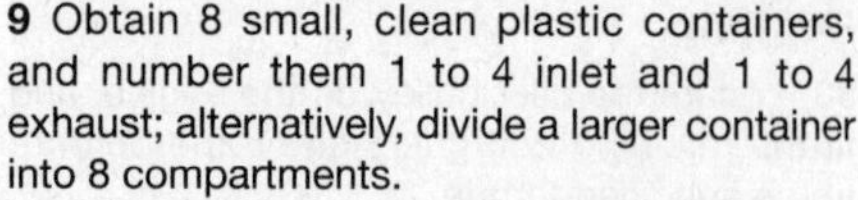

9 Obtain 8 small, clean plastic containers, and number them 1 to 4 inlet and 1 to 4 exhaust; alternatively, divide a larger container into 8 compartments.

10 Lift out each rocker arm. Place the rocker arms in their respective positions in the box or containers **(see illustration)**.

11 A compartmentalised container filled with engine oil is now required to retain the hydraulic tappets while they are removed from the cylinder head. Withdraw each hydraulic follower **(see illustration)** and place it in the container, keeping them each identified for correct refitting. The tappets must be totally submerged in the oil to prevent air entering them.

Inspection

12 Inspect the cam lobes and the camshaft bearing journals for scoring or other visible evidence of wear. Once the surface hardening of the cam lobes has been eroded, wear will occur at an accelerated rate. **Note:** *If these symptoms are visible on the tips of the camshaft lobes, check the corresponding rocker arm, as it will probably be worn as well.*

13 Examine the condition of the bearing surfaces in the cylinder head and camshaft bearing housing. If wear is evident, the cylinder head and bearing housing will both have to be renewed, as they are a matched assembly.

14 Inspect the rocker arms and tappets for scuffing, cracking or other damage and renew any components as necessary. Also check the condition of the tappet bores in the cylinder head. As with the camshafts, any wear in this area will necessitate cylinder head renewal.

Refitting

15 Thoroughly clean the sealant from the mating surfaces of the cylinder head and camshaft bearing housing. Use a suitable liquid gasket dissolving agent (available from Ford dealers) together with a soft putty knife; do not use a metal scraper or the faces will be damaged. As there is no conventional gasket used, the cleanliness of the mating faces is of the utmost importance.

16 Clean off any oil, dirt or grease from both components and dry with a clean lint-free cloth. Ensure that all the oilways are completely clean.

17 Liberally lubricate the hydraulic tappet bores in the cylinder head with clean engine oil.

18 Insert the hydraulic tappets into their original bores in the cylinder head unless they have been renewed.

19 Lubricate the rocker arms and place them over their respective tappets and valve stems. Lubricate the bearing surfaces **(see illustration)** and then refit the camshaft.

20 Apply a thin bead of silicone sealant (Ford part No WSE-M4G323-A4) to the mating surface of the camshaft cover/bearing ladder as shown **(see illustration)**.

21 Assemble the bearing ladder within 10 minutes of applying the sealant. Ford technicians use a special tool (303-245) to align the bearing ladder, however 2 suitable bolts (with their heads and threads cut off) can be used if the tool is not available.

22 Tighten the bolts to the specified torque in sequence **(see illustration)**.

23 Fit a new camshaft oil seal as described in Section 13.

24 Refit the camshaft sprocket, and tighten the retaining bolt.

25 Refit the timing belt and temporarily refit the crankshaft pulley bolt – use the old bolt. Rotate the engine at least 20 revolutions to allow the oil pump to deliver oil to the camshaft and associated components. Refit the timing belt cover.

26 Refit the remainder of the components in the reverse order of removal.

10 Cylinder head – removal and refitting

Removal

1 Apply the handbrake, then jack up the front of the vehicle and support it on axle stands (see *Jacking and vehicle support* Chapter 13 Section 5).

2 Disconnect the battery negative lead as described in Chapter 5A Section 3.

3 Remove the windscreen cowl panel and bulkhead closure panel as described in Chapter 12 Section 11.

4 Drain the cooling system as described in Chapter 1B Section 28.

5 Release the clamps, undo the 2 bolts, remove the air intake duct between the air cleaner housing and turbocharger, and disconnect the breather hose from the cylinder head cover **(see illustration)**.

9.20 Apply sealant to the camshaft housing

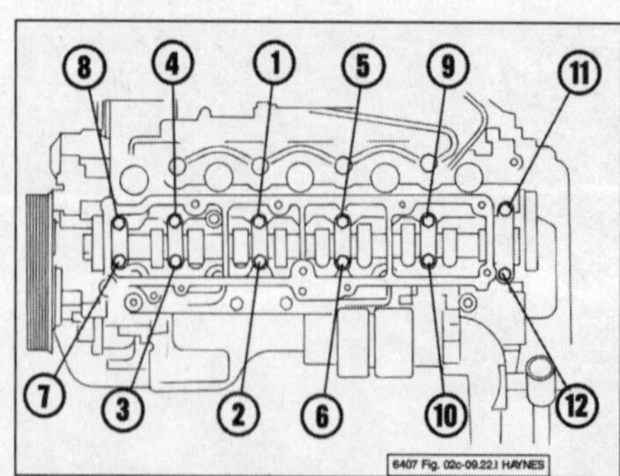

9.22 Bearing ladder bolts tightening sequence

10.5 Remove the air intake duct

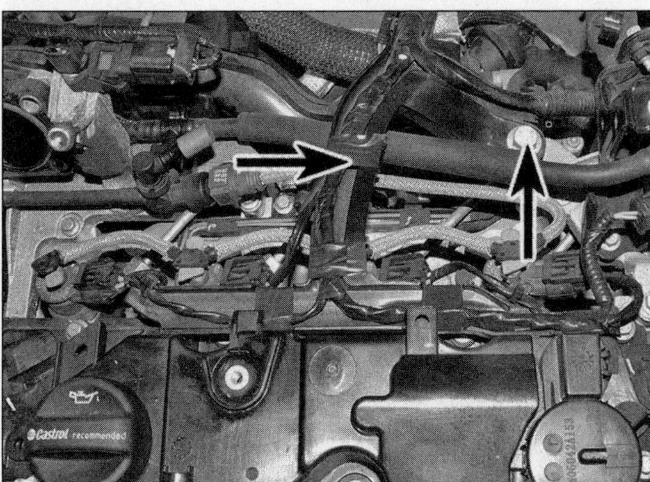

10.11 Undo the bolt, disconnect the wiring plugs, then unclip the harness duct

10.13 Depress the buttons, then disconnect the fuel supply and return hoses from the pump

6 Remove the timing belt, camshaft, rocker arms and hydraulic tappets as described in Section 9.

7 Remove the diesel particulate filter as described in Chapter 4B Section 17.

8 Remove the EGR cooler assembly as described in Chapter 4C Section 5.

9 Disconnect the hoses and unbolt the fuel filter assembly as described in Chapter 1B Section 21.

10 Undo the upper mounting bolts, and pivot the alternator away from the engine, undo the oil dipstick guide tube bolt, then undo the bolts securing the alternator mounting bracket to the cylinder head/block.

11 Note their fitted positions, then disconnect the wiring plugs as necessary, and unbolt the wiring harness duct from above the fuel rail and injectors **(see illustration)**.

12 Undo the unions and remove the high-pressure pipes between the fuel rail and the injectors. Counterhold the pipe unions with an open-ended spanner on the injector ports to prevent them from rotating. Discard the pipes, new ones must be fitted. Plug the openings to prevent contamination.

13 Disconnect the fuel supply and return hoses from the high-pressure fuel pump, then undo the bolts securing the pump mounting bracket to the cylinder head **(see illustration)**.

14 Remove the fuel injectors as described in Chapter 4B Section 10.

15 With reference to Chapter 4B Section 14, remove the turbocharger oil supply pipe, and disconnect the lower end of the oil return hose. Disconnect the vacuum hose from the wastegate actuator, and the variable vane position sensor.

16 Undo the coolant outlet housing (left-hand end of the cylinder head) retaining bolts, slacken the two bolts securing the housing support bracket to the top of the transmission bellhousing, and move the outlet housing away from the cylinder head a little **(see illustration)**. There is no need to disconnect the hoses.

17 Check that no components or electrical connectors are still fitted to the cylinder head.

18 Working in the reverse of the sequence shown **(see illustration 10.37)** undo the cylinder head bolts. Discard the bolts – new ones must be fitted.

19 Release the cylinder head from the cylinder block and location dowels by rocking it. The Ford tool for doing this consists simply of two metal rods with 90-degree angled ends **(see illustration)**. Do not prise between the mating faces of the cylinder head and block, as this may damage the gasket faces.

20 Lift the cylinder head from the block, and recover the gasket.

Preparation for refitting

21 The mating faces of the cylinder head and cylinder block must be perfectly clean before refitting the head. Ford recommend the use of a scouring agent for this purpose, but acceptable results can be achieved by using a hard plastic or wood scraper to remove all traces of gasket and carbon. The same method can be used to clean the piston crowns. Take particular care to avoid scoring or gouging the cylinder head/cylinder block mating surfaces during the cleaning operations, as aluminium alloy is easily damaged. Make sure that the carbon is not allowed to enter the oil and water passages – this is particularly important for the lubrication system, as carbon could block the oil supply to the engine's components. Using adhesive tape and paper, seal the water, oil and bolt holes in the cylinder block. To prevent carbon entering the gap between the pistons and bores, smear a little grease in the gap. After cleaning each piston, use a small brush to remove all traces of grease and carbon from the gap, then wipe away the remainder with a clean rag.

22 Check the mating surfaces of the cylinder block and the cylinder head for nicks, deep scratches and other damage. If slight, they may be removed carefully with a file, but if excessive, machining may be the only alternative to renewal. If warpage of the cylinder head gasket surface is suspected, use a straight-edge to check it for distortion. Refer to Part F of this Chapter if necessary.

23 Thoroughly clean the threads of the cylinder head bolt holes in the cylinder block. Ensure that the bolts run freely in their threads, and that all traces of oil and water are removed from each bolt hole.

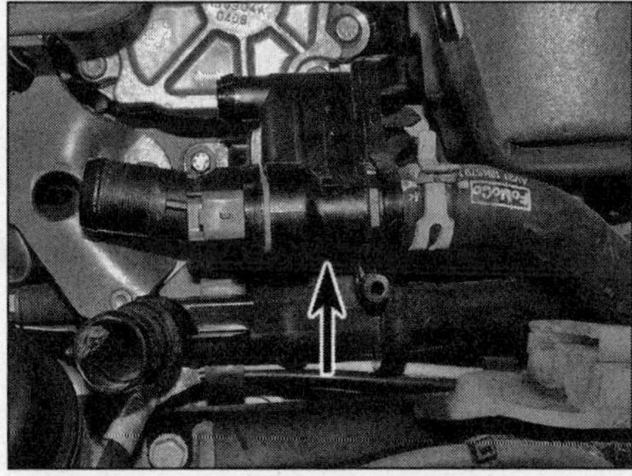

10.16 Remove the coolant outlet housing

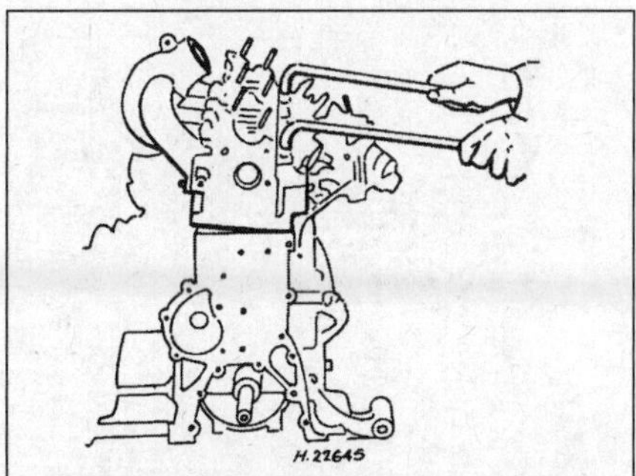

10.19 Free the cylinder head using angled rods

10.28 Measure the piston protrusion using a DTI gauge

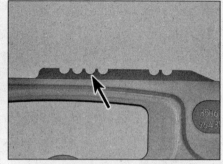

10.30 Cylinder head gasket thickness identification notches

Gasket selection

24 The gasket thickness is indicated by notches/holes on the front edge of the gasket. If the crankshaft or pistons/connecting rods have not been disturbed, fit a new gasket with the same number of notches/holes as the previous one. If the crankshaft/piston or connecting rods have been disturbed, it's necessary to work out the piston protrusion as follows:

25 Remove the crankshaft timing pin, then turn the crankshaft until pistons 1 and 4 are at TDC (Top Dead Centre). Position a dial test indicator (dial gauge) on the cylinder block adjacent to the rear of No 1 piston, and zero it on the block face. Transfer the probe to the crown of No 1 piston (10.0 mm in from the rear edge), then slowly turn the crankshaft back-and-forth past TDC, noting the highest reading on the indicator. Record this reading as protrusion A.

26 Repeat the check described in paragraph 25, this time 10.0 mm in from the front edge of the No 1 piston crown. Record this reading as protrusion B.

27 Add protrusion A to protrusion B, then divide the result by 2 to obtain an average reading for piston No 1.

28 Repeat the procedure described in paragraphs 25 to 27 on piston 4, then turn the crankshaft through 180° and carry out the procedure on the piston Nos 2 and 3 **(see illustration)**. Check that there is a maximum difference of 0.07 mm protrusion between any two pistons.

29 If a dial test indicator is not available, piston protrusion may be measured using a straight-edge and feeler blades or Vernier calipers. However, this is much less accurate, and cannot therefore be recommended.

30 Note the greatest piston protrusion measurement, and use this to determine the correct cylinder head gasket from the table below. The series of notches/holes on the side of the gasket are used for thickness identification **(see illustration)**.

Piston protrusion (mm)	Gasket thickness (mm)	Notches
0.533 to 0.634	1.25	2
0.634 to 0.684	1.30	3
0.684 to 0.734	1.35	1
0.734 to 0.784	1.40	4
0.784 to 0.886	1.45	5

Refitting

31 Turn the crankshaft and position Nos 1 and 4 pistons at TDC, then turn the crankshaft a quarter turn (90°) anti-clockwise.

32 Thoroughly clean the surfaces of the cylinder head and block.

33 Make sure that the locating dowels are in place, then fit the correct gasket the right way round on the cylinder block **(see illustration)**.

34 Carefully lower the cylinder head onto the gasket and block, making sure that it locates correctly onto the dowels.

35 Apply a smear of grease to the threads, and to the underside of the heads of the new cylinder head bolts.

36 Carefully insert the cylinder head bolts into their holes (do not drop them in) and initially finger-tighten them.

37 Working progressively and in sequence, tighten the cylinder head bolts to their Stage 1 torque setting, using a torque wrench and suitable socket **(see illustration)**.

38 Once all the bolts have been tightened to their Stage 1 torque setting, working again in the specified sequence, tighten each bolt to the specified Stage 2 setting. Finally, angle-tighten the bolts through the specified Stage 3 angle. It is recommended that an angle-measuring gauge is used during this stage of tightening, to ensure accuracy. **Note:** *Retightening of the cylinder head bolts after running the engine is not required.*

39 Refit the hydraulic tappets, rocker arms, and camshaft housing (complete with camshafts) as described in Section 9.

40 Refit the timing belt as described in Section 7.

41 The remainder of refitting is a reversal of removal, noting the following points.

a) *Use a new seal when refitting the coolant outlet housing.*
b) *When refitting a cylinder head, it is good practice to renew the thermostat.*
c) *Tighten all fasteners to the specified torque where given.*
d) *Refill the cooling system.*
e) *The engine may run erratically for the first few miles, until the engine management ECM relearns its stored values.*

11 Sump – removal and refitting

Removal

1 Drain the engine oil, then clean and refit the engine oil drain plug, tightening it securely. If the engine is nearing its service interval when the oil and filter are due for renewal, it is recommended that the filter is also removed, and a new one fitted. After reassembly, the engine can then be refilled with fresh oil. Refer to Chapter 1B Section 6 for further information.

2 Apply the handbrake, then jack up the front of the vehicle and support it on axle stands (see *Jacking and vehicle support*). Undo the bolts and remove the engine undershield.

3 Although not strictly necessary, remove the exhaust front pipe as described in Chapter 4B Section 17.

4 Where necessary, disconnect the wiring connector from the oil temperature sender unit, which is screwed into the sump.

5 Progressively slacken and remove all the sump retaining bolts/nuts. Since the sump bolts vary in length, remove each bolt in turn, and store it in its correct fitted order by pushing it through a clearly-marked cardboard template. This will avoid the possibility of installing the bolts in the wrong locations on refitting.

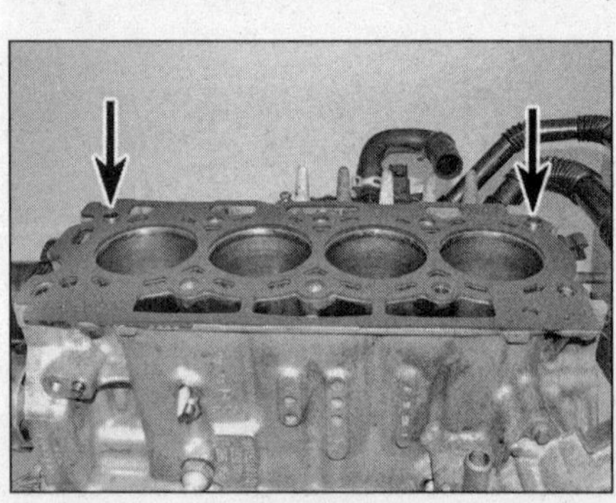
10.33 Ensure the gasket locates over the dowels

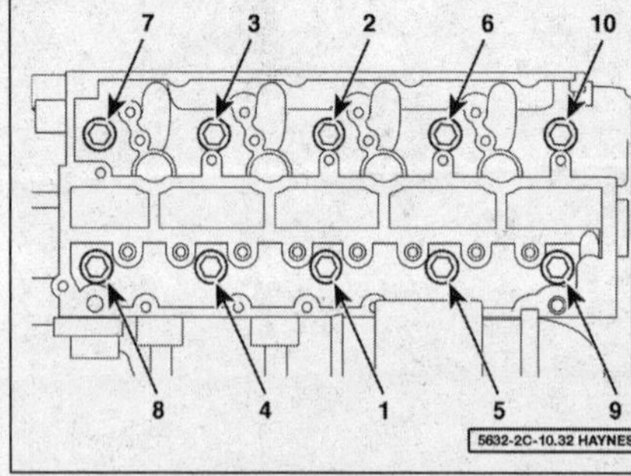

10.37 Cylinder head bolt tightening sequence

11.8 Apply a bead of sealant to the sump or crankcase mating surface. Ensure the sealant is applied to the inside of the retaining bolt holes

11.9 Refit the sump and tighten the bolts

6 Try to break the joint by striking the sump with the palm of your hand, then lower and withdraw the sump from under the car. If the sump is stuck (which is quite likely) use a putty knife or similar, carefully inserted between the sump and block. Ease the knife along the joint until the sump is released. While the sump is removed, take the opportunity to check the oil pump pick-up/strainer for signs of clogging or splitting. If necessary, remove the pump as described in Section 12, and clean or renew the strainer.

Refitting

7 Clean all traces of sealant from the mating surfaces of the cylinder block/crankcase and sump, then use a clean rag to wipe out the sump and the engine's interior.
8 Ensure that the sump mating surfaces are clean and dry, then apply a 3mm diameter bead of sealant (Ford part No WSE-M4G323-A4) to the sump mating surface **(see illustration)**. The sealant must be applied to the Inside of the bolt holes. Note that the sump must be installed within 10 minutes of applying the sealant, and the bolts tightened within a further 5 minutes.
9 Offer up the sump to the cylinder block/crankcase. Refit its retaining bolts/nuts, ensuring that each bolt is screwed into its original location. Tighten the bolts evenly and progressively to the specified torque setting **(see illustration)**.
10 Reconnect the wiring connector to the oil temperature sensor (where fitted).
11 Where applicable, refit the exhaust pipe.
12 Lower the vehicle to the ground, wait at least 30 minutes (for the sealant to set), and then refill the engine with oil as described in Chapter 1B Section 6.

12 Oil pump – removal, inspection and refitting

Removal

1 Remove the sump as described in Section 11.
2 Remove the crankshaft front oil seal as described in Section 13.
3 Disconnect the wiring plug, undo the bolts and remove the crankshaft position sensor, located on the right-hand end of the cylinder block.
4 Undo the three Torx security bolts and remove the oil pump pick-up tube from the pump/block **(see illustration)**. Discard the oil seal, a new one must be fitted.
5 Undo the 8 bolts, and remove the oil pump **(see illustration)**.

Inspection

6 Undo and remove the Torx bolts securing the cover to the oil pump **(see illustration)**.

12.4 Oil pick-up tube bolts

12.5 Oil pump retaining bolts

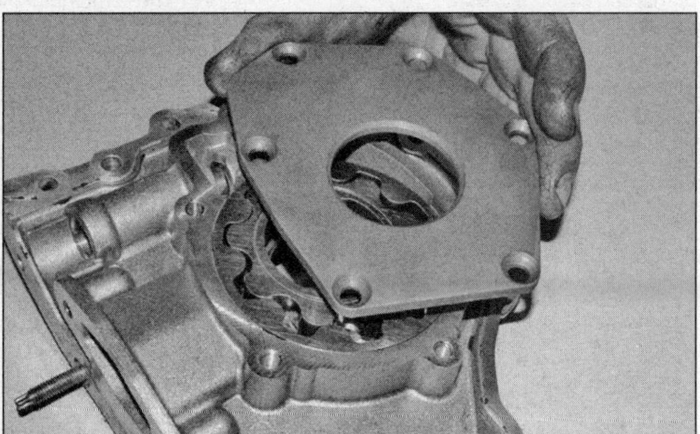
12.6 Undo the Torx bolts and remove the pump cover

12.7a Remove the circlip...

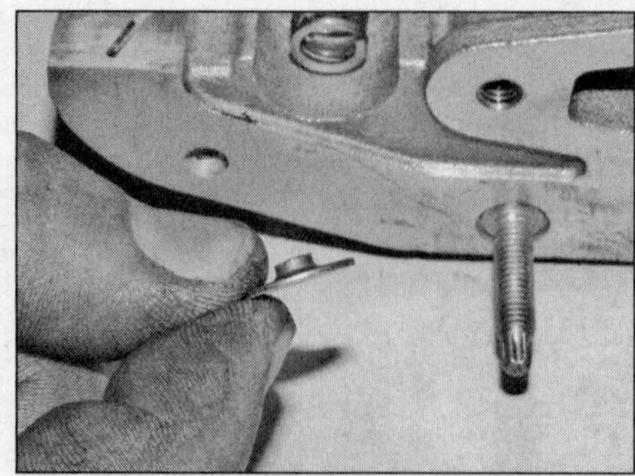

12.7b ...cap...

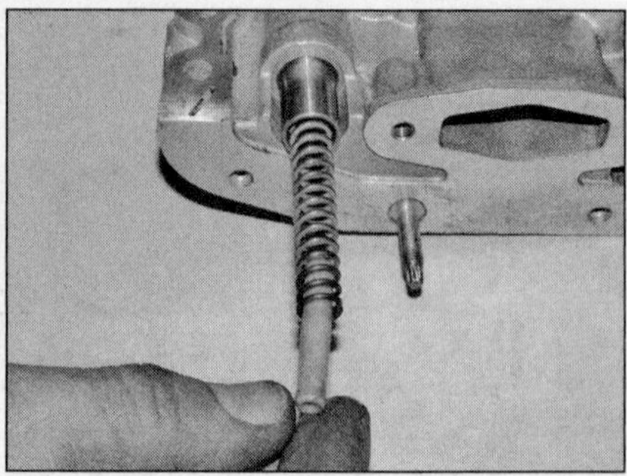

12.7c ...spring...

12.7d ...and piston

12.11 Apply a bead of sealant to the cylinder block mating surface

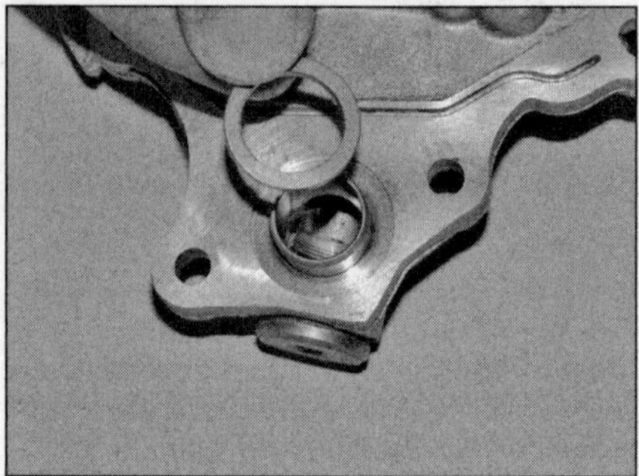

12.12a Fit a new seal...

Examine the pump rotors and body for signs of wear and damage. If worn, the complete pump must be renewed.

7 Remove the circlip, and extract the cap, valve piston and spring, noting which way around they are fitted **(see illustrations)**. The condition of the relief valve spring can only be measured by comparing it with a new one; if there is any doubt about its condition, it should also be renewed.

8 Refit the relief valve piston and spring, then secure them in place with the circlip.

9 Refit the cover to the oil pump, and tighten the Torx bolts securely.

Refitting

10 Remove all traces of sealant, and thoroughly clean the mating surfaces of the oil pump and cylinder block.

11 Apply a 4 mm diameter bead of silicone sealant to the mating face of the cylinder block **(see illustration)**. Ensure that no sealant enters any of the holes in the block.

12 With a new oil seal fitted, refit the oil pump over the end of the crankshaft, aligning the flats in the pump drive gear with the flats machined in the crankshaft **(see illustrations)**. Note that new oil pumps are supplied with the oil seal already fitted, and a seal protector sleeve. The sleeve fits over the end of the crankshaft to protect the seal as the pump is fitted.

13 Install the oil pump bolts and tighten them to the specified torque.

14 Refit the oil pick-up tube to the pump/cylinder block using a new O-ring seal. Ensure the oil dipstick guide tube is correctly refitted.

15 Refit the woodruff key to the crankshaft, and slide the crankshaft sprocket into place.

16 The remainder of refitting is a reversal of removal.

13 Oil seals – renewal

Crankshaft

Right-hand oil seal

1 Remove the crankshaft sprocket and Woodruff key as described in Section 8.

2 Measure and note the fitted depth of the oil seal.

3 Pull the oil seal from the housing using a screwdriver. Alternatively, drill a small hole in the oil seal, and use a self-tapping screw and a pair of pliers to remove it **(see illustration)**.

4 Clean the oil seal housing and the crankshaft sealing surface.

5 The new seal should be supplied with a

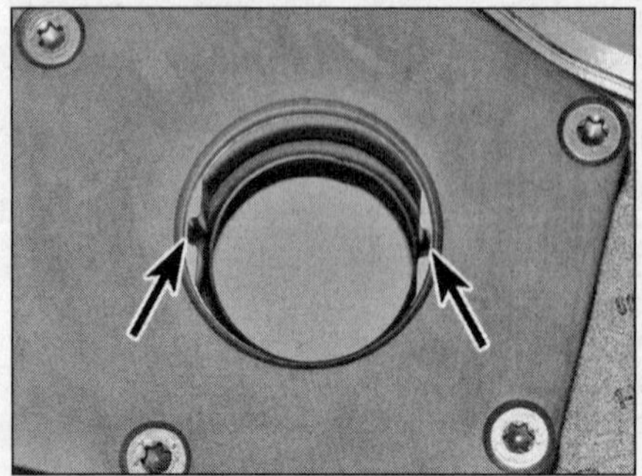

12.12b ...align the pump gear flats...

12.12c ...with those of the crankshaft

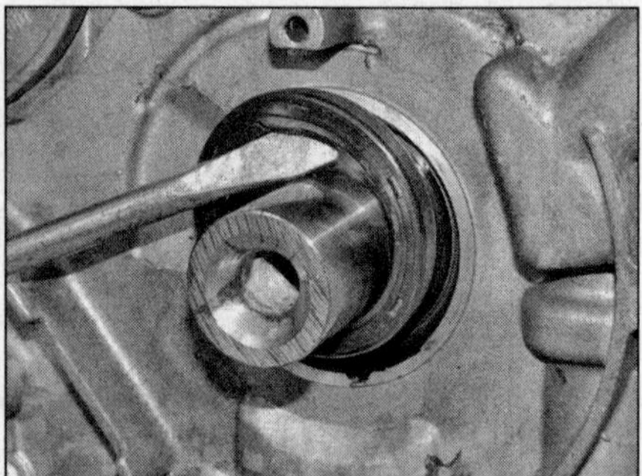

13.3 Take great care not to mark the crankshaft whilst levering out the oil seal

13.5a Slide the seal and protective sleeve over the end of the crankshaft...

13.5b ...and press the seal into place

13.12 Slide the seal and protective sleeve over the left-hand end of the crankshaft

13.16 Drill a hole, insert a self-tapping screw, and pull the seal from place using pliers

13.18a Use the correct tool to fit the seal...

13.18b ...or a suitable socket

protective sleeve, which fits over the end of the crankshaft to prevent any damage to the seal lip. With the sleeve in place, press the seal (open end first) into the pump to the previously-noted depth, using a suitable tube or socket **(see illustrations)**.

6 Where applicable, remove the plastic sleeve from the end of the crankshaft.

7 Refit the crankshaft sprocket as described in Section 8.

Left-hand oil seal

8 Remove the flywheel, as described in Section 15.

9 Measure and note the fitted depth of the oil seal.

10 Pull the oil seal from the housing using a screwdriver. Alternatively, drill a small hole in the oil seal, and use a self-tapping screw and a pair of pliers to remove it **(see illustration 13.3)**.

11 Clean the oil seal housing and the crankshaft sealing surface.

12 The new seal should be supplied with a protective sleeve, which fits over the end of the crankshaft to prevent any damage to the seal lip **(see illustration)**. With the sleeve in place, press the seal (open end first) into the housing to the previously-noted depth, using a suitable tube or socket.

13 Where applicable, remove the plastic sleeve from the end of the crankshaft.

14 Refit the flywheel, as described in Section 15.

Camshaft

15 Remove the camshaft sprocket as described in Section 8. In principle there is no need to remove the timing belt completely, but remember that if the belt has been contaminated with oil, it must be renewed.

16 Pull the oil seal from the housing using a hooked instrument. Alternatively, drill a small hole in the oil seal and use a self-tapping screw and a pair of pliers to remove it **(see illustration)**.

17 Clean the oil seal housing and the camshaft sealing surface.

18 Press the seal (open end first) into the housing to the previously-noted depth, using either the correct tool (303-684), a suitable tube or a socket which bears only of the outer edge of the seal **(see illustrations)**. If the seal was supplied with a protective sleeve, remove it.

19 Refit the camshaft sprocket as described in Section 8.

20 Where necessary, fit a new timing belt with reference to Section 7.

14 Oil pressure switch and level sensor – removal and refitting

Removal

Oil pressure switch

1 The oil pressure switch is located at the front of the cylinder block, adjacent to the oil dipstick guide tube. Note that on some models, access to the switch may be improved if the vehicle is jacked up and supported on axle stands, then undo the bolts and remove the engine undershield so that the switch can be reached from underneath (see *Jacking and vehicle support*).

2 Remove the protective sleeve from the wiring plug (where applicable), then disconnect the wiring from the switch.

3 Unscrew the switch from the cylinder block, and recover the sealing washer **(see illustration)**. Be prepared for oil spillage, and if the switch is to be left removed from the engine for any length of time, plug the hole in the cylinder block.

Oil level sensor

4 Where fitted, the oil level sensor is located at the rear of the cylinder block. Jack up the

14.3 The oil pressure switch is located on the front face of the cylinder block

front of the vehicle and support it securely on axle stands (see *Jacking and vehicle support*). Undo the bolts and remove the engine undershield.

5 Reach up between the driveshaft and the cylinder block, and disconnect the sensor wiring plug **(see illustration)**.

6 Using an open-ended spanner, unscrew the sensor and withdraw it from position.

Refitting

Oil pressure switch

7 Examine the sealing washer for any signs of damage or deterioration, and if necessary renew.

8 Refit the switch, complete with washer, and tighten it to the specified torque where given.

9 Refit the engine undershield, and lower the vehicle to the ground.

Oil level sensor

10 Smear a little silicone sealant on the threads and refit the sensor to the cylinder block, tightening it securely.

11 Reconnect the sensor wiring plug.

12 Refit the engine undershield, and lower the vehicle to the ground.

14.5 The oil level sensor is located on the rear face of the cylinder block (arrowed)

15 Flywheel – removal, inspection and refitting

Removal

1 Remove the transmission as described in Chapter 7 Section 7, then remove the clutch assembly as described in Chapter 6 Section 6.

2 Prevent the flywheel from turning. Do not attempt to lock the flywheel in position using the crankshaft pulley locking tool described in Section 3. Insert a 12 mm diameter rod or drill bit through the hole in the flywheel cover casting, and into a slot in the flywheel **(see illustration)**

3 Make alignment marks between the flywheel and crankshaft to aid refitment. Slacken and remove the flywheel retaining bolts, and remove the flywheel from the end of the crankshaft. Be careful not to drop it; it is heavy. If the flywheel locating dowel (where fitted) is a loose fit in the crankshaft end, remove it and store it with the flywheel for safe-keeping. Discard the flywheel bolts; new ones must be used on refitting.

Inspection

4 Examine the flywheel for scoring of the clutch face, and for wear or chipping of the ring gear teeth. If the clutch face is scored, the flywheel may be surface-ground, but renewal is preferable. Seek the advice of a Ford dealer or engine reconditioning specialist to see if machining is possible. If the ring gear is worn or damaged, the flywheel must be renewed, as it is not possible to renew the ring gear separately.

5 All engines maybe fitted with a dual-mass flywheel. The maximum travel of the primary mass in relation to the secondary must not exceed 15 teeth (or 20 degrees). If in doubt remove the flywheel and have a suitably equipped specialist check the flywheel. Inspect the flywheel for any grease or debris from the interface between the fixed part and the movable part of the flywheel. If any doubt to the condition of the flywheel exists, despite the expense we recommend replacing it.

Refitting

6 Clean the mating surfaces of the flywheel and crankshaft. Remove any remaining locking compound from the threads of the crankshaft holes, using the correct size of tap, if available.

7 If the new flywheel retaining bolts are not supplied with their threads already pre-coated, apply a suitable thread-locking compound to the threads of each bolt.

8 Ensure that the locating dowel is in position. Offer up the flywheel, locating it on the dowel (where fitted), and fit the new retaining bolts. Where no locating dowel is fitted, align the previously-made marks to ensure the flywheel is refitted in its original position.

9 Lock the flywheel using the method employed on dismantling, and tighten the retaining bolts to the specified torque **(see illustration)**.

10 Refit the clutch, then remove the flywheel locking tool, and refit the transmission.

16 Engine/transmission mountings – inspection and renewal

General

1 The engine/transmission mountings seldom require attention, but broken or deteriorated mountings should be renewed immediately, or the added strain placed on the driveline components may cause damage or wear.

2 While separate mountings may be removed and refitted individually, if more than one is disturbed at a time – such as if the engine/transmission unit is removed from its mountings – they must be reassembled and their fasteners tightened in the position marked on removal.

3 On reassembly, the complete weight of the engine/transmission unit must not be taken by the mountings until all are correctly aligned with the marks made on removal. Tighten the engine/transmission mounting fasteners to their specified torque wrench settings.

Inspection

4 During the check, the engine/transmission unit must be raised slightly, to remove its weight from the mountings.

5 Raise the front of the vehicle, and support it securely on axle stands. Position a jack under the sump, with a large block of wood between the jack head and the sump, then carefully raise the engine/transmission just enough to take the weight off the mountings.

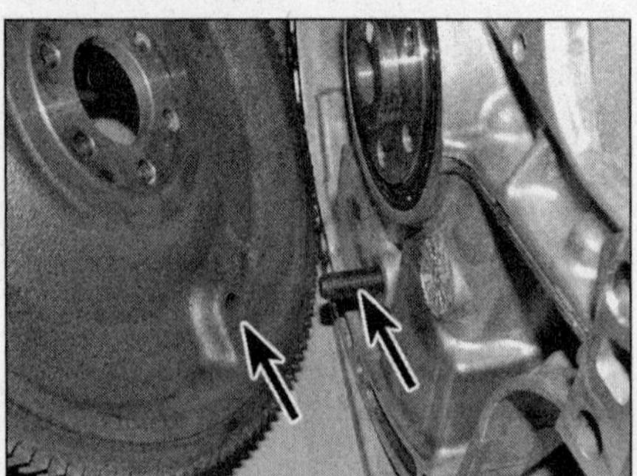

15.2 Lock the flywheel with a 12mm diameter rod or bolt

15.9 Flywheel retaining bolts

16.9 Right-hand engine mounting-to-engine bracket retaining nuts

Warning: DO NOT place any part of your body under the engine when it is supported only by a jack.

6 Check the mountings to see if the rubber is cracked, hardened or separated from the metal components. Sometimes the rubber will split right down the centre.

7 Check for relative movement between each mounting's brackets and the engine/transmission or body (use a large screwdriver or lever to attempt to move the mountings). If movement is noted, lower the engine and check-tighten the mounting fasteners.

Renewal

Note: *The following paragraphs assume the engine is supported beneath the sump as described earlier.*

Right-hand mounting

8 Release the clips, lift up the coolant expansion tank and position it to one side. Note there is no need to disconnect the coolant pipes.

9 Mark the position of the mounting on the vehicle, right-hand inner wing panel, then undo the three nuts securing the mounting to the engine bracket **(see illustration)**. Discard the nuts, new ones must be fitted.

10 Undo the three retaining bolts securing the mounting to the inner wing panel and withdraw the mounting from the vehicle **(see illustration)**.

11 On refitting, tighten all fasteners to the torque wrench settings specified. Re-align the marks made on removal, then tighten the new mounting bracket retaining nuts.

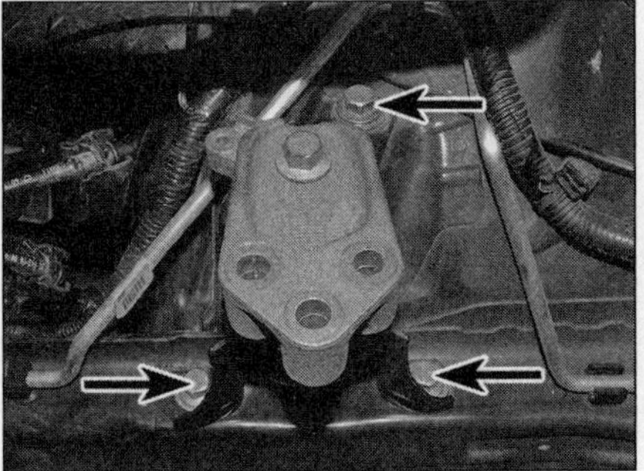

16.10 Right-hand engine mounting-to-inner wing panel retaining bolts

Left-hand mounting

12 Remove the battery and battery tray as described in Chapter 5A Section 3. Note that it is not necessary to remove the powertrain control module from the battery tray, just position the tray clear for access to the mounting.

13 Undo the three nuts securing the battery tray support bracket in position. Release the wiring loom from the support bracket and lift the support bracket out of the engine compartment **(see illustration)**.

14 With the transmission supported, mark the position of the mounting bracket on the transmission and on the body side member. Undo the three bolts securing the mounting bracket to the transmission and the two bolts securing the mounting to the body side member **(see illustrations)**. Remove the mounting from the engine compartment.

16.13 Undo the retaining nuts and lift out the battery tray support bracket

15 On refitting, re-align the mounting in the position noted on removal, then tighten all fasteners to the specified torque wrench settings. Refit the components disturbed for access using a reversal of the removal procedures.

Rear mounting (roll restrictor)

16 To remove the engine rear mounting, apply the handbrake, then jack up the front of the car and support it on axle stands (see *Jacking and vehicle support*). Unscrew the through-bolts and remove the engine rear mounting link from the bracket on the transmission and from the bracket on the subframe **(see illustration)**. Hold the engine stationary while the bolts are being removed, since the link will be under tension.

17 On refitting, ensure that the bolts are securely tightened to the specified torque wrench setting.

16.14a Left-hand engine mounting bracket-to-transmission retaining bolts (arrowed) ...

16.14b ... and mounting-to-body sidemember retaining bolts (arrowed)

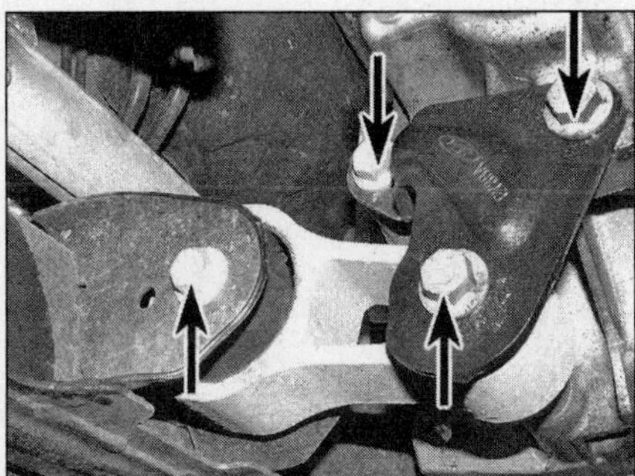

16.16 Rear mounting/roll restrictor retaining bolts

Notes

Chapter 2 Part D
1.6 litre SOHC diesel engine in-car repair procedures

Contents

Degrees of difficulty

Easy, suitable for novice with little experience

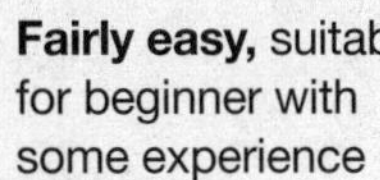

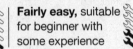

Fairly easy, suitable for beginner with some experience

Fairly difficult, suitable for competent DIY mechanic

Difficult, suitable for experienced DIY mechanic

Very difficult, suitable for expert DIY or professional

Specifications

General

Designation	Duratorq-TDCi
Engine codes*	T3DA, T3DB, T1DA and T1DB
Capacity	1560 cc
Bore	75.0 mm
Stroke	88.3 mm
Direction of crankshaft rotation	Clockwise (viewed from the right-hand side of vehicle)
No 1 cylinder location	At the transmission end of block
Maximum power output	
T3DA and T3DB engines	70 kW (95 PS) @ 3600 rpm
T1DA and T1DB engines	85 kW (115 PS) @ 3600 rpm
Maximum torque output	
T3DA and T3DB engines	230 Nm @ 2000 rpm
T1DA and T1DB engines	270 Nm @ 2500 rpm
Compression ratio	16 : 1

**The engine code is stamped onto a plate attached to the front of the cylinder block, next to the oil filter.*

Valves

Valve clearances (cold)	
Inlet	0.103 to 0.118 mm
Exhaust	0.113 to 0.128 mm

Compression pressures (engine hot, at cranking speed)

Normal	20 ± 5 bar
Minimum	15 bar
Maximum difference between any two cylinders	5 bar

Camshaft

Camshaft end float	0.195 – 0.3 mm

Lubrication system

Oil pump type	Gear-type, driven directly by the right-hand end of the crankshaft, by two flats machined along the crankshaft journal
Minimum oil pressure at 80°C:	
Idle speed	1.0 to 2.0 bar
2000 rpm	2.3 to 3.7 bar

Torque wrench settings

Torque wrench settings	Nm	lbf ft
Ancillary drivebelt tensioner roller	20	15
Big-end bolts: *		
Stage 1	10	7
Stage 2	Slacken 180°	
Stage 3	10	7
Stage 4	Angle-tighten a further 130°	
Camshaft bearing caps	10	7
Camshaft cover/bearing ladder:		
Studs	10	7
Bolts	10	7
Camshaft position sensor bolt	5	4
Camshaft sprocket bolt		
Stage 1	20	15
Stage 2	Angle-tighten a further 50°	
Coolant outlet housing bolts	8	6
Crankshaft position/speed sensor bolt	10	7
Crankshaft pulley/sprocket bolt: *		
Stage 1	35	26
Stage 2	Angle-tighten a further 190°	
Cylinder head bolts: *		
Stage 1	20	15
Stage 2	40	30
Stage 3	Angle-tighten a further 260°	
Cylinder head cover/manifold	13	10
EGR valve	10	7
Engine-to-transmission fixing bolts	47	35
Flywheel bolts: *		
Stage 1	30	22
Stage 2	Angle-tighten a further 90°	
Fuel pump sprocket	50	37
Left-hand engine/transmission mounting:		
Mounting-to-bracket centre nut	148	109
Mounting-to-bracket outer nuts	48	35
Mounting bracket to transmission	80	59
Main bearing ladder outer seam bolts:		
Stage 1	5	4
Stage 2	10	7
Main bearing ladder to cylinder block:		
Stage 1	10	7
Stage 2	Slacken 180°	
Stage 3	30	22
Stage 4	Angle-tighten a further 140°	
Piston oil jet spray tube bolt	20	15
Oil cooler retaining bolts	10	7
Oil filter cover	25	18
Oil pick-up pipe	10	7
Oil pressure switch	30	22
Oil pump to cylinder block:		
Stage 1	5	4
Stage 2	9	7
Rear engine/transmission mounting	25	18
Right-hand engine mounting:		
Mounting to Inner wing (nuts/bolts)	48	35
Mounting bracket to engine block	55	41
Sump drain plug	35	26
Sump bolts/nuts	10	7
Timing belt idler pulley	37	27
Timing belt tensioner pulley	30	22
Vacuum pump bolts	20	15

**Do not re-use*

1 General Information

How to use this Chapter

1 This Part of Chapter 2 describes the repair procedures that can reasonably be carried out on the engine while it remains in the vehicle. If the engine has been removed from the vehicle and is being dismantled as described in Part E, any preliminary dismantling procedures can be ignored.

2 Note that, while it may be possible physically to overhaul items such as the piston/connecting rod assemblies while the engine is in the car, such tasks are not usually carried out as separate operations. Usually, several additional procedures are required (not to mention the cleaning of components and oilways); for this reason, all such tasks are classed as major overhaul procedures, and are described in Part E of this Chapter.

3 Part E describes the removal of the engine/transmission from the car, and the full overhaul procedures that can then be carried out.

DV series engines

4 The 1.6 litre DV series of engines are the result of development collaboration between Citroën/Peugeot and Ford. Originally specified as a double overhead camshaft (DOHC) 16-valve design, the latest version fitted to the Ford Focus is a single overhead cam (SOHC), 8 valve variant. The direct injection, turbocharged, four-cylinder engine is mounted transversely, with the transmission mounted on the left-hand side.

5 A toothed timing belt drives the camshaft, high-pressure fuel pump and coolant pump. The camshaft operates the inlet and exhaust valves via rocker arms which are supported at their pivot ends by hydraulic self-adjusting tappets. The camshaft Is supported by bearings machined directly in the cylinder head and camshaft bearing housing.

6 The high-pressure fuel pump supplies fuel to the fuel rail, and subsequently to the electronically-controlled injectors which inject the fuel direct into the combustion chambers. This design differs from the previous type where an injection pump supplies the fuel at high pressure to each injector. The earlier, conventional type injection pump required fine calibration and timing, and these functions are now completed by the high-pressure pump, electronic injectors and engine management ECM.

7 The crankshaft runs in five main bearings of the usual shell type. Endfloat is controlled by thrustwashers either side of No 2 main bearing.

8 The pistons are selected to be of matching weight, and incorporate fully-floating gudgeon pins retained by circlips.

Repair operations precaution

9 The engine is a complex unit with numerous accessories and ancillary components. The design of the engine compartment is such that every conceivable space has been utilised, and access to virtually all of the engine components is extremely limited. In many cases, ancillary components will have to be removed, or moved to one side, and wiring, pipes and hoses will have to be disconnected or removed from various cable clips and support brackets.

10 When working on this engine, read through the entire procedure first, look at the car and engine at the same time, and establish whether you have the necessary tools, equipment, skill and patience to proceed. Allow considerable time for any operation, and be prepared for the unexpected.

11 Because of the limited access, many of the engine photographs appearing in this Chapter were, by necessity, taken with the engine removed from the vehicle.

Warning: It is essential to observe strict precautions when working on the fuel system components of the engine, particularly the high-pressure side of the system. Before carrying out any engine operations that entail working on, or near, any part of the fuel system, refer to the special information given in Chapter 4B Section 1.

12 Operations with engine in vehicle

a) Compression pressure – testing.
b) Cylinder head cover – removal and refitting.
c) Crankshaft pulley – removal and refitting.
d) Timing belt covers – removal and refitting.
e) Timing belt – removal, refitting and adjustment.
f) Timing belt tensioner and sprockets – removal and refitting.
g) Camshaft oil seal – renewal.
h) Camshaft, rocker arms and hydraulic tappets – removal, inspection and refitting.
i) Sump – removal and refitting.
j) Oil pump – removal and refitting.
k) Crankshaft oil seals – renewal.
l) Engine/transmission mountings – inspection and renewal.
m) Flywheel – removal, inspection and refitting.

2 Compression and leakdown tests – description and interpretation

Compression test

Note: *A compression tester specifically designed for diesel engines must be used for this test.*

1 When engine performance is down, or if misfiring occurs which cannot be attributed to the fuel system, a compression test can provide diagnostic clues as to the engine's condition. If the test is performed regularly, it can give warning of trouble before any other symptoms become apparent.

2 A compression tester specifically intended for diesel engines must be used, because of the higher pressures involved. The tester is connected to an adapter which screws into the glow plug or injector hole. On this engine, an adapter suitable for use in the glow plug holes will be required, so as not to disturb the fuel system components. It is unlikely to be worthwhile buying such a tester for occasional use, but it may be possible to borrow or hire one – if not, have the test performed by a garage.

3 Unless specific instructions to the contrary are supplied with the tester, observe the following points:

a) The battery must be in a good state of charge, the air filter must be clean, and the engine should be at normal operating temperature.
b) All the glow plugs should be removed as described in Chapter 5A Section 9 before starting the test.
c) Disconnect the fuel injector wiring plugs.

4 The compression pressures measured are not so important as the balance between cylinders. Values are given in the Specifications.

5 The cause of poor compression is less easy to establish on a diesel engine than on a petrol one. The effect of introducing oil into the cylinders ('wet' testing) is not conclusive, because there is a risk that the oil will sit in the swirl chamber or in the recess on the piston crown instead of passing to the rings. However, the following can be used as a rough guide to diagnosis.

6 All cylinders should produce very similar pressures; any difference greater than that specified indicates the existence of a fault. Note that the compression should build-up quickly in a healthy engine; low compression on the first stroke, followed by gradually-increasing pressure on successive strokes, indicates worn piston rings. A low compression reading on the first stroke, which does not build-up during successive strokes, indicates leaking valves or a blown head gasket (a cracked head could also be the cause). Deposits on the undersides of the valve heads can also cause low compression.

7 A low reading from two adjacent cylinders is almost certainly due to the head gasket having blown between them; the presence of coolant in the engine oil will confirm this.

8 If the compression reading is unusually high, the cylinder head surfaces, valves and pistons are probably coated with carbon deposits. If this is the case, the cylinder head should be removed and decarbonised.

Note: *After performing this test, a fault code may be generated and stored in the PCM memory. Have the PCM self-diagnosis facility interrogated by a Ford dealer or suitably-equipped specialist, and the fault code erased. Inexpensive fault code readers/scanners are readily available.*

3.9 Insert a 5.0 mm drill bit/bolt through the round hole in the sprocket flange into the hole in the oil pump housing (lower timing belt removed for clarity)

3.10 Insert an 8.0 mm bolt through the hole in the camshaft sprocket into the corresponding hole in the cylinder head

Leakdown test

9 A leakdown test measures the rate at which compressed air fed into the cylinder is lost. It is an alternative to a compression test, and in many ways it is better, since the escaping air provides easy identification of where pressure loss is occurring (piston rings, valves or head gasket).

10 The equipment needed for leakdown testing is unlikely to be available to the home mechanic. If poor compression is suspected, have the test performed by a suitably-equipped garage.

3 Engine assembly/valve timing holes – general information and usage

Note: *Do not attempt to rotate the engine whilst the crankshaft and camshaft are locked in position. If the engine is to be left in this state for a long period of time, it is a good idea to place suitable warning notices inside the vehicle, and in the engine compartment. This will reduce the possibility of the engine being accidentally cranked on the starter motor, which is likely to cause damage with the locking pins in place.*

1 Timing holes or slots are located only in the crankshaft pulley flange and camshaft sprocket hub. The holes/slots are used to position the pistons halfway up the cylinder bores. This will ensure that the valve timing is maintained during operations that require removal and refitting of the timing belt. When the holes/slots are aligned with their corresponding holes in the cylinder block and cylinder head, suitable diameter bolts/pins can be inserted to lock the crankshaft and camshaft in position, preventing rotation.

2 Note that the fuel system used on these engines does not have a conventional diesel injection pump, but instead uses a high-pressure fuel pump. However, the fuel pump sprocket must be pegged in position in a similar fashion to the camshaft sprocket.

3 To align the engine assembly/valve timing holes, proceed as follows.

4 Apply the handbrake, then jack up the front of the vehicle and support it on axle stands (see *Jacking and vehicle support*). Remove the right-hand front roadwheel.

5 To gain access to the crankshaft pulley, to enable the engine to be turned, the wheel arch plastic liner must be removed. The liner is secured by several plastic expanding rivets/nut/bolts. To remove the rivets, push in the centre pins a little, then prise the clips from place. Remove the liner from under the front wing.

6 Remove the starter motor and remove the crankshaft pulley as described in Section 5.

7 Remove the upper and lower timing belt covers as described in Section 6.

8 Temporarily refit the crankshaft pulley bolt (without the crankshaft pulley) and then remove the crankshaft locking tool.

9 Turn the crankshaft until the timing hole in the crankshaft sprocket aligns with the hole in the oil pump casing (this is at the 12 o'clock position). Fit the special tool 303-732, or a suitable alternative and lock the crankshaft in position **(see illustration)**.

10 With the crankshaft locked in position fit the camshaft locking tool (303-735 or similar). The hole in the camshaft sprocket should be at approximately the 1 o'clock position **(see illustration)**. If this is not the case remove the crankshaft locking pin and rotate the engine one revolution. Note that the crankshaft must always be turned in a clockwise direction (viewed from the right-hand side of vehicle).

11 When refitting the timing belt, insert Ford tool No 303-732 through the slot in the fuel pump sprocket and into the corresponding hole in the fuel pump mounting bracket. In the absence of this tool use a 5 mm bolt or drill bit.

12 The crankshaft and camshaft are now locked in position, preventing unnecessary rotation.

4 Cylinder head cover – removal and refitting

Removal

1 Disconnect the battery negative lead as described in Chapter 5A Section 3.

2 Pull the plastic cover upwards from the top of the engine.

3 Unbolt the fuel filter housing and move it to one side.

4 Release the hose clamp and remove the hose from the throttle body **(see illustration)**.

5 Unclip the fuel lines from the inlet manifold hose on top of the engine. Disconnect the wiring plug from the throttle body and then unbolt and remove the throttle body complete

4.4 Remove the hose from the throttle body

4.5a Disconnect the wiring plug and...

4.5b ...remove the hose complete with the throttle body

4.6a Remove the hose clamps and mounting bolt...

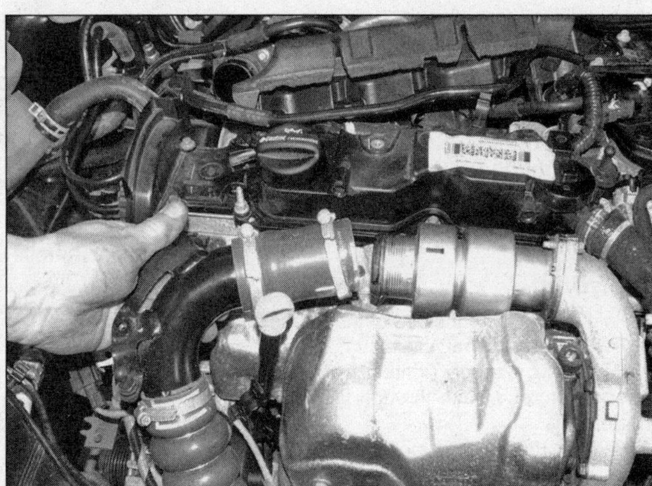
4.6b ... and then remove the hose

with the hose **(see illustrations)**. Plug the openings to prevent contamination.

6 Unbolt and then remove the turbocharger to intercooler hose **(see illustrations)**. Seal the opening to the turbocharger.

7 Remove the sound insulation from the top of the engine **(see illustration)**.

8 Disconnect the wiring plugs from the fuel injectors and camshaft position sensor and then remove the breather hose from the valve cover.

9 Unbolt and then remove the timing belt upper cover.

10 Remove the 9 bolts and then remove the cover **(see illustration)**. Recover the rubber seal.

Refitting

11 Refitting is a reversal of removal, but ensure that the valve cover seal is correctly located in the valve cover **(see illustration)**.

4.7 Remove the insulation

4.10 Remove the valve cover

4.11 Fit the seal correctly

5 Crankshaft pulley – removal and refitting

Removal

1 Jack up and support the front of the vehicle (see *Jacking and vehicle support*).
2 Disconnect the battery (Chapter 5A Section 3) and remove the engine undershield.
3 Remove the starter motor as described in Chapter 5A Section 7.
4 Remove wing liner and then remove the auxiliary drivebelt as described in Chapter 1B Section 24.
5 To lock the crankshaft, fit the Ford special tool 303-393 (or suitable equivalent) to the flywheel ring gear **(see illustration)**.
6 Using a suitable socket and extension bar, unscrew the retaining bolt, remove the washer, then slide the pulley off the end of the crankshaft **(see illustrations)**. If the pulley is tight fit, it can be drawn off the crankshaft using a suitable puller. If a puller is being used, refit the pulley retaining bolt without the washer, to avoid damaging the crankshaft as the puller is tightened.

Caution: Do not touch the outer magnetic sensor ring of the sprocket with your fingers, or allow metallic particles to come into contact with it.

Refitting

7 Refit the pulley to the end of the crankshaft.
8 Refit the crankshaft pulley. Fit a new bolt and retaining washer. Tighten the bolt to the specified torque, then through the specified angle.
9 Remove the locking tool and refit the starter motor
10 Refit and tension the auxiliary drivebelt as described in Chapter 1B Section 24
11 Refit the remaining components in reverse order of removal.

5.5 Install the flywheel locking tool (arrowed)

5.6a Where fitted remove the cover

5.6b Remove the bolt and...

5.6c ...then the pulley

6 Timing belt covers – removal and refitting

Warning: Refer to the precautionary information contained in Section 1 before proceeding.

Removal

Upper cover

1 Remove the engine cover from the top of the engine.
2 Remove the fuel lines and wiring loom from the support bracket next to the cover and then work the bracket free **(see illustrations)**.
3 Undo the 4 bolts and remove the timing belt upper cover **(see illustration)**.

Lower cover

4 Remove the crankshaft pulley as described in Section 5.
5 Position a trolley/workshop jack under the engine. Place a block of wood on the jack head (to help spread the load on the sump), then take the weight of the engine.
6 Prise up the coolant expansion tank and move it to one side – there is no need to drain the coolant.
7 Undo the nuts/bolts, and remove the right-hand engine mounting **(see illustration)**.

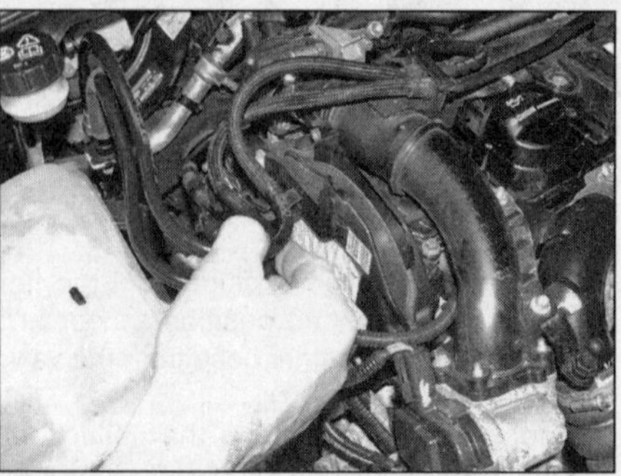

6.2a Release the fuel lines and...

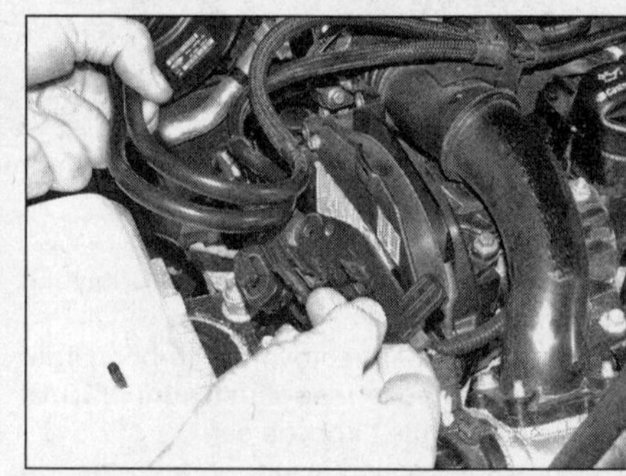

6.2b ...remove the bracket

6.3 Remove the upper cover

6.7 Remove the engine mounting

6.9 Remove the lower timing belt cover from below

7.4 Remove the wing liner

7.6 Undo the bolt (arrowed) and remove the crankshaft position sensor

8 Whilst not strictly necessary access is greatly improved if the mounting bracket is removed from the engine.

9 Undo the 4 bolts and remove the lower cover **(see illustration)**.

Refitting

10 Refitting of all the covers is a reversal of the relevant removal procedure, ensuring that each cover section is correctly located, and that the cover retaining bolts are securely tightened. Ensure that all disturbed hoses are reconnected and retained by their relevant clips.

7 Timing belt – removal, inspection, refitting and tensioning

General

1 The timing belt drives the camshaft, high-pressure fuel pump, and coolant pump from a toothed sprocket on the end of the crankshaft. If the belt breaks or slips in service, the pistons are likely to hit the valve heads, resulting in expensive damage.

2 The timing belt should be renewed at the specified intervals, or earlier if it is contaminated with oil, or at all noisy in operation (a 'scraping' noise due to uneven wear).

3 If the timing belt is being removed, it is a wise precaution to renew the coolant pump at the same time. This may avoid the need to remove the timing belt again at a later stage, should the coolant pump fail. The timing belt tensioner should always be replaced when a new timing belt is fitted.

Removal

4 Apply the handbrake, then jack up the front of the vehicle and support it on axle stands (see *Jacking and vehicle support*). Remove the front right-hand roadwheel, wing liner **(see illustration)** and the engine undershield.

5 Remove the upper and lower timing belt covers, as described in Section 6.

6 Undo the bolt and remove the crankshaft position sensor adjacent to the crankshaft sprocket flange, and move it to one side **(see illustration)**.

7 Undo the retaining bolt and remove the timing belt protection bracket, again, adjacent to the crankshaft sprocket flange **(see illustration)**.

8 Lock the crankshaft and camshaft in the correct position as described in Section 3. If necessary, temporarily refit the crankshaft pulley bolt to enable the crankshaft to be rotated.

9 Insert a hexagon key into the belt tensioner pulley centre, slacken the pulley bolt, and allow the tensioner to rotate, relieving the belt tension **(see illustration)**. With the belt slack, temporarily tighten the pulley bolt.

10 Note its routing, then remove the timing belt from the sprockets **(see illustration)**.

Inspection

11 Renew the belt as a matter of course, regardless of its apparent condition. The cost of a new belt is nothing compared with the cost of repairs should the belt break in service. If signs of oil contamination are found, trace the source of the oil leak and rectify it. Wash down the engine timing belt area and all related components, to remove all traces of oil. The tensioner must always be replaced. Check that the idler pulleys rotate freely without any sign of roughness, and also check that the coolant pump pulley rotates freely. It is highly recommended that both the coolant pump and the idler pulley are replaced at the same time as the timing belt and tensioner.

Refitting and tensioning

12 Commence refitting by ensuring that the crankshaft, camshaft and fuel pump sprocket timing pins are in position as described in Section 3.

13 Locate the timing belt on the crankshaft sprocket, then keeping it taut, locate it around the idler pulley, camshaft sprocket, high-pressure pump sprocket, coolant

7.7 Remove the timing belt protection bracket

7.9 Slacken the bolt and allow the tensioner to rotate, relieving the tension on the belt

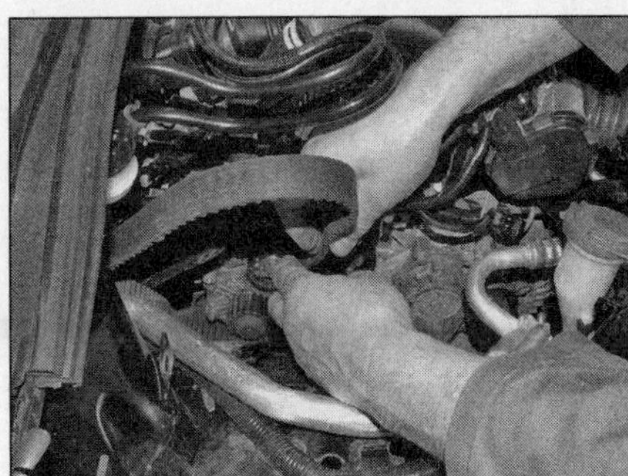
7.10 Remove the timing belt

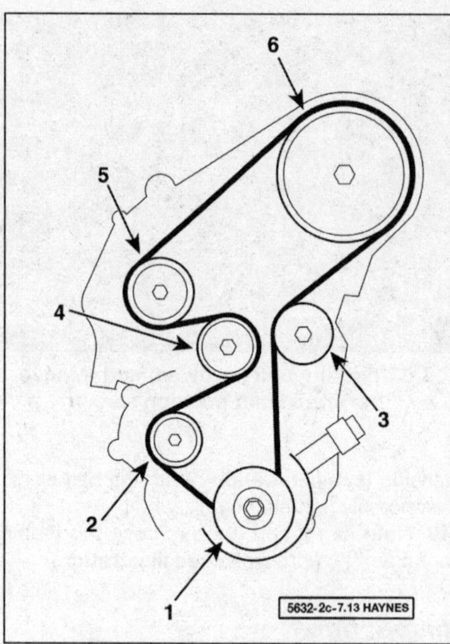

7.13 Timing belt routing

1 Crankshaft *4 Tensioner*
2 Waterpump *5 Fuel pump*
3 Idler *6 Camshaft*

pump sprocket, and the tensioner roller **(see illustration)**.

14 Refit the timing belt protection bracket and tighten the retaining bolt securely.

15 Slacken the tensioner pulley bolt, and using a hexagonal key, rotate the tensioner anti-clockwise, which moves the index arm clockwise, until the index arm is aligned as shown **(see illustration)**.

16 Remove the camshaft, crankshaft and fuel pump sprocket (where applicable) timing pins and, using a socket on the crankshaft pulley bolt, rotate the crankshaft clockwise 10 complete revolutions. Refit the crankshaft and camshaft locking pins.

17 Check that the tensioner index arm is still aligned between the edges of the area shown **(see illustration 7.15)**. If it is not, remove and belt and begin the refitting process again, starting at Paragraph 12.

18 The remainder of refitting is a reversal of removal. Tighten all fasteners to the specified torque where given.

7.15 The index arm must align with the lug (arrowed)

8 Timing belt sprockets and tensioner – removal and refitting

Camshaft sprocket

Removal

1 Remove the timing belt as described in Section 7.

2 Remove the locking tool from the camshaft sprocket/hub. Slacken the sprocket hub retaining bolt. To prevent the camshaft rotating as the bolt is slackened, a sprocket holding tool will be required. In the absence of the special Ford tool, an acceptable substitute can be fabricated at home (see **Tool Tip 1**). Do not attempt to use the engine assembly/valve timing locking tool to prevent the sprocket from rotating whilst the bolt is slackened.

3 Remove the sprocket hub retaining bolt, and slide the sprocket and hub off the end of the camshaft.

4 Clean the camshaft sprocket thoroughly, and renew it if there are any signs of wear, damage or cracks.

Refitting

5 Refit the camshaft sprocket to the camshaft **(see illustration)**.

6 Refit the sprocket hub retaining bolt. Tighten the bolt to the specified torque, preventing the camshaft from turning as during removal.

7 Align the engine assembly/valve timing slot in the camshaft sprocket hub with the hole in the cylinder head and refit the timing pin to lock the camshaft in position.

A sprocket holding tool can be made from two lengths of steel strip bolted together to form a forked end. Drill holes and insert bolts in the ends of the fork to engage with the sprocket spokes.

8 Fit the timing belt around the pump sprocket and camshaft sprocket, and tension the timing belt as described in Section 7.

Crankshaft sprocket

Removal

9 Remove the timing belt as described in Section 7.

10 Check that the engine assembly/valve timing holes are still aligned as described in Section 3, and the camshaft sprocket and flywheel are locked in position.

11 Slide the sprocket off the end of the crankshaft and collect the Woodruff key **(see illustrations)**.

12 Examine the crankshaft oil seal for signs of oil leakage and, if necessary, renew it as described in Section 14.

13 Clean the crankshaft sprocket thoroughly, and renew it if there are any signs of wear, damage or cracks. Recover the crankshaft locating key.

Refitting

14 Refit the key to the end of the crankshaft, then refit the crankshaft sprocket (with the flange facing the crankshaft pulley).

15 Fit the timing belt around the crankshaft

8.5 Ensure the lug on the sprocket hub engages with the slot on the end of the camshaft (arrowed)

8.11a Slide the sprocket from the crankshaft...

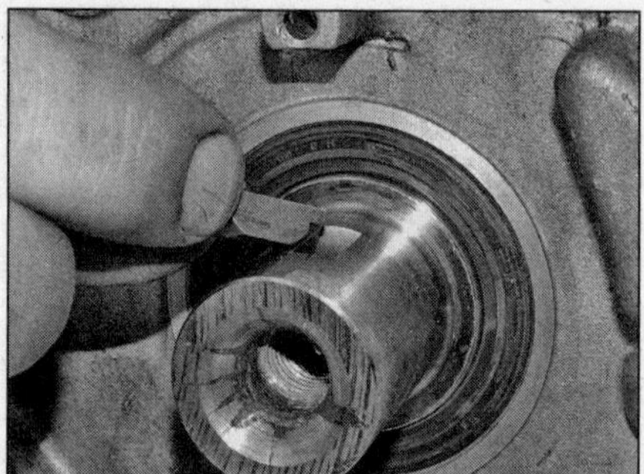

8.11b ...and recover the Woodruff key

TOOL TiP 2

Make a sprocket releasing tool from a short strip of steel. Drill two holes in the strip to correspond with the two holes in the sprocket. Drill a third hole just large enough to accept the flats of the sprocket retaining nut.

sprocket, and tension the timing belt as described in Section 7.

Fuel pump sprocket

Removal

16 Remove the timing belt as described in Section 7.

17 Using a suitable socket, undo the pump sprocket retaining nut. The sprocket can be held stationary by inserting a suitably-sized locking pin, drill or rod through the slot in the sprocket, and into the corresponding hole in the backplate, or by using a suitable forked tool engaged with the holes in the sprocket (see **Tool Tip 1**).

18 The pump sprocket is a taper fit on the pump shaft and it will be necessary to make up another tool to release it from the taper (see **Tool Tip 2**).

19 Partially unscrew the sprocket retaining nut, fit the home-made tool, and secure it to the sprocket with two suitable bolts. Prevent the sprocket from rotating as before, and unscrew the sprocket retaining nut. The nut will bear against the tool as it is undone, forcing the sprocket off the shaft taper. Once the taper is released, remove the tool, unscrew the nut fully, and remove the sprocket from the pump shaft.

9.4 Remove the vacuum pump

8.25 Remove the tensioner

20 Clean the sprocket thoroughly, and renew it if there are any signs of wear, damage or cracks.

Refitting

21 Refit the pump sprocket and retaining nut, and tighten the nut to the specified torque. Prevent the sprocket rotating as the nut is tightened using the sprocket holding tool.

22 Refit the timing belt as described in Section 7.

Coolant pump sprocket

23 The coolant pump sprocket is integral with the pump, and cannot be removed. Coolant pump removal is described in Chapter 3.

Tensioner pulley

Removal

24 Remove the timing belt as described in Section 7.

25 Remove the tensioner pulley retaining bolt, and then remove the tensioner **(see illustration)**.

26 Clean the tensioner pulley, but do not use any strong solvent which may enter the pulley bearings. Check that the pulley rotates freely, with no sign of stiffness or free play. The pulley should always be replaced when the timing belt is replaced.

27 Examine the pulley mounting stud for signs of damage and if necessary, renew it.

Refitting

28 Refitting is a reversal of removal.

9.6 Remove the camshaft position sensor (arrowed)

8.31 Timing belt idler pulley retaining nut (arrowed)

29 Refit the timing belt as described in Section 7.

Idler pulley

Removal

30 Remove the timing belt as described in Section 7.

31 Undo the retaining bolt/nut and withdraw the idler pulley from the engine **(see illustration)**.

32 Clean the idler pulley, but do not use any strong solvent which may enter the bearings. Check that the pulley rotates freely, with no sign of stiffness or free play. Renew the idler pulley if there is any doubt about its condition, or if there are any obvious signs of wear or damage.

Refitting

33 Locate the idler pulley on the engine, and fit the retaining bolt/nut. Tighten the bolt/nut to the specified torque.

34 Refit the timing belt as described in Section 7.

9 Camshaft, rocker arms and hydraulic tappets – removal, inspection and refitting

Removal

1 Remove the cylinder head cover/manifold as described in Section 4.

2 Remove the timing belt (Section 7) and the camshaft sprocket as described in Section 8.

3 Refit the right-hand engine mounting, but only tighten the bolts moderately; this will keep the engine supported during the camshaft removal.

4 Undo the bolts and remove the vacuum pump (see Chapter 9 Section 23). Recover the pump O-ring seals **(see illustration)**.

5 Unbolt the fuel filter (see Chapter 1B Section 21) and move it to one side.

6 Disconnect the wiring plug from the camshaft position sensor **(see illustration)**. Unbolt and remove the sensor from the bearing ladder.

7 Working in reverse order to that shown **(see illustration 9.22)** remove the retaining bolts

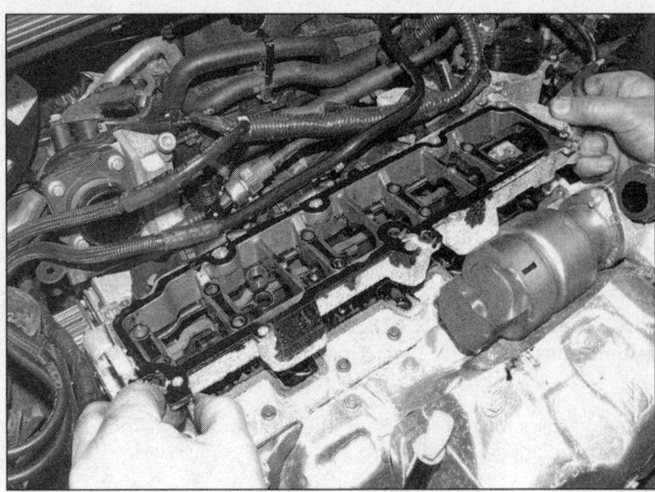

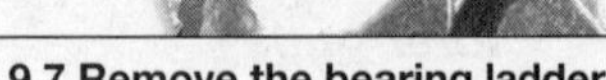

9.7 Remove the bearing ladder

9.8 Remove the camshaft

and then remove camshaft bearing cap ladder **(see illustration)**.

8 Lift out the camshaft **(see illustration)** and dispose of the oil seal. A new one will be required.

9 Obtain 8 small, clean plastic containers, and number them 1 to 4 inlet and 1 to 4 exhaust; alternatively, divide a larger container into 8 compartments.

10 Lift out each rocker arm. Place the rocker arms in their respective positions in the box or containers **(see illustration)**.

11 A compartmentalised container filled with engine oil is now required to retain the hydraulic tappets while they are removed from the cylinder head. Withdraw each hydraulic follower **(see illustration)** and place it in the container, keeping them each identified for correct refitting. The tappets must be totally submerged in the oil to prevent air entering them.

Inspection

12 Inspect the cam lobes and the camshaft bearing journals for scoring or other visible evidence of wear. Once the surface hardening of the cam lobes has been eroded, wear will occur at an accelerated rate. **Note:** *If these symptoms are visible on the tips of the camshaft lobes, check the corresponding rocker arm, as it will probably be worn as well.*

9.10 Remove the rocker arms (cam followers)

9.11 Use long nose pliers to remove the hydraulic tappets

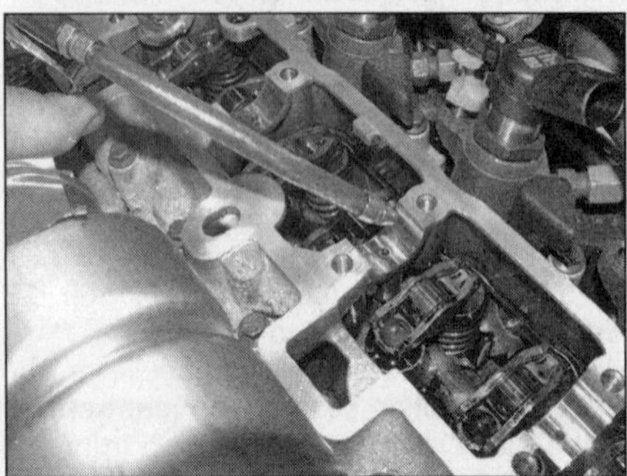

9.19 Lubricate the bearing surfaces

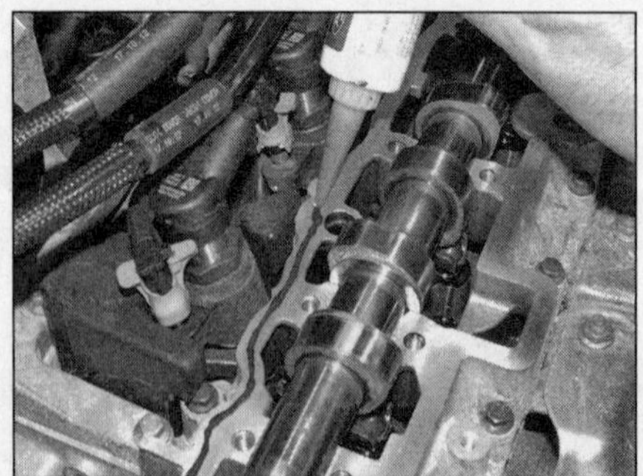

9.20 Apply sealant to the camshaft housing

13 Examine the condition of the bearing surfaces in the cylinder head and camshaft bearing housing. If wear is evident, the cylinder head and bearing housing will both have to be renewed, as they are a matched assembly.

14 Inspect the rocker arms and tappets for scuffing, cracking or other damage and renew any components as necessary. Also check the condition of the tappet bores in the cylinder head. As with the camshafts, any wear in this area will necessitate cylinder head renewal.

Refitting

15 Thoroughly clean the sealant from the mating surfaces of the cylinder head and camshaft bearing housing. Use a suitable liquid gasket dissolving agent (available from Ford dealers) together with a soft putty knife; do not use a metal scraper or the faces will be damaged. As there is no conventional gasket used, the cleanliness of the mating faces is of the utmost importance.

16 Clean off any oil, dirt or grease from both components and dry with a clean lint-free cloth. Ensure that all the oilways are completely clean.

17 Liberally lubricate the hydraulic tappet bores in the cylinder head with clean engine oil.

18 Insert the hydraulic tappets into their original bores in the cylinder head unless they have been renewed.

19 Lubricate the rocker arms and place them over their respective tappets and valve stems. Lubricate the bearing surfaces **(see illustration)** and then refit the camshaft.

20 Apply a thin bead of silicone sealant (Ford part No WSE-M4G323-A4) to the mating surface of the camshaft cover/bearing ladder as shown **(see illustration)**.

9.21 Refit the bearing ladder

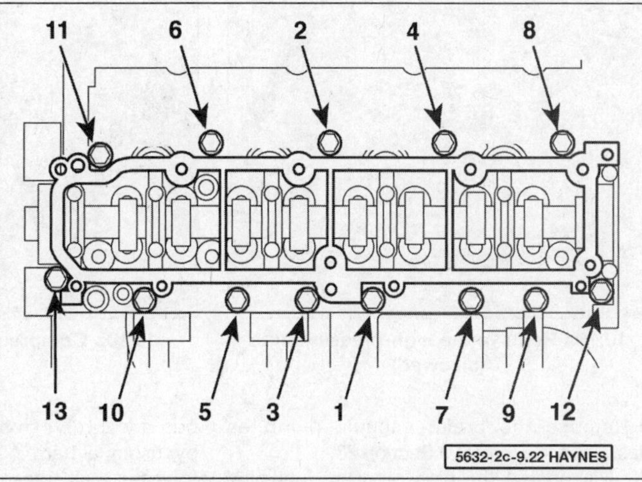

9.22 Tighten the bolts to the specified torque in the order shown

21 Assembly the bearing ladder within 10 minutes of applying the sealant **(see illustration)**. Ford technicians use a special tool (303-245) to align the bearing ladder, however 2 suitable bolts (with their heads and threads cut off) can be used if the tool is not available.

22 Tighten the bolts to the specified torque in sequence **(see illustration)**.

23 Fit a new camshaft oil seal as described in Section 14.

10.2 Remove the engine cover

24 Refit the camshaft sprocket, and tighten the retaining bolt.

25 Refit the timing belt and temporarily refit the crankshaft pulley bolt – use the old bolt. Rotate the engine at least 20 revolutions to allow the oil pump to deliver oil to the camshaft and associated components. Refit the timing belt cover.

26 Refit the remainder of the components in the reverse order of removal.

10 Cylinder head – removal and refitting

Removal

1 Apply the handbrake, then jack up the front of the vehicle and support it on axle stands (see *Jacking and vehicle support*). Remove the front right-hand roadwheel, the engine undershield, and the right-hand front wheel arch liner.

2 Remove the engine cover **(see illustration)** and then disconnect the battery negative lead as described in Chapter 5A Section 3. With reference to Chapter 12 Section 11 remove the wiper arms and screen cowl panel.

3 Drain the cooling system as described in Chapter 1B Section 28.

4 Remove the timing belt, camshaft, rocker arms and hydraulic tappets as described in Section 9.

5 Remove the turbocharger and exhaust manifold as described in Chapter 4B.

6 Unbolt the fuel filter assembly (and move it to one side) and the remove the glow plugs as described in Chapter 5A Section 9.

7 Undo the upper mounting bolts, and pivot the alternator away from the engine, undo the oil dipstick guide tube bolt, then undo the bolts securing the alternator mounting bracket to the cylinder head/block **(see illustration)**.

8 Undo the coolant outlet housing (left-hand end of the cylinder head) retaining bolts, slacken the two bolts securing the housing support bracket to the top of the transmission bellhousing, and move the outlet housing away from the cylinder head a little **(see illustration)**. There is no need to disconnect the hoses.

10.8 Access to the coolant outlet housing will be improved if the vacuum pump is removed first

10.7 The engine oil level dipstick guide tube is secured to the alternator bracket by a Torx bolt (arrowed)

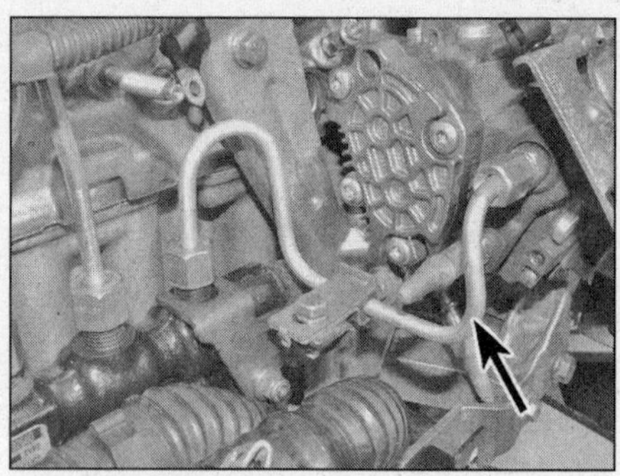
10.10a Remove the high-pressure pipe (arrowed)

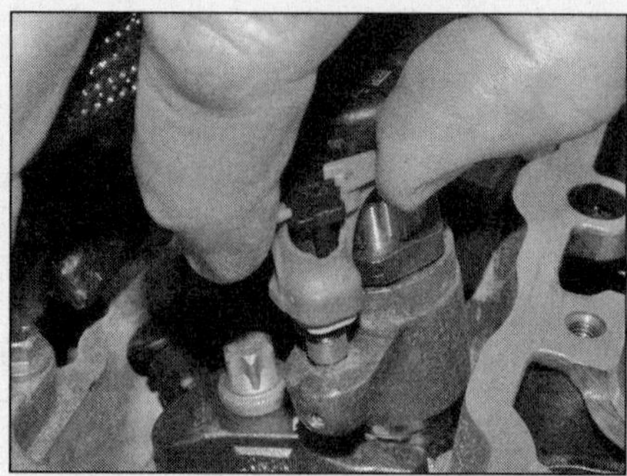
10.10b Compress the collars and...

10.10c ...remove the fuel bleed hoses from the injectors

9 Remove the brake vacuum pump as described in Chapter 9 Section 23.

10 Disconnect the high-pressure fuel pipe from the common rail to the pump, and disconnect the fuel supply and return hoses. Where fitted, remove the bracket at the rear of the pump, then undo the bolt/nut and remove the pump and mounting bracket as an assembly **(see illustrations)**. Immediately seal all the openings in the fuel system. Note that a new high-pressure pipe must be fitted – see Chapter 4B.

11 Unbolt the EGR pipe and inlet duct from the rear of the cylinder head.

12 Check that no components or electrical connectors are still fitted to the cylinder head.

13 Working in the reverse of the sequence shown **(see illustration 10.32)** undo the cylinder head bolts. Discard the bolts – new ones must be fitted.

14 Release the cylinder head from the cylinder block and location dowels by rocking it. The Ford tool for doing this consists simply of two metal rods with 90-degree angled ends **(see illustration)**. Do not prise between the mating faces of the cylinder head and block, as this may damage the gasket faces.

15 Lift the cylinder head from the block, and recover the gasket.

Preparation for refitting

16 The mating faces of the cylinder head and cylinder block must be perfectly clean before refitting the head. Ford recommend the use of a scouring agent for this purpose, but acceptable results can be achieved by using a hard plastic or wood scraper to remove all traces of gasket and carbon. The same method can be used to clean the piston crowns. Take particular care to avoid scoring or gouging the cylinder head/cylinder block mating surfaces during the cleaning operations, as aluminium alloy is easily damaged. Make sure that the carbon is not allowed to enter the oil and water passages – this is particularly important for the lubrication system, as carbon could block the oil supply to the engine's components. Using adhesive tape and paper, seal the water, oil and bolt holes in the cylinder block. To prevent carbon entering the gap between the pistons and bores, smear a little grease in the gap. After cleaning each piston, use a small brush to remove all traces of grease and carbon from the gap, then wipe away the remainder with a clean rag.

17 Check the mating surfaces of the cylinder block and the cylinder head for nicks, deep scratches and other damage. If slight, they may be removed carefully with a file, but if excessive, machining may be the only alternative to renewal. If warpage of the cylinder head gasket surface is suspected, use a straight-edge to check it for distortion. Refer to Part E of this Chapter if necessary.

18 Thoroughly clean the threads of the cylinder head bolt holes in the cylinder block. Ensure that the bolts run freely in their threads, and that all traces of oil and water are removed from each bolt hole. If required, pull the oil feed non-return valve from the cylinder head, and check the ball moves freely. Push a new valve into place if necessary **(see illustrations)**.

Gasket selection

19 The gasket thickness is indicated by notches/holes on the front edge of the gasket. If the crankshaft or pistons/connecting rods have not been disturbed, fit a new gasket with the same number of notches/holes as the previous one. If the crankshaft/piston or connecting rods have been disturbed, it's necessary to work out the piston protrusion as follows:

20 Remove the crankshaft timing pin, then turn the crankshaft until pistons 1 and 4 are at TDC (Top Dead Centre). Position a dial test indicator (dial gauge) on the cylinder block adjacent to the rear of No 1 piston, and zero it on the block face. Transfer the probe to the crown of No 1 piston (10.0 mm in from the rear edge), then slowly turn the crankshaft back-and-forth past TDC, noting the highest reading on the indicator. Record this reading as protrusion A.

21 Repeat the check described in paragraph 18, this time 10.0 mm in from the front edge of the No 1 piston crown. Record this reading as protrusion B.

22 Add protrusion A to protrusion B, then divide the result by 2 to obtain an average reading for piston No 1.

23 Repeat the procedure described in paragraphs 20 to 22 on piston 4, then turn

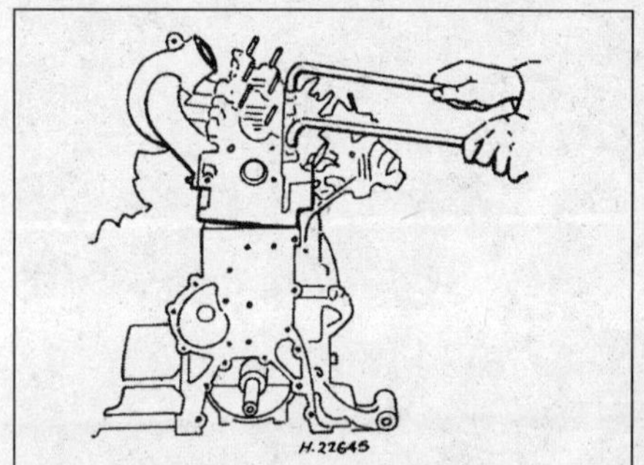

10.14 Free the cylinder head using angled rods

10.18a Pull the non-return valve from the cylinder head...

10.18b ...and push a new one into place

10.23 Measure the piston protrusion using a DTI gauge

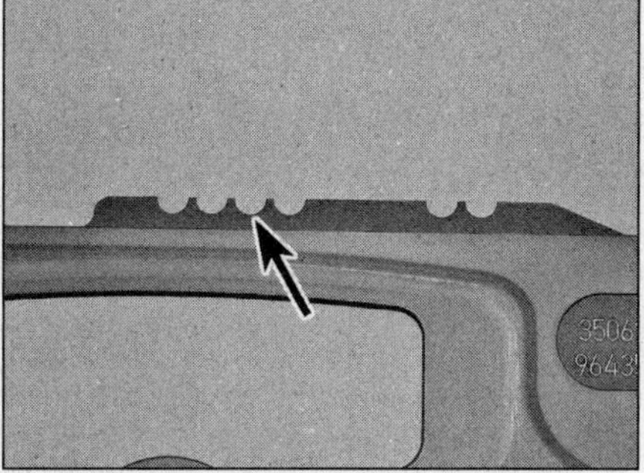
10.25 Cylinder head gasket thickness identification notches (arrowed)

10.28 Ensure the gasket locates over the dowels (arrowed)

the crankshaft through 180° and carry out the procedure on the piston Nos 2 and 3 **(see illustration)**. Check that there is a maximum difference of 0.07 mm protrusion between any two pistons.

24 If a dial test indicator is not available, piston protrusion may be measured using a straight-edge and feeler blades or Vernier calipers. However, this is much less accurate, and cannot therefore be recommended.

25 Note the greatest piston protrusion measurement, and use this to determine the correct cylinder head gasket from the table below. The series of notches/holes on the side of the gasket are used for thickness identification **(see illustration)**.

Refitting

26 Turn the crankshaft and position Nos 1 and 4 pistons at TDC, then turn the crankshaft a quarter turn (90°) anti-clockwise.

27 Thoroughly clean the surfaces of the cylinder head and block.

28 Make sure that the locating dowels are in place, then fit the correct gasket the right way round on the cylinder block **(see illustration)**.

29 Carefully lower the cylinder head onto the gasket and block, making sure that it locates correctly onto the dowels.

30 Apply a smear of grease to the threads, and to the underside of the heads of the new cylinder head bolts.

31 Carefully insert the cylinder head bolts into their holes (do not drop them in) and initially finger-tighten them.

32 Working progressively and in sequence, tighten the cylinder head bolts to their Stage 1 torque setting, using a torque wrench and suitable socket **(see illustration)**.

33 Once all the bolts have been tightened to their Stage 1 torque setting, working again in the specified sequence, tighten each bolt to the specified Stage 2 setting. Finally, angle-tighten the bolts through the specified Stage 3 angle. It is recommended that an angle-measuring gauge is used during this stage of tightening, to ensure accuracy. **Note:** *Retightening of the cylinder head bolts after running the engine is not required.*

34 Refit the hydraulic tappets, rocker arms, and camshaft housing (complete with camshafts) as described in Section 9.

35 Refit the timing belt as described in Section 7.

36 The remainder of refitting is a reversal of removal, noting the following points.

a) *Use a new seal when refitting the coolant outlet housing.*
b) *When refitting a cylinder head, it is good practice to renew the thermostat.*
c) *Refit the camshaft position sensor and set the air gap with reference to Chapter 4B Section 12.*
d) *Tighten all fasteners to the specified torque where given.*
e) *Refill the cooling system as described in Chapter 1B Section 28.*
f) *The engine may run erratically for the first few miles, until the engine management ECM relearns its stored values.*

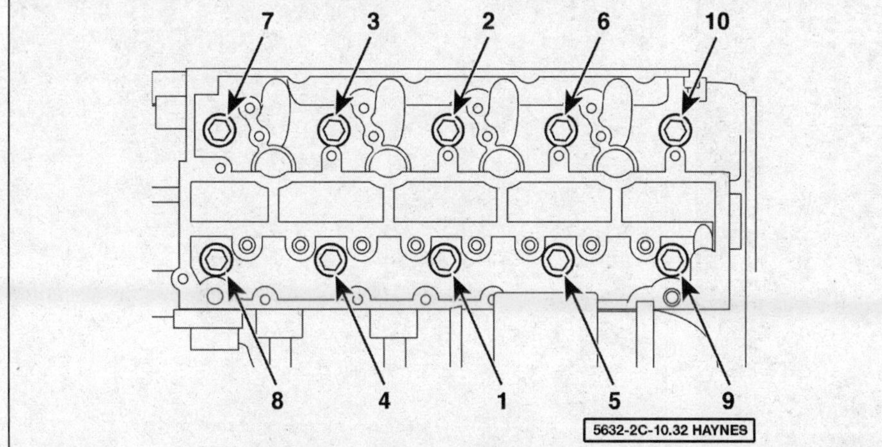

10.32 Cylinder head bolt tightening sequence

11 Sump – removal and refitting

Removal

1 Drain the engine oil, then clean and refit the engine oil drain plug, tightening it securely. If the engine is nearing its service interval when the oil and filter are due for renewal, it is recommended that the filter is also removed, and a new one fitted. After reassembly, the engine can then be refilled with fresh oil. Refer to Chapter 1B Section 6 for further information.

2 Apply the handbrake, then jack up the front of the vehicle and support it on axle stands (see *Jacking and vehicle support*). Undo the bolts and remove the engine undershield.

3 Remove the exhaust front pipe as described in Chapter 4B Section 17.

4 Where necessary, disconnect the wiring connector from the oil temperature sender unit, which is screwed into the sump.

5 Progressively slacken and remove all the sump retaining bolts/nuts. Since the sump bolts vary in length, remove each bolt in turn, and store it in its correct fitted order by pushing it through a clearly-marked cardboard template. This will avoid the possibility of installing the bolts in the wrong locations on refitting.

6 Try to break the joint by striking the sump with the palm of your hand, then lower and withdraw the sump from under the car. If the sump is stuck (which is quite likely) use a putty knife or similar, carefully inserted between the sump and block. Ease the knife along the joint until the sump is released. While the sump is removed, take the opportunity to check the oil pump pick-up/strainer for signs of clogging or splitting. If necessary, remove the pump as

11.8 Apply a bead of sealant to the sump or crankcase mating surface. Ensure the sealant is applied to the inside of the retaining bolt holes

11.9 Refit the sump and tighten the bolts

described in Section 12, and clean or renew the strainer.

Refitting

7 Clean all traces of sealant from the mating surfaces of the cylinder block/crankcase and sump, then use a clean rag to wipe out the sump and the engine's interior.

8 Ensure that the sump mating surfaces are clean and dry, then apply a 3mm diameter bead of sealant (Ford part No WSE-M4G323-A4) to the sump mating surface **(see illustration)**. The sealant must be applied to the Inside of the bolt holes. Note that the sump must be installed within 10 minutes of applying the sealant, and the bolts tightened within a further 5 minutes.

9 Offer up the sump to the cylinder block/crankcase. Refit its retaining bolts/nuts, ensuring that each bolt is screwed into its original location. Tighten the bolts evenly and progressively to the specified torque setting **(see illustration)**.

10 Reconnect the wiring connector to the oil temperature sensor (where fitted).

11 Lower the vehicle to the ground, wait at least 30 minutes (to allow the sealant to set) and then refill the engine with oil as described in Chapter 1B Section 6.

12 Oil pump – removal, inspection and refitting

Removal

1 Remove the sump as described in Section 11.

2 Remove the crankshaft sprocket as described in Section 8. Recover the locating key from the crankshaft.

3 Disconnect the wiring plug, undo the bolts and remove the crankshaft position sensor, located on the right-hand end of the cylinder block.

4 Undo the three bolts and remove the oil pump pick-up tube from the pump/block **(see illustration)**. Discard the oil seal, a new one must be fitted.

12.4 Oil pick-up tube bolts (arrowed)

5 Undo the 8 bolts, and remove the oil pump **(see illustration)**.

Inspection

6 Undo and remove the Torx bolts securing the cover to the oil pump **(see illustration)**.

12.5 Oil pump retaining bolts (arrowed)

12.6 Undo the Torx bolts and remove the pump cover

12.7a Remove the circlip...

12.7b ...cap...

12.7c ...spring...

12.7d ...and piston

12.11 Apply a bead of sealant to the cylinder block mating surface

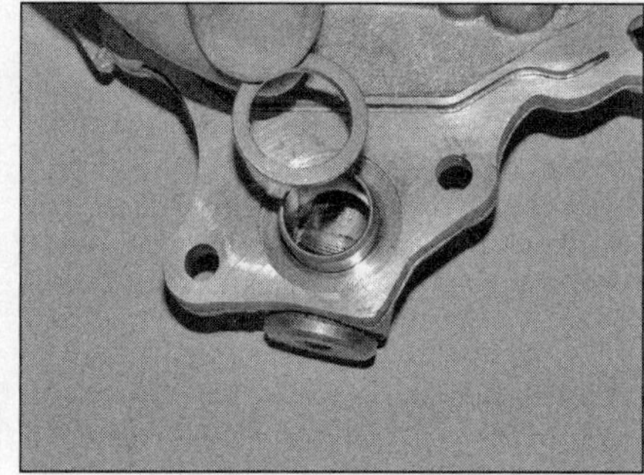

12.12a Fit a new seal...

Examine the pump rotors and body for signs of wear and damage. If worn, the complete pump must be renewed.

7 Remove the circlip, and extract the cap, valve piston and spring, noting which way around they are fitted **(see illustrations)**. The condition of the relief valve spring can only be measured by comparing it with a new one; if there is any doubt about its condition, it should also be renewed.

8 Refit the relief valve piston and spring, then secure them in place with the circlip.

9 Refit the cover to the oil pump, and tighten the Torx bolts securely.

Refitting

10 Remove all traces of sealant, and thoroughly clean the mating surfaces of the oil pump and cylinder block.

11 Apply a 4 mm diameter bead of silicone sealant to the mating face of the cylinder block **(see illustration)**. Ensure that no sealant enters any of the holes in the block.

12 With a new oil seal fitted, refit the oil pump over the end of the crankshaft, aligning the flats in the pump drive gear with the flats machined in the crankshaft **(see illustrations)**. Note that new oil pumps are supplied with the oil seal already fitted, and a seal protector sleeve. The sleeve fits over the end of the crankshaft to protect the seal as the pump is fitted.

13 Install the oil pump bolts and tighten them to the specified torque.

14 Refit the oil pick-up tube to the pump/cylinder block using a new O-ring seal. Ensure the oil dipstick guide tube is correctly refitted.

15 Refit the woodruff key to the crankshaft, and slide the crankshaft sprocket into place.

16 The remainder of refitting is a reversal of removal.

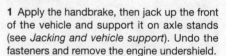

13 Oil cooler – removal and refitting

Removal

1 Apply the handbrake, then jack up the front of the vehicle and support it on axle stands (see *Jacking and vehicle support*). Undo the fasteners and remove the engine undershield.

2 The oil cooler is fitted to the front of the oil filter housing. Drain the coolant as described in Section 13.

3 Drain the engine oil as described in Chapter 1B Section 6, or be prepared for fluid spillage.

4 Undo the bolts/stud and remove the oil cooler **(see illustration)**. Recover the gasket.

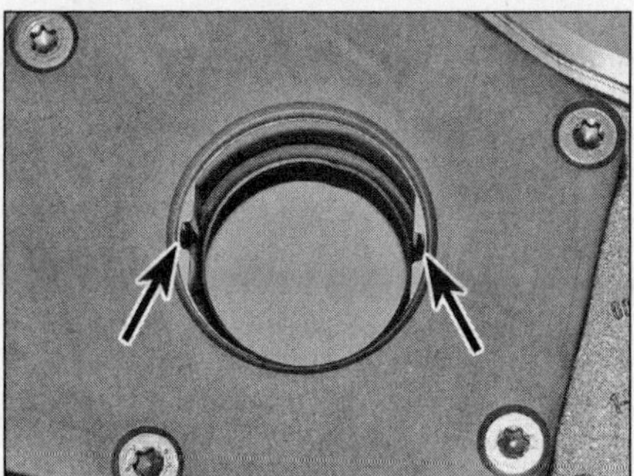

12.12b ...align the pump gear flats (arrowed)...

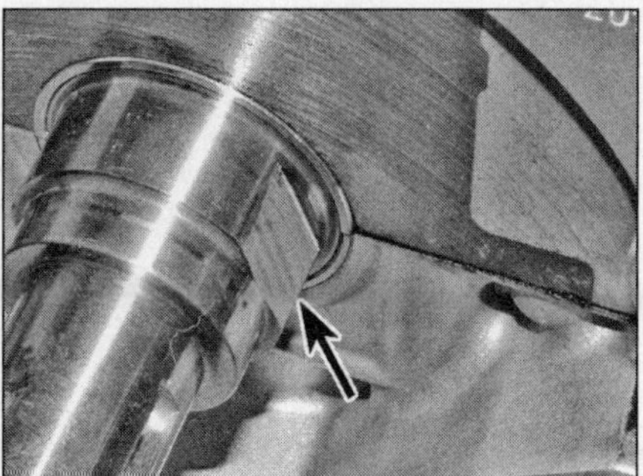

12.12c ...with those of the crankshaft (arrowed)

13.4 Undo the oil cooler bolts/stud (arrowed)

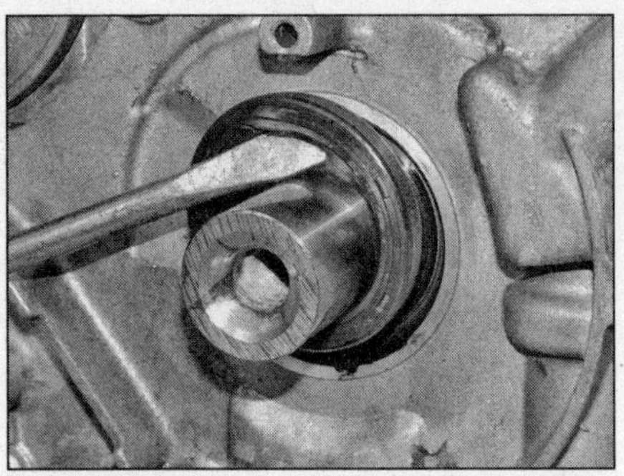
14.3 Take great care not to mark the crankshaft whilst levering out the oil seal

14.5a Slide the seal and protective sleeve over the end of the crankshaft...

14.5b ...and press the seal into place

Refitting

5 Fit a new gasket into the recesses in the oil filter housing, and refit the cooler. Tighten the bolts securely.

6 Refill or top-up the cooling system and engine oil level as described in Chapter 0 Section 5. Start the engine, and check the oil cooler for signs of leakage.

14 Oil seals – renewal

Crankshaft

Right-hand oil seal

1 Remove the crankshaft sprocket and Woodruff key as described in Section 8.

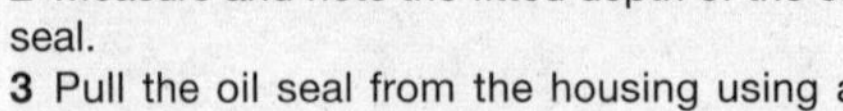

2 Measure and note the fitted depth of the oil seal.

3 Pull the oil seal from the housing using a screwdriver. Alternatively, drill a small hole in the oil seal, and use a self-tapping screw and a pair of pliers to remove it **(see illustration)**.

4 Clean the oil seal housing and the crankshaft sealing surface.

5 The new seal should be supplied with a protective sleeve, which fits over the end of the crankshaft to prevent any damage to the seal lip. With the sleeve in place, press the seal (open end first) into the pump to the previously-noted depth, using a suitable tube or socket **(see illustrations)**.

6 Where applicable, remove the plastic sleeve from the end of the crankshaft.

7 Refit the crankshaft sprocket as described in Section 8.

Left-hand oil seal

8 Remove the flywheel, as described in Section 16.

9 Measure and note the fitted depth of the oil seal.

10 Pull the oil seal from the housing using a screwdriver. Alternatively, drill a small hole in the oil seal, and use a self-tapping screw and a pair of pliers to remove it **(see illustration 14.3)**.

11 Clean the oil seal housing and the crankshaft sealing surface.

12 The new seal should be supplied with a protective sleeve, which fits over the end of the crankshaft to prevent any damage to the seal lip **(see illustration)**. With the sleeve in place, press the seal (open end first) into the housing to the previously-noted depth, using a suitable tube or socket.

13 Where applicable, remove the plastic sleeve from the end of the crankshaft.

14 Refit the flywheel, as described in Section 16.

Camshaft

15 Remove the camshaft sprocket as described in Section 8. In principle there is no need to remove the timing belt completely, but remember that if the belt has been contaminated with oil, it must be renewed.

16 Pull the oil seal from the housing using a hooked instrument. Alternatively, drill a small hole in the oil seal and use a self-tapping screw and a pair of pliers to remove it **(see illustration)**.

17 Clean the oil seal housing and the camshaft sealing surface.

18 Press the seal (open end first) into the housing to the previously-noted depth, using either the correct tool (303-684), a suitable tube or a socket which bears only of the outer edge of the seal **(see illustrations)**. If the seal was supplied with a protective sleeve, remove it.

19 Refit the camshaft sprocket as described in Section 8.

20 Where necessary, fit a new timing belt with reference to Section 7.

14.12 Slide the seal and protective sleeve over the left-hand end of the crankshaft

14.16 Drill a hole, insert a self-tapping screw, and pull the seal from place using pliers

14.18a Use the correct tool to fit the seal...

14.18b ...or a suitable socket

15 Oil pressure switch and level sensor – removal and refitting

Removal

Oil pressure switch

1 The oil pressure switch is located at the front of the cylinder block, adjacent to the oil dipstick guide tube. Note that on some models, access to the switch may be improved if the vehicle is jacked up and supported on axle stands, then undo the bolts and remove the engine undershield so that the switch can be reached from underneath (see *Jacking and vehicle support*).

2 Remove the protective sleeve from the wiring plug (where applicable), then disconnect the wiring from the switch.

3 Unscrew the switch from the cylinder block, and recover the sealing washer **(see illustration)**. Be prepared for oil spillage, and if the switch is to be left removed from the engine for any length of time, plug the hole in the cylinder block.

Oil level sensor

4 The oil level sensor is located at the rear of the cylinder block. Jack up the front of the vehicle and support it securely on axle stands (see *Jacking and vehicle support*). Undo the bolts and remove the engine undershield.

5 Reach up between the driveshaft and the cylinder block, and disconnect the sensor wiring plug **(see illustration)**.

6 Using an open-ended spanner, unscrew the sensor and withdraw it from position.

Refitting

Oil pressure switch

7 Examine the sealing washer for any signs of damage or deterioration, and if necessary renew.

8 Refit the switch, complete with washer, and tighten it to the specified torque where given.

9 Refit the engine undershield, and lower the vehicle to the ground.

Oil level sensor

10 Smear a little silicone sealant on the threads and refit the sensor to the cylinder block, tightening it securely.

11 Reconnect the sensor wiring plug.

12 Refit the engine undershield, and lower the vehicle to the ground.

15.3 The oil pressure switch is located on the front face of the cylinder block (arrowed)

15.5 The oil level sensor is located on the rear face of the cylinder block (arrowed)

16 Flywheel – removal, inspection and refitting

Removal

1 Remove the transmission as described in Chapter 7 Section 7, then remove the clutch assembly as described in Chapter 6 Section 6.

2 Prevent the flywheel from turning. Do not attempt to lock the flywheel in position using the crankshaft pulley locking tool described in Section 3. Insert a 12 mm diameter rod or drill bit through the hole in the flywheel cover casting, and into a slot in the flywheel **(see illustration)**

3 Make alignment marks between the flywheel and crankshaft to aid refitment. Slacken and remove the flywheel retaining bolts, and remove the flywheel from the end of the crankshaft. Be careful not to drop it; it is heavy. If the flywheel locating dowel (where fitted) is a loose fit in the crankshaft end, remove it and store it with the flywheel for safe-keeping. Discard the flywheel bolts; new ones must be used on refitting.

Inspection

4 Examine the flywheel for scoring of the clutch face, and for wear or chipping of the ring gear teeth. If the clutch face is scored, the flywheel may be surface-ground, but renewal is preferable. Seek the advice of a Ford dealer or engine reconditioning specialist to see if machining is possible. If the ring gear is worn or damaged, the flywheel must be renewed, as it is not possible to renew the ring gear separately.

5 All engines are fitted with a dual-mass flywheel. The maximum travel of the primary mass in relation to the secondary must not exceed 15 teeth (or 20 degrees). If in doubt remove the flywheel and have a suitably equipped specialist check the flywheel. Inspect the flywheel for any grease or debris from the interface between the fixed part and the movable part of the flywheel. If any doubt to the condition of the flywheel exists, despite the expense we recommend replacing it.

Refitting

6 Clean the mating surfaces of the flywheel and crankshaft. Remove any remaining locking compound from the threads of the crankshaft holes, using the correct size of tap, if available.

7 If the new flywheel retaining bolts are not supplied with their threads already pre-coated, apply a suitable thread-locking compound to the threads of each bolt.

8 Ensure that the locating dowel is in position. Offer up the flywheel, locating it on the dowel (where fitted), and fit the new retaining bolts. Where no locating dowel is fitted, align the previously-made marks to ensure the flywheel is refitted in its original position.

9 Lock the flywheel using the method employed on dismantling, and tighten the retaining bolts to the specified torque **(see illustration)**.

10 Refit the clutch as described in Chapter 6 Section 6. Remove the flywheel locking tool, and refit the transmission as described in Chapter 7 Section 7.

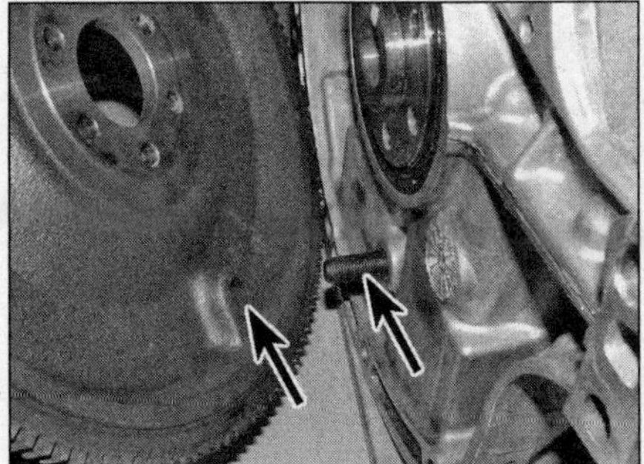

16.2 Lock the flywheel with a 12mm diameter rod or bolt (arrowed)

16.9 Flywheel retaining Torx bolts

17 Engine/transmission mountings – inspection and renewal

General

1 The engine/transmission mountings seldom require attention, but broken or deteriorated mountings should be renewed immediately, or the added strain placed on the driveline components may cause damage or wear.

2 While separate mountings may be removed and refitted individually, if more than one is disturbed at a time – such as if

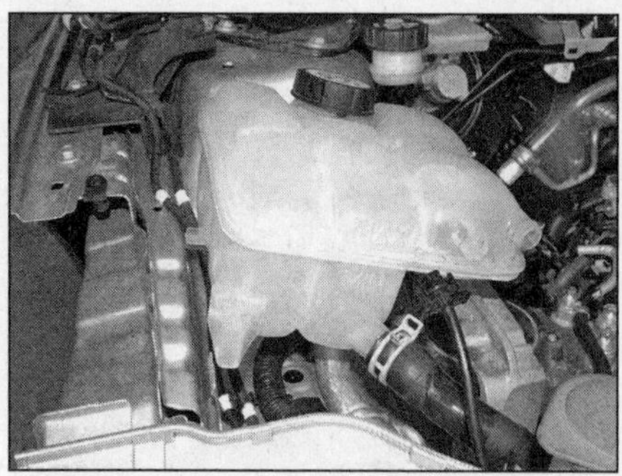
17.8 Move the coolant expansion bottle to the side

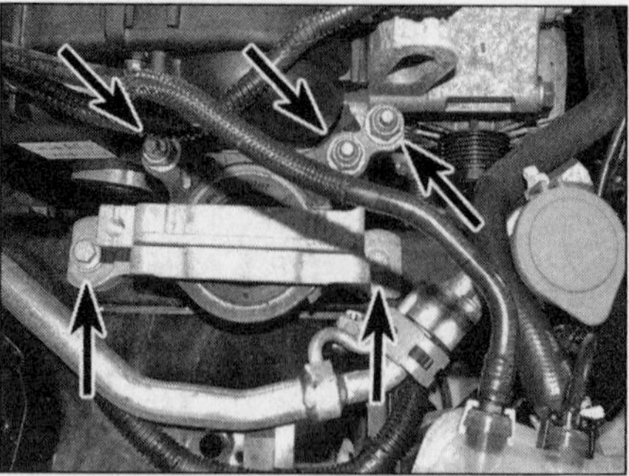
17.10a Undo the bolts (arrowed)...

17.10b ...and remove the mounting

17.14 Remove the battery support panel

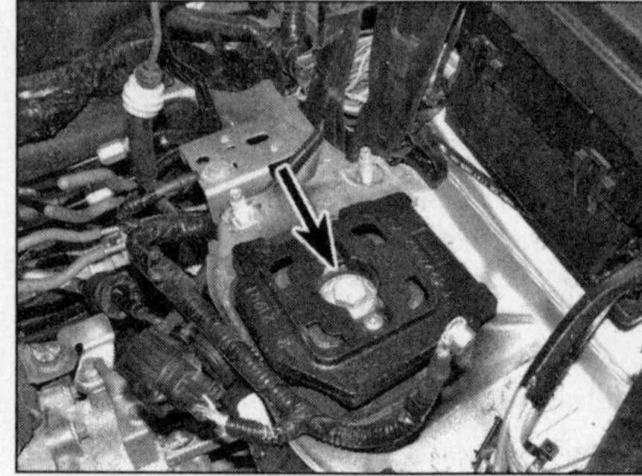
17.15 Remove the centre bolt (arrowed)

the engine/transmission unit is removed from its mountings – they must be reassembled and their fasteners tightened in the position marked on removal.

3 On reassembly, the complete weight of the engine/transmission unit must not be taken by the mountings until all are correctly aligned with the marks made on removal. Tighten the engine/transmission mounting fasteners to their specified torque wrench settings.

Inspection

4 During the check, the engine/transmission unit must be raised slightly, to remove its weight from the mountings.

5 Raise the front of the vehicle, and support it securely on axle stands. Position a jack under the sump, with a large block of wood between the jack head and the sump, then carefully raise the engine/transmission just enough to take the weight off the mountings.

Warning: DO NOT place any part of your body under the engine when it is supported only by a jack.

6 Check the mountings to see if the rubber is cracked, hardened or separated from the metal components. Sometimes the rubber will split right down the centre.

7 Check for relative movement between each mounting's brackets and the engine/transmission or body (use a large screwdriver or lever to attempt to move the mountings). If movement is noted, lower the engine and check-tighten the mounting fasteners.

Renewal

Note: *The following paragraphs assume the engine is supported beneath the sump as described earlier.*

Right-hand mounting

8 Lift up the coolant expansion tank and position it to one side **(see illustration)**. Note there is no need to disconnect the coolant pipes. On some models a vibration damper is fitted to the rear of the mounting. Where fitted unbolt and remove the damper.

9 Mark the position of the mounting on the vehicle on the right-hand inner wing panel, and then undo the 2 bolts securing the mounting.

10 Undo the 3 retaining bolts from the engine side of the mounting and then remove the mounting **(see illustrations)**.

11 Re-align the marks made on removal. Tighten all fasteners to the torque wrench settings specified.

Left-hand mounting

12 Remove the air filter housing as described in Chapter 4B Section 2.

13 Remove the battery as described in Chapter 5A Section 3, then undo the 3 bolts and remove the battery tray. Disconnect any wiring as the tray is withdrawn.

14 Unclip the wiring loom from the battery tray support panel, remove the 4 bolts and withdraw the support panel **(see illustration)**.

15 With the transmission supported, note the position of the mounting then unscrew the centre retaining bolt to release the upper half of the mounting from the transmission **(see illustration)**.

16 On six speed transmissions, lower the transmission slightly to access the 3 mounting bolts on the transmission **(see illustration)**. On five speed transmission access the bolts from the engine bay. Remove the bolts and recover the mounting.

17 Refitting is a reversal of removal. Re-align the mounting in the position noted on removal, then tighten all fasteners to the specified torque wrench settings.

Rear mounting (roll restrictor)

18 Remove the 3 mounting bolts from the transmission. Note, that the bolts are different lengths on five speed transmissions. Remove the single bolt from the subframe **(see illustration)**.

19 With the aid of an assistant pivot the engine (assuming the two main engine mountings are in position) and work the mounting free.

20 On refitting, ensure that the bolts are securely tightened to the specified torque wrench setting.

17.16 Lower the transmission and remove the bolts

17.18 Remove the bolts (arrowed)

Chapter 2 Part E
Engine removal and overhaul procedures

Contents

Degrees of difficulty

Easy, suitable for novice with little experience 	**Fairly easy,** suitable for beginner with some experience	**Fairly difficult,** suitable for competent DIY mechanic	**Difficult,** suitable for experienced DIY mechanic	**Very difficult,** suitable for expert DIY or professional

Specifications

Petrol engines

Valves	
Valve length:	
1.0 litre engines	Not available
1.6 litre engines:	
Inlet	96.95 mm
Exhaust	99.40 mm
Cylinder head	
Maximum permissible gasket surface distortion	0.05 mm
Camshaft endfloat (typical)	0.05 to 0.13 mm
Crankshaft end float:	
1.0 litre engines	0.13 to 0.38 mm
1.6 litre engines	Not available
Torque wrench settings	Refer to Chapter 2A or 2B Specifications

1.5 litre diesel engines

Cylinder head	
Maximum permissible gasket surface distortion	0.025 mm
Camshaft	
Endfloat	0.195 to 0.300 mm
Bearing journal diameter	23.959 to 23.980 mm
Crankshaft	
Endfloat	0.100 to 0.300 mm
Main bearing journal diameter	49.962 to 49.981 mm
Connecting rod journal diameter	44.975 to 44.991 mm
Cylinder block	
Cylinder bore diameter (reboring not possible)	73.5 mm
Main bearing radial clearance	0.017 to 0.043 mm
Connecting rods	
Big-end bore diameter	48.655 to 48.671 mm
Small-end bore diameter	25.000 mm
Connecting rod bearing clearance	0.024 to 0.070 mm
Gudgeon pin length	59.700 to 60.000 mm
Gudgeon pin diameter	24.995 to 25.000 mm
Pistons and piston rings	
Piston diameter	73.336 mm
Piston-to-bore clearance	0.164 to 0.196 mm
Piston ring end gaps – installed:	
Top compression ring	0.200 to 0.350 mm
Second compression ring	0.200 to 0.400 mm
Oil control ring	0.200 to 0.400 mm
Piston ring gap arrangement	120° to each other
Valve stem-to-guide clearance:	
Intake valve	0.103 to 0.118 mm
Exhaust valve	0.113 to 0.128 mm
Torque wrench settings	Refer to Chapter 2C Specifications

1.6 litre diesel engines

Valves	
Valve stem diameter:	
Inlet	5.485 +0.0, -0.015 mm
Exhaust	5.475 +0.0, -0.015 mm
Overall length:	
Inlet	96.43 ± 0.25 mm
Exhaust	96.65 ± 0.2 mm
Cylinder head	
Maximum gasket face distortion	0.025 mm
Crankshaft	
Endfloat	0.100 to 0.300 mm
Main bearing journal diameter	49.962 to 49.981mm
Connecting rod journal diameter	44.975 to 44.991 mm
Cylinder block	
Cylinder bore diameter (reboring not possible)	75.000 to 75.018 mm
Pistons and piston rings	
Piston diameter	74.104 to 74.128 mm
Piston-to-bore clearance	0.164 to 0.196 mm
Piston ring end gaps – installed:	
Top compression ring	0.20 to 0.35 mm
Second compression ring	0.20 to 0.40 mm
Oil control ring	0.85 to 1.00 mm
Piston ring gap arrangement	120° to each other
Torque wrench settings	Refer to Chapter 2D Specifications

1 General Information

1 Included in this Part of Chapter 2 are details of removing the engine/transmission from the car and general overhaul procedures for the cylinder head, cylinder block/crankcase and all other engine internal components.

2 The information given ranges from advice concerning preparation for an overhaul and the purchase of parts, to detailed step-by-step procedures covering removal, inspection, renovation and refitting of engine internal components.

3 After Section 8, all instructions are based on the assumption that the engine has been removed from the car. For information concerning in-car engine repair, as well as the removal and refitting of those external components necessary for full overhaul, refer to Part A, B, C or D of this Chapter (as applicable) and to Section 5. Ignore any preliminary dismantling operations described in Part A, B, C or D that are no longer relevant once the engine has been removed from the car.

4 It should be noted that a full strip down of the engine block on all petrol engines is not possible, since no specifications or torque wrench setting are provided by the manufacturer. On petrol engine therefore do not remove any parts of the engine block apart from the ancillaries (such as the thermostat housing) and those parts covered in the relevant section of Chapters 2A and 2B. Consequently most of this Chapter (apart from work on the cylinder head) is only applicable to diesel engines.

5 Apart from torque wrench settings, which are given at the beginning of Part A, B, C or D (as applicable), all specifications relating to engine overhaul are at the beginning of this Part of Chapter 2.

2 Engine overhaul – general information

1 It is not always easy to determine when, or if, an engine should be completely overhauled, as a number of factors must be considered.

2 High mileage is not necessarily an indication that an overhaul is needed, while low mileage does not preclude the need for an overhaul. Frequency of servicing is probably the most important consideration. An engine which has had regular and frequent oil and filter changes, as well as other required maintenance, should give many thousands of miles of reliable service. Conversely, a neglected engine may require an overhaul very early in its life.

3 Excessive oil consumption is an indication that piston rings, valve seals and/or valve guides are in need of attention. Make sure that oil leaks are not responsible before deciding that the rings and/or guides are worn. Perform a compression test, as described in Part A, B, C or D of this Chapter, to determine the likely cause of the problem.

4 Check the oil pressure with a gauge fitted in place of the oil pressure switch, and compare it with that specified. If it is extremely low, the main and big-end bearings, and/or the oil pump, are probably worn out.

5 Loss of power, rough running, knocking or metallic engine noises, excessive valve gear noise, and high fuel consumption may also point to the need for an overhaul, especially if they are all present at the same time. If a complete service does not cure the situation, major mechanical work is the only solution.

6 An engine overhaul involves restoring all internal parts to the specification of a new engine. During an overhaul, the pistons and the piston rings are renewed. New main and big-end bearings are generally fitted; if necessary, the crankshaft may be renewed to restore the journals. The valves are also serviced as well, since they are usually in less-than-perfect condition at this point. While the engine is being overhauled, other components, such as the distributor, starter and alternator, can be overhauled as well. The end result should be an as-new engine that will give many trouble-free miles.

Note: *Critical cooling system components such as the hoses, thermostat and coolant pump should be renewed when an engine is overhauled. The radiator should be checked carefully, to ensure that it is not clogged or leaking. Also, it is a good idea to renew the oil pump whenever the engine is overhauled.*

7 Before beginning the engine overhaul, read through the entire procedure, to familiarise yourself with the scope and requirements of the job. Overhauling an engine is not difficult if you follow carefully all of the instructions, have the necessary tools and equipment, and pay close attention to all specifications. It can, however, be time-consuming. Plan on the car being off the road for a minimum of two weeks, especially if parts must be taken to an engineering works for repair or reconditioning. Check on the availability of parts and make sure that any necessary special tools and equipment are obtained in advance. Most work can be done with typical hand tools, although a number of precision measuring tools are required for inspecting parts to determine if they must be renewed. Often the engineering works will handle the inspection of parts and offer advice concerning reconditioning and renewal.

8 Always wait until the engine has been completely dismantled, and until all components (especially the cylinder block/crankcase and the crankshaft) have been inspected, before deciding what service and repair operations must be performed by an engineering works. The condition of these components will be the major factor to consider when determining whether to overhaul the original engine, or to buy a reconditioned unit. Do not, therefore, purchase parts or have overhaul work done on other components until they have been thoroughly inspected. As a general rule, time is the primary cost of an overhaul, so it does not pay to fit worn or sub-standard parts.

9 As a final note, to ensure maximum life and minimum trouble from a reconditioned engine, everything must be assembled with care, in a spotlessly-clean environment.

3 Engine/transmission removal – methods and precautions

1 If you have decided that the engine must be removed for overhaul or major repair work, several preliminary steps should be taken.

2 Engine/transmission removal is extremely complicated and involved on these vehicles. It must be stated, that unless the vehicle can be positioned on a ramp, or raised and supported on axle stands over an inspection pit, it will be very difficult to carry out the work involved.

3 Cleaning the engine compartment and engine/transmission before beginning the removal procedure will help keep tools clean and organised.

4 An engine hoist will also be necessary. Make sure the equipment is rated in excess of the combined weight of the engine and transmission. Safety is of primary importance, considering the potential hazards involved in removing the engine/transmission from the car.

5 The help of an assistant is essential. Apart from the safety aspects involved, there are many instances when one person cannot simultaneously perform all of the operations required during engine/transmission removal.

6 Plan the operation ahead of time. Before starting work, arrange for the hire of, or obtain all of the tools and equipment you will need. Some of the equipment necessary to perform engine/transmission removal and installation safely (in addition to an engine hoist) is as follows: a heavy duty trolley jack, complete sets of spanners and sockets as described in the rear of this manual, wooden blocks, and plenty of rags and cleaning solvent for mopping-up spilled oil, coolant and fuel. If the hoist must be hired, make sure that you arrange for it in advance, and perform all of the operations possible without it beforehand. This will save you money and time.

7 Plan for the car to be out of use for quite a while. An engineering machine shop or engine reconditioning specialist will be required to perform some of the work which cannot be accomplished without special equipment. These places often have a busy schedule, so it would be a good idea to consult them before removing the engine, in order to accurately estimate the amount of time required to rebuild or repair components that may need work.

4.1 Remove the battery tray

4.3a Remove the upper section...

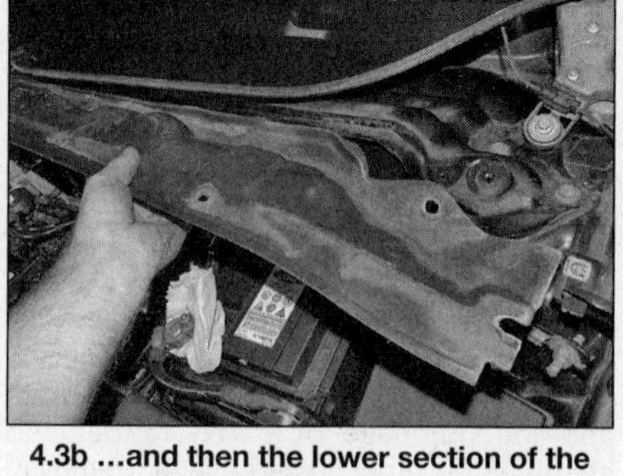
4.3b ...and then the lower section of the panel

8 During the engine/transmission removal procedure, it is advisable to make notes of the locations of all brackets, cable ties, earthing points, etc, as well as how the wiring harnesses, hoses and electrical connections are attached and routed around the engine and engine compartment. An effective way of doing this is to take a series of photographs of the various components before they are disconnected or removed; the resulting photographs will prove invaluable when the engine/transmission is refitted.

9 Always be extremely careful when removing and refitting the engine/transmission. Serious injury can result from careless actions. Plan ahead and take your time, and a job of this nature, although major, can be accomplished successfully.

10 On all Focus models, the engine must be removed complete with the transmission as an assembly. There is insufficient clearance in the engine compartment to remove the engine leaving the transmission in the vehicle. The assembly is removed by raising the front of the vehicle, and lowering the assembly from the engine compartment.

Note: *Such is the complexity of the power unit arrangement on these vehicles, and the variations that may be encountered according to model and optional equipment fitted, that the following should be regarded as a guide to the work involved, rather than a step-by-step procedure. Where differences are encountered, or additional component disconnection or removal is necessary, make notes of the work involved as an aid to refitting.*

4 Engine and transmission – removal, separation and refitting

Removal

1 Remove the battery (see Chapter 5A Section 3), then undo the bolts and remove the battery tray **(see illustration)**.

2 Remove the wiper arms as described in Chapter 12 Section 11.

3 Remove both sections of the windscreen cowl panel **(see illustrations)**.

4 Apply the handbrake, then jack up the front of the vehicle and support it on axle stands (see *Jacking and vehicle support*). Remove both front roadwheels and wheel arch liners. Also remove the undershield from beneath the engine and transmission where fitted.

5 Remove the engine top cover. To improve access, remove the bonnet.

6 Drain the cooling system with reference to Chapter 1A Section 28 or Chapter 1B Section 28.

7 Drain the transmission oil as described in Chapter 7 Section 6 **(see illustration)**. Refit the drain plug, and tighten it to the specified torque setting.

8 If the engine is to be dismantled, drain the engine oil and remove the oil filter as described in Chapter 1A or 1B. Clean and refit the drain plug, tightening it to the specified torque.

9 Refer to Chapter 8 Section 2 and remove both front driveshafts.

10 Remove the air cleaner assembly as described in Chapter 4A Section 5 or Chapter 4B Section 2 (if not already done so).

11 Remove the intercooler as described in Chapter 4A Section 11 or Chapter 4B Section 15.

12 Remove the radiator as described in Chapter 3 Section 7.

13 Refer to Chapter 1A Section 23 or Chapter 1B Section 24 and remove the auxiliary drivebelt.

14 Release the clamp and disconnect the coolant supply hose from the expansion tank.

15 Disconnect the fuel supply pipe(s) at the right-hand side or at the rear of the engine compartment. Plug/cover the openings to prevent contamination.

16 On models fitted with security bolts on the engine ECU, remove the engine management ECU as described in Chapter 4A Section 13 or Chapter 4B Section 12. Where no security bolts are fitted, open the cover and disconnect the wiring plugs.

17 Note their fitted positions, then disconnect the engine/transmission harness wiring plugs and earth connections from the fusebox on the left-hand side of the engine compartment **(see illustrations)**. Make a note of the harness routing. Also trace the wiring connectors back to the transmission and disconnect all engine related wiring and earth leads in this area, including the earth lead on the left-hand suspension turret, and the earth connections on the left-hand chassis member. Check that all the relevant connectors have been disconnected, and that the harness is

4.7 Drain the transmission oil

4.17a Disconnect the main engine wiring loom

4.17b Unbolt and remove the earth connections from the chassis

8.1c On some engines, the valve stem oil seal is integral with the spring seat

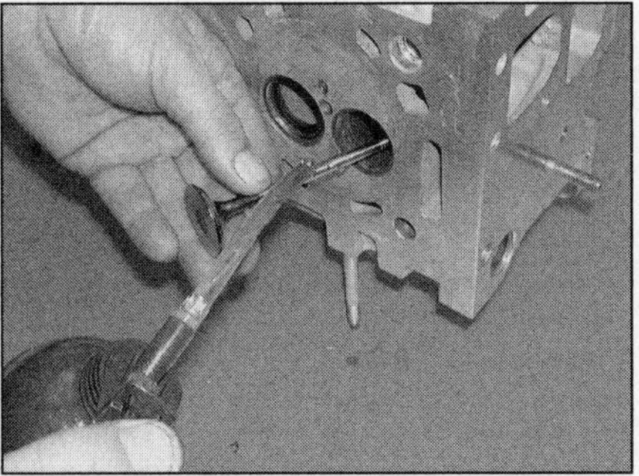
8.2 Lubricate the stem of the valve and insert it into the guide

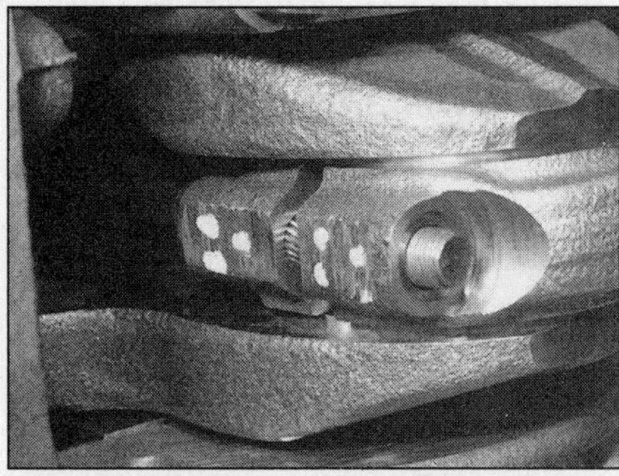
9.3 Connecting rod and big-end bearing cap identification marks (No 3 shown)

2 Lubricate the stem of the first valve, and insert it in the guide **(see illustration)**.

3 Locate the valve spring on top of its seat, then refit the spring retainer.

4 Compress the valve spring, and locate the split collets in the recess in the valve stem. Release the compressor, then repeat the procedure on the remaining valves. Ensure that each valve is inserted into its original location. If new valves are being fitted, insert them into the locations to which they have been ground.

5 With all the valves installed, support the cylinder head and, using a hammer and interposed block of wood, tap the end of each valve stem to settle the components.

6 Refit the camshafts, tappets and rocker arms (as applicable) as described in Part A, B, C or D of this Chapter.

7 Refit any remaining components using the reverse of the removal sequence and with new seals or gaskets as necessary.

8 The cylinder head can then be refitted as described in Part A, B, C or D of this Chapter.

9 Piston/connecting rod assembly – removal

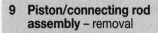

Caution: This procedure is only applicable to diesel engines. Do not remove the pistons or connecting rods from petrol engines.

1 Remove the cylinder head, sump and oil pump as described in Part C or D.

2 If there is a pronounced wear ridge at the top of any bore, it may be necessary to remove it with a scraper or ridge reamer, to avoid piston damage during removal. Such a ridge indicates excessive wear of the cylinder bore.

3 Using quick-drying paint, mark each connecting rod and big-end bearing cap with its respective cylinder number on the flat machined surface provided; if the engine has been dismantled before, note carefully any identifying marks made previously **(see illustration)**.

4 Turn the crankshaft to bring pistons 1 and 4 to BDC (bottom dead centre).

5 Unscrew the nuts or bolts, as applicable from No 1 piston big-end bearing cap. Take off the cap, and recover the bottom half bearing shell **(see illustration)**. If the bearing shells are to be re-used, tape the cap and the shell together.

6 Where applicable, to prevent the possibility of damage to the crankshaft bearing journals, tape over the connecting rod stud threads **(see illustration)**..

7 Using a hammer handle, push the piston up through the bore, and remove it from the top of the cylinder block. Recover the bearing shell, and tape it to the connecting rod for safe-keeping.

8 Loosely refit the big-end cap to the connecting rod, and secure with the nuts/bolts – this will help to keep the components in their correct order.

9 Remove No 4 piston assembly in the same way.

10 Turn the crankshaft through 180° to bring pistons 2 and 3 to BDC (bottom dead centre), and remove them in the same way.

10 Crankshaft – removal

Caution: This procedure is only applicable to diesel engines. Do not remove the crankshaft from petrol engines.

1 Remove the crankshaft sprocket and the oil pump as described in Part C or D, of this Chapter (as applicable).

2 Remove the pistons and connecting rods, as described in Section 9. If no work is to be done on the pistons and connecting rods, there is no need to remove the cylinder head, or to push the pistons out of the cylinder bores. The pistons should just be pushed far enough up the bores so that they are positioned clear of the crankshaft journals.

3 Check the crankshaft endfloat as described in Section 14, then proceed as follows.

4 Working around the inner periphery of the crankcase, unscrew the small bolts securing the crankshaft bearing cap housing to the base of the cylinder block. Note the correct fitted depth of the left-hand crankshaft oil seal in the cylinder block/bearing cap housing.

5 Working in the reverse of the tightening sequence, evenly and progressively slacken the ten large bearing cap housing retaining bolts by a turn at a time. Once all the bolts are loose, remove them from the housing. **Note:** *Prise up the two caps at the flywheel end of the housing to expose the two end main bearing bolts* **(see illustration)**.

9.5 Remove the big-end bearing shell and cap

9.6 To protect the crankshaft journals, tape over the connecting rod stud threads

10.5 Prise up the two caps to expose the main bearing bolts at the flywheel end

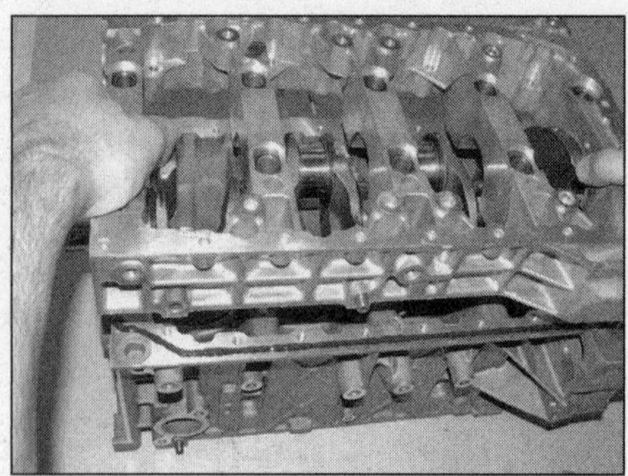
10.6 Remove the crankshaft bearing cap housing

6 With all the retaining bolts removed, tap around the outer periphery of the bearing cap housing using a soft-faced mallet to break the seal between the housing and cylinder block. Once the seal is released and the housing is clear of the locating dowels, lift it up and off the crankshaft and cylinder block **(see illustration)**. Recover the lower main bearing shells, and tape them to their respective locations in the housing. If the two locating dowels are a loose fit, remove them and store them with the housing for safe-keeping.
7 Lift out the crankshaft, and collect the left-hand oil seal.
8 Recover the upper main bearing shells, and store them along with the relevant lower bearing shell. Also recover the two thrustwashers (one fitted either side of No 2 main bearing) from the cylinder block.

11 Cylinder block/crankcase – cleaning and inspection

Cleaning

1 Remove all external components and electrical switches/sensors from the block. For complete cleaning, the core plugs should ideally be removed **(see illustrations)**. Drill a small hole in the plugs, then insert a self-tapping screw into the hole. Pull out the plugs by pulling on the screw with a pair of grips, or by using a slide hammer.
2 Where applicable, undo the retaining bolts and remove the piston oil jet spray tubes from inside the cylinder block **(see illustration)**.
3 Scrape all traces of gasket from the cylinder block/crankcase, and from the main bearing ladder (where fitted), taking care not to damage the gasket/sealing surfaces.
4 Remove all oil gallery plugs (where fitted). The plugs are usually very tight – they may have to be drilled out, and the holes retapped. Use new plugs when reassembling.
5 If any of the castings are extremely dirty, all should be steam-cleaned.
6 After the castings are returned, clean all oil holes and oil galleries one more time. Flush all internal passages with warm water until the water runs clear. Dry thoroughly, and apply a light film of oil to all mating surfaces, to prevent rusting. On cast-iron block engines, also oil the cylinder bores. If you have access to compressed air, use it to speed up the drying process, and to blow out all the oil holes and galleries.

Warning: Wear eye protection when using compressed air.

7 If the castings are not very dirty, you can do an adequate cleaning job with hot (as hot as you can stand), soapy water and a stiff brush. Take plenty of time, and do a thorough job. Regardless of the cleaning method used, be sure to clean all oil holes and galleries very thoroughly, and to dry all components well. On cast-iron block engines, protect the cylinder bores as described above, to prevent rusting.
8 All threaded holes must be clean, to ensure accurate torque readings during reassembly. To clean the threads, run the correct-size tap into each of the holes to remove rust, corrosion, thread sealant or sludge, and to restore damaged threads. If possible, use compressed air to clear the holes of debris produced by this operation.
9 Apply suitable sealant to the new oil gallery plugs, and insert them into the holes in the block. Tighten them securely. Apply suitable sealant to the new core plugs, and insert them into the holes in the block. Tap them into place with a close-fitting tube or socket.
10 Where applicable, clean the threads of the piston oil jet retaining bolt, and apply a drop of thread-locking compound to the bolt threads. Refit the piston oil jet spray tube to the cylinder block, and tighten its retaining bolt to the specified torque setting.
11 If the engine is not going to be reassembled right away, cover it with a large plastic bag to keep it clean; protect all mating surfaces and the cylinder bores as described above, to prevent rusting.

Inspection

12 Visually check the castings for cracks and corrosion. Look for stripped threads in the threaded holes. If there has been any history of internal water leakage, it may be worthwhile having an engine overhaul specialist check the cylinder block/crankcase with special equipment. If defects are found, have them repaired if possible, or renew the assembly.
13 Check each cylinder bore for scuffing and scoring. Check for signs of a wear ridge at the top of the cylinder, indicating that the bore is excessively worn.
14 If wear is suspected, have the cylinder bores measured by an automotive engineering workshop, who will be able to carry out the reboring, and supply suitable pistons/rings, etc, as applicable.
15 At the time of writing, it was not clear whether oversize pistons were available for all models. Consult your Ford dealer for the latest information on piston availability. If oversize pistons are available, then it may be possible to have the cylinder bores rebored and oversize pistons fitted. If oversize pistons are not available, and the bores are worn, renewal of the block is the only option.

11.1a Cylinder block core plugs (arrowed)

11.1b Remove the air conditioning compressor bracket

11.1c Remove the cylinder block ventilation/oil separator box

11.2 Piston cooling jets are fitted to the base of each cylinder bore

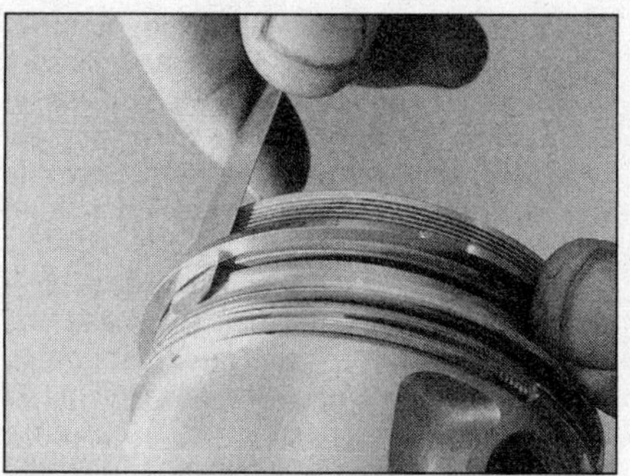
12.2 Remove the piston rings with the aid of feeler gauges

12.15a Prise out the circlip...

12.15b ...and withdraw the gudgeon pin

12 Piston/connecting rod assembly – inspection

1 Before the inspection process can begin, the piston/connecting rod assemblies must be cleaned, and the original piston rings removed from the pistons.

2 Carefully expand the old rings over the top of the pistons. The use of two or three old feeler blades will be helpful in preventing the rings dropping into empty grooves **(see illustration)**. Be careful not to scratch the piston with the ends of the ring. The rings are brittle, and will snap if they are spread too far. They are also very sharp – protect your hands and fingers. Note that the third ring incorporates an expander. Always remove the rings from the top of the piston.

3 Scrape away all traces of carbon from the top of the piston. A hand-held wire brush (or a piece of fine emery cloth) can be used, once the majority of the deposits have been scraped away.

4 Remove the carbon from the ring grooves in the piston, using an old ring. Break the ring in half to do this. Be careful to remove only the carbon deposits – do not remove any metal, and do not nick or scratch the sides of the ring grooves.

5 Once the deposits have been removed, clean the piston/connecting rod assembly with paraffin or a suitable solvent, and dry thoroughly. Make sure that the oil return holes in the ring grooves are clear.

6 If the pistons and cylinder bores are not damaged or worn excessively, and if the cylinder block does not need to be rebored, the original pistons can be refitted. Normal piston wear shows up as even vertical wear on the piston thrust surfaces, and slight looseness of the top ring in its groove. New piston rings should always be used when the engine is reassembled.

7 Carefully inspect each piston for cracks around the skirt, around the gudgeon pin holes, and at the piston ring 'lands' (between the ring grooves).

8 Look for scoring and scuffing on the piston skirt, holes in the piston crown, and burned areas at the edge of the crown. If the skirt is scored or scuffed, the engine may have been suffering from overheating, and/or abnormal combustion which caused excessively high operating temperatures. The cooling and lubrication systems should be checked thoroughly. Scorch marks on the sides of the pistons show that blow-by has occurred. A hole in the piston crown, or burned areas at the edge of the piston crown, indicates that abnormal combustion (pre-ignition, knocking, or detonation) has been occurring. If any of the above problems exist, the causes must be investigated and corrected, or the damage will occur again.

9 Corrosion of the piston, in the form of pitting, indicates that coolant has been leaking into the combustion chamber and/ or the crankcase. Again, the cause must be corrected, or the problem may persist in the rebuilt engine.

10 On aluminium-block engines with wet liners, it is not possible to renew the pistons separately; pistons are only supplied with piston rings and a liner, as a part of a matched assembly. On iron-block engines, pistons can be purchased from a Ford dealer.

11 Examine each connecting rod carefully for signs of damage, such as cracks around the big-end and small-end bearings. Check that the rod is not bent or distorted. Damage is highly unlikely, unless the engine has been seized or badly overheated. Detailed checking of the connecting rod assembly can only be carried out by a Ford dealer or engine repair specialist with the necessary equipment.

12 The big-end cap bolts/nuts must be renewed as a complete set prior to refitting. This should be done after the big-end bearing running clearance check has been carried out.

13 The gudgeon pins are of the floating type, secured in position by two circlips. The pistons and connecting rods can be separated as described in the following paragraphs.

14 Before separating the piston and connecting rod, check the position of the valve recesses or markings on the piston crown in relation to the connecting rod big-end bearing shell cut-outs and make a note of the orientation.

15 Using a small flat-bladed screwdriver, prise out the circlips, and push out the gudgeon pin **(see illustrations)**. Hand pressure should be sufficient to remove the pin. Identify the piston and rod to ensure correct reassembly. Discard the circlips – new ones must be used on refitting.

16 Examine the gudgeon pin and connecting rod small-end bearing for signs of wear or damage. Wear can be cured by renewing both the pin and bush. Bush renewal, however, is a specialist job – press facilities are required, and the new bush must be reamed accurately.

17 The connecting rods themselves should not be in need of renewal, unless seizure or some other major mechanical failure has occurred. Check the alignment of the connecting rods visually, and if the rods are not straight, take them to an engine overhaul specialist for a more detailed check.

18 Examine all components, and obtain any new parts from your Ford dealer. If new pistons are purchased, they will be supplied complete with gudgeon pins and circlips. Circlips can also be purchased individually.

19 Position the piston in relation to the connecting rod big-end bearing shell cut-outs as noted during separation.

20 Apply a smear of clean engine oil to the gudgeon pin and slide it into the piston and through the connecting rod small-end. Check that the piston pivots freely on the rod, then secure the gudgeon pin in position with two new circlips. Ensure that each circlip is correctly located in its groove in the piston.

13 Crankshaft – inspection

Checking endfloat

1 If the crankshaft endfloat is to be checked, this must be done when the crankshaft is installed in the cylinder block/crankcase, but is free to move.

2 Check the endfloat using a dial gauge in contact with the end of the crankshaft. Push the crankshaft fully one way, and then zero the gauge. Push the crankshaft fully the other way, and check the endfloat. The result can be compared with the specified amount,

13.2 Check the crankshaft endfloat using a DTI gauge...

13.3 ...or with feeler gauges

and will give an indication as to whether new thrustwashers are required **(see illustration)**.

3 If a dial gauge is not available, feeler gauges can be used. First push the crankshaft fully towards the flywheel end of the engine, then use feeler gauges to measure the gap between the web and the thrustwasher **(see illustration)**.

Inspection

4 Clean the crankshaft using paraffin or a suitable solvent, and dry it, preferably with compressed air if available. Be sure to clean the oil holes with a pipe cleaner or similar probe, to ensure that they are not obstructed.

Warning: Wear eye protection when using compressed air.

5 Check the main and big-end bearing journals for uneven wear, scoring, pitting and cracking.

6 Big-end bearing wear is accompanied by distinct metallic knocking when the engine is running (particularly noticeable when the engine is pulling from low speed) and by some loss of oil pressure.

7 Main bearing wear is accompanied by severe engine vibration and rumble – getting progressively worse as engine speed increases – and again by loss of oil pressure.

8 Check the bearing journal for roughness by running a finger lightly over the bearing surface. Any roughness (which will be accompanied by obvious bearing wear) indicates that the crankshaft requires regrinding (where possible) or renewal.

9 If the crankshaft has been reground, check for burrs around the crankshaft oil holes (the holes are usually chamfered, so burrs should not be a problem unless regrinding has been carried out carelessly). Remove any burrs with a fine file or scraper, and thoroughly clean the oil holes as described previously.

10 Have the crankshaft inspected and measured by an automotive engineering workshop, who will be able to carry out any necessary repairs, and supply relevant parts.

11 Check the oil seal contact surfaces at each end of the crankshaft for wear and damage. If the seal has worn a deep groove in the surface of the crankshaft, consult an engine overhaul specialist; repair may be possible, but otherwise a new crankshaft will be required.

12 Ford produce a set of undersize bearing shells for both the main and big-end bearings on most engines. Where the crankshaft journals have not already been reground, it may be possible to have the crankshaft reconditioned, and to fit undersize shells. If no undersize shells are available and the crankshaft has worn beyond the specified limits, the crankshaft will have to be renewed. Consult your Ford dealer or engine specialist for further information on parts availability.

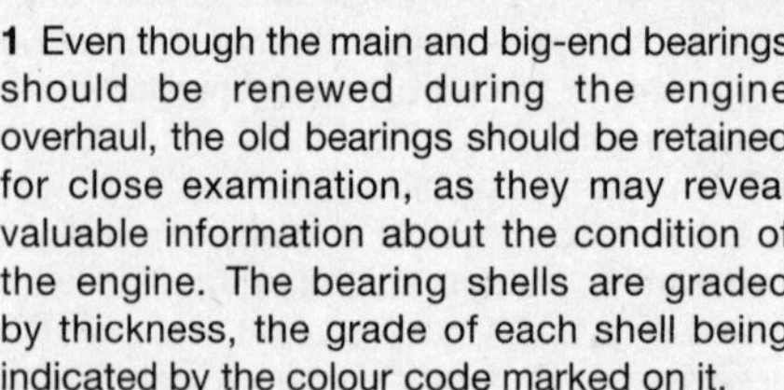

14 Main and big-end bearings – inspection

1 Even though the main and big-end bearings should be renewed during the engine overhaul, the old bearings should be retained for close examination, as they may reveal valuable information about the condition of the engine. The bearing shells are graded by thickness, the grade of each shell being indicated by the colour code marked on it.

2 Bearing failure can occur due to lack of lubrication, the presence of dirt or other foreign particles, overloading the engine, or corrosion **(see illustration)**. Regardless of the cause of bearing failure, the cause must be corrected (where applicable) before the engine is reassembled, to prevent it from happening again.

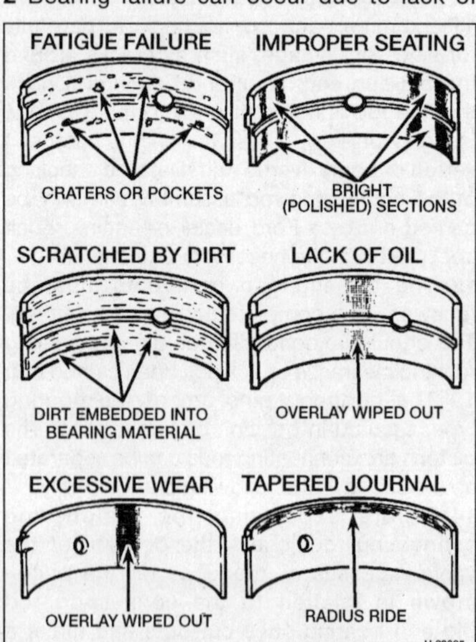

14.2 Typical bearing failures

3 When examining the bearing shells, remove them from the cylinder block/crankcase, the main bearing ladder/caps (as appropriate), the connecting rods and the connecting rod big-end bearing caps. Lay them out on a clean surface in the same general position as their location in the engine. This will enable you to match any bearing problems with the corresponding crankshaft journal. Do not touch any shell's bearing surface with your fingers while checking it, or the delicate surface may be scratched.

4 Dirt and other foreign matter gets into the engine in a variety of ways. It may be left in the engine during assembly, or it may pass through filters or the crankcase ventilation system. It may get into the oil, and from there into the bearings. Metal chips from machining operations and normal engine wear are often present. Abrasives are sometimes left in engine components after reconditioning, especially when parts are not thoroughly cleaned using the proper cleaning methods. Whatever the source, these foreign objects often end up embedded in the soft bearing material, and are easily recognised. Large particles will not embed in the bearing, and will score or gouge the bearing and journal. The best prevention for this cause of bearing failure is to clean all parts thoroughly, and keep everything spotlessly-clean during engine assembly. Frequent and regular engine oil and filter changes are also recommended.

5 Lack of lubrication (or lubrication breakdown) has a number of interrelated causes. Excessive heat (which thins the oil), overloading (which squeezes the oil from the bearing face) and oil leakage (from excessive bearing clearances, worn oil pump or high engine speeds) all contribute to lubrication breakdown. Blocked oil passages, which usually are the result of misaligned oil holes in a bearing shell, will also oil-starve a bearing, and destroy it. When lack of lubrication is the cause of bearing failure, the bearing material is wiped or extruded from the steel backing of the bearing. Temperatures may increase to the point where the steel backing turns blue from overheating.

6 Driving habits can have a definite effect on bearing life. Full-throttle, low-speed operation (labouring the engine) puts very high loads on bearings, tending to squeeze out the oil film. These loads cause the bearings to flex, which produces fine cracks in the bearing face (fatigue failure). Eventually, the bearing material will loosen in pieces, and tear away from the steel backing.

7 Short-distance driving leads to corrosion of bearings, because insufficient engine heat is produced to drive off the condensed water and corrosive gases. These products collect in the engine oil, forming acid and sludge. As the oil is carried to the engine bearings, the acid attacks and corrodes the bearing material.

8 Incorrect bearing installation during engine assembly will lead to bearing failure as well. Tight-fitting bearings leave insufficient bearing running clearance, and will result in oil starvation. Dirt or foreign particles trapped behind a bearing shell result in high spots on the bearing, which lead to failure.

9 Do not touch any shell's bearing surface with your fingers during reassembly; there is a risk of scratching the delicate surface, or of depositing particles of dirt on it.

10 As mentioned at the beginning of this Section, the bearing shells should be renewed as a matter of course during engine overhaul; to do otherwise is false economy.

15 Engine overhaul – reassembly sequence

1 Before reassembly begins, ensure that all new parts have been obtained, and that all necessary tools are available. Read through the entire procedure to familiarise yourself with the work involved, and to ensure that all items necessary for reassembly of the engine are at hand. In addition to all normal tools and materials, thread-locking compound will be needed. A suitable tube of liquid sealant will also be required for the joint faces that are fitted without gaskets. It is recommended that Ford's own products are used, which are specially formulated for this purpose; the relevant product names are quoted in the text of each Section where they are required.

2 In order to save time and avoid problems, engine reassembly can be carried out in the following order:

a) Crankshaft (Section 17).
b) Piston/connecting rod assemblies (Section 18).
c) Oil pump (see Part A, B, C or D – as applicable).
d) Sump (see Part A, B, C or D – as applicable).
e) Flywheel (see Part A, B, C or D – as applicable).
f) Cylinder head (see Part A, B, C or D – as applicable).
g) Timing belt tensioner and sprockets, and timing belt (see Part A, B, C or D – as applicable).
h) Engine external components.

3 At this stage, all engine components should be absolutely clean and dry, with all faults repaired. The components should be laid out (or in individual containers) on a completely clean work surface.

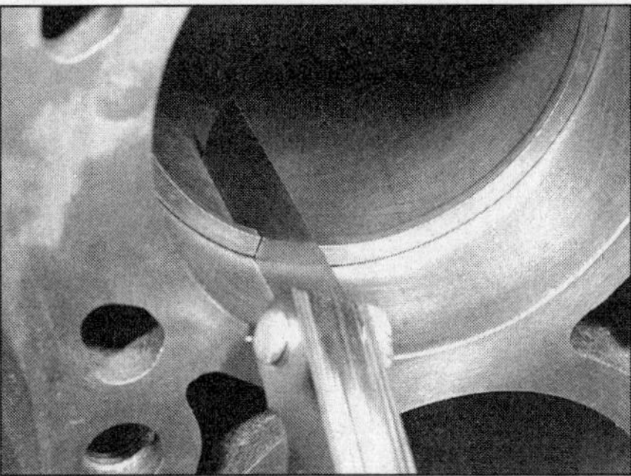

16.5 Measure the piston ring end gap with feeler gauges

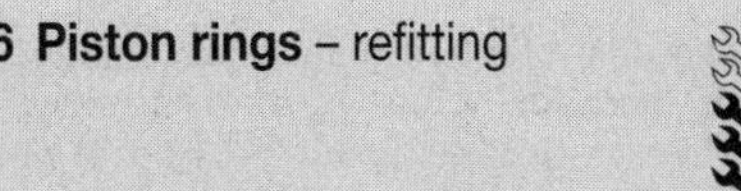

16 Piston rings – refitting

1 Before fitting new piston rings, the ring end gaps must be checked as follows.

2 Lay out the piston/connecting rod assemblies and the new piston ring sets, so that the ring sets will be matched with the same piston and cylinder during the end gap measurement and subsequent engine reassembly.

3 Insert the top ring into the first cylinder, and push it down the bore using the top of the piston. This will ensure that the ring remains square with the cylinder walls. Position the ring near the bottom of the cylinder bore, at the lower limit of ring travel. Note that the top and second compression rings are different. The second ring is easily identified by the step on its lower surface, and by the fact that its outer face is tapered.

4 Measure the end gap using feeler gauges.

5 Repeat the procedure with the ring at the top of the cylinder bore, at the upper limit of its travel, and compare the measurements with the figures given in the Specifications **(see illustration)**. Where no figures are given, seek the advice of a Ford dealer or engine reconditioning specialist.

6 If the gap is too small (unlikely if genuine Ford parts are used), it must be enlarged, or the ring ends may contact each other during engine operation, causing serious damage. Ideally, new piston rings providing the correct end gap should be fitted. As a last resort, the end gap can be increased by filing the ring ends very carefully with a fine file. Mount the file in a vice equipped with soft jaws, slip the ring over the file with the ends contacting the file face, and slowly move the ring to remove material from the ends. Take care, as piston rings are sharp, and are easily broken.

7 With new piston rings, it is unlikely that the end gap will be too large. If the gaps are too large, check that you have the correct rings for your engine and for the particular cylinder bore size.

8 Repeat the checking procedure for each ring in the first cylinder, and then for the rings in the remaining cylinders. Remember to keep rings, pistons and cylinders matched up.

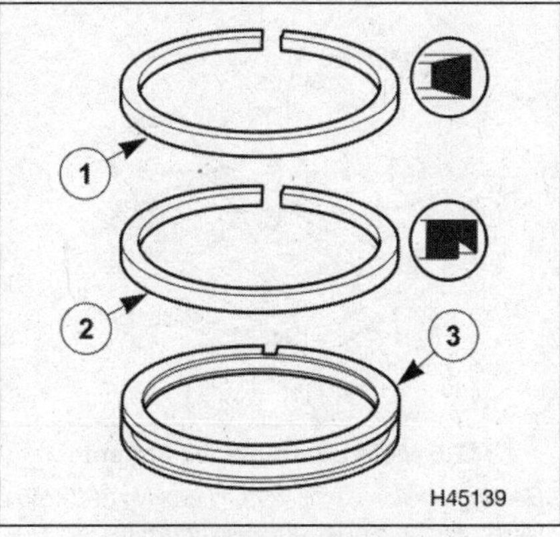

16.10 Piston ring details (typical)
1 Top compression ring
2 2nd compression ring
3 Oil scraper ring assembly

9 Once the ring end gaps have been checked and if necessary corrected, the rings can be fitted to the pistons.

10 Fit the piston rings using the same technique as for removal. Fit the bottom (oil control) ring first, and work up. When fitting the oil control ring, first insert the expander (where fitted), then fit the ring with its gap positioned 180° from the expander gap. Ensure that the second compression ring is fitted the correct way up, with its identification mark (either a dot of paint or the word TOP stamped on the ring surface) at the top, and the stepped surface at the bottom **(see illustration)**. Arrange the gaps of the top and second compression rings 120° either side of the oil control ring gap. **Note:** *Always follow any instructions supplied with the new piston ring sets – different manufacturers may specify different procedures. Do not mix up the top and second compression rings, as they have different cross-sections.*

17 Crankshaft – refitting

New main bearing shells

1 To ensure that the main bearing running clearance is correct, the bearing shells are supplied in various thicknesses or grades. The grades are indicated by a colour-coding marked on the edge of each shell. The grade of the new bearing shells required (either standard size or undersize) is selected using the reference marks on the cylinder block and on the crankshaft. The cylinder block marks identify the diameter of the bearing bores in the block, and the crankshaft marks identify the diameter of the crankshaft journals.

2 Note that on the engines described in this Manual, the upper shells are all of the same

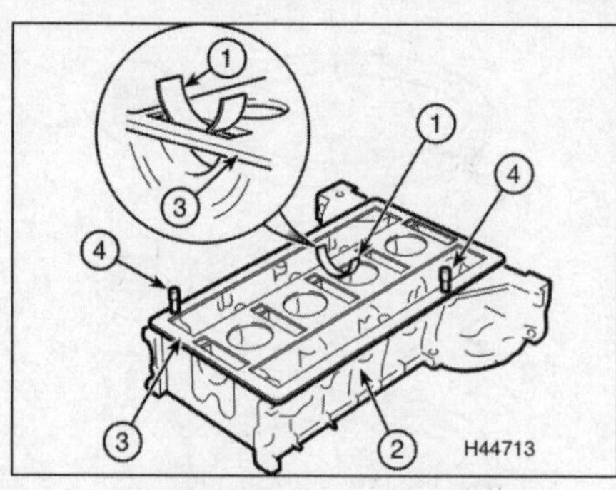

17.5 Main bearing shell fitment

1 Bearing shell *3 Ford tool No 303-245*
2 Main bearing ladder *4 Aligning pins*

17.7 Place the thrustwashers each side of the No 2 bearing upper location

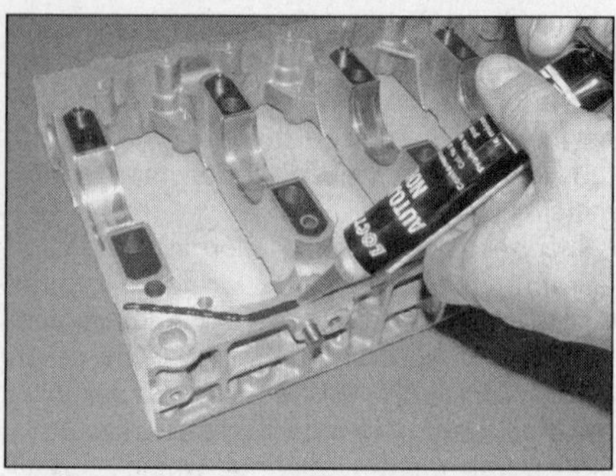

17.8 Apply a thin bead of RTV sealant to the bearing cap housing mating surface

size, and the running clearance is controlled by fitting a lower bearing shell of the required thickness.

3 Numerous grades of standard and oversize bearing shells are available, depending on the engine type, year of manufacture, and country of export. Using the cylinder block and crankshaft reference marks together with the crankshaft journal diameter, a Ford dealer or engine overhaul specialist will be able to supply the correct bearing shells to give the required bearing running clearance for each journal.

Final crankshaft refitting

4 Crankshaft refitting is the first major step in engine reassembly. It is assumed at this point that the cylinder block/crankcase and crankshaft have been cleaned, inspected and repaired or reconditioned as necessary. Position the engine upside-down.

5 Place the bearing shells in their locations. If new shells are being fitted, ensure that all traces of protective grease are cleaned off using paraffin. Wipe dry the shells with a lint-free cloth. The upper bearing shells all have a grooved surface, whereas the lower shells have a plain surface. It's essential that the lower bearing shells are centrally located in the bearing cap housing/ladder. To ensure this use a Ford tool (No 303-245) positioned over the housing/ladder, and insert the bearing shells through the slots in the tool **(see illustration)**.

6 Liberally lubricate each bearing shell in the cylinder block with clean engine oil then lower the crankshaft into position.

7 Insert the thrustwashers to either side of No 2 main bearing upper location and push them around the bearing journal until their edges are horizontal **(see illustration)**. Ensure that the oilway grooves on each thrustwasher face outwards (away from the bearing journal).

8 Thoroughly degrease the mating surfaces of the cylinder block and the crankshaft bearing cap housing. Apply a thin bead of silicone sealant (Ford part No WSE-M4G323-A4) to the bearing cap housing mating surface **(see illustration)**.

9 Lubricate the lower bearing shells with clean engine oil, then refit the bearing cap housing, ensuring that the shells are not displaced, and that the locating dowels engage correctly.

10 Install the ten large diameter, and sixteen smaller diameter crankshaft bearing cap housing retaining bolts, and screw them in until they are just making contact with the housing.

11 Working in sequence, tighten the bolts to the torque settings given in the Specifications **(see illustration)**.

12 With the bearing cap housing in place, check that the crankshaft rotates freely.

13 Refit the piston/connecting rod assemblies to the crankshaft as described in Section 18.

14 Refit the oil pump and sump.

15 Fit a new crankshaft left-hand oil seal, then refit the flywheel.

16 Where removed, refit the cylinder head, crankshaft sprocket and timing belt.

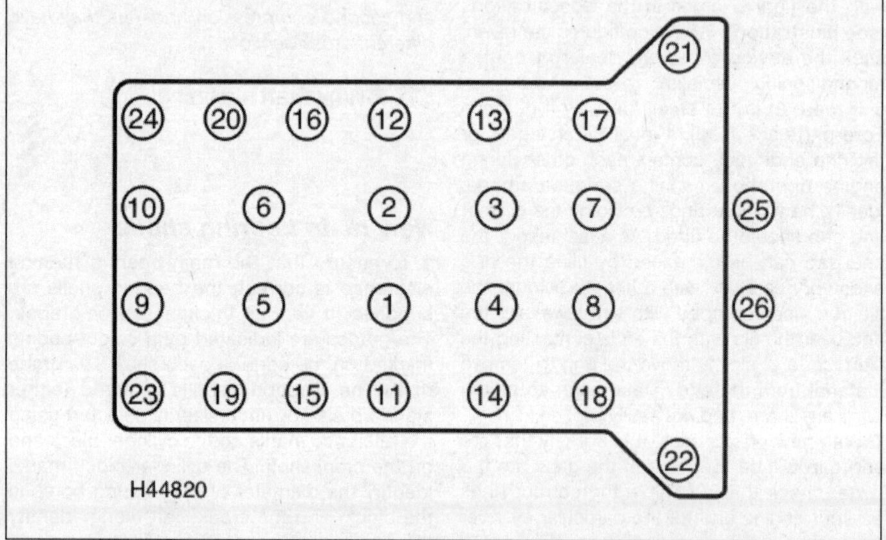

17.11 Main bearing cap housing/ladder retaining bolt tightening sequence

18 Pistons/connecting rods – refitting

Note: *New big-end cap nuts/bolts must be used on refitting.*

1 Note that the following procedure assumes that the crankshaft and main bearing ladder/caps are in place.

2 Clean the backs of the bearing shells, and the bearing locations in both the connecting rod and bearing cap.

3 Lubricate the cylinder bores, the pistons, and piston rings, then lay out each piston/connecting rod assembly in its respective position.

4 Start with assembly No 1. Make sure that the piston rings are still spaced as described in Section 16, then clamp them in position with a piston ring compressor.

5 Insert the piston/connecting rod assembly into the top of cylinder/liner No 1, ensuring the piston is correctly positioned – the DIST mark or arrow on the piston crown must be towards the timing belt end of the engine

6 Once the piston is correctly positioned, using a block of wood or hammer handle against the piston crown, tap the assembly into the cylinder/liner until the piston crown is flush with the top of the cylinder/liner **(see illustration)**.

7 On these engines, then connecting rod is made in one piece, then the big-end bearing cap is 'cracked' off. This ensures that the cap fits onto the connecting rod only in one position, and with maximum rigidity. Consequently, there are no locating notches for the bearing shells to fit into.

8 To ensure that the big-end bearing shells are centrally located in the connecting rod and cap, two special tools are available from Ford (part No 303-736). These half-moon shaped tools are pressed in from either side of the rod/cap and locate the shell exactly in the centre **(see illustration)**. Fit the shells into the connecting rods and big-end caps and lubricate them with plenty of clean engine oil.

9 Pull the connecting rods and pistons down the bores and onto the crankshaft journals. Fit the big-end caps – they will only fit properly one way round (see paragraph 10), and insert the new bolts.

10 Tighten the bolts to the specified torque settings.

11 Once the bearing cap retaining nuts have been correctly tightened, rotate the crankshaft. Check that it turns freely; some stiffness is to be expected if new components have been fitted, but there should be no signs of binding or tight spots.

12 Refit the cylinder head and oil pump as described in Part C of this Chapter.

18.6 Tap the piston into the bore using a hammer handle

19 Engine initial start-up after overhaul

1 With the engine refitted in the vehicle, double-check the engine oil and coolant levels. Make a final check that everything has been reconnected, and that there are no tools or rags left in the engine compartment.

2 Prime the fuel system (refer to Chapter 4A or 4B). Although the system is self-priming, it will help if the ignition is switched on and off several times before attempting to start the engine in order to purge air from the system.

3 Turn the engine on the starter until the oil pressure warning light goes out.

4 Fully depress the accelerator pedal, turn the ignition key to position M, and If necessary wait for the preheating warning light to go out.

5 Start the engine, noting that this may take a little longer than usual, due to the fuel system components having been disturbed.

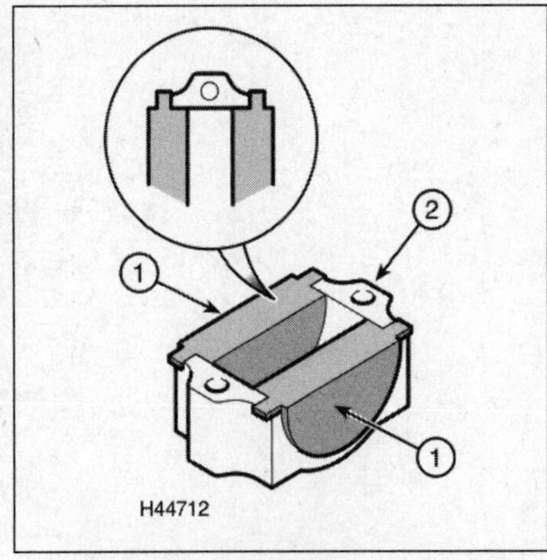

18.8 Big-end bearing shell positioning

1 Ford tool No 303-736
2 Bearing shell in the cap

6 While the engine is idling, check for fuel, water and oil leaks. Don't be alarmed if there are some odd smells and smoke from parts getting hot and burning off oil deposits.

7 Assuming all is well, keep the engine idling until hot water is felt circulating through the top hose, then switch off the engine.

8 After a few minutes, recheck the oil and coolant levels as described in *Weekly checks*, and top-up as necessary.

9 If new pistons, rings or crankshaft bearings have been fitted, the engine must be treated as new, and run-in for the first 500 miles. Do not operate the engine at full-throttle, or allow it to labour at low engine speeds in any gear. It is recommended that the oil and filter be changed at the end of this period.

Chapter 3
Cooling, heating and air conditioning systems

Contents

Degrees of difficulty

Easy, suitable for novice with little experience 	**Fairly easy,** suitable for beginner with some experience	**Fairly difficult,** suitable for competent DIY mechanic	**Difficult,** suitable for experienced DIY mechanic	**Very difficult,** suitable for expert DIY or professional 

Specifications

Coolant

Mixture type	See Lubricants and fluids on page 0•16
Cooling system capacity	See Chapter 1A or 1B

System pressure

Pressure test	1.3 to 1.75 bar approximately – see cap for actual value

Expansion tank filler cap

Pressure rating	1.3 to 1.5 bar approximately – see cap for actual value

Thermostat – opening temperature

Petrol engines	92°C
Diesel engines	88°C

Air conditioning system

Compressor clutch air gap:	
Sanden and Visteon compressors	0.35 to 0.70 mm
Denso compressor	0.35 to 0.60 mm
Refrigerant:	
Vehicles up to 16-08-2016:	R134a
Vehicles from 16-08-2016:	R1234yf
Refrigerant quantity:	
1.0 litre petrol engine	530 g
1.6 litre petrol engine	600 g
1.5 and 1.6 litre diesel engines	530 g
Refrigerant oil:	
Vehicles up to 16-08-2016 (with R134a refrigerant):	
Visteon and Sanden compressors	Ford WSH-M1C231-B
Denso compressor	Denso ND8
Vehicles from 16-08-2016 (with R1234yf refrigerant):	
All models	Ford WSS-M2C300-A2
Refrigerant oil quantity (when refilling after a system flush):	
1.0 litre petrol engine	130 ml
1.6 litre petrol engine	150 ml
1.5 and 1.6 litre diesel engines	130 ml
When renewing the condenser	30 ml
When renewing the evaporator	30 ml
When renewing the accumulator/dehydrator	90 ml
When renewing the compressor:	
If the oil drained from the faulty compressor is more than 110 ml	Add the total quantity of oil, as for system flush

Torque wrench settings

	Nm	lbf ft
Air conditioning accumulator/dehydrator-to condenser bolt	7	5
Air conditioning compressor mounting bolts	24	18
Air conditioning high-pressure cut-off switch	10	7
Auxiliary drivebelt tensioner bolts	25	18
Coolant pump bolts		
1.6 litre engines*	10	7
1.0 litre petrol		
Short bolts	10	7
Long bolts;		
Stage 1	15	11
Stage 2	Angle-tighten a further 90°	
Coolant pump pulley bolts	24	18
Radiator mounting bracket-to-body bolts	25	18
Refrigerant line connection	11	8
Refrigerant line to compressor	20	15
Refrigerant line to evaporator	20	15
Thermostat housing bolts	10	7

**Use new fasteners – 1.6 litre petrol engines only*

1 General Information

Warning: DO NOT attempt to remove the expansion tank filler cap, or to disturb any part of the cooling system, while it or the engine is hot, as there is a very great risk of scalding. If the expansion tank filler cap must be removed before the engine and radiator have fully cooled down (even though this is not recommended) the pressure in the cooling system must first be released. Cover the cap with a thick layer of cloth, to avoid scalding, and slowly unscrew the filler cap until a hissing sound can be heard. When the hissing has stopped, showing that pressure is released, slowly unscrew the filler cap further until it can be removed; if more hissing sounds are heard, wait until they have stopped before unscrewing the cap completely. At all times, keep well away from the filler opening.

Warning: Do not allow coolant to come in contact with your skin, or with the painted surfaces of the vehicle. Rinse off spills immediately with plenty of water. Never leave coolant lying around in an open container, or in a puddle in the driveway or on the garage floor. Children and pets are attracted by its sweet smell, but coolant is fatal if ingested.

Warning: If the engine is hot, the electric cooling fan may start rotating even if the engine is not running, so be careful to keep hands, hair and loose clothing well clear when working in the engine compartment.

Engine cooling system

1 All vehicles covered by this manual employ a pressurised engine cooling system with thermostatically-controlled coolant circulation. The coolant is circulated by an impeller-type pump, bolted to the right-hand end of the cylinder block. On all petrol models the pump is driven by the crankshaft pulley via the auxiliary drivebelt. On diesel models the pump is driven by the timing belt.

2 The coolant flows through the cylinder block around each cylinder; in the cylinder head, cast-in coolant passages direct coolant around the inlet and exhaust ports, near the spark plug areas and close to the exhaust valve guides.

3 A wax type thermostat is located in a housing attached to the engine. During warm-up, the closed thermostat prevents coolant from circulating through the radiator. Instead, it returns through the coolant pipe running across the front of the engine to the radiator or expansion bottle. The supply to the heater is made from the rear of the thermostat housing. As the engine nears normal operating temperature, the thermostat opens and allows hot coolant to travel through the radiator, where it is cooled before returning to the engine. On some models, an electrically-heated thermostat is fitted, where the engine management ECM controls the position of the thermostat to improve engine efficiency and reduce harmful exhaust emissions.

4 EcoBoost engines feature a thermostat housing that that incorporates a dual thermostat and a by pass valve. This allows control of the coolant temperature in three phases: In stage 1 with the coolant below 70 degrees coolant only flows through the exhaust side of the cylinder head. Stage 2 operates as a conventional system when the coolant temperature is between 70 and 80 degrees centigrade. Stage 3 operates at coolant temperatures between 92 to 106 degrees. At these temperatures the thermostat is fully open and all coolant passes through the radiator. Some models also have an electric coolant pump (located on the radiator) fitted. The electric pump operates if the coolant temperature rises excessively after engine shut down.

5 The cooling system is sealed by a pressure-type filler cap in the expansion tank. The pressure in the system raises the boiling point of the coolant, and increases the cooling efficiency of the radiator. When the engine is at normal operating temperature, the coolant expands, and the surplus is displaced into the expansion tank. When the system cools, the surplus coolant is automatically drawn back from the tank into the radiator.

6 The temperature gauge and cooling fan(s) are controlled by the engine coolant temperature sensor that transmits a signal to the engine electronic control module (ECM) to operate them.

Heating/ventilation system

7 The heating system consists of a blower fan and heater matrix (radiator) located in the heater unit, with hoses connecting the heater matrix to the engine cooling system. Hot engine coolant is circulated through the heater matrix. When the heater temperature control on the facia is operated, a flap door opens to expose the heater box to the passenger compartment. When the blower control is operated, the blower fan forces air through the unit according to the setting selected. The heater controls are linked to the flap doors by cables.

8 Incoming fresh air for the ventilation system passes through a pollen filter mounted at the front of the heater housing (see Chapter 1A Section 25 or Chapter 1B Section 25) – this ensures that most particles will be removed before the air enters the cabin. However, it is vital that the pollen filter is changed regularly, since a blocked filter will significantly reduce airflow to the cabin, leading to ineffective de-misting.

9 The ventilation system air distribution is controlled by flap doors on the heater housing. All the vehicles have a recirculated air function, with the flap being controlled by a servo motor.

Air conditioning system

10 See Section 11.

2 Engine coolant (antifreeze) – general information

Warning: Engine coolant (antifreeze) contains monoethylene glycol and other constituents, which are toxic if taken internally. They can also be absorbed into the skin after prolonged contact.

Note: *Refer to Chapter 1A or 1B for further information on coolant renewal.*

1 The cooling system should be filled with a water/monoethylene glycol-based coolant solution, of a strength which will prevent freezing down to at least –25°C, or lower if the local climate requires it. Coolant also provides protection against corrosion, and increases the boiling point.

2 The cooling system should be maintained according to the schedule described in Chapter 1A or 1B. If the engine coolant used is old or contaminated it is likely to cause damage, and encourage the formation of corrosion and scale in the system. Use coolant which is to Ford's specification and to the correct concentration.

3 Before adding the coolant, check all hoses and hose connections, because coolant tends to leak through very small openings. Engines don't normally consume coolant, so if the level goes down, find the cause and correct it.

4 The engine coolant concentration should be between 40% and 55%. If the concentration drops below 40% there will be insufficient protection, this must then be brought back to specification. Hydrometers are available at most automotive accessory shops to test the coolant concentration.

3 Cooling system hoses – disconnection and renewal

Note: *Refer to the warnings given in Section 1 of this Chapter before starting work.*

1 If the checks described in Chapter 1A or 1B reveal a faulty hose, it must be renewed as follows.

2 First drain the cooling system (see Chapter 1A or 1B); if the coolant is not due for renewal, the drained coolant may be re-used, if it is collected in a clean container.

3 To disconnect any hose, use a pair of pliers to release the spring clamps (or a screwdriver to slacken screw-type clamps), then move them along the hose clear of the union. Carefully work the hose off its stubs **(see illustration)**. The hoses can be removed with relative ease when new – on an older car, they may have stuck.

4 If a hose proves stubborn, try to release it by rotating it on its unions before attempting to work it off. Gently prise the end of the hose with a blunt instrument (such as a flat-bladed screwdriver), but do not apply too much force, and take care not to damage the pipe stubs or hoses. Note in particular that the radiator hose unions are fragile; do not use excessive force when attempting to remove the hoses. If all else fails, cut the hose with a sharp knife, then slit it so that it can be peeled off in two pieces. While expensive, this is preferable to buying a new radiator. Check first, however, that a new hose is readily available.

5 When refitting a hose, first slide the clamps onto the hose, then work the hose onto its unions. If the hose is stiff, use soap (or washing-up liquid) as a lubricant, or soften it by soaking it in boiling water, but take care to prevent scalding.

6 Work each hose end fully onto its union, then check that the hose is settled correctly and is properly routed. Slide each clip along the hose until it is behind the union flared end, before tightening it securely.

7 Refill the system with coolant (see Chapter 1A or 1B).

8 Check carefully for leaks as soon as possible after disturbing any part of the cooling system.

3.3 You can buy special tools specifically designed to release spring type hose clamps

4.6 Disconnect the wiring plug

4.7a A quick release connector is fitted to the rear inboard hose. Depress the button to release the hose

4.7b Release the spring clamps from the hoses

4 Thermostat – removal, testing and refitting

Note: *Refer to the warnings given in Section 1 of this Chapter before starting work.*

1 On 1.0 litre petrol and diesel models the thermostat is located within a housing on the left-hand end of the cylinder head. On 1.6 petrol models the thermostat is located on the front, right-hand end of the engine block. 1.0 litre EcoBoost models have a secondary thermostat fitted in this position as well. Note also that 1.6 litre EcoBoost models have additional electronically controlled diverter valves fitted to the thermostat housing and on the left-hand end of the cylinder head.

Removal

2 Disconnect the battery negative (earth) lead (see Chapter 5A Section 3).

3 Drain the cooling system (see Chapter 1A or 1B). If the coolant is relatively new or in good condition, drain it into a clean container and re-use it.

4 Remove the engine cover

1.0 litre petrol models – main thermostat

Note: *At the time of writing the thermostat was not available as a separate item. If it is faulty the complete housing must be replaced.*

5 Remove the air filter housing and intercooler pipe from the front left-hand side of the engine bay.

6 Disconnect the wiring plug from the coolant temperature sensor **(see illustration)** and then unclip the loom. Move the wiring loom to one side.

7 Anticipating some coolant spillage release the hoses from the housing. These are held in place by spring clips and a quick release connector **(see illustrations)**.

4.8 Remove the housing from the cylinder head

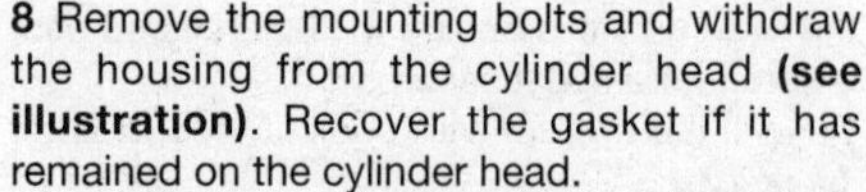

4.10 The block mounted thermostat (arrowed). Note turbocharger removed for clarity

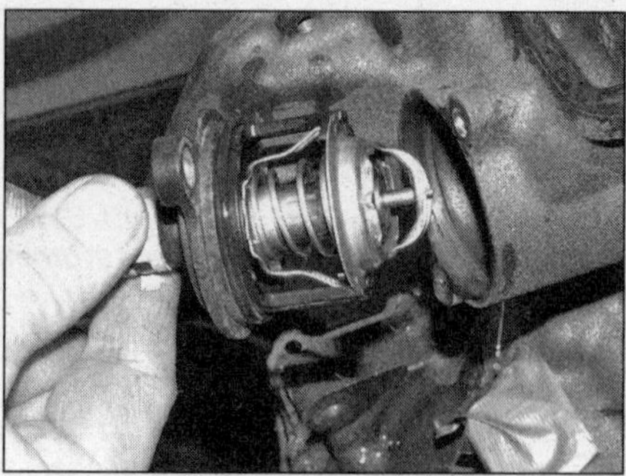
4.12 Remove the thermostat

8 Remove the mounting bolts and withdraw the housing from the cylinder head **(see illustration)**. Recover the gasket if it has remained on the cylinder head.

9 If required the thermostat can be removed from the housing for testing. Aftermarket motor factors may supply the thermostat as a separate item.

1.0 litre petrol models – engine block mounted thermostat

10 The secondary thermostat is located on the from of the engine **(see illustration)**. Access can be improved by removing the alternator (Chapter 5A Section 5) and the coolant distribution pipe from the rear of the coolant pump.

11 Access is also possible from beneath if the engine is raised at the front (see *Jacking and vehicle support* in the reference section) and the engine undershield removed.

12 Unbolt and then remove the thermostat **(see illustration)**.

1.6 litre petrol models

13 Remove the alternator as described in Chapter 5A Section 5.

14 On EcoBoost models disconnect the wiring plug from the control valve.

15 Release the spring clamps and then on EcoBoost models remove the bolts and remove the control valve **(see illustration)**. Recover the gasket.

16 Remove the 4 main mounting bolts and then withdraw the housing. Recover the gasket.

4.15 Remove the control valve

17 If the thermostat has remained in the engine block, remove the thermostat. Note that on thermostats fitted with a 'jiggle pin' (a small hole and pin in the outer section of the thermostat) the jiggle pin should be in the 12 o'clock position.

Diesel models

18 Remove the air filter housing and intercooler pipe from the front left-hand side of the engine bay.

19 Unbolt the fuel filter housing and move it to one side.

20 Disconnect the wiring plug from the temperature sensor.

21 Release the spring clips and remove the coolant hoses.

22 Remove the bolts and then remove the housing **(see illustration)**. Recover the gasket.

Testing

General

23 Before assuming the thermostat is to blame for a cooling system problem, check the coolant level (see *Weekly checks*), the auxiliary drivebelt tension and condition (see Chapter 1A or 1B) and the temperature gauge operation.

24 If the engine seems to be taking a long time to warm up (based on heater output or temperature gauge operation), the thermostat may be stuck open. Renew the thermostat.

25 Equally, a lengthy warm-up period might suggest that the thermostat is missing – it may have been removed or inadvertently omitted by a previous owner or mechanic. Don't drive the vehicle without a thermostat – the engine management system's ECM will stay in warm-up mode for longer than necessary, causing emissions and fuel economy to suffer.

4.22 Undo the bolts (arrowed) and detach the thermostat housing

26 If the engine runs hot, use your hand to check the temperature of the radiator top hose. If the hose isn't hot, but the engine is, the thermostat is probably stuck closed, preventing the coolant inside the engine from escaping to the radiator – renew the thermostat.

27 If the radiator top hose is hot, it means that the coolant is flowing and the thermostat is open. Consult the Fault finding Section at the end of this manual to assist in tracing possible cooling system faults.

Thermostat test

Note: *If there is any doubt as to the operation of the thermostat it should always be replaced.*

28 If the thermostat remains in the open position at room temperature, it is faulty, and must be renewed as a matter of course.

29 To test it fully, suspend the thermostat (or the complete housing) on a length of string in a container of cold water, with a thermometer beside it; ensure that neither touches the side of the container.

30 Heat the water, and check the temperature at which the thermostat begins to open; compare this value with that specified. Checking the fully-open temperature may not be possible in an open container if it is higher than the boiling point of water at atmospheric pressure. Remove the thermostat and allow it to cool down; check that it closes fully.

31 If the thermostat does not open and close as described, if it sticks in either position, or if it does not open at the specified temperature, it must be renewed.

Refitting

32 Refitting is the reverse of the removal procedure, noting the following points:

a) *Clean the mating surfaces carefully, and renew the thermostat's sealing ring/gasket.*
b) *Fit the thermostat in the same position as noted on removal.*
c) *Tighten the thermostat cover/housing bolts to the specified torque wrench setting.*

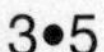

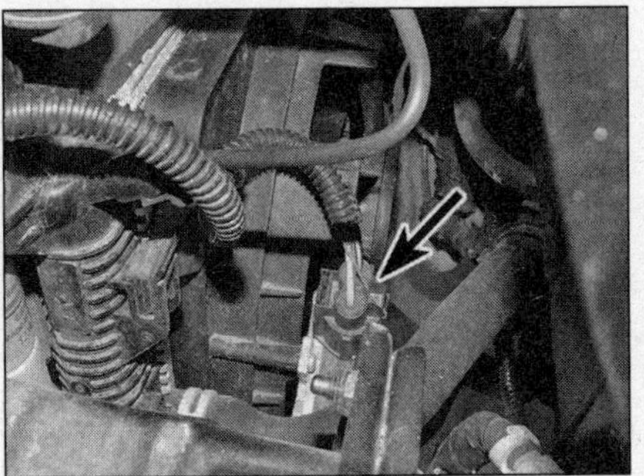

5.7 Disconnect the wiring plug connector

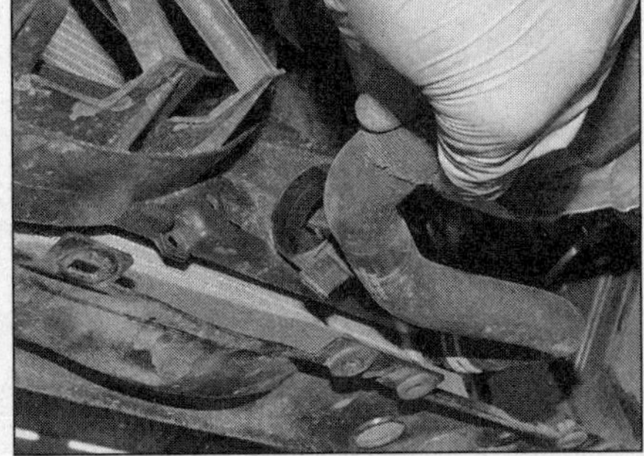

5.9 Unclip the hose from the bracket – diesel engine shown

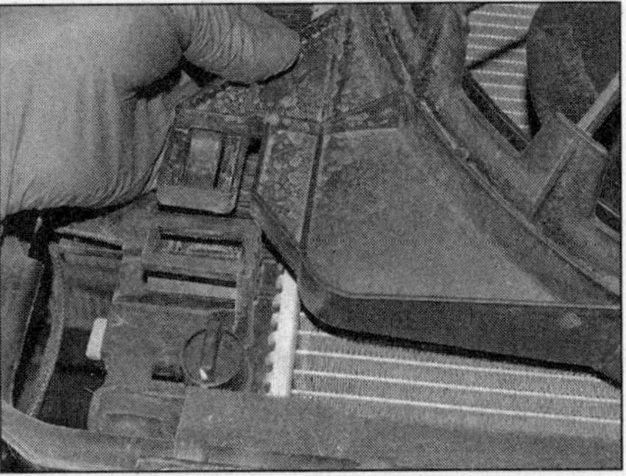

5.10a Release the lower...

d) Remake all the coolant hose connections, then refill the cooling system as described in the relevant part of Chapter 1A or 1B.

e) Start the engine and allow it to reach normal operating temperature, then check for leaks and proper thermostat operation.

5 Radiator electric cooling fan(s) – testing, removal and refitting

Note: *Refer to the warnings given in Section 1 of this Chapter before starting work.*

Testing

1 The radiator cooling fan is controlled by the engine management system's ECM, acting on the information received primarily from the engine coolant temperature sensor.

2 First, check the relevant fuses and relays (see Chapter 12 Section 3).

3 To test the fan motor, unplug the electrical connector, and use fused jumper wires to connect the fan directly to the battery. If the fan still does not work, renew the motor.

4 If the motor proved sound, the fault lies in the engine coolant temperature sensor (see Section 6), in the wiring loom (see Chapter 12 for testing details) or in the engine management system.

Removal

5 Disconnect the battery and remove the air filter housing and air inlet duct. Jack up the front of the vehicle (see *Jacking and vehicle support*). Undo the fasteners and remove the engine undershield.

6 On 1.0 litre petrol engine models, remove the electric coolant pump from the lower part of the fan cowling, as described in Section 8.

7 Disconnect the wiring plug from the cooling fan and then unclip the loom from the support bracket on the shroud **(see illustration)**.

8 On models fitted with an electric coolant pump, remove the single bolt and move the pump to one side. There is no need to disconnect the coolant hoses.

9 Depending on model, it will be necessary to unclip the coolant hose from the support bracket, on the fan cowling **(see illustration)**.

10 Use a screwdriver to slightly open the retaining clips and then push the fan assembly

5.10b ...and upper retaining clips

5.10c Retaining clip with fan assembly removed

upwards to release it from the mounting brackets **(see illustrations)**. Depending on model, it may be easier to lower the fan assembly from the vehicle, or lift it out from the engine compartment.

11 If required the fan can now be removed from the cowling assembly by removing the securing screws.

Refitting

12 Refitting is the reverse of the removal procedure.

6 Coolant temperature sensor – removal and refitting

Note: *Refer to the warnings given in Section 1 of this Chapter before starting work.*

1 On all models, the sensor is located at the coolant outlet housing at the left-hand end of the cylinder head.

Removal

Warning: Ensure the coolant is cold before attempting this procedure.

2 Remove the engine cover and then remove the air filter housing and inlet duct from the left-hand side of the engine bay.

3 Disconnect the wiring plug from the sensor.

4 The sensor is clipped into place with a horseshoe shaped retaining clip. Pull out the clip and if necessary recover the seal from the thermostat housing – it will normally come away with the sensor **(see illustrations)**. Be prepared for coolant spillage and have rag or a rubber plug handy to force into the sensor aperture – or better still have a replacement sensor to hand. This way only a little coolant will be lost.

5 If required the sensor operation can be

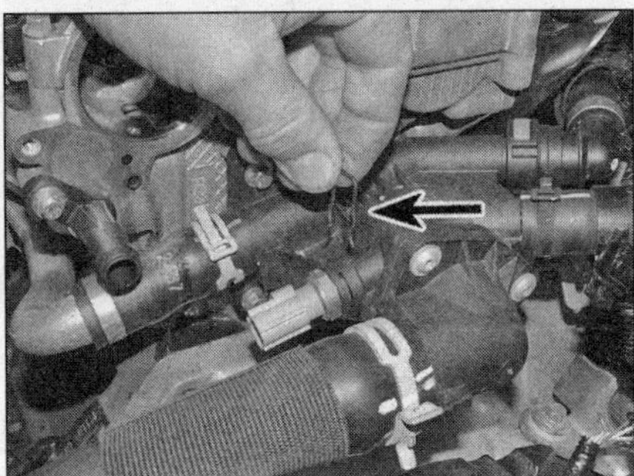

6.4a Pull out the retaining clip (arrowed)...

6.4b ... followed by the sensor

7.5a Remove the main coolant hoses...

7.5b ...and the vent hose

7.7 Unclip the wiring loom

checked by using a multi-meter (set to the ohms scale) to check the resistance of the sensor. Connect the meter to the sensor and gently warm the sensor with a hot air gun (or suspend the sensor in a pan of water that can be brought up to the boil). As the temperature changes the resistance will change. The normal failure mode will be either open circuit (very high resistance) or short circuit (very low resistance). Note however this is not a definitive test, as the sensor may still respond to temperature changes, but the change in resistance may not track the change in coolant temperature.

Refitting

6 Refitting is the reverse of the removal procedure.

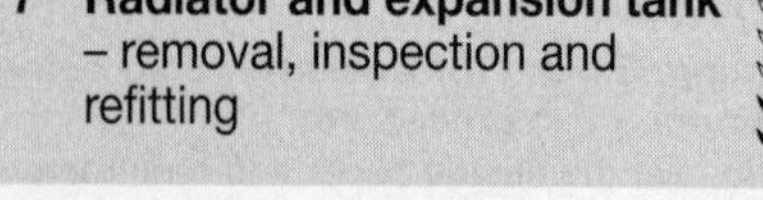

7 Radiator and expansion tank – removal, inspection and refitting

Note: *Refer to the warnings given in Section 1 of this Chapter before starting work.*

Radiator removal

Note: *If leakage is the reason for removing the radiator, bear in mind that minor leaks can often be cured using a radiator sealant added to the coolant with the radiator in situ.*

1 Drain the coolant system as described in Chapter 1A or 1B.

2 To provide greater clearance for the radiator to be lowered and removed, ensure that the handbrake is firmly applied, then raise and support the front of the car on axle stands (see *Jacking and vehicle support*).

3 Remove the radiator fan and shroud assembly as described in Section 5.

4 Whilst not strictly necessary, removal of the front bumper cover (as described in Chapter 11 Section 6) is highly recommended, as this allows better access to the coolant hoses and the condenser retaining clips.

5 Release the clamps and disconnect the radiator upper, lower and vent hoses **(see illustrations)**.

6 Remove the cooling fan and shroud as described in Section 5 of this Chapter.

7 Unclip the two wiring loom connectors from the radiator support panel **(see illustration)**.

8 On turbo models, remove the intercooler as described in Chapter 4A or 4B. Note this is not essential, but it avoids any possibility of damaging the intercooler as the radiator is removed.

9 Using straps or cable ties secure the radiator and condenser. They should be supported separately, so that the radiator can be removed whilst leaving the condenser in place.

10 Unbolt and then remove the radiator/condenser support panel **(see illustration)**.

11 Remove the 2 bolts one from each side of the radiator **(see illustration)**.

12 Working with care and crucially ensuring that no strain is placed on the condenser or AC refrigerant lines work the radiator free from the locating clips at each end. The radiator must be pushed up, to release it from the lower retaining clips, before it can be lowered from the vehicle.

13 With the radiator released carefully lower it and then remove it from the vehicle **(see illustration)**. Anticipate some coolant spillage as the radiator is removed.

Radiator inspection

14 With the radiator removed, it can be inspected for leaks and damage. If it leaks or is damaged the radiator should be replaced – repair is not usually an option.

15 Insects and dirt can be removed from the radiator with a garden hose or a soft brush. Take care not to damage the cooling fins as this is being done.

Radiator refitting

16 Refitting is the reverse of the removal procedure, noting the following points:

a) *Be sure the mounting rubbers are seated properly at the base of the radiator.*
b) *After refitting, refill the cooling system with the recommended coolant (see Chapter 1A or 1B).*
c) *Start the engine, and check for leaks. Allow the engine to reach normal operating temperature, indicated by the radiator top hose becoming hot. Once the engine has cooled (ideally, leave overnight), recheck the coolant level, and add more if required.*

Expansion tank

Removal

17 With the engine completely cool, remove the expansion tank filler cap to release any pressure, then refit the cap.

7.10 Remove the support panel

7.11 Remove the bolt (arrowed)

7.13 Lower the radiator

7.18 Remove the upper coolant hoses – 1.0 litre petrol shown

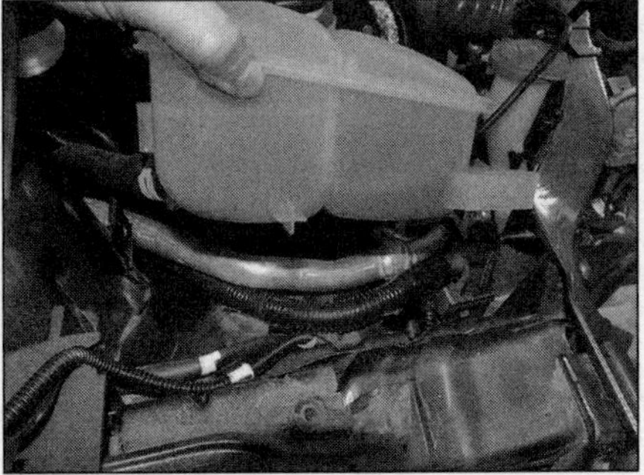

7.19 Release the expansion tank by pulling it upwards

8.10 Remove the coolant pump

18 Disconnect the upper hoses from the tank **(see illustration)**, depending on model, there may be more than one hose.

19 Pull the expansion tank upwards to release it from the mounting lugs **(see illustration)**.

20 Have a suitable container ready and then release the main outlet hose from the base of the expansion tank.

21 Wash out the tank, and inspect it for cracks and chafing – renew it if damaged.

Refitting

22 Refitting is the reverse of the removal procedure. Refill the cooling system with the recommended coolant, then start the engine and allow it to reach normal operating temperature, indicated by the radiator top hose becoming hot. Recheck the coolant level and add more if required, then check for leaks.

8 Coolant pump – checking, removal and refitting

Note: *Refer to the warnings given in Section 1 of this Chapter before starting work.*

Checking

1 A failure in the coolant pump can cause serious engine damage due to overheating and in the case of the diesel engine valve train damage as the coolant pump is driven by the timing belt.

2 There are three ways to check the operation of the coolant pump while it's installed on the engine. If the pump is defective, fit a new or rebuilt unit.

3 With the engine running at normal operating temperature, squeeze the radiator top hose. If the coolant pump is working properly, a pressure surge should be felt as the hose is released.

Warning: Keep your hands away from the radiator electric cooling fan blades.

4 Coolant pumps are usually equipped with weep or vent holes. If a failure occurs in the pump seal, coolant will leak from the hole. In most cases you'll need an torch to find the hole on the coolant pump from underneath to check for leaks.

5 If the coolant pump shaft bearings fail, there may be a howling sound at the drivebelt end of the engine while it's running. Shaft wear can be felt if the coolant pump pulley is rocked up and down.

6 Don't mistake drivebelt slippage, which causes a squealing sound, for coolant pump bearing failure.

Removal – all models

7 Drain the cooling system (see Chapter 1A Section 28 for petrol engines and Chapter 1B Section 28 for diesel engines).

8 Remove the auxiliary drive belt (s) and the drive belt pulley as described in Chapter 1A Section 23 for petrol engines and Chapter 1B Section 24 for diesel engines.

1.0 litre petrol models

9 Unbolt and remove the 7 bolts, noting their positions. Dispose of the 2 longer bolts as the must be replaced.

10 Remove the pump and clean the mounting surface **(see illustration)**. The replacement pump should be supplied with a new gasket, if not, or if you intend to replace the original pump, obtain a replacement gasket.

11 Fit the new pump and tighten the 5 short bolts in a diagonal sequence to the specified torque. Tighten the remaining 2 long bolts to the specified torque **(see illustration)**. On completion refill the cooling system as described in Chapter 1A Section 28 and check for leaks.

1.6 litre petrol models

12 Remove the timing belt and tensioner as described in Chapter 1A Section 22.

13 Undo the bolts and remove the coolant pump **(see illustration)**.

14 Clean the mounting surface. The replacement pump should be supplied with a new gasket, if not, or if you intend to replace the original pump, obtain a replacement gasket **(see illustration)**. If the coolant pump has been replaced the timing belt and tensioner should always be replaced. On completion refill the cooling system as described in Chapter 1A Section 28 and check for leaks.

Diesel models

15 Remove the timing belt as described in Chapter 1B Section 23.

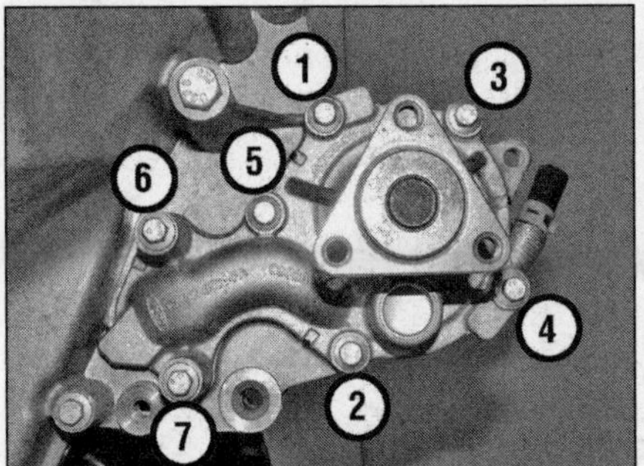

8.11 Tighten the bolts 1-5 in the order shown and then tighten bolts 6 and 7

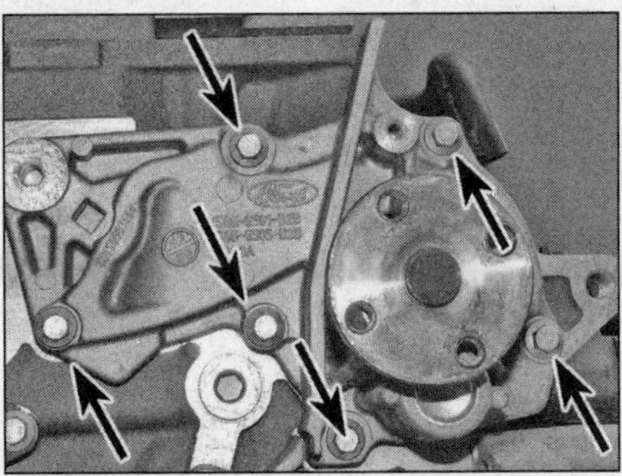

8.13 Undo the bolts (arrowed) and remove the coolant pump

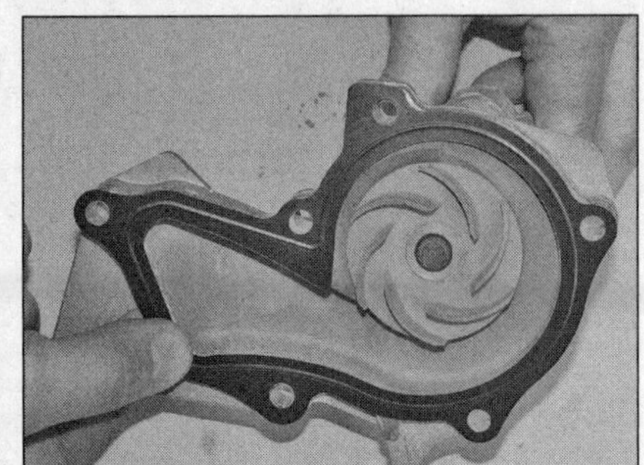

8.14 Renew the gasket

8.16 Undo the bolts (arrowed) and remove the coolant pump

8.17 Renew the coolant pump gasket

16 Unscrew the bolts and remove the coolant pump pulley **(see illustration)**.

17 Clean the pump mating surfaces carefully. The gasket must be renewed whenever it is disturbed **(see illustration)**. Refit the pump and tighten the bolts to the specified torque wrench setting. If the coolant pump has been replaced the timing belt and tensioner should always be replaced. On completion refill the cooling system as described in Chapter 1B Section 28 and check for leaks.

8.19 Location of electric coolant pump

Auxiliary electric coolant pump

Note: *1.0 litre Ecoboost engines only*

18 Raise the front of the vehicle and support it securely on axle stands (see *Jacking and vehicle support*). Where fitted, undo the fasteners and remove the engine undershield.

19 The pump is located at the rear, lower part of the cooling fan shroud **(see illustration)**.

20 Working underneath, disconnect the wiring connector, and then release the clamps and disconnect the hoses from the pump **(see illustration)**.

21 Undo the bolt securing the mounting bracket to the fan shroud, and lower the pump from place.

22 Refitting is a reversal of removal.

23 On completion, refill the cooling system.

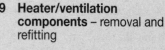

9 Heater/ventilation components – removal and refitting

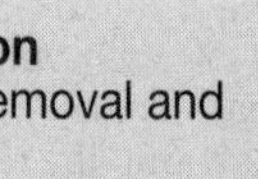

Warning: The air conditioning system is under high pressure. Do not loosen any fittings or remove any components until after the system has been discharged. Air conditioning refrigerant should be properly discharged at a dealer service department or an automotive air conditioning repair facility capable of handling R134a (up to 08-2016) or R1234yf (from 08-2016) refrigerant. Always wear eye protection when disconnecting air conditioning system fittings

Heater blower motor

1 Ford suggest that the blower motor can be removed with the use of Ford special tool 412-131. This tool locks on to the fan and allows the complete fan assembly to be rotated with the facia still in place **(see illustration)**.

8.20 Disconnect wiring connector and hoses from the pump

9.1 Even with the facia removed access to the blower motor (arrowed) is limited

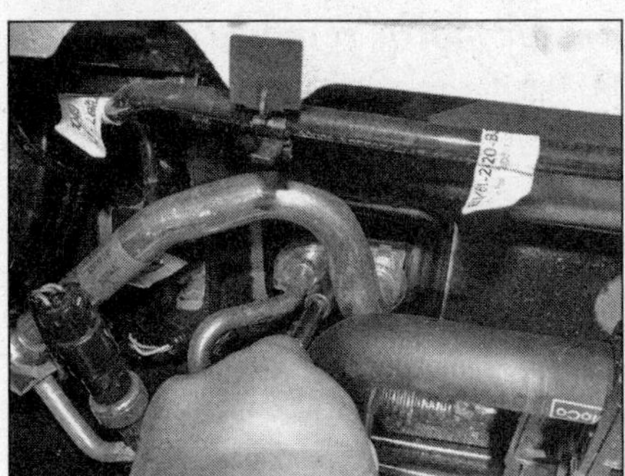
9.5a Release the refrigerant pipes and recover the O-ring seals

9.5b Align the locking collars with the arrow marks (arrowed) to release the coolant hoses

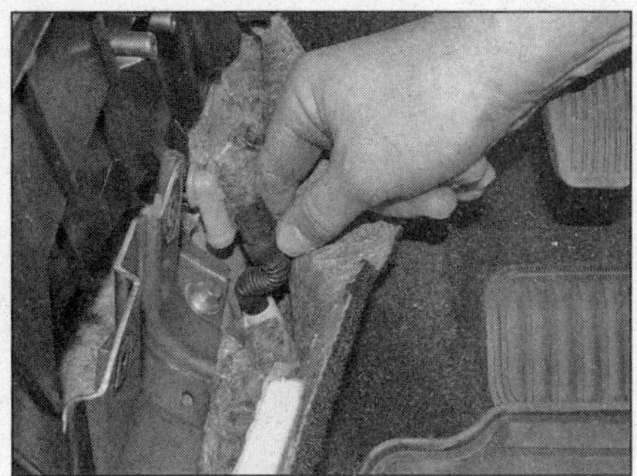
9.6 Remove the drain hose

However we found this impossible, so resorted to removing the facia and cross member as described in Chapter 11 Section 30.

2 Before starting work the Air Conditioning (AC) system, must be discharged by a suitably equipped garage or mobile AC specialist. It is a criminal offence to knowingly discharge refrigerant to the atmosphere.

3 Disconnect the battery negative lead as described in Chapter 5A Section 3.

4 Remove the complete facia and cross member as described in Chapter 11 Section 30.

9.8a Remove the screws (arrowed) and...

9.8b ...remove the housing

9.9a Depress the locking clip

9.9b Remove the blower fan and motor

5 Working under the bonnet release the AC refrigerant pipes and then disconnect the flow and return coolant hoses **(see illustrations)**.

6 Disconnect any remaining wiring plugs and then remove the evaporator drain pipe **(see illustration)**.

7 With the aid of an assistant pull the heater box away from the bulkhead and then remove the assembly from the vehicle.

8 With the heater box on the bench remove the 3 screws and remove the air recirculation flap housing **(see illustrations)**.

9 Disconnect the blower motor wiring plug, then depress the release clip, and rotate the blower motor clockwise (RHD) or anti-clockwise (LHD) and pull the motor from the housing **(see illustrations)**. Take great care not to damage the motor fan – it's extremely delicate. Do not pull on the fan, or allow the motor to rest on the fan.

10 Refitting is the reverse of the removal procedure.

Blower motor resistor

11 The resistor is located behind the pollen filter housing. Access is gained by removing the glovebox as described in Chapter 11 Section 29.

12 With the glovebox removed, reach up behind the heater housing and disconnect the wiring plug connectors. Undo the single screw at the lower part of the resistor and remove it releasing the upper part from the locating clip **(see illustrations)**.

13 Refitting is a reversal of removal.

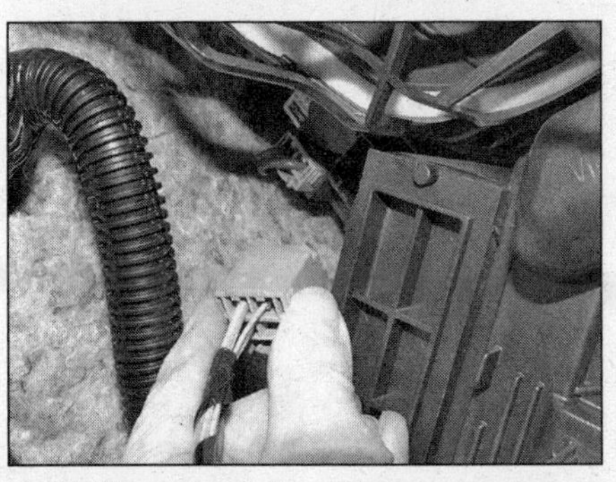
9.12a Disconnect the wiring connectors...

9.12b ...undo the retaining screw...

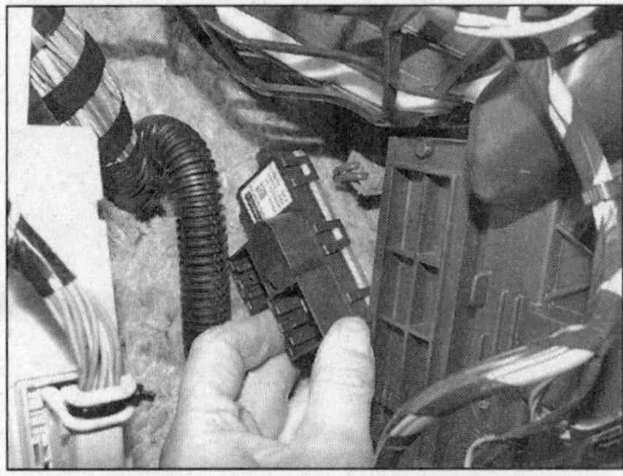
9.12c ...and release the resistor from the housing

9.16a Remove the upper screw (arrowed)...

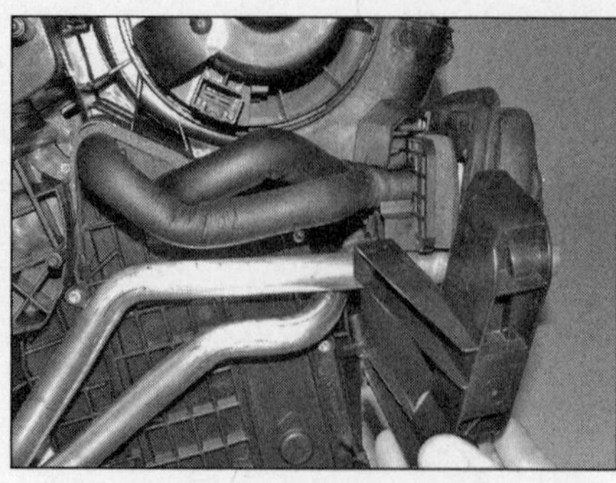
9.16b ...and then the cover

9.17a Remove the screws (arrowed) and...

9.17b ...lift off the cover

10.2a Unscrew the gear knob...

10.2b ...unclip the gaiter...

Heater matrix removal

14 The heater matrix can only be removed once the heater box has been removed. Follow the procedure in paragraphs 1-7 of this Section and remove the heater box from the vehicle.

15 With the heater box on the bench release the cover from the pollen filter housing and remove the filter.

16 Remove the 2 screws that lock the inlet and outlet pipes in position **(see illustrations)** and then remove the foam insulation.

17 Turn the heater box over and remove the screws from the lower section. Separate the lower section and lift out the heater matrix **(see illustrations)**.

18 Refitting is the reverse of the removal procedure. Refill the cooling system with the recommended coolant (see Chapter 1A or 1B). Start the engine and allow it to reach normal operating temperature, indicated by the radiator top hose becoming hot. Recheck the coolant level and add more if required, then check for leaks. Check the operation of the heater.

Pollen filter

19 Refer to Chapter 1A Section 25 or Chapter 1B Section 25.

10 Heater/air conditioning controls – removal and refitting

Heater control panel

1 Disconnect the battery negative (earth) lead (see Chapter 5A Section 3).

2 Unscrew the gear knob from the top of the gear lever, then unclip and remove the gaiter from the centre console, releasing the reverse gear linkage rod from the gear lever housing as it is removed **(see illustrations)**.

3 Using a trim tool, carefully unclip the finishing trim from the left-hand side of the centre console, followed by the finishing trim from around the front of the centre console **(see illustrations)**.

10.2c ...and release the linkage rod

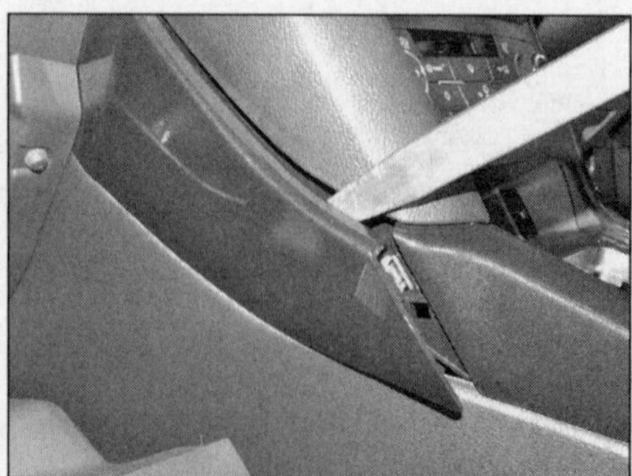
10.3a Using a trim tool...

10.3b ...to carefully unclip the finishing trims

10.4a Unclip the trim panel...

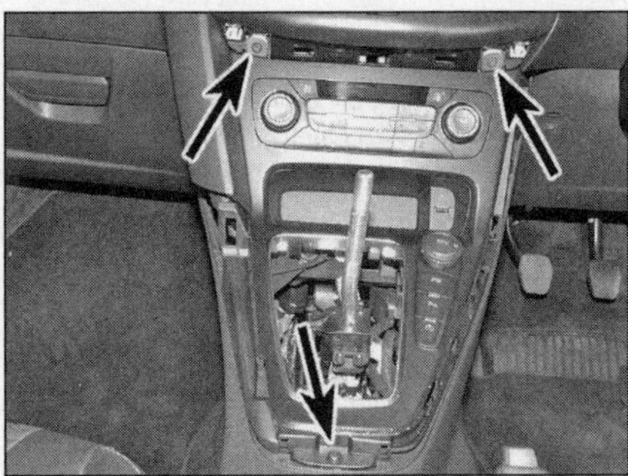

10.4b ...remove the three screws...

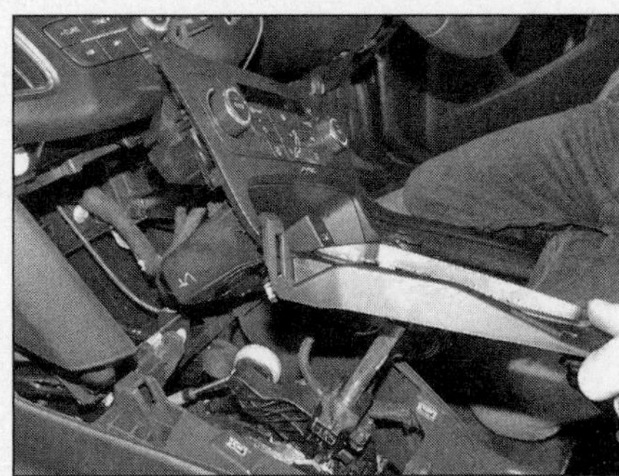

10.4c ...then withdraw the control panel...

4 Unclip the trim panel from above the heater control panel, then undo the three mounting screws and remove the control panel from the facia, disconnecting the wiring plugs as it is withdrawn **(see illustrations)**.

5 If required undo the four mounting screws and remove the control panel from the facia panel **(see illustration)**.

6 Individual components of the control panel are not available. If any of the switches or rotary controls are faulty then the complete panel must be replaced.

7 Refitting is the reverse of the removal procedure.

10.4d ...and disconnect the wiring plugs

10.5 Remove the heater control panel

11 Air conditioning system – general information and precautions

General information

1 The air conditioning system consists of a condenser mounted in front of the radiator, an evaporator mounted adjacent to the heater matrix, a compressor driven by an auxiliary drivebelt, an accumulator/ dehydrator, and the plumbing connecting all of the above components – this contains a choke (or 'venturi') mounted in the inlet to the evaporator, which creates the drop in pressure required to produce the cooling effect.

2 A blower fan forces the warmer air of the passenger compartment through the evaporator core (rather like a radiator in reverse), transferring the heat from the air to the refrigerant. The liquid refrigerant boils off into low-pressure vapour, taking the heat with it when it leaves the evaporator.

3 The refrigerant circuit high- and low-pressure service ports are located on the right-hand side of the engine compartment **(see illustrations)**. The low pressure service port is at the right-hand rear of the engine compartment and the high-pressure service port is at the front of the engine compartment to the rear of the right-hand side headlight unit.

Precautions

Warning: The air conditioning system is under high pressure. Do not loosen any fittings or remove any components until after the system has been discharged. Air conditioning refrigerant should be properly discharged at a dealer service department or an automotive air conditioning repair facility capable of handling R134a refrigerant (models up to 16/08/16) or R1234yf refrigerant (models from 16/08/16). Always wear eye protection when disconnecting air conditioning system fittings.

4 When an air conditioning system is fitted, it is necessary to observe the following special

11.3a High pressure service port

11.3b Low pressure service port – 1.0 litre petrol model

11.3c Low pressure service port – 1.5 litre diesel model

precautions whenever dealing with any part of the system, its associated components, and any items which necessitate disconnection of the system:

a) *While the refrigerants used are less damaging to the environment than the previously-used R12, it is still a very dangerous substance. It must not be allowed into contact with the skin or eyes, or there is a risk of frostbite. It must also not be discharged in an enclosed space – while it is not toxic, there is a risk of suffocation. The refrigerant is heavier than air, and so must never be discharged over a pit.*
b) *The refrigerant must not be allowed to come in contact with a naked flame, otherwise a poisonous gas will be created – under certain circumstances, this can form an explosive mixture with air. For similar reasons, smoking in the presence of refrigerant is highly dangerous, particularly if the vapour is inhaled through a lighted cigarette.*
c) *Never discharge the system to the atmosphere – R134a is not an ozone-depleting ChloroFluoroCarbon (CFC) like R12, but is instead a hydrofluorocarbon, which causes environmental damage by contributing to the 'greenhouse effect' if released into the atmosphere.*
d) *Refrigerants must not be mixed; the system uses different seals (now green-coloured, previously black) and has different fittings requiring different tools, so that there is no chance of the refrigerants becoming mixed accidentally.*

12.6 Disconnect the refrigerant pipes

e) *If for any reason the system must be discharged, entrust this task to your Ford dealer or an air conditioning specialist.*
f) *It is essential that the system be professionally discharged prior to using any form of heat – welding, soldering, brazing, etc – in the vicinity of the system, before having the vehicle oven-dried at a temperature exceeding 70°C after repainting, and before disconnecting any part of the system.*

12 Air conditioning system components – removal and refitting

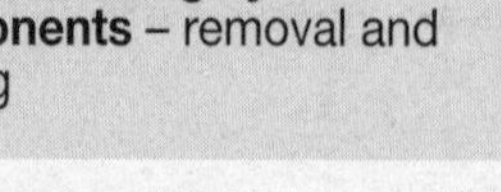

Warning: The air conditioning system is under high pressure. Do not loosen any fittings or remove any components until after the system has been discharged. Air conditioning refrigerant should be properly discharged into an approved type of container at a dealer service department or an automotive air conditioning repair facility capable of handling R134a refrigerant (models up to 16/08/16) or R1234yf refrigerant (models from 16/08/16). Cap or plug the pipe lines as soon as they are disconnected to prevent the entry of moisture. Always wear eye protection when disconnecting air conditioning system fittings.

Note: *This Section refers to the components of the air conditioning system itself – refer to Sections 9 and 10 for details of components common to the heating/ventilation system.*

Condenser

Caution: Before starting work the Air Conditioning (AC) system, must be discharged by a suitably equipped garage or mobile AC specialist. It is a criminal offence to knowingly discharge refrigerant to the atmosphere.

1 Disconnect the battery negative (earth) lead (see Chapter 5A Section 3).

2 Apply the handbrake, then raise the front of the vehicle and support on axle stands.

3 Remove the engine undershield and the air deflector from beneath the front bumper.

4 The condenser is fitted between the radiator and the active shutter grille, remove the front bumper and active shutter grille, as described in Chapter 11 Section 6 and Chapter 11 Section 7.

5 On turbo models, remove the intercooler as described in Chapter 4A Section 11 or Chapter 4B Section 15. Note this is not essential, but it avoids any possibility of damaging the intercooler as the condenser is removed.

6 With the system discharged, disconnect the two refrigerant lines from the right-hand side of the condenser **(see illustration)**. Immediately cap the open fittings, to prevent the entry of dirt and moisture.

7 Undo the two mounting bolts (one at each side) securing the condenser to the radiator, then lift the condenser to release it from the retaining clips on the lower part of the radiator **(see illustrations)**. Take care not to damage the radiator as the condenser is withdrawn.

8 Refitting is the reverse of removal. Renew the O-rings and lubricate with refrigerant oil.

9 Have the system evacuated, charged and leak-tested by the specialist who discharged it.

Evaporator

10 The evaporator is mounted inside the heater housing with the heater matrix. In order to remove the evaporator, the complete heater housing must be removed.

Caution: Before starting work the Air Conditioning (AC) system, must be discharged by a suitably equipped garage or mobile AC specialist. It is a criminal offence to knowingly discharge refrigerant to the atmosphere.

11 Disconnect the battery negative (earth) lead (see Chapter 5A Section 3).

12 Drain the cooling system as described in Chapter 1A or 1B.

13 Follow the procedure described in Section 9 (paragraphs 1-7) and remove the complete heater box assembly from the vehicle.

14 With the assembly on the bench remove the heater matrix **(see illustrations 9.17a and 9.17b)**.

15 Remove the end panel from the housing **(see illustration)**.

12.7a Undo the mounting bolts (one side shown)

12.7b Release the lower retaining clips (one side shown)

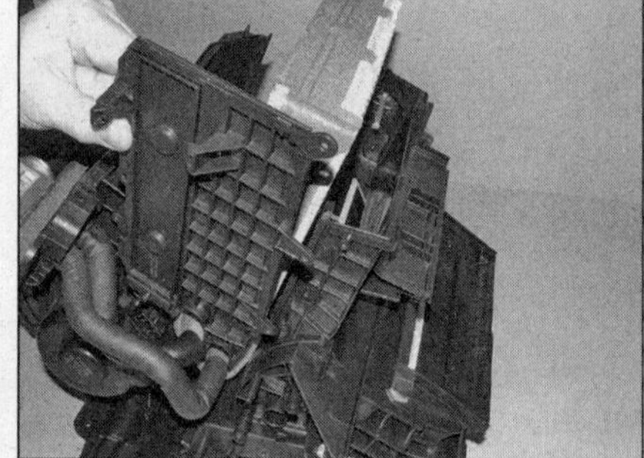
12.15 Remove the end panel

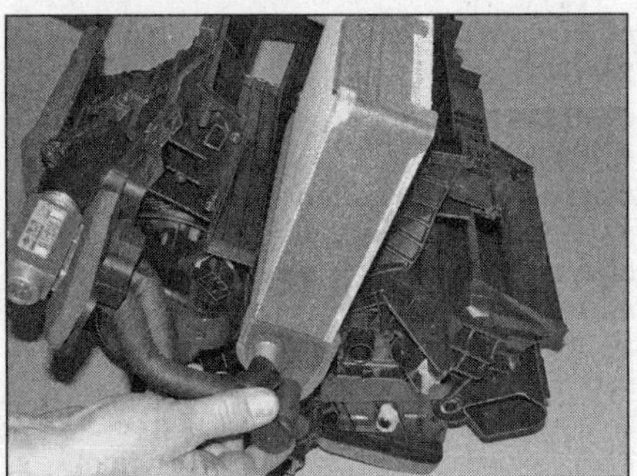
12.16 Remove the evaporator core

12.22a Remove the refrigerant lines (arrowed) and...

12.22b ...immediately seal the openings

16 Lift out the evaporator core, complete with the expansion valve **(see illustration)**. Remove the expansion vale.

17 Refitting is the reverse of removal, noting the following points:

a) Fit new O-rings seals and lubricate them with compressor oil before assembly.

b) Tighten all fasteners to the specified torque where given.

c) Have the system evacuated, charged and leak-tested by the specialist who discharged it.

Compressor

Caution: Before starting work the Air Conditioning (AC) system, must be discharged by a suitably equipped garage or mobile AC specialist. It is a criminal offence to knowingly discharge refrigerant to the atmosphere.

18 Disconnect the battery negative (earth) lead (see Chapter 5A Section 3).

19 Apply the handbrake, then raise the front of the vehicle and support on axle stands. Remove the right-hand front roadwheel.

20 Remove the right-hand front wheel arch liner, and engine undershield.

21 Remove the auxiliary drive belt as described in Chapter 1A Section 23 for petrol engines and Chapter 1B Section 24 for diesel engines.

22 Unscrew the clamping bolt(s) to disconnect the refrigerant lines from the compressor **(see illustrations)**. Plug the line connections to prevent entry of any dirt or moisture. Discard the O-ring seals, new ones must be fitted.

23 Unbolt the compressor from the cylinder block/crankcase, unplug its electrical connector, then withdraw the compressor from the vehicle **(see illustration)**.

Note: *Keep the compressor level during handling and storage. If the compressor has seized, or if you find metal particles in the refrigerant lines, the system must be flushed out by an air conditioning technician, and the accumulator/dehydrator must be renewed.*

24 Prior to installation, turn the compressor clutch centre six times, to disperse any oil that has collected in the head.

25 Refit the compressor in the reverse order of removal; renew all seals disturbed.

26 If you are installing a new compressor, refer to the compressor manufacturer's instructions (and the specifications at the start of this Chapter) for adding refrigerant oil to the system.

27 Refit the wheel arch liner, undershield and roadwheel. Lower the vehicle to the ground.

28 Have the system evacuated, charged and leak-tested by the specialist that discharged it.

Accumulator/dehydrator (Receiver drier)

Caution: Before starting work the Air Conditioning (AC) system, must be discharged by a suitably equipped garage or mobile AC specialist. It is a criminal offence to knowingly discharge refrigerant to the atmosphere.

29 Apply the handbrake, then raise the front of the vehicle and support on axle stands.

30 Remove the engine undershield and the air deflector from beneath the bumper cover.

31 The Accumulator/dehydrator (Receiver drier) is fitted to the end of the condenser, remove the front bumper and active shutter grille, as described in Chapter 11 Section 6 and Chapter 11 Section 7.

1.0 litre petrol and diesel models

32 Reach up and remove the 2 upper mounting bolts and then remove the lower mounting bolt **(see illustration)**.

33 Work the accumulator free from the

12.23 Remove the compressor

12.32 Undo the lower mounting bolt

12.39 The AC pressure switch (arrowed)

condenser and then lower it from the vehicle. Immediately plug the openings in the condenser.

34 Refit the accumulator/dehydrator in the reverse order of removal. Renew all seals disturbed and lubricate then with compressor oil before refitting. Refit the remainder of the components and then have the AC system leak tested and recharged with the correct quantity of refrigerant.

1.6 litre petrol models

35 On these models the accumulator housing is part of the condenser assembly.

36 Remove the blanking plug from the base of the accumulator and then using suitable circlip pliers remove the now exposed circlip.

37 Screw a suitable long bolt into the base of the accumulator and pull the accumulator free from the housing.

38 Refit the accumulator/dehydrator in the reverse order of removal. Renew all seals disturbed and lubricate then with compressor oil before refitting. Refit the remainder of the components and then have the AC system leak tested and recharged with the correct quantity of refrigerant.

High- and low-pressure cut-off switch

Caution: Before starting work the Air Conditioning (AC) system, must be discharged by a suitably equipped garage or mobile AC specialist. It is a criminal offence to knowingly discharge refrigerant to the atmosphere.

39 The switch is located to the rear of the radiator, on the right-hand side of the engine compartment. Disconnect the wiring connector from the pressure switch **(see illustration)**.

40 With the system discharged and the wiring connector disconnected, the switch can then be unscrewed from the refrigerant pipe.

41 Refitting is the reverse of the removal procedure. Renew the O-ring on the switch and lubricate with refrigerant oil.

42 Have the system leak-tested and charged by the specialist that discharged it, then check the operation of the air conditioning system.

Chapter 4 Part A
Fuel and exhaust systems – petrol engines

Contents

Degrees of difficulty

Easy, suitable for novice with little experience 	**Fairly easy,** suitable for beginner with some experience	**Fairly difficult,** suitable for competent DIY mechanic	**Difficult,** suitable for experienced DIY mechanic	**Very difficult,** suitable for expert DIY or professional 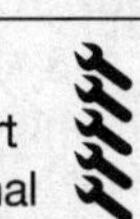

Specifications

General

System type	Sequential multiport fuel indirect injection
Fuel octane requirement	95 RON unleaded

Torque wrench settings

	Nm	lbf ft
Accelerator pedal assembly nuts	8	6
Camshaft position sensor	8	6
Catalytic converter support bracket bolts:		
1.6 EcoBoost engines:		
Stage 1 (to convertor)	7	5
Stage 2	Loosen 360°	
To transmission	48	35
1.6 Ti-VCt engines	25	18
Crankshaft position sensor	8	6
Exhaust heat shield bolts	10	7
Exhaust manifold:		
1.6 EcoBoost engine (to cylinder head)	21	16
1.6 Ti-VCT engine (to cylinder head):		
Stage1	20	15
Stage 2	55	41
Manifold to exhaust flexible section (Ti-VCT engines)	48	35
Floor panel brace bolts	70	51
Fuel pulse damper (Ti-VCT engines only)	10	7
Fuel rail high pressure pipe (EcoBoost engines only)		
Stage 1	21	16
Stage 2	Wait 5 minutes	
Stage 3	21	16
Fuel rail mounting bolts:		
EcoBoost engines	23	17
1.6 litre engines	15	11
Fuel tank strap retaining bolts	25	18

Torque wrench settings (continued)	Nm	lbf ft
Inlet manifold nuts/bolts:		
1.0 litre engines	10	7
1.6 EcoBoost engines:		
Upper bolts	18	13
Lower bolts	10	7
1.6 litre Ti-VCT engines	18	13
Oxygen sensors	48	35
Throttle body retaining bolts	10	7
Turbocharger oil drain pipe bolts	10	7
Turbocharger oil supply pipe bolt	30	22
Turbocharger to exhaust manifold (1.6 litre EcoBoost engines)	30	22
Turbocharger to cylinder head nuts (1.0 litre EcoBoost engine):		
Stage 1	19	14
Stage 2	24	17
Stage 3	Wait 30 seconds	
Stage 4	24	17
Variable camshaft timing oil control solenoid	10	7

1 General information and precautions

General information

1 The fuel system consists of a fuel tank (mounted under the floor, beneath the rear seats), fuel hoses, an electric fuel pump mounted in the fuel tank, and a sequential electronic fuel injection system controlled by an engine management electronic control unit (Powertrain Control Module).

2 On Ti-VCT models the electric fuel pump supplies fuel under pressure to the fuel rail, which distributes fuel to the injectors. A pressure regulator integral with the pump controls the system pressure. From the fuel rail, fuel is injected into the inlet ports, just above the inlet valves, by four fuel injectors. The fuel rail is mounted to the cylinder head, just above the plastic inlet manifold.

3 EcoBoost models feature a high pressure direct injection fuel system. Fuel is supplied by the tank mounted pump to a camshaft driven high pressure fuel pump. From here fuel is supplied (via a fuel rail) to fuel injectors mounted in the cylinder head.

4 The amount of fuel supplied by the injectors is precisely controlled by the Powertrain Control Module (PCM). The module uses the signals from the crankshaft position sensor and the camshaft position sensor to trigger each injector separately in cylinder firing order (sequential injection), with benefits in terms of better fuel economy and leaner exhaust emissions.

5 The Powertrain Control Module is the heart of the entire engine management system, controlling the fuel injection, ignition and emissions control systems. The module receives information from various sensors which is then computed and compared with preset values stored in its memory to determine the required period of injection.

6 Information on crankshaft position and engine speed is generated by a crankshaft position sensor. On Ti-VCT models the inductive head of the sensor runs just above the engine flywheel and scans a series of protrusions on the flywheel periphery. On EcoBoost models the sensor is located behind the crankshaft pulley. On Ti-VCT models, as the crankshaft rotates, the sensor transmits a pulse to the system's ignition module every time a protrusion passes it. There is one missing protrusion in the flywheel periphery at a point corresponding to 90° BTDC. The ignition module recognises the absence of a pulse from the crankshaft position sensor at this point to establish a reference mark for crankshaft position. Similarly, the time interval between absent pulses is used to determine engine speed. On Ecoboost models an inductive sensor is fitted that picks up the variation in the magnetic field in the pick up ring fitted to the rear of the crankshaft pulley. The information from the crankshaft position sensors is then fed to the Powertrain Control Module for further processing.

7 On all engines 2 camshaft position sensors are fitted, as each camshaft is fitted with variable timing units. The camshaft position sensor functions in the same way as the crankshaft position sensor, producing a series of pulses. The output from the sensors provides the Powertrain Control Module with a reference point, to enable it to determine the firing order and operate the injectors in the appropriate sequence.

8 Engine temperature information is supplied by the coolant temperature sensor. The sensor is an NTC (Negative Temperature Coefficient) thermistor – that is, a semi-conductor whose electrical resistance decreases as its temperature increases. The sensor provides the Powertrain Control Module with a constantly-varying (analogue) voltage signal, corresponding to the temperature of the engine coolant. This is used to refine the calculations made by the module when determining the correct amount of fuel required to achieve the ideal air/fuel mixture ratio.

9 Inlet air temperature and density information for air/fuel mixture ratio calculations is provided by a temperature and manifold absolute pressure (TMAP) sensor. The TMAP sensor is located on the throttle housing, and consists of a pressure transducer and a temperature sensor which directly supersedes the mass airflow and inlet air temperature sensors. The TMAP sensor provides information to the Powertrain Control Module relating to inlet manifold vacuum and barometric pressure, and the temperature of the air in the inlet manifold. When the ignition is switched on with the engine stopped, the sensor calculates barometric pressure and, when the engine is running, the sensor calculates inlet manifold vacuum. All engines are fitted with a mass airflow sensor in the outlet duct from the air cleaner housing.

10 The throttle valve inside the throttle housing is controlled by the driver with the accelerator pedal. As the valve opens, the amount of air that can pass through the system increases. As the throttle valve opens further, the TMAP sensor signal alters, and the Powertrain Control Module opens each injector for a longer duration, to increase the amount of fuel delivered to the inlet ports.

11 All models features a throttle which is electronically-controlled – an accelerator cable is not fitted. Instead, a throttle position sensor fitted to the accelerator pedal provides the Powertrain Control Module with the throttle opening signal, and this is relayed to a motor-driven throttle valve. This system also enables the PCM to control the engine idle speed, varying the throttle opening as required by changes in engine temperature and load.

12 To improve performance and economy all EcoBoost models have a low inertia turbocharger and intercooler fitted.

13 On all models, road speed is monitored by the ABS wheel sensors.

14 The clutch pedal position is monitored by a switch fitted to the pedal bracket. This sends a signal to the Powertrain Control Module.

15 Oxygen sensors in the exhaust system provides the module with constant feedback – 'closed-loop' control – which enables it to adjust the mixture to provide the best possible operating conditions for the catalytic converter. A further sensor is fitted, downstream of the converter, to monitor the converter's operation, and this provides an even finer degree of emission control.

16 The air inlet side of the system consists of an air cleaner housing, an inlet hose, a throttle housing and on EcoBoost models a turbocharger.

17 Both the idle speed and mixture are under the control of the Powertrain Control Module, and cannot be adjusted.

Precautions

18 Before disconnecting any of the fuel injection system sensor wiring plugs, ensure at least that the ignition is switched off (ideally, disconnect the battery). If this is not done, it could result in a fault code being logged in the system memory, and may even cause damage to the component concerned.

19 Residual pressure will remain in the fuel lines long after the car was last used. When disconnecting any fuel line, first depressurise the fuel system as described in Section 2.

Warning: Many of the procedures in this Chapter require the removal of fuel lines and connections, which may result in some fuel spillage. Before carrying out any operation on the fuel system, refer to the precautions given in ' Safety first, !' at the beginning of this manual, and follow them implicitly. Petrol is a highly-dangerous and volatile liquid, and the precautions necessary when handling it cannot be overstressed.

2 Fuel system – depressurisation

Warning: The following procedure will merely relieve the pressure in the fuel system – remember that fuel will still be present in the system components, and take precautions accordingly before disconnecting any of them.

Note: *Refer to the warning note in Section 1 before proceeding.*

1 The fuel system referred to in this Chapter is defined as the fuel tank and tank-mounted fuel pump/fuel gauge sender unit, the fuel injector, and the metal pipes and flexible hoses of the fuel lines between these components. On EcoBoost engines this also includes the high pressure fuel pump. All these contain fuel, which will be under pressure while the engine is running and/or while the ignition is switched on.

2 The pressure will remain for some time after the ignition has been switched off, and must be relieved before any of these components is disturbed for servicing work.

3 The simplest depressurisation method is to disconnect the fuel pump electrical supply by removing the fuel pump fuse from the fusebox located inside the vehicle, behind the glovebox **(see illustration)** (refer to the wiring diagrams or vehicle handbook for exact location) and starting the engine; allow the engine to idle until it stops through lack of fuel. Turn the engine over once or twice on the starter to ensure that all pressure is released, then switch off the ignition; do not forget to refit the fuse when work is complete.

4 On Ti-VCT models an adapter is available to fit the Schrader-type valve on the fuel rail pressure test/release fitting (identifiable by its blue plastic cap, and located on the union of the fuel feed line and the fuel rail), this may be used to release the fuel pressure. The Ford adapter (tool number 23-033) operates like to a drain tap – turning the tap clockwise releases the pressure. If the adapter is not available, place cloth rags around the valve, then remove the cap and allow the fuel pressure to dissipate. Refit the cap on completion.

5 Note that, once the fuel system has been depressurised and drained (even partially), it will take significantly longer to restart the engine – perhaps several seconds of cranking – before the system is refilled and pressure restored.

3 Unleaded petrol – general information and usage

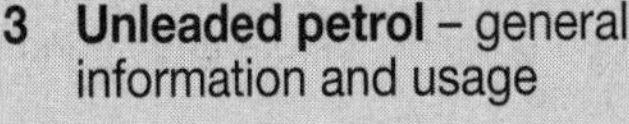

1 All petrol models are designed to run on fuel with a minimum octane rating of 95 (RON). All models have a catalytic converter, and so must be run on unleaded fuel only. Under no circumstances should leaded fuel (UK '4-star' or LRP) be used, as this will damage the converter.

2 Super unleaded petrol (98 octane) can also be used in all models if wished, though there is no advantage in doing so.

4 Fuel lines and fittings – general information

Note: *Refer to the warning note in Section 1 before proceeding.*

Quick-release couplings

1 A variety of quick-release couplings are employed at many of the unions in the fuel feed and return lines.

2 Before disconnecting any fuel system component, relieve the residual pressure in the system (see Section 2), and equalise tank pressure by removing the fuel filler cap.

Warning: This procedure will merely relieve the increased pressure necessary for the engine to run – remember that fuel will still be present in the system components, and take precautions accordingly before disconnecting any of them.

3 Release the protruding locking lugs on each union by squeezing them together and carefully pulling the coupling apart **(see illustrations)**. Use rag to soak up any spilt fuel. Where the unions are colour-coded, the pipes cannot be confused. Where both unions are the same colour, note carefully which pipe is connected to which, and ensure that they are correctly reconnected on refitting.

4 To reconnect one of these couplings, press them firmly together. Switch the ignition on and off five times to pressurise the system,

2.3 Fusebox inside the vehicle

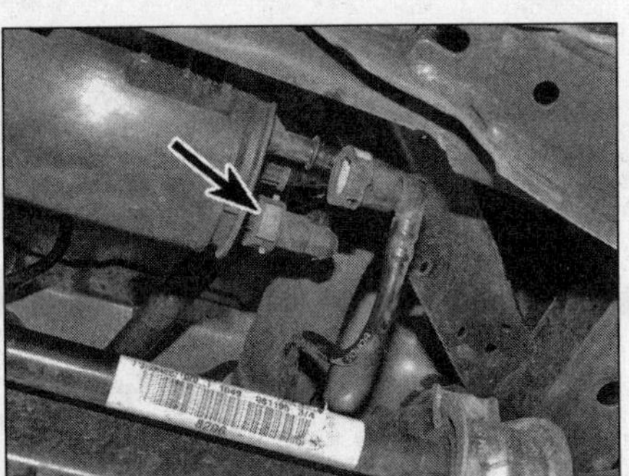

4.3a Squeeze the quick-release connectors to release them (arrowed)...

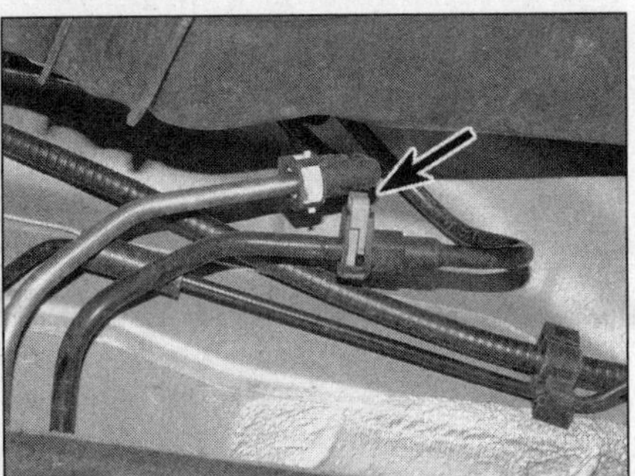

4.3b ...or slide up the locking clip (arrowed)

and check for any sign of fuel leakage around the disturbed coupling before attempting to start the engine.

Checking fuel lines

5 Checking procedures for the fuel lines are included in Chapter 1A Section 8.

Component renewal

6 If any damaged sections are to be renewed, use original-equipment hoses or pipes, constructed from exactly the same material as the section being renewed. Do not install substitutes constructed from inferior or inappropriate material; this could cause a fuel leak or a fire.

7 Before detaching or disconnecting any part of the fuel system, note the routing of all hoses and pipes, and the orientation of all clamps and clips. New sections must be installed in exactly the same manner.

8 Before disconnecting any part of the fuel system, be sure to relieve the fuel system pressure, and equalise tank pressure by removing the fuel filler cap. Also disconnect the battery negative (earth) lead – see Chapter 5A Section 3. Cover the fitting being disconnected with a rag, to absorb any fuel that may spray out.

5 Air cleaner assembly – removal and refitting

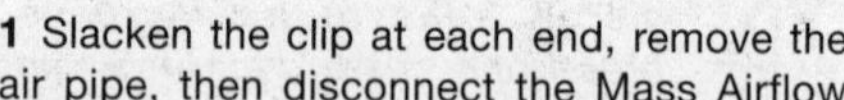

1 Slacken the clip at each end, remove the air pipe, then disconnect the Mass Airflow Sensor (MAF) wiring plug and remove the cable clip **(see illustrations)**.

2 Unhook the rubber retaining ring **(see illustration)**.

3 Pull the air cleaner upwards to remove it **(see illustration)**. The pegs on the base of the cleaner fit into rubber grommets. These pegs may prove troublesome to release, and some effort may be needed – take care to avoid personal injury.

4 When refitting, locate the air cleaner pegs into the grommets and push down firmly to engage them in the grommets. Lubricate them with a silicon type grease if necessary. Make sure the air cleaner duct clamps are securely refitted/tightened to prevent air leaks.

6 Accelerator pedal – removal and refitting

Removal

1 Remove the driver's side facia lower panel, as described in Chapter 11 Section 30.

2 Disconnect the battery negative lead as described in Chapter 5A Section 3.

3 Disconnect the wiring plug from the throttle position sensor, then unscrew the 2 mounting nuts and remove the pedal/sensor assembly from the bulkhead studs **(see illustration)**. Note that the sensor is not available separately from the pedal assembly.

Note: *Ford insist that the sensor wiring plug can only be disconnected 10 times before is becomes irreversibly damaged. Use a marker pen to record each disconnection on the side of the connector. Only disconnect the plug if it is absolutely necessary.*

Refitting

4 Refit in the reverse order of removal. On completion, check the action of the pedal to ensure that the throttle has full unrestricted movement, and fully returns when released.

5 Reconnect the battery as described in Chapter 5A Section 3.

7 Fuel tank – removal, inspection and refitting

Note: *Refer to the warning note in Section 1 before proceeding.*

Removal

1 Run the fuel level as low as possible prior to removing the tank. There is no drain plug fitted (and syphoning may prove difficult) but it may be possible to partially drain the tank.

2 Relieve the residual pressure in the fuel system (see Section 2), and equalise tank pressure by removing the fuel filler cap.

3 Disconnect the battery negative (earth) lead (see Chapter 5A Section 3).

4 Chock the front wheels, then jack up the rear of the car and support it on axle stands (see *Jacking and vehicle support*). Remove the rear roadwheels.

5 Unhook the exhaust system mounting rubbers from the centre and rear hangers, and allow the exhaust system to rest on the rear suspension crossmember.

6 Undo the nuts securing the flange of the exhaust system rear section, then manoeuvre the rear section to one side, and secure it in place using cable ties/wire/string.

7 Undo the 3 bolts and pull the left-hand side air deflector shield rearwards to release its retaining clip and then remove the centre protective cover from under the EVAP canister **(see illustrations)**.

8 Undo the nuts and remove the exhaust

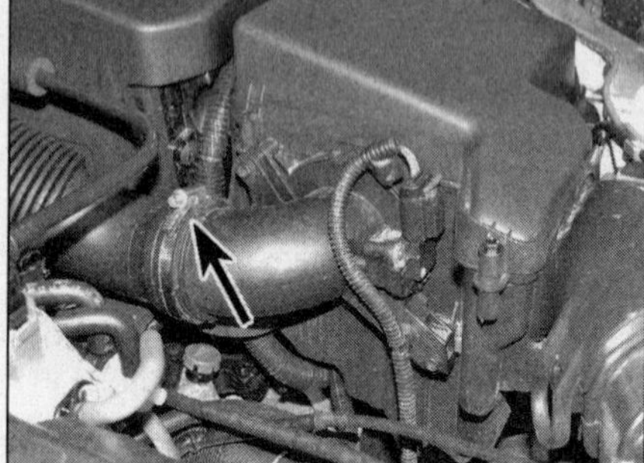

5.1a Slacken the hose clips at each end, remove the air pipe, ...

5.1b ...and disconnect the wiring plug from the MAF sensor

5.2 Unhook the rubber ring

5.3 Remove the air filter housing

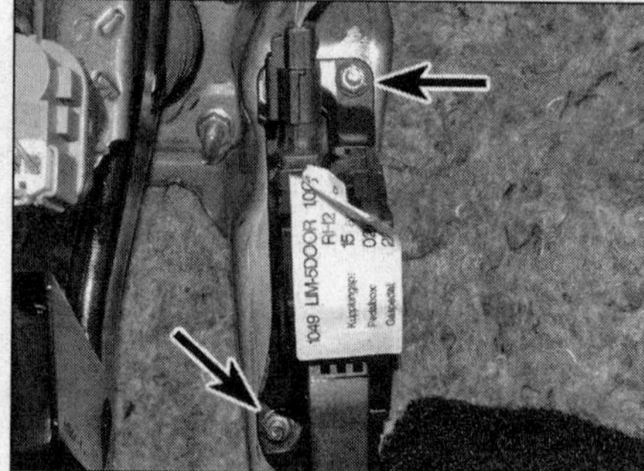

6.3 Accelerator pedal/sensor assembly mounting nuts (arrowed)

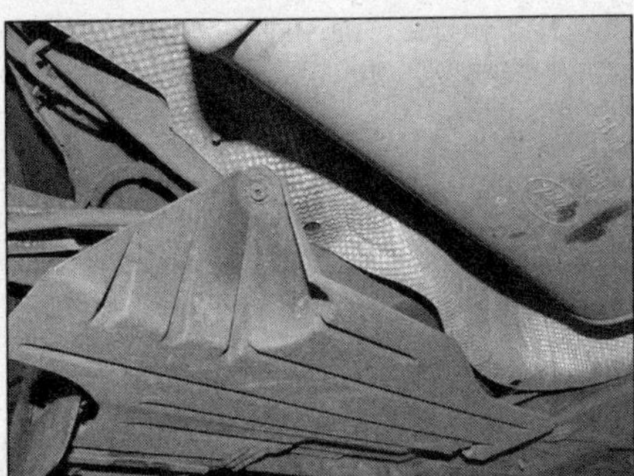
7.7a Undo the bolts and remove the left-hand side air deflector shield...

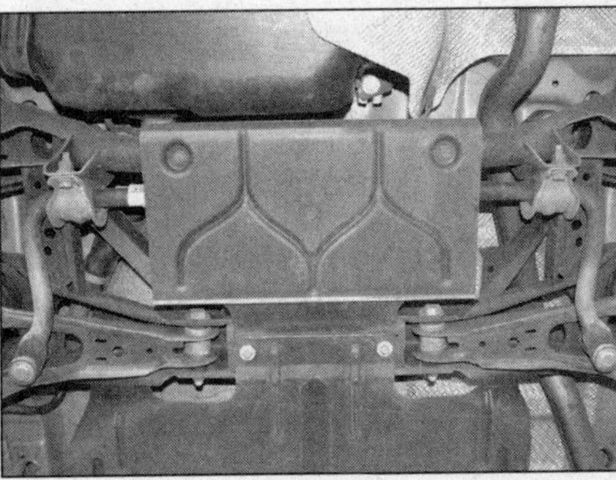
7.7b ... and remove the centre protective cover

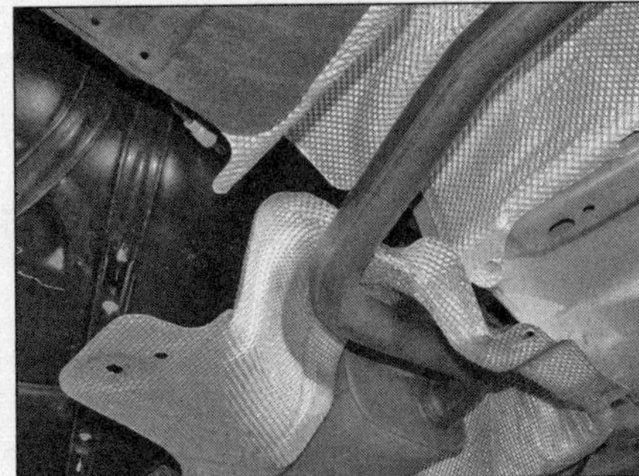
7.8 Undo the nuts and remove the heat shields beneath the fuel tank

centre and rear section heat shields from the vehicle underside **(see illustration)**.

9 Release the clips and disconnect the fuel tank filler pipes **(see illustration)**. Do not use any sharp-edged tools to release the pipes from their stub, as the pipe is easily damaged.

10 Depress the release button and disconnect the fuel tank vent pipe from the rear of the tank to the evaporative emissions **(see illustration)**.

11 Disconnect the fuel supply pipe and EVAP canister purge valve pipe from the front of the tank **(see illustration)**.

12 Support the tank using a trolley jack and a large sheet of wood to spread the load.

13 Note exactly how the fuel tank retaining straps are arranged to make refitting easier. In particular, note their fitted order under the retaining bolt heads, where applicable. The left-hand side strap is on top at the front fixing.

14 Unbolt and remove the fuel tank retaining straps **(see illustrations)**, but do not lower the tank at this stage.

15 Partially lower the tank on the jack, taking care that no strain is placed on any fuel lines or wiring. As soon as the wiring connector for the fuel pump/gauge sender on top of the tank is accessible, reach in and disconnect it, then release the clip and disconnect the breather hose from the top of the tank **(see illustrations)**. Where applicable, unclip the EVAP canister hose from the top of the tank.

7.9 Remove the filler pipe

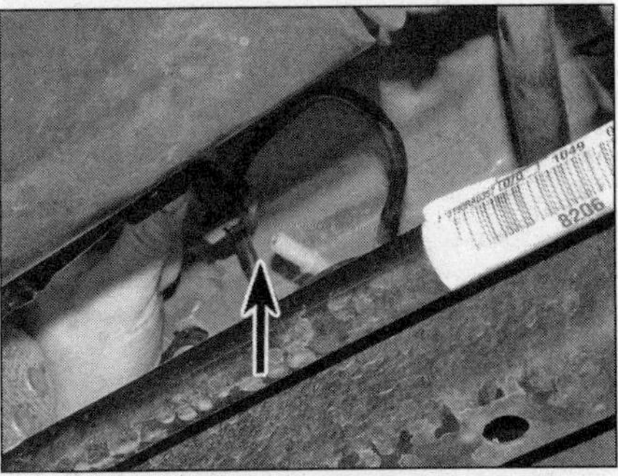
7.10 Depress the release button (arrowed) and disconnect the vent pipe from the rear of the tank

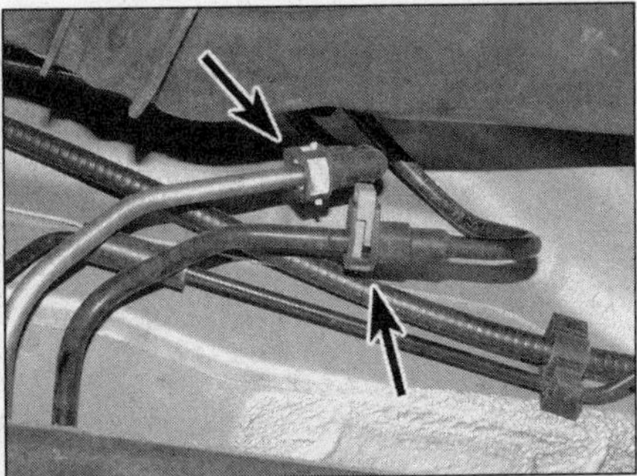
7.11 Disconnect the fuel supply and purge valve pipe at the front of the tank (arrowed)

7.14a Undo the bolts at the rear (arrowed)...

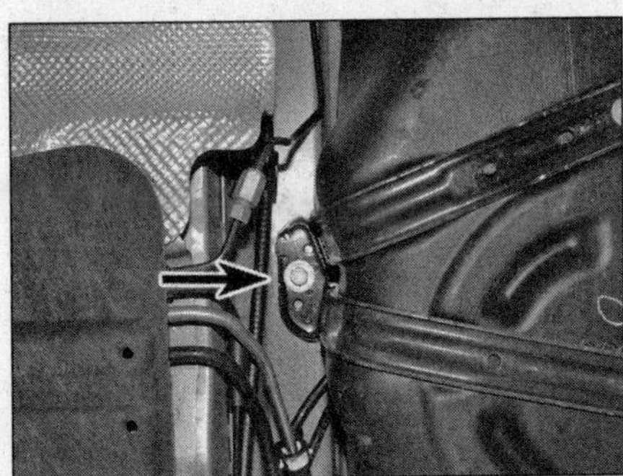
7.14b ...and at the front (arrowed)

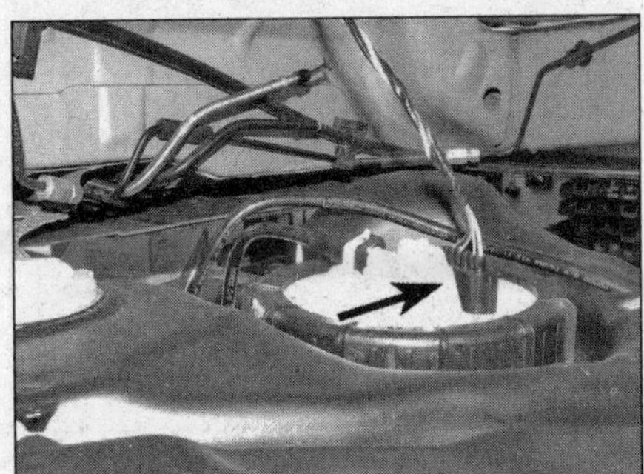
7.15a Disconnect the wiring plug (arrowed)...

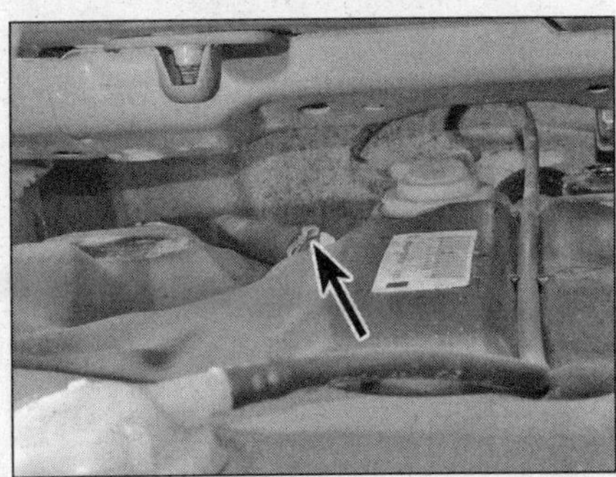
7.15b ...then release the clip and disconnect the breather pipe (arrowed)

16 Lower the fuel tank to the ground, checking all the way down that no pipes or wiring are under any strain. Remove the tank from under the car.

Inspection

17 Whilst removed, the fuel tank can be inspected for damage or deterioration. Removal of the fuel pump/fuel gauge sender unit (see Section 8) will allow a partial inspection of the interior. If the tank is contaminated with sediment or water, swill it out with clean fuel. Do not under any circumstances undertake any repairs on a leaking or damaged fuel tank; this work must be carried out by a professional who has experience in this critical and potentially dangerous work.

18 Whilst the fuel tank is removed from the car, it should be placed in a safe area where sparks or open flames cannot ignite the fumes coming out of the tank. Be especially careful inside garages where a natural-gas type appliance is located, because the pilot light could cause an explosion.

19 Check the condition of the lower filler pipe and renew it if necessary.

Refitting

20 Refitting is a reversal of the removal procedure, noting the following points:

a) *Ensure that all pipe and wiring connections are securely fitted.*
b) *When refitting the quick-release couplings, press them together until the locking lugs snap into their groove.*
c) *Tighten the tank strap retaining bolts to the specified torque.*
d) *If evidence of contamination was found, do not return any previously-drained fuel to the tank unless it is carefully filtered first.*

8 Fuel pump/fuel gauge sender unit – removal and refitting

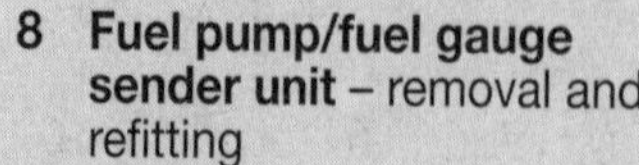
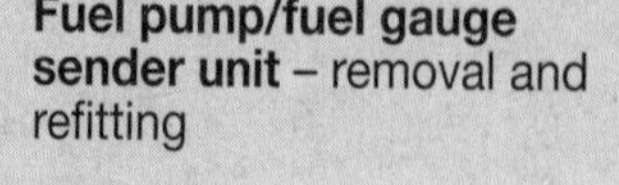

Note: *Refer to the warning note in Section 1 before proceeding.*

Removal

1 A combined fuel pump and fuel gauge sender unit is located in the top face of the fuel tank. The combined unit can only be detached and withdrawn from the tank after the tank is released and lowered from under the car. Refer to Section 7 and remove the fuel tank, then proceed as follows.

2 With the fuel tank removed, disconnect the fuel supply pipe (if still attached to the tank) from the stub by squeezing the quick-release lugs.

3 Unscrew and remove the special retaining ring, either by unscrewing it with a special locking collar tool – these are widely available from tool suppliers such as Draper, or by fabricating a home made tool **(see illustrations)**.

4 Take out the rubber seal, then carefully lift out the fuel pump/gauge sender unit from the tank. Take care that the sender unit float and arm are not damaged as the unit is removed. To avoid any possibility of the tank distorting immediately refit the locking collar back onto the fuel tank

5 The level sender unit can be tested by connecting an ohmmeter across the sender terminals, and measuring its resistance **(see illustration)**. Check that the resistance changes smoothly and progressively as the arm is moved through the full range of travel.

Refitting

6 Refitting is a reversal of removal, but fit a new rubber seal and tighten the retaining ring securely, aligning the arrow on the top of the module with the mark on the top of the tank **(see illustrations)**. Refit the fuel tank as described in Section 7.

9 Fuel tank roll-over valve – removal and refitting

1 The roll-over valve is built into the top of the fuel tank. It is not possible to access the valve. Its purpose is to prevent fuel loss if the car becomes inverted in a crash.

10 Turbocharger – removal and refitting

Note: *The 1.6 Ti-VCT engine does not have a turbocharger fitted.*

Removal

1 Disconnect the battery as described in Chapter 5A Section 3 and allow the engine to fully cool. Remove the engine cover.

2 Jack up and support the front of the vehicle (see *Jacking and vehicle support* in the reference section).

3 Remove the engine undershield.

4 Remove the catalytic converter as described in Section 15.

5 Drain the cooling system as described in Chapter 1A Section 28.

1.0 litre models

6 Release the hose clamps and the mounting bracket and remove the air inlet duct.

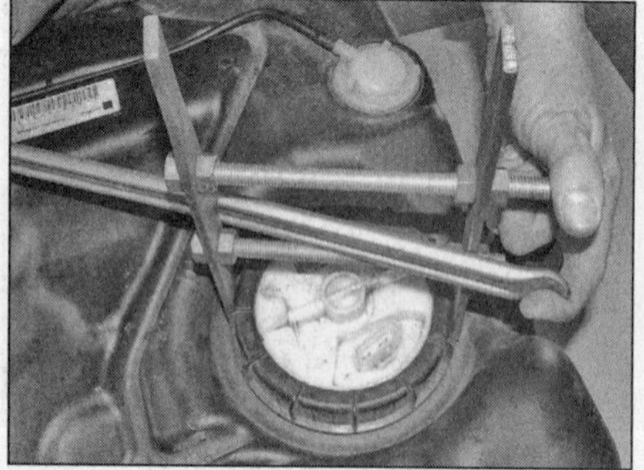

8.3a Using a home-made tool to slacken the retaining ring...

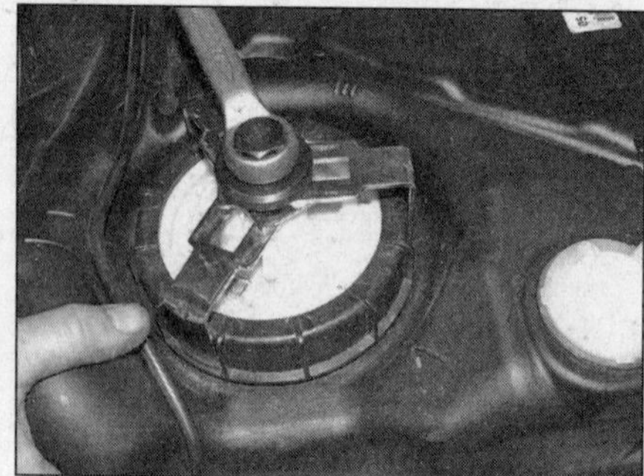

8.3b ...or a commercially available one

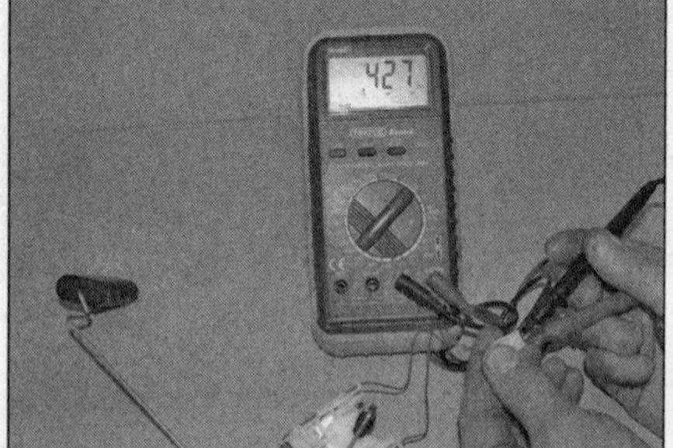

8.5 Measure the resistance of the sender unit at full and zero float arm deflection

8.6a Align the arrow on the top of the module with the mark on the tank (arrowed)

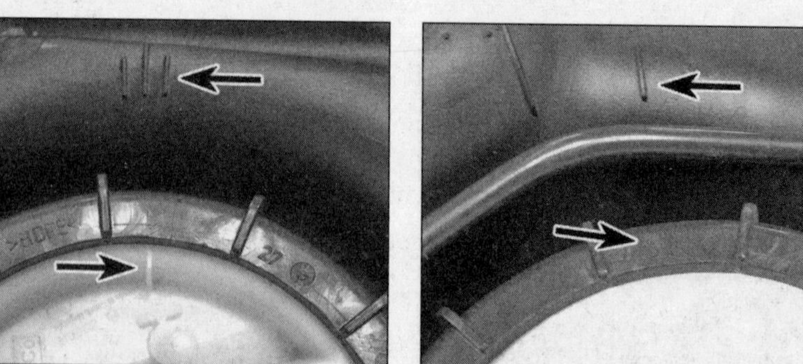

8.6b Tighten the locking collar so that the marks (arrowed) align

10.7 Remove the coolant hoses

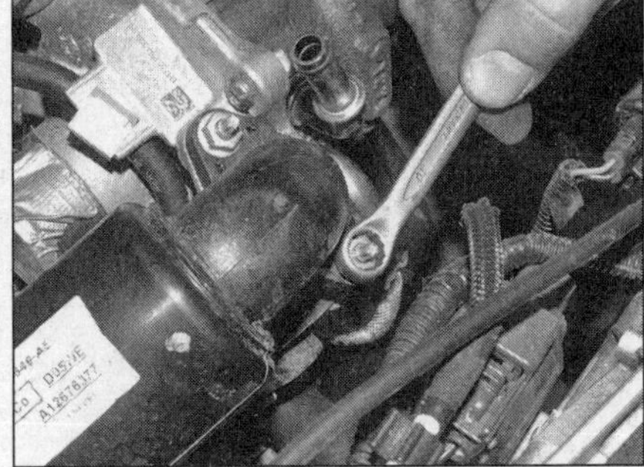

10.8a Unbolt the outlet pipe...

10.8b ...and remove it

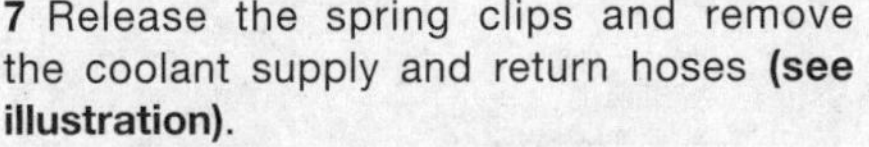

7 Release the spring clips and remove the coolant supply and return hoses **(see illustration)**.

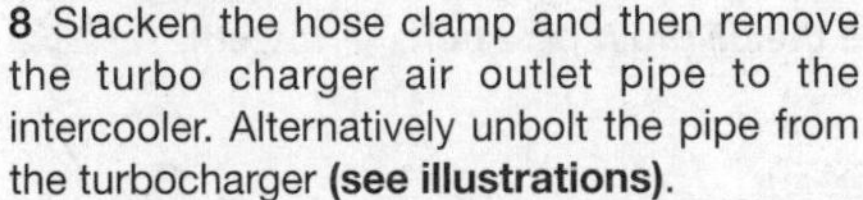

8 Slacken the hose clamp and then remove the turbo charger air outlet pipe to the intercooler. Alternatively unbolt the pipe from the turbocharger **(see illustrations)**.

9 From below the turbocharger remove the 2 bolts and release the oil drain pipe.

10 Unbolt and remove the oil supply pipe **(see illustration)**. Dispose of the pipe – a new one must be fitted.

11 Compress the spring clamp and remove the vacuum hoses from the diverter valve and waste gate **(see illustration)**.

12 Remove the 4 main mounting bolts, check that all components have been disconnected and then remove the turbocharger **(see illustrations)**.

13 Unbolt and recover the combined heat shield and cylinder head to turbocharger gasket **(see illustration)**. Dispose of the gasket, a new one must be fitted.

14 Refitting is a reversal of removal. Tighten the main turbocharger to cylinder head nuts in a diagonal sequence to the specified torque. Refill the cooling system, check the oil level and then restart the engine, checking for coolant and oil leaks.

10.10 Remove the 'banjo' bolt from the oil feed pipe

10.11 Remove the vacuum hose

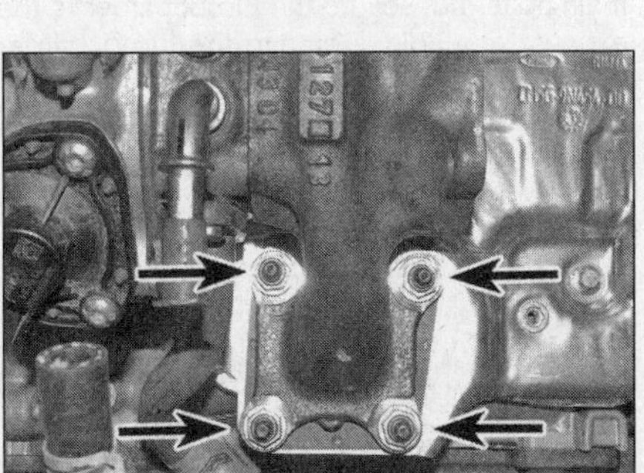

10.12a Remove the main mounting nuts (arrowed)

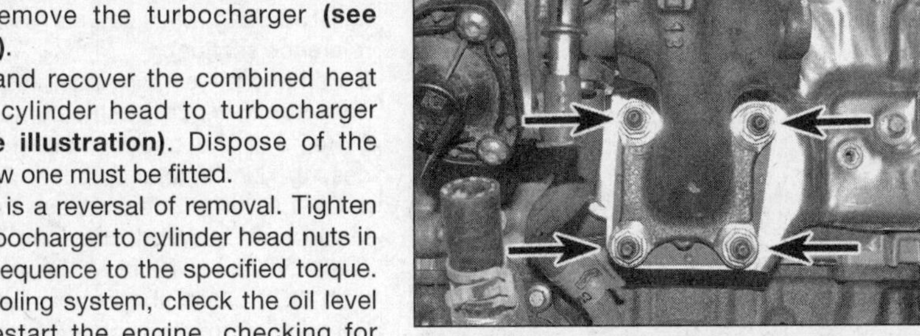

10.12b Remove the turbocharger

1.6 litre models

Note: *Access to the turbocharger is limited and awkward. Whilst not strictly necessary access can be improved by removing the right-hand drive shaft. If other major work is being undertakes at the same time – such as clutch replacement, then consider removing the entire engine and transmission to access the turbocharger.*

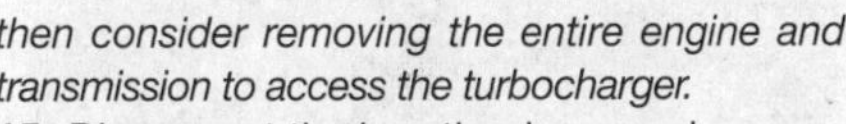

15 Disconnect the breather hose and remove the inlet pipe from the top of the engine **(see illustration)**.

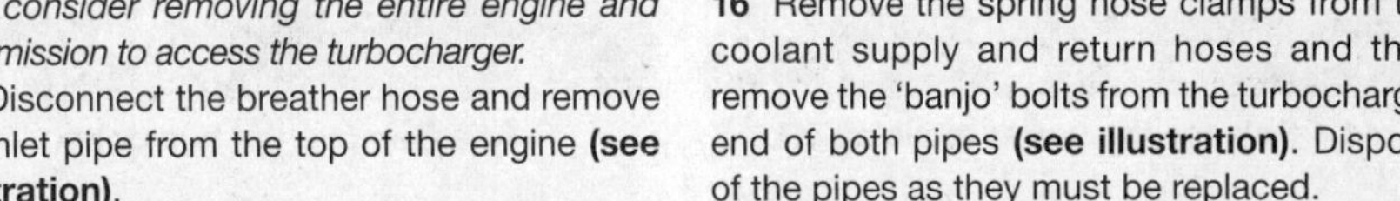

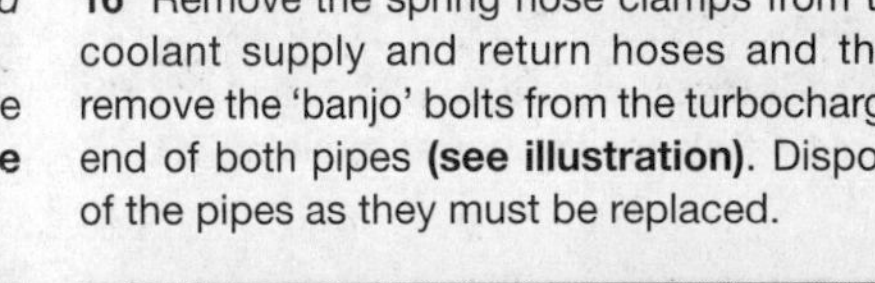

16 Remove the spring hose clamps from the coolant supply and return hoses and then remove the 'banjo' bolts from the turbocharger end of both pipes **(see illustration)**. Dispose of the pipes as they must be replaced.

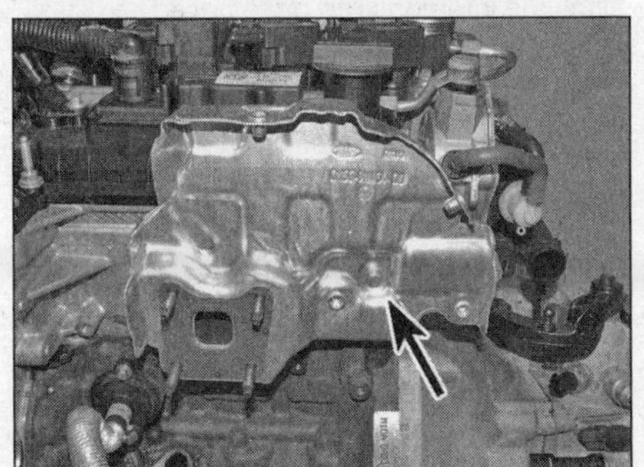

10.13 Remove the combined heat shield and gasket mounting bolt (arrowed)

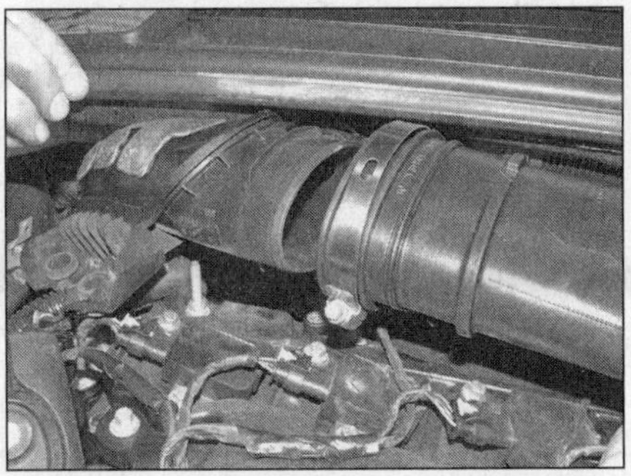

10.15 Remove the turbocharger air inlet pipe

10.16 Remove the coolant pipes

10.17 Remove the heat shield

10.19 Remove the oil drain pipe bolts (arrowed)

17 Remove the 4 bolts from the heat shield and manoeuvre the shield out from top of the engine **(see illustration)**.

18 Unbolt the turbocharger oil supply pipe from the engine block.

19 Remove the turbocharger oil drain pipe **(see illustration)**. Recover the gaskets/O-rings. Where O-rings are fitted they can be reused if they are in good condition. On models fitted with gaskets the gaskets must be replaced. Anticipate some oil loss as the pipe is removed.

20 Release the vacuum hose from the waste gate control valve and then release the vacuum hose to the control solenoid. Disconnect the wiring plug from the solenoid and then remove the control solenoid from the vehicle.

21 Check that all pipes and connections have been removed and then remove the 3 main bolts that secure the turbocharger to the exhaust manifold. Remove the turbocharger from below.

22 Refitting is a reversal of removal. Where indicated fit new components. Tighten the main turbocharger to cylinder head nuts in a diagonal sequence to the specified torque. Refill the cooling system, check the oil level and then restart the engine, checking for coolant and oil leaks.

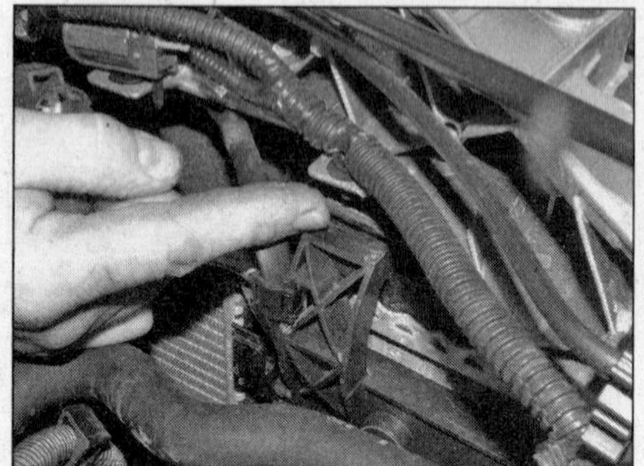

11.4 Release the upper retaining clip

11.6a Remove the two bolts...

11.6b ...and fit longer bolts

11.8 Lower the intercooler (1.0 litre shown)

11 Intercooler – removal and refitting

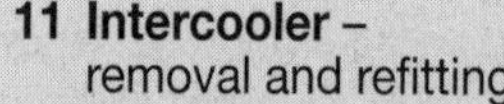

1 Jack up and support the front of the vehicle (see *Jacking and vehicle support* in the reference section).

2 Remove the engine undershield and the air deflector from beneath the bumper cover.

3 Remove the cooling fan and shroud as described in Chapter 3 Section 5.

4 On 1.0 litre models release the intercooler fan upper retaining clip **(see illustration)**, pivot the fan away from the intercooler and then lift it out of the bottom retaining clips. Remove it from the vehicle.

5 Support the radiator and condenser assembly with suitable straps. On 1.6 litre models, disconnect the wiring plug from the boost pressure sensor.

6 Remove the support panel bolts (two at each side) and replace them with some extra long bolts **(see illustrations)**. This will allow the crossmember to be lowered enough to allow the intercooler to be removed.

7 Slacken the hose clamps and remove the inlet and outlet hoses from the intercooler.

8 Lower the intercooler from the vehicle **(see illustration)**.

9 Refitting is a reversal of removal.

12 Fuel injection system – checking

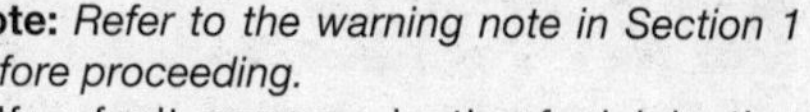

Note: *Refer to the warning note in Section 1 before proceeding.*

1 If a fault appears in the fuel injection system, first ensure that all the system wiring

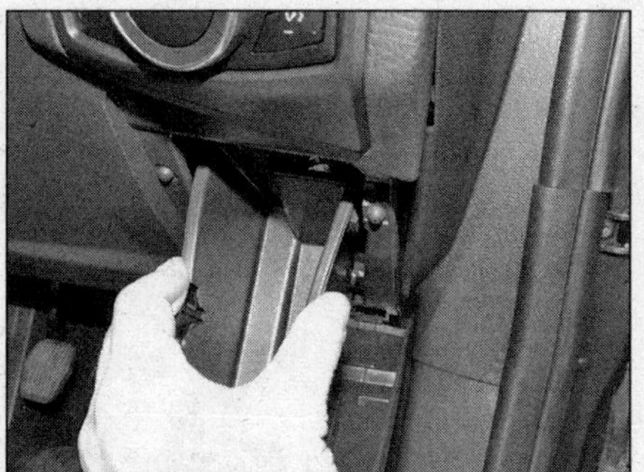
12.2a Compress the sides of the storage compartment and pull downwards...

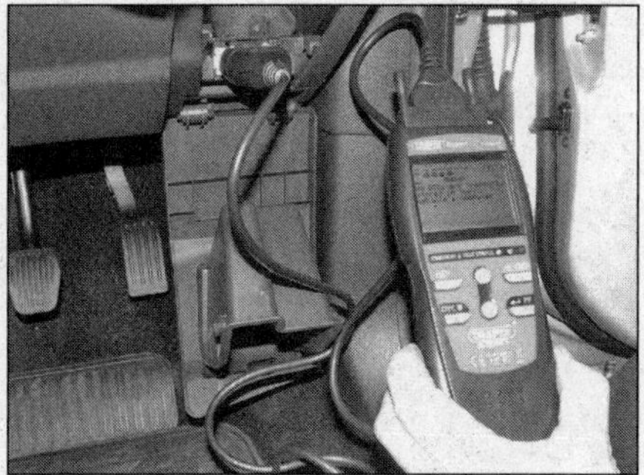
12.2b ...to access the diagnostic plug

13.2 Remove the inlet hose

connectors are securely connected and free of corrosion – also refer to paragraphs 6 to 9 below. Then ensure that the fault is not due to poor maintenance; ie, check that the air cleaner filter element is clean, the spark plugs are in good condition and correctly gapped, the cylinder compression pressures are correct, the ignition system wiring is in good condition and securely connected, and the engine breather hoses are clear and undamaged, referring to Chapter 1A, Chapter 2A or 2B and Chapter 5B.

2 If these checks fail to reveal the cause of the problem, the car should be taken to a suitably-equipped Ford dealer or garage for testing. A diagnostic connector is fitted below the steering column, into which dedicated electronic test equipment can be plugged **(see illustrations)**. The test equipment is capable of 'interrogating' the engine management system ECM (Powertrain Control Module) electronically and accessing its internal fault log (reading fault codes).

3 Fault codes can only be extracted from the ECM using a dedicated fault code reader. A Ford dealer will obviously have such a reader, but they are also available from other suppliers. Code readers are becoming increasingly affordable for the home mechanic, however their scope is often limited to displaying the mandatory emissions related fault codes.

4 Using this equipment, faults can be pinpointed quickly and simply, even if their occurrence is intermittent. Testing all the system components individually in an attempt to locate the fault by elimination is a time-consuming operation that is unlikely to be fruitful (particularly if the fault occurs dynamically), and carries a high risk of damage to the ECM's internal components. Note however that fault codes may be logged as symptom of the fault, not the cause of the fault.

Limited Operation Strategy

5 Certain faults, such as failure of one of the engine management system sensors, will cause the system will revert to a backup (or 'limp-home') mode, referred to by Ford as 'Limited Operation Strategy' (LOS). This is intended to be a 'get-you-home' facility only – the engine management warning light will come on when this mode is in operation.

6 In this mode, the signal from the defective sensor is substituted with a fixed value (it would normally vary), which may lead to loss of power, poor idling, and generally-poor running, especially when the engine is cold.

7 However, the engine may in fact run quite well in this situation, and the only clue (other than the warning light) would be that the exhaust CO emissions (for example) will be higher than they should be.

8 Bear in mind that, even if the defective sensor is correctly identified and renewed, the engine may not return to normal running until the fault code is erased, taking the system out of LOS. This also applies even if the cause of the fault was a loose connection or damaged piece of wire – until the fault code is erased, the system will continue in LOS.

13 Fuel injection system components – removal and refitting

Note: *Refer to the precautions in Section 1 before proceeding.*

Throttle body

1.0 litre EcoBoost engines

1 Remove the engine cover and then slacken the hose clamps and disconnect the breather hosed from the turbocharger inlet hose.

2 Disconnect the wiring plug from the boost pressure sensor and remove the inlet hose **(see illustration)**.

3 Slacken the hose clamps in the outlet pipe from the intercooler at the intercooler and at the throttle body **(see illustration)**.

4 Remove the 2 bolts from the support bracket and then remove the hose **(see illustrations)**.

5 Disconnect the wiring plug and then remove the 3 bolts from the throttle body. Remove the

13.3 Slacken the hose at the intercooler

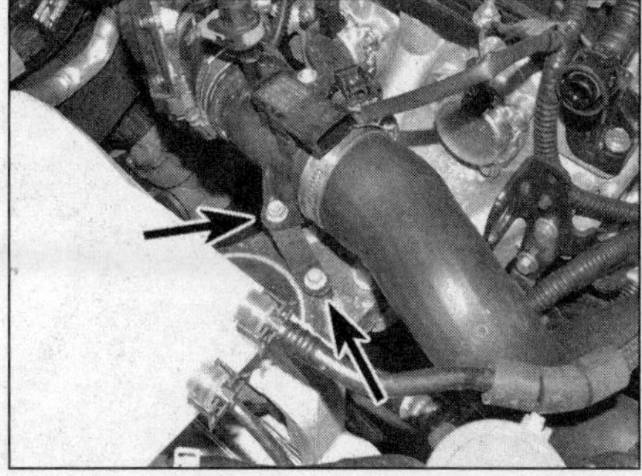
13.4a Remove the bolts (arrowed)...

13.4b ...and then remove the hose

13.5a Disconnect the wiring plug

13.5b Remove the bolts (arrowed)...

13.5c ...and then remove the throttle body

throttle body and recover the O-ring seal **(see illustrations)**.

6 Refitting is a reversal of removal, but renew the O-ring seal if it is damaged or in poor condition.

7 After refitting the throttle body, turn the ignition key to position II and wait for 1 minute for the throttle body to initialise, then turn the ignition off. Do not press the accelerator pedal during this procedure.

13.9 Remove the damper

13.10 Remove the breather pipe

13.11a Disconnect the wiring plug

13.11b Remove the bolts (arrowed)

1.6 litre EcoBoost engines

8 Remove the engine cover.

9 At the front of the engine remove the hose from the pulse damper and then remove the damper **(see illustration)**.

10 Release the breather pipes from the inlet manifold **(see illustration)** and then slacken the hose clip from the inlet hose. Remove the hose from the throttle body.

11 Disconnect the wiring plug and then remove the 4 torx head screws from the throttle body **(see illustrations)**. Remove the throttle body from the vehicle and recover the seal.

12 Refitting is a reversal of removal. Use a new seal, and tighten the mounting bolts to the specified torque.

13 After refitting the throttle body, turn the ignition key to position II and wait for 1 minute for the throttle body to initialise, then turn the ignition off. Do not press the accelerator pedal during this procedure.

1.6 litre Ti-VCT engines

14 Slacken the clamps and remove the air cleaner outlet tube **(see illustration)**.

15 Slide up the locking catch, and disconnect the wiring plug from the throttle body **(see illustration)**.

16 Detach the engine breather pipe from the cylinder head cover.

17 Undo the 4 bolts and remove the throttle body **(see illustration)**.

18 Refitting is a reversal of removal. Use a new gasket/seal, and tighten the mounting bolts to the specified torque.

13.14 Release the hose clamp

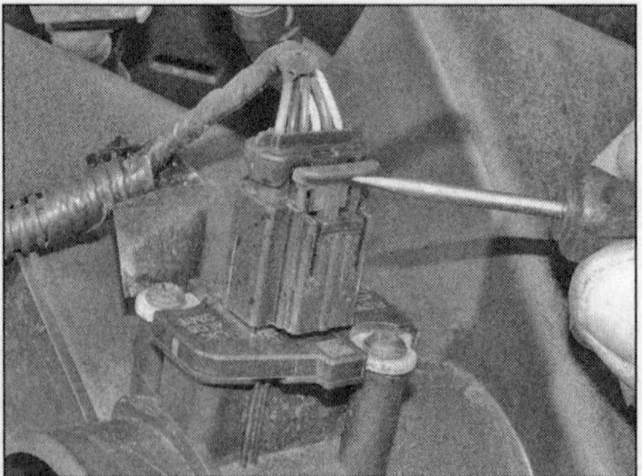
13.15 Slide up the locking catch

13.17 Undo the 4 bolts and remove the throttle body

13.25a Slacken and then...

13.25b ...remove the high pressure pipe

13.26 Disconnect the wiring plug from the fuel rail pressure sensor

19 After refitting the throttle body, turn the ignition key to position II and wait for 1 minute for the throttle body to initialise, then turn the ignition off. Do not press the accelerator pedal during this procedure.

Fuel rail and injectors

20 Relieve the residual pressure in the fuel system (see Section 2), and equalise tank pressure by removing the fuel filler cap.

Warning: This procedure will merely relieve the increased pressure necessary for the engine to run – remember that fuel will still be present in the system components, and take precautions accordingly before disconnecting any of them.

21 Disconnect the battery negative (earth) lead (see Chapter 5A Section 3).

1.0 litre and 1.6 EcoBoost engines

Note: *Removal of the high pressure fuel pump is covered in Chapter 2A, Section 4.*

22 EcoBoost engines feature high pressure 'direct' fuel injection. On these engines fuel is injected directly into the combustion chamber.

23 Remove the engine cover and then remove the turbocharger inlet pipe from the top of the engine.

24 Disconnect the wiring plugs from the ignition coils and then remove the coils. On 1.6 engines remove the coil support panel.

25 Place an absorbent cloth beneath the fuel pipe and disconnect the pipe at the fuel rail and the fuel pump **(see illustrations)**. Dispose of the pipe – it must be replaced.

13.27 Remove the fuel rail bolts

13.29 Remove the injectors

26 Disconnect the wiring plug from the fuel rail pressure sensor **(see illustration)**.

27 Remove the 2 bolts from the fuel rail **(see illustration)** – the injectors will stay in place. If the injectors start to come out with the rail, ease them back into the cylinder head. Seal the injectors with suitable blanking plugs.

28 Disconnect the wiring loom from the injectors. This can either be done at the injector, or at the multi-plug at the rear of the valve cover.

29 Pull up the injectors to remove them **(see illustration)**. Ford list a set of special tools (205-047, 205-047-08 and 310-206) to aid removal of the injectors. These tools are a small slide hammer and an adapter that locks over the injector. We removed then using a small pry bar (to lever the injector out) and a block of wood to act as a fulcrum for the pry bar. The block of wood also helps to spread the load over the valve cover.

30 With the injectors on the bench cut off the seal with a sharp knife **(see illustration)**. The seals must always be replaced if the injectors are removed.

31 Ford special tool 310-128 (or equivalent) will be required to fit the new seal **(see illustrations)**. Fit the new seal to the taper and holding the taper against the injector use the other half of the tool to push the seal up the taper and on to the injector. Push the seal into the groove and then use the special tool to settle the seal into position.

32 Replace the upper seals and fit a new spring clip. Fit the injectors to the fuel rail

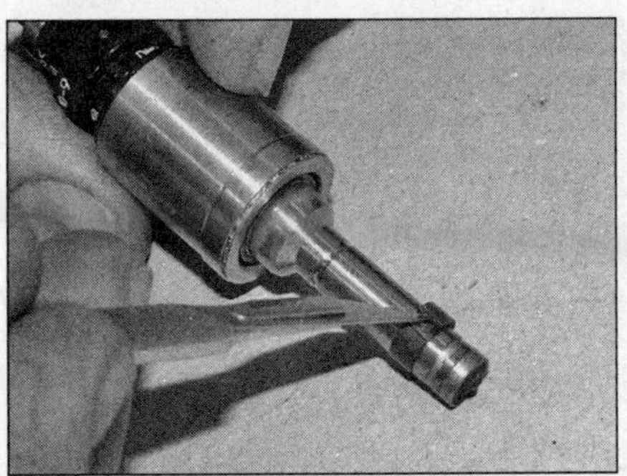
13.30 Cut off the old seal

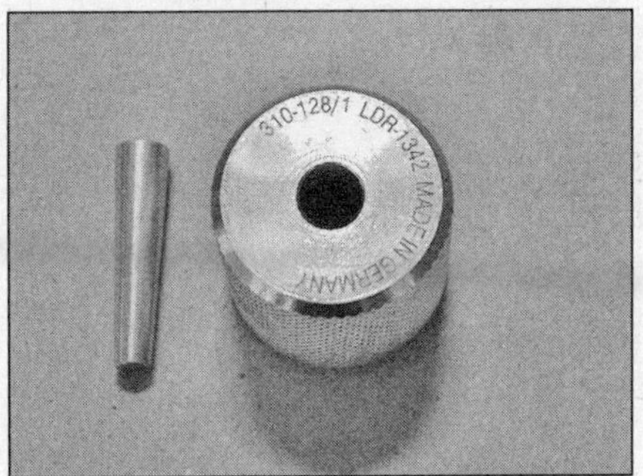

13.31a The special tool needed to fit the new seals

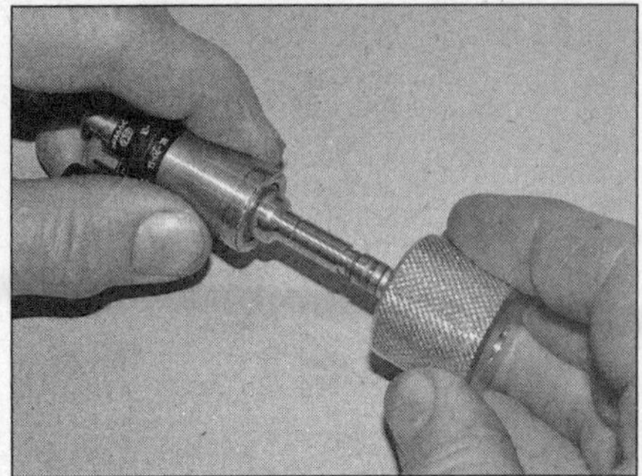
13.31b Slide the seal into position with a rotary motion

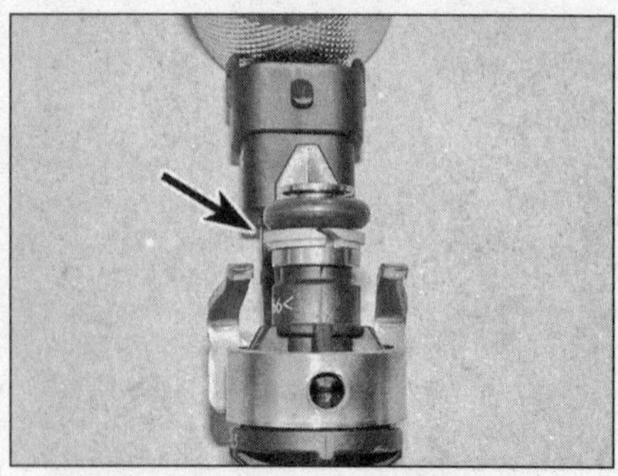
13.32a The washer (arrowed) must be fitted with the narrow side towards the injector

13.32b Fit the refurbished injectors to the fuel rail

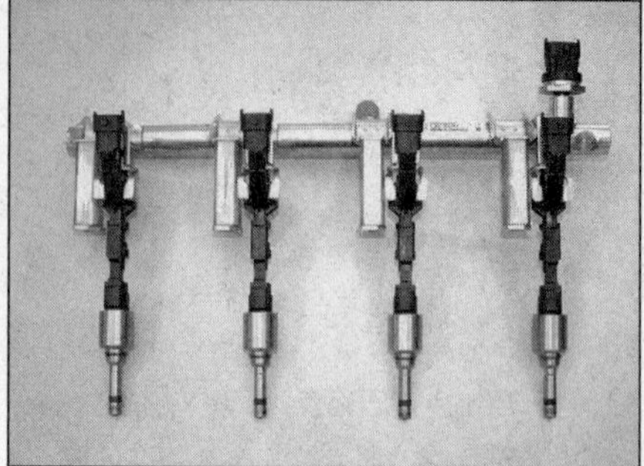
13.32c The injectors fitted to the rail (1.6 litre engine shown)

ensuring that the cut out in the rail aligns with the electrical connector **(see illustrations)**.

33 Check that the injector holes in the cylinder head are clean and free of debris before refitting the fuel rail and injectors.

34 Align the injectors with the holes in the cylinder head **(see illustration)** and push down evenly on the fuel rail. Tighten the fuel rail bolts to the specified torque.

35 Fit a new high pressure pipe to the fuel rail and tighten it to the specified torque **(see illustration)**.

36 Refit the remainder of the components in reverse order to removal. Start the engine and check carefully for fuel leaks.

1.6 Ti-VCT engines

37 Disconnect the engine breather hose from the cylinder head cover.

38 Unclip the fuel supply pipe from the support bracket, then prise out the locking catch, depress the release button and disconnect the pipe from the fuel rail **(see illustration)**.

39 Depress the wire locking clips and pull the wiring connectors assembly up from the injectors **(see illustrations)**. If necessary, disconnect the wiring plug from the oil pressure switch to allow the harness assembly to be moved to one side.

40 Disconnect the wiring plugs from the throttle body, camshaft variable timing oil control solenoid at the right-hand end of the cylinder head, and the inlet camshaft position sensor at the left-hand end of the cylinder head.

41 Unscrew and remove the two fuel rail mounting bolts. Carefully pull the fuel rail upwards to release the injectors from place – there will be some resistance from the injector O-ring seals **(see illustrations)**.

42 Remove the retaining clips and carefully

13.34 Fit the fuel rail to the cylinder head

13.35 A crows foot wrench will be required to tighten the fuel pipe

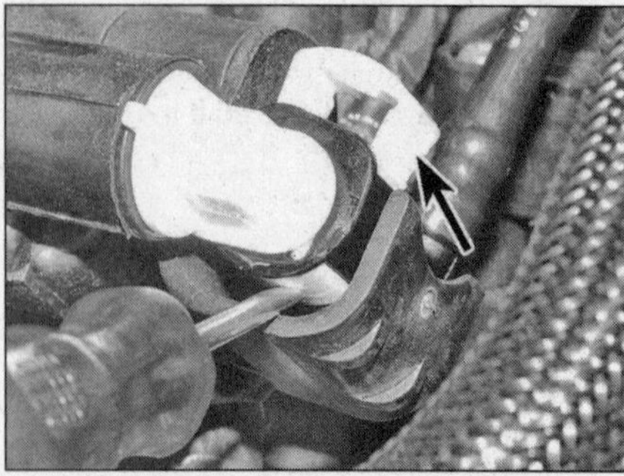
13.38 Prise out the locking catch (arrowed) then depress the release button

13.39a Push the locking clips (arrowed) forwards ...

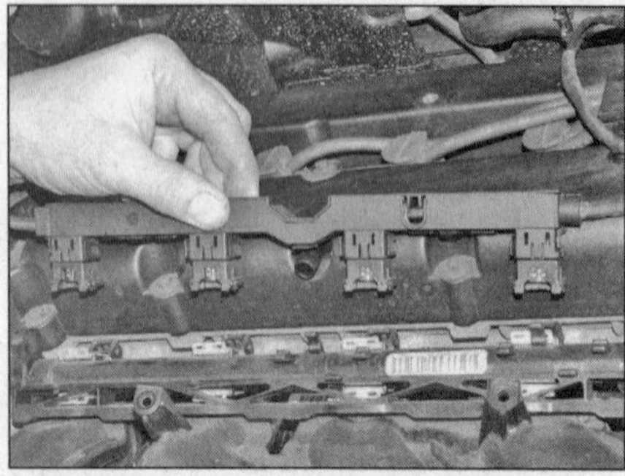
13.39b ... and gently pull the connector assembly from the injectors

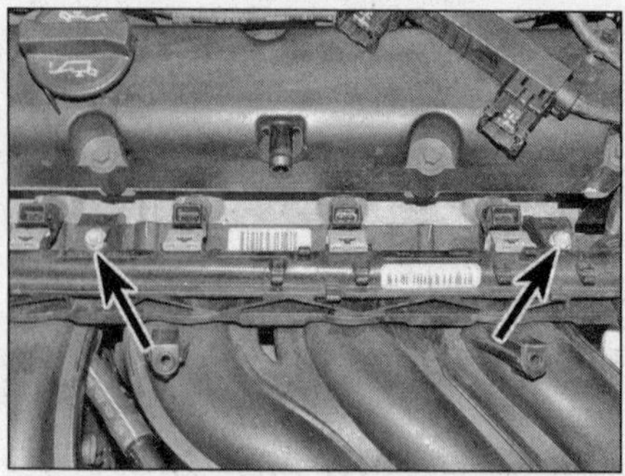
13.41a Undo the fuel rail mounting bolts (arrowed) ...

13.41b ... and pull the fuel upwards from place

pull the injectors from the fuel rail **(see illustrations)**.

43 Using a screwdriver, prise the O-rings from the grooves at each end of the injectors **(see illustration)**. Discard the O-rings and obtain new ones.

44 If required, the fuel pulse damper can be removed after the retaining clip/bolts have been removed **(see illustration)**. When refitting the damper, lubricate the new O-ring seals with clean engine oil.

45 Refitting is the reverse of the removal procedure, noting the following points:

a) *Fit new injector O-rings, and lubricate them with clean engine oil to aid refitting.*
b) *Tighten the fuel rail mounting bolts to the specified torque.*
c) *Ensure that the hoses and wiring are routed correctly, and secured on reconnection by any clips or ties provided.*
d) *On completion, switch the ignition on to activate the fuel pump and pressurise the system, without cranking the engine. Check for signs of fuel leaks around all disturbed unions and joints before attempting to start the engine.*

13.42a Release the retaining clips from the rail ...

13.42b ... and pull the injector from the rail

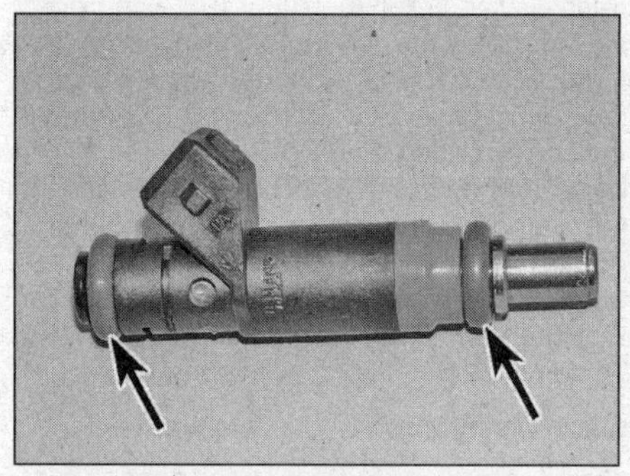

13.43 Renew the injector O-rings seals (arrowed)

13.44 Prise out the clip and remove the fuel pulse damper

Mass airflow sensor

46 A Mass Air Flow (MAF) sensor is fitted to all models. The sensor is located in the inlet ducting close to the air filter housing **(see illustration)**.

47 Disconnect the wiring plug and remove the screw or screws depending on the model. Pull the sensor free from the housing.

48 Refitting is a reversal of removal. Note the arrow on the top of the sensor indicating airflow.

Manifold Absolute Pressure Sensor

49 EcoBoost models have a Manifold Absolute Pressure (MAP) sensor fitted to the output side of the turbocharger and to the inlet manifold.

50 On 1.0 litre engines one sensor is mounted just before the throttle body **(see illustration)** and the other is mounted in the inlet manifold. In both case, disconnect the wiring plug, remove the screw and pull the sensor from the housing.

51 On 1.6 litre engines one sensor is fitted to the left-hand end of the intercooler and the other to the inlet manifold. To remove the intercooler mounted sensor, follow the procedure for intercooler removal as described in Section 11 of this Chapter, but do not completely remove the intercooler. Disconnect the wiring plug, remove the screw and pull the sensor from the housing.

52 Refitting is a reversal of removal.

Powertrain Control Module

Note: *If a new PCM is to be fitted, the configuration information stored within the module must be uploaded to Ford diagnostic equipment prior to the module being removed, and downloaded to the new PCM once installed. Entrust this task to a Ford dealer or suitably-equipped specialist.*

53 Disconnect the battery negative lead as described in Chapter 5A Section 3.

54 Jack up and support the front of the vehicle (see *Jacking and vehicle support* in the reference section).

55 Remove the left-hand road wheel and inner wing liner to access the control module **(see illustration)**, which is located inside a plastic housing.

56 The PCM is protected from theft by shear bolts. The remains of the shear bolts must be drilled out to access the PCM.

57 Drill out the shear bolts, open the cover and disconnect the wiring plug(s). Remove the PCM.

58 Refitting is a reversal of removal, but fit new shear bolts and tighten them until the head breaks off.

13.46 The MAF sensor on 1.0 litre engines (arrowed)

13.50 The MAP sensor on 1.0 litre engines (arrowed)

13.55 Location of control module – bumper removed for clarity

13.59 The 1.0 litre crankshaft position sensor (arrowed)

13.61a Disconnect the wiring plug...

13.61b ...unbolt and remove the sensor (1.6 litre engine)

Crankshaft position sensor

1.0 and 1.6 litre EcoBoost engines

59 The sensor on both engines is fitted behind the crankshaft pulley **(see illustration)**. Jack up the front of the car and support it on axle stands (see *Jacking and vehicle support*).

60 Remove the right-hand road wheel and the right-hand wing liner.

61 With the ignition switched off, disconnect the wiring plug, then unscrew the mounting bolt and withdraw the sensor **(see illustrations)**.

62 Refitting is a reversal of removal. Ensure that the sensor is clean when refitting, and tighten the bolt to the specified torque.

1.6 litre Ti-VCT engines

63 The sensor is located on the front left-hand side of the engine, close to the transmission **(see illustration)**. For improved access, apply the handbrake, then jack up the front of the car and support it on axle stands (see *Jacking and vehicle support*). Remove the engine undershield (where fitted).

64 With the ignition switched off, disconnect the wiring plug, then unscrew the mounting bolt and withdraw the sensor.

65 Refitting is a reversal of removal. Ensure that the sensor is clean when refitting, and tighten the bolt to the specified torque.

Camshaft position sensor

66 All engines feature one sensor per camshaft. On 1.0 litre engines the sensors are at the right-hand end on the engine **(see illustration)**, on 1.6 litre engines the sensors are at the left-hand end of the valve cover.

67 With the engine switched off, remove the engine cover.

68 On 1.0 litre engines disconnect the wiring plug **(see illustration)** and unbolt the sensor. Remove the sensor from the housing.

69 On 1.6 litre EcoBoost engines, remove the ignition coils and the coil support bracket to access the sensors. Disconnect the wiring plug, remove the bolt and pull the sensor from the housing **(see illustrations)**.

70 On 1.6 litre Ti-VCT engines, disconnect the wiring plug from the camshaft position sensors, remove the bolt and pull the sensor from the housing **(see illustration)**.

71 Refitting is a reversal of removal, but use a new seal. Smear a little engine oil on the seal before fitting the sensor, and tighten the bolt(s) to the specified torque.

Coolant temperature sensor

72 See Chapter 3 Section 6.

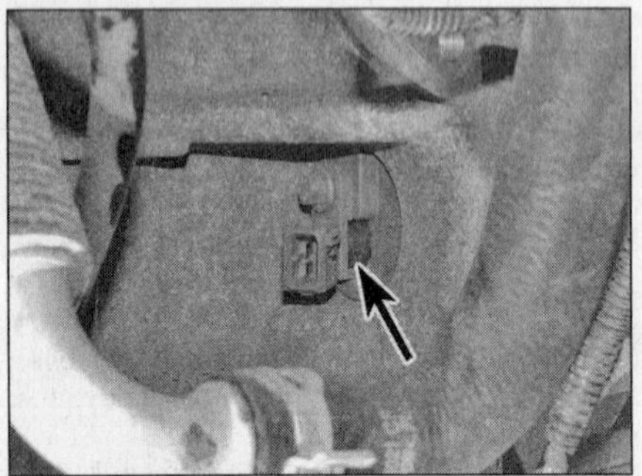
13.63 Crankshaft position sensor (arrowed)

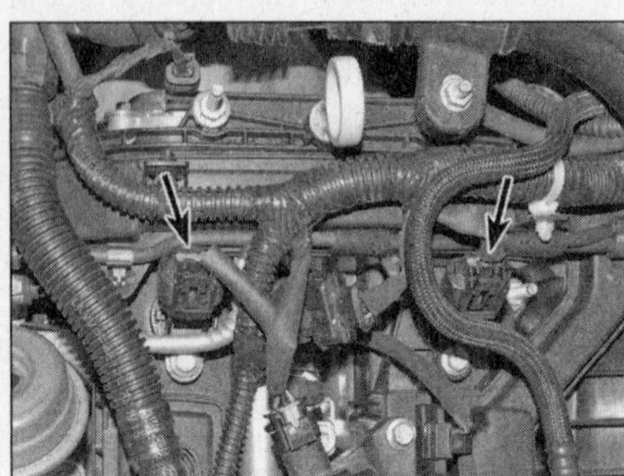
13.66 Location of the two camshaft sensors – 1.0 litre engine

13.68 Disconnect the wiring plug

13.69a Remove the bolt and...

13.69b ...pull the sensor from the housing

13.70 Disconnect the camshaft position sensor wiring plug

13.74 Remove the solenoid (1.0 litre engine)

13.75 Disconnect the wiring plug

13.76 Remove the solenoid from the housing

Variable camshaft timing oil control solenoids

73 The solenoids on the 1.0 litre engine are fitted to the extreme right-hand end of the engine in the timing belt cover.

74 Disconnect the wiring plug, remove the 3 bolts and withdraw the solenoid **(see illustration)**. Recover the seal if it remains in the timing belt cover.

75 The solenoids are located at the front, right-hand end of the cylinder head cover. Disconnect the solenoid wiring plug **(see illustration)**.

76 Undo the retaining bolt and pull the solenoid from place **(see illustration)**.

77 Refitting is a reversal of removal. Ensure the solenoid and aperture are scrupulously clean prior to refitting. Tighten the bolt to the specified torque.

Clutch pedal position switch

78 Remove the driver's side facia lower panel as described in Chapter 11 Section 30.

79 With the ignition switched off, disconnect the wiring from the clutch switch **(see illustration)**.

80 Rotate the switch anti-clockwise and remove it **(see illustration)**.

81 Refitting is a reversal of removal.

Power steering pressure switch

82 Refer to Chapter 10 Section 18.

Oxygen sensor

83 Refer to Chapter 4C Section 5.

13.79 Disconnect the wiring plug

13.80 Rotate the switch to remove it

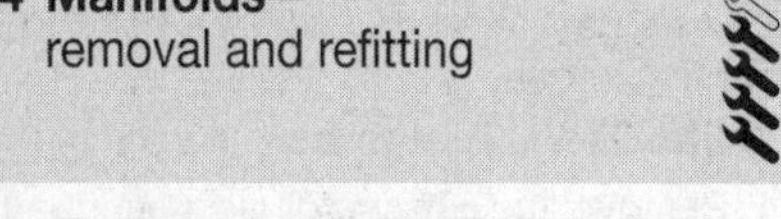

14 Manifolds – removal and refitting

Note: *Refer to the warning note in Section 1 before proceeding.*

Inlet manifold

1 Depressurise the fuel system as described in Section 2. On completion, disconnect the battery negative lead (refer to Chapter 5A Section 3).

2 Remove the engine cover.

1.0 Litre engines

3 Slacken the hose clamps and remove the air ducts from the top of the engine (from the air filter to the turbocharger) and then remove the inlet air duct from the throttle body – as described for throttle body in Section 13 of this Chapter. Remove the throttle body from the manifold inlet duct and then remove the duct **(see illustration)**.

4 Trace the pipe work and remove the EVAP pipe work from the valve cover **(see illustration)**. Release the vacuum pipes from the control solenoid at the rear of the inlet manifold.

5 Disconnect the breather pipes from the inlet manifold **(see illustration)** and then unclip the coolant hoses. Disconnect the wiring plug from the MAP sensor.

6 Remove the support bracket from the right-hand end of the manifold and then remove the main manifold bolts in the reverse order to that shown **(see illustration 14.8)**.

7 Remove the seals and inspect the manifold for cracks or damage.

14.3 Remove the inlet duct

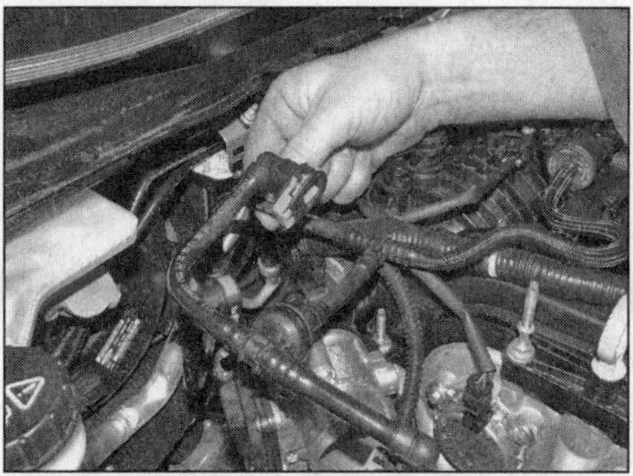
14.4 Remove the EVAP pipe work

14.5 Remove the breather pipes

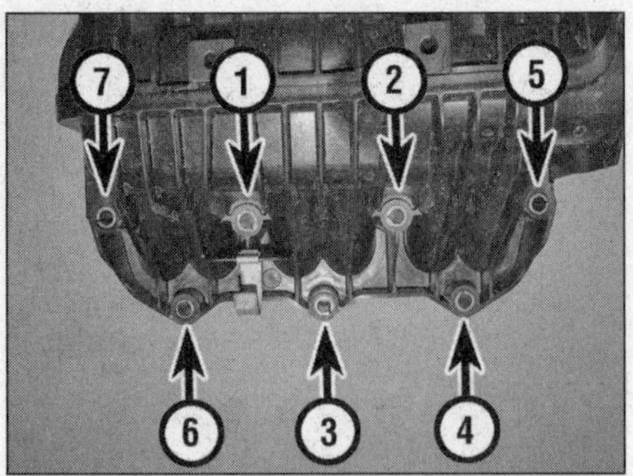

14.8 Tighten the manifold bolts in the order shown

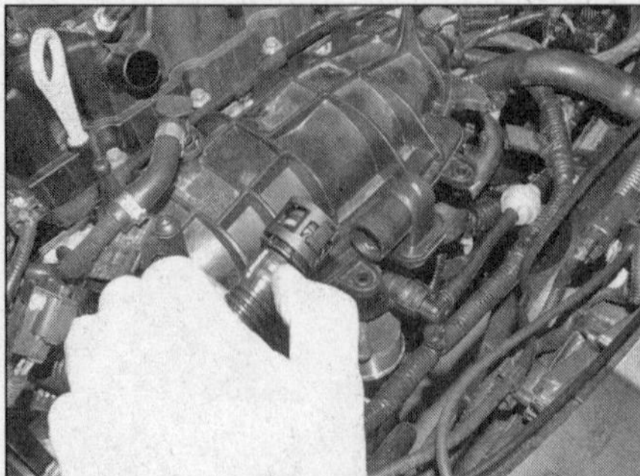

14.10 Remove the breather pipe

14.11a Disconnect the wiring plug from the MAP sensor...

14.11b ...and release the loom from the manifold

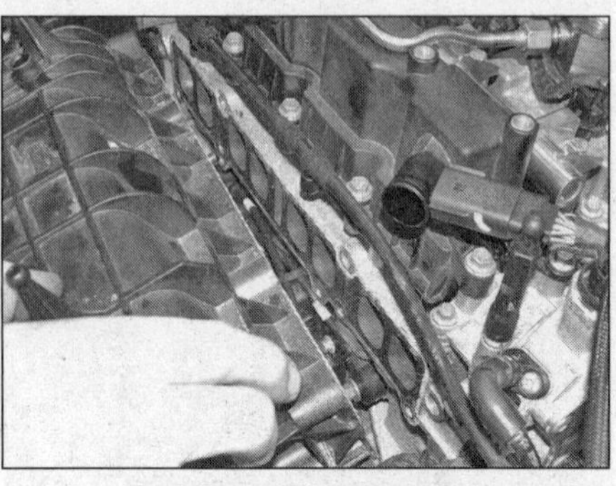

14.12 Remove the manifold

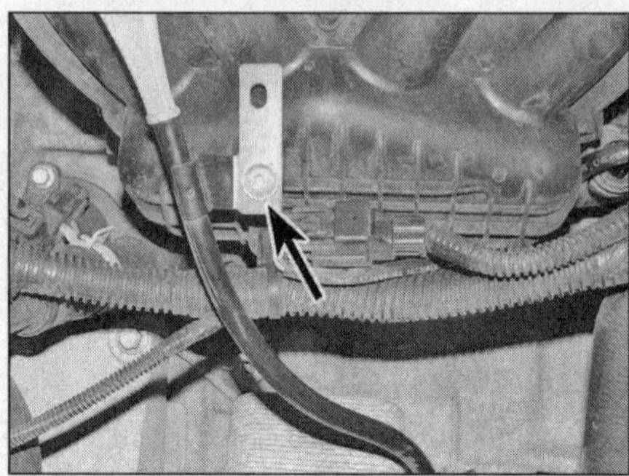

14.17 Undo the engine oil level dipstick guide tube bolt (arrowed)

8 Fit new seals and then tighten the manifold bolts in the order shown **(see illustration)** to the specified torque.

1.6 litre EcoBoost engines

9 With reference to Section 13 of this Chapter remove the inlet pipe from the throttle body. There is no need to remove the throttle body – this can be removed after the inlet manifold has been removed if required.

10 Remove the breather pipes from the manifold **(see illustration)**.

11 Disconnect the wiring plugs from the throttle body and the MAP sensor. Unclip the loom from the retaining clips on the manifold **(see illustrations)**.

12 Check that all components have been removed then unbolt the manifold from the cylinder head **(see illustration)**. Note the different lengths of the bolts.

13 Refitting is a reversal of removal, but fit a new gasket and tighten the bolts to the specified torque.

1.6 litre Ti-VCT engines

14 Remove the alternator as described in Chapter 5A Section 5.

15 Remove the fuel rail with injectors as described in Section 13.

16 Remove the throttle body as described in Section 13.

17 Undo the bolt securing the engine oil level dipstick guide tube to the manifold **(see illustration)**.

18 Note their fitted locations and disconnect any vacuum hoses/pipes/wiring harnesses attached to the manifold **(see illustration)**.

19 Undo the retaining bolts and remove the manifold. Renew the manifold-to-cylinder head seals/gasket **(see illustration)**.

20 Refitting is a reversal of removal, noting the following points:

a) Ensure that the mating faces are clean, and use a new manifold-to-cylinder head seals/gasket.

b) Tighten all fixings to the specified torque in the order shown **(see illustration)**.

c) On completion, switch the ignition on to activate the fuel pump and pressurize the system, without cranking the engine. Check for signs of fuel leaks around all disturbed unions and joints before attempting to start the engine.

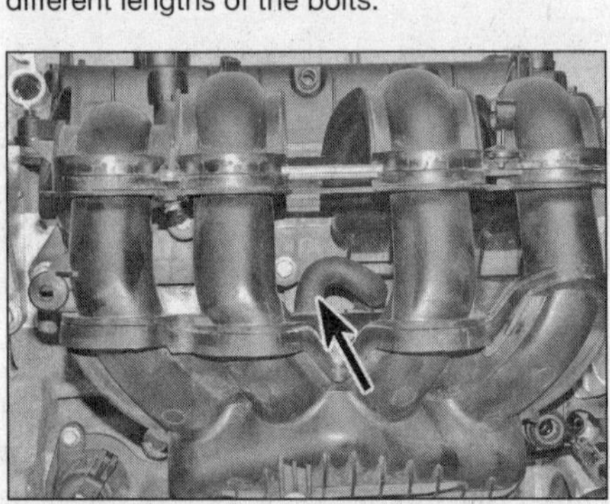

14.18 Disconnect the breather hose (arrowed)

14.19 Renew the manifold-to-cylinder head seals

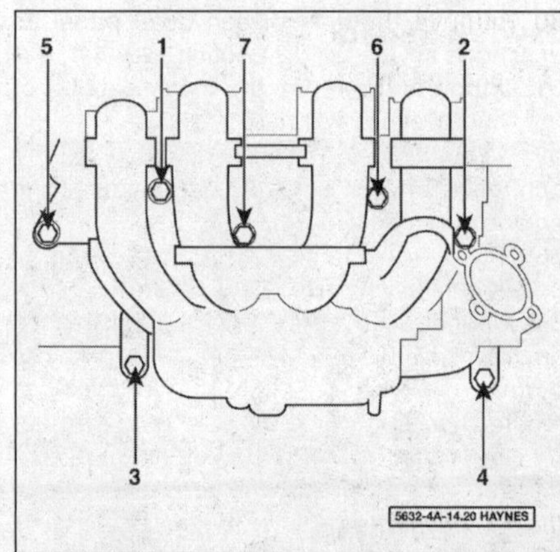

14.20 Tighten the bolts in the order shown

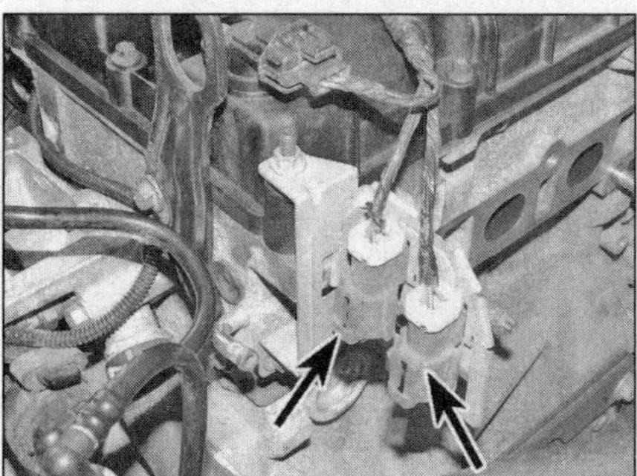
14.32 Disconnect the oxygen sensor wiring plugs (arrowed)

14.33 Remove the heat shield from over the exhaust manifold (arrowed)

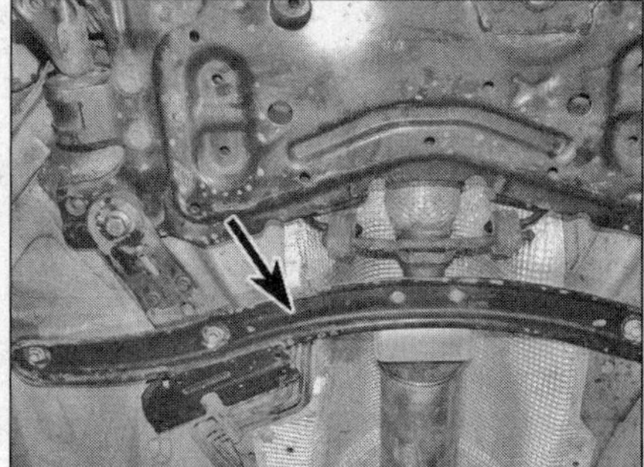
14.35 Remove the floor panel brace (arrowed)

Exhaust manifold

21 Disconnect the battery negative lead as described in Chapter 5A Section 3.

Warning: Do not attempt this procedure until the engine is completely cool – ideally, the car should be left overnight before starting work.

1.0 litre EcoBoost engines

22 On these engines the exhaust manifold is integrated into the cylinder head. If a fault develops then the cylinder head will have to be removed and replaced.

1.6 EcoBoost engines

23 Remove the turbocharger as described in Section 10 of this Chapter.

24 Working from the outside in slacken the 9 retaining bolts evenly.

25 Recover the gasket.

26 Clean and inspect the cylinder head and the manifold mounting surfaces. Replace any worm or damaged cylinder head studs.

27 Fit a new gasket and working from the inside to the outside tighten the exhaust manifold bolts to the specified torque.

1.6 Ti-VCT models

28 The exhaust manifold is integral with the front catalytic converter. Remove the front subframe as described in Section 15.

29 Remove the wiper arms as described in Chapter 12 Section 11.

30 Remove the windscreen cowl panel as described in Chapter 12 Section 11.

31 Unbolt and remove the lower section of the windscreen cowl panel

32 Disconnect the oxygen sensors' wiring connectors behind the left-hand side of the engine **(see illustration)**.

33 Remove the bolts securing the exhaust manifold heat shield **(see illustration)**.

34 Working in a diagonal sequence, loosen and remove the exhaust manifold nuts. The manifold will remain in position for now, located on the cylinder head studs – do not try and slide it off the studs yet. **Note:** *If all of the studs come out with the nuts, leave two of them in place to support the manifold.*

35 Undo the bolts and remove the floor panel brace beneath the front of the exhaust system **(see illustration)**.

36 Undo the 2 bolts securing the catalytic converter to the support bracket on its underside, and with the help of an assistant, slide the manifold off the cylinder head studs (or completely unscrew any remaining studs), and lower it down to remove it, taking care not to damage the sensors or their wiring. Recover and discard the gasket **(see illustration)**.

37 Unscrew the oxygen sensors from the manifold and catalytic converter.

38 Refitting is a reversal of removal, noting the following points:

a) *Ensure that the mating faces are clean, and use new manifold gaskets.*
b) *Use new manifold/catalytic converter nuts/bolt.*
c) *Do not fully tighten the manifold/catalytic converter mounting nuts/bolts until the front subframe has been refitted as described in Chapter 10 Section 21.*
d) *Tighten the manifold nuts in a diagonal sequence, in the two stages specified.*
e) *Tighten all fixings to the specified torque.*

15 Exhaust system – general information, removal and refitting

Caution: Any work on the exhaust system should only be attempted once the system is completely cool – this may take several hours, especially in the case of the forward sections, such as the manifold and catalytic converter.

14.36 Undo the bolts and remove the support bracket under the catalytic converter

General information

1 All models have a centre exhaust silencer and a separate rear silencer. At the front, where the centre section joins the manifold, a flexible ('mesh') section is fitted, to allow for engine movement.

2 The system is suspended throughout its entire length by rubber mountings.

Removal

3 To remove a part of the system, first jack up the front or rear of the car, and support it on axle stands (see *Jacking and vehicle support*). Alternatively, position the car over an inspection pit, or on car ramps.

Centre section

4 To prevent damage to the exhaust flexible section, support it by attaching a pair of splints either side (two scrap strips of wood, plant canes, etc) using some cable-ties **(see illustration)**. If a new centre section is being fitted, this precaution only applies to the new section of exhaust.

5 Unscrew the nuts securing the centre section to the flexible joint, and separate the joint. Recover the gasket.

6 Even if just the centre section is being removed, it still has to be separated from the rear silencer. Unbolt the clamp where the centre section joins the silencer, and separate the pipes (bear in mind that a corroded rear silencer may be damaged during removal – see paragraph 9).

15.4 Make a 'splint' to support the flexible section of the exhaust

7 Unhook the centre section's two rubber mountings, and remove it from under the car.

Rear silencer

8 When fitted in the factory, the exhaust system from the front section flange to the end of the tail pipe is one piece. However, if the rear silencer is to be renewed, new silencers should be available – check with your parts supplier. Using a hacksaw, cut through the exhaust pipe 150 mm behind the mounting, in front of the rear silencer.

9 Unhook the silencer rubber mountings, and remove it from under the car.

Heat shields

10 The heat shields are secured to the underside of the body by special nuts. Each shield can be removed separately, but note that they may overlap, making it necessary to loosen another section first. If a shield is being removed to gain access to a component located behind it, it may prove sufficient in some cases to remove the retaining nuts and/or bolts, and simply lower the shield, without disturbing the exhaust system. Otherwise, remove the exhaust section as described earlier.

Refitting

11 In all cases, refitting is a reversal of removal, but note the following points:

a) *Always use new gaskets, nuts and clamps (as applicable), and coat all threads with copper grease. Make sure any new clamps are the same size as the original – overtightening a clamp which is too big will not seal the joint.*

b) *On a sleeved joint (such as that between the centre section and rear silencer), use a smear of exhaust jointing paste to achieve a gas-tight seal.*

c) *If any of the exhaust mounting rubbers are in poor condition, fit new ones.*

d) *Make sure that the exhaust is suspended properly on its mountings, and will not come into contact with the floor or any suspension parts. The rear silencer especially must be aligned correctly before tightening the clamp nuts.*

e) *Tighten all nuts/bolts to the specified torque, where given.*

Chapter 4 Part B
Fuel and exhaust systems – diesel engines

Contents

Degrees of difficulty

Easy, suitable for novice with little experience 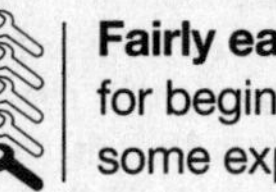	**Fairly easy,** suitable for beginner with some experience	**Fairly difficult,** suitable for competent DIY mechanic	**Difficult,** suitable for experienced DIY mechanic	**Very difficult,** suitable for expert DIY or professional 

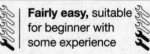

Specifications

General

System type: Bosch direct injection common rail, with timing belt driven high-pressure delivery pump, variable nozzle turbocharger, and intercooler

Torque wrench settings	**Nm**	**lbf ft**
Camshaft position sensor:	10	7
Catalytic converter/DPF to engine block	25	18
Common rail mounting bolts	22	16
Crankshaft position sensor	8	6
Exhaust manifold to cylinder head	25	18
Fuel high-pressure pipe union nuts: *		
Stage 1	20	15
Stage 2	25	18
Fuel injector clamp bolts (cast clamp):		
Stage 1	7	5
Stage 2	Angle-tighten a further 85°	
Fuel injector clamp bolts (pressed clamp):		
Stage 1	7	5
Stage 2	Angle-tighten a further 80°	
Fuel injection pump mounting bolts	20	15
Fuel injection pump sprocket nut	50	37
Fuel tank sender unit collar	85	63
Throttle body bolts	8	6
Turbocharger to catalytic converter/DPF clamp*	25	18
Turbocharger oil supply banjo bolt	30	22
Turbocharger support bracket bolt	25	18
Turbocharger to exhaust manifold*	25	18

**Do not re-use*

1 General information and precautions

General information

1 The operation of the fuel injection system is described in more detail in Section 5.

2 Fuel is drawn from a tank under the rear of the vehicle by a tank-immersed electric pump, and then forced through a filter to the injection pump.

3 The camshaft-driven injection pump is a tandem pump – a low pressure vane-type pump which supplies the high-pressure pump with fuel at a constant pressure, and a high-pressure piston-type pump which supplies fuel to the common fuel rail at variable pressure.

4 Fuel is supplied from the common fuel rail to the injectors. Also inside the injection pump assembly is a pressure control valve which regulates the pressure of fuel from the high-pressure pump, and a fuel volume control valve which regulates the fuel flow to the high-pressure side of the pump. The injectors are operated by solenoids controlled by the PCM, based on information supplied by various sensors. The engine PCM also controls the preheating side of the system – refer to Chapter 5A Section 1 for more details.

5 The engine management system fitted, incorporates a 'drive-by-wire' system, where the traditional accelerator cable is replaced by an accelerator pedal position sensor. The position and rate-of-change of the accelerator pedal is reported by the position sensor to the PCM, which then adjusts the fuel injectors and fuel pressure to deliver the required amount of fuel and optimum combustion efficiency.

6 The exhaust system incorporates a turbocharger and an EGR system. Further detail of the emission control systems can be found in Chapter 4C Section 2.

Precautions

- When working on diesel fuel system components, scrupulous cleanliness must be observed, and care must be taken not to introduce any foreign matter into fuel lines or components.
- After carrying out any work involving disconnection of fuel lines, it is advisable to check the connections for leaks; pressurise the system by cranking the engine several times.
- Electronic control units are very sensitive components, and certain precautions must be taken to avoid damage to these units.
- When carrying out welding operations on the vehicle using electric welding equipment, the battery and alternator should be disconnected.
- Although the underbonnet-mounted modules will tolerate normal underbonnet conditions, they can be adversely affected by excess heat or moisture. If using welding equipment or pressure-washing equipment in the vicinity of an electronic module, take care not to direct heat, or jets of water or steam, at the module. If this cannot be avoided, remove the module from the vehicle, and protect its wiring plug with a plastic bag.
- Before disconnecting any wiring, or removing components, always ensure that the ignition is switched off.
- Do not attempt to improvise PCM fault diagnosis procedures using a test lamp or multimeter, as irreparable damage could be caused to the module.

After working on fuel injection/engine management system components, ensure that all wiring is correctly reconnected before reconnecting the battery or switching on the ignition.

2 Air cleaner assembly – removal and refitting

Removal

1 Slacken the retaining clip and disconnect the air outlet hose **(see illustration)**, from the Mass Airflow Sensor (MAF).

2 Disconnect the wiring connector from the MAF sensor, and unclip the wiring loom from the air cleaner housing **(see illustrations)**.

3 Disconnect the vacuum hose from the rear of the MAF sensor **(see illustration)**.

4 Unhook the rubber retaining strap, and then pull the air cleaner upwards to release the locating pegs, on the lower part of the air cleaner housing **(see illustrations)**. The pegs on the base of the cleaner fit into

2.1 Disconnect the air intake hose

2.2a Disconnect the wiring plug from the MAF sensor...

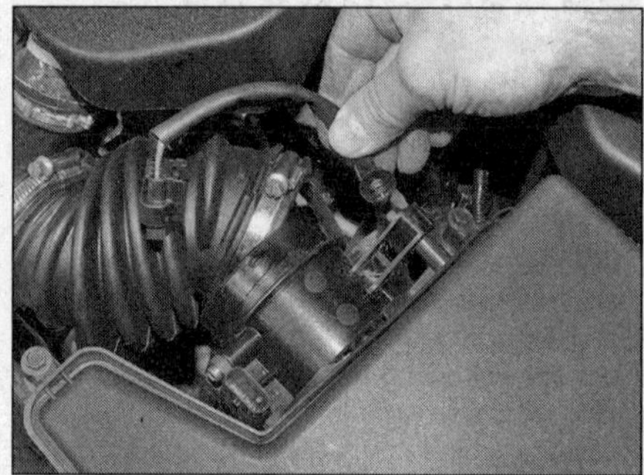

2.2b ...and unclip the wiring loom

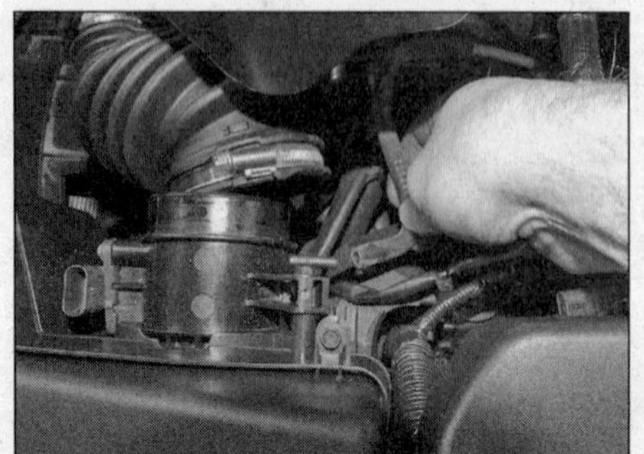

2.3 Disconnect the vacuum hose

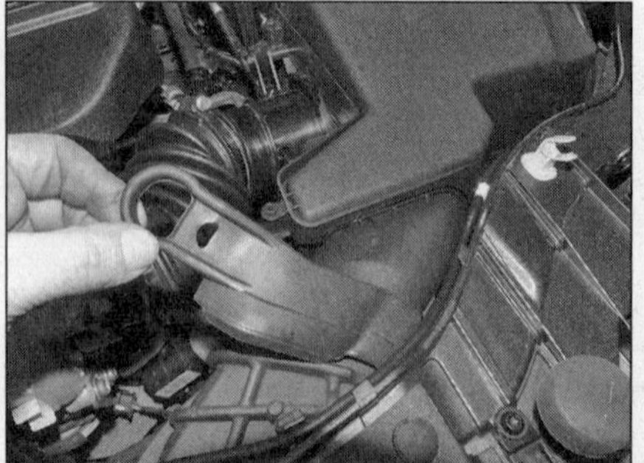

2.4a Release the securing strap...

2.4b ...and remove the air cleaner housing

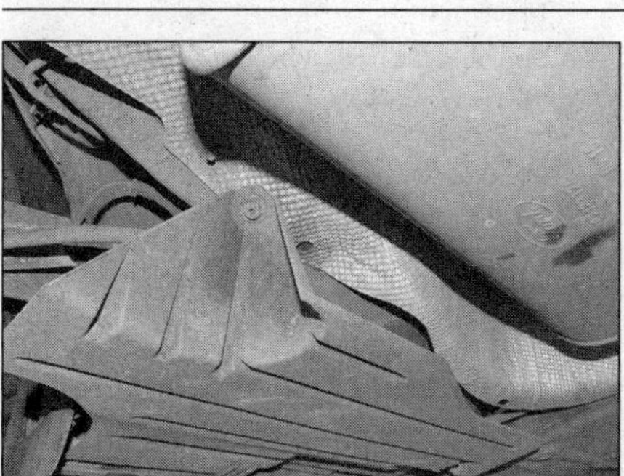
3.7a Undo the bolts and remove the left-hand side air deflector shield...

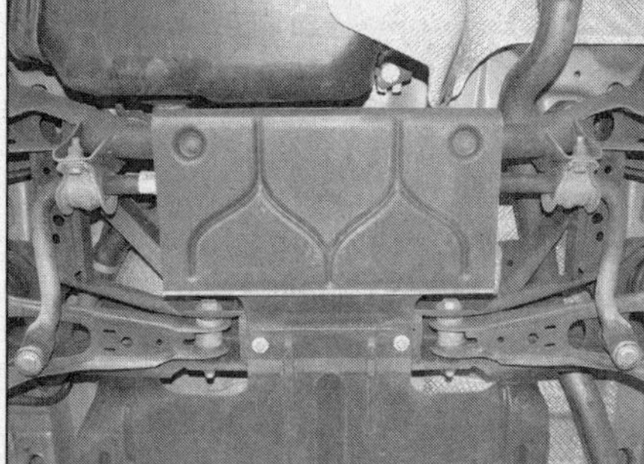
3.7b ...and the rear centre protective cover

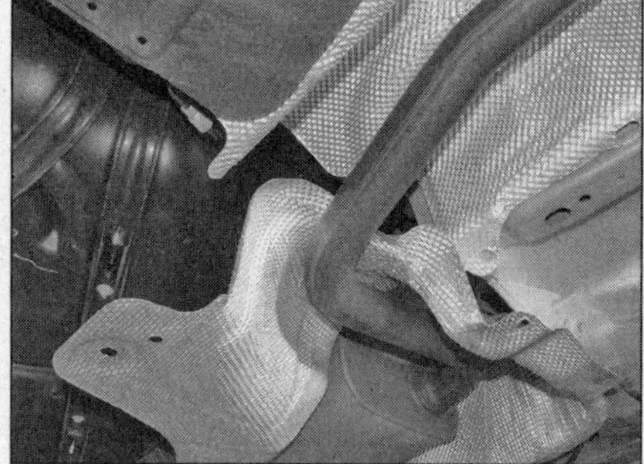
3.8 Undo the nuts and remove the heat shields beneath the fuel tank

rubber grommets. These pegs may prove troublesome to release, and some effort may be needed – take care to avoid personal injury.

Refitting

5 When refitting, locate the air cleaner pegs into the grommets and push down firmly to engage them in the grommets. Lubricate them with a silicon type grease if necessary. Make sure the air cleaner duct clamps are securely refitted/tightened to prevent air leaks.

3 Fuel tank – removal and refitting

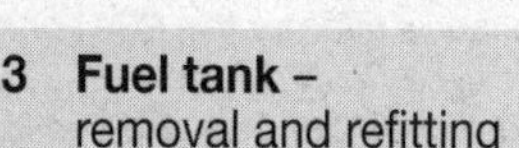

Note: *Observe the precautions in Section 1 before working on any component in the fuel system.*

Note: *Refer to the warning note in Section 1 before proceeding.*

Removal

1 Run the fuel level as low as possible prior to removing the tank. There is no drain plug fitted (and syphoning may prove difficult) but it may be possible to partially drain the tank.

2 Relieve the residual pressure in the fuel system (see Section 2), and equalise tank pressure by removing the fuel filler cap.

3 Disconnect the battery negative (earth) lead (see Chapter 5A Section 3).

4 Chock the front wheels, then jack up the rear of the car and support it on axle stands (see *Jacking and vehicle support*). Remove the rear roadwheels.

3.9 Remove the filler pipe

3.10 Depress the release button (arrowed) and disconnect the vent pipe from the rear of the tank

5 Unhook the exhaust system mounting rubbers from the centre and rear hangers, and allow the exhaust system to rest on the rear suspension crossmember.

6 Undo the nuts securing the flange of the exhaust system rear section, then manoeuvre the rear section to one side, and secure it in place using cable ties/wire/string.

7 Undo the 3 bolts and pull the left-hand side air deflector shield rearwards to release its retaining clip and then remove the protective cover from the rear **(see illustrations)**.

8 Undo the nuts and remove the exhaust centre and rear section heat shields from the vehicle underside **(see illustration)**.

9 Release the clips and disconnect the fuel tank filler pipes **(see illustration)**. Do not use any sharp-edged tools to release the pipes from their stub, as the pipe is easily damaged.

10 Depress the release button and disconnect the fuel tank vent pipe from the rear of the tank to the evaporative emissions **(see illustration)**.

11 Disconnect the fuel supply pipe and return pipe from the front of the tank **(see illustration)**.

12 Support the tank using a trolley jack and a large sheet of wood to spread the load.

13 Note exactly how the fuel tank retaining straps are arranged to make refitting easier. In particular, note their fitted order under the retaining bolt heads, where applicable. The left-hand side strap is on top at the front fixing.

14 Unbolt and remove the fuel tank retaining straps **(see illustrations)**, but do not lower the tank at this stage.

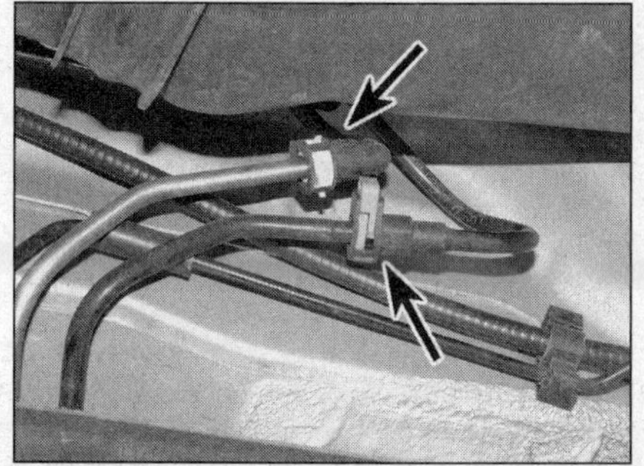
3.11 Disconnect the fuel supply and purge valve pipe at the front of the tank (arrowed)

3.14a Undo the bolts at the rear (arrowed)...

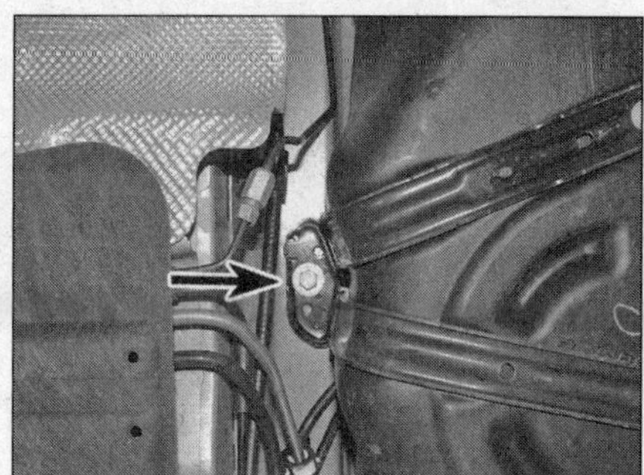
3.14b ...and at the front (arrowed)

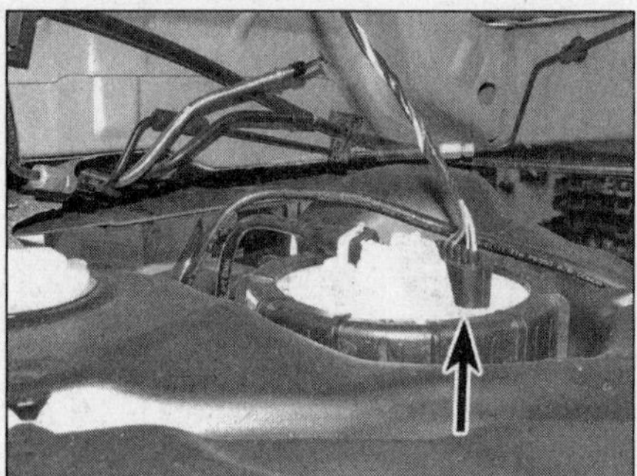
3.15a Disconnect the wiring plug (arrowed)...

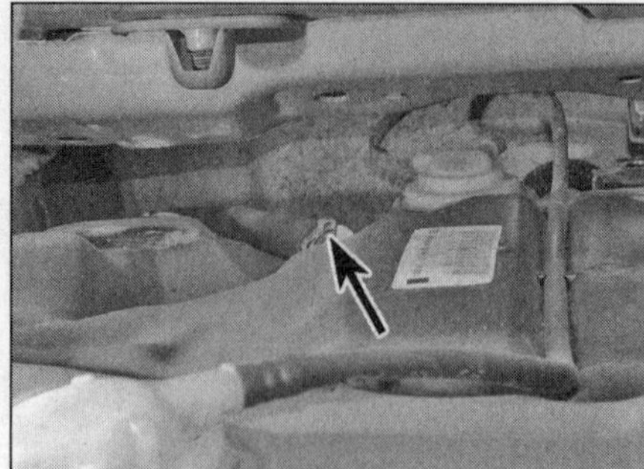
3.15b ...then release the clip and disconnect the breather pipe (arrowed)

15 Partially lower the tank on the jack, taking care that no strain is placed on any fuel lines or wiring. As soon as the wiring connector for the fuel pump/gauge sender on top of the tank is accessible, reach in and disconnect it, then release the clip and disconnect the breather hose from the top of the tank **(see illustrations)**.

16 Lower the fuel tank to the ground, checking all the way down that no pipes or wiring are under any strain. Remove the tank from under the car.

Inspection

17 Whilst removed, the fuel tank can be inspected for damage or deterioration. Removal of the fuel pump/fuel gauge sender unit (see Section 7) will allow a partial inspection of the interior. If the tank is contaminated with sediment or water, swill it out with clean fuel. Do not under any circumstances undertake any repairs on a leaking or damaged fuel tank; this work must be carried out by a professional who has experience in this critical and potentially dangerous work.

18 Whilst the fuel tank is removed from the car, it should be placed in a safe area where sparks or open flames cannot ignite the fumes coming out of the tank. Be especially careful inside garages where a natural-gas type appliance is located, because the pilot light could cause an explosion.

19 Check the condition of the lower filler pipe and renew it if necessary.

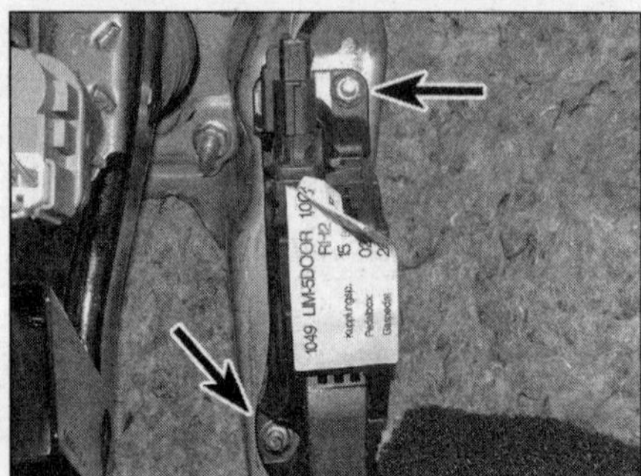
4.3 Accelerator pedal/sensor assembly mounting nuts (arrowed)

Refitting

20 Refitting is a reversal of the removal procedure, noting the following points:

a) *Ensure that all pipe and wiring connections are securely fitted.*
b) *When refitting the quick-release couplings, press them together until the locking lugs snap into their groove.*
c) *Tighten the tank strap retaining bolts to the specified torque.*
d) *If evidence of contamination was found, do not return any previously-drained fuel to the tank unless it is carefully filtered first.*

4 Accelerator pedal – removal and refitting

Removal

1 Remove the driver's side facia lower panel, as described in Chapter 11 Section 30.

2 Disconnect the battery negative lead as described in Chapter 5A Section 3.

3 Disconnect the wiring plug from the throttle position sensor, then unscrew the 2 mounting nuts and remove the pedal/sensor assembly from the bulkhead studs **(see illustration)**. Note that the sensor is not available separately from the pedal assembly. **Note:** *Ford insist that the sensor wiring plug can only be disconnected 10 times before is becomes irreversibly damaged. Use a marker pen to record each disconnection on the side of the connector. Only disconnect the plug if it is absolutely necessary.*

Refitting

4 Refit in the reverse order of removal. On completion, check the action of the pedal to ensure that the throttle has full unrestricted movement, and fully returns when released.

5 Reconnect the battery as described in Chapter 5A Section 3.

5 Fuel Injection system – general information

1 The system is under the overall control of the engine management PCM (Powertrain Control Module), which also controls the preheating system.

2 Fuel is supplied from the rear-mounted fuel tank, via an electrically-powered lift pump and the fuel filter, to the fuel injection pump. The fuel injection pump supplies fuel under high pressure to the common fuel rail. The fuel rail provides a reservoir of fuel under pressure ready for the injectors to deliver direct to the combustion chamber. The individual fuel injectors incorporate piezoelectrical/electromagnetic elements, which when operated, allow the high-pressure fuel to be injected. The elements are controlled by the PCM. The fuel injection pump purely provides high-pressure fuel. The timing and duration of the injection is controlled by the PCM based, on the information received from the various sensors. In order to increase combustion efficiency and reduce combustion noise (diesel 'knock'), a small amount of fuel is injected before the main injection takes place – this is known as Pre- or Pilot-injection. The fuel filter incorporates a heater element.

3 Additionally, the engine management PCM activates the preheating system, and the exhaust gas recirculation (EGR) system.

4 The system uses the following sensors.

a) *Crankshaft sensor – informs the PCM of the crankshaft speed and position.*
b) *Coolant/cylinder head temperature sensor – informs the PCM of engine temperature.*
c) *Mass airflow sensor – informs the PCM of the mass air entering the inlet tract.*
d) *Wheel speed sensor – informs the PCM of the vehicle speed.*
e) *Accelerator pedal position sensor – informs the PCM of throttle position, and the rate of throttle opening/closing.*
f) *Fuel high-pressure sensor – informs the PCM of the pressure of the fuel in the common rail.*
g) *Camshaft position sensor – informs the PCM of the camshaft position so that the engine firing sequence can be established.*
h) *Stop-light switch – informs the PCM when the brakes are being applied*
i) *Boost pressure sensor – informs the PCM of the boost pressure generated by the turbocharger.*
j) *Air conditioning pressure sensor – informs the PCM of the high-pressure side of the air conditioning circuit, in case a raised idle speed is required to compensate for compressor load.*
k) *Inlet air temperature sensor – informs the PCM of the inlet air temperature.*
l) *Clutch pedal switch – informs the PCM of the clutch pedal position.*
m) *Turbocharger position sensor – informs the PCM of the position of the variable in take nozzle guide rails.*

5 On all models, a 'drive-by-wire' throttle control system is used. The accelerator pedal is not physically connected to the fuel injection pump with a traditional cable, but instead is monitored by a dual potentiometer mounted on the pedal assembly, which provides the

5.9a Compress sides of the storage compartment and pull down...

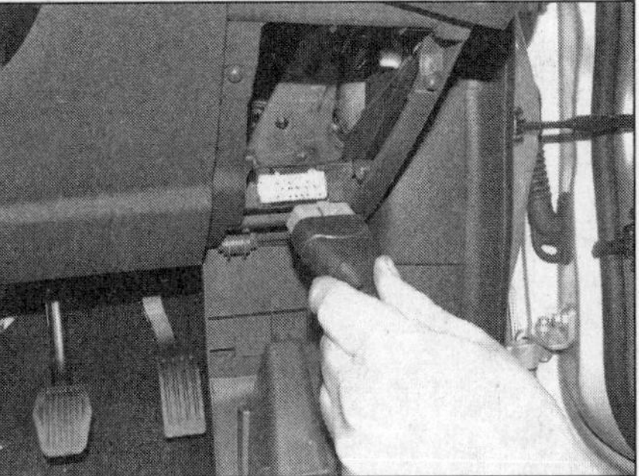

5.9b ...to access the diagnostic socket

6.11 Using a hand priming pump kit to assist with fuel system bleeding

powertrain control module (PCM) with a signal relating to accelerator pedal movement.

6 The signals from the various sensors are processed by the PCM, and the optimum fuel quantity and injection timing settings are selected for the prevailing engine operating conditions.

7 A catalytic converter, a particulate filter and an exhaust gas recirculation (EGR) system are fitted, to reduce harmful exhaust gas emissions. Details of this and other emissions control system equipment are given in Chapter 4C.

8 If there is an abnormality in any of the readings obtained from any sensor, the PCM enters its back-up mode. In this event, the PCM ignores the abnormal sensor signal, and assumes a preprogrammed value which will allow the engine to continue running (albeit at reduced efficiency). If the PCM enters this back-up mode, the warning light on the instrument panel will come on, and the relevant fault code will be stored in the PCM memory.

9 If the warning light comes on, the vehicle should be taken to a Ford dealer or specialist at the earliest opportunity. A complete test of the system can then be carried out, using a special electronic test unit which is simply plugged into the system's diagnostic connector. The connector is located behind the driver's side storage compartment **(see illustrations)**.

6 Fuel system – priming and bleeding

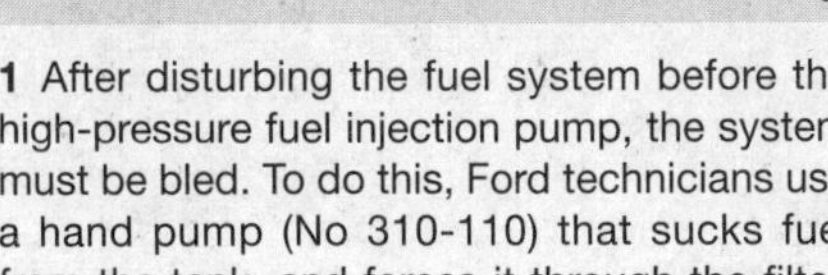

1 After disturbing the fuel system before the high-pressure fuel injection pump, the system must be bled. To do this, Ford technicians use a hand pump (No 310-110) that sucks fuel from the tank, and forces it through the filter. In the absence of this tool, use a hand-held vacuum pump.

2 Remove the plastic cover on the top of the engine.

Using the Ford pump

3 Disconnect the fuel supply pipe quick-release connector from the high-pressure fuel injection pump, and place the end of the pipe in a suitable container to catch the emerging fuel.

4 Disconnect the fuel supply hose to the fuel filter, and connect the hand pump (or equivalent) between the hose and the filter. Ensure the arrow on the pump is pointing towards the fuel filter.

5 Operate the pump until there is a continuous flow of fuel into the container. Squeeze and hold the hand pump for 10 seconds.

6 Release the pump, then squeeze and hold the pump for a further 10 seconds.

7 Reattach the pipe to the high-pressure pump, then operate the pump until strong resistance is felt.

8 Operate the starter motor and run the engine until it reaches normal operating temperature.

Caution: Do not operate the starter motor for more than 10 seconds, then wait 30 seconds before trying again.

9 Stop the engine, and remove the hand pump. Wipe up any fuel spillage, and refit the engine cover.

Using a hand-held vacuum pump

10 Release the securing clip and disconnect the fuel outlet hose from the top of the fuel filter.

11 Connect the vacuum pump pipe to the outlet on the filter, and continue to pull a vacuum until bubble-free fuel emerges from the hose **(see illustration)**.

12 Reconnect the fuel hose.

13 Operate the starter motor and run the engine until it reaches normal operating temperature.

Caution: Do not operate the starter motor for more than 10 seconds, then wait 30 seconds before trying again.

14 Stop the engine. Wipe up any fuel spillage, and refit the engine cover.

7 Fuel gauge sender unit – removal and refitting

Note: *Observe the precautions in Section 1 before working on any component in the fuel system.*

Removal

1 A combined fuel pump and fuel gauge sender unit is located in the top face of the fuel tank. The combined unit can only be detached and withdrawn from the tank after the tank is released and lowered from under the car. Refer to Section 3 and remove the fuel tank, then proceed as follows.

2 With the fuel tank removed, disconnect the fuel supply pipe (if still attached to the tank) from the stub by squeezing the quick-release lugs.

3 Unscrew and remove the special retaining ring, either by unscrewing it with a special locking collar tool – these are widely available from tool suppliers such as Draper, or by fabricating a home made tool **(see illustrations)**.

4 Take out the rubber seal, then carefully lift

7.3a Using a home-made tool to slacken the retaining ring...

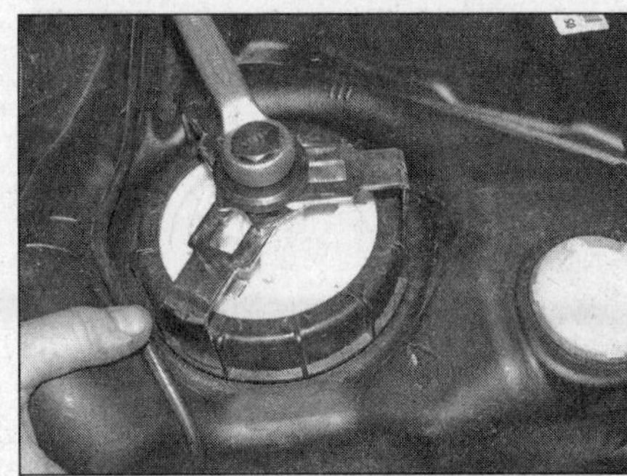

7.3b ...or a commercially available one

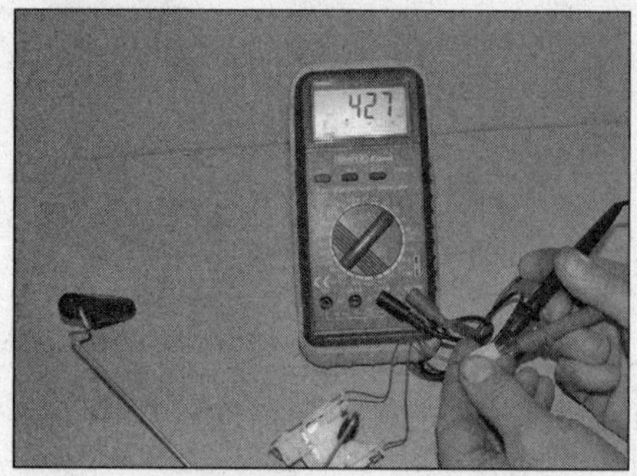

7.5 Measure the resistance of the sender unit at full and zero float arm deflection

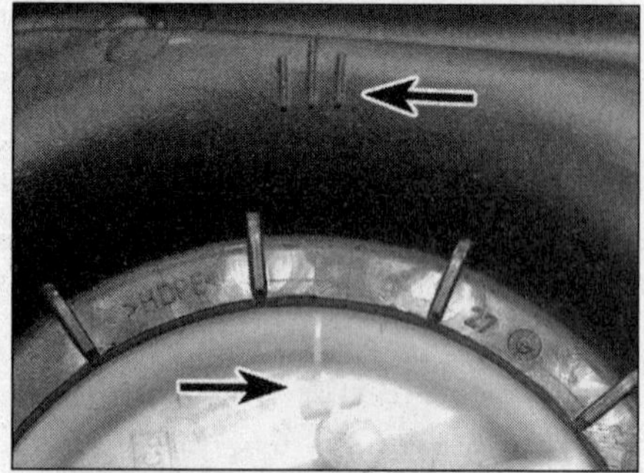

7.6b Align the arrow on the top of the module with the mark on the tank (arrowed)

out the fuel pump/gauge sender unit from the tank. Take care that the sender unit float and arm are not damaged as the unit is removed. To avoid any possibility of the tank distorting immediately refit the locking collar back onto the fuel tank

5 The level sender unit can be tested by connecting an ohmmeter across the sender terminals, and measuring its resistance **(see illustration)**. Check that the resistance changes smoothly and progressively as the arm is moved through the full range of travel.

Refitting

6 Refitting is a reversal of removal, but fit a new rubber seal and tighten the retaining ring securely, aligning the arrow on the top of the module with the mark on the top of the tank **(see illustrations)**. Refit the fuel tank as described in Section 3.

7.6a Renew the rubber seal

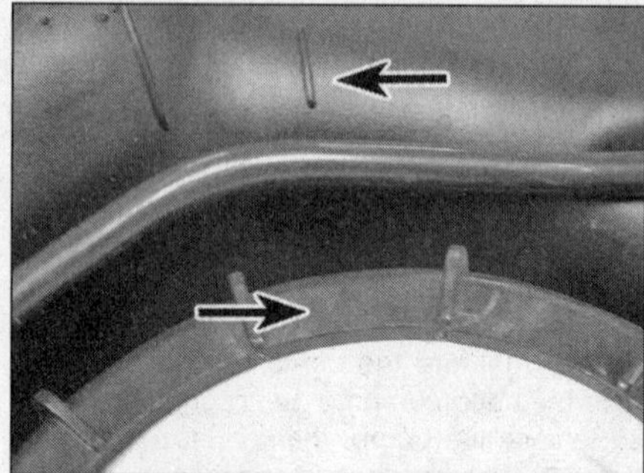

7.6c Tighten the locking collar so that the marks (arrowed) align

8 Fuel injection system – testing and adjustment

Testing

1 If a fault appears in the fuel injection system, first ensure that all the system wiring connectors are securely connected and free from corrosion. Ensure that the fault is not due to poor maintenance; ie, check that the air cleaner filter element is clean, that the cylinder compression pressures are correct (see Chapter 1B, 2D or 2E), and that the engine breather hoses are clear and undamaged.

2 If the engine will not start, check the condition of the glow plugs (see Chapter 5A Section 9).

3 If these checks fail to reveal the cause of the problem, the vehicle should be taken to a Ford dealer or specialist for testing using special electronic equipment which is plugged into the diagnostic connector (see Section 5). The tester should locate the fault quickly and simply, avoiding the need to test all the system components individually, which is time-consuming, and also carries a risk of damaging the PCM.

Adjustment

4 The engine idle speed, maximum speed and fuel injection pump timing are all controlled by the PCM. Whilst in theory it is possible to check the settings, if they are found to be in need of adjustment, the car will have to be taken to a suitably-equipped Ford dealer or specialist. They will have access to the necessary diagnostic equipment required to test and (where possible) adjust the settings.

9 Fuel injection pump – removal and refitting

Caution: Cleanliness is essential. Be careful not to allow dirt into the injection pump or injector pipes during this procedure.

Note: *A new fuel pump to common rail high-pressure fuel pipe will be required for refitting.*

Removal

1 Disconnect the battery and remove the timing belt as described in Chapter 2C Section 7 or Chapter 2D Section 7. After removal of the timing belt, temporarily refit the right-hand engine mounting but do not fully tighten the bolts.

2 Remove the air filter assembly as described in Section 2.

3 Remove the EGR cooler as described in Chapter 4C Section 5, or on models without a cooler, undo the bolts, release the clamps and remove the EGR pipe **(see illustrations)**.

4 Undo the bolts/nuts and remove the support brackets above the fuel common rail and the high-pressure pump.

5 Undo the union nuts and remove the high-pressure fuel pipe between the fuel common rail and the high-pressure pump. Plug the openings to prevent contamination.

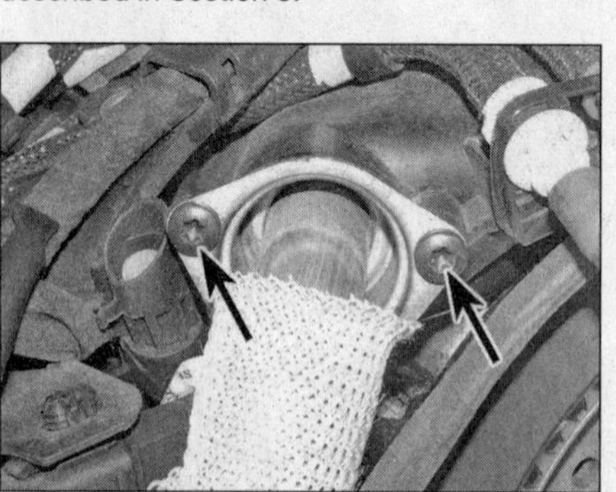

9.3a Undo the 2 bolts (arrowed) securing the EGR pipe to the manifold/cover ...

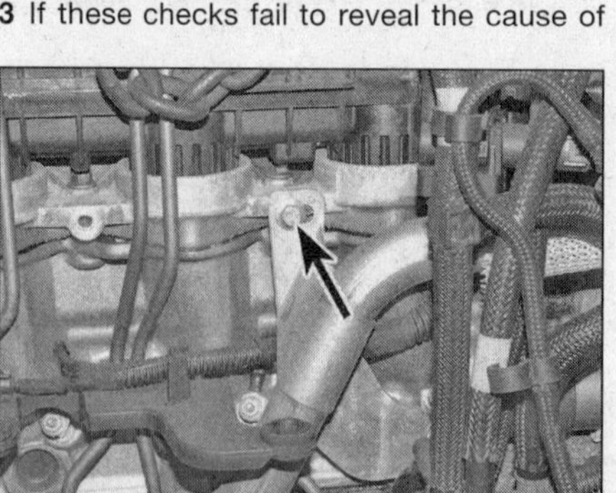

9.3b ... then the bolt (arrowed) securing the pipe to the head ...

9.3c ... then release the clamp (arrowed) and remove the EGR pipe

6 Disconnect the wiring plug from the high-pressure fuel pump.

7 Depress the release buttons and disconnect the fuel supply and return hoses from the pump. Note that the hoses may have a release button on each side of the fitting. Plug the openings to prevent contamination.

8 Hold the pump sprocket stationary, and loosen the centre nut securing it to the pump shaft (see **Tool Tip 1**).

9 The fuel pump sprocket is a taper fit on the pump shaft and it will be necessary to make up a tool to release it from the taper (see **Tool Tip 2**). Partially unscrew the sprocket retaining nut, fit the home-made tool, and secure it to the sprocket with two 7.0 mm bolts and nuts. Prevent the sprocket from rotating as before, and screw down the nuts, forcing the sprocket off the shaft taper.

10 Once the taper is released, remove the tool, unscrew the nut fully, and remove the sprocket from the pump shaft.

11 Undo the three bolts, and remove the pump from the mounting bracket.

Caution: The high-pressure fuel pump is manufactured to extremely close tolerances and must not be dismantled in any way. Do not unscrew the fuel pipe male union on the rear of the pump, or attempt to remove the sensor, piston de-activator switch, or the seal on the pump shaft. No parts for the pump are available separately and if the unit is in any way suspect, it must be renewed.

Refitting

12 Refitting is a reversal of removal, noting the following points:

a) Always renew the pump-to-common rail high-pressure pipe.

b) With everything reassembled and reconnected, and observing the precautions listed in Section 1, start the engine and allow it to idle. Check for leaks at the high-pressure fuel pipe unions with the engine idling. If satisfactory, increase the engine speed to 3000 rpm and check again for leaks.

c) Take the car for a short road test and check for leaks once again on return. If any leaks are detected, obtain and fit another new high-pressure fuel pipe. Do not attempt to cure even the slightest leak by further tightening of the pipe unions.

10 Fuel injectors – removal and refitting

Warning: Refer to the information contained in Section 1 before proceeding.

Note: *The following procedure describes the removal and refitting of the injectors as a complete set. However, each injector may be removed individually if required. New copper washers, upper seals, injector clamp retaining nuts/bolts and a high-pressure fuel pipe will be required for each disturbed injector when refitting.*

A sprocket holding tool can be made from two lengths of steel strip bolted together to form a forked end. Bend the ends of the strip through 90° to form the 'prongs'.

Make a sprocket releasing tool from a short strip of steel. Drill two holes in the strip to correspond with the two holes in the sprocket. Drill a third hole just large enough to accept the flats of the sprocket retaining nut.

Removal

1 Disconnect the battery as described in Chapter 5A Section 3.

2 Release the clamp, undo the nuts/bolt and move the intake ducting/throttle body from above the cylinder head cover to one side.

3 Disconnect the wiring plugs from the injectors **(see illustration)**.

4 Undo the retaining bolt, then unclip the wiring harness tray and move it to one side for access to the injectors.

5 Hold down the black central union, pull up the green collar, and pull the fuel return hose from the top of each injector. Plug the openings to prevent dirt ingress then move the return hose assembly to one side **(see illustrations)**. Plug the openings to prevent contamination.

6 Remove the starter motor as described in Chapter 5A Section 7.

7 Clean the area around the high-pressure fuel pipe unions on the accumulator rail-to-injector fuel pipes then unscrew the pipe unions. Use a second spanner to counterhold the unions screwed into the injectors – these unions must not be allowed to move **(see illustration)**. Note their fitted locations and remove the pipes.

10.3 Disconnect the wiring plugs

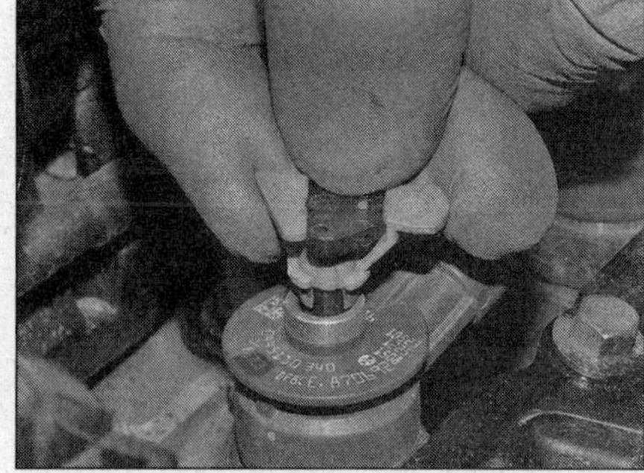

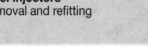

10.5a Pull up the green collar …

10.5b … then pull the return union from each injector

10.7 Use a second spanner to prevent the injector port from rotating

10.9a Injector clamp retaining bolt

10.9b Carefully remove the injector

8 Plug the openings in the accumulator rail and fuel injectors to prevent dirt ingress.

9 Unscrew the injector retaining bolt, remove the clamp and carefully pull or lever the injector from place. If necessary, use an open-ended spanner and twist the injector to free it from position **(see illustrations)**. Do not lever against or pull on the solenoid housing at the top of the injector. Note down the injectors position – if the injectors are to be refitted, they must be refitted to their original locations.

10 Remove the copper washer from each injector, or from the cylinder head if they remained in place during injector removal. New copper washers will be required for refitting. Cover the injector hole in the cylinder head to prevent dirt ingress.

11 Remove the seal from each of the cylinder head injector recesses or injector body. New ones will be required.

12 Examine each injector visually for any signs of obvious damage or deterioration. If any defects are apparent, renew the injector(s). Note down the injector classification number – this may be needed during the refitting procedure if the injectors have been renewed.

Caution: The injectors are manufactured to extremely close tolerances and must not be dismantled in any way. Do not unscrew the fuel pipe union on the side of the injector, or separate any parts of the injector body. Do not attempt to clean carbon deposits from the injector nozzle or carry out any form of ultrasonic or pressure testing.

13 Use a vacuum cleaner to remove any debris from the cylinder head recesses, and the surrounding areas.

Refitting

14 Renew the copper seals on the injectors, and the seals in the cylinder head recesses **(see illustrations)**.

15 Insert the injectors into the cylinder head. If the injectors are being refitted, they must be inserted into their original locations.

16 Refit the injector clamps, but don't tighten the retaining bolts at this stage.

17 Working on one fuel injector at a time, remove the blanking plugs from the fuel pipe unions on the accumulator rail and the relevant injector. Locate a new high-pressure fuel pipe over the unions and screw on the union nuts. Take care not to cross-thread the nuts or strain the fuel pipes as they are fitted. Once the union nut threads have started, finger-tighten the nuts only at this stage, to the ends of the threads.

18 When all the fuel pipes are in place, tighten the injector clamp retaining bolts to the specified torque and through the specified angle.

19 Using an open-ended spanner, hold each fuel pipe union in turn and tighten the union nut to the specified torque using a torque wrench and crow's-foot adapter **(see illustration)**. Tighten all the union nuts in the same way.

20 If new injectors have been fitted, their classification numbers must be programmed into the engine management PCM using dedicated diagnostic equipment/scanner. If this equipment is not available, entrust this task to a Ford dealer or suitably-equipped repairer. Note that it should be possible to drive the vehicle, albeit with reduced performance/increased emissions, to a repairer for the numbers to be programmed.

21 The remainder of refitting is a reversal of removal.

11 Accumulator (common) rail – removal and refitting

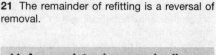

Warning: Refer to the information contained in Section 1 before proceeding.

Note: *A complete new set of high-pressure fuel pipes will be required for refitting.*

Removal

1.5 litre engines

1 Remove the starter motor as described in Chapter 5A Section 7.

1.6 litre engines

2 Disconnect the battery negative lead as described in Chapter 5A Section 3.

3 Remove the windscreen grille cowl as described in Chapter 12 Section 11.

4 Remove the air cleaner as described in Section 2.

5 Slacken the clamps, undo the retaining bolts/nuts and remove the air intake ducting assembly from the top of the engine.

6 Remove the fuel filter as described in Chapter 1B Section 21 then undo the retaining bolts and remove the fuel filter mounting bracket.

7 Remove the EGR valve assembly as described in Chapter 4C Section 5.

8 Undo the bolts/nut and remove the throttle body/duct assembly from the intake manifold.

All engines

9 Clean the area around the high-pressure fuel pipes to and from the accumulator rail, then unscrew the pump-to-accumulator rail pipe unions. Use a second spanner to counterhold the union screwed in to the

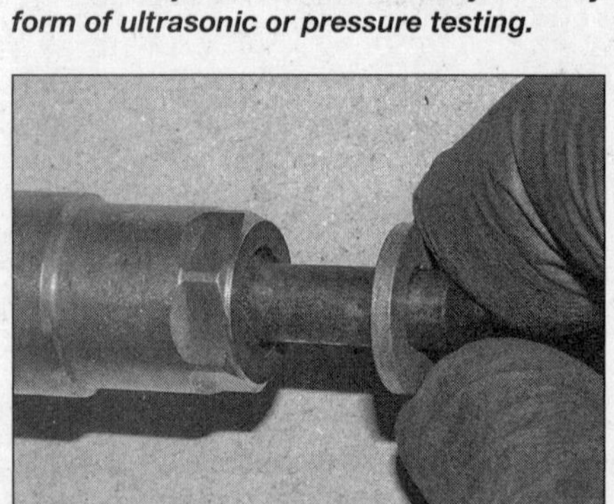

10.14a Renew the copper seals on the injectors...

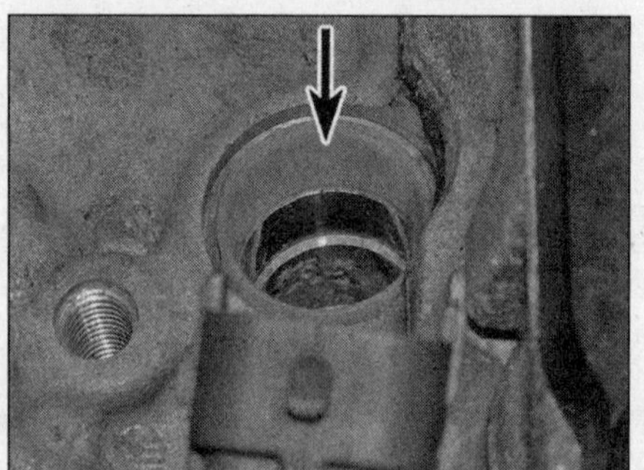

10.14b ...and the seals in the cylinder head

10.19 Use a crow's-foot adapter to tighten the fuel pipe union

11.10 Use a second spanner to counterhold the fuel injector unions whilst slackening the pipe unions

11.12 Pressure sensor – arrowed

11.13 Fuel rail mounting bolts – arrowed

pump body as described in Section 9. The screwed-in union must not be allowed to move. Remove the pipe and discard it – a new one must be fitted. Plug the openings to prevent contamination.

10 Repeat the procedure on the accumulator rail-to-injector fuel pipes. Use a second spanner to counterhold the unions screwed into the injectors **(see illustration)** – these unions must not be allowed to move. Note their fitted locations and remove the pipes.

11 Plug the openings in the accumulator rail and fuel pump to prevent dirt ingress.

12 Disconnect the pressure sensor wiring plug from the accumulator rail **(see illustration)**.

13 Unscrew the two accumulator rail mounting bolts/nuts **(see illustration)**, and manoeuvre it out. **Note:** *The fuel pressure sensor on the accumulator rail must not be removed.*

Refitting

14 Locate the accumulator rail in position, refit and finger-tighten the mounting bolts.

15 Reconnect the accumulator pressure sensor wiring plug.

16 Fit the new pump-to-rail high-pressure pipe, and only finger-tighten the unions at first, then tighten the unions to the Stage 1 torque setting, followed by the Stage 2 torque setting. Use a second spanner to counterhold the union screwed into the pump body.

17 Fit the new set of rail-to-injector high-pressure pipes, and finger-tighten the unions.

18 Tighten the accumulator mounting bolts to the specified torque.

19 Tighten the rail-to-injector pipe unions to the Stage 1 torque setting, followed by the Stage 2 setting. Use a second spanner to counterhold the injector unions.

20 The remainder of refitting is a reversal of removal, noting the following points:

a) *Ensure all wiring connectors and harnesses are correctly refitting and secured.*

b) *Prime and bleed the fuel system as described in Section 3.*

c) *Observing the precautions listed in Section 2, start the engine and allow it to idle. Check for leaks at the high-pressure fuel pipe unions with the engine idling. If satisfactory, increase the engine speed to 4000 rpm and check again for leaks. Take the car for a short road test, and check for leaks once again on return. If any leaks are detected, obtain and fit additional new high-pressure fuel pipes as required. Do not attempt to cure even the slightest leak by further tightening of the pipe unions. During the road test, initialise the engine management PCM as follows – engage third gear and stabilise the engine at 1000 rpm, then accelerate fully up to 3500 rpm.*

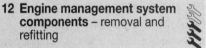

12 Engine management system components – removal and refitting

Crankshaft position/ speed sensor

1 The crankshaft position sensor is located adjacent to the crankshaft pulley on the right-hand end of the engine. Slacken the right-hand front roadwheel bolts, then jack the front of the vehicle up and support it on axle stands (see *Jacking and vehicle support*). Remove the right-hand front roadwheel.

2 Release the fasteners and remove the right-hand front wheel arch liner.

3 Disconnect the wiring connector from the crankshaft speed sensor **(see illustration)**.

4 Undo the retaining bolt and remove the sensor from the cylinder block.

5 Refitting is a reversal of removal, tightening the sensor retaining bolt to the specified torque.

Mass airflow sensor

6 The Mass Air Flow (MAF) sensor is fitted to the side of the air cleaner housing. Disconnect the retaining clips and remove the outlet hose from the sensor **(see illustration)**.

7 Disconnect the sensor wiring connector and also disconnect the vacuum pipe **(see illustrations 2.2a and 2.3)**.

8 Undo the two retaining screws and remove the mass air flow sensor from the air cleaner assembly **(see illustration)**.

12.3 The crankshaft position sensor

12.6 Remove the air outlet hose

12.8 Undo the sensor retaining screws

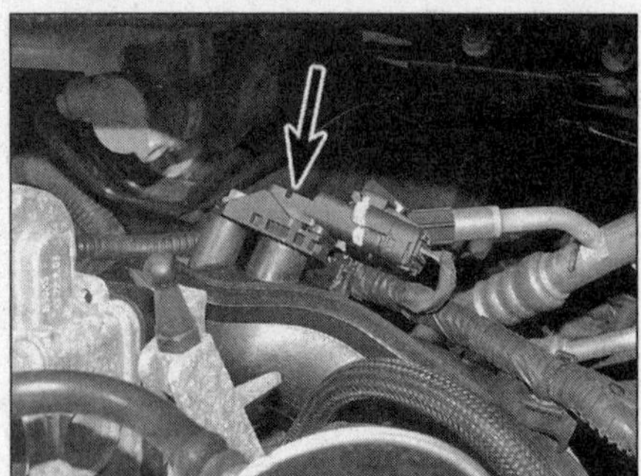
12.12 The air temperature sensor

12.20 Location of Powertrain control module – bumper removed for clarity

12.26 Remove the intercooler hose/pipe

9 Refitting is the reverse of removal, lubricating the sealing ring.

Coolant temperature sensor

10 Refer to Chapter 3 Section 6 for removal and refitting details.

Accelerator pedal position sensor

11 The sensor is secured to the accelerator pedal. Refer to Section 4 of this Chapter for pedal removal. Note that at the time of writing, the sensor was not available separately from the pedal assembly.

Charge air temperature sensor

12 The sensor is mounted on the inlet manifold **(see illustration)**.

13 Remove the engine cover by pulling it straight up.

14 Ensure the ignition is switched off then disconnect the wiring connector from the sensor.

15 Slacken and remove the retaining bolt and remove the sensor from the vehicle.

16 Refitting is the reverse of removal, tightening the sensor retaining securely.

Stop-light switch

17 The powertrain control module receives a signal from the stop-light switch which indicates when the brakes are being applied. Stop-light switch removal and refitting details can be found in Chapter 9 Section 20.

Powertrain control module (PCM)

Note: *If a new control module is fitted, it must be programmed using dedicated Ford test equipment. Entrust this task to a Ford dealer or suitably-equipped specialist.*

18 Disconnect the battery negative lead as described in Chapter 5A Section 3.

19 Jack up and support the front of the vehicle (see *Jacking and vehicle support* in the reference section).

20 Remove the left-hand road wheel and inner wheel arch liner to access the control module, which is located inside a plastic housing **(see illustration)**.

21 The PCM may be protected from theft by shear bolts. The remains of the shear bolts must be drilled out to access the PCM.

22 Where applicable, drill out the shear bolts, open the cover and disconnect the wiring plug(s). Remove the PCM.

23 Refitting is a reversal of removal, but fit new shear bolts and tighten them until the head breaks off.

Fuel pressure sensor

24 It is not possible to replace the sensor separately from the fuel rail. Ford advise that no attempt should be made to remove it. If the sensor is faulty, renew the fuel rail as described in this Section.

Camshaft position sensor

25 The camshaft position sensor is mounted on the right-hand end of the cylinder head cover, directly behind the camshaft sprocket.

26 Slacken the retaining clips, undo the mounting bolt(s) and remove the turbo intercooler pipe **(see illustration)**.

27 Release the securing clip and disconnect the sensor wiring connector **(see illustration)**.

28 Undo the bolt and pull the sensor from position **(see illustration)**.

29 Upon refitting, position the sensor so that the nipple of the sensor is just in contact with the camshaft signal wheel. Tighten the sensor retaining bolt to the specified torque.

30 The remainder of refitting is a reversal of removal.

Turbocharger boost pressure control valve

31 Remove engine cover from over the top of the engine

32 Disconnect the wiring plug, then undo the 2 regulator retaining nuts **(see illustration)**.

33 Note their fitted locations and disconnect the vacuum hoses as the regulator is withdrawn.

34 Refitting is a reversal of removal.

Fuel pressure control valve and fuel volume control valve

35 These valves are fitted to the high-pressure injection pump. They are not available as separate items, and can only be renewed along with the pump. Ford advise that no attempt should be made to remove the valves.

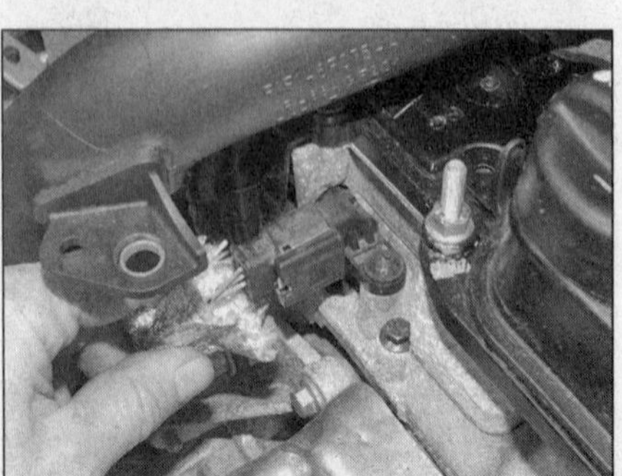
12.27 Disconnect the sensor wiring connector

12.28 Remove the camshaft position sensor

12.32 Turbocharger boost pressure control valve (arrowed)

13 Turbocharger – description and precautions

Description

1 A turbocharger increases engine efficiency by raising the pressure in the inlet manifold above atmospheric pressure. Instead of the air simply being sucked into the cylinders, it is forced in. Additional fuel is supplied by the injection pump in proportion to the increased air inlet.

2 Energy for the operation of the turbocharger comes from the exhaust gas. The gas flows through a specially-shaped housing (the turbine housing) and in so doing, spins the turbine wheel. The turbine wheel is attached to a shaft, at the end of which is another vaned wheel known as the compressor wheel. The compressor wheel spins in its own housing and compresses the inducted air on the way to the inlet manifold.

3 The compressed air passes through an intercooler. This is an air-to-air heat exchanger, mounted with the radiator at the front of the vehicle. The purpose of the intercooler is to remove from the inducted air some of the heat gained in being compressed. Because cooler air is denser, removal of this heat further increases engine efficiency.

4 The turbocharger has adjustable guide vanes controlling the flow of exhaust gas into the turbine. The vanes are swivelled by a vacuum unit on the turbocharger, controlled by the boost pressure regulator valve, controlled in turn by the engine management PCM. At lower engine speeds, the vanes close together, giving a smaller exhaust gas entry port, and therefore higher gas speed, which increases boost pressure at low engine speed. At high engine speed, the vanes are turned to give a larger exhaust gas entry port, and therefore lower gas speed, effectively maintaining a reasonably constant boost pressure over the engine rev range. This is known as a Variable Nozzle Turbocharger (VNT).

14.2a Remove the air Intake hose

14.2b Undo the bolts securing the outlet duct to the turbocharger...

5 The turbo shaft is pressure-lubricated by an oil feed pipe from the main oil gallery. The shaft 'floats' on a cushion of oil. A drain pipe returns the oil to the sump.

Precautions

6 The turbocharger operates at extremely high speeds and temperatures. Certain precautions must be observed to avoid premature failure of the turbo or injury to the operator.

- Do not operate the turbo with any parts exposed. Foreign objects falling onto the rotating vanes could cause excessive damage and (if ejected) personal injury.
- Do not race the engine immediately after start-up, especially if it is cold. Give the oil a few seconds to circulate.
- Always allow the engine to return to idle speed before switching it off – do not blip the throttle and switch off, as this will leave the turbo spinning without lubrication.
- Allow the engine to idle for several minutes before switching off after a high-speed run.
- Observe the recommended intervals for oil and filter changing, and use a reputable oil of the specified quality (see Lubricants and fluids). Neglect of oil changing, or use of inferior oil, can cause carbon formation on the turbo shaft and subsequent failure.

14 Turbocharger – removal, inspection and refitting

Removal

1 Remove the particulate filter/catalytic converter as described in Section 17.

2 Slacken the clamps and remove the air inlet hose, then undo the retaining bolts/nut to disconnect the turbocharger alloy outlet air duct **(see illustrations)**.

3 Slacken the retaining clips and remove the intercooler air hose, then undo the mounting bolt/nut and remove the air outlet pipe **(see illustrations)**.

4 Release the clamps and disconnect the

14.3a Remove the intercooler hose...

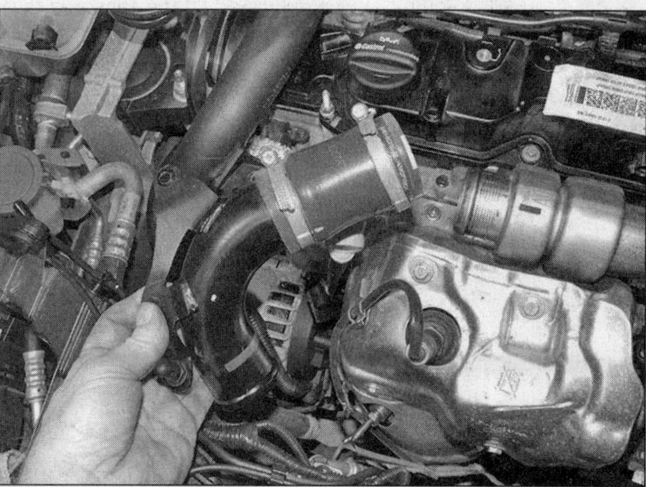
14.3b ...then undo the bolt/nut, and release the pipe

14.4 Disconnect the breather pipe

14.5a Undo the 3 nuts along the top...

14.5b ...and slacken the nut at the front of the heatshield

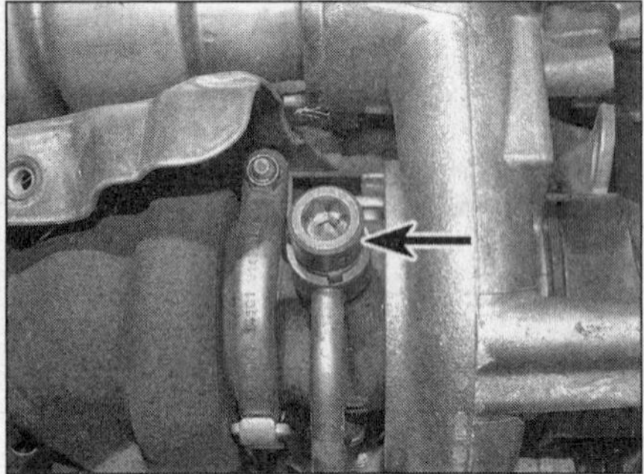
14.6a Oil supply pipe-to-turbocharger banjo bolt

14.6b Oil supply pipe-to-cylinder block banjo bolt

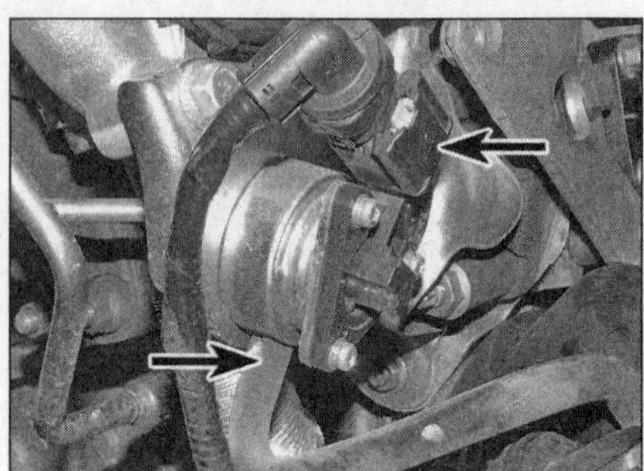
14.8 Disconnect the wiring plug and vacuum hose

breather pipe from the cylinder head cover to the turbocharger intake duct **(see illustration)**.

5 Undo the nuts and remove the heatshield above the turbocharger **(see illustrations)**.

6 Unscrew the oil supply pipe banjo bolts and remove the pipe from the turbocharger and cylinder block **(see illustrations)**. Recover the sealing washers.

7 Slacken the hose clip and disconnect the turbocharger oil return hose from the cylinder block.

8 Disconnect the vacuum hose and wiring plug from the turbocharger wastegate capsule **(see illustration)**.

9 Unscrew the four nuts, and remove the turbocharger from the exhaust manifold **(see illustrations)**. Discard the nuts – new ones must be fitted.

Inspection

10 With the turbocharger removed, inspect the housing for cracks or other visible damage.

11 Spin the turbine or the compressor wheel, to verify that the shaft is intact and to feel for excessive shake or roughness. Some play is normal, since in use the shaft is 'floating' on a film of oil. Check that the wheel vanes are undamaged.

12 If oil contamination of the exhaust or induction passages is apparent, it is likely that turbo shaft oil seals have failed.

13 No DIY repair of the turbo is possible, and none of the internal or external parts are available separately. If the turbocharger is suspect in any way, a complete new (or reconditioned) unit must be obtained.

Refitting

14 Refitting is a reverse of the removal procedure, bearing in mind the following points:

a) *Renew the turbocharger retaining nuts/bolts and gaskets.*
b) *If a new turbocharger is being fitted, change the engine oil and filter. Also renew the filter in the oil feed pipe.*
c) *Prime the turbocharger by injecting clean engine oil through the oil feed pipe union before reconnecting the union.*

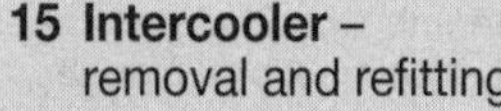

15 Intercooler – removal and refitting

Removal

1 Raise the front of the vehicle and support it securely on axle stands (see *Jacking and vehicle support*).

2 Undo the fasteners and remove the front bumper, as described in Chapter 11 Section 6

3 Slacken the hose clamps and remove the upper hose from the intercooler **(see illustration)**.

14.9a The turbocharger is secured by 2 nuts below...

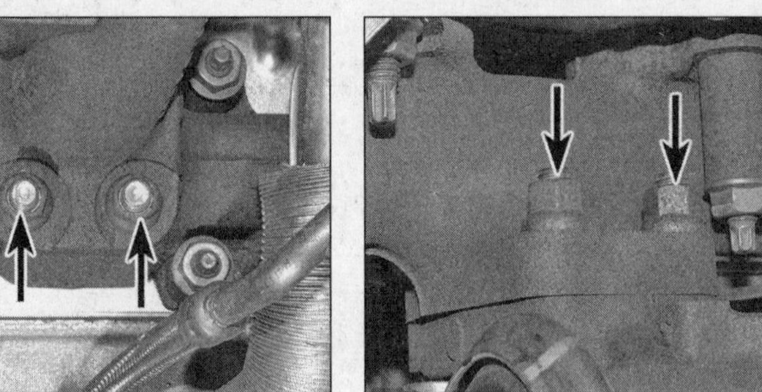
14.9b ...and 2 nuts above

15.3 Remove the upper intercooler hose

15.4 Remove the plastic shield

15.6a Remove the two bolts...

15.6b ...and fit longer bolts

15.7a Release the locating clips...

15.7b ...and remove the air duct

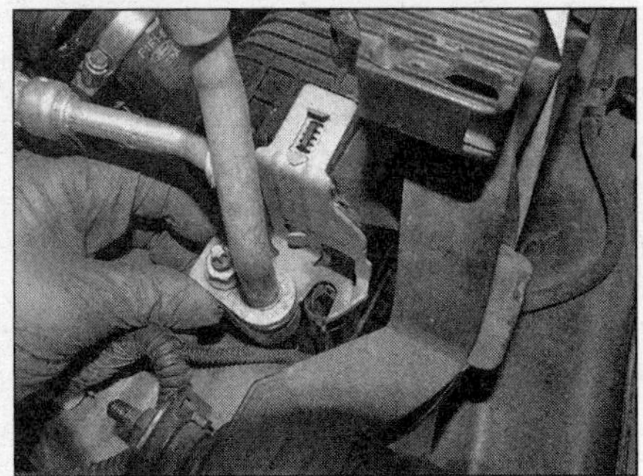
15.8 Unclip the A/C pipe from the intercooler

4 Undo the retaining bolt and remove the plastic shield from the upper crossmember **(see illustration)**.

5 Arrange straps or cable ties and support the radiator and condenser assembly, so that the main support crossmember below the assembly can be lowered.

6 Remove the support panel bolts (two at each side) and replace them with some extra long bolts **(see illustrations)**. This will allow the crossmember to be lowered enough to allow the intercooler to be removed.

7 Release the locating clips, then remove the air duct from the front of the intercooler **(see illustrations)**.

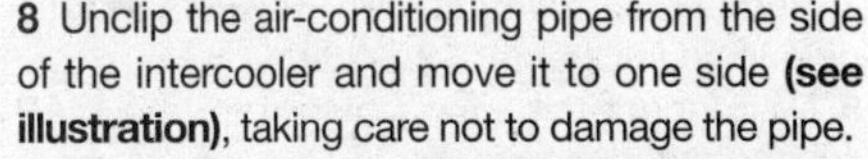

8 Unclip the air-conditioning pipe from the side of the intercooler and move it to one side **(see illustration)**, taking care not to damage the pipe.

9 Slacken the hose clamps and release the lower hose from the intercooler **(see illustration)**.

10 Release the locating peg on the top of the intercooler from the upper crossmember, then unclip the retaining clip **(see illustrations)**.

11 Release the two locating lugs on the bottom of the intercooler from the lower crossmember, then lower the intercooler out from the engine compartment **(see illustrations)**.

Refitting

12 Refitting is a reversal of removal. Ensure the inside of the inlet and outlet hoses are clean where they attach to the intercooler.

15.9 Release the lower intercooler hose

15.10a Release the upper locating peg...

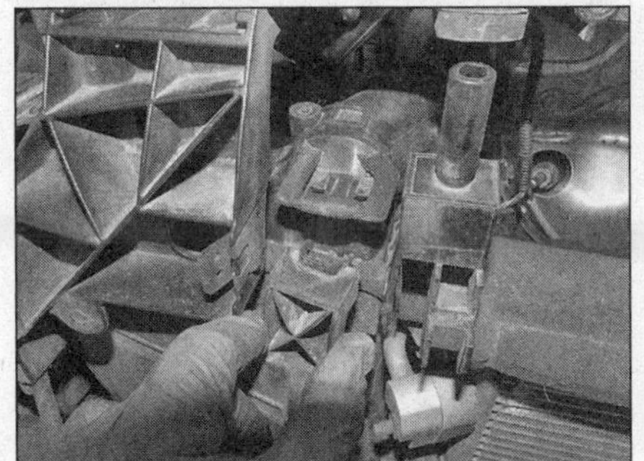
15.10b ...then unclip the retaining clip

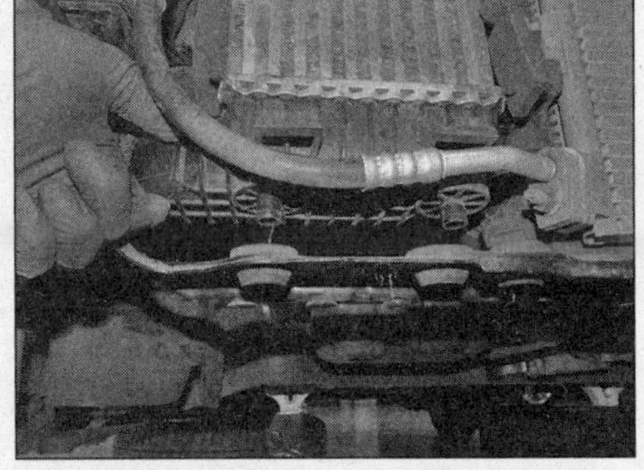
15.11a Release the lower locating pegs...

15.11b ...and remove the intercooler

17.2 The differential pressure sensor

16 Manifolds – removal and refitting

Inlet manifold

1 The inlet manifold is integral with the cylinder head – refer to Chapter 2C Section 10 or Chapter 2D Section 10.

Removal

2 Pull up and remove plastic cover from the top of the engine.

3 Slacken the clamp, undo the nuts/bolts and remove the air intake pipe from the top of the engine.

4 Remove the windscreen cowl panels as described in Chapter 12 Section 11.

5 Disconnect the wiring plug from the MAP sensor on the manifold.

6 Remove the EGR valve as described in Chapter 4C Section 5.

7 Undo the 3 retaining bolts/studs securing the manifold to the cylinder head, and manoeuvre it from place.

Exhaust manifold

Removal

8 Remove the turbocharger as described in Section 14.

9 Undo the nuts securing the exhaust manifold to the cylinder head, and recover the spacers. Pull the manifold from the mounting studs. If the manifold is being removed to renew the gasket, no further dismantling is required. Remove the gasket.

Refitting

10 Examine the studs for signs of damage and corrosion; remove traces of corrosion, and repair or renew any damaged studs.

11 Ensure the mating surfaces of the exhaust manifold and cylinder head are clean and dry.

17.8 Support the flexible section with wooden splints

Position the new gasket, and refit the exhaust manifold to the cylinder head. Tighten the nuts to the specified torque.

12 The remainder of refitting is a reversal of removal, noting the following points:

a) *Tighten all fasteners to their specified torque where available.*
b) *Apply a little high-temperature anti-seize grease (Copperslip) to the manifold studs.*

17 Exhaust system – general information and component renewal

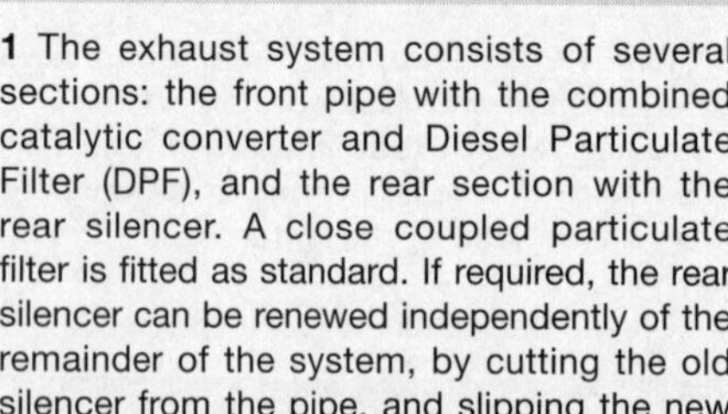

1 The exhaust system consists of several sections: the front pipe with the combined catalytic converter and Diesel Particulate Filter (DPF), and the rear section with the rear silencer. A close coupled particulate filter is fitted as standard. If required, the rear silencer can be renewed independently of the remainder of the system, by cutting the old silencer from the pipe, and slipping the new one over the cut end – details are given in this Section.

2 The DPF will 'regenerate' when certain driving conditions are met. By regenerating, the captured soot particulates in the DPF are burnt off. A diesel vehicle that is only used for short journeys may never meet the conditions required for regeneration of the DPF to take place. If the DPF becomes blocked (sensed by the differential pressure sensors and indicated by the engine management warning light) it will have to be replaced **(see illustration)**. To avoid this situation it is important that the vehicle is fully warmed up and driven at higher road speed every 1000 miles or so. Ford do not give exact figures, but a 20 minute journey at motorway speeds should ensure that regeneration takes place.

3 The exhaust system is joined together by a mixture of flanged, or sliding joints. Apply plenty of penetrating fluid to the fasteners prior to removal, undo the fasteners, unhook the rubber mountings, and manoeuvre the system from under the vehicle.

4 Each section is refitted by reversing the removal sequence, noting the following points:

a) *Ensure that all traces of corrosion have been removed from the flanges and renew all gaskets.*
b) *Inspect the rubber mountings for signs of damage or deterioration, and renew as necessary.*
c) *Prior to tightening the exhaust system fasteners to the specified torque, ensure that all rubber mountings are correctly located, and that there is adequate clearance between the exhaust system and vehicle underbody.*

Catalytic converter and particulate filter

5 The catalytic converter and particulate filter are a single unit.

6 Remove the engine cover by pulling it up.

7 Raise the front of the vehicle and support it securely on axle stands (see *Jacking and vehicle support*). Remove the engine undershield.

8 Attach wooden 'splints' to each side of the exhaust flexible section using cable ties **(see illustration)**. This is to prevent excessive bending of the section as it's disconnected. Undo the 2 nuts securing the flexible section to the exhaust.

9 Undo the 2 nuts securing the catalytic converter/DPF to the support bracket, and the bolts securing the catalytic converter/DPF to the cylinder block.

10 Disconnect the wiring plugs from the temperature sensor and the oxygen sensor

11 Note their fitted positions, and disconnect the pressure take-off hoses from the catalytic converter/particulate filter.

12 Undo the bolts and remove the heat shield over the catalytic converter.

13 Slacken the clamp securing the catalytic converter to the turbocharger. Note its fitted position to aid refitting and then dispose of it – a new one will be required for refitting.

14 Remove the heat shield bracket.

15 Manoeuvre the catalytic converter/DPF from place.

16 Refitting is a reversal of removal, but remember to fit new gaskets and replace the filter to turbocharger clamp.

Rear silencer

17 Slacken the various clamps securing the exhaust pipe/silencer, then release it from the rubber mountings.

Chapter 4 Part C
Emission control systems

Contents

Degrees of difficulty

Easy, suitable for novice with little experience 	**Fairly easy,** suitable for beginner with some experience	**Fairly difficult,** suitable for competent DIY mechanic	**Difficult,** suitable for experienced DIY mechanic	**Very difficult,** suitable for expert DIY or professional

Specifications

Torque wrench settings

Torque wrench settings	Nm	lbf ft
Catalytic converter (to exhaust nuts)	48	35
EGR cooler (main bolts)	20	15
EGR mounting bolts (diesel engines)	10	7
Oxygen sensor (petrol engines)	42	31

1 General Information

1 All models covered by this manual have various features built into the fuel and exhaust systems to help minimise harmful emissions. These features fall broadly into three categories; crankcase emission control, evaporative emission control (petrol engines only), and exhaust emission control. The main features of these systems are as follows.

Crankcase emission control

2 To reduce the emissions of unburned hydrocarbons from the crankcase into the atmosphere, a Positive Crankcase Ventilation (PCV) system is used. The engine is sealed, and the blow-by gases and oil vapour are drawn from inside the crankcase, through an oil separator, into the inlet tract, to be burned by the engine during normal combustion.

3 Under conditions of high manifold depression (idling, deceleration) the gases will be sucked positively out of the crankcase. Under conditions of low manifold depression (acceleration, full-throttle running) the gases are forced out of the crankcase by the (relatively) higher crankcase pressure; if the engine is worn, the raised crankcase pressure (due to increased blow-by) will cause some of the flow to return under all manifold conditions.

Evaporative emission control

4 The evaporative emission control (EVAP) system is only fitted to petrol engines and is used to minimise the escape of unburned hydrocarbons into the atmosphere. To do this, the fuel tank filler cap is sealed, and a carbon canister is used to collect and store petrol vapours generated in the tank. When the engine is running, the vapours are cleared from the canister by an ECM-controlled electrically-operated EVAP purge valve into the inlet tract, to be burned by the engine during normal combustion.

5 To ensure that the engine runs correctly when idling, the valve only opens when the engine is running under load; the valve then opens to allow the stored vapour to pass into the inlet tract.

Exhaust emission control

Oxygen (lambda) sensors

6 To minimise the amount of pollutants which escape into the atmosphere, all models are fitted with a catalytic converter in the exhaust system. The system is of the closed-loop type, in which two heated oxygen sensors in the exhaust system provide the engine management ECM with constant feedback on the oxygen content of the exhaust gases. The pre catalytic converter sensor is used for mixture control and the post catalytic converter is used to monitor the catalytic converter efficiency. This enables the ECM to adjust the mixture by altering injector opening time, thus providing the best possible conditions for the converter to operate. The system functions in the following way.

7 The oxygen sensors (also known as a lambda sensors) have built-in heating elements, activated by the ECM to quickly bring the sensor's tip to an efficient operating temperature. The sensor's tip is sensitive to oxygen, and sends the control module a varying voltage depending on the amount of oxygen in the exhaust gases; if the inlet air/fuel mixture is too rich, the exhaust gases are low in oxygen, so the sensor sends a voltage signal proportional to the oxygen detected, the voltage altering as the mixture weakens and the amount of oxygen in the exhaust gases rises. Peak conversion efficiency of all major pollutants occurs if the inlet air/fuel mixture is maintained at the chemically-correct ratio for complete combustion of petrol – 14.7 parts (by weight) of air to 1 part of fuel (the stoichiometric ratio). The sensor output voltage alters in a large step at this point, the ECM using the signal change as a reference point, and correcting the inlet air/fuel mixture accordingly, by altering the fuel injector opening time.

8 On diesel engines a single pre catalytic convertor oxygen sensor is fitted. The sensor provides combustion information to the ECM and this information is used (primarily) to control the position of the EGR (Exhaust Gas Recirculation) valve and therefore the amount of exhaust gas fed back into the combustion chamber.

Exhaust gas recirculation (EGR)

9 This system is only fitted diesel models, and is designed to recirculate small quantities of exhaust gas into the inlet tract, and therefore into the combustion process. This reduces the level of oxides of nitrogen present in the final exhaust gas which is released into the atmosphere.

10 The volume of exhaust gas recirculated is controlled by a vacuum operated control valve. The EGR system is controlled by the engine management ECM, which receives information on engine operating parameters from its various sensors.

Catalytic converters

11 Catalytic converters are fitted to all models. On 1.6 Ti-VCT engines the catalytic converter is integral with the exhaust manifold. On all other engines the converter is a separate item mounted as close as possible to the turbocharger. On diesel engines the catalytic converter is combined with the particulate filter to form one common part.

Particulate filter

12 Only fitted to diesel engines and combined in one unit with the catalytic converter the Diesel Particulate Filter (DPF) traps soot particles produced by the combustion process. Differential pressure sensors are fitted fore and aft of the DPF, and as the filter becomes full the drop in pressure measured by the sensors is monitored by the engine management ECM. When certain driving conditions are met the filter will be 'regenerated'. By controlling the point of injection, combined with glow plug control and EGR control the temperature in the filter can be raised and the accumulated soot particles are then burnt. Regeneration only takes place when certain driving conditions are met. A car that is used mostly for stop/start town driving may never meet the required conditions for regeneration. It is therefore recommended that at least once every 1000 miles or so that all diesel vehicle are driven at reasonable speed for a minimum of 20 minutes. The engine should be fully up to normal operating temperature before starting. A short motorway or dual carriageway drive is ideal for the purpose.

2 Catalytic converter – general information and precautions

1 On all petrol models, a three-way catalytic converter is incorporated into the exhaust. The catalytic converter is a reliable and simple device, which needs no maintenance in itself, but there are some facts of which an owner should be aware if the converter is to function properly for its full service life.

a) *DO NOT use leaded petrol or LRP – the lead will coat the precious metals, reducing their converting efficiency, and will eventually destroy the converter.*
b) *Always keep the ignition and fuel systems well-maintained in accordance with the manufacturer's schedule (see Chapter 1A or 1B).*
c) *If the engine develops a misfire, do not drive the vehicle at all (or at least as little as possible) until the fault is cured.*
d) *DO NOT push – or tow-start the vehicle – this will soak the catalytic converter in unburned fuel, causing it to overheat when the engine does start.*
e) *DO NOT switch off the ignition at high engine speeds, ie, do not blip the throttle immediately before switching off.*
f) *DO NOT use fuel or engine oil additives – these may contain substances harmful to the catalytic converter.*
g) *DO NOT continue to use the vehicle if the engine burns oil to the extent of leaving a visible trail of blue smoke.*
h) *Remember that the catalytic converter operates at very high temperatures. DO NOT, therefore, park the vehicle in dry undergrowth, over long grass or piles of dead leaves, after a long run.*
i) *Remember that the catalytic converter is FRAGILE. Do not strike it with tools during servicing work.*
j) *In some cases, a sulphurous smell (like that of rotten eggs) may be noticed from the exhaust. This is common to many catalytic converter-equipped vehicles. Once the vehicle has covered a few thousand miles, the problem should disappear – in the meantime, try changing the brand of petrol used.*
k) *The catalytic converter used on a well-maintained and well-driven vehicle should last for between 50 000 and 100 000 miles. If the converter is no longer effective, it must be renewed.*

3 Crankcase emission control system – checking and component renewal

Checking

1 The components of this system require no attention other than to check that the hoses are clear and undamaged.

Oil separator renewal

2 Only the 1.6 petrol engines feature an external oil separator and crankcase breather system.

3 Remove the inlet manifold as described in Chapter 4A Section 14

4 The oil separator is located on the front facing side of the cylinder block, below the inlet manifold. Disconnect the breather hose from the top of the separator.

5 On 1.6 Ti-VCT engines only, pull the PCV valve from the top of the separator **(see illustration)**.

6 Undo the bolts and remove the separator **(see illustration)**. Recover the gasket.

7 On reassembly, fit a new gasket and tighten the bolts securely.

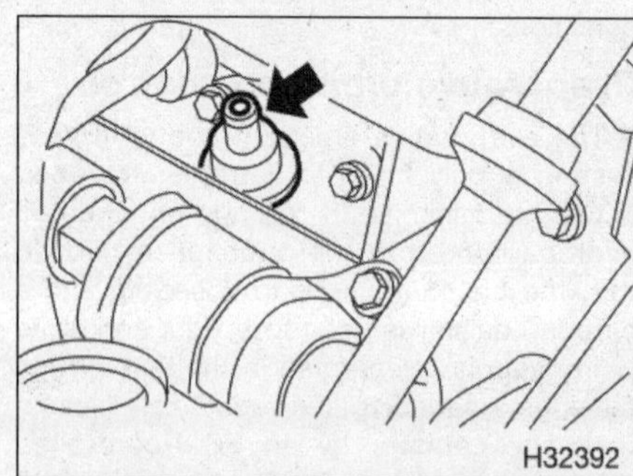

3.5 PCV valve location – 1.6 litre Ti-VCT engines

3.6 Oil separator – 1.6 litre EcoBoost engines

4.5a Remove the protective cover

4.5b The carbon canister is attached to the rear subframe

4 Evaporative emission control system – checking and component renewal

Checking

1 Poor idle, stalling and poor driveability can be caused by an inoperative canister vacuum valve, a damaged canister, split or cracked hoses, or hoses connected to the wrong fittings. Check the fuel filler cap for a damaged or deformed gasket.

2 Fuel loss or fuel odour can be caused by liquid fuel leaking from fuel lines, a cracked or damaged canister, an inoperative canister vacuum valve, and disconnected, misrouted, kinked or damaged vapour or control hoses.

3 Inspect each hose attached to the canister for kinks, leaks and cracks along its entire length. Repair or renew as necessary.

4 Inspect the canister. If it is cracked or damaged, renew it. Look for fuel leaking from the bottom of the canister. If fuel is leaking, renew the canister, and check the hoses and hose routing.

4.6 Disconnect the hoses from the canister

4.7 Remove the canister

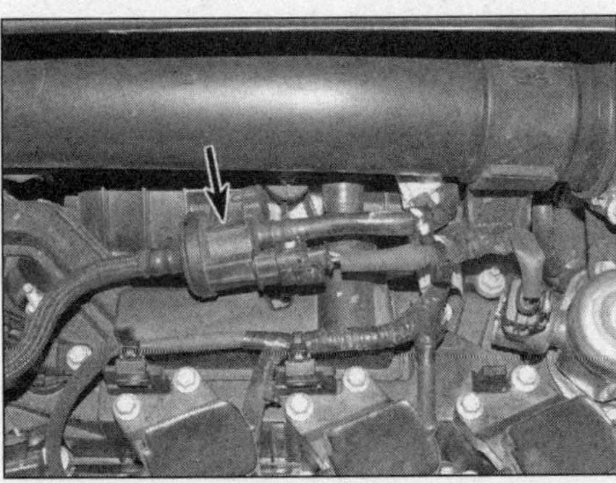
4.9 Location of purge valve – 1.0 litre engines

4.10 Disconnect the wiring plug from the purge valve

Component renewal

Carbon canister

5 The canister is located under the rear of the vehicle, attached to the rear subframe **(see illustrations)**.

6 Note their fitted locations, then press in the release buttons, and disconnect the hoses from the canister **(see illustration)**.

7 Undo the two retaining screws and lower the canister from place **(see illustration)**.

8 Refitting is a reversal of removal.

Canister purge valve (EVAP)

9 The canister purge valve is mounted in the engine compartment on the valve cover on 1.0 litre engines **(see illustration)**, and at the left-hand end of the cylinder head on 1.6 litre engines.

10 Note their fitted positions, then disconnect the vacuum pipes and wiring plug from the valve **(see illustration)**.

11 Unclip the valve from the bracket.

12 Refitting is a reversal of removal.

5 Exhaust emission control systems – checking and component renewal

Checking

1 Checking of the system as a whole entails a close visual inspection of all hoses, pipes and connections for condition and security. Apart from this, any known or suspected faults should be attended to by a Ford dealer or suitably-equipped specialist.

Component renewal

Heated oxygen (lambda) sensors

Note: *The sensor is delicate, and will not work if it is dropped or knocked, or if any cleaning materials are used on it.*

2 Disconnect the oxygen sensor wiring plugs at the rear of the engine (1.6 litre models) or

5.2 Oxygen sensor wiring plugs (arrowed) at the left-hand end of the cylinder head – 1.0 litre engines

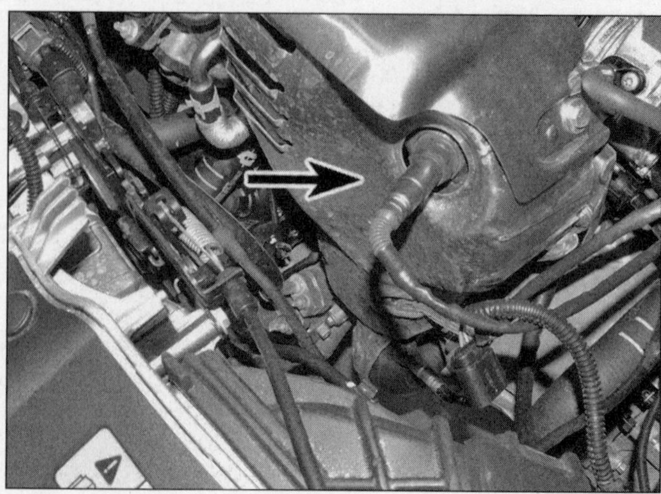
5.3a The pre-converter oxygen sensor (arrowed)...

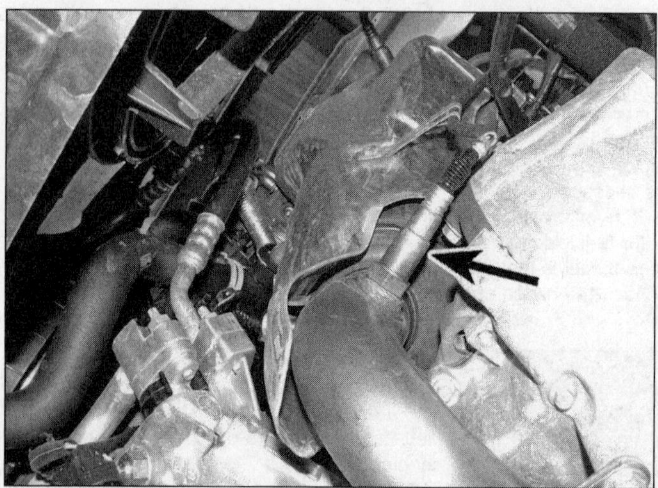
5.3b ...and the post converter sensor (1.0 litre engines)

5.9 Remove the bolts (arrowed)

at the left-hand end of the cylinder head **(see illustration)**.

3 Unscrew the sensors from place **(see illustrations)**.

4 On refitting, clean the sealing washer (where fitted) and renew it if it is damaged or worn. Apply a smear of anti-seize compound to the sensor's threads, then refit the sensor, tightening it to the specified torque. Reconnect the wiring and secure with cable-ties where applicable.

Catalytic converter(s)

5 The catalytic converter(s) is part of the exhaust manifold on 1.6 Ti-VCT engines. Refer to Chapter 4A Section 14 for renewal procedures and additional information.

6 On diesel engines the converter is part of the particulate filter. Removal and refitting of the DPF is covered in Chapter 4B Section 17.

Removal

7 Jack up and support the front of the vehicle (see *Jacking and vehicle support* in the reference section). Remove the engine undershield.

1.0 litre engines

8 Remove the heat shield from the turbocharger and disconnect the oxygen sensor wiring plugs.

9 Remove the 3 bolts and single nut from the manifold at the turbocharger **(see illustration)** and then remove the 2 nuts from the junction with the main exhaust.

10 Working beneath the engine remove the mounting bracket from the sump and then support the flexible section of the converter with a suitable wooden splint **(see illustrations)**.

5.10a Remove the support bracket nuts (arrowed)...

5.10b ...and then support the flexible section

5.12a Remove the nuts and bolts from the support bracket (arrowed)...

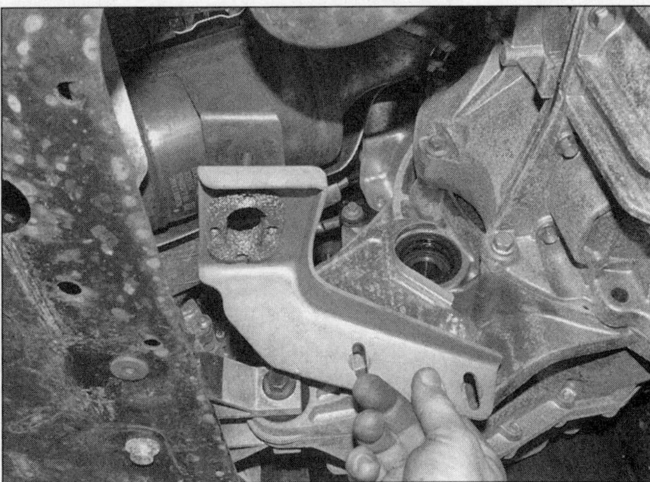
5.12b ...and then remove it

11 Remove the convertor and recover the gaskets. With the converter on the bench, remove the heat shield and then remove the oxygen sensors.

1.6 litre engines

12 Unbolt and remove the support bracket from the engine **(see illustrations)**.

13 Remove the windscreen wipers and windscreen cowl panel as described in Chapter 12 Section 11.

14 Working from the engine bay remove the heat shield **(see illustration)** and then remove the upper mounting bolt from the converter.

15 From beneath the engine reach up and remove the remaining 2 bolts from the converter **(see illustration)**. Access is limited.

Refitting

16 Clean all mounting surfaces and inspect the catalytic converter for damage. Check that the monolith is secure in the converter by shaking it gently. Examine the oxygen sensor mounting bosses – cracks in the welds here will let in air and confuse the oxygen sensor.

17 Fit new gaskets and then refit the converter. Refitting of the rest of the components is a reversal of removal.

EGR cooler/valve – diesel engines only

18 Disconnect the battery negative lead as described in Chapter 5A Section 3.

19 Pull up and remove the engine cover

Control valve

20 Disconnect the wiring plug from the control valve and then remove the 2 mounting bolts. Remove the control valve and recover the seal/gasket.

21 Refitting is a reversal of removal. Remember to replace the gasket.

EGR cooler

22 Remove the wiper arms and windscreen cowl panel as described in Chapter 12 Section 11.

23 Remove the air filter housing (Chapter 4B Section 2) and the battery (Chapter 5A Section 3).

24 Anticipating some fuel spillage, remove the fuel lines from the fuel filter and from the rear of the cylinder head

25 Disconnect the wiring plugs from the fuel injectors, the fuel pressure sensor, the EGR control valve and the fuel filter. Release the wiring loom from the various cable clips and then move the loom t o the side.

26 Unplug the vacuum lines from the control valve at the rear of the cylinder head.

27 Drain the coolant (Chapter 1B Section 28) and then disconnect the coolant hoses from the EGR cooler. Anticipate some coolant spillage.

28 Unbolt the EGR pipe from inlet pipe and then remove the remove the 4 mounting bolts and single nut. Withdraw the cooler from the engine and recover the gaskets.

29 Refitting is a reversal of removal, but remember to replace the gasket and tighten the bolts to the specified torque where given.

5.14 Remove the heat shield

5.15 Remove the lower mounting bolts (arrowed)

Chapter 5 Part A
Starting and charging systems

Contents

Degrees of difficulty

Easy, suitable for novice with little experience 

Fairly easy, suitable for beginner with some experience

Fairly difficult, suitable for competent DIY mechanic

Difficult, suitable for experienced DIY mechanic

Very difficult, suitable for expert DIY or professional 

Specifications

System type	12 volt, negative earth	
Battery		
Type	Low-maintenance or maintenance-free sealed for life	
Capacity	43, 50, 60, 70 or 80 Ah (depending on model)	
Charge condition:		
Poor	12.5 volts	
Normal	12.6 volts	
Good	12.7 volts	
Torque wrench settings	**Nm**	**lbf ft**
Accessory drive belt tensioner bolts	25	18
Alternator mounting bolts:		
1.0 litre engines	48	35
1.6 litre engines	45	33
Diesel engines		
Front (auxiliary belt side) bolts	45	33
Rear (cylinder block side) bolts	39	29
Alternator pulley	80	59
Glow Plugs	8	6
Starter motor mounting bolts		
Petrol engines	35	26
Diesel engines	25	18

1 General information and precautions

General information

1 The engine electrical system consists mainly of the charging and starting systems. Because of their engine-related functions, these components are covered separately from the body electrical devices such as the lights, instruments, etc (which are covered in Chapter 12). Information on the ignition system (petrol engines only) is covered in Part B of this Chapter.

2 The electrical system is of the 12 volt negative earth type.

3 The battery is of the low-maintenance or maintenance-free (sealed for life) type, and is charged by the alternator, which is belt-driven from the crankshaft pulley. Models that have a Stop/Start option are fitted with an advanced EFB (Enhanced Flooded Battery) battery specifically designed to cope with the high load demanded of the system.

4 The starter motor is of the pre-engaged type, incorporating an integral solenoid. On starting, the solenoid moves the drive pinion into engagement with the flywheel ring gear before the starter motor is energised. Once the engine has started, a one-way clutch prevents the motor armature being driven by the engine until the pinion disengages from the flywheel.

5 Further details of the various systems are given in the relevant Sections of this Chapter. While some repair procedures are given, the usual course of action is to renew the component concerned.

Precautions

Warning: It is necessary to take extra care when working on the electrical system to avoid damage to semi-conductor devices (diodes and transistors), and to avoid the risk of personal injury. In addition to the precautions given in Safety first!, observe the following when working on the system:

- ***Always remove rings, watches, etc, before working on the electrical system. Even with the battery disconnected, capacitive discharge could occur if a component's live terminal is earthed through a metal object. This could cause a shock or nasty burn.***
- ***Do not reverse the battery connections. Components such as the alternator, electronic control units, or any other components having semi-conductor circuitry could be irreparably damaged.***
- ***Never disconnect the battery terminals, the alternator, any electrical wiring or any test instruments when the engine is running.***
- ***Do not allow the engine to turn the alternator when the alternator is not connected.***
- ***Never test for alternator output by 'flashing' the output lead to earth.***
- ***Always ensure that the battery negative lead is disconnected when working on the electrical system.***
- ***If the engine is being started using jump leads and a slave battery, connect the batteries positive-to-positive and negative-to-negative (see Jump starting). This also applies when connecting a battery charger.***
- ***Never use an ohmmeter of the type incorporating a hand-cranked generator for circuit or continuity testing.***
- ***Before using electric-arc welding equipment on the car, disconnect the battery, alternator and components such as the electronic control units (where applicable) to protect them from the risk of damage.***

2 Battery – testing and charging

Testing

Standard and low-maintenance battery

1 If the vehicle covers a small annual mileage, it is worthwhile checking the specific gravity of the electrolyte every three months to determine the state of charge of the battery. Use a hydrometer to make the check, and compare the results with the following table. Note that the specific gravity readings assume an electrolyte temperature of 15°C; for every 10°C below 15°C subtract 0.007. For every 10°C above 15°C add 0.007.

	Ambient temperature	
	Above 25°C	Below 25°C
Fully-charged	1.210 to 1.230	1.270 to 1.290
70% charged	1.170 to 1.190	1.230 to 1.250
Discharged	1.050 to 1.070	1.110 to 1.130

2 If the battery condition is suspect, first check the specific gravity of electrolyte in each cell. A variation of 0.040 or more between any cells indicates loss of electrolyte or deterioration of the internal plates.

3 If the specific gravity variation is 0.040 or more, the battery should be renewed. If the cell variation is satisfactory but the battery is discharged, it should be charged as described later in this Section.

Maintenance-free battery

4 In cases where a sealed for life maintenance-free battery is fitted, topping-up and testing of the electrolyte in each cell may not be possible. The condition of the battery can therefore only be tested using a battery condition indicator or a voltmeter.

5 Certain models may be fitted with a maintenance-free battery, with a built-in charge condition indicator. The indicator is located in the top of the battery casing, and indicates the condition of the battery from its colour. The charge conditions denoted by the colour of the indicator should be printed on a label attached to the battery – if not, consult a Ford dealer or automotive electrician for advice.

All types

6 If testing the battery using a voltmeter, connect the voltmeter across the battery and note the voltage. The test is only accurate if the battery has not been subjected to any kind of charge for the previous six hours. If this is not the case, switch on the headlights for 30 seconds, then wait four to five minutes before testing the battery after switching off the headlights. All other electrical circuits must be switched off, so check that the doors and tailgate are fully shut when making the test.

7 If the voltage reading is less than 12.2 volts, then the battery is discharged, whilst a reading of 12.2 to 12.4 volts indicates a partially-discharged condition.

8 If the battery is to be charged, remove it from the vehicle and charge it as described later in this Section.

Charging

Note: *The following is intended as a guide only. Always refer to the manufacturer's recommendations (often printed on a label attached to the battery) before charging a battery.*

Standard and low-maintenance battery

9 Charge the battery at a rate equivalent to 10% of the battery capacity (eg, for a 45 Ah battery charge at 4.5 A) and continue to charge the battery at this rate until no further rise in specific gravity is noted over a four-hour period.

10 Alternatively, a trickle charger charging at the rate of 1.5 amps can safely be used overnight.

11 Specially rapid boost charges which are claimed to restore the power of the battery in 1 to 2 hours are not recommended, as they can cause serious damage to the battery plates through overheating. If the battery is completely flat, recharging should take at least 24 hours.

12 While charging the battery, note that the temperature of the electrolyte should never exceed 38°C.

Maintenance-free battery

13 This battery type takes considerably longer to fully recharge than the standard type, the time taken being dependent on the extent of discharge, but it can take anything up to three days.

14 A constant voltage type charger is required, to be set, when connected, to 13.9 to 14.9 volts with a charger current below 25 amps. Using this method, the battery should be useable within three hours, giving a voltage reading of 12.5 volts, but this is for a partially-

discharged battery and, as mentioned, full charging can take far longer.

15 If the battery is to be charged from a fully-discharged state (condition reading less than 12.2 volts), have it recharged by your Ford dealer or local automotive electrician, as the charge rate is higher, and constant supervision during charging is necessary.

3 Battery – disconnecting, removal and refitting

Caution: Wait at least 5 minutes after turning off the ignition switch before disconnecting the battery. This is to allow sufficient time for the various control modules to store information.

Note: *Ensure you have the audio unit security code. This code will need to be inputted after reconnecting the battery – refer to the owner's handbook supplied with the vehicle.*

Disconnecting

1 Open the bonnet and lower the drivers side window. Remove the key (or keyless fob) from the vehicle.

2 Wait at least 5 minutes and then disconnect the battery at the negative (earth) terminal provided on the left-hand suspension tower **(see illustration)**.

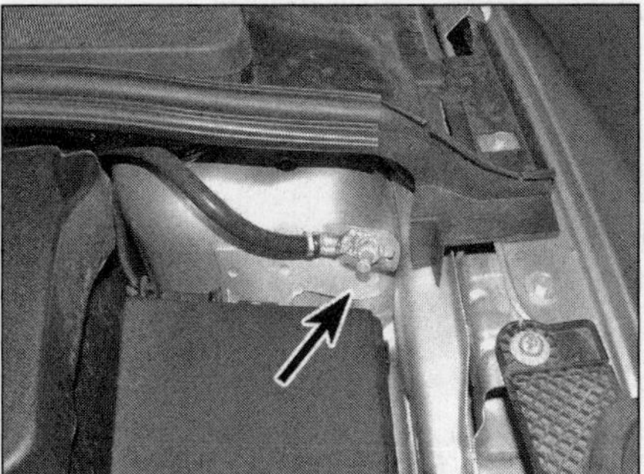

3.2 Disconnect the battery at the main earth (negative) terminal (arrowed)

3 Reconnect the battery when all work is complete. Reach through the open drivers window and turn the side lights on for a few minutes. This will allow any accumulated surface charge on the battery to dissipate. Enter the vehicle and turn the ignition on. Wait for a minute or so before starting the car. The short waiting time will allow all the modules in the vehicle time to 'boot ' up and stabilise. Note that it may take several drive cycles for the engine management system to fully re-learn the optimum operating strategy. Where one touch power windows are fitted initialise them as described in paragraph 18.

Removal

4 Disconnect the battery as described above.

5 Release the clip and remove the battery cover **(see illustration)**.

3.5 Release the clip and remove the battery cover

6 Remove the air cleaner assembly as described in Chapter 4A Section 5 or Chapter 4B Section 2.

7 Slacken the clamp nut and disconnect the battery positive lead terminal **(see illustration)**.

8 Unclip the wiring loom from across the front of the battery box **(see illustration)**.

9 Using a screwdriver release the two upper clips and remove the front wall of the battery box **(see illustrations)**.

10 Unscrew the nuts and remove the battery retaining clamp **(see illustration)**.

11 Pull the battery forward slightly and disconnect the battery earth lead and remove the battery from the engine compartment **(see illustration)**. Take care as the battery is a heavy item. If required the main earth lead can be left connected to the battery post, as the other end has been disconnected from the inner wing panel.

12 With the battery removed the battery tray

3.7 Disconnect battery positive lead

3.8 Unclip the wiring loom

3.9a Release the securing clips...

3.9b ... and unclip the battery box front cover

3.10 Remove the battery clamp

3.11 Disconnect the earth lead

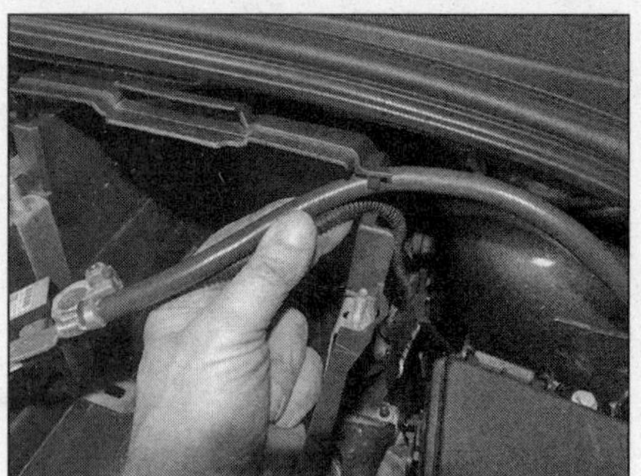
3.12a Unclip the earth lead...

3.12b ...undo the nut to remove the sensor (1.5 diesel shown)...

3.12c ...and remove the battery tray mounting bolts

can be removed. Release the wiring loom/ sensor/relay from the side of the battery tray (depending on model). Remove the mounting bolts and lift out the battery tray **(see illustrations)**.

13 If required the battery tray support bracket can now be removed **(see illustration)**.

Refitting

14 With the battery box bolted securely in position, place the battery into the battery box, making sure the earth lead is secure.

15 Refit the battery retaining clamp and tighten the retaining nuts.

16 Reconnect the battery positive lead and then the battery box front panel and cover. Refit the other end of the negative (earth) lead to the vehicle body.

17 Refit the air cleaner assembly as described in Chapter 4A Section 5 or Chapter 4B Section 2.

18 After reconnecting the battery, the engine may run erratically until it's been driven for a few minutes to allow the PCM to relearn. Also the electric windows may need to be re-initialised as follows:

a) *Press and hold the window control close button until the window is fully closed.*
b) *Release the button, then press it again for 3 seconds.*
c) *Briefly press the open button to the second detent, then release it. The window should open automatically.*
d) *Briefly press the close button to the second detent, then release it. If the window does not close automatically, repeat the complete procedure.*
e) *Repeat this procedure on each window.*

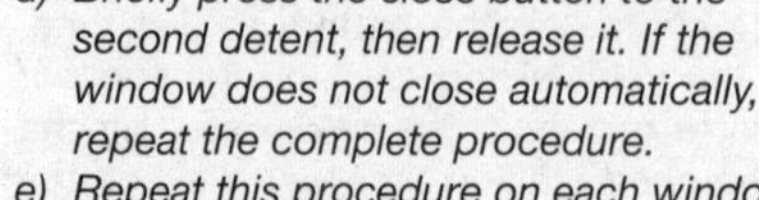

4 Charging system – testing

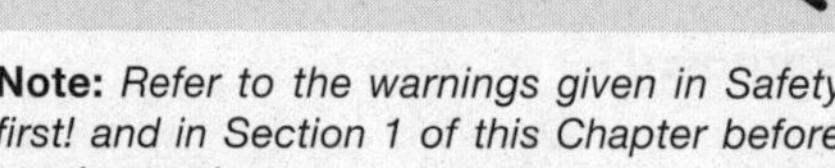

Note: *Refer to the warnings given in Safety first! and in Section 1 of this Chapter before starting work.*

1 If the ignition/no-charge warning light fails to illuminate when the ignition is switched on, first check the alternator wiring connections for security. If all is satisfactory, the alternator maybe at fault and should be renewed or taken to an auto-electrician for testing and repair.

2 If the ignition warning light illuminates when the engine is running, stop the engine and check that the drivebelt is correctly tensioned (see Chapter 1A Section 23 for petrol engines or Chapter 1B Section 24 for diesel engines) and that the alternator connections are secure. If all is so far satisfactory, have the alternator checked by an auto-electrician for testing and repair.

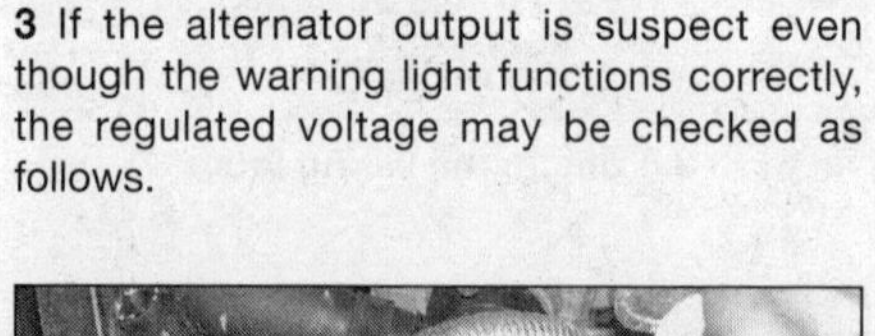

3 If the alternator output is suspect even though the warning light functions correctly, the regulated voltage may be checked as follows.

4 Connect a voltmeter across the battery terminals and start the engine.

5 Increase the engine speed until the voltmeter reading remains steady; the reading should be between 13.5 and 14.8 volts.

6 Switch on as many electrical accessories (eg, the headlights, heated rear window and heater blower) as possible, and check that the alternator maintains the regulated voltage between 13.5 and 14.8 volts.

7 If the regulated voltage is not as stated, the fault may be due to worn brushes, weak brush springs, a faulty voltage regulator, a faulty diode, a severed phase winding, or worn or damaged slip-rings. At the time of writing, it would appear that no parts were available for the alternator. If faulty the complete assembly must be renewed. If in doubt, the alternator should be renewed or taken to an auto-electrician for testing.

5 Alternator – removal and refitting

Removal

1 Disconnect the battery negative lead (see Section 3).

2 On models with hydraulic power steering, undo the bolt and move the power steering reservoir to one side.

3 Jack up and support the front of the vehicle (see *Jacking and vehicle support* in the reference section).

4 Remove the engine undershield and the inner wing liner.

5 Remove the auxiliary drivebelt as described in Chapter 1A Section 23 or Chapter 1B Section 24.

1.0 litre engines

6 Remove the protective cap from the rear of the alternator and then unbolt the main output cable **(see illustration)**. Unplug the control cable.

7 Unbolt and then remove the auxiliary belt tensioner.

8 Remove the upper and lower mounting

3.13 Battery tray support bracket

5.6 Remove the protective cap

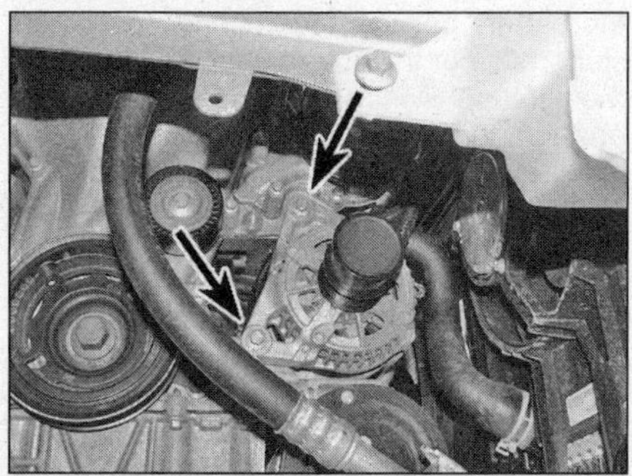
5.8a Remove the bolts (arrowed)...

5.8b ...and lower the alternator from the vehicle

5.9 Alternator upper mounting (arrowed) on the 1.6 Ti-VCT engine

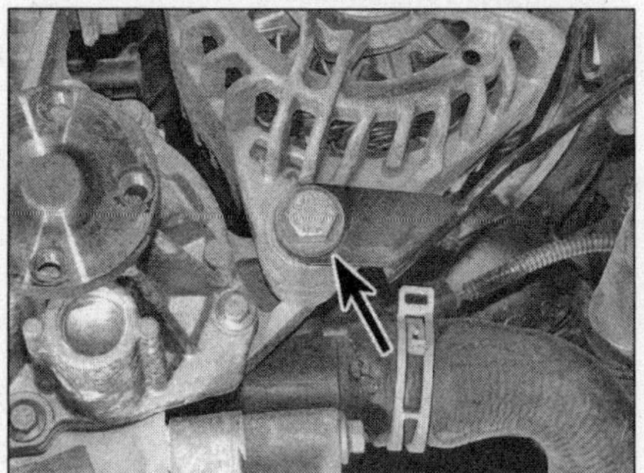
5.10 Alternator lower mounting bolt (arrowed)

5.13 Remove the alternator (1.6 EcoBoost engine shown)

5.14 Remove the intercooler hoses

bolts and then lower the alternator from the vehicle **(see illustrations)**.

1.6 litre engines

9 Undo and remove the alternator upper mounting nut and bolt **(see illustration)**. On models with hydraulic power steering, the reservoir mounting bracket is held in place with the mounting bolts also.

10 Undo the alternator lower retaining bolt **(see illustration)**.

11 Unclip the alternator wiring harness, then disconnect the power steering pressure switch, and the plug from the rear of the alternator.

12 Prise off the plastic cap, then undo the nut and disconnect the remaining cable from the rear of the alternator.

13 Unscrew the alternator upper mounting stud. This can be done using two nuts locked together on the stud's threads, or pull the alternator forwards a little and use a pair of self-grip pliers to unscrew the stud. Support the alternator as the stud is removed, then lift the alternator from place **(see illustration)**.

Diesel engines

14 Slacken the clamps and remove the intercooler supply and return hoses **(see illustration)**, as described in Chapter 4B Section 15.

15 Prise up the rubber cap and undo the cable securing nut, then disconnect the battery positive cable and wiring plug from the alternator **(see illustrations)**.

16 Unbolt and remove the auxiliary belt tensioner. **Note:** *Depending on model, there may be two or three bolts securing the tensioner in place.*

17 Unbolt the air conditioning compressor from the cylinder block mounting bracket and move it to one side, with reference to Chapter 3 Section 12. The refrigerant pipes will not have to be disconnected to move the compressor, but take care not to damage the pipes as it is moved to one side. Secure the compressor in position with cable ties.

18 Slacken the alternator upper and lower rear mounting bolts. These do not have to be completely removed, as they only open the slotted bush to secure the alternator in place **(see illustration)**.

19 Remove the upper and lower mounting

5.15a Prise out the rubber cap and undo the securing nut

5.15b Disconnect the wiring plug connector

5.18 Alternator rear bolts and slotted bushes

5.19 Lower mounting bolt arrowed – upper bolt behind tensioner

bolts from the auxiliary belt end of the alternator **(see illustration)** and lift the alternator upwards from it's position in the engine compartment.

Refitting

20 Refitting is a reversal of removal. Remembering to tighten the various fasteners to their specified torque where given.

6 Starting system – testing

Note: *Refer to the precautions given in Safety first! and in Section 1 of this Chapter before starting work.*

1 If the starter motor fails to operate when the ignition key is turned to the appropriate position, the following possible causes may be to blame:

a) The battery is faulty.

b) The electrical connections between the switch, solenoid, battery and starter motor are somewhere failing to pass the necessary current from the battery through the starter to earth.

c) The solenoid is faulty.

d) The starter motor is mechanically or electrically defective.

2 To check the battery, switch on the headlights. If they dim after a few seconds, this indicates that the battery is discharged – recharge (see Section 2) or renew the battery. If the headlights glow brightly, operate the ignition switch and observe the lights. If they dim, then this indicates that current is reaching the starter motor, therefore the fault must lie in the starter motor. If the lights continue to glow brightly (and no clicking sound can be heard from the starter motor solenoid), this indicates that there is a fault in the circuit or solenoid – see following paragraphs. If the starter motor turns slowly when operated, but the battery is in good condition, then this indicates that either the starter motor is faulty, or there is considerable resistance somewhere in the circuit.

3 If a fault in the circuit is suspected, disconnect the battery leads (including the earth connection to the body), the starter/solenoid wiring and the engine/transmission earth strap. Thoroughly clean the connections, and reconnect the leads and wiring, then use a voltmeter or test light to check that full battery voltage is available at the battery positive lead connection to the solenoid, and that the earth is sound. Smear petroleum jelly around the battery terminals to prevent corrosion – corroded connections are amongst the most frequent causes of electrical system faults.

4 If the battery and all connections are in good condition, check the circuit by disconnecting the wire from the solenoid blade terminal. Connect a voltmeter or test light between the wire end and a good earth (such as the battery negative terminal), and check that the wire is live when the ignition switch is turned to the start position. If it is, then the circuit is sound – if not, the circuit wiring can be checked as described in Chapter 12.

5 The solenoid contacts can be checked by connecting a voltmeter or test light between the battery positive feed connection on the starter side of the solenoid, and earth. When the ignition switch is turned to the start position, there should be a reading or lighted bulb, as applicable. If there is no reading or lighted bulb, the solenoid is faulty and should be renewed.

6 If the circuit and solenoid are proved sound, the fault must lie in the starter motor. In this event, it may be possible to have the starter motor overhauled by a specialist, but check on the cost of spares before proceeding, as it may prove more economical to obtain a new or exchange motor.

7 Starter motor – removal and refitting

Removal

1 Disconnect the battery negative lead (see Section 3).

2 Jack up and support the front of the vehicle (see *Jacking and vehicle support* in the reference section).

3 Remove the engine undershield.

1.0 litre engines

4 To make access easier, remove the battery and battery tray, as described in Section 3.

5 Working from below remove the wiring connectors from the rear of the starter motor and the remove the lower mounting bolt **(see illustration)**.

6 From the engine bay remove the upper mounting bolt and withdraw the starter from below **(see illustration)**. When removing the upper mounting bolt, have an assistant support the starter from underneath to prevent it falling out.

1.6 litre engines

7 The starter motor is located on the front of the cylinder block. Remove the air cleaner

7.5 Disconnect the wiring connectors (A) and lower mounting bolt (B)

7.6 Remove the starter motor

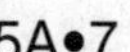

7.9 Undo the 2 nuts (arrowed) and disconnect the starter motor wiring

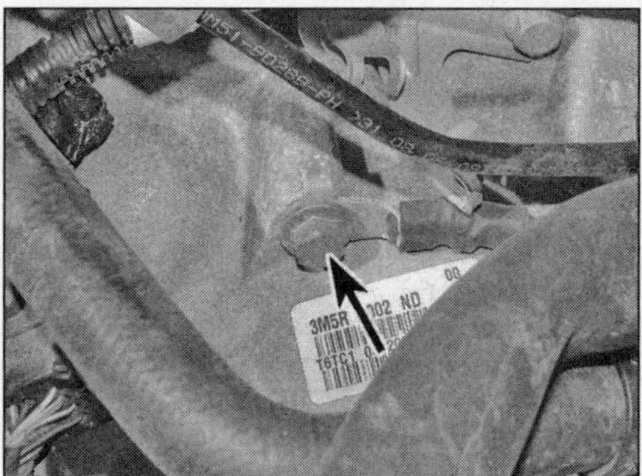

7.10 Note the earth connection on the rearmost starter mounting bolt (arrowed)

7.11 Location of starter motor

7.13 Note location of wiring loom bracket

7.14 Undo the two wiring securing nuts

assembly as described in Chapter 4A Section 5.

8 Unclip the wiring connector securing clips and move the wiring over the starter motor to one side.

9 Disconnect the starter motor wiring connections **(see illustration)**.

10 Support the starter motor, then undo the 3 retaining bolts and manoeuvre it from place. Note the earth connection on the rearmost bolt and the bracket on the lower bolt **(see illustration)**.

Diesel engines

11 The starter motor is located on the rear of the cylinder block **(see illustration)**.

12 Remove the battery and tray, as described in Section 3.

13 Undo the starter motor lower mounting bolt from underneath, noting the wiring loom mounting bracket located on the bolt **(see illustration)**.

14 Note their fitted positions, then undo the two securing nuts and disconnect the wiring connections from the starter motor **(see illustration)**.

15 Unclip the wiring loom retaining clip from one of the upper mounting bolts, then undo the upper mounting bolts, and remove the starter motor. The starter motor will need to be lowered down and out from under the vehicle. As the upper bolts are removed, an assistant will be required to support the starter from underneath. To make removal easier, disconnect the wiring connector from the oxygen sensor to make more room for the starter to be lowered and removed.

Refitting

16 Refitting is a reversal of removal. Make sure mounting bolts are all in correctly and the starter is sitting squarely with the transmission housing, then tighten to their specified torque.

8 Starter motor – testing and overhaul

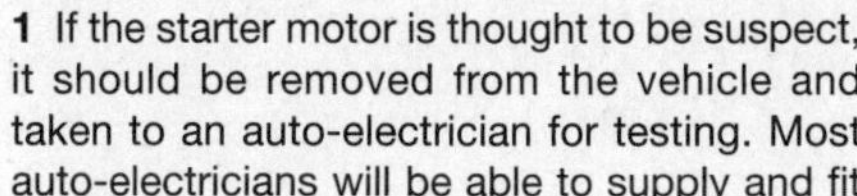

1 If the starter motor is thought to be suspect, it should be removed from the vehicle and taken to an auto-electrician for testing. Most auto-electricians will be able to supply and fit brushes at a reasonable cost. However, check on the cost of repairs before proceeding, as it may prove more economical to obtain a new or exchange motor.

9 Glow plugs – removal and refitting

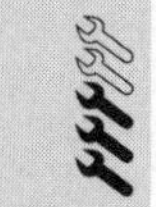

General information

1 To assist cold starting at sub zero temperatures, diesel engine models are fitted with a preheating system, which comprises a relay, and four glow plugs. The system is controlled by the engine management PCM (Powertrain Control Module), using information provided by the coolant temperature sensor.

2 The duration of the preheating period is governed by the engine management Powertrain Control Module (PCM), using information provided by the coolant temperature sensor. A warning light informs the driver that preheating is taking place. The lamp extinguishes when sufficient preheating has taken place to allow the engine to be started, but power will still be supplied to the glow plugs for a further period, known as post-heating, to reduce exhaust emissions. The glow plugs are also energized by the PCM during particulate filter regeneration.

Removal

3 Disconnect the battery negative lead as described in Section 3.

4 Remove the engine cover from the top of the engine and then (where fitted) remove the sound insulation panel **(see illustrations)**.

5 Reach down the back of the engine, pull the

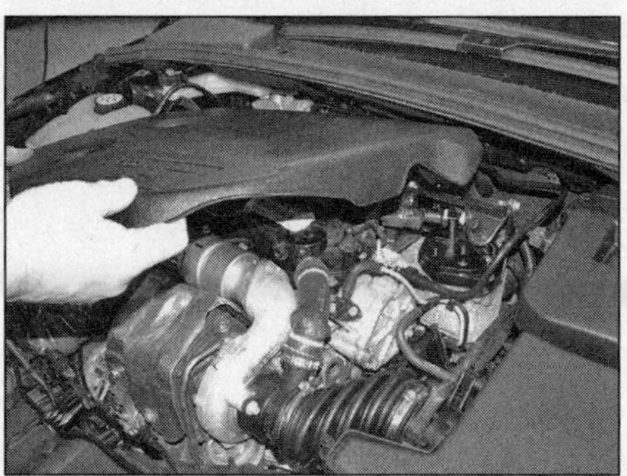

9.4a Remove the engine cover...

9.4b ...and the sound insulation panel (where fitted)

electrical connector from each glow plug, and move the supply cable to one side.

6 Using a deep socket, carefully unscrew each glow plug from the cylinder head.

Inspection

7 Inspect the glow plugs for signs of damage. Burt or eroded glow plug tips can be caused by a bad injector spray pattern. Have the injectors checked if this sort of damage is found.

8 The glow plugs can be energized by applying 12 volts to them to verify that they heat up evenly and in the required time. Observe the following precautions:

a) Support the glow plug by clamping it carefully in a vice or self-locking pliers. Remember it will be red hot.

b) Make sure that the power supply or test lead incorporates a fuse or overload trip to protect against damage from a short-circuit.

c) After testing, allow the glow plug to cool for several minutes before attempting to handle it.

9 A glow plug in good condition will start to glow red at the tip after drawing current for 5 seconds or so. Any plug which takes much longer to start glowing, or which starts glowing in the middle instead of at the tip, is probably defective.

Refitting

10 Thoroughly clean the glow plugs, and the glow plug seating areas in the cylinder head.

11 Apply a smear of anti-seize compound to the glow plug threads, then refit the glow plug and tighten it to the specified torque.

12 Reconnect the wiring to the glow plug and tighten the nut securely.

13 The remainder of refitting is a reversal of removal.

Chapter 5 Part B
Ignition system – petrol models

Contents

Degrees of difficulty

Easy, suitable for novice with little experience	Fairly easy, suitable for beginner with some experience	Fairly difficult, suitable for competent DIY mechanic	Difficult, suitable for experienced DIY mechanic	Very difficult, suitable for expert DIY or professional

Specifications

General

System type	Electronic distributorless ignition system controlled by engine management system (Powertrain Control Module)
Firing order	1-3-4-2 or 1-2-3
Location of No 1 cylinder	Timing belt end

Ignition system data

Ignition timing	Controlled by the Powertrain Control Module (PCM)
Ignition coil resistances	Not available

Torque wrench settings

	Nm	lbf ft
Ignition coil	10	7
Knock sensors	20	15

1 Ignition system – general information and precautions

General information

1 The ignition system is integrated with the fuel injection system to form a combined engine management system under the control of the Powertrain control module (PCM) (see Chapter 4A for further information). The main ignition system components include the ignition switch, the battery, the crankshaft speed/position sensor, the ignition coil (or coils), the camshaft position sensor(s), the knock sensor(s), and the spark plugs.

2 A Distributorless Ignition System (DIS) is fitted where the main functions of the conventional distributor are superseded by a computerised module within the Powertrain Control Module. On 1.6 litre Ti-VCT engines, the remote ignition coil unit combines a double-ended pair of coils – each time a coil receives an ignition signal, two sparks are produced, one at each end of the secondary windings. One spark goes to a cylinder on its compression stroke and the other goes to the corresponding cylinder on its exhaust stroke. The first will give the correct power stroke, but the second spark will have no effect (a 'wasted spark'), occurring as it does during exhaust conditions. On 1.0 and 1.6 litre EcoBoost engines, one coil is fitted for each spark plug. The coil fits above the spark plug, and has an integral power stage and HT cap. This system is often referred as a 'COP' (Coil On Plug) ignition system.

3 The information contained in this Chapter concentrates on the ignition-related components of the engine management system. Information covering the fuel, exhaust and emission control components can be found in the applicable Parts of Chapter 4A.

Precautions

4 The following precautions must be observed, to prevent damage to the ignition system components and to reduce risk of personal injury.

a) *Do not keep the ignition on for more than 10 seconds if the engine will not start.*
b) *Ensure that the ignition is switched off before disconnecting any of the ignition wiring.*
c) *Ensure that the ignition is switched off before connecting or disconnecting any ignition test equipment, such as a timing light.*
d) *Do not earth the coil primary or secondary circuits.*

Warning: Voltages produced by an electronic ignition system are considerably higher than those produced by conventional ignition systems. Extreme care must be taken when working on the system with the ignition switched on. Persons with surgically-implanted cardiac pacemaker devices should keep well clear of the ignition circuits, components and test equipment.

2 Ignition system – testing

Warning: Voltages produced by an electronic ignition system are considerably higher than those produced by conventional ignition systems. Extreme care must be taken when working on the system if the ignition is switched on. Persons with surgically-implanted cardiac pacemaker devices should keep well clear of the ignition circuits, components and test equipment.

General

1 The components of the ignition system are normally very reliable; most faults are far more likely to be due to loose or dirty connections, or to tracking of HT voltage due to dirt, dampness or damaged insulation, than to the failure of any of the system's components. Always check all wiring thoroughly before condemning an electrical component, and work methodically to eliminate all other possibilities before deciding that a particular component is faulty.

2 The old practice of checking for a spark by holding the live end of an HT cap a short distance away from the engine is not recommended; not only is there a high risk of a powerful electric shock, but the PCM or HT coil may be damaged. Similarly, never try to diagnose misfires by pulling off one HT coil at a time.

3 The following tests should be carried out when an obvious fault such as non-starting or a clearly detectable misfire exists. Some faults, however, are more obscure and are often disguised by the fact that the PCM will adopt an emergency program (limp-home) mode to maintain as much driveability as possible. Faults of this nature usually appear in the form of excessive fuel consumption, poor idling characteristics, lack of performance, knocking or pinking noises from the engine under certain conditions, or a combination of these conditions. Where problems such as this are experienced, the best course is to refer the car to a suitably-equipped garage for diagnostic testing using dedicated test equipment.

Engine will not start

Note: *Remember that a fault with the anti-theft alarm or immobiliser will give rise to apparent starting problems. Make sure that the alarm or immobiliser has been deactivated, referring to the vehicle handbook for details.*

4 If the engine either will not turn over at all, or only turns very slowly, check the battery and starter motor. Connect a voltmeter across the battery terminals (meter positive probe to battery positive terminal) then note the voltage reading obtained while turning the engine over on the starter for (no more than) ten seconds. If the reading obtained is less than approximately 9.5 volts, first check the battery, starter motor and charging system as described in Part A of this Chapter.

Engine misfires

5 An irregular misfire is probably due to a loose connection to one of the ignition coils or system sensors.

6 With the ignition switched off, check carefully through the system, ensuring that all connections are clean and securely fastened.

7 Regular misfiring indicates a problem with one of the ignition coils or spark plugs. As no resistance values are available, testing the coils is best left to a Ford dealer or suitably-equipped specialist.

8 Any further checking of the system components should be carried out after first checking the PCM for fault codes.

3 Electronic ignition HT coil(s) – removal and refitting

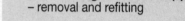

Removal

1.0 litre and 1.6 litre EcoBoost engines

1 Pull up and remove the engine cover. Ensure the ignition is switched off. Ideally disconnect the battery (Chapter 5A Section 3).

2 Disconnect the ignition coil(s) wiring plug(s) **(see illustration)**. It is safest to work on one coil at a time. However, if the coils and the wiring plugs are marked for position, all 4 could be removed at once.

3 Each coil is secured by 2 bolts. Undo the bolts and pull the coil from the cylinder head **(see illustrations)**.

3.2 Disconnect the ignition coil wiring plug

3.3a Remove the bolts and...

3.3b ...pull off the coil (1.0 litre engine)

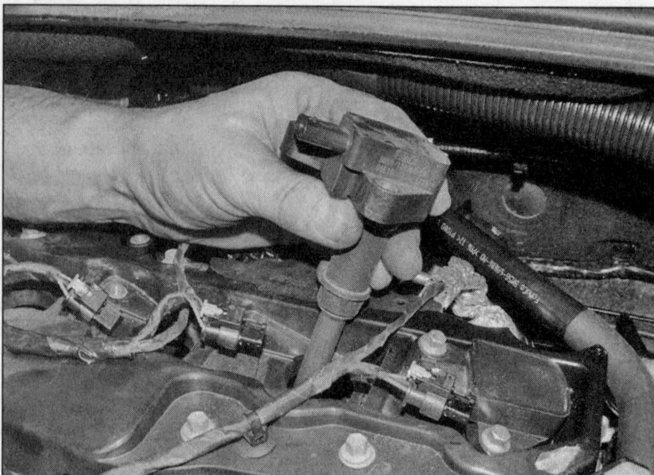

3.3c Remove the coil (1.6 engines)

3.5 Disconnect the ignition coil wiring plug (arrowed)

3.6 Pull the HT leads (arrowed) from the terminals on the coil

1.6 litre Ti-VCT engines

4 The ignition coil is bolted to the coolant outlet elbow on the left-hand end of the cylinder head.

5 Make sure the ignition is switched off, then disconnect the main wiring plug from the coil **(see illustration)**.

6 Identify the HT leads for position (mark the leads and the coil terminals) then carefully pull them from the terminals on the coil **(see illustration)**.

7 Unscrew the four mounting bolts and remove the ignition coil from the engine compartment. Where applicable, recover the heat shield/mounting plate.

Refitting

8 Refitting is a reversal of removal. Tighten the retaining bolts to the specified torque.

4 Ignition timing – checking and adjustment

1 Due to the nature of the ignition system, the ignition timing is constantly being monitored and adjusted by the engine management PCM, and nominal values cannot be given. Therefore, it is not possible for the home mechanic to check the ignition timing.

2 The only way in which the ignition timing can be checked is using special electronic test equipment, connected to the engine management system diagnostic connector. No adjustment of the ignition timing is possible. Should the ignition timing be incorrect, then a fault must be present in the engine management system.

5 Knock sensor – removal and refitting

Removal

1.0 litre engines

1 The knock sensor is located on the rear of the engine above the starter motor, to the left of the oil filter **(see illustration)**.

2 Jack up and support the front of the vehicle (see *Jacking and vehicle support* in the reference section).

3 Remove the starter motor as described in Chapter 5A Section 7.

4 Disconnect the wiring plug and unbolt the sensor.

1.6 litre engines

5 The knock sensors are located on the front facing side of the cylinder block under the inlet manifold.

6 Remove the inlet manifold as described in Chapter 4A Section 14.

7 Trace the wiring back from the sensor to the connector, then slide the retaining clip down and disconnect the wiring plug.

8 Note its fitted position, then undo the bolt and remove the sensor **(see illustration)**.

Refitting

9 Refitting is a reversal of removal, noting the following points:

a) The sensor(s) must be refitted in their original positions, with the wiring harness angle exactly as before.

b) Tightening the retaining bolt to the specified torque is absolutely essential. Failure to do so could impair the performance of the sensor, causing engine damage.

5.1 Location of knock sensor on 1.0 litre engines

5.8 The knock sensors on 1.6 litre Ti-VCT engines (arrowed)

Chapter 6
Clutch

Contents

Degrees of difficulty

Easy, suitable for novice with little experience 	**Fairly easy,** suitable for beginner with some experience	**Fairly difficult,** suitable for competent DIY mechanic	**Difficult,** suitable for experienced DIY mechanic	**Very difficult,** suitable for expert DIY or professional 

Specifications

General

Clutch type	Single dry plate, diaphragm spring, hydraulic actuation

Driven plate

Warp limit	0.2 mm

Torque wrench settings

	Nm	lbf ft
Pressure plate retaining bolts	29	21
Release bearing and slave cylinder mounting bolts	10	7

1 General Information

1 A single dry plate diaphragm spring clutch is fitted to all manual transmission models. The clutch is hydraulically operated via a master and slave cylinder. All models have an internally-mounted slave cylinder and release bearing combined into one unit.

2 The main components of the clutch are the pressure plate, the driven plate (sometimes called the friction plate or disc) and the release bearing. The pressure plate is bolted to the flywheel, with the driven plate sandwiched between them. The centre of the driven plate carries female splines which mate with the splines on the transmission input shaft. The release bearing acts on the diaphragm spring fingers of the pressure plate.

3 When the engine is running and the clutch pedal is released, the diaphragm spring clamps the pressure plate, driven plate and flywheel firmly together. Drive is transmitted through the friction surfaces of the flywheel and pressure plate to the linings of the driven plate, and thus to the transmission input shaft.

4 The slave cylinder is incorporated into the release bearing – when the slave cylinder operates, the release bearing moves against the diaphragm spring fingers. As the spring pressure on the pressure plate is relieved, the flywheel and pressure plate spin without moving the driven plate. As the pedal is released, spring pressure is restored and the drive is gradually taken up.

5 The clutch hydraulic system consists of a master cylinder, a slave cylinder and the associated pipes and hoses. The fluid reservoir is shared with the brake master cylinder.

2 Clutch pedal – removal and refitting

Warning: Hydraulic fluid is poisonous; wash off immediately and thoroughly in the case of skin contact, and seek immediate medical advice if any fluid is swallowed or gets into the eyes. Certain types of hydraulic fluid are inflammable, and may ignite when allowed into contact with hot components; when servicing any hydraulic system, it is safest to assume that the fluid IS inflammable, and to take precautions against the risk of fire as though it is petrol that is being handled. Hydraulic fluid is also an effective paint stripper, and will attack plastics; if any is spilt, it should be washed off immediately, using copious quantities

2.2 Remove the bolts from the suspension brace (arrowed)

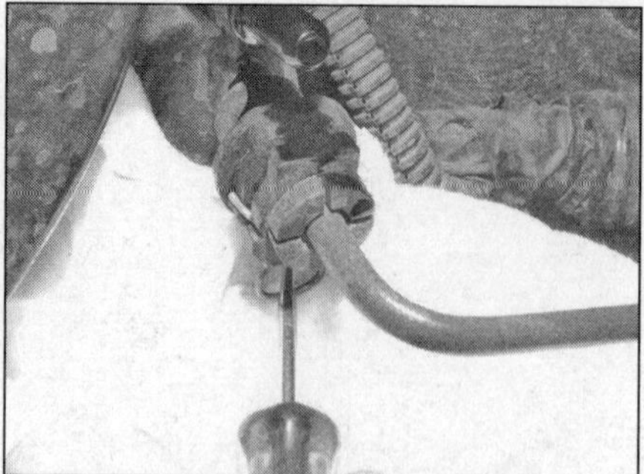
2.3a Prise down the clip and pull the pressure pipe from the clutch master cylinder

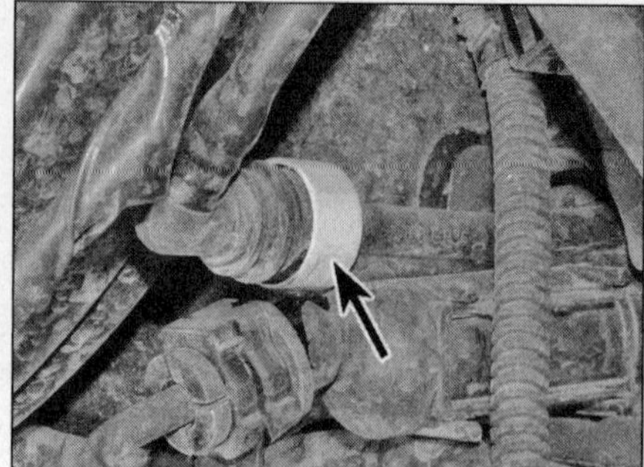
2.3b Pull back the collar (arrowed) and disconnect the fluid supply pipe

of clean water. Finally, it is hygroscopic (it absorbs moisture from the air) – old fluid may be contaminated and unfit for further use. When topping-up or renewing the fluid, always use the recommended type, and ensure that it comes from a freshly-opened sealed container.

Removal

1 Remove the facia as described in Chapter 11 Section 30, then remove the steering column as described in Chapter 10 Section 14.

2 Remove the wiper arms, windscreen cowl panel and wiper motors (as described in Chapter 12 Section 11) and then remove the strut brace from the suspension towers **(see illustration)**. With the brace removed temporarily refit the bolts to the suspension towers.

3 Depress the release buttons/prise out the clip and disconnect the pressure pipe from the clutch master cylinder connection at the engine compartment bulkhead, then disconnect the fluid supply hose from the master cylinder **(see illustrations)**. Be prepared for fluid spillage – wipe up any spills immediately – the fluid could damage paintwork, etc.

4 Disconnect the wiring plug connector(s) from the clutch pedal position switch(es). Depending on model, there may be two sensors fitted to the clutch pedal bracket, the lower is the clutch pedal switch and the upper one being the starter inhibitor switch**(see illustrations)**.

5 Undo the retaining nuts and manoeuvre the clutch pedal complete with the bracket and master cylinder from place **(see illustration)**.

6 To separate the master cylinder from the pedal bracket, begin by squeezing the sides of the retaining clip and pull the pushrod from the pedal **(see illustration)**.

7 Rotate the master cylinder 60° clockwise and pull it from the bracket **(see illustration)**.

Refitting

8 Refit by reversing the removal operations. Note the following points:

a) Tighten all fasteners securely.

b) Renew the seal between the master cylinder and the bulkhead if necessary.

c) Bleed the clutch hydraulic system as described in Section 5.

d) Check the operation of the clutch before refitting the lower facia panel.

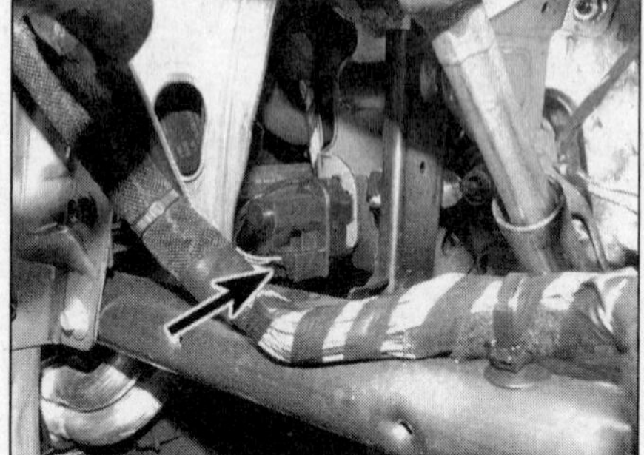
2.4a Disconnect the wiring plug from the clutch pedal position switch...

2.4b ...and the starter inhibitor switch

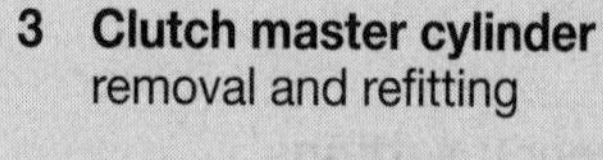

3 Clutch master cylinder – removal and refitting

Note: *No repair or overhaul of the cylinder is possible. In the event of a hydraulic system fault, or any sign of visible fluid leakage on or around the master cylinder or clutch pedal, the unit should be renewed.*

1 Removal and refitting of the master cylinder is included in the pedal removal and refitting procedure described previously.

2.5 Undo the nuts (arrowed) and remove the pedal/master cylinder assembly

2.6 Squeeze the sides of the clip (arrowed) and pull the pushrod from the pedal

2.7 Rotate the master cylinder 60° clockwise and pull it from the bracket

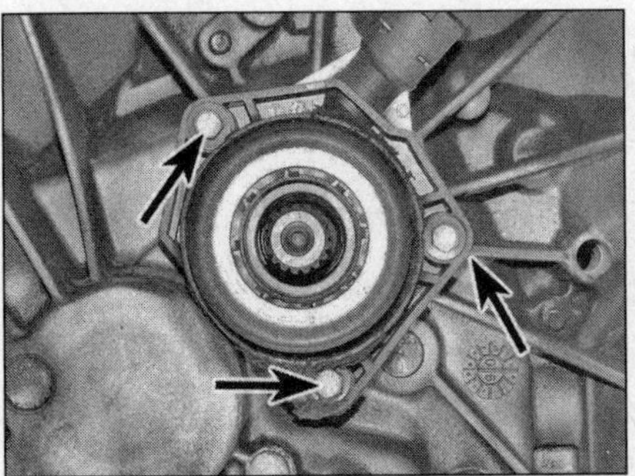

4.3 Slave cylinder mounting bolts (arrowed)

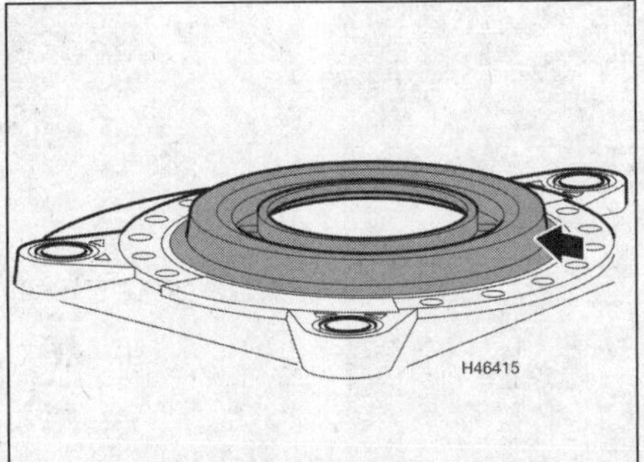

4.4 Apply a bead of sealant to the slave cylinder around the edge (arrowed)

5.3 Connect the hose to the bleed screw on the top of the transmission housing

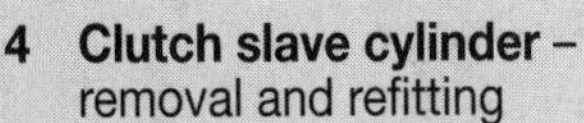

4 Clutch slave cylinder – removal and refitting

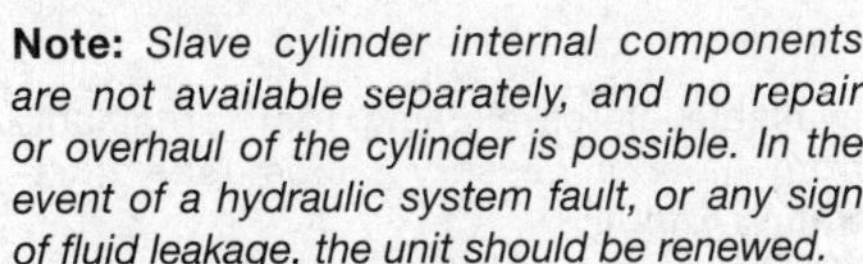

Note: *Slave cylinder internal components are not available separately, and no repair or overhaul of the cylinder is possible. In the event of a hydraulic system fault, or any sign of fluid leakage, the unit should be renewed.*

Note: *Refer to the warning at the beginning of Section 2 before proceeding.*

Removal

1 Remove the transmission as described in Chapter 7 Section 7. The internal slave cylinder cannot be removed with the transmission in place.

2 Release the rubber seal from the transmission.

3 Remove the mounting bolts securing the cylinder and release bearing assembly to the transmission **(see illustration)**, and remove the assembly, feeding the fluid pipe in through the transmission aperture.

Refitting

4 Ensure the release bearing/slave cylinder and transmission casing mating surfaces are clean. Apply a bead of sealant (Ford No ESK-M4G269-A) to the rear of the bearing/cylinder as shown **(see illustration)**.

5 Lubricate the inner lips of the seal with a little grease, then position the release bearing/slave cylinder on the input shaft, and tighten the bolts to the specified torque. Take care not to damage the seal lips with the input shaft splines – wrap adhesive tape around the splines prior to fitting the cylinder.

6 Refit the rubber seal around the pipes, ensuring it is correctly positioned.

7 The remainder of refitting is a reversal of removal, noting the following points:

a) Refit the transmission.

b) Remove the adhesive tape from the input shaft splines.

c) Bleed the clutch hydraulic system on completion (Section 5).

5 Clutch hydraulic system – bleeding

Note: *Refer to the warning at the beginning of Section 2 before proceeding.*

1 Top-up the hydraulic fluid reservoir on the brake master cylinder with fresh clean fluid of the specified type (see *Weekly checks*).

2 Remove the air cleaner assembly as described in Chapter 4A Section 5 for petrol engines or Chapter 4B Section 2 for diesel engines.

3 Remove the dust cover, and fit a length of clear hose over the bleed screw on the slave cylinder **(see illustration)**. Place the other end of the hose in a jar containing a small amount of hydraulic fluid.

4 Slacken the bleed screw half a turn, then have an assistant depress the clutch pedal. Tighten the bleed screw when the pedal is depressed. Have the assistant release the pedal, then slacken the bleed screw again.

5 Repeat the process until clean fluid, free of air bubbles, emerges from the bleed screw. Tighten the screw at the end of a pedal downstroke, and remove the hose and jar. Refit the dust cover.

6 Top-up the hydraulic fluid reservoir.

7 Pressure bleeding equipment may be used if preferred.

6 Clutch assembly – removal, inspection and refitting

Warning: Dust created by clutch wear and deposited on the clutch components may contain asbestos, which is a health hazard. DO NOT blow it out with compressed air or inhale any of it. DO NOT use petrol or petroleum-based solvents to clean off the dust. Brake system cleaner or methylated spirit should be used to flush the dust into a suitable receptacle. After the clutch components are wiped clean with rags, dispose of the contaminated rags and the used cleaner in a sealed, marked container.

Removal

1 Access to the clutch may be gained in one of two ways. Either the engine/transmission assembly can be removed as described in Chapter 2E Section 4, and the transmission then separated from the engine, or the engine may be left in the car and the transmission removed independently as described in Chapter 7 Section 7. If the clutch is to be refitted, use paint or marker pen to mark the position of the pressure plate relative to the flywheel.

2 Having separated the transmission from the flywheel, check if there are any marks identifying the relation of the pressure plate to the flywheel. If not, make your own marks using a dab of paint or a scriber. These marks will be used if the original pressure plate is refitted, and will help to maintain the balance of the unit. A new pressure plate may be fitted in any position allowed by the locating dowels.

3 Unscrew and remove the 6 pressure plate retaining bolts, working in a diagonal sequence, and slackening the bolts only a turn at a time. If necessary, the flywheel may be held stationary using a home-made locking tool **(see illustrations)**.

6.3a Undo the pressure plate retaining bolts

6.3b Using a home-made tool to lock the flywheel

6.14a The clutch driven plate should be marked to indicate which side faces the transmission or flywheel

6.14b Position the driven plate using a clutch aligning tool

4 Ease the pressure plate off its locating dowels. Be prepared to catch the driven plate, which will drop out as the pressure plate is removed. Note which way round the driven plate is fitted.

Inspection

5 With the clutch assembly removed, clean off all traces of clutch dust using a dry cloth. This is best done outside or in a well-ventilated area.

6 Examine the linings of the driven plate for wear and loose rivets, and the rim for distortion, cracks, broken torsion springs and worn splines. The surface of the friction linings may be highly glazed, but, as long as the friction material pattern can be clearly seen, this is satisfactory.

7 If there is any sign of oil contamination, indicated by a continuous or patchy, shiny black discolouration, the plate must be renewed and the source of the contamination traced and rectified. This will be either a leaking crankshaft oil seal or transmission input shaft oil seal – or both.

8 The driven plate must also be renewed if the lining thickness has worn down to, or just above, the level of the rivet heads. Given the amount of dismantling work necessary to gain access to the driven plate, it may be wise to fit a new plate regardless of the old one's condition.

9 Check the machined faces of the flywheel and pressure plate. If either is grooved, or heavily scored, renewal is necessary. Providing the damage is not too serious, the flywheel can be removed as described in Chapter 2A, 2B, 2C or 2D and taken to an engineering works, who may be able to clean up the surface by machining.

10 The pressure plate must be renewed if any cracks are apparent, if the diaphragm spring is damaged or its pressure suspect, or if there is excessive warpage of the pressure plate face.

11 With the transmission removed, check the condition of the release bearing, as described in Section 7.

Refitting

12 It is advisable to refit the clutch assembly with clean hands, and to wipe down the pressure plate and flywheel faces with a clean dry rag before assembly begins.

13 Fit an appropriate centring tool into the hole at the end of the crankshaft. The tool must be a sliding fit in the crankshaft hole and the driven plate centre. Ford centring tool No 308-204 may also be available, or a suitable equivalent may be fabricated.

14 Place the friction plate in position as noted on removal. Note that the new driven plate will be marked to indicate which side faces the flywheel **(see illustrations)**.

15 Place the pressure plate over the dowels. Refit the retaining bolts, and tighten them finger-tight so that the driven plate is gripped lightly, but can still be moved.

16 The driven plate must now be centralised so that, when the engine and transmission are mated, the splines of the gearbox input shaft will pass through the splines in the centre of the driven plate hub.

17 Centralisation can be carried out by inserting a round bar through the hole in the centre of the driven plate, so that the end of the bar rests in the hole in the rear end of the crankshaft. Move the bar sideways or up-and-down, to move the plate in whichever direction is necessary to achieve centralisation. Centralisation can then be checked by removing the bar and viewing the driven plate hub in relation to the diaphragm spring fingers, or by viewing through the side apertures of the pressure plate, and checking that the driven plate is central in relation to the outer edge of the pressure plate.

18 An alternative and more accurate method of centralisation is to use a commercially-available clutch-aligning tool, obtainable from most accessory shops **(see illustration 6.14b)**.

19 Once the clutch is centralised, progressively tighten the pressure plate bolts in a diagonal sequence to the specified torque setting.

20 The engine and/or transmission can now be refitted by referring to the appropriate Chapters of this manual.

7 Clutch release bearing – removal, inspection and refitting

Removal

1 Access to the clutch release bearing may be gained in one of two ways. Either the engine/transmission assembly can be removed as described in Chapter 2E Section 4, and the transmission then separated from the engine, or the engine may be left in the car and the transmission removed independently as described in Chapter 7 Section 7.

2 The release bearing and slave cylinder are combined into one unit, and cannot be separated. Refer to the slave cylinder removal procedure in Section 4.

Inspection

3 Check the bearing for smoothness of operation, and renew it if there is any roughness or harshness as the bearing is spun. It is a good idea to renew the bearing as a matter of course during clutch overhaul, regardless of its apparent condition, considering the amount of dismantling work necessary to gain access to it.

Refitting

4 Refer to Section 4.

Chapter 7
Manual transmission

Contents

Degrees of difficulty

Easy, suitable for novice with little experience	**Fairly easy,** suitable for beginner with some experience	**Fairly difficult,** suitable for competent DIY mechanic	**Difficult,** suitable for experienced DIY mechanic	**Very difficult,** suitable for expert DIY or professional

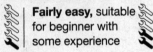

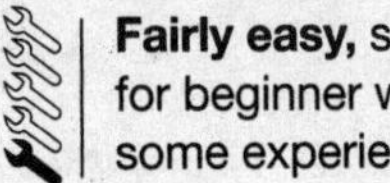

Specifications

General

Transmission type	Five or six forward speeds, one reverse. Synchromesh on all forward gears. Gearchange linkage operated by twin cables
Transmission code	B5/iB5 (5 speed) or B6 (6 speed)
Transmission oil type	Ford WSS-M2C200-D2
Transmission oil capacity:	
B5/iB5 transmission	2.30 litres
B6 transmission	1.67 litres
B6 transmission removal quantity	0.50 litres

Gear ratios (typical)

	B5/iB5 transmission	B6 transmission
1st	3.58: 1	3.727: 1
2nd	1.93: 1	2.048: 1
3rd	1.28: 1	1.258: 1
4th	0.95: 1	0.919: 1
5th	0.76: 1	0.738: 1
6th	N/A	0.622: 1
Reverse	3.62: 1	3.818: 1

Final drive ratios

B5/iB5 transmission:	
1.0 litre petrol engine (70kW/95ps)	4.06: 1
1.0 litre petrol engine (110kW/150ps)	4.25: 1
B6 transmission:	
1.0 litre petrol engine	4.067: 1
1.6 litre petrol engine	3.824: 1
1.5 & 1.6 litre diesel engines	3.611: 1

Torque wrench settings

	Nm	lbf ft
Battery tray bolts	10	7
Battery tray support bracket	48	35
Catalytic converter support bracket (compressible mounting):		
Stage 1	7	5
Stage 2	Loosen 360°	
Engine/transmission left-hand mounting upper section:		
Centre bolt*	148	109
Four outer nuts	48	35
Engine/transmission rear mounting (to transmission)	63	46
Engine/transmission rear mounting (to subframe)		
Stage 1	30	22
Stage 2	Angle tighten a further 270°	
Exhaust to Catalytic converter nuts	48	35
Gearchange cable bracket bolts	20	15
Gearchange cable bushing	9	7
Gearchange mechanism to floor	9	7
Oil filler/level plug – B5/iB5 transmissions	35	26
Oil filler/level/drain plug – B6 transmissions	40	30
Reversing light switch:		
B5/iB5 transmissions	12	9
B6 transmissions	24	18
Transmission mounting bracket (on transmission)	80	59
Transmission to engine bolts	48	35

**Do not re-use*

1 General Information

1 The transmission is contained in a cast-aluminium alloy casing bolted to the engine's left-hand end, and consists of the gearbox and final drive differential – often called a transaxle. The transmission unit type is stamped on a plate attached to the transmission. The manual transmissions used in the Focus (covered by this manual) are the B5/iB5 (5 speed) and the B6 (6 speed).

2 Drive is transmitted from the crankshaft via the clutch to the input shaft, which has a splined extension to accept the clutch driven plate. From the input shaft, drive is transmitted to the output shaft, from where the drive is transmitted to the differential crownwheel, which rotates with the differential and planetary gears, thus driving the sun gears and driveshafts. The rotation of the planetary gears on their shaft allows the inner roadwheel to rotate at a slower speed than the outer roadwheel when the car is cornering.

3 The input and output shafts are arranged side-by-side, parallel to the crankshaft and driveshafts, so that their gear pinion teeth are in constant mesh. In the neutral position, the output shaft gear pinions rotate freely, so that drive cannot be transmitted to the crownwheel.

4 Gear selection is via a floor-mounted lever and selector cable mechanism.

5 The transmission selector mechanism causes the appropriate selector fork to move its respective synchro-sleeve along the output shaft, to lock the gear pinion to the synchro-hub. Since the synchro-hubs are splined to the output shaft, this locks the pinion to the shaft, so that drive can be transmitted. To ensure that gearchanging can be made quickly and quietly, a synchromesh system is fitted to all forward gears, consisting of baulk rings and spring-loaded fingers, as well as the gear pinions and synchro-hubs. The synchromesh cones are formed on the mating faces of the baulk rings and gear pinions.

Transmission overhaul

6 Because of the complexity of the assembly, possible unavailability of new parts and special tools necessary, internal repair procedures for the transmission are not recommended for the home mechanic. The bulk of the information in this Chapter is devoted to removal and refitting procedures.

2.1 Prise up the gear lever gaiter

2 Gearchange cables – adjustment

Note: *A 4 mm drill bit will be required for this adjustment.*

1 Working inside the vehicle, put the gear lever into neutral and carefully unclip the trim panel at the base of the gear lever gaiter, and move the gaiter to one side, for access to the base of the gear lever **(see illustration)**.

2 Move the gear lever to the 4th gear position, then insert a 4 mm drill bit into the gear lever base mechanism, making sure that it is fully inserted **(see illustration)**.

B5/iB5 (5-speed) transmission

3 Apply the handbrake, then jack up the front of the car, supporting it on axle stands (see *Jacking and vehicle support*). Remove the engine undershield.

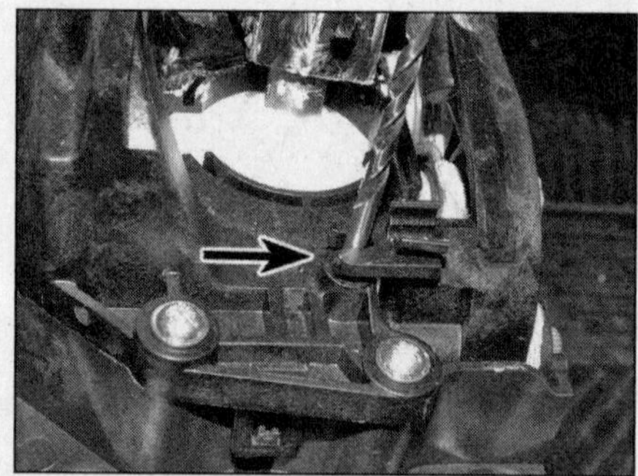

2.2 Insert a 4.0 mm drill bit (arrowed) to hold the lever in 4th gear

2.4 Unclip the cover from the front of the transmission

2.6 Prise out the locking insert

2.13 Prise the coloured insert (arrowed) upwards to unlock the selector cable

4 At the front face of the transmission housing, remove the selector mechanism cover by working around the edge, releasing a total of seven clips **(see illustration)**.

5 Only the selector cable is to be adjusted during this procedure – this is the cable which comes to the lowest point on the front of the transmission, with its end fitting nearest the engine.

6 Unlock the selector cable by pressing the coloured insert towards the engine, and move the transmission selector lever (not the gear lever inside the car) to the 4th gear position by moving it up or down as necessary **(see illustration)**.

7 Lock the selector cable in position by moving the coloured insert away from the engine.

8 Refit the selector mechanism cover, ensuring that the clips engage correctly, and lower the car to the ground.

9 Inside the car, remove the drill bit from the gear lever base mechanism, and refit the gear lever gaiter trim panel.

10 Start the engine, keeping the clutch pedal depressed, and check for correct gear selection.

B6 (6-speed) transmission

11 Remove the air filter housing as described in Chapter 4A Section 5 4A for petrol engines or Chapter 4B Section 2 4B for diesel engines.

12 Only the selector cable is to be adjusted during this procedure – this is the left-hand cable, nearest to the inner wing.

13 Release the cable from the ball joint and then unlock the selector cable by prising the coloured insert upwards **(see illustration)**. Move the transmission selector lever (not the gear lever inside the car) to the 4th gear position by moving it forwards or backwards as necessary.

14 Refit the cable to the ball joint and then press the selector cable locking insert down to lock the cable.

15 Remove the drill bit from the gear lever base mechanism, and refit the gaiter trim panel. Start the engine, keeping the clutch pedal depressed, and check for correct gear selection.

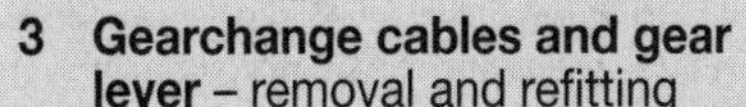

3 Gearchange cables and gear lever – removal and refitting

Removal

1 Remove the air cleaner assembly as described in Chapter 4A Section 5 4A for petrol engine or Chapter 4B Section 2 4B for diesel engines.

2 Apply the handbrake, then jack up the front of the car, supporting it on axle stands (see *Jacking and vehicle support*). Remove the engine undershield.

3 On B5/iB5 (5-speed) transmissions, remove the trim cover from over the selector cable mechanism on the front of the transmission **(see illustration 2.4)**.

3.4a Where no release button is fitted prise off the inner cable...

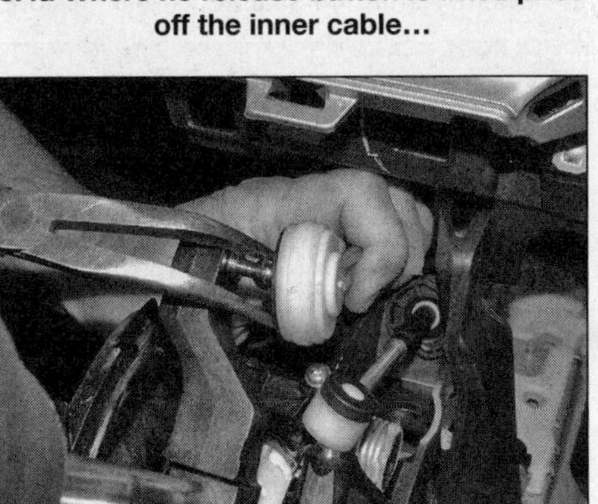

3.8a Prise off the selector cable...

4 Remove the cables from the support brackets by twisting the spring-loaded knurled collars anti-clockwise. Depress the release button (where fitted) and detach the selector cable from the lever on the transmission, then prise the shift cable end fitting from the its lever on the transmission – note their fitted locations **(see illustrations)**. Unclip the cables from the clips on the transmission casing.

5 Working under the vehicle, remove the washer-type fasteners, and slide the exhaust heat shield rearwards.

6 Follow the routing of the cables and unclip them from the vehicle body underside.

7 Remove the centre console as described in Chapter 11 Section 27.

8 Prise off the selector cable and press the release button on the shift cable **(see illustrations)**.

3.4b ...and then release the outer

3.8b ...and release the shift cable

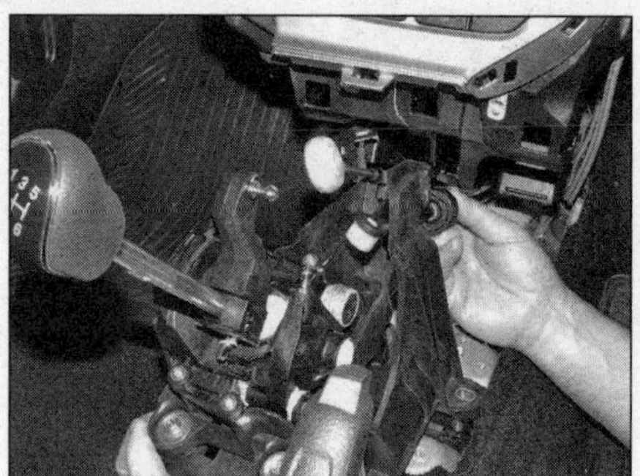

3.9 Release the outer cables

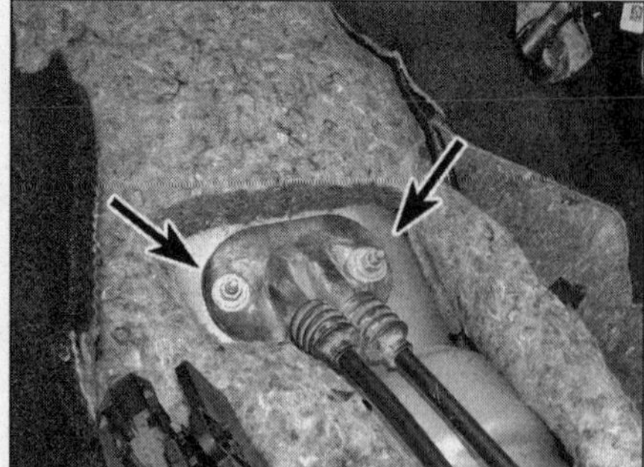

3.10 Undo the nuts (arrowed) to release the grommet – shown with the heater removed for clarity

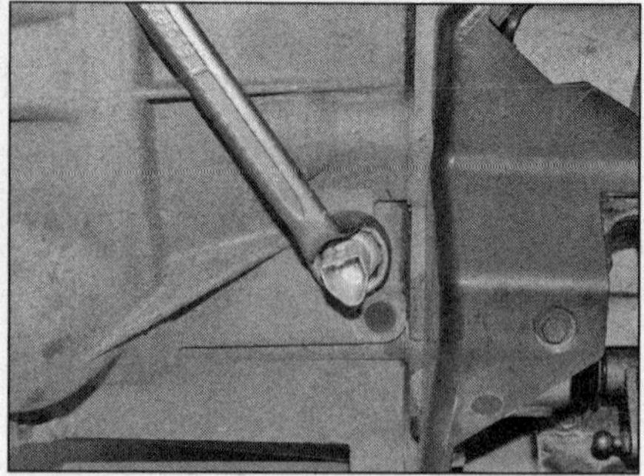

4.3 Unscrew the reversing light switch – B5/iB5 transmission

9 Disconnect the cable outers from the gear lever housing by twisting the collars and sliding them from the housing **(see illustration)**. If required, the gear lever housing assembly can be removed by unscrewing the mounting bolts.

10 Fold back the carpet and insulation material under the centre part of the facia for access to the selector cable floor grommet. Remove the two nuts and release the grommet from the floor **(see illustration)**.

11 Pass the cables up through the floor.

Refitting

12 Refitting is a reversal of removal. Use new clips when reconnecting the gearchange cables, and adjust the cables as described in Section 2.

4 Reversing light switch – removal and refitting

B5/iB5 (5-speed) transmission

1 The switch is located on the front of the transmission, next to the selector cable mounting bracket on the front cover. To improve access, jack up the front left-hand side of the car (see *Jacking and vehicle support*). Where fitted, remove the engine undershield.

2 Disconnect the wiring plug from the switch.

3 Unscrew and remove the switch from the front of the transmission **(see illustration)** – as the switch is higher than the level of the transmission filler level plug **(see illustration 6.5)**, there should be no oil spillage as the switch is removed.

4 Refitting is a reversal of removal. Before refitting, make sure the switch is clean, including the mating faces. Tighten the switch to the specified torque.

B6 (6-speed) transmission

5 The switch is located on top of the transmission in the gear selector housing. Remove the air cleaner as described in Chapter 4A Section 5 4A or Chapter 4B Section 2.

6 Select 4th gear before removing the reversing light switch from the gear selector housing.

7 Disconnect the wiring leading to the reversing light switch **(see illustration)**.

8 Unscrew the reversing light switch from the gear selector housing.

9 Refitting is a reversal of the removal procedure. Before refitting, make sure the switch is clean, including the mating faces. Tighten the switch to the specified torque.

5 Oil seals – renewal

1 Oil leaks frequently occur due to wear or deterioration of the driveshaft oil seals, or the selector shaft oil seal (iB5 transmission). Renewal of these seals is relatively easy, since the repairs can be performed without removing the transmission from the vehicle.

Driveshaft oil seals

2 The driveshaft oil seals are located at the sides of the transmission, where the driveshafts enter the transmission. If leakage at the seal is suspected, raise the vehicle and support it securely on axle stands. If the seal is leaking, oil will be found on the side of the transmission below the driveshaft.

3 Refer to Chapter 8 Section 2 and remove the appropriate driveshaft.

4 Using a large screwdriver or lever, carefully prise the oil seal out of the transmission casing, taking care not to damage the transmission casing **(see illustration)**.

5 Wipe clean the oil seal seating in the transmission casing.

6 Dip the new oil seal in clean oil, then press it a little way into the casing by hand, making sure that it is square to its seating.

7 Using suitable tubing or a large socket, carefully drive the oil seal fully into the casing until it contacts the seating **(see illustration)**.

8 When refitting the left-hand driveshaft on the B5/iB5 transmission, use the protective sleeve which should be provided with Ford parts. The sleeve is fitted into the seal, and the driveshaft is then fitted through it – the sleeve is then withdrawn and cut free.

9 Refit the driveshaft (see Chapter 8 Section 2).

4.7 Disconnecting the wiring connector from the reverse light switch – B6 transmissions

5.4 A special oil seal removal tool can be used to prise the driveshaft oil seal from place

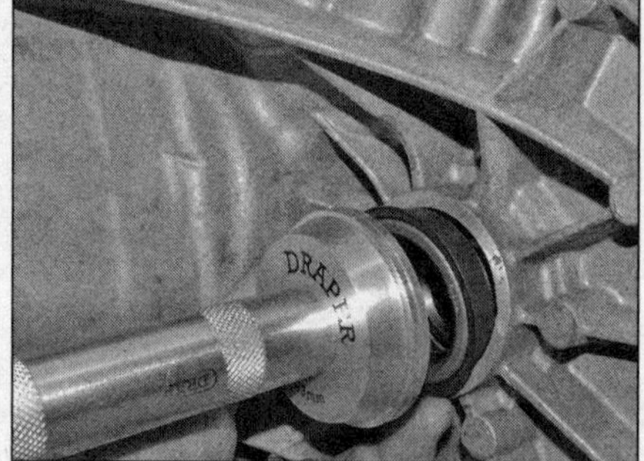

5.7 Drive the oil seal into place using a socket, or as shown here a special seal installation tool

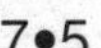

6.5 The 5 speed transmission filler plug

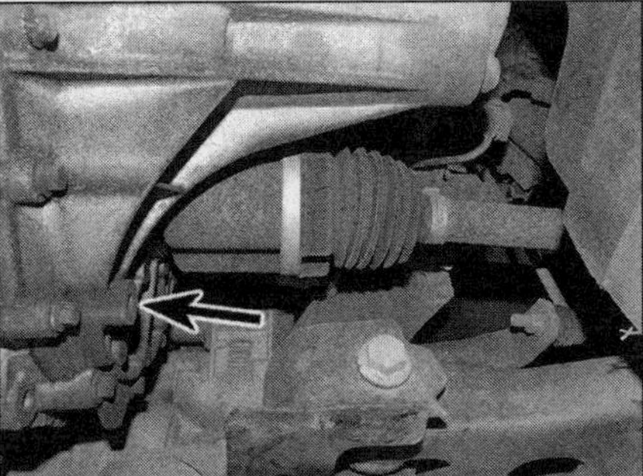
6.7 Transmission drain plug

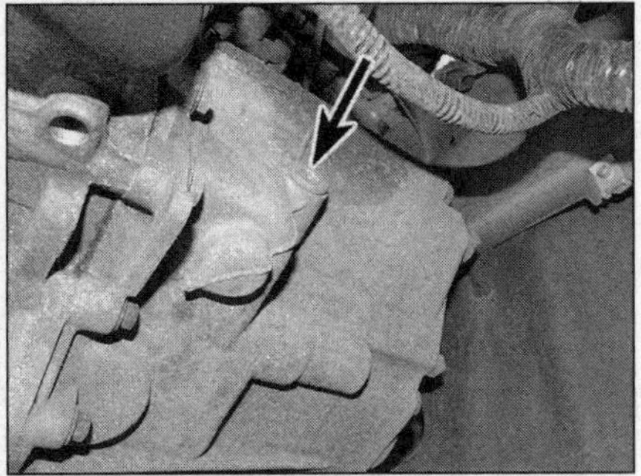
6.11 Transmission filler/level plug

Selector shaft oil seal (B5/iB5 transmission)

10 Apply the handbrake, then jack up the front of the car, supporting it on axle stands (see *Jacking and vehicle support*). Where fitted, remove the engine undershield.

11 At the front face of the transmission housing, remove the selector mechanism cover by working around the edge, releasing a total of seven clips.

12 Prise off the retaining clips, then pull the shift and selector cables from the transmission levers, and detach them from the cable support brackets by turning the knurled collars clockwise.

13 Unscrew and remove the four bolts securing the selector mechanism rear cover to the transmission housing.

14 Remove the transmission shift lever by prising off the protective cap and extracting the retaining clip.

15 With the shift lever removed, unscrew the securing bolt and take off the selector lever and dust cover.

16 The selector shaft oil seal can now be prised out of its location. If using a screwdriver or similar sharp tool, take great care not to mark or gouge the selector shaft or the seal housing as this is done, or the new seal will also leak.

17 Before fitting the new oil seal, carefully clean the visible part of the selector shaft, and the oil seal housing. Wrap a little tape around the end of the shaft, to protect the seal lips as they pass over it.

18 Smear the new oil seal with a little oil, then carefully fit it over the end of the selector shaft, lips facing inwards (towards the transmission).

19 Making sure that the seal stays square to the shaft, press it fully along the shaft (if available, a 16 mm ring spanner is ideal for this).

20 Press the seal fully into its housing, again using the ring spanner or perhaps a deep socket. Remove the tape from the end of the shaft.

21 Further refitting is a reversal of removal. Tighten the selector lever securing bolt to the specified torque, and use new clips when reconnecting the gearchange cables.

22 On completion, check and if necessary adjust the cables as described in Section 2.

6 Transmission oil – draining and refilling

Note: *Although not included in the maintenance schedule by the manufacturers, it is a good idea to drain and renew the manual transmission oil on a regular basis. The frequency with which this needs to carried out can be left to the individual, but it is certainly advisable on a vehicle that has covered a high mileage.*

1 The oil is best drained when the transmission is hot, but bear in mind the risk of burning yourself on hot exhaust components, etc. Apply the handbrake, then jack up the front of the car, and support it on axle stands (See *Jacking and vehicle support*).

2 Remove the engine undershield, then position a container under the transmission driveshafts (B5/iB5 transmission) or drain plug (B6 transmission), to catch the transmission oil.

B5/iB5 (5-speed) transmission

3 The iB5 transmission has no drain plug; the most effective way to drain the oil is to remove one or both driveshafts, as described in Chapter 8 Section 2.

4 When refilling the transmission, remember that the vehicle must be level for the oil level to be correct, so the front of the vehicle will need to be lowered down of the jack and axle stands.

5 Refill the transmission until the level is 5-10 mm below the filler plug **(see illustration)**.

6 When the transmission oil level is correct (with the vehicle level), refit the filler plug and tighten it to the torque specified at the beginning of this Chapter. When completed, refit the engine undershield.

B6 (6-speed) transmission

7 The drain plug is located in the base of the differential housing **(see illustration)** – like the oil filler/level plug, a special hexagonal socket (or large Allen key) will be required for removal.

8 Remove the drain plug and allow the oil to drain completely into the container, when the flow of oil stops clean and refit the drain plug, using a new washer, as required. Tighten the drain plug to the torque specified at the beginning of this Chapter.

9 When refilling the transmission, remember that the vehicle must be level for the oil level to be correct, so the front of the vehicle will need to be lowered down of the jack and axle stands.

10 Refill the transmission until the oil starts to flow from the filler hole and then remove the amount specified (0.5 litres), in the specifications section of this Chapter.

11 When the transmission oil level is correct (with the vehicle level), refit the filler plug **(see illustration)**, and tighten it to the torque specified at the beginning of this Chapter. When completed, refit the engine undershield.

7 Transmission – removal and refitting

Warning: The hydraulic fluid used in the clutch system is brake fluid, which is poisonous. Take care to keep it off bare skin, and in particular out of your eyes. The fluid also attacks paintwork, and may discolour carpets, etc – keep spillages to a minimum, and wash any off immediately with cold water. Finally, brake fluid is highly inflammable, and should be handled with the same care as petrol.

Note: *Read through this procedure before starting work to see what is involved, particularly in terms of lifting equipment. Depending on the facilities available, the home mechanic may prefer to remove the engine and transmission together, then separate them on the bench, as described in Chapter 2E. The help of an assistant is highly recommended if the transmission is to be removed (and later refitted) on its own.*

Removal

1 Pull up and remove the engine cover.

2 Remove the air cleaner and inlet duct as described in Chapter 4A Section 5 or Chapter 4B Section 2

3 Remove the battery, as described in Chapter 5A Section 3.

4 Undo the 3 bolts and remove the battery tray.

7.6 Remove the clutch hydraulic fluid line

7.8a Release the wiring loom from the top of the transmission

5 Make sure that the gear lever is in neutral. Taking adequate precautions against brake fluid spillage (refer to the Warning at the start of this Section), pull out the securing clip, then pull the pipe fitting out of the clutch slave cylinder at the top of the transmission. Plug or tape over the pipe end, to avoid losing fluid, and to prevent dirt entry.

6 Unclip the slave cylinder fluid pipe from the support bracket **(see illustration)**, and move it clear of the transmission.

7 Where fitted remove the cover from the gearchange selector cables and then disconnect the gearchange cables from the transmission as described in Section 3.

8 Disconnect the wiring connector from the reversing light switch (see Section 4). Unclip the wiring harness cable(s), and then disconnect the transmission earth **(see illustrations)**.

9 Jack up and support the front of the vehicle (see *Jacking and vehicle support* in the reference section).

10 Remove the engine undershield.

11 Remove both driveshafts from the transmission as described in Chapter 8 Section 2 8.

12 On 1.6 EcoBoost engines and 1.6 diesel engines remove the air inlet pipe from beneath the engine.

13 Where fitted remove the exhaust/catalytic converter support bracket from above the rear engine mounting **(see illustration)**.

14 Remove the starter motor as described in Chapter 5A Section 7.

15 Separate the exhaust pipe at the front subframe. On 1.0 litre engines remove the exhaust bracket from the bell housing.

16 Unbolt and remove the rear engine mounting/torque strap from the rear of the transmission bell housing.

17 Work round the transmission bell housing and move the remaining hoses and wiring loom to one side.

18 Secure the coolant hoses with cable ties as required.

19 The engine/transmission must now be supported, as the left-hand mounting must be dismantled and removed. Ford technicians use a support bar which locates on the front subframe. The engine can be supported (just) with a proprietary engine support bar fitted to the inner wings, this method is not recommended.

20 We used a large trolley jack (with a block of wood to spread the load) under the sump to support the engine and then to stabilise the engine we used a support bar resting on the inner wings. The support bar was there just in case the trolley jack moved. With the trolley jack and support bar in place we supported the transmission with a scissor type transmission jack. **Note:** *Always take care when using a hydraulic jack, as it is possible for this type to collapse under load – generally, a scissor-type jack avoids this problem, but is also less stable, and offers no manoeuvrability.*

21 An alternative method is to use an engine hoist (with one leg placed outside the right-hand wheel) to support the engine. This allows the engine and transmission to be lowered and manoeuvred easily, but (depending on the type of hoist) limits access to the bell housing bolts. Again depending on the design of the engine hoist the placing of a suitable jack under the transmission may prove to be problematic.

22 Undo the 2 upper transmission-to-engine retaining bolts.

23 With the engine securely supported,

7.8b Remove the earth cable

7.13 Remove the support bracket

7.23 Remove the central bolt (arrowed)

7.24 Remove the mounting

progressively unscrew and remove the left-hand mounting central bolt **(see illustration)**.

24 Remove three further nuts/bolts, and remove the lower section of the engine left-hand mounting **(see illustration)**.

25 Taking care that nothing which is still attached to the engine is placed under strain, lower the transmission so that it will clear the left-hand chassis leg.

26 Remove the lower transmission-to-engine bolts. The bell housing bolts are of different lengths, so note their positions carefully for refitting.

27 Check that, apart from the remaining bell housing bolts, there is nothing preventing the transmission from being removed. Make sure that any wiring or hoses lying on top of the transmission are not going to get caught up and stretched as the transmission is lowered.

28 Unscrew the remaining bell housing bolts. If the transmission does not separate on its own, it must be rocked from side-to-side, to free it from the locating dowels. As the transmission is withdrawn from the engine, make sure its weight is supported at all times – the transmission input shaft (or the clutch) may otherwise be damaged as it is withdrawn through the clutch assembly bolted to the engine flywheel.

29 Keeping the transmission steady, carefully lower it down and remove it from under the car.

30 The clutch components can now be inspected with reference to Chapter 6, and renewed if necessary. Unless they are virtually new, it is worth renewing the clutch components as a matter of course, even if the transmission has been removed for some other reason.

Refitting

31 If removed, refit the clutch components (see Chapter 6 Section 6). Also ensure that the engine-to-transmission adapter plates (where fitted) are in position on the engine.

32 Lightly oil the splines of the transmission input shaft. Take care not to apply too much or the clutch plates may become contaminated.

33 With the transmission secured to the hoist/trolley jack as on removal, raise it into position, and then carefully slide it onto the engine, at the same time engaging the input shaft with the clutch driven plate splines. If marks were made between the transmission and engine on removal, these can be used as a guide to correct alignment.

34 Do not use excessive force to refit the transmission – if the input shaft does not slide into place easily, readjust the angle of the transmission so that it is level, and/or turn the input shaft so that the splines engage properly with the plate. If problems are still experienced, check that the clutch driven plate is correctly centred (Chapter 6 Section 6).

35 Once the transmission is successfully mated to the engine, insert as many of the flange bolts as possible, and tighten them progressively to draw the transmission fully onto the locating dowels.

36 Refit the lower section of the engine left-hand mounting, and tighten the nuts to the specified torque.

37 Raise the transmission into position, then refit the upper section of the engine left-hand mounting. Tighten the nuts to the specified torque, noting that the centre nut is tightened considerably more than the four outer ones.

38 Refit the remaining transmission-to-engine bolts, and tighten all of them to the specified torque.

39 Refit the engine/transmission rear mounting to the subframe, and tighten the through-bolts to the specified torque.

40 Once the engine/transmission mountings have been refitted, the support bar, engine hoist or supporting jack can be removed.

41 Further refitting is a reversal of removal, noting the following points:

a) *Refit the starter motor as described in Chapter 5A Section 7.*
b) *Refit the driveshafts as described in Chapter 8 Section 2.*
c) *On completion, adjust the gearchange cables as described in Section 2.*

8 Transmission overhaul – general information

1 The overhaul of a manual transmission is a complex (and often expensive) engineering task for the DIY home mechanic to undertake, which requires access to specialist equipment. It involves dismantling and reassembly of many small components, measuring clearances precisely and if necessary, adjusting them by the selection shims and spacers. Internal transmission components are also often difficult to obtain and in many instances, extremely expensive. Because of this, if the transmission develops a fault or becomes noisy, the best course of action is to have the unit overhauled by a specialist repairer or to obtain an exchange reconditioned unit.

2 Nevertheless, it is not impossible for the more experienced mechanic to overhaul the transmission if the special tools are available and the job is carried out in a deliberate step-by-step manner, to ensure that nothing is overlooked.

3 The tools necessary for an overhaul include internal and external circlip pliers, bearing pullers, a slide hammer, a set of pin punches, a dial test indicator, and possibly a hydraulic press. In addition, a large, sturdy workbench and a vice will be required.

4 During dismantling of the transmission, make careful notes of how each component is fitted to make reassembly easier and accurate.

5 Before dismantling the transmission, it will help if you have some idea of where the problem lies. Certain problems can be closely related to specific areas in the transmission which can make component examination and renewal easier. Refer to Fault finding at the end of this manual for more information.

Chapter 8
Driveshafts

Contents

Degrees of difficulty

Easy, suitable for novice with little experience 	**Fairly easy,** suitable for beginner with some experience	**Fairly difficult,** suitable for competent DIY mechanic	**Difficult,** suitable for experienced DIY mechanic	**Very difficult,** suitable for expert DIY or professional

Specifications

General

Driveshaft type	Solid steel shafts with inner and outer constant velocity (CV) joints, both outer joints are of the ball-and-cage type and the inner joints of the tripod (spider-and-yoke) type. Right-hand driveshaft is fitted with a support bearing
Outer constant velocity joint type	Ball-and-cage
Inner constant velocity joint type	Tripod

Lubrication

Lubricant type	Special grease supplied in repair kit, or suitable molybdenum disulphide grease – consult a Ford dealer or parts specialist
CV joint grease capacity (approximate):	
Outboard joint	100 g
Inboard joint	100 g

Torque wrench settings

	Nm	lbf ft
Brake flexible hose (to suspension strut)	10	7
Driveshaft Nut: *		
Stage 1	80	60
Stage 2	Angle-tighten a further 90°	
Headlight levelling sensor bracket to lower arm	11	8
Lower arm balljoint to hub carrier bolt*	83	61
Right-hand driveshaft support bearing cap nuts*		
Stage 1	6	4
Stage 2	25	18
Roadwheel nuts	135	100

**Do not re-use*

1 General Information

1 Drive is transmitted from the differential to the front wheels by means of two solid-steel, equal-length driveshafts equipped with constant velocity (CV) joints at their inner and outer ends. Due to the position of the transmission, an intermediate shaft and support bearing are incorporated into the right-hand driveshaft assembly.
2 A ball-and-cage type CV joint is fitted to the outer end of each driveshaft. The joint has an outer member, which is splined at its outer end to accept the wheel hub, and is threaded so that it can be fastened to the hub by a large bolt. The joint contains six balls within a cage, which engage with the inner member. The complete assembly is protected by a flexible gaiter secured to the driveshaft and joint outer member.
3 At the inner end, the driveshaft is splined to engage a tripod type CV joint, containing needle roller bearings and cups. On the left-hand side, the driveshaft inner CV joint engages directly with the differential sun wheel. On the right-hand side, the inner joint is integral with the intermediate shaft, the inner end of which engages with the differential sun wheel. As on the outer joints, a flexible gaiter secured to the driveshaft and CV joint outer member protects the complete assembly.

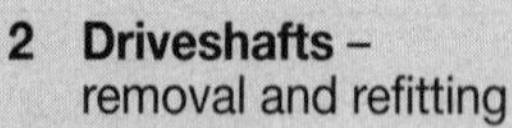

2 Driveshafts – removal and refitting

Removal

1 Firmly apply the handbrake and chock the rear wheels. When the driveshaft nut is to be loosened (or tightened), it is preferable to do so with the car resting on its wheels. If the car is jacked up, this places a high load on the jack, and the car could slip off.
2 If the car has steel wheels, remove the wheel trim on the side being worked on – the driveshaft nut can then be loosened with the wheel on the ground. On models with alloy wheels remove the centre cap from the wheel to access the driveshaft nut – if a suitable socket is available. The other option is to remove the wheel on the side being worked on, and to fit the temporary spare (see Wheel changing at the front of this Manual) – this wheel allows easy access to the driveshaft nut.

2.3a Slacken the driveshaft retaining nut

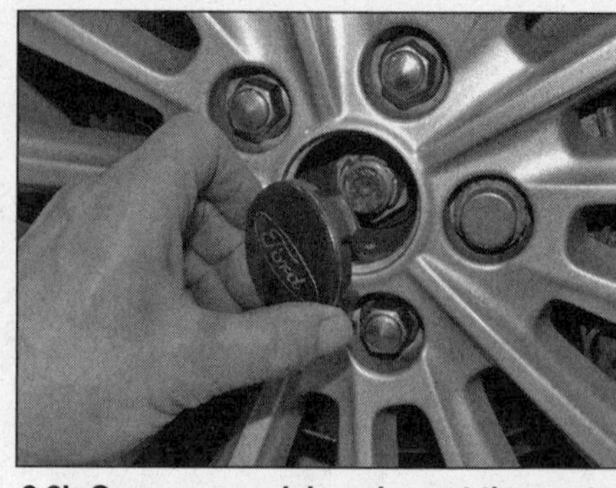

2.3b On some models, prise out the centre cap...

2.3c ...and slacken the nut

2.4 Undo the bolts (arrowed) and remove the engine undershield

3 With an assistant firmly depressing the brake pedal, slacken the driveshaft retaining nut using a socket and a long extension bar **(see illustrations)**. Note that this nut is extremely tight – ensure that the tools used to loosen it are of good quality, and a good fit.
4 Loosen the front wheel nuts, then jack up the front of the car and support it on axle stands (see *Jacking and vehicle support*). Remove the appropriate front roadwheel, then undo the fasteners and remove the engine undershield **(see illustration)**.
5 Remove the previously-slackened driveshaft retaining nut. Discard the nut – a new one must be fitted.
6 Tap or press the end of the driveshaft approximately 15 to 20 mm into the wheel hub. The splines on the shaft may be a tight fit in the hub, use a special tool to press the shaft out from the hub, as required.
7 Where fitted, undo the bolt and detach the headlight leveling sensor bracket from the lower arm **(see illustration)**.
8 Unbolt the brake flexible hose from the suspension strut **(see illustration)**.
9 Slacken the lower control arm balljoint bolt and detach the lower control arm balljoint from the hub carrier **(see illustration)**.
10 Pull down on the suspension lower arm

2.7 Undo the leveling sensor bracket securing bolt

2.8 Undo the brake hose securing bolt

2.9 Undo the balljoint securing bolt from the hub carrier

2.10 Using a bar, block of wood and chain to release the balljoint

2.11 Pull the hub carrier outwards, and withdraw the driveshaft

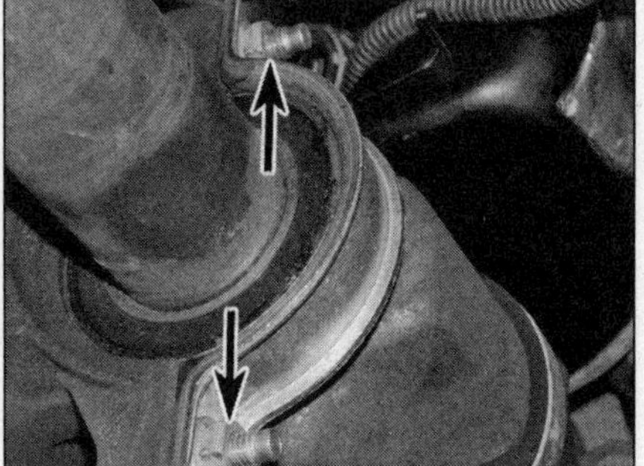
2.13 Undo the 2 nuts (arrowed) and remove the intermediate bearing cap

using a strong bar to release the balljoint shank from the hub carrier **(see illustration)**. Take care not to damage the balljoint dust cover during and after disconnection.

11 Swivel the suspension strut and hub carrier assembly outwards, and then withdraw the driveshaft CV joint completely from the hub flange **(see illustration)**.

12 If removing the left-hand driveshaft, free the inner CV joint from the transmission by levering between the edge of the joint and the transmission casing with a large screwdriver or similar tool. Take care not to damage the transmission oil seal or the inner CV joint gaiter. Withdraw the driveshaft from under the wheel arch.

13 If removing the right-hand driveshaft, undo the two nuts and remove the cap from the intermediate shaft support bearing **(see illustration)**. Dispose of the cap and nuts – new ones must be fitted. Pull the intermediate shaft out of the transmission, and remove the driveshaft assembly from under the wheel arch. **Note:** *Do not pull the outer shaft from the intermediate shaft – the coupling will separate.*

Refitting

14 Refitting is a reversal of removal, but observe the following points.

a) *Prior to refitting, remove all traces, rust, oil and dirt from the splines of the outer CV joint, and lubricate the splines of the inner joint with wheel bearing grease.*
b) *Apply a little grease to the driveshaft seal lips in the transmission casing.*
c) *If working on the left-hand driveshaft, ensure that the inner CV joint is pushed fully into the transmission, so that the retaining circlip locks into place in the differential gear.*
d) *Always use a new driveshaft-to-hub retaining nut.*
e) *Fit the same wheel as was used for loosening the driveshaft bolt, and lower the car to the ground.*
f) *Tighten all nuts and bolts to the specified torque (see Chapters 9 and 10 for brake and suspension component torque settings). When tightening the driveshaft bolt, tighten first using a torque wrench, then further, through the specified angle, using an angle-tightening gauge.*
g) *Ford insist that when refitting the right-hand driveshaft the intermediate shaft bearing cap and nuts must be renewed.*
h) *Where applicable, refit the alloy wheel on completion. Tighten the roadwheel nuts to the specified torque.*

3 Outer constant velocity joint gaiter – renewal

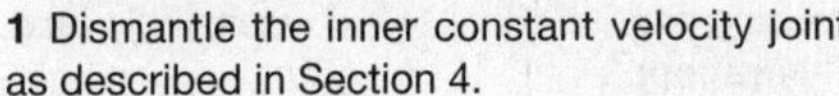

1 Dismantle the inner constant velocity joint as described in Section 4.

Models with a vibration damper fitted

2 On these vehicles, after removing the inner CV joint, measure and note the distance from the end of the shaft to the edge of the damper. The damper must then be pressed from the shaft, the outer joint boot renewed, then the damper pressed back into its original position using the dimensions previously-noted. If access to a hydraulic press in not available, most engineering workshops (automotive or otherwise) would be prepared to carry out this task.

All models

3 Cut off the gaiter retaining clips, then slide the gaiter down the shaft to expose the outer constant velocity joint **(see illustration)**.

Caution: Do not disassemble the outer CV joint.

4 Scoop out as much grease as possible from the joint.

5 Inspect the ball tracks on the inner and outer members. If the tracks have widened, the balls will no longer be a tight fit. At the same time, check the ball cage windows for wear or cracking between the windows. If the joints appear worn, complete renewal may be the only option – check with a Ford dealer or specialist.

6 If the joint is in satisfactory condition, obtain a repair kit from your Ford dealer, consisting of a new gaiter, retaining clips, driveshaft bolt, circlip and grease.

7 Pack the joint with the half of the grease supplied, working it well into the ball tracks, and into the driveshaft opening in the inner member **(see illustration)**.

8 Slide the rubber gaiter onto the shaft.

9 Apply the remaining grease to the joint and the inside of the gaiter.

10 Locate the outer lip of the gaiter in the groove on the joint outer member, then fit the retaining clip. Remove any slack in the clips by carefully compressing the raised section using a special pair of pincers **(see illus-**

3.3 Cut the gaiter retaining clips

3.7 Pack the outer CV joint with about half the grease supplied

3.10a Locate the outer clip on the gaiter ...

3.10b ... then using a special pair of pliers ...

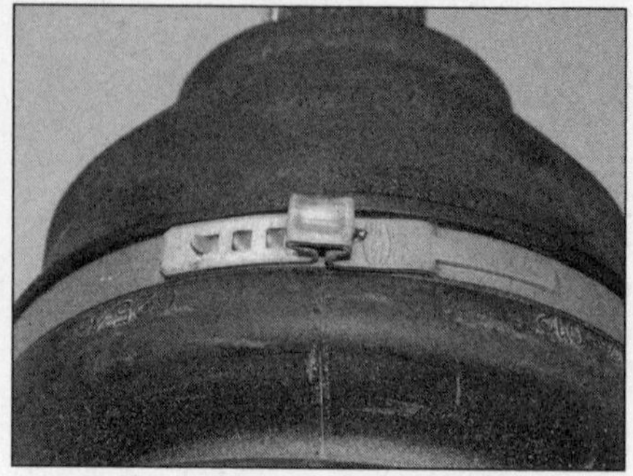
3.10c ... remove any slack in the clip

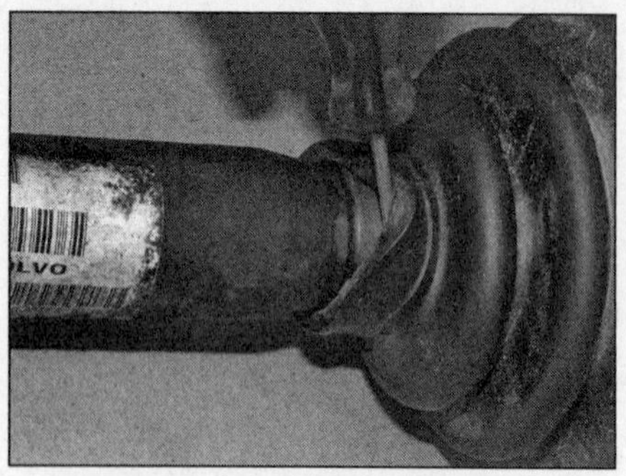

3.11 Lift the inner edge of the gaiter to equalise the air pressure

trations). **Note:** *Ensure no grease is on the surfaces between the gaiter and the joint housing.*

11 Use a small screwdriver to lift the inner lip of the gaiter, allowing the air pressure inside the gaiter to equalise, then fit the inner clip to the gaiter **(see illustration)**.

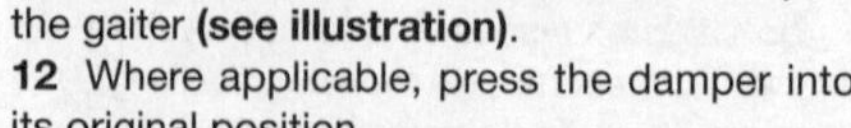

12 Where applicable, press the damper into its original position.

13 Reassembly the inner constant velocity joint as described in Section 4.

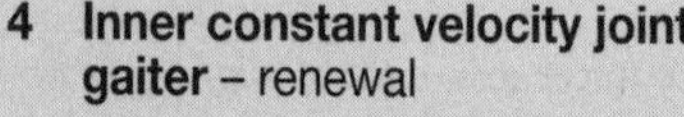

4 Inner constant velocity joint gaiter – renewal

1 Remove the driveshaft(s) as described in Section 2.

2 Cut through the metal clips, and slide the gaiter from the inner CV joint.

3 Clean out some of the grease from the joint, then make alignment marks between the housing and the shaft, to aid reassembly **(see illustration)**.

4 Carefully pull the housing from the tripod, twisting the housing so the tripod rollers come out one at a time. If necessary, use a soft-faced hammer or mallet to tap the housing off.

5 Clean the grease from the tripod and housing.

6 Remove the circlip, and carefully drive the tripod from the end of the shaft **(see illustrations)**. Discard the circlip, a new one (supplied in the repair kit) must be fitted. Remove the gaiter if still on the shaft.

7 Slide the new gaiter onto the shaft along with the smaller clip **(see illustration)**.

8 Refit the tripod with the bevelled edge towards the driveshaft, and drive it fully into place, until the new circlip can be installed **(see illustrations)**.

9 Lubricate the tripod rollers with some of the grease supplied in the gaiter kit, then fill the housing and gaiter with the remainder.

10 Refit the housing to the tripod, tapping

4.3 Make alignment marks between the shaft and housing

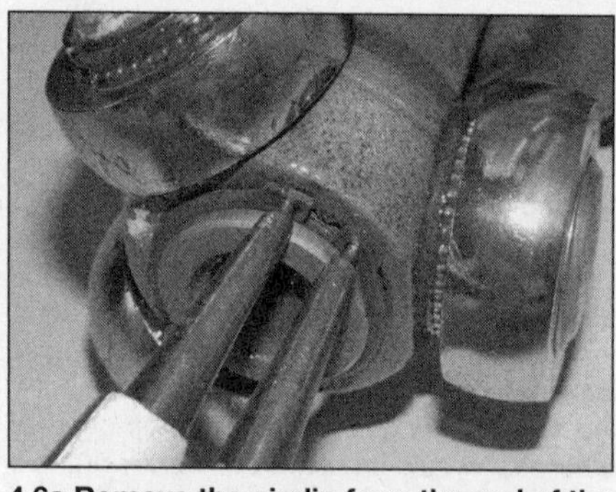
4.6a Remove the circlip from the end of the shaft ...

4.6b ... then carefully drive the tripod from the shaft

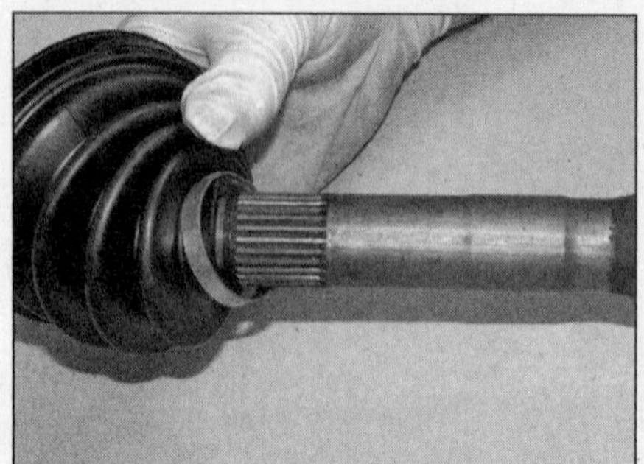
4.7 Slide the new gaiter and smaller diameter clip onto the shaft

4.8a Fit the tripod with the bevelled edge (arrowed) towards the shaft ...

4.8b ... then fit the new circlip

4.11 The smaller diameter of the gaiter must locate over the groove in the shaft (arrowed)

4.12 Equalise the air pressure before tightening the gaiter clip

it gently into place using a soft-hammer or mallet if necessary.

11 Slide the new gaiter into place ensuring the smaller diameter of the gaiter locates over the grooves in the shaft **(see illustration)**.

12 Fit the new retaining clips **(see illustration)**.

13 Fit the new circlip to the end of the shaft **(see illustration)**.

14 Refit the driveshaft(s) as described in Section 2.

5 Right-hand driveshaft support bearing – removal and refitting

1 If the bearing is suspect it can be replaced. Note however that a driveshaft with a faulty bearing will normally have covered a high mileage. It may be more cost effective to replace the complete driveshaft with an exchange, reconditioned assembly as the constant velocity joints are likely to be worn anyway.

2 Remove the outer CV joint as described in Section 3. The bearing must be pressed from the shaft using a hydraulic press. If access to a hydraulic press in not available, most engineering workshops (automotive or otherwise) would be prepared to carry out this task for a modest fee.

3 Press the replacement bearing into position and then fit a new outer CV boot gaiter as described in Section 3.

6 Driveshaft overhaul – general information

1 Road test the car, and listen for a metallic clicking from the front as the car is driven slowly in a circle with the steering on full-lock. Repeat the check on full-left and full-right lock. This noise may also be apparent when pulling away from a standstill with lock applied. If a clicking noise is heard, this indicates wear in the outer constant velocity joints.

2 If vibration, consistent with road speed, is felt through the car when accelerating, there is a possibility of wear in the inner constant velocity joints.

3 If the joints are worn or damaged, it would appear at the time of writing that no parts are available, other then boot renewal kits, and the complete driveshaft must be renewed. Exchange driveshafts are available – check with a Ford dealer or specialist.

4.13 The circlip on the end of the shaft must be renewed

Notes

Chapter 9
Braking system

Contents

Degrees of difficulty

Easy, suitable for novice with little experience 	**Fairly easy,** suitable for beginner with some experience	**Fairly difficult,** suitable for competent DIY mechanic	**Difficult,** suitable for experienced DIY mechanic	**Very difficult,** suitable for expert DIY or professional 

Specifications

Front brakes

Type	Ventilated disc, with single sliding piston caliper
Disc diameter	278 mm, 300 mm or 320 mm (depending on model)
Disc thickness:	
New	25.0 mm
Minimum	23.0 mm
Maximum disc thickness variation	0.020 mm
Maximum disc/hub run-out (installed)	0.070 mm
Brake pad friction material minimum thickness	1.5 mm

Rear drum brakes

Type	Leading and trailing shoes, with automatic adjusters
Drum diameter:	
New	228.3 mm
Maximum	230.2 mm
Brake shoe friction material minimum thickness	1.0 mm

Rear disc brakes

Type	Solid disc, with single-piston floating caliper
Disc diameter	271 mm
Disc thickness:	
New	11.0 mm
Minimum	9.0 mm
Maximum disc thickness variation	0.025 mm
Maximum disc/hub runout (installed)	0.1 mm
Brake pad friction material minimum thickness	1.5 mm

Torque wrench settings

	Nm	lbf ft
ABS wheel sensor securing bolts	5	4
Brake pipe to master cylinder	18	14
Brake pipe to hydraulic control unit	11	8
Brake pipe unions	15	11
Front caliper guide bolts	28	21
Front caliper mounting bracket bolts	175	130
Handbrake lever mountings	35	26
Master cylinder to servo mountings*	25	18
Pedal bracket to servo mountings*	24	18
Rear caliper bracket	70	52
Rear caliper guide bolts	35	26
Rear wheel cylinder bolts	10	7
Roadwheel nuts	135	100
Suspension strut brace bolts*	35	26

**Use new bolts*

1 General Information

1 The braking system is of diagonally-split, dual-circuit design, with ventilated discs at the front, and drum or disc brakes (according to model) at the rear. The front calipers are of single sliding piston design, and (where fitted) the rear calipers are of a single-piston floating design, using asbestos-free pads. The rear drum brakes are of the leading and trailing shoe type, and are self-adjusting during footbrake operation. The rear brake shoe linings are of different thicknesses, in order to allow for the different proportional rates of wear.

2 The vacuum servo unit uses vacuum supplied by a camshaft driven vacuum pump, except on Ti-VCT models where inlet manifold depression (generated only when a petrol engine is running) is used. The vacuum servo unit boosts the effort applied by the driver at the brake pedal and transmits this increased effort to the master cylinder pistons.

3 The handbrake is cable-operated, and acts on the rear brakes. On rear drum brake models, the cables operate on the rear trailing brake shoe operating levers; on rear disc brake models, they operate on levers on the rear calipers. The handbrake lever incorporates an automatic adjuster, which will adjust the cable when the handbrake is operated several times.

4 The anti-lock braking system (ABS) uses the basic conventional brake system, together with an ABS hydraulic unit fitted between the master cylinder and the four brake units at each wheel. The hydraulic unit consists of a hydraulic actuator, an ABS brake pressure pump, and an ABS module. Braking at each of the four wheels is controlled by separate solenoid valves in the hydraulic actuator. If wheel lock-up is detected by one of the wheel sensors, when the vehicle speed is above 3 mph, the valve opens; releasing pressure to the relevant brake until the wheel regains a rotational speed corresponding to the speed of the vehicle. The cycle can be repeated many times a second. In the event of a fault in the ABS system, the conventional braking system is not affected. Diagnosis of a fault in the ABS system requires the use of special equipment, and this work should therefore be left to a Ford dealer or suitably-equipped specialist. The wheel speed sensor signal rings are built-into the oil seals of the wheel bearings.

5 Where fitted, the traction control systems are integrated with the ABS, and use the same wheel sensors. The hydraulic control unit has additional solenoid valves incorporated to enable control of the wheel brake pressure. The system is only active at speeds up to 53 mph – when the system is active the warning light on the instrument panel illuminates to warn the driver. This uses controlled braking of the spinning driving wheel when the grip at the driven wheels are different. The spinning wheel is braked by the ABS system, transferring a greater proportion of the engine torque through the differential to the other wheel, which increases the use of the available traction control.

6 On several models in the range, there is an Electronic Stability Program (ESP) available. This system supports the vehicle's stability and steering through a combination of ABS and traction control operations. There is a switch on the centre console, so that if required the system can be switched off. This will then illuminate the warning light on the instrument panel, to inform the driver that the ESP is not in operation. The stability of the vehicle is measured by Yaw rate and Accelerometer sensors, which sense the movement of the vehicle about its vertical axis, and also lateral acceleration.

Note: *When servicing any part of the system, work carefully and methodically; also observe scrupulous cleanliness when overhauling any part of the hydraulic system. Always renew components (in axle sets, where applicable) if in doubt about their condition, and use only genuine Ford parts, or at least those of known good quality. Note the warnings given in 'Safety first!' and at relevant points in this Chapter concerning the dangers of asbestos dust and hydraulic fluid.*

2 Front brake pads – renewal

Warning: Renew both sets of front brake pads at the same time – never renew the pads on only one wheel, as uneven braking may result. Note that the dust created by wear of the pads may contain asbestos, which is a health hazard. Never blow it out with compressed air, and don't inhale any of it. An approved filtering mask should be worn when working on the brakes. DO NOT use petrol or petroleum-based solvents to clean brake parts; use brake cleaner or methylated spirit only.

1 Apply the handbrake, then slacken the front roadwheel nuts. Jack up the front of the vehicle and support it on axle stands. Remove both front roadwheels.

2 Follow the accompanying photos **(illustrations 2.2a to 2.2p)** for the actual pad renewal procedure. Be sure to stay in order and read the caption under each illustration, and note the following points:

a) *New pads may have an adhesive foil on the backplates. Remove this foil prior to installation.*

b) *Thoroughly clean the caliper guide surfaces, and apply a little brake assembly (polycarbamide) grease.*

c) *When pushing the caliper piston back to accommodate new pads, keep a close eye on the fluid level in the reservoir.*

3 Depress the brake pedal repeatedly, until the pads are pressed into firm contact with the brake disc, and normal (non-assisted) pedal pressure is restored.

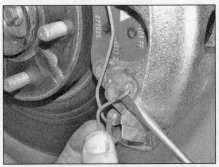

2.2a Use a flat-bladed screwdriver to carefully prise off the caliper retaining spring

2.2b Prise out the rubber caps ...

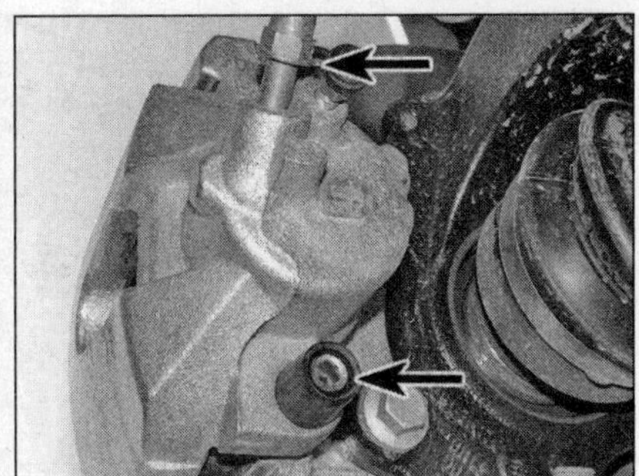

2.2c ... and use an Allen key to undo the caliper guide bolts (arrowed)

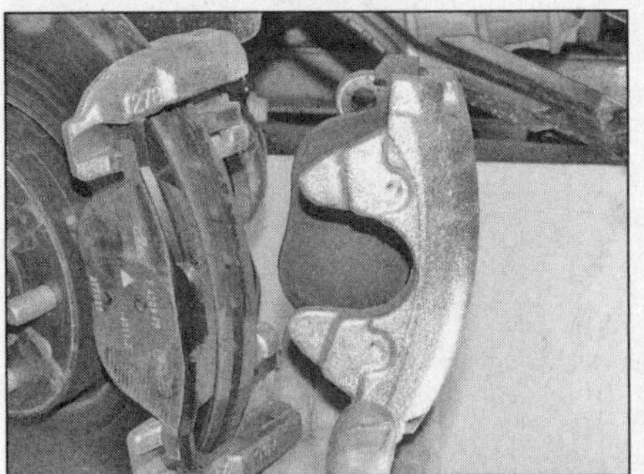

2.2d Slide the caliper and inner pad from the disc

2.2e Pull the inner brake pad from the caliper piston ...

2.2f ... and lift the outer pad from the caliper bracket

2.2g If you're fitting new pads, push the piston back into the caliper using a piston retraction tool or G-clamp. Keep an eye on the fluid level in the reservoir. Remove any surplus with a syringe

2.2h Clean the pad mounting surfaces with a wire brush

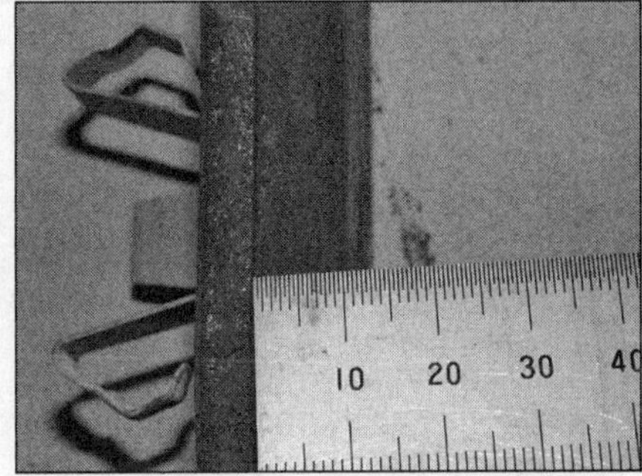

2.2i Measure the thickness of the pad's friction material. If it's 1.5 mm or less, renew all the front pads

2.2j Fit the outer pad to the caliper mounting bracket ...

2.2k ... then fit the inner pad to the caliper piston

2.2l Slide the caliper with the inner panel fitted over the disc and outer pad

2.2m Refit the caliper guide bolts and tighten them to the specified torque

2.2n Press the rubber caps into position

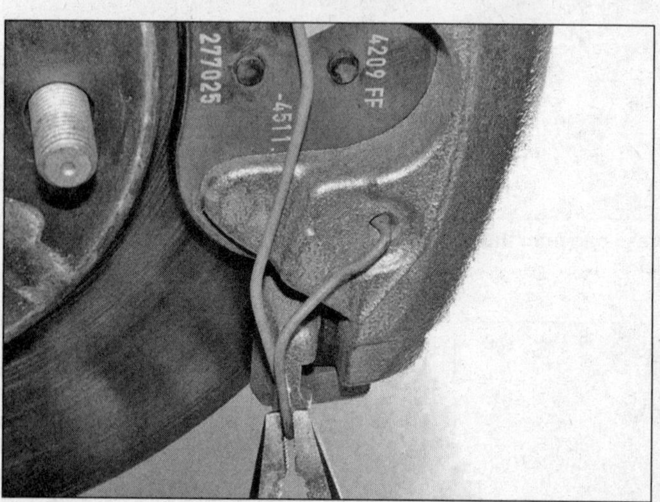

2.2o Use a pair of pliers ...

2.2p ... to refit the caliper retaining spring

4 Repeat the above procedure on the remaining front brake caliper.

5 Refit the roadwheels, then lower the vehicle to the ground and tighten the roadwheel nuts to the specified torque.

6 Check the hydraulic fluid level as described in *Weekly checks*.

Caution: New pads will not give full braking efficiency until they have bedded-in. Be prepared for this, and avoid hard braking as far as possible for the first hundred miles or so after pad renewal.

3 Front brake caliper – removal, overhaul and refitting

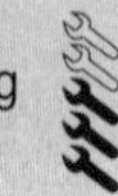

Note: *Refer to the warning at the beginning of the previous Section before proceeding.*

Removal

1 Apply the handbrake. Loosen the front wheel nuts, then jack up the front of the vehicle and support it on axle stands. Remove the appropriate front wheel.

2 Fit a brake hose clamp to the flexible hose leading to the caliper **(see illustration)**. This will minimise brake fluid loss during subsequent operations.

3 Loosen the union on the caliper end of the flexible brake hose **(see illustration)**. Once loosened, do not try to unscrew the hose at this stage.

4 Remove the brake pads as described in Section 2.

5 Support the caliper in one hand, and prevent the hydraulic hose from turning with the other hand. Unscrew the caliper from the hose, making sure that the hose is not twisted unduly

3.2 Use a hose clamp on the flexible hoses

3.3 Slacken the flexible hose union (arrowed)

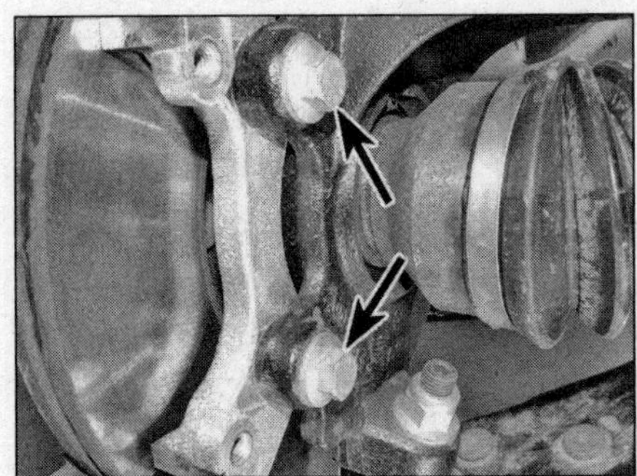
3.6 Caliper bracket bolts (arrowed)

or strained. Once the caliper is detached, plug the open hydraulic unions in the caliper and hose, to keep out dust and dirt.

6 If required, the caliper bracket can be unbolted from the hub carrier **(see illustration)**.

Overhaul

Note: *Before starting work, check on the availability of parts (caliper overhaul kit/seals).*

7 With the caliper on the bench, brush away all traces of dust and dirt, but take care not to inhale any dust, as it may be harmful to your health.

8 Pull the dust cover rubber seal from the end of the piston.

9 Apply low air pressure to the fluid inlet union, to eject the piston. Only low air pressure is required for this, such as is produced by a foot-operated tyre pump.

Caution: The piston may be ejected with some force. Position a thin piece of wood between the piston and the caliper body to prevent damage to the end face of the piston in the event of it being ejected suddenly.

10 Using a suitable blunt instrument, prise the piston seal from the groove in the cylinder bore. Take care not to scratch the surface of the bore.

11 Clean the piston and caliper body with methylated spirit, and allow to dry. Examine the surfaces of the piston and cylinder bore for wear, damage and corrosion. If the piston alone is unserviceable, a new piston must be obtained, along with seals. If the cylinder bore is unserviceable, the complete caliper must be renewed. The seals must be renewed, regardless of the condition of the other components.

12 Coat the piston and seals with clean brake fluid, then manipulate the piston seal into the groove in the cylinder bore.

13 Push the piston squarely into its bore, taking care not to damage the seal.

14 Fit the dust cover rubber seal onto the piston and caliper, then depress the piston fully.

Refitting

15 If removed, refit the caliper bracket and tighten the bolts to the specified torque.

16 Refit the brake pads as described in Section 2, but screw the caliper onto the flexible hose before refitting it to the caliper bracket.

17 Tighten the flexible hose union ensuring the hose is not kinked/twisted.

18 Bleed the brake circuit according to the procedure given in Section 14, remembering to remove the brake hose clamp from the flexible hose. Make sure there are no leaks from the hose connections. Test the brakes carefully before returning the vehicle to normal service.

4 Front brake disc – inspection, removal and refitting

Note: *To prevent uneven braking, BOTH front brake discs must be renewed or reground at the same time.*

Inspection

1 Apply the handbrake. Loosen the relevant wheel nuts, jack up the front of the vehicle and support it on axle stands. Remove the appropriate front wheel.

2 Remove the front brake caliper from the disc with reference to Section 3, and undo the two caliper bracket securing bolts. Do not disconnect the flexible hose. Support the caliper on an axle stand, or suspend it out of the way with a piece of wire, taking care to avoid straining the flexible hose **(see illustration)**.

3 Temporarily refit two of the wheel nuts to diagonally-opposite studs, with the flat sides of the nuts against the disc. Tighten the nuts progressively, to hold the disc firmly.

4 Scrape any corrosion from the disc. Rotate the disc, and examine it for deep scoring, grooving or cracks. Using a micrometer, measure the thickness of the disc in several places **(see illustration)**. The minimum thickness is stamped on the disc hub. Light wear and scoring is normal, but if excessive, the disc should be removed, and either reground by a specialist, or renewed. If regrinding is undertaken, the minimum thickness must be maintained. Obviously, if the disc is cracked, it must be renewed.

5 Using a dial gauge or a flat metal block and feeler gauges, check that the disc run-out 10 mm from the outer edge does not exceed the limit given in the Specifications. To do this, fix the measuring equipment, and rotate the disc, noting the variation in measurement as the disc is rotated. The difference between the minimum and maximum measurements recorded is the disc run-out.

6 If the run-out is greater than the specified amount, check for variations of the disc thickness as follows. Mark the disc at eight positions 45° apart then, using a micrometer, measure the disc thickness at the eight positions, 15 mm in from the outer edge. If the variation between the minimum and maximum readings is greater than the specified amount, the disc should be renewed.

7 The hub face run-out can also be checked in a similar way. First remove the disc as described later in this Section, fix the measuring equipment, then slowly rotate the hub, and check that the run-out does not exceed the amount given in the Specifications. If the hub face run-out is excessive, this should be corrected (by renewing the hub bearings – see Chapter 10 Section 2) before rechecking the disc run-out.

Removal

8 With the wheel, caliper and bracket removed, remove the wheel nuts which were temporarily refitted in paragraph 3.

9 Mark the disc in relation to the hub, if it is to be refitted.

10 Remove the washer/retaining clip(s) (where fitted), and withdraw the disc over the wheel studs **(see illustration)**.

4.2 Suspend the caliper from the spring using wire or string

4.4 Measure the thickness of the disc using a micrometer

4.10 Lift the brake disc from the studs

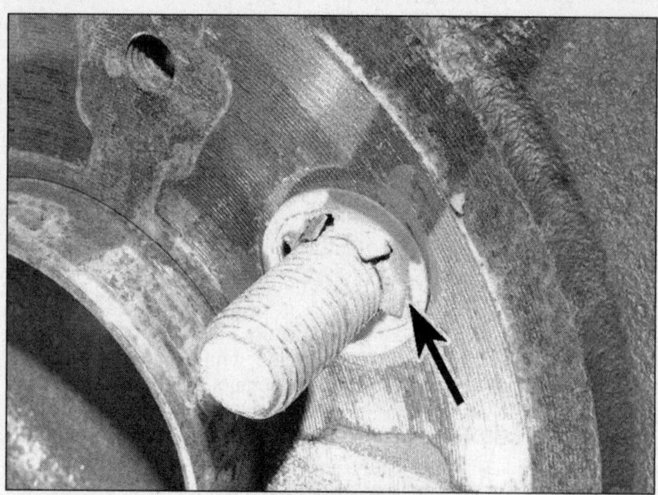

5.2a Prise off the clip (arrowed)

5.2b Use 2 x 8 mm bolts to force the drum from place

Refitting

11 Make sure that the disc and hub mating surfaces are clean, then locate the disc on the wheel studs. Align the previously-made marks if the original disc is being refitted.

12 Refit the washer/retaining clip(s), where fitted.

13 Refit the brake caliper and bracket with reference to Section 3.

14 Refit the wheel, and lower the vehicle to the ground. Tighten wheel nuts to their specified torque.

15 Test the brakes carefully before returning the vehicle to normal service.

5 Rear brake drum – removal, inspection and refitting

Note: *Refer to the warning at the beginning of Section 6 before proceeding.*

Note: *To prevent uneven braking, BOTH rear brake drums must be renewed at the same time.*

Removal

1 Chock the front wheels, release the handbrake and engage 1st gear (or P). Loosen the relevant wheel nuts, jack up the rear of the vehicle and support it on axle stands. Remove the appropriate rear wheel.

2 Prise off the spring clip (where fitted), and pull the drum from place. If the drum is reluctant to move, use two 8.0 mm bolts screwed into the threaded holes provided, and draw the drum from place **(see illustrations)**. If the brake drum is still reluctant to remove, slacken the handbrake cable as described in Section 22 and try again.

3 With the brake drum removed, clean the dust from the drum, brake shoes, wheel cylinder and backplate, using brake cleaner or methylated spirit. Take care not to inhale the dust, as it may contain asbestos.

Inspection

4 Clean the inside surfaces of the brake drum, then examine the internal friction surface for signs of scoring or cracks. If it is cracked, deeply scored, or has worn to a diameter greater than the maximum given in the Specifications, then it should be renewed, together with the drum on the other side.

5 Regrinding of the brake drum is not recommended.

Refitting

6 Refitting is a reversal of removal, tightening relevant bolts to their specified torque. Where necessary, adjust the handbrake as described in Section 22.

7 Test the brakes carefully before returning the vehicle to normal service.

6 Rear brake shoes – renewal

Warning: Drum brake shoes must be renewed on BOTH rear wheels at the same time – never renew the shoes on only one wheel, as uneven braking may result. Also, the dust created by wear of the shoes may contain asbestos, which is a health hazard. Never blow it out with compressed air, and don't inhale any of it. An approved filtering mask should be worn when working on the brakes. DO NOT use petroleum-based solvents to clean brake parts; use brake cleaner or methylated spirit only.

1 Chock the front wheels, release the handbrake and engage 1st gear. Loosen the relevant wheel nuts, jack up the rear of the vehicle and support it on axle stands. Remove the rear wheels. Work on one brake assembly at a time, using the assembled brake for reference if necessary.

2 Remove the rear brake drum as described in Section 5.

3 Note the fitted position of the springs and the brake shoes, then clean the components with brake cleaner, and allow to dry **(see illustration)** ; position a tray beneath the backplate, to catch the cleaner and residue.

4 Remove the two shoe hold-down springs, use a pair of pliers to depress the ends so that they can be withdrawn off the pins. If required, remove the hold-down pins from the backplate **(see illustration)**. Note that on some models, it's not possible to remove the rearmost hold-down pin with the backplate in place.

6.3 Clean the components with brake cleaner

6.4 Depress the hold-down spring, and slide it from under the head of the pin

6.5 Pull the top end of the shoe assembly outwards from the wheel cylinder

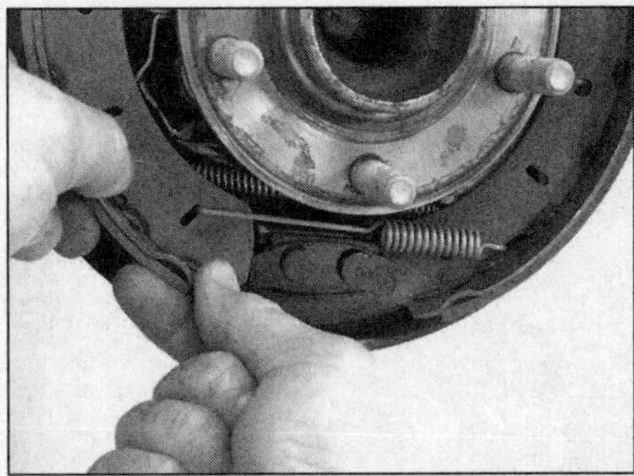
6.7a Pull the bottom end of the shoes from the anchor ...

6.7b ... then pivot the whole brake shoe assembly outwards

6.8 Pull the spring back and disengage the handbrake lever cable end fitting from the lever on the shoe

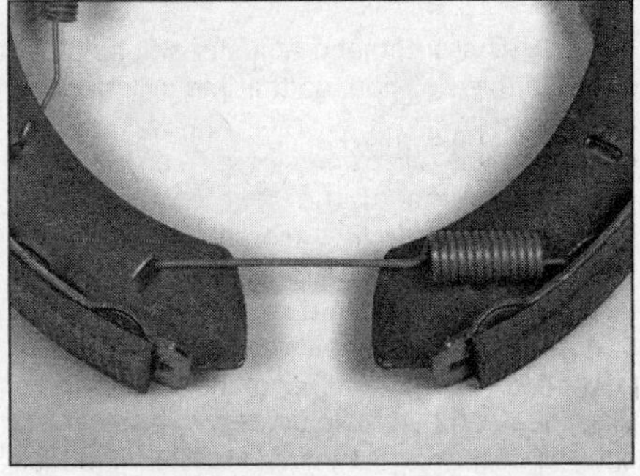
6.9 Unhook the lower return spring

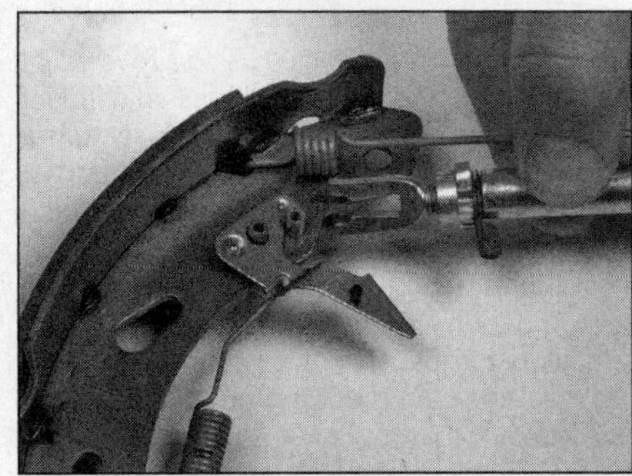
6.10 Pull the shoe from the strut and brake shoe adjuster

5 Disconnect the top ends of the shoes from the wheel cylinder, taking care not to damage the rubber boots **(see illustration).**

6 To prevent the wheel cylinder pistons from being accidentally ejected, fit a suitable elastic band or wire lengthways over the cylinder/pistons. DO NOT press the brake pedal while the shoes are removed.

7 Pull the bottom end of the brake shoes from the bottom anchor **(see illustrations)**. Use pliers or an adjustable spanner over the edge of the shoe to lever it away, if required.

8 Pull the handbrake cable spring back from the operating lever on the rear of the trailing shoe. Unhook the cable end from the cut-out in the lever, and remove the brake shoes **(see illustration).**

9 Working on a clean bench, move the bottom ends of the brake shoes together, and unhook the lower return spring from the shoes, noting the location holes **(see illustration).**

10 Pull the leading shoe from the strut and brake shoe adjuster **(see illustration).**

11 Pull the adjustment strut to release it from the trailing brake shoe, then unhook the upper return spring from the shoes, noting the location holes **(see illustrations).** Ford insist that the upper return spring is renewed.

12 If the wheel cylinder shows signs of fluid leakage, or if there is any reason to suspect it of being defective, inspect it now, as described in the next Section.

13 Clean the backplate, and apply small amounts of high melting-point brake grease to the brake shoe contact points. Be careful not to get grease on any friction surfaces.

14 Lubricate the sliding components of the brake shoe adjuster with a little high melting-point brake grease.

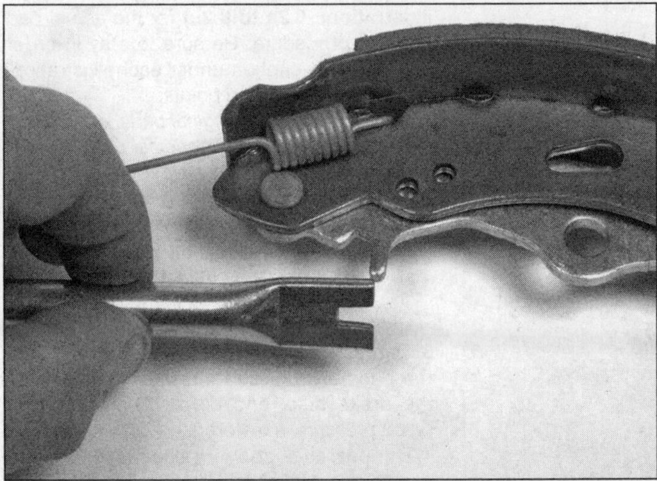
6.11a Pull the adjustment strut from the trailing shoe ...

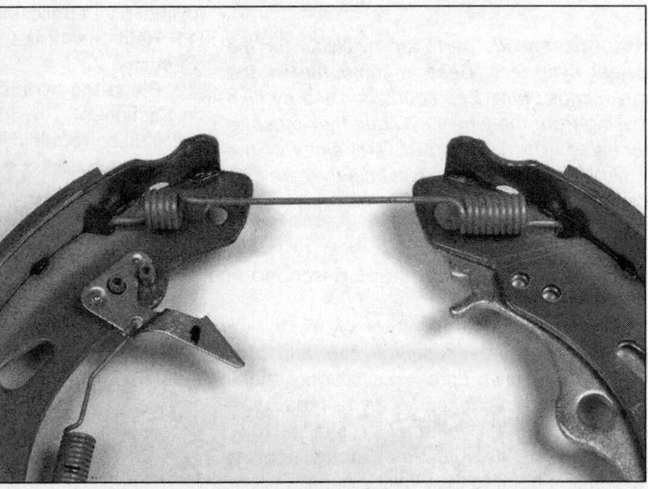
6.11b ... then unhook the upper return spring

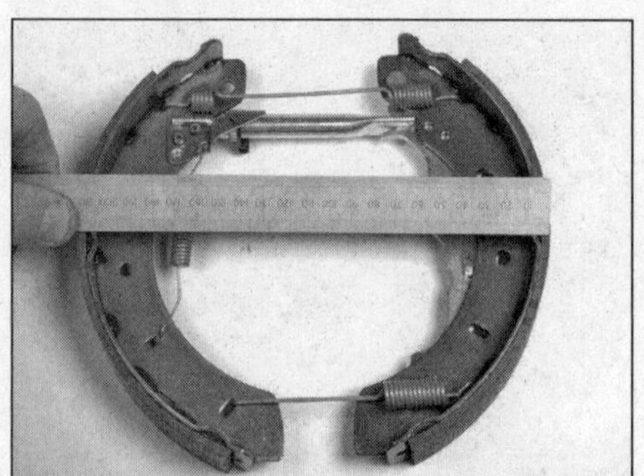
6.15a Set the adjustment strut so the diameter of the shoe assembly is 228 mm

6.15b When reassembled, the top of the assembly should look like this ...

6.15c ... and the lower end should look like this

15 Fit the new brake shoes using a reversal of the removal procedure, but set the adjustment strut so the diameter of the shoe assembly is approximately 228 mm **(see illustrations)**.

16 Before refitting the brake drum, it should be inspected as described in Section 5.

17 With the drum in position and all the securing bolts and nuts tightened to their specified torque, refit the wheel, then carry out the renewal procedure on the remaining rear brake.

18 Lower the vehicle to the ground, and tighten the wheel nuts to the specified torque.

19 Depress the brake pedal several times, in order to operate the self-adjusting mechanism and set the shoes at their normal operating position.

20 Make several forward and reverse stops, and operate the handbrake fully two or three times (adjust the handbrake as required). Give the vehicle a road test, to make sure that the brakes are functioning correctly, and to bed-in the new shoes to the contours of the drum. Remember that the new shoes will not give full braking efficiency until they have bedded-in.

7 Rear wheel cylinder – removal and refitting

Note: *No service parts are available for the wheel cylinders. Bear in mind that if the brake shoes have been contaminated by fluid leaking from the wheel cylinder, they must be renewed. The shoes on BOTH sides of the vehicle must be renewed, even if they are only contaminated on one side.*

Removal

1 Remove the brake drum as described in Section 5.

2 Minimise fluid loss either by removing the master cylinder reservoir cap, and then tightening it down onto a piece of polythene to obtain an airtight seal, or by using a brake hose clamp, a G-clamp, or similar tool, to clamp the flexible hose at the nearest convenient point to the wheel cylinder.

3 Pull the brake shoes apart at their top ends, so that they are just clear of the wheel cylinder. The automatic adjuster will hold the shoes in this position, so that the cylinder can be withdrawn.

4 Wipe away all traces of dirt around the hydraulic union at the rear of the wheel cylinder, then undo the union nut.

5 Unscrew the two bolts securing the wheel cylinder to the backplate **(see illustration)**.

6 Withdraw the wheel cylinder from the backplate so that it is clear of the brake shoes. Plug the open hydraulic unions, to prevent the entry of dirt, and to minimise further fluid loss whilst the cylinder is detached.

Refitting

7 Wipe clean the backplate and remove the plug from the end of the hydraulic pipe. Fit the cylinder onto the backplate and screw in the hydraulic union nut by hand, being careful not to cross-thread it.

8 Tighten the mounting bolts, then fully tighten the hydraulic union nut.

9 Retract the automatic brake adjuster mechanism, so that the brake shoes engage with the pistons of the wheel cylinder. To do this, prise the shoes apart slightly, turn the automatic adjuster to its minimum position, and release the shoes.

10 Remove the clamp from the flexible brake hose, or the polythene from the master cylinder (as applicable).

11 Refit the brake drum with reference to Section 5.

12 Bleed the hydraulic system as described in Section 14. Providing suitable precautions were taken to minimise loss of fluid, it should only be necessary to bleed the relevant rear brake.

7.5 Undo the 2 bolts and remove the wheel cylinder

13 Test the brakes carefully before returning the vehicle to normal service.

8 Rear brake pads – renewal

Warning: Renew both sets of rear brake pads at the same time – never renew the pads on only one wheel, as uneven braking may result. Note that the dust created by wear of the pads may contain asbestos, which is a health hazard. Never blow it out with compressed air, and don't inhale any of it. An approved filtering mask should be worn when working on the brakes. DO NOT use petrol or petroleum-based solvents to clean brake parts; use brake cleaner or methylated spirit only.

1 Chock the front wheels, slacken the rear road- wheel nuts, then jack up the rear of the vehicle and support it on axle stands (see *Jacking and vehicle support*). Remove the rear wheels.

2 With the handbrake lever fully released, follow the accompanying photos **(see illustrations 8.2a to 8.2u)** for the actual pad renewal procedure. Be sure to stay in order and read the caption under each illustration, and note the following points:

a) *If re-installing the original pads, ensure they are fitted to their original position.*
b) *Thoroughly clean the caliper guide surfaces and guide bolts.*
c) *If new pads are to be fitted, use a piston retraction tool to push the piston back and twist it clockwise at the same time – keep an eye on the fluid level in the reservoir whilst retracting the piston.*

3 Depress the brake pedal repeatedly, until the pads are pressed into firm contact with the brake disc, and normal (non-assisted) pedal pressure is restored.

4 Repeat the above procedure on the remaining brake caliper.

5 If necessary, adjust the handbrake as described in Section 22.

8.2a Prise away the retaining spring

8.2b Pull out the rubber caps ...

8.2c ... and use a 7 mm Allen key or bit to unscrew the guide bolts

8.2d Unclip the brake hose from the bracket

8.2e Lift away the caliper ...

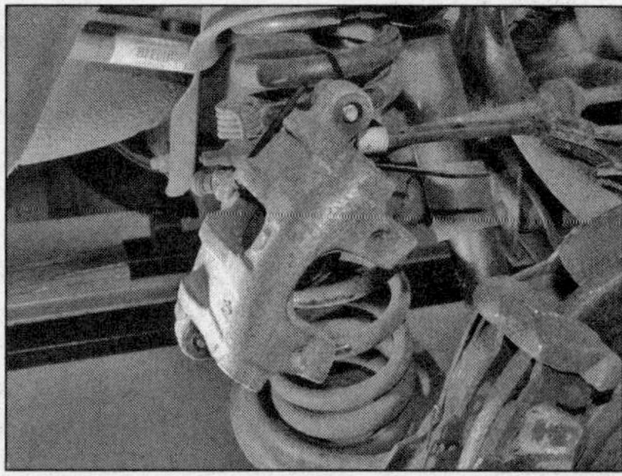
8.2f ... and suspend it from the suspension using cable ties/string

8.2g Remove the outer brake pad ...

8.2h ... and the inner pad

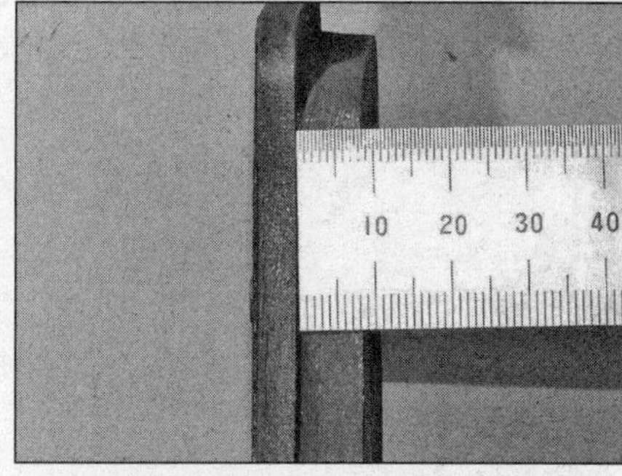

8.2i Measure the thickness of the pad friction material

8.2j Use a wire brush to clean the pad mounting bracket

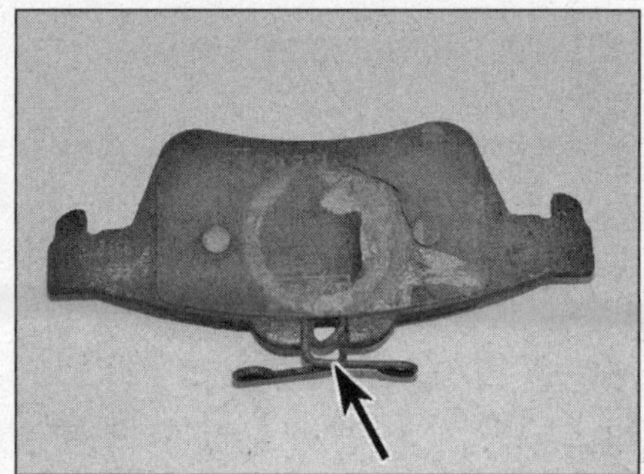
8.2k Note that the inner pad has an anti-rattle spring (arrowed)

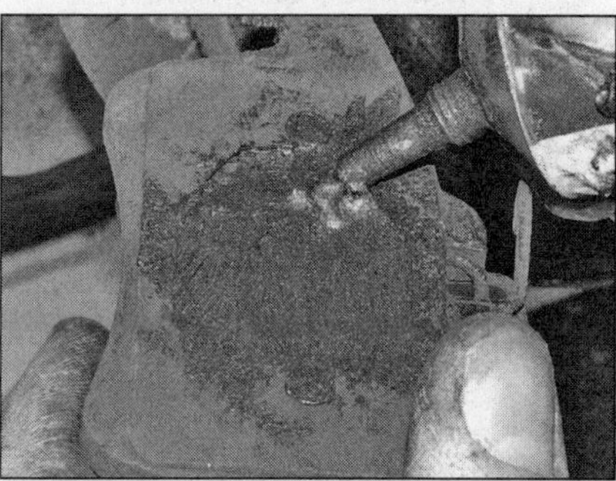
8.2l Apply a little high-temperature anti-seize grease (Copperslip) to the rear of the pad ...

8.2m ... and the areas where the pad backing plate contacts the mounting bracket

8.2n Fit the inner pad – friction material side against the disc ...

8.2o ... followed by the outer pad

8.2p If new pads have been fitted, use a retraction tool to rotate the caliper piston clockwise, at the same time as pushing it into the caliper. Keep an eye on the fluid level in the reservoir. Remove any surplus with a syringe.

8.2q Refit the caliper over the pads ...

8.2r ... then refit and tighten the guide bolts to the specified torque

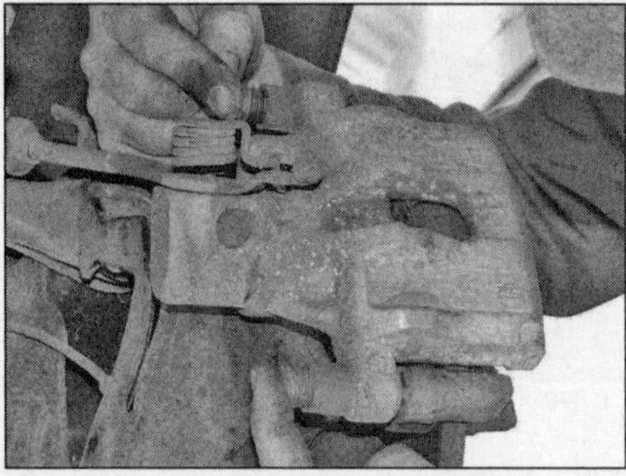
8.2s Refit the rubber caps

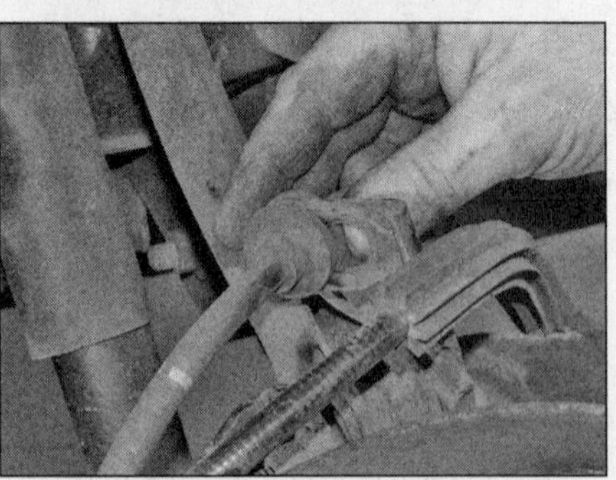
8.2t Clip the brake hose back into the bracket

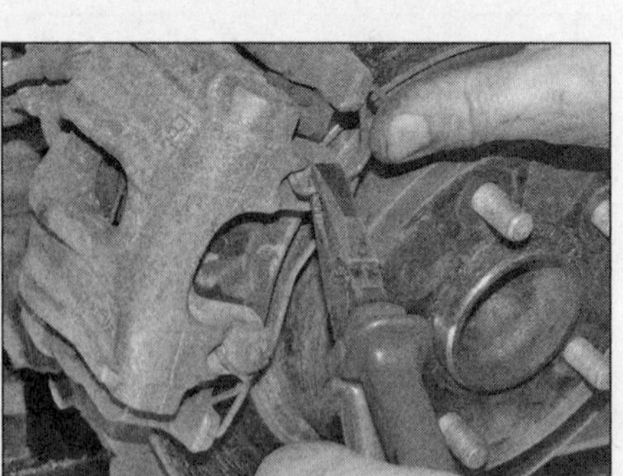
8.2u Use pliers to refit the caliper retaining spring

6 Refit the roadwheels, then lower the vehicle to the ground and tighten the roadwheel nuts to the specified torque.

7 Check the hydraulic fluid level as described in *Weekly checks*.

Caution: New pads will not give full braking efficiency until they have bedded-in. Be prepared for this, and avoid hard braking as far as possible for the first hundred miles or so after pad renewal.

9 Rear brake caliper – removal, overhaul and refitting

Removal

1 Chock the front wheels, and engage 1st gear. Loosen the rear wheel nuts, jack up the rear of the vehicle and support it on axle stands. Remove the appropriate rear wheel.

2 Fit a brake hose clamp to the flexible hose leading to the caliper **(see illustration 3.2)**. This will minimise brake fluid loss during subsequent operations.

3 Slacken (but do not completely unscrew) the union on the caliper end of the flexible hose.

4 Unclip the handbrake inner cable fitting

9.4 Unclip the cable end fitting (arrowed) from the caliper lever

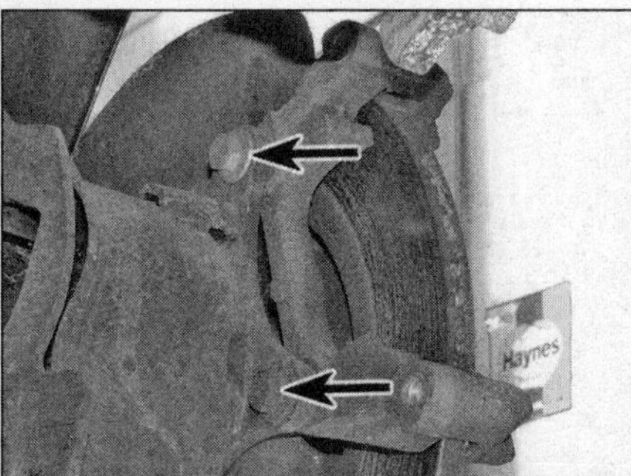

9.6 Undo the caliper mounting bracket bolts (arrowed)

10.3 Pull the rear brake disc over the wheel studs

from the lever on the caliper, then detach the outer cable from the bracket **(see illustration)**.

5 Unscrew the caliper from the hydraulic brake hose, making sure that the hose is not twisted or strained unduly. Plug the open hydraulic unions to keep dust and dirt out.

6 If necessary, unbolt the caliper bracket from the hub carrier **(see illustration)**.

Overhaul

7 No overhaul procedures, or parts, were available at the time of writing. Check the availability of spares before dismantling the caliper. Do not attempt to dismantle the handbrake mechanism inside the caliper; if the mechanism is faulty, the complete caliper assembly must be renewed.

Refitting

8 Refit the caliper, and where applicable the bracket, by reversing the removal operations. Refer to the points made in Section 22 when reconnecting the handbrake cable. Tighten the mounting bolts and wheel nuts to the specified torque, and do not forget to remove the brake hose clamp from the flexible brake hose.

9 Bleed the brake circuit according to the procedure given in Section 14. Make sure there are no leaks from the hose connections. Test the brakes carefully before returning the vehicle to normal service.

10 Rear brake disc – inspection, removal and refitting

Removal

1 Remove the rear caliper and pads as described in Section 9 and Section 8.

2 Unbolt the caliper carrier bracket from the hub **(see illustration 9.6)**, then mark the disc in relation to the hub, if it is to be refitted.

3 Remove the retaining clip from the wheel stud (where fitted), and withdraw the disc over the wheel studs **(see illustration)**.

4 Procedures for inspection of the rear brake discs are the same as the front brake discs as described in Section 4.

Refitting

5 Refitting is a reversal of removal, as described in the relevant Sections. Apply a little thread locking compound to the caliper bracket-to-hub carrier bolts.

11 Master cylinder – removal and refitting

Warning: Brake fluid is poisonous. Take care to keep it off bare skin, and in particular not to get splashes in your eyes. The fluid also attacks paintwork and plastics – wash off spillages immediately with cold water. Finally, brake fluid is highly inflammable, and should be handled with the same care as petrol.

Removal

1 Exhaust the vacuum in the servo by pressing the brake pedal a few times, with the engine switched off.

2 Disconnect the battery negative lead. **Note:** *Before disconnecting the battery, refer to Chapter 5A Section 3 for precautions.*

Warning: Do not syphon the fluid by mouth; it is poisonous. Any brake fluid spilt on paintwork should be washed off with clean water, without delay – brake fluid is also a highly-effective paint-stripper.

3 Raise the vehicle and remove the wheels. Slacken the front bleed nipples, attach a rubber hose to the nipple, and place the other end of the hose in a suitable container. Operate the brake pedal until the fluid level is down to the base of the reservoir.

4 Depress the release button and detach the clutch master cylinder fluid supply hose from the side of the brake fluid reservoir **(see illustration)**. Plug the openings to prevent contamination.

5 Disconnect the wiring plug from the fluid level sensor on the side of the reservoir **(see illustration 11.4)**.

6 Identify the locations of each brake pipe on the master cylinder, then place rags beneath the master cylinder to catch spilt hydraulic fluid.

7 Clean around the hydraulic union nuts. Unscrew the nuts, and disconnect the hydraulic lines from the master cylinder **(see illustration)**. If the nuts are tight, a split ring spanner should be used in preference to an open-ended spanner. Cap the end of the pipes and the master cylinder to prevent any dirt contamination.

8 Undo the master cylinder securing nuts, and withdraw the master cylinder from the studs on the servo unit **(see illustration)**.

11.4 Depress the release button (on the reverse of the connector – 1), and disconnect the clutch fluid supply hose, then disconnect the level warning sensor wiring plug (2)

11.7 Undo the brake pipe unions (arrowed)

11.8 Master cylinder retaining nuts (arrowed)

Discard the nuts – new ones must be fitted.

9 Recover the gasket/seal from the master cylinder.

10 If the master cylinder is faulty, it must be renewed. At the time of writing, no overhaul kits were available.

Refitting

11 Refitting is a reversal of the removal procedure, noting the following points:

a) Clean the contact surfaces of the master cylinder and servo, and locate a new gasket on the master cylinder.

b) Refit and tighten the nuts to the specified torque.

c) Carefully insert the brake pipes in the apertures in the master cylinder, then tighten the union nuts. Make sure that the nuts enter their threads correctly.

d) Fill the reservoir with fresh brake fluid.

e) Bleed the brake hydraulic system as described in Section 14.

f) Test the brakes carefully before returning the vehicle to normal service.

Brake fluid reservoir

12 Carry out the procedure described in Paragraph 3 to 7 of this Section.

13 Disconnect the wiring plug from the fluid level sensor on the side of the reservoir.

14 Remove the retaining pin and detach the reservoir from the master cylinder **(see illustration)**.

11.14 Pull out the reservoir retaining pin (arrowed – viewed from underneath)

12 Brake pedal – removal and refitting

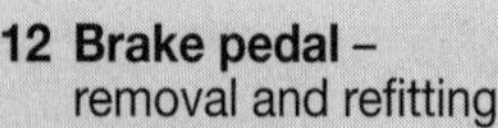

Removal

1 Working inside the vehicle, move the driver's seat fully to the rear, to allow maximum working area.

2 Remove the driver's side lower facia panel as described in Chapter 11 Section 30.

3 Remove the accelerator pedal as described in Chapter 4A Section 6.

4 Disconnect the electrical connectors to the brake pedal switches. Remove the switches by turning them, then pulling them out of the pedal bracket **(see illustration)**.

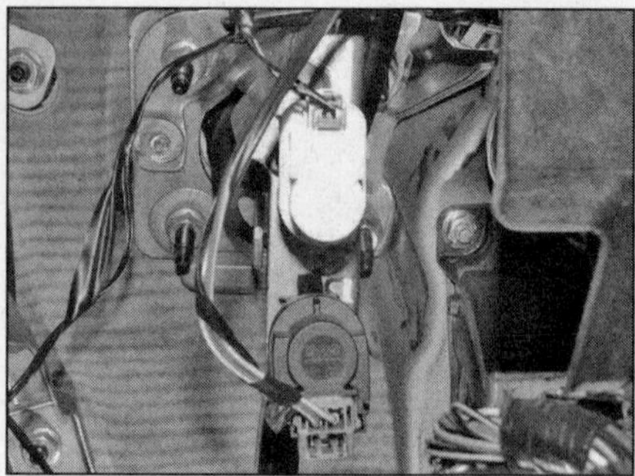

12.4 Disconnect the wiring plugs from the brake pedal switches

5 Prise out the pin securing the servo pushrod to the pedal **(see illustration)**. Discard the pin – a new one must be fitted.

6 Slacken the 5 retaining nuts on the pedal bracket assembly **(see illustration)**.

7 Manoeuvre the pedal assembly rearwards, and down from under the facia. No further dismantling of the assembly is recommended – it would appear that only the complete assembly is available.

Refitting

8 Refitting is a reversal of the removal procedure.

9 Refit the brake pedal switches as described in Section 20.

13 Hydraulic pipes and hoses – inspection, removal and refitting

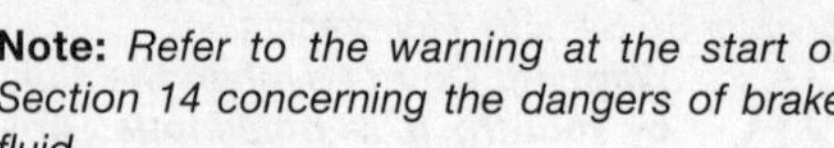

Note: *Refer to the warning at the start of Section 14 concerning the dangers of brake fluid.*

Inspection

1 Jack up the front and rear of the vehicle, and support on axle stands (see *Jacking and vehicle support*). Making sure the vehicle is safely supported on a level surface.

2 Check for signs of leakage at the pipe unions, then examine the flexible hoses for signs of cracking, chafing and fraying.

3 The brake pipes should be examined carefully for signs of dents, corrosion or other damage. Corrosion should be scraped off, and if the depth of pitting is significant, the pipes renewed. This is particularly likely in those areas underneath the vehicle body where the pipes are exposed and unprotected.

4 Renew any defective brake pipes and/or hoses.

Removal

5 If a section of pipe or hose is to be removed, loss of brake fluid can be reduced by unscrewing the filler cap, and completely sealing the top of the reservoir with cling film or adhesive tape. Alternatively, the reservoir can be emptied (see Section 11).

6 To remove a section of pipe, hold the adjoining hose union nut with a spanner to prevent it from turning, then unscrew the union nut at the end of the pipe, and release it. Repeat the procedure at the other end of the pipe, then release the pipe by pulling out the clips attaching it to the body.

7 Where the union nuts are exposed to the full force of the weather, they can sometimes be quite tight. If an open-ended spanner is used, burring of the flats on the nuts is not uncommon, and for this reason, it is preferable to use a split ring (brake) spanner **(see illustration)**, which will engage all the flats. If such a spanner is not available, self-locking grips may be used as a last resort; these may well damage the nuts, but if the pipe is to be renewed, this does not matter.

8 To further minimise the loss of fluid when

12.5 Prise out and discard the servo pushrod pin

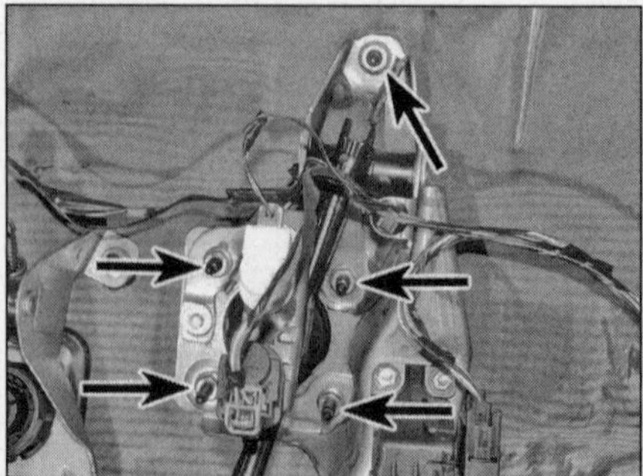

12.6 Brake pedal bracket assembly retaining nuts (arrowed)

13.7 Use a brake pipe spanner to slacken the union nuts

disconnecting a flexible brake line from a rigid pipe, clamp the hose as near as possible to the pipe to be detached, using a brake hose clamp or a pair of self-locking grips with protected jaws.

9 To remove a flexible hose, first clean the ends of the hose and the surrounding area, then unscrew the union nuts from the hose ends. Remove the spring clip, and withdraw the hose from the serrated mounting in the support bracket. Where applicable, unscrew the hose from the caliper.

10 Brake pipes supplied with flared ends and union nuts can be obtained individually or in sets from Ford dealers or accessory shops. The pipe is then bent to shape, using the old pipe as a guide, and is ready for fitting. Be careful not to kink or crimp the pipe when bending it; ideally, a proper pipe-bending tool should be used.

Refitting

11 Refitting of the pipes and hoses is a reversal of removal. Make sure that all brake pipes are securely supported in their clips, and ensure that the hoses are not kinked. Check also that the hoses are clear of all suspension components and underbody fittings, and will remain clear during movement of the suspension and steering.

12 On completion, bleed the hydraulic system as described in Section 14.

14 Hydraulic system – bleeding

Warning: Brake fluid contains polyglycol ethers and polyglycols which are poisonous. Take care to keep it off bare skin, and in particular not to get splashes in your eyes. Wash hands thoroughly after handling and if fluid contacts the eyes, flush out with cold running water. If irritation persists get medical attention immediately. The fluid also attacks paintwork and plastics – wash off spillages immediately with cold water. Finally, brake fluid is highly inflammable, and should be handled with the same care as petrol.

Note: *On models that have the ESP (Electronic Stability Programme) option, if air enters the ABS valve block, diagnostic equipment (such as Ford's IDS tool) will be required to successfully bleed the brakes.*

1 If the master cylinder has been disconnected and reconnected, then the complete system (all circuits) must be bled of air. If a component of one circuit has been disturbed, then only that particular circuit need be bled.

2 Bleeding should commence on the furthest bleed nipple from the master cylinder, followed by the next one until the bleed nipple remaining nearest to the master cylinder is bled last.

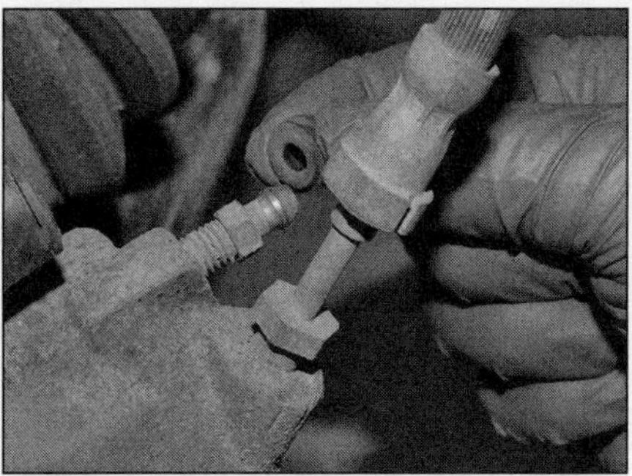

14.7a Prise off the dust cap from the bleed screw (arrowed)

14.7b Connect the kit and open the bleed screw

3 There are a variety of do-it-yourself 'one-man' brake bleeding kits available from motor accessory shops, and it is recommended that one of these kits be used wherever possible, as they greatly simplify the brake bleeding operation. Follow the kit manufacturer's instructions in conjunction with the following procedure. If a pressure-bleeding kit is obtained, then it will not be necessary to depress the brake pedal in the following procedure.

4 During the bleeding operation, do not allow the brake fluid level in the reservoir to drop below the minimum mark. If the level is allowed to fall so far that air is drawn in, the whole procedure will have to be started again from scratch. Only use new fluid for topping-up, preferably from a freshly-opened container. Never re-use fluid bled from the system.

5 Before starting, check that all rigid pipes and flexible hoses are in good condition, and that all hydraulic unions are tight. Take great care not to allow hydraulic fluid to come into contact with the vehicle paintwork, otherwise the finish will be seriously damaged. Wash off any spilt fluid immediately with cold water.

6 If a brake bleeding kit is not being used, gather together a clean jar, a length of plastic or rubber tubing which is a tight fit over the bleed screw, and a new container of the specified brake fluid (see Lubricants and fluids). The help of an assistant will also be required.

7 Clean the area around the bleed screw on the rear brake unit to be bled (it is important that no dirt be allowed to enter the hydraulic system), and remove the dust cap. Connect one end of the tubing to the bleed screw, and immerse the other end in the jar **(see illustrations)**. The jar should be filled with sufficient brake fluid to keep the end of the tube submerged.

8 Open the bleed screw by half a turn, and have the assistant depress the brake pedal to the floor. Tighten the bleed screw at the end of the down stroke, then have the assistant release the pedal. Continue this procedure until clean brake fluid, free from air bubbles, can be seen flowing into the jar. Finally tighten the bleed screw with the pedal in the fully-depressed position.

9 Remove the tube, and refit the dust cap. Top-up the master cylinder reservoir if necessary, then repeat the procedure on the opposite rear brake.

10 Repeat the procedure on the front brake furthest from the master cylinder, followed by the brake nearest to the master cylinder.

11 Check the feel of the brake pedal – it should be firm. If it is spongy, there is still some air in the system, and the bleeding procedure should be repeated.

12 When bleeding is complete, top-up the master cylinder reservoir and refit the cap.

13 Check the clutch operation on completion; it may be necessary to bleed the clutch hydraulic system as described in Chapter 6 Section 5.

15 Vacuum servo unit – testing, removal and refitting

Testing

1 To test the operation of the servo unit, depress the footbrake four or five times to dissipate the vacuum, then start the engine while keeping the footbrake depressed. As the engine starts, there should be a noticeable give in the brake pedal as vacuum builds-up. Allow the engine to run for at least two minutes, and then switch it off. If the brake pedal is now depressed again, it should be possible to hear a hiss from the servo when the pedal is depressed. After four or five applications, no further hissing should be heard, and the pedal should feel harder.

2 Before assuming that a problem exists in the servo unit itself, inspect the non-return valve as described in the next Section.

Removal

3 Remove the wipers and windscreen cowl panel as described in Chapter 12 Section 11 and then remove the suspension strut brace. Replace the bolts temporarily back in the suspension strut

4 Remove the engine cover and where necessary remove the air intake pipe from above the timing belt.

5 Refer to Section 11 and remove the master

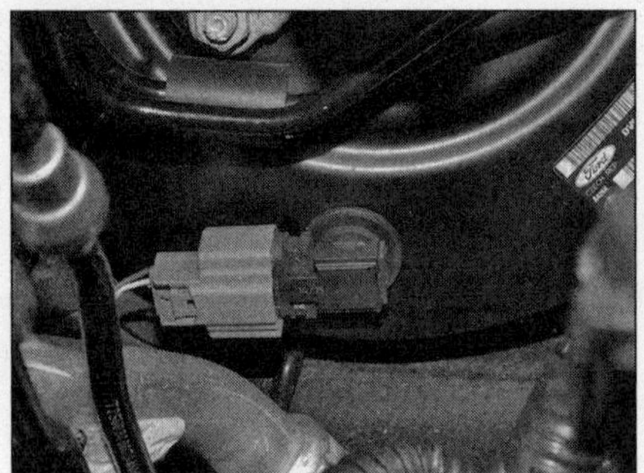

15.9 Disconnect the wiring plug (arrowed)

cylinder and then unclip the brake lines from the bulkhead.

6 Detach the coolant expansion tank from the right-hand side inner wing and move it to one side.

7 Disconnect the wiring plug from the AC pressure switch in the refrigerant pipes.

8 Carefully prise the vacuum line from the brake servo.

9 Disconnect the wiring plug from the brake vacuum sensor **(see illustration)** and where fitted the ABS brake pedal travel sensor.

10 Jack up and support the front of the vehicle (see *Jacking and vehicle support* in the reference section) and then remove the engine undershield.

11 To allow removal of the brake servo the engine must be moved forward slightly. Place a heavy duty trolley jack (with a block of wood on the jack head to spread the load) beneath the sump and take the weight of the engine.

12 Remove the right-hand engine mounting as described in Chapter 2A, 2B, 2C or 2D, depending on engine. With care drag the engine forward on the trolley jack at the right-hand end.

13 Remove the driver's side lower facia panel as described in Chapter 11 Section 30.

14 Disconnect their wiring plugs, then remove the brake pedal position switch and the brake light switch from the bracket. Rotate the position switch anti-clockwise, and the light switch clockwise. Do not move the brake pedal during this procedure.

15 Carefully prise the pin from the servo actuator rod **(see illustration 12.5)**. Discard the pin – a new one must be fitted

16 Undo the 4 nuts securing the servo to the bulkhead/pedal bracket and manoeuvre it from the engine compartment.

17 Note that the servo unit cannot be dismantled for repair or overhaul and, if faulty, must be renewed.

Refitting

18 Refitting is a reversal of the removal procedure, noting the following points:

a) Refer to the relevant Sections/Chapters for details of refitting the other components removed.

b) Compress the actuator rod into the brake servo, before refitting.

c) Make sure the gasket is correctly positioned on the servo.

d) Fir t new bolts to the suspension tower and the brake pedal assembly.

e) Test the brakes carefully before returning the vehicle to normal service.

16 Vacuum servo unit vacuum hose and non-return valve – removal, testing and refitting

Note: *The non return valve is fitted to the servo end of the vacuum pipe, and is supplied complete with the brake servo vacuum hose.*

Removal

1 With the engine switched off, depress the brake pedal four or five times, to dissipate any remaining vacuum from the servo unit.

2 Disconnect the vacuum hose adapter at the servo unit, by pulling it free from the rubber grommet. If it is reluctant to move, prise it free, using a screwdriver with its blade inserted under the flange.

3 Detach the vacuum hose from the inlet manifold connection, pressing in the collar to disengage the tabs, then withdrawing the collar slowly.

4 If the hose or the fixings are damaged or in poor condition, they must be renewed.

Testing

5 Examine the non-return valve for damage and signs of deterioration, and renew it if necessary. The valve may be tested by blowing through its connecting hoses in both directions. It should only be possible to blow from the servo end towards the inlet manifold.

Refitting

6 Refitting is a reversal of the removal procedure. If fitting a new non-return valve, ensure that it is fitted the correct way round.

17 ABS hydraulic unit – removal and refitting

1 Renewal of the ABS unit assembly requires access to specialist diagnostic and testing equipment in order to purge air from the system, initilise and code the ECM. Consequently, we recommend this task is entrusted to Ford dealer or suitably-equipped specialist.The ABS unit is located in the left-hand rear corner of the engine compartment, behind the battery **(see illustration)**.

18 ABS wheel sensor – testing, removal and refitting

Testing

1 Checking of the sensors is done either by substitution for a known good unit, or interrogating the ABS ECU for stored fault codes, using dedicated test equipment found at Ford dealers or suitably-equipped specialists.

Removal

Front wheel sensor

2 Apply the handbrake and loosen the relevant front wheel nuts. Jack up the front of the vehicle and support it on axle stands. Remove the wheel.

3 Disconnect the sensor wiring plug.

4 Unscrew the sensor mounting bolt from the hub carrier and withdraw the sensor **(see illustration)**. Withdraw the O-ring seal.

Rear wheel sensor

5 Chock the front wheels, and engage 1st gear (or P). Jack up the rear of the vehicle and support it on axle stands. Remove the relevant wheel.

6 Disconnect the sensor wiring plug.

7 Unscrew the sensor mounting bolt, and withdraw the sensor **(see illustration)**. Withdraw the O-ring seal.

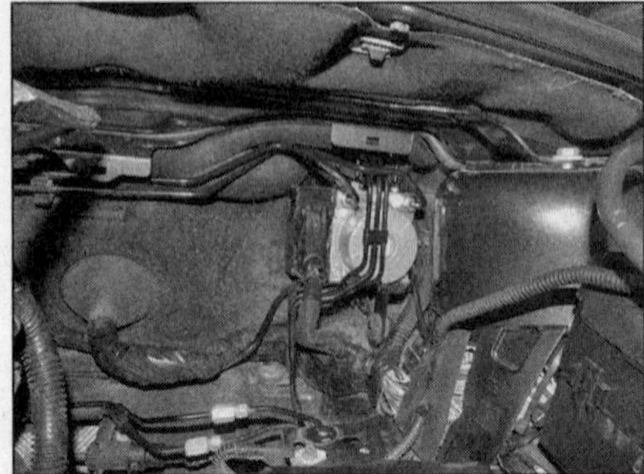

17.1 Location of ABS unit

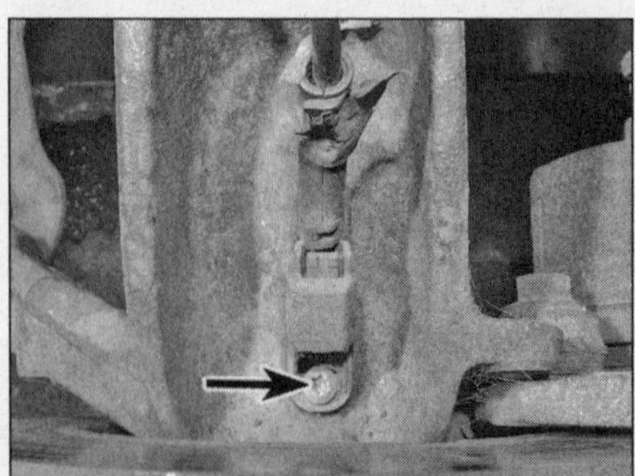

18.4 Front ABS sensor mounting bolt (arrowed)

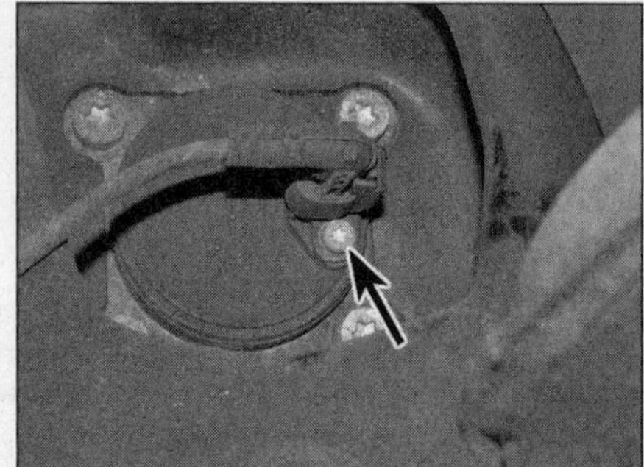

18.7 Rear ABS sensor retaining bolt (arrowed) – disc brake model

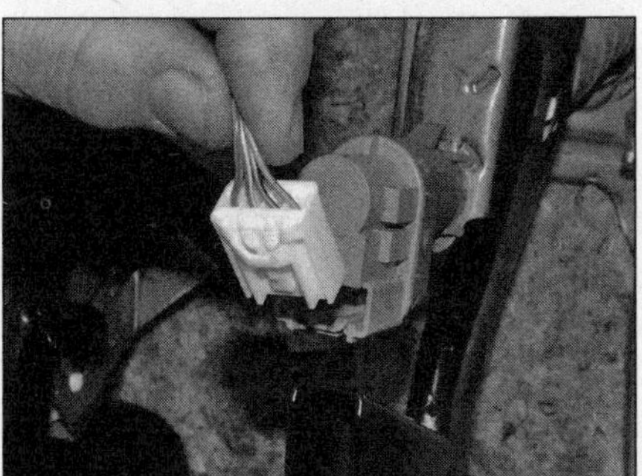

20.3 Disconnect the wiring plug

20.4 Remove the switch

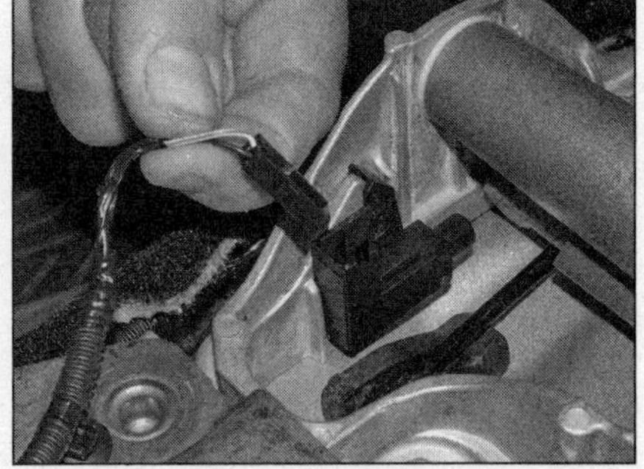

21.3 Disconnect the handbrake warning light switch (arrowed)

Refitting

8 Refitting is a reversal of the removal procedure. Fit a new O-ring seal to the hub carrier – not the sensor.

19 Traction control system – general information

1 The Traction control system is an expanded version of the ABS system. It is integrated with the ABS, and uses the same wheel sensors. It also uses the hydraulic control unit, which incorporates additional internal solenoid valves.

2 To remove the wheel sensors, carry out the procedure as described in Section 18.

3 Renewal of the ABS unit assembly requires access to specialist diagnostic and testing equipment in order to purge air from the system, initilise and code the ECM. Consequently, we recommend this task is entrusted to Ford dealer or suitably-equipped specialist.

20 Brake pedal switch – removal and refitting

Removal

1 Disconnect the battery negative (earth) lead (see Chapter 5A Section 3).

2 Remove the driver's side lower facia panel as described in Chapter 11 Section 30.

3 Disconnect the wiring connector from the brake light switch. This is the blue and white switch **(see illustration)**.

4 Rotate the switch anti-clockwise by a quarter-turn, and withdraw it from the pedal bracket **(see illustration)**. Do not depress the brake pedal during the removal or refitting procedure – the pedal must be 'at rest'.

Refitting and adjustment

5 Refitting is a reversal of the removal procedure. **Note:** *If both switches have been removed, the brake pedal position switch must be installed before the light switch.*

21 Handbrake lever – removal and refitting

Removal

1 Chock the front wheels, and engage 1st gear.

2 Remove the centre console as described in Chapter 11 Section 27.

3 Disconnect the electrical connector from the handbrake warning switch **(see illustration)**.

4 Slacken the locknut, then undo the handbrake adjusting nut **(see illustrations)**.

5 Unscrew the mounting bolts securing the handbrake lever to the floor **(see illustration)**.

6 Withdraw the handbrake from inside the vehicle.

21.4a Slacken the cable (models with no armrest) and...

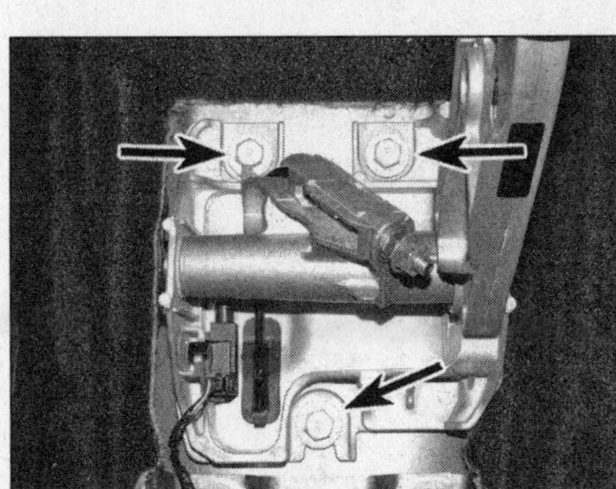

21.5 Handbrake lever mounting bolts (arrowed). Models without and armrest shown, models with and armrest are similar

Refitting and adjustment

7 Refitting is a reversal of removal, ensuring the cable retaining tab is positioned away from the cable.

8 When refitting the lever, it will be necessary to adjust the mechanism, as follows. **Note:** *The handbrake should only be adjusted when the brakes are cool.*

9 Tighten the cable adjustment nut finger-tight, then raise the handbrake lever 12 notches.

10 Fully release the handbrake, then slacken the adjustment nut to the end of the threads.

Disc brake models

11 Insert a 0.7 mm feeler gauge between the handbrake lever and the caliper abutment on both sides **(see illustration)**.

12 With the help of an assistant, tighten the adjustment nut, until movement is observed

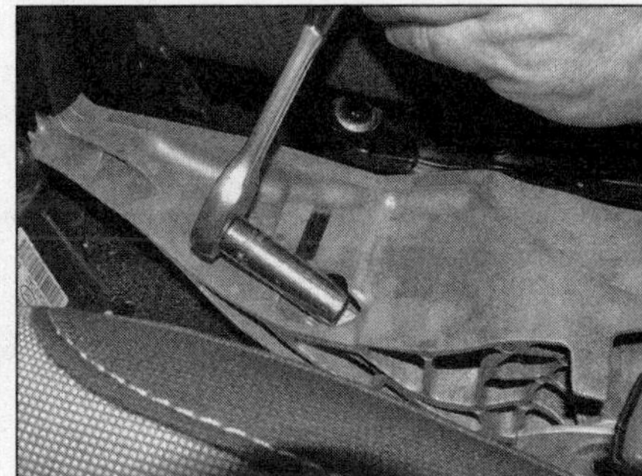

21.4b ... on models with and armrest

21.11 Insert a 0.7 mm feeler gauge between the caliper lever and the abutment (stop)

21.12a Unclip the gaiter...

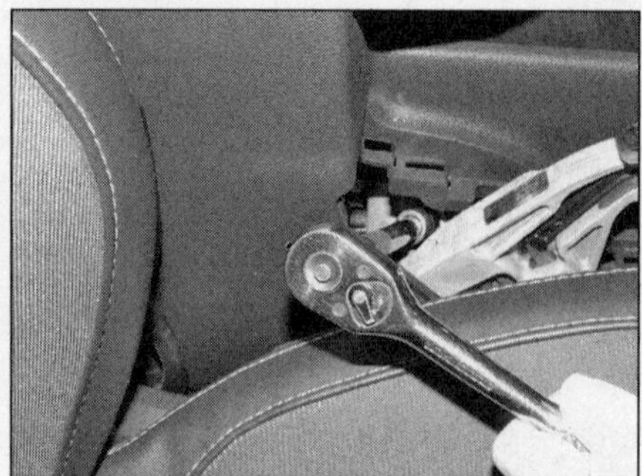
21.12b ...and adjust the handbrake cable

21.15 Insert a 2.0 mm feeler gauge between the lever end stop and the side of the shoe

on one of the caliper handbrake levers. If the centre console has been refitted, unclip the gaiter from around the handbrake lever and adjust the nut with a ratchet and deep socket **(see illustrations)**

13 Remove the feeler gauges from both sides, then check the wheels rotate freely with no excess friction or drag caused by the brake. Tighten the adjustment locknut.

Drum brake models

14 Remove the brake drums as described in Section 5.

15 Ensure the handbrake lever is fully released, then insert a 2.0 mm feeler gauge (or hex key) between the handbrake lever end stop and the rear brake shoe on each side **(see illustration)**.

16 With the help of an assistant, tighten the cable adjustment nut until movement is observed on one of the handbrake levers.

17 Remove the feeler gauges, and refit the drum brakes as described in Section 5.

18 Check the wheels rotate freely with no excess friction or drag caused by the brake. Tighten the cable locknut.

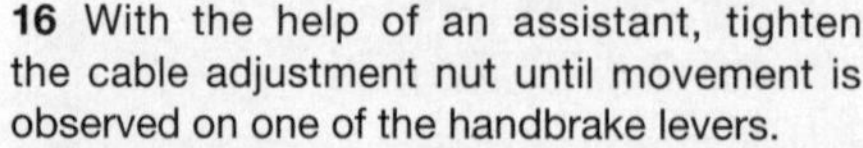

22 Handbrake cables – removal and refitting

Removal

1 Starting at the rear, prise up and remove the gaiter/trim around the handbrake lever.

2 Slacken the handbrake adjustment nut to the end of the threads.

3 Chock the front wheels and engage 1st gear. Loosen the wheel nuts on the relevant rear wheel, then jack up the rear of the vehicle and support it on axle stands. Fully release the handbrake lever.

4 Release the fasteners and remove the air deflector panel on each side **(see illustration)**.

5 Remove the exhaust system as described in Chapter 4A Section 15 for petrol engines, and Chapter 4B Section 17 for diesel engines.

6 Undo the fasteners and remove the exhaust front and centre heat shields.

7 Remove the relevant rear wheel and unclip the handbrake outer cable from its retaining clips **(see illustration)**.

Disc brake models

8 Unbolt the cable guide from the arm on both sides **(see illustration)**.

9 Use a pair of pliers to detach the handbrake cable inner fitting from the lever on each caliper **(see illustration 9.4)**.

10 Detach each outer cable from the bracket on the vehicle underbody, then disengage them from the equaliser bracket **(see illustrations)**. Note that the left-hand cable has a black sleeve, and the right-hand cable has a white sleeve.

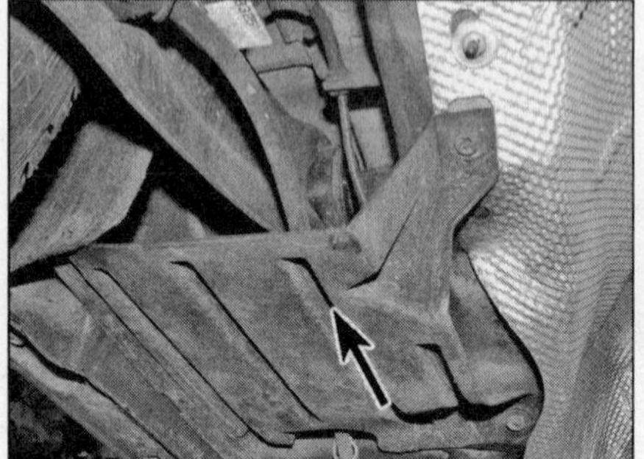
22.4 Remove the air deflector panel each side (arrowed)

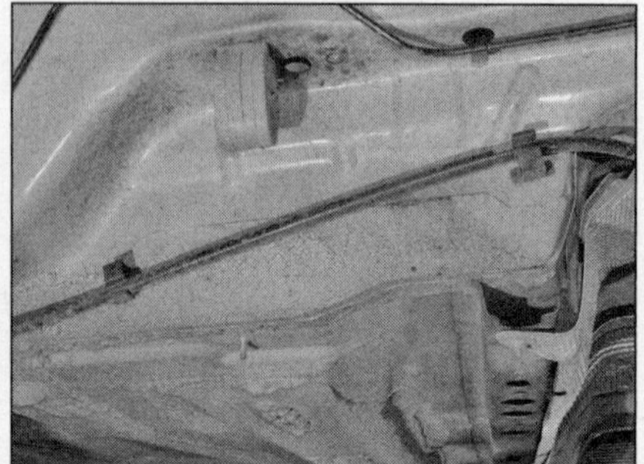
22.7 Release the handbrake cable from the retaining clips

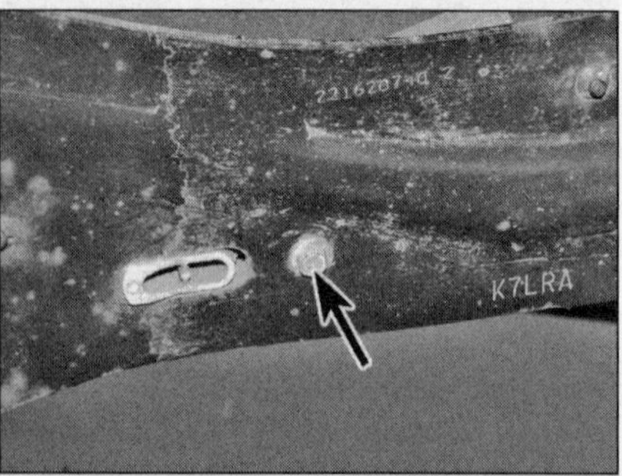

22.8 Undo the bolt (arrowed) securing the cable guide to the tie-bar

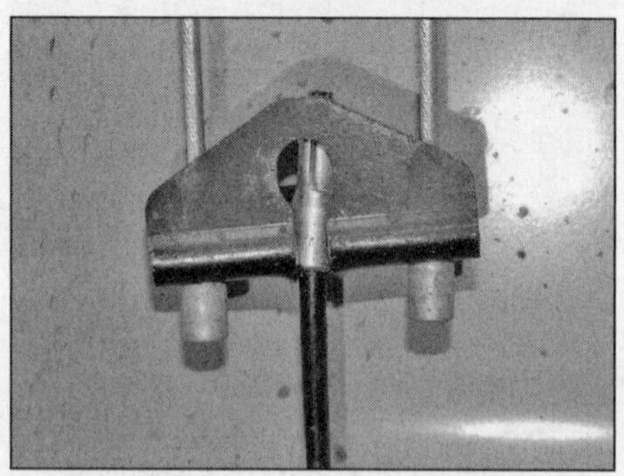
22.10a Disconnect the cables from the equaliser bracket

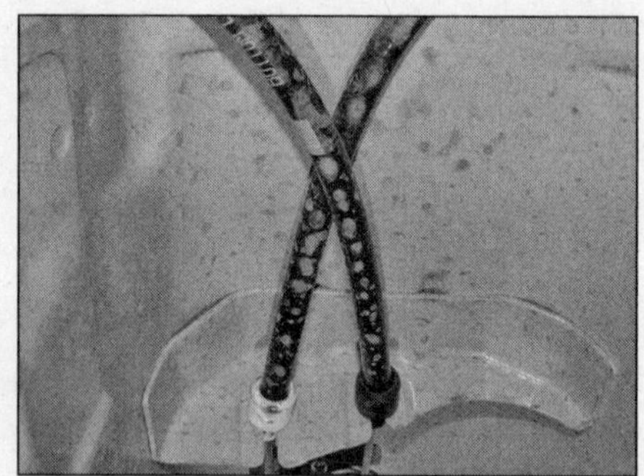
22.10b Note that the cables cross over when fitted correctly

Drum brake models

11 Unbolt the outer cable guide from the tie-bar on both sides **(see illustration)**.

12 Unclip the handbrake cable from the arm both sides. Pull the cable through the tie-bar on both sides.

13 Unclip the cable from the support hangers. Note that there are marks on the cable outer sleeve to indicate the clip positions.

14 Rotate each cable through 90° and detach them from the equaliser, then depress the clips and pull the outer cables from the bracket **(see illustrations 22.10a and 22.10b)**. Withdraw the cables from beneath the vehicle. Note that the left-hand cable has a black sleeve, whilst the right-hand cable has a white sleeve.

Refitting

15 Refitting is a reversal of the removal procedure, noting the following points:

a) Adjust the cable as described in Section 21.

b) Make sure that the cable end fittings are correctly located

c) Check the operation of the handbrake. Make sure that both wheels are locked, then free to turn, as the handbrake is operated.

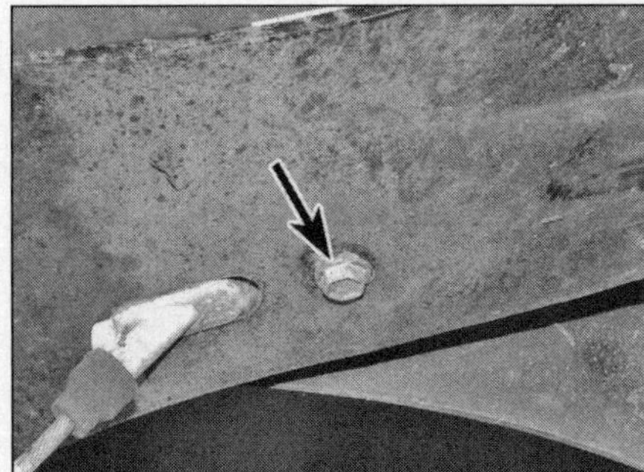

22.11 Undo the bolt (arrowed) securing the handbrake cable to the tie-bar

23.3 The boost pressure solenoid valve – 1.0 litre petrol engine

23.5a Release the brake servo hose...

23.5b ...and disconnect the vacuum hose

23 Vacuum pump – removal and refitting

1 A camshaft driven vacuum pump is fitted to all models except 1.6 Ti-VCT petrol models. The pump primarily supplies vacuum for the brake servo, but it can also supplies vacuum to the various engine controls (depending on model), that are vacuum operated, e.g. the turbocharger wastegate.

Removal

2 Pull up and remove the engine cover.

1.0 litre petrol engines

3 Disconnect the wiring connector, then undo the retaining nuts and remove the turbocharger boost pressure control solenoid valve from the bracket on the brake vacuum pump **(see illustration)**.

4 To improve access remove the air filter housing and associated pipe work – as described in Chapter 4A Section 5.

5 Pull the vacuum hose from the top of vacuum pump, then release the securing clip and disconnect the main vacuum hose to the brake servo unit **(see illustrations)**.

6 Undo the retaining bolts and remove the vacuum pump **(see illustrations)**. Discard the gasket/seal, new ones must be fitted.

Diesel engines

7 To improve access remove the air filter housing and associated pipe work – as described in Chapter 4B Section 2.

23.6a Remove the bolts (arrowed)...

23.6b ...and then remove the pump

23.8a Disconnect the vacuum hose...

23.8b ...and release the brake servo hose

23.9 Remove the two securing nuts

8 Pull the vacuum hose from the top of vacuum pump, then release the securing clip and disconnect the main vacuum hose to the brake servo unit **(see illustrations)**.

9 Undo the retaining nuts and remove the vacuum pump **(see illustration)**. Discard the gasket/seal, new ones must be fitted.

Refitting

10 Refitting is a reversal of removal, noting the following points:

a) Ensure the pump and cylinder head mating surfaces are clean and dry. Fit a new gasket/seal.

*b) Ensure the drive coupling is aligned with the slot in the camshaft **(see illustration 23.6b).***

c) Start the engine and check for correct operation of the pump (check brakes have servo action) as described in Section 15.

d) Make sure all the hose connections are secure, and check for leaks.

Chapter 10
Suspension and steering

Contents

Degrees of difficulty

Easy, suitable for novice with little experience 	**Fairly easy,** suitable for beginner with some experience	**Fairly difficult,** suitable for competent DIY mechanic	**Difficult,** suitable for experienced DIY mechanic	**Very difficult,** suitable for expert DIY or professional

Specifications

Front suspension

Type . . . . Independent, with MacPherson struts incorporating coil springs and telescopic shock absorbers. Anti-roll bar fitted to all models

Rear suspension

Type . . . . Fully-independent, multi-link with separate coil springs and hydraulic telescopic shock absorbers. Anti-roll bar fitted to all models

Steering

Type . . . . Electric power-assisted rack-and-pinion. Hydraulic on some early models

Steering fluid type . . . . See *Lubricants and fluids*

Wheel alignment and steering angles

Front wheel (at curb weight):	
Hatchback models:	
Camber angle	- 0.78° ± 1.25°
Castor angle	4.18° ± 1.00°
Toe setting	0.20° ± 0.20° toe-in
Hatchback Sport models:	
Camber angle	- 0.80° ± 0.75°
Caster angle	4.23° ± 0.75°
Toe setting	0.20° ± 0.20° toe-in
Estate models:	
Camber angle	- 0.78° ± 1.25°
Caster angle	4.01° ± 1.00°
Toe setting	0.20° ± 0.20° toe-in
Estate Sport models:	
Camber angle	- 0.78° ± 1.25°
Caster angle	4.14° ± 1.00°
Toe setting	0.20° ± 0.20° toe-in
Rear wheel (at curb weight):	
Hatchback models:	
Camber angle	- 1.35° ± 1.25°
Toe setting	0.38° ± 0.20° toe-in
Hatchback Sport models:	
Camber angle	- 1.40° ± 1.25°
Toe setting	0.38° ± 0.20° toe-in
Estate models:	
Camber	- 1.23° ± 1.25°
Toe setting	0.38° ± 0.20° toe-in
Estate Sport models:	
Camber angle	- 1.33° ± 1.25°
Toe setting	0.38° ± 0.20° toe-in

Tyres

Tyre pressures	See *Weekly checks*

Torque wrench settings

	Nm	lbf ft
Front suspension		
ABS sensor	10	7
Anti-roll bar clamp bolts*		
Stage 1	115	85
Stage 2	Angle tighten a further 90°	
Anti-roll bar drop link nuts*	48	35
Balljoint-to-control arm bolts	70	52
Balljoint to control arm (pinch bolt)	83	61
Control arm to subframe: *		
Rear bolt		
Stage 1	115	85
Stage 2	Angle tighten a further 90°	
Front bolt		
Stage 1	150	111
Stage 2	Angle tighten a further 90°	
Driveshaft bolt	See Chapter 8	
Lower torque rod bolts (engine side):		
Stage 1	35	26
Stage 2	Loosen 360°	
Stage 3	85	63
Subframe front and rear mounting bolts: *		
Upper	115	85
Front:		
Stage 1	140	103
Stage 2	Angle tighten a further 180°	
Subframe rear mounting brackets 63	46	
Suspension strut piston nut* 55	41	
Suspension strut to hub carrier*		
Stage 1	80	59
Stage 2	Angle tighten a further 180°	
Suspension strut upper mounting/brace to body	35	26

Torque wrench settings (continued)

	Nm	lbf ft
Rear suspension		
Anti-roll bar link to lower control arms	62	45
Anti-roll bar link to lower arm (solid link)	30	22
Anti-roll bar link to anti-roll bar (link with balljoints)	120	89
Anti-roll bar-to-subframe bolts	60	44
Lateral link/hub carrier to body	115	85
Lower control arm to hub carrier	115	85
Lower control arm to subframe	90	66
Rear hub bearing assembly	110	81
Shock absorber lower mounting bolt	115	85
Shock absorber upper mounting nut*	25	18
Shock absorber upper mounting bolts	25	18
Subframe bolts	115	85
Tie-rod bolts	115	85
Upper control arm to hub carrier/lateral link and subframe	115	85
Steering		
Power steering pump bolts	23	17
Steering column mounting bolts*	25	18
Steering rack mounting bolts		
Stage 1	40	30
Stage 2	Angle tighten a further 60°	
Steering rack mounting bolts (EPS)		
Stage 1	110	81
Stage 2	Loosen 360°	
Stage 3	55	41
Stage 4	Angle tighten a further 180°	
Steering wheel bolt	48	35
Steering shaft universal joint pinch-bolt*	28	21
Track rod end balljoint nuts*	48	35
Track rod locknuts	90	66
Roadwheel nuts	135	100

Do not re-use

1 General Information

1 The independent front suspension is of the MacPherson strut type, incorporating coil springs and integral telescopic shock absorbers. The struts are located by transverse control arms, which are attached to the front subframe via rubber bushes at their inner ends, and incorporate a balljoint at their outer ends. The hub carriers, which carry the hub bearings, brake calipers and the hub/disc assemblies, are bolted to the MacPherson struts, and connected to the control arms through the balljoints. A front anti-roll bar is fitted to all models, and is attached to the subframe and to the MacPherson struts via link arms **(see illustration)**.

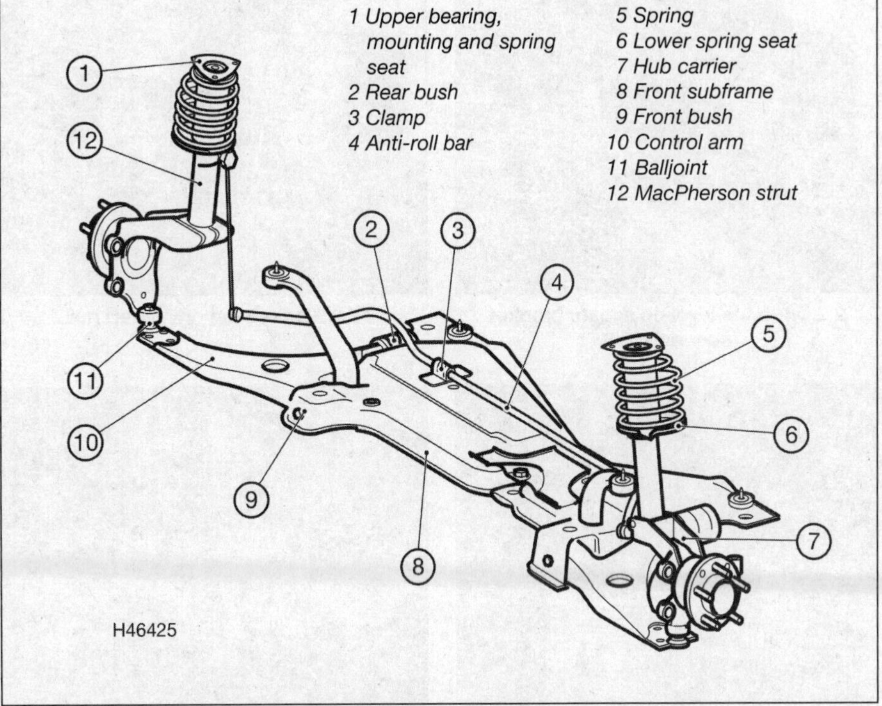

1.1 Front suspension

2 The rear suspension is of the fully independent, multilink type, consisting of an upper and lower control arm mounted via rubber bushes, to the lateral link/hub carrier and rear subframe. The lateral link is attached to the vehicle body at the front end and incorporate the hub carrier at the rear. The assembly is located by a tie rod each side. Coil springs are fitted between the lower control arm and the subframe. Separate hydraulic

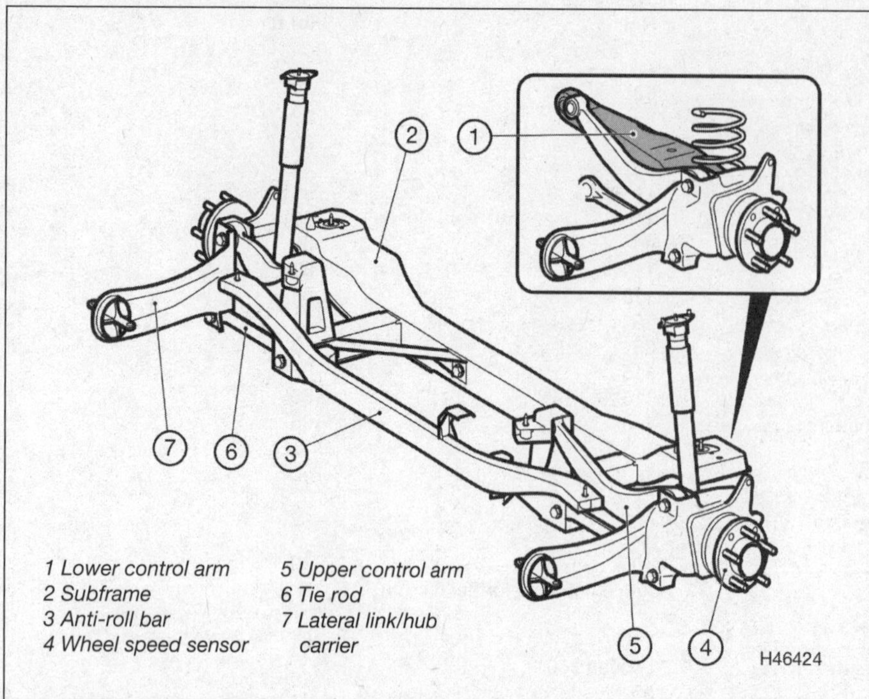

1.2 Rear suspension

telescopic shock absorbers are fitted between the hub carrier between the lower control arm and the vehicle body **(see illustration)**.

3 Power-assisted rack and pinion steering is fitted as standard equipment. On most models, power assistance is derived from an electric motor mounted on the steering rack. This is Ford's first use of Electric Power Steering (EPS) on a production vehicle. Some models use standard power steering with a hydraulic pump driven by the auxiliary drivebelt.

2.2 Undo the leveling sensor bracket securing bolt

2.3 Slacken the driveshaft nut

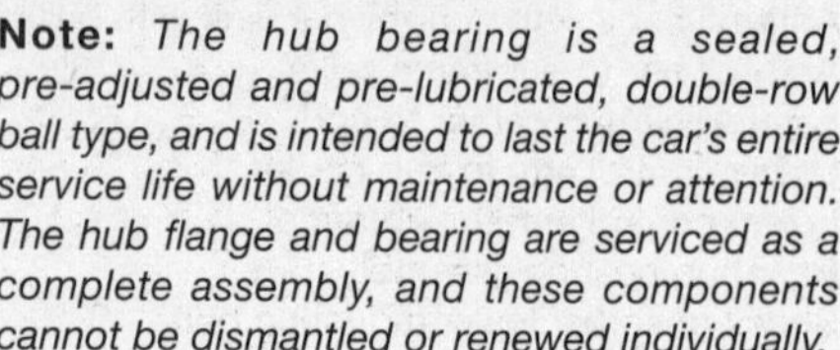

2 Front hub carrier and bearing – removal and refitting

Note: *The hub bearing is a sealed, pre-adjusted and pre-lubricated, double-row ball type, and is intended to last the car's entire service life without maintenance or attention. The hub flange and bearing are serviced as a complete assembly, and these components cannot be dismantled or renewed individually.*

Removal

1 Loosen the appropriate front wheel nuts, then jack up the front of the car and support it on axle stands (see *Jacking and vehicle support*). Remove the appropriate front roadwheel.

2 Undo the bolt securing the headlight levelling sensor bracket to the right-hand front lower arm **(see illustration)**.

3 Slacken and remove the nut securing the driveshaft to the hub **(see illustration).** Have an assistant depress the brake pedal to prevent the hub from rotating. Discard the nut, a new one must be used.

4 Remove the front brake disc as described in Chapter 9 Section 4.

5 Disconnect the wiring plug, undo the bolt and remove the ABS wheel sensor from the hub carrier – refer to Chapter 9 Section 18 if necessary.

6 Undo the retaining nut, then disconnect the steering track rod end balljoint from the hub carrier. If necessary, use a balljoint separator tool **(see illustrations 19.3a and 19.3b)**.

7 Unbolt the brake flexible hose from the suspension strut **(see illustration)**.

8 Tap or press the end of the driveshaft approximately 15 to 20 mm into the wheel hub. The splines on the shaft may be a tight fit in the hub, use a special tool to press the shaft out from the hub, as required.

9 Slacken the lower control arm balljoint bolt and detach the lower control arm balljoint from the hub carrier **(see illustration)**.

10 Pull down on the suspension lower arm using a strong bar to release the balljoint shank from the hub carrier **(see illustration).** Take care not to damage the balljoint dust cover during and after disconnection.

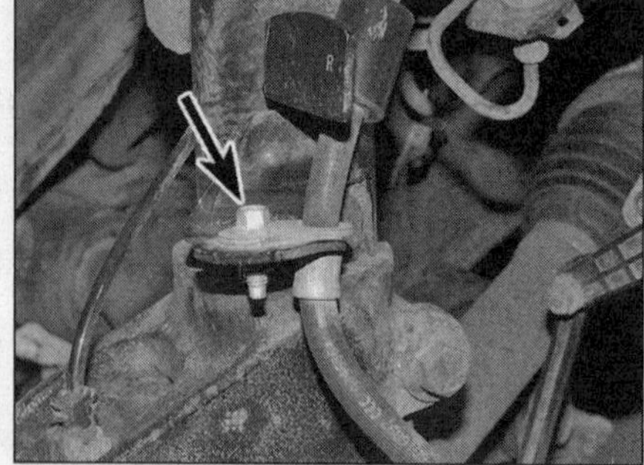

2.7 Undo the brake hose securing bolt

2.9 Undo the lower arm balljoint securing bolt

2.10 Using a bar, block of wood and chain to release the balljoint

2.11 Withdraw the end of the driveshaft from the hub flange

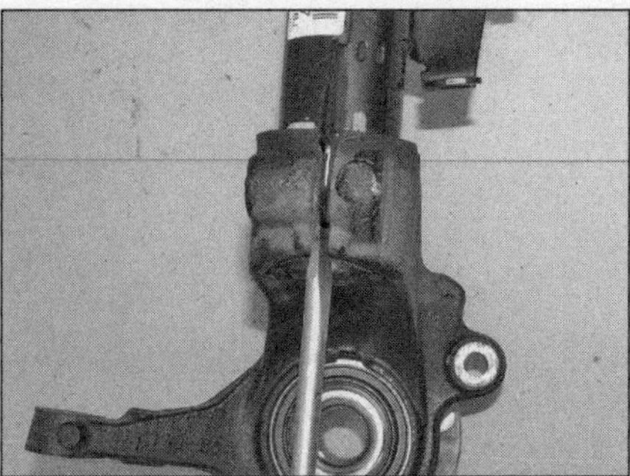

2.12a With the bolt removed, spread the hub carrier slightly using a large screwdriver ...

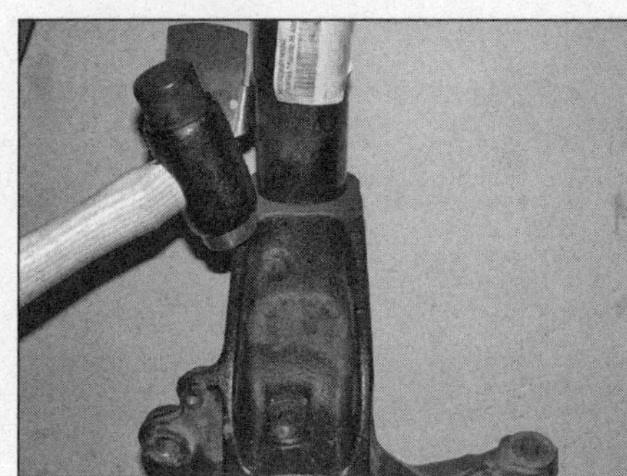

2.12b ... then gently tap the hub carrier downwards from the shock absorber

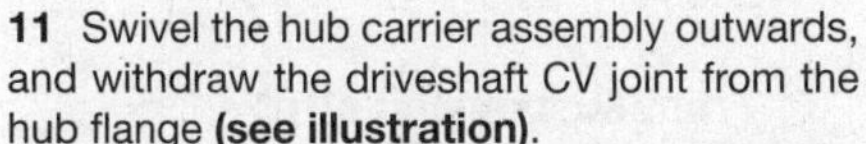

11 Swivel the hub carrier assembly outwards, and withdraw the driveshaft CV joint from the hub flange **(see illustration)**.

12 Remove the bolt securing the hub carrier to the shock absorber. Insert a flat-bladed tool into the gap and very slightly spread the hub carrier where it clamps onto the lower end of the shock absorber. Tap the hub carrier downwards from the shock absorber at the same time. Note which way the bolt is inserted – from the front **(see illustrations)**.

13 The hub and bearing must now be removed from the hub carrier as an assembly. Due to the design of the assembly, we found it impossible to press the new hub/bearing into the carrier without using Ford special tool No 204-348 **(see illustrations)**. The bearing will be rendered unserviceable by removal and cannot be re-used.

Refitting

14 Prior to refitting, remove all traces of metal adhesive, rust, oil and dirt from the splines and threads of the driveshaft outer CV joint and the bearing housing mating surface on the hub carrier.

15 The remainder of refitting is a reversal of removal, but observe the following points:

a) Ensure that the hub and brake disc mating faces are spotlessly clean, and refit the disc with the orientation marks aligned.

b) A new driveshaft retaining bolt should be used.

c) Ensure that the ABS sensor, and the sensor location in the hub carrier, are perfectly clean before refitting.

d) Tighten all nuts and bolts to the specified torque (see Chapter 9 for brake component torque settings).

2.13a Using the Ford special tool to support the hub carrier, press the hub flange and bearing out ...

2.13b ... then assembly the special tool around the new bearing/flange assembly ...

2.13c ... position the hub carrier over the new bearing, and the special tool in place on the hub carrier...

2.13d ... then press the hub carrier ...

2.13e ... fully onto the bearing

3.4a Remove the screws...

3.4b ...and the plastic rivets...

3.4c ...then unclip the two grille panels

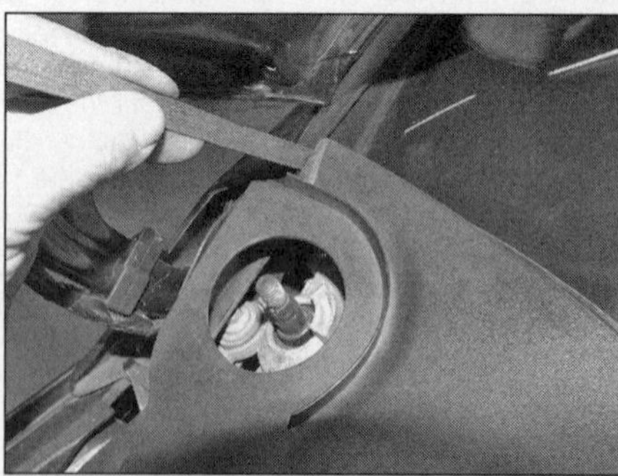
3.5a Unclip the ends of the panel...

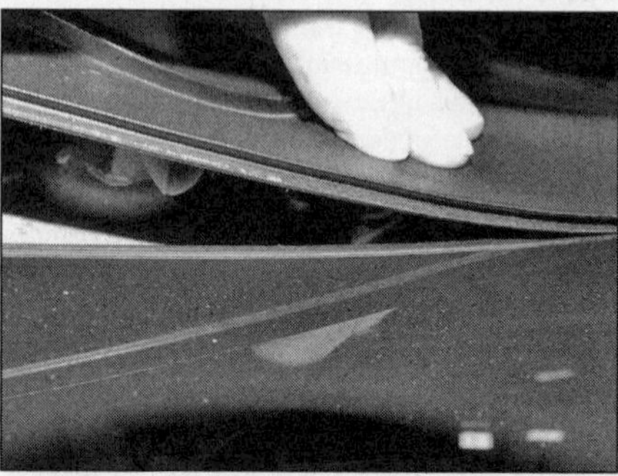
3.5b ...release it from the windscreen seal...

3.5c ...then remove trim panel

3.6a Undo the retaining bolts...

3 Front suspension strut – removal and refitting

Removal

1 Loosen the appropriate front wheel nuts, then jack up the front of the car and support it on axle stands (see *Jacking and vehicle support*). Remove the appropriate front roadwheel.

2 Pull up and remove the engine cover.

3 Remove the wiper arms as described in Chapter 12 Section 11.

4 Undo the retaining screws (one at each end) and plastic rivets along the length of the windscreen cowl panel, then unclip the grille panels **(see illustrations)**.

5 Carefully unclip the both upper ends of the plastic windscreen cowl panel, then carefully release the trim panel from the seal along the lower edge of the windscreen and remove it from the rear of the engine compartment **(see illustrations)**.

6 Undo the retaining bolts and remove the lower metal windscreen panel from the rear of the engine compartment **(see illustrations)**.

7 Undo the nut securing the anti-roll bar link balljoint to the suspension strut. Use an Allen key to counterhold the balljoint shank **(see illustrations)**. A new nut will be required.

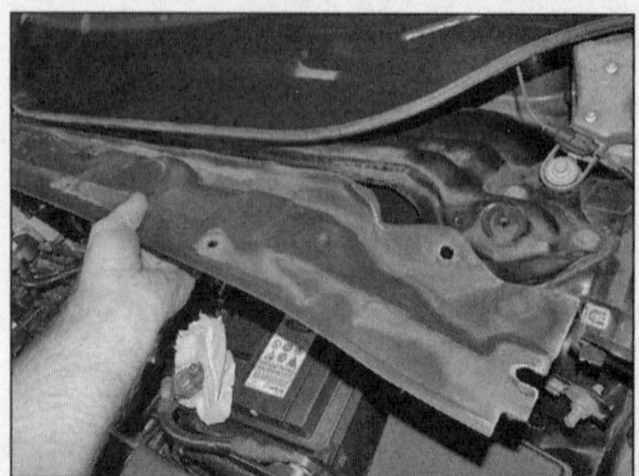
3.6b ...and remove the lower metal panel

3.7a Disconnect the upper part of the link bar...

3.7b ...using an Allen key to counterhold the anti-roll bar link balljoint

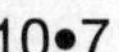

3.8 Unbolt the brake hose bracket

3.10 Undo the 3 bolts from the top of the strut

4.2 Hold the strut piston rod with an Allen key, and slacken the retaining nut

8 Unbolt the brake hose from the bracket on the lower part of the suspension strut **(see illustration)**.

9 Remove the bolt securing the hub carrier to the shock absorber. Insert a flat-bladed tool into the gap and very slightly spread the hub carrier where it clamps onto the lower end of the shock absorber. Tap the hub carrier downwards from the shock absorber at the same time. Note which way the bolt is inserted – from the front **(see illustrations 2.12a and 2.12b)**. A new bolt will be required.

10 Support the strut and remove the bolts from the top of the suspension strut top mounting **(see illustration)**. Dispose of the bolts – they must be replaced. If required, have an assistant support the strut assembly.

11 Manoeuvre the strut out from underneath the wheel arch.

Refitting

12 Refitting is a reversal of removal, but tighten all nuts and bolts to the specified torque, using new nuts/bolts where necessary.

4 Front suspension strut – dismantling, inspection and reassembly

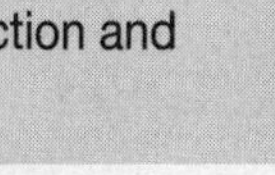

Warning: Before attempting to dismantle the suspension strut, a suitable tool to hold the coil spring in compression must be obtained. Adjustable coil spring compressors which can be positively secured to the spring coils are readily available, and are recommended for this operation. Any attempt to dismantle the strut without such a tool is likely to result in damage or personal injury.

Dismantling

1 Remove the strut from the car as described in Section 3.

2 Slacken the strut mounting nut 1/2 a turn, while holding the protruding portion of the piston rod with an Allen key **(see illustration)**. DO NOT remove the nut completely at this stage.

3 Fit the spring compressors to the coil springs, and tighten the compressors until the load is taken off the spring seats **(see illustration)**.

4 Remove the piston nut, then make alignment marks where the ends of the spring contact the upper and lower seats **(see illustration)**. Discard the nut – a new one must be fitted.

5 Remove the upper mounting/spring seat, bump stop and gaiter followed by the spring **(see illustration)**. Do not attempt to separate the spring seat from the mounting or the bearing balls will fall out.

Inspection

6 With the strut assembly now completely dismantled, examine all the components for wear, damage or deformation. Renew any of the components as necessary.

7 Examine the shock absorber for signs of fluid leakage, and check the strut piston for signs of pitting along its entire length. Test the operation of the shock absorber, while holding it in an upright position, by moving the piston through a full stroke and then through short strokes of 50 to 100 mm. In both cases, the resistance felt should be smooth and continuous. If the resistance is jerky, or uneven, or if there is any visible sign of wear or damage, renewal is necessary.

8 If any doubt exists about the condition of the coil spring, gradually release the spring compressor, and check the spring for distortion and signs of cracking. Since no minimum free length is specified by Ford, the only way to check the tension of the spring is to compare it to a new component. Renew the spring if it is damaged or distorted, or if there is any doubt as to its condition.

9 Inspect all other components for signs of damage or deterioration, and renew any that are suspect.

10 If a new shock absorber is being fitted, hold it vertically and pump the piston a few times to prime it.

Reassembly

11 Reassembly is a reversal of dismantling, but ensure that the spring is fully compressed before fitting. Make sure that the spring ends are correctly located in the upper and lower

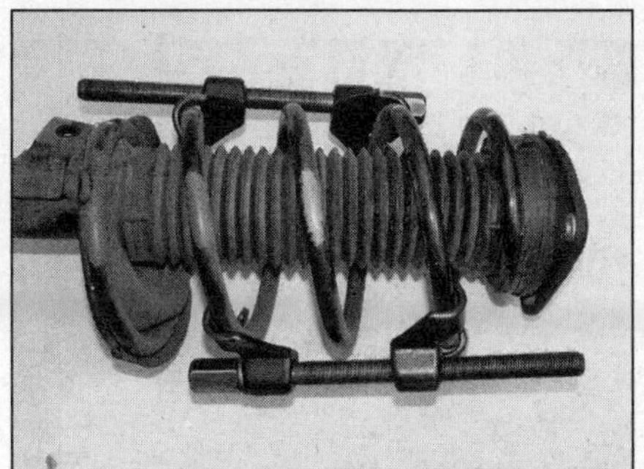

4.3 Fit the compressors to the springs

4.4 Make alignment marks between the spring and seats

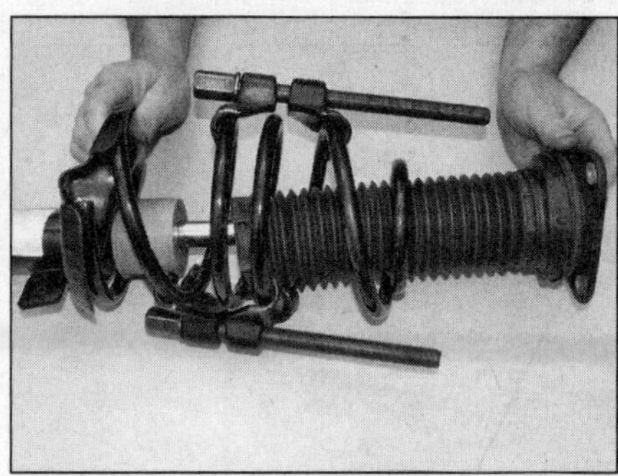

4.5 With the springs fully compressed, remove the mounting/seat/bump stop and gaiter, followed by the spring

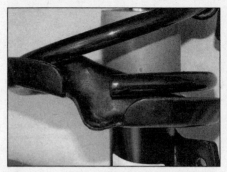

4.11a Ensure the spring ends are correctly located in their seats

seats, aligning the marks made on removal, then tighten the new shock absorber piston retaining nut and strut mounting bolts to the specified torque **(see illustrations)**.

5 Front suspension control arm and balljoint – removal, overhaul and refitting

Balljoint

Note: *At the time of writing Ford do not supply the balljoint separately from the control arm. However replacements are available from after market suppliers.*

Removal

1 Loosen the appropriate front wheel nuts. Chock the rear wheels and apply the handbrake, then jack up the front of the vehicle

4.11b Tighten the new piston rod nut to the specified torque

and support it on axle stands (see *Jacking and vehicle support*). Remove the appropriate front roadwheel, then release the fasteners and remove the engine undershield (where fitted).

2 Undo the bolt securing the headlight levelling sensor bracket to the control arm (where fitted).

3 Slacken the nut until it is level with the end of the balljoint shank, then using a balljoint separator tool, detach the suspension control arm balljoint from the hub carrier. Use an Allen key in the end of the balljoint shank to prevent it from rotating as the nut is slackened. Discard the nut – a new one must be fitted.

4 Use a stout bar to lever the control arm downwards and over the end of the balljoint shank. Take care not to damage the balljoint dust cover during and after disconnection.

5 If the original balljoint is being removed, use a drill to remove the 3 balljoint-to-control arm retaining rivets **(see illustrations)**. Pull the balljoint from the control arm.

6 If the balljoint being removed is not the original, undo the 3 bolts and pull the balljoint from the control arm.

Refitting

7 New balljoints should be supplied with suitable retaining bolts. Position the new balljoint in the end of the control arm, insert the bolts from underneath, and tighten the nuts to the specified torque **(see illustrations)**.

8 The remainder of refitting is a reversal of removal. Tighten all fasteners to their specified torque, where given.

Control arm

Removal

9 Proceed as described in Paragraphs 1 to 4.

10 Undo the two bolts securing the control arm rear mounting and the single bolt securing the front mounting and manoeuvre the control arm from under the vehicle **(see illustrations)**. Discard the bolts, new one must be fitted.

Overhaul

11 Thoroughly clean the control arm and the area around the control arm mountings. Inspect the arm for any signs of cracks, damage or distortion, and carefully check the inner pivot bushes for signs of swelling, cracks or deterioration of the rubber.

12 If either bush requires renewal, the work should be entrusted to a Ford dealer or specialist. A hydraulic press and suitable

5.5a Drill out the 3 rivets ...

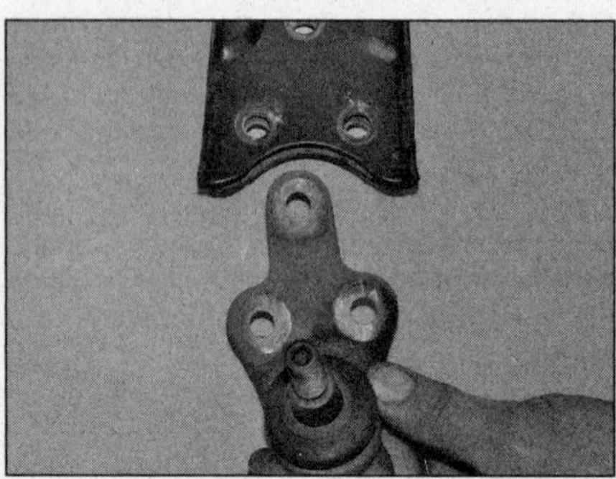

5.5b ... and pull the balljoint from the control arm

5.7a Insert the bolts from the underside of the control arm ...

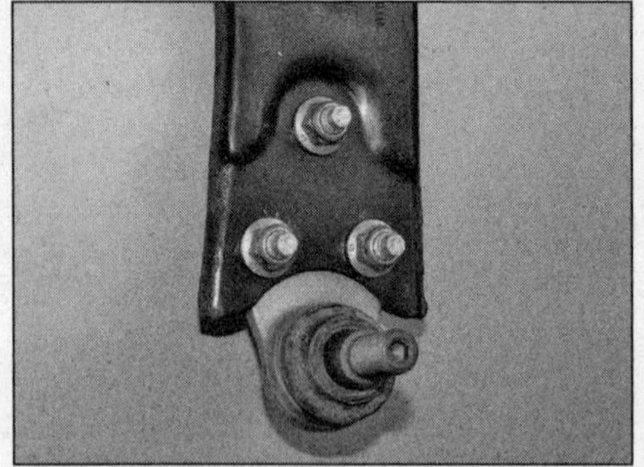

5.7b ... and fit the self-locking nuts on the upper side

5.10a Control arm rear mounting bolts (arrowed) ...

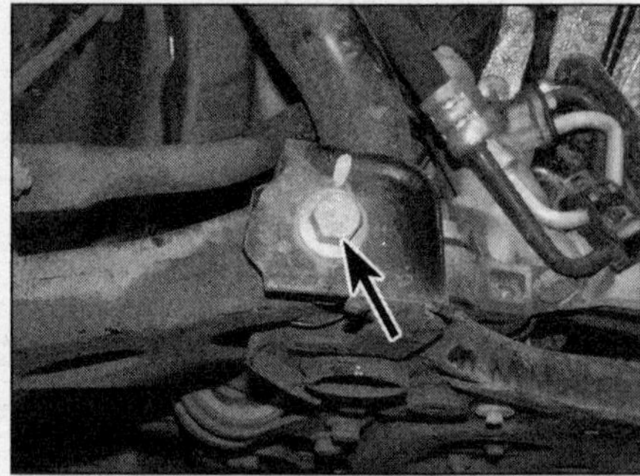

5.10b ... and front mounting bolt (arrowed)

6.1 Undo the fasteners (arrowed) and remove the engine undershield

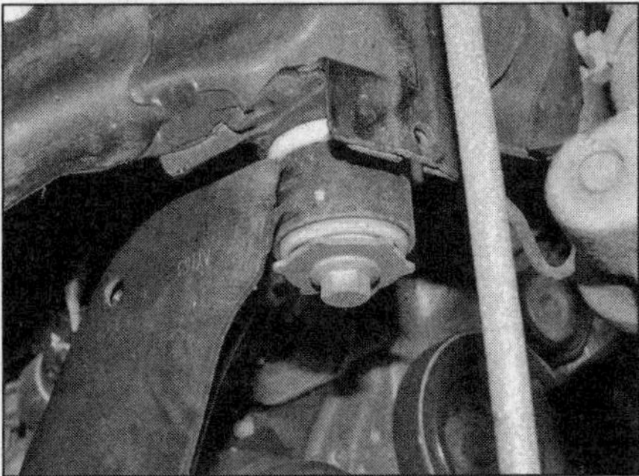
6.11 Slacken the subframe front mounting bolt each side, about 6 turns

6.12 Undo the subframe rear mounting bolts (arrowed)

spacers are required to remove and refit the bushes and a setting gauge is needed for accurate positioning of the bushes in the arm.

Refitting

13 Locate the arm in its mountings, and starting at the rear, fit the new mounting bolts finger-tight only. Fully tighten the rear bolts to the specified torque.

14 Engage the balljoint shank in the control arm, then tighten the new nut to the specified torque.

15 Place an axle stand under the control arm and then raise the vehicle on the jack, so that the original axle stand can be removed. If not already done so as a safety measure, place the road wheel under the sill next to the jack. Carefully lower the jack so that the weight of the vehicle comes onto the axle stand under the control arm. When all the weight of the vehicle is on the control arm tighten the rear bolt of the control arm to the specified torque.

16 The remainder of refitting is a reversal of removal. Have the front wheel alignment checked at the earliest opportunity.

6 Front anti-roll bar – removal and refitting

Removal

1 Loosen the appropriate front wheel nuts. Chock the rear wheels and apply the handbrake, then jack up the front of the vehicle and support it on axle stands (see *Jacking and vehicle support*). Remove the appropriate front roadwheel, then release the fasteners and remove the engine undershield (where fitted) **(see illustration)**

2 Slacken the nut until it is level with the end of the balljoint shank, then using a balljoint separator tool, detach the suspension control arm balljoint from the hub carrier. Use an Allen key in the end of the balljoint shank to prevent it from rotating as the nut is slackened.

3 Use a stout bar to lever the control arm downwards and over the end of the balljoint shank. Take care not to damage the balljoint dust cover during and after disconnection.

4 Ensure the wheels are in the straight-ahead position, then working under the facia, undo and remove the steering column lower universal joint pinch-bolt **(see illustration 14.8)**. Discard the bolt – a new one must be fitted.

5 Undo the nut each side securing the lower end of the anti-roll bar links to the bar. Use a Torx bit to counterhold the nut.

6 Undo the nut and detach the track rod end balljoint from the hub carrier each side, using a balljoint separator tool as described in Section 19.

7 Undo the bolt at the lower rear of the engine securing the lower torque rod to the bracket on the transmission/engine.

8 Attach splints each side of the exhaust flexible section (two wooden strips secured by cable tie will suffice) to prevent excessive bending, then undo the bolts/nuts securing the centre exhaust section to the front section.

9 Unhook the exhaust mounting rubbers at the front.

10 Position a sturdy trolley jack beneath, and in contact with, the rear of the subframe.

11 Undo the bolt each side securing the front of the subframe to the body approximately 6 turns **(see illustration)**. Note that new subframe front mounting bolts will be required for refitting.

12 Undo the bolts each side securing the rear mounting brackets to the subframe and vehicle body, and recover the washers **(see illustration)**. Note that new subframe mounting bolts will be required for refitting.

13 Carefully lower the jack and allow the subframe to drop slightly at the rear, so that the anti-roll bar clamp bolts are accessible. On models fitted with hydraulic power steering take care not to damage the power steering hoses.

14 Undo the bolts securing the anti-roll bar clamps on each side of the subframe, and manipulate the anti-roll bar out from under the car **(see illustration)**. Discard the bolts, new ones must be fitted.

15 Examine the anti-roll bar for signs of damage or distortion, and the connecting links and mounting bushes for signs of deterioration of the rubber. The bushes are split along their length and must be fitted in their original positions **(see illustration)**.

Refitting

16 Manipulate the anti-roll bar into position on the subframe. Fit the new clamp bolts and tighten to the specified torque.

17 Raise the subframe at the rear, fit the rear mounting brackets to the body, and tighten the bolts (new where applicable) hand-tight only at this stage.

18 The alignment of the subframe must be checked by inserting round tools can be inserted through the holes in the side members. Ford tools (part No 205-880) may

6.14 Anti-roll bar clamp bolts (arrowed)

6.15 The anti-roll bar bushes are split to facilitate renewal, and are shaped to fit the bar profile

6.18 Align the front subframe by inserting aligning tools (arrowed) through the holes in the subframe into the corresponding holes in the vehicle body

be available. Alternatively, using two lengths of wooden dowel, 20 mm in diameter, and approximately 150 mm in length **(see illustration)**.

19 With the subframe correctly aligned, fit new front subframe mounting bolts, and tighten all subframe bolts to the specified torque.

20 The remainder of refitting is a reversal of removal. Have the front wheel alignment checked at the earliest opportunity.

7 Rear hub bearings – renewal

1 The rear hub bearings cannot be renewed separately, and are supplied with the rear hub as a complete assembly.

2 Remove the brake disc or drum (as applicable) as described in Chapter 9 Section 5 or 10.

3 Undo the bolt and remove the ABS wheel speed sensor from the hub carrier, as described in Chapter 9 Section 18.

4 Undo the four Torx bolts and withdrawn the bearing assembly from the hub carrier.

5 Fit the new assembly to the hub carrier then insert and tighten the bolts to the specified torque.

6 Refit the ABS wheel speed sensor and brake disc or drum.

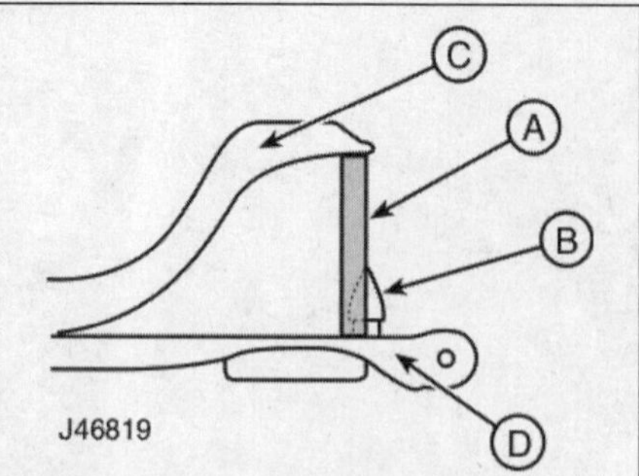

8.7 Remove the bump stop (B), and insert the spacer (A) between the lower control arm (D) and the spring upper seat (C)

8 Rear hub carrier/lateral link – removal and refitting

Removal

1 Remove the rear hub as described in the previous Section. On models with disc brakes, unbolt and remove the disc shield.

2 Undo the bolt securing the handbrake cable retaining clip to the lateral link, then unhook the cable from the connecting sleeve. Pull the cable through the lateral link/hub carrier.

3 Unclip the brake hose from the hub carrier.

4 Unclip the handbrake cable from the hub carrier.

5 Release the ABS wheel speed sensor wiring harness from the clips on the lateral link.

6 Remove the relevant rear coil spring as described in Section 10.

7 Fabricate a spacer, 40 mm in diameter, and 179 mm long. Unscrew the suspension bump stop, insert the spacer between the lower control arm and the coil spring upper seat, then raise the lower control arm with a trolley jack until the spacer is lightly trapped **(see illustration)**. Ensure the spacer is vertical.

8 Undo the fasteners and remove the air baffle plate from the relevant side **(see illustration)**.

9 Undo the retaining bolt and withdraw the ABS wheel sensor from hub carrier/lateral link. Do not disconnect the wheel sensor wiring plug.

8.8 Remove the air baffle plate (arrowed)

10 Undo the bolts securing the upper control arm and tie rod to the lateral link/hub carrier **(see illustrations 11.4 and 11.10b)**.

11 Undo the bolt and detach the lower control arm from the lateral link/hub carrier **(see illustration 11.14a)**.

12 Undo the 2 bolts securing the front mounting to the vehicle body, and withdrawn the lateral link from under the vehicle **(see illustration)**.

13 Renewal of the bush at the front of the lateral link requires the use of special tools. With the front of the arm lowered from the vehicle body, a special tool can be used to push the bush from the lateral link arm **(see illustrations)**. if this work is carried out whilst the lateral arm is still fitted to the vehicle, take care there is no stress/damage to any wiring, brake hoses/pipes or handbrake cables, as the arm is lowered.

Refitting

14 Manoeuvre the lateral link into position and tighten the 2 front mounting bolts to the specified torque.

15 Refit the ABS wheel speed sensor wiring harness clips to the link.

16 Position the handbrake cable and refit the cable retaining clip.

17 Refit the upper control arm, lower control arm and tie rod, but don't tighten the bolts yet.

18 Ensure the fabricated spacer (paragraph 7) is still in place between the lower control arm and the spring seat **(see illustration 8.7)**.

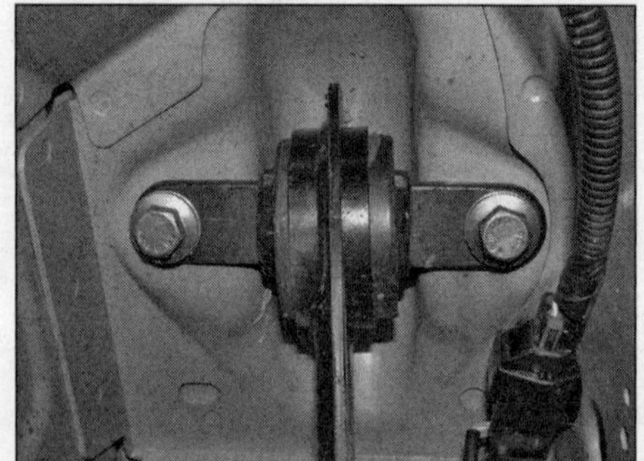
8.12 Lateral link/hub carrier front mounting bolts

8.13a Using special tool...

8.13b ...to remove the front bush

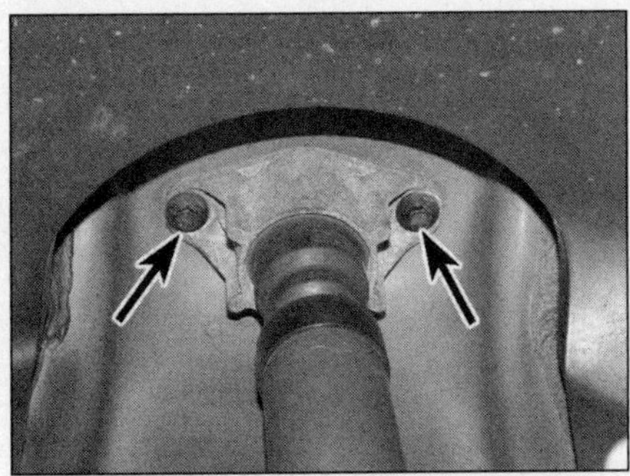
9.3 Shock absorber upper mounting bolts (arrowed)

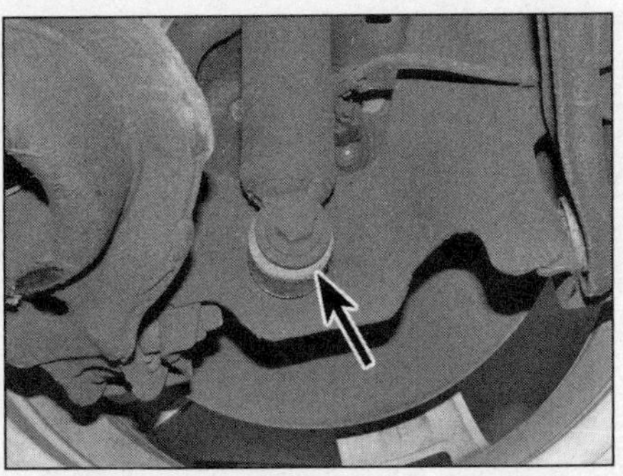
9.4 Shock absorber lower mounting bolt (arrowed)

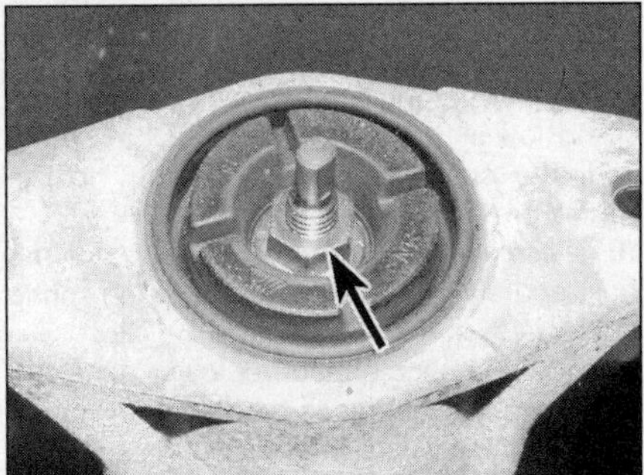
9.5 Undo the shock absorber upper mounting nut (arrowed)

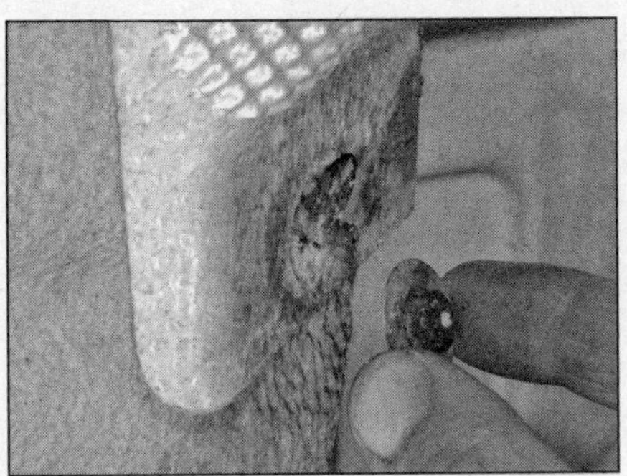
9.7 Undo the nuts securing the heat shield

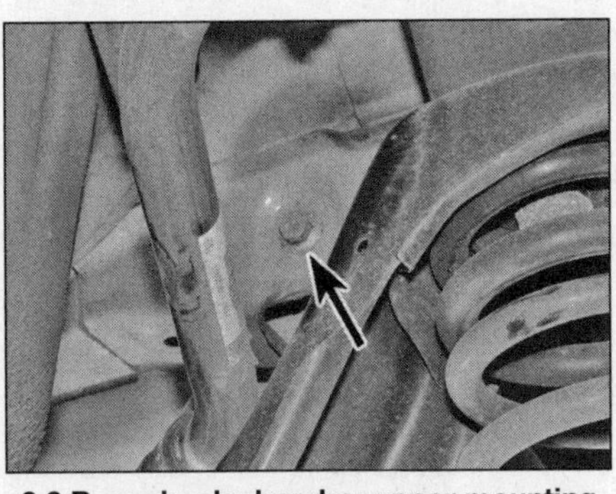
9.8 Rear shock absorber upper mounting bolt (arrowed)

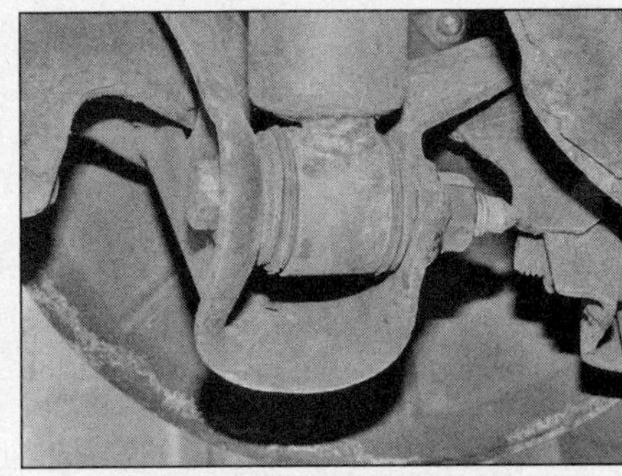
9.9 Rear shock absorber lower mounting bolt

19 Tighten the upper control arm, lower control arm and tie rod bolts to their specified torque. Remove the spacer, and refit the bump stop.

20 The remainder of refitting is a reversal of removal. Have the rear wheel alignment checked at the earliest opportunity.

9 Rear shock absorber – removal and refitting

Removal

1 Slacken the rear roadwheel nuts, then chock the front wheels then jack up the rear of the vehicle and support it on axle stands (see *Jacking and vehicle support*). Remove the rear wheels.

2 Place a trolley jack under the hub carrier and raise the suspension a little to take the load off the shock absorber.

Hatchback models

3 Undo the 2 bolts securing the upper end of the shock absorber to the vehicle body **(see illustration)**.

4 Undo the lower mounting bolt, and pull the shock absorber from the hub carrier **(see illustration)**.

5 If required, undo the nut and pull the upper mounting from the shock absorber **(see illustration)**.

6 Check the condition of the shock absorber and renew as necessary.

Estate models

7 If removing the left-hand shock absorber, unhook the rear silencer from the rubber mountings, undo the fasteners, and remove the exhaust heat shield **(see illustration)**.

8 Undo the shock absorber upper mounting bolt **(see illustration)**.

9 Undo and remove the shock absorber lower mounting bolt **(see illustration)**. Manoeuvre the shock absorber from under the vehicle.

Refitting

10 Refitting is a reversal of removal, tightening all nuts and bolts to the specified torques.

10 Rear coil spring – removal and refitting

Removal

1 Slacken the road wheel nuts, then chock the front wheels and raise the rear of the vehicle. Support it securely on axle stands (see *Jacking and vehicle support*). Remove the roadwheels.

2 Undo the nut securing the anti-roll bar link to the lower control arm **(see illustration 12.2)**.

3 Position a trolley jack under the hub carrier, and take the weight.

4 Remove the shock absorber lower mounting bolt.

5 Attach spring compressors to the spring and compress the spring. Ford specify tools No 204-167 and 204-167-01. Alternative spring compressors may be available **(see illustration)**.

6 Remove the trolley jack, and remove the spring.

7 Examine all the components for wear or damage, and renew as necessary.

Refitting

8 Refit the rubbers seats to the control arm

10.5 Remove the rear springs using spring compressors

and spring, ensuring the ends of the spring locate correctly **(see illustrations)**.

9 Refit the compressed spring onto the seat in the lower control arm. Rotate the spring until the spring engages correctly in the control arm grooves.

10 Raise the control arm by means of the jack, and engage the upper end of the spring in its recess in the body.

11 Refit the shock absorber lower mounting bolt, securing it in place before removing the jack. Tighten all nuts and bolts to the specified torque.

12 Release and remove the spring compressor.

13 Remainder of refitting is a reversal of removal.

10.8a The lug (arrowed) on the underside of the seat must locate in the hole in the arm

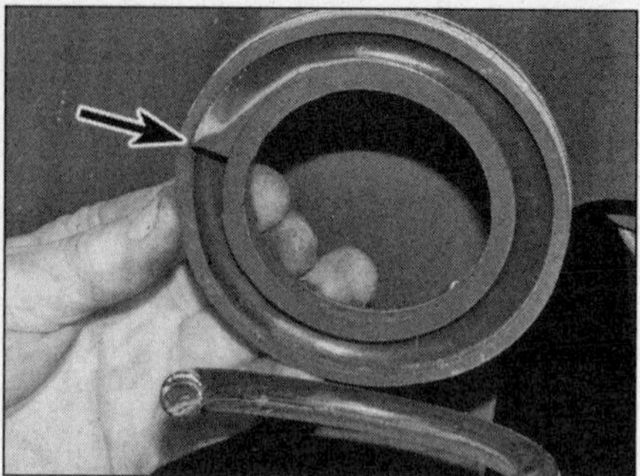

10.8b The end of the spring must fit against the stop in the rubber seat (arrowed)

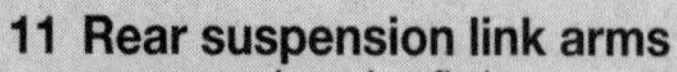

11 Rear suspension link arms – removal and refitting

Removal

1 Loosen the rear wheel bolts. Chock the front wheels, then jack up the rear of the vehicle and support it on axle stands (see *Jacking and vehicle support*). Remove the appropriate rear roadwheel(s).

Tie-rod – Hatchback models

2 Remove the rear spring as described in Section 10.

3 Fabricate a spacer, 40 mm in diameter, and 179 mm long. Unscrew the suspension bump stop, insert the spacer between the lower control arm and the coil spring upper seat, then raise the lower control arm with a trolley jack until the spacer is lightly trapped **(see illustration 8.7)**. Ensure the spacer is vertical.

4 Undo the outer and inner bolts, then remove the tie-rod **(see illustration)**. Note that the tie-rod is marked FRONT on one side.

Tie-rod – Estate models

5 Remove the rear spring as described in Section 10.

6 Fabricate a spacer, 40 mm in diameter, and 179 mm long. Insert the spacer between the lower control arm and the coil spring upper seat, then raise the lower control arm with a trolley jack until the spacer is lightly trapped **(see illustration 8.7)**. Ensure the spacer is vertical.

7 Undo the outer and inner bolts, then remove the tie-rod **(see illustration 11.4)**. Note that the tie-rod is marked FRONT on one side.

Upper control arm – Hatchback models

8 Remove the rear spring as described in Section 10.

9 Fabricate a spacer, 40 mm in diameter, and 179 mm long. Unscrew the suspension bump stop, insert the spacer between the lower control arm and the coil spring upper seat, then raise the lower control arm with a trolley jack until the spacer is lightly trapped **(see illustration 8.7)**. Ensure the spacer is vertical.

10 Undo the outer and inner bolts, then remove the control arm **(see illustrations)**.

Upper control arm – Estate models

11 Fabricate a spacer, 40 mm in diameter, and 179 mm long. Insert the spacer between the lower control arm and the coil spring upper seat, then raise the lower control arm with a trolley jack until the spacer is lightly trapped **(see illustration 8.7)**. Ensure the spacer is vertical.

12 Undo the outer and inner bolts, then remove the control arm **(see illustrations 11.10a and 11.10b)**.

Lower control arm

13 Remove the coil spring as described in Section 10.

14 Mark the position of the inner bolt eccentric washer in relation to the arm, then undo the inner and outer control arm bolts, rotate the anti-roll bar approximately 30° and remove the control arm **(see illustrations)**.

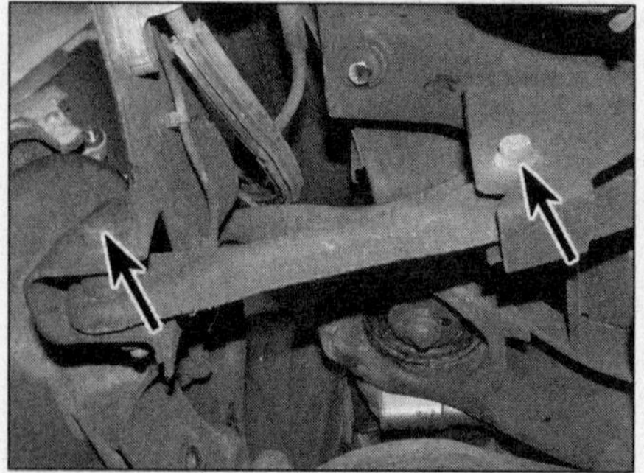

11.4 Tie-rod mounting bolts (arrowed)

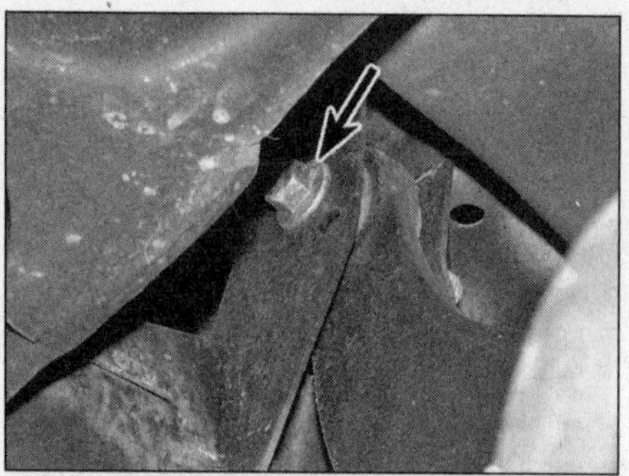

11.10a Upper control arm inner bolt (arrowed) ...

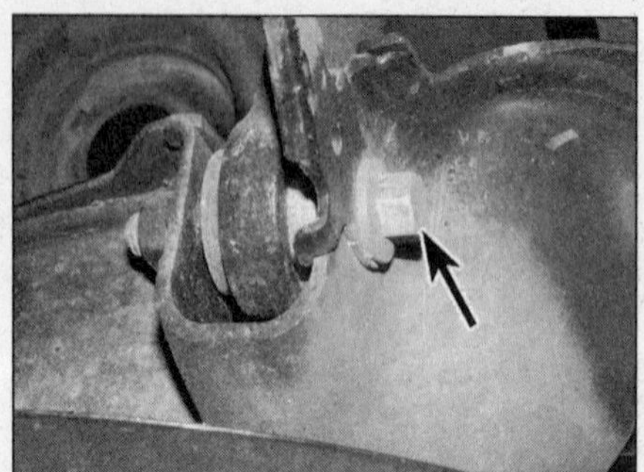

11.10b ... and outer bolt (arrowed)

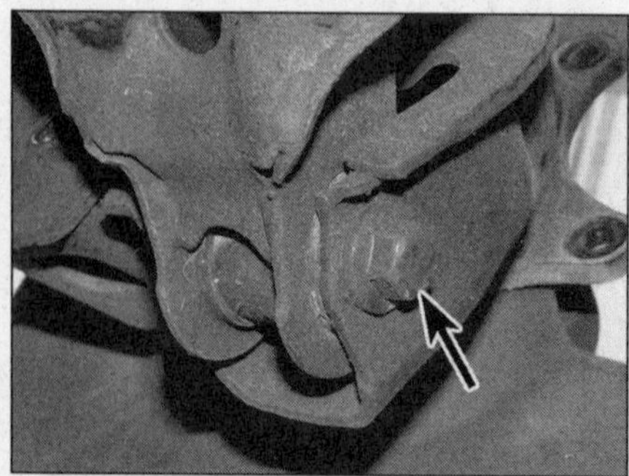

11.14a Undo the lower control arm outer bolt (arrowed) ...

11.14b ... then mark the position of the eccentric washer (arrowed) and remove the bolt

15 Examine the condition of the metal-elastic bushes in the control arm. If renewal is necessary, the bushes must be pressed from the arm and new ones pressed into place. This necessitates the use of an hydraulic press. Entrust this task to a Ford dealer or suitably-equipped garage.

Refitting

16 Refitting any of the control arms/tie rods is essentially a reversal of removal, noting the following points:

a) *Tighten all fasteners to their specified torque where given, using a little thread-locking compound.*
b) *Before tightening any control arm/tie rod mounting bolts, ensure the suspension is in the 'normal' position using the fabricated spacers as described in the removal procedures.*

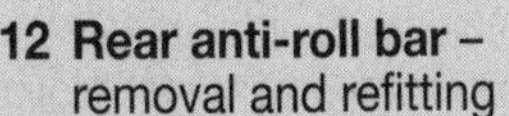

12 Rear anti-roll bar – removal and refitting

Removal

1 Chock the front wheels, then jack up the rear of the vehicle and support it on axle stands (see *Jacking and vehicle support*).

2 Undo the nuts securing the outer ends of the anti-roll bar to the links **(see illustration)**. Take care not to damage the rubber boots.

3 Undo the bolts securing the anti-roll bar clamps to the subframe, manoeuvre the anti-roll bar from under the vehicle **(see illustration)**.

4 Examine the anti-roll bar for signs of damage or distortion, and the connecting links and mounting bushes for signs of deterioration of the rubber. The bushes are split along their length and must be fitted in their original positions.

Refitting

5 Position the anti-roll bar, then fit and tighten the bolts securing the anti-roll bar clamps to the subframe.

6 Refit the anti-roll bar links and tighten the nuts to the specified torque, using a Torx bit to counterhold the nuts.

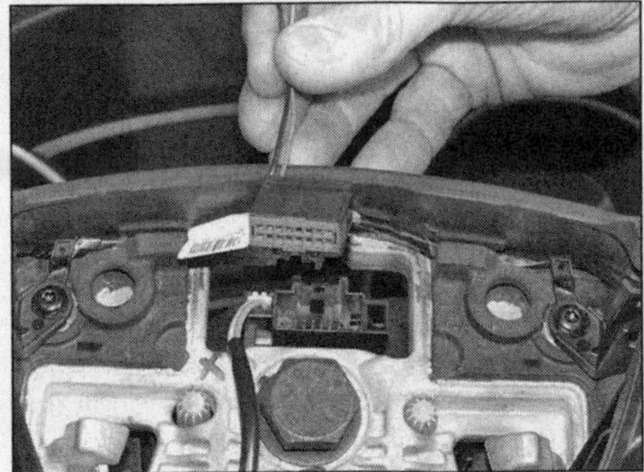

13.3 Steering wheel retaining bolt (arrowed)

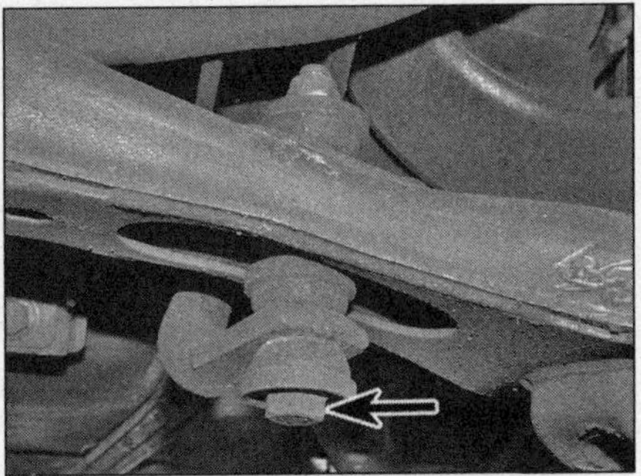

12.2 Rear anti-roll bar-to-control arm bolt (arrowed)

7 The remainder of refitting is a reversal of removal.

13 Steering wheel – removal and refitting

Warning: Handle the airbag unit with extreme care as a precaution against personal injury, and always hold it with the cover facing away from the body. If in doubt concerning any proposed work involving the airbag unit or its control circuitry, consult a Ford dealer.

Removal

1 Drive the car forwards, and park it with the front wheels in the straight-ahead position.

2 Remove the driver's airbag as described in Chapter 12 Section 22. Secure the rotary contact unit in place using tape to prevent any rotation.

3 Disconnect the wiring plug at the top of the steering wheel aperture, then undo the steering wheel centre retaining bolt **(see illustration)**.

4 Make alignment marks between the steering wheel centre and the column shaft **(see illustration)**, then lift the steering wheel off the column shaft, and feed the wiring through the hole in the wheel, as it is removed.

Refitting

5 Ensure that the front wheels are still in the straight-ahead position.

13.4 Make alignment marks

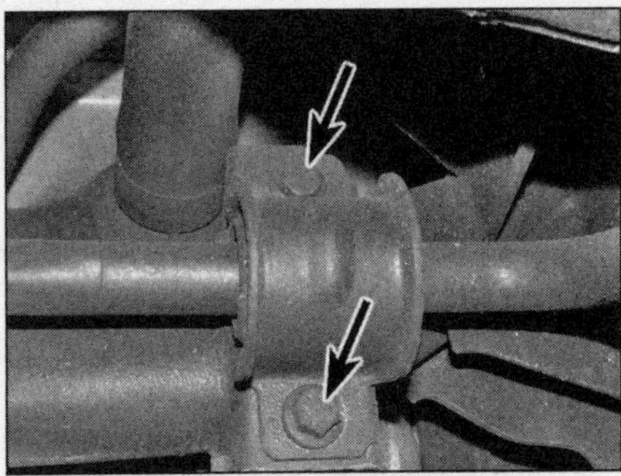

12.3 Undo the bolts (arrowed) securing the anti-roll bar clamps

6 Check the airbag rotary contact unit is still aligned. Refer to Chapter 12 Section 22, if necessary.

7 Feed the wiring through the hole in the steering wheel, then engage the wheel with the steering column shaft. Ensure that the marks made on removal are aligned, and that the pegs on the contact reel engage with the recesses on the steering wheel hub.

8 Refit the steering wheel retaining bolt, and tighten it to the specified torque.

9 Refit the airbag unit to the steering wheel as described in Chapter 12 Section 22.

14 Steering column – removal and refitting

Removal

1 Disconnect the battery negative lead – see Chapter 5A Section 3.

2 Fully extend and then lower the steering column.

3 Undo the fasteners and remove the lower facia panel on the driver's side – see Chapter 11 Section 30.

4 Turn the steering wheel for access, then release the retaining clips and remove the steering column upper shroud **(see illustration)**. Turn the steering wheel back to the straight-ahead position.

5 Undo the 2 retaining screws, in the recesses

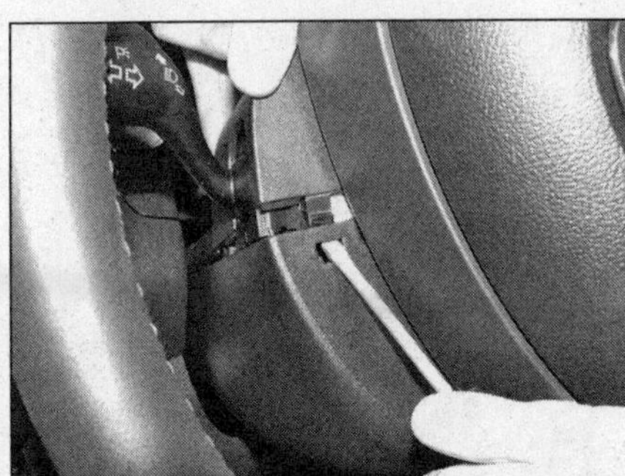

14.4 Release the clip each side securing the column upper shroud to the lower

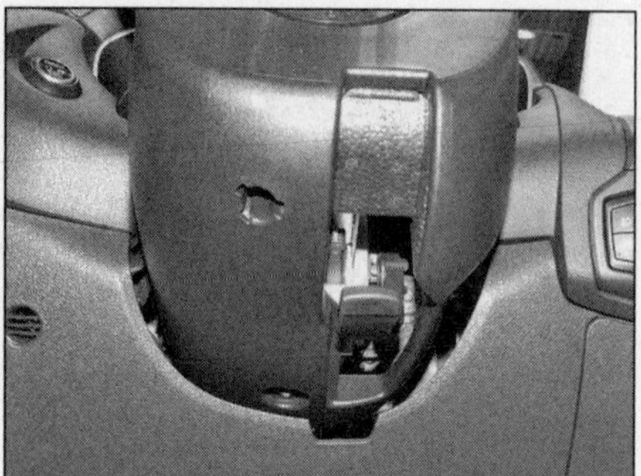

14.5 Undo the screws securing the column lower shroud

14.8 Steering column lower pinch-bolt (arrowed)

14.9 Steering column mounting bolts (arrowed)

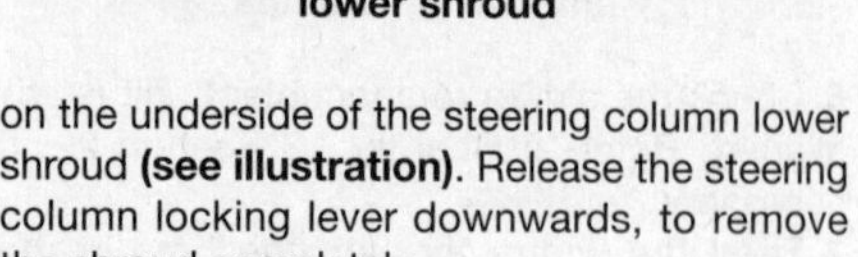

on the underside of the steering column lower shroud **(see illustration)**. Release the steering column locking lever downwards, to remove the shroud completely.

6 Remove the steering wheel as described in Section 13.

7 Note their fitted positions and routing, then disconnect the various column wiring plugs and release the loom retaining clips.

8 Undo the steering column lower pinch-bolt and pull the joint upwards from the pinion **(see illustration)**. Ensure the column adjustment lever is released before detaching the joint from the pinion. Discard the pinch-bolt, a new one must be fitted.

9 Undo the 4 retaining bolts and manoeuvre the column from the vehicle **(see illustration)**. Discard the bolts, new ones must be fitted.

10 If required, drill out the security bolts, and remove the steering lock from the column. No further dismantling of the assembly is recommended.

Refitting

11 Refitting is a reversal of removal, bearing in mind the following points:

a) *Lubricate universal joint splines with grease before engaging the steering column.*

b) *When fitting the new column retaining bolts, the shortest bolts are nearest the bulkhead.*

c) *Use a new universal joint pinch-bolt.*

d) *If refitting the steering lock, tighten the new security bolts until their heads snap off.*

e) *If the steering column has been rotated, or the front wheels turned from straight-ahead, reset the airbag contact reel as described in Chapter 12 Section 22.*

15 Steering rack – removal and refitting

Removal

1 Drive the car forwards and park it with the steering wheels in the straight-ahead position. Remove the ignition key to lock the steering in this position.

2 Remove the lower facia panel on the driver's side as described in Chapter 11 Section 30.

3 Remove the steering column pinch-bolt and pull the joint upwards from the pinion **(see illustration 14.8)**. Ensure the column adjustment lever is released before detaching the joint from the pinion. Discard the pinch-bolt, a new one must be fitted.

4 Loosen the front wheel nuts. Chock the rear wheels then jack up the front of the vehicle and support it on axle stands (see *Jacking and vehicle support*). Remove both front roadwheels.

5 Undo the fasteners and remove the engine undershield **(see illustration 6.1)**.

6 Undo the bolt securing the headlight levelling sensor bracket to the lower control arm (where applicable).

7 On some models, disconnect the steering angle sensor wiring plug (located at the steering column pinion in the engine compartment).

8 Attach splints each side of the exhaust flexible section (two wooden strips secured by cable tie will suffice) to prevent excessive bending, then undo the bolts/nuts securing the centre exhaust section to the front section.

9 Unhook the exhaust mounting rubbers at the front.

10 Slacken the nut until it is level with the end of the balljoint shank, then using a balljoint separator tool, detach the suspension control arm balljoint from the hub carrier. Use an Allen key in the end of the balljoint shank to prevent it from rotating as the nut is slackened **(see illustration 2.8)**.

11 Use a stout bar to lever the control arm downwards and over the end of the balljoint shank. Take care not to damage the balljoint dust cover during and after disconnection.

12 Undo the nut each side securing the lower end of the anti-roll bar links to the bar. Use a Torx bit to counterhold the nut.

13 Undo the nut and detach the track rod end balljoint from the hub carrier each side, using a balljoint separator tool as described in Section 19.

14 Undo the bolt at the lower rear of the engine securing the lower torque rod to the bracket on the transmission/engine.

15 On models with standard power steering, remove the bolt and unclip the power steering pipes from the steering rack. Undo the bolt, rotate the clamp plate and disconnect the pipes from the steering rack pinion. On models fitted with electric power steering disconnect the wiring plugs **(see illustrations)**.

16 Position a sturdy trolley jack beneath, and in contact with, the rear of the subframe.

17 Undo the bolt each side securing the front of the subframe **(see illustration 6.11)**. Note that new subframe front mounting bolts will be required for refitting.

18 Undo the bolts each side securing the rear mounting brackets to the subframe and vehicle body, and recover the washers **(see illustration 6.12)**. Note that new subframe mounting bolts will be required for refitting.

19 Carefully lower the jack and subframe. Take care not to damage the power steering hoses.

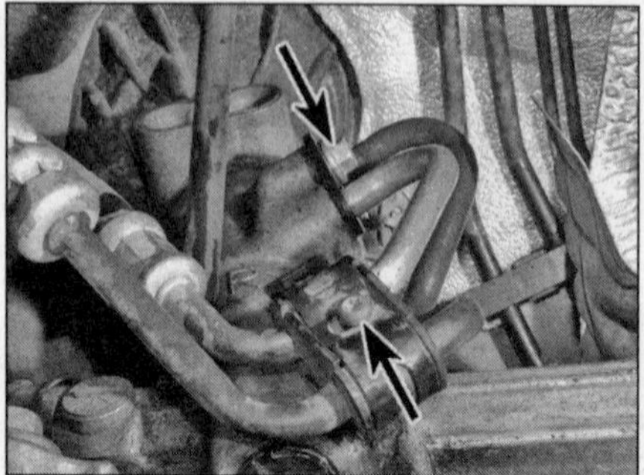

15.15a Steering rack pipes clamp bolts (arrowed)

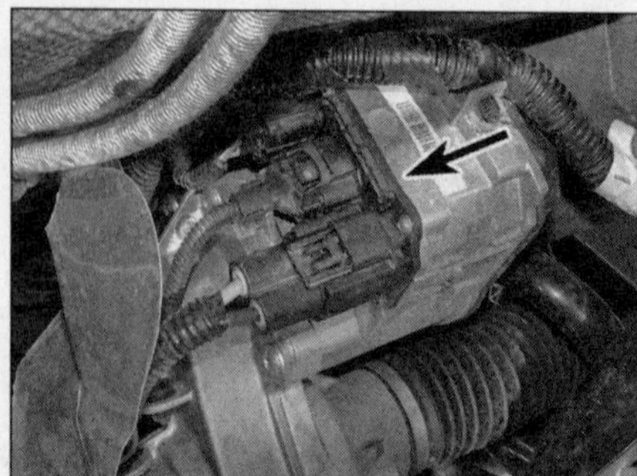

15.15b Disconnect the wiring plugs (arrowed)

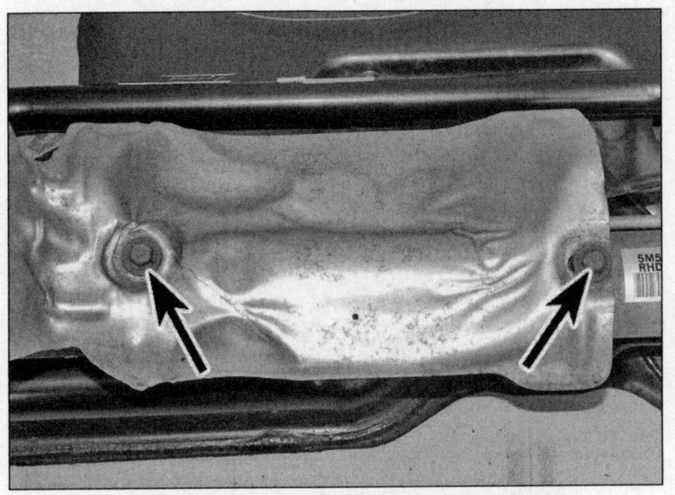

15.21 Steering rack heat shield bolts (arrowed)

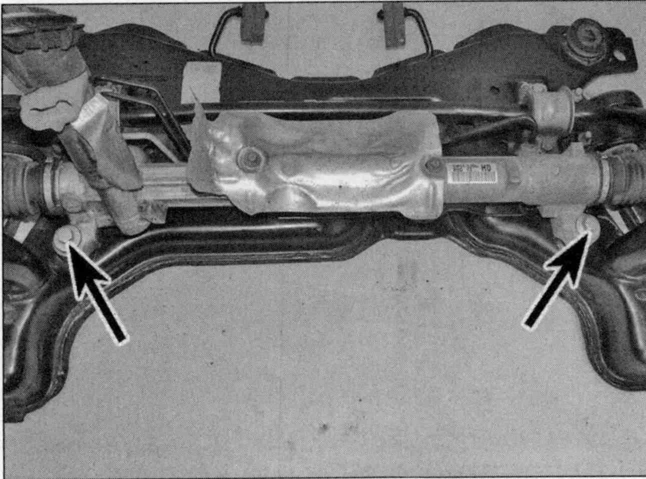
15.22 Steering rack retaining bolts (arrowed)

20 Undo the bolts and remove the anti-roll bar **(see illustration 6.14)**. Discard the bolts – new ones must be fitted.
21 Undo the bolts and remove the steering rack heat shield **(see illustration)**.
22 Undo the retaining bolts, and lift the steering rack from the subframe **(see illustration)**. Note that electric power steering models have a third bolt securing the steering rack to the subframe.

Refitting

23 Manipulate the steering rack into position and tighten the bolts to the specified torque.
24 Refit the steering rack heat shield and tighten the bolts securely.
25 Refit the anti-roll bar to the subframe and tighten the new bolts to the specified torque.
26 Ensure the steering rack pinion bulkhead seal is in place, then raise the subframe into position.
27 Fit the subframe rear mounting brackets to the body, then insert the new front and rear subframe mounting bolts. Only hand tighten them at this stage.
28 The alignment of the subframe must be checked by inserting round tools though the holes in the side members. Ford tools (part No 205-880) may be available. Alternatively, using two lengths of wooden dowel, 20 mm in diameter, and approximately 150 mm in length **(see illustration 6.18)**.
29 With the subframe correctly aligned, tighten all subframe bolts to the specified torque.
30 Engage the steering shaft universal joint with the pinion shaft, and push it fully home.
31 Fit the new universal joint pinch-bolt and tighten it to the specified torque.
32 Refit the fluid pipes to the steering rack using new O-ring seals, and tighten the retaining bolt securely.
33 The remainder of refitting is a reversal of removal, noting the following points:

a) Tighten all fasteners to their specified torque where given.
b) Have the front wheel alignment checked at the earliest opportunity.

16 Steering rack gaiters – renewal

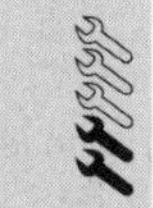

1 Remove the track rod end on the side concerned as described in Section 19. Unscrew the locknut from the track rod.
2 Release the two clips and peel off the gaiter. Disconnect the breather hose as the gaiter is withdrawn **(see illustration)**
3 Clean out any dirt and grit from the inner end of the track rod and (when accessible) the rack.
4 Wrap insulating tape around the track rod threads to protect the new gaiter whilst installing.
5 Refit the track rod end locknut.
6 Refit the track rod end as described in Section 19.

17 Steering system – bleeding

Note: *This section only applies to models fitted with hydraulic power steering.*
1 Wipe clean the area around the reservoir filler neck, and unscrew the filler cap/dipstick from the reservoir.
2 If topping-up is necessary, use clean fluid of the specified type (see *Weekly checks*). Check for leaks if frequent topping-up is required. Do not run the engine without fluid in the reservoir.
3 After component renewal, or if the fluid level has been allowed to fall so low that air has entered the hydraulic system, bleeding must be carried out as follows.
4 Fill the reservoir to the MAX mark as described in *Weekly checks*. Note that the power steering fluid should be cold, and poured slowly to minimise aeration.
5 Raise the front of the vehicle until the tyres are just clear of the ground, then support the vehicle securely on axle stands (see *Jacking and vehicle support*).
6 Without starting the engine, slowly turn the steering wheel from lock to lock, and add power steering fluid until the fluid level ceases to drop.
7 Start the engine and turn the steering wheel repeatedly from full lock one way, to full lock the other way, then top-up the fluid level as necessary.
8 Turn the steering wheel slowly to the full right lock position, and hold it there for 2 seconds.
9 Now turn the steering wheel slowly to the full left lock position, and hold it there for 2 seconds.
10 Top-up the fluid level again if necessary.
11 Repeat paragraphs 8 and 9 until the steering operation is satisfactory.
12 If the steering is still noisy (indicating air in the system), leave the vehicle overnight, and then try again. If this still fails to remove the air, the vehicle must be taken to a Ford dealer or suitably-equipped specialist, who will be

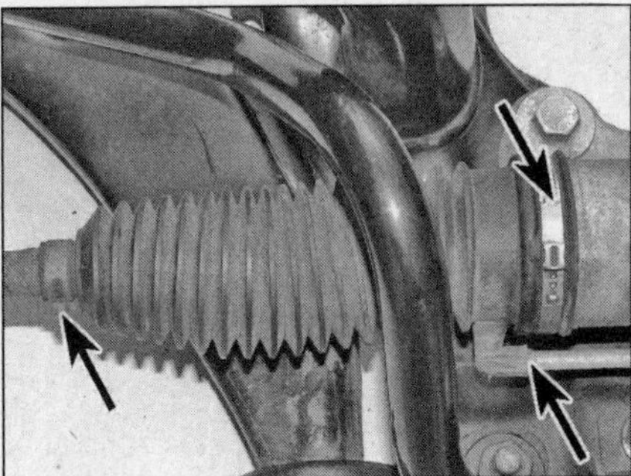
16.2 Steering rack gaiter clips and breather hose (arrowed) – shown with the rack removed for clarity

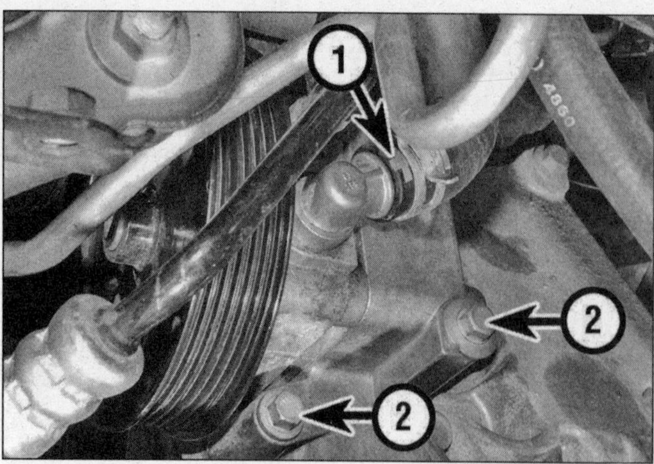

18.6 Power steering pump fluid supply hose (1) and lower mounting bolts (2)

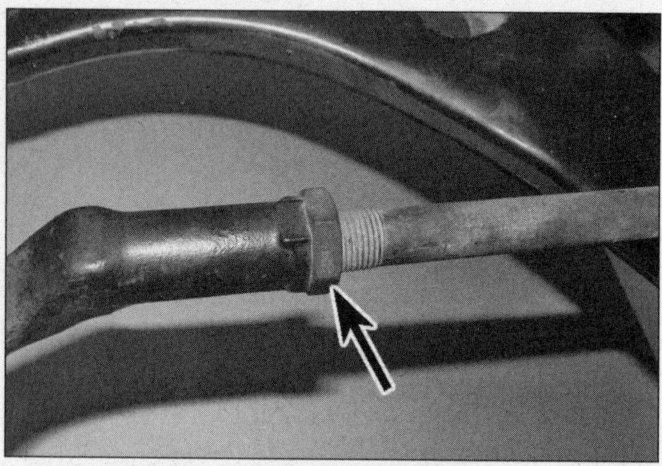
19.2 Slacken the track rod end locknut (arrowed)

able to apply a vacuum to the reservoir using special tools.

13 On completion, stop the engine, lower the vehicle to the ground, and recheck the fluid level.

18 Power steering pump – removal and refitting

Note: *This section only applies to models fitted with hydraulic power steering.*

Removal

1 Remove the auxiliary drivebelt as described in Chapter 1A Section 23 or Chapter 1B Section 24.

2 Jack up the front of the vehicle and support it securely on axle stands (see *Jacking and vehicle support*).

3 Undo the fasteners and remove the splash shield under the radiator.

4 Undo the bolts and remove the right-hand wheel arch liner.

5 Release the clamp and disconnect the hose from the power steering cooler to the pump. Be prepared for fluid spillage. Plug the openings to prevent contamination.

6 Disconnect the fluid supply hose from the pump **(see illustration)**. Be prepared for fluid spillage. Plug the openings to prevent contamination.

7 Undo the 2 lower mounting bolts from the pump **(see illustration 18.6)**.

8 Remove the alternator as described in Chapter 5A Section 5.

9 Disconnect the power steering pump pressure switch wiring plug.

10 Slacken the power steering pump pressure pipe union nut.

11 Undo the upper mounting bolts and remove the pump. Disconnect the pressure pipe as the pump is withdrawn.

Refitting

12 Refitting is a reversal of removal, bearing in mind the following points:

a) Use a new O-ring on pressure pipe union.

b) Tighten the mounting bolts to the specified torque.

c) Refill/top-up the fluid reservoir, and bleed the system as described in Section 17.

19 Track rod end – removal and refitting

Removal

1 Loosen the appropriate front wheel nuts. Chock the rear wheels, then jack up the front of the vehicle and support it on axle stands (see *Jacking and vehicle support*). Remove the appropriate front roadwheel.

2 Counterhold the track rod, and slacken the track rod end locknut by half a turn **(see illustration)**. If the locknut is now left in this position, it will act as a further guide for refitting.

3 Unscrew the track rod end balljoint nut, using and Allen key to counterhold the balljoint shank. Separate the balljoint from the steering arm with a proprietary balljoint separator, then remove the nut and disengage the balljoint from the arm **(see illustrations)**.

19.3a Use an Allen key to counterhold the track rod end balljoint shank

19.3b Use a separator tool to detach the track rod end from the hub carrier

4 Unscrew the track rod end from the track rod, counting the number of turns needed to remove it. Make a note of the number of turns, so that the tracking can be reset (or at least approximated) on refitting.

Refitting

5 Screw the track rod end onto the track rod by the same number of turns noted during removal.

6 Engage the balljoint in the steering arm. Fit a new nut and tighten it to the specified torque.

7 Counterhold the track rod and tighten the locknut.

8 Refit the front wheel, lower the car and tighten the wheel bolts in a diagonal sequence to the specified torque.

9 Have the front wheel toe-in (tracking) checked and adjusted by a Ford dealer or suitably-equipped repairer.

20 Wheel alignment and steering angles – general information

1 A car's steering and suspension geometry is defined in four basic settings – all angles are expressed in degrees (toe settings are also expressed as a measurement); the relevant settings are camber, castor, steering axis inclination, and toe setting **(see illustration)**. On the models covered by this manual, only the front and rear wheel toe settings are adjustable.

2 Camber is the angle at which the front wheels are set from the vertical when viewed from the front or rear of the car. Negative camber is the amount (in degrees) that the wheels are tilted inward at the top from the vertical.

3 The front camber angle is adjusted by slackening the steering knuckle-to-suspension strut mounting bolts and repositioning the hub carrier assemblies as necessary.

4 Castor is the angle between the steering axis and a vertical line when viewed from each side of the car. Positive castor is when the steering axis is inclined rearward at the top.

5 Steering axis inclination is the angle (when viewed from the front of the vehicle) between the vertical and an imaginary line drawn through the front suspension strut upper mounting and the control arm balljoint.

6 Toe setting is the amount by which the distance between the front inside edges of the roadwheels (measured at hub height) differs from the diametrically opposite distance measured between the rear inside edges of the roadwheels. Toe-in is when the roadwheels point inwards, towards each other at the front, while toe-out is when they splay outwards from each other at the front.

7 The front wheel toe setting is adjusted by altering the length of the steering track rods on both sides. This adjustment is normally referred to as the tracking.

8 The rear wheel toe setting is adjusted by rotating the lateral link front mounting bolt in the chassis. The bolt incorporates an eccentric washer, and the pivot point for the link varies as the bolt is rotated.

9 All other suspension and steering angles are set during manufacture, and no adjustment is possible. It can be assumed, therefore, that unless the vehicle has suffered accident damage, all the preset angles will be correct.

10 Special optical measuring equipment is necessary to accurately check and adjust the front and rear toe settings and front camber angles, and this work should be carried out by a Ford dealer or similar expert. Most tyre-fitting centres have the expertise and equipment to carry out at least a front wheel toe setting (tracking) check for a nominal charge.

21 Front subframe – removal and refitting

1 The front subframe removal and refitting is described within the steering rack removal and refitting procedure, as described in Section 15. If the subframe is to be removed as part of another procedure (eg, catalytic converter renewal), the steering rack and anti-roll bar can be left in place on the subframe.

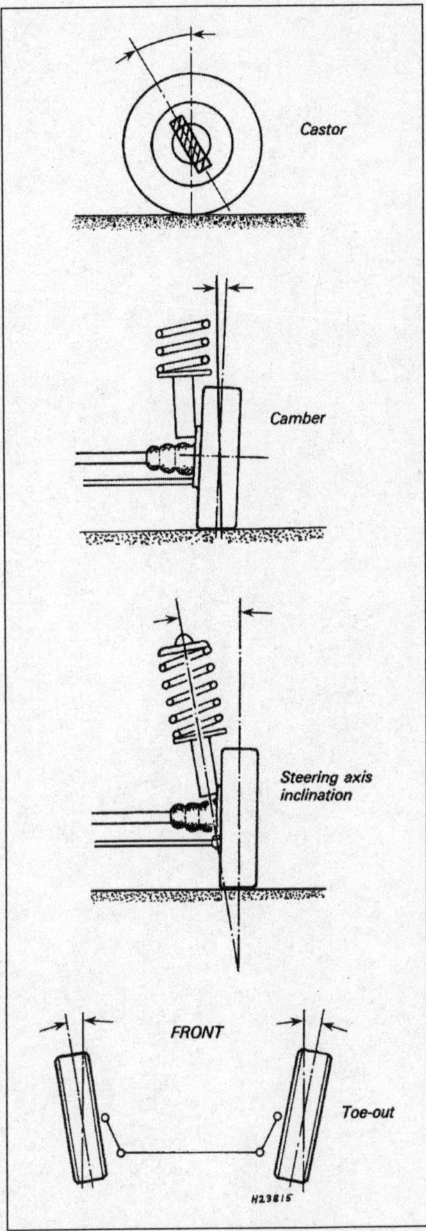

20.1 Front wheel geometry

Notes

Chapter 11
Bodywork and fittings

Contents

Degrees of difficulty

Easy, suitable for novice with little experience 	**Fairly easy,** suitable for beginner with some experience	**Fairly difficult,** suitable for competent DIY mechanic	**Difficult,** suitable for experienced DIY mechanic	**Very difficult,** suitable for expert DIY or professional 

Specifications

Torque wrench settings

	Nm	lbf ft
Crossmember A-pillar bolts	40	30
Crossmember bolts	25	18
Front seat mounting bolts	35	26
Heater box to crossmember bolts	10	7
Passenger's airbag module lower support bracket:		
Bolts	9	6
Nuts	7	5
Rear seat cushion bolts	24	18
Rear seat backrest catch retaining bolts	23	17
Rear seat hinge	24	18
Seat belt mounting nuts and bolts:		
Front inertia reel bolt	35	26
Front lower anchorage	35	26
Front seat belt buckle stake	47	35
Front seat bolts shoulder height adjuster	35	26
Front upper anchorage	35	26
Rear belt buckle stalks	55	41
Rear centre inertia reel	47	35
Rear centre lower anchorage	55	41
Rear outer inertia reel	47	35
Rear outer lower anchorage	40	30

1 General Information

1 The bodyshell and underframe on all models feature variable thickness steel. Achieved by laser-welded technology, used to join steel panels of different gauges. This gives a stiffer structure, with mounting points being more rigid, which I turn gives an improved crash performance.

2 An additional safety crossmember is incorporated between the A-pillars in the upper area of the bulkhead, and the facia and steering column are secured to it. The lower bulkhead area is reinforced by additional systems of members connected to the front of the vehicle.

3 The body side rocker panels (sills) are constructed from high strength martensitic steel. The A-pillars and B-pillars are made from high strength manganese boron steel. Partial repair of these panels is forbidden, if they are accident damaged they must be replaced as complete sections.

4 All doors are reinforced and incorporate side impact protection, which is secured in the door structure. There are additional impact absorbers to the front and rear of the vehicle, behind the bumper assemblies.

5 All sheet metal surfaces which are prone to corrosion are galvanised. The painting process includes a base colour which closely matches the final topcoat, so that any stone damage is not as noticeable. The front wings are of a bolt-on type to ease their renewal if required.

6 Automatic seat belts are fitted to all models, and the front seat safety belts are equipped with a pyrotechnic pretension seat belt buckle, which is attached to the seat frame of each front seat. In the event of a serious front impact, the system is triggered and pulls the stalk buckle downwards to tension the seat belt. It is not possible to reset the tensioner once fired, and it must therefore be renewed. The tensioners are fired by an explosive charge similar to that used in the airbag, and are triggered via the airbag control module. The safety belt retractor, which is fitted in the base of the B-pillar, has a device to control the seat belt, if the deceleration force is enough to activate the airbags.

7 Central locking is standard on all models. Where double-locking is fitted, the lock mechanism is disconnected (when the system is in use) from the interior door handles, making it impossible to open any of the doors or the tailgate/boot lid from inside the vehicle. This means that, even if a thief should break a side window, he will not be able to open the door using the interior handle. In the event of a serious accident, a crash sensor unlocks all doors if they were previously locked.

8 Many of the procedures in this Chapter require the battery to be disconnected; refer to Chapter 5A Section 3.

2 Maintenance – bodywork and underframe

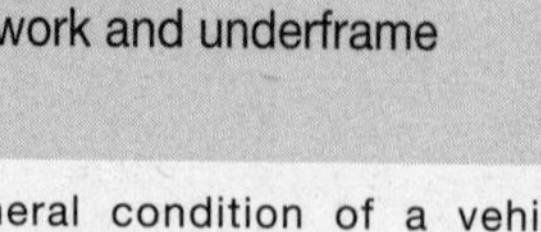

1 The general condition of a vehicle's bodywork is the one thing that significantly affects its value. Maintenance is easy, but needs to be regular. Neglect, particularly after minor damage, can lead quickly to further deterioration and costly repair bills. It is important also to keep watch on those parts of the vehicle not immediately visible, for instance the underside, inside all the wheel arches, and the lower part of the engine compartment.

2 The basic maintenance routine for the bodywork is washing – preferably with a lot of water, from a hose. This will remove all the loose solids which may have stuck to the vehicle. It is important to flush these off in such a way as to prevent grit from scratching the finish. The wheel arches and underframe need washing in the same way, to remove any accumulated mud, which will retain moisture and tend to encourage rust. Paradoxically enough, the best time to clean the underframe and wheel arches is in wet weather, when the mud is thoroughly wet and soft. In very wet weather, the underframe is usually cleaned of large accumulations automatically, and this is a good time for inspection.

3 Periodically, except on vehicles with a wax-based underbody protective coating, it is a good idea to have the whole of the underframe of the vehicle steam-cleaned, engine compartment included, so that a thorough inspection can be carried out to see what minor repairs and renovations are necessary. Steam-cleaning is available at many garages, and is necessary for the removal of the accumulation of oily grime, which sometimes is allowed to become thick in certain areas. If steam-cleaning facilities are not available, there are some excellent grease solvents available which can be brush-applied; the dirt can then be simply hosed off. Note that these methods should not be used on vehicles with wax-based underbody protective coating, or the coating will be removed. Such vehicles should be inspected annually, preferably just prior to Winter, when the underbody should be washed down, and any damage to the wax coating repaired. Ideally, a completely fresh coat should be applied. It would also be worth considering the use of such wax-based protection for injection into door panels, sills, box sections, etc, as an additional safeguard against rust damage, where such protection is not provided by the vehicle manufacturer.

4 After washing paintwork, wipe off with a chamois leather to give an unspotted clear finish. A coat of clear protective wax polish will give added protection against chemical pollutants in the air. If the paintwork sheen has dulled or oxidised, use a cleaner/polisher combination to restore the brilliance of the shine. This requires a little effort, but such dulling is usually caused because regular washing has been neglected. Care needs to be taken with metallic paintwork, as special non-abrasive cleaner/polisher is required to avoid damage to the finish. Always check that the door and ventilator opening drain holes and pipes are completely clear, so that water can be drained out. Brightwork should be treated in the same way as paintwork. Windscreens and windows can be kept clear of the smeary film which often appears, by the use of proprietary glass cleaner. Never use any form of wax or other body or chromium polish on glass.

3 Maintenance – upholstery and carpets

1 Mats and carpets should be brushed or vacuum-cleaned regularly, to keep them free of grit. If they are badly stained, remove them from the vehicle for scrubbing or sponging, and make quite sure they are dry before refitting. Seats and interior trim panels can be kept clean by wiping with a damp cloth. If they do become stained (which can be more apparent on light-coloured upholstery), use a little liquid detergent and a soft nail brush to scour the grime out of the grain of the material. Do not forget to keep the headlining clean in the same way as the upholstery. When using liquid cleaners inside the vehicle, do not over-wet the surfaces being cleaned. Excessive damp could get into the seams and padded interior, causing stains, offensive odours or even rot.

Caution: If the inside of the vehicle gets wet accidentally, it is worthwhile taking some trouble to dry it out properly, particularly where carpets are involved. Do not leave oil or electric heaters inside the vehicle for this purpose.

4 Minor body damage – repair

Minor scratches in bodywork

1 If the scratch is very superficial, and does not penetrate to the metal of the bodywork, repair is very simple. Lightly rub the area of the scratch with a paintwork renovator, or a very fine cutting paste, to remove loose paint from the scratch, and to clear the surrounding bodywork of wax polish. Rinse the area with clean water.

2 Apply touch-up paint to the scratch using a fine paint brush; continue to apply fine layers of paint until the surface of the paint in the scratch is level with the surrounding paintwork. Allow the new paint at least two weeks to harden, then blend it into the surrounding paintwork by rubbing the scratch area with a paintwork renovator or a very fine cutting paste. Finally, apply wax polish.

3 Where the scratch has penetrated right through to the metal of the bodywork, causing the metal to rust, a different repair technique is required. Remove any loose rust from the bottom of the scratch with a penknife, then apply rust-inhibiting paint to prevent the formation of rust in the future. Using a rubber or nylon applicator, fill the scratch with bodystopper paste. If required, this paste can be mixed with cellulose thinners to provide a very thin paste which is ideal for filling narrow scratches. Before the stopper-paste in the scratch hardens, wrap a piece of smooth cotton rag around the top of a finger. Dip the finger in cellulose thinners, and quickly sweep it across the surface of the stopper-paste in the scratch; this will ensure that the surface of the stopper-paste is slightly hollowed. The scratch can now be painted over as described earlier in this Section.

Dents in bodywork

4 When deep denting of the vehicle's bodywork has taken place, the first task is to pull the dent out, until the affected bodywork almost attains its original shape. There is little point in trying to restore the original shape completely, as the metal in the damaged area will have stretched on impact, and cannot be reshaped fully to its original contour. It is better to bring the level of the dent up to a point which is about 3 mm below the level of the surrounding bodywork. In cases where the dent is very shallow anyway, it is not worth trying to pull it out at all. If the underside of the dent is accessible, it can be hammered out gently from behind, using a mallet with a wooden or plastic head. Whilst doing this, hold a suitable block of wood firmly against the outside of the panel, to absorb the impact from the hammer blows and thus prevent a large area of the bodywork from being 'belled-out'.

5 Should the dent be in a section of the bodywork which has a double skin, or some other factor making it inaccessible from behind, a different technique is called for. Drill several small holes through the metal inside the area – particularly in the deeper section. Then screw long self-tapping screws into the holes, just sufficiently for them to gain a good purchase in the metal. Now the dent can be pulled out by pulling on the protruding heads of the screws with a pair of pliers.

6 The next stage of the repair is the removal of the paint from the damaged area, and from an inch or so of the surrounding 'sound' bodywork. This is accomplished most easily by using a wire brush or abrasive pad on a power drill, although it can be done just as effectively by hand, using sheets of abrasive paper. To complete the preparation for filling, score the surface of the bare metal with a screwdriver or the tang of a file, or alternatively, drill small holes in the affected area. This will provide a really good 'key' for the filler paste.

7 To complete the repair, see the Section on filling and respraying.

Rust holes or gashes in bodywork

8 Remove all paint from the affected area, and from an inch or so of the surrounding 'sound' bodywork, using an abrasive pad or a wire brush on a power drill. If these are not available, a few sheets of abrasive paper will do the job most effectively. With the paint removed, you will be able to judge the severity of the corrosion, and therefore decide whether to renew the whole panel (if this is possible) or to repair the affected area. New body panels are not as expensive as most people think, and it is often quicker and more satisfactory to fit a new panel than to attempt to repair large areas of corrosion.

9 Remove all fittings from the affected area, except those which will act as a guide to the original shape of the damaged bodywork (e.g. headlight shells etc). Then, using tin snips or a hacksaw blade, remove all loose metal and any other metal badly affected by corrosion. Hammer the edges of the hole inwards, in order to create a slight depression for the filler paste.

10 Wire-brush the affected area to remove the powdery rust from the surface of the remaining metal. Paint the affected area with rust-inhibiting paint, if the back of the rusted area is accessible, treat this also.

11 Before filling can take place, it will be necessary to block the hole in some way. This can be achieved by the use of aluminium or plastic mesh, or aluminium tape.

12 Aluminium or plastic mesh, or glass-fibre matting, is probably the best material to use for a large hole. Cut a piece to the approximate size and shape of the hole to be filled, then position it in the hole so that its edges are below the level of the surrounding bodywork. It can be retained in position by several blobs of filler paste around its periphery.

13 Aluminium tape should be used for small or very narrow holes. Pull a piece off the roll, trim it to the approximate size and shape required, then pull off the backing paper (if used) and stick the tape over the hole; it can be overlapped if the thickness of one piece is insufficient. Burnish down the edges of the tape with the handle of a screwdriver or similar, to ensure that the tape is securely attached to the metal underneath.

Filling and respraying

14 Before using this Section, see the Sections on dent, deep scratch, rust holes and gash repairs.

15 Many types of bodyfiller are available, but generally speaking, those proprietary kits which contain a tin of filler paste and a tube of resin hardener are best for this type of repair. A wide, flexible plastic or nylon applicator will be found invaluable for imparting a smooth and well-contoured finish to the surface of the filler.

16 Mix up a little filler on a clean piece of card or board – measure the hardener carefully (follow the maker's instructions on the pack), otherwise the filler will set too rapidly or too slowly. Using the applicator, apply the filler paste to the prepared area; draw the applicator across the surface of the filler to achieve the correct contour and to level the surface. As soon as a contour that approximates to the correct one is achieved, stop working the paste – if you carry on too long, the paste will become sticky and begin to 'pick-up' on the applicator. Continue to add thin layers of filler paste at 20-minute intervals, until the level of the filler is just proud of the surrounding bodywork.

17 Once the filler has hardened, the excess can be removed using a metal plane or file. From then on, progressively-finer grades of abrasive paper should be used, starting with a 40-grade production paper, and finishing with a 400-grade wet-and-dry paper. Always wrap the abrasive paper around a flat rubber, cork, or wooden block – otherwise the surface of the filler will not be completely flat. During the smoothing of the filler surface, the wet-and-dry paper should be periodically rinsed in water. This will ensure that a very smooth finish is imparted to the filler at the final stage.

18 At this stage, the 'dent' should be surrounded by a ring of bare metal, which in turn should be encircled by the finely 'feathered' edge of the good paintwork. Rinse the repair area with clean water, until all of the dust produced by the rubbing-down operation has gone.

19 Spray the whole area with a light coat of primer – this will show up any imperfections in the surface of the filler. Repair these imperfections with fresh filler paste or bodystopper, and once more smooth the surface with abrasive paper. Repeat this spray-and-repair procedure until you are satisfied that the surface of the filler, and the feathered edge of the paintwork, are perfect. Clean the repair area with clean water, and allow to dry fully.

20 The repair area is now ready for final spraying. Paint spraying must be carried out in a warm, dry, windless and dust-free atmosphere. This condition can be created artificially if you have access to a large indoor working area, but if you are forced to work in the open, you will have to pick your day very carefully. If you are working indoors, dousing the floor in the work area with water will help to settle the dust which would otherwise be in the atmosphere. If the repair area is confined to one body panel, mask off the surrounding panels; this will help to minimise the effects of a slight mis-match in paint colours. Bodywork fittings (e.g. chrome strips, door handles etc) will also need to be masked off. Use genuine masking tape, and several thicknesses of newspaper, for the masking operations.

21 Before commencing to spray, agitate the aerosol can thoroughly, then spray a test area (an old tin, or similar) until the technique is mastered. Cover the repair area with a thick coat of primer; the thickness should be built up using several thin layers of paint, rather than one thick one. Using 400-grade wet-and-dry paper, rub down the surface of the primer until it is really smooth. While doing this, the work area should be thoroughly doused with water, and the wet-and-dry paper periodically rinsed in water. Allow to dry before spraying on more paint.

22 Spray on the top coat, again building up the thickness by using several thin layers of paint. Start spraying at one edge of the repair area, and then, using a side-to-side motion, work until the whole repair area and about 2 inches of the surrounding original paintwork is covered. Remove all masking material 10 to 15 minutes after spraying on the final coat of paint.

23 Allow the new paint at least two weeks to harden, then, using a paintwork renovator, or a very fine cutting paste, blend the edges of the paint into the existing paintwork. Finally, apply wax polish.

Plastic components

24 With the use of more and more plastic body components by the vehicle manufacturers (e.g. bumpers. spoilers, and in some cases major body panels), rectification of more serious damage to such items has become a matter of either entrusting repair work to a specialist in this field, or renewing complete components. Repair of such damage by the DIY owner is not really feasible, owing to the cost of the equipment and materials required for effecting such repairs. The basic technique involves making a groove along the line of the crack in the plastic, using a rotary burr in a power drill. The damaged part is then welded back together, using a hot-air gun to heat up and fuse a plastic filler rod into the groove. Any excess plastic is then removed, and the area rubbed down to a smooth finish. It is important that a filler rod of the correct plastic is used, as body components can be made of a variety of different types (e.g. polycarbonate, ABS, polypropylene).

25 Damage of a less serious nature (abrasions, minor cracks etc) can be repaired by the DIY owner using a two-part epoxy filler repair material. Once mixed in equal proportions, this is used in similar fashion to the bodywork filler used on metal panels. The filler is usually cured in twenty to thirty minutes, ready for sanding and painting.

26 If the owner is renewing a complete component himself, or if he has repaired it with epoxy filler, he will be left with the problem of finding a suitable paint for finishing which is compatible with the type of plastic used. At one time, the use of a universal paint was not possible, owing to the complex range of plastics encountered in body component applications. Standard paints, generally speaking, will not bond to plastic or rubber satisfactorily. However, it is now possible to obtain a plastic body parts finishing kit which consists of a pre-primer treatment, a primer and coloured top coat. Full instructions are normally supplied with a kit, but basically, the method of use is to first apply the pre-primer to the component concerned, and allow it to dry for up to 30 minutes. Then the primer is applied, and left to dry for about an hour before finally applying the special-coloured top coat. The result is a correctly-coloured component, where the paint will flex with the plastic or rubber, a property that standard paint does not normally posses.

5 Major body damage – repair

1 Where serious damage has occurred, or large areas need renewal due to neglect, it means that complete new panels will need welding-in; this is best left to professionals. If the damage is due to impact, it will also be necessary to check completely the alignment of the bodyshell; this can only be carried out accurately by a Ford dealer or suitably equipped body shop, using special jigs. If the body is left misaligned, it is primarily dangerous, as the car will not handle properly, and secondly, uneven stresses will be imposed on the steering, suspension and possibly transmission, causing abnormal wear or complete failure, particularly to items such as the tyres.

6 Bumper covers – removal and refitting

Front bumper cover removal

1 Apply the handbrake, jack up the front of the vehicle and support it on axle stands (see *Jacking and vehicle support* in the reference section). if required, remove the front wheels for easier access.

2 Undo the fasteners and remove the engine undershield, remove the front deflector trim first to access the screws in the front of the undershield **(see illustrations)**.

3 Still working from below remove the air deflector from the base of the bumper cover **(see illustrations)**.

4 Remove both front headlights as described in Chapter 12 Section 8.

6.2a Remove the deflector trim...

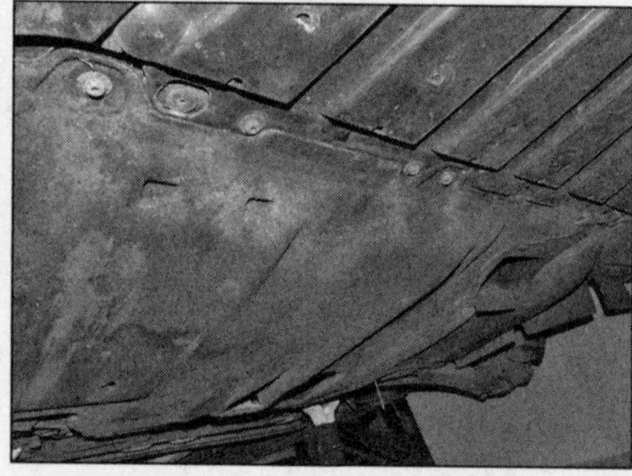

6.2b ...then undo the undershield fasteners

6.3a Remove the plastic rivets...

6.3b ...and the rear securing screws

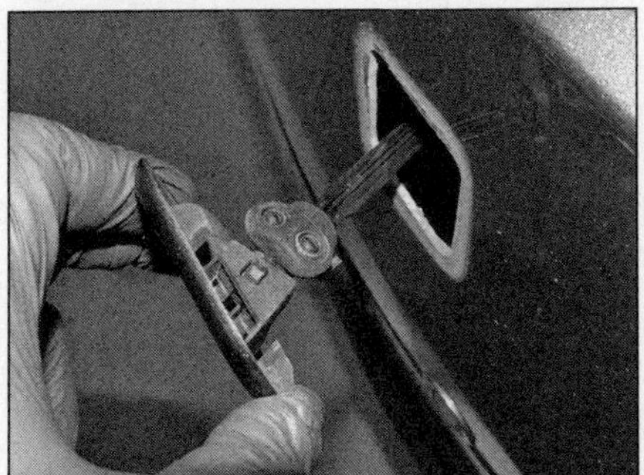

6.5a Pull out the washer jet...

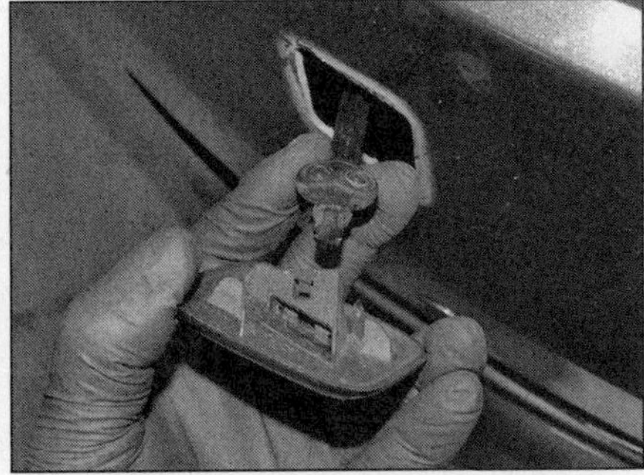

6.5b ...and unclip the trim cover

6.5c Using a cable tie to secure cover

6.6a Unclip the release handle...

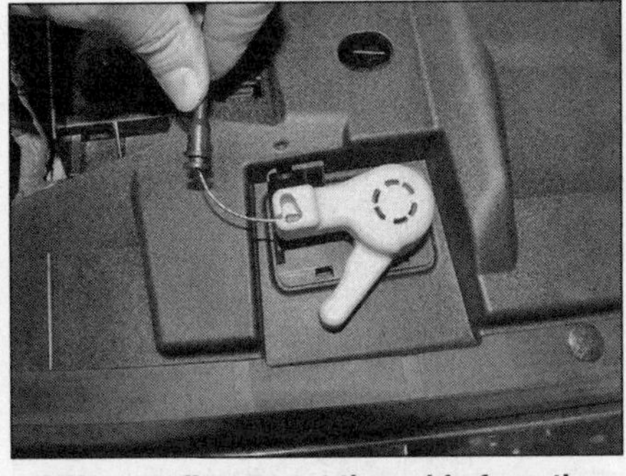

6.6b ...or disconnect the cable from the handle

6.7a Prise out the two rivets...

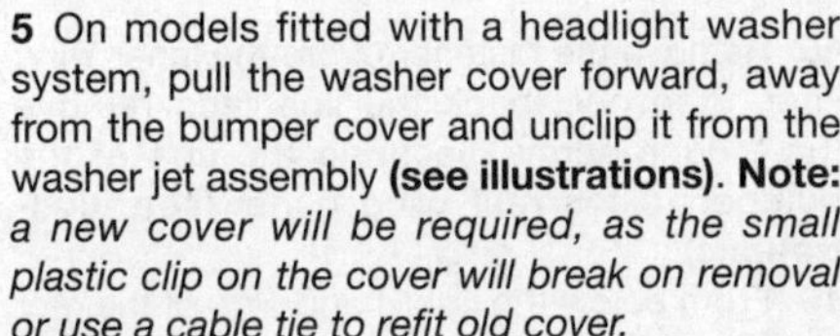

5 On models fitted with a headlight washer system, pull the washer cover forward, away from the bumper cover and unclip it from the washer jet assembly **(see illustrations)**. **Note:** *a new cover will be required, as the small plastic clip on the cover will break on removal or use a cable tie to refit old cover.*

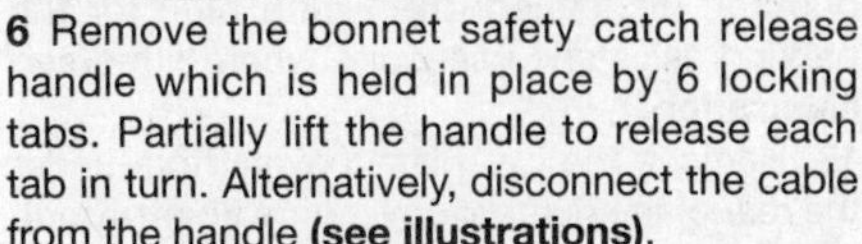

6 Remove the bonnet safety catch release handle which is held in place by 6 locking tabs. Partially lift the handle to release each tab in turn. Alternatively, disconnect the cable from the handle **(see illustrations)**.

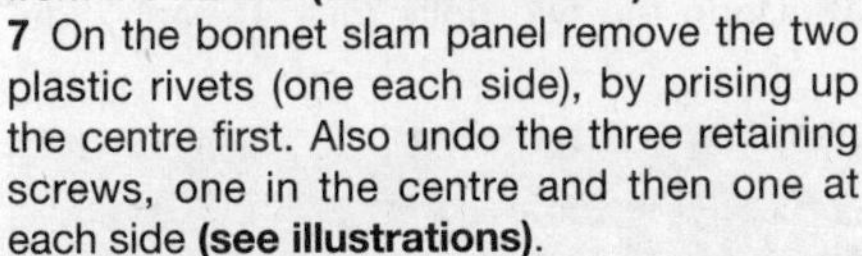

7 On the bonnet slam panel remove the two plastic rivets (one each side), by prising up the centre first. Also undo the three retaining screws, one in the centre and then one at each side **(see illustrations)**.

8 Working in each wheel arch in turn remove the fasteners that secure the front edge of the inner wing liner to the bumper cover **(see illustration)**.

9 On both sides release the plastic rivet from the end of the wing panel, then work the ends of the bumper cover free from the front wings **(see illustrations)**.

6.7b ...undo the centre screw...

6.7c ...and the two outer screws

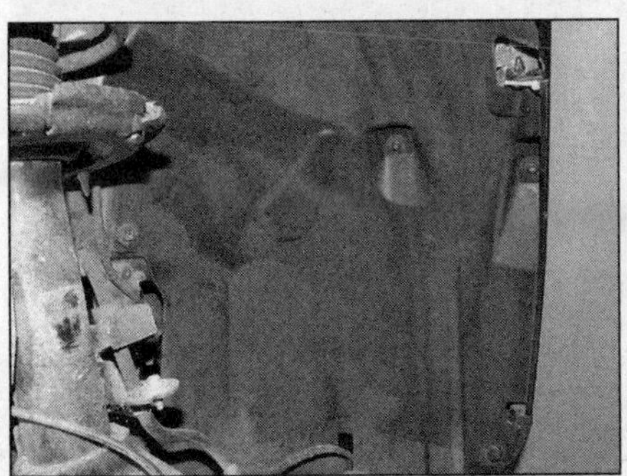

6.8 Undo the inner wing panel fasteners

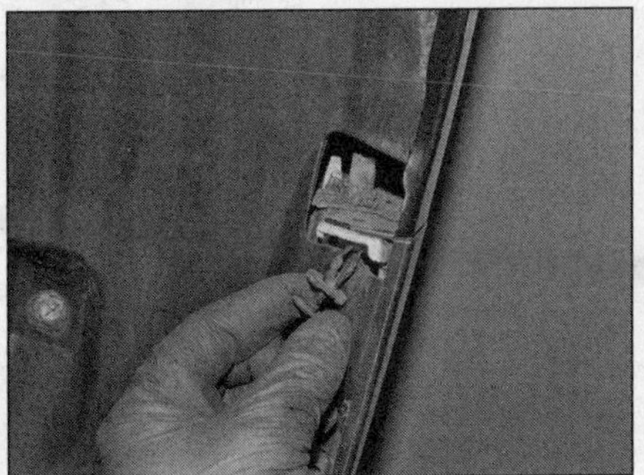

6.9a Remove the plastic rivet...

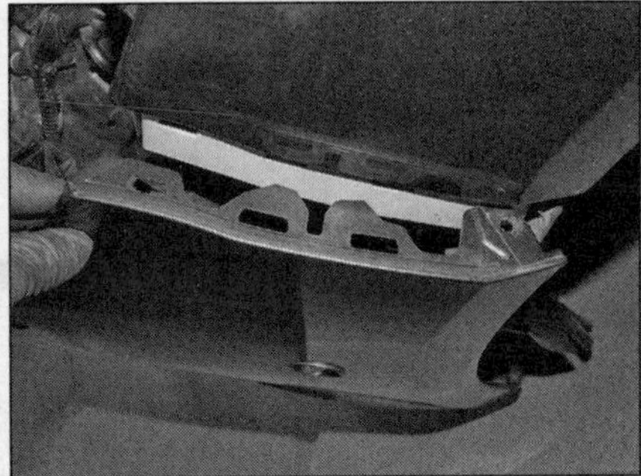

6.9b ...and release the bumper from the front wing

6.10a Remove the torx screws...

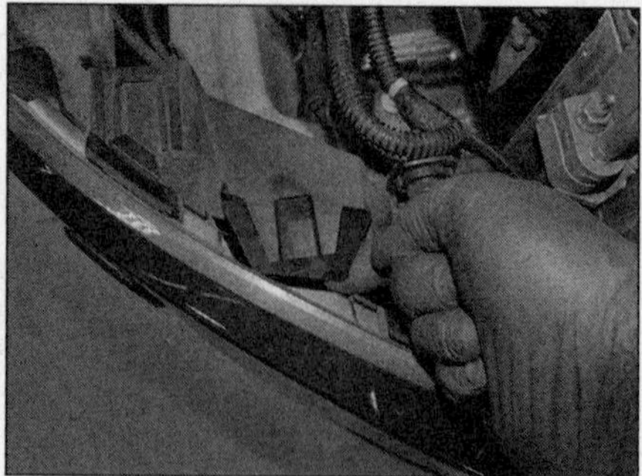
6.10b ...and release the locking tabs

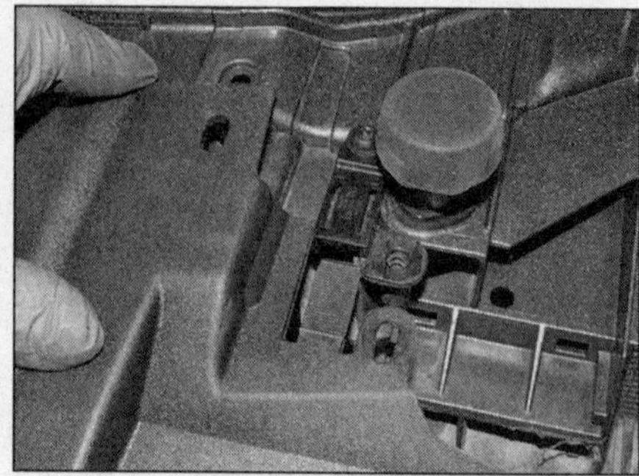
6.11a Unclip the upper part of the cover...

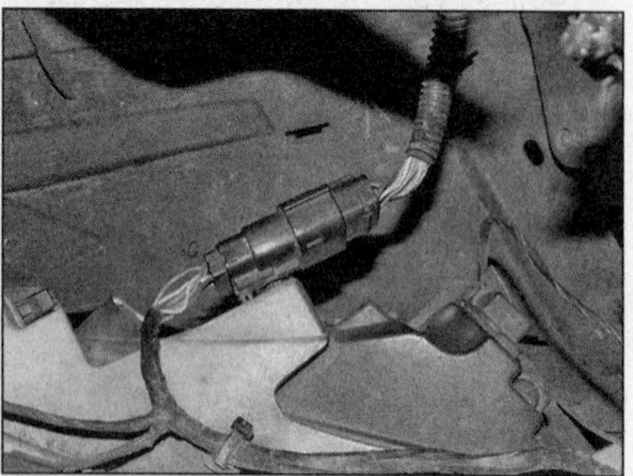
6.11b ...and disconnect the wiring connector

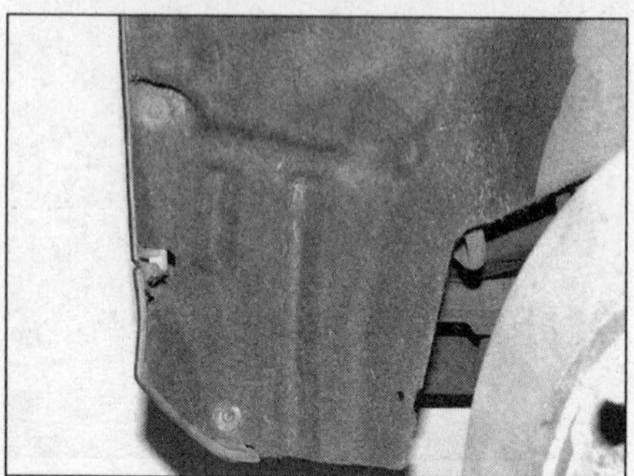
6.15a Remove the liner fasteners...

6.15b ...and remove the hidden screw

10 Remove the torx headed screws (one at each side) and then unhook the bumper from the locking tabs in each headlight aperture **(see illustrations)**.

11 With the aid of and assistant remove the bumper cover, unclipping the top of the bumber from the locating clips, then reach behind the left-hand side of the bumper cover to disconnect the wiring plug(s) for the fog lights and headlight washer system (where fitted), as it is removed **(see illustrations)**.

Rear bumper cover removal

Hatchback models

12 Chock the front wheels, jack up the rear of the vehicle and support it on axle stands (see *Jacking and vehicle support*). Open up the boot/tailgate.

13 Remove both rear lamps as described in Chapter 12 Section 8.

14 Where fitted, undo the two securing bolts and remove the rear mudflaps from the lower edges of the bumper.

15 Remove the fasteners from the inner wing liner, then peel back the liner and remove the hidden screw, securing the end of the bumper to the rear wing panel **(see illustrations)**.

16 From below the right-hand side of the rear bumper, disconnect the wiring plug for the parking assistance sensors, where fitted**(see illustration)**.

17 Remove the two plastic rivets from under the rear of the bumper cover **(see illustration)**.

18 Undo the two bolts (one at each side)

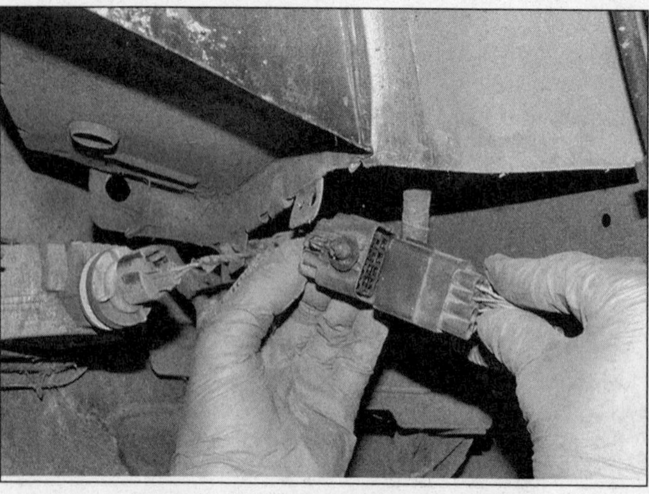
6.16 Disconnect the wiring connector

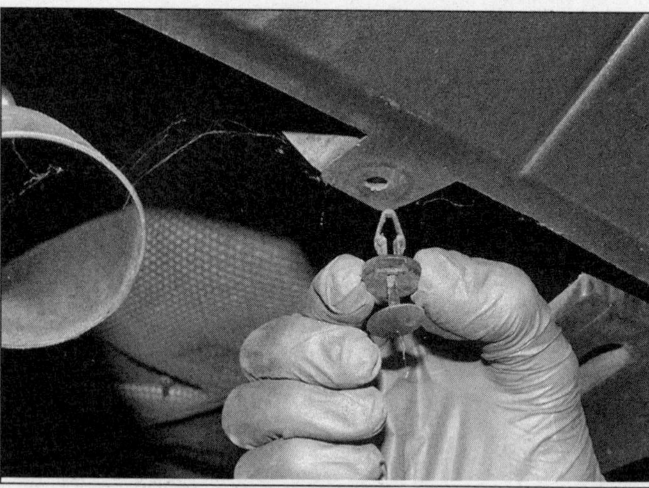
6.17 Remove the plastic rivets

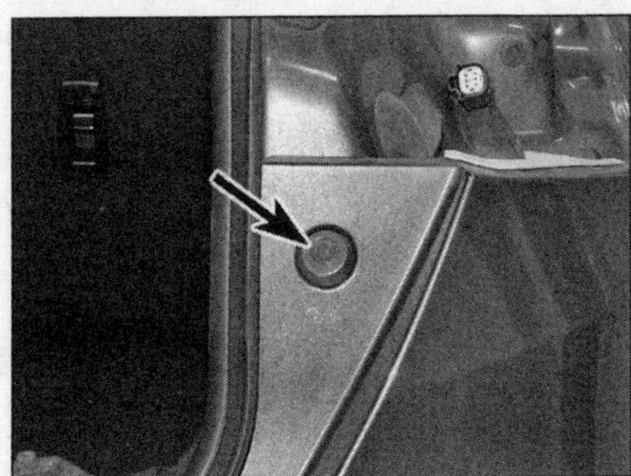
6.18 Undo the upper mounting bolts

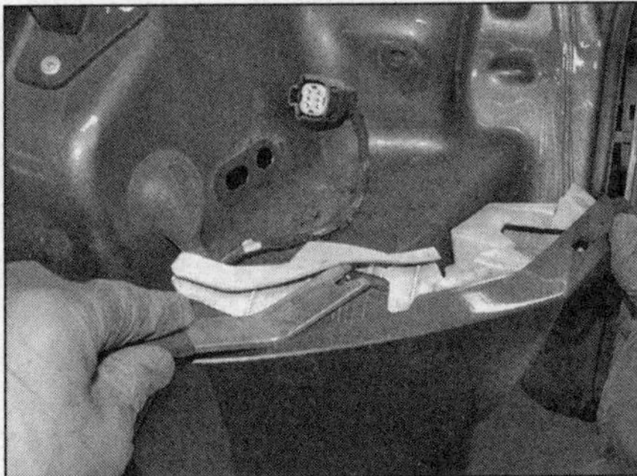
6.19a Release the locking clips...

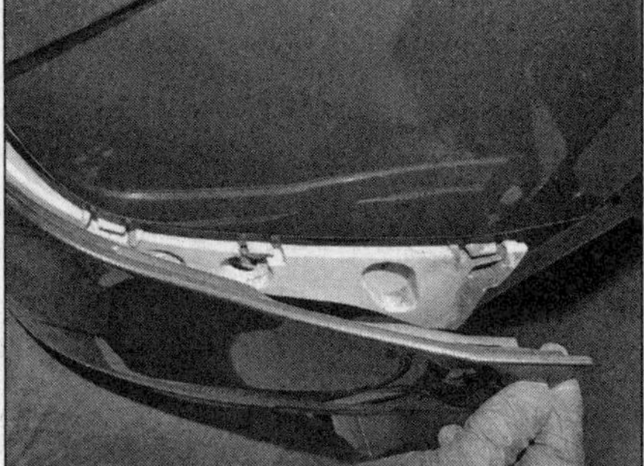
6.19b ...and unclip the bumper from the wing panel

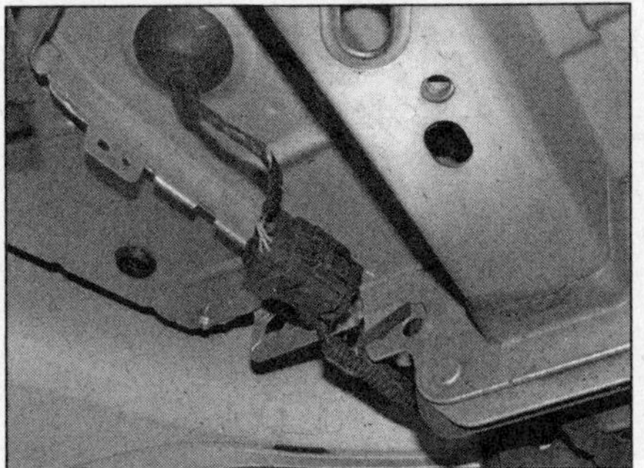
6.23 Disconnect the wiring plug

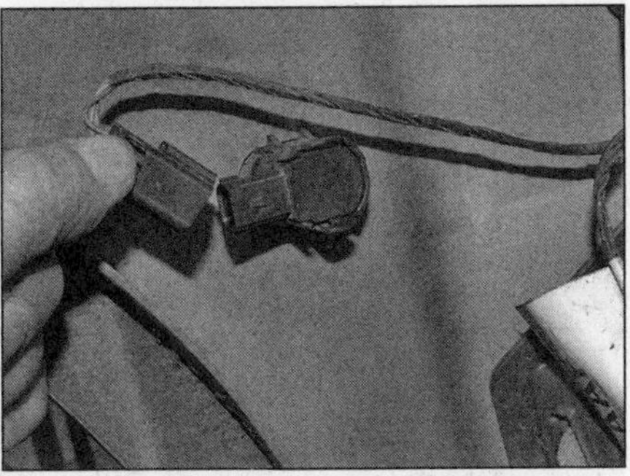
6.27a Disconnect the wiring connector...

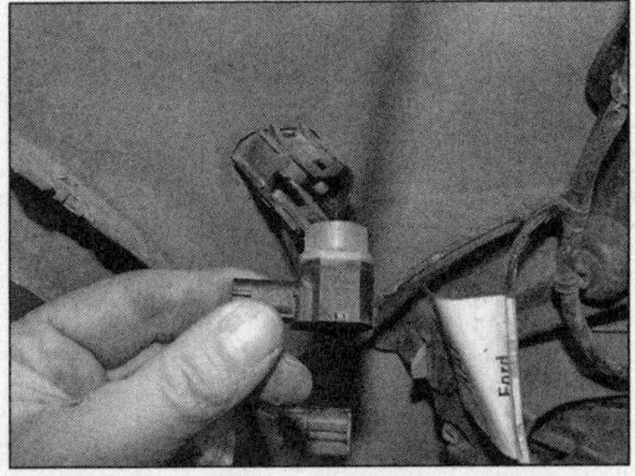
6.27b ...and unclip the sensor

from the top of the bumper cover, inside the tailgate aperture **(see illustration)**.

19 Release the locating clips inside the rear light aperture, then unclip the edges of the bumper from the rear wing panels **(see illustrations)**. Then with the aid of an assistant remove the bumper cover.

Estate models

20 Chock the front wheels, jack up the rear of the vehicle and support it on axle stands (see *Jacking and vehicle support*).

21 Undo the bolts and retaining clips from each side and remove the mudflaps.

22 On both sides partially fold back the wheel arch liner to access the hidden bolt. Remove the bolt.

23 From below, disconnect the wiring plug for the rear foglamp/reversing light/parking assistance sensors (as applicable) **(see illustration)**.

24 Remove the plastic expanding rivets from the bumper underside.

25 Remove the 4 bolts from the tailgate aperture and with the aid of an assistant release the bumper edges from the rear wing. Remove the bumper.

26 If required, drill out the rivet s (5mm drill bit) and remove the bumper cover support panel.

All models

27 If required, the parking distance sensors can be removed from the bumper cover, by disconnecting the wiring connector, releasing the retaining tangs and withdrawing the sensor from the cover **(see illustrations)**.

Refitting

28 Refitting is a reversal of the removal procedure. Make sure that, where applicable, the bumper guides are located correctly. Check all electrical components that have been disconnected.

7 Active shutter grille – removal and refitting

1 Several models feature a motorised grille, fitted in front of the radiator/condenser assembly. The opening and closing of the slats in the grille is controlled by the Power Control Module (PCM). The position of the slats is calculated from various parameters including vehicle speed, ambient temperature and AC compressor operation. The default position is open. The PCM will open and shut the grille slats at engine start to calibrate the position of the slats. A single stepper motor is used to control the slats in the grille.

Removal

2 Jack up and support the front of the vehicle, with reference to Chapter 13 Section 5.

3 Remove the front bumper cover as described in Section 6 of this Chapter.

4 Undo the retaining bolt and remove the small plastic cover from the upper cross member**(see illustration)**.

7.4 Remove the trim panel

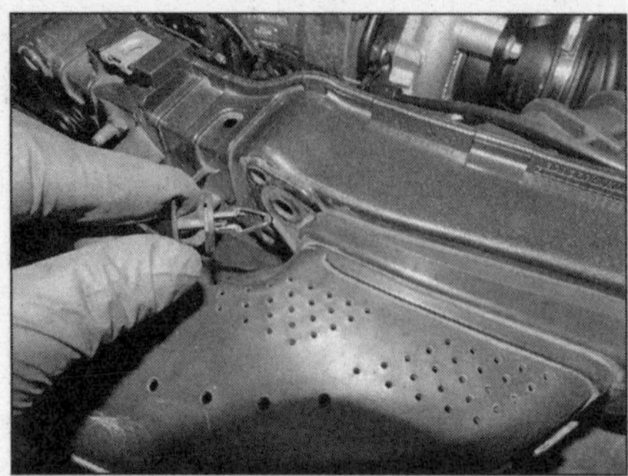
7.5a Release the fasteners...

7.5b ...and remove the air duct

7.6 Unclip the upper air scoop

7.7a Undo the upper screws...

7.7b ...and unclip the lower part

7.8 Unclip the wiring connectors

7.10a Undo the mounting bolts...

5 Remove the plastic rivets and remove the air intake duct from the upper cross member**(see illustrations)**.

6 Unclip the air scoop cowling from above the front bumper bar **(see illustration)**.

7 Undo the upper retaining screws, then unclip the lower part of the lower air scoop from below the bumper bar **(see illustrations)**.

8 Unclip the two wiring loom connectors from the left-hand side of the radiator support panel **(see illustration)**.

9 Arrange straps or cable ties and support the radiator and condenser assembly, so that the main support crossmember below the assembly can be lowered.

10 Remove the support panel bolts (two at each side) and replace them with some extra long bolts **(see illustrations)**. This will allow the crossmember to be lowered enough to allow the intercooler to be removed.

11 Remove the securing clips (one at each side) from the top of the active shutter grille, then lift the assembly up to release it from the lower retaining clips on the side of the radiator **(see illustrations)**.

12 Disconnect the wiring plug from the grille stepper motor and unclip the wiring loom from the cowling **(see illustrations)**.

7.10b ...and replace them with longer bolts

7.11a Release the upper securing clips...

7.11b ...then lift to release lower retaining clips

7.12a Disconnect the wiring plug...

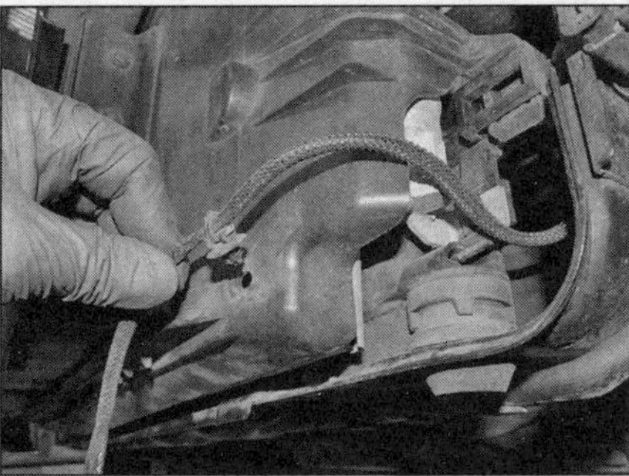
7.12b ...and unclip the wiring loom

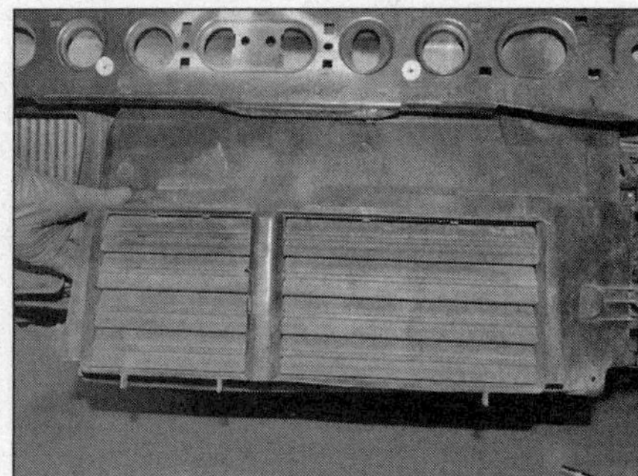
7.13 Remove the active shutter grille

13 Lower the active shutter grille assembly downwards, and out from the front of the vehicle **(see illustration)**.

14 If required the stepper motor can be removed from the grille, by releasing the securing clip **(see illustrations)**.

Refitting

15 Refitting is a reversal of the removal procedure.

8 Bonnet – removal, refitting and adjustment

Removal

1 Open the bonnet, and support it in the open position using the stay. Release the clips and remove the bonnet insulation panel **(see illustrations)**.

2 Disconnect the windscreen washer hoses from the bottom of the jets, and unclip them from the bonnet **(see illustration)**.

3 On models with heated washer jets, disconnect the windscreen washer wiring connector from the bottom of the jets **(see illustration)**, and unclip the loom from the bonnet.

4 To assist in correctly realigning the bonnet when refitting it, mark the outline of the hinges with a soft pencil. Loosen the two hinge retaining nuts on each side.

5 With the help of an assistant, unscrew the four nuts, release the stay, and lift the bonnet from the vehicle.

Refitting and adjustment

6 Refitting is a reversal of the removal procedure, noting the following points:

a) Position the bonnet hinges within the outline marks made during removal, but if necessary, alter its position to provide a uniform gap all round.

b) Adjust the front height by re-positioning the lock and turning the rubber buffers on the engine compartment front cross panel up or down to support the bonnet.

7.14a Remove the securing clip...

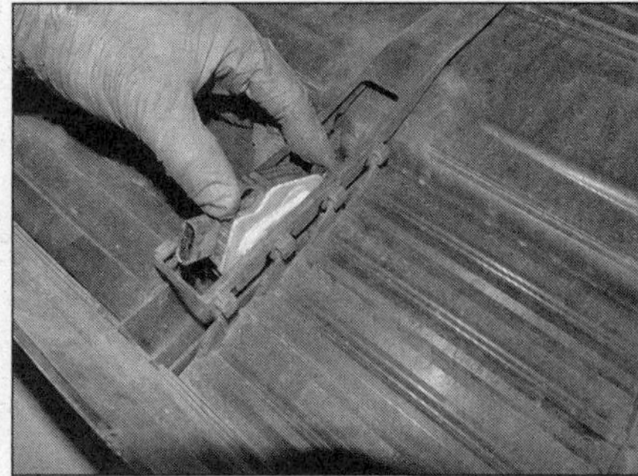
7.14b ...turn over grille and remove motor

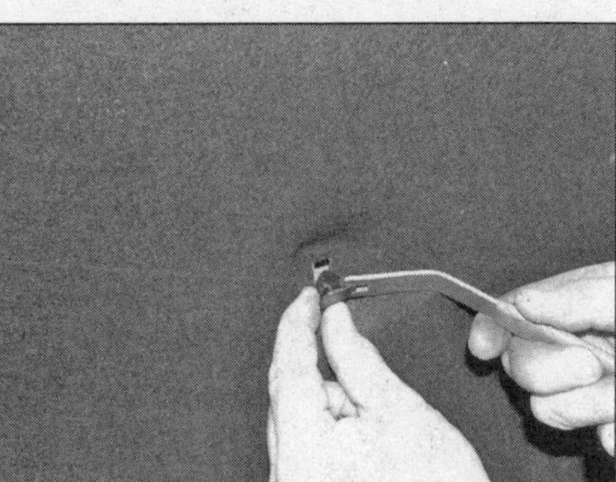
8.1a Release the retaining clips...

8.1b ...and then remove the insulation panel

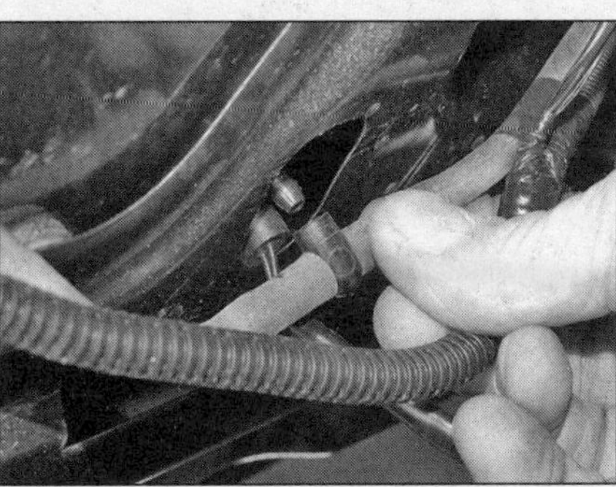
8.2 Disconnect the washer jets

8.3 Disconnect the wiring connector

9.1 Disconnect the switch wiring plug

9.2 Unclip the release cable

9.3 Remove the mounting bolts

9 Bonnet lock and release lever – removal, refitting and adjustment

Bonnet lock

1 Open the bonnet and disconnect the wiring plug from the bonnet open warning switch **(see illustration)**.

2 Unclip the cable to the bonnet release handle on the front crossmember, from the front of the lock assembly **(see illustration)**.

3 Make alignment marks between the lock and panel, then undo the two mounting bolts securing the lock assembly to the bonnet slam panel **(see illustration)**. Disconnect the release cable (which goes to the release handle in the passenger compartment), from the lock, if required.

4 Refitting is a reversal of the removal procedure, starting by positioning the lock as noted before removal. **Note:** *Make sure both release cables are fitted correctly before shutting the bonnet.*

5 If the front of the bonnet is not level with the front wings, the lock may be moved up or down within the mounting holes. After making an adjustment, raise or lower the rubber buffers to support the bonnet correctly.

Release lever

6 Working inside the front passenger footwell, unclip the plastic cover from the release lever **(see illustration)**.

7 Using a 10mm deep socket, slide it through the centre of the lever pivot to release the locking clips, then withdraw the lever **(see illustrations)**.

8 Unclip the trim panel, then undo the two retaining screws to remove the release lever linkage from the inner panel **(see illustrations)**. Unclip the cable from the release linkage, if required.

9 Refitting is a reversal of the removal procedure, making sure release cable is fitted correctly.

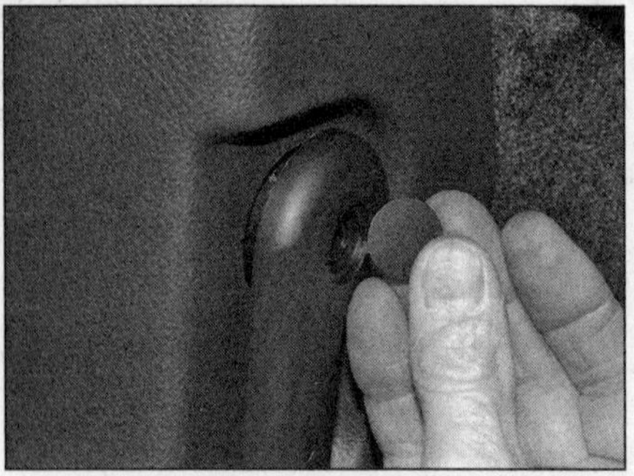
9.6 Unclip the trim cover

9.7a Insert socket to release clips...

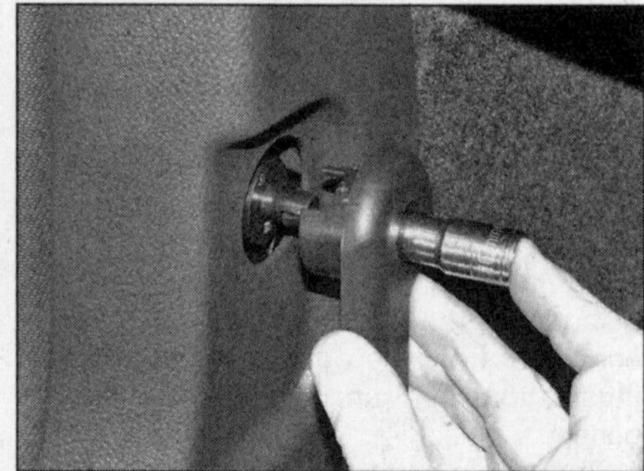
9.7b ...and withdraw the bonnet release lever

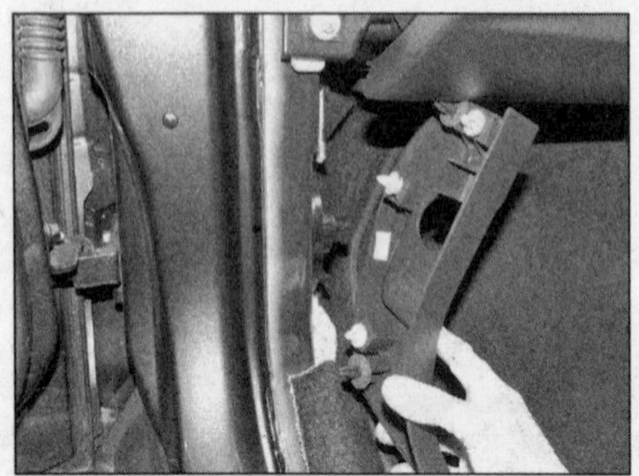
9.8a Unclip the sill trim...

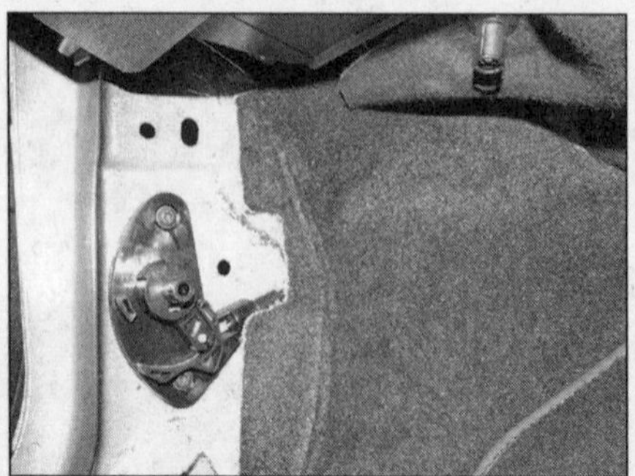
9.8b ...undo the screws...

9.8c ...and remove the release linkage

10.2a Remove the cover...

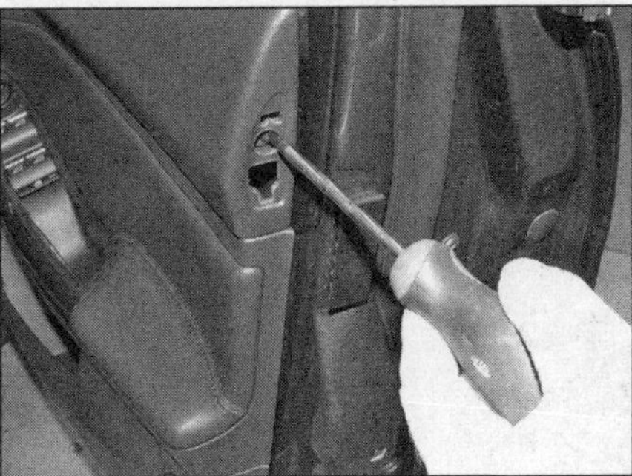

10.2b ...and then the screw

10.3 Remove the reflector and then the screw

10 Door inner trim panel – removal and refitting

Removal

1 Disconnect the battery negative (earth) lead (Chapter 5A Section 3).

Front door

2 Use a plastic type trim tool and remove the small trim piece from the end of the panel. Remove the now exposed screw **(see illustrations)**.

3 At the rear edge of the panel, remove the door ajar reflector and then remove the screw **(see illustrations)**.

4 Remove the cover from the centre of the door release handle and then remove the now exposed screw **(see illustration)**.

5 Again using a plastic trim tool prise free the trim piece from around the door switch panel. Work the upper end free first and then release the locating peg at the lower end **(see illustrations)**.

6 Release the switch panel disconnecting the wiring plugs as the panel is removed **(see illustrations)**.

7 Remove the two screws from behind the switch panel **(see illustration)**.

8 At the top of the door prise free the audio system tweeter speaker panel **(see illustration)**. Disconnect the wiring plug as the panel is removed.

10.4 Remove the cover and the now exposed screw

10.5a Unclip the upper part of the trim...

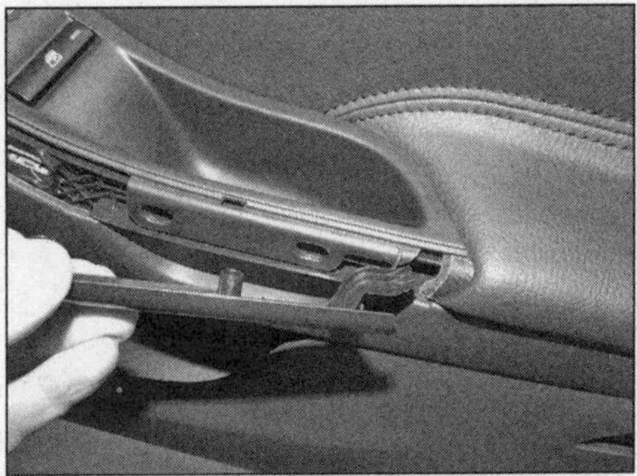

10.5b ...and release the locating pegs at the lower end

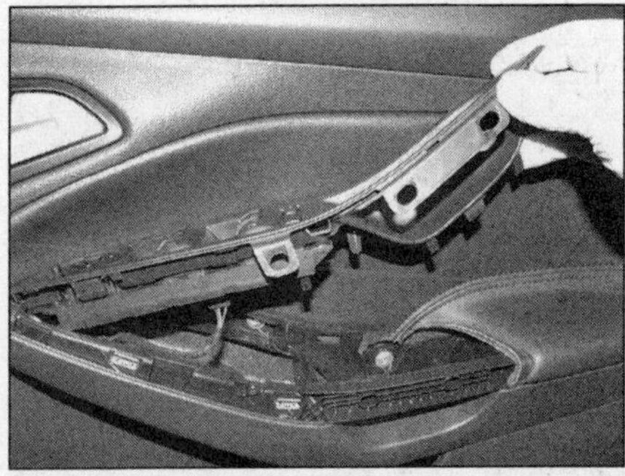

10.6a Release the panel and...

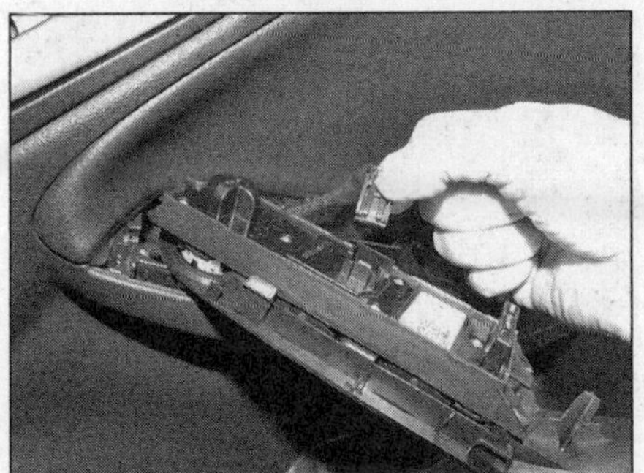

10.6b ...disconnect the wiring plug

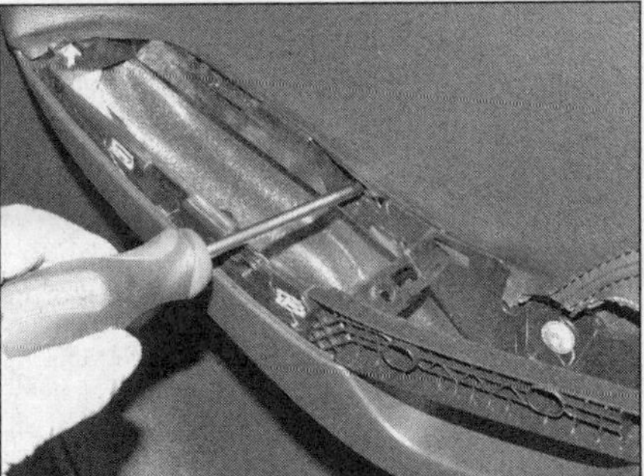

10.7 Remove the two screws

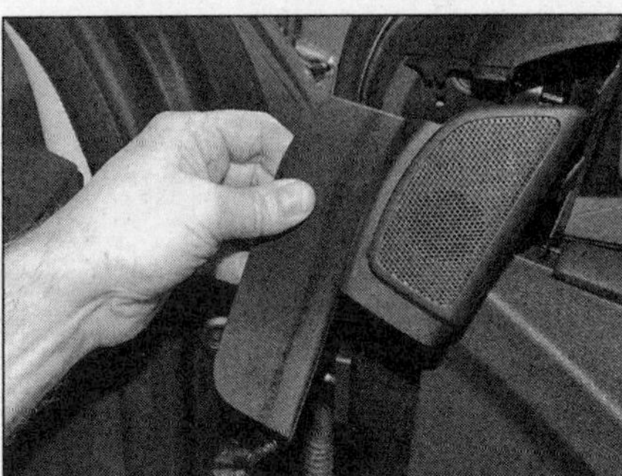

10.8 Unclip the speaker trim panel

10.9 Using trim tool to release clips

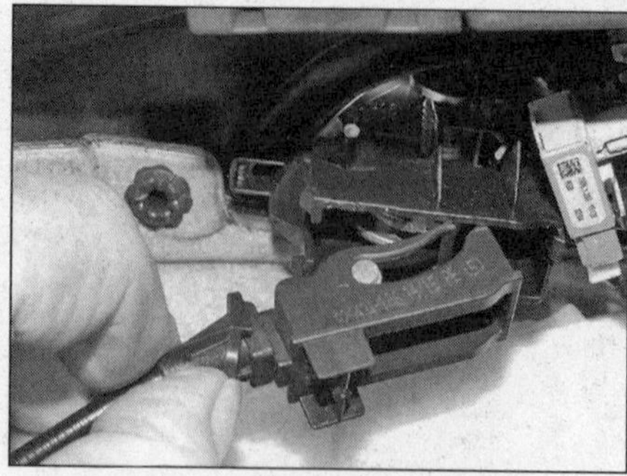
10.10a Unclip the release cable...

10.10b ...disconnect the wiring connector...

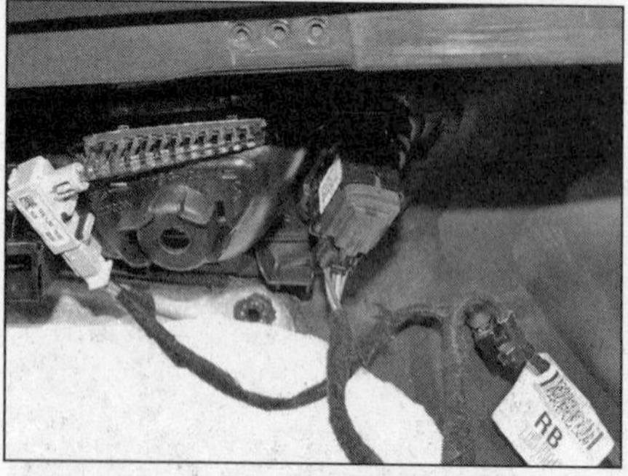

10.10c ...and disconnect switch/light connectors, where fitted

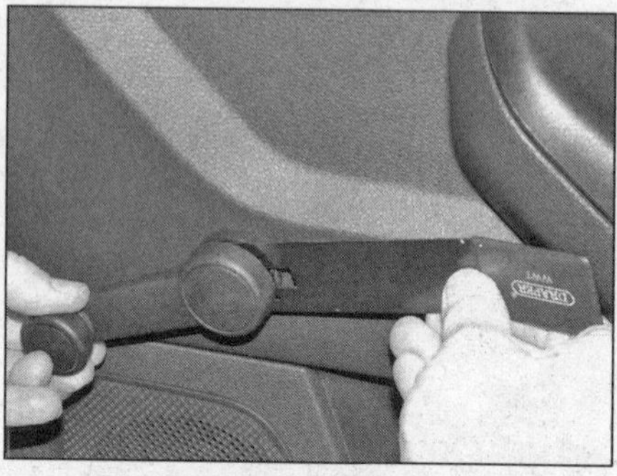
10.11a Release the spring clip

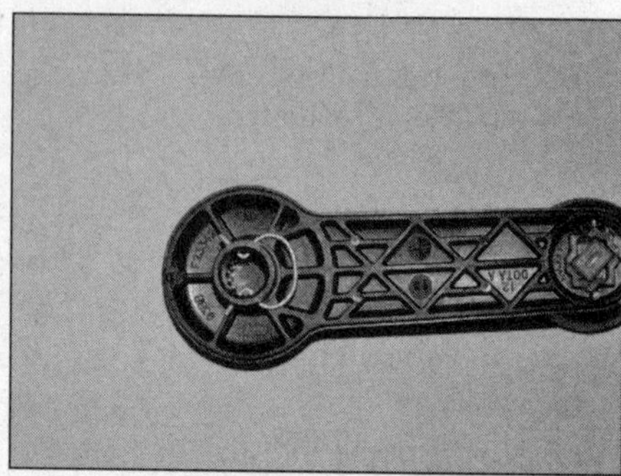
10.11b Note its orientation

9 Working around the outer edge, use a plastic trim tool to release the retaining clips securing the trim panel **(see illustration)**.

10 Lift the panel slightly to release it from the door panel, then disconnect the cable from the release handle. Also disconnect the wiring connectors (depending on model), as the trim panel is removed **(see illustrations)**.

Rear door

11 On models fitted with manual windows use a suitable tool to release the spring clip **(see illustrations)**. Alternatively the spring clip can be released using a polishing cloth dragged around the handle and moved in a sawing action to release securing clip. With handle removed, recover the washer.

12 Prise free the door pull handle upper trim piece. On models with power windows disconnect the wiring plug as the handle is removed **(see illustrations)**.

13 Remove the two torx head screws from inside the door pull aperture **(see illustration)**.

14 Unclip the cover from the door release

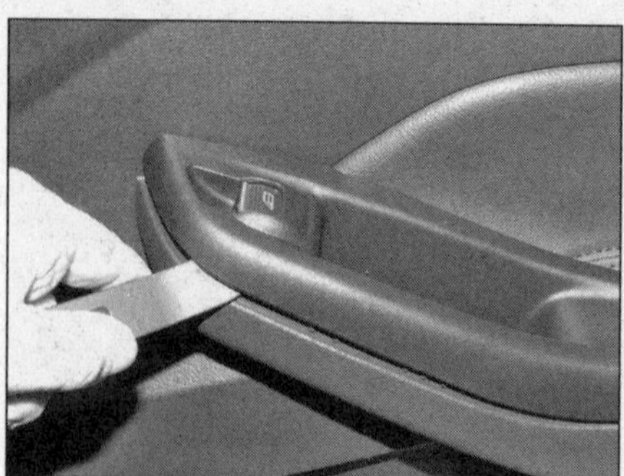
10.12a Prise up the upper part of the trim...

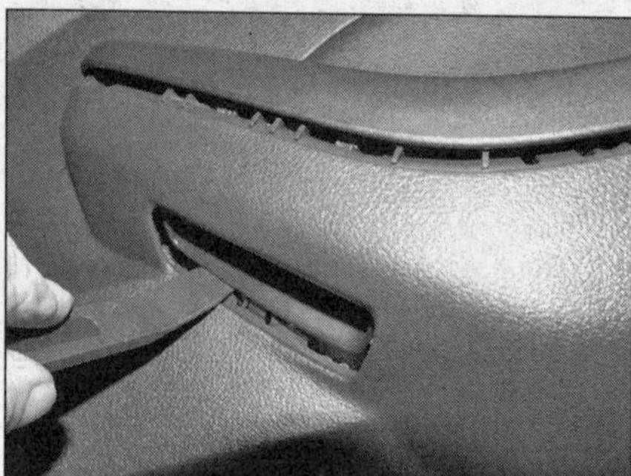
10.12b ...and the lower part...

10.12c ...to release the securing clip...

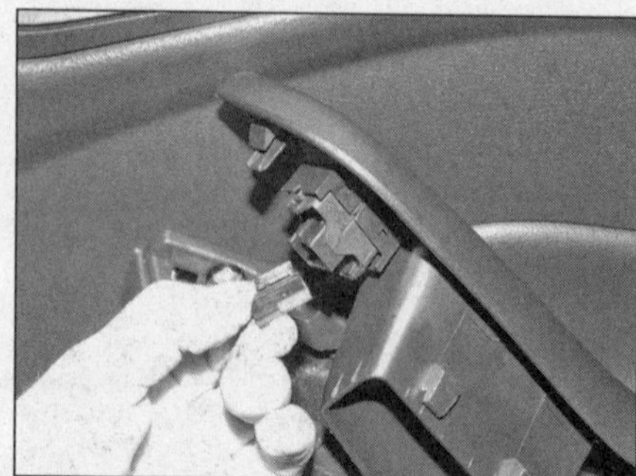
10.12d ...then on models with power windows disconnect the wiring plug

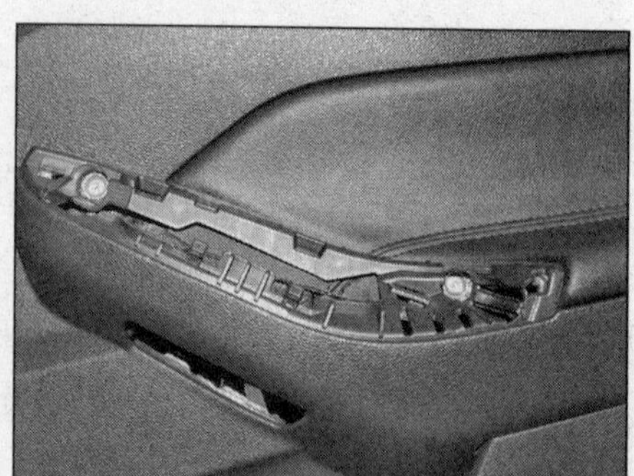
10.13 Remove the screws

10.14 Remove the cover

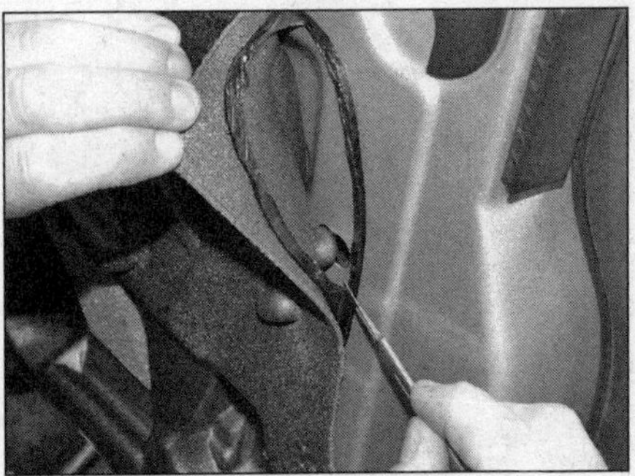
11.2 Remove the membrane

11.4 Release the glass clamp

handle and remove the now exposed screw **(see illustration)**.

15 Working around the outer edge of the panel, use a forked trim tool to release the retaining clips securing the trim panel.

16 Disconnect the door handle release cable and any wiring plug connectors, as the panel is withdrawn **(see illustrations 10.10a, 10.10b & 10.10c)**.

Refitting

17 Refitting is a reversal of the removal procedure.

11 Door window glass – removal and refitting

Removal

Front door

1 Remove the door inner trim panel as described in Section 10.

2 Use a sharp knife and carefully remove the door membrane **(see illustration)**.

3 Refit the power window switch panel and lower the window to access the glass retaining clamps.

4 Use a suitable screwdriver or punch and release the glass clamps **(see illustration)**.

5 With the glass free from the clamps, push the glass up and remove it from the outside of the door **(see illustration)**. The aid of an assistant is recommended here.

Rear door

6 Remove the door inner trim panel as described in Section 10.

7 Remove the inner panel membrane by carefully cutting through the sealant **(see illustration 11.2)**.

8 On power window models refit the switch, on manual windows refit the winder handle. Fully lower the window.

9 Carefully remove the outer weather strip. Protect the door paint work with masking tape if necessary.

10 Prise free and remove the 2 sections of the trim panel from around the upper door frame **(see illustration)**.

11 Prise free the inner weather strip and then pull up and remove the rear rubber seal from the glass guide channel.

12 At the rear edge of the door remove the outer trim panel. It is held in place by 3 screws **(see illustration)**.

13 Lower the window to access the glass retaining clamp.

14 Use a suitable screwdriver and release the glass clamp.

15 With the glass free from the clamps, push the glass up and remove it from the outside. The aid of an assistant is recommended here.

Refitting

16 Refitting is a reversal of the removal procedure, but note the following:

a) Make sure that the glass is correctly located in the clamp.

b) Start the vehicle and initialise the window by fully lowering the appropriate window and holding the switch in the down position for a few seconds. Fully raise the window and hold the switch in the up position for several seconds.

c) Repeat the above procedure once more.

12 Door window regulator – removal and refitting

Removal

Front door

1 Follow the procedure for glass removal in Section 11, but do not fully remove the glass, simply tape it in the up position using strong adhesive tape.

2 Remove the front door speaker, reach through the opening and disconnect the wiring plug. Unclip the wiring loom from the cable clip below the motor

3 Release the cable guide clip from the regulator and then partially undo the 5

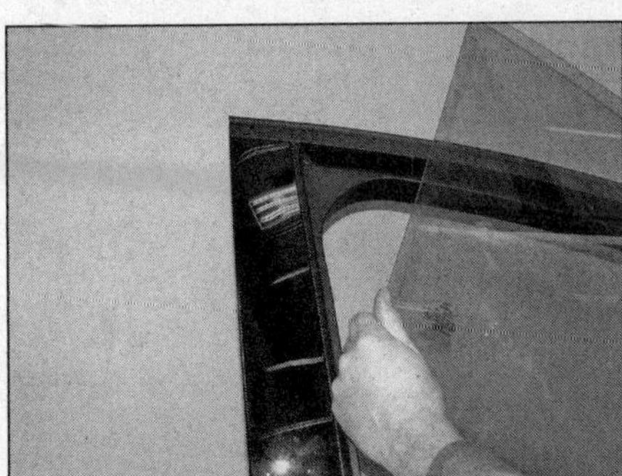
11.5 Remove the glass

11.10 Remove the upper trim panel

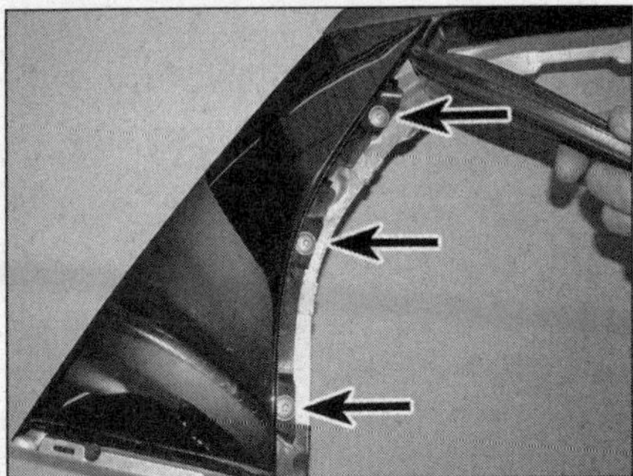
11.12 Remove the screws (arrowed)

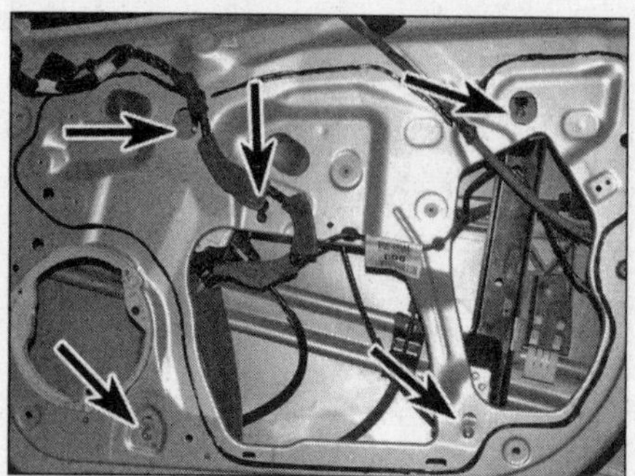
12.3a Release the screws (arrowed)...

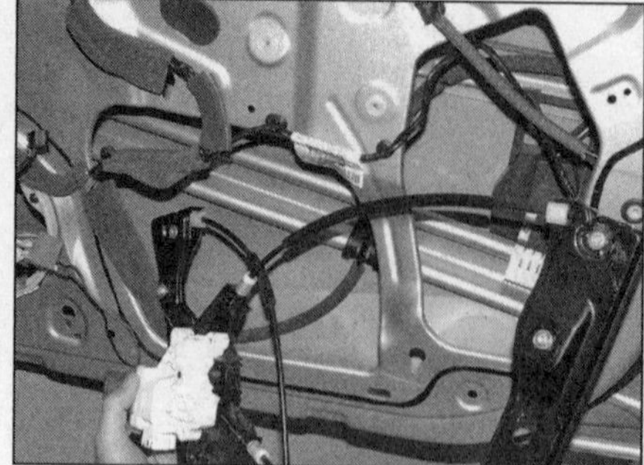
12.3b ...and work the regulator free from the door frame

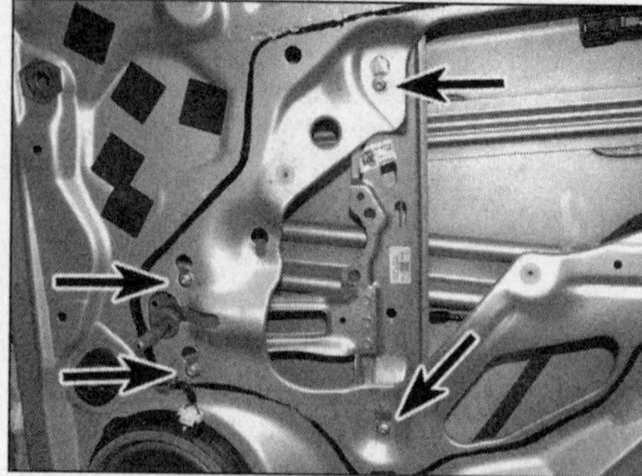
12.6 The regulator mounting screws (arrowed)

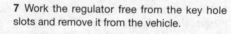

retaining screws. Work the guide channels and motor free from the key hole slots and remove the channels, cables and motor as a single item **(see illustrations)**.

4 If required the motor can now be removed from the regulator.

Rear door

5 Follow the procedure for glass removal in Section 11, but do not remove any of the door frame upper trim panels or fully remove the glass. Tape the glass in the fully closed position using strong adhesive tape (eg. Duct tape).

6 Where fitted, disconnect the wiring plug form the motor and then slacken (but do not remove) the 4 regulator mounting bolts **(see illustration)**.

13.2 Slacken the screw

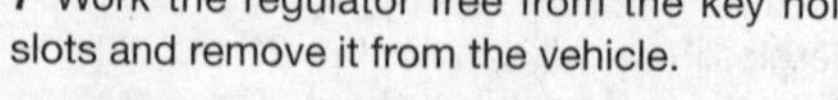

7 Work the regulator free from the key hole slots and remove it from the vehicle.

Refitting

8 Refitting is a reversal of the removal procedure, but note the following:

a) Make sure that the glass is correctly located in the clamps.

b) Start the vehicle and initialise the window by fully lowering the appropriate window and holding the switch in the down position for a few seconds. Fully raise the window and hold the switch in the up position for several seconds.

c) Repeat the above procedure once more.

13.3 Remove the smaller section of the handle

13 Door handle and lock components – removal and refitting

Removal

Exterior handle – front

1 Prise out the rubber grommet from the end of the door adjacent to the exterior handle.

2 Working through the aperture, slacken the handle retaining bolt approximately 22 turns **(see illustration)**.

3 Where fitted, carefully pull the trim and lock cylinder from the door **(see illustration)**. On all other handles, remove the trim at the rear of the handle (where the lock cylinder would be on conventional systems).

4 Pull the exterior handle rearwards, and manoeuvre it from the door **(see illustration)**.

5 Recover the seals between the handle and the door skin.

Exterior handle – rear

6 Prise out the rubber grommet from the end of the door adjacent to the exterior handle.

7 Working through the aperture, slacken the handle retaining bolt approximately 7 turns **(see illustration 13.2)**.

8 Pull the trim at the rear of the handle outwards **(see illustration)**.

9 Pull the exterior handle rearwards, and manoeuvre it from the door. Recover the seals between the handle and the door skin **(see illustration)**.

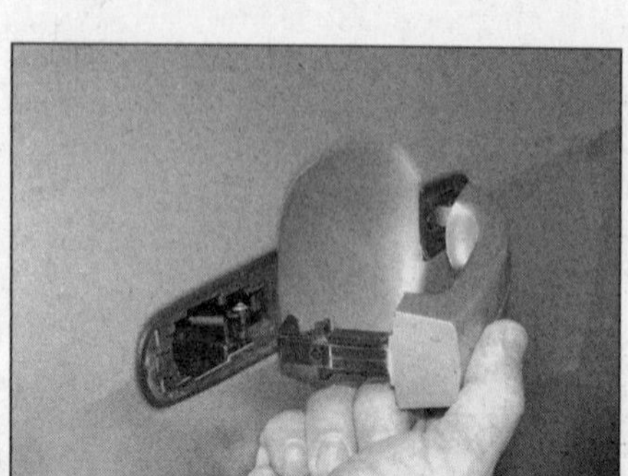
13.4 Remove the main section of the exterior handle

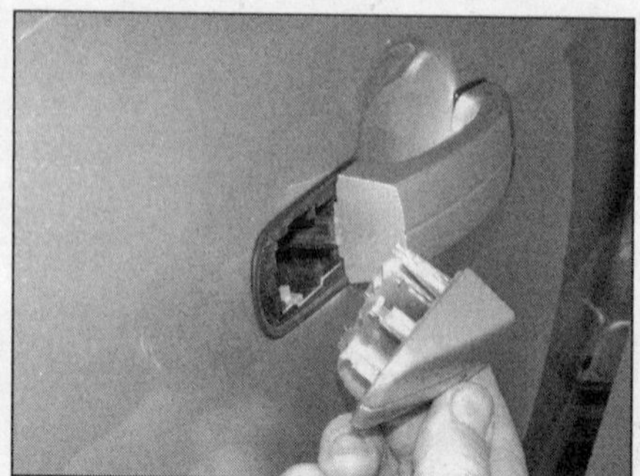
13.8 Release the smaller section of the handle

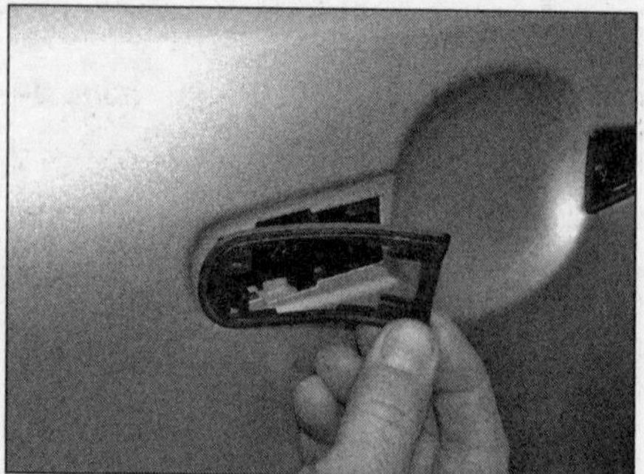
13.9 Recover the seals

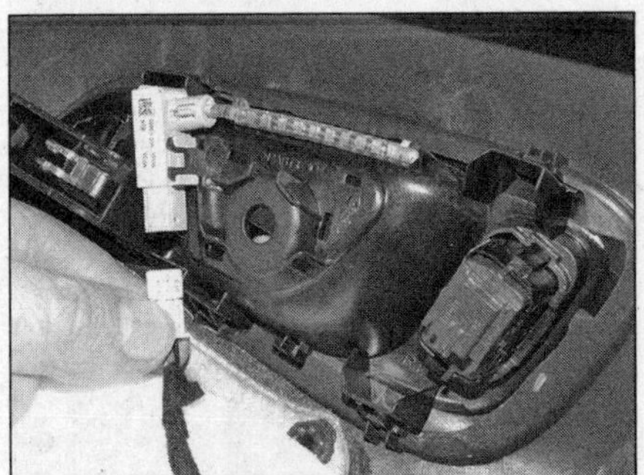
13.11a Disconnect the wiring connector...

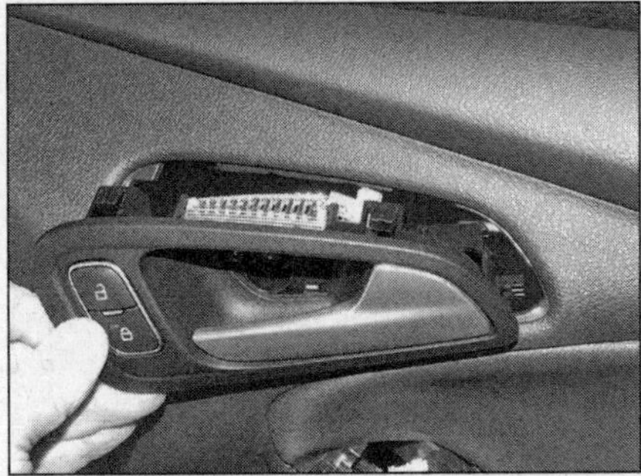
13.11b ...and withdraw the interior handle

13.14a Remove the screw from the door skin...

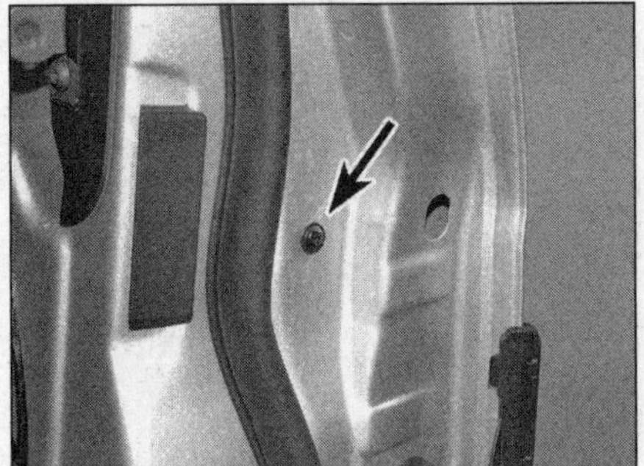
13.14b ...and from the door shut (arrowed)

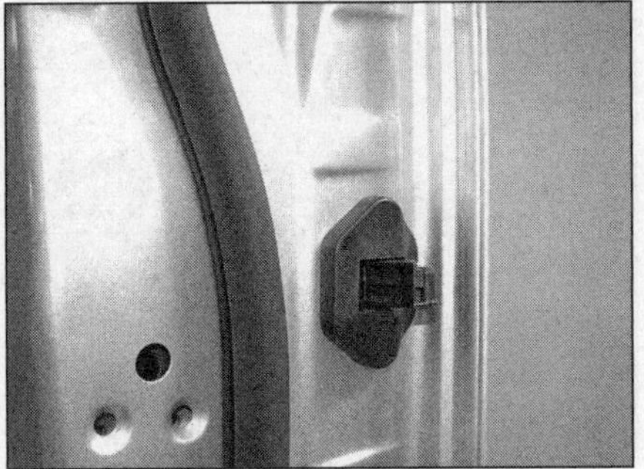
13.15a Remove the cover...

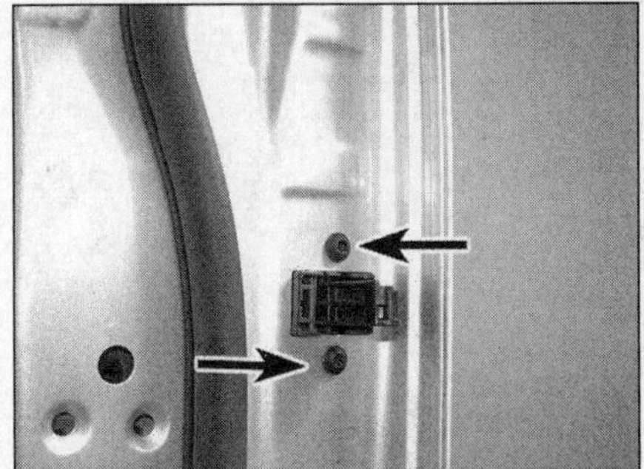
13.15b ...and the screws (arrowed)

Interior handle

10 Remove the door inner trim panel as described in Section 10.

11 Where applicable, disconnect the wiring connector from the handle illumination light, then detach the door release handle from the door trim panel by depressing the locking tabs and withdrawing the handle **(see illustrations)**.

Latch – front

12 Remove the window regulator as described in Section 12.

13 Remove the exterior handle as described in this Section.

14 Unclip the inner section of the door handle assembly from the door skin and then remove the single upper screw from the door shut **(see illustrations)**.

15 On models fitted with door edge protectors, unclip the door edge protector and then remove the operating rod cover from the edge protector. Remove the 2 screws and push the edge protector inside the door frame **(see illustrations)**.

16 Remove the 3 main bolts from the latch and manoeuvre the complete assembly from the door frame **(see illustrations)**. Disconnect the wiring plug as the latch is removed.

17 If the latch assembly is to be replaced, disconnect the interior release cable from the latch.

Lock cylinder

18 Prise out the rubber grommet from the end of the door adjacent to the exterior handle.

19 Working through the aperture, slacken the handle retaining bolt approximately 22 turns **(see illustration 13.2)**.

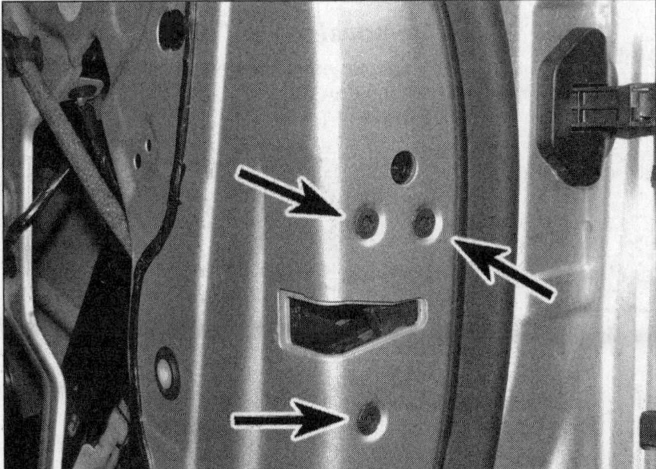
13.16a Remove the screws (arrowed)...

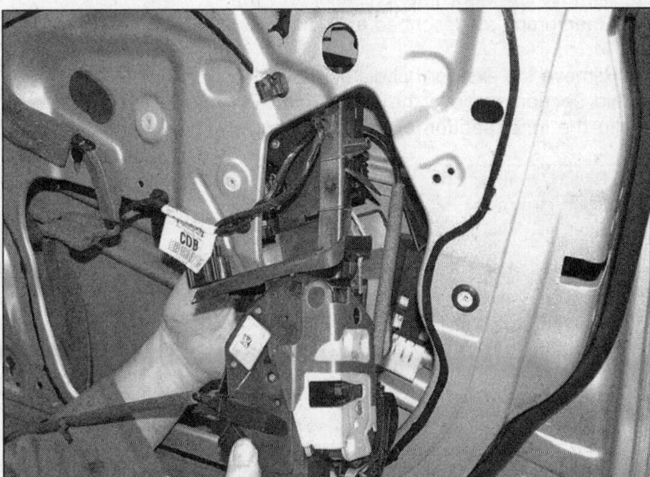

13.16b ...and manoeuvre the assembly from the door

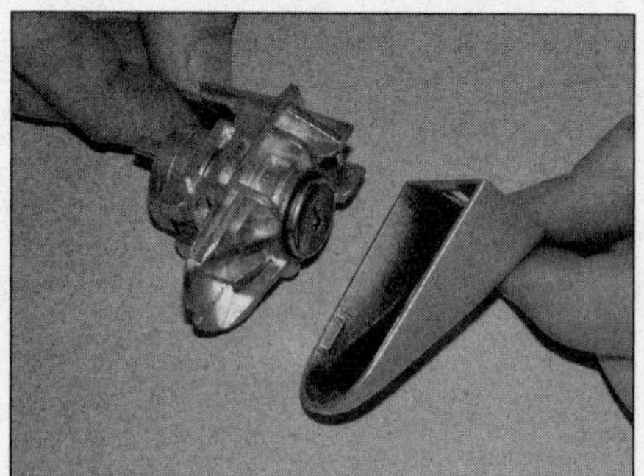
13.21a Remove the cover...

13.21b and then the circlip

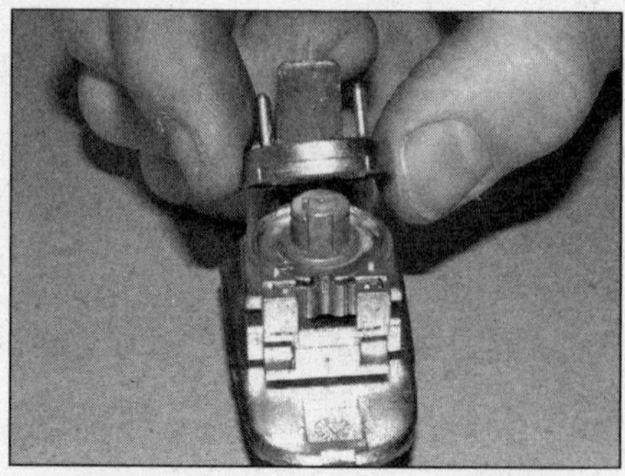
13.21c Remove the cover and then...

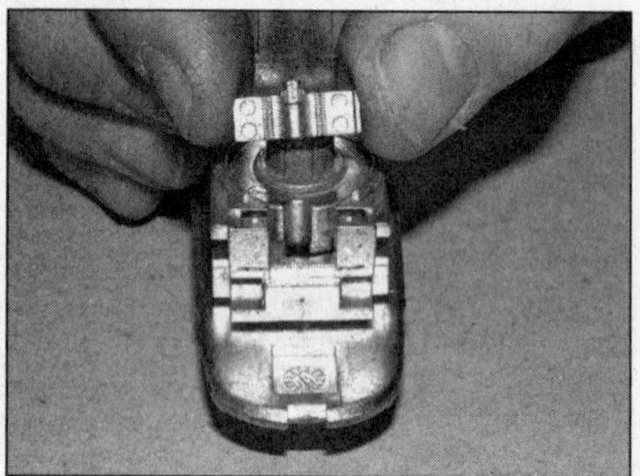
13.21d ...slide out the locking plate

13.21e Drill out the locking pin cover and...

13.21f ...then drive out the locking pin

20 Pull the trim and lock cylinder from the door **(see illustration 13.3)**.

21 The key barrel can now be removed from the housing by prising off the circlip, the barrel cover and the locking plate. Next, using a 4mm drill bit partially drill out the locking pin housing and then driving out the locking pin with a 2mm punch **(see illustrations)**. Remove the cylinder whilst covering the tumblers with one hand. Immediately insert the key to lock the tumblers in place.

Latch – rear

22 Remove the door interior panel and the door membrane as described in Sections 10 and 11.

23 Remove the exterior handle as described in this Section, remove the screw and then unclip the inner section of the door handle assembly from the door skin **(see illustration)**.

24 Release the cable clip from the inner handle cable and then remove the single screw from the latch **(see illustration)**.

25 Remove the 3 mounting bolts from the door shut and partially remove the latch, so that the wiring plug can be disconnected **(see illustration)**. Manoeuvre the latch from the door frame.

26 If required the inner release cable, the outer handle cable and the glass guide channel can now be removed from the latch assembly.

Refitting

Handles (exterior and interior)

27 Refitting is a reversal of the removal procedure.

Lock cylinder

28 Refitting is a reversal of removal.

Latch

29 Refitting is a reversal of the removal procedure.

14 Door – removal and refitting

Removal

1 Disconnect the battery negative (earth) lead (Chapter 5A Section 3).

2 Using a Torx key, unscrew and remove the

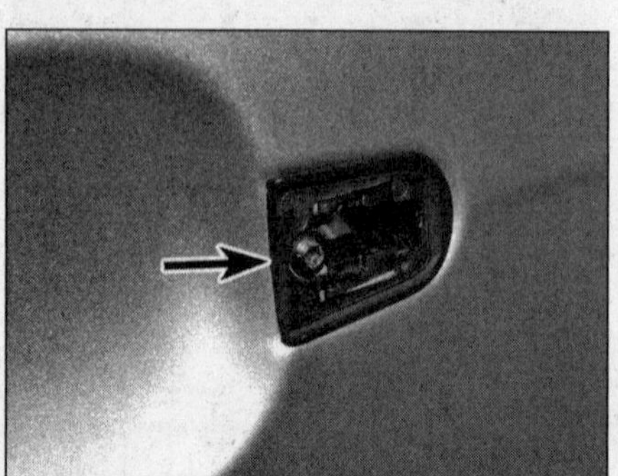
13.23 Remove the screw (arrowed)

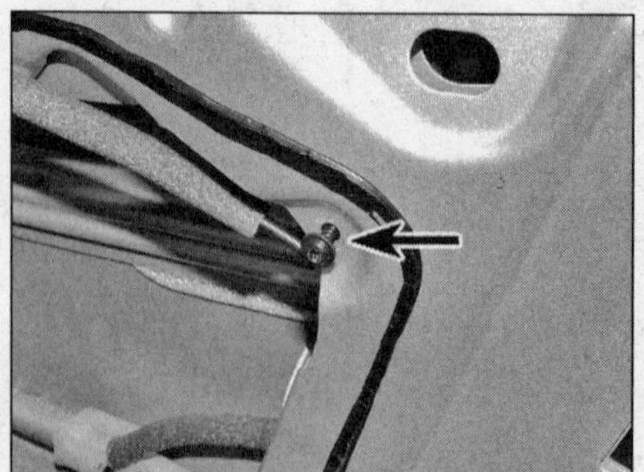
13.24 Remove the screw (arrowed)

13.25 Disconnect the wiring plug

check strap mounting bolt from the door pillar **(see illustration)**.

3 Prise out the rubber gaiter, and disconnect the wiring block connector **(see illustration)**.

4 Position a trolley jack under the door. The head of the jack should be covered with a suitable material to avoid damage to the door.

5 Have an assistant support the door, then undo the retaining bolts in the top and bottom hinge pins **(see illustrations)**.

6 Carefully lift the door from the hinges, and with the aid of the trolley jack (and an assistant) remove the door from the vehicle.

Refitting

7 Refitting is a reversal of the removal procedure, but check that the door lock passes over the striker centrally. If necessary, reposition the striker.

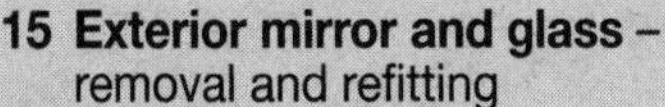

15 Exterior mirror and glass – removal and refitting

Removal

Mirror

1 Unclip the speaker trim panel from the front of the window opening and disconnect the wiring plug, as it is withdrawn **(see illustration)**.

2 Disconnect the wiring plug and then remove the blanking grommet **(see illustrations)**.

3 Unscrew the mirror mounting bolts **(see illustration)**, then release the clip and withdraw the mirror from the outside of the door. Recover the mirror seal as the wiring/cable is being drawn through the rubber grommet.

Mirror glass

4 Pull the outer edge of the glass rearwards, insert a broad plastic type trim tool behind the glass and gently prise the glass from place **(see illustration)**.

5 Withdraw the mirror glass and disconnect

14.2 Undo the check strap Torx bolt

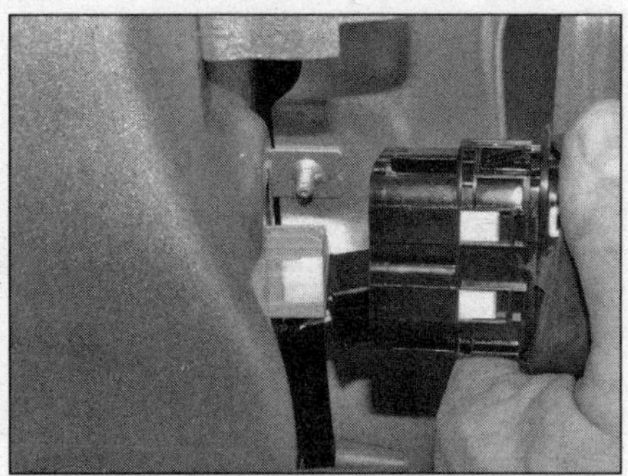

14.3 Disconnect the wiring plug

14.5a Undo the upper hinge bolt...

14.5b ...and the lower hinge bolt

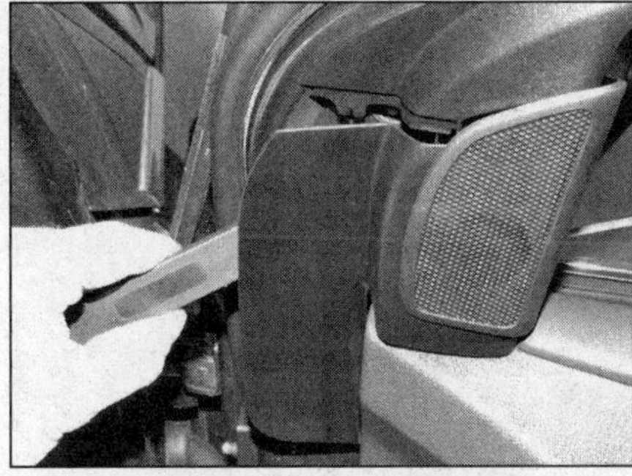

15.1 Remove the speaker panel

15.2a Disconnect the wiring plug...

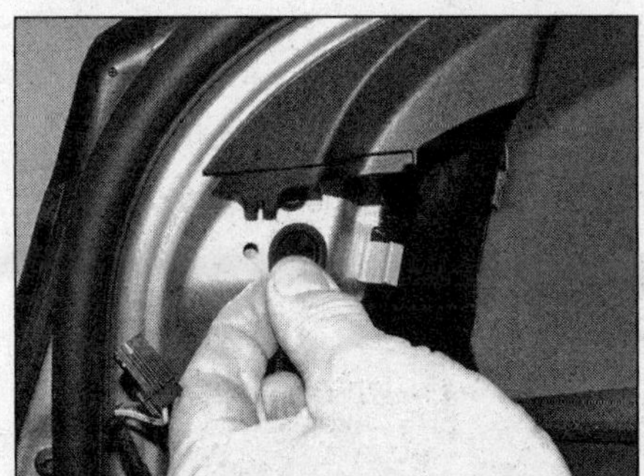

15.2b ...and remove the grommet

15.3 Remove the mounting screws (arrowed)

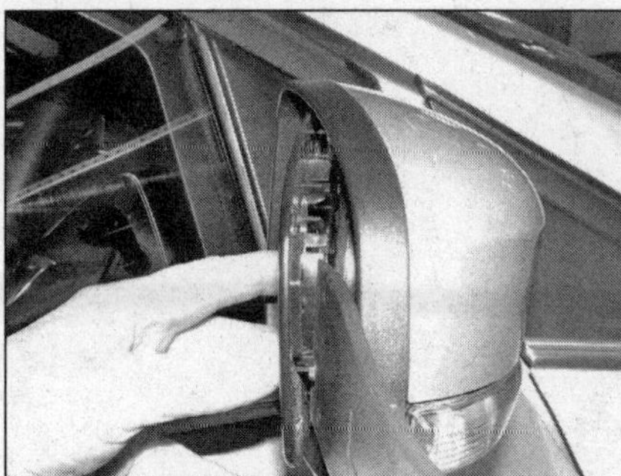

15.4 Prise the glass from the housing

15.5 Disconnect the wiring plugs

the wiring connectors for the heated mirrors **(see illustration)**.

Refitting

6 Refitting is a reversal of the removal procedure.

16.3a Unclip the left-hand side trim panel...

16.1a Push the clip at the base of the mirror rearwards, and slide it up from the windscreen mounting

16 Interior mirror – removal and refitting

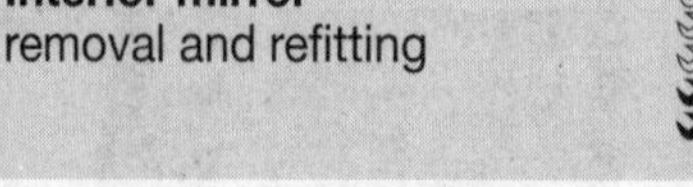

Basic mirror

1 Press the retaining clip away from the windscreen, then slide the mirror up from the base **(see illustrations)**.

2 Refitting is a reversal of removal.

Auto-dimming mirror

3 Release the securing clips and remove the left-hand side trim panel fro around the mirror base, followed by the right-hand side **(see illustrations)**.

4 Disconnect the mirror wiring plug connector at the top of the mirror stem**(see illustration)**.

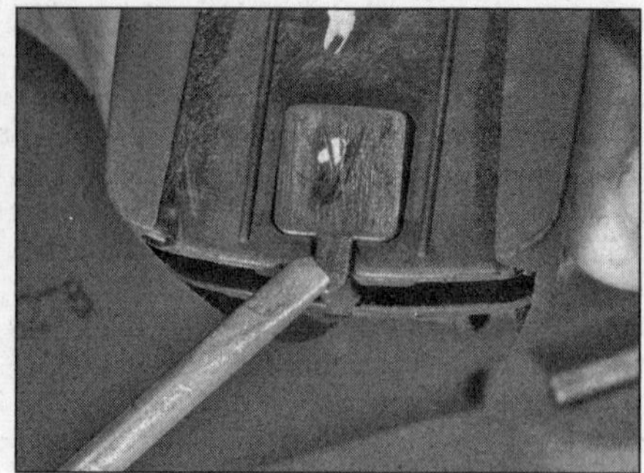
16.1b Mirror retaining clip – viewed from the front face of the mirror base

5 Rotate the mirror base 60° anti-clockwise and detach it from the mounting **(see illustrations)**.

6 Refitting is the reversal of the removal procedure.

17 Tailgate – removal and refitting

Removal

1 Disconnect the battery negative (earth) lead (Chapter 5A Section 3).

2 Remove the tailgate inner trim panels as described in Section 26.

3 Remove the high level brake light as described in Chapter 12 Section 8, and disconnect the washer hose **(see illustration)**.

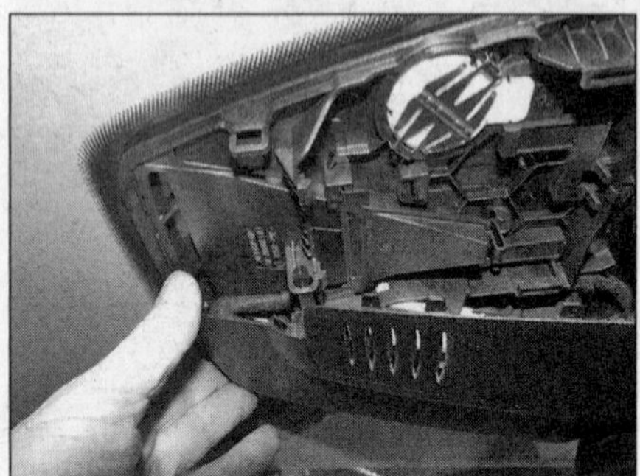
16.3b ...then release the locating pegs...

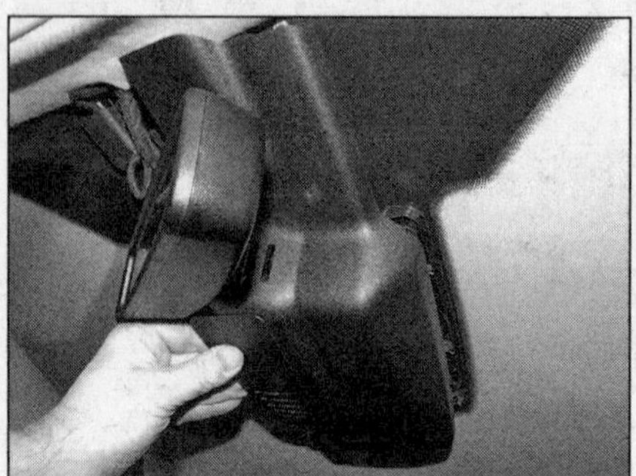
16.3c ...and remove the right-hand side trim panel

16.4 Disconnect the wiring connector

16.5a Rotate the mirror 60° anti-clockwise...

16.5b ...to release it from the mounting bracket

17.3 Disconnect the washer hose

4 Undo the retaining bolts in the handle recesses, then pull trim panel away from the tailgate to release the retaining clips.

5 Carefully unclip the upper central tailgate trim and then pull the rear window side trims inwards to release the clips.

6 With all the tailgate trim panels removed, work around the tailgate and disconnect the various wiring loom connectors. If necessary label the wiring loom connectors as they are disconnected.

7 Unbolt the earth connections **(see illustration)** and unclip the wiring loom from the multiple cable clips.

8 Prise the rubber grommet **(see illustration)** from the tailgate aperture, and pull out the wiring loom.

9 Mark the position of the tailgate hinge and then slacken but do not remove the hinge bolts.

10 Have an assistant support the tailgate in its open position.

11 Using a small screwdriver, prise off the clip securing the struts to the tailgate **(see illustration)**. Pull the sockets from the ball-studs, and move the struts downwards.

12 Unscrew and remove the hinge bolts (two each side) from the tailgate **(see illustration)**. Withdraw the tailgate from the body aperture, taking care not to damage the paintwork.

17.7 Unbolt the earth connections

17.8 Prise the grommet free

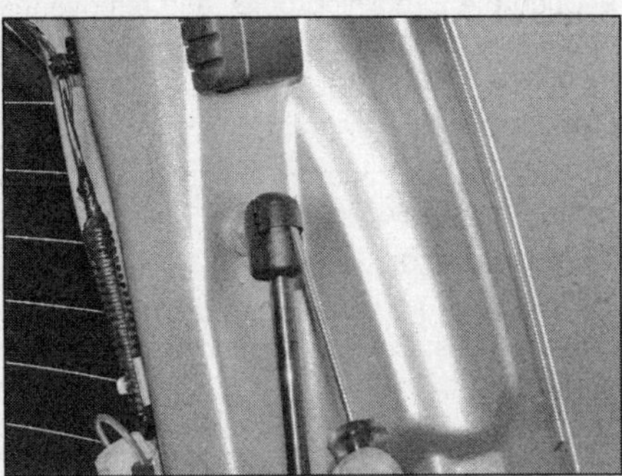

17.11 Unclip the tailgate struts

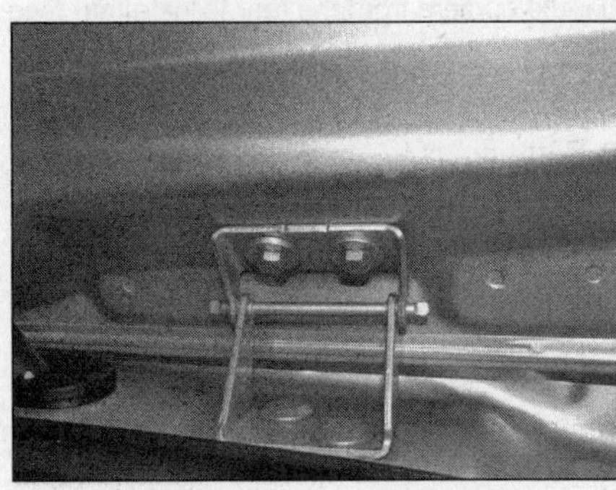

17.12 Remove the hinge bolts

Refitting

13 Refitting is a reversal of the removal procedure, but check that the tailgate is located centrally in the body aperture, and that the striker enters the lock centrally. If necessary, loosen the mounting nuts and reposition the tailgate as required.

18 Support struts – removal and refitting

Removal

1 Have an assistant support the tailgate or bonnet in its open position.

2 Prise off the upper spring clip securing the strut to the tailgate, boot or bonnet. Pull the socket from the ball-stud **(see illustration 17.11)**.

3 Similarly prise off the bottom clip, and pull the socket from the ball-stud. Withdraw the strut.

Refitting

4 Refitting is a reversal of the removal procedure, making sure that the strut is fitted the same way up as when it was removed.

19 Tailgate lock components – removal and refitting

Removal

Latch

1 Remove the tailgate interior trim panel as described in Section 26.

2 Disconnect the electrical connector from the tailgate latch assembly **(see illustration)**.

3 Undo the 3 lock securing bolts and remove the lock assembly **(see illustration)**.

Release switch

4 Remove the tailgate interior trim panel as described in Section 26.

5 Unbolt the switch mounting bolts from the tailgate (6 in total). On Estate models disconnect the wiring plugs. Remove the panel complete with the switch.

6 Disconnect the electrical connector from the switch.

7 Depress the locking tabs and remove the release switch **(see illustration)**.

8 On models with rear facing camera, release the locking tabs and unclip the release

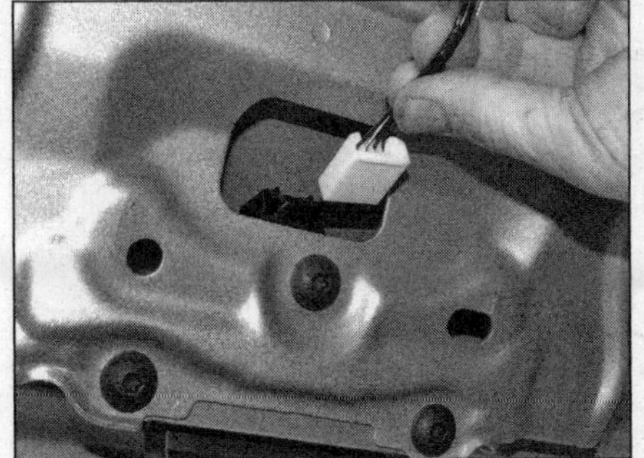

19.2 Disconnect the wiring plug

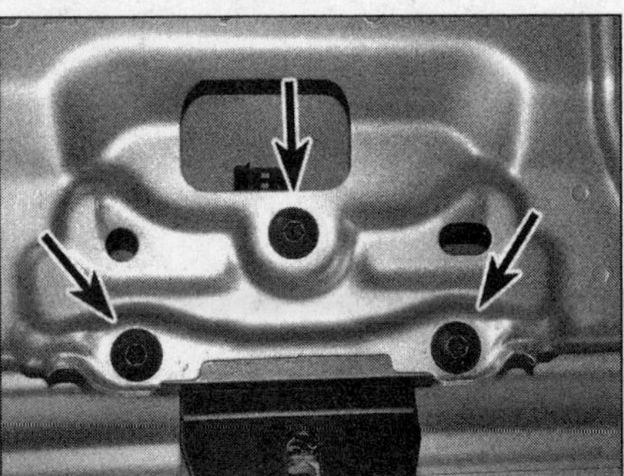

19.3 Remove the bolts (arrowed)

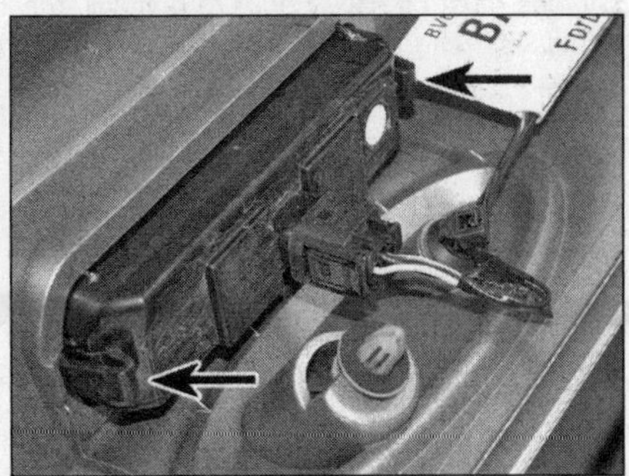

19.7 Depress the locking tabs (arrowed)

19.8a Release the locking tabs...

19.8b ...and withdraw the release switch/ camera housing

handle/camera from the rear tailgate trim **(see illustrations)**.

Refitting

9 Refitting is a reversal of the removal procedure.

20 Central locking system – testing, reprogramming, removal and refitting

Testing/reprogramming

1 Testing of the central locking/alarm system can only be carried out using Ford's IDS diagnostic tester.

2 Prior to reprogramming a remote locking transmitter, ensure the vehicle battery is fully-charged, and the alarm is not armed or triggered. Fasten all seat belts, and close all doors.

3 Turn the ignition switch from position I to position II four times within 6 seconds, then turn it to position 0 (off).

4 A chime will be heard to indicate that the 'learning mode' has begun.

5 Within 10 seconds of the previous step, press any button on the remote transmitter until a further chime is heard. This indicates the process has been successful. Turn the ignition switch to position II to exit the learning mode.

Removal

Body Control Module (BCM)

Note: *If the BCM is to be renewed, the unit settings must be saved prior to removal, then initialised using the FORD IDS diagnostic tester.*

6 Removal and refitting of the BCM is described in Chapter 12.

Keyless entry system module

Note: *If the module is to be renewed, the unit settings must be saved prior to removal, then initialised using the FORD IDS diagnostic tester.*

7 Disconnect the battery negative lead as described in Chapter 5A.

8 Remove the left-hand luggage compartment side panel, C-pillar panel and parcel shelf support as described in Section 28.

9 Undo the 2 retaining bolts, and remove the module. Disconnect the wiring plugs as the module is withdrawn.

Door motors

10 The door lock motors are integral with the locks. Refer to Section 13.

Tailgate motor

11 The boot lid/tailgate motors are integral with the locks. Refer to Section 19.

Refitting

12 In all cases, refitting is a reversal of the removal procedure.

21 Windscreen and fixed windows – removal and refitting

1 The windscreen and rear window on all models are bonded in place with special mastic, as are the rear side windows. Special tools are required to cut free the old units and fit new ones; special cleaning solutions and primer are also required. It is therefore recommended that this work is entrusted to a Ford dealer or windscreen replacement specialist.

22 Body side-trim mouldings and adhesive emblems – removal and refitting

Removal

1 Body side trims and mouldings are attached either by retaining clips or adhesive bonding. On bonded mouldings, insert a length of strong cord (fishing line is ideal) behind the moulding or emblem concerned. With a sawing action, break the adhesive bond between the moulding or emblem and the panel.

2 Thoroughly clean all traces of adhesive from the panel using methylated spirit, and allow the location to dry.

3 On mouldings with retaining clips, unclip the mouldings from the panel, taking care not to damage the paintwork.

Refitting

4 Peel back the protective paper from the rear face of the new moulding or emblem. Carefully fit it into position on the panel concerned, but take care not to touch the adhesive. When in position, apply hand pressure to the moulding/emblem for a short period, to ensure maximum adhesion to the panel.

5 Renew any broken retaining clips before refitting trims or mouldings.

23 Sunroof – general information and adjustment

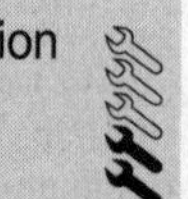

Glass panel

1 Slide back the sun blind, and set the glass panel in the closed position.

2 Pull the panel guide arm covers inwards and remove them **(see illustration)**.

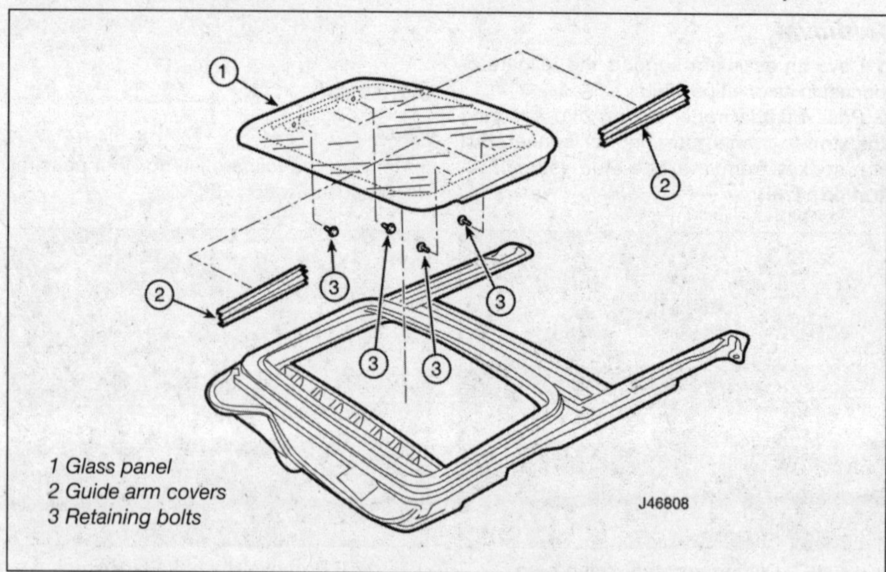

23.2 Sunroof glass panel details

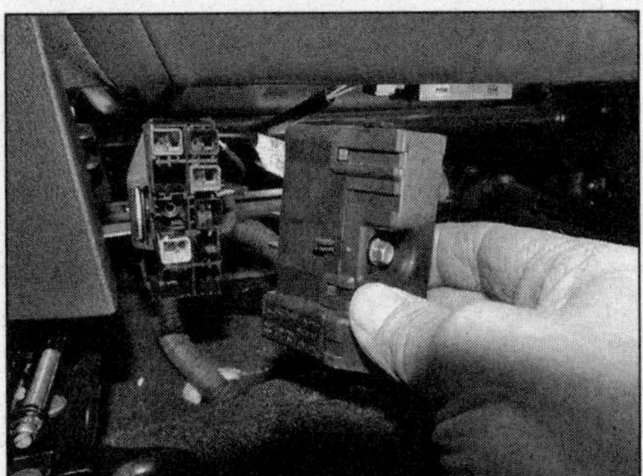

24.2 Remove the bolt and disconnect the wiring plug

3 Undo the 2 retaining bolts each side, then lift the sunroof glass panel out from the vehicle.

4 When refitting, adjust the position of the rear edge of the panel so that it is flush with the roof, then tighten the bolts.

5 The remainder of refitting is a reversal of removal.

Sun blind

6 Remove the glass panel as described in paragraphs 1 to 3.

7 Close the sun blind, then undo the bolts each side securing the blind.

8 Manoeuvre the blind from the vehicle.

9 Refitting is a reversal of removal.

Sunroof mechanism and motor

10 Removal of the sunroof mechanism and/or motor involves removal of the headlining. This is a complex task, which requires patience and dexterity, and is considered to be beyond the scope of a DIYer. Consequently, we recommend this task be entrusted to a Ford dealer or upholstery specialist.

Adjustment

11 The sunroof should operate freely, without sticking or binding, as it is opened and closed. When in the closed position, check that the panel is flush with the surrounding roof panel.

12 If adjustment is required, slide back the sun blind, but leave the glass panel in the closed position.

13 Loosen the rear securing bolts (one each side). Adjust the glass panel up or down, so that it is flush at its back edge with the roof panel.

14 Loosen the front securing bolts (one each side). Adjust the glass panel up or down, so that it is flush at its front edge with the roof panel.

15 Retighten the four securing bolts.

16 Check the roof seal for wind noise and water leaks.

Drain tubes

17 There are four drain tubes, one located in each corner of the sunroof aperture.

18 To remove any obstruction insert a length of suitable nylon wire down through the tubes. If the obstruction cannot be cleared, access the drain tubes as follows:

24.3 Remove the front bolts...

19 The front drain tubes go down the front A-pillars; remove the lower trim panel to gain access to the drain tube.

20 The rear drain tubes go down the C-pillars (Hatchback) or D-pillars (Estate); remove the rear side trims to gain access.

24 Seats – removal and refitting

Removal

Front seat

1 Disconnect the battery negative lead, and position the lead away from the battery (see Chapter 5A Section 3).

Warning: Before proceeding, wait a minimum of 5 minutes, as a precaution against accidental firing of the airbag unit or seat belt pretensioner. This period ensures that any residual electrical energy is dissipated.

2 Push the seat fully rear-ward and undo the security bolt from the wiring plug at the front of the seat, then disconnect the wiring plug **(see illustration)**.

3 Remove the front seat mounting bolts **(see illustration)**.

4 Move the seat fully forward and undo the two rear bolts **(see illustration)**.

5 To ease removal, depress the locking clip and remove the seat headrest, and then with the help of an assistant, manoeuvre the seat from the vehicle. Note that the seat is extremely heavy, take care not to damage the paintwork on the vehicle, with the seat runners as the seat is withdrawn.

Rear seat cushion

6 Unclip the plastic trim from the hinges at the front of each seat cushion.

7 Unscrew and remove the Torx mounting bolts from the hinges**(see illustration)**, and then withdraw the seat cushion from inside the vehicle.

Rear seat backrest

8 Fold the rear seat cushion forwards (if not already removed). Unbolt and remove the centre seatbelt and latch. Disconnect the wiring plug (where fitted). Fold the backrest forward.

9 Use a screwdriver to force rearwards the locking catch, and lift the outer end of the backrest from the hinge **(see illustration)**.

10 Pull the backrest from the centre pivot to disengage the mounting pin **(see illustration)**.

24.4 ...and the rear bolts

24.7 Undo the torx bolts

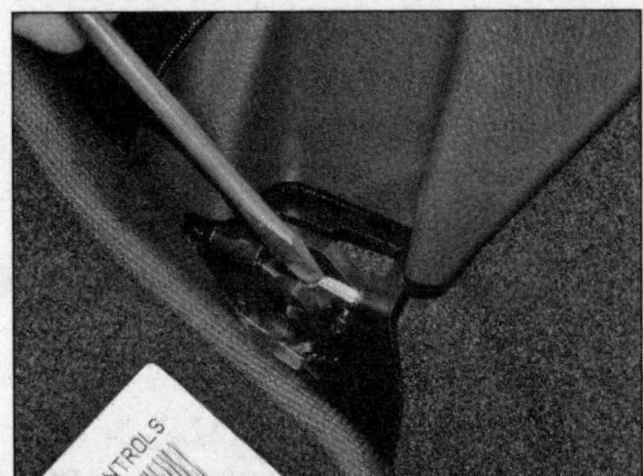

24.9 Release the catch and lift the outer end of the backrest

24.10 Pull the backrest from the pivot to disengage the mounting pin

25.2 Remove the lower bolt

25.3 Remove the upper mounting bolt

If necessary, undo the seat belt stalk mounting bolt and manoeuvre the backrest from the vehicle.

Refitting

11 Refitting is a reversal of the removal procedure, tighten the mounting bolts to the specified torque.

25 Seat belts – removal and refitting

Warning: Be careful when handling the seat belt tensioning device, it contains a small explosive charge (pyrotechnic device) similar to the one used to deploy the airbag(s). Clearly, injury could be caused if these are released in an uncontrolled fashion. Once fired, the tensioner cannot be reset, and must be renewed. Note also that seat belts and associated components which have been subject to impact loads must be renewed.

Removal

Front seat belt

1 Disconnect the battery negative lead, and position the lead away from the battery (see Chapter 5A Section 3).

Warning: Before proceeding, wait a minimum of 5 minutes, as a precaution against accidental firing of the seat belt tensioner. This period ensures that any residual electrical energy is dissipated.

Warning: There is a potential risk of the seat belt tensioning device firing during removal, so it should be handled carefully. Once removed, treat it with care – do not allow use chemicals on or near it, and do not expose it to high temperatures, or it may detonate.

2 Remove the lower mounting bolt **(see illustration)** and then remove B-pillar trim panel as described in Section 26.

3 Undo the seat belt upper anchorage bolt from the height adjuster **(see illustration)**.

4 Unscrew the mounting bolt, and lift seat belt reel unit to remove from the base of the pillar. Disconnect the wiring plug as the reel is removed. **(see illustrations)**.

5 If required the seat belt shoulder strap height adjuster can now be removed.

Rear side seat belt

6 Remove the C-pillar, shelf support panel (part of the C-pillar panel) and where necessary the smaller D-pillar panel as described in Section 26.

7 Unbolt the lower mounting and feed the belt through the C-pillar/shelf support panel **(see illustrations)**.

8 Remove the mounting bolt securing the seat belt reel **(see illustration)**.

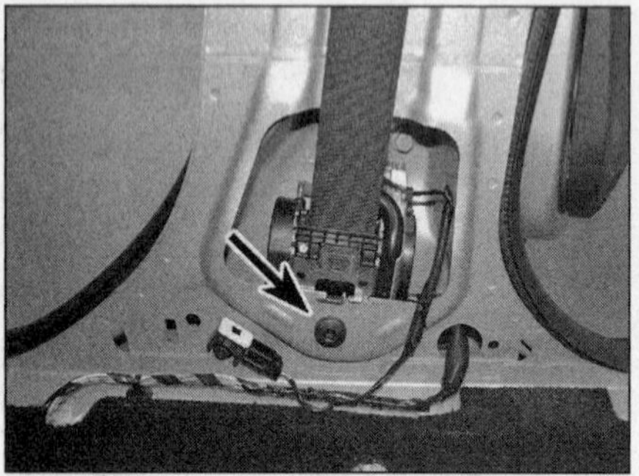
25.4a Remove the inertia reel mounting bolt (arrowed)...

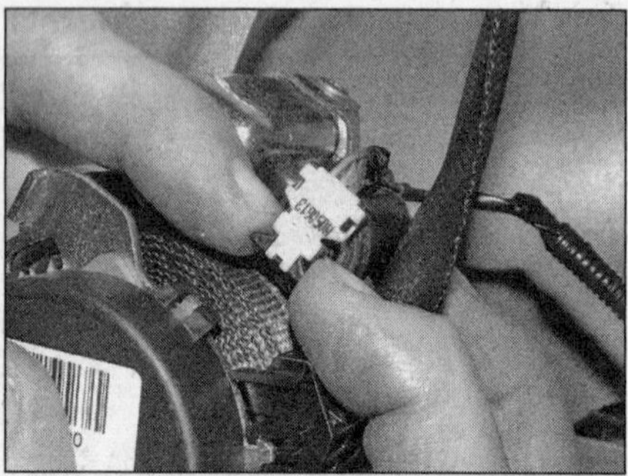
25.4b ...and disconnect the wiring plug

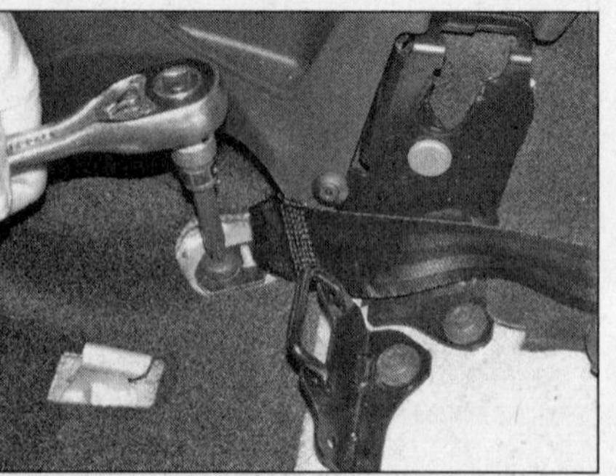
25.7a Remove the lower mounting...

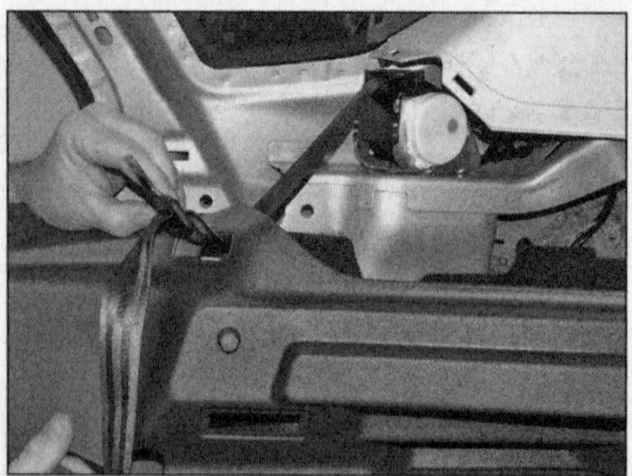
25.7b ...and feed the belt through the panel

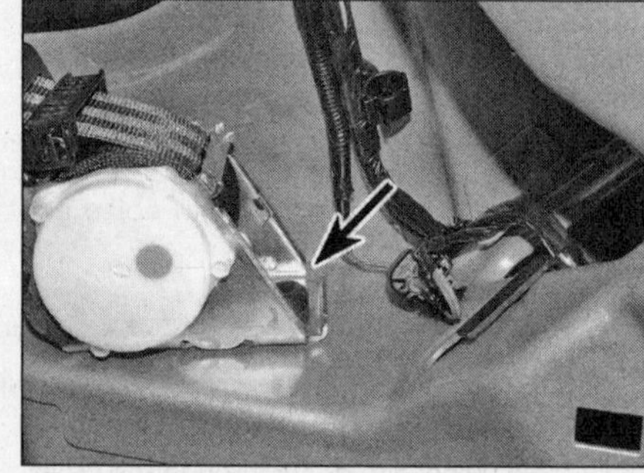
25.8 Remove the bolt (arrowed)

Rear centre seat belt

9 The centre rear seat belt reel is attached to the rear seat backrest. Remove the backrest as described in Section 26.

10 Do not allow the seatbelt webbing to fully retract. To avoid this fit a suitable clip around the webbing above the plastic belt stop rivet. A 'Bulldog' style stationary clip is ideal for this task.

11 Use a screwdriver to prise up the backrest release button surround trim, releasing the clips. When refitting the trim, align the notch with the slot **(see illustrations)**.

12 Push down the backrest padding and use a screwdriver to depress the clip on the side of the headrest guide tubes **(see illustrations)**. Pull the guide tubes from the backrest.

13 Depress the clips and remove the seat belt guide trim from the top of the backrest **(see illustration)**. Feed the seat belt through the slot in the trim.

14 Gently prise out the beading securing the top half of the backrest seat fabric **(see illustration)**.

15 Carefully pull the seat foam padding from the top part of the backrest **(see illustrations)**.

16 Peel away the top part of the backrest fabric covering, which is glued in place **(see illustration)**.

17 Undo the Torx bolt and manoeuvre the seat belt reel from the seat backrest. Feed the seat belt through the seat backrest bracket as the reel is withdrawn.

Seat belt stalks

18 The front seat belt stalks are bolted to the seat frame **(see illustration)** and can be removed after removing the front seat as described in Section 24.

19 Note its routing, then unclip the pretensioner wiring harness from the underside of the seat.

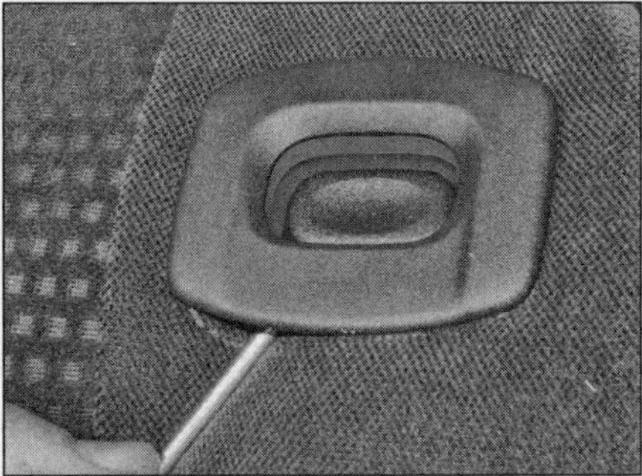

25.11a Prise up the backrest release button surround

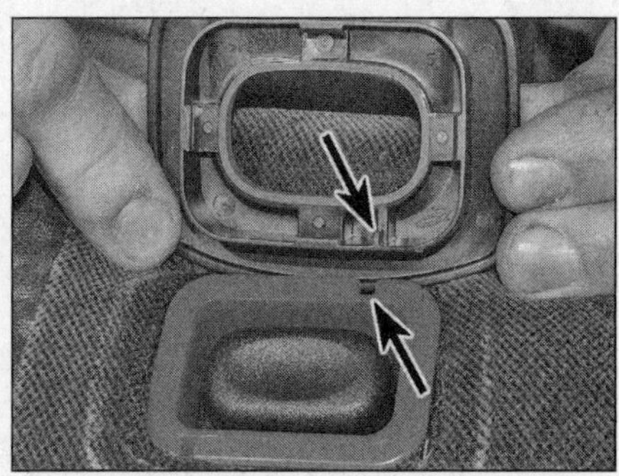

25.11b Align the notch with the slot (arrowed)

25.12a Push-in the clip and pull the headrest guide tube from the backrest

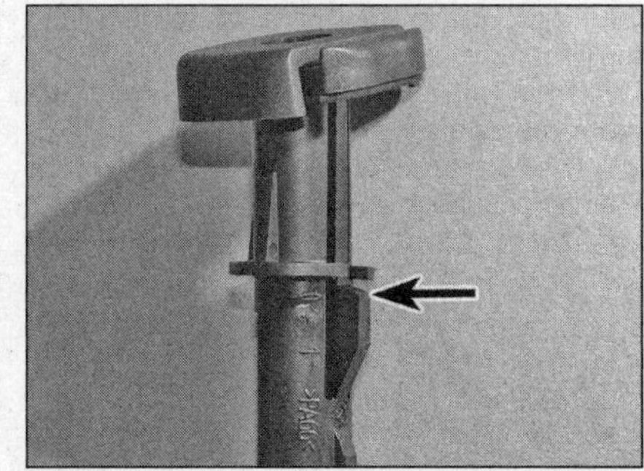

25.12b Depress the headrest guide tube clip (arrowed) – shown with the tube removed

25.13 Depress the clips and remove the belt guide trim

25.14 Prise out the beading securing the top part of the backrest fabric

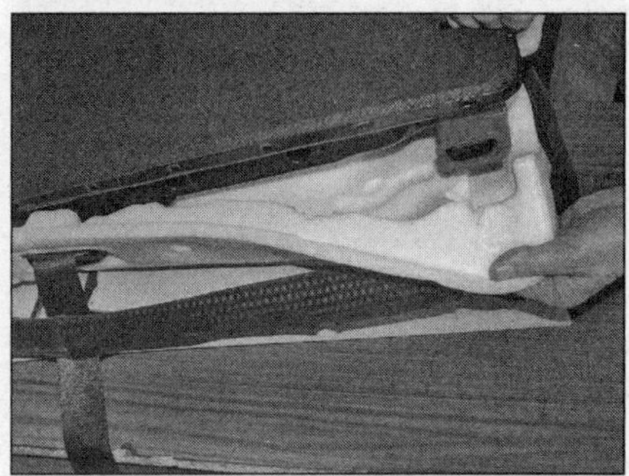

25.15a Pull the foam padding from the top part of the backrest ...

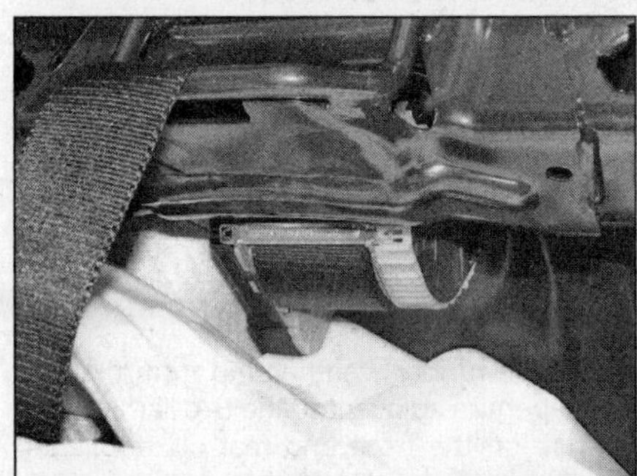

25.15b ... to access the inertia seat belt reel

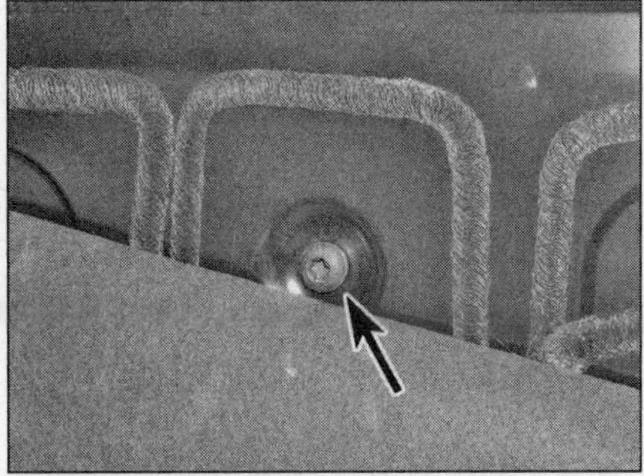

25.16 Peel away the top part of the seat backrest fabric to expose the inertia reel retaining bolt (arrowed)

25.18 Seat belt pretensioner retaining bolt (arrowed)

25.23 The rear seatbelts centre stalks

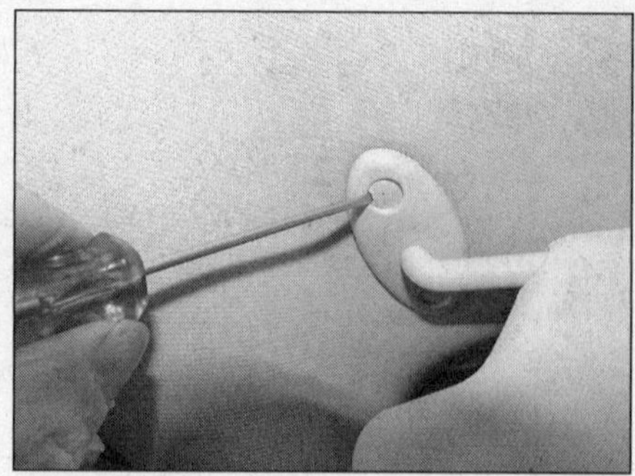
26.1 Remove the covers to access screws

26.3 Prise up the cover

20 Unclip the pretensioner wiring plug from the seat frame.
21 Undo the Torx bolt and remove the pretensioner/stalk.
22 The rear stalks are bolted to the floor. Tip the rear seat cushion forward.
23 Where fitted, disconnect the wiring plug and unbolt the appropriate stalk **(see illustration)**.

Refitting

24 Refitting is a reversal of the removal procedure, noting the following points:

a) Tighten the mounting nuts and bolts to the specified torque.
b) Make sure the seat belt reel locating dowel is correctly positioned.
c) Refit spacers in their correct position.

26 Interior trim panels – removal and refitting

Note: *This section covers the removal and installation of the interior trim panels. It may be necessary to remove an overlapping trim before you can remove the one required. For more information on trim removal, look at the relevant Chapters and Sections, where the trims may need to be removed to carry out any other procedures (eg, to remove the steering column you will need to remove the shrouds).*

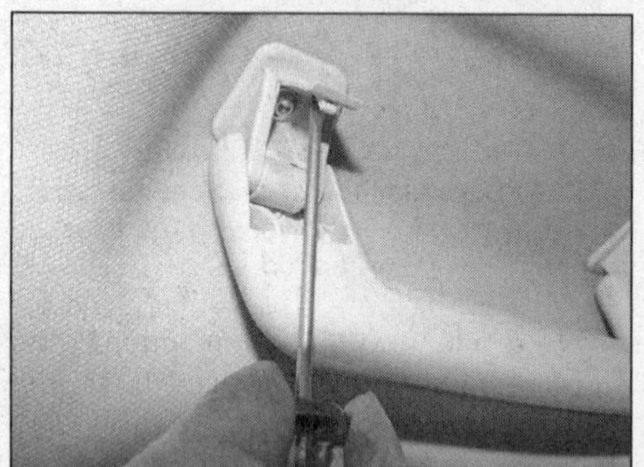
26.4 Prise up the covers

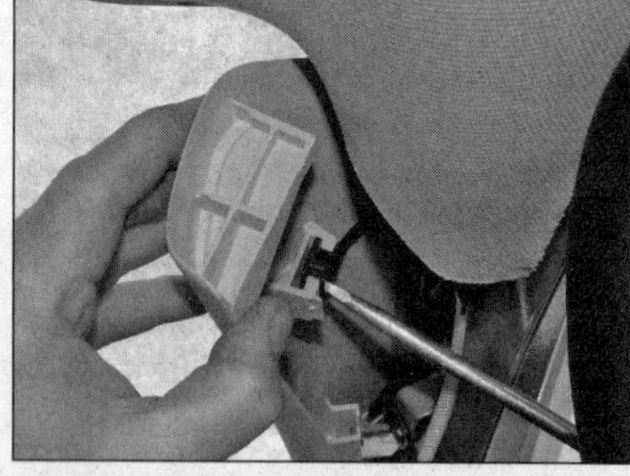
26.6a Prise the panel free...

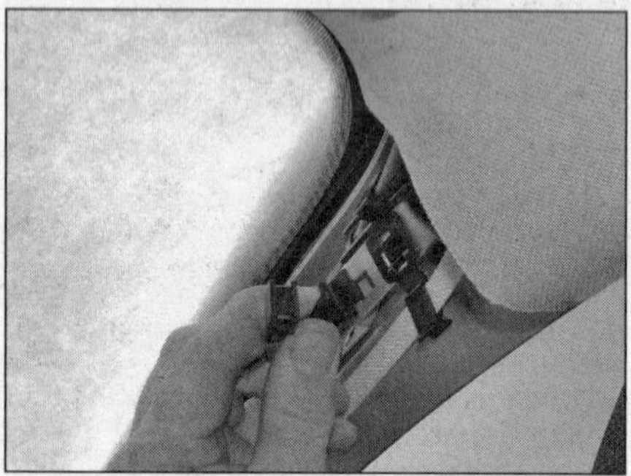
26.6b ...recover the upper trim clip...

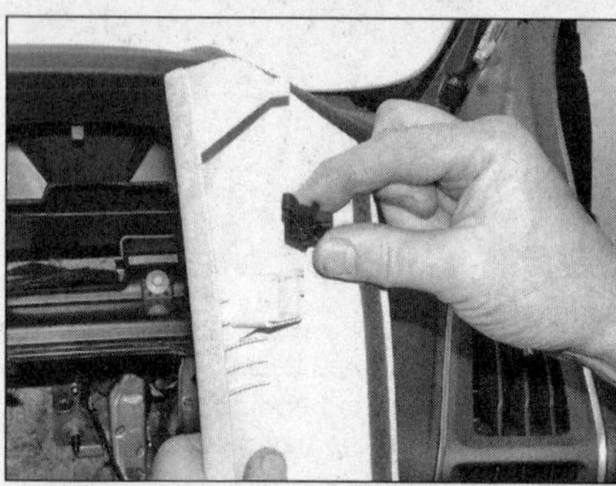
26.6c ...and transfer it to the panel

26.8 Pull up the door step panels

26.9 Remove cover and undo screw

Sunvisor removal

1 Remove the screw covers, unscrew the mounting bolts and remove the visor **(see illustration)**.
2 Disconnect the wiring for the vanity mirror light, where fitted.
3 Prise up the cover, unscrew the inner bracket mounting bolts, and remove the bracket **(see illustration)**.

Passenger grab handle removal

4 Prise up the covers, then unscrew the mounting bolts and remove the grab handle **(see illustration)**.

A-pillar trim removal

5 Pull the rubber weatherstrip away from the area adjacent to the pillar.
6 Starting at the top, carefully pull the A-pillar trim inwards to release the retaining clips **(see illustrations)**. Note that it is quite likely that some of the clips will be damaged during the removal procedure.

B-pillar trim removal

7 Pull the rubber weatherstrip from the rear door aperture adjacent to the B-pillar trim.
8 Prise up the front and rear sill door step panels **(see illustration)**.
9 Prise out the cover and undo the screw at the top of the B-pillar trim upper section **(see illustrations)**.

26.11 Remove the upper section of the panel

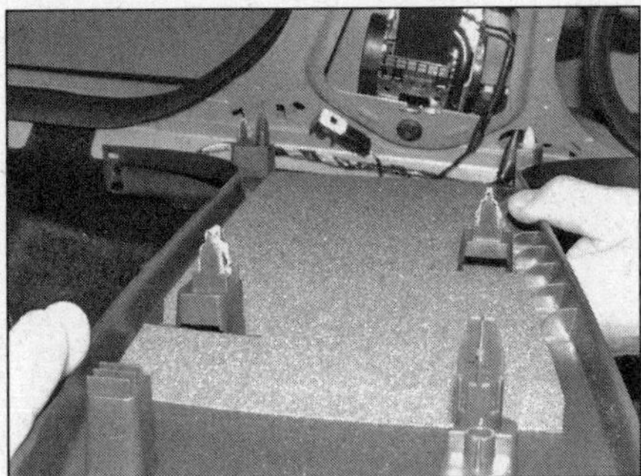
26.13 Note the position of the retaining clips

26.17 Remove the panel

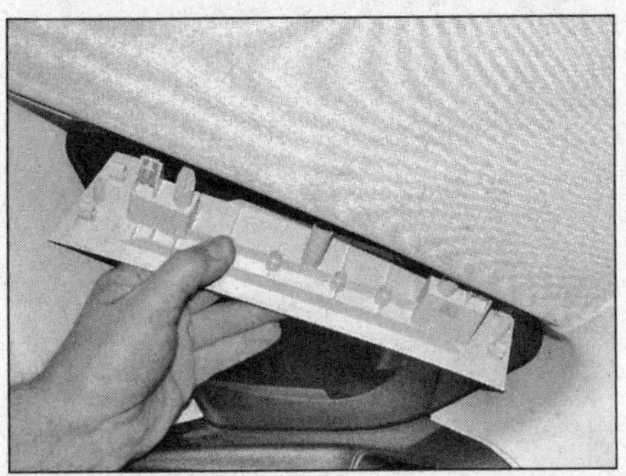
26.18a Remove the roof panel

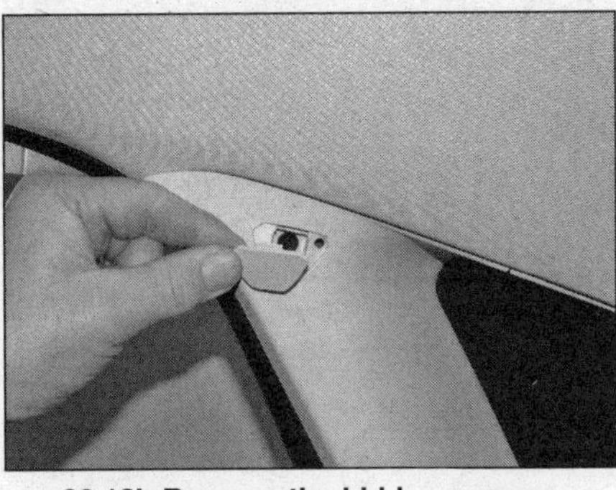
26.18b Remove the hidden screw...

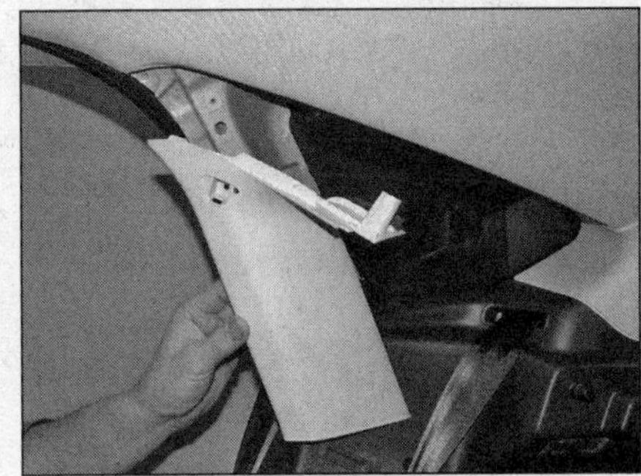
26.18c ...and prise the panel free

10 Unscrew the seat belt mounting bolt from its lower anchorage point.

11 Carefully pull the upper B-pillar trim from the pillar **(see illustration)**.

12 Feed the seatbelt webbing through the panel as it is removed.

13 Prise free the lower section of the B-pillar trim panel **(see illustration)**.

C-pillar trim removal

Hatchback models

14 Remove the rear parcel shelf and then fold the rear seat back forwards.

15 Remove the rear seat back as described in Section 24 of this Chapter.

16 Pull the rubber weatherstrip from the tailgate aperture adjacent to the C-pillar.

17 Remove the trim clip and then pull up the rear door step panel **(see illustration)**.

18 Prise down the panel from above the rear side window glass and then remove the cover from the upper section of the C-pillar panel. Remove the bolt and then remove the panel **(see illustrations)**.

19 Unbolt the rear seat belt mounting from beneath the seat cushion.

20 Locate and remove the 2 screws from the parcel shelf support panel **(see illustration)**. Feed the seat belt through the panel as it is removed and then disconnect the wiring plug from the lamp as the panel is removed.

21 Remove the 2 trim clips and the pull the main section of the C-pillar trim downwards and inwards to release the retaining clips **(see illustration)**.

Estate models

22 Fold the rear seat backrest cushion forwards.

23 Pull the rubber weatherstrip from the door aperture adjacent to the C-pillar.

24 Remove the cover from the upper section of the trim by inserting a thin plastic trim tool from the rear of the panel. Remove the now exposed bolt.

25 Pull the C-pillar trim inwards to release the retaining clips.

D-pillar trim removal

Hatchback models

26 Remove the parcel shelf and the shelf support panel as described above.

27 Pull the rubber weatherstrip from the rear of the D-pillar and then prise the trim panel from the pillar.

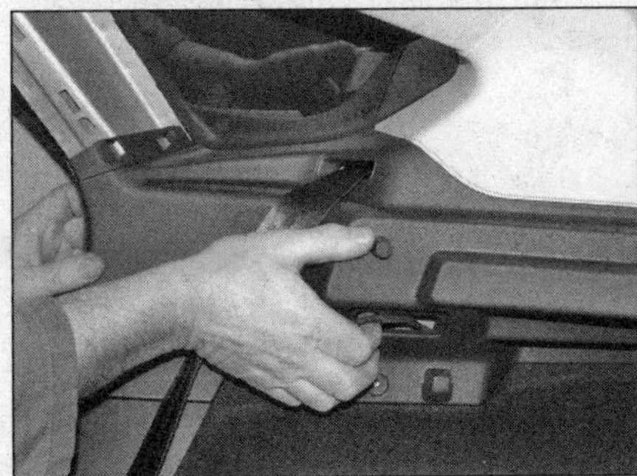
26.20 Remove the shelf support panel

Estate models

28 Tilt the rear seat backrest forwards, then remove the C-pillar trim as described previously in this Section.

29 Pull the rubber weatherstrip from the tailgate aperture adjacent to the D-pillar

30 Undo the 2 screws and pull the parcel shelf support panel inwards to release the retaining clips.

31 Disconnect the wiring plugs from the load area lamp and the 12 volt power outlet as the panel is removed.

32 Pull the D-pillar trim forwards and downwards to release it.

Steering column shrouds removal

33 Fully extend and lower the column.

34 To release the upper shroud from the

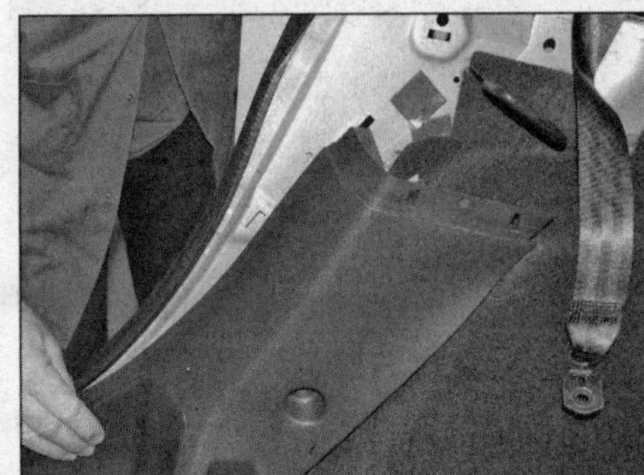
26.21 Remove the C-pillar trim panel

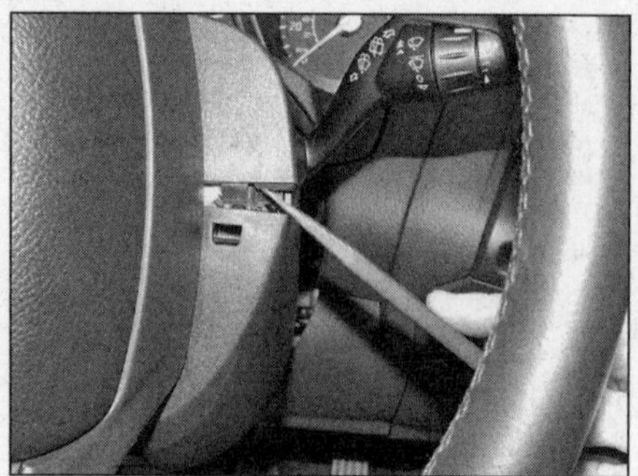
26.34a Release the retaining clips...

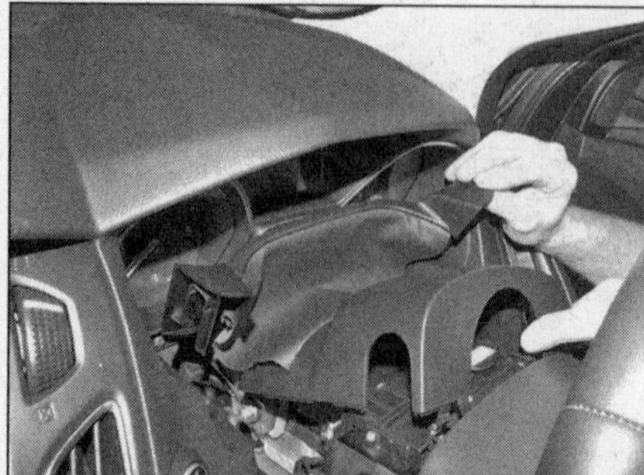
26.34b ...and remove the upper shroud

26.35 Remove the screws (arrowed)

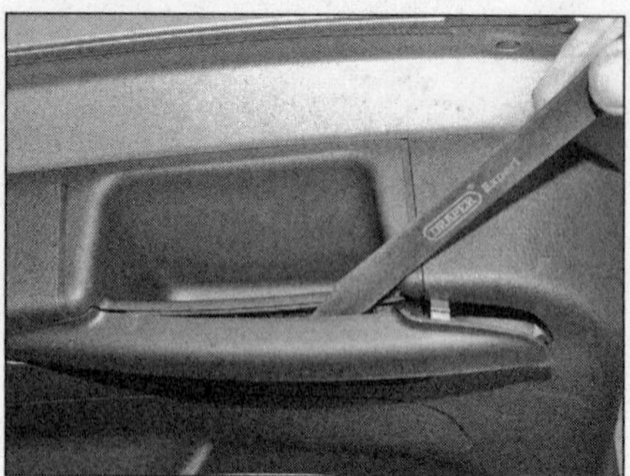
26.44a Remove the handle cover

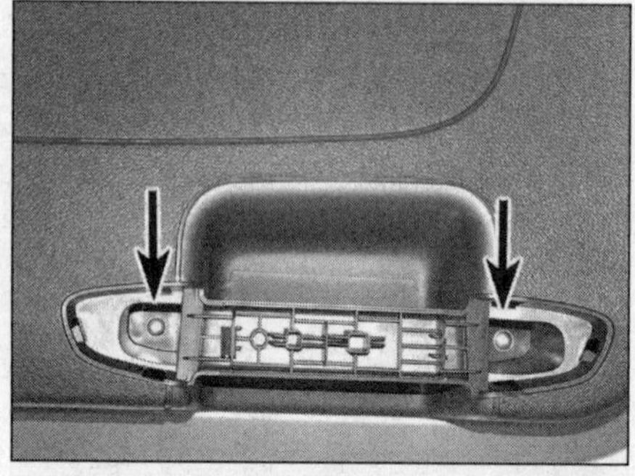
26.44b Remove the screws (arrowed)

26.45 Remove the main panel

lower shroud, turn the steering wheel 90°, insert a thin screwdriver into a hole at each side of the column. Lift the upper shroud from the column and unclip it from the bottom of the instrument panel **(see illustrations)**.

35 Undo the two retaining screws from the lower shroud, and remove it from under the steering column **(see illustration)**. Release the steering column adjustment lever to remove the shroud.

Luggage area side panel removal

Note: *The procedure is the same for both Hatchback and Estate models.*

36 Remove the parcel shelf and the luggage compartment floor covering.

37 Pull up the rear seat cushion and then remove the rear seat backrest (see Section 24).

38 Remove the C-pillar trim as described previously in this Section.

39 Remove the parcel shelf support panel – as described above and then prise up and remove the rear door step scuff panel.

40 Pull the rubber weatherstrip from the tailgate aperture.

41 Remove the trim clips and then prise up the tailgate slam panel trim panel.

42 Pull the panel free and disconnect the power outlet wiring plug (if working on the left-hand panel and where fitted).

Tailgate trim panel

43 On both the Hatchback and Estate models, removal of the tailgate trim panels is similar.

44 Open the tailgate and remove the covers from the pull handles. Remove the now exposed screws **(see illustrations)**.

45 Prise free the main panel section **(see illustration)**.

46 Use a suitable plastic trim tool and release the upper trim panel **(see illustration)**.

47 With the upper and lower panels removed the side sections can now be prised free **(see illustration)**.

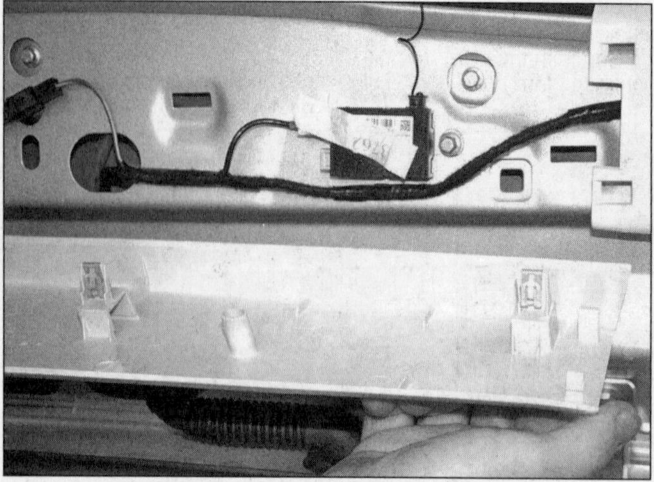
26.46 Remove the upper trim panel

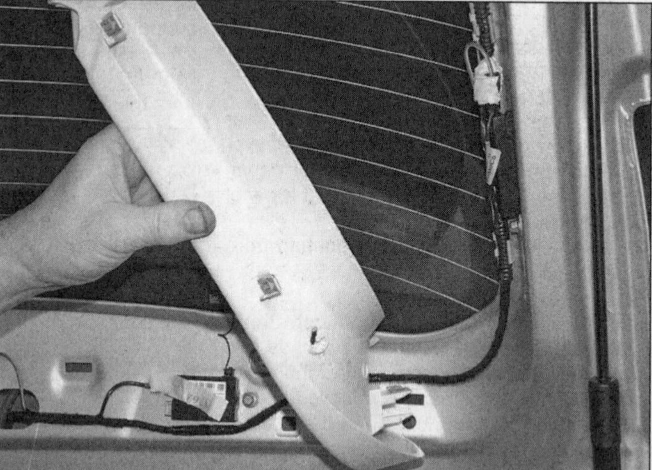
26.47 Prise free the side panels

27.2a Unscrew the gear knob...

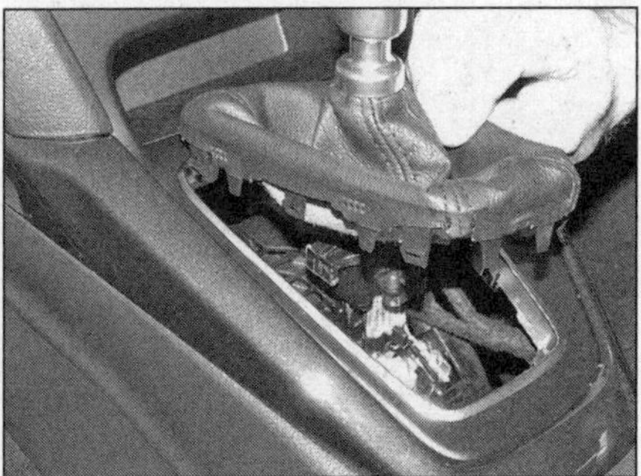
27.2b ... unclip the gaiter...

27.2c ...and release linkage rod

27 Centre console – removal and refitting

27.3a Unclip the left-hand trim...

27.3b ...followed by the surround trim

Removal

1 Removal is considerably easier if both front seats are removed as described in Section 24.

2 Unscrew the gear lever knob, then unclip the gear lever gaiter and trim panel, unclip the reverse linkage rod and withdraw the gaiter completely from the gear lever **(see illustrations)**.

3 Using a trim tool, carefully unclip the finishing trim from the left-hand side of the centre console, followed by the finishing trim surrounding the gear lever **(see illustrations)**.

4 Using a trim tool, carefully unclip the small trim panel from above the heater control panel and undo the two retaining screws from the top of the centre control panel, then undo the screw at the lower end of the centre trim panel and withdraw it from the console. Disconnect the wiring connectors, as the trim panel is removed **(see illustrations)**.

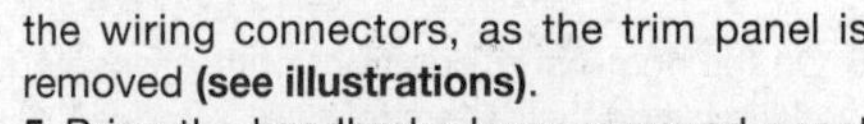

5 Prise the handbrake lever surround panel free, then withdraw and remove the gaiter from over the handbrake lever **(see illustrations)**.

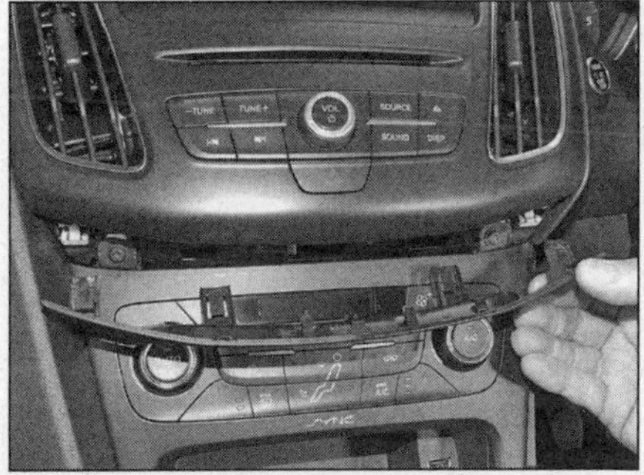
27.4a Unclip the trim to access upper screws...

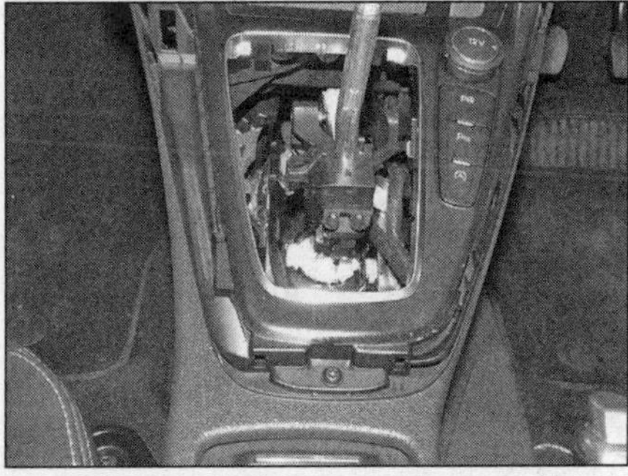
27.4b ...undo lower centre screw...

27.4c ...and withdraw the centre panel...

27.4d ...disconnecting wiring connectors

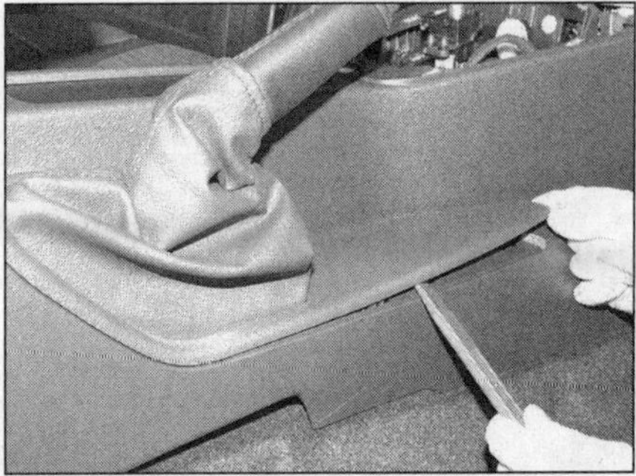
27.5a Unclip the trim panel...

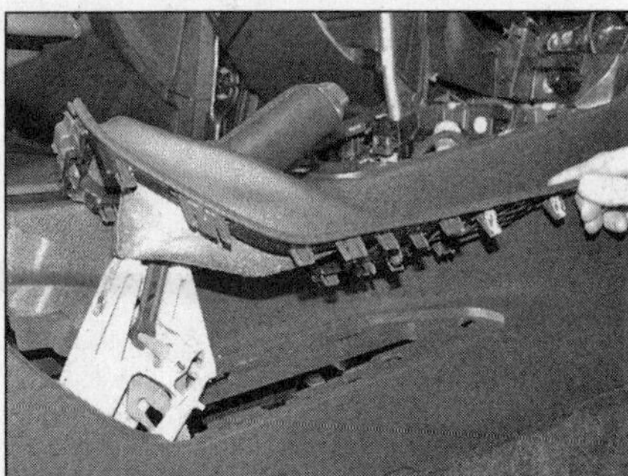
27.5b ...and withdraw the gaiter from the lever

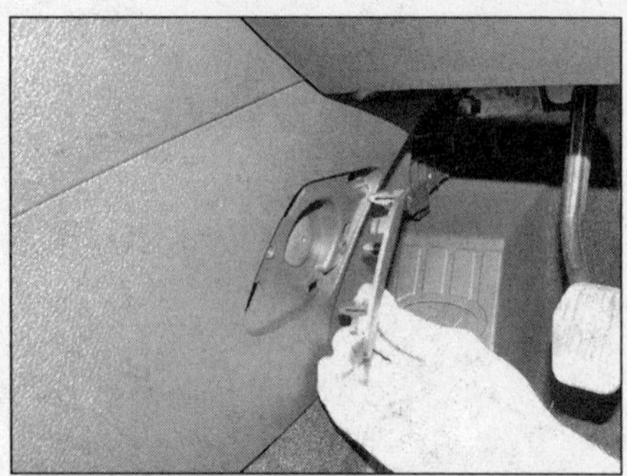
27.6a Remove the cover...

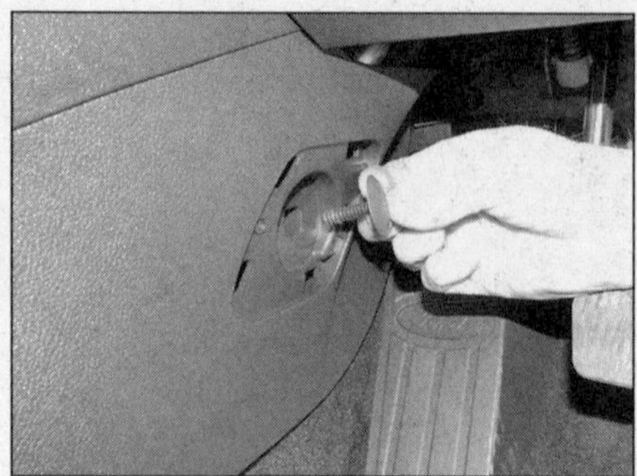
27.6b ...the trim clip...

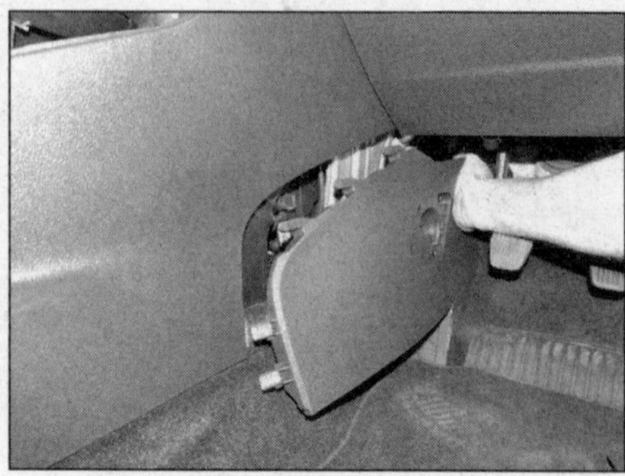
27.6c ...and then the panel

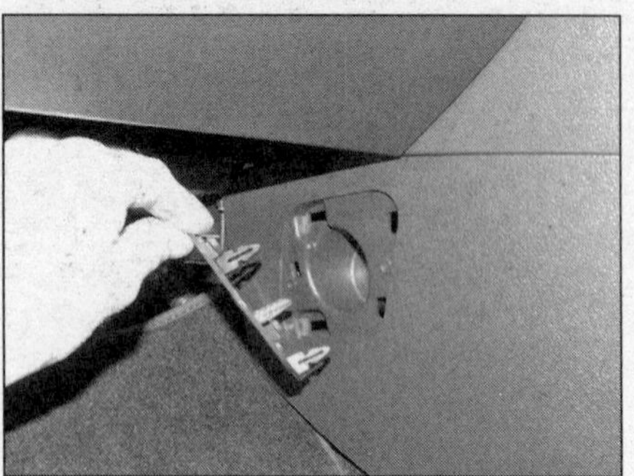
27.7a Remove the cover...

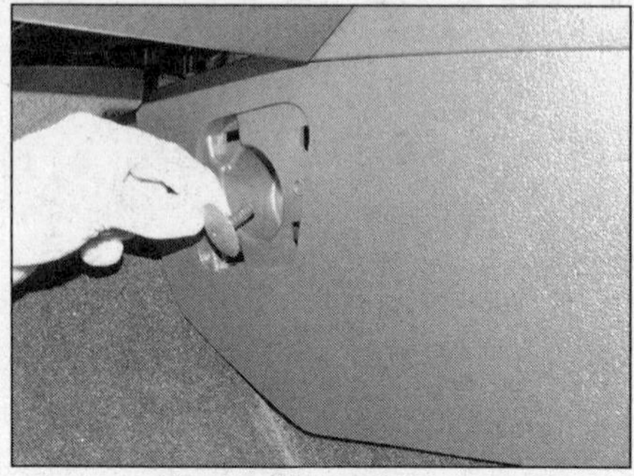
27.7b ...the trim clip...

27.7c ...and then the panel

6 On the right-hand side front of the console, working inside the drivers footwell, remove the cover at the front edge of the panel. Remove the now exposed trim clip and remove the trim panel from the front of the centre console **(see illustrations)**.

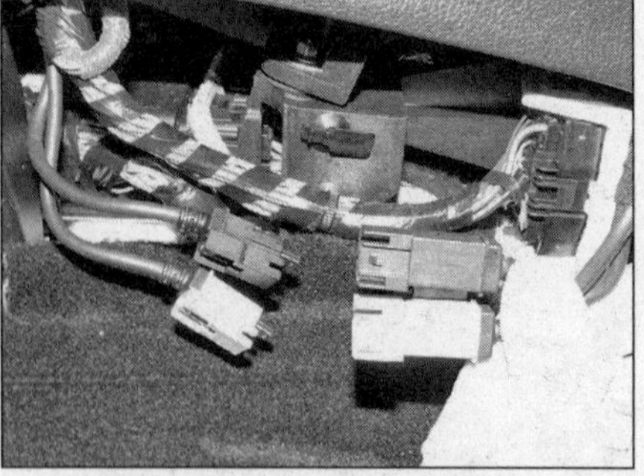
27.8a Disconnect and cables...

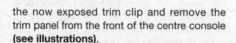

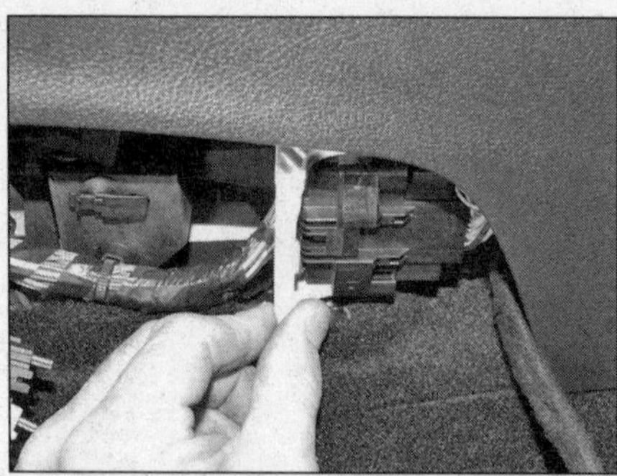
27.8b ...release the locking lever...

7 On the left-hand side front of the console, working inside the passenger front footwell, remove the cover at the front edge of the panel. Remove the now exposed trim clip and remove the trim panel from the front of the centre console **(see illustrations)**.

8 Still working on the left-hand side front of the console, inside the passenger footwell, disconnect the wiring connectors, and release the wiring loom clips from the centre console**(see illustrations)**.

9 If the front seats have not been removed, then move both seats fully forwards and remove the two bolts (one at each side) at the rear of the console **(see illustration)**.

10 Remove the two bolts, and one screw at the right-hand side from the front of the console, then lift up the console from over the

27.8c ...and disconnect the wiring block connector...

27.8d ...and unclip from console

27.9 Remove the bolts at the rear

27.10a Undo the two bolts and one screw...

27.10b ...then remove the centre console

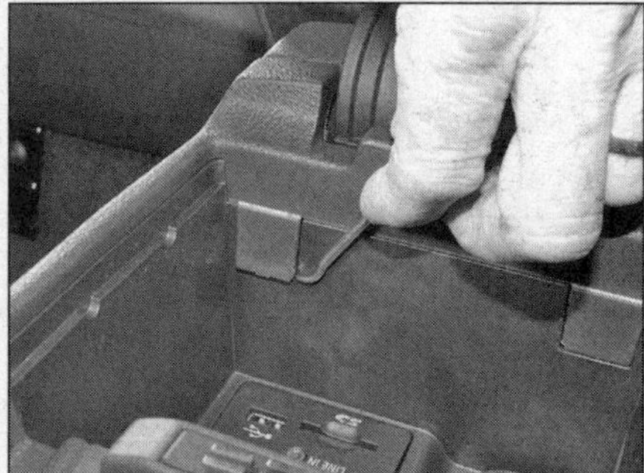
27.11a Unclip the covers...

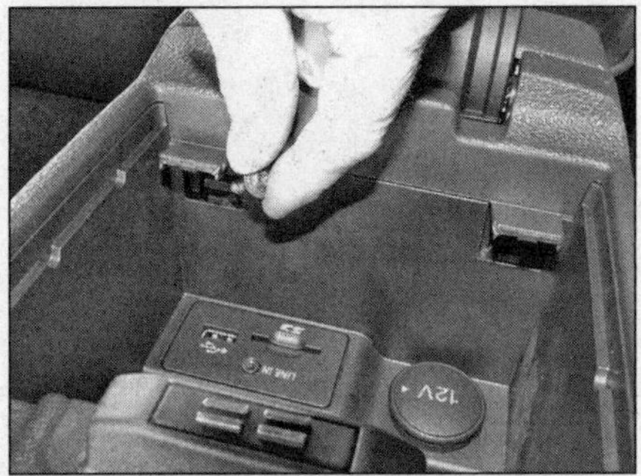
27.11b ...remove the screws...

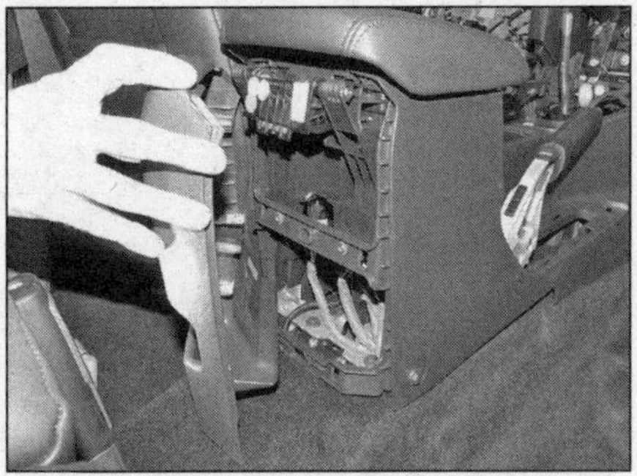
27.11c ...and release the rear trim panel...

27.11d ...to access the wiring connector(s)

handbrake lever **(see illustrations)**. As the console is withdrawn, check for any wiring connectors still attached to the underside of the console.

11 Where an armrest if fitted, if required the rear section can be removed to access rear wiring connectors. Open the top of the armrest and unclip the two plastic covers inside the rear of the console. Undo the two retaining screws and unclip the rear trim from the rear of the centre console, the wiring connectors can now be accessed **(see illustrations)**.

12 Refitting is a reversal of the removal procedure, making sure that all the trim panels are clipped together correctly and all wiring connectors have been connected securely.

28 Overhead console – removal and refitting

Removal

1 Carefully prise free the switch panel from the overhead console (taking care not to damage the plastic trim), and then disconnect the wiring plug as the switch panel is removed**(see illustrations)**.

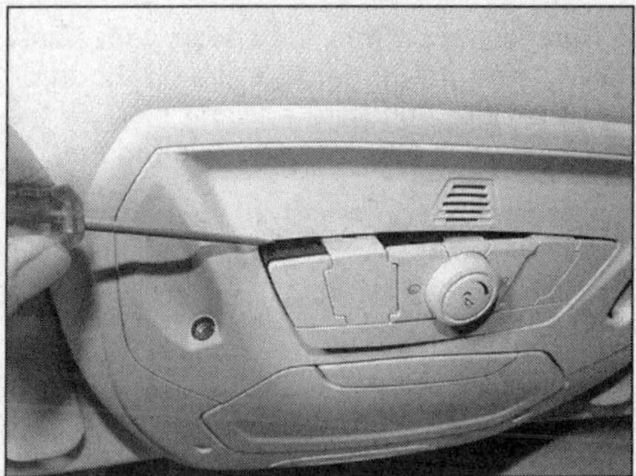
28.1a Prise out the switch panel...

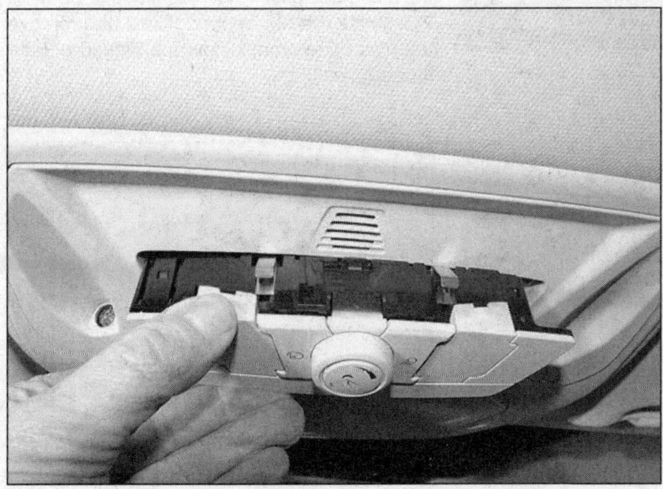
28.1b ...from the console...

28.1c ...and disconnect the wiring connector

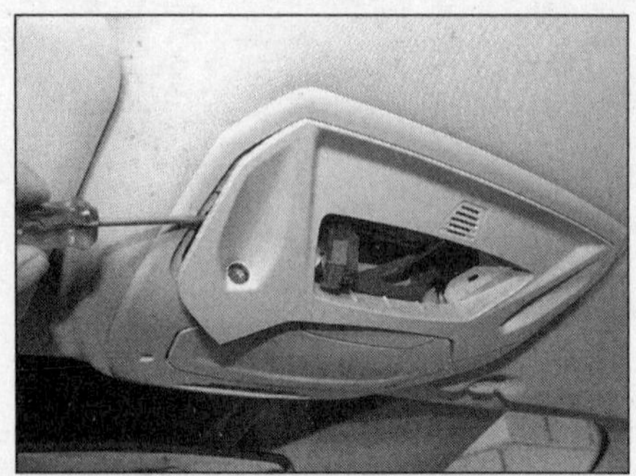
28.2a Prise out the sensor panel...

28.2b ...from the console...

28.2c ...and disconnect the wiring connectors

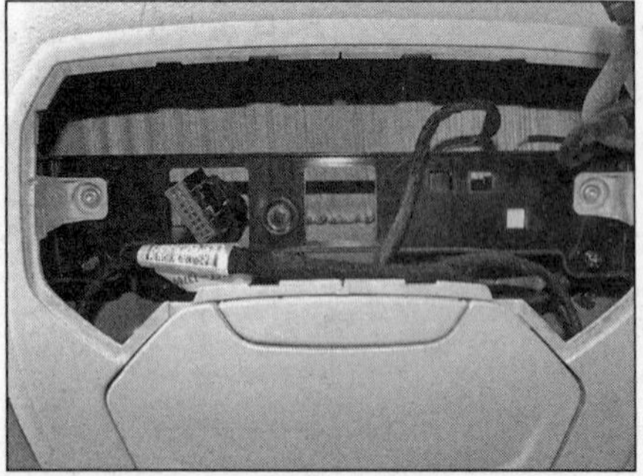
28.3a Undo the two retaining screws...

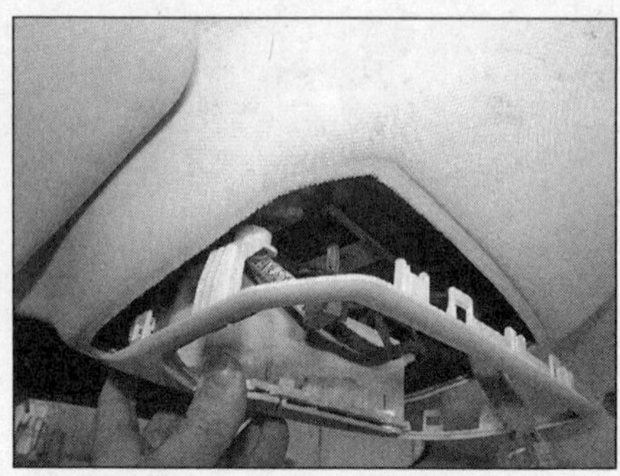
28.3b ...and unclip the console...

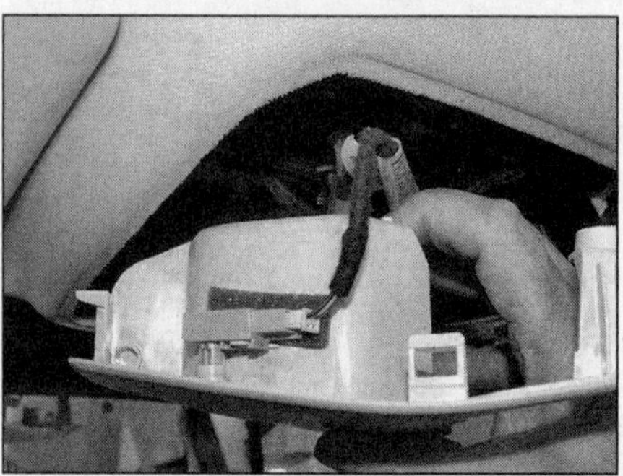
28.3c ...and disconnect the wiring connectors

2 Carefully prise free the sensor trim panel (taking care not to damage the plastic trim), and then disconnect the wiring plug as the sensor panel is removed**(see illustrations)**.

29.1a Peel back the door seal...

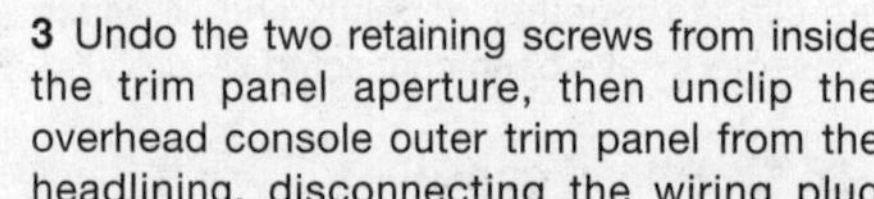

3 Undo the two retaining screws from inside the trim panel aperture, then unclip the overhead console outer trim panel from the headlining, disconnecting the wiring plug connectors from the sensors, as the panel is removed **(see illustrations)**.

29.1b ...remove the facia end panel...

Refitting

4 Refitting is a reversal of the removal procedure.

29 Glovebox – removal and refitting

1 Peel back the door seal and prise the end panel from the end of the facia panel, then remove the screw from the left-hand end of the glove box assembly **(see illustrations)**.

2 Release the two securing clips and remove the trim panel from below the glovebox **(see illustrations)**.

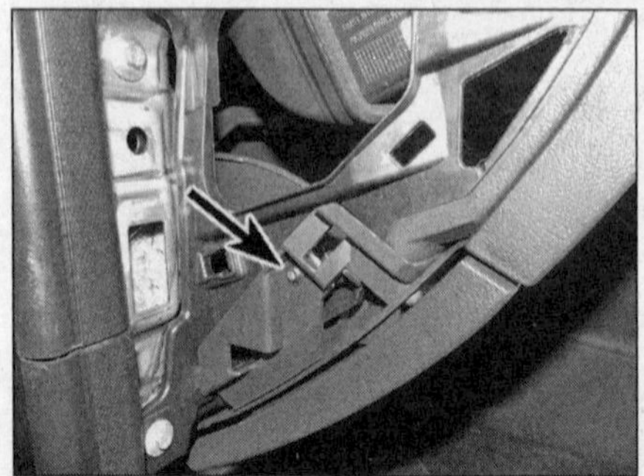
29.1c ...and undo the retaining screw

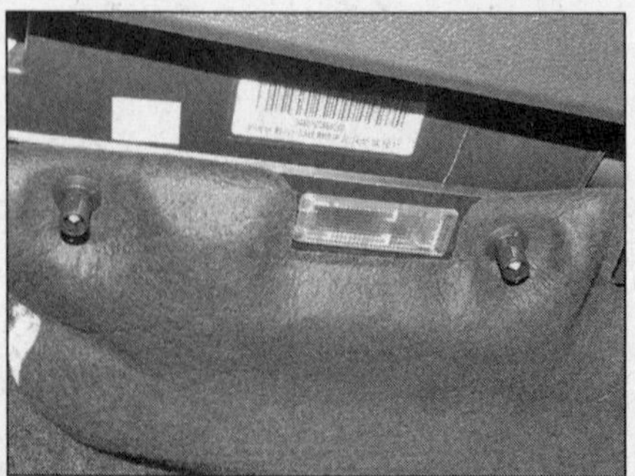
29.2a Remove the two securing clips...

29.2b ...and withdraw the trim panel

3 Open the glovebox and remove the two upper mounting screws **(see illustration)**.

4 Remove the two lower mounting screws. Note that the lower mounting screws are difficult to locate, and are up behind the footwell light panel **(see illustration)**.

5 Partially remove the glovebox, and then disconnect the wiring plugs from the rear of the glovebox assembly, as it is being withdrawn from the facia panel **(see illustrations)**.

6 Refitting is a reversal of the removal procedure, making sure that the glovebox is located correctly before tightening the mounting screws.

30 Facia and crossmember – removal and refitting

Facia

Removal

1 Disconnect the battery negative (earth) lead (Chapter 5A Section 3).

2 Whilst not strictly necessary, access to the centre console, steering column and facia will be greatly improved if both front seats are removed first, as described in Section 24.

3 Remove the centre console as described in Section 27, and remove the glovebox, as described in Section 29.

4 Working up inside the glovebox aperture, unbolt the passenger side airbag from the crossmember, then disconnect the wiring plug from the passenger airbag. Also disconnect the wiring connectors from the proximity entry/keyless start module, which is up to the right-hand side front of the airbag unit**(see illustrations)**. Release the wiring loom from any retaining clips on the facia panel.

5 Working below the glovebox, unclip the footwell light unit and disconnect the wiring connector, then remove the single bolt and remove the air duct pipe from the heater unit **(see illustrations)**.

6 Remove the Audio unit and air vent trim panel, as described in Chapter 12 Section 18.

7 Release the wiring loom from the clips directly behind the now removed HeaterAudio

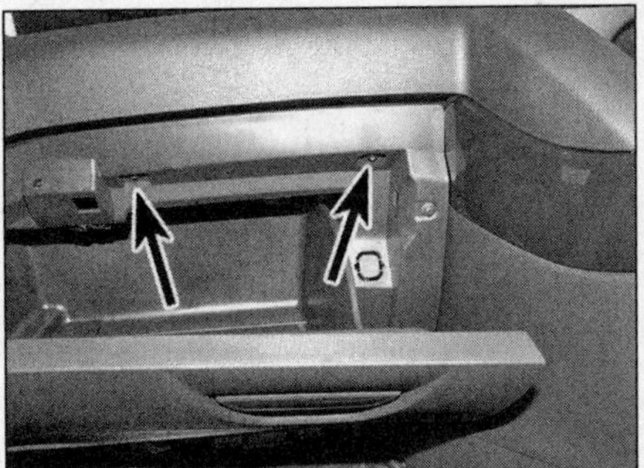

29.3 Remove the upper mounting screws

29.4 Undo the two mounting screws up behind footwell light panel

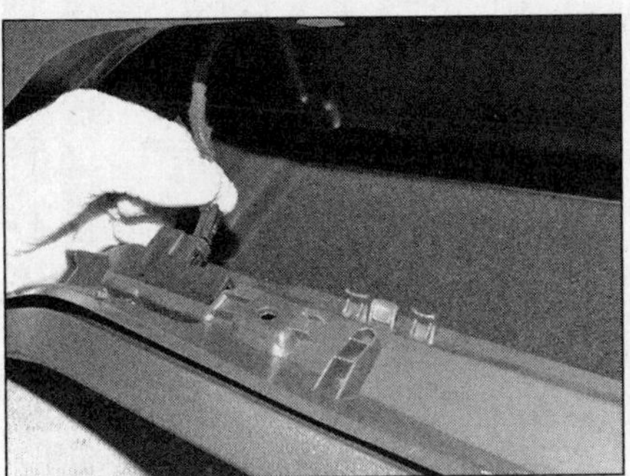

29.5a Disconnect the wiring connectors...

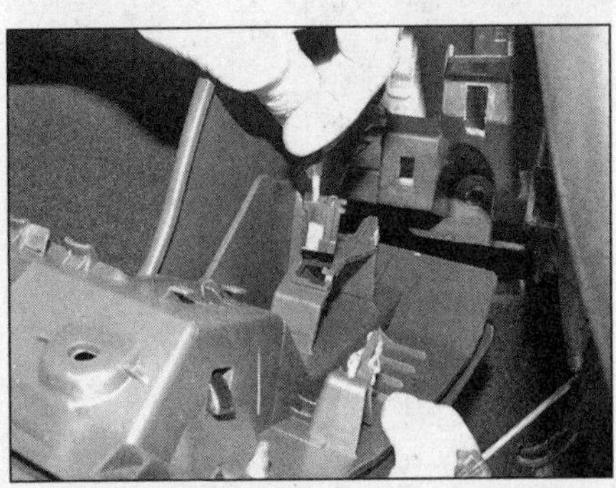

29.5b ...as the glovebox is removed

30.4a Undo the airbag securing bolts and disconnect the wiring connector

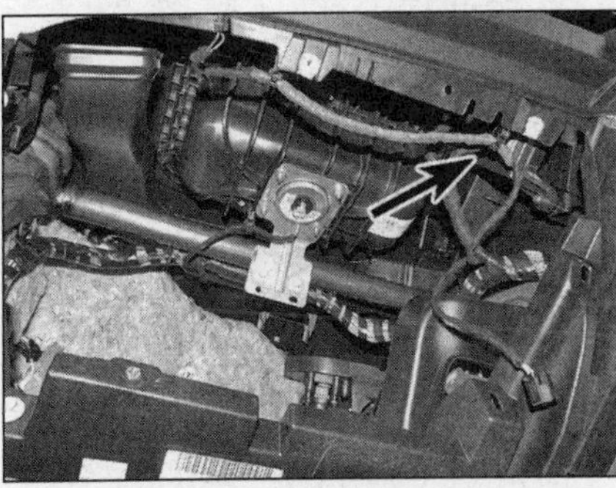

30.4b Disconnect the wiring connectors from the module

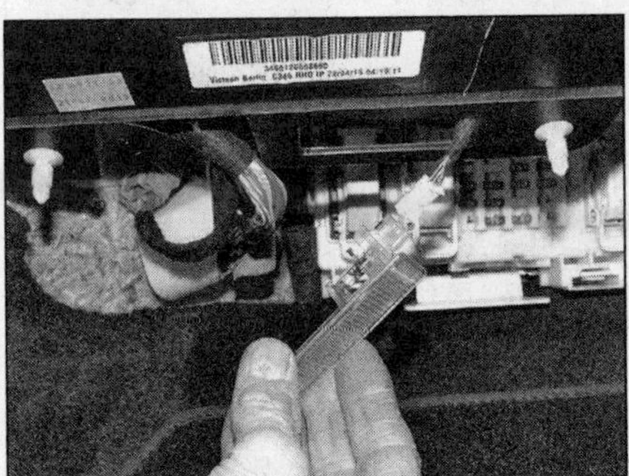

30.5a Remove the footwell light...

30.5b ...undo the retaining bolt...

30.5c ...and remove the air ducting

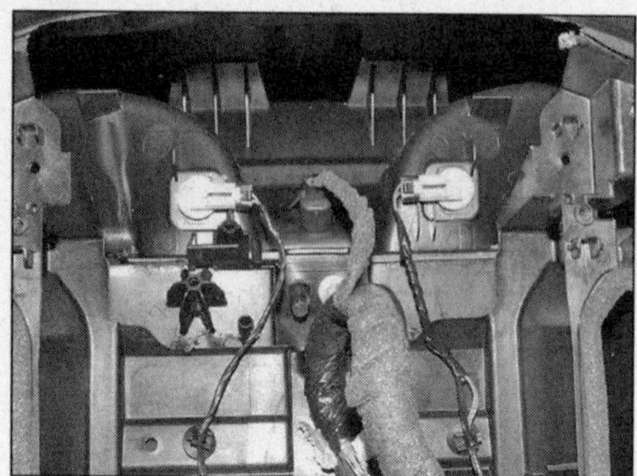
30.7a Disconnect the wiring connectors...

30.7b ...and release the wiring loom clips

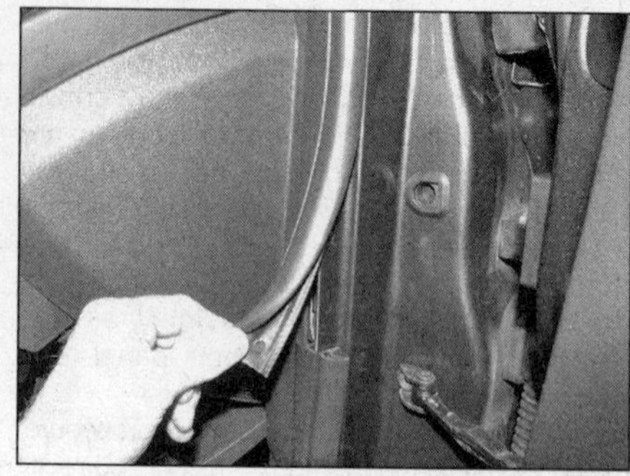
30.8a Peel back the door seal...

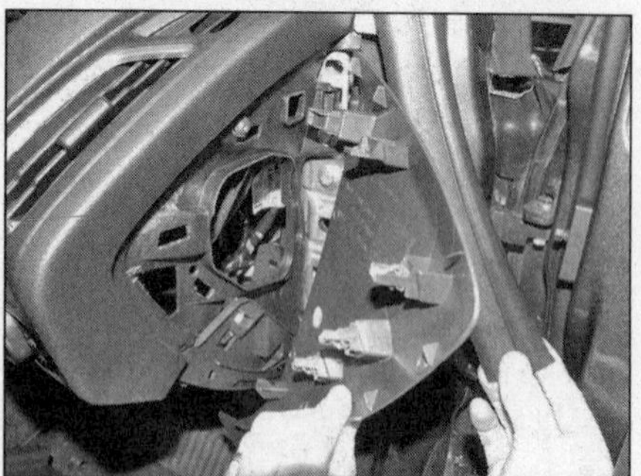
30.8b ...remove the end panel...

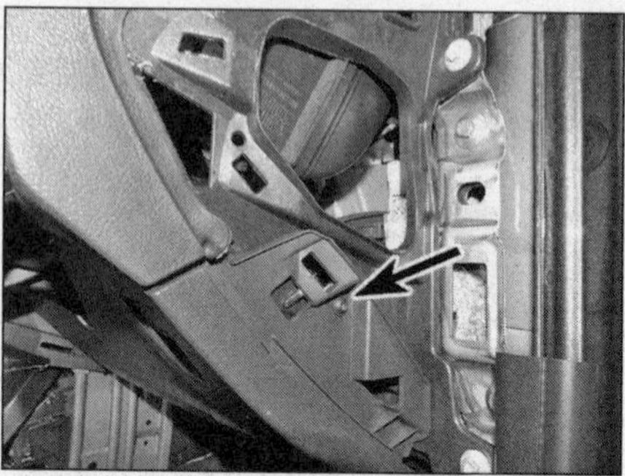
30.8c ...and undo the lower trim panel securing screw

30.9 Unclip the compartment from the facia

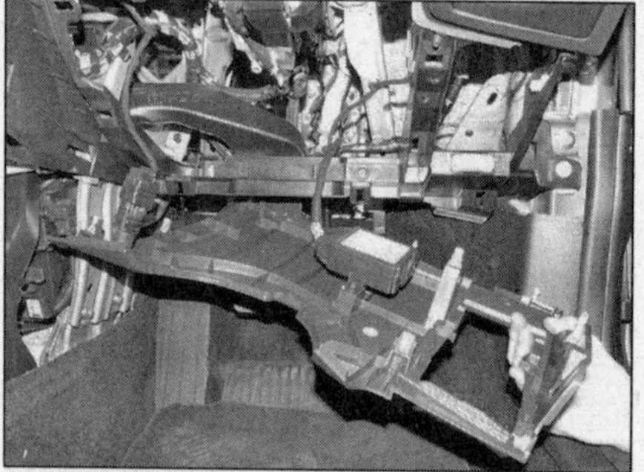
30.10 Remove the lower trim panel

control panel, and disconnect from the sensors in the heater unit **(see illustrations)**.

8 Peel back the door seal and prise the end panel from the driver's side end of the facia panel, then remove the screw from the right-hand end of the lower facia panel **(see illustrations)**.

9 Open the compartment in the lower trim panel, then squeeze the sides together and pull down to remove it from the facia panel **(see illustration)**.

10 Unclip the driver's side lower facia trim panel from below the steering column, disconnect the wiring electrical connectors from the module and sensor, as the trim panel is withdrawn **(see illustration)**.

11 Fully extend and lower the steering column and then remove the upper and lower steering column shrouds (Section 26).

12 Disconnect the wiring loom and electrical connectors from the steering column switches, or remove the column switches, as described in Chapter 12 Section 5.

13 Reach behind the upper trim panel and unclip the stop/start switch from the facia, then disconnect the wiring connector **(see illustration)**.

14 Remove the instrument panel as described in Chapter 12 Section 10.

15 Release the main light switch from the right-hand side of the facia panel, disconnect the wiring connector and remove the switch **(see illustration)**.

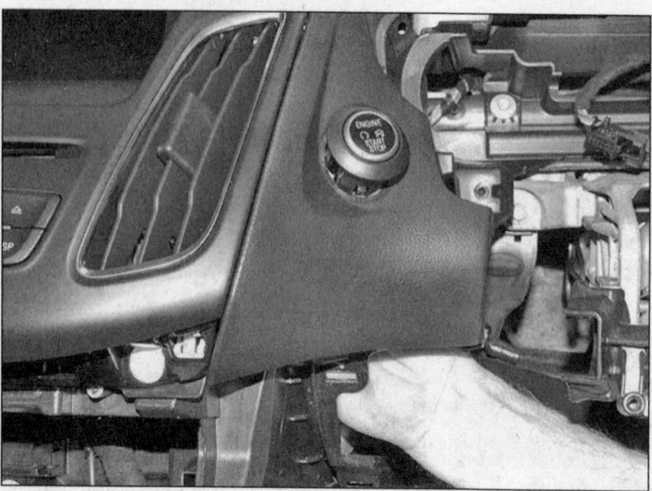

30.13 Remove the stop/start switch

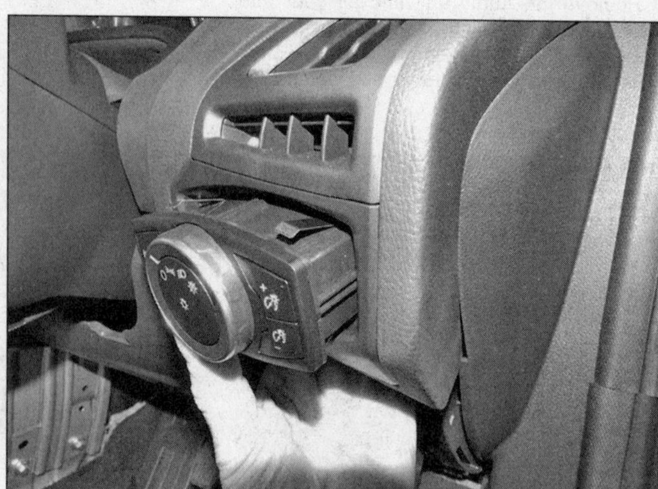
30.15 Remove the light switch unit

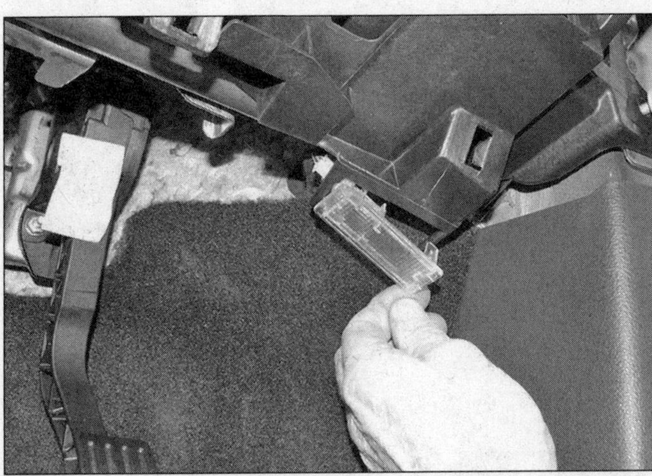
30.16a Remove the footwell light...

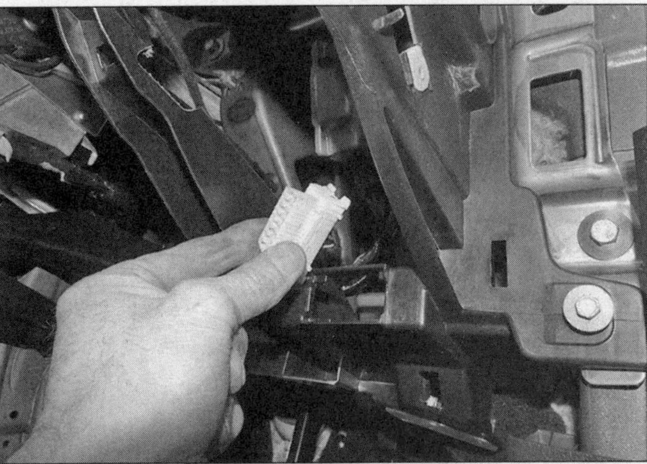
30.16b ...and release the diagnostic socket

30.17a Undo the retaining bolt...

30.17b ...and remove the air ducting

16 Working in the drivers side footwell, remove the footwell light and unclip the diagnostic socket from the lower part of the facia panel **(see illustrations)**.

17 Undo the retaining bolt from the lower part of the facia panel, then release the air distribution ducting from the heater unit and remove it from the driver's side footwell **(see illustrations)**.

18 Remove both A-pillar trims, as described in Section 26.

19 Working around the facia panel check for any wiring loom retaining clips, and then detach them from the facia panel, noting there fitted position **(see illustrations)**.

20 Unclip the sunlight sensor from the top of

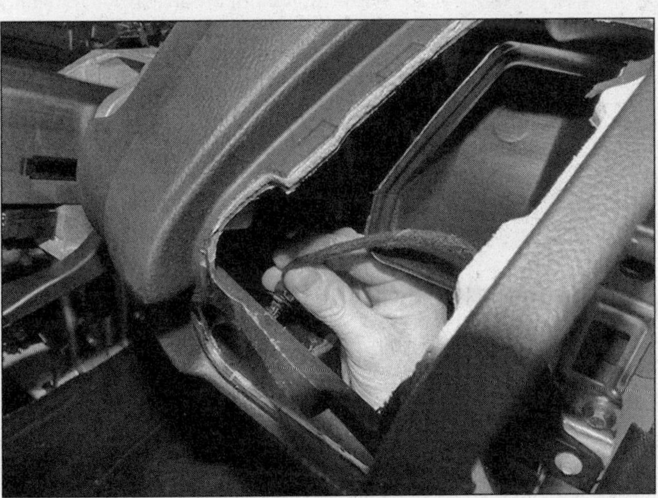
30.19a Detach the wiring loom retaining clips...

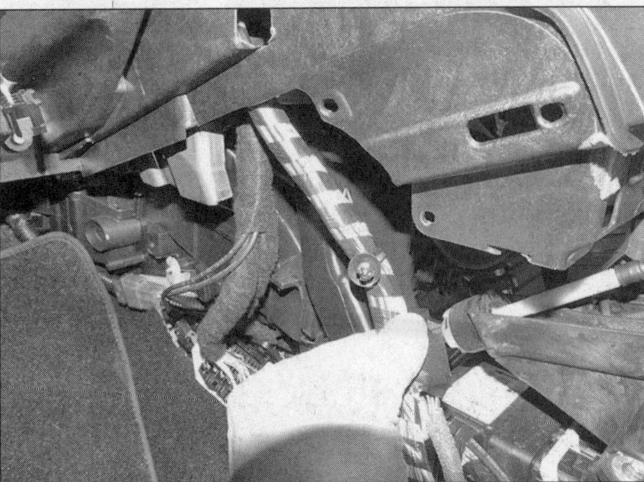
30.19b ...noting there fitted position

30.20 Remove the sunlight sensor from the facia

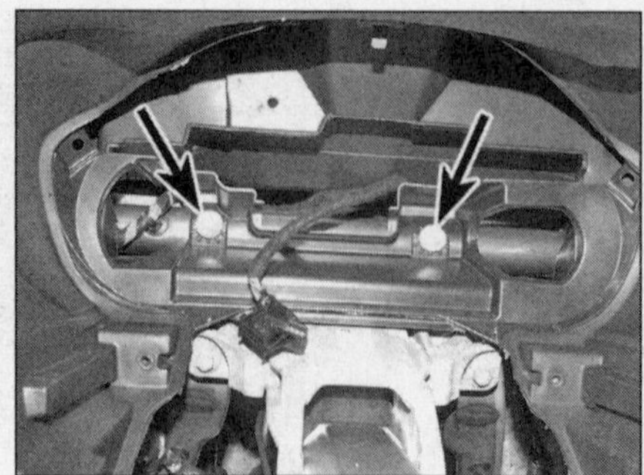

30.21a Remove the two bolts from inside the instrument aperture...

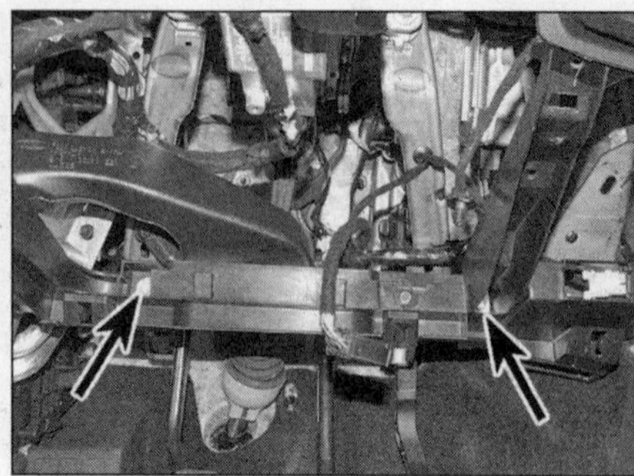

30.21b ...two bolts from driver's side lower edge...

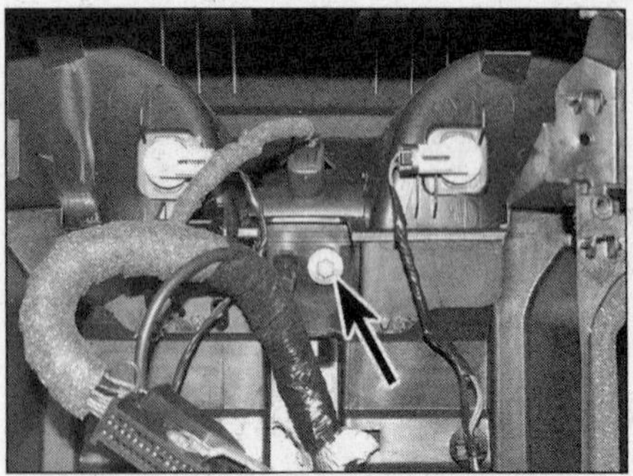

30.21c ...one bolt at the upper centre of the facia...

30.21d ...and two bolts at the lower centre of the facia...

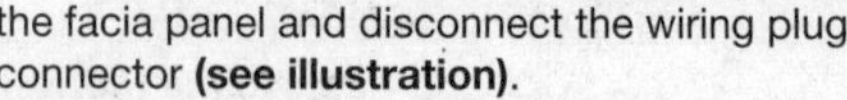

the facia panel and disconnect the wiring plug connector **(see illustration)**.

21 Remove the the facia panel mounting bolts, following the accompanying photos **(see illustrations)**.

22 With the aid of an assistant remove the four bolts from the end of the facia (two at each end) and partially remove the facia panel by pulling it forward, to release it from the upper locating clips **(see illustrations)**. As the facia is withdrawn, the sunlight sensor wiring will need to be guided out through the top of the facia, remembering its location for refitting.

Refitting

23 Refitting is a reversal of the removal procedure. On completion, check the operation of all the electrical components. See precautions in Chapter 12 Section 21, before refitting the driver and passenger airbags and re-connecting the battery.

Crossmember

Removal

24 Remove the facia, as described above, then remove wiper arms and the windscreen cowling upper panel, as described in Chapter 12 Section 11.

25 With the windscreen upper cowling removed, undo the retaining bolts and remove the metal lower section of the scuttle panel **(see illustration)**.

30.21e ...then one bolt to the right of the gear lever housing...

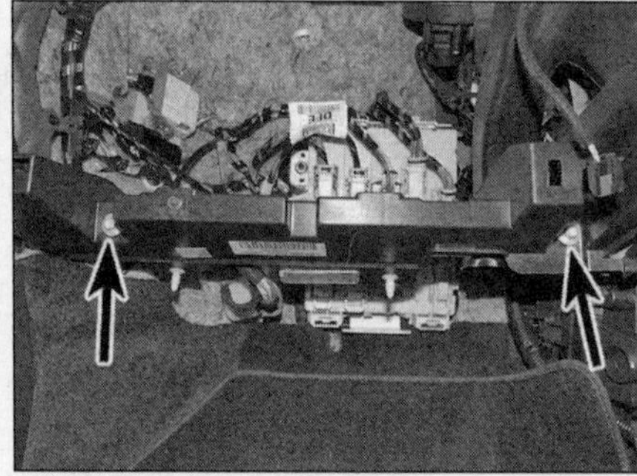

30.21f ...and two bolts from passenger side lower edge

30.22a Undo the bolts and pull the facia rearwards...

30.22b ...to release it from the upper locating clips

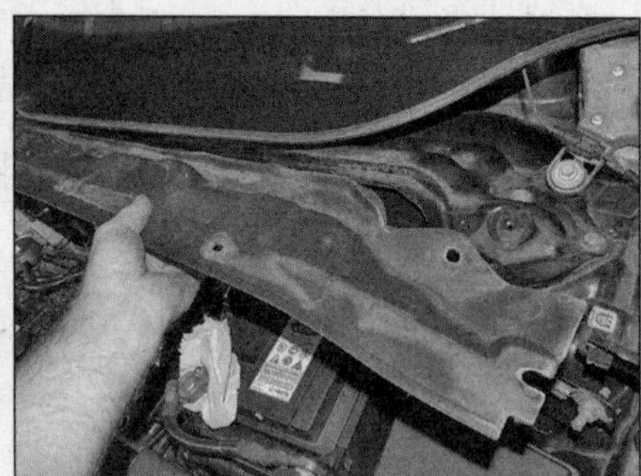

30.25 Remove the lower metal section

30.27a Remove the blanking plug...

30.27b ...and then the bolt

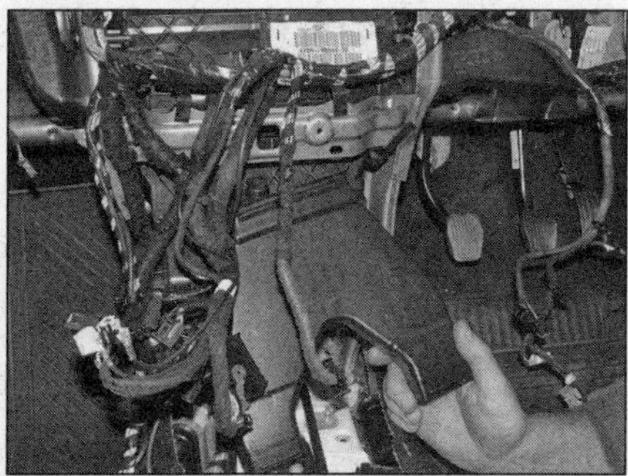
30.28a Remove the air distribution ducts...

30.28b ...and then the support bracket

30.30 Remove the bolts (uppers shown)

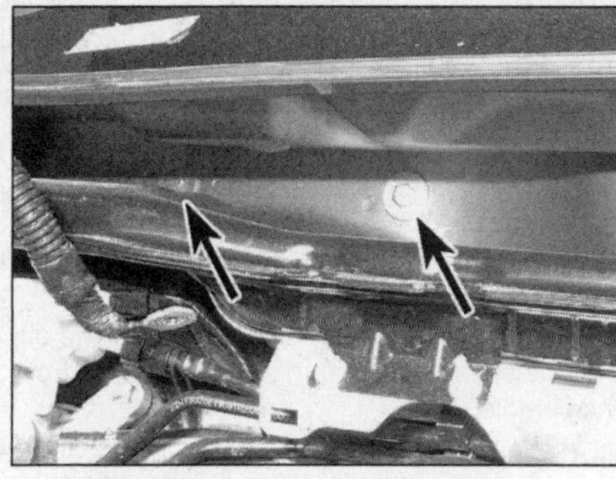
30.31 Remove the bolts (arrowed)

26 With reference to Section 14 of this Chapter remove both front doors.

27 Remove the mounting bolts from both A-pillars **(see illustrations)**.

28 At the transmission tunnel, remove the air distribution ducts and then remove the support brackets from each side of the transmission tunnel **(see illustrations)**.

29 Remove the 4 lower bolts from the lower section of the heater box. Remove the lower section from the vehicle.

30 Unbolt the heater box from the crossmember (4 bolts) **(see illustration)**.

31 Working under the bonnet remove the 2 bolts from the scuttle **(see illustration)**.

32 Disconnect the wiring loom from the crossmember as required. Note the position and layout of the wiring loom and label the loom as required in order to aid refitting.

33 Remove the bonnet release handle and the scuff panel from the base of the A-pillar. Fold back the carpet and remove the earth connections from the sill **(see illustrations)**. Repeat the procedure on the drivers side, for the scuff panel.

34 Disconnect the wiring plugs from the Body Control Module (BCM) and from the A-pillar **(see illustrations)**.

30.33a Remove the handle...

30.33b ...and then the panel

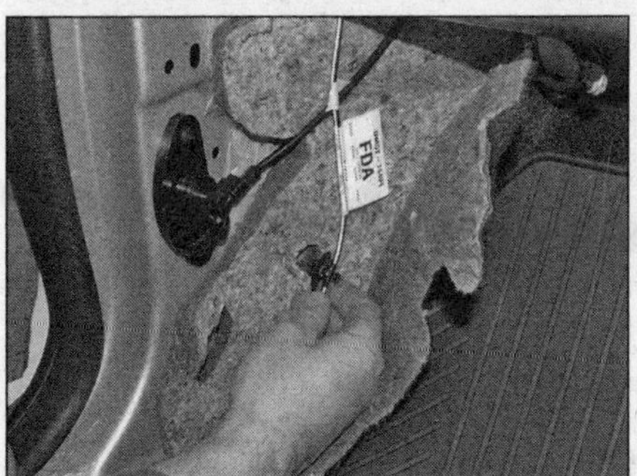

30.33c Release the wiring loom

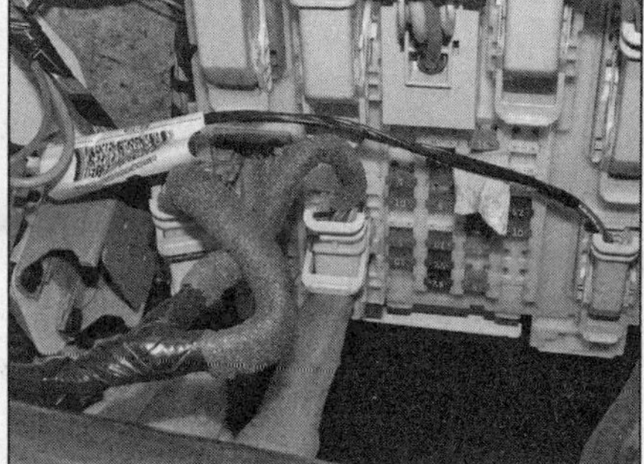
30.34a Disconnect the wiring plugs from the BCM...

30.34b ...and the A-pillar

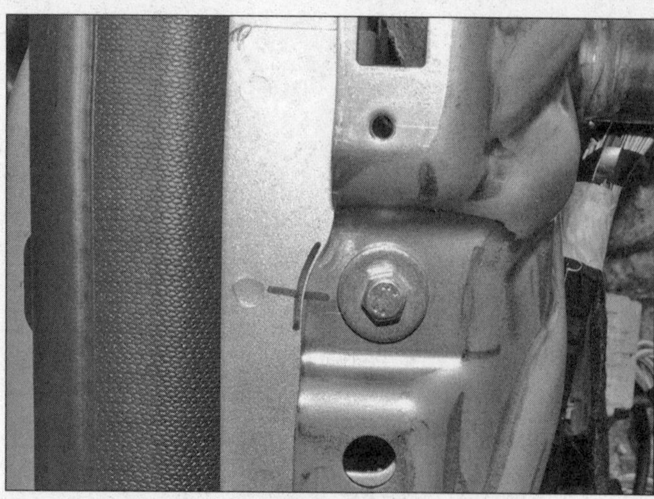
30.35 Mark the position on the crossmember

30.38 The adjuster (arrowed) must contact the A-pillar

35 Mark the position of the crossmember in relation to the A-pillars **(see illustration)**.

36 Remove the 4 bolts and then with the aid of an assistant remove the crossmember from the vehicle.

Refitting

37 Before refitting the crossmember fully unwind, and then turn back one revolution the tolerance adjusters at both ends of the crossmember.

38 Refit the crossmember, ensuring that the tolerance adjuster are in contact with the A-pillars **(see illustration)** and that the previously made marks all line up correctly.

31.2 Release the fasteners and remove the mudflap

31.3a Undo the screws...

39 The remainder of refitting is a reversal of the removal procedure.

31 Wheel arch liner – removal and refitting

Removal

Front

1 Apply the handbrake. If the wheel is to be removed (to improve access), loosen the wheel nuts. Jack up the front of the vehicle and support it on axle stands (see *Jacking and vehicle support*). Remove the front wheel.

2 Where fitted remove the mudflap, these are held in place with various retaining clips **(see illustration)**.

3 Unscrew the screws securing the liner to the inner wing panel, and also release the securing clips from the wheel arch liner **(see illustrations)**.

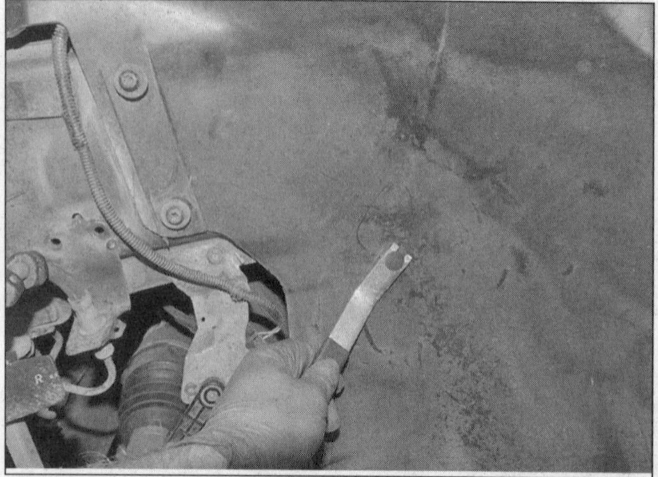
31.3b ...and using a trim tool...

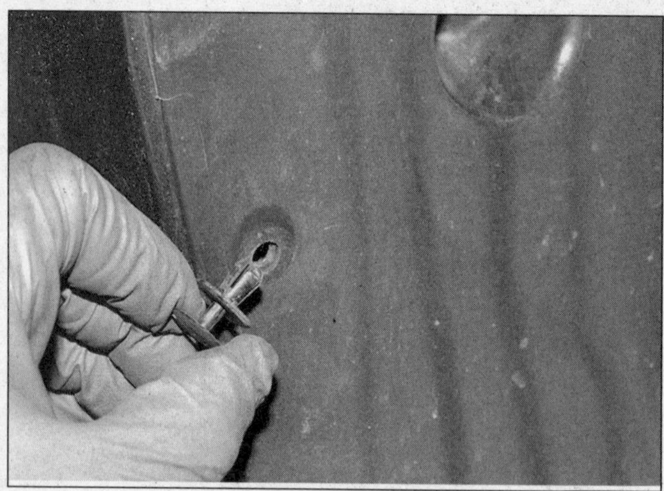
31.3c ...remove the securing clips

31.4a Remove the securing clips...

31.4b ...and pull back the front of the liner...

4 Remove the two securing clips from the lower front edge of the liner, then pull back the liner and withdraw the liner from under the wheel arch **(see illustrations)**.

Rear

5 Chock the front wheels, and engage 1st gear. If the wheel is to be removed (to improve access), loosen the wheel nuts. Jack up the rear of the vehicle and support it on axle stands (see *Jacking and vehicle support*). Remove the rear wheel.

6 Where fitted remove the mudflap **(see illustration)**.

7 Unscrew the screws securing the liner to the inner wing panel, and also release the securing clips from the wheel arch liner, then withdraw the liner from under the wheel arch **(see illustrations)**.

Refitting

8 Refitting is a reversal of the removal procedure. If the wheels were removed, tighten the wheel nuts to the specified torque.

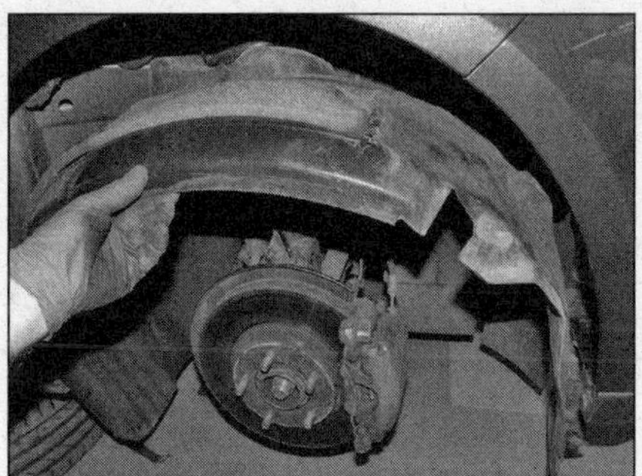

31.4c ...then withdraw the liner

31.6 Note how the rear mudflap clips in position (arrowed)

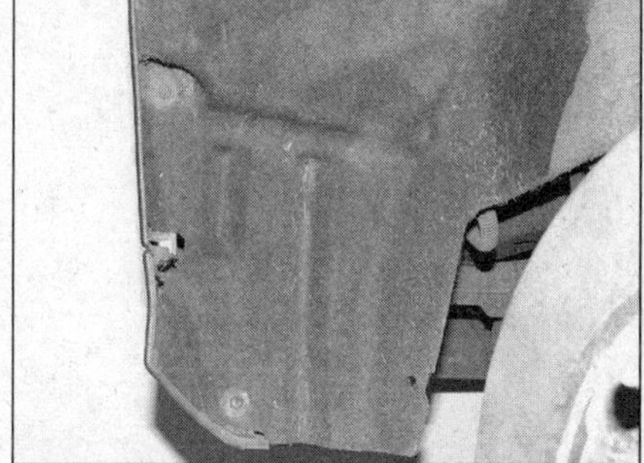

31.7a Undo the screws at the rear...

31.7b ...release the centre securing clips...

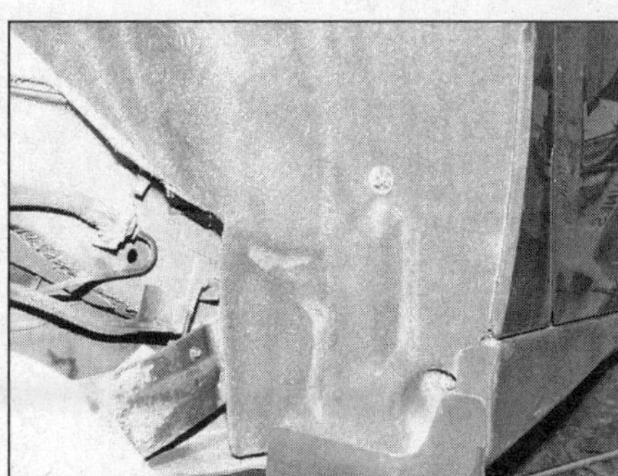

31.7c ...also the front fasteners...

31.7d ...then withdraw the liner

Chapter 12
Body electrical systems

Contents

Degrees of difficulty

Easy, suitable for novice with little experience 

Fairly easy, suitable for beginner with some experience

Fairly difficult, suitable for competent DIY mechanic

Difficult, suitable for experienced DIY mechanic

Very difficult, suitable for expert DIY or professional

Specifications

System type . . . 12 volt, negative earth

Bulbs	**Power rating (watts)**	**Type**
Approach light	5	W5W
Direction indicators	21	PY21W
Direction indicator side repeaters	5	WY5W
Foglamp:		
Front	55	H8
Rear	21	P21W
Headlight:		
Halogen:		
Dipped	55*	H7
Main	55	H1 or H15
Gas discharge (Xenon):		
Dipped	35	D3S
Main	55	H7
Glovebox light	5	W5W
High-level brake light	LED	
Interior light	5	W5W
Number plate light	LED	
Luggage compartment light	5	W5W
Reading light	5	W5W
Reversing light	16	W16W
Sidelights	5	W5W
Stop/tail light	21/5	P21/5W
Tail light 5	W5W	
Vanity mirror	5	W5W

**Check the wattage of the existing bulb and replace like for like.*

Note: *Some models have LEDs (light emitting diodes) fitted to the side and tail lights instead of conventional bulbs.*

Torque wrench settings

	Nm	lbf ft
Airbag control unit nuts	7	5
Crash sensor bolts	6	4
Passenger airbag bolts:		
To facia	6	4
To cross member	8	6

1 General information and precautions

Warning: Before carrying out any work on the electrical system, read through the precautions given in 'Safety first!' at the beginning of this manual, and in Chapter 5A.

1 The electrical system is of 12 volt negative earth type. Power for the lights and all electrical accessories is supplied by a lead-acid type battery which is charged by the alternator.

2 This Chapter covers repair and service procedures for the various electrical components not associated with the engine. Information on the battery, alternator and starter motor can be found in Chapter 5A.

3 It should be noted that prior to working on any component in the electrical system, the battery negative terminal should first be disconnected to prevent the possibility of electrical short-circuits and/or fires. **Note:** *If the vehicle has a security-coded radio, check that you have a copy of the code number before disconnecting the battery. Refer to your Ford dealer if in doubt.*

2 Electrical fault finding – general information

Note: *Refer to the precautions given in 'Safety first!' and in Chapter 5A before starting work. The following tests relate to testing of the main electrical circuits, and should not be used to test delicate electronic circuits (such as anti-lock braking systems), particularly where an electronic control unit is used.*

Caution: The Ford Focus electrical system is extremely complex. Many of the Electronic Control Modules (ECMs) are connected via a 'Databus' system, where they are able to share information from the various sensors, and communicate with each other. Due to the design of the Databus system, it is not advisable to backprobe the ECMs with a multimeter in the traditional manner. Instead, the electrical systems are equipped with a sophisticated self-diagnosis system, which can interrogate the various ECMs to reveal stored fault codes, and help pinpoint faults. In order to access the self-diagnosis system, specialist test equipment (fault code reader/scanner) is required.

General

1 Typically, electrical circuit consists of an electrical component, any switches, relays, motors, fuses, fusible links or circuit breakers related to that component, and the wiring and connectors which link the component to both the battery and the chassis. To help to pinpoint a problem in an electrical circuit, wiring diagrams are included at the end of this Chapter.

2 Have a good look at the appropriate wiring diagram before attempting to diagnose an electrical fault, to obtain a complete understanding of the components included in the particular circuit concerned. The possible sources of a fault can be narrowed down by noting if other components related to the circuit are operating properly. If several components or circuits fail at one time, the problem is likely to be related to a shared fuse or earth connection.

3 An electrical problem will usually stem from simple cause, such as loose or corroded connections, a faulty earth connection, a blown fuse, a melted fusible link, or a faulty relay (refer to Section 3 for details of testing relays). Visually inspect the condition of all fuses, wires and connections in a problem circuit before testing the components. Use the wiring diagrams to determine which terminal connections will need to be checked in order to pinpoint the trouble-spot.

4 The basic tools required for electrical fault finding include a circuit tester or voltmeter (a 12 volt bulb with a set of test leads can also be used for certain tests); a self-powered test light (sometimes known as a continuity tester); an ohmmeter (to measure resistance); a battery and set of test leads; and a jumper wire, preferably with a circuit breaker or fuse incorporated, which can be used to bypass suspect wires or electrical components. Before attempting to locate a problem with test instruments, use the wiring diagram to determine where to make the connections.

5 Sometimes, an intermittent wiring fault (usually caused to a poor or dirty connection, or damaged wiring insulation) can be pinpointed by performing a wiggle test on the wiring. This involves wiggling the wiring by hand to see if the fault occurs as the wiring is moved. It should be possible to narrow down the source of the fault to a particular section of wiring. This method of testing can be used in conjunction with any of the tests described in the following sub-Sections.

6 Apart from problems due to poor connections, two basic types of fault can occur in an electrical circuit: open-circuit, or short-circuit.

7 Largely, open-circuit faults are caused by a break somewhere in the circuit, which prevents current from flowing. An open-circuit fault will prevent a component from working, but will not cause the relevant circuit fuse to blow.

8 Low resistance or short-circuit faults are caused by a 'short'; a failure point which allows the current flowing in the circuit to 'escape' along an alternative route, somewhere in the circuit. This typically occurs when a positive supply wire touches either an earth wire, or an earthed component such as the bodyshell. Such faults are normally caused by a breakdown in wiring insulation, A short circuit fault will normally cause the relevant circuit fuse to blow.

9 Fuses are designed to protect a circuit from being overloaded. A blown fuse indicates that there may be problem in that particular circuit and it is important to identify and rectify the problem before renewing the fuse. Always renew a blown fuse with one of the correct current rating; fitting a fuse of a different rating may cause an overloaded circuit to overheat and even catch fire.

Finding an open-circuit

10 One of the most straightforward ways of finding an open-circuit fault is by using a circuit test meter or voltmeter. Connect one lead of the meter to either the negative battery terminal or a known good earth. Connect the other lead to a connector in the circuit being tested, preferably nearest to the battery or fuse. Switch on the circuit, bearing in mind that some circuits are live only when the ignition switch is moved to a particular position. If voltage is present (indicated either by the tester bulb lighting or a voltmeter reading, as applicable), this means that the section of the circuit between the relevant connector and the battery is problem-free. Continue to check the remainder of the circuit in the same fashion. When a point is reached at which no voltage is present, the problem must lie between that point and the previous test point with voltage. Most problems can be traced to a broken, corroded or loose connection.

⚠ ***Warning: Under no circumstances may live measuring instruments such as ohmmeters, voltmeters or a bulb and test lead be used to test any of the airbag circuitry. Any testing of these components must be left to a Ford dealer or specialist, as there is a danger of activating the system if the correct procedures are not followed.***

Finding a short-circuit

11 Loading the circuit during testing will produce false results and may damage your test equipment, so all electrical loads must be disconnected from the circuit before it can be checked for short circuits. Loads are the components which draw current from a circuit, such as bulbs, motors, heating elements, etc.

12 Keep both the ignition and the circuit under test switched off, then remove the relevant fuse from the circuit, and connect a circuit test meter or voltmeter to the fuse connections.

13 Switch on the circuit, bearing in mind that some circuits are live only when the ignition switch is moved to a particular position. If voltage is present (indicated either by the tester bulb lighting or a voltmeter reading, as applicable), this means that there is a short-circuit. If no voltage is present, but the fuse still blows with the load(s) connected, this indicates an internal fault in the load(s).

Finding an earth fault

14 The battery negative terminal is connected to 'earth': the metal of the engine/transmission and the car body – and most systems are wired so that they only receive a positive feed, the current returning through the metal of the car body. This means that the component mounting and the body form part of that circuit. Loose or corroded mountings can therefore cause a range of electrical faults, ranging from total failure of a circuit, to a puzzling partial fault. In particular, lights may shine dimly (especially when another circuit sharing the same earth point is in operation), motors (eg, wiper motors or the radiator auxiliary cooling fan motor) may run slowly, and the operation of one circuit may have an apparently unrelated effect on another. Note that on many vehicles, earth straps are used between certain components, such as the engine/transmission and the body, usually where there is no metal-to-metal contact between components due to flexible rubber mountings, etc **(see illustrations)**.

15 To check whether a component is properly earthed, disconnect the battery and connect one lead of an ohmmeter to a known good earth point. Connect the other lead to the wire or earth connection being tested. The resistance reading should be zero; if not, check the connection as follows.

16 If an earth connection is thought to be faulty, dismantle the connection and clean back to bare metal both the bodyshell and the wire terminal or the component earth connection mating surface. Be careful to remove all traces of dirt and corrosion, then use a knife to trim away any paint, so that a clean metal-to-metal joint is made. On reassembly, tighten the joint fasteners securely; if a wire terminal is being refitted, use serrated washers between the terminal and the bodyshell to ensure a clean and secure connection. When the connection is remade, prevent the onset of corrosion in the future by applying a coat of petroleum jelly or silicone-based grease or by spraying on (at regular intervals) a proprietary ignition sealer or a water dispersant lubricant.

3 Fuses and relays – general information

Main fuses

1 Fuse are located under and behind the glovebox, in the engine compartment and at the rear left-hand side of the load area.

2 Access to the passenger side glovebox

2.14a Earth connection on the left-hand side suspension turret in the engine compartment...

2.14b ...on the left-hand chassis leg in the engine compartment (under the air filter)...

2.14c ...on the transmission bell housing (arrowed)...

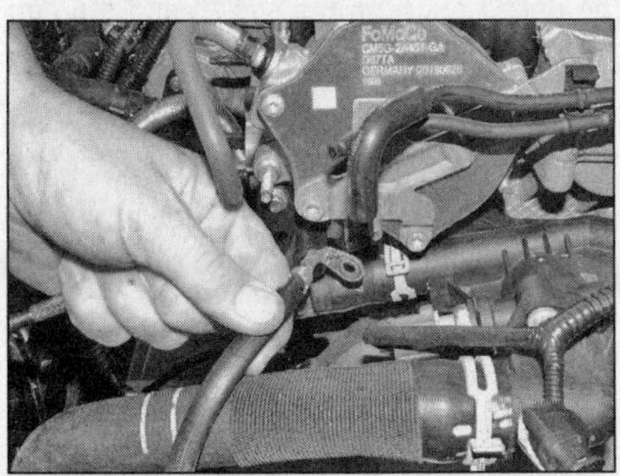

2.14d ...on the vacuum pump stud...

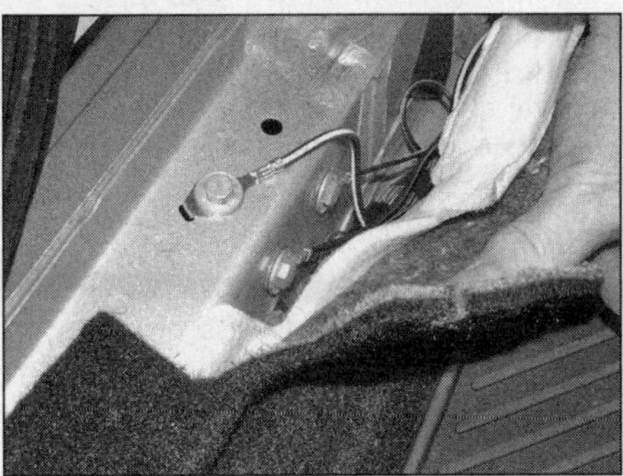

2.14e ...on the left-hand...

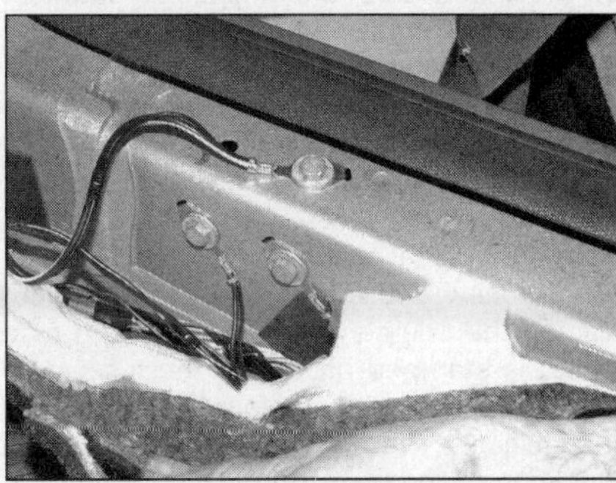

2.14f ...and right-hand front door sills (under the sill trims)

3.2a Remove the trim panel...

3.2b.. to access the passenger compartment fusebox

3.3a Release the clip at the rear...

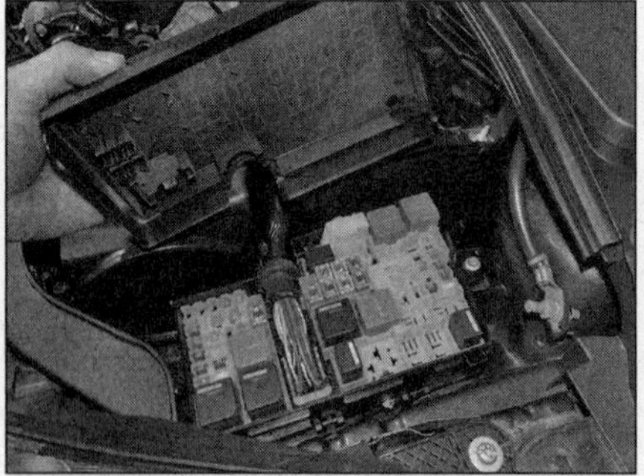

3.3b ...then lift off the fusebox cover

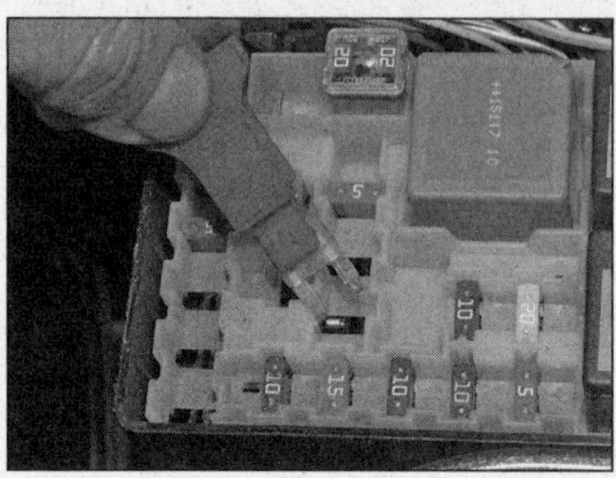

3.5 Removing a fuse

3.9 Fusible links are fitted behind plastic cover

fuses is gained by removing the trim panel below the glovebox. The panel is secured by 2 fasteners. Undo the fasteners and allow the panel to drop down **(see illustrations)**. Access can be greatly improved by removing the glovebox as described in Chapter 11 Section 29.

3 To access the engine compartment fusebox, open the bonnet, then release the securing clip at the rear of the fusebox cover and pull it upwards to open the fusebox **(see illustrations)**.

4 Each fuse is numbered; the fuses' ratings and circuits they protect are listed on the rear face of the cover panel. A list of fuses is given with the wiring diagrams.

5 To remove a fuse, first switch off the circuit concerned (or the ignition), then pull the fuse out of its terminals – a pair of tweezers provided specifically for this purpose are fitted on the underside of the engine compartment fusebox cover **(see illustration)**. The wire within the fuse should be visible; if the fuse is blown the wire will have a break in it, which will be visible through the plastic casing.

6 Always renew a fuse with one of an identical rating; never use a fuse with a different rating from the original or substitute anything else. Never renew a fuse more than once without tracing the source of the trouble. The fuse rating is stamped on top of the fuse; note that the fuses are also colour-coded for easy recognition.

7 If a new fuse blows immediately, find the cause before renewing it again; a short to earth as a result of faulty insulation is most likely. Where a fuse protects more than one circuit, try to isolate the defect by switching on each circuit in turn (if possible) until the fuse blows again. Always carry a supply of spare fuses of each relevant rating on the vehicle, a spare of each rating should be clipped into the base of the fusebox.

8 Note that some circuits are protected by 'maxi' fuses fitted in the engine compartment fusebox. These fuses are physically much bigger than the normal fuses, and have correspondingly higher ratings. Should one of these fuses fail, have the circuit examined a Ford dealer or specialist prior to renewing the fuse.

9 Multiple fusible links are fitted under a plastic cover in front of the battery **(see illustration)**. They can be accessed by prising the loom free and cutting through the cable ties. Failure of any of the fusible links indicates a major fault. Do not attempt to replace the links until the cause of the problem has been rectified. Note, depending on model, the removal of the air cleaner assembly will be required to access the fusible links.

Relays

10 The main relays are located in the engine compartment fusebox. The location and function of the relays is given on the underside of the fusebox lid. Additional relays (dependant on the trim level) are also located in the load area fusebox.

11 The relays are of sealed construction, and cannot be repaired if faulty. The relays are of the plug-in type, and may be removed by pulling directly from their terminals. In some cases, it will be necessary to prise the two plastic clips outwards before removing the relay.

12 If a circuit or system controlled by a relay develops a fault and the relay is suspect, operate the system; if the relay is functioning, it should be possible to hear it click as it is energised. If this is the case, the fault lies with the components or wiring of the system. If the relay is not being energised, then either the relay is not receiving a main supply or a switching voltage, or the relay itself is faulty. Testing is by the substitution of a known good unit, but be careful; while some relays are identical in appearance and in operation, others look similar but perform different functions.

13 To renew a relay, first ensure that the ignition switch is off. The relay can then simply be pulled out from the socket and the new relay pressed in.

4 Ignition/stop start switch – removal and refitting

1 Ensure the battery negative lead has been disconnected as described in Chapter 5A Section 3.

2 Fully extend and lower the steering column.

Ignition switch – early models

3 Turn the ignition switch to position I, then rotate the steering wheel as necessary to

4.3 Rotate the steering wheel and release the upper shroud retaining clip each side

4.4 Lower steering column shroud bolts (arrowed)

access the column upper shroud retaining clips. Release the clips and remove the shroud **(see illustration)**.

4 Undo the bolts and remove the steering column lower shroud **(see illustration)**. Release the steering column adjustment lever to remove the shroud.

5 Disconnect the wiring plug, then depress the clips and remove the ignition switch **(see illustration)**. Do not turn the lock cylinder (key) from position I whilst the ignition switch is removed.

6 Disconnect the wiring plug from the key reader coil and then prise the coil assembly from the lock cylinder housing **(see illustration)**.

7 Remove the circlip, cover plate and small interlock plate from the rear of the lock cylinder.

8 With the key still in position I, insert a thin rod into the hole in the lower part of the cylinder housing and depress the spring-loaded locking lug, and pull the cylinder from the housing **(see illustrations)**.

9 Refitting is a reversal of removal. Note that the lock cylinder (key) must be in position I prior to refitting the ignition switch.

Stop/start switch – later models

10 Remove the facia lower trim panel on the driver's side, as described in Chapter 11 Section 30.

11 Reach up behind the facia and unclip the stop/start switch from the facia trim panel **(see illustrations)**. Disconnect the wiring connector as the switch is withdrawn.

12 Refitting is a reversal of removal.

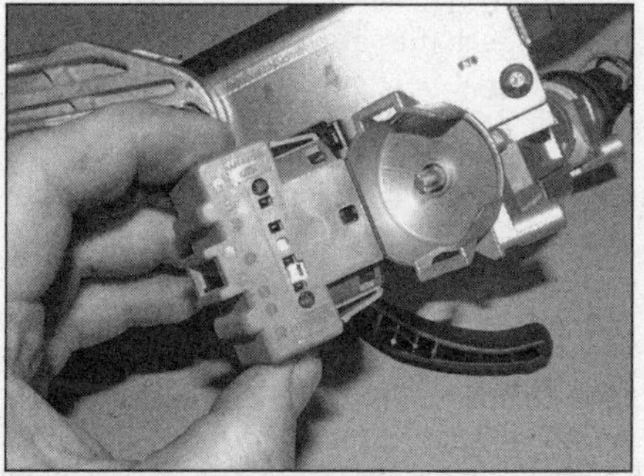

4.5 Release the clips and pull the switch from the lock

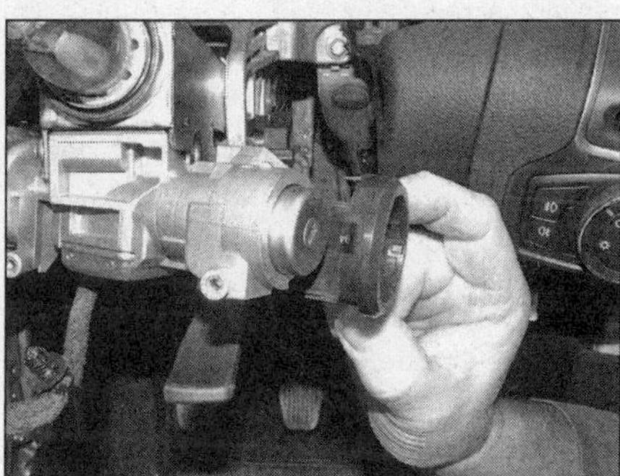

4.6 Remove the key reader coil

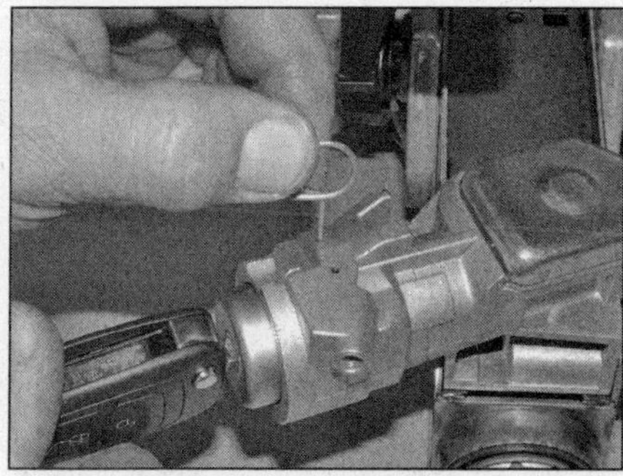

4.8a Release the lock cylinder...

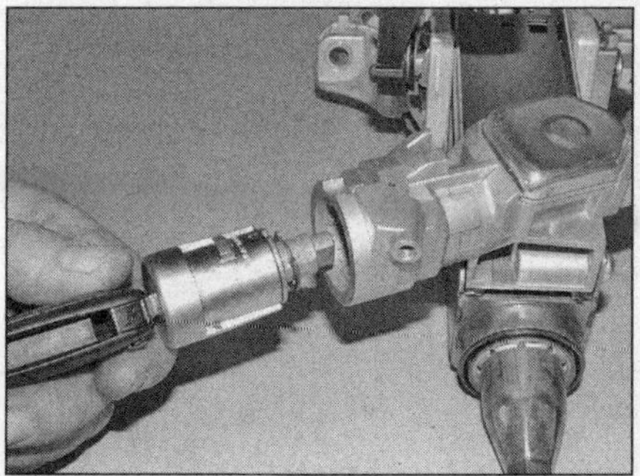

4.8b ...and withdraw it from the housing

4.11a Release the securing clips...

4.11b ...and withdraw the switch

5.3a Undo the two screws...

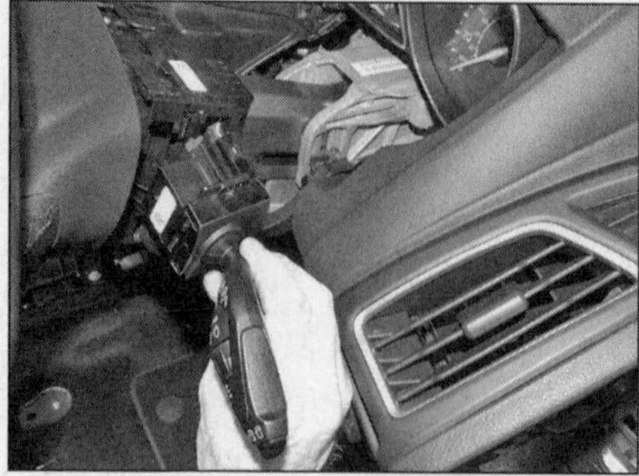
5.3b ...and slide the relevant switch from place

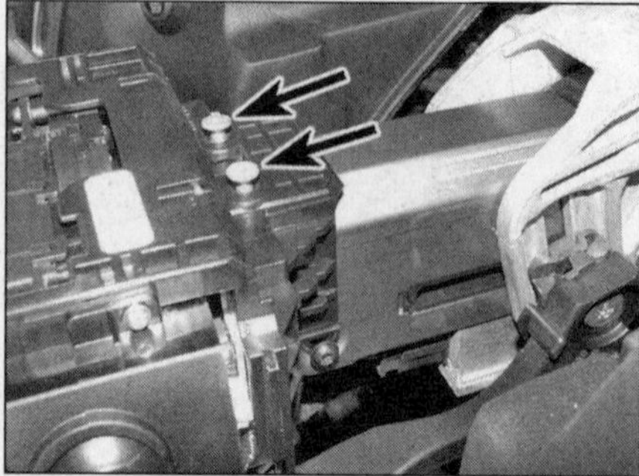
5.5a Undo the two upper screws...

5.5b ...disconnect the lower wiring connector...

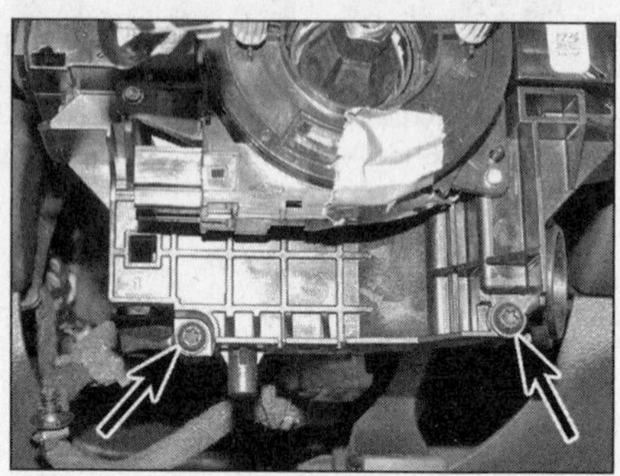
5.5c ...undo the two lower screws...

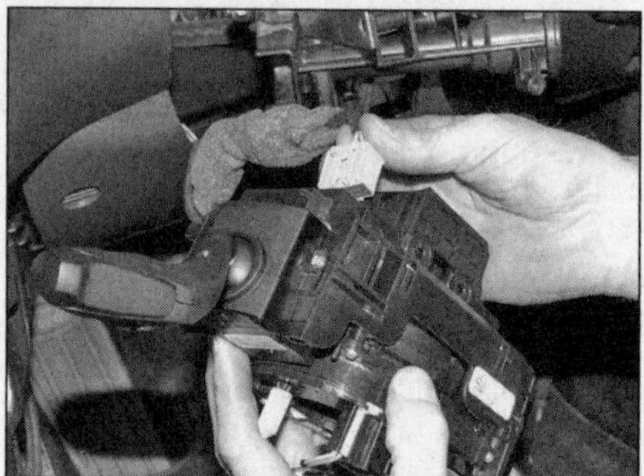
5.5d ...and disconnect the wiring connectors at the rear

5 Switches – removal and refitting

Steering column switches

1 Release the locking lever and fully extend and lower the steering column.

2 Rotate the steering wheel as necessary to access the shroud retaining clips, then undo the lower shroud retaining screws and remove shrouds from around steering column **(see illustrations 4.3 and 4.4)**. Release the steering column adjustment lever to remove the shroud.

3 Undo the two securing screws and slide the relevant switch from the assembly **(see illustrations)**.

4 If the multifunction switch/rotary contact carrier is to be removed as a complete assembly, begin by removing the steering wheel as described in Chapter 10 Section 13.

5 Disconnect the wiring plugs, undo the four retaining screws and slide the assembly from the steering column **(see illustrations)**.

6 Refitting is a reversal of removal.

Multifunction light switch

7 Open the compartment in the lower trim panel, then squeeze the sides together and pull down to unclip it from the facia panel **(see illustration)**.

8 Reaching inside the compartment aperture, release the retaining clips and remove the switch from the facia panel **(see illustration)**. Disconnect the wiring connector from the light switch, as it is removed.

9 Refitting is a reversal of removal.

Glovebox light switch

10 Remove the glovebox as described in Chapter 11 Section 29.

11 Using a small screwdriver, pull up the locking clip from the switch assembly.

12 Release the clips and remove the switch.

13 Refitting is a reversal of removal.

Door mirror adjuster

14 The door mirror adjusters are integral with the window switch assemblies fitted to the door panels.

15 To remove the switch assemblies, carefully prise away the grab handle outer trim **(see illustration)**.

16 Prise fee the switch panel and detach the wiring connector. With the assembly on the bench remove the screws and release the

5.7 Unclip the compartment from the facia

5.8 Remove the switch

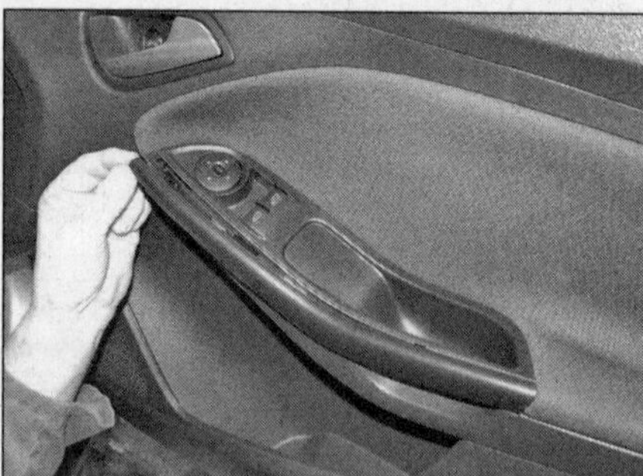
5.15 Release the trim

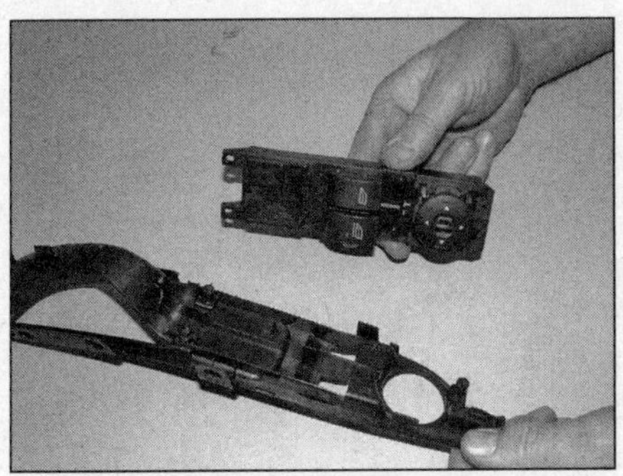
5.16 Remove the switch assembly from the panel

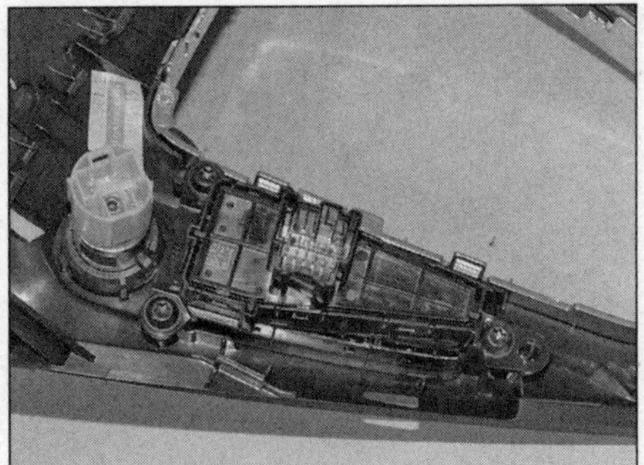
5.19 Undo the three screws

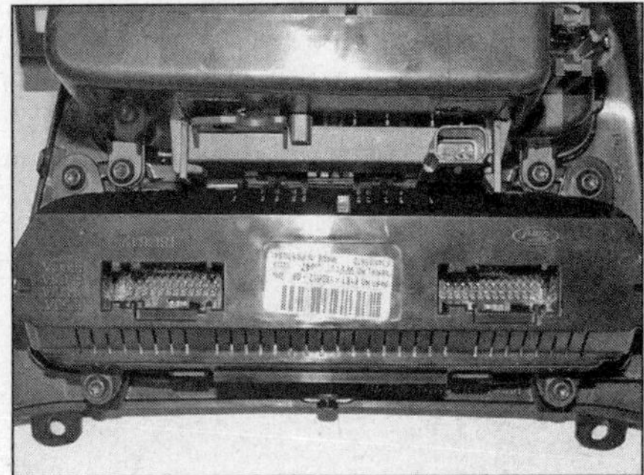
5.22 Undo the four screws

switch panel from the door pull handle trim **(see illustration)**.

17 Refit in the reverse order of removal.

Centre console switches

18 Remove the trim panel from the top of the centre console, as described in Chapter 11 Section 27.

19 Undo the three retaining screws and remove the switch assembly from the rear of the trim panel **(see illustration)**.

20 Refitting is a reversal of removal.

Heater control switches

21 Remove the heater control trim panel from the top of the centre console, as described in Chapter 11 Section 27.

22 The switches are part of the heater control panel. Undo the four retaining screws and remove the heater control panel/switches from the rear of the trim panel **(see illustration)**.

23 Refitting is a reversal of removal.

Audio and hazard warning light switches

24 Remove the Audio unit, as described in Section 18.

25 The switches are part of the Audio control panel. Undo the four retaining screws and remove the switch panel from the rear of the trim **(see illustration)**.

26 Refitting is a reversal of removal.

Sunroof control switch

27 Remove the switch from the overhead console, as described in Chapter 11 Section 28.

Central locking switch

28 The switch is located in the drivers side door pull handle surround, remove the drivers door trim panel, as described in Chapter 11 Section 10.

29 Release the securing clips at the rear of the switch, and then withdraw the switch from the front of the trim panel **(see illustrations)**.

30 Refitting is a reversal of removal.

Window switches

31 Removal is the same procedure as described for the removal of the exterior mirror switch, earlier in this Section **(see illustrations 5.15 and 5.16)**.

32 On rear window switches, remove the switch panel, release the securing clips and withdraw the switch from the rear of the switch panel **(see illustrations)**.

33 Refitting is a reversal of removal.

Courtesy light switches

34 The courtesy lights are controlled by microswitches incorporated into the door locks. The switches are not available separately. If defective, the door lock assembly must be renewed (see Chapter 11 Section 13).

Handbrake warning switch

35 Remove the centre console as described in Chapter 11 Section 27.

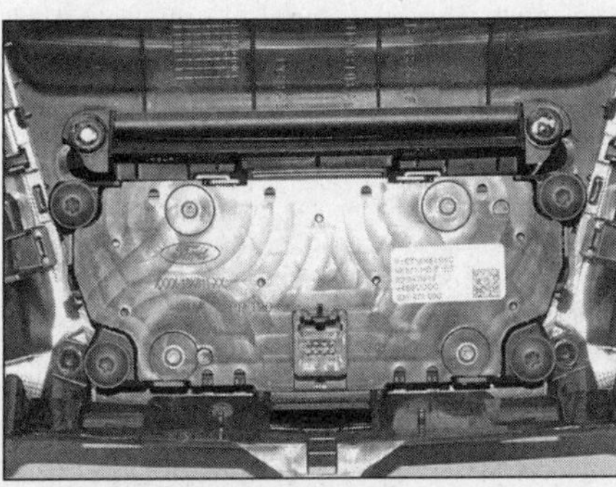
5.25 Undo the four screws

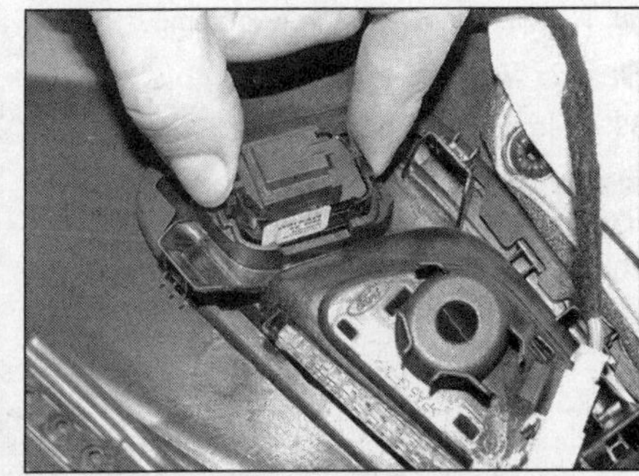
5.29a Release the securing clips...

5.29b ...and remove the switch

5.32a Release the securing clips...

5.32b ...and remove the switch

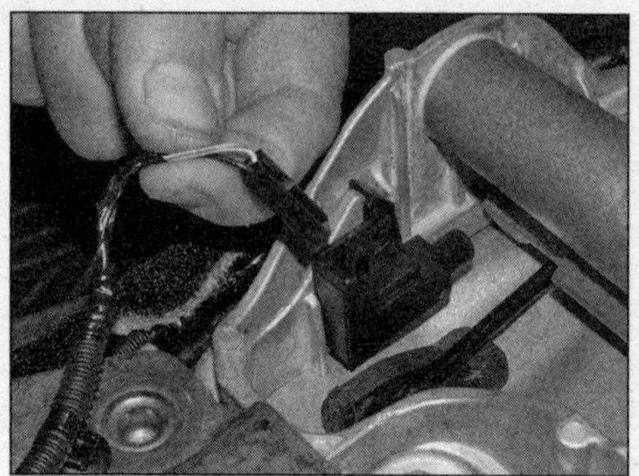
5.36 Disconnect the wiring plug

5.37 Release the switch

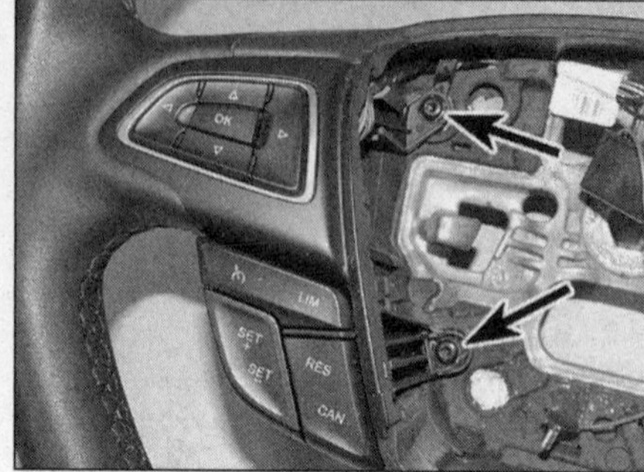

5.43a Remove the two screws...

5.43b ...and withdraw the switch

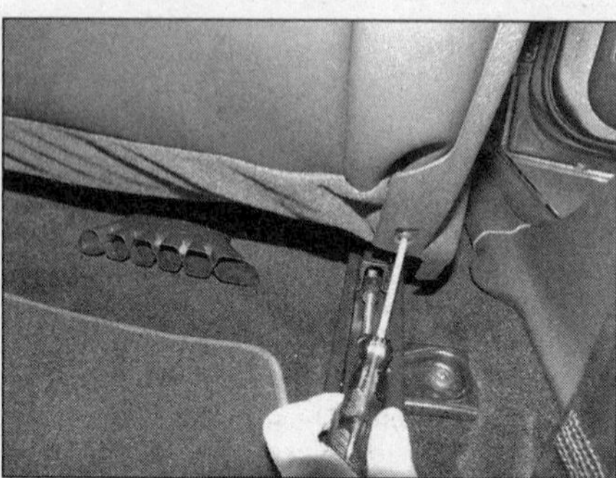
5.46 Undo the retaining screw

36 Detach the wiring connector from the switch **(see illustration)**.

37 Release the locking tab and detach the switch **(see illustration)**.

38 Refit in the reverse order of removal.

Brake light switch

39 Refer to Chapter 9 Section 20.

Headlight control/foglamp/ instrument illumination

40 These switches are integral with the multi-function light switch. Removal is described earlier in this Section.

Hazard warning switch

41 The hazard warning switch is an integral part of the audio control panel. If it is faulty, the audio control panel must be replaced.

Steering wheel switches

42 Remove the driver's airbag as described in Section 22.

43 Undo the retaining screws and remove the relevant switch pad, then disconnect the wiring plug as it is removed**(see illustrations)**.

44 Refitting is a reversal of removal.

Seat heating switches

45 These switches are integral with the Audio switch assembly, removal is described earlier in this Section.

Seat adjustment switches

46 Slide the seat forwards and undo the securing screw at the rear of the seat side trim panel **(see illustration)**.

47 Unclip the trim from the side of the seat frame, and then unclip the switches from the trim panel **(see illustrations)**.

48 Disconnect the wiring connector from the switches, as it is removed.

49 Refitting is a reversal of removal.

6 Exterior light bulbs – renewal

Note: *This section does not cover bulb renewal on models fitted with gas discharge headlights; refer to Section 9 for renewal details.*

1 Whenever a bulb is renewed, note the following points:

a) Remember that if the light has just been in use, the bulb may be extremely hot.

5.47a Unclip the trim panel...

5.47b ...and release the switch assembly

6.3a Remove the cover...

6.3b ...release the lower locking clip...

6.3c ...and disconnect the wiring plug

6.4 Remove the bulb

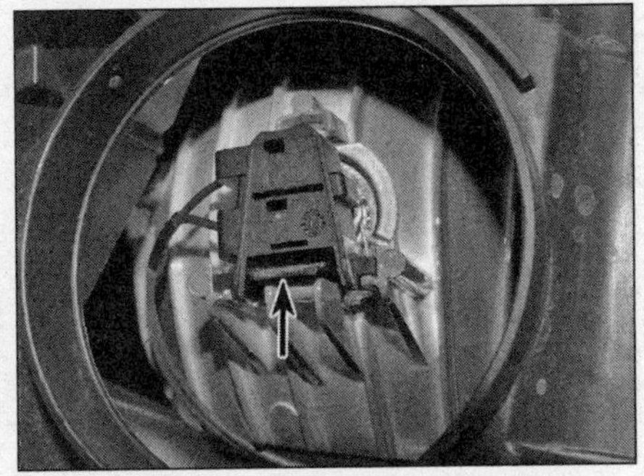
6.7 Release the lower locking clip...

6.8 ...and withdraw the bulb and holder

b) *Do not touch the bulb glass with the fingers, as the small deposits can cause the bulb to cloud over. If the bulb is accidentally touched with bare hands clean it with methylated spirits before fitting.*

c) *Always check the bulb contacts and holder, ensuring that there is clean metal-to-metal contact. Clean off any corrosion or dirt before fitting a new bulb.*

d) *Wherever bayonet-type bulbs are fitted, ensure that the live contacts bear firmly against the bulb contact.*

e) *Always ensure that the new bulb is of the correct rating and that it is completely clean before fitting it.*

Halogen main beam

2 Remove the headlight unit as described in Section 8.

3 Remove the rubber cover, press the locking clip at the bottom of the connector and disconnect the locking/wiring plug from the rear of the light unit **(see illustrations)**.

4 Note the orientation of the bulb and then withdraw it from the light unit **(see illustration)**.

5 Fit the new bulb using a reversal of the removal procedure.

Halogen dipped beam

6 Remove the headlight as described in Section 8.

7 Remove the rubber cover and release the bulb holder locking clip at the lower part of the wiring connector **(see illustration)**.

8 Note the orientation of the bulb holder and unclip it from the headlight unit **(see illustration)**.Pull the bulb from the holder to renew.

9 Fit the new bulb using a reversal of the removal procedure. Do not touch the glass part of the halogen bulb on refitting.

Sidelight

Note: *On models fitted with Xenon headlights the sidelights are LED type bulbs. These are not replaceable. If they are faulty the entire headlamp must be replaced.*

10 Remove the headlight unit as described in Section 8, then remove the cover from the rear of the headlight.

11 Remove the bulb holder complete with the bulb **(see illustration)**. Note that this is difficult to access and it may prove easier to remove the bulb and holder with a pair of long nose pliers.

12 Remove the bulb from the bulb holder **(see illustration)**.

Front direction indicator

13 Remove the headlight as described in Section 8.

14 Remove the rubber cover from the end of the headlamp **(see illustration)**.

6.11 Remove the bulb complete with the bulb holder

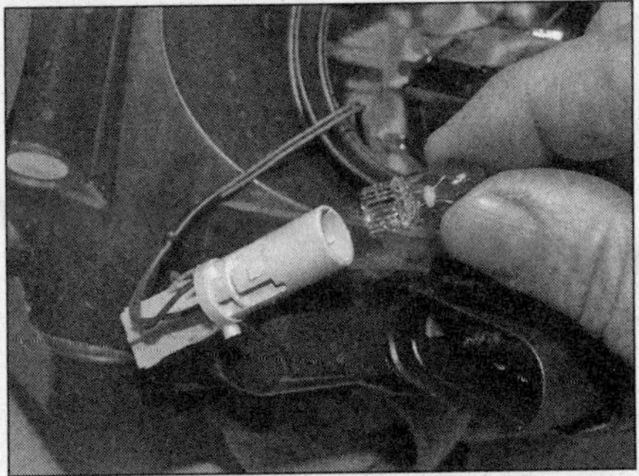
6.12 Remove the bulb from the bulb holder

6.14 Remove the cover

6.15 Remove the bulb holder

6.16 Remove the bayonet type bulb

6.19 Pull back the wheel arch liner

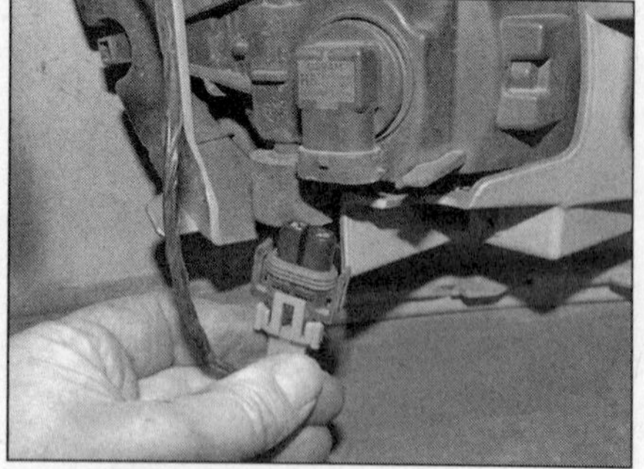
6.20 Disconnect the wiring connector

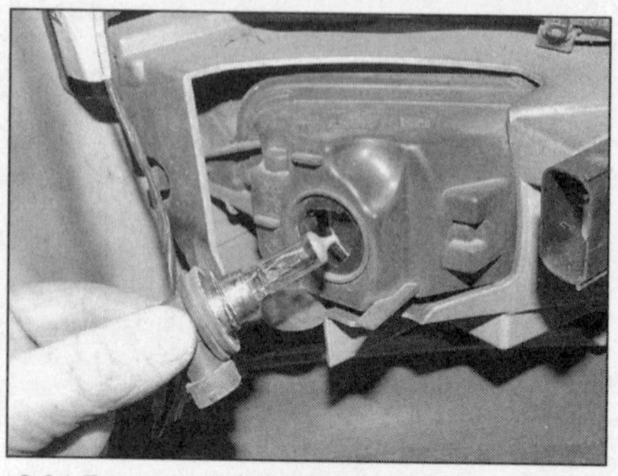
6.21 Remove the integrated bulb and bulb holder

6.25 Pull out the bulb holder

15 Rotate the bulb holder anti-clockwise and pull it from the headlight unit **(see illustration).**

16 Carefully press the bulb in slightly, and then twist it anti-clockwise to remove it from the bulb holder **(see illustration).**

17 Fit the new bulb using a reversal of the removal procedure.

Front foglamp

18 Access to the front foglamp bulbs can be gained from above, by removing the headlight, or from below by jacking up the vehicle (see *Jacking and vehicle support* in the reference section).

19 If working from below release the fasteners and pull back the front of the inner wheel arch liner from below the bumper cover **(see illustration).**

20 Reach up behind the bumper and disconnect the wiring connector from the rear of the light unit **(see illustration).**

21 Rotate the bulbholder anti-clockwise and pull it from the foglamp unit **(see illustration).** Note that the bulb is integral with the bulbholder.

22 Fit the new bulb using a reversal of the removal procedure.

Direction indicator side repeater

23 The side repeater is located in the door mirror.

24 Access to the bulb is possible by removing the mirror glass, as described in Chapter 11 Section 15.

25 Pull the bulb and holder from the side repeater, inside the mirror housing, and then remove the bulb **(see illustration).**

26 Refitting is a reversal of removal.

Approach light

27 The approach light is located in the base of the door mirror, remove the door mirror glass as described in Chapter 11 Section 15.

28 Pull the bulb and holder from the approach light, inside the mirror housing **(see illustration).**

29 Pull the wedge-type bulb from the bulbholder **(see illustration).**

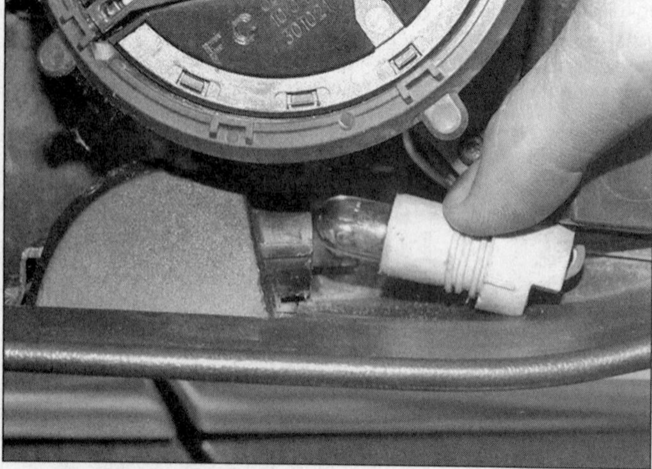
6.28 Pull out the bulb holder

6.29 Pull out the bulb

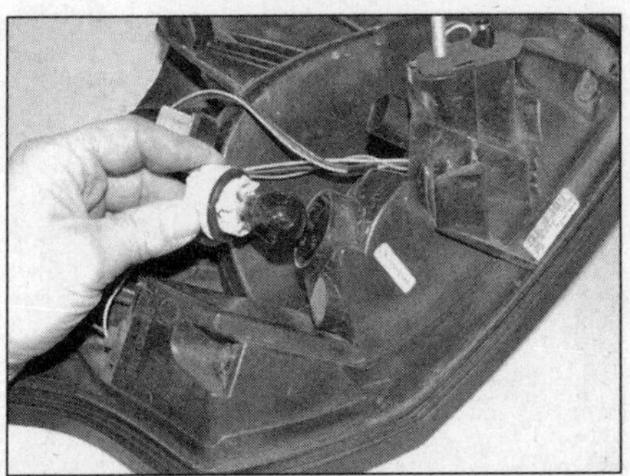
6.32a Remove the bulb holder – indicator

6.32b Remove the bulb holder – reversing light

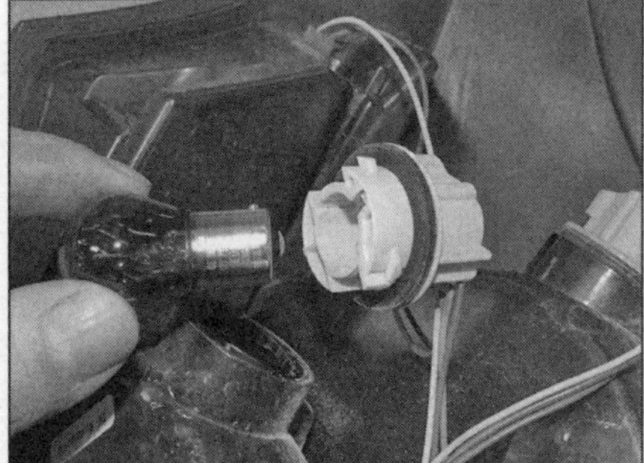
6.33 Remove the bayonet type bulb – indicator shown

30 Fit the new bulb using a reversal of the removal procedure.

Rear combination light

Note: *On models fitted with Xenon headlights the sidelights are LED type bulbs. These are not replaceable. If they are faulty the entire lamp must be replaced.*

Hatchback models

31 Remove the rear light unit as described in Section 8.

32 Rotate the relevant bulbholder anti-clockwise and pull it from the lamp **(see illustrations)**.

33 Where a bayonet type bulb is fitted (indicator, brake and side light), push and twist the bulb anti-clockwise to remove it **(see illustration)**.

34 Where a capless bulb is fitted (reversing light), pull the bulb straight out from the bulb holder**(see illustration)**.

35 Refitting is a reversal of removal.

Estate models

36 Remove the rear light unit as described in Section 8.

37 Undo the bolts, and remove the bulbholder.

38 Press and twist the relevant bulb anti-clockwise, and withdraw it from the bulbholder.

39 Fit the new bulb using a reversal of the removal procedure.

Rear foglamp/reversing light

40 Reach up behind the bumper and rotate the bulbholder anti-clockwise and pull it from the rear of the light unit **(see illustration)**. If required, release the fasteners at the rear of the inner wheel arch liner and pull it away from the rear bumper to give better access to the light unit.

6.34 Remove the wedge type bulb – reversing light

41 Push and twist the bulb anti-clockwise, and pull it from the bulbholder **(see illustration)**.

42 Refitting is a reversal of removal.

Number plate light

43 The number plate light uses LED type bulbs. If a fault develops with the lamp the complete assembly (including the tailgate release switch) must be replaced.

44 To replace the lamp remove the tailgate handle as described in Chapter 11, Section 19.

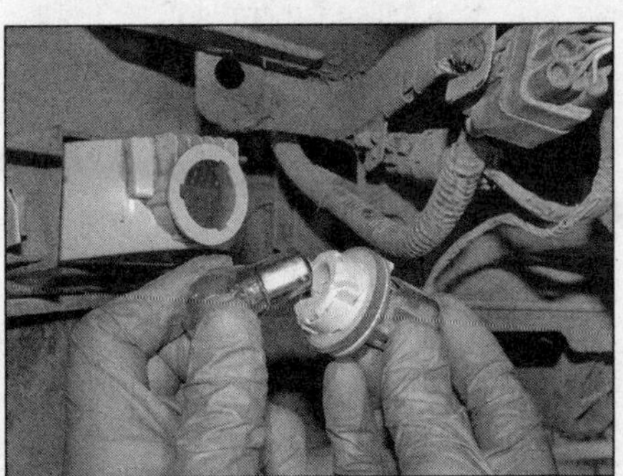
6.41 Remove the bayonet type bulb

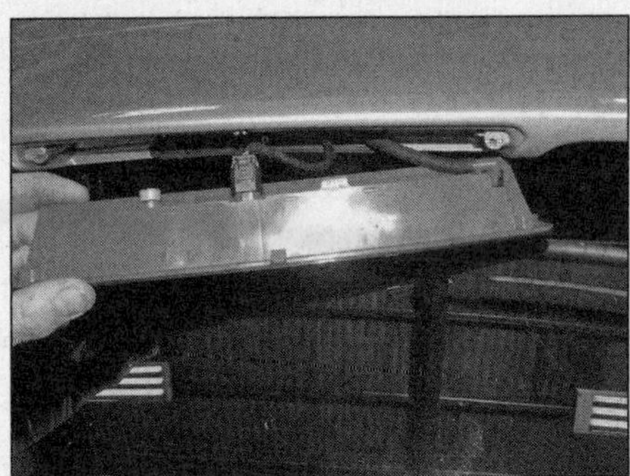
6.45 Remove the lamp

6.40 Disconnect the wiring connector

High-level brake light

Hatchback and Estate models

45 Undo the screws and remove the light unit **(see illustration)**.

46 The high level brake light uses LED type bulbs. If a fault develops with the lamp the entire assembly must be replaced

7 Interior light bulbs – renewal

1 Whenever a bulb is renewed, note the following points:

a) *Remember that if the light has just been in use, the bulb may be extremely hot.*

b) *Always check the bulb contacts and holder, ensuring that there is clean metal-to-metal contact between the bulb and its live and earth. Clean off any corrosion or dirt before fitting a new bulb.*

c) *Wherever bayonet-type bulbs are fitted, ensure that the live contact(s) bear firmly against the bulb contact.*

d) *Always ensure that the new bulb is of the correct rating and that it is completely clean before fitting it.*

e) *Some vehicles feature LED type bulbs. If these fail the entire lamp will require replacement.*

Interior lights

2 Prise free the lamp, ensuring that the metal frame stays fixed to the roof liner. Remove

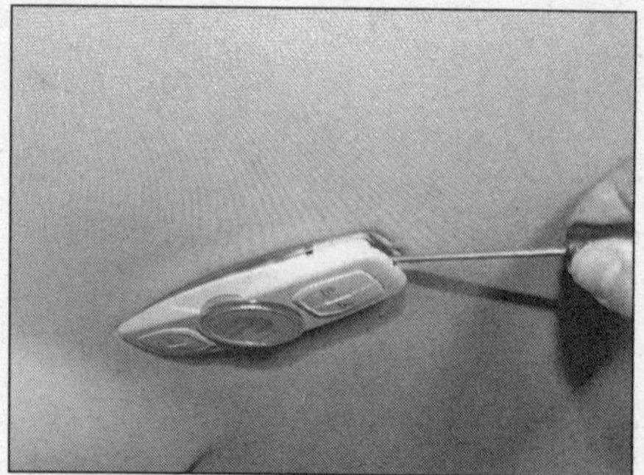
7.2a Prise the lamp free

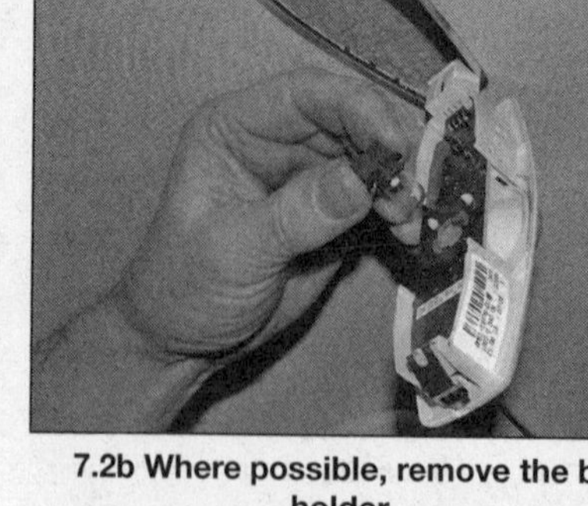
7.2b Where possible, remove the bulb holder...

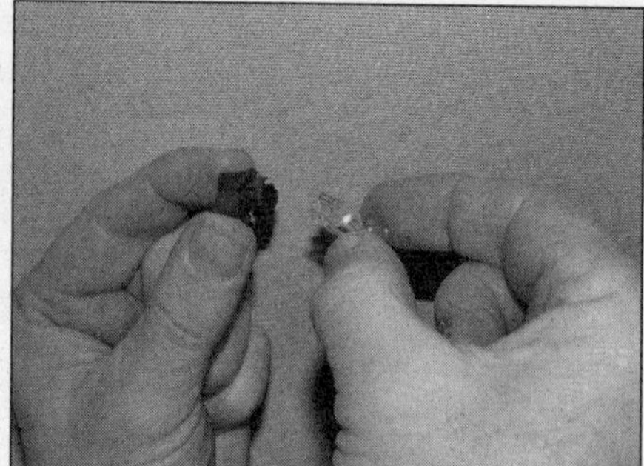
7.2c ... and then remove the bulb from the holder

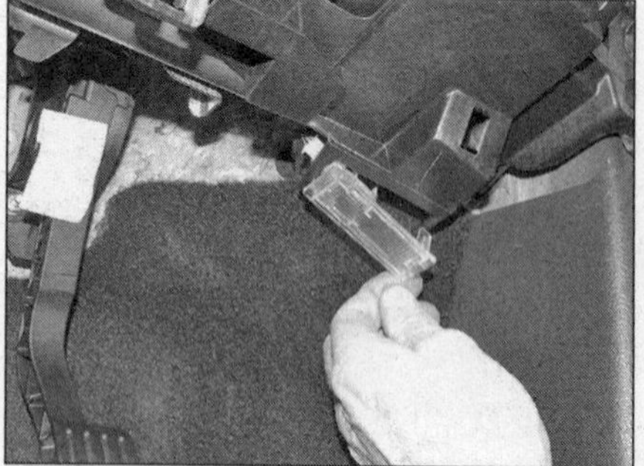
7.8a Prise the lamp free (drivers side footwell)...

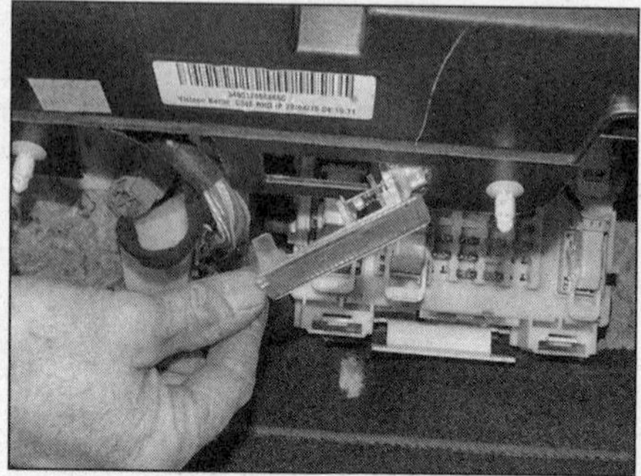
7.8b ...and passenger side footwell (LED type bulb)...

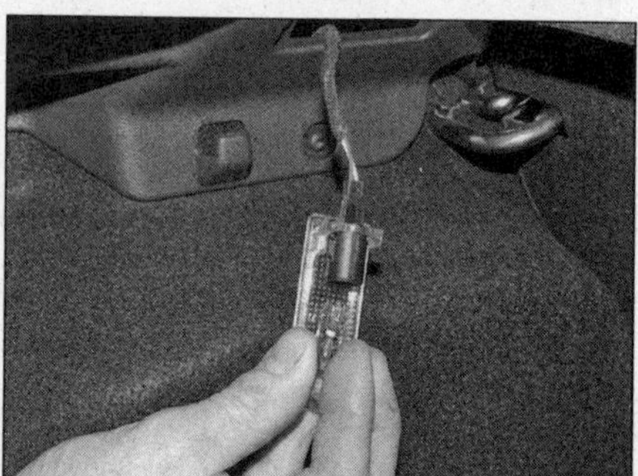
7.8c ...or remove the wedge type bulb (luggage compartment)

the bulb holder and then pull the capless style bulb from the bulb holder. **(see illustrations)**.

3 Fit a new bulb using a reversal of the removal procedure.

Glovebox

4 Remove the glovebox as described in Chapter 11 Section 29.

5 Disconnect the wiring plug, work the locking clip free and, where applicable, pull the wedge-type bulb from its holder.

6 Fit the new bulb using a reversal of the removal procedure.

Footwell lights/ luggage area light

7 The footwell lights and the load area lights are identical.

8 Reach under the facia (or open the tailgate) and prise free the lamp/lens from the trim panel. Where applicable, pull the wedge-type capless bulb from the holder **(see illustrations)**.

9 Fit the new bulb using a reversal of the removal procedure.

Instrument panel bulbs

10 On all models covered by this Manual, it is not possible to renew the instrument panel bulbs individually as they are of LED design and soldered to a printed circuit board. It is not possible to renew a single LED. Where an LED is not functioning, the complete instrument panel must be renewed.

Switch illumination

11 The switches are illuminated by LEDs, and cannot be renewed separately. Refer to Section 5 and remove the switch.

Heater/air conditioning control panel illumination

12 The control panel is illuminated by non-renewable LEDs. If defective, the control panel may need to be renewed.

8 Exterior light units – removal, refitting and beam adjustment

Headlight unit

Removal

Caution: On models equipped with gas discharge headlights, disconnect the battery negative lead, as described in Chapter 5A Section 3, prior to working on the headlights.

1 Open the bonnet and undo the two headlight retaining screws **(see illustrations)**.

2 With the screws removed, pull the headlamp forward, whilst slightly lifting the rear to remove it **(see illustration)**.

8.1a Undo the rear screw...

8.1b ...the front screw...

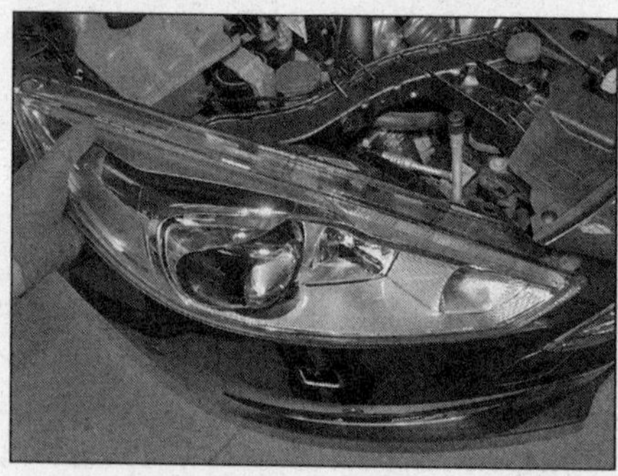
8.2 ...withdraw the headlight forward...

8.3 ...and disconnect the wiring plug connector

8.5 Unclip the trim cover...

8.6 ...and remove the screws

3 Disconnect the wiring plug(s) from the rear of the headlight, as it's withdrawn from the vehicle **(see illustration)**.

Refitting

4 Refitting is a reversal of the removal procedure. On completion check for satisfactory operation, and have the headlight beam adjustment checked as soon as possible (see below).

Front foglamp

Removal

5 Carefully unclip the trim cover from the front bumper cover, taking care not to damage the paintwork **(see illustration)**.

6 Undo the three mounting screws, withdraw the foglamp from the front bumper, and disconnect the wiring **(see illustration)**.

Refitting

7 Refitting is a reversal of removal, but have the foglamp beam setting checked at the earliest opportunity. An approximate adjustment can be made by positioning the car 10 metres in front of a wall marked with the centre point of the foglamp lens. Turn the adjustment screw as required. Note that only height adjustment is possible – there is no lateral adjustment.

Direction indicator side repeater

8 The side repeater is located in the door mirror.

9 Access is possible by removing the mirror glass, as described in Chapter 11 Section 15.

10 Remove the bulb holder from inside the mirror housing **(see illustration 6.25)**.

11 Remove the cover by depressing the locking tabs inside the mirror housing **(see illustrations)**.

12 Release the securing clip inside the mirror housing and remove the side repeater light from the mirror **(see illustrations)**.

13 Refitting is a reversal of removal.

Approach light

14 The approach light is located in the base of the door mirror, remove the door mirror glass as described in Chapter 11 Section 15.

15 Remove the bulb holder from inside the mirror housing **(see illustration 6.28)**.

16 Release the clip and manoeuvre the lens from the base of the mirror housing **(see illustration)**.

17 Refitting is the reversal of the removal procedure.

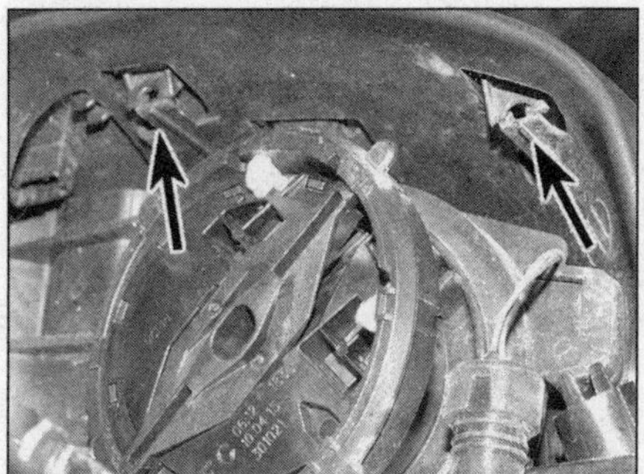
8.11a Release the upper securing clips...

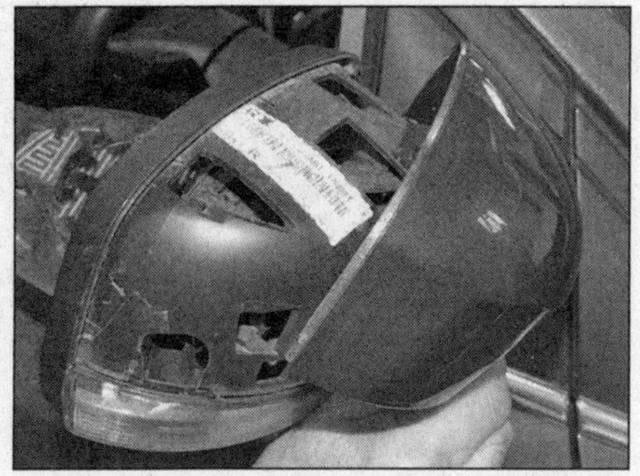
8.11b ...and remove outer cover

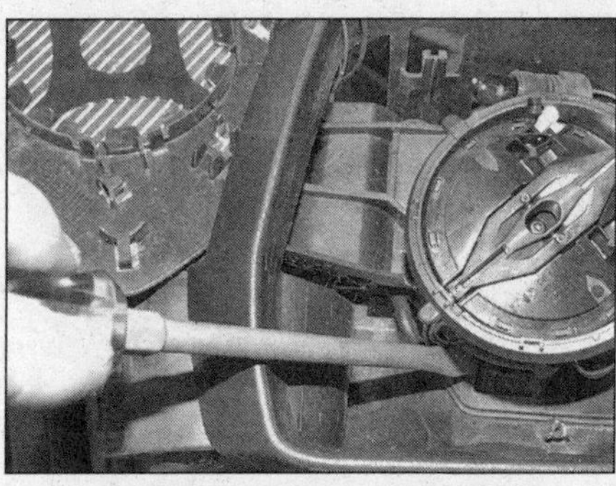
8.12a Release the securing clip...

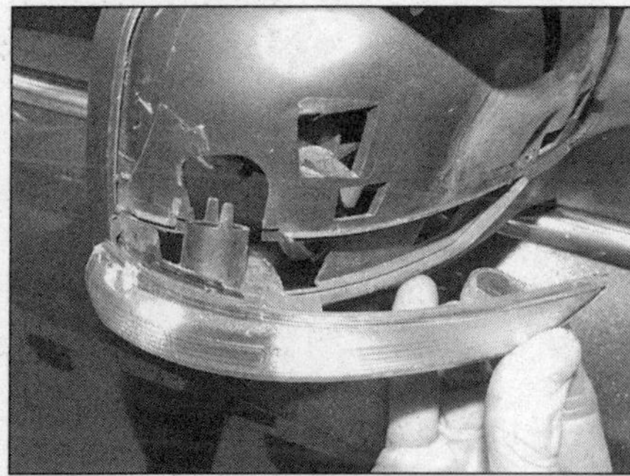
8.12b ...and remove the side repeater light unit

8.16 Remove the approach light unit

Rear combination light

Hatchback and Estate models

18 Open the tailgate and then remove the small cover from inside the load area, behind the rear light unit **(see illustration)**.

8.18 Unclip the trim cover

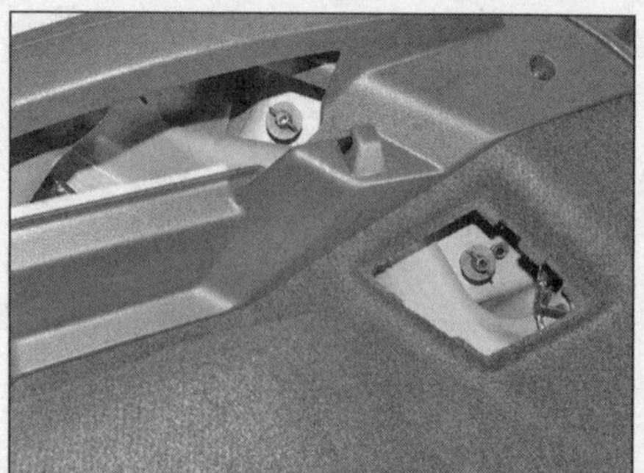

8.19 The light unit thumbwheels (Hatchback model shown)

19 Undo the upper and lower light unit retaining thumbwheels **(see illustration)**. These are difficult to access and often very tight. If required, use a flat screwdriver in the slot to slacken the thumbwheels.

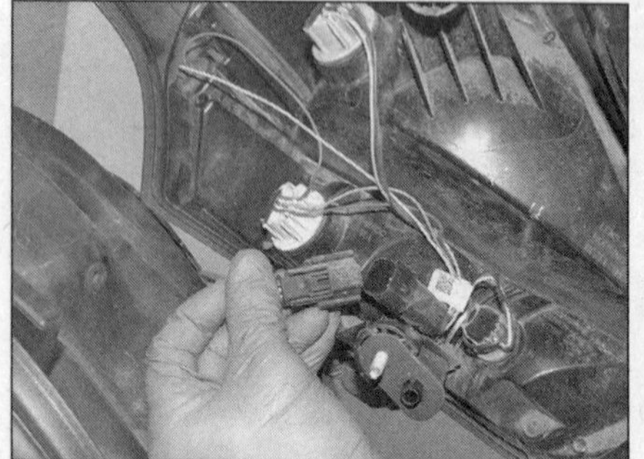

8.20c Disconnect the wiring plug

8.23a Disconnect the wiring plug...

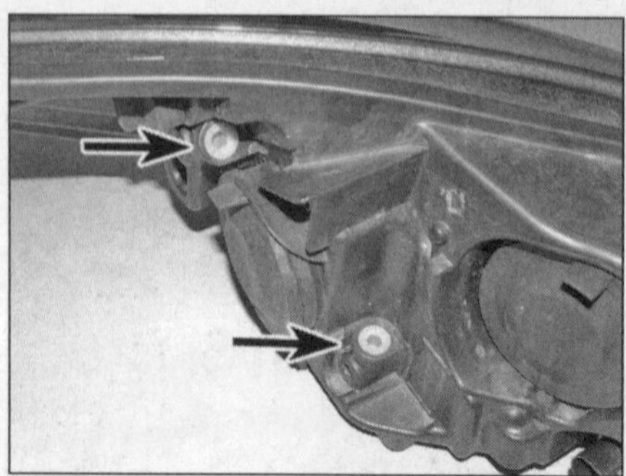

8.29a Headlight beam adjustment screws (arrowed)

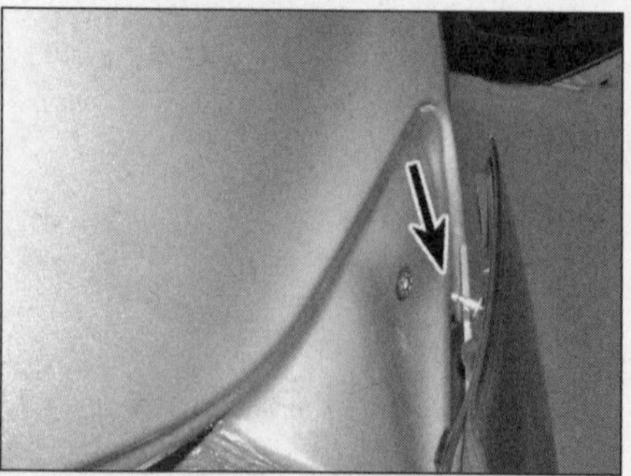

8.20a The locating peg (arrowed) on Hatchback models...

20 Pull the light unit outward at the side (to release the unit from the locating peg) and then rearwards, disconnecting the wiring plug as it is removed **(see illustrations)**.

21 Refitting is a reversal of removal.

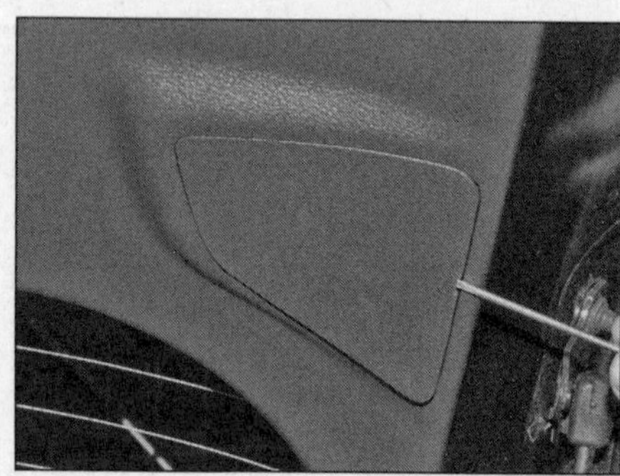

8.22 Use a screwdriver to remove the cover

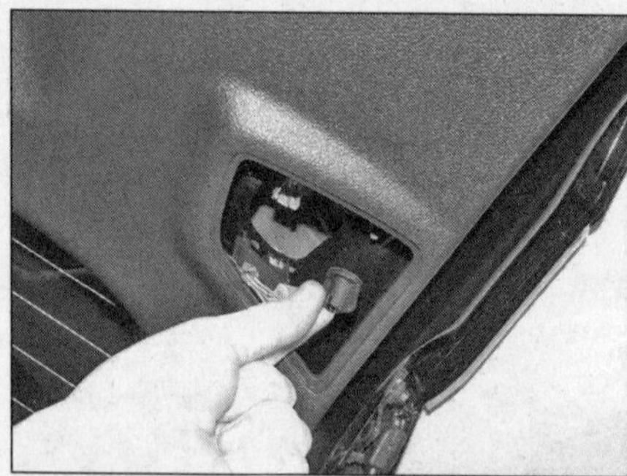

8.23b ...and remove the thumbwheel

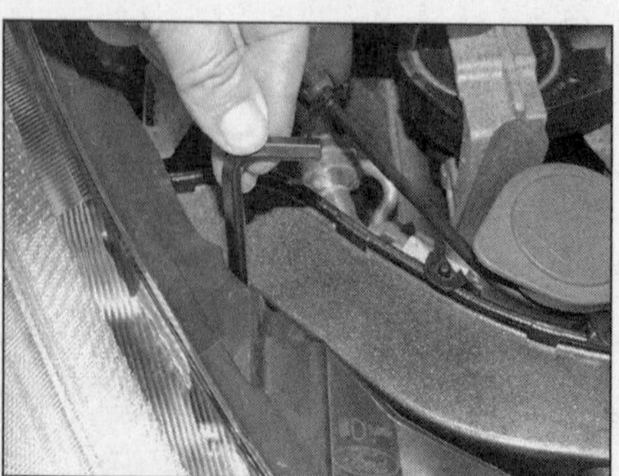

8.29b Using an Allen key...

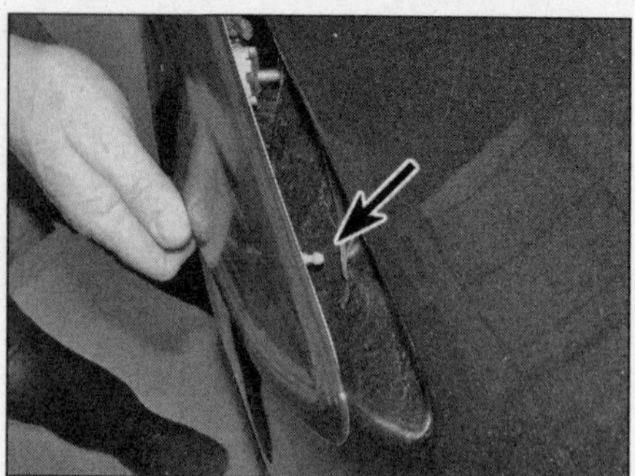

8.20b ...and on Estate models (arrowed)

Tailgate lamp – Estate models

22 Open the tailgate and remove the cover from the tailgate trim panel **(see illustration)**.

23 Disconnect the wiring plug. Release the thumbwheel **(see illustrations)** and remove the lamp.

24 Refitting is a reversal of removal.

Number plate light

25 To replace the lamp remove the tailgate handle as described in Chapter 11, Section 19.

High-level brake light

26 Remove the screws, release the lamp, disconnect the wiring plug and the screen washer jet **(see illustration 6.45)**.

27 Refitting is a reversal of removal.

Beam adjustment

Halogen headlights

28 Accurate adjustment of the headlight beam is only possible using optical beam setting equipment, and this work should therefore be carried out by a Ford dealer or suitably-equipped workshop.

29 For reference, the headlights can be adjusted using the adjuster screws, accessible via the top of each light unit **(see illustrations)**.

30 All models are equipped with an electrically-operated headlight beam adjustment system which is controlled through the switch in the facia. Ensure that the switch is set to the basic O position before adjusting the headlight aim.

8.29c ...to turn the adjustment screws

9 Xenon gas discharge headlight system – removal, refitting and adjustment

General information

1 Xenon gas discharge headlights are fitted to certain higher specification models. The headlights dipped beam bulbs produce light by means of an electric arc, rather than by heating a metal filament as in conventional halogen bulbs. An electronically-operated shutter is fitted in front of the bulb which angles the light for dipped beam, then re-angles the light for main beam. A conventional halogen bulb is also fitted to augment the main beam light output. The arc is generated by a control circuit which operates at voltages of above 28 000 volts. The intensity of the emitted light means that the headlight beam has to be controlled dynamically to avoid dazzling other road users. An electronic control unit monitors the vehicle's pitch and overall ride height by sensors mounted on the front and rear suspension and adjusts the beam range accordingly, using the range control motors built into the headlight units.

2 All bulbs apart from the Xenon dipped beam bulbs are removed in the same manner as the bulbs fitted to the conventional halogen headlights. Note that where Xenon headlights are fitted, LED style bulbs provide the sidelight illumination. If a fault develops with the LED type of sidelight, then the entire headlight will require replacement.

Warning: The discharge bulb starter circuitry operates at extremely high voltages. To avoid the risk of electric shock, ensure that the battery negative cable is disconnected before working on the headlight units (see Chapter 5A Section 3), then additionally switch the dipped beam on and off to discharge any residual voltage.

Headlight dipped beam

Caution: The dipped beam bulb is under gas pressure of at least 10 bar, therefore it is recommended that protective glasses and suitable gloves are worn during this procedure.

9.4a Remove the cover...

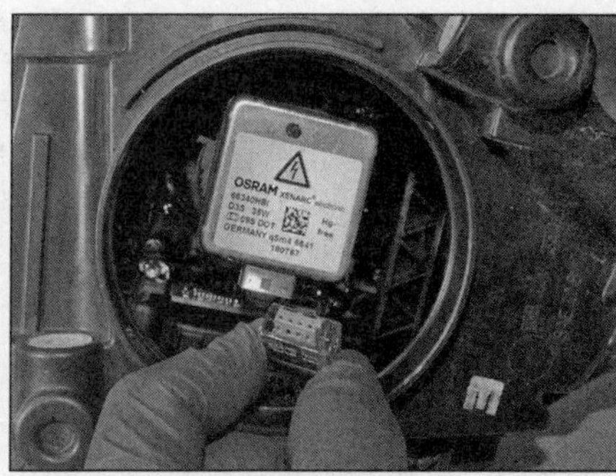

9.4b ...and disconnect the wiring connector

9.5a Remove the bulb assembly...

9.5b ...by turning the outer collar anti-clockwise

3 Remove the headlight as described in Section 8.

4 Remove the rear cover and disconnect the wiring plug **(see illustrations)**.

5 Rotate the outer plastic locking collar anti-clockwise and remove the bulb assembly **(see illustrations)**. Store the bulb in a safe place if it is not to be immediately refitted.

6 Refitting is a reversal of removal.

Front ride height sensor

Removal

7 The sensor is mounted via a link-rod to the lower control arm of the right-hand front wheel **(see illustration)**. Apply the handbrake, then jack up the front of the vehicle and support it on axle stands (see *Jacking and vehicle support*). Remove the right-hand front wheel.

8 Undo the nut securing the link-rod arm to the sensor **(see illustration)**.

9 Drill out the 2 rivets securing the sensor bracket to the vehicle body.

10 Disconnect the wiring plug as the sensor is withdrawn.

Refitting

11 Refitting is a reversal of removal. Note that if a new sensor has been fitted, then a calibration procedure must be carrier out. This requires access to Ford diagnostic equipment – entrust this task to a Ford dealer or suitably-equipped specialist.

Rear ride height sensor

Removal

12 The sensor is secured to the right-hand lower control arm and the rear subframe **(see illustration)**. Chock the front wheels, then jack up the rear of the vehicle and support it on axle stands (see *Jacking and vehicle support*).

9.7 Location of ride height sensor

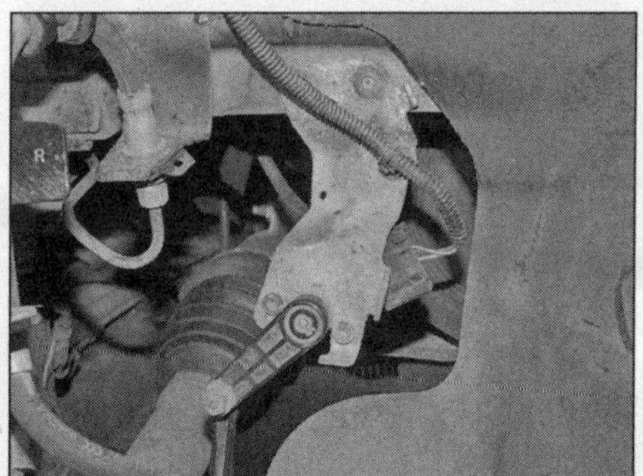

9.8 Undo the link-arm securing nut

9.12 Location of ride height sensor

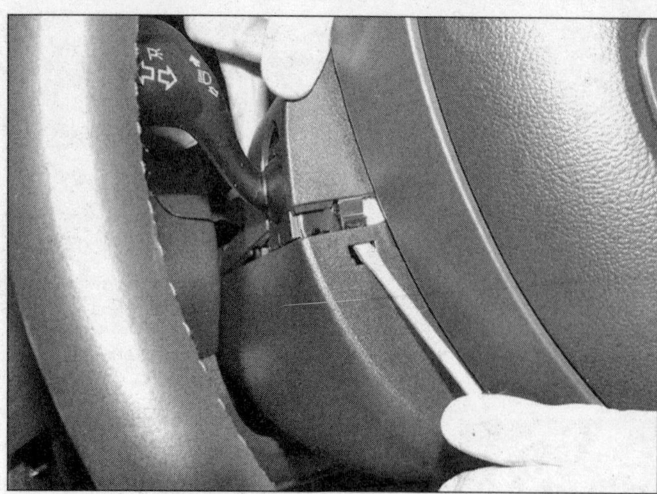

10.3 Release the retaining clips...

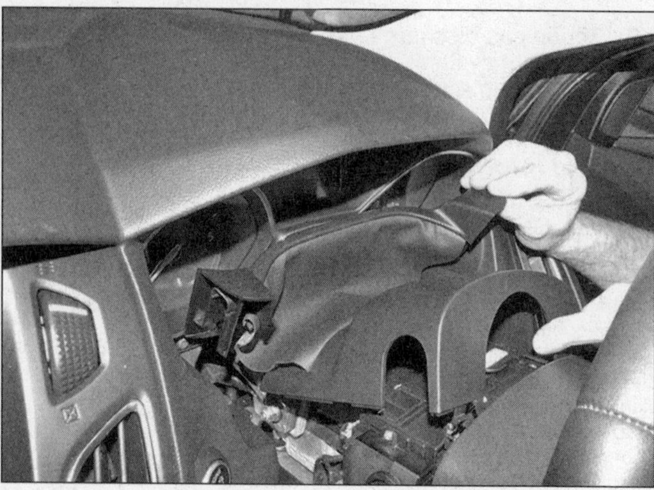

10.4 ...and unclip the upper shroud

13 Disconnect the sensor wiring plug, then undo the bolts and remove the sensor, bracket and lever arm assembly.

Refitting

14 Refitting is a reversal of removal. Note that if a new sensor has been fitted, then a calibration procedure must be carried out. This requires access to Ford diagnostic equipment – entrust this task to a Ford dealer or suitably-equipped specialist.

10.5a Undo the lower mounting screws...

Beam adjustment

15 The basic alignment procedure of the headlights is the same as normal halogen headlights. However, before the procedure is attempted, the ride height sensors must be calibrated using dedicated Ford test equipment. Therefore this task should be entrusted to a Ford dealer or suitably-equipped specialist.

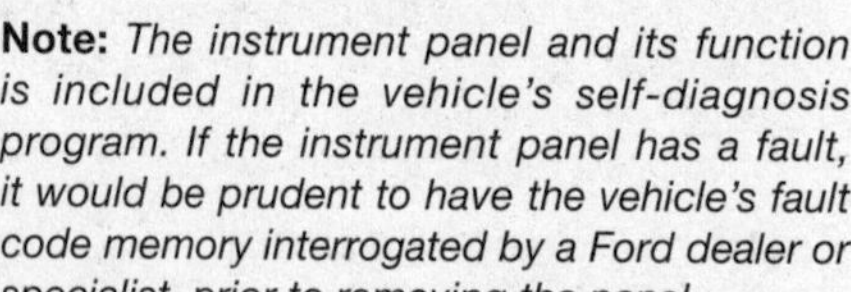

10 Instrument panel – removal and refitting

Note: *The instrument panel and its function is included in the vehicle's self-diagnosis program. If the instrument panel has a fault, it would be prudent to have the vehicle's fault code memory interrogated by a Ford dealer or specialist, prior to removing the panel.*

Note: *If the instrument panel is being substituted with a new or exchange unit, the assistance of a Ford dealer or specialist is required to download necessary software, and initialise/adapt the various instrument panel functions.*

Removal

1 Disconnect the battery negative lead as described in Chapter 5A Section 3.

2 Fully extend the steering column, and move it to its lowest position.

3 Rotate the steering wheel and release the two retaining clips to remove the upper shroud from the lower shroud **(see illustration)**.

4 Remove the upper shroud complete with the trim panel from below the instrument panel **(see illustration)**.

5 Undo the two retaining screws on the lower edge of the instrument panel, then using a trim tool, release the upper mounting clip and carefully pull the top edge of the panel rearwards. Manoeuvre the instrument panel from the facia, and then disconnect the wiring plug connector as it is withdrawn **(see illustrations)**.

Refitting

6 Refitting is a reversal of removal, but see the note at the beginning of this section.

10.5b ...release the upper part of the panel

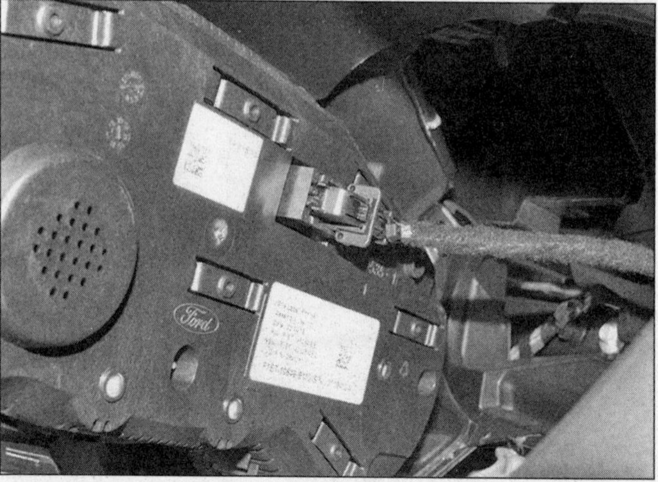

10.5c Disconnect the wiring connector

11.3a Pull off the rubber cap...

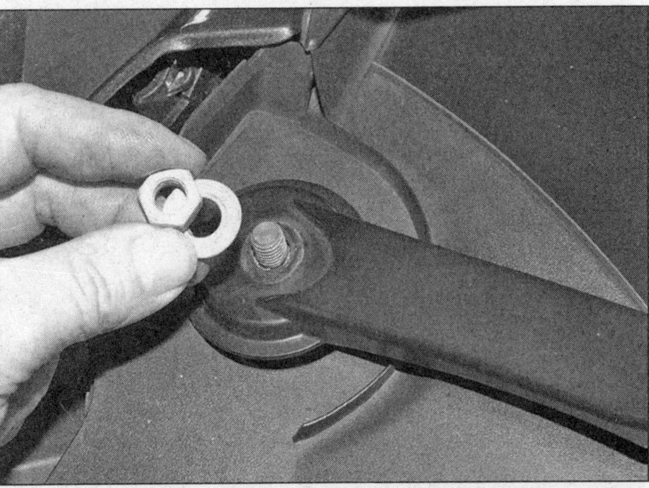
11.3b ...remove the nut and washer...

11.3c ...then remove the wiper arm

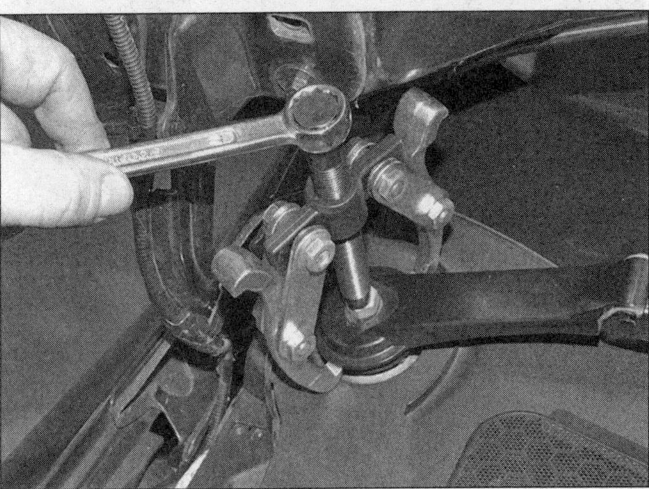
11.3d A small two legged puller can be used to remove the arm if necessary

11 Windscreen wiper components – removal and refitting

Wiper blades

1 Refer to *Weekly checks*.

Wiper arms

Removal

2 If the wipers are not in their parked position, switch on the ignition, and allow the motor to automatically park.

3 Before removing an arm, mark its parked position on the glass with a strip of adhesive tape. Prise off the cover and unscrew the spindle nut **(see illustrations)**. Ease the arm from the spindle by rocking it slowly from side-to-side. Note that the drivers arm must be fitted above the passenger side arm.

Refitting

4 Refitting is a reversal of removal, but before tightening the spindle nuts, position the wiper blades as marked before removal.

Wiper motors

Note: *If the wiper motors are replaced they must be initialised using a suitable diagnostic tool. Entrust this task to a Ford dealer or suitably equipped specialist.*

Note: *Whilst the motors are physically identical, they are programmed differently. This means it is not possible to swap the motors over from side to side.*

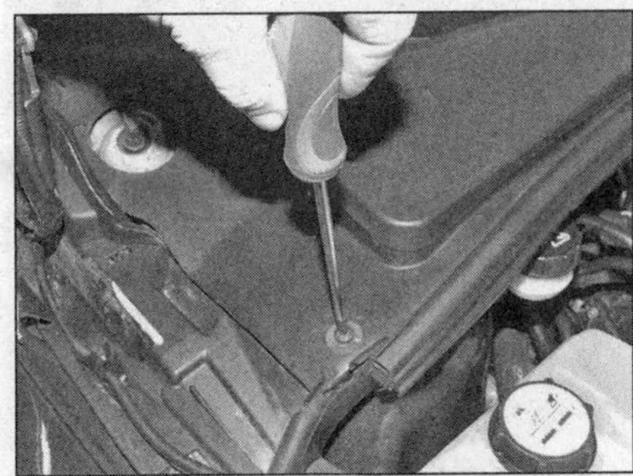
11.7 Undo the retaining screws

Removal

5 Remove the wiper arms as described in the previous above.

6 Disconnect the battery as described in Chapter 5A Section 3).

7 Open the bonnet, and then undo the two retaining screws (one a each side), from the scuttle cowling panel **(see illustration)**.

8 Unclip the two grille panels from the top of the scuttle cowling panel **(see illustration)**.

11.8 Unclip the grille panels

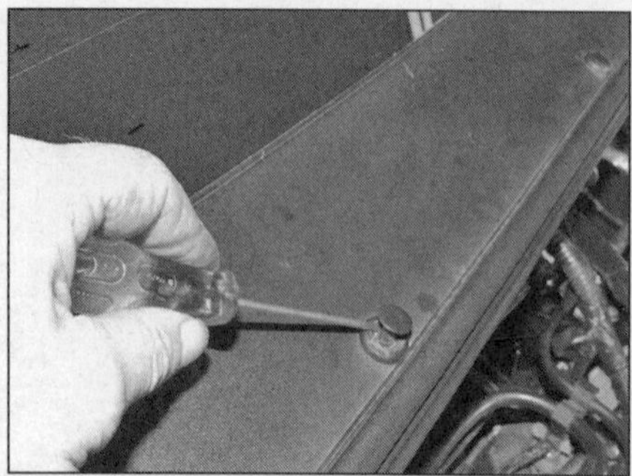

11.9a Lift up the centre pin...

11.9b ...and remove the plastic rivets

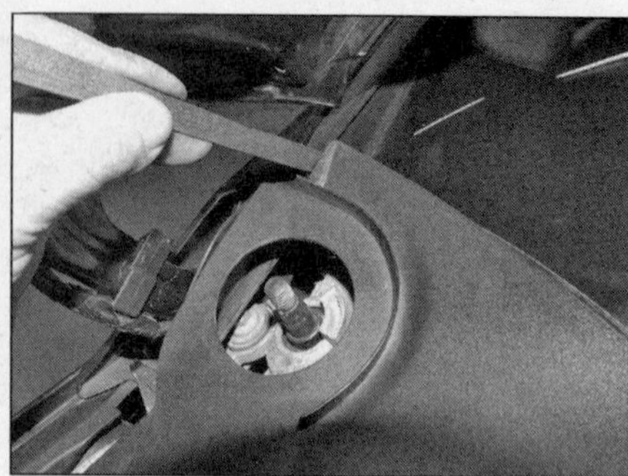

11.9c Using a hooked tool...

11.9d ...unclip the panel from the windscreen...

11.9e ...and remove the scuttle panel

11.10a Release the securing clip...

11.10b ...and remove the end trim panel

9 Remove the clips at the front edge of the scuttle cowling panel, then using a hooked tool starting at the outer edges, pull the panel upwards to release it from the base of the windscreen **(see illustrations)**. The panel is a tight fit at the base of the windscreen and is best released by working it free at one end first.

10 At the appropriate side, release the securing clip and remove the plastic end trim panel **(see illustrations)**.

11 Where fitted unclip the wiring plug for the heated windscreen from the wiper motor support bracket **(see illustration)**.

12 Unbolt the wiper motor support bracket (two bolts). Pull the motor and bracket free, disconnecting the wiring plug as the motor is withdrawn. **(see illustrations)**.

13 Recover the mounting grommet from the locating peg on the rear of the wiper motor, if necessary.

14 Undo the three screws securing the motor to the bracket and remove the motor from the bracket, as required.

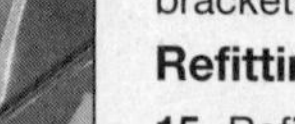

Refitting

15 Refitting is a reversal of removal, making sure the locating peg/mounting on the rear of the motor is positioned in the bulkhead correctly and the wiring connector is secure. Note however that if replacement motor (or motors) have been fitted that the wipers must be initialised using suitable diagnostic equipment.

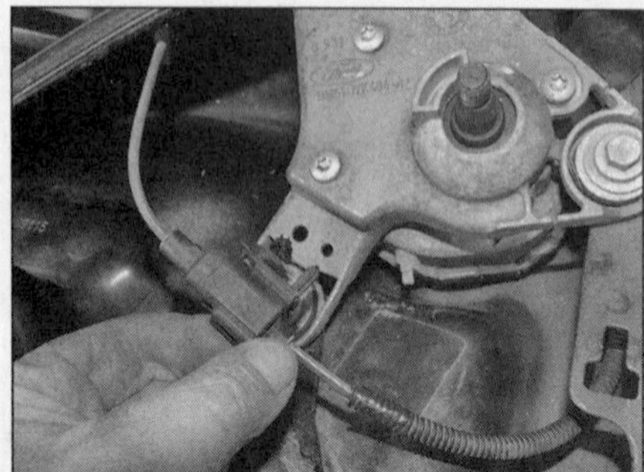

11.11 Unclip the wiring clip

11.12a Undo the mounting bolts...

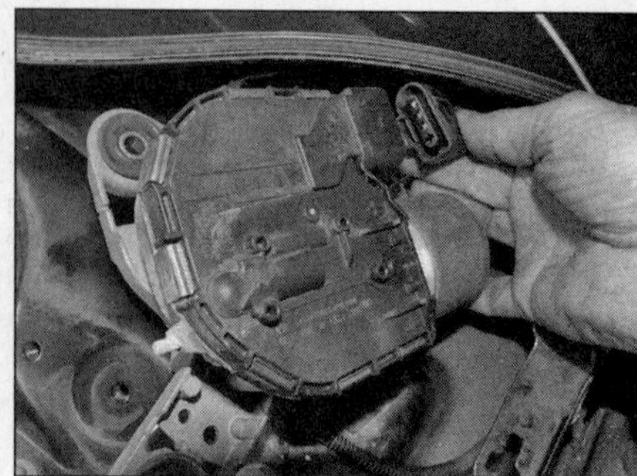

11.12b ...and disconnect the wiring connector on removal

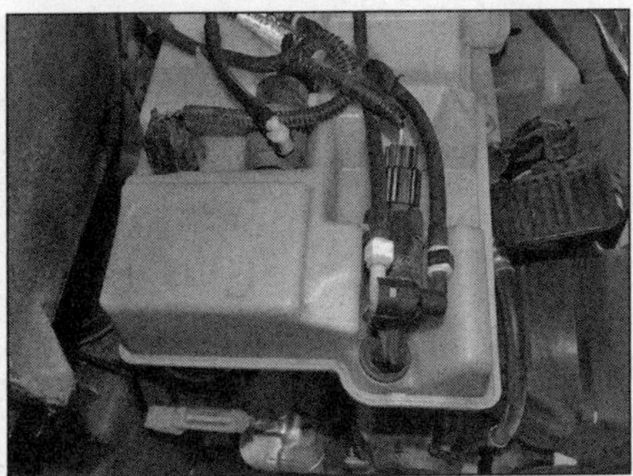

12.2 The screen washer pumps

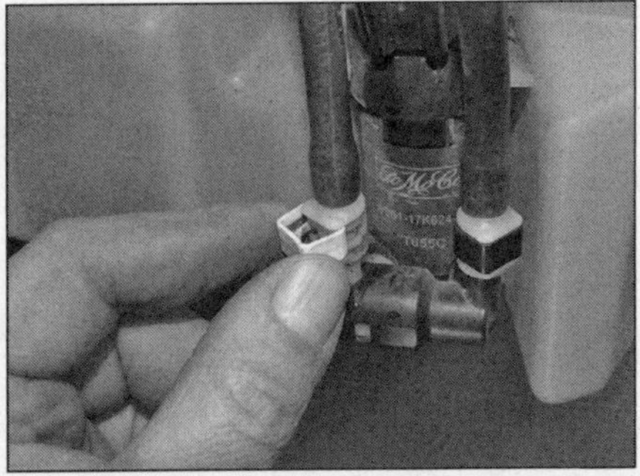

12.5a Release the locking clips...

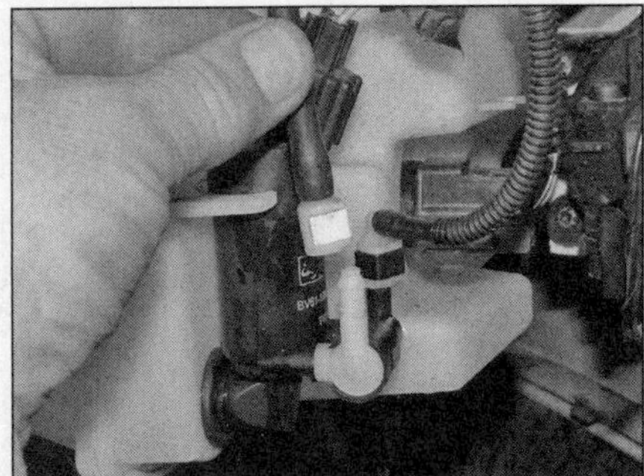

12.5b ...and release the hoses

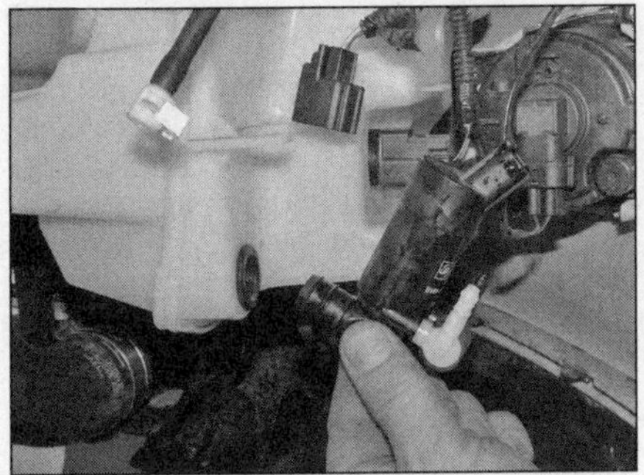

12.6 Pull the pump from the grommet in the reservoir

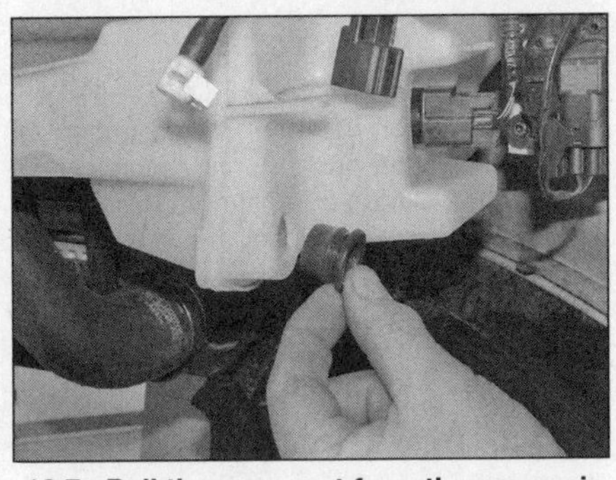

12.7a Pull the grommet from the reservoir

12.7b The grommet incorporates a coarse filter

12 Washer system – removal and refitting

1 All models covered by this manual are fitted with both a windscreen washer system and a tailgate washer. Some models are also fitted with headlight washers.

2 The fluid reservoir for the windscreen/headlight washer is located behind the right-hand end of the bumper cover. The windscreen washer fluid pump(s) are attached to the side of the reservoir body **(see illustration)**. The tailgate washer is fed by the same reservoir, with a dual output pump. Models fitted with a headlight washer system have an additional pump fitted to the reservoir. Access to the reservoir and pump(s) is made from below.

3 The reservoir fluid level must be regularly topped-up with windscreen washer fluid containing an antifreeze agent, but not cooling system antifreeze – see *Weekly checks*.

Washer pump

4 To remove the pump, jack up and support the front of the vehicle (see *Jacking and vehicle support* in the reference section). Remove the right-hand road wheel and the wing liner.

5 The supply hoses are attached by quick release connectors. Have a suitable container ready beneath the washer reservoir, release the locking clip and pull off the appropriate hose connector **(see illustrations)**.

6 Work the pump free from the retaining grommet **(see illustration)**.

7 Remove the grommet and check that the filter is clear **(see illustrations)**.

Reservoir

8 To remove the reservoir, remove the front bumper cover and then remove the reservoir filler neck. Disconnect the wiring plugs from the pump(s) and where fitted the fluid level sensor. Release the washer hoses and then remove the two mounting bolts **(see illustrations)**. Unhook the reservoir form the upper mounting and remove it from the vehicle.

12.8a Remove the filler neck...

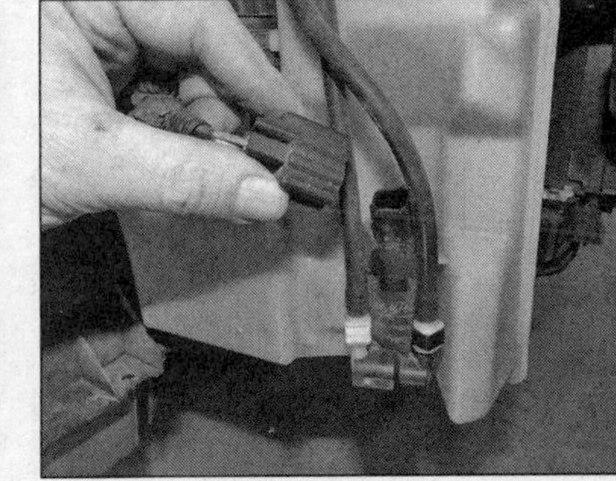

12.8b ...disconnect the pump wiring connector(s)...

12.8c ...and level sensor wiring

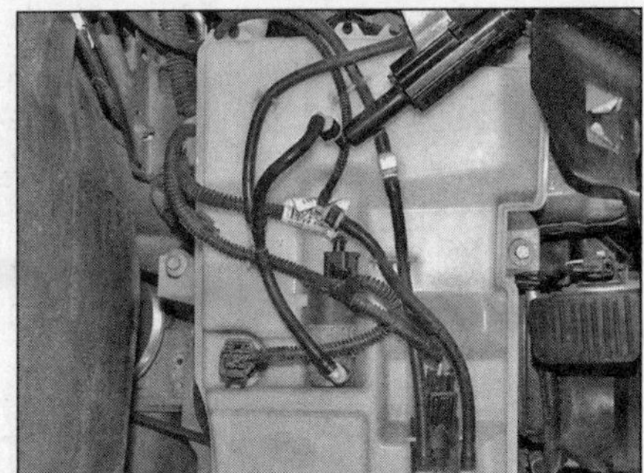

12.8d Reservoir mounting bolts

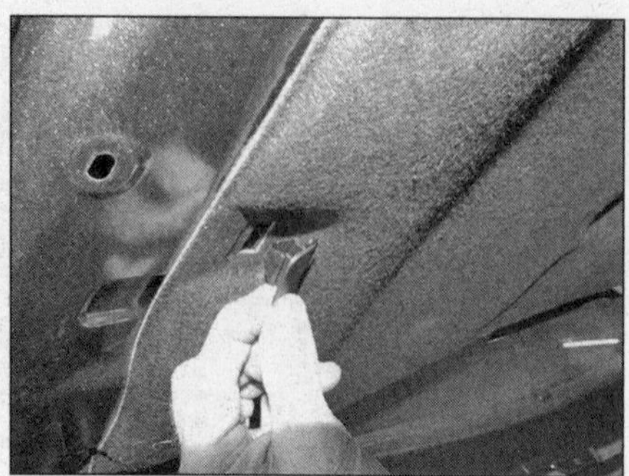
12.9a Unclip the insulation panel...

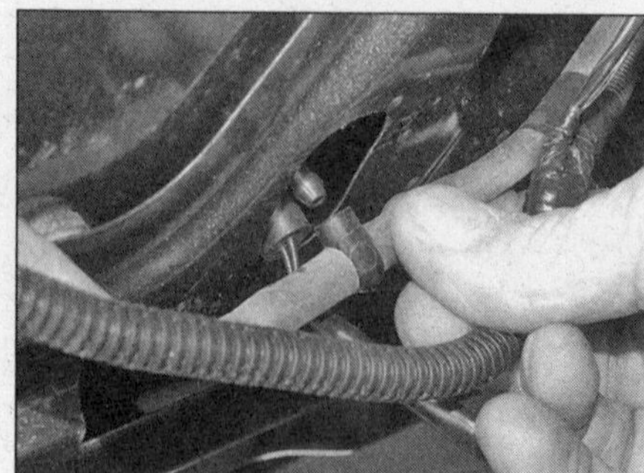
12.9b ...disconnect the washer hose...

12.9c ...and wiring connector

Windscreen washer jets

9 The windscreen washer jets can be adjusted by inserting a pin into the jet and altering the aim as required. To remove a washer jet, open the bonnet and unclip the bonnet insulation panel, then disconnect the hose from the washer jet, and on models with heated washer jets, disconnect the wiring connector **(see illustrations)**.

10 Push the jet forwards, and lift the rear edge, to manoeuvre the jet out from the bonnet **(see illustration)**.

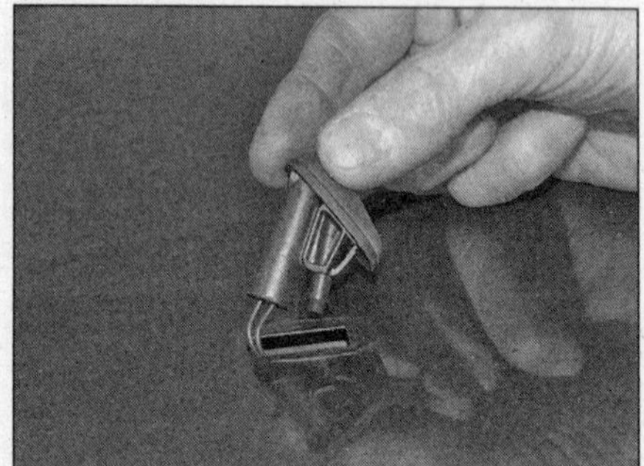
12.10 Press the jet forwards and lift the rear edge

Headlight washer jets

11 Pull the washer cover forward, away from the bumper cover and unclip it from the washer jet assembly **(see illustrations)**. **Note:** *a new cover will be required, as the small plastic clip on the cover will break on removal or use a cable tie to secure it back to the jet assembly.*

12 Remove the fasteners at the front edge of the inner wheel arch liner, and then pull back the liner to access the washer jet assembly **(see illustration)**.

13 Release the locking clip and disconnect the washer hose from the rear of the washer jet assembly, then depress the locating tabs and remove the jet assembly from the front panel **(see illustration)**. If required, remove the front bumper cover, as described in Chapter 11 Section 6, to give better access.

Rear screen washer jet

14 The rear screen washer jet is located in the high level brake light. If a fault develops with the washer jet, remove the high level brake light, as described in Section 8 of this Chapter, then unclip the jet from the light unit **(see illustration)**.

12.11a Pull out the washer jet...

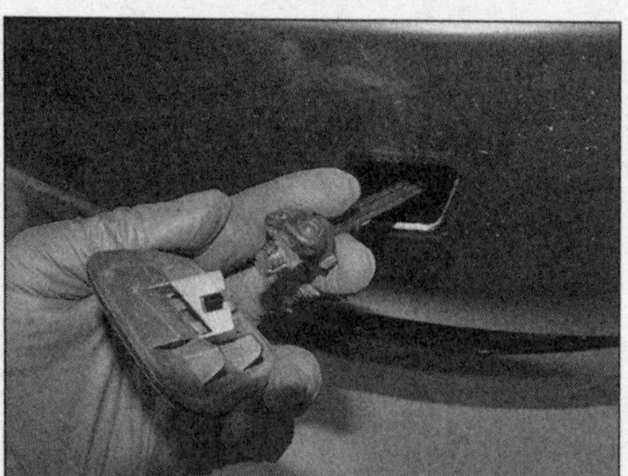
12.11b ...and unclip the trim cover

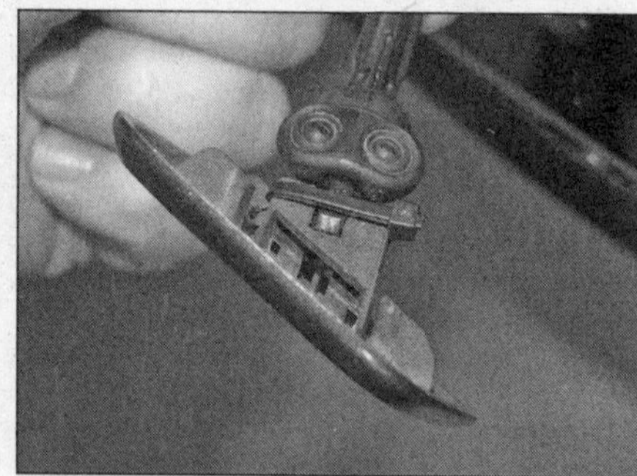
12.11c Using a cable tie to secure cover

12.12 Pull back the wheel arch liner

12.13 Unclip the washer jet assembly

12.14 Unclip the jet from the light unit

13.2a Remove the cover...

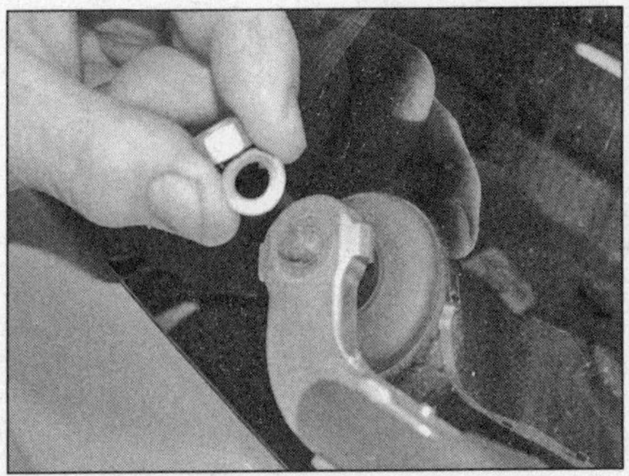
13.2b..nut and washer

13.3a Rock the wiper arm free or...

13.3b..use a suitable puller

13.6a Remove the bolts (arrowed)...

13.6b ...and remove the wiper motor

13 Tailgate wiper motor – removal and refitting

Removal

1 Make sure the tailgate wiper is switched off and in its rest position. Mark the position of the wiper blade on the tailgate window glass using masking tape.

2 Remove the wiper arm cover, nut and washer **(see illustrations)**.

3 Gently rock the wiper arm free from the spindle. If necessary use a puller to free the arm from the spindle **(see illustrations)**.

4 Open the tailgate and remove the trim panel as described in Chapter 11.

5 Detach the wiring connector from the wiper motor.

6 Undo the three wiper motor mounting bolts and remove the wiper motor from the tailgate **(see illustrations)**. Check the condition of the spindle rubber grommet in the tailgate, and if necessary, renew it.

Refitting

7 Refit in the reverse order of removal. Refit the wiper arm and blade so that the arm is parked correctly.

14 Horns – removal and refitting

Removal

1 There are two horns fitted, and are located behind the front bumper cover on the right and left-hand side **(see illustrations)**. Raise the front of the vehicle and support it securely on axle stands (see *Jacking and vehicle support*).

14.1a Horn located on the left-hand side...

14.1b ...and the right-hand side

2 Access is possible if the front of the inner wheel arch liner is pulled back to access the rear of the bumper at each end **(see illustration 12.12)**. Alternatively remove the front bumper cover as described in Chapter 11 Section 6.

3 Disconnect the horn wiring plug, undo the mounting bolt and remove the horn from the vehicle.

Refitting

4 Refit in the reverse order of removal. Check operation of horn, before refitting the wheel arch liner/bumper.

15 Sunroof motor – removal and refitting

1 Removal of the sunroof motor requires the headlining to be removed. This is an involved task, requiring patience and dexterity. Consequently, we recommend you entrust this task to a Ford dealer or upholstery specialist.

16 Central locking system – general information

1 All models are equipped with a central door locking system, which automatically locks all doors and the rear tailgate/boot lid in unison with the manual locking of the driver's front door. The system is operated electronically with motors/switches incorporated into the

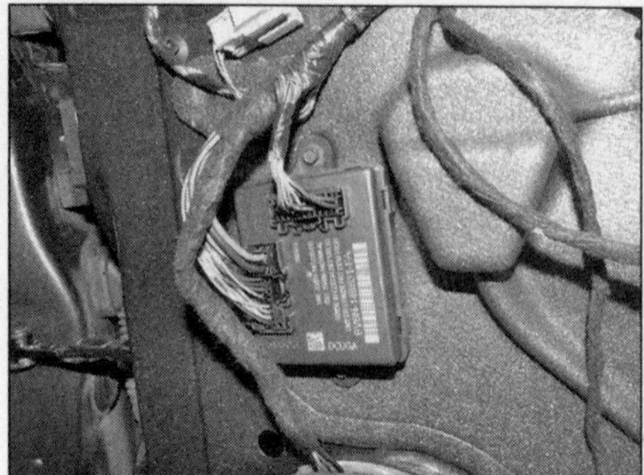

16.2a Drivers door control module...

16.2b ...rear door control module

door lock assemblies. The system is controlled by the BCM (Body Control Module – formerly referred to by Ford as the Generic Electronic Module – GEM) and the Keyless Vehicle Module (KVM) – where fitted. The BCM and the KVM communicate with the vehicle's other control modules via an information network known as a Databus. Control modules integral with electric window motors receive signals from the BCM via the databus, and directly control the operation of the door locks. The tailgate/boot lid has its own control module, integral with the lock assembly. If any module is renewed, new software for the unit must be downloaded from Ford. Entrust this task to a Ford dealer or suitably-equipped specialist.

2 There are door control modules fitted to the inside of each door, behind the door trim panel **(see illustrations)**. These can be accessed by removing the door trim panels, as described in Chapter 11 Section 10.

3 The control unit is equipped with a self-diagnosis capability. Should the system develop a fault, have the control unit interrogated by a Ford dealer or suitably-equipped specialist. Once the fault has been established, refer to the relevant Section of Chapter to renew a door module or tailgate/boot lid lock as applicable.

17 Parking aid components – general, removal and refitting

General information

1 The parking aid system is fitted as standard on higher specification models. It is also an optional extra on most models within the range. Top of the range models also have a parking assist system fitted. Ford call this system 'Active park assist'. The system uses ultra sound sensors, a control module and the ability of the electric power steering system to turn the vehicles wheels with no driver assistance. Under the right conditions the system will identify a suitable parking space and reverse the car into the space with no driver control of the steering wheel

2 Four ultrasound sensors located in the bumpers measure the distance to the closest object behind or in front the car, and inform the driver using acoustic signals from the audio system speakers. The information display will also show a moving graphic or text message. The nearer the object, the more frequent the acoustic signals. The system includes a control module and self-diagnosis program, and therefore, in the event of a fault, the vehicle should be taken to a Ford dealer or suitably-equipped specialist who will be able to interrogate the system.

3 On models with rear facing camera, the camera is built into the release switch assembly in the tailgate, above the number plate. To remove the camera, see Chapter 11 Section 19.

Parking Aid Module (PAM)

Removal

4 The control unit is located behind the right-hand luggage compartment side trim panel. Remove the luggage compartment side panel trim as described in Chapter 11, and remove the foam padding behind the panel.

5 Undo the 2 retaining bolts, and remove the PAM **(see illustrations)**. As the unit is removed, disconnect the wiring plugs.

Refitting

6 Refitting is a reversal of removal.

Range/distance sensor

Removal

7 Remove the relevant bumper as described in Chapter 11 Section 6.

8 Disconnect the sensor wiring plug, then push the retaining clips apart, and pull the sensor from position **(see illustrations)**.

Refitting

9 Refitting is a reversal of removal. Press the sensor firmly into position until the retaining clips engage.

18 Audio system – removal and refitting

Note: *This Section applies only to standard-fit audio equipment.*

Note: *If a new audio unit is to be fitted, it must be configured using Ford diagnostic equipment (IDS). Entrust this task to a Ford dealer or suitably equipped specialist.*

17.5a The parking aid module on hatchback models...

17.5b ...and on estate models

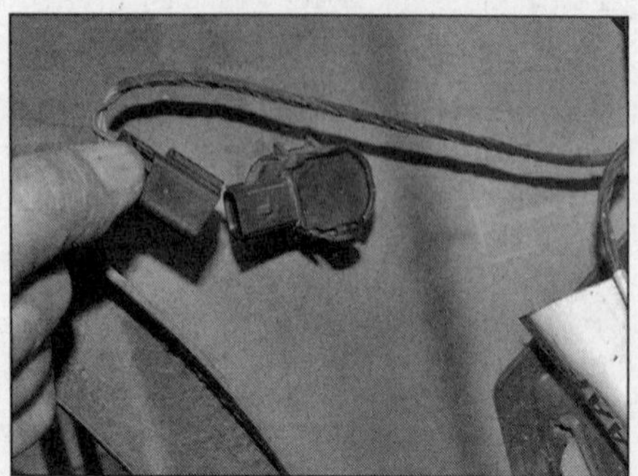

17.8a Disconnect the wiring connector...

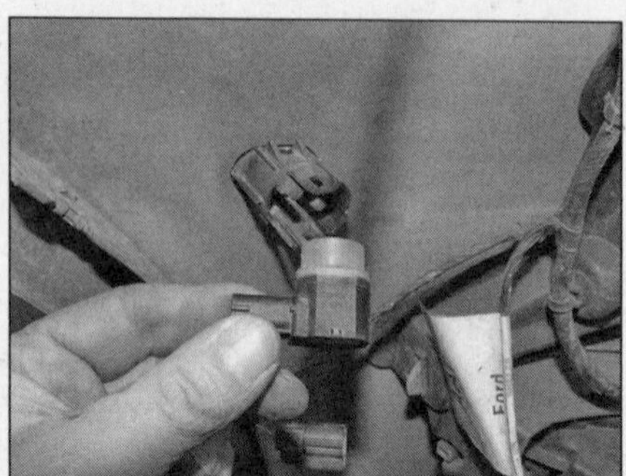

17.8b ...and unclip the parking sensor

18.4a Remove the two screws...

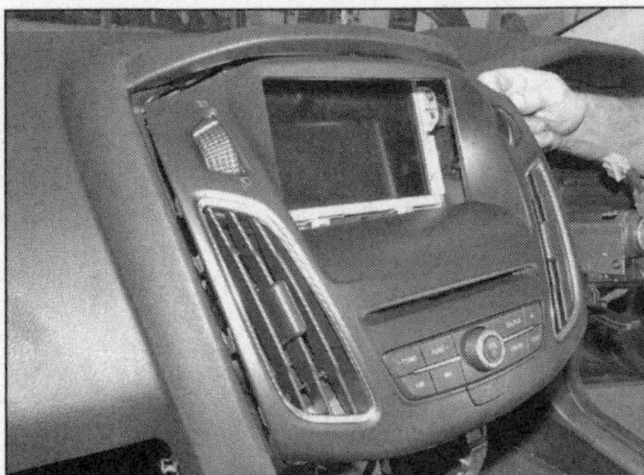
18.4b ...release the control panel...

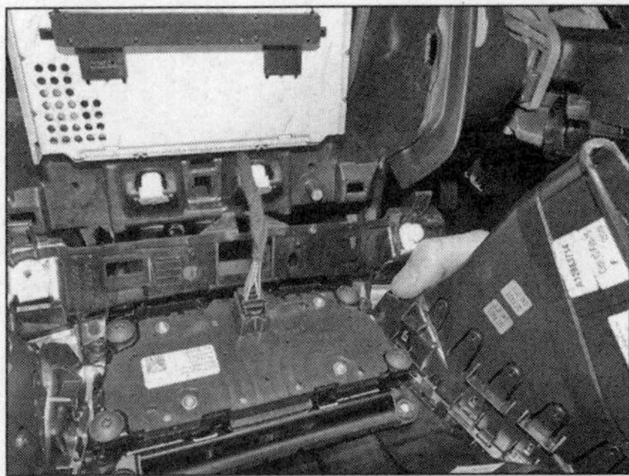
18.4c ...and disconnect the wiring plug

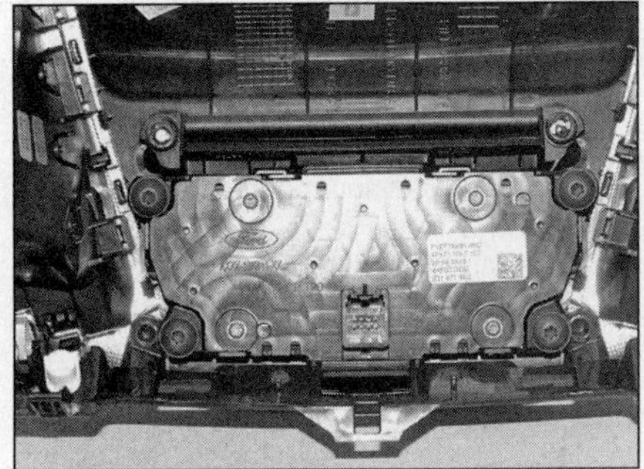
18.5 Undo the four mounting screws

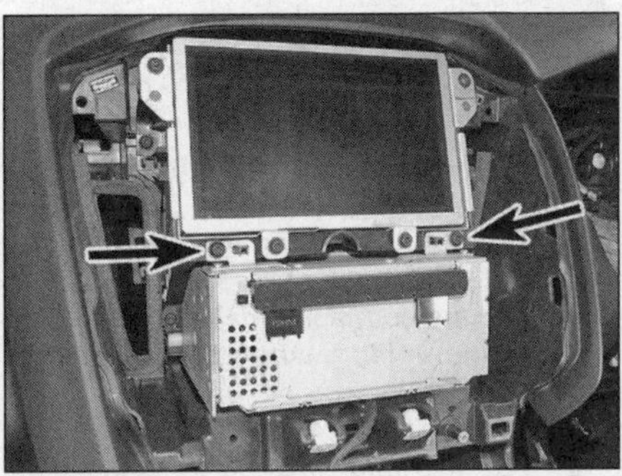
18.7a Remove the two upper screws...

18.7b ...and disconnect the wiring plugs

1 All Audio units fitted the Ford focus feature a front control panel, an information display unit and the main audio unit. All models have a minimum of 6 speakers. Higher specification models also have additional rear 'tweeters' and on some models a spare wheel well mounted 'Subwoofer' speaker.

Removal

2 Disconnect the battery negative lead as described in Chapter 5A Section 3.

3 Remove the heater control trim panel from the front of the centre console, as described in Chapter 3 Section 10.

Front control panel

4 Remove the two retaining screws and gently work the control panel free from the facia, disconnecting the wiring connector from the Audio control panel **(see illustrations)**.

5 Place the panel on a soft surface and remove the 4 mounting screws to release the control panel from the surround **(see illustration)**.

Audio unit

6 Remove the control panel as described above.

7 Remove the two upper mounting screws, then pull the unit forward to release it from the lower locating clips. As the unit is withdrawn, remove the wiring plugs **(see illustrations)**.

Information display unit

8 Remove the control panel and Audio unit, as described above.

9 Remove the four screws from the plastic mounting bracket, then pull the display unit complete with mounting bracket out from the facia, disconnecting the wiring plugs, as it is removed **(see illustrations)**.

10 If required the display can now be removed from the mounting bracket by removing the four retaining screws **(see illustration)**.

Refitting

11 Refitting is a reversal of removal, but if a new unit has been fitted, suitable software must be downloaded from Ford. Entrust this task to a Ford dealer or suitably-equipped specialist.

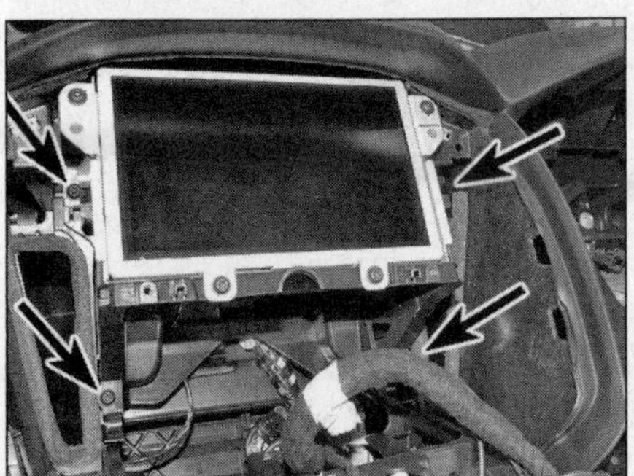
18.9a Remove the four mounting screws...

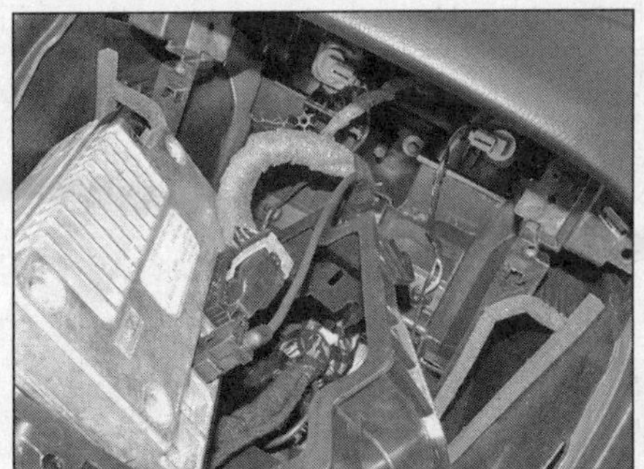
18.9b ...and disconnect the wiring connectors

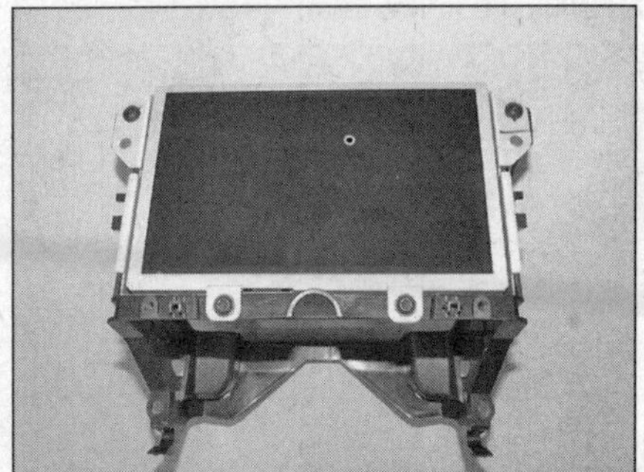
18.10 Undo the four retaining screws

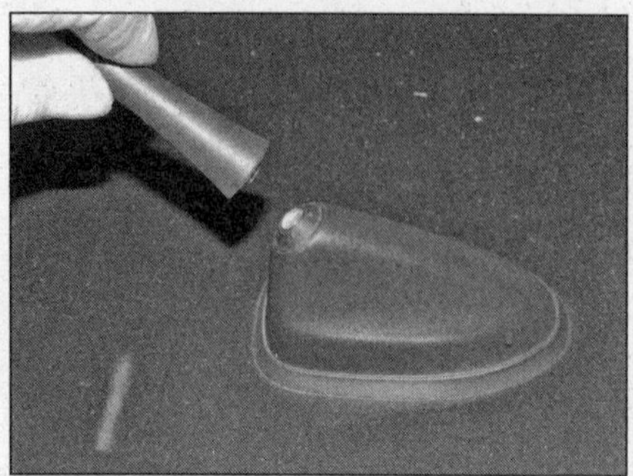
19.2 Unscrew the aerial mast from the base

20.2a Disconnect the wiring connector...

20.2b ...then undo the screws and remove the speaker

19 Aerial – removal and refitting

1 Removal and refitting of the aerial requires the headlining to be removed. This is an involved task, requiring patience and dexterity. Consequently, we recommend you entrust this task to a Ford dealer or upholstery specialist.

2 If required, the aerial mast can be unscrewed from the base **(see illustration)**.

20 Speakers – removal and refitting

Door speakers

1 To remove a door-mounted speaker, remove the appropriate door trim as described in Chapter 11 Section 10.

2 Disconnect the wiring connector, the remove the three screws (or on some models drill out the rivets) securing the speaker to the door **(see illustrations)**.

3 Refit in the reverse order of removal.

Front tweeter speakers

4 Unclip the speaker grille trim panel from the top of the door trim panel **(see illustration)**.

5 Disconnect the wiring plug **(see illustration)**.

6 Release the retaining clips and remove the speaker from the trim panel.

7 Refitting is a reversal of removal.

20.4 Remove the trim panel

21 Airbag system – general information and precautions

⚠ ***Warning: Before carrying out any operations on the airbag system, disconnect the battery negative terminal (see Chapter 5A). When operations are complete, make sure no one is inside the vehicle when the battery is reconnected.***

- ***Note that the airbag(s) must not be subjected to temperatures in excess of 90°C. When the airbag is removed, ensure that it is stored the correct way up (pad upwards) to prevent possible inflation.***
- ***Do not allow any solvents or cleaning agents to contact the airbag assemblies. They must be cleaned using only a damp cloth.***
- ***The airbags and control unit are both sensitive to impact. If either is dropped or damaged they should be renewed.***
- ***Disconnect the airbag control unit wiring plug prior to using arc-welding equipment on the vehicle.***

1 A driver's and passenger's airbag, side airbags (seat mounted) and overhead curtain airbags are fitted as standard equipment to all models in the Ford Focus range. The driver's airbag is fitted to the centre of the steering wheel. The passenger's airbag is fitted to the upper surface of the facia, above the glovebox. The airbag system comprises the airbag unit(s) (complete with gas generators), impact sensors, the control unit and a warning light in the instrument panel.

20.5 Disconnect the wiring plug

2 The airbag system is triggered in the event of a direct or offset frontal impact above a predetermined force. The airbag is inflated within milliseconds, and forms a safety cushion between the driver and the steering wheel or (where applicable) the passenger and the facia. This prevents contact between the upper body and the steering wheel, column and facia, and therefore greatly reduces the risk of injury. The airbag then deflates almost immediately through vents in the side of the airbag. The side airbags and overhead curtain airbags are triggered by side impacts, registered by the sensors fitted to the base of the B-pillars on each side.

3 Every time the ignition is switched on, the airbag control unit performs a self-test. The self-test takes approximately 7 seconds, and during this time the airbag warning light on the facia is illuminated. After the self-test has been completed, the warning light should go out. If the warning light fails to come on, remains illuminated after the initial 7 second period, or comes on at any time when the vehicle is being driven, there is a fault in the airbag system. The vehicle should then be taken to a Ford dealer or specialist for examination at the earliest possible opportunity.

22 Airbag system components – removal and refitting

Note: *Refer to the warnings in Section 21 before carrying out the following operations.*

1 Disconnect the battery negative terminal (see Chapter 5A Section 3). Wait at least 5 minutes for any residual electrical energy to dissipate before commencing work. **Note:** *If removing the driver's airbag, turn the steering wheel 90° from straight-ahead before disconnecting the battery, otherwise the steering lock will engage.*

Driver's airbag

2 Set the steering wheel and front wheels in the 'straight-ahead' position.

3 Rotate the steering wheel 90° in each direction to access the steering column upper shroud retaining clips. Release the clips and remove the shroud **(see illustration 10.3 and 10.4)**.

22.4a Insert a flat-bladed screwdriver and push the handle down...

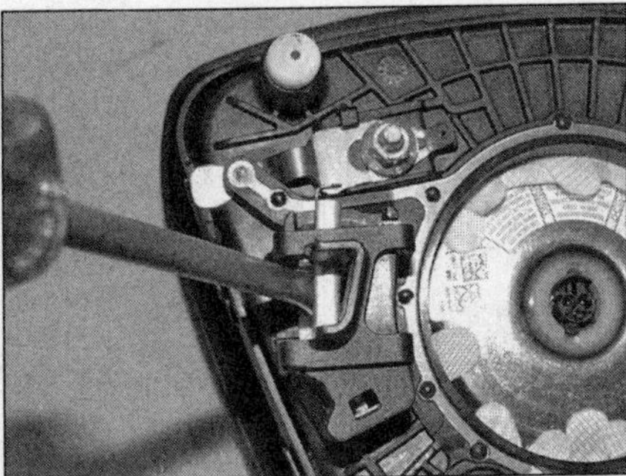
22.4b ...to release the airbag retaining clips...

22.4c ...on both sides of the airbag

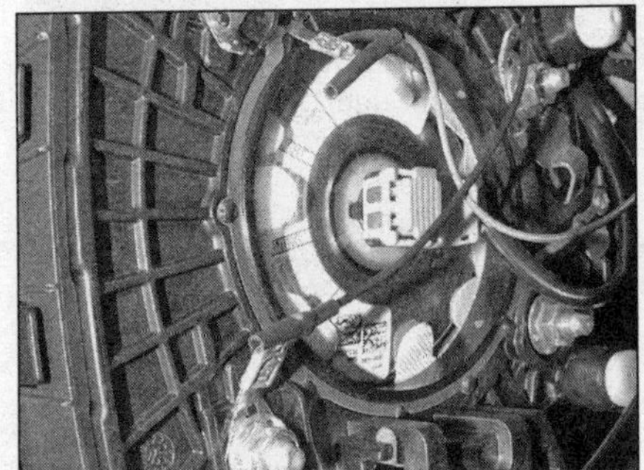
22.5a Disconnect the two outer single wiring connectors...

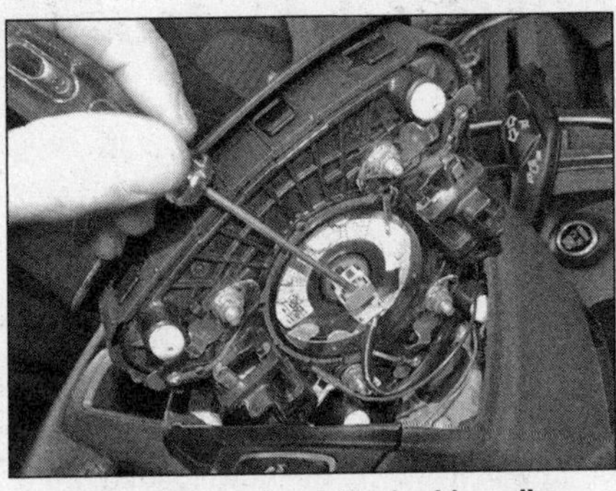
22.5b ...then release the locking clip...

22.5c ...and disconnect the airbag wiring plug

4 Locate the access hole in the reverse side of the steering wheel, and insert a flat-bladed screwdriver into the hole, then push the handle downwards to release the retaining clip **(see illustrations)**. Turn the steering wheel 180° and release the clip on the other side.

5 Temporarily touch the striker plate of the front door to discharge any electrostatic electricity. Return the steering wheel to the straight-ahead position, then carefully lift the airbag assembly away from the steering wheel and disconnect the wiring connectors from the rear of the unit **(see illustrations)**. Note that the airbag must not be knocked or dropped, and should be stored the correct way up with its padded surface uppermost, in a safe place.

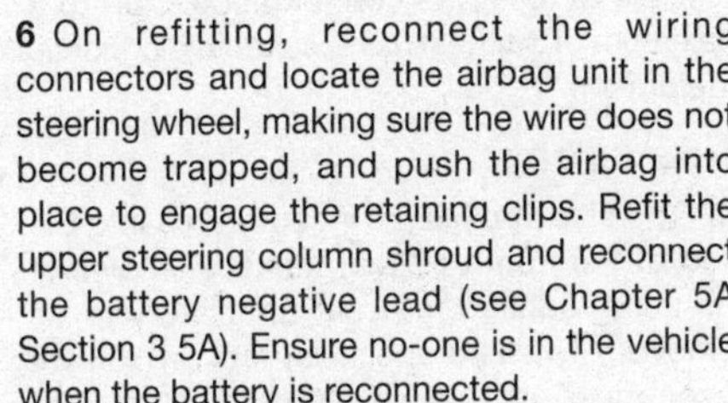

6 On refitting, reconnect the wiring connectors and locate the airbag unit in the steering wheel, making sure the wire does not become trapped, and push the airbag into place to engage the retaining clips. Refit the upper steering column shroud and reconnect the battery negative lead (see Chapter 5A Section 3 5A). Ensure no-one is in the vehicle when the battery is reconnected.

Passenger airbag

7 Remove the passenger side glovebox, as described in Chapter 11 Section 29.

8 Disconnect the airbag wiring plug **(see illustration)**.

9 Remove the two bolts from the support bracket, then remove the six nuts that hold the airbag up under the facia panel **(see illustration)**.

10 Refitting is a reversal of removal. Ensure that no one is inside the vehicle and then reconnect the battery negative lead.

Airbag wiring contact unit (clockspring)

11 Remove the airbag and then the steering wheel as described in Chapter 10 Section 13.

12 With reference to Chapter 11 remove the upper and lower steering column shrouds.

13 Ensure that the coloured mark is visible through the window in the clockspring **(see illustration)**.

14 Disconnect the wiring plug from the

22.8 Disconnect the wiring plug

22.9 Undo the six airbag mounting nuts

22.13 Ensure the yellow mark is visible in the window (arrowed)

22.16 Remove the clockspring

22.19 Unclip the air duct

contact unit and the steering angle sensor (where fitted).

15 If the contact unit is to be refitted, apply tape to lock the unit in position. Do not attempt to rotate the unit.

16 Undo the screws and remove the contact unit **(see illustration)**.

17 Refitting is a reversal of removal, but if there is any doubt as to the correct position of the clock spring it must be centralised as follows:.

a) *Rotate the clockspring unit rotor clockwise until a resistance is felt.*

b) *Rotate the rotor anti-clockwise 2 and a half turns – the coloured marking will be visible in the window at the 7 o'clock position.*

c) *Tape the clockspring in position.*

Restraint Control Module (RCM)

18 Refer to Chapte 11 Section 27 and remove the centre console, as the control module is located in front of the gear lever assembly.

19 Unclip the air duct from the right-hand side of the control module for better access **(see illustration)**.

20 Release the locking devices and disconnect the wiring plugs for the control unit.

21 Undo the retaining bolts and remove the control unit **(see illustration)**.

22 Refitting is a reversal of removal, ensuring the module is refitted with the arrow mark on the top pointing forwards. Note that if a new module has been fitted, software for it will need to be downloaded from Ford. Entrust this task to a Ford dealer or suitably-equipped specialist. Note also that if the any of the airbags have deployed it is possible to reset the control module (up to a maximum of 5 times) using suitable diagnostic equipment.

Side airbags

23 The side airbags are incorporated into the side of the front and rear seats. Removal of the units requires the seat upholstery to be removed. This is a specialist task, which we recommend should be entrusted to a Ford dealer or specialist.

Head/overhead curtain airbags

24 Renewal of the head airbags/inflatable curtain requires removal of the headlining. This is a specialist task, and should be entrusted to a Ford dealer or specialist.

Crash/lateral acceleration sensors

Front sensor

25 Open the bonnet, undo the 2 bolts and remove the bonnet catch.

26 Undo the retaining bolt and remove the sensor.

27 Refitting is a reversal of removal.

Side sensors

28 The side sensors are located in the vehicle's B-pillars each side.

29 Remove the B-pillar trim panel (see Chapter 11) and then unbolt the seatbelt lower mounting.

30 Disconnect the sensor wiring pug, then undo the bolt and remove the sensor **(see illustration)**. Take great care not to damage the sensor wiring harness. Note that the sensor must be handled carefully. Do not refit a sensor that has been dropped or knocked.

31 Refitting is a reversal of removal.

23 Anti-theft alarm system – general information

1 An anti-theft alarm and immobiliser system is fitted as standard equipment. Should the system become faulty, the vehicle should be taken to a Ford dealer or specialist for examination. They will have access to a special diagnostic tester which will quickly trace any fault present in the system.

24 Electronic control modules – removal and refitting

Note: *All of these modules are included in the vehicle's sophisticated self-diagnosis system. Should a fault occur, have the system interrogated using a fault code reader/*

22.21 Remove the control module

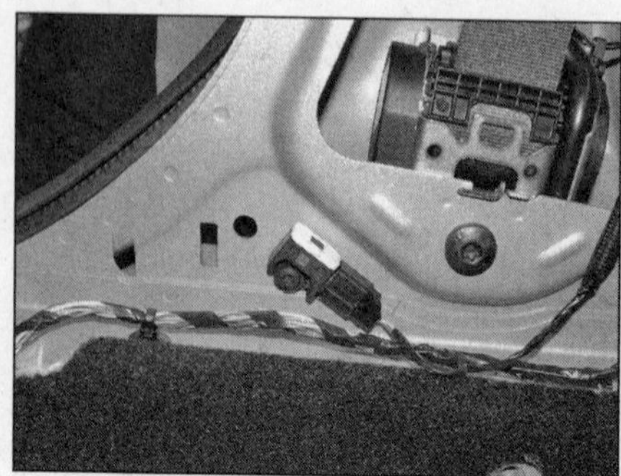
22.30 The B-pillar crash sensor

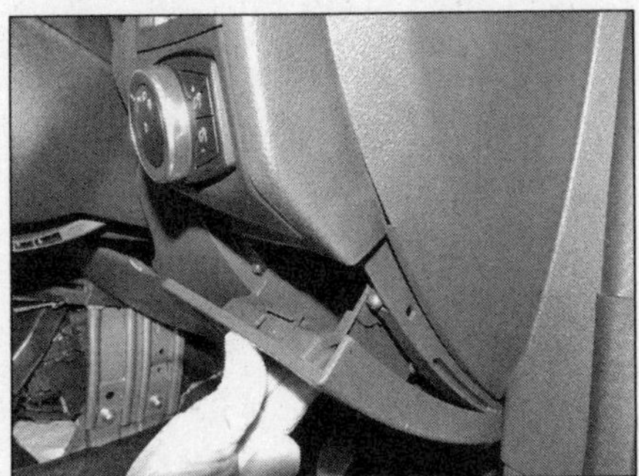
24.0a Open the small compartment...

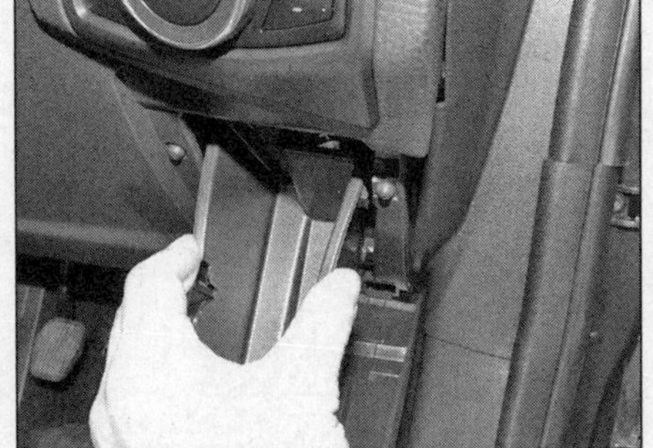
24.0b ...squeeze the sides inwards and pull down...

24.0c ...to access the diagnostic plug

Ford test equipment, via the diagnostic plug located under the driver's side of the facia, above the pedals **(see illustration).**

Removal

1 Disconnect the battery negative lead as described in Chapter 5A.

Body control module (BCM)

2 The body control module is located behind the glovebox on the passenger side of the vehicle.

3 Remove the glovebox as described in Chapter 11 Section 29.

4 Note their fitted positions, and disconnect the wiring plugs **(see illustration).**

5 Release the locking pegs at the lower part of the module, and then withdraw downwards and out from the bulkhead **(see illustration).**

6 If a new BCM is to be fitted, the unit must be configured and initialised using Ford diagnostic equipment (IDS). Entrust this task to a Ford dealer or suitably-equipped specialist.

Keyless vehicle module (KVM)

7 The proximity entry and keyless start module is located behind the facia, above the glovebox on the passenger side of the facia **(see illustration).**

8 Remove the glovebox, as described in Chapter 11 Section 29.

9 Note the locations of the wiring connectors and disconnect them.

10 Remove the two mounting screws and remove the module from under the facia **(see illustration).**

Headlamp control module

11 The headlamp control module is located behind the lower trim panel on the driver's side of the facia.

12 Remove the trim panel, as described in Chapter 11 Section 30.

13 Disconnect the wiring connector **(see illustration).**

14 Remove the two mounting screws and remove the module from the lower trim panel **(see illustration).**

Climate control module (CCM)

15 Removal of the CCM is described in Chapter 3, Section 10.

Refitting

16 Refitting is a reversal of removal. If a new module has been fitted, software will need to be downloaded from Ford. Entrust this task to a Ford dealer or suitably-equipped specialist.

24.4 Disconnect the wiring plugs, noting their position

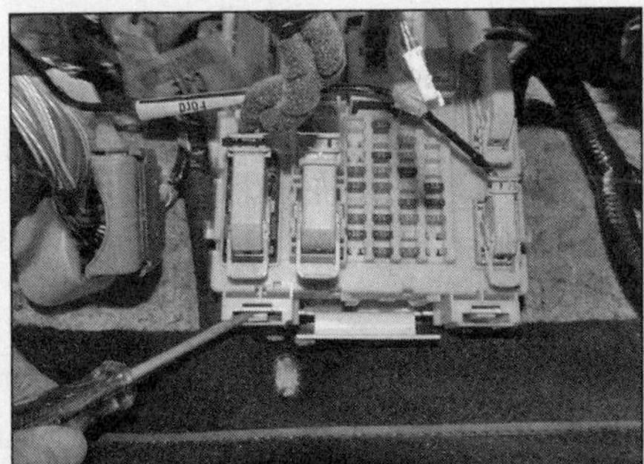
24.5 Release the locking pegs

24.7 Location of control module

24.10 Undo the mounting screws

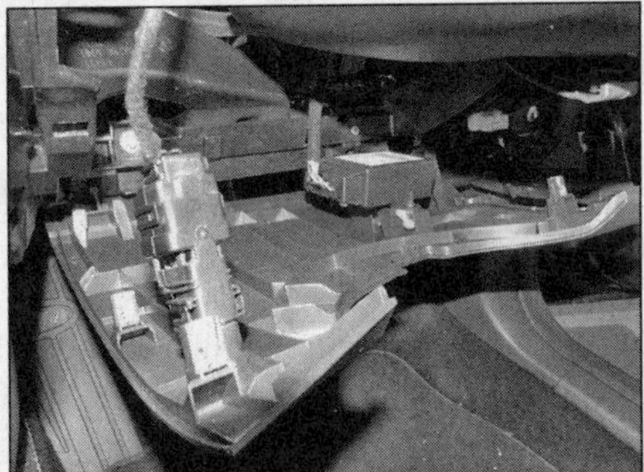
24.13 Disconnect the wiring connector

24.14 Undo the mounting screws

BATTERY JUNCTION BOX (BJB)

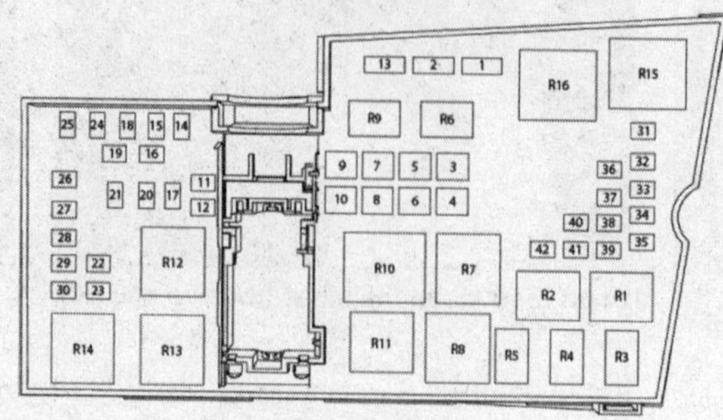

FUSE/RELAY	VALUE	DESCRIPTION	OEM NAME
1	40 A	Anti-lock braking system (ABS) module	F7
2	30 A	Anti-lock braking system (ABS) module	F8
3	30 A	Rear window defrost relay	F9
4	40 A	Blower motor relay	F10
5	30 A	Low voltage DC/DC converter	F11
6	30 A	PCM power relay	F12
7	30 A	Starter relay, Battery charge control module (BCCM)	F13
8	40 A	Heated windshield element right	F14
9	25 A	Transmission control module (TCM)	F15
10	40 A	Heated windshield element left	F16
11	20 A	All wheel drive control module, Fuel fired booster heater module	F17
12	20 A	Windshield wiper motor left and right front	F18
13	5 A	Anti-lock braking system (ABS) module	F19
14	15 A	Horn relay	F20
15	5 A	Brake pedal positioning (BPP) switch	F21
16	15 A	Battery monitoring sensor	F22
17	5 A	Headlamp switch, Battery junction box(BJB) - F11, F48, Ignition relay, Heater element 3 relay, Horn relay, A/C clutch relay, Rear and front window defrost relay, PCM power relay, Contactor relay	F23
18	5 A	Rear window defrost relay	F24
19	-	Not used	-
20	15 A	Transmission control module (TCM), Body control module (BCM)	F26
21	15 A	A/C clutch relay	F27
22	10 A	DC/DC converter	F28
23	20 A	Headlamp washer, Delayed accessory relay, Ignition relay, Front window defrost relay	F29
24	20 A	Battery junction box (BJB), Powertrain control module (PCM)	F30
25	10 A	Data link connector (DLC), Smart data link connector (SDLC) module	F31
26	10 A	Engine cooling fan relay, Universal Oxygen sensors, Variable camshaft timing 12 solenoid, Powertrain control module (PCM), Electric motor coolant diverter valve, Cabin air conditioning isolator solenoid valve, Cabin heater coolant diverter valve, High voltage battery coolant diverter valve, High voltage battery coolant, Catalyst monitor sensor, Evaporative emission purge valve	F32
27	10 A	Coil-on-plug 1,2,3,4, Powertrain control module (PCM)	F33
28	10 A	Contactor relay, Powertrain control module (PCM), Evaporative emission (EVAP) purge valve	F34

Fuses and relays

29	10 A	Universal heated oxygen sensors, Variable camshaft timing 11 solenoid, Powertrain control module (PCM), Evaporative emission purge valve, Variable camshaft timing	F35
30	5 A	Cabin heater coolant pump, Electric motor coolant pump, High voltage battery coolant pump, Grille shutter actuator	F36
31	20 A	Dashboard voltage outlet	F37
32	15 A	Coil on plug 1,2,3,4, Powertrain control module (PCM)	F38
33	5 A	Headlamp assembly left and right	F39
34	5 A	Power steering control module (PSCM)	F40
35	20 A	Body control module (BCM) - F85, F87	F41
36	15 A	Rear wiper relay, Rear window wiper motor	F42
37	15 A	Headlamp control module (HCM), Headlamp assembly left and right	F43
38	5 A	Proximity warning radar unit	F44
39	20A	Windshield heater washer jet, left and right	F45
40	-	Not used	-
41	5 A	In-vehicle temperature / humidity sensor	F47
42	5 A	Vacuum pump cut-off relay	F48
R1	-	Not used	-
R2	-	Not used	-
R3	-	Horn relay	-
R4	-	Contactor relay	-
R5	-	Not used	-
R6	-	Not used	-
R7	-	Heater element 3	-
R8	-	Heater element 1 and 2 relay	-
R9	-	Not used	-
R10	-	Starter relay	-
R11	-	A/C clutch relay	-
R12	-	Engine cooling fan relay	-
R13	-	Blower motor relay	-
R14	-	PCM power relay	-
R15	-	Vacuum pump cut-off relay	-
R16	-	Ignition relay	-

Fuses and relays (continued)

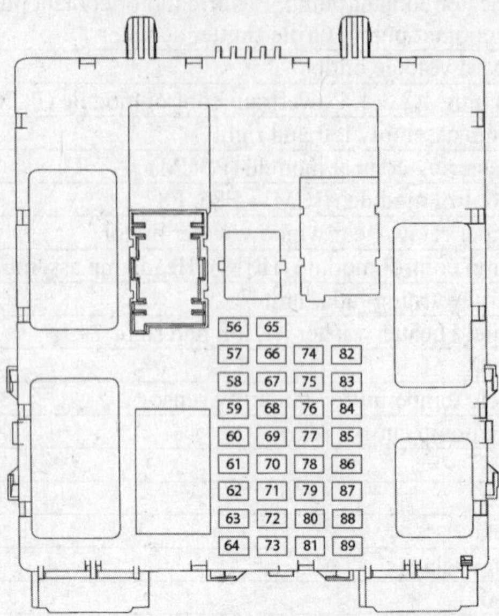

FUSE	VALUE	DESCRIPTION	OEM NAME
56	20 A	Fuel pump relay, Fuel pump control module	F56
57	-	Not used	-
58	-	Not used	-
59	5 A	Passive anti-theft transceiver	F59
60	10 A	Luggage compartment lamp left and right, Master window control switch, Luggage compartment lamp	F60
61	20 A	Cigar lighter front, Power point rear	F61
62	5 A	Electrochromatic inside mirror unit, Rain sensor	F62
63	10 A	Null relay	F63
64	-	Not used	-
65	10 A	Liftgate / decklid release relay, Liftgate / Decklid latch assembly	F65
66	20 A	Driver door unlock relay, Central double lock relay, Driver door unlock relay	F66
67	7.5 A	Front control / display interface module (FCDIM), Global positioning system module (GPSM), Accessory protocol interface module (APIM)	F67
68	15 A	Spare relay	F68
69	5 A	Instrument panel cluster (IPC), Information center module (ICM)	F69
70	20 A	Passenger door unlock relay, All unlock relay, Door latch left and right front, Door latch left and right rear	F70
71	10 A	HVAC control module, EMTC and DATC	F71
72	7.5 A	Steering angle sensor module (SASM)	F72
73	7.5 A	Data link connector (DLC), Anti-theft alarm horn with integral battery smart data link connector (SDLC) module	F73
74	15 A	High beam relay, Headlamp assembly left and right	F74
75	15 A	Fog lamp relay, Fog lamp left and right front	F75
76	10 A	Reversing lamp relay, Reversing lamp left and right, Electrochromatic inside mirror unit	F76
77	20 A	Front washer relay, Rear washer relay, Windshield washer pump motor	F77

Fuses and relays (continued)

78	5 A	Telematic control unit (TCU) module, Remote function actuator (RFA) module, Start-stop switch	F78
79	15 A	Audio control module (ACM), Front controls interface module (FCIM)	F79
80	20 A	Roof opening panel module	F80
81	5 A	Remote functions receiver (RFR) module, intrusion sensor	F81
82	-	Not used	-
83	-	Not used	-
84	-	Not used	-
85	7.5 A	DC/DC converter module, Audio control module, Roof opening panel module, HVAC module, DATC, Telematic control unit (TCU) module, All wheel drive control module, Rear wiper relay	F85
86	10 A	Passenger airbag deactivation indicator, Overhead console switch assembly, Restraints control module (RCM)	F86
87	15 A	Steering angle sensor module (SASM), Clockspring	F87
88	-	Not used	-
89	-	Not used	-

REAR JUNCTION BOX (RJB)

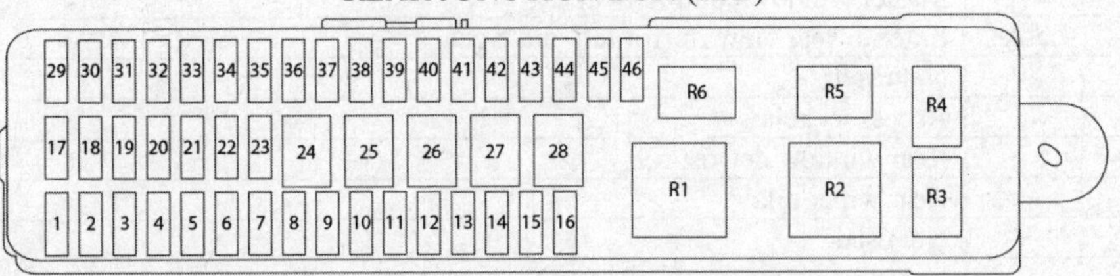

FUSE/RELAY	VALUE	DESCRIPTION	OEM NAME
1	5 A	Accessory relay, Rear window defrost relay, Ignition relay	F1
2	-	Not used	-
3	5 A	Exterior doors handles	F3
4	25 A	Driver door module (DDM)	F4
5	25 A	Passenger door module (PDM)	F5
6	25 A	Door module left rear	F6
7	25 A	Door module right rear	F7
8	10 A	Security horn relay	F8
9	25 A	Driver seat control switch	F9
10	25 A	Audio digital signal processing (DSP) module	F10
11	5 A	High voltage battery pack upper	F11
12	-	Not used	-
13	-	Not used	-
14	-	Not used	-
15	-	Not used	-
16	-	Not used	-
17	-	Not used	-
18	-	Not used	-
19	-	Not used	-
20	-	Not used	-
21	5 A	Null relay	F21
22	10 A	Digital audio control module	F22
23	-	Not used	-
24	30 A	Rear window defrost relay	F24
25	20 A	Power point cargo area	F25

Fuses and relays (continued)

26	-	Not used	-
27	-	Not used	-
28	40 A	Trailer tow module	F28
29	5 A	Video camera, Low voltage DC/DC converter	F29
30	5 A	Parking aid module (PAM)	F30
31	-	Not used	-
32	-	Not used	-
33	15 A	Rear wiper relay, Rear window wiper motor	F33
34	15 A	Driver seat, Heated seat module driver front	F34
35	15 A	HVAC module, Heated sear module, Passenger side front passenger seat	F35
36	-	Not used	-
37	-	Not used	-
38	-	Not used	-
39	15 A	Fuel and damper control module	F39
40	-	Not used	-
41	5 A	Trailer tow module	F41
42	-	Not used	-
43	-	Not used	-
44	10 A	Master window control switch	F44
45	7.5 A	Exterior rear view mirror left and right	F45
46	-	Not used	-
R1	-	Accessory relay	-
R2	-	Rear window defrost relay	-
R3	-	Rear wiper relay	-
R4	-	Not used	-
R5	-	Not used	-
R6	-	Not used	-

HIGH CURRENT BATTERY JUNCTION BOX (BJB)

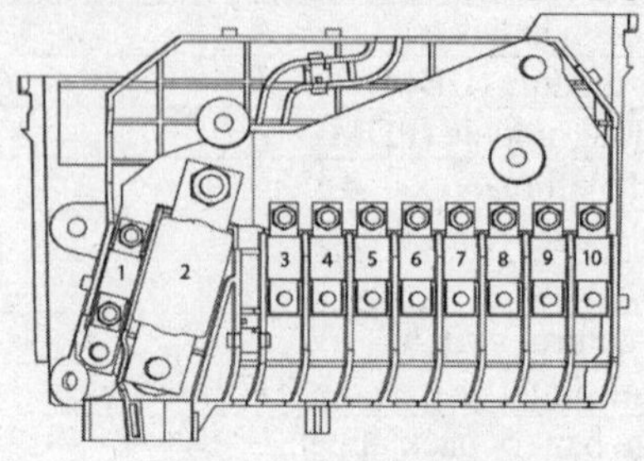

FUSE	VALUE	DESCRIPTION	OEM NAME
1	80 A	Power steering control module (PSCM)	MEGA 1
2	150 A	DC / DC converter control module, Starter motor, Generator	MEGA 2
3	100 A	Battery junction box (BJB)	MEGA 3
4	50 A	Body control module (BCM)	MEGA 4
5	70 A	Heater element 1 and 2 relay	MEGA 5
6	70 A	Rear junction box (RJB) - Accessory relay	MEGA 6
7	40 A	Engine cooling fan 1	MEGA 7
8	50 A	Engine cooling fan 1 and 3 or Engine cooling fan 3 with fan control module (40 A)	MEGA 8
9	50 A	Body control module (BCM)	MEGA 9
10	60 A	Glow plug module, Engine cooling fan relay 3	MEGA 10

Fuses and relays (continued)

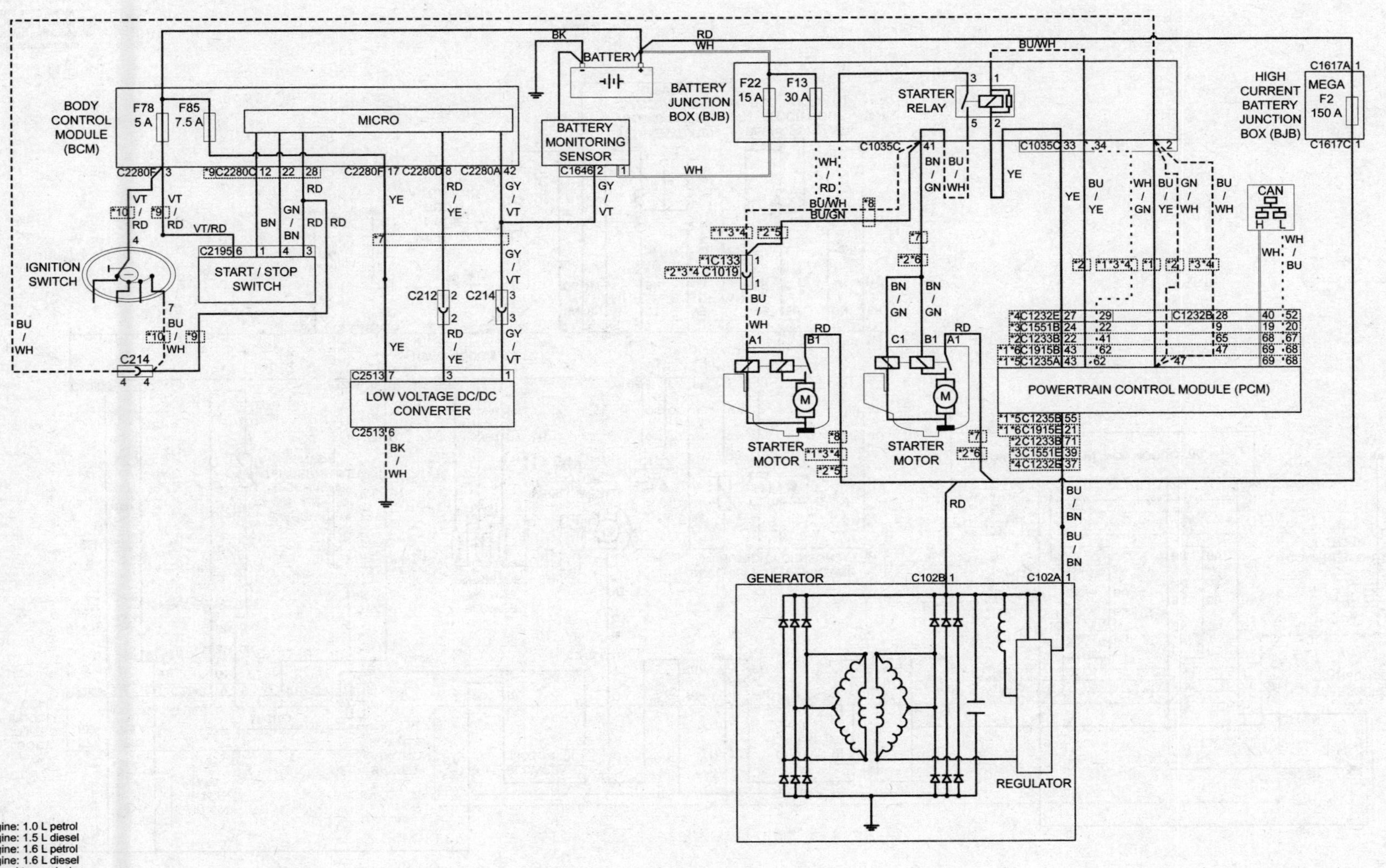

*1 Engine: 1.0 L petrol
*2 Engine: 1.5 L diesel
*3 Engine: 1.6 L petrol
*4 Engine: 1.6 L diesel
*5 Manual transmission
*6 Automatic transmission
*7 With start stop
*8 Without start stop
*9 With keyless
*10 Without keyless

Starting and charging

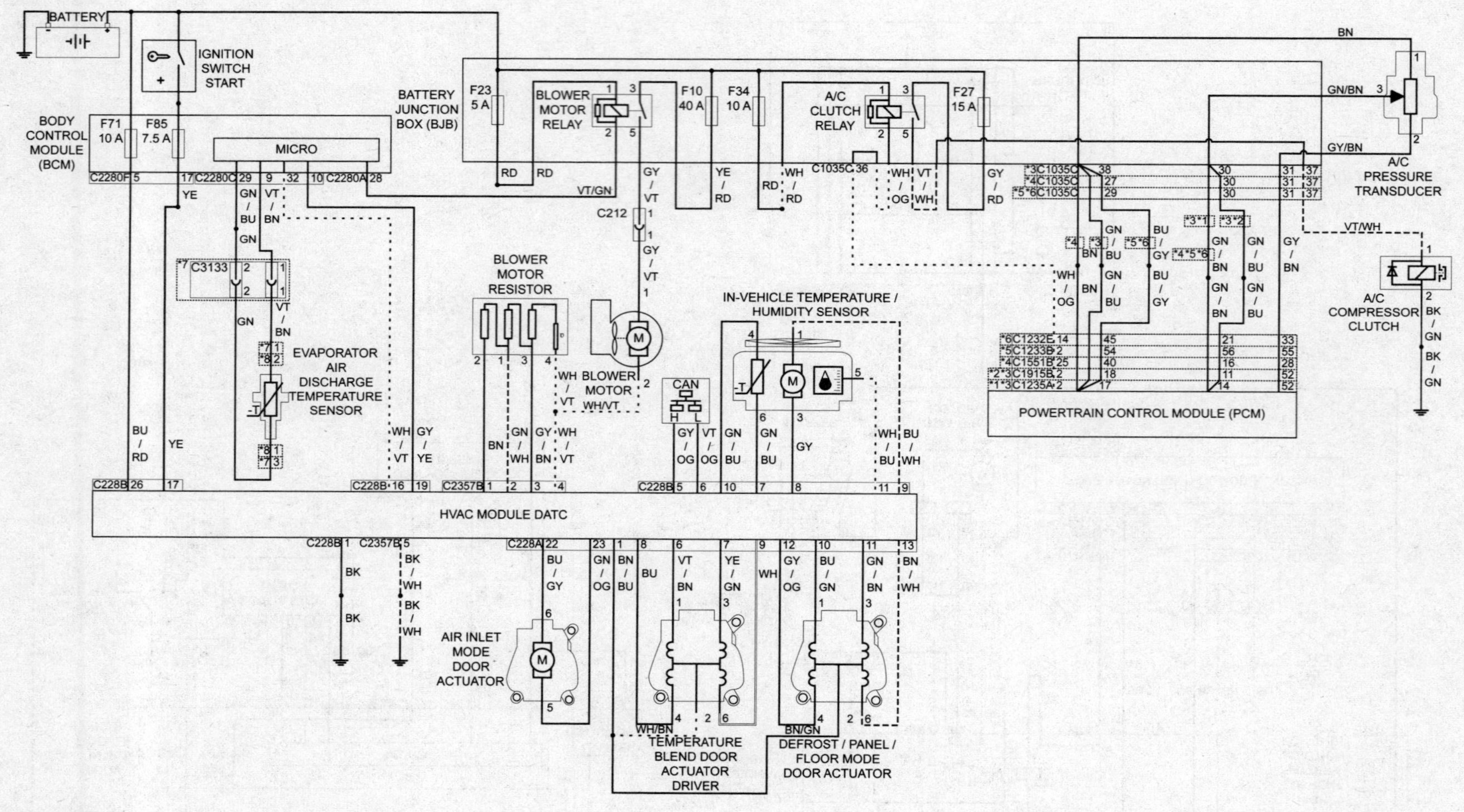

*1 Manual transmission
*2 Automatic transmission
*3 Engine: 1.0 L petrol
*4 Engine: 1.6 L petrol
*5 Engine: 1.5 L diesel
*6 Engine: 1.6 L diesel
*7 With R134A refrigerant
*8 Without R134A refrigerant

Air conditioning, heating and cooling – manual air conditioning

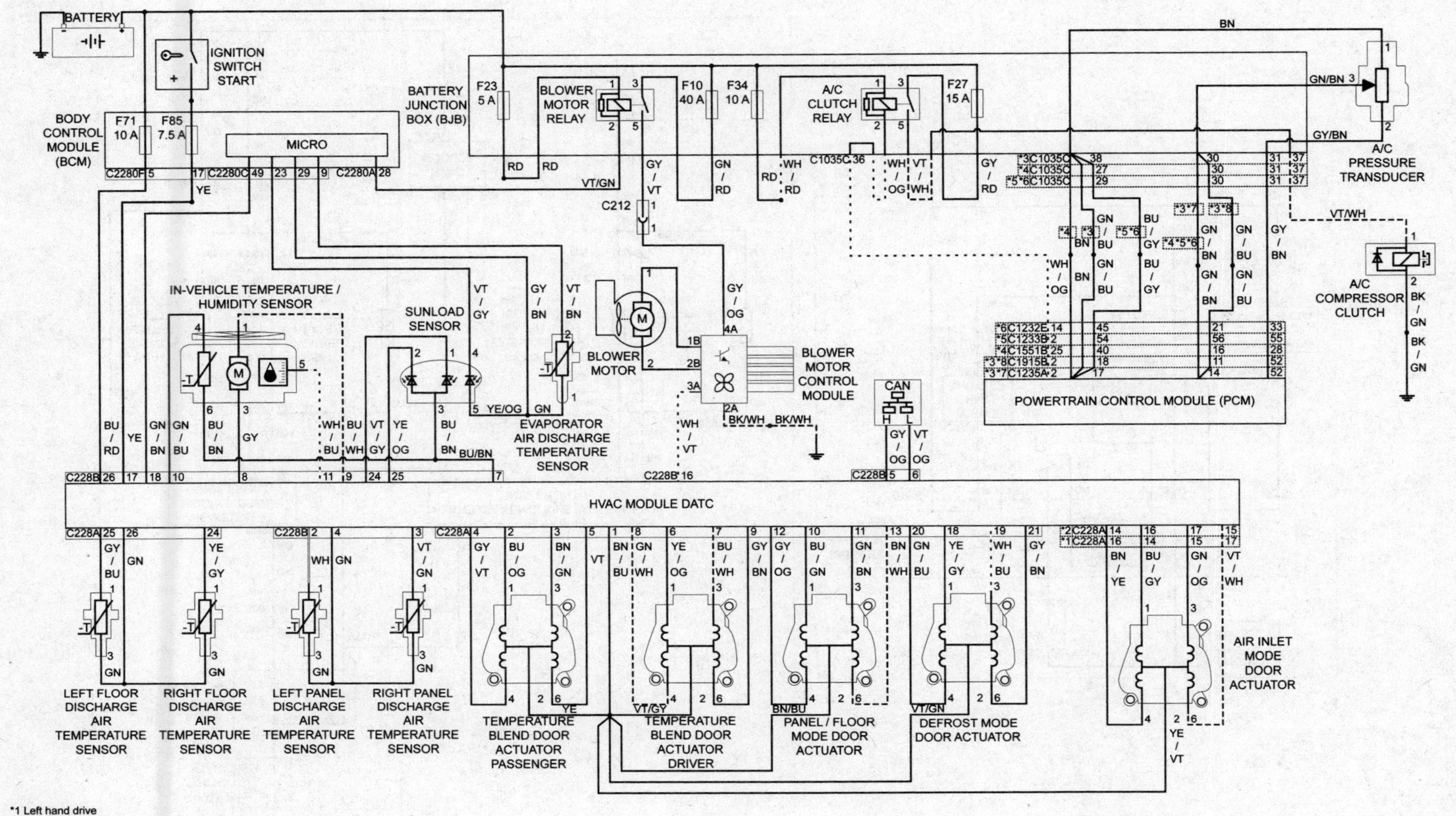

*1 Left hand drive
*2 Right hand drive
*3 Engine: 1.0 L petrol
*4 Engine: 1.6 L petrol
*5 Engine: 1.5 L diesel
*6 Engine: 1.6 L diesel
*7 Manual transmission
*8 Automatic transmission

Air conditioning, heating and cooling – automatic air conditioning

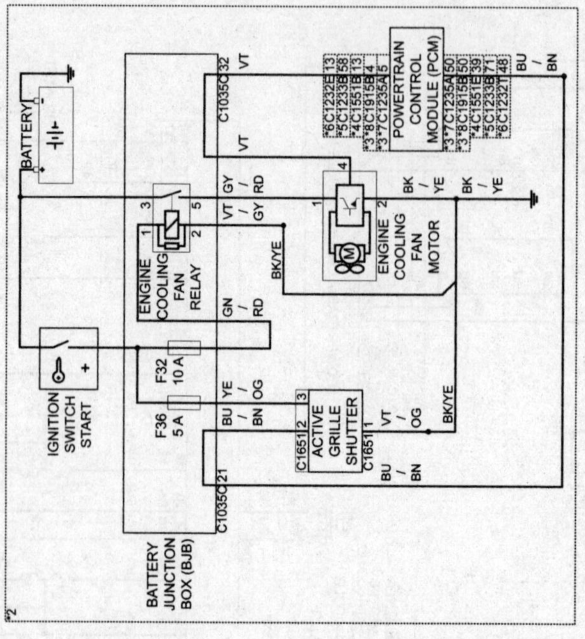

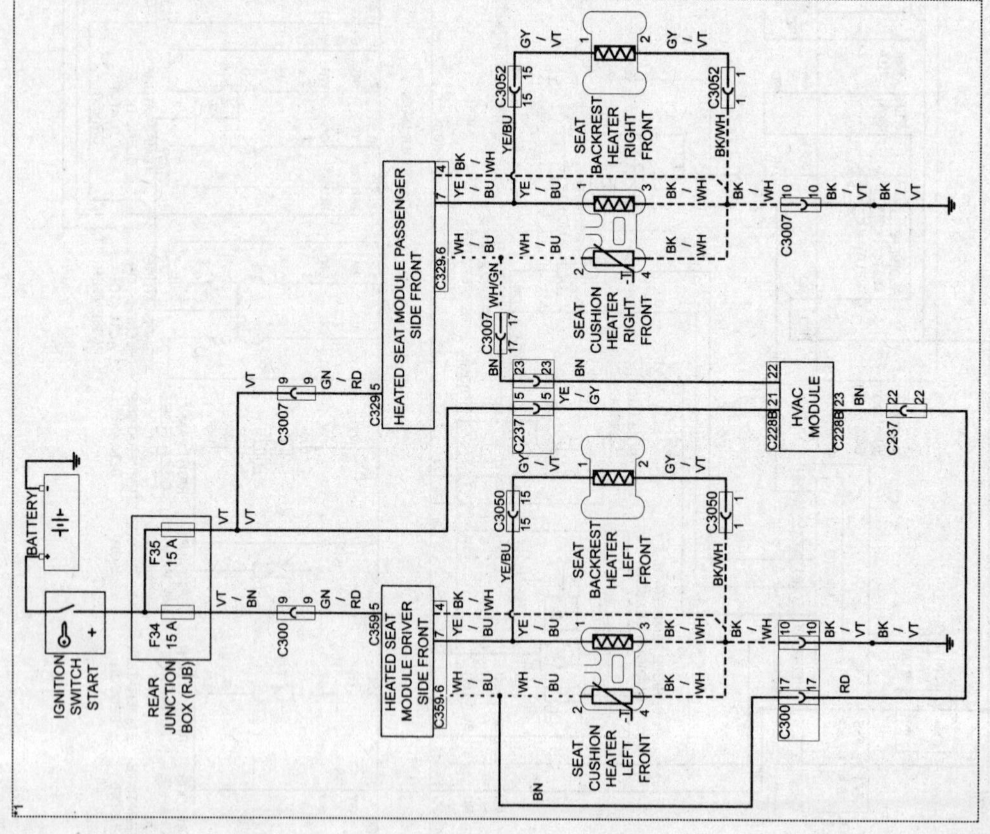

Heated seats and cooling fan

*1 Heated seats
*2 Cooling fan
*3 Engine: 1.0 L petrol
*4 Engine: 1.6 L petrol
*5 Engine: 1.5 L diesel
*6 Engine: 1.6 L diesel
*7 Manual transmission
*8 Automatic transmission

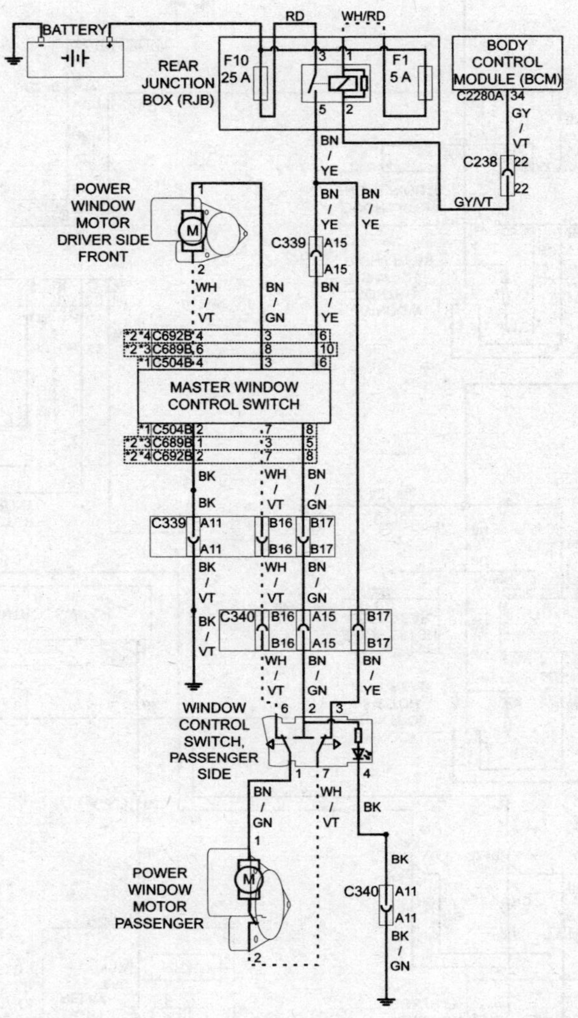

Power windows – without door module and without rear power windows

*1 Left hand drive
*2 Right hand drive
*3 Version 1
*4 Version 2

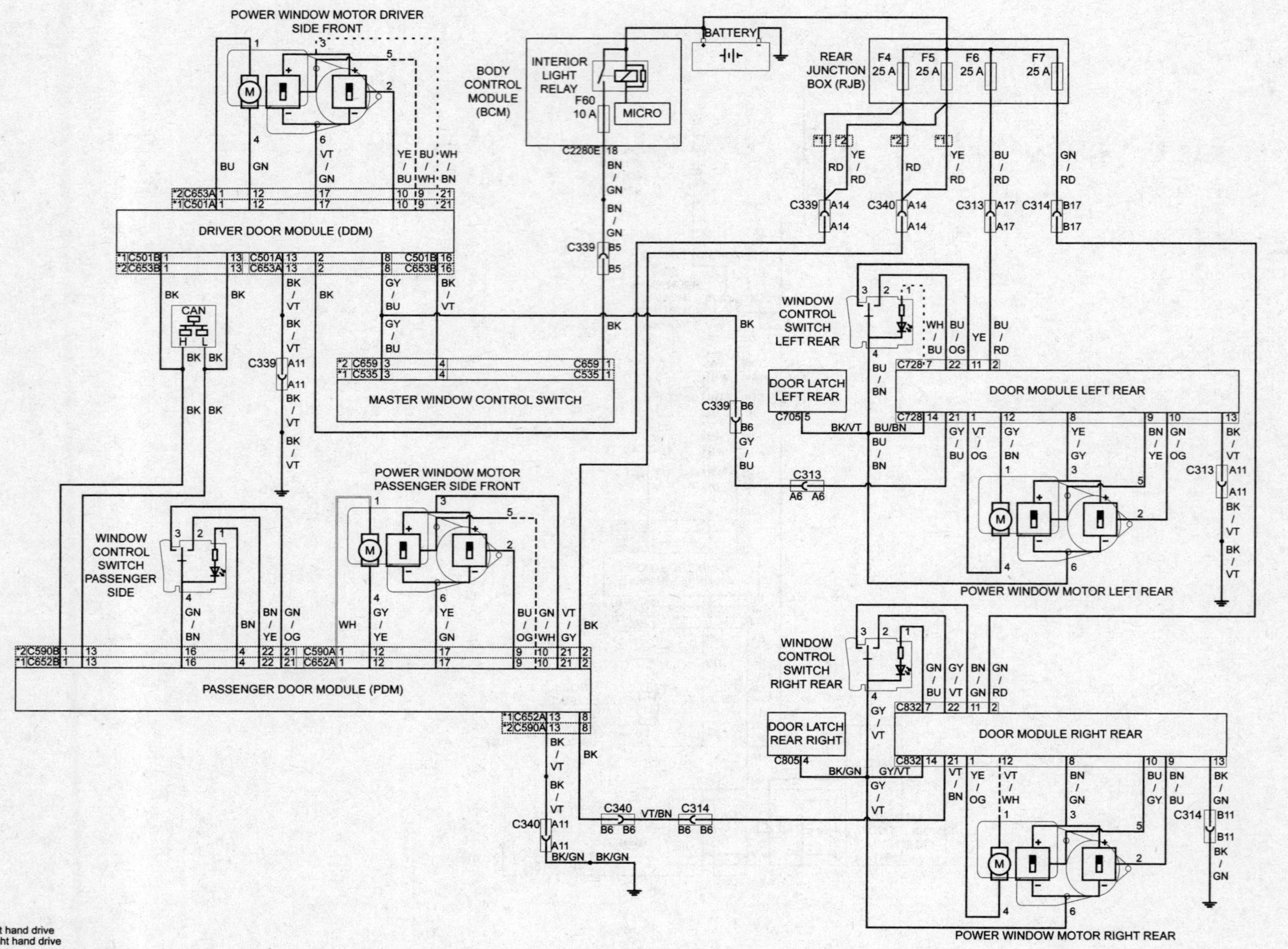

Power windows – with door modules

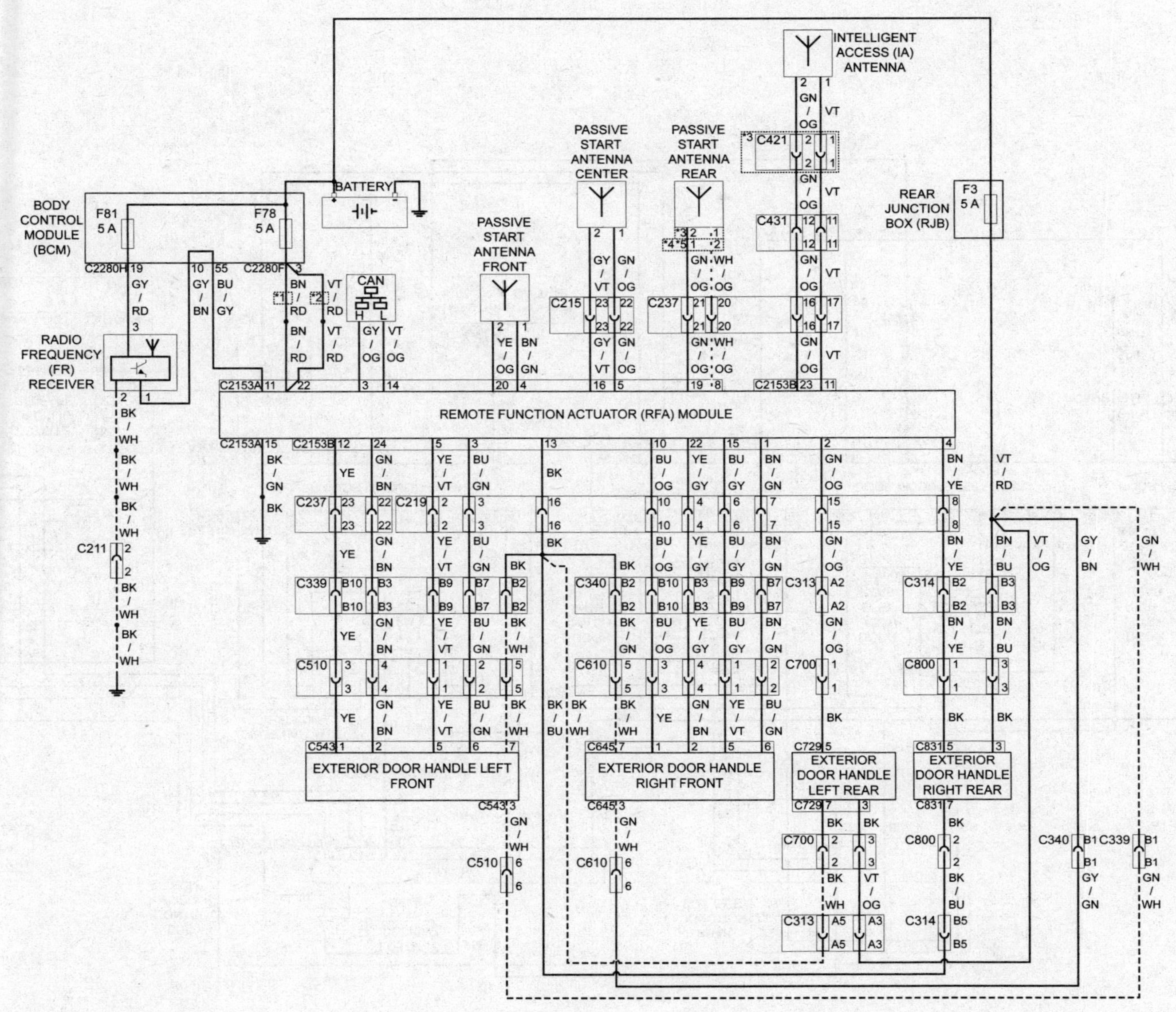

*1 With electric
*2 Without electric
*3 Body type: Wagon
*4 Body type: 4 doors
*5 Body type: 5 doors

Power door locks – keyless

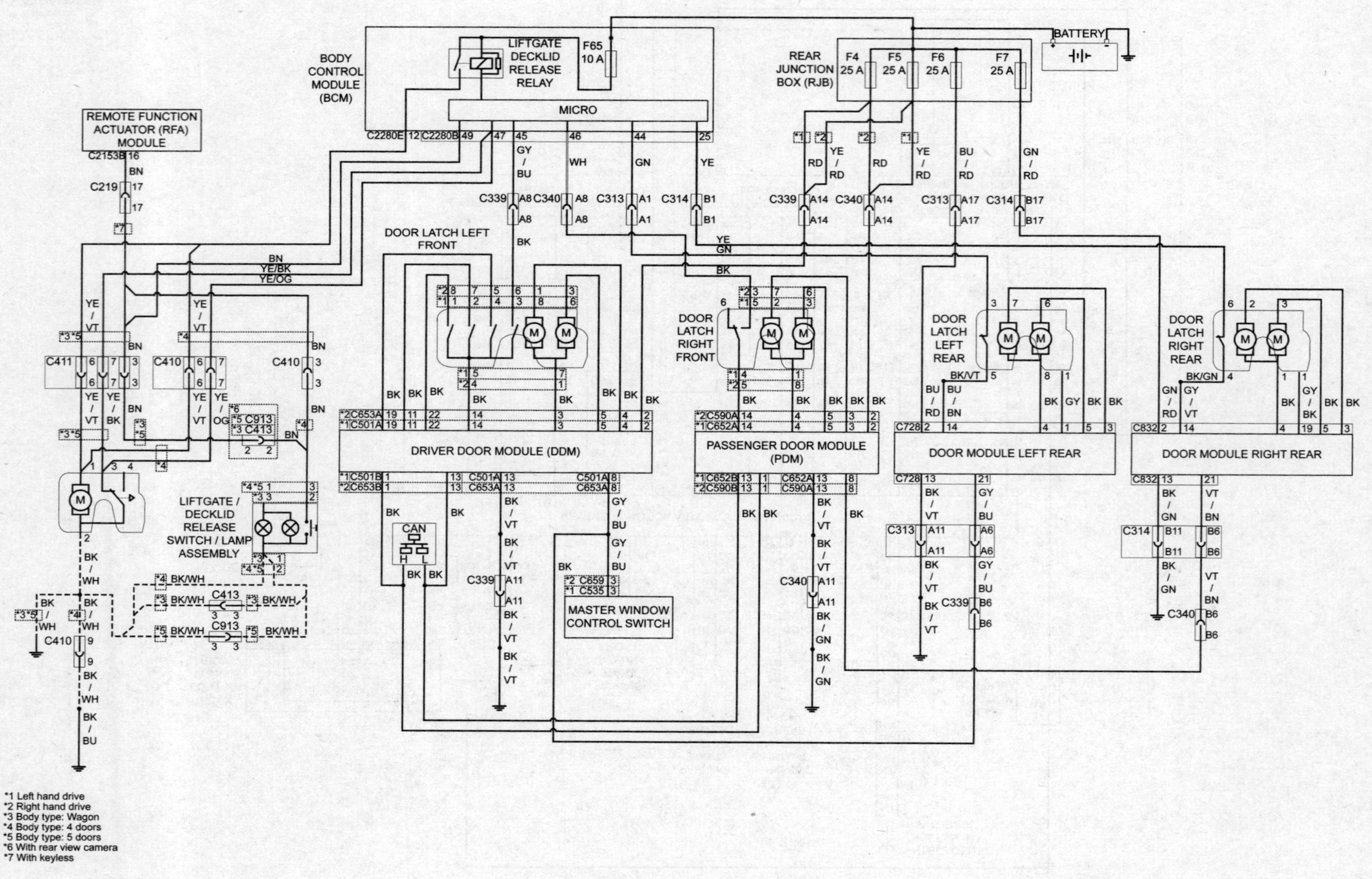

*1 Left hand drive
*2 Right hand drive
*3 Body type: Wagon
*4 Body type: 4 doors
*5 Body type: 5 doors
*6 With rear view camera
*7 With keyless

Power door locks – with door modules

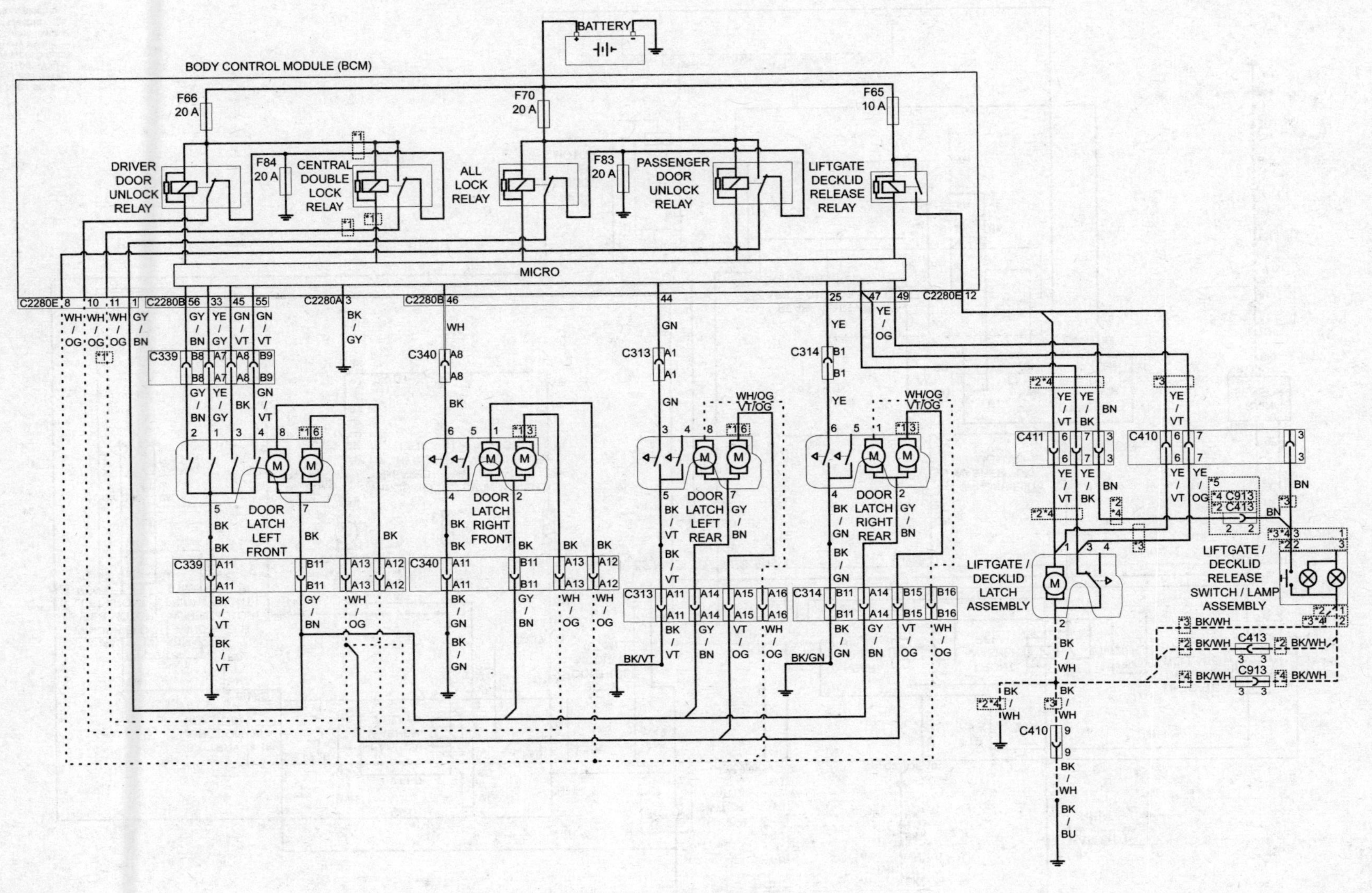

*1 Left hand drive
*2 Body type: Wagon
*3 Body type: 4 doors
*4 Body type: 5 doors
*5 With rear view camera

Power door locks – without door modules

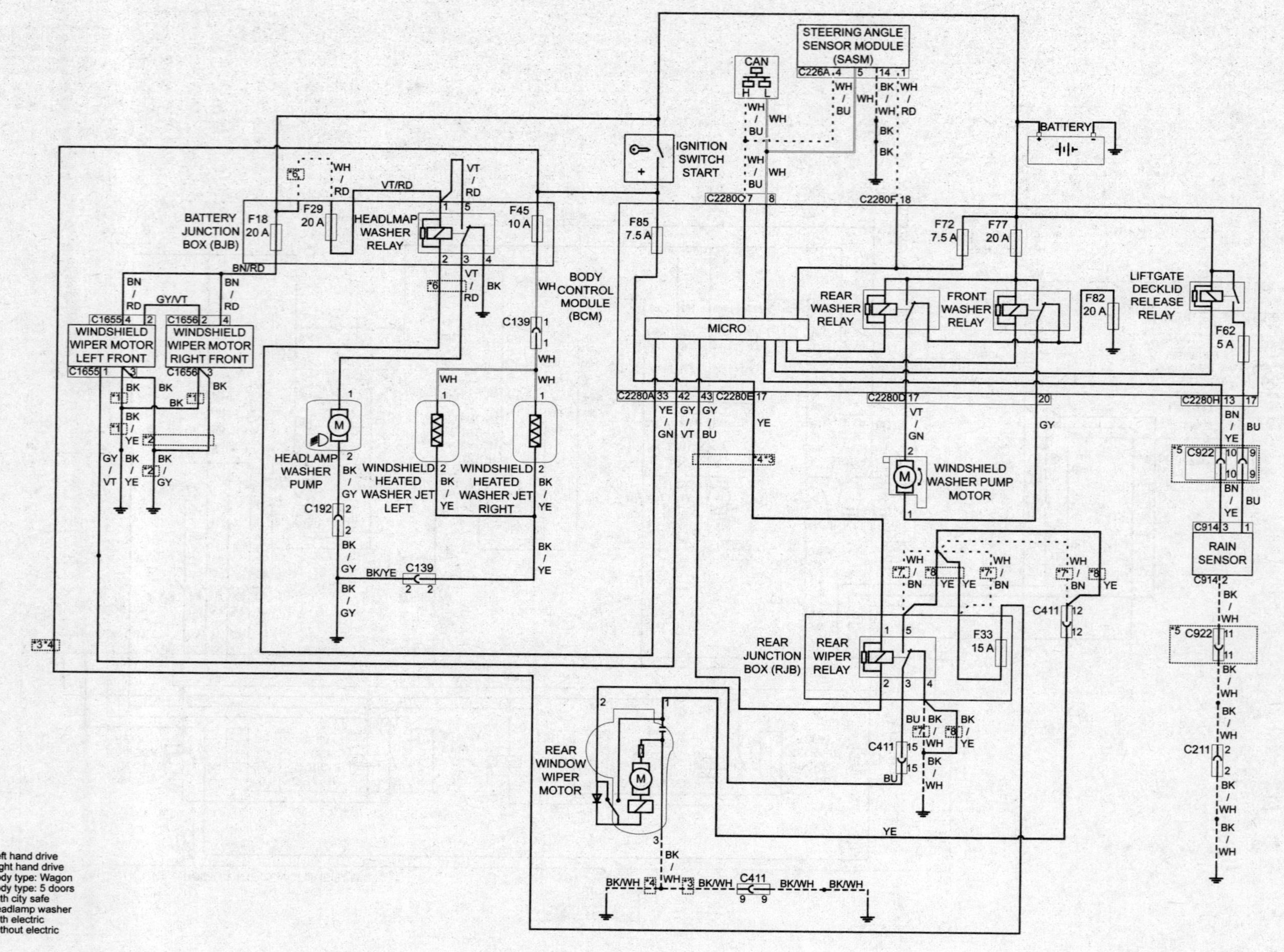

Wiper washer

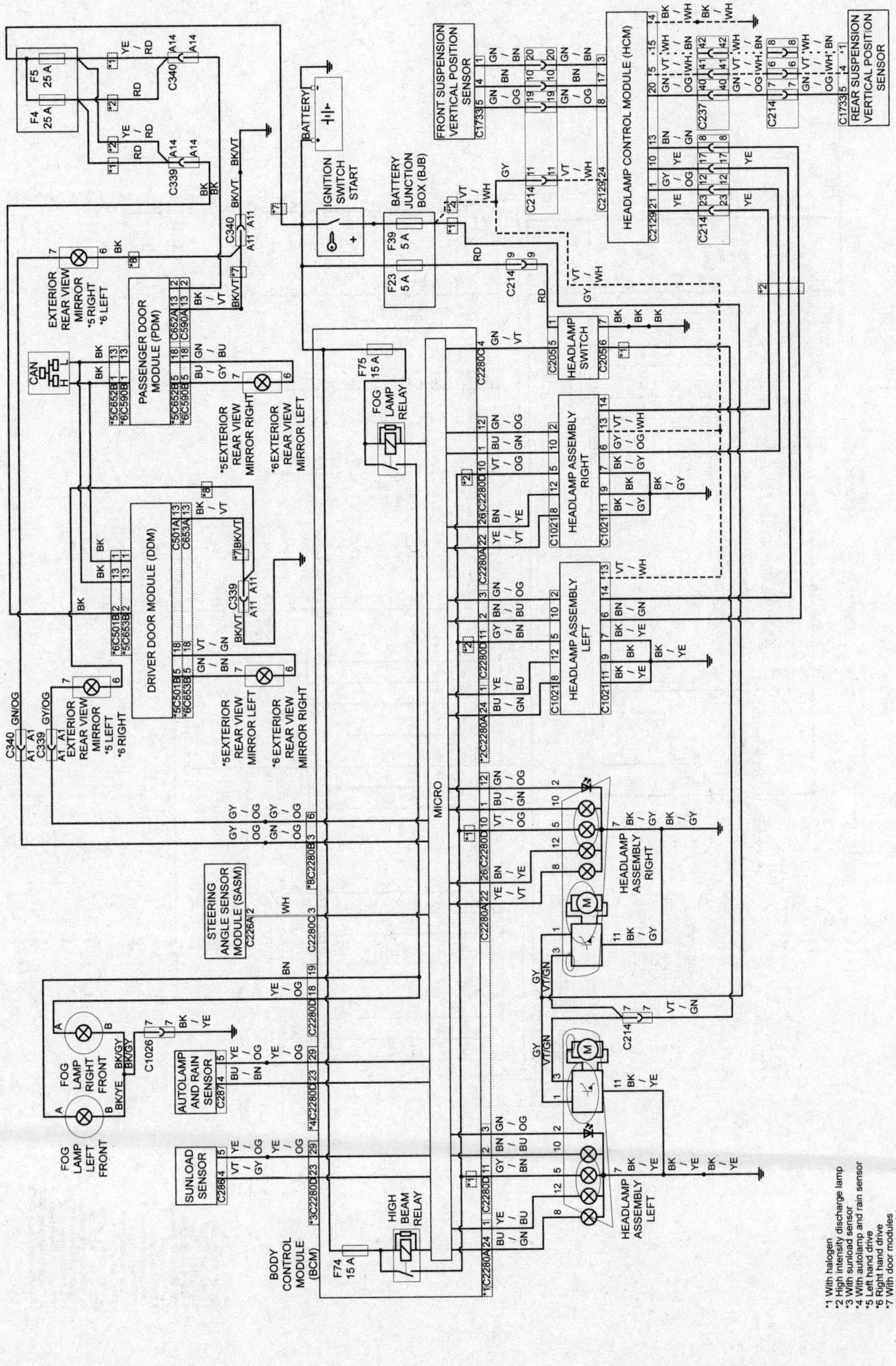

*1 With halogen
*2 High intensity discharge lamp
*3 With sunload sensor
*4 With autolamp and rain sensor
*5 Left hand drive
*6 Right hand drive
*7 With door modules
*8 Without door modules

Exterior lights – front

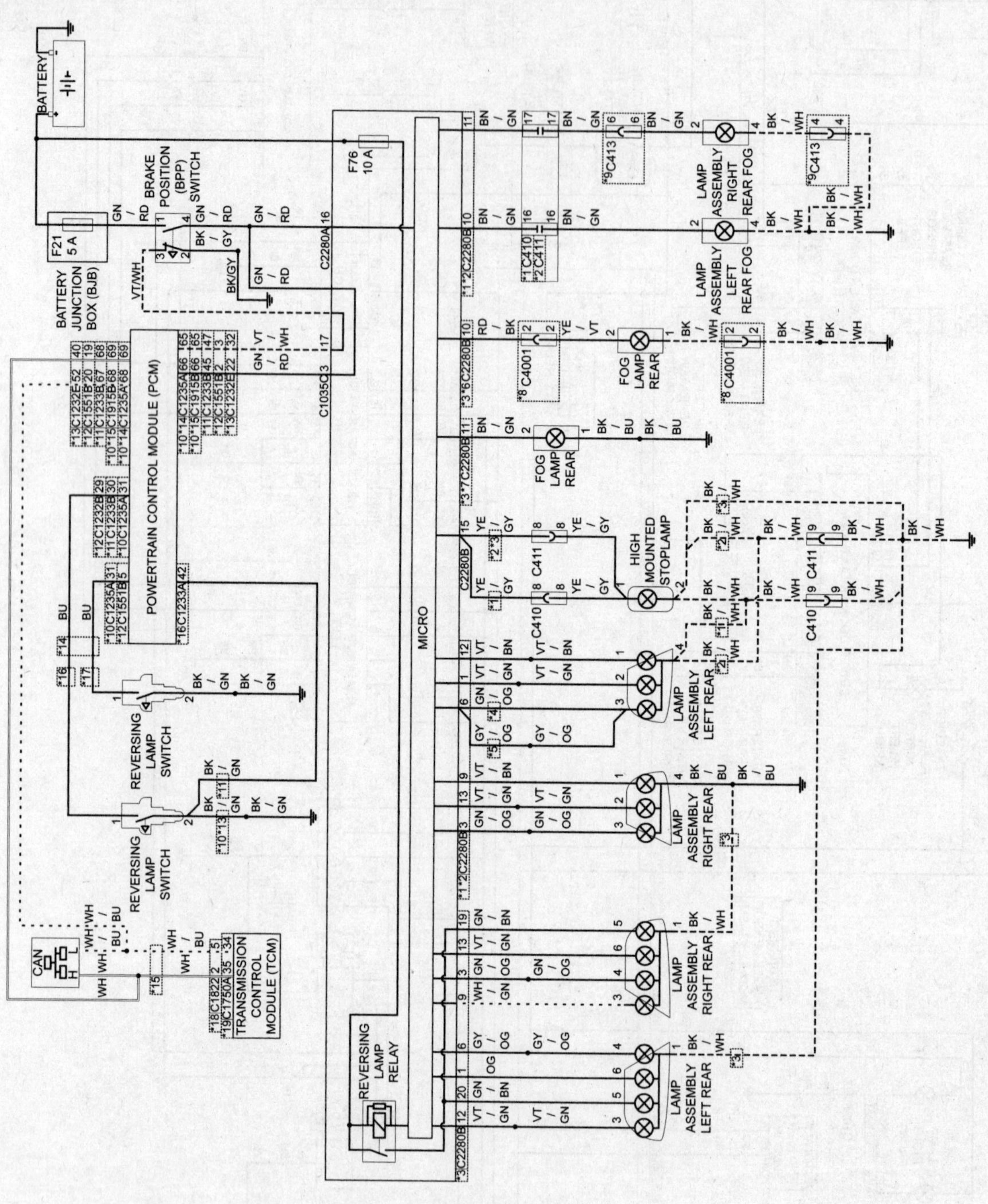

Exterior lights – rear

*1 Body type: 4 doors
*2 Body type: Wagon
*3 Body type: 5 doors
*4 With door modules
*5 Without door modules
*6 Left hand drive
*7 Right hand drive
*8 With door modules
*9 With rear camera
*10 Engine: 1.0 L petrol
*11 Engine: 1.5 L diesel
*12 Engine: 1.6 L petrol
*13 Engine: 1.6 L diesel
*14 Manual transmission
*15 Automatic transmission
*16 6 speed transmission
*17 5 speed transmission
*18 Transmission type: MPS6
*19 Transmission type: DPS6

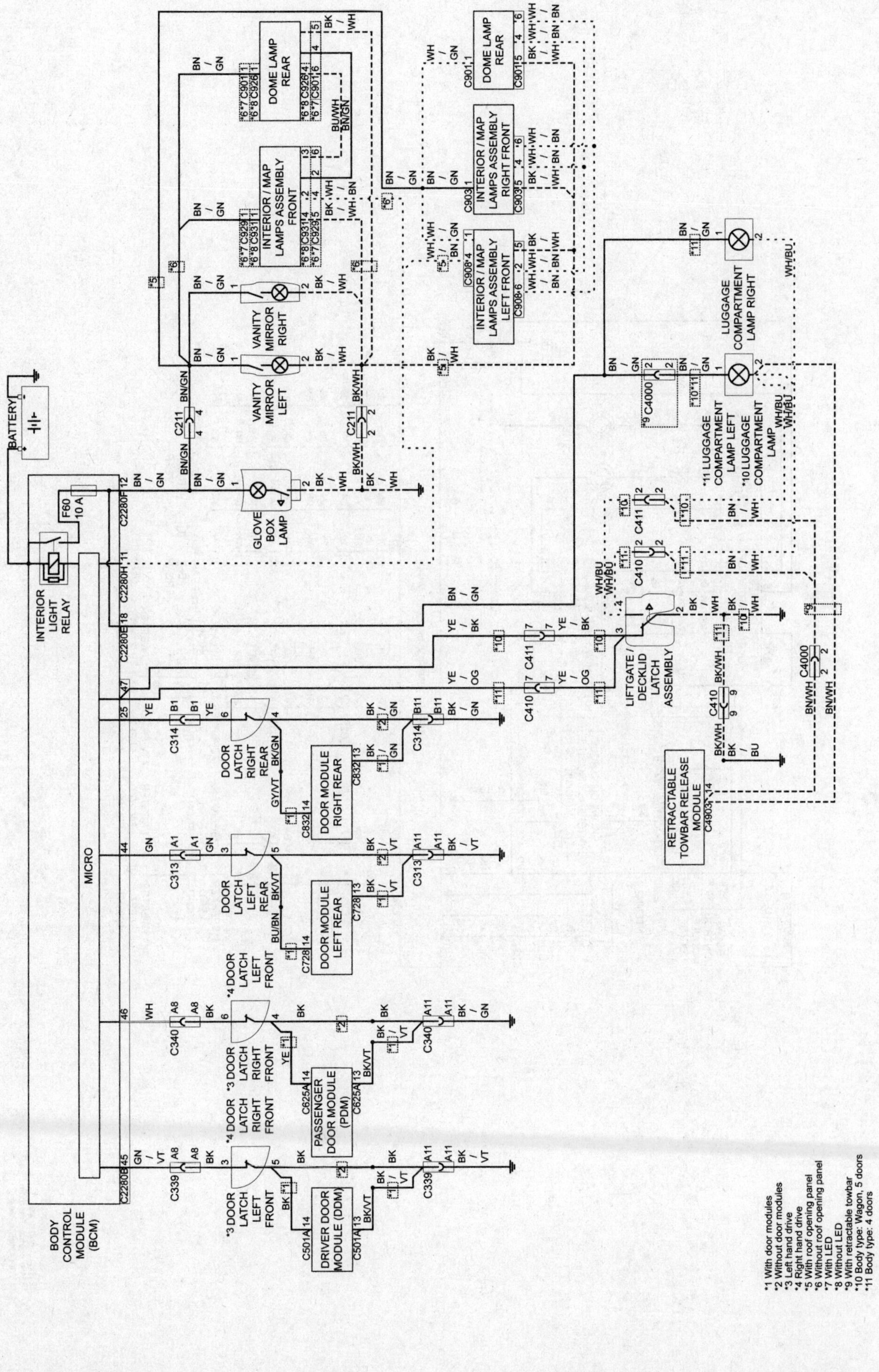
BATTERY
INTERIOR LIGHT RELAY
F60 10 A
BODY CONTROL MODULE (BCM)
MICRO
GLOVE BOX LAMP
VANITY MIRROR LEFT
VANITY MIRROR RIGHT
INTERIOR / MAP LAMPS ASSEMBLY FRONT
DOME LAMP REAR
INTERIOR / MAP LAMPS ASSEMBLY LEFT FRONT
INTERIOR / MAP LAMPS ASSEMBLY RIGHT FRONT
LUGGAGE COMPARTMENT LAMP RIGHT
*11 LUGGAGE COMPARTMENT LAMP LEFT
*10 LUGGAGE COMPARTMENT LAMP
LIFTGATE / DECKLID LATCH ASSEMBLY
RETRACTABLE TOWBAR RELEASE MODULE
*3 DOOR LATCH LEFT FRONT
*4 DOOR LATCH RIGHT FRONT
*3 DOOR LATCH RIGHT FRONT
*4 DOOR LATCH LEFT FRONT
DOOR LATCH LEFT REAR
DOOR LATCH RIGHT REAR
DRIVER DOOR MODULE (DDM)
PASSENGER DOOR MODULE (PDM)
DOOR MODULE LEFT REAR
DOOR MODULE RIGHT REAR
*1 With door modules
*2 Without door modules
*3 Left hand drive
*4 Right hand drive
*5 With roof opening panel
*6 Without roof opening panel
*7 With LED
*8 Without LED
*9 With retractable towbar
*10 Body type: Wagon, 5 doors
*11 Body type: 4 doors

Interior lights

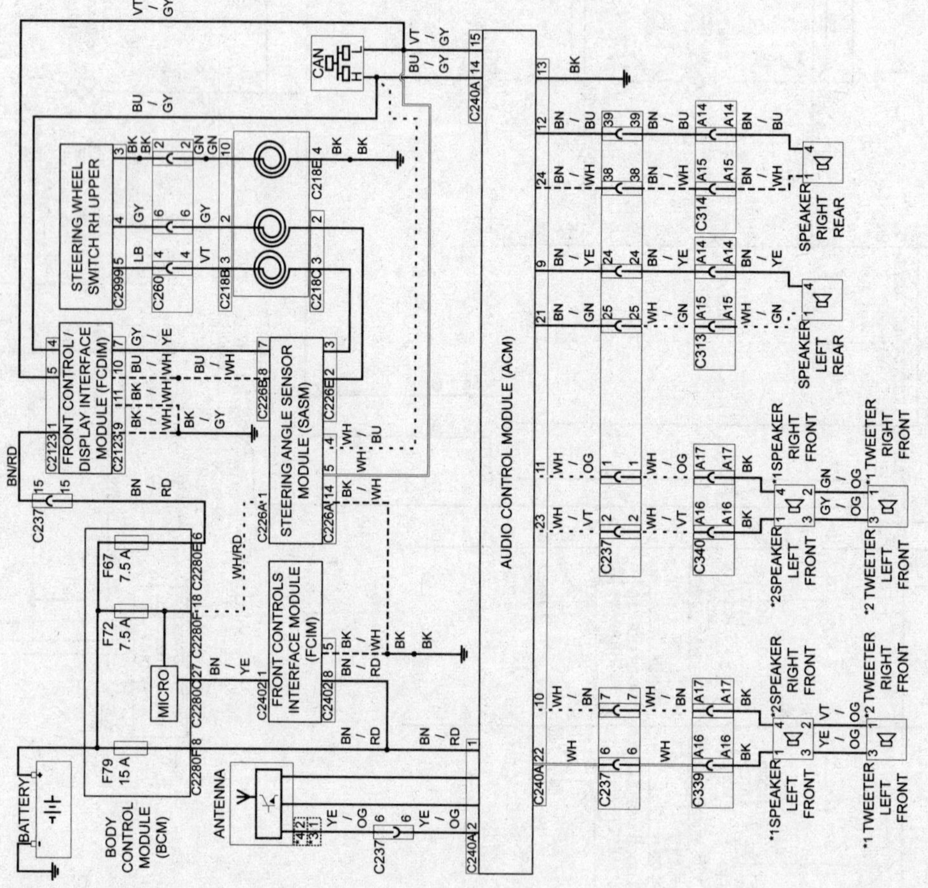

Sound system – standard audio

*1 Left hand drive
*2 Right hand drive
*3 Without satellite radio
*4 With satellite radio

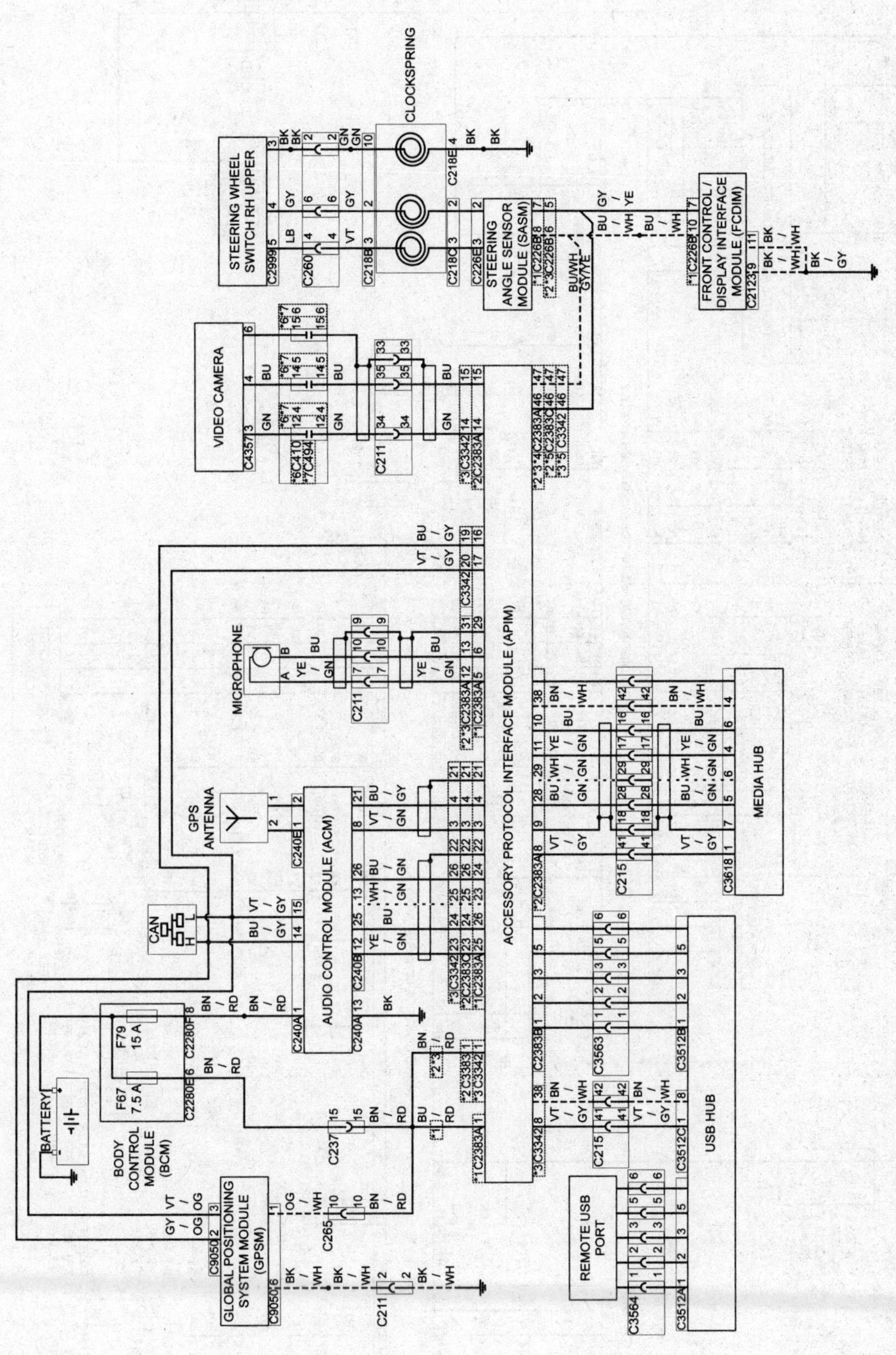

*1 With SYNC generation 1
*2 With SYNC generation 2
*3 With SYNC generation 3
*4 Version 1
*5 Version 2
*6 Body type: 4 doors
*7 Body type: 5 doors

Sound system - premium audio - SYNC

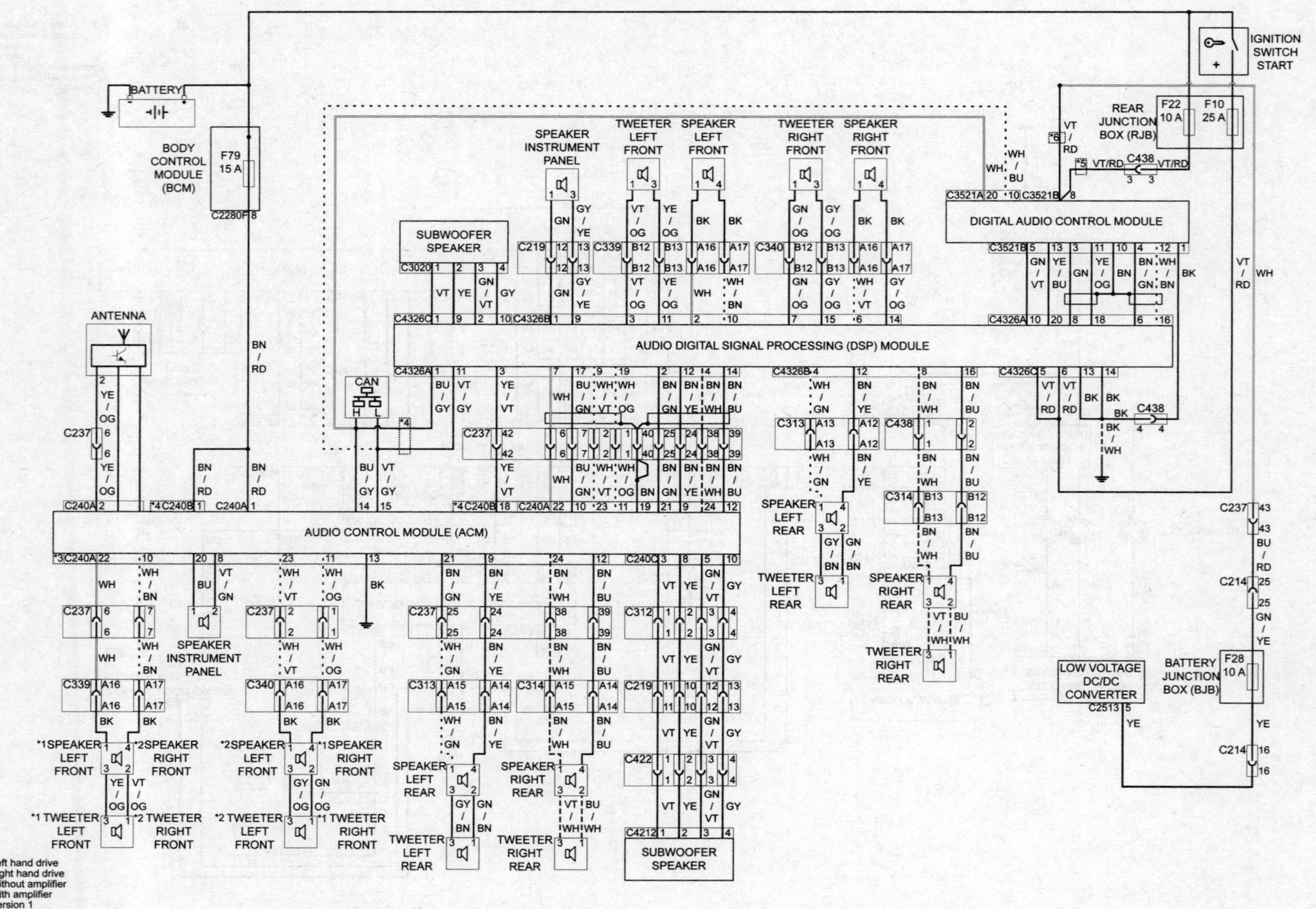

Sound system – premium audio – speakers

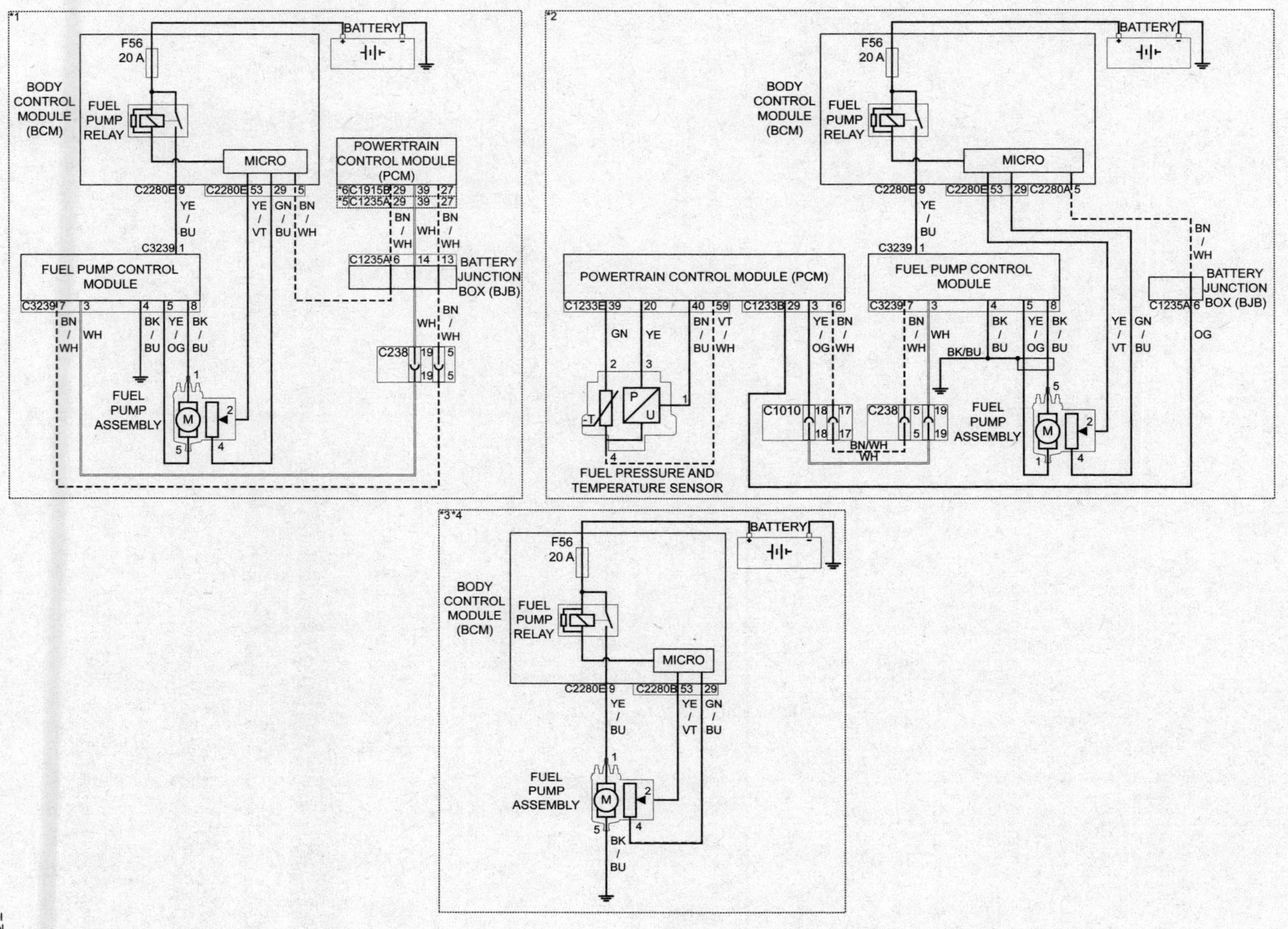

*1 Engine: 1.0 L petrol
*2 Engine: 1.5 L diesel
*3 Engine: 1.6 L petrol
*4 Engine: 1.6 L diesel
*5 Manual transmission
*6 Automatic transmission

Fuel pump

Dimensions and weights

Note: *All figures are approximate, and may vary according to model. Refer to manufacturer's data for exact figures.*

Dimensions

Overall length:	
Hatchback models	4360-4399 mm
Estate models	4538 mm
Overall width (including mirrors)	2010 mm
Wheelbase	2648 mm
Track:	
Front	1544 to 1559 mm
Rear	1534 to 1549 mm
Height (without roof bars):	
Hatchback models	1455 to 1485 mm
Estate models	1456 to 1488 mm

Weights

Gross vehicle weight	See Vehicle identification plate on page REF•7
Maximum towing weight	See Vehicle identification plate on page REF•7

Fuel economy

Although depreciation is still the biggest part of the cost of motoring for most car owners, the cost of fuel is more immediately noticeable. These pages give some tips on how to get the best fuel economy.

Working it out

Manufacturer's figures

Car manufacturers are required by law to provide fuel consumption information on all new vehicles sold. These 'official' figures are obtained by simulating various driving conditions on a rolling road or a test track. Real life conditions are different, so the fuel consumption actually achieved may not bear much resemblance to the quoted figures.

How to calculate it

Many cars now have trip computers which will display fuel consumption, both instantaneous and average. Refer to the owner's handbook for details of how to use these.

To calculate consumption yourself (and maybe to check that the trip computer is accurate), proceed as follows.

1. Fill up with fuel and note the mileage, or zero the trip recorder.
2. Drive as usual until you need to fill up again.
3. Note the amount of fuel required to refill the tank, and the mileage covered since the previous fill-up.
4. Divide the mileage by the amount of fuel used to obtain the consumption figure.

For example:

Mileage at first fill-up (a) = 27,903
Mileage at second fill-up (b) = 28,346
Mileage covered (b - a) = 443
Fuel required at second fill-up = 48.6 litres

The half-completed changeover to metric units in the UK means that we buy our fuel in litres, measure distances in miles and talk about fuel consumption in miles per gallon. There are two ways round this: the first is to convert the litres to gallons before doing the calculation (by dividing by 4.546, or see Table 1). So in the example:

48.6 litres ÷ 4.546 = 10.69 gallons
443 miles ÷ 10.69 gallons = 41.4 mpg

The second way is to calculate the consumption in miles per litre, then multiply that figure by 4.546 (or see Table 2).

So in the example, fuel consumption is:

443 miles ÷ 48.6 litres = 9.1 mpl
9.1 mpl x 4.546 = 41.4 mpg

The rest of Europe expresses fuel consumption in litres of fuel required to travel 100 km (l/100 km). For interest, the conversions are given in Table 3. In practice it doesn't matter what units you use, provided you know what your normal consumption is and can spot if it's getting better or worse.

Table 1: conversion of litres to Imperial gallons

litres	1	2	3	4	5	10	20	30	40	50	60	70
gallons	0.22	0.44	0.66	0.88	1.10	2.24	4.49	6.73	8.98	11.22	13.47	15.71

Table 2: conversion of miles per litre to miles per gallon

miles per litre	5	6	7	8	9	10	11	12	13	14
miles per gallon	23	27	32	36	41	46	50	55	59	64

Table 3: conversion of litres per 100 km to miles per gallon

litres per 100 km	4	4.5	5	5.5	6	6.5	7	8	9	10
miles per gallon	71	63	56	51	47	43	40	35	31	28

Maintenance

A well-maintained car uses less fuel and creates less pollution. In particular:

Filters

Change air and fuel filters at the specified intervals.

Oil

Use a good quality oil of the lowest viscosity specified by the vehicle manufacturer (see *Lubricants and fluids*). Check the level often and be careful not to overfill.

Spark plugs

When applicable, renew at the specified intervals.

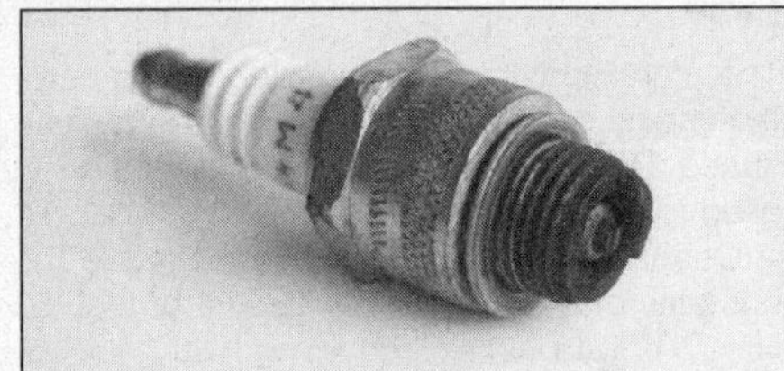

Tyres

Check tyre pressures regularly. Under-inflated tyres have an increased rolling resistance. It is generally safe to use the higher pressures specified for full load conditions even when not fully laden, but keep an eye on the centre band of tread for signs of wear due to over-inflation.

When buying new tyres, consider the 'fuel saving' models which most manufacturers include in their ranges.

Driving style

Acceleration

Acceleration uses more fuel than driving at a steady speed. The best technique with modern cars is to accelerate reasonably briskly to the desired speed, changing up through the gears as soon as possible without making the engine labour.

Air conditioning

Air conditioning absorbs quite a bit of energy from the engine – typically 3 kW (4 hp) or so. The effect on fuel consumption is at its worst in slow traffic. Switch it off when not required.

Anticipation

Drive smoothly and try to read the traffic flow so as to avoid unnecessary acceleration and braking.

Automatic transmission

When accelerating in an automatic, avoid depressing the throttle so far as to make the transmission hold onto lower gears at higher speeds. Don't use the 'Sport' setting, if applicable.

When stationary with the engine running, select 'N' or 'P'. When moving, keep your left foot away from the brake.

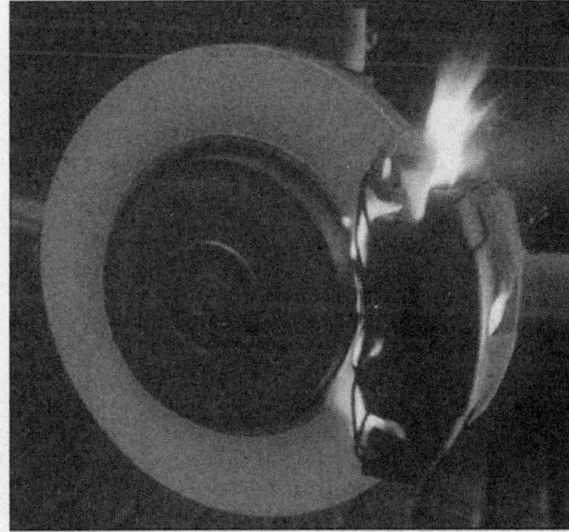

Braking

Braking converts the car's energy of motion into heat – essentially, it is wasted. Obviously some braking is always going to be necessary, but with good anticipation it is surprising how much can be avoided, especially on routes that you know well.

Carshare

Consider sharing lifts to work or to the shops. Even once a week will make a difference.

Electrical loads

Electricity is 'fuel' too; the alternator which charges the battery does so by converting some of the engine's energy of motion into electrical energy. The more electrical accessories are in use, the greater the load on the alternator. Switch off big consumers like the heated rear window when not required.

Freewheeling

Freewheeling (coasting) in neutral with the engine switched off is dangerous. The effort required to operate power-assisted brakes and steering increases when the engine is not running, with a potential lack of control in emergency situations.

In any case, modern fuel injection systems automatically cut off the engine's fuel supply on the overrun (moving and in gear, but with the accelerator pedal released).

Gadgets

Bolt-on devices claiming to save fuel have been around for nearly as long as the motor car itself. Those which worked were rapidly adopted as standard equipment by the vehicle manufacturers. Others worked only in certain situations, or saved fuel only at the expense of unacceptable effects on performance, driveability or the life of engine components.

The most effective fuel saving gadget is the driver's right foot.

Journey planning

Combine (eg) a trip to the supermarket with a visit to the recycling centre and the DIY store, rather than making separate journeys.

When possible choose a travelling time outside rush hours.

Load

The more heavily a car is laden, the greater the energy required to accelerate it to a given speed. Remove heavy items which you don't need to carry.

One load which is often overlooked is the contents of the fuel tank. A tankful of fuel (55 litres / 12 gallons) weighs 45 kg (100 lb) or so. Just half filling it may be worthwhile.

Lost?

At the risk of stating the obvious, if you're going somewhere new, have details of the route to hand. There's not much point in achieving record mpg if you also go miles out of your way.

Parking

If possible, carry out any reversing or turning manoeuvres when you arrive at a parking space so that you can drive straight out when you leave. Manoeuvering when the engine is cold uses a lot more fuel.

Driving around looking for free on-street parking may cost more in fuel than buying a car park ticket.

Premium fuel

Most major oil companies (and some supermarkets) have premium grades of fuel which are several pence a litre dearer than the standard grades. Reports vary, but the consensus seems to be that if these fuels improve economy at all, they do not do so by enough to justify their extra cost.

Roof rack

When loading a roof rack, try to produce a wedge shape with the narrow end at the front. Any cover should be securely fastened – if it flaps it's creating turbulence and absorbing energy.

Remove roof racks and boxes when not in use – they increase air resistance and can create a surprising amount of noise.

Short journeys

The engine is at its least efficient, and wear is highest, during the first few miles after a cold start. Consider walking, cycling or using public transport.

Speed

The engine is at its most efficient when running at a steady speed and load at the rpm where it develops maximum torque. (You can find this figure in the car's handbook.) For most cars this corresponds to between 55 and 65 mph in top gear.

Above the optimum cruising speed, fuel consumption starts to rise quite sharply. A car travelling at 80 mph will typically be using 30% more fuel than at 60 mph.

Supermarket fuel

It may be cheap but is it any good? In the UK all supermarket fuel must meet the relevant British Standard. The major oil companies will say that their branded fuels have better additive packages which may stop carbon and other deposits building up. A reasonable compromise might be to use one tank of branded fuel to three or four from the supermarket.

Switch off when stationary

Switch off the engine if you look like being stationary for more than 30 seconds or so. This is good for the environment as well as for your pocket. Be aware though that frequent restarts are hard on the battery and the starter motor.

Windows

Driving with the windows open increases air turbulence around the vehicle. Closing the windows promotes smooth airflow and reduced resistance. The faster you go, the more significant this is.

And finally . . .

Driving techniques associated with good fuel economy tend to involve moderate acceleration and low top speeds. Be considerate to the needs of other road users who may need to make brisker progress; even if you do not agree with them this is not an excuse to be obstructive.

Safety must always take precedence over economy, whether it is a question of accelerating hard to complete an overtaking manoeuvre, killing your speed when confronted with a potential hazard or switching the lights on when it starts to get dark.

Conversion factors

Length (distance)

Inches (in)	x 25.4	= Millimetres (mm)	x 0.0394	= Inches (in)
Feet (ft)	x 0.305	= Metres (m)	x 3.281	= Feet (ft)
Miles	x 1.609	= Kilometres (km)	x 0.621	= Miles

Volume (capacity)

Cubic inches (cu in; in^3)	x 16.387	= Cubic centimetres (cc; cm^3)	x 0.061	= Cubic inches (cu in; in^3)
Imperial pints (Imp pt)	x 0.568	= Litres (l)	x 1.76	= Imperial pints (Imp pt)
Imperial quarts (Imp qt)	x 1.137	= Litres (l)	x 0.88	= Imperial quarts (Imp qt)
Imperial quarts (Imp qt)	x 1.201	= US quarts (US qt)	x 0.833	= Imperial quarts (Imp qt)
US quarts (US qt)	x 0.946	= Litres (l)	x 1.057	= US quarts (US qt)
Imperial gallons (Imp gal)	x 4.546	= Litres (l)	x 0.22	= Imperial gallons (Imp gal)
Imperial gallons (Imp gal)	x 1.201	= US gallons (US gal)	x 0.833	= Imperial gallons (Imp gal)
US gallons (US gal)	x 3.785	= Litres (l)	x 0.264	= US gallons (US gal)

Mass (weight)

Ounces (oz)	x 28.35	= Grams (g)	x 0.035	= Ounces (oz)
Pounds (lb)	x 0.454	= Kilograms (kg)	x 2.205	= Pounds (lb)

Force

Ounces-force (ozf; oz)	x 0.278	= Newtons (N)	x 3.6	= Ounces-force (ozf; oz)
Pounds-force (lbf; lb)	x 4.448	= Newtons (N)	x 0.225	= Pounds-force (lbf; lb)
Newtons (N)	x 0.1	= Kilograms-force (kgf; kg)	x 9.81	= Newtons (N)

Pressure

Pounds-force per square inch (psi; lbf/in^2; lb/in^2)	x 0.070	= Kilograms-force per square centimetre (kgf/cm^2; kg/cm^2)	x 14.223	= Pounds-force per square inch (psi; lbf/in^2; lb/in^2)
Pounds-force per square inch (psi; lbf/in^2; lb/in^2)	x 0.068	= Atmospheres (atm)	x 14.696	= Pounds-force per square inch (psi; lbf/in^2; lb/in^2)
Pounds-force per square inch (psi; lbf/in^2; lb/in^2)	x 0.069	= Bars	x 14.5	= Pounds-force per square inch (psi; lbf/in^2; lb/in^2)
Pounds-force per square inch (psi; lbf/in^2; lb/in^2)	x 6.895	= Kilopascals (kPa)	x 0.145	= Pounds-force per square inch (psi; lbf/in^2; lb/in^2)
Kilopascals (kPa)	x 0.01	= Kilograms-force per square centimetre (kgf/cm^2; kg/cm^2)	x 98.1	= Kilopascals (kPa)
Millibar (mbar)	x 100	= Pascals (Pa)	x 0.01	= Millibar (mbar)
Millibar (mbar)	x 0.0145	= Pounds-force per square inch (psi; lbf/in^2; lb/in^2)	x 68.947	= Millibar (mbar)
Millibar (mbar)	x 0.75	= Millimetres of mercury (mmHg)	x 1.333	= Millibar (mbar)
Millibar (mbar)	x 0.401	= Inches of water (inH$_2$O)	x 2.491	= Millibar (mbar)
Millimetres of mercury (mmHg)	x 0.535	= Inches of water (inH$_2$O)	x 1.868	= Millimetres of mercury (mmHg)
Inches of water (inH$_2$O)	x 0.036	= Pounds-force per square inch (psi; lbf/in^2; lb/in^2)	x 27.68	= Inches of water (inH$_2$O)

Torque (moment of force)

Pounds-force inches (lbf in; lb in)	x 1.152	= Kilograms-force centimetre (kgf cm; kg cm)	x 0.868	= Pounds-force inches (lbf in; lb in)
Pounds-force inches (lbf in; lb in)	x 0.113	= Newton metres (Nm)	x 8.85	= Pounds-force inches (lbf in; lb in)
Pounds-force inches (lbf in; lb in)	x 0.083	= Pounds-force feet (lbf ft; lb ft)	x 12	= Pounds-force inches (lbf in; lb in)
Pounds-force feet (lbf ft; lb ft)	x 0.138	= Kilograms-force metres (kgf m; kg m)	x 7.233	= Pounds-force feet (lbf ft; lb ft)
Pounds-force feet (lbf ft; lb ft)	x 1.356	= Newton metres (Nm)	x 0.738	= Pounds-force feet (lbf ft; lb ft)
Newton metres (Nm)	x 0.102	= Kilograms-force metres (kgf m; kg m)	x 9.804	= Newton metres (Nm)

Power

Horsepower (hp)	x 745.7	= Watts (W)	x 0.0013	= Horsepower (hp)

Velocity (speed)

Miles per hour (miles/hr; mph)	x 1.609	= Kilometres per hour (km/hr; kph)	x 0.621	= Miles per hour (miles/hr; mph)

Fuel consumption*

Miles per gallon, Imperial (mpg)	x 0.354	= Kilometres per litre (km/l)	x 2.825	= Miles per gallon, Imperial (mpg)
Miles per gallon, US (mpg)	x 0.425	= Kilometres per litre (km/l)	x 2.352	= Miles per gallon, US (mpg)

Temperature

Degrees Fahrenheit = (°C x 1.8) + 32

Degrees Celsius (Degrees Centigrade; °C) = (°F - 32) x 0.56

** It is common practice to convert from miles per gallon (mpg) to litres/100 kilometres (l/100km), where mpg x l/100 km = 282*

Spare parts are available from many sources, including maker's appointed garages, accessory shops, and motor factors. To be sure of obtaining the correct parts, it will sometimes be necessary to quote the vehicle identification number. If possible, it can also be useful to take the old parts along for positive identification. Items such as starter motors and alternators may be available under a service exchange scheme – any parts returned should be clean.

Our advice regarding spare parts is as follows.

Officially appointed garages

This is the best source of parts which are peculiar to your car, and which are not otherwise generally available (eg, badges, interior trim, certain body panels, etc). It is also the only place at which you should buy parts if the vehicle is still under warranty.

Accessory shops

These are very good places to buy materials and components needed for the maintenance of your car (oil, air and fuel filters, light bulbs, drivebelts, greases, brake pads, touch-up paint, etc). Components of this nature sold by a reputable shop are usually of the same standard as those used by the car manufacturer.

Besides components, these shops also sell tools and general accessories, usually have convenient opening hours, charge lower prices, and can often be found close to home. Some accessory shops have parts counters where components needed for almost any repair job can be purchased or ordered.

Motor factors

Good factors will stock all the more important components which wear out comparatively quickly, and can sometimes supply individual components needed for the overhaul of a larger assembly (eg, brake seals and hydraulic parts, bearing shells, pistons, valves). They may also handle work such as cylinder block reboring, crankshaft regrinding, etc.

Tyre and exhaust specialists

These outlets may be independent, or members of a local or national chain. They frequently offer competitive prices when compared with a main dealer or local garage, but it will pay to obtain several quotes before making a decision. When researching prices, also ask what extras may be added – for instance fitting a new valve and balancing the wheel are both commonly charged on top of the price of a new tyre.

Other sources

Beware of parts or materials obtained from market stalls, car boot sales or similar outlets. Such items are not invariably sub-standard, but there is little chance of compensation if they do prove unsatisfactory. in the case of safety-critical components such as brake pads, there is the risk not only of financial loss, but also of an accident causing injury or death.

Second-hand components or assemblies obtained from a car breaker can be a good buy in some circumstances, but this sort of purchase is best made by the experienced DIY mechanic.

Vehicle identification numbers

1 Modifications are a continuing and unpublicised process in vehicle manufacture, quite apart from major model changes. Spare parts manuals and lists are compiled upon a numerical basis, the individual vehicle identification numbers being essential to correct identification of the component concerned.

2 When ordering spare parts, always give as much information as possible. Quote the car model, year of manufacture, body and engine numbers as appropriate.

3 The vehicle identification plate is situated on the driver's side B-pillar **(see illustration)**. The vehicle identification number is also repeated in the form of plate visible through the windscreen on the passenger's side **(see illustration)**, And it can also be seen under the bonnet, stamped into the front right hand inner wing panel.

4 The engine number is located on the left-hand front side of the engine cylinder block. Other identification numbers or codes are stamped on major items such as the gearbox, etc.

5 The vehicle weights are also located on the VIN plate, which is attached to the driver's side door B-pillar. They are listed under the chassis number, in the following order:

Gross vehicle weight
Gross train weight
Maximum permissible front axle load
Maximum permissible rear axle load

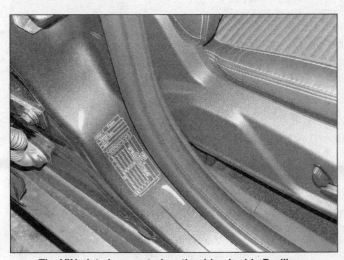

The VIN plate is mounted on the driver's side B-pillar...

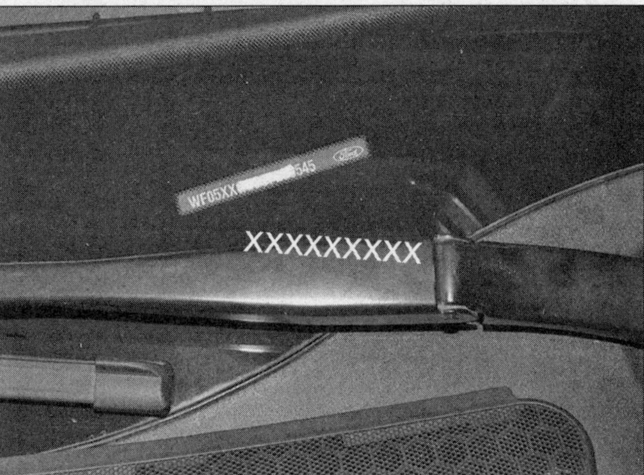

...and on a plate on the facia (visible through the windscreen)

Whenever servicing, repair or overhaul work is carried out on the car or its components, observe the following procedures and instructions. This will assist in carrying out the operation efficiently and to a professional standard of workmanship.

Joint mating faces and gaskets

When separating components at their mating faces, never insert screwdrivers or similar implements into the joint between the faces in order to prise them apart. This can cause severe damage which results in oil leaks, coolant leaks, etc upon reassembly. Separation is usually achieved by tapping along the joint with a soft-faced hammer in order to break the seal. However, note that this method may not be suitable where dowels are used for component location.

Where a gasket is used between the mating faces of two components, a new one must be fitted on reassembly; fit it dry unless otherwise stated in the repair procedure. Make sure that the mating faces are clean and dry, with all traces of old gasket removed. When cleaning a joint face, use a tool which is unlikely to score or damage the face, and remove any burrs or nicks with an oilstone or fine file.

Make sure that tapped holes are cleaned with a pipe cleaner, and keep them free of jointing compound, if this is being used, unless specifically instructed otherwise.

Ensure that all orifices, channels or pipes are clear, and blow through them, preferably using compressed air.

Oil seals

Oil seals can be removed by levering them out with a wide flat-bladed screwdriver or similar implement. Alternatively, a number of self-tapping screws may be screwed into the seal, and these used as a purchase for pliers or some similar device in order to pull the seal free.

Whenever an oil seal is removed from its working location, either individually or as part of an assembly, it should be renewed.

The very fine sealing lip of the seal is easily damaged, and will not seal if the surface it contacts is not completely clean and free from scratches, nicks or grooves. If the original sealing surface of the component cannot be restored, and the manufacturer has not made provision for slight relocation of the seal relative to the sealing surface, the component should be renewed.

Protect the lips of the seal from any surface which may damage them in the course of fitting. Use tape or a conical sleeve where possible. Where indicated, lubricate the seal lips with oil before fitting and, on dual-lipped seals, fill the space between the lips with grease.

Unless otherwise stated, oil seals must be fitted with their sealing lips toward the lubricant to be sealed.

Use a tubular drift or block of wood of the appropriate size to install the seal and, if the seal housing is shouldered, drive the seal down to the shoulder. If the seal housing is unshouldered, the seal should be fitted with its face flush with the housing top face (unless otherwise instructed).

Screw threads and fastenings

Seized nuts, bolts and screws are quite a common occurrence where corrosion has set in, and the use of penetrating oil or releasing fluid will often overcome this problem if the offending item is soaked for a while before attempting to release it. The use of an impact driver may also provide a means of releasing such stubborn fastening devices, when used in conjunction with the appropriate screwdriver bit or socket. If none of these methods works, it may be necessary to resort to the careful application of heat, or the use of a hacksaw or nut splitter device. Before resorting to extreme methods, check that you are not dealing with a left-hand thread!

Studs are usually removed by locking two nuts together on the threaded part, and then using a spanner on the lower nut to unscrew the stud. Studs or bolts which have broken off below the surface of the component in which they are mounted can sometimes be removed using a stud extractor.

Always ensure that a blind tapped hole is completely free from oil, grease, water or other fluid before installing the bolt or stud. Failure to do this could cause the housing to crack due to the hydraulic action of the bolt or stud as it is screwed in.

For some screw fastenings, notably cylinder head bolts or nuts, torque wrench settings are no longer specified for the latter stages of tightening, "angle-tightening" being called up instead. Typically, a fairly low torque wrench setting will be applied to the bolts/nuts in the correct sequence, followed by one or more stages of tightening through specified angles.

When checking or retightening a nut or bolt to a specified torque setting, slacken the nut or bolt by a quarter of a turn, and then retighten to the specified setting. However, this should not be attempted where angular tightening has been used.

Locknuts, locktabs and washers

Any fastening which will rotate against a component or housing during tightening should always have a washer between it and the relevant component or housing.

Spring or split washers should always be renewed when they are used to lock a critical component such as a big-end bearing retaining bolt or nut. Locktabs which are folded over to retain a nut or bolt should always be renewed.

Self-locking nuts can be re-used in non-critical areas, providing resistance can be felt when the locking portion passes over the bolt or stud thread. However, it should be noted that self-locking stiffnuts tend to lose their effectiveness after long periods of use, and should then be renewed as a matter of course.

Split pins must always be replaced with new ones of the correct size for the hole.

When thread-locking compound is found on the threads of a fastener which is to be re-used, it should be cleaned off with a wire brush and solvent, and fresh compound applied on reassembly.

Special tools

Some repair procedures in this manual entail the use of special tools such as a press, two or three-legged pullers, spring compressors, etc. Wherever possible, suitable readily-available alternatives to the manufacturer's special tools are described, and are shown in use. In some instances, where no alternative is possible, it has been necessary to resort to the use of a manufacturer's tool, and this has been done for reasons of safety as well as the efficient completion of the repair operation. Unless you are highly-skilled and have a thorough understanding of the procedures described, never attempt to bypass the use of any special tool when the procedure described specifies its use. Not only is there a very great risk of personal injury, but expensive damage could be caused to the components involved.

Environmental considerations

When disposing of used engine oil, brake fluid, antifreeze, etc, give due consideration to any detrimental environmental effects. Do not, for instance, pour any of the above liquids down drains into the general sewage system, or onto the ground to soak away. Many local council refuse tips provide a facility for waste oil disposal, as do some garages. You can find your nearest disposal point by calling the Environment Agency on 08708 506 506 or by visiting www.oilbankline.org.uk.

Note: It is illegal and anti-social to dump oil down the drain. To find the location of your local oil recycling bank, call 08708 506 506 or visit www.oilbankline.org.uk.

The jack supplied with the vehicle tool kit should only be used for changing the roadwheels – see Wheel changing at the front of this manual. When carrying out any other kind of work, raise the vehicle using a hydraulic trolley jack, and always supplement the jack with axle stands positioned under the vehicle jacking points.

When using a trolley jack or axle stands, position the jack head or axle stand head adjacent to one of the relevant wheel changing jacking points under the sills **(see illustration)**. Use a block of wood between the jack or axle stand and the sill.

Do not attempt to jack the vehicle under the sump, or any of the suspension components.

The jack supplied with the vehicle locates in the jacking points on the underside of the sills – see Wheel changing at the front of this manual. Ensure that the jack head is correctly engaged before attempting to raise the vehicle.

Never work under, around, or near a raised vehicle, unless it is adequately supported in at least two places.

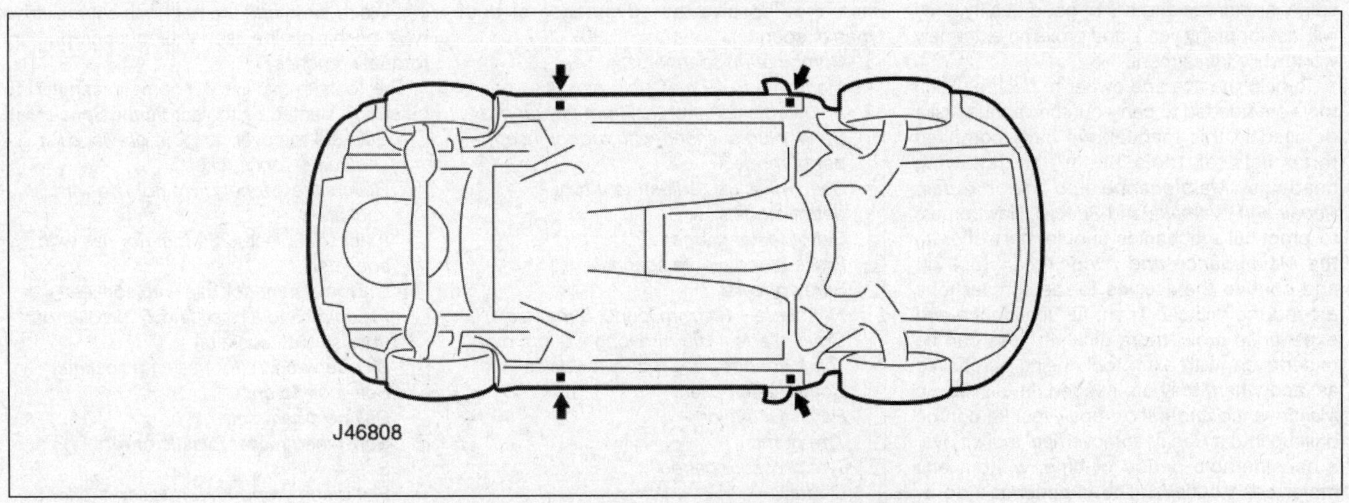

Use a workshop/trolley jack at the points indicated

Tools and working facilities

Introduction

A selection of good tools is a fundamental requirement for anyone contemplating the maintenance and repair of a motor vehicle. For the owner who does not possess any, their purchase will prove a considerable expense, offsetting some of the savings made by doing-it-yourself. However, provided that the tools purchased meet the relevant national safety standards and are of good quality, they will last for many years and prove an extremely worthwhile investment.

To help the average owner to decide which tools are needed to carry out the various tasks detailed in this manual, we have compiled three lists of tools under the following headings: *Maintenance and minor repair*, *Repair and overhaul*, and *Special*. Newcomers to practical mechanics should start off with the *Maintenance and minor repair* tool kit, and confine themselves to the simpler jobs around the vehicle. Then, as confidence and experience grow, more difficult tasks can be undertaken, with extra tools being purchased as, and when, they are needed. In this way, a *Maintenance and minor repair* tool kit can be built up into a *Repair and overhaul* tool kit over a considerable period of time, without any major cash outlays. The experienced do-it-yourselfer will have a tool kit good enough for most repair and overhaul procedures, and will add tools from the *Special* category when it is felt that the expense is justified by the amount of use to which these tools will be put.

Maintenance and minor repair tool kit

The tools given in this list should be considered as a minimum requirement if routine maintenance, servicing and minor repair operations are to be undertaken. We recommend the purchase of combination spanners (ring one end, open-ended the other); although more expensive than open-ended ones, they do give the advantages of both types of spanner.

☐ *Combination spanners:*
Metric - 8 to 19 mm inclusive
☐ *Adjustable spanner - 35 mm jaw (approx.)*
☐ *Spark plug spanner (with rubber insert) - petrol models*
☐ *Spark plug gap adjustment tool - petrol models*
☐ *Set of feeler gauges*
☐ *Brake bleed nipple spanner*
☐ *Screwdrivers:*
Flat blade - 100 mm long x 6 mm dia
Cross blade - 100 mm long x 6 mm dia
Torx - various sizes (not all vehicles)
☐ *Combination pliers*
☐ *Hacksaw (junior)*
☐ *Tyre pump*
☐ *Tyre pressure gauge*
☐ *Oil can*
☐ *Oil filter removal tool (if applicable)*
☐ *Fine emery cloth*
☐ *Wire brush (small)*
☐ *Funnel (medium size)*
☐ *Sump drain plug key (not all vehicles)*

Repair and overhaul tool kit

These tools are virtually essential for anyone undertaking any major repairs to a motor vehicle, and are additional to those given in the *Maintenance and minor repair* list. Included in this list is a comprehensive set of sockets. Although these are expensive, they will be found invaluable as they are so versatile - particularly if various drives are included in the set. We recommend the half-inch square-drive type, as this can be used with most proprietary torque wrenches.

The tools in this list will sometimes need to be supplemented by tools from the *Special* list:

☐ *Sockets to cover range in previous list (including Torx sockets)*
☐ *Reversible ratchet drive (for use with sockets)*
☐ *Extension piece, 250 mm (for use with sockets)*
☐ *Universal joint (for use with sockets)*
☐ *Flexible handle or sliding T "breaker bar" (for use with sockets)*
☐ *Torque wrench (for use with sockets)*
☐ *Self-locking grips*
☐ *Ball pein hammer*
☐ *Soft-faced mallet (plastic or rubber)*
☐ *Screwdrivers:*
Flat blade - long & sturdy, short (chubby), and narrow (electrician's) types
Cross blade – long & sturdy, and short (chubby) types
☐ *Pliers:*
Long-nosed
Side cutters (electrician's)
Circlip (internal and external)
☐ *Cold chisel - 25 mm*
☐ *Scriber*
☐ *Scraper*
☐ *Centre-punch*
☐ *Pin punch*
☐ *Hacksaw*
☐ *Brake hose clamp*
☐ *Brake/clutch bleeding kit*
☐ *Selection of twist drills*
☐ *Steel rule/straight-edge*
☐ *Allen keys (inc. splined/Torx type)*
☐ *Selection of files*
☐ *Wire brush*
☐ *Axle stands*
☐ *Jack (strong trolley or hydraulic type)*
☐ *Light with extension lead*
☐ *Universal electrical multi-meter*

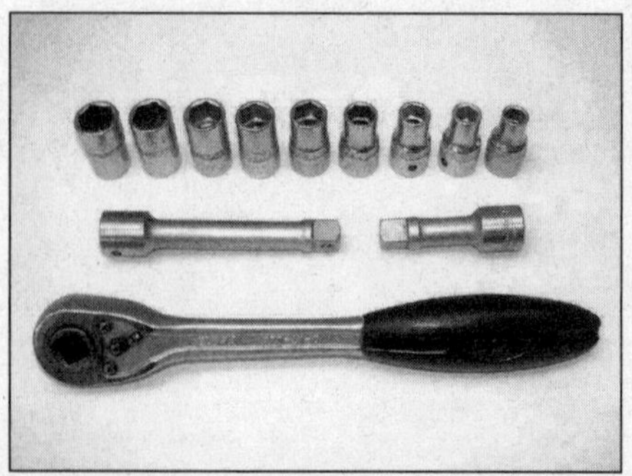

Sockets and reversible ratchet drive

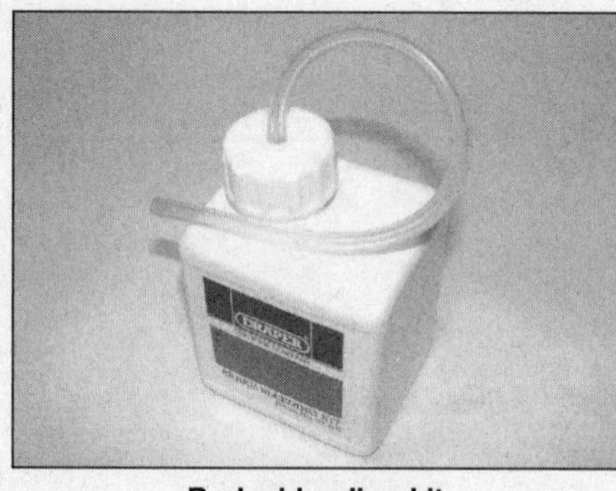

Brake bleeding kit

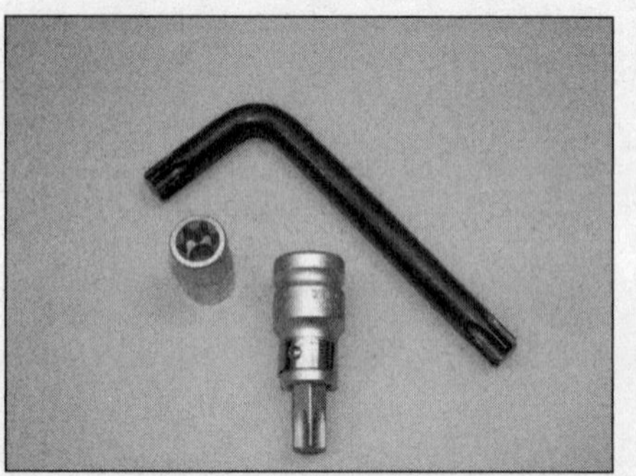

Torx key, socket and bit

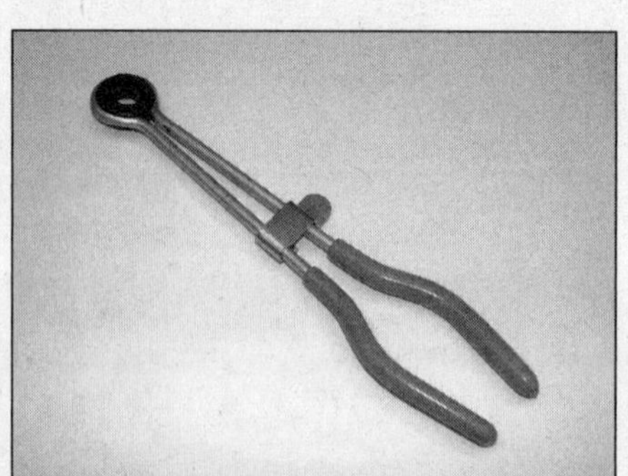

Hose clamp

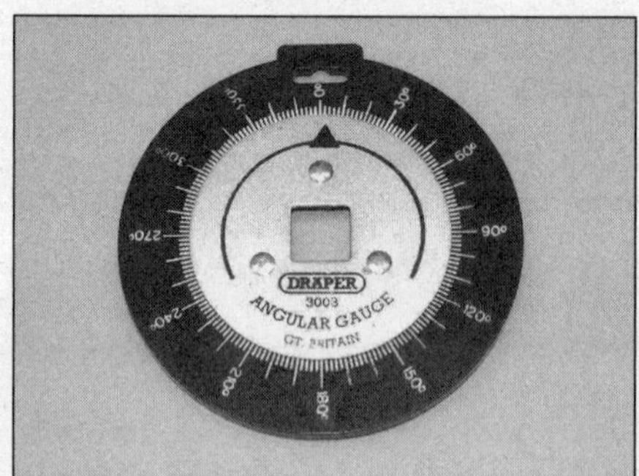

Angular-tightening gauge

Special tools

The tools in this list are those which are not used regularly, are expensive to buy, or which need to be used in accordance with their manufacturers' instructions. Unless relatively difficult mechanical jobs are undertaken frequently, it will not be economic to buy many of these tools. Where this is the case, you could consider clubbing together with friends (or joining a motorists' club) to make a joint purchase, or borrowing the tools against a deposit from a local garage or tool hire specialist.

The following list contains only those tools and instruments freely available to the public, and not those special tools produced by the vehicle manufacturer specifically for its dealer network. You will find occasional references to these manufacturers' special tools in the text of this manual. Generally, an alternative method of doing the job without the vehicle manufacturers' special tool is given. However, sometimes there is no alternative to using them. Where this is the case and the relevant tool cannot be bought or borrowed, you will have to entrust the work to a dealer.

☐ *Angular-tightening gauge*
☐ *Valve spring compressor*
☐ *Valve grinding tool*
☐ *Piston ring compressor*
☐ *Piston ring removal/installation tool*
☐ *Cylinder bore hone*
☐ *Balljoint separator*
☐ *Coil spring compressors (where applicable)*
☐ *Two/three-legged hub and bearing puller*
☐ *Impact screwdriver*
☐ *Micrometer and/or vernier calipers*
☐ *Dial gauge*
☐ *Tachometer*
☐ *Fault code reader*
☐ *Cylinder compression gauge*
☐ *Hand-operated vacuum pump and gauge*
☐ *Clutch plate alignment set*
☐ *Brake shoe steady spring cup removal tool*
☐ *Bush and bearing removal/installation set*
☐ *Stud extractors*
☐ *Tap and die set*
☐ *Lifting tackle*

Buying tools

Reputable motor accessory shops and superstores often offer excellent quality tools at discount prices, so it pays to shop around.

Remember, you don't have to buy the most expensive items on the shelf, but it is always advisable to steer clear of the very cheap tools. Beware of 'bargains' offered on market stalls, on-line or at car boot sales. There are plenty of good tools around at reasonable prices, but always aim to purchase items which meet the relevant national safety standards. If in doubt, ask the proprietor or manager of the shop for advice before making a purchase.

Care and maintenance of tools

Having purchased a reasonable tool kit, it is necessary to keep the tools in a clean and serviceable condition. After use, always wipe off any dirt, grease and metal particles using a clean, dry cloth, before putting the tools away. Never leave them lying around after they have been used. A simple tool rack on the garage or workshop wall for items such as screwdrivers and pliers is a good idea. Store all normal spanners and sockets in a metal box. Any measuring instruments, gauges, meters, etc, must be carefully stored where they cannot be damaged or become rusty.

Take a little care when tools are used. Hammer heads inevitably become marked, and screwdrivers lose the keen edge on their blades from time to time. A little timely attention with emery cloth or a file will soon restore items like this to a good finish.

Working facilities

Not to be forgotten when discussing tools is the workshop itself. If anything more than routine maintenance is to be carried out, a suitable working area becomes essential.

It is appreciated that many an owner-mechanic is forced by circumstances to remove an engine or similar item without the benefit of a garage or workshop. Having done this, any repairs should always be done under the cover of a roof.

Wherever possible, any dismantling should be done on a clean, flat workbench or table at a suitable working height.

Any workbench needs a vice; one with a jaw opening of 100 mm is suitable for most jobs. As mentioned previously, some clean dry storage space is also required for tools, as well as for any lubricants, cleaning fluids, touch-up paints etc, which become necessary.

Another item which may be required, and which has a much more general usage, is an electric drill with a chuck capacity of at least 8 mm. This, together with a good range of twist drills, is virtually essential for fitting accessories.

Last, but not least, always keep a supply of old newspapers and clean, lint-free rags available, and try to keep any working area as clean as possible.

Micrometers

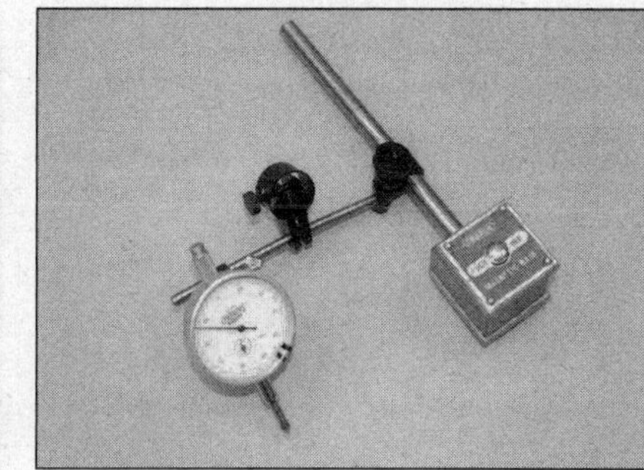

Dial test indicator ("dial gauge")

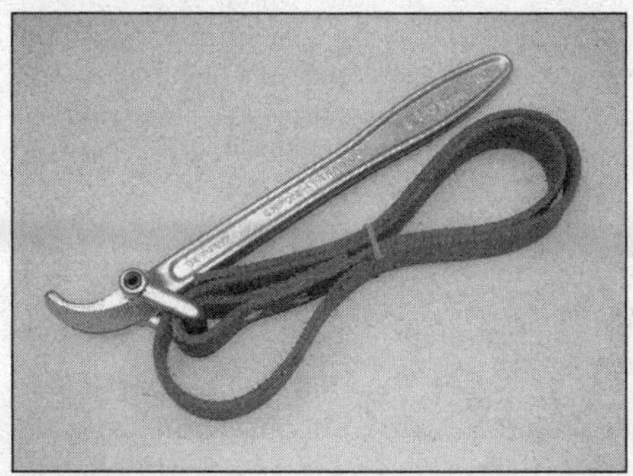

Oil filter removal tool (strap wrench type)

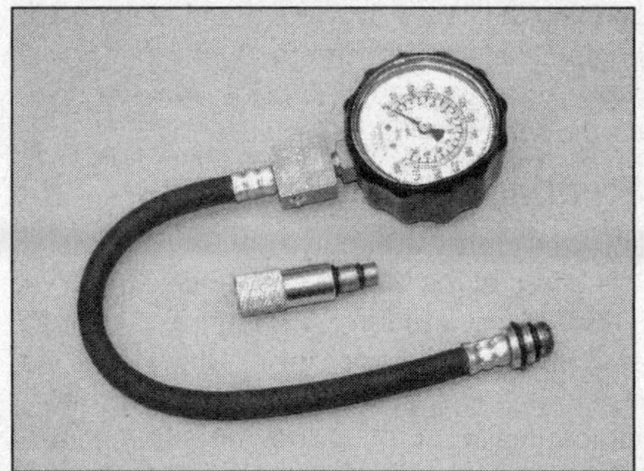

Compression tester

Bearing puller

MOT test checks

This is a guide to getting your vehicle through the MOT test. Obviously it will not be possible to examine the vehicle to the same standard as the professional MOT tester. However, working through the following checks will enable you to identify any problem areas before submitting the vehicle for the test.

It has only been possible to summarise the test requirements here, based on the regulations in force at the time of printing. Test standards are becoming increasingly stringent, although there are some exemptions for older vehicles.

An assistant will be needed to help carry out some of these checks.

The checks have been sub-divided into four categories, as follows:

1 Checks carried out **FROM THE DRIVER'S SEAT**

2 Checks carried out **WITH THE VEHICLE ON THE GROUND**

3 Checks carried out **WITH THE VEHICLE RAISED AND THE WHEELS FREE TO TURN**

4 Checks carried out on **YOUR VEHICLE'S EXHAUST EMISSION SYSTEM**

1 Checks carried out FROM THE DRIVER'S SEAT

Handbrake (parking brake)

☐ Test the operation of the handbrake. Excessive travel (too many clicks) indicates incorrect brake or cable adjustment.

☐ Check that the handbrake cannot be released by tapping the lever sideways. Check the security of the lever mountings.

☐ If the parking brake is foot-operated, check that the pedal is secure and without excessive travel, and that the release mechanism operates correctly.

☐ Where applicable, test the operation of the electronic handbrake. The brake should engage and disengage without excessive delay. If the warning light does not extinguish when the brake is disengaged, this could indicate a fault which will need further investigation.

Footbrake

☐ Depress the brake pedal and check that it does not creep down to the floor, indicating a master cylinder fault. Release the pedal, wait a few seconds, then depress it again. If the pedal travels nearly to the floor before firm resistance is felt, brake adjustment or repair is necessary. If the pedal feels spongy, there is air in the hydraulic system which must be removed by bleeding.

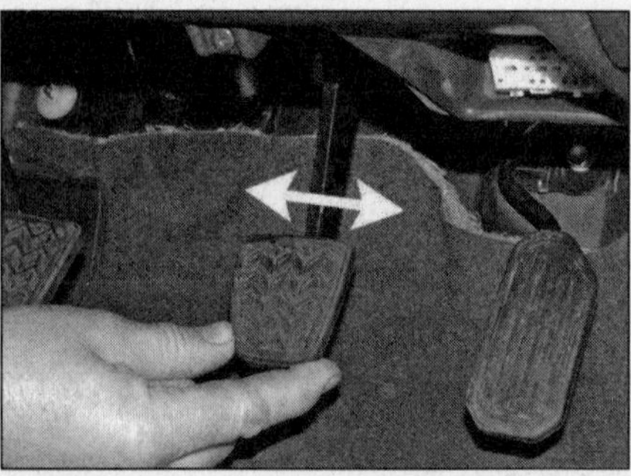

☐ Check that the brake pedal is secure and in good condition. Check also for signs of fluid leaks on the pedal, floor or carpets, which would indicate failed seals in the brake master cylinder.

☐ Check the servo unit (when applicable) by operating the brake pedal several times, then keeping the pedal depressed and starting the engine. As the engine starts, the pedal will move down slightly. If not, the vacuum hose or the servo itself may be faulty.

Steering wheel and column

☐ Examine the steering wheel for fractures or looseness of the hub, spokes or rim.

☐ Move the steering wheel from side to side and then up and down. Check that the steering wheel is not loose on the column, indicating wear or a loose retaining nut. Continue moving the steering wheel as before, but also turn it slightly from left to right.

☐ Check that the steering wheel is not loose on the column, and that there is no abnormal movement of the steering wheel, indicating wear in the column support bearings or couplings.

☐ Check that the ignition lock (where fitted) engages and disengages correctly.

☐ Steering column adjustment mechanisms (where fitted) must be able to lock the column securely in place with no play evident.

Windscreen, mirrors and sunvisor

☐ The windscreen must be free of cracks or other significant damage within the driver's field of view. (Small stone chips are acceptable.) Rear view mirrors must be secure, intact, and capable of being adjusted.

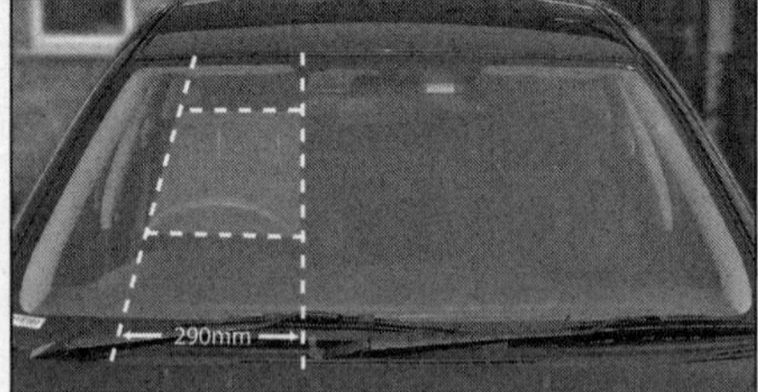

☐ The driver's sunvisor must be capable of being stored in the "up" position.

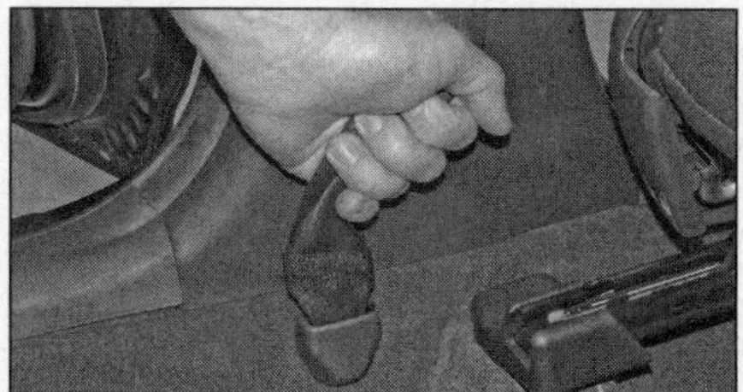

Seat belts and seats

Note: *The following checks are applicable to all seat belts, front and rear.*

☐ Examine the webbing of all the belts (including rear belts if fitted) for cuts, serious fraying or deterioration. Fasten and unfasten each belt to check the buckles. If applicable, check the retracting mechanism. Check the security of all seat belt mountings accessible from inside the vehicle, ensuring any height adjustable mountings lock securely in place.

☐ Seat belts with pre-tensioners, once activated, have a "flag" or similar showing on the seat belt stalk. This, in itself, is not a reason for test failure.

☐ The front seats themselves must be securely attached and the backrests must lock in the upright position.

Doors

☐ Both front doors must be able to be opened and closed from outside and inside, and must latch securely when closed.

Bonnet and boot/tailgate

☐ The bonnet and boot/tailgate must latch securely when closed.

2 Checks carried out WITH THE VEHICLE ON THE GROUND

Vehicle identification

☐ Number plates must be in good condition, secure and legible, with letters and numbers correctly spaced – spacing at (A) should be 33 mm and at (B) 11 mm. At the front, digits must be black on a white background and at the rear black on a yellow background. Other background designs (such as honeycomb) are not permitted.

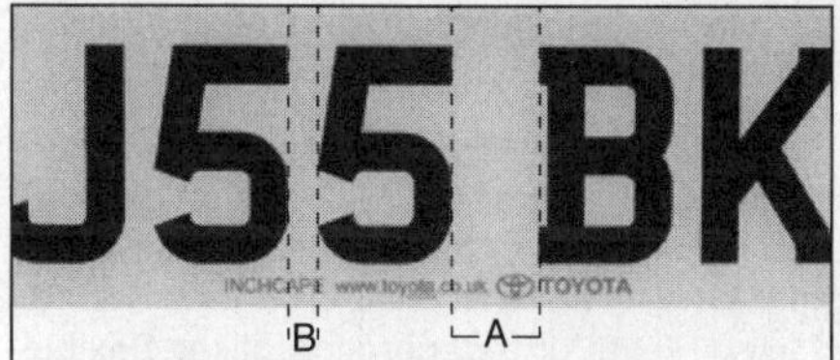

☐ The VIN plate and/or homologation plate must be permanently displayed and legible.

Electrical equipment

☐ Switch on the ignition and check the operation of the horn.

☐ Check the windscreen washers and wipers, examining the wiper blades; renew damaged or perished blades. Also check the operation of the stop-lights.

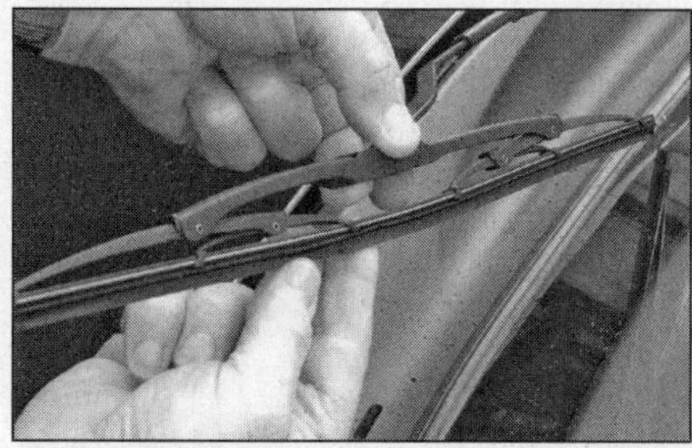

☐ Check the operation of the sidelights and number plate lights. The lenses and reflectors must be secure, clean and undamaged.

☐ Check the operation and alignment of the headlights. The headlight reflectors must not be tarnished and the lenses must be undamaged.

☐ Switch on the ignition and check the operation of the direction indicators (including the instrument panel tell-tale) and the hazard warning lights. Operation of the sidelights and stop-lights must not affect the indicators - if it does, the cause is usually a bad earth at the rear light cluster. Indicators should flash at a rate of between 60 and 120 times per minute – faster or slower than this could indicate a fault with the flasher unit or a bad earth at one of the light units.

☐ Check the operation of the rear foglight(s), including the warning light on the instrument panel or in the switch.

☐ The warning lights must illuminate in accordance with the manufacturer's design. For most vehicles, the ABS and other warning lights should illuminate when the ignition is switched on, and (if the system is operating properly) extinguish after a few seconds. Refer to the owner's handbook.

Footbrake

☐ Examine the master cylinder, brake pipes and servo unit for leaks, loose mountings, corrosion or other damage. If ABS is fitted, this unit should also be examined for signs of leaks or corrosion.

☐ The fluid reservoir must be secure and the fluid level must be between the upper (**A**) and lower (**B**) markings.

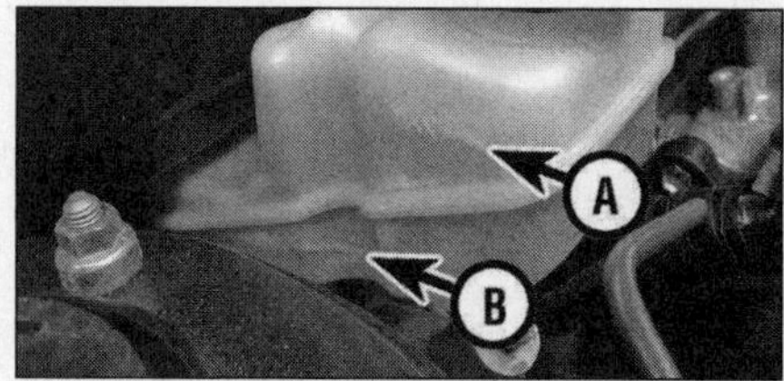

☐ Inspect both front brake flexible hoses for cracks or deterioration of the rubber. Turn the steering from lock to lock, and ensure that the hoses do not contact the wheel, tyre, or any part of the steering or suspension mechanism. With the brake pedal firmly depressed, check the hoses for bulges or leaks under pressure.

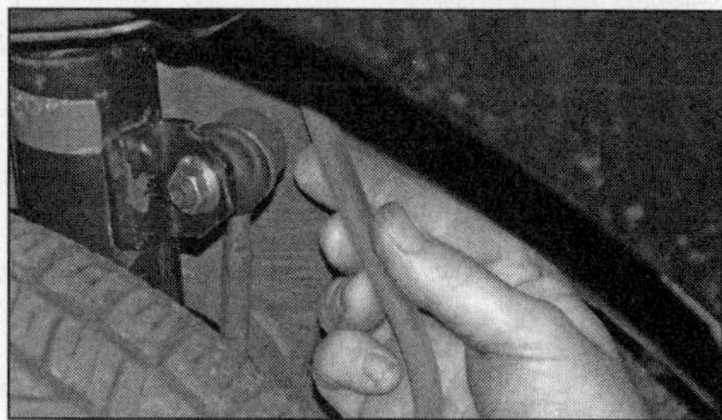

Steering and suspension

☐ Have your assistant turn the steering wheel from side to side slightly, up to the point where the steering gear just begins to transmit this movement to the roadwheels. Check for excessive free play between the steering wheel and the steering gear, indicating wear or insecurity of the steering column joints, the column-to-steering gear coupling, or the steering gear itself.

☐ Have your assistant turn the steering wheel more vigorously in each direction, so that the roadwheels just begin to turn. As this is done, examine all the steering joints, linkages, fittings and attachments. Renew any component that shows signs of wear or damage. On vehicles with power steering, check the security and condition of the steering pump, drivebelt and hoses.

☐ Check that the vehicle is standing level, and at approximately the correct ride height.

Shock absorbers

☐ Depress each corner of the vehicle in turn, then release it. The vehicle should rise and then settle in its normal position. If the vehicle continues to rise and fall, the shock absorber is defective. A shock absorber which has seized will also cause the vehicle to fail.

Exhaust system

☐ Start the engine. With your assistant holding a rag over the tailpipe, check the entire system for leaks. Repair or renew leaking sections.

3 Checks carried out WITH THE VEHICLE RAISED AND THE WHEELS FREE TO TURN

Jack up the front and rear of the vehicle, and securely support it on axle stands. Position the stands clear of the suspension assemblies. Ensure that the wheels are clear of the ground and that the steering can be turned from lock to lock.

Steering mechanism

☐ Have your assistant turn the steering from lock to lock. Check that the steering turns smoothly, and that no part of the steering mechanism, including a wheel or tyre, fouls any brake hose or pipe or any part of the body structure.

☐ Examine the steering rack rubber gaiters for damage or insecurity of the retaining clips. If power steering is fitted, check for signs of damage or leakage of the fluid hoses, pipes or connections. Also check for excessive stiffness or binding of the steering, a missing split pin or locking device, or severe corrosion of the body structure within 30 cm of any steering component attachment point.

Front and rear suspension and wheel bearings

☐ Starting at the front right-hand side, grasp the roadwheel at the 3 o'clock and 9 o'clock positions and rock gently but firmly. Check for free play or insecurity at the wheel bearings, suspension balljoints, or suspension mount-ings, pivots and attachments.

☐ Now grasp the wheel at the 12 o'clock and 6 o'clock positions and repeat the previous inspection. Spin the wheel, and check for roughness or tightness of the front wheel bearing.

☐ If excess free play is suspected at a component pivot point, this can be confirmed by using a large screwdriver or similar tool and levering between the mounting and the component attachment. This will confirm whether the wear is in the pivot bush, its retaining bolt, or in the mounting itself (the bolt holes can often become elongated).

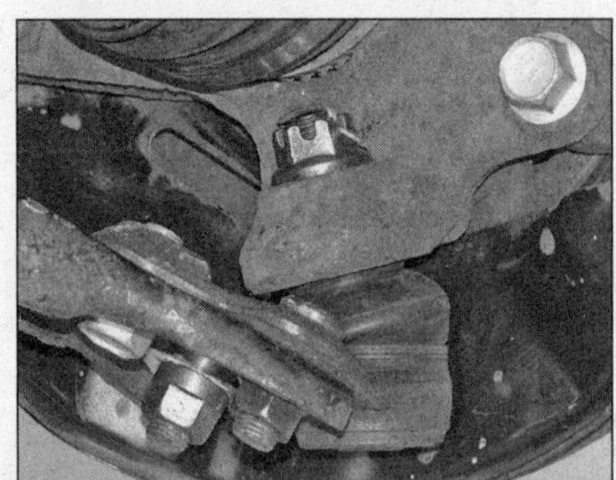

☐ Carry out all the above checks at the other front wheel, and then at both rear wheels.

Springs and shock absorbers

☐ Examine the suspension struts (when applicable) for serious fluid leakage, corrosion, or damage to the casing. Also check the security of the mounting points.

☐ If coil springs are fitted, check that the spring ends locate in their seats, and that the spring is not corroded, cracked or broken.

☐ If leaf springs are fitted, check that all leaves are intact, that the axle is securely attached to each spring, and that there is no deterioration of the spring eye mountings, bushes, and shackles.

☐ The same general checks apply to vehicles fitted with other suspension types, such as torsion bars, hydraulic displacer units, etc. Ensure that all mountings and attachments are secure, that there are no signs of excessive wear, corrosion or damage, and (on hydraulic types) that there are no fluid leaks or damaged pipes.

☐ Inspect the shock absorbers for signs of serious fluid leakage. Check for wear of the mounting bushes or attachments, or damage to the body of the unit.

Driveshafts (fwd vehicles only)

☐ Rotate each front wheel in turn and inspect the constant velocity joint gaiters for splits or damage. Also check that each driveshaft is straight and undamaged.

Braking system

☐ If possible without dismantling, check brake pad wear and disc condition. Ensure that the friction lining material has not worn excessively, (A) and that the discs are not fractured, pitted, scored or badly worn (B).

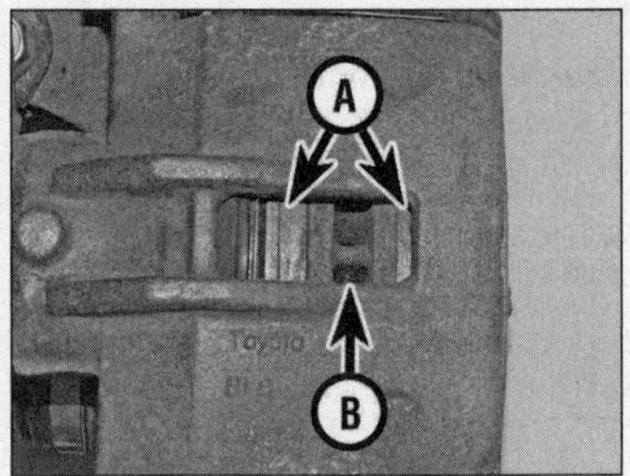

☐ Examine all the rigid brake pipes underneath the vehicle, and the flexible hose(s) at the rear. Look for corrosion, chafing or insecurity of the pipes, and for signs of bulging under pressure, chafing, splits or deterioration of the flexible hoses.

☐ Look for signs of fluid leaks at the brake calipers or on the brake backplates. Repair or renew leaking components.

☐ Slowly spin each wheel, while your assistant depresses and releases the footbrake. Ensure that each brake is operating and does not bind when the pedal is released.

□Examine the handbrake mechanism, checking for frayed or broken cables, excessive corrosion, or wear or insecurity of the linkage. Check that the mechanism works on each relevant wheel, and releases fully, without binding.

□It is not possible to test brake efficiency without special equipment, but a road test can be carried out later to check that the vehicle pulls up in a straight line.

Fuel and exhaust systems

□Inspect the fuel tank (including the filler cap), fuel pipes, hoses and unions. All components must be secure and free from leaks. Locking fuel caps must lock securely and the key must be provided for the MOT test.

□Examine the exhaust system over its entire length, checking for any damaged, broken or missing mountings, security of the retaining clamps and rust or corrosion.

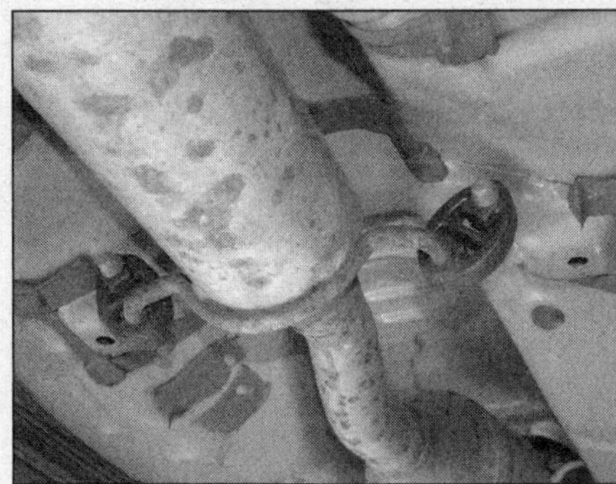

Wheels and tyres

□Examine the sidewalls and tread area of each tyre in turn. Check for cuts, tears, lumps, bulges, separation of the tread, and exposure of the ply or cord due to wear or damage. Check that the tyre bead is correctly seated on the wheel rim, that the valve is sound and properly seated, and that the wheel is not distorted or damaged.

□Check that the tyres are of the correct size for the vehicle, that they are of the same size and type on each axle, and that the pressures are correct.

□Check the tyre tread depth. The legal minimum at the time of writing is 1.6 mm over the central three-quarters of the tread width. Abnormal tread wear may indicate incorrect front wheel alignment or wear in steering or suspension components.

□If the spare wheel is fitted externally or in a separate carrier beneath the vehicle, check that mountings are secure and free of excessive corrosion.

Body corrosion

□Check the condition of the entire vehicle structure for signs of corrosion in load-bearing areas. (These include chassis box sections, side sills, cross-members, pillars, and all suspension, steering, braking system and seat belt mountings and anchorages.) Any corrosion which has seriously reduced the thickness of a load-bearing area (or is within 30 cm of safety-related components such as steering or suspension) is likely to cause the vehicle to fail. In this case professional repairs are likely to be needed.

□Damage or corrosion which causes sharp or otherwise dangerous edges to be exposed will also cause the vehicle to fail.

Towbars

□Check the condition of mounting points (both beneath the vehicle and within boot/ hatchback areas) for signs of corrosion, ensuring that all fixings are secure and not worn or damaged. There must be no excessive play in detachable tow ball arms or quick-release mechanisms.

4 Checks carried out on **YOUR VEHICLE'S EXHAUST EMISSION SYSTEM**

Petrol models

□The engine should be warmed up, and running well (ignition system in good order, air filter element clean, etc).

□Before testing, run the engine at around 2500 rpm for 20 seconds. Let the engine drop to idle, and watch for smoke from the exhaust. If the idle speed is too high, or if dense blue or black smoke emerges for more than 5 seconds, the vehicle will fail. Typically, blue smoke signifies oil burning (engine wear); black smoke means unburnt fuel (dirty air cleaner element, or other fuel system fault).

□An exhaust gas analyser for measuring carbon monoxide (CO) and hydrocarbons (HC) is now needed. If one cannot be hired or borrowed, have a local garage perform the check.

CO emissions (mixture)

□The MOT tester has access to the CO limits for all vehicles. The CO level is measured at idle speed, and at 'fast idle' (2500 to 3000 rpm). The following limits are given as a general guide:

At idle speed – Less than 0.5% CO
At 'fast idle' – Less than 0.3% CO
Lambda reading – 0.97 to 1.03

□If the CO level is too high, this may point to poor maintenance, a fuel injection system problem, faulty lambda (oxygen) sensor or catalytic converter. Try an injector cleaning treatment, and check the vehicle's ECU for fault codes.

HC emissions

□The MOT tester has access to HC limits for all vehicles. The HC level is measured at 'fast idle' (2500 to 3000 rpm). The following limits are given as a general guide:

At 'fast idle' – Less then 200 ppm

□Excessive HC emissions are typically caused by oil being burnt (worn engine), or by a blocked crankcase ventilation system ('breather'). If the engine oil is old and thin, an oil change may help. If the engine is running badly, check the vehicle's ECU for fault codes.

Diesel models

□The only emission test for diesel engines is measuring exhaust smoke density, using a calibrated smoke meter. The test involves accelerating the engine at least 3 times to its maximum unloaded speed.

Note: *On engines with a timing belt, it is VITAL that the belt is in good condition before the test is carried out.*

□With the engine warmed up, it is first purged by running at around 2500 rpm for 20 seconds. A governor check is then carried out, by slowly accelerating the engine to its maximum speed. After this, the smoke meter is connected, and the engine is accelerated quickly to maximum speed three times. If the smoke density is less than the limits given below, the vehicle will pass:

Non-turbo vehicles: 2.5m-1
Turbocharged vehicles: 3.0m-1

□If excess smoke is produced, try fitting a new air cleaner element, or using an injector cleaning treatment. If the engine is running badly, where applicable, check the vehicle's ECU for fault codes. Also check the vehicle's EGR system, where applicable. At high mileages, the injectors may require professional attention.

Engine

- ☐ Engine fails to rotate when attempting to start
- ☐ Engine rotates, but will not start
- ☐ Engine difficult to start when cold
- ☐ Engine difficult to start when hot
- ☐ Starter motor noisy or excessively-rough in engagement
- ☐ Engine starts, but stops immediately
- ☐ Engine idles erratically
- ☐ Engine misfires at idle speed
- ☐ Engine misfires throughout the driving speed range
- ☐ Engine hesitates on acceleration
- ☐ Engine stalls
- ☐ Engine lacks power
- ☐ Engine backfires
- ☐ Oil pressure warning light illuminated with engine running
- ☐ Engine runs-on after switching off
- ☐ Engine noises

Cooling system

- ☐ Overheating
- ☐ Overcooling
- ☐ External coolant leakage
- ☐ Internal coolant leakage
- ☐ Corrosion

Fuel and exhaust systems

- ☐ Excessive fuel consumption
- ☐ Fuel leakage and/or fuel odour
- ☐ Excessive noise or fumes from exhaust system

Clutch

- ☐ Pedal travels to floor – no pressure or very little resistance
- ☐ Clutch fails to disengage (unable to select gears)
- ☐ Clutch slips (engine speed increases, with no increase in vehicle speed)
- ☐ Judder as clutch is engaged
- ☐ Noise when depressing or releasing clutch pedal

Manual transmission

- ☐ Noisy in neutral with engine running
- ☐ Noisy in one particular gear
- ☐ Difficulty engaging gears
- ☐ Jumps out of gear
- ☐ Vibration
- ☐ Lubricant leaks

Driveshafts

- ☐ Vibration when accelerating or decelerating
- ☐ Clicking or knocking noise on turns (at slow speed on full-lock)

Braking system

- ☐ Vehicle pulls to one side under braking
- ☐ Noise (grinding or high-pitched squeal) when brakes applied
- ☐ Excessive brake pedal travel
- ☐ Brake pedal feels spongy when depressed
- ☐ Excessive brake pedal effort required to stop vehicle
- ☐ Judder felt through brake pedal or steering wheel when braking
- ☐ Pedal pulsates when braking hard
- ☐ Brakes binding
- ☐ Rear wheels locking under normal braking

Steering and suspension

- ☐ Vehicle pulls to one side
- ☐ Wheel wobble and vibration
- ☐ Excessive pitching and/or rolling around corners, or during braking
- ☐ Wandering or general instability
- ☐ Excessively-stiff steering
- ☐ Excessive play in steering
- ☐ Lack of power assistance
- ☐ Tyre wear excessive

Electrical system

- ☐ Battery will not hold a charge more than a few days
- ☐ Ignition/no-charge warning light remains illuminated with engine running
- ☐ Ignition/no-charge warning light fails to come on
- ☐ Lights inoperative
- ☐ Instrument readings inaccurate or erratic
- ☐ Horn inoperative, or unsatisfactory in operation
- ☐ Windscreen/tailgate wipers inoperative, or unsatisfactory in operation
- ☐ Windscreen washers inoperative, or unsatisfactory in operation
- ☐ Electric windows inoperative, or unsatisfactory in operation
- ☐ Central locking system inoperative, or unsatisfactory in operation

Introduction

The vehicle owner who does his or her own maintenance according to the recommended service schedules should not have to use this section of the manual very often. Modern component reliability is such that, provided those items subject to wear or deterioration are inspected or renewed at the specified intervals, sudden failure is comparatively rare. Faults do not usually just happen as a result of sudden failure, but develop over a period of time. Major mechanical failures in particular are usually preceded by characteristic symptoms over hundreds or even thousands of miles. Those components which do occasionally fail without warning are often small and easily carried in the vehicle.

With any fault-finding, the first step is to decide where to begin investigations. Sometimes this is obvious, but on other occasions, a little detective work will be necessary. The owner who makes half a dozen haphazard adjustments or replacements may be successful in curing a fault (or its symptoms), but will be none the wiser if the fault recurs, and ultimately may have spent more time and money than was necessary. A calm and logical approach will be found to be more satisfactory in the long run. Always take into account any warning signs or abnormalities that may have been noticed in the period preceding the fault – power loss, high or low gauge readings, unusual smells, etc – and remember that failure of components such as fuses or spark plugs may only be pointers to some underlying fault.

The pages which follow provide an easy-reference guide to the more common problems which may occur during the operation of the vehicle. These problems and their possible causes are grouped under headings denoting various components or systems, such as Engine, Cooling system, etc. The general

Chapter which deals with the problem is also shown in brackets; refer to the relevant part of that Chapter for system-specific information. Whatever the fault, certain basic principles apply. These are as follows:

Verify the fault. This is simply a matter of being sure that you know what the symptoms are before starting work. This is particularly important if you are investigating a fault for someone else, who may not have described it very accurately.

Don't overlook the obvious. For example, if the vehicle won't start, is there fuel in the tank? (Don't take anyone else's word on this particular point, and don't trust the fuel gauge either!) If an electrical fault is indicated, look for loose or broken wires before digging out the test gear.

Cure the disease, not the symptom. Substituting a flat battery with a fully-charged one will get you off the hard shoulder, but if the underlying cause is not attended to, the new battery will go the same way. Similarly, changing oil-fouled spark plugs for a new set will get you moving again, but remember that the reason for the fouling (if it wasn't simply an incorrect grade of plug) will have to be established and corrected.

Don't take anything for granted. Particularly, don't forget that a new component may itself be defective (especially if its been rattling around in the boot for months), and don't leave components out of a fault diagnosis sequence just because they are new or recently-fitted. When you do finally diagnose a difficult fault, you'll probably realise that all the evidence was there from the start.

Engine

Engine fails to rotate when attempting to start

- ☐ Battery terminal connections loose or corroded (see *Weekly checks*).
- ☐ Battery discharged or faulty (Chapter 5A Section 2).
- ☐ Broken, loose or disconnected wiring in the starting circuit (Chapter 5A Section 8).
- ☐ Defective starter solenoid or switch (Chapter 5A Section 8).
- ☐ Defective starter motor (Chapter 5A Section 8).
- ☐ Starter pinion or flywheel/driveplate ring gear teeth loose or broken (Chapter 2A, 2B or 2D and 5A).
- ☐ Engine earth strap broken or disconnected (Chapter 5A or 12).

Engine rotates, but will not start

- ☐ Fuel tank empty.
- ☐ Battery discharged (engine rotates slowly) (Chapter 5A Section 2).
- ☐ Battery terminal connections loose or corroded (see *Weekly checks*).
- ☐ Ignition components damp or damaged (Chapters 1A and 5B).
- ☐ Broken, loose or disconnected wiring in the ignition circuit (Chapters 1A and 5B).
- ☐ Worn, faulty or incorrectly-gapped spark plugs (Chapter 1A Section 21).
- ☐ Fuel injection system fault (Chapter 4A or 4B).
- ☐ Major mechanical failure (eg, timing belt/chain) (Chapter 2A, 2B or 2D).

Engine difficult to start when cold

- ☐ Battery discharged (Chapter 5A Section 2).
- ☐ Battery terminal connections loose or corroded (see *Weekly checks*).
- ☐ Worn, faulty or incorrectly-gapped spark plugs (Chapter 1A Section 21).
- ☐ Fuel injection system fault (Chapter 4A or 4B).
- ☐ Other ignition system fault (Chapters 1A or1B and 5B).
- ☐ Low cylinder compressions (Chapter 2A, 2B or 2D).

Engine difficult to start when hot

- ☐ Air filter element dirty or clogged (Chapter 1A or 1B).
- ☐ Fuel injection system fault (Chapter 4A or 4B).
- ☐ Low cylinder compressions (Chapter 2A, 2B or 2D).

Starter motor noisy or excessively-rough in engagement

- ☐ Starter pinion or flywheel ring gear teeth loose or broken (Chapter 2A, 2B or 2D and 5A).
- ☐ Starter motor mounting bolts loose or missing (Chapter 5A Section 7).
- ☐ Starter motor internal components worn or damaged (Chapter 5A Section 8).

Engine starts, but stops immediately

- ☐ Loose or faulty electrical connections in the ignition circuit (Chapters 1A or 1B and 5B).
- ☐ Vacuum leak at the throttle body or intake manifold (Chapter 4A or 4B).
- ☐ Blocked injector/fuel injection system fault (Chapter 4A or 4B).

Engine idles erratically

- ☐ Air filter element clogged (Chapter 1A or 1B).
- ☐ Vacuum leak at the throttle body, intake manifold or associated hoses (Chapter 4A or 4B).
- ☐ Worn, faulty or incorrectly-gapped spark plugs (Chapter 1A Section 21).
- ☐ Uneven or low cylinder compressions (Chapter 2A, 2B or 2D).
- ☐ Camshaft lobes worn (Chapter 2A, 2B or 2D).
- ☐ Timing belt incorrectly fitted (Chapter 2A, 2B or 2D).
- ☐ Blocked injector/fuel injection system fault (Chapter 4A or 4B).

Engine misfires at idle speed

- ☐ Worn, faulty or incorrectly-gapped spark plugs (Chapter 1A Section 21).
- ☐ Vacuum leak at the throttle body, intake manifold or associated hoses (Chapter 4A or 4B).
- ☐ Blocked injector/fuel injection system fault (Chapter 4A or 4B).
- ☐ Uneven or low cylinder compressions (Chapter 2A, 2B or 2D).
- ☐ Disconnected, leaking, or perished crankcase ventilation hoses (Chapter 4C Section 3).

Engine misfires throughout the driving speed range

- ☐ Fuel pump faulty, or delivery pressure low (Chapter 4A or 4B).
- ☐ Fuel tank vent blocked, or fuel pipes restricted (Chapter 4A or 4B).
- ☐ Vacuum leak at the throttle body, intake manifold or associated hoses (Chapter 4A or 4B).
- ☐ Worn, faulty or incorrectly-gapped spark plugs (Chapter 1A Section 21).
- ☐ Faulty ignition coil (Chapter 5B Section 3).
- ☐ Uneven or low cylinder compressions (Chapter 2A, 2B or 2D).
- ☐ Blocked injector/fuel injection system fault (Chapter 4A or 4B).

Engine hesitates on acceleration

- ☐ Worn, faulty or incorrectly-gapped spark plugs (Chapter 1A Section 21).
- ☐ Vacuum leak at the throttle body, intake manifold or associated hoses (Chapter 4A or 4B).
- ☐ Blocked injector/fuel injection system fault (Chapter 4A or 4B).

Engine (continued)

Engine stalls

- ☐ Vacuum leak at the throttle body, intake manifold or associated hoses (Chapter 4A or 4B).
- ☐ Fuel pump faulty, or delivery pressure low (Chapter 4A or 4B).
- ☐ Fuel tank vent blocked, or fuel pipes restricted (Chapter 4A or 4B).
- ☐ Blocked injector/fuel injection system fault (Chapter 4A or 4B).
- ☐ Faulty injector(s) (Chapter 4A or 4B).

Engine lacks power

- ☐ Timing belt incorrectly fitted or tensioned (Chapter 2A, 2B or 2D).
- ☐ Fuel pump faulty, or delivery pressure low Chapter 4A or 4B).
- ☐ Uneven or low cylinder compressions (Chapter 2A a, 2B or 2C).
- ☐ Worn, faulty or incorrectly-gapped spark plugs (Chapter 1A Section 21).
- ☐ Vacuum leak at the throttle body, intake manifold or associated hoses (Chapter 4A or 4B).
- ☐ Blocked injector/fuel injection system fault (Chapter 4A or 4B).
- ☐ Brakes binding (Chapter 9 Section 1).
- ☐ Clutch slipping (Chapter 6 Section 5).
- ☐ Air filter element clogged (Chapter 1A or 1B).

Engine backfires

- ☐ Timing belt incorrectly fitted or tensioned (Chapter 2A, 2B or 2D).
- ☐ Vacuum leak at the throttle body, intake manifold or associated hoses (Chapter 4A or 4B).
- ☐ Blocked injector/fuel injection system fault (Chapter 4A or 2B).

Oil pressure warning light illuminated with engine running

- ☐ Low oil level, or incorrect oil grade (*Weekly checks*).
- ☐ Faulty oil pressure switch (Chapter 5A).
- ☐ Worn engine bearings and/or oil pump (Chapter 2A, 2B or 2D).
- ☐ High engine operating temperature (Chapter 3).
- ☐ Oil pressure relief valve defective (Chapter 2A, 2B or 2D).
- ☐ Oil pick-up strainer clogged (Chapter 2A, 2B or 2D).

Engine runs-on after switching off

- ☐ Excessive carbon build-up in engine (Chapter 2A, 2B or 2D).
- ☐ High engine operating temperature (Chapter 3).
- ☐ Fuel injection system fault (Chapter 4A or 4B).

Engine noises

Pre-ignition (pinking) or knocking during acceleration or under load

- ☐ Ignition system fault (Chapters 1A and 5B).
- ☐ Incorrect grade of spark plug (Chapter 1A Section 21).
- ☐ Vacuum leak at the throttle body, intake manifold or associated hoses (Chapter 4A or 4B).
- ☐ Excessive carbon build-up in engine (Chapter 2A, 2B or 2D).
- ☐ Blocked injector/fuel injection system fault (Chapter 4A or 4B).

Whistling or wheezing noises

- ☐ Leaking intake manifold or throttle body gasket (Chapter 4A or 4B).
- ☐ Leaking exhaust manifold gasket or pipe-to-manifold joint (Chapter 4A or 4B).
- ☐ Leaking vacuum hose (Chapters 4A, 4B and 9).
- ☐ Blowing cylinder head gasket (Chapter 2A, 2B or 2D).

Tapping or rattling noises

- ☐ Worn valve gear or camshaft (Chapter 2A, 2B or 2D).
- ☐ Ancillary component fault (coolant pump, alternator, etc) (Chapters 3, 5A, etc).

Knocking or thumping noises

- ☐ Worn big-end bearings (regular heavy knocking, perhaps less under load) (Chapter 2A, 2B or 2D).
- ☐ Worn main bearings (rumbling and knocking, perhaps worsening under load) (Chapter 2A, 2B or 2D).
- ☐ Piston slap (most noticeable when cold) (Chapter 2A, 2B or 2D).
- ☐ Ancillary component fault (coolant pump, alternator, etc) (Chapters 3, 5A, etc).

Cooling system

Overheating

- ☐ Insufficient coolant in system (*Weekly checks*).
- ☐ Thermostat faulty (Chapter 3 Section 4).
- ☐ Radiator core blocked, or grille restricted (Chapter 3 Section 7).
- ☐ Electric cooling fan or thermostatic switch faulty (Chapter 3 Section 5).
- ☐ Inaccurate temperature gauge sender unit (Chapter 3).
- ☐ Airlock in cooling system (Chapter 3 Section 2).
- ☐ Expansion tank pressure cap faulty (Chapter 3 Section 7).

Overcooling

- ☐ Thermostat faulty (Chapter 3 Section 4).
- ☐ Inaccurate engine coolant temperature sensor (Chapter 3 Section 6).

External coolant leakage

- ☐ Deteriorated or damaged hoses or hose clips (Chapter 1A or 1B).
- ☐ Radiator core or heater matrix leaking (Chapter 3 Section 9).
- ☐ Pressure cap faulty (Chapter 3 Section 7).
- ☐ Coolant pump internal seal leaking (Chapter 3 Section 8).
- ☐ Coolant pump-to-housing seal leaking (Chapter 3 Section 8).
- ☐ Boiling due to overheating (Chapter 3 Section 1).
- ☐ Core plug leaking (Chapter 2A, 2B or 2D).

Internal coolant leakage

- ☐ Leaking cylinder head gasket (Chapter 2A, 2B or 2D).
- ☐ Cracked cylinder head or cylinder block (Chapter 2A, 2B or 2D).

Corrosion

- ☐ Infrequent draining and flushing (Chapter 1A or 1B).
- ☐ Incorrect coolant mixture or inappropriate coolant type (see *Weekly checks*).

Fuel and exhaust systems

Excessive fuel consumption

- ☐ Air filter element dirty or clogged (Chapter 1A or 1B).
- ☐ Fuel injection system fault (Chapter 4A or 4B).
- ☐ Ignition system fault (Chapters 1A and 5B).
- ☐ Tyres under-inflated (see *Weekly checks*).

Fuel leakage and/or fuel odour

- ☐ Damaged fuel tank, pipes or connections (Chapter 4A or 4B).

Excessive noise or fumes from exhaust system

- ☐ Leaking exhaust system or manifold joints (Chapters 1A, 1B and 4A and 4B).
- ☐ Leaking, corroded or damaged silencers or pipe (Chapters 1A, 1B, 4A and 4B).
- ☐ Broken mountings causing body or suspension contact (Chapter 1A or 1B).

Clutch

Pedal travels to floor – no pressure or very little resistance

- ☐ Faulty master or slave cylinder (Chapter 6 Section 3 and 4).
- ☐ Faulty hydraulic release system (Chapter 6 Section 5, 7).
- ☐ Broken clutch release bearing or arm (Chapter 6 Section 7).
- ☐ Broken diaphragm spring in clutch pressure plate (Chapter 6 Section 6).

Clutch fails to disengage (unable to select gears)

- ☐ Faulty master or slave cylinder (Chapter 6 Section 3 and 4).
- ☐ Faulty hydraulic release system (Chapter 6 Section 7).
- ☐ Clutch disc sticking on gearbox input shaft splines (Chapter 6 Section 6).
- ☐ Clutch disc sticking to flywheel or pressure plate (Chapter 6 Section 6).
- ☐ Faulty pressure plate assembly (Chapter 6 Section 6).
- ☐ Clutch release mechanism worn or incorrectly assembled (Chapter 6 Section 7).

Clutch slips (engine speed increases, with no increase in vehicle speed)

- ☐ Faulty hydraulic release system (Chapter 6 Section 7).
- ☐ Clutch disc linings excessively worn (Chapter 6 Section 6).
- ☐ Clutch disc linings contaminated with oil or grease (Chapter 6 Section 6).
- ☐ Faulty pressure plate or weak diaphragm spring (Chapter 6 Section 6).

Judder as clutch is engaged

- ☐ Clutch disc linings contaminated with oil or grease (Chapter 6 Section 6).
- ☐ Clutch disc linings excessively worn (Chapter 6 Section 6).
- ☐ Faulty or distorted pressure plate or diaphragm spring (Chapter 6 Section 6).
- ☐ Worn or loose engine or gearbox mountings (Chapter 2A, 2B 2B, 2C 2C or 2D 2D).
- ☐ Clutch disc hub or gearbox input shaft splines worn (Chapter 6 Section 6).

Noise when depressing or releasing clutch pedal

- ☐ Worn clutch release bearing (Chapter 6 Section 6, 7).
- ☐ Worn or dry clutch pedal pivot (Chapter 6 Section 2).
- ☐ Faulty pressure plate assembly (Chapter 6 Section 6).
- ☐ Pressure plate diaphragm spring broken (Chapter 6 Section 6).
- ☐ Broken clutch friction plate cushioning springs (Chapter 6 Section 6).

Manual transmission

Noisy in neutral with engine running

- ☐ Input shaft bearings worn (noise apparent with clutch pedal released, but not when depressed) (Chapter 7 Section 8).*
- ☐ Clutch release bearing worn (noise apparent with clutch pedal depressed, possibly less when released) (Chapter 6 Section 7).

Noisy in one particular gear

- ☐ Worn, damaged or chipped gear teeth (Chapter 7 Section 8).*

Difficulty engaging gears

- ☐ Clutch fault (Chapter 6 Section 6).
- ☐ Worn or damaged gear linkage (Chapter 7 Section 3).
- ☐ Worn synchroniser units (Chapter 7 Section 8).*

Jumps out of gear

- ☐ Worn or damaged gear linkage (Chapter 7 Section 3).
- ☐ Worn synchroniser units (Chapter 7 Section 8).*
- ☐ Worn selector forks (Chapter 7 Section 8).*

Vibration

- ☐ Lack of oil (Chapter 7 Section 6).
- ☐ Worn bearings (Chapter 7 Section 8).*

Lubricant leaks

- ☐ Leaking oil seal (Chapter 7 Section 5).
- ☐ Leaking housing joint (Chapter7 Section 8).*
- ☐ Leaking input shaft oil seal (Chapter 7 Section 5).

Note: **Although the corrective action necessary to remedy the symptoms described is beyond the scope of the home mechanic, the above information should be helpful in isolating the cause of the condition, so that the owner can communicate clearly with a professional mechanic.*

Driveshafts

Vibration when accelerating or decelerating

- ☐ Worn inner constant velocity joint (Chapter 8 Section 4).
- ☐ Bent or distorted driveshaft (Chapter 8 Section 2).

Clicking or knocking noise on turns (at slow speed on full-lock)

- ☐ Worn outer constant velocity joint (Chapter 8 Section 3).
- ☐ Lack of constant velocity joint lubricant, possibly due to damaged gaiter (Chapter 8 Section 3, 4).

Braking system

Vehicle pulls to one side under braking

- ☐ Worn, defective, damaged or contaminated front or rear brake pads/shoes on one side (Chapters 1A or 1B and 9).
- ☐ Seized or partially-seized front or rear brake caliper or wheel cylinder (Chapter 9 Section 7, 9).
- ☐ A mixture of brake pad/shoe lining materials fitted between sides (Chapter 9 Section 2, 6, 8).
- ☐ Brake caliper mounting bolts loose (Chapter 9 Section 3).
- ☐ Worn or damaged steering or suspension components (Chapters 1A or 1B and 10).

Noise (grinding or high-pitched squeal) when brakes applied

- ☐ Brake pad/shoe friction lining material worn down to metal backing (Chapters 1A or 1B and 9).
- ☐ Excessive corrosion of brake disc/drum – may be apparent after the vehicle has been standing for some time (Chapters 1A or 1B and 9).
- ☐ Foreign object (stone chipping, etc) trapped between brake disc and shield (Chapters 1A or 1B and 9).

Excessive brake pedal travel

- ☐ Faulty master cylinder (Chapter 9 Section 11).
- ☐ Air in hydraulic system (Chapter 9 Section 14).
- ☐ Faulty vacuum servo unit (Chapter 9 Section 15, 16).
- ☐ Faulty vacuum pump, where fitted (Chapter 9 Section 23).

Brake pedal feels spongy when depressed

- ☐ Air in hydraulic system (Chapter 9 Section 14).
- ☐ Deteriorated flexible rubber brake hoses (Chapters 1A or 1B and 9).
- ☐ Master cylinder mountings loose (Chapter 9 Section 11).
- ☐ Faulty master cylinder (Chapter 9 Section 11).

Excessive brake pedal effort required to stop vehicle

- ☐ Faulty vacuum servo unit (Chapter 9 Section 15).
- ☐ Disconnected, damaged or insecure brake servo vacuum hose (Chapters 1A or 1B and 9).
- ☐ Faulty vacuum pump, where fitted (Chapter 9 Section 23).
- ☐ Primary or secondary hydraulic circuit failure (Chapter 9 Section 14).
- ☐ Seized brake caliper/wheel cylinder (Chapter 9 Section 3, 7).
- ☐ Brake pads/shoes incorrectly fitted (Chapter 9 Section 2, 6, 8).
- ☐ Incorrect grade of brake pads/shoes fitted (Chapter 9 Section 2, 6, 8).
- ☐ Brake pads/shoes contaminated (Chapter 9 Section 2, 6, 8).

Judder felt through brake pedal or steering wheel when braking

- ☐ Excessive run-out or distortion of brake disc(s)/drums (Chapter 9 Section 4, 5, 10).
- ☐ Brake pad/shoe linings worn (Chapters 1A or 1B and 9).
- ☐ Brake caliper mounting bolts loose (Chapter 9 Section 3, 9).
- ☐ Wear in suspension or steering components or mountings (Chapter 1A Section 12, Chapter 1B Section 14 or Chapter 10).

Pedal pulsates when braking hard

Normal feature of ABS – no fault

Brakes binding

- ☐ Seized brake caliper piston(s)/wheel cylinder (Chapter 9 Section 3, 7, 9).
- ☐ Incorrectly-adjusted handbrake mechanism (Chapter 9 Section 21).
- ☐ Faulty master cylinder (Chapter 9 Section 11).

Rear wheels locking under normal braking

- ☐ Rear brake pad/shoe linings contaminated (Chapters 1A or 1B and 9).
- ☐ Rear brake discs/drums warped (Chapter 1A Section 10, Chapter 1B Section 12 or Chapter 9).

Steering and suspension

Vehicle pulls to one side

- ☐ Defective tyre (see *Weekly checks*).
- ☐ Excessive wear in suspension or steering components (Chapters 1A or 1B and 10).
- ☐ Incorrect front wheel alignment (Chapter 10 Section 20).
- ☐ Accident damage to steering or suspension components (Chapters 1A or 1B and 10).

Wheel wobble and vibration

- ☐ Front roadwheels out of balance (vibration felt mainly through the steering wheel) (*Weekly checks*).
- ☐ Rear roadwheels out of balance (vibration felt throughout the vehicle) (*Weekly checks*).
- ☐ Roadwheels damaged or distorted (*Weekly checks*).
- ☐ Faulty or damaged tyre (*Weekly checks*).
- ☐ Worn steering or suspension joints, bushes or components (Chapters 1A or 1B and 10).
- ☐ Wheel nuts loose (Chapters 1A or 1B and 10).

Excessive pitching and/or rolling around corners, or during braking

- ☐ Defective shock absorbers (Chapters 1A or 1B and 10).
- ☐ Broken or weak coil spring and/or suspension component (Chapters 1A or 1B and 10).
- ☐ Worn or damaged anti-roll bar or mountings (Chapter 10 Section 6, 12).

Wandering or general instability

- ☐ Incorrect front wheel alignment (Chapter 10 Section 20).
- ☐ Worn steering or suspension joints, bushes or components (Chapters 1A or 1B and 10).
- ☐ Roadwheels out of balance (*Weekly checks*).
- ☐ Faulty or damaged tyre (*Weekly checks*).
- ☐ Wheel nuts loose (Chapter 1A Section 16).
- ☐ Defective shock absorbers (Chapters 1A or 1B and 10).

Excessively-stiff steering

- ☐ Seized track rod end balljoint or suspension balljoint (Chapters 1A or 1B and 10).
- ☐ Broken or incorrectly adjusted auxiliary drivebelt (Chapters 1A or 1B and 10).
- ☐ Incorrect front wheel alignment (Chapter 10 Section 20).
- ☐ Steering gear damaged (Chapter 10 Section 15).

Steering and suspension (continued)

Excessive play in steering

- ☐ Worn steering column universal joint(s) (Chapter 10 Section 14).
- ☐ Worn steering track rod end balljoints (Chapters 1A or 1B and 10).
- ☐ Worn steering gear (Chapter 10 Section 15).
- ☐ Worn steering or suspension joints, bushes or components (Chapters 1A or 1B and 10).

Lack of power assistance

- ☐ Broken or incorrectly-adjusted auxiliary drivebelt (Chapters 1A or 1B).
- ☐ Incorrect power steering fluid level (*Weekly checks*).
- ☐ Restriction in power steering fluid hoses – models with hydraulic power steering systems (Chapter 10 Section 17).
- ☐ Faulty power steering pump – models with hydraulic power steering systems (Chapter 10 Section 18).
- ☐ Faulty steering gear (Chapter 10 Section 15

Tyre wear excessive

Tyres worn on inside or outside edges

- ☐ Incorrect camber or castor angles (Chapter 10 Section 20).
- ☐ Worn steering or suspension joints, bushes or components (Chapters 1A or 1B and 10).
- ☐ Excessively-hard cornering.Accident damage.

Tyre treads exhibit feathered edges

- ☐ Incorrect toe setting (Chapter 10 Section 20).

Tyres worn in centre of tread

- ☐ Tyres over-inflated (*Weekly checks*).

Tyres worn on inside and outside edges

- ☐ Tyres under-inflated (*Weekly checks*).
- ☐ Worn shock absorbers (Chapter 10 Section 3, 9).

Tyres worn unevenly

- ☐ Tyres/wheels out of balance (*Weekly checks*).
- ☐ Excessive wheel or tyre run-out (Chapter 10 Section 20).
- ☐ Worn shock absorbers (Chapters 1A or 1B and 10).
- ☐ Faulty tyre (*Weekly checks*).

Electrical system

Battery will not hold a charge more than a few days

- ☐ Battery defective internally (Chapter 5A Section 2).
- ☐ Battery electrolyte level low – where applicable (*Weekly checks*).
- ☐ Battery terminal connections loose or corroded (*Weekly checks*).
- ☐ Auxiliary drivebelt worn – or incorrectly adjusted, where applicable (Chapter 1A Section 23)(Chapter 1B Section 24).
- ☐ Alternator not charging at correct output (Chapter 5A Section 4).
- ☐ Alternator or voltage regulator faulty (Chapter 5A Section 4).
- ☐ Short-circuit causing continual battery drain (Chapters 5A and 12).

Ignition/no-charge warning light remains illuminated with engine running

- ☐ Auxiliary drivebelt broken, worn, or incorrectly adjusted (Chapter 1A or 1B).
- ☐ Internal fault in alternator or voltage regulator (Chapter 5A Section 4).
- ☐ Broken, disconnected, or loose wiring in charging circuit (Chapter 5A Section 4).

Ignition/no-charge warning light fails to come on

- ☐ Broken, disconnected, or loose wiring in warning light circuit (Chapter 5A Section 4).
- ☐ Alternator faulty (Chapter 5A Section 5).

Lights inoperative

- ☐ Bulb blown (Chapter 12 Section 6).
- ☐ Corrosion of bulb or bulbholder contacts (Chapter 12 Section 6).
- ☐ Blown fuse (Chapter 12 Section 3).
- ☐ Faulty relay (Chapter 12 Section 3).
- ☐ Broken, loose, or disconnected wiring (Chapter 12 Section 2).
- ☐ Faulty switch (Chapter 12 Section 5).

Instrument readings inaccurate or erratic

Fuel or temperature gauges give no reading

- ☐ Faulty coolant temperature sensor (Chapter 3 Section 6).
- ☐ Wiring open-circuit (Chapter 12 Section 2).
- ☐ Faulty gauge (Chapter 12 Section 10).

Fuel or temperature gauges give continuous maximum reading

- ☐ Faulty coolant temperature sensor (Chapter 3 Section 6).
- ☐ Wiring short-circuit (Chapter 12 Section 2).
- ☐ Faulty gauge (Chapter 12 Section 10).

Horn inoperative, or unsatisfactory in operation

Horn operates all the time

- ☐ Horn contacts permanently bridged or horn push stuck down (Chapter 12 Section 5).

Horn fails to operate

- ☐ Blown fuse (Chapter 12 Section 3).
- ☐ Cable or cable connections loose, broken or disconnected (Chapter 12 Section 2).
- ☐ Faulty horn (Chapter 12 Section 5).

Horn emits intermittent or unsatisfactory sound

- ☐ Cable connections loose (Chapter 12 Section 2).
- ☐ Horn mountings loose (Chapter 12 Section 14).
- ☐ Faulty horn (Chapter 12 Section 14).

Electrical system (continued)

Windscreen/tailgate wipers inoperative, or unsatisfactory in operation

Wipers fail to operate, or operate very slowly

- ☐ Wiper blades stuck to screen, or linkage seized or binding (*Weekly checks* and Chapter 12 Section 11).
- ☐ Blown fuse (Chapter 12 Section 3).
- ☐ Cable or cable connections loose, broken or disconnected (Chapter 12 Section 2).
- ☐ Faulty relay (Chapter 12 Section 3).
- ☐ Faulty wiper motor (Chapter 12 Section 11).

Wiper blades sweep over too large or too small an area of the glass

- ☐ Wiper arms incorrectly positioned on spindles (Chapter 12 Section 11).
- ☐ Excessive wear of wiper linkage (Chapter 12 Section 11).
- ☐ Wiper motor or linkage mountings loose or insecure (Chapter 12 Section 11).

Wiper blades fail to clean the glass effectively

- ☐ Wiper blade rubbers worn or perished (*Weekly checks*).
- ☐ Wiper arm tension springs broken, or arm pivots seized (Chapter 12 Section 11).
- ☐ Insufficient windscreen washer additive to adequately remove road film (*Weekly checks*).

Windscreen washers inoperative, or unsatisfactory in operation

One or more washer jets inoperative

- ☐ Blocked washer jet (Chapter 12 Section 12).
- ☐ Disconnected, kinked or restricted fluid hose (Chapter 12 Section 12).
- ☐ Insufficient fluid in washer reservoir (*Weekly checks*).

Washer pump fails to operate

- ☐ Broken or disconnected wiring or connections (Chapter 12 Section 12).
- ☐ Blown fuse (Chapter 12 Section 3).
- ☐ Faulty washer switch (Chapter 12 Section 5).
- ☐ Faulty washer pump (Chapter 12 Section 12).

Electric windows inoperative, or unsatisfactory in operation

Window glass will only move in one direction

- ☐ Faulty switch (Chapter 12 Section 5).

Window glass slow to move

- ☐ Regulator seized or damaged, or in need of lubrication (Chapter 11 Section 12).
- ☐ Door internal components or trim fouling regulator (Chapter 11 Section 12).
- ☐ Faulty motor (Chapter 11 Section 12).

Window glass fails to move

- ☐ Blown fuse (Chapter 12 Section 3).
- ☐ Faulty relay (Chapter 12 Section 3).
- ☐ Broken or disconnected wiring or connections (Chapter 12 Section 2).
- ☐ Faulty motor (Chapter 11 Section 12).
- ☐ Faulty BCM (Chapter 12 Section 24).

Central locking system inoperative, or unsatisfactory in operation

Complete system failure

- ☐ Blown fuse (Chapter 12 Section 3).
- ☐ Faulty BCM (Chapter 12 Section 24).
- ☐ Broken or disconnected wiring or connections (Chapter 12 Section 2).

Latch locks but will not unlock, or unlocks but will not lock

- ☐ Faulty switch (Chapter 12 Section 5).
- ☐ Broken or disconnected latch operating rods or levers (Chapter 11 Section 13).
- ☐ Faulty BCM (Chapter 12 Section 24).

One lock fails to operate

- ☐ Broken or disconnected wiring or connections (Chapter 12 Section 2).
- ☐ Faulty motor (Chapter 11 Section 13).
- ☐ Broken, binding or disconnected lock operating rods or levers (Chapter 11 Section 13).
- ☐ Fault in door lock (Chapter 11 Section 13).

A

ABS (Anti-lock brake system) A system, usually electronically controlled, that senses incipient wheel lockup during braking and relieves hydraulic pressure at wheels that are about to skid.

Air bag An inflatable bag hidden in the steering wheel (driver's side) or the dash or glovebox (passenger side). In a head-on collision, the bags inflate, preventing the driver and front passenger from being thrown forward into the steering wheel or windscreen.

Air cleaner A metal or plastic housing, containing a filter element, which removes dust and dirt from the air being drawn into the engine.

Air filter element The actual filter in an air cleaner system, usually manufactured from pleated paper and requiring renewal at regular intervals.

Air filter

Allen key A hexagonal wrench which fits into a recessed hexagonal hole.

Alligator clip A long-nosed spring-loaded metal clip with meshing teeth. Used to make temporary electrical connections.

Alternator A component in the electrical system which converts mechanical energy from a drivebelt into electrical energy to charge the battery and to operate the starting system, ignition system and electrical accessories.

Ampere (amp) A unit of measurement for the flow of electric current. One amp is the amount of current produced by one volt acting through a resistance of one ohm.

Anaerobic sealer A substance used to prevent bolts and screws from loosening. Anaerobic means that it does not require oxygen for activation. The Loctite brand is widely used.

Antifreeze A substance (usually ethylene glycol) mixed with water, and added to a vehicle's cooling system, to prevent freezing of the coolant in winter. Antifreeze also contains chemicals to inhibit corrosion and the formation of rust and other deposits that would tend to clog the radiator and coolant passages and reduce cooling efficiency.

Anti-seize compound A coating that reduces the risk of seizing on fasteners that are subjected to high temperatures, such as exhaust manifold bolts and nuts.

Asbestos A natural fibrous mineral with great heat resistance, commonly used in the composition of brake friction materials. Asbestos is a health hazard and the dust created by brake systems should never be inhaled or ingested.

Axle A shaft on which a wheel revolves, or which revolves with a wheel. Also, a solid beam that connects the two wheels at one end of the vehicle. An axle which also transmits power to the wheels is known as a live axle.

Axleshaft A single rotating shaft, on either side of the differential, which delivers power from the final drive assembly to the drive wheels. Also called a driveshaft or a halfshaft.

B

Ball bearing An anti-friction bearing consisting of a hardened inner and outer race with hardened steel balls between two races.

Bearing The curved surface on a shaft or in a bore, or the part assembled into either, that permits relative motion between them with minimum wear and friction.

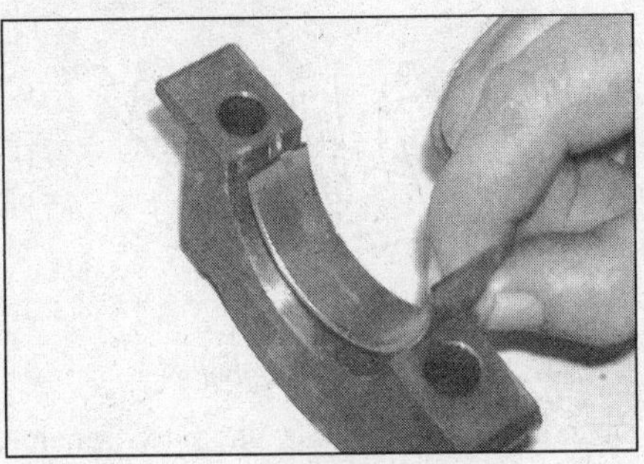

Bearing

Big-end bearing The bearing in the end of the connecting rod that's attached to the crankshaft.

Bleed nipple A valve on a brake wheel cylinder, caliper or other hydraulic component that is opened to purge the hydraulic system of air. Also called a bleed screw.

Brake bleeding Procedure for removing air from lines of a hydraulic brake system.

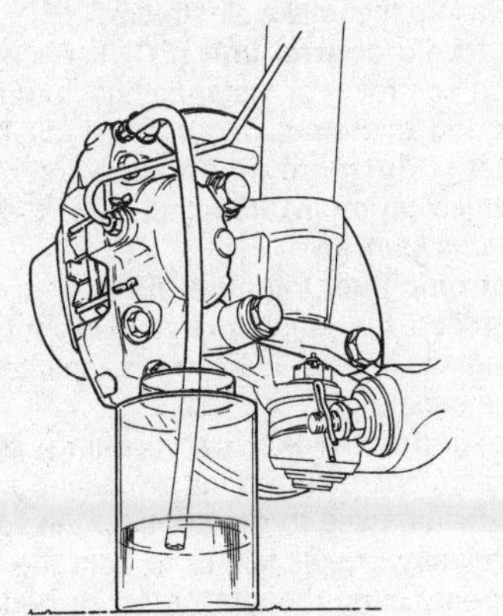

Brake bleeding

Brake disc The component of a disc brake that rotates with the wheels.

Brake drum The component of a drum brake that rotates with the wheels.

Brake linings The friction material which contacts the brake disc or drum to retard the vehicle's speed. The linings are bonded or riveted to the brake pads or shoes.

Brake pads The replaceable friction pads that pinch the brake disc when the brakes are applied. Brake pads consist of a friction material bonded or riveted to a rigid backing plate.

Brake shoe The crescent-shaped carrier to which the brake linings are mounted and which forces the lining against the rotating drum during braking.

Braking systems For more information on braking systems, consult the *Haynes Automotive Brake Manual*.

Breaker bar A long socket wrench handle providing greater leverage.

Bulkhead The insulated partition between the engine and the passenger compartment.

C

Caliper The non-rotating part of a disc-brake assembly that straddles the disc and carries the brake pads. The caliper also contains the hydraulic components that cause the pads to pinch the disc when the brakes are applied. A caliper is also a measuring tool that can be set to measure inside or outside dimensions of an object.

Camshaft A rotating shaft on which a series of cam lobes operate the valve mechanisms. The camshaft may be driven by gears, by sprockets and chain or by sprockets and a belt.

Canister A container in an evaporative emission control system; contains activated charcoal granules to trap vapours from the fuel system.

Canister

Carburettor A device which mixes fuel with air in the proper proportions to provide a desired power output from a spark ignition internal combustion engine.

Castellated Resembling the parapets along the top of a castle wall. For example, a castellated balljoint stud nut.

Castor In wheel alignment, the backward or forward tilt of the steering axis. Castor is positive when the steering axis is inclined rearward at the top.

Catalytic converter A silencer-like device in the exhaust system which converts certain pollutants in the exhaust gases into less harmful substances.

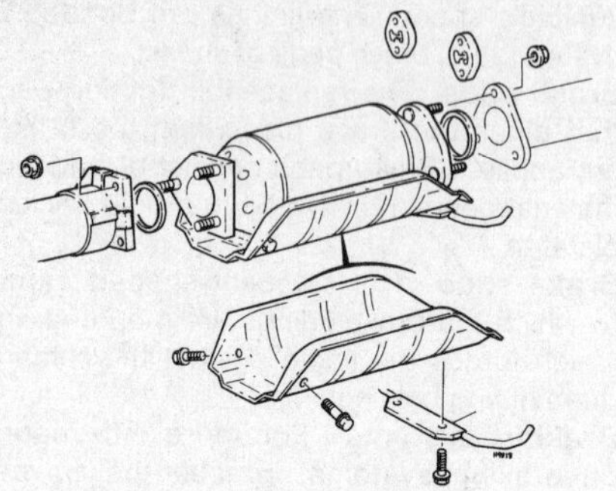
Catalytic converter

Circlip A ring-shaped clip used to prevent endwise movement of cylindrical parts and shafts. An internal circlip is installed in a groove in a housing; an external circlip fits into a groove on the outside of a cylindrical piece such as a shaft.

Clearance The amount of space between two parts. For example, between a piston and a cylinder, between a bearing and a journal, etc.

Coil spring A spiral of elastic steel found in various sizes throughout a vehicle, for example as a springing medium in the suspension and in the valve train.

Compression Reduction in volume, and increase in pressure and temperature, of a gas, caused by squeezing it into a smaller space.

Compression ratio The relationship between cylinder volume when the piston is at top dead centre and cylinder volume when the piston is at bottom dead centre.

Constant velocity (CV) joint A type of universal joint that cancels out vibrations caused by driving power being transmitted through an angle.

Core plug A disc or cup-shaped metal device inserted in a hole in a casting through which core was removed when the casting was formed. Also known as a freeze plug or expansion plug.

Crankcase The lower part of the engine block in which the crankshaft rotates.

Crankshaft The main rotating member, or shaft, running the length of the crankcase, with offset "throws" to which the connecting rods are attached.

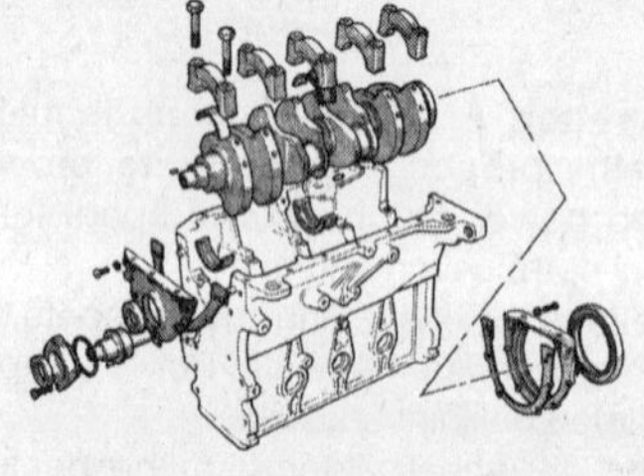
Crankshaft assembly

Crocodile clip See Alligator clip

D

Diagnostic code Code numbers obtained by accessing the diagnostic mode of an engine management computer. This code can be used to determine the area in the system where a malfunction may be located.

Disc brake A brake design incorporating a rotating disc onto which brake pads are squeezed. The resulting friction converts the energy of a moving vehicle into heat.

Double-overhead cam (DOHC) An engine that uses two overhead camshafts, usually one for the intake valves and one for the exhaust valves.

Drivebelt(s) The belt(s) used to drive accessories such as the alternator, water pump, power steering pump, air conditioning compressor, etc. off the crankshaft pulley.

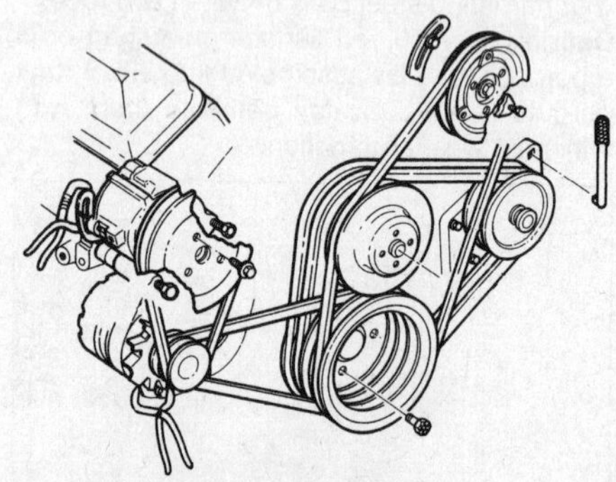
Accessory drivebelts

Driveshaft Any shaft used to transmit motion. Commonly used when referring to the axleshafts on a front wheel drive vehicle.

Drum brake A type of brake using a drum-shaped metal cylinder attached to the inner surface of the wheel. When the brake pedal is pressed, curved brake shoes with friction linings press against the inside of the drum to slow or stop the vehicle.

E

EGR valve A valve used to introduce exhaust gases into the intake air stream.

Electronic control unit (ECU) A computer which controls (for instance) ignition and fuel injection systems, or an anti-lock braking system. For more information refer to the *Haynes Automotive Electrical and Electronic Systems Manual*.

Electronic Fuel Injection (EFI) A computer controlled fuel system that distributes fuel through an injector located in each intake port of the engine.

Emergency brake A braking system, independent of the main hydraulic system, that can be used to slow or stop the vehicle if the primary brakes fail, or to hold the vehicle stationary even though the brake pedal isn't depressed. It usually consists of a hand lever that actuates either front or rear brakes mechanically through a series of cables and linkages. Also known as a handbrake or parking brake.

Endfloat The amount of lengthwise movement between two parts. As applied to a crankshaft, the distance that the crankshaft can move forward and back in the cylinder block.

Engine management system (EMS) A computer controlled system which manages the fuel injection and the ignition systems in an integrated fashion.

Exhaust manifold A part with several passages through which exhaust gases leave the engine combustion chambers and enter the exhaust pipe.

F

Fan clutch A viscous (fluid) drive coupling device which permits variable engine fan speeds in relation to engine speeds.

Feeler blade A thin strip or blade of hardened steel, ground to an exact thickness, used to check or measure clearances between parts.

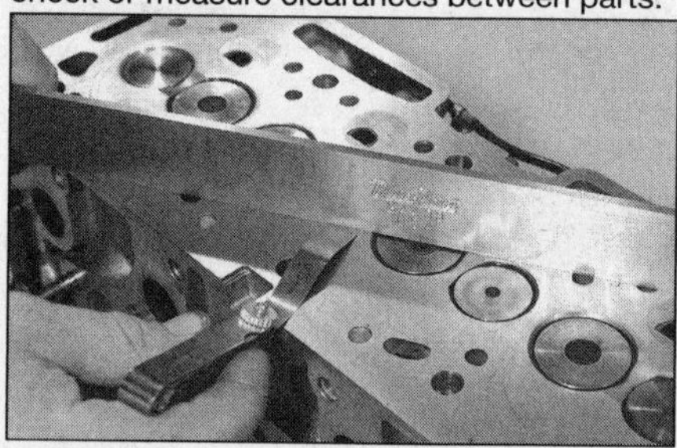
Feeler blade

Firing order The order in which the engine cylinders fire, or deliver their power strokes, beginning with the number one cylinder.

Flywheel A heavy spinning wheel in which energy is absorbed and stored by means of momentum. On cars, the flywheel is attached to the crankshaft to smooth out firing impulses.

Free play The amount of travel before any action takes place. The "looseness" in a linkage, or an assembly of parts, between the initial application of force and actual movement. For example, the distance the brake pedal moves before the pistons in the master cylinder are actuated.

Fuse An electrical device which protects a circuit against accidental overload. The typical fuse contains a soft piece of metal which is calibrated to melt at a predetermined current flow (expressed as amps) and break the circuit.

Fusible link A circuit protection device consisting of a conductor surrounded by heat-resistant insulation. The conductor is smaller than the wire it protects, so it acts as the weakest link in the circuit. Unlike a blown fuse, a failed fusible link must frequently be cut from the wire for replacement.

G

Gap The distance the spark must travel in jumping from the centre electrode to the side electrode in a spark plug. Also refers to the spacing between the points in a contact breaker assembly in a conventional points-type ignition, or to the distance between the reluctor or rotor and the pickup coil in an electronic ignition.

Adjusting spark plug gap

Gasket Any thin, soft material - usually cork, cardboard, asbestos or soft metal - installed between two metal surfaces to ensure a good seal. For instance, the cylinder head gasket seals the joint between the block and the cylinder head.

Gasket

Gauge An instrument panel display used to monitor engine conditions. A gauge with a movable pointer on a dial or a fixed scale is an analogue gauge. A gauge with a numerical readout is called a digital gauge.

H

Halfshaft A rotating shaft that transmits power from the final drive unit to a drive wheel, usually when referring to a live rear axle.

Harmonic balancer A device designed to reduce torsion or twisting vibration in the crankshaft. May be incorporated in the crankshaft pulley. Also known as a vibration damper.

Hone An abrasive tool for correcting small irregularities or differences in diameter in an engine cylinder, brake cylinder, etc.

Hydraulic tappet A tappet that utilises hydraulic pressure from the engine's lubrication system to maintain zero clearance (constant contact with both camshaft and valve stem). Automatically adjusts to variation in valve stem length. Hydraulic tappets also reduce valve noise.

I

Ignition timing The moment at which the spark plug fires, usually expressed in the number of crankshaft degrees before the piston reaches the top of its stroke.

Inlet manifold A tube or housing with passages through which flows the air-fuel mixture (carburettor vehicles and vehicles with throttle body injection) or air only (port fuel-injected vehicles) to the port openings in the cylinder head.

J

Jump start Starting the engine of a vehicle with a discharged or weak battery by attaching jump leads from the weak battery to a charged or helper battery.

L

Load Sensing Proportioning Valve (LSPV) A brake hydraulic system control valve that works like a proportioning valve, but also takes into consideration the amount of weight carried by the rear axle.

Locknut A nut used to lock an adjustment nut, or other threaded component, in place. For example, a locknut is employed to keep the adjusting nut on the rocker arm in position.

Lockwasher A form of washer designed to prevent an attaching nut from working loose.

M

MacPherson strut A type of front suspension system devised by Earle MacPherson at Ford of England. In its original form, a simple lateral link with the anti-roll bar creates the lower control arm. A long strut - an integral coil spring and shock absorber - is mounted between the body and the steering knuckle. Many modern so-called MacPherson strut systems use a conventional lower A-arm and don't rely on the anti-roll bar for location.

Multimeter An electrical test instrument with the capability to measure voltage, current and resistance.

N

NOx Oxides of Nitrogen. A common toxic pollutant emitted by petrol and diesel engines at higher temperatures.

O

Ohm The unit of electrical resistance. One volt applied to a resistance of one ohm will produce a current of one amp.

Ohmmeter An instrument for measuring electrical resistance.

O-ring A type of sealing ring made of a special rubber-like material; in use, the O-ring is compressed into a groove to provide the sealing action.

Overhead cam (ohc) engine An engine with the camshaft(s) located on top of the cylinder head(s).

Overhead valve (ohv) engine An engine with the valves located in the cylinder head, but with the camshaft located in the engine block.

Oxygen sensor A device installed in the engine exhaust manifold, which senses the oxygen content in the exhaust and converts this information into an electric current. Also called a Lambda sensor.

P

Phillips screw A type of screw head having a cross instead of a slot for a corresponding type of screwdriver.

Plastigage A thin strip of plastic thread, available in different sizes, used for measuring clearances. For example, a strip of Plastigage is laid across a bearing journal. The parts are assembled and dismantled; the width of the crushed strip indicates the clearance between journal and bearing.

Plastigage

Propeller shaft The long hollow tube with universal joints at both ends that carries power from the transmission to the differential on front-engined rear wheel drive vehicles.

Proportioning valve A hydraulic control valve which limits the amount of pressure to the rear brakes during panic stops to prevent wheel lock-up.

R

Rack-and-pinion steering A steering system with a pinion gear on the end of the steering shaft that mates with a rack (think of a geared wheel opened up and laid flat). When the steering wheel is turned, the pinion turns, moving the rack to the left or right. This movement is transmitted through the track rods to the steering arms at the wheels.

Radiator A liquid-to-air heat transfer device designed to reduce the temperature of the coolant in an internal combustion engine cooling system.

Refrigerant Any substance used as a heat transfer agent in an air-conditioning system. R-12 has been the principle refrigerant for many years; recently, however, manufacturers have begun using R-134a, a non-CFC substance that is considered less harmful to the ozone in the upper atmosphere.

Rocker arm A lever arm that rocks on a shaft or pivots on a stud. In an overhead valve engine, the rocker arm converts the upward movement of the pushrod into a downward movement to open a valve.

Rotor In a distributor, the rotating device inside the cap that connects the centre electrode and the outer terminals as it turns, distributing the high voltage from the coil secondary winding to the proper spark plug. Also, that part of an alternator which rotates inside the stator. Also, the rotating assembly of a turbocharger, including the compressor wheel, shaft and turbine wheel.

Runout The amount of wobble (in-and-out movement) of a gear or wheel as it's rotated. The amount a shaft rotates "out-of-true." The out-of-round condition of a rotating part.

S

Sealant A liquid or paste used to prevent leakage at a joint. Sometimes used in conjunction with a gasket.

Sealed beam lamp An older headlight design which integrates the reflector, lens and filaments into a hermetically-sealed one-piece unit. When a filament burns out or the lens cracks, the entire unit is simply replaced.

Serpentine drivebelt A single, long, wide accessory drivebelt that's used on some newer vehicles to drive all the accessories, instead of a series of smaller, shorter belts. Serpentine drivebelts are usually tensioned by an automatic tensioner.

Serpentine drivebelt

Shim Thin spacer, commonly used to adjust the clearance or relative positions between two parts. For example, shims inserted into or under bucket tappets control valve clearances. Clearance is adjusted by changing the thickness of the shim.

Slide hammer A special puller that screws into or hooks onto a component such as a shaft or bearing; a heavy sliding handle on the shaft bottoms against the end of the shaft to knock the component free.

Sprocket A tooth or projection on the periphery of a wheel, shaped to engage with a chain or drivebelt. Commonly used to refer to the sprocket wheel itself.

Starter inhibitor switch On vehicles with an automatic transmission, a switch that prevents starting if the vehicle is not in Neutral or Park.

Strut See MacPherson strut.

T

Tappet A cylindrical component which transmits motion from the cam to the valve stem, either directly or via a pushrod and rocker arm. Also called a cam follower.

Thermostat A heat-controlled valve that regulates the flow of coolant between the cylinder block and the radiator, so maintaining optimum engine operating temperature. A thermostat is also used in some air cleaners in which the temperature is regulated.

Thrust bearing The bearing in the clutch assembly that is moved in to the release levers by clutch pedal action to disengage the clutch. Also referred to as a release bearing.

Timing belt A toothed belt which drives the camshaft. Serious engine damage may result if it breaks in service.

Timing chain A chain which drives the camshaft.

Toe-in The amount the front wheels are closer together at the front than at the rear. On rear wheel drive vehicles, a slight amount of toe-in is usually specified to keep the front wheels running parallel on the road by offsetting other forces that tend to spread the wheels apart.

Toe-out The amount the front wheels are closer together at the rear than at the front. On front wheel drive vehicles, a slight amount of toe-out is usually specified.

Tools For full information on choosing and using tools, refer to the *Haynes Automotive Tools Manual*.

Tracer A stripe of a second colour applied to a wire insulator to distinguish that wire from another one with the same colour insulator.

Tune-up A process of accurate and careful adjustments and parts replacement to obtain the best possible engine performance.

Turbocharger A centrifugal device, driven by exhaust gases, that pressurises the intake air. Normally used to increase the power output from a given engine displacement, but can also be used primarily to reduce exhaust emissions (as on VW's "Umwelt" Diesel engine).

U

Universal joint or U-joint A double-pivoted connection for transmitting power from a driving to a driven shaft through an angle. A U-joint consists of two Y-shaped yokes and a cross-shaped member called the spider.

V

Valve A device through which the flow of liquid, gas, vacuum, or loose material in bulk may be started, stopped, or regulated by a movable part that opens, shuts, or partially obstructs one or more ports or passageways. A valve is also the movable part of such a device.

Valve clearance The clearance between the valve tip (the end of the valve stem) and the rocker arm or tappet. The valve clearance is measured when the valve is closed.

Vernier caliper A precision measuring instrument that measures inside and outside dimensions. Not quite as accurate as a micrometer, but more convenient.

Viscosity The thickness of a liquid or its resistance to flow.

Volt A unit for expressing electrical "pressure" in a circuit. One volt that will produce a current of one ampere through a resistance of one ohm.

W

Welding Various processes used to join metal items by heating the areas to be joined to a molten state and fusing them together. For more information refer to the *Haynes Automotive Welding Manual*.

Wiring diagram A drawing portraying the components and wires in a vehicle's electrical system, using standardised symbols. For more information refer to the *Haynes Automotive Electrical and Electronic Systems Manual*.

Note: *References throughout this index are in the form* "**Chapter number**" • "**Page number**". *So, for example, 2C•15 refers to page 15 of Chapter 2C.*

Note: *References throughout this index are in the form* **"Chapter number" • "Page number"**. *So, for example, 2C•15 refers to page 15 of Chapter 2C.*

Note: *References throughout this index are in the form* **"Chapter number" • "Page number"**. *So, for example, 2C•15 refers to page 15 of Chapter 2C.*

Note: References throughout this index are in the form **"Chapter number" • "Page number"***. So, for example, 2C•15 refers to page 15 of Chapter 2C.*